THE
HARSHACARITA
OF BĀṆABHAṬṬA

THE HARSHACARITA OF BĀṆABHAṬṬA

(Text of Uchchhvāsas I — VIII)

Edited with an Introduction and Notes
by
MAHĀMAHOPĀDHYĀYA
P. V. KANE

MOTILAL BANARSIDASS PUBLISHERS
PRIVATE LIMITED • DELHI

First Edition: Bombay, 1918
Reprint: Delhi, 1965, 1973, 1986, 1997

ISBN: 81-208-0032-x (Cloth)
ISBN: 81-208-0051-6 (Paper)

Also available at:

MOTILAL BANARSIDASS
41 U.A. Bungalow Road, Jawahar Nagar, Delhi 110 007
8, Mahalaxmi Chamber, Warden Road, Mumbai 400 026
120 Royapettah High Road, Mylapore, Madras 600 004
Sanas Plaza, Subhash Nagar, Pune 411 002
16 St. Mark's Road, Bangalore 560 001
8 Camac Street, Calcutta 700 017
Ashok Rajpath, Patna 800 004
Chowk, Varanasi 221 001

PRINTED IN INDIA
BY JAINENDRA PRAKASH JAIN AT SHRI JAINENDRA PRESS,
A-45 NARAINA, PHASE I, NEW DELHI 110 028
AND PUBLISHED BY NARENDRA PRAKASH JAIN FOR
MOTILAL BANARSIDASS PUBLISHERS PRIVATE LIMITED,
BUNGALOW ROAD, DELHI 110 007

PREFACE.

The present edition contains the whole of the text of he Harshacharita (Uchchhvāsas I–VIII). As there is at present no other annotated edition of the Harshacharita in the market, the present edition needs no apology. This edition will, it is hoped, meet all the requirements of the University student. No pains have been spared to make the book useful not only to the college student, but also to the general reader. As the work was published in two parts in two years, the paging of one part is independent of the other.

The commentary of S'aṃkara published by the Nirṇayasāgara Press has been highly useful to me. The elegant and spirited translation of the Harshacharita by Prof. Cowell and Mr. Thomas is a monument of skill and learning. Though I have unfortunately had frequent occasion to differ from them, my sincerest thanks are due to them, particularly for happy renderings of words and phrases. The Harshacharita is a difficult book and I am afraid that many passages have still remained obscure. I crave the indulgence of the reader and will most thankfully receive all suggestions and criticisms.

P. V. KANE.

A list of some of the abbreviations employed in the work.

अ०—The Nirṇaya-sāgara edition of the हर्षचरित.

अम०—अमरकोश.

अलं०—अलंकारसर्वस्व of रुय्यक.

उत्तरराम०—उत्तररामचरित of भवभूति.

क—The Calcutta edition of the Harshacharita by Īsvara-chandra Vidyāsāgara.

का० or काम०—कामन्दकीयनीतिसार.

काद०—कादम्बरी (Dr. Peterson's edition).

क्षीर०—क्षीरस्वामी, commentator of the अमरकोश.

चतु०—चतुर्वर्गचिन्तामणि of हेमाद्रि.

पा०—पाणिनि's अष्टाध्यायी.

ब—The edition of the Harshacharita in the Bombay Sanskrit Series.

बृह०—बृहत्संहिता of वराहमिहिर (edited by Prof. Kern).

भागवतपु०—भागवतपुराण. महा०—महाभारत (Bombay edition).

मनु०—मनुस्मृति. मे०—मेदिनीकोश.

याज्ञ० or याज्ञवल्क्य०—याज्ञवल्क्यस्मृति. रघु०—रघुवंश.

वायु०—वायुपुराण (Ānandās'rama ed.).

विष्णुपु० or विष्णु०—विष्णुपुराण. शब्द०—शब्दकल्पद्रुम.

सं०—संकेत, commentary on the हर्षचरित. सि. कौ. = सिद्धान्तकौमुदी.

A—The Nirṇaya-sāgara edition of the Harshacharita.

Anand. ed.—Ānandās'rama edition.

B—The edition of the Harshacharita in the Bombay Sanskrit Series.

B. R. W. W.—Beal's Buddhist records of the Western World.

C—Is'varachandra's edition of the Harshacharita.

C. I. or *C. I. I.*—Corpus Inscriptionum Indicarum.

C and *T.*—The translation of the Harshacharita by Prof. Cowell and Mr. Thomas.

E. I.—Epigraphia Indica.

I. A.—Indian Antiquary.

J. B. B. R. A. S.—Journal of the Bombay Branch of the Royal Asiatic Society.

J. R. A. S.—Journal of the Royal Asiatic Society.

P—Dr. Peterson's edition of the Kādambarī.

TABLE OF CONTENTS

Introduction.

I. Personal History of Bâṇa.

About the personal history of Sanskrit authors and especially poets, our knowledge is generally very meagre. In the case of many Sanskrit poets, we know next to nothing beyond their names. Around the names of some (*e. g.* Kâlidâsa), tradition has been busy in weaving such fanciful and bewildering stories that it is no easy task to separate the solid grain of truth from the chaff. In the case of some, the meagre account of themselves contained in their own works has to be eked out with information derived from contemporary or subsequent records in literature, grants and inscriptions. There are a few who have left to posterity a tolerably full account of themselves in their works*. Bâṇa perhaps stands at the head of such Sanskrit authors. To his Kâdambarî is prefixed a brief account of his family. But in his Harshacharita, we find a much fuller account of his ancestors and himself. The first two Uchchhvâsas of the Harshacharita are taken up with the history of Bâṇa's forefathers and Bâṇa himself. The personal narrative is continued even in the third Uchchhvâsa. Space does not permit us to give in detail a full account of Bâṇa as gathered from the Harshacharita. We propose to dwell upon only a few salient points of the narrative of Bâṇa's personal history.

The genealogical tree of Bâṇa's family as constructed

---

* In this connection we may mention Bilhaṇa and Mankha, who, in the Vikramânkadevacharita and the S'rîkaṇṭhacharita respectively, furnish a full account of their lives, their contemporaries &c.

from the Harshacharita* is given in the footnote below. In the introductory verses to the Kâdambarî the genealogy is given as follows. Kubera was a Brâhmaṇa of the Vâtsyâyana gotra and was honoured by many Gupta kings. His son was Arthapati, whose son was Chitrabhânu who was Bâṇa's father. The student will notice that in this narrative, Pâs'upata, who appears to have been the great-grand-father of Bâṇa, if we are to rely upon the Harshacharita, is omitted. It is strange that Bâṇa (or his son who is supposed by some to have written the introductory verses to the Kâdambarî) should have forgotten his own great-grand-father. The only explanation that we offer (of course with great hesitation) is that the verses containing the reference to Pâs'upata were not to be found in the Mss. used for preparing the printed editions of the Kâdambarî.

The progenitor of Bâṇa's family, Vatsa, lived in a place called Prîtikûṭa on the banks of the Hiraṇyabâhu, otherwise called S'oṇa. Bâṇa's mother, Râjadevî, died while he was yet a child. He was all the more dear to his father, who was a very mother to him. Bâṇa had the misfortune to lose his father when he was about fourteen years old. Bâṇa tells us that he thereafter led a wandering life. He mentions as the

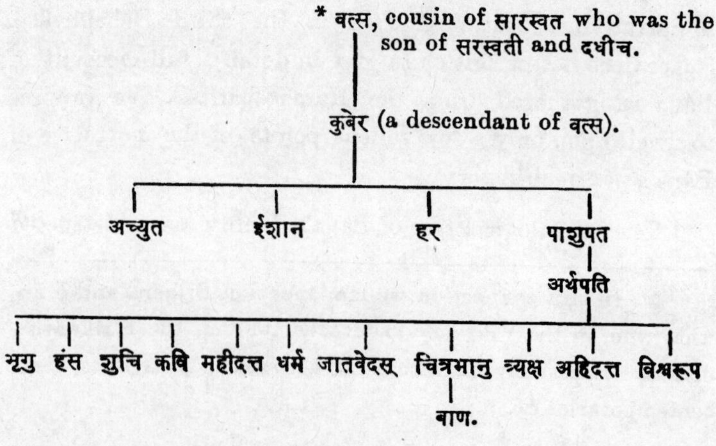

companions of his wanderings a number of persons*. Although Bâṇa had ancestral wealth sufficient to maintain him in ease and comfort, yet his strong curiosity to see differen' lands impelled him to wander from place to place and made him an object of ridicule in the eyes of his elderly contemporaries. After finishing his wanderings in which he gathered a rich harvest of wisdom and experience, he returned to his native place Brâhmaṇâdhivâsa (or Prîtikûṭa) with broadened sympathies and a widened outlook.

One day in the height of summer, when Bâṇa sat in his house after the midday meal his cousin (born of a S'ûdra woman) Chandrasena ushered in a courier who brought a letter from Kṛishṇa, a brother (cousin) of Emperor Harsha. In the letter Kṛishṇa referred Bâṇa to the messenger Mekhalaka and bade him lose no time in carrying out the wishes of the writer. The message was:—"Emperor Harsha's ears have been poisoned against you by some wicked people. But I knew the truth about you and interceded on your behalf with the king and told him that you (Bâṇa) must not have been guilty of anything beyond youthful rashness and folly. The king admits this and so you should come to the emperor's court without delay."

After a good deal of misgiving as to how he would be received at the court of Harsha, Bâṇa performed some auspicious rites and set out from his native place Prîtikûṭa. On the third day he reached the camp of Harsha which was then on the Ajirâvatî near the town Maṇitâra.

---

* "अभवंश्चास्य वयसा समानाः सुहृदः सहायाश्च । तथा च । भ्रातरौ पारशवौ चन्द्रसेनमातृषेणौ, भाषाकविरीशानः परं मित्रं, प्रणयिनौ रुद्रनारायणौ, विद्वांसौ वारबाणवासबाणौ, वर्णकविर्वेणीभारतः, प्राकृतकृत्कुलपुत्रो वायुविकारः, बन्दिनावनङ्गबाणसूचिबाणौ, कात्यायनिका चक्रवाकिका, जाङ्गुलिको मयूरकः, ताम्बूलदायकश्चण्डकः, भिषक्पुत्रो मन्दारकः, पुस्तकवाचकः सुदृष्टिः, कलादश्चामीकरः, हैरिकः सिन्धुषेणः, लेखको गोविन्दकः, चित्रकृद्वीरवर्मा, पुस्तकृत्कुमारदत्तः, मार्दङ्गिको जीमूतः, गायनौ सोमिलग्रहादित्यौ, सैरन्ध्री कुरङ्गिका, वांशिकौ मधुकरपारावतौ, गान्धर्वोपाध्यायो दर्दुरकः, संवाहिका केरलिका, लासकयुवा ताण्डविकः, आक्षिक आखण्डलः, कितवो भीमकः, शैलालियुवा शिखण्डकः, नर्तकी हरिणिका, पाराशरी सुमतिः, क्षपणको वीरदेवः, कथको जयसेनः, शैवो वक्रघोणः, मन्त्रसाधकः करालः, असुरविवरव्यसनी लोहिताक्षः, धातुवादविद्विहङ्गमः, दार्दुरिको दामोदरः, ऐन्द्रजालिकश्चकोराक्षः, मस्करी ताम्रचूडः ।"

When Bâṇa was presented to Harsha who had with him the son of the king of Mâlvâ, the emperor received him at first with mock signs of anger, but afterwards showed him much favour. After basking in the sunshine of royal favour, Bâṇa returned to his native place. He was greeted with a cordial welcome by his friends and relatives. The reader Sudṛishṭi entertained him with a recital of the Vâyupurâṇa. Then the bard Sûchîbâṇa recited two verses (Âryâs), which pointedly referred to the life of Harsha. All were charmed and Bâṇa's cousins (sons of his paternal uncles), Gaṇapati, Adhipaṭi, Târâpati and S'yâmala, looked at one another and the youngest of them, S'yâmala, made bold to ask Bâṇa to tell them from the beginning the wondrous story of Harsha's life. Bâṇa expressed his inability to do justice to the mighty deeds of the emperor and, as the day was far advanced, began the narrative the next morning.

Here ends the autobiographical part of the Harshacharita with which alone we are concerned at present.

As to the later stages of Bâṇa's life we have no account left. He died leaving his romance of Kâdambarî unfinished. Bâṇa's son tells us in the introduction to the Uttarabhâga that he finished the Kâdambarî as a work of filial duty and not out of pride*. Dr. Buhler says that the name of Bâṇa's son was Bhûshaṇabâṇa†. In some MSS. of the Kâdambarî, the son is called Pulinda‡ or Pulina. Dhanapâla, while praising Bâṇa in his introduction to the Tilakamanjarî, seems to suggest that Pulinda was the name of his son§.

---

* "याते दिवं पितरि तद्वचसैव सार्धं विच्छेदमाप भुवि यस्तु कथाप्रबन्धः । दुःखं सतां तदसमाप्तिकृतं विलोक्य प्रारब्ध एव स मया न कवित्वदर्पात् ॥"

† See Dr. Peterson's Introduction to Kâdambarî p. 40.

‡ *Vide* Prof. S. R. Bhandarkar's report on the search for MSS. 1904–5, 1905–6 p. 39; see also Dr. Stein's catalogue of Sanskrit MSS. at Jammu p. 299.

§ केवलोऽपि स्फुरन्बाणः करोति विमदान्कवीन् ।
किं पुनः क्लृप्तसन्धानपुलिन्ध्र (न्द?) कृतसन्निधिः ॥ verse 26.

(It will be noticed that the verse has two meanings).

It is said that the poet Mayûra was a contemporary and father-in-law of Bâṇa. Mayûra praised the sun in hundred verses, which make up the Sûryas'ataka and became free from leprosy. Bâṇa became jealous of him, maimed himself, composed the Chaṇḍîs'ataka in honour of Durgâ, who made him all right. The story of Mayûra's freedom from disease is alluded to in the Kâvyaprakâs'a*. There are Subhâshitas in which Bâṇa and Mayûra are spoken of as contemporaries and as patronized by king Harsha†. Verses from the Sûryas'ataka are quoted in the Dhvanyâloka (latter half of 9th century A. D.)‡. The Kavikaṇṭhâbharaṇa of Kshemendra mentions Mayûra by name and quotes a verse as his which is found in the Sûryas'ataka§. So it is not beyond the bounds of probability that Bâṇa and Mayûra were contemporaries. A Mayûraka is mentioned as one of the companions of Bâṇa in his wanderings (see the passage quoted above on p. III). But as he is mentioned there as a snake-doctor ('Jângulika' = Vishavaidya), it seems to us that he is not the same as the poet Mayûra. The commentators of the Bhaktâmarastotra of the Jain Mânatungâchârya say that Mânatunga lived at the court of Bhoja in Ujjayinî and was a contemporary of Bâṇa and Mayûra. They further narrate various stories about Bâṇa and Mayûra. We believe that those stories have no historic basis and are purely imaginary. We therefore refrain from reproducing them here.

II The date of Bâṇa.

As we are fortunate in possessing some account of Bâṇa from his own pen, so also we are lucky in being able to fix

---

* 'आदित्यादेर्मयूरादीनामिवानर्थनिवारणम्'

† 'अहो प्रभावो वाग्देव्या यन्मातङ्गदिवाकरः ।
श्रीहर्षस्याभवत्सभ्यः समो बाणमयूरयोः ॥'

This verse is ascribed to Râjas'ekhara and is quoted in the Subhâshitâvali and the S'ârngadharapaddhati.

'स चित्रवर्णविच्छित्तिहारिणोरवनीपतिः ।
श्रीहर्ष इव सङ्घट्टं चक्रे बाणमयूरयोः ॥'
नवसाहसाङ्कचरित II. 18.

‡ The verse 'दत्तानन्दाः' &c. (9th in the Nir. ed. of सूर्यशतक.)

§ In the fourth सन्धि of the कविकण्ठाभरण the verse 'अस्तव्यस्तत्वशून्यो' &c. is quoted as Mayūra's (verse 18 of the सूर्यशतक).

the date of Bâṇa beyond the possibility of cavil. As a matter of fact Bâṇa's date is one of the surest planks in the tottering structure of ancient India Chronology.

This is not the place to set out in detail how Bâṇa's date has been fixed. Suffice it to say that a famous Chinese traveller, Hiouen Thsang, was in India from 629 A. D. to 645 A. D. He has left extensive memoirs of his travels, in which he speaks in detail about a king Harsha who was the emperor of northern India. Although there are slight discrepancies in the accounts of Harsha furnished by Bâṇa and the Chinese pilgrim, the points of agreement are so many and so striking that there is not the least doubt that the Emperor Harsha, the patron of Bâṇa, is the same as the great monarch of whom the Chinese pilgrim has left extensive notices. Harsha is said to have reigned from 606 A. D. to 648 A. D. Therefore Bâṇa must have flourished towards the end of the 6th and in the first half of the 7th century of the Christian era.

We shall set forth below a good deal of evidence which strongly corroborates the above conclusion. We believe that a part of this evidence is for the first time brought to the notice of Sanskrit scholars by us.

(1) The Harshacharita of Bâṇa is mentioned by Ruyyaka in his Alamkârasarvasva a number of times.* We are told by him that he wrote a work called Harshacharitavârtika †. Ruyyaka wrote his Alamkârasarvasva about 1150 A. D.

(2) Kshemendra, in his voluminous writings, men-

---

* " 'यस्तपोवनमिति मुनिभिः...' इत्यादि हर्षचरिते श्रीकण्ठाख्यजनपदवर्णने" p. 47 of अलंकारसर्वस्व; "तथा च हर्षचरिते 'अनुरूपो देव्या इत्यात्मसम्भावना' इत्यादौ, तथा 'यामीति न स्नेहसदृशम्' इत्यादावुक्तविषय आक्षेपः" p. 117 of अलं०; "यथा हर्षचरिते राज्यवर्धनं प्रति श्रीहर्षोक्तिषु 'यदि बाल इति सुतरामपरित्याज्योऽस्मि ...' " p. 139; 'नमन्तु शिरांसि धनूंषि वा कर्णपूरीक्रियन्तामाज्ञा मौर्व्यो वा' p. 158 of अलं० (this occurs in the 6th उच्छ्वास); "यथा वा हर्षचरितप्रारम्भे ब्रह्मसदसि वेदस्वरूपवर्णने । ...एवं तत्रैव मुनिक्रोधवर्णने, पुलिन्दवर्णनादौ ज्ञेयम्" p. 182. He quotes from the Kâdambarî also. 'चित्रकर्मसु वर्णसङ्करो यतिषु दण्डग्रहणानि' p. 154 of अलं० (see कादम्बरी p. 6 of P.)

† 'एषा (उत्प्रेक्षा) च समस्तोपमाप्रतिपादकविषयेऽपि **हर्षचरितवार्तिके साहित्यमीमांसायां** च तेषु तेषु प्रदेशेषूदाहृता' p. 61 of अलंकारसर्वस्व.

tions Bâṇa by name a number of times *. Kshemendra tells us that he wrote his Kavikaṇṭhâbharaṇa and Suvṛittatilaka in the reign of king Anantarâja (1028-1063 A. D.) of Kashmîr, and quotes a verse of king Kalas'a (1080 A. D.—1088 A. D.). So he flourished in the latter half of the 11th century A. D. Kshemendra seems to have written a work called 'Padyakâdambarî' based on Bâṇa's romance.†

(3) Namisâdhu, the commentator of Rudraṭa's Kâvyâlamkâra, mentions the Kâdambarî and the Harshacharita as specimens of the two types of prose compositions, *viz.*, Kathâ and Âkhyâyikâ‡. From the last verse of his comment, we learn that Namisâdhu wrote in 1069 A. D.

(4) Bhoja in his Sarasvatîkaṇṭhâbharaṇa has a few references to Bâṇa. In one place we are told that Bâṇa does not excel so much in poetry as in prose¶. The exact dates of Bhoja's reign (which was very long, extending over 50 years) are not yet fixed. But he seems to have come to the throne in the second decade of the 11th century.

(5) The Das'arûpa of Dhanamjaya mentions Bâṇa by name§. Dhanamjaya was patronized by king Munja.$ If Munja is the uncle of the great Bhoja, as it seems to be the case, Dhanamjaya flourished before 1000 A. D.

---

* In his औचित्यविचारचर्चा he quotes the verse 'स्तनयुगमश्रुस्नातं' &c. and says in the same work "न तु यथा भट्टबाणस्य 'जयत्युपेन्द्रः स चकार' ". In his कविकण्ठाभरण (सन्धि II) he says "यथा च भट्टबाणस्य 'कटु क्वणन्तो मलदायकाः' " (which occurs in the Introduction to the कादम्बरी).

† In his कविकण्ठाभरण, क्षेमेन्द्र cites no less than seven verses from his पद्यकादम्बरी. One of them is 'तत्कालोपनते वयस्यनिधने हा पुण्डरीकेति तन्मोहव्यञ्जनमश्मभञ्जनमलं जीवस्य सन्तर्जनम् । कुञ्जव्यापि कपिञ्जलेन करुणं निस्पदमाक्रन्दितं येनाद्यापि च तैः स्मृतेन हरिणैः शष्पं परित्यज्यते ॥' (this is cited as an instance of शब्दवैमल्य in the 4th सन्धि).

‡ See comment on काव्यालङ्कार of रुद्रट XVI. 22 and 26.

¶ 'यादृग्गद्यविधौ बाणः पद्यबन्धे न तादृशः ।' p. 142 of the 1st Vol. of the Benares edition. See p. 146 of the same volume for a quotation from Bâṇa 'हर इव जितमन्मथः गुह इवाप्रतिहतशक्तिः'.

§ 'यथा हि महाश्वेतावर्णनावसरे भट्टबाणस्य' under II. 35 (निर्णय० ed.); 'यथा कादम्बर्यां वैशम्पायनस्य' under IV. 66.

$ 'आविष्कृतं मुञ्जमहीशगोष्ठीवैदग्ध्यभाजा दशरूपमेतत् ' last verse of the दशरूप.

(6) Abhinanda wrote the Kâdambarîkathâsâra, in which he faithfully versifies the story of Bâṇa's Kâdambarî. Abhinanda tells us that his great-great-grand-father, S'aktisvâmin was a minister of Muktâpîḍa, a king of the Karkoṭa family*. Abhinanda is praised for the excellence of his Anushṭubh verses by Kshemendra in his Suvṛitta-tilaka†.

(7) The author of the Dhvanyâloka, Ânandavardhana, flourished in the reign of king Avantivarman (855-883 A. D.)‡ of Kashmir. In the Dhvanyâloka, Bâṇa and his two prose compositions are mentioned by name$. From this it follows that in the latter half of the 9th century Bâṇa's works had attained a pre-eminent position in the world of letters.

(8) Vâmana, in his Kâvyâlaṃkârasûtravṛitti seems to quote a few words from the Kâdambarî§. Vâmana flour-

---

* स **शक्तिस्वामिनं** पुत्रमवाप श्रुतशालिनम् । राज्ञः **कर्कोटवंशस्य मुक्तापीडस्य मन्त्रिणम्** ॥ verse 7 of **कादम्बरीकथासार.**

† 'अनुष्टुप्सततासक्ता साभिनन्दस्य नन्दिनी । विद्याधरस्य वदने गुलिकेव प्रभावभूः ॥'

We wish here to call the attention of the reader to a curious fact. Abhinava-gupta says in his Dhvanyâlokalochana that Bhaṭṭajayantaka wrote Kâdambarîkathâ-sâra; p. 142 "कथातात्पर्ये सर्गबन्धो यथा भट्टजयन्तकस्य कादम्बरीकथासारम्." The question arises whether this is a different work from that of Abhinanda or whether it is a slip on the part of the learned author of the Lochana or whether it is a mistake of the scribe's. We know that Abhinanda was the son of Bhaṭṭajayanta, called Vṛittikâra.

‡ 'मुक्ताकणः शिवस्वामी कविरानन्दवर्धनः । प्रथां रत्नाकरश्चागात्साम्राज्येऽवन्तिवर्मणः ॥' राजतरङ्गिणी V. 34.

$ यथा स्थाण्वीश्वराख्यजनपदवर्णने **भट्टबाणस्य** 'यत्र च मत्तमातङ्गगामिन्यः' ध्वन्यालोक p. 100; यथा **हर्षचरिते** 'समवाय इव विरोधिनां पदार्थानाम्' p. 101; "यथा **हर्षचरिते** सिंहनादवाक्येषु—'वृत्तेऽस्मिन्महाप्रलये' p. 127; 'यथा **कादम्बर्यां** कादम्बरीदर्शनावसरे' p. 87. On p. 99 of the ध्वन्यालोक a passage is quoted from the Harshacharita (उच्छ्वास II) without naming it.

§ "'**अनुकरोति भगवतो नारायणस्य**' इत्यत्रापि, मन्ये, सशब्दः कविना प्रयुक्तो लेखकैस्तु प्रमादान्न लिखित इति" on 'आहेति भूतेऽन्यणलन्तभ्रमाद् ब्रुवो लटि' काव्यालंकारसूत्र V. 2. 44. For the words 'अनुकरोति भगवतो नारायणस्य' see कादम्बरी p. 6 of Dr. Peterson's edition.

ished in the latter half of the 8th century. We shall briefly indicate the data that enable us to arrive at this date for Vâmana. (a) Vâmana quotes from the Uttararâmacharita of Bhavabhûti a verse*. Bhavabhûti flourished before 700 A. D†. So Vâmana is later than 700 A. D. (b) He is often quoted by Pratîhârendurâja, the commentator of Udbhaṭa's Kavyâlaṃkâra‡. Pratîhârendurâja, who was a pupil of Mukula, son of Kallaṭa, flourished in the first half of the 10th century. Therefore Vâmana is earlier than 900 A. D. (c) Abhinavagupta says § that Ânandavardhana, bearing in mind the conflicting views of Vâmana and Bhâmaha as regards Samâsokti and Âkshepa, gave the verse 'Anurâgavatî sandhyâ' (p. 37 Dhvanyâloka) as an example. So according to Abhinavagupta, Vâmana flourished before Ânandavardhana *i. e.* before the latter half of 9th century A. D. (d) A Vâmana is mentioned as the minister ¶ of king Jayâpîḍa (745—776 A. D.) of Kashmir and is identified by Kashmirian Pandits with the author of the Kâvyâlaṃkârasûtra. These four lines of inquiry make it highly probable, if not certain, that Vâmana flourished in the latter half of the 8th century. Bâṇa's Kâdambarî was well-known, as shown above, in the latter half of the 8th century.

Thus from the 12th century backwards to the 8th, we have a host of writers who refer in unmistakable terms to Bâṇa and his works. Besides those mentioned by us above, there are writers of less note such as the authors of the Nalachampû and the Kîrtikaumudî that refer to Bâṇa. We refrain from quoting them for want of space.

The date of Bâṇa is of paramount importance for the chronology of Sanskrit writers. Bâṇa in the introduction to his Harshacharita mentions a number of Sanskrit works

---

* 'इयं गेहे लक्ष्मीरियममृतवर्तिर्नयनयोः' &c. on काव्यालंकारसूत्र IV. 3. 2. (रूपक).

† See Dr. Bhandarkar's preface to the Mâlatîmâdhava p. IX.

‡ See Folios 12, 55, 56, &c. of the Deccan College Ms. of Pratîhârendurâja's commentary.

§ 'वामनाभिप्रायेणायमाक्षेपः, भामहाभिप्रायेण तु समासोक्तिरित्यमुमाशयं हृदये गृहीत्वा समासोक्त्याक्षेपयोरिदमेकमेवोदाहरणं व्यतरद्ग्रन्थकृत् ।' लोचन p. 37.

¶ 'मनोरथः शङ्खदत्तश्चटकः सन्धिमांस्तथा । बभूवुः कवयस्तस्य वामनाद्याश्च मन्त्रिणः ॥' राजतरंगिणी IV. 497.

and poets*. The first half of the 7th century is the *terminus ad quem* of these poets. In this connection we strongly recommend that the student should read Dr. Peterson's valuable and instructive Introduction to his edition of the Kâdambarî. Although we have the misfortune to differ from the learned author of the Indroduction on a number of points, we feel confident that the Introduction will surely rouse the student's critical faculty†.

As one point (*viz.* the relative position of Subandhu and Bâṇa) on which we differ from Dr. Peterson is of great importance in connection with the date of Bâṇa, we shall discuss it here.

---

* The works and poets mentioned by name are:–Vyâsa, Vâsavadattâ, Bhaṭṭâra–Harichandra, Sâtavâhana, the Setu of Pravarasena, Bhâsa, Kâlidâsa, Bṛihatkathâ and Âḍhyarâja.

† The following are the most important among the points on which we differ from Dr. Peterson, though with the greatest diffidence:—(1) 'it is clear that by *Akhyâyikâ* in the present passage, Bâṇa refers *to metrical stories*, such as furnished him with the material of his own romance' (p. 70); (2) Bhâsa being the contemporary or immediate predecessor of Bâṇa (p. 71); (3) the Vâsavadattâ mentioned in the Harshacharita is not the one that was written by Subandhu; (4) the Nâṭakas, with a sûtradhâra in their beginning, were novelties in Bâṇa's day (p. 80); (5) Kâlidâsa was a contemporary of Bâṇa (p. 81); (6) Aḍhyarâja, mentioned in the Harshacharita, is not a proper noun (p. 96); (7) that Indian Astronomy, as taught by Âryabhaṭa and Varâhamihira and as known to Kâlidâsa and Bâṇa, is of Greek origin. About Âkhyâyikâ, we shall speak later on. It should be noted that in the Mâlavikâgnimitra, Kâlidâsa calls himself 'Vartamânakavi' and styles Bhâsa as of world-wide fame. So Bhâsa, who must have preceded Kâlidâsa by some generations, could not have been a contemporary or immediate predecessor of Bâṇa. We shall try to show that Subandhu preceded Bâṇa. That Âḍhyarâja was a name we know from a verse that occurs in the Sarasvatîkaṇthâbharaṇa (vol.I.p.136 Benares edition) 'केऽभूवन्नाढ्यराजस्य काले प्राकृतभाषिणः। काले श्रीसाहसाङ्कस्य के न संस्कृतभाषिणः॥'. The commentary explains that आढ्यराज stands for शालिवाहन and साहसाङ्क for विक्रम. It is not possible to dismiss the other points briefly.

Dr. Peterson was inclined to place Subandhu, the author of the extant Vâsavadattâ, after Bâṇa. His reasons are given on pp. 71—73 of his introduction. 'For that after the graceless string of extravagant and indecent puns presented by the present Vâsavadattâ had been received with approval into the national literature, a reversion should have been possible to the chastity, alike of sentiment and of diction, of Bâṇa and Bhavabhûti would be a literary miracle almost incredible.' We have to strike here a note of caution. We should always beware of foisting our modern conceptions of literary style and beauty on authors and critics that flourished centuries before us. How are we to know that the skill of Subandhu in stringing together puns might not have kindled the admiration of Bâṇa who seems to have himself thought very highly of such puzzles as Prahelikâs? It is curious to note that Dr. Peterson, in his preface to the Subhâshitâvali of Vallabhadeva (p. 133), abandons the position taken up by him as to the relative position of Subandhu and Bâṇa in his introduction to the Kâdambarî.

We think that the Vâsavadattâ praised in the Harshacharita so * eloquently is the present work of that name written by Subandhu. Our reasons are:—

(1) In Vâmana's Kâvyâlamkârasûtravṛitti, a passage is quoted which is found in the Harshacharita and the extant Vâsavadattâ of Subandhu with very slight variations †.

---

* कवीनामगलद्दर्पो नूनं **वासवदत्तया** । शक्त्येव पाण्डुपुत्राणां गतया कर्णगोचरम् ॥. The महाभाष्य commenting on the वार्तिक 'अधिकृत्य कृत्ये ग्रन्थे लुबाख्यायिकाभ्यो बहुलम्' mentions three works of the आख्यायिका class, *viz.* वासवदत्ता, सुमनोत्तरा and भैमरथी (Kielhorn vol. II p. 313). In another place he speaks of a person who studies the आख्यायिका वासवदत्ता (vol II p. 284). It is not probable that Bâṇa refers to this work. It is to be noted that the extant वासवदत्ता would have to be called a कथा and not an आख्यायिका as defined below.

† 'कुलिशशिखरखरनखरप्रचयप्रचण्डचपेटापाटितमत्तमातङ्गकुम्भस्थलगलन्मदच्छटाच्छुरितचारुकेसरभारभासुरमुखे केसरिणि' काव्यालंकारसूत्रवृत्ति I. 3. 25. See Vâsavadattâ (p. 331 of the S'rîrangam edition and p. 266 of Hall's). See हर्षचरित (उच्छ्वास VI) p. 40 of our text. In the वासवदत्ता the words are '०चपेटपाटितमत्तमातङ्गकुम्भस्थलरुधिरच्छटाच्छुरितचारुकेसरभारभासुरकेसरिकदम्बेन.' This correspondence between the वासवदत्ता and the हर्षचरित opens up the question whether Bâṇa

We have seen above that Vâmana probably flourished in the latter half of the 8th century and that he quotes the Kâdambarî also. It is difficult to say from what author Vâmana takes his quotation. But from the locative 'Kesariṇi' it seems that the Harshacharita is drawn upon.

(2) Kavirâja, the author of the Râghavapâṇḍavîya, mentions Subandhu, Bâṇa and himself as the masters of Vakrokti *. We think that the three are mentioned by the author in chronological order, placing himself last of all.

(3) Vākpatirâja, the author of Gauḍavaho, a Prakrit poem, refers to the composition of Subandhu †. No other poet bearing the name of Subandhu, except the author of the Vâsavadattâ, is known to us. Therefore we are justified in holding that Vâkpatirâja refers to the author of the extant Vâsavadattâ. Vâkpatirâja was a protégé of Yas'ovarman of Kânyakubja and an admirer (and perhaps friend and pupil) of Bhavabhûti. Pandit comes to the conclusion (Introduction to Gauḍavaho, p. 100) that Vâkpatirâja wrote his poem between 700-725 A. D. It is curious to note that while Vâkpatirâja mentions the work of Subandhu in the same breath with Bhâsa and Kâlidâsa, he is silent as regards Bâṇa who wrote a prose work similar to Subandhu's. What then is the probable conclusion ? It is that when Vâkpatirâja wrote Subandhu was a famous author while Bâṇa was yet unknown to fame.

From the foregoing it seems very probable that Subandhu, the author of the present Vâsavadattâ, preceded Bâṇa.

In Mankha's S'rikaṇṭhacharita we find a verse where both Bâṇa and Subandhu are praised together ‡.

---

actually borrowed the words of the वासवदत्ता. There are many passages where Bâṇa's words and ideas coincide with those of the Vâsavadattâ. For want of space we refrain from quoting them.

* 'सुबन्धुर्बाणभट्टश्च कविराज इति त्रयः । वक्रोक्तिमार्गनिपुणाश्चतुर्थो विद्यते न वा ॥' राघवपाण्डवीय I. 41.

† 'भासम्मि जलणमित्ते कन्तीदेवे अ जस्स रहुआरे । सोबन्धवे अ बन्धम्मि हारियन्दे अ आणन्दो ॥'

Pandit's Gaudavaho, verse 800.

‡ 'मेण्ठे स्वर्दिरदाधिरोहिणि वशं याते सुबन्धौ विधेः शान्ते हन्त च भारवौ विघटिते बाणे विषादस्पृशः ।' श्रीकण्ठचरित II. 53.

III Bâṇa's works.

Before proceeding with the subject of this section, a few remarks concerning the origin and development of Sanskrit Rhetoric and of Kathâ and Âkhyâyikâ in particular would not be out of place here.

The oldest writer who specifically mentions Âkhyâyikâs is Kâtyâyana*. Kâtyâyana seems to intimate that the Âkhyâyikâs he refers to were not the episodes contained in such books as the Mahâbhârata, but that they were independent and distinct works. Patanjali in his Mahâbhâshya, while commenting upon the above-mentioned Vârtika, gives the names of three Âkhyâyikâs, *viz.* Vâsavadattâ, Sumanottarâ and Bhaimarathî†. In another place Patanjali speaks of one who knows or studies the Âkhyâyikâ Vâsavadattâ or Sumanottarâ‡. Subandhu, who, we saw above, preceded Bâṇa, alludes to some canons of the art of poetry. In one place§ he says that the composition of a good poet should not contain superfluous words such as 'tu', 'hi' &c. In another place he says that the utterances of a good poet should be divided into Uchchhvâsas (chapters) and should contain fine puns and verses in the Vaktra metre¶. This seems to refer to what are called Âkhyâyikâs, as we shall see later on. Daṇḍin,|| who is gene-

---

* 'लुबाख्यायिकाभ्यो बहुलम्' a वार्तिक on 'अधिकृत्य कृते ग्रन्थे' पा॰IV.3. 87.; 'आख्यानाख्यायिकेतिहासपुराणेभ्यश्च' वार्तिक on पा॰ IV. 2. 60.

† "'अधिकृत्य कृते ग्रन्थे' बहुलं लुग्वक्तव्यः । वासवदत्ता सुमनोत्तरा । न च भवति । भैमरथी ।"

‡ Mahâbhâshya (Kielhorn) vol. II. p. 284 'वासवदत्तिकः सौमनोत्तरिकः'. Vide p. XI above.

§ 'सत्कविकाव्यबन्ध इवाबद्धतुहिनः' वासवदत्ता p. 134 (Hall).

¶ 'दीर्घोच्छ्वासरचनाकुलं सुश्लेषवक्त्रघटनापटु सत्कविवचनमिव' वासवदत्ता p. 184 (Hall).

|| A few scholars are inclined to place Daṇḍin later. This is not the place to discuss at length the question. Our reasons for placing him in the 6th century are briefly these:—(1) he is mentioned as an ancient writer along with Bhâmaha and Udbhaṭa (latter half of 8th century) by Jayaratha (p. 3. अलङ्कारसर्वस्व); (2) Namisâdhu speaks of Daṇḍin as follows:— 'ननु दण्डि-मेधाविरुद्र-भामहादिकृतानि सन्त्येवालङ्कारशास्त्राणि' (p. 2 of रुद्रटकाव्यालङ्कार). We believe the authors are arranged chrono-

rally assigned to the 6th century A. D., refers to the distinction drawn between Kathâ and Âkhyâyikâ by certain writers, disapproves of it and finally says that both are different names for the same class of composition*. Daṇḍin further says that an Âkhyâyikâ should exhibit a profusion of compounds†. The lexicon of Amarasimha defines‡ Kathâ and Âkhyâyikâ, pointing out that the former is imaginary and has very little historical value, while the latter deals with matters of history. Bâṇa himself often alludes to the two classes of prose compositions§. Bâṇa offers a glowing tribute of praise to the writers of Âkhyâyikâs that preceded him¶. He refers to some peculiarities that distinguished the Âkhyâyikâ from other classes of compositions, *viz.* division into Uchchhvâsas and the occurrence of the Vaktra metre. Bâṇa himself clearly intimates that his Harshacharita is an Âkhyâyikâ‖. The introductory verses to the Pûrvabhâga clearly indicate that the Kâdambarî was intended to be a Kathâ ☙ (technically so called). This makes it clear that Bâṇa *did not* strike out a new path in writing his two prose works, that he had before him certain works which went under the name of Âkhyâyikâ and that criticism had been busy in laying down canons for regulating the two classes of prose compositions.

---

logically, as मेधाविरुद्र is mentioned in Bhâmaha's work; (3) Daṇḍin's treatment appears crude and unscientific as compared with Bhâmaha's; (4) Bhâmaha in a few places refers to the opinions of some (अपरे, अन्ये &c.) and these are found in Daṇḍin's work. (5) Tamil and Canarese writers belonging to the 8th century refer to him.

* See Kâvyâdars'a I. 23–30.

† 'तद्गुरूणां लघूनां च बाहुल्याल्पत्वमिश्रणैः । उच्चावचप्रकारं तद् दृश्यमाख्यायिकादिषु ॥' काव्यादर्श I. 81.

‡ 'आख्यायिकोपलब्धार्था' अमर० I. 6. 5; 'प्रबन्धकल्पना कथा'.

§ 'काव्यनाटकाख्यानकाख्यायिकालेख्यव्याख्यानादिक्रियानिपुणैः' p. 3 of कादम्बरी (Peterson); 'कथासु नाटकेषु आख्यायिकासु काव्येषु' p. 75 (Peterson).

¶ उच्छ्वासान्तेऽप्यखिन्नास्ते येषां वक्त्रे सरस्वती । कथमाख्यायिकाकारा न ते वन्द्याः कवीश्वराः ॥' हर्षचरित.

‖ 'तथापि नृपतेर्भक्त्याभीतो निर्वहणाकुलः । करोम्याख्यायिकाम्भोधौ जिह्वाप्लवनचापलम् ॥' हर्षचरित.

☙ 'द्विजेन तेनाक्षतकण्ठकौण्ठ्यया महामनोमोहमलीमसान्धया । अलब्धवैदग्ध्यविलासमुग्धया धिया निबद्धेयमतिद्वयी कथा ॥'

It is believed by some Sanskrit scholars that Bâṇa wrote before Sanskrit rhetoricians had done their best to degrade the sublime art of poetry to a pedantic enumeration of set similes and metaphors (*vide* Dr. Peterson's Introduction p. 43). We hold, with the greatest deference, that this is, to a great extent, fallacious. We possess ample evidence to establish that long before Bâṇa flourished, the science of Rhetoric had made great progress. We find that an inscription of Rudradâman (150 A. D.) exhibits a prose containing very long compounds, alliteration (Anuprâsa) and other figures*. In the same inscription reference is made to prose (Gadya) and poetry (Padya) that are ornate, fine on account of the (poetic) conventions observed in them and that contain perspicuous, short, sweet, striking and charming words†. An inscription of the time of Samudragupta (4th century A. D.) contains a prose that vies with that of Bâṇa himself‡. The Mandasor inscription dated in the Mâlava era 529 (*i. e.* 473 A. D.) contains verses that rival in diction and imagery the best efforts of Kâlidâsa, Bhavabhûti and other masters of classical Sanskrit. § Daṇḍin, who, as we said above, is not placed later than the 6th century A. D., gives a tolerably full treatment of Rhetoric. He says that he only improves upon what other Âchâryas that preceded him

---

* See Archaeological Survey, Western India. vol. II (about Kathiawad) p. 128.

† 'स्फुटलघुमधुरचित्रकान्तशब्दसमयोदारालङ्कृतंगद्यपद्य'

‡ Dr. Fleet's Corpus Inscriptionum Indicarum vol. III. p. 8. Mark the following 'कृपणदीनानाथातुरजनोद्धरणसमन्त्रदीक्षाद्युपगतमनसः समिद्धस्य विग्रहवतो लोकानुग्रहस्य धनदवरुणेन्द्रान्तकसमस्य स्वभुजबलविजितानेकनरपतिविभवप्रत्यर्पणनित्यव्यापृतायुक्तपुरुषस्य निशितविदग्धमतिगान्धर्वललितैर्व्रीडितत्रिदशपतिगुरुतुम्बुरुनारदादेर्विद्वज्जनोपजीव्यानेककाव्यक्रियाभिः प्रतिष्ठितकविराजशब्दस्य' &c.

§ See Dr. Fleet's Corpus Inscriptionum vol. III p. 76ff. We shall quote only two verses. 'चतुःसमुद्रान्तविलोलमेखलां सुमेरुकैलासबृहत्पयोधराम् । वनान्तवान्तस्फुटपुष्पहासिनीं कुमारगुप्ते पृथिवीं प्रशासति ॥ स्मरवशगतरुणजनवल्लभाङ्गनाविपुलकान्तपीनोरु-स्तनजघनघनालिङ्गननिर्भर्त्सिततुहिन-हिमपाते ॥' It will be noticed that the second verse (an Ârya) forms a single compound.

had laid down*. Daṇḍin asserts that a profusion of compounds is the very life of prose†. This dictum has been followed by later prose-writers only too well. Bhaṭṭi devotes four *sargas* of his Bhaṭṭikâvya to the illustration of subjects that properly fall to be treated under Rhetoric. He exemplifies more than thirty figures of speech. He wrote in Valabhi under a king named Dharasena. Four kings of the Valabhi dynasty bore the name Dharasena. The dates of the four kings fall between about 500 A. D. and 651 A. D. So Bhaṭṭi was a predecessor or at least a contemporary of Bâṇa. In Subhandhu's Vâsavadattâ we meet with a number of allusions to Rhetoric. Subandhu boasts of his skill in composing a work full of paronomasia on each syllable‡. He refers to S'ṛinkhalâbandha (a peculiar arrangement of words) and mentions the figures of speech Utprekshâ and Âkshepa§. Bâṇa refers to such puzzles and conundrums as Prahelikâ and mentions in the introduction to the Harshacharita a few figures of speech such as Jâti (Svabhâvokti), Utprekshâ and S'lesha¶. In the Introduction to the Kâdambarî are mentioned the figures Dîpaka, Upamâ, S'lesha and Jâti.

In this brief *resume* we have shown that, before Bâṇa flourished, Rhetoric had made great progress, though it had not reached perfection.

The Harshacharita $ and the Kâdambarî are well-known as the works of Bâṇa. A third work, the Chaṇḍîs'ataka,

---

* 'किं तु बीजं विकल्पानां **पूर्वाचार्यैः** प्रकल्पितम् । तदेव परिसंस्कर्तुमयमसत्परिश्रमः ॥' काव्यादर्श II. 2.

† 'ओजः समासभूयस्त्वमेतद्गद्यस्य जीवितम् ।' काव्यादर्श I. 80.

‡ सरस्वतीदत्तवरप्रसादश्चक्रे **सुबन्धुः** सुजनैकबन्धुः । प्रत्यक्षर**श्लेष**मयप्रबन्धविन्यासवैदग्ध्यनिधिर्निबन्धम् ॥

§ 'शृङ्खलाबन्धो वर्णग्रथनासु उत्प्रेक्षाक्षेपौ काव्यालङ्कारेषु' वासवदत्ता p. 126 (Hall).

¶ 'अक्षरच्युतकमात्राच्युतकबिन्दुमतीगूढचतुर्थपादप्रहेलिकाप्रदानादिभिः' p. 3 of कादम्बरी (Peterson); 'बिन्दुमतीं चिन्तयता प्रहेलिकां भावयता' p. 88 of कादम्बरी.

$ The learned translators of the Harshacharita intimate that the Harshacharita was forgotten by Indian writers, though rare copies existed unknown in libraries. They mention only the साहित्यदर्पण and the काव्यप्रकाश as referring to the हर्षचरित. We is ascribed to him. There is nothing improbable in Bâṇa's authorship of a century of verses in honour of Chaṇḍî. We know that he gives in the Kâdambarî a powerful and picturesque description of the temple of Chaṇḍikâ. Still many hesitate to assert that Bâṇa *was* the author of the Chaṇḍîs'ataka*. A drama styled Pârvatîpariṇaya is also ascribed to Bâṇa. In the prelude to the Pârvatîpariṇaya, we are told that the drama was composed by Bâṇa of the Vatsa Gotra†. The author of the Kâdambarî also was descended from Vatsa. The drama, though not of the highest order of merit, has some excellences of its own. The subject is the same as that of the Kumârasambhava of Kâlidâsa. There are remarkable coincidences, both of phrase and thought, between the two works. Hence it is said by some scholars that the Pârvatîpariṇaya is only the work of a plagiarist and not of an eminent author like Bâṇa. We think, however, that this argument does not possess much force. We know that the fine verses of Kâlidâsa were the delight of Bâṇa and had kindled his admiration‡. When the subject was the same, it was quite natural that Bâṇa should unconsciously imitate in thought and expression his favourite author. Even in Kâlidâsa we recognise the words of the Mahâbhârata and the Bhagvatgîtâ. It is further argued that the Pârvatîpariṇaya is, as compared with the Harshacharita and the Kâdambarî, quite common-place. We

---

have quoted above passages from आनन्दवर्धन, नमिसाधु and रुय्यक that mention the हर्षचरित by name. It is clear that, at all events in Kashmir, the Harshacharita was carefully preserved and studied. For Kalhaṇa's indebtedness to the Harshacharita, see Dr. Stein's Kalhaṇa vol. I p. 133.

* We may draw the attention of the reader to the fact that verses from the Chaṇḍîs'ataka occur in the सरस्वतीकण्ठाभरण, in the काव्यप्रकाश and in अर्जुनवर्मदेव's टीका on अमरुशतक. अर्जुनवर्मदेव (p. 3) expressly ascribes the authorship of the चण्डीशतक to बाण "उपनिबद्धं च भट्टबाणेनैवंविध एव संग्रामप्रस्तावे देव्यास्तद्भङ्गिभिर्भगवता भर्गेण सह प्रीतिप्रतिपादनाय बहुधा नर्म-यथा 'दृष्टावासक्तदृष्टिः' &c." (verse 37 of चण्डी०)

† 'अस्ति कविसार्वभौमो वत्सान्वयजलधिसम्भवो बाणः । नृत्यति यद्रसनायां वेधोमुखलासिका वाणी ॥' 4th verse, Act I.

‡ 'निर्गतासु न वा कस्य कालिदासस्य सूक्तिषु । प्रीतिर्मधुरसान्द्रासु मञ्जरीष्विव जायते ॥' Introduction to हर्षचरित.

think that this, even if entirely true, would not militate against Bâṇa's authorship of the work. The work might have been written before Bâṇa had attained the mastery of his mature years. In the Pârvatîpariṇaya we find that Bâṇa is feeling his way. His prose in the drama reminds us of the Kâdambarî and the Harshacharita. Many ideas and turns of expression are common to the drama and the two prose works of Bâṇa. We cite below only one of them for want of space*. Besides we must not forget that Bâṇa was handicapped in verse. We have quoted above a critic's opinion that Bâṇa does not excel so much in verse as in prose. That remark could not have been based on the few verses that occur in the two prose works of Bâṇa. They rather refer to some compositions in verse written by Bâṇa. We suggest that the Pârvatîpariṇaya may be one of them. Chaṇḍapâla and Guṇavinayagaṇi, the commentators of the Nalachampû of Trivikramabhaṭṭa, inform us that Bâna wrote a drama entitled Mukuṭatâḍitaka†. We know nothing about this drama from other sources. Kshemendra quotes a verse as Bâṇa's‡, in which the sad plight of Kâdambarî due to separation from her lover is described. It seems therefore that Bâṇa wrote, according to Kshemendra, the story of Kâdambarî in verse also.

In the Kâvyaprakâs'a we read that Bâṇa obtained money from king Harsha§. A few scholars relying upon Kashmir tradition are of opinion that the drama Ratnâvali was really

---

* Act I 'हिमवान्—देवि कन्यापितृत्वं खलु गृहमेधिनामधिकतरं दुःखमावहति ।...कुचयुगलं परिणद्धं यथा यथा वृद्धिमेति तन्वङ्ग्याः । वरचिन्ताहृतमनसस्तथा तथा कार्श्यमेति मे गात्रम् ॥'. Compare this with the passage in the हर्षचरित (उच्छ्वास IV) 'हृदयमन्धकारयति मे दिवसमिव पयोधरोन्नतिरस्याः ।...सेयं सर्वाभिभाविनी शोकाग्नेर्दाह शक्तिर्यदपत्यत्वे समानेऽपि जातायां दुहितरि दूयन्ते सन्तः' (p. 13 of our text).

† "यदाह मुकुटताडितकनाटके बाणः 'आशाः प्रोषितदिग्गजा इव गुहाः प्रध्वस्तसिंहा इव द्रोण्यः कृत्तमहाद्रुमा इव भुवः प्रोत्खातशैला इव । बिभ्राणाः क्षयकालरिक्तसकलत्रैलोक्यकष्टां दशां जाताः क्षीणमहारथाः कुरुपतेर्देवस्य शून्याः सभाः ॥' "

‡ "यथा वा भट्टबाणस्य–'हारो जलार्द्रवसनं नलिनीदलानि प्रालेयशीकरमुचस्तुहिनांशुभासः। यस्येन्धनानि सरसानि च चन्दनानि निर्वाणमेष्यति कथं स मनोभवाग्निः ॥' अत्र विप्रलम्भभरभग्नधैर्यायाः कादम्बर्या विरहव्यथावर्णना &c." औचित्यविचारचर्चा.

§ 'श्रीहर्षादेर्बाणादीनामिव धनम्.' Many MSS. read धावकादीनाम्.

the work of Bâṇa, who, in return for the money bestowed by king Harsha upon him, published the work in his patron's name. This view seems to us to be entirely wrong. In the first place, there are three dramas, the Ratnâvali, the Priyadars'ikâ and the Nâgânanda, the authorship of which is claimed by Harsha. The Prastâvanâs to all the three dramas are identical almost word for word. In the Prastâvanâ of each of the three dramas Harsha is said to be the author. No one ascribes the Priyadars'ikâ and the Nâgânanda to Bâṇa. Hence the Ratnāvali also is not the work of Bâṇa. The Ratnâvali is quoted by Damodaragupta in his Kuṭṭanîmata (8th century A. D.). The Ratnâvali and the Nâgânanda are quoted by name in the Dhvanyâloka (p. 150, p. 176 respectively). The Ratnâvali is quoted at least a score of times in the Das'arûpa. The Nâgânanda and the Priyadars'ikâ are also quoted in the Das'arûpa but not so frequently. But in none of these writings is there the slightest hint that the author of the Ratnâvali was Bâṇa and not Harsha. It is remarkable that Kshemendra, himself a very erudite Kashmirian scholar, quotes some verses from the Ratnāvali and attributes them to S'rîharsha*.

The introductory verses attached to the Kâdambarî are supposed by some scholars to be the composition not of Bâṇa, but of his son or some one else. We demur to this conclusion on the following grounds. (a) If the verses had been written by Bâṇa's son, he would have referred to his authorship of them, as he does in the case of the introductory verses prefixed to the Uttarabhâga. Moreover he would not have mentioned his father in the colourless way in which the last verse (of the Pûrvabhâga) speaks of Bâṇa as 'Dvijena tena &c.' (b) Kshemendra quotes in his works at least four verses of the Introduction and twice distinctly says that they are Bâṇa's (in Auchityavichâracharchâ†

* In the कविकण्ठाभरण (सन्धि V) "इन्द्रजालपरिचयो यथा श्रीहर्षस्य 'एष ब्रह्मा सरोजे' &c. (रत्नावलि IV. 11). In the औचित्यविचारचर्चा he quotes the following verses as श्रीहर्ष's:—'परिम्लानं &c.' (रत्ना॰ II. 12); 'विश्रान्तविग्रहकथः &c.' (रत्ना॰ I. 8); 'उद्दामोत्कलिकां &c.' (रत्ना॰ II. 4); भयानके यथा श्रीहर्षस्य 'कण्ठे कृत्तावशेषं &c.', अपि च 'नष्टं वर्षवरैः' (रत्ना॰ II. 2–3).

† न तु यथा भट्टबाणस्य 'जयत्युपेन्द्रः स चकार दूरतः' &c.; the कविकण्ठाभरण quotes the verse 'कट्ठु कणन्तो' &c. as Bāṇa's.

and the Kavikaṇṭhâbharaṇa). (c) It is next to impossible that Bâṇa, an orthodox writer, should have commenced his work without any kind of salutation at the beginning.

IV Kathâ and Âkhyâyikâ.

We shall now briefly indicate the characteristics of these two classes of writings as defined by Sankrit rhetoricians.

The earliest known writer. who puts down the points of difference between Kathâ and Âkhyâyikâ as defined by some rhetoricians (although he himself disapproves of them), is Daṇḍin. (1) In an Âkhyâyikâ, it is the hero himself who tells the whole story; while in a Kathâ, the story is told either by the hero or by someone else. (2) An Âkhyâyikâ is divided into sections named Uchchhvâsas and contains verses in the Vaktra and Aparavaktra metres, while in a Kathâ it is not so. (3) In a Kathâ, such topics as the kidnapping of a girl, battles, separation, the rise of the sun and the moon are described; in an Âkhyâyikâ it is not so. (4) A Kathâ is distinguished by possessing certain catchwords which the author intentionally puts in. Daṇḍin remarks that no hard and fast line of demarcation can be drawn between the two classes of works, and that the points mentioned above have not been invariably followed by writers and that hence Kathâ and Âkhyâyikâ are but two names for the same species of prose composition. Bhâmaha's definitions of Kathâ and Âkhyâyikâ are given below.* In Rudraṭa's Kâvyâlaṃkâra, Kathâ and Âkhyâyikâ are defined†. The author seems to have had in mind the Kâdambarî and the Harshacharita in defining the two species of prose composition. We have seen above that a profusion of compounds was said by Daṇḍin to constitute the very essence of prose and hence long compounds form the ruling characteristic of Kathâ and Âkhyâyikâ. But certain restrictions were laid

* प्रकृतानाकुलश्राव्यं शब्दार्थपदवृत्तिना । गद्येन युक्तोदात्तार्था सोच्छ्वासाऽऽख्यायिका मता ॥ वृत्तमाख्यायते तस्यां नायकेन स्वचेष्टितम् । वक्त्रं चापरवक्त्रं च काले भाव्यर्थशंसि च ॥ कवेरभिप्रायकृतैरङ्कनैः कैश्चिदङ्किता । कन्याहरणसंग्रामविप्रलम्भोदयान्विता ॥ न वक्त्रापरवक्त्राभ्यां युक्ता नोच्छ्वासवत्यपि । संस्कृतं संस्कृता चेष्टा कथाऽपभ्रंशभाक् तथा ॥ अन्यैः स्वचरितं तस्यां नायकेन तु नोच्यते । स्वगुणाविष्कृतिं कुर्यादभिजातः कथं जनः ॥ भामह I. 25–29.

† See Rudraṭa's Kâvyâlaṃkâra XVI. 20–30.

down by the author of the Dhvanyâloka. He says* that even in an Âkhyâyikâ very long compounds should not occur in depicting pathos and the love of separated lovers.

† Abhinavagupta distinguishes Âkhyâyikâ from Kathâ by saying that the former is divided into sections called Uchchhvâsas and contains verses in the Vaktra and Aparavaktra metres; while the latter lacks these features. The Sâhityadarpaṇa says:—a Kathâ contains a fine plot in prose, with a verse in the Âryâ, Vaktra or Aparavaktra metre here and there; a Kathâ is introduced by a salutation in verse and reference is made to the conduct of the wicked &c‡. It further says that an Âkhyâyikâ is just like a Kathâ with this addition that the former contains a narrative of the poet himself and of other poets, that its divisions are styled Âs'vâsas and that it contains verses at the beginning of each Âs'vâsa that suggest future events.§

In passing we wish to notice one question of interest. Is Bâṇa indebted to anybody for the materials of his Kâdambarî ? It seems that Bâṇa derived the dry bones of his story from the Bṛihatkathâ of Guṇâḍhya. That work, said to have been written in the Pais'âchî language, is

---

* 'आख्यायिकायां तु भूम्ना मध्यमसमासादीर्घसमासे एव सङ्घटने। गद्यस्य विकटनिबन्धाश्रयेण च्छायावत्त्वात् । तत्र च तस्य प्रकृष्यमाणत्वात् । कथायां तु विकटबन्धप्राचुर्येऽपि गद्यस्य रसबन्धोक्तमौचित्यमनुसर्तव्यम्। ...गद्यबन्धेऽपि अतिदीर्घसमासा रचना न विप्रलम्भशृङ्गारकरुणयोराख्यायिकायामपि शोभते'। ध्वन्यालोक p. 143.

† 'आख्यायिकोच्छ्वासादिना वक्त्रापरवक्त्रादिना च युक्ता। कथा तद्विरहिता' p. 143 of लोचन.

‡ कथायां सरसं वस्तु **गद्यैरेव** विनिर्मितम् ॥
क्वचिदत्र भवेदार्या क्वचिद्वक्त्रापवक्त्रके ॥
आदौ पद्यैर्नमस्कारः खलादेर्वृत्तकीर्तनम् ॥

साहित्यदर्पण 6th Parichchheda.

Dr. Peterson read पद्यैरेव विनिर्मितम् and translated 'A Kathâ...is a narration in prose of matter already existing in a metrical form' p. 69 of Introduction to the Kâdambarî.

§ 'आख्यायिका कथावत्स्यात्कवेर्वंशानुकीर्तनम्। अस्यामन्यकवीनां च वृत्तं पद्यं क्वचित्क्वचित् ॥ कथांशानां व्यवच्छेद आश्वास इति बध्यते । आर्यावक्त्रापवक्त्राणां छन्दसा येन केनचित्। अन्यापदेशेनाश्वासमुखे भाव्यर्थसूचनम्।'

now lost*. But there exist two Sankrit renderings of that Bṛihatkathâ, the one by Kshemendra called Bṛihatkathâ-manjarî and the other by Somadeva called Kathâsaritsâgara. The story of Sumanas (Sumânasa in Bṛihatkathâmanjarî) bears a remarkable resemblance to the Kâdambarî in the matter of incidents. As the story is a long one we forbear from reproducing it here. The curious reader may refer to the works of Kshemendra and Somadeva.† Bâṇa of course exercised the poet's privilege in moulding the narrative so as to suit his own purpose. He infused life and vigour into the dry-as-dust narrative of the Bṛihatkathâ.

V Literary Estimate.

Bâṇa is one of the brightest stars in the galaxy of Sanskrit poets. Ancient Sanskrit writers and modern European critics are at one in bestowing on Bâṇa an unstinted meed of praise. By Sanskrit critics, his works were regarded as the finest specimens of the Pânchâlî style of composition.‡ He is easily the first among the writers of classical Sanskrit

---

* That the Bṛihatkathâ of Guṇâḍhya was in existence before 600 A. D. can be proved by numerous quotations from ancient authors. We shall cite a few. कथा हि सर्वभाषाभिः संस्कृतेन च बध्यते। भूतभाषामयीं प्राहुरद्भुतार्थां बृहत्कथाम् ॥ काव्यादर्श I. 38.; समुद्दीपितकन्दर्पा कृतगौरीप्रसाधना । हरलीलेव नो कस्य विस्मयाय बृहत्कथा ॥ Introduction to हर्षचरित; 'बृहत्कथारम्भैरिव शालभञ्जिकोपेतैः' 'केचिद् बृहत्कथानुबन्धिनो गुणाढ्याः' (both from वासवदत्ता); 'बृहत्कथाकुशलेन' (कादम्बरी Peterson p. 51. l. 15); 'इत्याद्यशेषमिह वस्तुविभेदजातं रामायणादि च विभाव्य बृहत्कथां च । आसूत्रयेत्तदनु नेतृरसानुगुण्याच्चित्रां कथामुचितचारुवचःप्रपञ्चैः ॥' दशरूप of धनञ्जय; नमिसाधु commenting upon Rudraṭa II. 10 says "तथा प्राकृतमेव किंचिद्विशेषात् पैशाचिकम् ।...इत्यादयोऽन्येपि प्राकृतविहिता व्यञ्जनादेशा न क्रियन्ते ते च बृहत्कथादिलक्ष्यदर्शनाज्ज्ञेयाः'. The Nalachampû and Govardhana's Saptas'atî praise Guṇâḍhya.

† See बृहत्कथामञ्जरी (निर्णयसागर ed.) XVI. 183–251 and कथासरित्सागर X. 3. (शक्तियशोलम्बक 3rd तरङ्ग).

‡ शब्दार्थयोः समो गुम्फः पाञ्चाली रीतिरिष्यते ।
शीलाभट्टारिकावाचि बाणोक्तिषु च सा यदि ॥

i. e. In the Pânchâlî style word and sense should be equally balanced.

prose.* We give below a few verses containing appreciations of Bâṇa by various Sanskrit writers.†

We shall briefly point out some of the merits and defects of Bâṇa's writings. The student will do well to read Dr. Peterson's eloquent appreciation of Bâṇa in his Introduction to the Kâdambarî (pp. 36-43).

1. He shows great skill and discrimination in characterization. All the characters in the Kâdambarî are life-like and consistent. The gentle and youthful Hârîta; the generous and loving king Târâpîḍa; the trusted S'ukanâsa whose first thought was always for the king; the tender queen Vilâsavatî; the devoted Patralekhâ, who followed the prince Chandrâpîḍa like his shadow; the affectionate yet stern Kapinjala; Mahâs'vetâ, holy in mind as she was fair in body, who serves as the foil for the heroine; these are characters that are bound to make a deep impression on the heart of the reader. Bâṇa, however, lavished all his skill in depicting the hero and the heroine of his romance. We think that Bâṇa, as has been remarked in the case of Shakespeare, was more successful in delineating his heroine than his hero. 'On Kâdambarî in particular, Bâṇa has spent all his wealth of observation, fullness of imagery, and keenness of sympathy.' 'From the moment when for the first

---

* It was said by rhetoricians that prose was the touchstone of poets 'गद्यं कवीनां निकषं वदन्ति' quoted by वामन in his काव्यालङ्कारसूत्रवृत्ति on का. सू. I. 3. 21.

† शश्वद्बाणद्वितीयेन नमदाकारधारिणा ।
धनुषेव गुणाढ्येन निःशेषो रञ्जितो जनः ॥—नलचम्पू.
युक्तं कादम्बरीं श्रुत्वा कवयो मौनमाश्रिताः ।
बाणध्वनावनध्यायो भवतीति स्मृतिर्यतः ॥—कीर्तिकौमुदी I. 15.
जाता शिखण्डिनी प्राग्यथा शिखण्डी तथावगच्छामि ।
प्रागल्भ्यमधिकमाप्तुं वाणी बाणो बभूवेति ॥—आर्यासप्तशती of गोवर्धन.
केवलोपि स्फुरन्बाणः &c. quoted above from धनपाल's तिलकमञ्जरी.
सुबन्धुर्बाणभट्टश्च कविराज इति त्रयः ।
वक्रोक्तिमार्गनिपुणाश्चतुर्थो विद्यते न वा ॥—राघवपाण्डवीय I. 41.
श्लेषे केचन शब्दगुम्फविषये केचिद्रसे चापरेऽ-
लंकारे कतिचित्सदर्थविषये चान्ये कथावर्णने ।
आ सर्वत्र गभीरधीरकविताविन्ध्याटवीचातुरी-
सञ्चारी कविकुम्भिकुम्भभिदुरो बाणस्तु पञ्चाननः ॥—श्रीचन्द्रदेव,
(the last) quoted from Mr. Parakhi's work.

time her eye falls and rests on Chandrâpîḍa, this image of a maiden heart, torn by the conflicting emotions af love and virgin shame, of hope and despondency, of cherished filial duty and a new-born longing, of fear of the world's scorn and the knowledge that a world given in exchange for this will be a world well lost, takes full possession of the reader.

2. Though the Kâdambarî contains glowing descriptions of love, they are chaste and free from grossness of any kind. In this respect the Das akumâracharita contrasts most unfavourably with the Kâdambarî. In the former, the reader is disgusted with the filthy intrigues of the ruffian heroes of that book.

3. Although Bâṇa was fettered by the canons of Rhetoric which laid down that long compounds were of the essence of prose, he displays considerable variety of style. His diction is generally smooth and graceful and he could write with force and brevity when it suited his purpose to do so. In this connection we may refer to the stern advice of Kapinjala to Punḍarîka. Bâṇa's prose is generally ornate and full of poetic fancies. He revels in the jingling assonance of sounds. Upamâ, Rûpaka and Utprekshâ are met with at every step. Among the other figures of speech may be mentioned Dîpaka, Sahokti, Virodha, Nidars'anâ and Vishama.

4. He seems to have been a close observer not only of courts and kings, but even of the less bright aspects of human life. His description of the old Draviḍa ascetic, though somewhat long-drawn and tedious, shows that he had an eye for the ridiculous and the bizarre. His descriptions of court and life in cities present a vivid picture of the time in which he lived. The advice of S'ukanâsa to Chandrâpîḍa is a masterpiece. It sets out very clearly all the evils that beset not only the path of Chandrâpîḍa, but of all princes in all climes. The Harshacharita of Bâṇa possesses great interest for the antiquarian from the fact that it affords a vivid picture of Indian society in the 7th century and of the manners and customs of those far-off days.

5. Bâṇa seems to have been a great lover of Nature. He is never tired of using for poetic purposes the flora and fauna of India. His references to plants and flowers, though sometimes overdrawn and fanciful, are generally charming.

6. Although most of the characters of the Kâdambarî are shadowy and some of them are in their second or even third birth, the poet's genius is so superb and his power of developing love and pathos is so great that the reader soon forgets the unreal character of the work and his mind is enthralled by the engrossing interest of the woes and happiness of the characters. 'We find ourselves face to face with the story of human sorrow and divine consolation, of death and the passionate longing for a union after death that goes straight from the heart of one who had himself felt the pang and nursed the hope, to us who are of like frame with him'. In the Harshacharita the hero is a historic personage. The author's task is thereby rendered more difficult. Yet Bâṇa acquits himself most creditably. It will be seen later on that he has nowhere stretched any point in favour of his hero and that his version is generally corroborated by independent evidence.

His defects.

One of the greatest flaws of Bâṇa's writings is that they abound in puns on words and recondite allusions. The reader is often at a loss, amidst the array of double-meaning words, bold and fanciful allusions, to grasp the exact meaning of the author. Though this is a blemish according to modern ideas of criticism, ancient India thought otherwise. These by-ways of puns were called Vakrokti (crooked speech), which was raised to the position of an Alaṃkâra. Subandhu, we have seen above, boasts of his skill in puns on each letter.

Another serious blemish is that in the Kâdambarî we meet with a defect in constructive art, which is due to the device of weaving stories within stories. The reader is unable to carry in his head the bewildering turns and convolutions of the story and the confusion of curses and counter curses. The fact that the greater part of the story is put in the mouth of a parrot is a serious drawback to the verisimilitude of the work.

Bâṇa seems to have had very little sense of proportion. In his descriptions of Mahâs'vetā and the temple of Chaṇḍikâ he tires the reader by dwelling too much on every detail. The patience of the reader is exhausted by the overloading of single words with epithets and of the epithets to these epithets. It sometimes so seems that the poet cares only for the gorgeous description of the evening, morning, moonrise or the limbs of the heroine and leaves the plot to take care of itself.

It is necessary to say a few words about Bâṇa's son. It may be at once admitted that the highest praise is due to the dutiful son of Bâṇa for having creditably performed his self-imposed task. He possesses not a few of the excellences of his father. He has almost the same command over the Sanskrit language as his father. His style is as ornate and as full of figures of speech as his father's. But we must not forget that in the son's work the defects of his father are exaggerated and others peculiar to the son alone are added. We miss in the Uttarabhâga the bold and striking fancies of Bâṇa with which we become familiar in the Pûrvabhâga. The description of the love torment of Kâdambarī is insipid and drawn out to a tedious length. The references to mythological and other lore are few and far between in the Uttarabhâga. The different lines of the story are made to converge far more rapidly than Bâṇa would have done. The picturesque descriptions of flora and fauna in which Bâṇa is profuse are lacking in the Uttarabhâga. Such masterpieces of realism as the advice of S'ukanâsa to Chandrâpîḍa are conspicuous by their absence in the Uttarabhâga. The perusal of the Uttarabhâga leaves the reader under the impression that the author was only anxious to bring the story to a close somehow. The touch of genius that appeals to the mind and makes the characters live before the eyes of the reader is altogether wanting.

VI The Harshacharita.

A comparison of the Harshacharita with the Kādambarī is instructive and interesting. Both works are composed in the same ornate and elaborate style. Both exhibit, more or less, the same merits and defects. But the Harshacharita is very much inferior to the Kādambarī as a literary work In the Harshacharita the author cares more for the jingling repetition of the same letters than in the Kādambarī. The puns are generally more laboured in the Harshacharita.

The Kādambarī is much more free from the use of provincial expressions than the Harshacharita. In the Harshacharita the author seems to have consciously employed a very large number of words that are found only in the lexicons. In the Harshacharita we never come across that subtle analysis of human nature that we meet with at every step in the Kādambarī. The characters of the Kādambarī are all of them painted with a finer brush than those in the Harshacharita. In the ease and flow of speech, in the force and vigour of thought and expression, and in the happy description of impulses, emotions and sentiments that sway human conduct, the Kādambarī vastly excels the Harshacharita. In the whole of the Harshacharita there is hardly any passage that approaches, in elegance and grace of language, in the keen observation of human nature and the springs of human action, in apt and happy sentiments, the advice of S'ukanāsa to Chandrāpîḍa or the friendly exhortation of Kapinjala to Puṇḍarîka. But the Harshacharita enjoys certain advantages over the Kādambarī. The Harshacharita is of prime importance to the historian of ancient India. It contains a mass of information on the state of ancient Indian society, on social and religious observances and practices, on military organization, on the actualities of life in camp and city, on the progress of medicine and the various arts and industries.

There is one striking point in which both the Kādambarī and the Harshacharita are similar. The hand of Death prevented the former work from being completed. The latter also comes to an abrupt conclusion. We can only speculate as to the reason why Bāṇa left only a partial account of the career of Harsha. Probably the author never intended to offer to the world a complete account of his patron's life.* Perhaps Bāṇa was swayed by the consideration that the glorious career of his patron after he re-

---

* It should be noted that Bāṇa expressed his inability to do justice to the whole of the career of Harsha and promised his cousins that he would deal only with a portion of it. 'कः खलु पुरुषायुषशतेनापि शक्नुयादविकलमस्य चरितं वर्णयितुम् । एकदेशे तु यदि कुतूहलं वः, सज्जा वयम्' 3rd उच्छ्वास.

covered his sister Rājyas'rī was very fresh in the memory of the people when he wrote and needed no words of praise from him. Bāṇa wrote the Harshacharita rather as a literary work than as a history of Harsha's reign and was satisfied when his Muse had taken a sufficiently long flight. Whatever may have been the reason, the student of Indian antiquities cannot but express his regret and mortification that the work was left incomplete.

Besides the Harshacharita, the writings of Chinese authors, particularly of Hiuen Tsang, supply reliable information about Harsha and his times. Moreover there are several inscriptions of Harsha himself and his contemporaries that shed a flood of light on the topics which the Harshacharita deals with. All this information, when put together, gives us a fairly accurate and life-like picture of the times of Harsha. But several considerations, particularly of space and utility, prevent us from entering into a detailed examination of the data furnished by the authorities indicated above. To those that desire a full treatment of this subject, we would recommend the standard work of Mr. V. A. Smith on the early History of India. All that we can endeavour to do here is to dwell upon some of the salient features of the life and career of Harsha as delineated in the Harshacharita, to note the important points of divergence between the Harshacharita and our other authorities and to supplement the information furnished by the Harshacharita from the other materials mentioned above.

VII The predecessors of Harsha.

The Harshacharita tells us that the remote ancestor of Harsha was Pushpabhūti. Between him and Prabhākaravardhana, father of Harsha, intervened several unnamed kings. The Madhuban and Banskhera copper-plates* of Harsha furnish the following genealogy:—

---

* The following is the text of the Madhuban copper-plate inscription of Harsha (See E. I. vol VII. p. 155 and also E. I. vol. I p. 67). ओम् । स्वस्ति महानौहस्त्यश्वजयस्कन्धावारात् **कपित्थिकाया:** महाराजश्री**नरवर्धन**स्तस्य पुत्रस्तत्पादानुध्यातः श्री**वज्रिणीदेव्या**मुत्पन्नः परमादित्यभक्तो महाराजश्री**राज्यवर्धन**स्तस्य पुत्रस्तत्पादानुध्यातः श्री**अप्सरोदेव्या**मुत्पन्नः परमादित्यभक्तो महाराजश्रीम**दादित्यवर्धन**स्तस्य पुत्रस्तत्पादानुध्यातः श्री**महासेनगुप्तादेव्या**मुत्पन्नश्चतुःसमुद्रातिक्रान्तकीर्तिः प्रतापानुरागोपनतान्यराजो वर्णाश्रमव्यवस्थापनप्रवृत्तचक्र एकचक्ररथ इव प्रजानामार्तिहरः परमादित्यभक्तः परमभट्टारकमहाराजाधिराज-

श्री**प्रभाकरवर्धन**स्तस्य पुत्रस्तत्पादानुध्यातः सितयशःप्रतानविच्छुरितसकलभुवनमण्डलः परिगृहीतधनदवरुणेन्द्रप्रभृतिलोकपालतेजाः सत्पथोपार्जितानेकद्रविणभूमिप्रदानसंप्रीणितार्थिहृदयोऽतिशयितपूर्वराजचरितो देव्याममलयशोमत्यां श्री**यशोमत्या**मुत्पन्नः परमसौगतः सुगत इव परहितैकरतः परमभट्टारकमहाराजाधिराजश्री**राज्यवर्धनः**

राजानो युधि दुष्टवाजिन इव श्री**देवगुप्ता**दयः
कृत्वा येन कशाप्रहारविमुखाः सर्वे समं संयताः ।
उत्खाय द्विषतो विजित्य वसुधां कृत्वा प्रजानां प्रियं
प्राणानुज्झितवानरातिभवने सत्यानुरोधेन यः ॥

तस्यानुजस्तत्पादानुध्यातः परममाहेश्वरो महेश्वर इव सर्वसत्त्वानुकम्पी परमभट्टारकमहाराजाधिराजश्री**हर्षः श्रावस्तीभुक्तौ कुण्डधानी**वैषयिक**सोमकुण्डका**ग्रामे समुपगतान् महासामन्त—महाराज—दौःसाधसाधनिक—प्रमातार—राजस्थानीय—कुमारामात्योपरिक—विषयपति—भटचाटसेवकादीन् प्रतिवासिजनपदांश्च समाज्ञापयति । अस्तु वः संविदितम् । अयं **सोमकुण्डका**ग्रामो ब्राह्मणवामरथ्येन कूटशासनेन भुक्तक इति विचार्य यतस्तच्छासनं भङ्क्त्वा तस्मादाक्षिप्य च स्वसीमापर्यन्तः सोद्रङ्गः सर्वराजकुलाभाव्यप्रत्यायसमेतः सर्वपरिहृतपरिहारो विषयादुद्धृतपिण्डः पुत्रपौत्रानुगश्चन्द्रार्कक्षितिसमकालीनो भूमिच्छिद्रन्यायेन मया पितुः परमभट्टारकमहाराजाधिराजश्री**प्रभाकरवर्धनदेवस्य** मातुः परमभट्टारिकामहादेवीराज्ञीश्री**यशोमतीदेव्याः** ज्येष्ठभ्रातृपरमभट्टारकमहाराजाधिराजश्री**राज्यवर्धनदेव**पादानां च पुण्ययशोभिवृद्धये सावर्णिसगोत्रच्छन्दोगसब्रह्मचारिभट्टवातस्वामि—विष्णुवृद्धसगोत्रबह्वृचसब्रह्मचारि-भट्टशिवदेवस्वामिभ्यां प्रतिग्रहधर्मणाग्रहारत्वेन प्रतिपादितः । विदित्वा भवद्भिः समनुमन्तव्यः प्रतिवासिजनपदैरप्याज्ञाश्रवणविधेयैर्भूत्वा यथासमुचिततुल्यमेयभागभोगकरहिरण्यादिप्रत्याया अनयोरेवोपनेयाः सेवोपस्थानं च करणीयमिति । अपि च

अस्मत्कुलक्रममुदारमुदाहरद्भिरन्यैश्च दानमिदमभ्यनुमोदनीयम् ।
लक्ष्म्यास्तडित्सलिलबुद्बुदचञ्चलाया दानं फलं परयशःपरिपालनं च ॥
कर्मणा मनसा वाचा कर्तव्यं प्राणिने हितम् ।
हर्षेणैतत्समाख्यातं धर्मार्जनमनुत्तमम् ॥

दूतकोऽत्र महाप्रमातार-महासामन्त-श्री**स्कन्दगुप्तः** महाक्षपटलाधिकरणाधिकृतसामन्तमहाराजेश्वरगुप्तसमादेशाच्चोत्कीर्णं गर्जरेण (गुर्जरेण?) । संवत् २० ५ मार्गशीर्ष वदि ६. The Banskhera plate of Harsha (see E. I. vol. IV p. 208 ff) contains the same details as above, except the following:—The charter is issued from Vardhamānakoṭî; the donees are Bālachandra, a Rigvedin of the Bharadvājagotra and Bhadrasvāmin, a Sāmavedin; the village granted is Markaṭasāgara, which was in the *Bhukti* of Ahichchhatrā and in the western *Pathaka* of the Angadîya *Vishaya*; the keeper of the records is one Bhāna or Bhānu and the concluding words are 'उत्कीर्णमीश्वरेणेदमिति संवत् २० २ कार्ति वदि १ स्वहस्तो मम महाराजाधिराजश्रीहर्षस्य ।'.

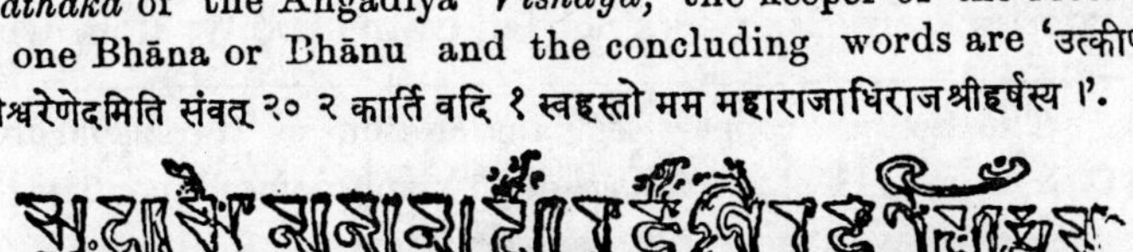

स्व ह स्तो म म म हा रा जा धि रा ज श्री ह र्ष स्य

Autograph of Harsha from the Banskhera plate.

Naravardhana=Vajriṇîdevî
|
Rājyavardhana=Apsarodevī
|
Âdityavardhana=Mahāsenaguptā
|
Prabhākaravardhana=Yas'omatī
|
Rājyavardhana | Harsha | Rājyas'rī

Hiuen Tsang begins with Prabhākaravardhana and informs us that Rājyavardhana was the elder brother of Harsha.* Bāṇa tells us that Harsha's ancestors ruled at Sthāṇvîs'vara (modern Thanesar), while Hiuen Tsang makes Kānyakubja the capital of Harsha.† The explanation probably lies in this fact that when Hiuen Tsang visited Harsha (which was about 643 A. D.), Kānyakubja was one of the capitals of Harsha's vast empire. When Rājyas'ri's husband Grahavarman was killed and she became a Buddhist nun, Harsha might have taken over the kingdom of Kanoj and made the latter his capital as being more in the centre of his dominions than Thanesar.

Hiuen Tsang tells us that the family of Harsha belonged to the Vais'ya caste. It has been rightly pointed out that the learned Chinese traveller confounds the third of the four principal castes with the Bais clan of Rajputs (who were Kshatriyas).‡ Bâṇa nowhere gives the slightest hint that the family of Harsha was not of Kshatriya descent. There are moreover indications to the contrary. Harsha's sister was married to Grahavarman, who came of the ancient Kshatriya family of the Maukharis (for whom see below). Prabhākaravardhana was the son of Mahāsenaguptā, who seems to have been the sister of Mahāsenagupta of Magadha. Unfortunately Bāṇa does not tell us the family from which

The Sonpat copper seal inscription of Harshavardhana (C. I. I. vol. III p. 231 ff), though much defaced, confirms the statements made in the two copperplates.

* See B. R. W. W. vol. I p. 210.

† B. R. W. W. vol. I p. 209.

‡ B. R. W. W. Vol. I p. 209 n. 12.

Harsha's mother came. Dr. Hoernle* thinks that her very name indicates that Yas'omatî must have been the daughter of the famous king of Mālava, Yas'odharma Vikramāditya. One fails to see how her very name shows that she was the daughter of Yas'odharman. Some support may be lent to the conjecture of Dr. Hoernle by the words of Yas'omatî that she was born in a family 'rendered glorious by Dharma'.† It further appears from certain words in the Harshacharita that Yas'omatî's father was a mighty warrior and that her parents were living at the time of her death.‡

The kingdom of Thanesar must not originally have been very large. It was surrounded on all sides by petty states, which waged constant wars among themselves. There is small wonder in this. Even Great Britain, which is such a small country, was divided only a few centuries ago into three kingdoms the rulers of which indulged in sanguinary feuds on the slightest pretexts. The inscriptions of Harsha style his ancestors (except Prabhākaravardhana) 'mahārāja'. It is only Prabhākaravardhana who is styled 'Mahārājādhirāja' which was one of the *birudas* of an aspirant for universal sovereignty. The Harshacharita informs us that Prabhākaravardhana fought successfully against the Hûṇas, the kings of Sindhu, Gurjara, Gāndhāra, Lāṭa (Bróach) and Mālava. The conquest of the Hûṇas, if effected by Prabhâkaravardhana, must have been very perfunctory, as, a short time before his death, he had to send Râjyavardhana against them.

When Râjyavardhana came to the throne he must have been a very young man (about 19 or 20). We are told in the Harshacharita that the elder of the two Gupta princes named Kumāragupta, who was a companion of Rājyavardhana and Harsha, was about 18 years old. So Rājyavardhana was also of the same age at the time. Further we see that when Rājyavardhana returned after vanquishing

* See J. R. A. S. for 1903 p. 556.

† 'धर्मधवले कुले जाता' text p. 30 (5th उच्छ्वास).

‡ 'वीरजा वीरजाया &c.' text p. 30; 'अम्ब तात न पश्यतं पापां परलोकप्रस्थितां माम् &c.' same page.

the Hûṇas, there was a slight growth of hair on his chin. Harsha was the junior of Rājyavardhana by about four years and Rājyasrî was younger by about six years than her eldest brother. So Harsha and Rājyasrî were respectively about sixteen and fourteen years old when their father died. This is confirmed by the fact that Harsha is in several places* spoken of as '*Bāla*' and Rājyas'rî as 'Bālā.'† It seems that Prabhâkaravardhana died in 605 A. D. and therefore it follows that Harsha was born about 590 A. D. and ascended the throne in 606 A. D.‡ From the astronomical data furnished by Bāṇa about the birth of Harsha, Mr. C.V.Vaidya shows that Harsha was born on 4th June 590 A. D.§ Grahavarmā, the husband of Rājyas'rî, was killed by a king of Mālava. Who this Mālava king was is not quite clear. We are told in the Harshacharita that Rājyavardhana marched against this king with a small but picked force of cavalry under Bhaṇḍin and utterly routed him. In the inscriptions of Harsha we read that Rājyavardhana vanquished a certain king named Devagupta. As Rājyavardhana died very young he could not have waged many wars. Buhler conjectured with great probability that it was this Devagupta that had killed Grahavarman and was therefore chastised by Rājyavardhana. This conjecture is to some extent supported by the fact that the Harshacharita mentions a certain Gupta as having seized Kānyakubja.$ Dr Hoernle does not approve of the conjecture of Buhler. ¶ There are no doubt difficulties in the way of Buhler's guess. The two companions of Harsha and his elder brother are Mālava princes. Harsha is represented in the Harshacharita as very intimate with the younger of the two Mālava princes *viz.* Mâdhavagupta. ‖ In another place we find Harsha talking to 'the son of the

* See text p. 42 'यदि बाल इति नितरां तर्हि न परित्याज्योऽस्मि'; p. 56 'बाल एवाखण्डलभूमिमारूढः'; p. 85 'इयं नः स्वसा बाला च बहुदुःखखेदिता च.'

† See V. A. Smith's Early History of India p. 312 (2nd edition).

‡ See above p. IV.

§ See J. B. B. R. A. S. vol. 24 pp. 252–254.

$ See text p. 67 'गुप्तनाम्ना गृहीते कुशस्थले'.

¶ J. R. A. S. 1903 p. 561.

‖ See text p. 72 'अवलम्ब्य दक्षिणेन हस्तेन च माधवगुप्तमंसे'.

Mālava king that sat behind (Harsha)'.* So then it could not have been possible that these two princes were in any way related to the Mālava king that killed Grahavarmā. If they had been, they would naturally have been objects of suspicion rather than of trust. It is to be noted that Rājyas'rî is let off from imprisonment by a *certain noble* called Gupta.. † It is remarkable that he is not designated 'Rājaputra' or 'Rāja' but only 'Kulaputra.' So obviously he is not the king of Mālava that killed Grahavarmā nor can he be one of the two Gupta princes, the companions of Harsha, that were 'Rājaputras.' If it was Devagupta that killed Grahavarmā, he could not have been the same as the Mahārājādhirāja Devagupta of Magadha, whose approximate dates according to Dr. Fleet are 680–700 A. D. (see Deo Baranark Inscription pp. 213, 215) and who was the maternal grand-father of the Vākāṭaka king Pravarasena II (*vide* Chammak and Sivani copperplate inscriptions in C. I. vol. III pp. 240 and 247).

Rājyavardhana, young and confiding, was treacherously murdered, according to the Harshacharita, by a Gauḍa king. One MS. of the Harshacharita calls him Narendragupta. ‡ The commentator of the Harshacharita tells us that his name was S'as'ānka. He is corroborated by the statement of Hiuen Tsang that She-shang-kia (S'as'ānka) king of Karṇasuvarṇa (Bengal) murdered Rājyavardhana. § Bāṇa perhaps purposely omitted the express mention of the murderer of the reigning emperor's elder brother.$ But there are passages containing veiled allusions to the name S'as'ānka which we have pointed out in the notes (see *e. g.* text p. 38).

VIII The accession of Harsha and his relations with his contemporaries.

Bāṇa tells us that Harsha quietly ascended the throne

* 'पृष्ठतो निषण्णस्य मालवराजसूनोरकथयत्' 2nd उच्छ्वास.

† 'कान्यकुब्जाद्गौडसंभ्रमे गुप्तितो गुप्तनाम्ना कुलपुत्रेण निष्कासनम्' text p. 81.

‡ See E. I. vol. I. p. 70.

§ B. R. W. W. vol. I. p. 210.

$ Note the verse 'आत्मनाम गुरोर्नाम नामातिकृपणस्य च । श्रेयस्कामो न गृह्णीयाज्ज्येष्ठापत्यकलत्रयोः ॥'.

after the murder of his elder brother. But Hiuen Tsang has surrounded the accession of Harsha in an atmosphere of mystery and suspicion. We are told that the minister Bhaṇḍī asked the ministers to choose Harsha as king and that they accepted his advice; but Harsha had his own scruples and wanted to consult a statue of Avalokites'vara Bodhisattva on the Ganges before accepting the crown offered to him.* It is this account that leads Mr. V. A. Smith to remark that 'some unknown obstacle stood in the way of Harsha's accession and compelled him to rely for his title to the crown upon election by the nobles rather than upon his hereditary claims'.† We believe that the story was probably invented by the Buddhist admirers of Harsha to show that the latter was under the particular care of the Bodhisattva Avalokites'vara. We know from the Harshacharita that Bhaṇḍī, instead of being merely a great minister as Hiuen Tsang says, was a first cousin, being the mother's brother's son of Harsha and a very intimate friend. Bhaṇḍī was about eight years of age when Rājyas'rī was born and was thus slightly senior to Rājyavardhana. After ascending the throne Harsha started on his brilliant career of conquest and within a few years (about six) made himself the overlord of the whole of Northern India including Gujarat from the Himālayas to the Narmadā and from the bay of Bengal to Sindh. He had a long reign of about forty-two years and may fitly be styled the last Hindu Emperor of Northern India.

The Harshacharita contains a few references to these conquests. We are told in the third Uchchhvāsa that he vanquished the king of Sindhu and that he levied tribute from the Himālayan territory which is difficult of access.‡ On his relations with the Guptas we have already made a few remarks above. It seems that Harsha crowned Kumāragupta,§ the elder of the two Mālava princes, the companions

---

* See B. R. W. W. vol. I pp. 211-213.

† See Early History of India p. 312 (2nd edition).

‡ 'अत्र पुरुषोत्तमेन सिन्धुराजं प्रमथ्य लक्ष्मीरात्मीकृता।...अत्र परमेश्वरेण तुषारशैलभुवो दुर्गाया गृहीतः करः'.

§ 'अत्र देवेनाभिषिक्तः कुमारः' 3rd उच्छ्वास and com. thereon.

of his boyhood. What became of this Kumāragupta we do not know. We saw above that the younger of the two Mālava princes, Mādhavagupta, was in high favour with Harsha. The Aphsad stone Inscription speaks of Mādhavagupta of Magadha who was anxious to meet the glorious Harsha.* The former was most probably the same as the favourite companion of Harsha's early years. Further particulars of the Guptas of Magadha may be learnt from Dr. Fleet's Gupta Inscriptions (pp. 200–218).† Another royal family with whom Harsha came in close contact was the Maukhari. His sister Rājyas'rî was married to Grahavarmā, son of Avantivarman. His capital was Kānyakubja. Bāṇa intimates that the Maukhari family was very ancient and highly honoured and that the Maukharis were great devotees of S'iva. ‡ Particulars of the Maukhari kings and their genealogy will be found in Dr. Fleet's Gupta Inscriptions pp. 219–230. The Maukharis and the Guptas of Magadha went often to war.§ The Harshacharita tells us that Kumāra alias Bhāskaravarman, king of Prāgjyotisha (Assam), formed a close friendship with Harsha on the eve of the latter's career of world conquest. Hiuen Tsang confirms this and tells us how once Harsha followed on the southern bank of the Ganges towards Kanoj while Kumāra-rāja kept pace with him on the northern. $

Harsha's glorious career of conquest suffered one memorable check. Pulakes'in II, the greatest of the

* See C. I. vol. III p. 200, 204 'श्रीहर्षदेवनिजसङ्गमवाञ्छया च.'

† Bāṇa says that one of his ancestors was honoured by several Guptas 'अनेकगुप्तार्चितपादपङ्कजः कुबेरनामांश इव स्वयम्भुवः' Introductory verses to the Kādambarî.

‡ The correct form seems to be मौखरि. Mark 'नमामि भर्वोश्चरणाम्बुजद्वयं सशेखरैर्मौखरिभिः कृतार्चनम् ।' Introductory verses to काद०. The Asirgad copper seal of S'arvavarman uses the words 'शर्ववर्मा मौखरिः' (C. I. vol. III. p. 220). But the Jaunpur stone inscription of ईश्वरवर्मन् sanctions the form मौखर 'मौखराणां भूभुजाम्' (C. I. vol. III p. 229).

§ See *e. g.* Aphsad Stone Inscription (C. I. vol. III p. 200, 203).

$ B. R. W. W. vol. I pp. 217–218; see also vol. II pp. 196–198, where Hiuen Tsang relates how he went to the court of Kāmarūpa.

Chālukyas of Badami, became the overlord of the Deccan south of the Narmadā, as Harsha had become emperor of Northern India. Harsha wanted to break down his supremacy but failed. * The Chālukya emperor claims to have inflicted a crushing defeat on the emperor Harsha. †

Harsha established an era of his own which commenced in 606 A. D. Several inscriptions dated in this era have been recovered. ‡ This is not the place to go into that question. We may mention that Alberuni's account of this era is most confusing. He says that the era of Harsha is used in Mathurā and the country of Kanoj, that between S'rîharsha and Vikramāditya there is an interval of four hundred years; but that according to the Kashmirian calendar the era of S'rîharsha was 664 years later than Vikramāditya. §

IX Harsha as a poet and a patron of literature.

Not only was Harsha great as a conqueror and ruler, but he is an author of considerable distinction. We have discussed above the question of the authorship of the Ratnāvali and come to the conclusion that it is the work of Harsha. This is not the place to enter upon a critical examination of the three plays of Harsha. It may be said that they do not show the highest flights of imagination and fancy and are much inferior to the masterpieces of Kālidāsa and Bhavabhūti. They have however a peculiar simplicity, correctness and charm which have endeared them to the writers of works on dramaturgy. In the Nāgānanda, the author takes up the story of Jîmûtavāhana famous in Buddhist legend.

---

* See B. R. W. W. vol. II pp. 256–257 and Mr. V. A. Smith's Early History of India p. 313.

† Note the verse 'अपरिमितविभूतिस्फीतसामन्तसेनामकुटमणिमयूखाक्रान्तपादारविन्दः । युधि पतितगजेन्द्रानीकबीभत्सभूतो भयविगलितहर्षो येन चाकारि हर्षः ॥' E. I. vol. 6 p. 6 and I. A. vol. VIII p. 242; I.A. vol. VI p. 76 'समरसंसक्तसकलोत्तरापथेश्वरश्रीहर्षवर्धनपराजयोपलब्धपरमेश्वरापरनामधेयस्य सत्याश्रयश्रीपृथिवीवल्लभमहाराजाधिराजपरमेश्वरस्य प्रियतनयः.' At p. 86 the words 'समर...नामधेयः' recur. In I. A. vol. VIII p. 13 सत्याश्रय is spoken of as 'जेतुर्दिशां विजितहर्षमहानृपस्य.'

‡ See I. A. vol. 26 p. 32 and E. I. vol. V Appendix p. 73 ff

§ Vide Alberuni (ed. by Sachau) vol. II p. 5 (Trubner) and Cunningham's Indian Eras pp. 64–65.

Besides these three plays Harsha is credited by some with the authorship of the Suprabhāta stotra (for which see Appendix B) and the Ashṭamahās'rîchaityastotra. But in the Tibetan Tanjur and in Minayeff's MSS. the former is ascribed to king Harshadeva of Kashmir.* In the Madhuban inscription a verse composed by Harsha is quoted and it is not unlikely that the verse about Rājyavardhana is Harsha's own composition. Kshîrasvāmin in his commentary on the Amarakos'a † quotes a lexicographer S'rîharsha. The Subhāshitāvali cites a verse of S'rîharshadeva which is not found in his extant works. ‡ In the Prasannarāghava of Jayadeva (I. 22) Harsha is styled the 'joy of poesy'. Harsha, as has been usual with almost all great Indian kings, was a patron of literature. His munificence was enjoyed by poets like Bāṇa, Mayûra and Mātangadivâkara. The Subhâshitâvali quotes a verse of Mayûra in which a certain unnamed king is praised. § It is not unlikely that the king referred to is Harsha. The commentary on the Kāvyaprakās'a called Sârasamuchchaya praises the liberality of Harsha towards Bâṇa. $

X. The State of religious beliefs under Harsha.

There are several points of interest on which a close study of the Harshacharita yields valuable information; but for want of space we pass them over. It would however be improper not to say a few words on the state of religion under Harsha.

Our authorities show that there were three competing

---

* *Vide* J. R. A. S. for 1903 p. 704

† 'सङ्घातमृत्युर्मरकं मारिर्मारी च देवतेति **श्रीहर्पः**' on 'आतुरोऽभ्यमितोऽभ्यान्तः'.

‡ No. 233 'अशठमलोलमजिह्मं त्यागिनमनुरागिणं विशेपज्ञम् । यदि नाश्रयति नरं श्रीः श्रीरेव हि वञ्चिता तत्र ॥'. The same verse is No. 470 in the शार्ङ्गधरपद्धति, but the author is not specified.

§ No. 2515 'भूपालाः शशिभास्करान्वयभुवः के नाम नासादिता भर्तारं पुनरेकमेव हि भुवस्त्वां देव मन्यामहे । येनाङ्गं परिमृष्य कुन्तलमथाकृष्य व्युदस्यायतं चोलं प्राप्य च मध्यदेशमधुना काञ्च्यां करः पातितः ॥'. It will be noticed that the words अङ्ग, कुन्तल, चोल, मध्यदेश and काञ्ची are paronomastic.

$ 'हेम्नो भारशतानि वा मदमुचां वृन्दानि वा दन्तिनां श्रीहर्षेण समर्पितानि कवये बाणाय कुत्राद्य तत् । या बाणेन तु तस्य सूक्तिनिकरैरुट्टङ्किताः कीर्तयस्ताः कल्पप्रलयेऽपि यान्ति न मनाङ्मन्ये परिम्लानताम् ॥.'

religions in the times of Harsha, viz. Brahmanism, Buddhism and Jainism. Of these the last (particularly the Digambara sect of it) does not appear to have been popular in Northern India. The sight of a naked Jain ascetic is cited as a very bad omen.* The two other religions were in a flourishing state. It should not be supposed that ordinarily Buddhism was looked upon by orthodox Hindus as something to be abhorred. On the contrary Bāṇa everywhere speaks of things Buddhist with fairness and tolerance.† People passed from one persuasion to the other without much fear of persecution. So Divākaramitra is represented as originally being a student of the Maitrāyaṇîya recension of the Yajurveda and as passing over to Buddhism while still young. In spite of his Buddhistic predilections, he is waited upon by persons of various shades of opinions and beliefs, such as S'aivas, Bhāgavatas, Jainas, Paurāṇikas, Mîmāṇsakas, all intent upon arriving at the truth in the giddy whirlpool of opposing doctrines. Bāṇa, though himself an orthodox Brahmin writer, does not gloss over the fact that Rājyavardhana had strong leanings in favour of Buddhism. The companions of Rājyas'rî are represented as invoking the Buddha in their distress.‡ Bāṇa makes even Harsha say that he would don the red robes of the Buddhist order along with his sister after he had fulfilled his vow.§ Harsha describes in his inscription his brother Rājyavardhana as a very devout Buddhist (Paramasaugataḥ) and speaks of him more reverently than even his own father. The inscriptions of Harsha show that even in the royal family there was no strict adherence to a particular deity or form of faith. The three immediate ancestors of Harsha are described as great devotees of the sun (Paramādityabhaktaḥ). Bāṇa tells us that Pushpabhūti, the remote ancestor of Harsha, was a devout worshipper of S'iva.$ But Bāṇa himself describes how Prabhākara-

* *Vide* text p. 20 'अभिमुखमाजगाम शिखिपिच्छलाञ्छनो नग्नाटकः.'

† See *e. g.* text p. 78 ll 4–7.

‡ भगवन् भक्तजने सञ्वरिणि **सुगत** सुप्तोऽसि' text p. 79.

§ 'इयं तु ग्रहीष्यति मयैव समं समाप्तकृत्येन काषायाणि' text p. 85.

$ 'तस्य...सहजैव...अन्यदेवताविमुखी...भगवति...भवे भूयसी भक्तिरभूत्' 3rd उच्छ्वास.

vardhana everyday devoutly worshipped the sun with red flowers. Harsha calls himself a devout worshipper of S'iva (Paramamāhes'varaḥ). The Sonpat seal of Harsha has the emblem of a Nandī. Bāṇa informs us that Harsha set out on his expedition after worshipping S'iva* and that the head accountant of the village where Harsha put up on the first day presented a golden seal with the crest of a bull. From these data one may say that between Brahmin and Buddhist and between the devotee of one deity and that of another there did not exist that great gulf which minds brought up in other environments are apt to suppose as having existed. There were certain root-ideas, certain habits of thought and modes of life, that were common to all. Coming to matters of detail, we find that Prabhākaravardhana celebrated many and elaborate sacrifices.† In describing the houses of his cousins, Bāṇa gives us an instructive picture of their surroundings in the 7th century A. D.‡ When Harsha made fun of Bāṇa by dwelling upon the wild years of his youth, Bāṇa in self-defence mentioned several things which entitled him to be better treated by the king.§ On his return from the court of Harsha, Bāṇa questions his kinsmen on matters that were vital to the Brahmins of his day, viz. the performances of sacrifices. the incessant study of the Vedas, of grammar, logic, the Mīmāṇsā and poetry. Bāṇa tells us that Paurāṇikas were as popular in those days as in these. His friend Sudṛishṭi treated him to a recital of the Vāyupurāṇa. We are told that Paurāṇikas clever in comforting those striken with grief surrounded Harsha after the death of his father. From the Kādambarī we learn that then as now the Mahābhārata was a favourite book with all, especially with women. The Harshacharita also dwells upon the popularity of the great

---

* 'विरच्य्य परमया भक्त्या भगवतो नीललोहितस्यार्चाम्' text p. 53.

† Vide text pp. 2 and 38.

‡ Note the first paragraph of the 2nd उच्छ्वास.

§ 'ब्राह्मणोऽस्मि जातः सोमपायिनां वंशे वात्स्यायनानाम् । यथाकालमुपनयनादयः कृताः संस्काराः । सम्यक्पठितः साङ्गो वेदः । श्रुतानि यथाशक्ति शास्त्राणि । दारपरिग्रहादभ्यागारिकोऽस्मि ।...लोकद्वयाविरोधिभिस्तु चापलैः शैशवमशून्यमासीत् । अत्रानपलापोऽस्मि ।' 2nd उच्छ्वास.

epic.* The description of the rites performed when Prabhâkaravardhana was on his deathbed, though somewhat weird, shows us what popular Hindu religious practices and observances were in the 7th century A. D.† When Bâṇa started on his visit to Harsha, he gives us a graphic and entertaining description of the way in which an orthodox Brahmin should make preparations to leave his home on an important undertaking. The long and rather curious list of the companions of Bâṇa in his youth (p. III above) shows us with what a strange medley of people an orthodox Brâhmaṇa could associate without running any serious risk of losing caste or position. It is to be noted that two of his most intimate associates were his cousins born of a S'ûdra mother. We may draw the attention of the student to the elaborate descriptions of the festivities on the birth of Harsha‡ and the marriage of Rājyas'rī. §

Hiuen Tsang dwells at great length on the condition of religion in the times of Harsha. He mentions that towards the end of his career Harsha became a very devout Buddhist and once in every five years he held a great assembly when he emptied his treasury to give away all in charity. $ We hope that the student of the Harshacharita will not fail to read the curious incidents and ancedotes that the Chinese traveller relates conecrning Harsha.

XI. The text of the Harshacharita.

The present edition is based on three editions of the Harshacharita, *viz.* the Nirṇayasāgara edition, that in the Bombay Sanskrit Series and the Calcutta edition of Is'varachandra. The first and third agree closely. The edition of Dr. Fuhrer contains in the footnotes very valuable material derived from eight MSS. We do not follow any particular edition. All important readings have been discussed in the notes. In a few cases the punctuation is wrong in the text, but has been corrected in the notes.

---

* 'महाभारतभावितात्मानः' 3rd उच्छ्वास; 'कस्य न द्वितीयमहाभारते भत्रेदस्य चरिते कुतूहलम्' 3rd उच्छ्वास; 'विविधवीररसवृत्तान्तरामणीयकेन महाभारतमपि लघयन्निव' text p. 45.

† *Vide* text p. 21.

‡ Text pp. 7–9.

§ Text pp. 13–14.

$ B. R. W. W. Vol. I. pp. 214–215.

XII. Commentaries.

The only commentary available is the Sanketa written by S'ankara. The commentary so far as it goes is very valuable, particularly in the explanation of obscure words and puns. But it is very often meagre and passes over whole pages with scarcely a word of comment. So we did not include it in our edition. We know very little concerning the age or native place of the commentator. As the commentary has only been found in Kashmir, it is not unreasonable to suppose that S'ankara was a native of Kashmir. His father's name was Puṇyākara and he invokes Ganes'a at the beginning of his work. Among the authors and works named by him are:—Amarasiṃha, Kālidāsa, Kātyāyana author of the Vārtikas, Kṛishṇa (a Prakrit poet), Kauṭilya, Gāruḍas'āstra, Chāṇakya, Bharatamuni, Bhāmaha, Manu, Mahābhārata, Rājas'ekhara, Lāṭāchārya (an astronomical writer), Vātsyāyana (author of Kāmasūtra), Vyāḍi (author of the grammatical work Saṃgraha). Among the works from which quotations are taken without specifying the author are (besides those mentioned above):—Kāvyālaṃkâra of Udbhaṭa, Dhvanyâloka, Bhagavatgîtā, Meghadūta, Raghuvaṃs'a. The commentator very frequently refers to previous commentators in the words 'kechit', 'anye', 'apare' &c. At the end of his commentary S'ankara tells us that he follows tradition in explaining the difficult Harshacharita.* Hence it is clear that he was preceded by a number of commentaries.

As to the age of the commentator, we can give only an approximate result. As he either names or quotes from Rājas'ekhara, Udbhaṭa and the Dhvanyāloka, he is later than the 9th century A. D. But he is comparatively an early writer. One of the Mss of the commentary was, we are told by Dr. Fuhrer, dated Saṃvat 1520 i. e. 1464 A. D. if it is the Vikrama era to which the date refers, as is likely Besides the fact that, instead of quoting such eminent Âlaṃkārikas as Mammaṭa and Ruyyaka (both Kashmirians), he quotes the ancient Kashmirian rhetoricians Bhāmaha and

---

* 'दुर्बोधे हर्षचरिते संप्रदायानुरोधतः। गूढार्थोन्मुद्रणां चक्रे शङ्करो विदुषां कृते ॥'.

Udbhaṭa goes to strengthen the view that he was an early writer. He may therefore have flourished before the 12th century A. D.

It is to be noted that S'ankara cites a few vernacular words in explaining the Harshacharita. These may furnish some clue to his nationality.*

It appears that Ruyyaka, the famous author of the Alaṃkārasarvasva, wrote a commentary on the Harshacharita called Harshacharitavārtika.† The author of the commentary on the Vyaktiviveka of Mahimabhaṭṭa, who is generally regarded to be the same as Ruyyaka, also refers to his own commentary on the Harshacharita called Harshacharitavārtika.‡ It is a pity that this ancient commentary on the Harshacharita by so able and eminent a critic as Ruyyaka has not yet been brought to light. If it ever comes to light, it will be of great help in explaining many of the difficulties in the Harshacharita and in settling the text which is very corrupt in several places.

XIII The plan of the Notes.

The method adopted in the notes is as follows:—First of all a long passage is taken and is split up into clauses. Each difficult clause in then translated. In order to indicate clearly the meanings of words, Sanskrit words are often enclosed in brackets after their English equivalents. If a clause be difficult, the idea is expanded and clearly explained. Difficult compounds occurring in that clause are dissolved, quotations from kos'as such as that of Amarasiṃha are cited, references to mythology are dealt with at length and difficult words are traced to their origin. All grammatical peculiarities have been carefully noted. Parallel passages from the author's work or from the works of other authors

---

* *e. g.* on the word गुञ्जा he remarks 'सन्ना इति यस्य प्रसिद्धिः' notes p. 168; on प्रौढिक he says 'योग्याशनार्थं प्रसेवकः यो बुक्कण इति प्रसिद्धः'; on लम्बापटहाः he says 'तमिला इति प्रसिद्धाः' notes p. 175.

† p. 61 of अलङ्कारसर्वस्व. *Vide* p. VI above.

‡ 'एतदस्माभिर्हर्षचरितवार्तिके विस्तृत्य प्रतिपादितं तत एवावसेयम्' p. 44 of the commentary of the व्यक्तिविवेक (Trivandrum Sanskrit series).

are given to further elucidate the meaning. Bold type has been employed in the notes to draw attention to important citations. Only easy passages have not been fully translated.

XIV The Appendices.

The first appendix contains an abstract of the Harsha-charita. The second appendix contains the Suprabhâta-stotra. The third appendix is a general index dealing with proper names, mythological references, information of general interest and other kindred matters occurring in the notes.

हर्षचरितम् ।

प्रथम उच्छ्वासः ।

[1]नमस्तुङ्गशिरश्चुम्बिचन्द्रचामरचारवे ।
त्रैलोक्यनगरारम्भमूलस्तम्भाय शम्भवे ॥ १ ॥
हरकण्ठग्रहानन्दमीलिताक्षीं नमाम्युमाम् ।
कालकूटविषस्पर्शजातमूर्छागमामिव ॥ २ ॥
नमः सर्वविदे तस्मै व्यासाय कविवेधसे ।
चक्रे पुण्यं सरस्वत्या यो वर्षमिव भारतम् ॥ ३ ॥
प्रायः कुकवयो लोके रागाधिष्ठितदृष्टयः ।
कोकिला इव जायन्ते वाचालाः कामकारिणः ॥ ४ ॥
सन्ति श्वान इवासंख्या जातिभाजो गृहे गृहे ।
उत्पादका न बहवः कवयः शरभा इव ॥ ५ ॥
अन्यवर्णपरावृत्त्या बन्धचिह्ननिगूहनैः ।
अनाख्यातः सतां मध्ये कविश्चौरो विभाव्यते ॥ ६ ॥
श्लेषप्रायमुदीच्येषु प्रतीच्येष्वर्थमात्रकम् ।
उत्प्रेक्षा दाक्षिणात्येषु गौडेष्वक्षरडम्बरः[2] ॥ ७ ॥
नवोऽर्थो जातिरग्राम्या श्लेषोऽक्लिष्टः स्फुटो रसः ।
विकटाक्षरबन्धश्च कृत्स्नमेकत्र दुष्करम् ॥ ८ ॥
किं कवेस्तस्य काव्येन सर्ववृत्तान्तगामिनी ।
कथेव भारती यस्य न [3]व्याप्नोति जगत्त्रयम् ॥ ९ ॥
उच्छ्वासान्तेऽप्यखिन्नास्ते येषां वक्त्रे सरस्वती ।
कथमाख्यायिकाकारा न ते वन्द्याः कवीश्वराः ॥ १० ॥
कवीनामगलद्दर्पो नूनं वासवदत्तया ।
शक्त्येव पाण्डुपुत्राणां गतया कर्णगोचरम् ॥ ११ ॥

---

१ अस्मात्प्राक् 'इच्छादिशक्तिनिचयप्रसरक्रमेण विश्वावभासनविधौ प्रथितप्रभावा। याध्यायिनां हृदयकोकनदप्रतिष्ठा रूपं प्रकाशयति नौमि सरस्वतीं ताम्' इत्ययं श्लोको ब-पुस्तके दृश्यते. २ 'डम्बरम्' ब. ३ 'प्राप्नोति दिगन्तरम्' क.

पदबन्धोज्ज्वलो हारी कृतवर्णक्रमस्थितिः ।
भट्टारहरिचन्द्रस्य गद्यबन्धो नृपायते ॥ १२ ॥
अविनाशिनमग्राम्यमकरोत्सातवाहनः ।
विशुद्धजातिभिः कोशं रत्नैरिव सुभाषितैः ॥ १३ ॥
कीर्तिः प्रवरसेनस्य प्रयाता कुमुदोज्ज्वला ।
सागरस्य परं पारं कपिसेनेव सेतुना ॥ १४ ॥
सूत्रधारकृतारम्भैर्नाटकैर्बहुभूमिकैः ।
सपताकैर्यशो लेभे भासो देवकुलैरिव ॥ १५ ॥
निर्गतासु न वा कस्य कालिदासस्य सूक्तिषु ।
प्रीतिर्मधुरसान्द्रा[1]सु मञ्जरीष्विव जायते ॥ १६ ॥
समुद्दीपितकन्दर्पा कृतगौरीप्रसाधना ।
हरलीलेव नो कस्य विस्मयाय बृहत्कथा ॥ १७ ॥
आढ्यराजकृतोत्साहैर्हृदयस्थैः स्मृतैरपि ॥
जिह्वान्तः कृष्यमाणेव न कवित्वे प्रवर्तते ॥ १८ ॥
तथापि नृपतेर्भक्त्याभीतो निर्वहणाकुलः ।
करोम्याख्यायिकाम्भोधौ जिह्वाप्लवनचापलम् ॥ १९ ॥
सुखप्रबोधललिता सुवर्णघटनोज्ज्वलैः ।
शब्दैराख्यायिका भाति शय्येव प्रतिपादकैः ॥ २० ॥
जयति ज्वलत्प्रतापज्वलनप्राकारकृतजगद्रक्षः ।
सकलप्रणयिमनोरथसिद्धिश्रीपर्वतो हर्षः ॥ २१ ॥

एवमनुश्रूयते—पुरा किल भगवान्स्वलोकमधितिष्ठन्परमेष्ठी विकासिनि पद्मविष्टरे समुपविष्टः सुनासीरप्रमुखैर्गीर्वाणैः परिवृतो ब्रह्मोद्याः कथाः कुर्वन्नन्याश्च निरवद्या विद्यागोष्ठीर्भावयन्कदाचिदासाञ्चक्रे । तथासीनं च तं त्रिभुवनप्रतीक्ष्यं मनुदक्षचाक्षुषप्रभृतयः प्रजापतयः सर्वे च सप्तर्षिपुरःसरा महर्षयः सिषेविरे । केचिदृचः स्तुतिचतुराः समुदचारयन् । केचिदपचितिभाञ्जि यजूंष्यपठन् । केचित्प्रशंसासामानि जगुः । अपरे विवृतक्रतुक्रियातन्त्रान्मन्त्रान्व्याचचक्षिरे । विद्याविसंवादकृताश्च तत्र तेषामन्योन्यस्य विद्या[2]विवादाः प्रादुरभवन् ।

अथातिरोषणः प्रकृत्या महातपा मुनिरत्रेस्तनयस्तारापतेर्भ्राता नाम्ना दुर्वासा द्वितीयेन[3] मन्दपालनाम्ना मुनिना सह कलहायमानः साम गायन्क्रोधान्धो विस्वरमकरोत् । सर्वेषु च शापभयप्रतिपन्नमौनेषु मुनिष्वन्यालापलीलयावधीरयति कमलसम्भवे भगवती कुमारी किञ्चिदुन्मुक्तबालभावे

१ '०सार्द्रासु' क–ब. २ 'अन्योन्यस्य विवादाः' ब. ३ 'द्वितीयेनोपमन्युनाम्ना' ब.

भूषितनवयौवने वयसि[1] वर्तमाना, गृहीतचामरप्रचलद्भुजलता पितामहमुपवीजयन्ती, निर्भर्त्सनताडनजातरागाभ्यामिव स्वभावारुणाभ्यां पादपल्लवाभ्यां समुद्भासमाना, शिष्यद्वयेनेव पदक्रममुखरेण नूपुरयुगलेन वाचालितचरणा, मर्दन[2]नगरतोरणस्तम्भविभ्रमं बिभ्राणा जङ्घाद्वितयम्, सलीलमुत्कलहंसकुलकलालापप्रलापिनि मेखलादाम्नि[3] विन्यस्तवामहस्तकिसलया, विद्वन्मानसनिवासलग्नेन गुणकलापेनेवांसावलम्बिना ब्रह्मसूत्रेण पवित्रीकृतकाया, भास्वन्मध्यनायकमनेकमुक्तानुयातमपवर्गमार्गमिव हारमुद्वहन्ती, वदनप्रविष्टसर्वविद्या[4]चरणालक्तकरसेनेव पाटलेन स्फुरता दशनच्छदेन विराजमाना, संक्रान्तकमलासनकृष्णाजिनप्रतिमां साममधुरगीताकर्णनावतीर्णशशिहरिणामिव कपोलस्थलीं दधाना, तिर्यक्सावज्ञमुन्नमितैकभ्रूलता, श्रोत्रमेकं विस्वरश्रवणकलुषितं प्रक्षालयन्तीवापाङ्गनिर्गतेन लोचनाश्रुजलप्रवाहेणेतरश्रवणेन च विकसितसितसिन्धुवारमञ्जरीजुषा हसतेव प्रकटितविद्यामदा, श्रुतिप्रणयिभिः प्रणवैरिव कर्णावतंसकुसुममधुकरकुलैरुपास्यमाना, सूक्ष्मविमलेन प्रज्ञाप्रतानेनेवांशुकेनाच्छादितशरीरा, वाङ्मयमिव निर्मलं दिक्षु दशनज्योत्स्नालोकं विकिरन्ती देवी सरस्वती श्रुत्वा जहास।

दृष्ट्वा च तां तथा हसन्तीं स मुनिः 'आः पापकारिणि, दुर्गृहीतविद्यालवावलेपदुर्विदग्धे, मामुपहससि' इत्युक्त्वा शिरःकम्पशीर्यमाणबन्धविशरारोरुन्मिषत्पिङ्गलिम्नो जटाकलापस्य रोचिषा[5] सिञ्चन्निव रोषदहनद्रवेण दश दिशः, कृतकालसन्निधानामिवान्धकारितललाटपट्टाष्टापदामन्तः[6]पुरमण्डनपत्रभङ्गमकरिकां भ्रुकुटिमाबध्नन्, अतिलोहितेन चक्षुषामर्षदेवतायै स्वरुधिरोपहारमिव प्रयच्छन्, निर्दयदष्टदशनच्छदभयपलायमानामिव वाचं रुन्धन्दन्तांशुच्छलेन, अंसावस्रंसिनः शापशासनपट्टस्येव ग्रभ्नन्ग्रन्थिमन्यथा कृष्णाजिनस्य, स्वेदकणप्रतिबिम्बितैः शापशङ्काशरणागतैरिव सुरासुरमुनिभिः प्रतिपन्नसर्वावयवः, कोपकम्पतरलिताङ्गुलिना करेण प्रसादनलग्नामक्षरमालामिवाक्षमालामाक्षिप्य कामण्डलवेन वारिणा समुपस्पृश्य शापजलं जग्राह।

अत्रान्तरे स्वयम्भुवोऽभ्याशे समुपविष्टा देवी मूर्तिमती पीयूषफेनपटलपाण्डरं कल्पद्रुमदुकूलवल्कलं वसाना, बिसतन्तुमयेनांशुकेनोन्नतस्तनमध्यबद्धगात्रिकाग्रन्थिः, तपोबलनिर्जितत्रिभुवनजयपताकाभिरिव तिसृभिर्भस्मपुण्ड्रकराजिभिर्विराजितललाटाजिरा, स्कन्धावलम्बिना[7] सुधाफेनधवलेन तपःप्रभावकुण्डलीकृतेन गङ्गा[8]स्रोतसेव योगपट्टकेन विरचितवैकक्ष्यका, सव्येन ब्रह्मोत्पत्तिपुण्डरीकमुकुलमिव स्फटिककमण्डलुं करेण कलयन्ती, दक्षिणम-

---

१ '०यौवने नवे वयसि' अ–क. २ 'धर्मनगर' ब. ३ 'धाम्नि' ब. ४ '०विद्यालक्तक०' अ–क. ५ 'शोचिषा' ज–क्. ६ 'अन्तकमण्डन०' ब. ७ '०लम्बिना फेन०' ब. ८ 'गगनगङ्गा०' ब.

क्षमालाकृतपरिक्षेपं कम्बुनिर्मितोर्मिकादन्तुरितं तर्जनतरङ्गिततर्जनीकमुत्क्षिपन्ती करम्, 'आः पाप, क्रोधोपहत, दुरात्मन्, अज्ञ, अनात्मज्ञ, ब्रह्मबन्धो, मुनिखेट, अपसद, निराकृत, कथमात्मस्खलितविलक्षः सुरासुरमुनिमनुजवृन्दवन्दनीयां त्रिभुवनमातरं भगवतीं सरस्वतीं शप्तुमभिलषसि' इत्यभिदधाना, रोषविमुक्तवेत्रासनैरोङ्कारमुखरितमुखैरूरु[१]क्षेपदोलायमानजटाभारभरितदिग्भिः परिकरबन्धभ्रमितकृष्णाजिनाटोप[२]च्छायाश्यामायमानदिवसैरमर्षनिःश्वासदोलाप्रेङ्खोलितब्रह्मलोकैः सोमरसमिव स्वेदविसरव्याजेन स्रवद्भिरग्निहोत्रपवित्रभस्मस्मेरललाटैः कुशतन्तुचारुचामरचीरचीवरिभिराषाढिभिः प्रहरणीकृतकमण्डलुमण्डलैर्मूर्तैश्चतुर्भिर्वेदैः सह वृषीमपहाय सावित्री समुत्तस्थौ।

ततो 'मर्षय भगवन्, अभूमिरेषा शापस्य' इत्यनुनाथ्यमानोऽपि विबुधैः, 'उपाध्याय, स्खलितमेकं क्षमस्व' इति बद्धाञ्जलिपुटैः प्रसाद्यमानोऽपि स्वशिष्यैः, 'पुत्र, मा कृथास्तपसः प्रत्यूहम्' इति निवार्यमाणोऽप्यत्रिणा, रोषावेशविवशो दुर्वासाः 'दुर्विनीते, व्यपनयामि ते विद्याजनितामुन्नतिमिमाम्, अधस्ताद्गच्छ मर्त्यलोकम्' इत्युक्त्वा तच्छापोदकं विससर्ज। प्रतिशापदानोद्यतां सावित्रीं 'सखि, संहर रोषम्, असंस्कृतमतयोऽपि जात्यैव द्विजन्मानो माननीयाः' इत्यभिदधाना सरस्वत्येव न्यवारयत्।

अथ तां तथा शप्तां सरस्वतीं दृष्ट्वा पितामहो भगवान्कमलोत्पत्तिलग्नमृणालसूत्रामिव धवलयज्ञोपवीतिनीं तनुमुद्वहन्, उद्गच्छदच्छाङ्गुलीयकमरकतमयूखलताकलापेन त्रिभुवनोपप्लवप्रशमकुशापीडधारिणेव दक्षिणेन करेण निवार्य शापकलकलम्, अतिविमलदीर्घैर्भाविकृतयुगारम्भसूत्रपातमिव दिक्षु पातयन् दशनकिरणैः, सरस्वतीप्रस्थानमङ्गलपटहेनेव पूरयन्नाशाः स्वरेण, सुधीरमुवाच—'ब्रह्मन्, न खलु साधुसेवितोऽयं पन्था येनासि प्रवृत्तः। निहन्त्येष परस्तात्। उद्दामप्रसृतेन्द्रियाश्वसमुत्थापितं हि रजः कलुषयति दृष्टिमनक्षजिताम्। कियद्दूरं वा चक्षुरीक्षते। विशुद्धया हि धिया पश्यन्ति कृतबुद्धयः सर्वानर्थानसतः सतो वा। निसर्गविरोधिनी चेयं पयःपावकयोरिव धर्मक्रोधयोरेकत्र वृत्तिः। आलोकमपहाय कथं तमसि निमज्जसि। क्षमा हि मूलं सर्वतपसाम्। परदोषदर्शनदक्षा दृष्टिरिव कुपिता बुद्धिर्न त आत्मरागदोषं पश्यति। क्व महातपोभारवैवधिकता, क्व पुरोभागित्वम्। अतिरोषणश्चक्षुष्मानन्ध एव जनः। नहि कोपकलुषिता विमृशति मतिः कर्तव्यमकर्तव्यं वा। कुपितस्य प्रथममन्धकारीभवति विद्या, ततो भ्रुकुटिः। आदाविन्द्रियाणि[३] रागः समास्कन्दति, चरमं चक्षुः। आरम्भे तपो गलति, पश्चात्स्वेदसलिलम्। पूर्वमयशः स्फुरति, अनन्तरमधरः। कथं लोकविनाशाय

१ 'आक्षेप' ब. २ 'कृष्णाजिनपटच्छाया' क. ३ 'इन्द्रियाधिष्ठानं रागः' ब.

ते विषपादपस्येव जटावल्कलानि जातानि। अनुचिता खल्वस्य मुनिवेशस्य हारयष्टिरिव वृत्तमुक्ता चित्तवृत्तिः। शैलूष इव वृथा वहसि कृत्रिममुपशमशून्येन चेतसा तापसाकल्पम्। अल्पमपि न ते पश्यामि कुशलजातम्। अनेनातिलघिम्नाद्याप्युपर्येव प्लवसे ज्ञानोदन्वतः। न खल्वनेलमूका एडा[1] जडा वा सर्वे एते महर्षयः। रोषदोषनिषद्ये स्वहृदये निग्राह्ये किमर्थमसि निगृहीतवाननागसं सरस्वतीम्। एतानि तान्यात्मप्रमाद[2]स्खलितवैलक्ष्याणि, यैर्याति[3] वाच्यतामविदग्धो जनः' इत्युक्त्वा पुनराह—'वत्से सरस्वति विषादं मा गाः। एषा त्वामनुयास्यति सावित्री विनोदयिष्यति चास्मद्विरहदुःखिताम्। आत्मजमुखकमलावलोकनावधिश्च ते शापोऽयं भविष्यति' इति। एतावदभिधाय विसर्जितसुरासुरमुनिमनुजमण्डलः ससंभ्रमोपगतनारदस्कन्धविन्यस्तहस्तः समुचिताह्निककरणायोदतिष्ठत्। सरस्वत्यपि शप्ता किञ्चिदधोमुखी धवलकृष्णशारां कृष्णाजिनलेखामिव[4] दृष्टिमुरसि पातयन्ती, सुरभिनिःश्वासपरिमललग्नैर्मूर्तैः शापाक्षरैरिव षट्चरणचक्रैराकृष्यमाणा, शापशोकशिथिलितहस्ता, अधोमुखीभूतेनोपदिश्यमानमर्त्यलोकावतरणमार्गेव नखमयूखजालकेन, नूपुरव्याहाराहूतैर्भवनकलहंसकुलैर्ब्रह्मलोकनिवासिहृदयैरिवानुगम्यमाना समं सावित्र्या गृहमगात्।

अत्रान्तरे सरस्वत्यवतरणवार्तामिव कथयितुं मध्यमं लोकमवततारांशुमाली। क्रमेण च मन्दायमाने मुकुलितबिसिनीविसरव्यसनविषण्णसरसि वासरे, मधुमदमुदितकामिनीकोपकुटिलकटाक्षक्षिप्यमाण इव क्षेपीयः क्षितिधरशिखरमवतरति तरुणतरकपिलपनलोहिते लोकैकचक्षुषि भगवति, प्रस्नुत[5]मुखमाहेयीयूथक्षरत्क्षीरधाराधवलितेष्वासन्नचन्द्रोदयोद्दामक्षीरोदलहरीक्षालितेष्विव दिव्याश्रमोपशल्येषु, अपराह्णप्रचारचलिते चामरिणि चामीकरतटताडना[6]रुणितरदने रदति सुरस्रवन्तीरोधांसि स्वैरमैरावते, प्रसृतानेकविद्याधराभिसारिकासहस्रचरणालक्तकरसानुलिप्त इव प्रकटयति च तारापथे पाटलताम्, तारापथप्रस्थितसिद्धदत्तदिनकरास्तमयार्घ्यावर्जिते रञ्जितककुभि कुसुम्भभासि स्रवति पिनाकिप्रणतिमुदितसंध्यास्वेदसलिल इव रक्तचन्दनद्रवे, वन्दारुमुनिवृन्दारकवृन्दबध्यमानसंध्याञ्जलिवने ब्रह्मोत्पत्तिकमलसेवागतसकलकमलाकर इव राजति ब्रह्मलोके, समुच्चारिततृतीयसवन[7]ब्रह्मणि ब्रह्मणि, ज्वलितवैतानज्वलनज्वालाजटालाजिरेष्वारब्धधर्मसाधनशिबिरनीराजनेष्विव सप्तर्षिमन्दिरेषु, अघमर्षणमुषितकिल्बिषविषगदोल्लाघलघुषु यतिषु, संध्योपासनासीनतपस्विपङ्क्तिपूतपुलिने प्लवमाननलिनयोनियानहंसहासदन्तुरितोर्मिणि मन्दाकिनीजले, जलदेवतातपत्रे पत्ररथकुलकलत्रान्तःपुरसौधे

---

१ 'पण्डा जडा वा' क. २ 'प्रसाद' ब. ३ 'याप्यतां यात्यविदग्धो' अ–क. ४ अस्मात्परं 'तपसे' इत्यधिकं ब–पुस्तके. ५ 'प्रस्तुतमखमाहेयी' ब. ६ '०ताडनरणितरदने' अ–क. ७ 'सवनव्रतब्रह्मणि' ब.

निजमधुमधुरामोदिनि कृतमधुपमुदि मुमुदिषमाणे कुमुदवने, दिवसावसानताम्यत्तामरसमधुरमधुसपीतिप्रीते सुषुप्सति मृदुमृणालकाण्डकण्डूयनकुण्डलितकन्धरे धुतपक्षराजिवीजितराजीव[१]सरसि राजहंसयूथे, तटलताकुसुमधूलिधूसरितसरिति [२]सरति सिद्धपुरपुरंध्रिधम्मिल्लमल्लिकागन्धग्राहिणि सायन्तने तनीयसि निशानिःश्वासनिभे नभस्वति, सङ्कोचोदञ्चदुच्चकेसरकोटिसङ्कटकुशेशय[३]कोशकोटरकुटीशायिनि षट्चरणचक्रे, नृत्तोद्धूतधूर्जटिजटाटवीकुटजकुड्मलनिकरनिभे नभस्थलं स्तबकयति तारागणे, संध्यानुबन्धताम्रे परिणमत्तालफलत्वक्त्विषि कालमेवमेदुरे मेदिनीं मीलयति नववयसि तमसि, तरुणतरतिमिरपटलपाटनपटीयसि समुन्मिषति यामिनीकामिनीकर्णपूरचम्पककलिकाकदम्बके प्रदीपप्रकरे, प्रतनुतुहिनकिरणकिरणलावण्यालोकपाण्डुन्याश्यानलीनीरमुक्तकालिन्दीकूल[४]वालुकापुलिनायमाने शातक्रतवे क्रश[५]यति तिमिरमाशामुखे, खमुचि मेचकितविकचितकुवलयसरसि शशधरकरनिकरकचग्रहाविले विलीयमाने मानिनीमनसीव शर्वरीशवरीचिकुरचये चापपक्षत्विषि तमसि, उदिते भगवत्युदयगिरिशिखरकटककुहरहरिखरनखरनिवहहेतिनिहतनिजहरिणगलितरुधिरनिचयनिचितमिव लोहितं वपुरुदयरागधरमधरमिव विभावरीवध्वा धारयति श्वेतभानौ, अचलच्युतचन्द्रकान्तजलधाराधौत इव ध्वस्ते ध्वान्ते, गोलोकगलितदुग्धविसरवाहिनि दन्तमयमकरमुखमहाप्रणाल इवापूरयितुं प्रवृत्ते पयोधिमिन्दुमण्डले, स्पष्टे प्रदोषसमये सावित्री शून्यहृदयामिव किमपि ध्यायन्तीं सास्रां सरस्वतीमवादीत्—

'सखि, त्रिभुवनोपदेशदानदक्षायास्तव पुरो जिह्वा जिह्रेति मे जल्पन्ती। जानास्येव यादृश्यो विसंस्थुला गुणवत्यपि जने दुर्जनवन्निर्दाक्षिण्याः क्षणभङ्गिन्यो दुरतिक्रमणीया[६] न रमणीया दैवस्य वामा वृत्तयः। निष्कारणा च निकारकणिकापि कलु[७]षयति मनस्विनोऽपि मानसमसदृशजनादापतन्ती। अनवरतनयनजलसिच्यमानश्च तरुरिव विपल्लवोऽपि सहस्रधा प्ररोहति शो[८]कः। अतिसुकुमारं च जनं सन्तापपरमाणवो मालतीकुसुममिव म्लानिमानयन्ति। महतां चोपरि निपतन्नणुरपि सृणिरिव करिणां क्लेशः कदर्थनायालम्। सहजस्नेहपाशग्रन्थिबन्धनाश्च बान्धवभूता दुस्त्यजा जन्मभूमयः। दारयति दारुणः क्रकचपात इव हृदयं संस्तुतजनविरहः। सा नार्हस्येवं भवितुम्। अभूमिः खल्वसि दुःखक्ष्वेडाङ्कुरप्रसवा[९]नाम्। अपि च पुराकृते कर्मणि बलवति शुभेऽशुभे वा फलकृति तिष्ठत्यधिष्ठातरि प्रष्ठे पृष्ठतश्च कोऽ-

---

१ 'राजीवरजसि' ब. २ एतन्नास्ति अ–क–पुस्तकयोः. ३ 'कुशेशयकोटर०' क; 'कुटीकोटर०' ब. ४ 'बालपुलिना०' अ–क. ५ 'कृशयति' अ. ६ 'क्रमणीया दैवस्य' ब. ७ 'क्लेशयति' ब. ८ एतन्नास्ति अ–क–पुस्तकयोः. ९ 'प्रभावानाम्' ब–क.

वसरो विदुषि शुचाम्। इदं च ते त्रिभुवनमङ्गलैककमलममङ्गलभूताः कथमिव मुखमपवित्रयन्त्यश्रुबिन्दवः । तदलम्। अधुना कथय कतमं भुवो भागमलङ्कर्तुमिच्छसि। कस्मिन्नवतितीर्षति ते पुण्यभाजि प्रदेशे हृदयम्। कानि वा तीर्थान्यनुग्रहीतुमभिलषसि केषु वा धन्येषु तपोवनधामसु तपस्यन्ती स्थातुमिच्छसि। सज्जोऽयमुप[1]चरणचतुरः सहपांशुक्रीडापरिचयपेशलः प्रेयान्सखीजनः क्षितितलावतरणाय। अनन्यशरणा चाद्यैव प्रभृति प्रतिपद्यस्व मनसा वाचा क्रियया च सर्वविद्याविधातारं [2]धातारं च स्व[3]श्रेयसे स्वचरणरजःपवित्रितत्रिदशासुरं सुधासूतिकलिकाकल्पितकर्णावतंसं देवदेवं त्रिभुवनगुरुं त्र्यम्बकम्। अल्पीयसैव कालेन स ते शापशोकविरतिं वितरिष्यति'। इति।

एवमुक्ता मुक्तमुक्ताफलधवललोचनजललवा सरस्वती प्रत्यवादीत्—'प्रियसखि, त्वया सह विचरन्त्या न मे काञ्चिदपि पीडामुत्पादयिष्यति ब्रह्मलोकविरहः शापशोको वा। केवलं कमलासनसेवासुखमार्द्रयति मे हृदयम्। अपि च त्वमेव वेत्सि ये भुवि धर्मधामानि समाधिसाधनानि योगयोग्यानि च स्थानानि स्थातुम्' इत्येवमभिधाय विरराम रणरणकोपनीतप्रजागरा [4]चानिमीलितलोचनैव तां निशामनयत्।

अपरेद्युरुदिते भगवति त्रिभुवनशेखरे खणखणायमान[5]खरखलीनक्षतनिजतुरग[6]मुखक्षिप्तेन क्षतजेनेव पाटलितवपुष्युदयाचलचूडामणौ जरत्कृकवाकुचूडारुणारुणपुरःसरे विरोचने नातिदूरवर्ती विविच्य पितामहवि[7]मानहंसकुलपालः पर्यटन्नपरवक्त्रमुच्चैरगायत्—

'तरलयसि दृशं किमुत्सुकामकलुषमानसवासलालिते।
अवतर कलहंसि वापिकां पुनरपि यास्यसि पङ्कजालयम्'

तच्छ्रुत्वा सरस्वती पुनरचिन्तयत्—'अहमिवानेन पर्यनुयुक्ता। भवतु। मानयामि मुनेर्वचनम्' इत्युक्त्वोत्थाय कृतमहीतलावतरणसङ्कल्पा परित्यज्य वियोगविक्लवं स्वपरिजनं ज्ञातिवर्गमवगणय्यावगणा त्रिः प्रदक्षिणीकृत्य चतुर्मुखं कथमप्यनुनयनिवर्तितानुयायिव्रतिव्राता ब्रह्मलोकतः सावित्रीद्वितीया निर्जगाम।

ततः क्रमेण ध्रुवप्रवृत्तां धर्मधेनुमिवाधोधावमानधवलपयोधराम्, उद्धुरध्वनिम्, अन्धकमथनमौलिमालतीमालिकाम्, आलीयमानवालखिल्यरुद्धरोधसम्, अरुन्धतीधौततारत्वचम्, [8]त्वङ्गत्तुङ्गतरङ्गतरत्तरलतरतारतारकाम्,

---

१ 'अनुचरण०' ब. २ 'दातारम्' अ–क. ३ 'श्वःश्रेयसस्य चरणरजः०' अ–क. ४ 'चामीलित' ब. ५ 'स्खलत्खलीन' अ–क. ६ 'मुखक्षरक्षतजेनेव' ब. ७ 'पितामहवाहनहंस०' ब. ८ 'तङ्गत्तुङ्गतरङ्गतरलिततारकाम्' ब.

तापसविकीर्ण[1]विरलतिलोदकपुलकितपुलिनाम्, आप्लवनपूतपितामहपातितपितृपिण्डपाण्डुरितपाराम्, पर्यन्तसुप्तसप्तर्षिकुशशयनसूचितसूर्यग्रहसूतकोपवासाम्, आचमनशुचिशचीपतिमुच्यमानार्चनकुसुमनिकरशाराम्, शिवपुरापतितनिर्माल्यमन्दारदामकाम्, अनादरदारितमन्दरदरीदृषदम्, अनेकनाकनायकनिकायकामिनीकुचकलशविलुलितविग्रहाम्, ग्राह[2]ग्रावग्रामस्खलनमुखरितस्रोतसम्, सुषुम्णास्रुतशशिसुधाशीकरस्तबकतारकिततीराम्, धिषणाग्निकार्यधूमधूसरितसैकताम्, सिद्धविरचितवालुकालिङ्गलङ्घनत्रासविद्रुतविद्याधराम्, निर्मोकमुक्तिमिव गगनोरगस्य, लीलाललाटिकामिव त्रिविष्टपविटस्य, विक्रयवीथीमिव पुण्यपण्यस्य, दन्तार्गला[3]मिव नरकनगरद्वारस्य, अंशुकोष्णीषपट्टिकामिव सुमेरुनृपस्य, दुकूलकदलिकामिव कैलासकुञ्जरस्य, पद्धतिमिवापवर्गस्य, नेमिमिव कृतयुगचक्रस्य, सप्तसागरराजमहिषीं मन्दाकिनीमनुसरन्ती मर्त्यलोकमवततार। अपश्यच्चाम्बरतलस्थितैव हारमिव वरुणस्य, अमृतनिर्झरमिव चन्द्राचलस्य, शशिमणिनिष्यन्दमिव विन्ध्यस्य, कर्पूरद्रुमद्रवप्रवाहमिव दण्डकारण्यस्य, लावण्यरसप्रस्रवणमिव दिशाम्, स्फाटिकशिलापट्टशयनमिवाम्बरश्रियाः, स्वच्छशिशिरसुरसवारिपूर्णं भगवतः पितामहस्यापत्यं हिरण्यबाहु[4]नामानं महानदम्, यं जनाः शोण इति कथयन्ति। दृष्ट्वा च तं रामणीयकहृतहृदया तस्यैव तीरे वासमरोचयत्[5]। उवाच च सावित्रीम्—'सखि, मधुरमयूरविरुतयः कुसुमपांशुपटलसिकतिलतरुतलाः परिमलमत्तमधुपवेणीवीणारणितरमणीया रमयन्ति मां मन्दीकृतमन्दाकीनीद्युतेरस्य महानदस्योपकण्ठभूमयः। पक्षपाति च हृदयमत्रैव स्थातुं मे' इति। अभिनन्दितवचना च तथेति तया तस्य पश्चिमे तीरे समवातरत्। एकस्मिंश्च शुचौ शिलातलसनाथे तटलतामण्डपे गृहबुद्धिं बबन्ध। विश्रान्ता च नातिचिरादुत्थाय सावित्र्या सार्धमुच्चितार्चनकुसुमा सस्नौ। पुलिनपृष्ठप्रतिष्ठा[6]पितसैकतशिवलिङ्गा च भक्त्या परमया पञ्चब्रह्मपुरःसरां सम्यङ्मुद्राबन्धविहितपरिकरां ध्रुवागीतिगर्भामवनिपवनवनगगनदहनतपनतुहिनकिरणयजमानमयीर्मूर्तीरष्टावपि ध्यायन्ती सुचिरमष्टपुष्पिकामदात्। अयत्नोपनतेन फलमूलेनामृतरसमप्यतिशिशयिषमाणेन च स्वादिम्ना शिशिरेण शोणवारिणा शरीरस्थितिमकरोत्। अतिवाहितदिवसा च तस्मिंल्लतामण्डपशिलातले कल्पितपल्लवशयना सुष्वाप। अन्येद्युरप्यनेनैव क्रमेण नक्तन्दिनमत्यवाहयत्।

एवमतिक्रामत्सु दिवसेषु गच्छति च काले कदाचिद्यामामात्रोद्गते च रवावुत्तरस्यां ककुभि प्रतिशब्दपूरितवनगह्वरं गम्भीरतारतरं तुरङ्गहेषितह्रादमश्र-

---

१ '०वितीर्णतरल०' अ–क. २ 'ग्रहग्रावस्खलन' ब. ३ 'दत्तार्गला०' अ–क. ४ 'हिरण्यवाह' अ–क. ५ 'अरचयत्' अ–क. ६ 'प्रतिष्ठित' अ–क.

णोत् । उपजातकुतूहला च निर्गत्य लतामण्डपाद्विलोकयन्ती विकचकेतकीगर्भपत्रपाण्डुरं रजःसङ्घातं नातिदवीयसि संमुखमापतन्तमपश्यत् । क्रमेण च सामीप्योपजायमानामिव्यक्ति तस्मिन्महति शफरोदरधूसरे रजसि पयसीव मकरचक्रं प्लवमानं पुरः प्रधावमानेन, प्रलम्बकुटिलकचपल्लवघटितललाटजूटकेन, धवलदन्तपत्रिकाद्युतिहसितकपोलभित्तिना, पिनद्धकृष्णागुरुपङ्कल्कच्छुरणकृष्णशबलकषायकञ्चुकेन, उत्तरीयकृतशिरोवेष्टनेन, वामप्रकोष्ठनिविष्टस्पष्टहाटककटकेन, द्विगुणपट्टपट्टिकागाढग्रन्थिग्रथितासिधेनुना, अनवरतव्यायामकृशकर्कशशरीरेण, वातहरिणयूथेनेव मुहुर्मुहुः खमुड्डीयमानेन, लङ्घितसमविषमावटविटपेन, कोणधारिणा, कृपाणपाणिना, सेवागृहीतविविधवनकुसुमफलमूलपर्णेन, 'चल चल, याहि याहि, अपसर्पापसर्प, पुरः प्रयच्छ पन्थानम्' इत्यनवरतकृतकलकलेन, युवप्रायेण, सहस्रमात्रेण पदातिबलेन सनाथमश्ववृन्दं सन्ददर्श ।

मध्ये च तस्य सार्धचन्द्रेण मुक्ताफलजालमालिना विविधरत्नखण्डखचितेन शङ्खक्षीरफेनपाण्डुरेण क्षीरोदेनेव स्वयं लक्ष्मीं दातुमागतेन गगनगतेनातपत्रेण कृतच्छायम्, अच्छाच्छेनाभरणद्युतीनां निवहेन दिशामिव दर्शनानुरागलग्नेन चक्रवालेनानुगम्यमानम्, आनितम्बविलम्बिन्या मालतीशेखरस्रजा सकलभुवनविजयार्जितया रूपपताकयेव विराजमानम्, उत्सर्पिभिः शिखण्डखण्डिका[1]पद्मरागमणेररुणैरंशुजालैरदृश्यमानवनदेवताविधृतैर्बालपल्लवैरिव प्रमृज्यमानमार्गरेणु[2]परुषवपुषम्, बकुलकुड्मलमण्डलीमुण्डमालामण्डनमनोहरेण कुटिलकुन्तलस्तबकमालिना मौलिना मीलितातपं पिबन्तमिव दिवसम्, पशुपतिजटामुकुटमृगाङ्कद्वितीयशकलघटितस्येव सहजलक्ष्मीसमालिङ्गितस्य ललाटपट्टस्य मनःशिलापङ्कपिङ्गलेन लावण्येन लिम्पन्तमिवान्तरिक्षम्, अभिनवयौवनारम्भावष्टम्भप्रगल्भदृष्टिपाततृणीकृतत्रिभुवनस्य चक्षुषः प्रथिम्ना विकचकुमुदकुवलयकमलसरःसहस्रसञ्छादितदशदिशं शरदमिव प्रवर्तयन्तम्, आयतनयननदीसीमान्तसेतुबन्धेन ललाटतटशशिमणिशिलातलगलितेन कान्तिसलिलस्रोतसेव द्राघीयसा घोणावंशेन शोभमानम्, अतिसुरभिसहकारकर्पूरकक्कोललवङ्गपारिजातकपरिमलमुचा मत्तमधुकरकुलकोलाहलमुखरेण मुखेन सनन्दनवनं वसन्तमिव [3]वमन्तम्, आसन्नसुहृत्परिहासभावनोत्तानितमुखमुग्धहसितैर्दशनज्योत्स्नास्नपितदिङ्मुखैः पुनःपुनर्नभसि सञ्चारिणं चन्द्रालोकमिव कल्पयन्तम्, कदम्बमुकुलस्थूलमुक्ताफलयुगलमध्याध्यासितमरकतस्य त्रिकण्टककर्णाभरणस्य प्रेङ्खतः प्रभया समुत्सर्पन्त्या कृतसकुसुमहरितकुन्दपल्लवकर्णावतंसमिवोपलक्ष्यमाणम्, आमोदितमृगमदपङ्कलिखितपत्रभङ्गभास्वरं भुजयुगलमुद्दाममकराक्रान्तशिखरमिव म-

१ 'गण्डिका' क–ब. २ 'रेणुरूषितपरुष' ब. ३ 'अवतारयन्तम्' ब.

करकेतुकेतुदण्डद्वयं दधानम्, धवलब्रह्मसूत्रसीमन्तितं सागरमथनसामर्षगङ्गास्रोतःसन्दानितमिव मन्दरं देहमुद्वहन्तम्, कर्पूरक्षोदमुष्टिच्छुरणपांशुलेनेव कान्तोच्चकुचचक्रवाकयुगलविपुलपुलिनेनोरःस्थलेन स्थूलभुजायामपुञ्जितं पुरो विस्तारयन्तमिव दिक्चक्रम्, पुरस्तादीषदधोनाभिनिहितैककोणकमनीयेन पृष्ठतः कक्ष्याधिकक्षिप्तपल्लवेनोभयतः संवलनप्रकटितोरुत्रिभागेन हारीतहरिता निबिडनिपीडितेनाधरवाससा विभज्यमानतनुतरमध्यभागम्, अनवरतश्रमोपचितमांस[1]कठिनविकटमकरमुखसंलग्नजानुभ्यां विशालवक्षःस्थलोपलवेदिकोत्तम्भनशिलास्तम्भाभ्यां चारुचन्दनस्थासकस्थूलकान्तिभ्यामूरुदण्डाभ्यामुपहसन्तमिवैरावतकरायामम्, अतिभरितोरुभारवहनखेदेनेव तनुतरजङ्घाकाण्डम्, कल्पपादपपल्लवद्वयस्येव पाटलस्योभयपार्श्वावलम्बिनः पादद्वयस्य दोलायमानैर्नखमयूखैरश्वमण्डनचामरमालामिव रचयन्तम्, अभिमुखमुच्चरुदञ्चद्भिरतिचिरमुपरि विश्राम्यद्भिरिव वलितविकटं पतद्भिः खुरैः खण्डितभुवि प्रतिक्षणदशन[2]ग्रहमुक्तिखणखणायितखरखलीने दीर्घघ्राण[3]लीनलालिकललाटलुलितचारुचामीकरचक्रके शिञ्जानशात[4]कौम्भजयनशोभिनि मनोरंहसि गोलाङ्गूलकपोलकालकायलोम्नि नीलसिन्धुवारवर्णे वाजिनि महति समारूढम्, उभयतः पर्याणपट्टश्लिष्टहस्ताभ्यामासन्नपरिचारकाभ्यां दोधूयमानधवलचामरिकायुगलम्, अग्रतः पठतो बन्दिनः सुभाषितमुत्कण्टकितकपोलफलकेन लग्नकर्णोत्पलकेसरपक्ष्मशकलेनेव मुखशशिना भावयन्तम्, अनङ्गयुगावतारमिव दर्शयन्तम्, चन्द्रमयीमिव सृष्टिमुत्पादयन्तम्, विलासप्रायमिव जीवलोकं जनयन्तम्, अनुरागमयमिव सर्गान्त[5]रमारचयन्तम्, शृङ्गारमयमिव दिवसमापादयन्तम्, रागराज्यमिव प्रवर्तयन्तम्, आकर्षणाञ्जनमिव चक्षुषोः, वशीकरणमन्त्रमिव मनसः, स्वस्थावेशचूर्णमिवेन्द्रियाणाम्, असन्तोषमिव कौतुकस्य, सिद्धयोगमिव सौभाग्यस्य, पुनर्जन्मदिवसमिव मन्मथस्य, रसायनमिव यौवनस्य, एकराज्यमिव रामणीयकस्य कीर्तिस्तम्भमिव रूपस्य, मूलकोषमिव लावण्यस्य, पुण्यकर्मपरिणाममिव संसारस्य, प्रथमाङ्कुरमिव कान्तिलतायाः, सर्गाभ्यासफलमिव प्रजापतेः; प्रतापमिव विभ्रमस्य, यशःप्रवाहमिव वैदग्ध्यस्य, अष्टादशवर्षदेशीयं युवानमद्राक्षीत्। पार्श्वे च तस्य द्वितीयमपरसंश्लिष्टतुरङ्गम्, प्रांशुमुत्तप्तपनीयस्तम्भाकारम्, परिणतवयसमपि व्यायामकठिनकायम्, नीचनखश्मश्रुकचम्, शुक्तिखलतिम्, ईषत्तुन्दिलम्, रोमशोरःस्थलम्, अनुल्बणोदारवेशतया जरामपि विनयमिव शिक्षयन्तम्, गुणानपि गरिमाणमिवानयन्तम्, महानुभावतामपि शिष्यतामिवानयन्तम्, आचारस्याचार्यकमिव कुर्वाणम्, धवलवारबाणधारिणम्, धौतदुकूलपट्टिकापरिवेष्टितमौलिं पुरुषम्।

---

१ 'मांसबन्धविकट' ब. २ 'दशनविमुक्त' अ-क. ३ 'घ्राणालीनलालिकेललाटपट्टलुठित' ब. ४ 'कुम्भायान' ब. ५ 'मार्गान्तरमानयन्तम्' अ-क.

अथ स युवा पुरोयायिनां यथादर्शनं प्रतिनिवृत्य[1] विस्मितमनसां कथयतां पदातीनां सकाशादुपलभ्य दिव्याकृति तत्कन्यायुगलमुपजातकुतूहलः प्रतूर्णतुरगो दिदृक्षुस्तं लतामण्डपोद्देशमाजगाम दूरादेव च तुरगादवततार। निवारितपरिजनश्च तेन द्वितीयेन साधुना सह चरणाभ्यामेव सविनयमुपससर्प। कृतोपसंग्रहणौ तौ सावित्री समं सरस्वत्या किसलयासनदानादिना सकुसुमफलार्घावसानेन वनवासोचितेनातिथ्येन यथाक्रममुपजग्राह। आसीनयोश्च तयोरासीना नातिचिरमिव स्थित्वा तं द्वितीयं प्रवयसमुद्दिश्यावादीत्—'आर्य, सहजलज्जाधनस्य प्रमदाजनस्य प्रथमाभिभाषणमशालीनता, विशेषतो वनमृगीमुग्धस्य कुलकुमारीजनस्य। केवलमियमालोकनकृतार्थाय चक्षुषे स्पृहयन्ती प्रेरयत्युदन्तश्रवणकुतूहलिनी श्रोत्रवृत्तिः। प्रथमदर्शने चोपायनमिवोपनयति[2] सज्जनः प्रणयम्। अप्रगल्भमपि जनं प्रभवता प्रश्रयेणार्पितं मनो मध्विव वाचालयति। अयत्नेनैव चातिनम्रे साधौ धनुषीव गुणः परां कोटिमारोपयति[3] विस्रम्भः। जनयन्ति च विस्मयमतिधीरधियामप्यदृष्टपूर्वा दृश्यमाना जगति स्रष्टुः सृष्टयतिशयाः, यतस्त्रिभुवनाभिभावि रूपमिदमस्य महानुभावस्य। सौजन्यपरतन्त्रा चेयं देवानांप्रियस्यातिभद्रता कारयति कथां न तु युवतिजने सहोत्था तरलता। तत्कथयागमनेनापुण्यभाक्तमो विजृम्भितविरहव्यथः शून्यतां नीतो देशः। क्व वा गन्तव्यम्। कस्य वायमपहृतहरहुङ्काराहङ्कारोऽपर इवानन्यजो युवा। किंनाम्नः समृद्धतपसः पितुरयममृतवर्षी कौस्तुभमणिरिव हरेर्हृदयमाह्लादयति। का चास्य त्रिभुवननमस्या प्रभातसंध्येव महतस्तेजसो जननी। कानि वास्य पुण्यभाञ्जि भजन्त्यभिख्यामक्षराणि। आर्यपरिज्ञानेऽप्ययमेव क्रमः कौतुकानुरोधिनो हृदयस्य'। इत्युक्तवत्यां तस्यां प्रकटितप्रश्रयोऽसौ प्रतिव्याजहार—'आयुष्मति, सतां हि प्रियंवदता कुलविद्या। न केवलमाननं हृदयमपि च ते चन्द्रमयमिव सुधाशीकरशीतलैरानन्दयति वचोभिः। सौजन्यजन्मभूमयो भूयसा शुभेन सज्जननिर्माणशिल्पकला[4] भवादृश्यो जायन्ते। दूरे तावदन्योन्यस्यालापनमभिजातैः सह दृशोऽपि मिश्रीभूता[5] महतीं भूमिमारोपयन्ति। श्रूयताम्—अयं खलु भूषणं भार्गववंशस्य भगवतो भूर्भुवःस्वस्त्रितयतिलकस्य, अदभ्रप्रभावस्तम्भितजम्भारिभुजस्तम्भस्य, सुरासुरमुकुटमणिशिलाशयनदुर्ललितपादपङ्केरुहस्य, निजतेजःप्रसरप्लुष्टपुलोम्नश्च्यवनस्य बहिर्वृत्ति जीवितं दधीचो नाम तनयः। जनन्यस्य जितजगतोऽनेकपार्थिवसहस्रानुयातस्य शर्यातस्य सुता राजपुत्री त्रिभुवनकन्यारत्नं सुकन्या नाम। तां खलु देवीमन्तर्वत्नीं विदित्वा वैजनने मासि प्रसवाय पिता पत्युः पार्श्वात्स्वगृहमानाययत्। असूत च सा तत्र देवी

---

१ 'प्रतीत्य' अ. २ '०नयन्ति सज्जनाः' क. ३ 'कटिमारोहन्ति' ब. ४ 'शिल्पकला इव' ब. ५ 'मिश्रीकृता महतीं...पयन्ति प्रणयम्' ब.

दीर्घायुषमेनम्। अनेहसावर्धत तत्रैवायमानन्दितज्ञातिवर्गो बालस्तारकाराज इव राजीवलोचनो राजगृहे। भर्तृभवनमागच्छन्त्यामपि दुहितरि नासेचनकदर्शनमिमममुञ्चन्मातामहो मनोविनोदनं नप्तारम्। अशिक्षतायं तत्रैव सर्वा विद्याः सकलाश्च कलाः। कालेन चोपारूढयौवनमिममालोक्याहमिवासावप्यनुभवतु मुखकमलावलोकनानन्दमस्येति मातामहः कथंकथमप्येनं पितुरन्तिकमधुना व्यसर्जयत्। मामपि तस्य देवस्य सुगृहीतनाम्नः शर्यातस्याज्ञाकारिणं विकुक्षिनामानं भृत्यपरमाणुमवधारयतु भवती। पितुः पादमूलमायान्तं मया साभिसारमकरोत्स्वामी। तद्धि नः कुलक्रमागतं राजकुलम्। उत्तमानां च चिरन्तनता जनयत्यनुजीविन्यपि जने कियन्मात्रमपि मन्दाक्षम्। अक्षीणः खलु दाक्षिण्यकोशो महताम्। इतश्च गव्यूतिमात्रमिव पारेशोणं तस्य भगवतश्च्यवनस्य स्वनाम्ना निर्मितव्यपदेशं च्यावनं नाम चैत्ररथकल्पं काननं निवासः। तदवधिश्चेयं नौ यात्रा। यदि च गृहीतक्षणं दाक्षिण्यमनवहेलं वा हृदयमस्माकमुपरि भूमिर्वा प्रसादानामयं जनः श्रवणार्हो वा, ततो न विमाननीयोऽयं नः प्रथमः प्रणयः कुतूहलस्य। वयमपि शुश्रूषवो वृत्तान्तमायुष्मत्योः। नेयमाकृतिर्दिव्यतां व्यभिचरति। गोत्रनामनी तु श्रोतुमभिलषति नौ हृदयम्। तत्कथय कतमो वंशः स्पृहणीयतां जन्मना नीतः। का चेयमत्रभवती भवत्याः समीपे समवाय इव विरोधिनां पदार्थानाम्। तथा हि। सन्निहितबालान्धकारा भास्वन्मूर्तिश्च, पुण्डरीकमुखी हरिणलोचना च, बालातपप्रभाधरा कुमुदहासिनी च, कलहंसस्वना समुन्नतपयोधरा च, कमलकोमलकरा हिमगिरिशिलापृथुनितम्बा च, करभोरुर्विलम्बितगमना च, अमुक्तकुमारभावा स्निग्धतारका च' इति। सा त्ववादीत्—'आर्य, श्रोष्यसि कालेन। भूयसो दिवसानत्र स्थातुमभिलषति नौ हृदयम्। अल्पीयांश्चायमध्वा। परिचय एव प्रकटीकरिष्यति। आर्येण न विस्मरणीयोऽयमनुषङ्गदृष्टो जनः' इत्यभिधाय तूष्णीमभूत्। दधीचस्तु नवाम्भोभरगम्भीराम्भोधरध्वाननिभया भारत्या नर्तयन्वनलताभवनभाजो भुजगभुजः सुधीरमुवाच—'आर्ये, करिष्यति प्रसादमार्याराध्यमाना। पश्यामस्तावत्तातम्। उत्तिष्ठ। व्रजामः' इति। तथेति च तेनाभ्यनुज्ञातः शनकैरुत्थाय कृतनमस्कृतिरुच्चचाल। तुरगारूढं च तं प्रयान्तं सरस्वती सुचिरमुत्तम्भितपक्ष्मणा निश्चलतारकेण लिखितेनेव चक्षुषा व्यलोकयत्। उत्तीर्य शोणमचिरेणैव कालेन दधीचः पितुराश्रमपदं जगाम। गते च तस्मिन्सा तामेव दिशमालोकयन्ती सुचिरमतिष्ठत्। कृच्छ्रादिव च सञ्जहार दृशम्।

अथ मुहूर्तमिव स्थित्वा स्मृत्वा च तां तस्य रूपसम्पदं पुनः पुनर्व्यस्मयतास्या हृदयम्। भूयोऽपि चक्षुराचकाङ्क्ष तद्दर्शनम्। अवशेव केनाप्य-

नीयत तामेव दिशं दृष्टिः। अप्रहितमपि मनस्तेनैव सार्धमगात्। अजायत च नवपल्लव इव बालवनलतायाः कुतोऽप्यस्या अनुरागश्चेतसि। ततः प्रभृति सालस्येव शून्येव सनिद्रेव दिवसमनयत्। अस्तमुपयाति च प्रत्यक्पर्यस्तमण्डले लाङ्गलिकास्तबकताम्रत्विषि कमलिनीकामुके कठोरसारसशिरःशोणशोचिषि सवित्रे त्रयीमये तेजसि, तरुणतरतमालश्यामले च मलिनयति व्योम व्योमव्यापिनि तिमिरसञ्चये, सञ्चरत्सिद्धसुन्दरीनूपुररवानुसारिणि च मन्दं मन्दं मन्दाकिनीहंस इव समुत्सर्पति शशिनि गगनतलम्, कृतसंध्याप्रणामा निशामुख एव निपत्य विमुक्ताङ्गी पल्लवशयने तस्थौ। सावित्र्यपि कृत्वा यथाक्रियमाणं सायन्तनं क्रियाकलापमुचिते शयनकाले किसलयशयनमभजत। जातनिद्रा च सुष्वाप।

इतरा तु मुहुर्मुहुरङ्गवलनैर्विलुलितकिसलयशयनतला निमीलितलोचनापि नाभजत निद्राम्। अचिन्तयच्च—'मर्त्यलोकः खलु सर्वलोकानामुपरि, यस्मिन्नेवंविधानि सम्भवन्ति त्रिभुवनभूषणानि सकलगुणग्रामगुरूणि रत्नानि। तथा हि। तस्य मुखलावण्यप्रवाहस्य निष्यन्दबिन्दुरिन्दुः। तस्य च चक्षुषो विक्षेपा विकचकुमुदकुवलयकमलाकराः। तस्य चाधरमणेर्दीधितयो विकसितबन्धूकवनराजयः। तस्य चाङ्गस्य परभागोपकरणमनङ्गः। पुण्यभाञ्जि तानि चक्षूंषि चेतांसि यौवनानि वा स्त्रैणानि, येषामसौ[1] विषयो दर्शनस्य। क्षणं नु दर्शयता च तमन्यजन्मजनितेनेव मे फलितमधर्मेण। का प्रतिपत्तिरिदानीम्' इति चिन्तयन्त्येव कथंकथमप्युपजातनिद्रा चिरात्क्षणमशेत। सुप्ता च तं दीर्घलोचनं स्वप्ने ददर्श। स्वप्नासादितद्वितीयदर्शना चाकर्णाकृष्टकार्मुकेण मनसि निर्दयमताड्यत[2] प्रतिबुद्धा मकरकेतुना। मदनशरताडितायाश्च तस्या वार्तामिवोपलब्धुमरतिराजगाम। तथा हि। ततः प्रभृति कुसुमधूलिधवलाभिर्वनलताभिरताडितापि वेदनामधत्त। मन्दमन्दमारुतविधुतैः कुसुमरजोभिरदूषितलोचनाप्यश्रुजलं मुमोच। हंसपक्षतालवृन्तैवा[3]न्तवातविततैः शोणशीकरैरसिक्ताप्यार्द्रतामगात्। प्रेङ्खत्कादम्बमिथुनै[4]रनूढाप्यघूर्णत वनकमलिनीकल्लोलदोलाभिः। विघटमानचक्रवाकयुगलविसृष्टैरस्पृष्टापि श्यामतामाससाद विरहनिःश्वासधूमैः। पुष्पधूलिधूसरैरदष्टापि व्यचेष्टत मधुकरकुलैः।

अथ गणरात्रापगमे निवर्तमानस्तेनैव वर्त्मना तं देशमागत्य तथैव निवारितपरिजनश्छत्रधारद्वितीयो विकुक्षिर्ढुढौके। सरस्वती तु तं दूरादेव संमुखमागच्छन्तं प्रीत्या ससंभ्रममुत्थाय वनमृगीवोद्ग्रीवा विलोकयन्ती मार्गपरिश्रान्तमस्नपयदिव धवलितदशदिशा दृशा। कृतासनपरिग्रहं तु तं प्रीत्या सावित्री पप्रच्छ—'आर्य, कच्चित्कुशली कुमारः' इति। सोऽब्रवीत्—

१ 'येषामसावविषयः' ब. २ 'अताड्यत मकरकेतुना प्रतिबुद्धाया मदन०' अ-क.
३ '०वृन्तव्रात' अ-क. ४ 'मिथुनाभिरनूढा' अ-ब.

'आयुष्मति, कुशली । स्मरति च भवत्योः । केवलममीषु दिवसेषु तनीयसीमिव तनुं बिभर्ति । अविज्ञायमानां चानिमित्तां शून्यतामिवाधत्ते । अपि च । अन्व[1]क्षमागमिष्यत्येव मालतीति नाम्ना वाणिनी वार्तां वो विज्ञातुम् । उच्छ्वसितं सा कुमारस्य' इति । तच्छ्रुत्वा पुनरपि सावित्री समभाषत—'अतिमहानुभावः खलु कुमारो यदेवमविज्ञायमाने क्षणदृष्टेऽपि जने परिचितिमनुबध्नाति । तस्य हि गच्छतो यदृच्छया कथमप्यंशुकमिव मार्गलतासु मानसमस्मासु मुहूर्तमासक्तमासीत् । अशून्यं हि सौजन्यमाभिजात्येन वः स्वामिसूनोः । अलसः खलु लोको यदेवं सुलभसौहार्दानि येनकेनचिन्न क्रीणाति महतां मनांसि । सोऽयमौदार्यातिशयः कोऽपि महात्मनामितरजनदुर्लभो येनोपकरणीकुर्वन्ति त्रिभुवनम्' इति । विकुक्षिरुच्चावचैरालापैः सुचिरमिव स्थित्वा यथाभिलषितं देशमयासीत् ।

अपरेद्युरुद्यति भगवति द्युमणावुद्दामद्युतावभिद्रुततारके तिरस्कृततमसि तामरसव्[2]यासव्यसनिनि सहस्ररश्मौ शोणमुत्तीर्यायान्ती, तरलदेहप्रभावितानच्छलेनात्यच्छं सकलं शोणसलिलमिवानयन्ती, स्फुटितातिमुक्तककुसुमस्तबकसमत्विषि सटाले महति मृगपताविव गौरी तुरङ्गमे स्थिता, सलीलमुरोब[3]न्धारोपितस्य तिर्यगुत्कर्णतुरगाकर्ण्यमाननूपुरपटुरणितस्यातिबहलेन पिण्डालक्तकेन पल्लवितस्य कुङ्कुमपिञ्जरितपृष्ठस्य चरणयुगलस्य प्रसरद्भिरतिलोहितैः प्रभाप्रवाहैरुभयतस्ताडनदोहदलोभागतानि किसलयितानि रक्ताशोकवनानीवाकर्षयन्ती, सकलजीवलोकहृदयहठहरणाघोषणयेव रशनया शिञ्जानजघनस्थला, धौतधवलनेत्रनिर्मितेन निर्मोकलघुतरेणाप्रपदीनेन कञ्चुकेन तिरोहिततनुलता, छातकञ्चुकान्तरदृश्यमानैराश्यानचन्दनधवलैरवयवैः स्वच्छसलिलाभ्यन्तरविभाव्यमानमृणालकाण्डेव सरसी, कुसुम्भरागपाटलं पुलकबन्धचित्रं चण्डातकमन्तः[4]स्फुटं स्फटिकभूमिरिव रत्ननिधानमादधाना, हारेणामलकीफलनिस्[5]तलमुक्ताफलेन स्फुरितस्थूलग्रहगणशारा शारदीव श्वेतविरलजलधरपटलावृता द्यौः, कुचपूर्णकलशयोरुपरि रत्नप्रालम्बमालिकामरुणहरितकिरणकिसलयिनीं कस्यापि पुण्यवतो हृदयप्रवेशव[6]नमालिकामिव बद्धां धारयन्ती, प्रकोष्ठनिविष्टस्यैकैकस्य हाटककटकस्य मरकतमकरवेदिकासनाथस्य हरितीकृतदिगन्ताभिर्मयूखसन्ततिभिः स्थलकमलिनीभिरिव लक्ष्मीशङ्कयानुगम्यमाना, बहलताम्बूलकृष्णिकान्धकारितेनाधरसम्पुटेन मुखशशिपीतं ससंध्यारागं तिमिरमिव वमन्ती, विकचनयनकुवलयकुतूहलालीनयालिकुलसंहत्या नीलांशुकजालिकयेव निरुद्धार्धवदना, नीलीरागनिहितनीलिम्ना शिखिगलशितिना वामश्रवणाश्रयिणा दन्तपत्रेण कालमेघपल्लवेन विद्यु-

---

१ 'अन्वक्षमागमिष्यत्येव' क. २ 'तामरसव्याकोश०' क. ३ 'उरोबन्धारोपित०' ब. ४ 'अन्तःस्फुरस्फटिक' ब. ५ 'निस्तुल०' अ. ६ 'वन्दनमालिका०' ब. ७ 'प्रबाल०' ब. ८ 'शिति' अ–क.

दिव द्योतमाना, बकुलफलानुकारिणीभिस्तिसृभिर्मुक्ताभिः कल्पितेन बालिकायुगलेनाधोमुखेनालोकजलवर्षिणा सिञ्चन्तीवातिकोमले भुजलते, दक्षिणकर्णावतंसितया केतकीगर्भपलाशलेखया रजनिकरजिह्वालतयेव लावण्यलोभेन लिह्यमानकपोलतला, तमालश्यामलेन मृगमदामोदनिष्यन्दिना तिलकबिन्दुना मुद्रितमिव मनोभवसर्वस्वं वदनमुद्वहन्ती, ललाटलासकस्य सीमन्तचुम्बिनश्चटुलतिलकमणेरुदञ्चता चटुलेनांशुजालेन रक्तांशुकेनेव कृतशिरोवगुण्ठना, पृष्ठप्रेङ्खदनादरसंयमनशिथिलजूटिकाबन्धा नीलचामरावचूलिनीव चूडामणिमकरिकासनाथा मकरकेतुकेतुपताका, कुलदेवतेव चन्द्रमसः, पुनःसञ्जीवनौषधिरिव पुष्पधनुषः, वेलेव रागसागरस्य, ज्योत्स्नेव यौवनचन्द्रोदयस्य, महानदीव रतिरसामृतस्य, कुसुमोद्गतिरिव सुरततरोः, बालविद्येव वैदग्ध्यस्य, कौमुदीव कान्तेः, धृतिरिव धैर्यस्य, गुरुशालेव गौरवस्य, बीजभूमिरिव विनयस्य, गोष्ठीव गुणानाम्, मनस्वितेव महानुभावतायाः, तृप्तिरिव तारुण्यस्य, कुवलयदलदामदीर्घलोचनया पाटलाधरया कुन्दकुड्मलस्फुटदशनया शिरीषमालासुकुमारभुजयुगलया कमलकोमलकरया बकुलसुरभिनिःश्वसितया चम्पकावदातया कुसुममय्येव ताम्बूलकरङ्कवाहिन्या महाप्रमाणाश्वतरारूढयानुगम्यमाना, कतिपयपरिचारकपरिकरा मालती समदृश्यत। दूरादेव च दधीचप्रेम्णा सरस्वत्या लुण्ठितेव मनोरथैः, आकृष्टेव कुतूहलेन, प्रत्युद्गतेवोत्कलिकाभिः, आलिङ्गितेवोत्कण्ठया, अन्तःप्रवेशितेव हृदयेन, स्नपितेवानन्दाश्रुभिः, विलुप्तेव स्मितेन, वीजितेवोच्छ्वसितैः, आच्छादितेव चक्षुषा, अभ्यर्चितेव वदनपुण्डरीकेण, सखीकृतेवाशया सविधमुपययौ। अवतीर्य च तुरगाद्दूरादेवावनतेन मूर्ध्ना प्रणाममकरोत्। आलिङ्गिता च ताभ्यां सविनयमुपाविशत्। सप्रश्रयं ताभ्यां सम्भाषिता च पुण्यभाजमात्मानममन्यत। अकथयच्च दधीचसन्दिष्टं शिरसि विनिहितेनाञ्जलिना नमस्कारम्। अगृह्णाच्चाकारतः प्रभृत्यग्राम्यतया तैस्तैरपि पेशलैरालापैः सावित्रीसरस्वत्योर्मनसी।

क्रमेण चातीते मध्यन्दिनसमये शोणमवतीर्णायां सावित्र्यां स्नातुमुत्सारितपरिजना साकूता मालती कुसुमप्रस्तरशायिनीं समुपसृत्य सरस्वतीमाबभाषे—'देवि, विज्ञप्यं नः किञ्चिदस्ति रहसि। अतो मुहूर्तमवधानदानेन प्रसादं क्रियमाणमिच्छामि' इति। सरस्वती तु दधीचसन्देशाशङ्किनी किं वक्ष्यतीति स्तनविनिहितवामकरनखकिरणदन्तुरितमुद्भिद्यमानकुतूहलाङ्कुरनिकरमिव हृदयमुत्तरीयदुकूलवल्कलैकदेशेन सञ्छादयन्ती, गलतावतंसपल्लवेन श्रोतुं श्रवणेनेव धावमानेनानवरतश्वाससन्दोहदोलायितां जीविताशामिव समासन्नलतामवलम्बमाना, समुत्फुल्लस्य मुखशशिनो लावण्यप्रवाहेण शृङ्गाररसेनेव प्लावयन्ती जीवलोकम्, शयनकुसुमपरिमलमग्नैर्मधुकरकदम्बकैर्म-

---

१ 'चटुलातिलक' अ-क.

दनानलदाहश्यामलैर्मनोरथैरिव निर्गत्य मूर्तैरुत्क्षिप्यमाणा, कुसुमशयनीयात्स्मरशरसंज्वरिणी मन्दं मन्दमुदगात्। 'उपांशु कथय' इति कपोलतलप्रतिबिम्बितां लज्जयेव कर्णमूलं मालतीं प्रवेशयन्ती मधुरया गिरा सुधीरमुवाच—'सखि मालति किमर्थमेवममिदधासि। काहमवधानदानस्य शरीरस्य प्राणानां वा। सर्वस्या[1]प्रार्थितोऽपि प्रभवत्येवा[2]तिवेलं चक्षुष्यो जनः। सा न काचिद्या न भवसि मे स्वसा सखी प्रणयिनी प्राणसमा च। नियुज्यतां यावतः कार्यस्य क्षमं क्षोदीयसो गरीयसो वा शरीरकमिदम्। अनवस्करमाश्रवं मे त्वयि हृदयम्। प्रीत्या प्रतिसे[3]रा विधेयास्मि ते। व्यावृणु वरवर्णिनि विवक्षितम्' इति। सा त्ववादीत्—'देवि, जानास्येव माधुर्यं विषयाणाम्, लोलुपतां चेन्द्रियग्रामस्य, उन्मादितां च नवयौवनस्य, पारिप्लवतां च मनसः। प्रख्यातैव मन्मथस्य दुर्निवारता। अतो न मामुपालम्भेनोपस्थातुमर्हसि। न च बालिशता चपलता चारणता वा वाचालतायाः कारणम्। न किंचिन्न कारयत्यसाधारणा स्वामिभक्तिः। सा त्वं देवि यदैव दृष्टासि देवेन तत एवारभ्यास्य कामो गुरुः, चन्द्रमा जीवितेशः, मलयमरुदुच्छ्वासहेतुः, आधयोऽन्तरङ्गस्थानेषु, सन्तापः परमसुहृत्, प्रजागर आप्तः, मनोरथाः सर्वगताः, निःश्वासा विग्रहाग्रेसराः, मृत्युः पार्श्ववर्ती, रणरणकः सञ्चारकः, सङ्कल्पा बुद्ध्युपदेशवृद्धाः। किं वा विज्ञापयामि। अनुरूपो दे[4]व्या इत्यात्मसम्भावना, शीलवानिति प्रक्रमविरुद्धम्, धीर इत्यवस्थाविपरीतम्, सुभग इति त्वदायत्तम्, स्थिरप्रीतिरिति निपुणोपक्षेपः, जानाति सेवितुमित्यस्वामिभावोचितम्, इच्छति दासभावमामरणात्कर्तुमिति धूर्तालापः, भवनस्वामिनी भवसीत्युपप्रलोभनम्, पुण्यभागिनी भजति भर्तारं तादृशमिति स्वामिपक्षपातः, त्वं तस्य मृत्युरित्यप्रियम्, अगुणज्ञासीत्यधिक्षेपः, स्वप्नेऽस्य बहुशः कृतप्रसादासीत्यसाक्षिकम्, प्राणरक्षार्थमर्थयत इति कातरता, तत्रागम्यतामित्याज्ञा, वारितोऽपि बलादागच्छतीति परिभवः। तदेवमगोचरे गिरामसीति श्रुत्वा देवी प्रमाणम्' इत्यभिधाय तूष्णीमभूत्।

अथ सरस्वती प्रीतिविस्फारितेन चक्षुषा प्रत्यवादीत्—'अयि, न शक्नोमि बहु भाषितुम्। एषास्मि ते स्मितवादिनि वचसि स्थिता। गृह्यन्ताममी प्राणाः' इति। मालती तु 'यदाज्ञापयि[5]ष्यतिप्रसादः' इति व्याहृत्य प्रहर्षपरवशा प्रणम्य प्रजविना तुरगेण ततार शोणम्। अगाच्च दधीचमानेतुं च्यवनाश्रमपदम्। इतरा तु सखीस्नेहेन सावित्रीमपि विदितवृत्तान्तामकरोत्। उत्कण्ठाभारभृता च ताम्यता चेतसा कल्पायितं कथंकथमपि दिवसशेषमनैषीत्। अस्तमुपगतवति भगवति गभस्तिमति, स्तिमिततरमवतरति तमसि, प्रहसितामिव सितां दिशं पौरन्दरीं दरीमिव केसरिणि मुञ्चति चन्द्रमसि,

---

१ 'प्रार्थितेऽपि' ब. २ 'प्रभवत्यवातिपेशलः' क–ब. ३ 'प्रतिसरास्मि ते' ब. ४ 'देव' ब. ५ 'यथाज्ञापयिष्यसि प्रसादः' ब.

सरस्वती शुचिनि चीनांशुकसुकुमारे तरङ्गिणि दुकूलकोमले शयन इव शोण-सैकते समुपविष्टा स्वप्नकृतप्रार्थनापादपतनलग्नां दधीचचरणनखचन्द्रिकामिव ललाटिकां दधाना, गण्डस्थलादर्शप्रतिबिम्बितेन 'चारुहासिनि, अयमसावाहृतो हृदयदयितो जनः' इति श्रवणसमीपवर्तिना निवेद्यमानमदनसन्देशेवेन्दुना, विकीर्यमाणनखकिरणचक्रवालेन बालव्यजनीकृतचन्द्रकलाकलापेनेव[1] करेण वीजयन्ती स्वेदिनं स्पष्टकपोलपट्टम्, 'अत्र दधीचादृते न केनचित्प्रवेष्टव्यम्' इति तिरश्चीनं चित्तभुवा पातितां विलासवेत्रलतामिव बालमृणालिकामधिस्तनं स्तनयन्ती[2] कथमपि हृदयेन वहन्ती प्रतिपालयामास। आसीच्चास्या मनसि—'अहमपि नाम सरस्वती यत्रामुना मनोजन्मना जघन्येव[3] परवशीकृता। तत्र का गणनेतरासु तपस्विनीष्वतितरलासु तरुणीषु' इति।

आजगाम च मधुमास इव सुरभिगन्धवहः, हंस इव कृतमृणालधृतिः[4], शिखण्डीव घनप्रीत्युन्मुखः, मलयानिल इवाहितसरसचन्दनधवलतनुलतोत्कम्पः, कृष्यमाण इव कृतकरकचग्रहेण ग्रहपतिना, प्रेर्यमाण इव कन्दर्पोद्दीपनदक्षेण दक्षिणानिलेन, उह्यमान इवोत्कलिकाबहलेन रतिरसेन, परिमलसम्पातिना मधुपपटलेन पटेनेव नीलेनाच्छादिताङ्गयष्टिः, अन्तःस्फुरत मत्तमदनकरिकर्णशङ्खायमानेन प्रतिमेन्दुना प्रथमसमागमविलासविलक्षस्मितेनेव धवलीक्रियमाणैककपोलोदरो मालतीद्वितीयो दधीचः। आगत्य च हृदयगतदयितानूपुररवमिश्रयेव हंसगद्गदया गिरा कृतसम्भाषणो यथा मन्मथः समाज्ञापयति, यथा यौवनमुपदिशति, यथानुरागः शिक्षयति, यथा विदग्धताध्यापयति, तथा तामभिरामां रामामरमयत्। उपजातविस्रम्भा चात्मानमकथयदस्य सरस्वती। तेन[5] तु सार्धमेकं दिवसमिवानयत्संवत्सरमधिकम्।

अथ दैवयोगात्सरस्वती बभार गर्भम्। असूत चानेहसा सर्वलक्षणाभिरामं तनयम्। तस्मै च जातमात्रायैव 'सम्यक्सरहस्याः सर्वे वेदाः सर्वाणि च शास्त्राणि सकलाश्च कलाः मत्प्रसादात्स्वयमाविर्भविष्यन्ति' इति वरमदात्। सद्भर्तृश्लाघया दर्शयितुमिव हृदयेनादाय दधीचं पितामहादेशात्समं सावित्र्या ब्रह्मलोकमारुरोह। गतायां च तस्यां दधीचोऽपि हृदये ह्रादिन्येवाभिहतो भार्गववंशसम्भूतस्य भ्रातुर्ब्राह्मणस्य जायामक्षमालाभिधानां मुनिकन्यकामात्मसूनोः संवर्धनाय नियुज्य विरहातुरस्तपसे वनमगात्। यस्मिन्नेवावसरे सरस्वत्यसूत तनयं तस्मिन्नेवाक्षमालापि सुतं प्रसूतवती। तौ तु सा निर्विशेषं सामान्यस्तन्या शनैः शनैः शिशू समवर्धयत्। एकस्तयोः सारस्वताख्य

---

१ 'कृतचन्द्रकरेणेव करेण' ब. २ 'स्तनयन्तीम्' क; 'स्तनन्ती' ब. ३ 'जानत्येव' ब. ४ 'धृतिः' ब. ५ 'तया' अ—क.

एवाभवत्, द्वितीयोऽपि वत्सनामाभवत् । आसीच्च तयोः सोदर्ययोरिव स्पृहणीया प्रीतिः ।

अथ सारस्वतो मातुर्महिम्ना यौवनारम्भ एवाविर्भूताशेषविद्यासम्भारस्तस्मिन्सवयसि भ्रातरि प्रेयसि प्राणसमे सुहृदि वत्से वाङ्मयं समस्तमेव सञ्चारयामास । चकार च कृतदारपरिग्रहस्यास्य तस्मिन्नेव प्रदेशे प्रीत्या प्रीतिकूटनामानं निवासम् । आत्मनाप्याषाढी, कृष्णाजिनी, वल्कली, अक्षवलयी, मेखली, जटी च भूत्वा तपस्यतो जनयितुरेव जगामान्तिकम् ।

अथ तस्मात्[1]प्रवर्धमानादिपुरुषजनितात्मचरणोन्नतिनिर्गतप्रघोषः, परमेश्वरशिरोधृतः, सकलकलागमगम्भीरः, महामुनिमान्यः, विपक्षक्षोभक्षमः, क्षितितललब्धायतिः, अस्खलितप्रवृत्तो भागीरथीप्रवाह इव पावनः प्रावर्तत विपुलो[2] वंशः । यस्मादजायन्त वात्स्यायना नाम गृहमुनयः, आश्रितश्रौता अप्यनालम्बितालीकबककाकवः, कृतकुक्कुटवृत्ता अप्यबैडालवृत्तयः, विवर्जितजनपङ्क्तयः, परिहृतकपटकीरै[3]कुचीकूर्चाकूताः, अगृहीतगह्वराः, न्यक्कृतनिकृतयः, प्रसन्नप्रकृतयः, विगतविकृतयः, परपरिवादपराचीनचेतसः, वर्णत्रयव्यावृत्तिविशुद्धान्धसः, धीरधिषणो[4]वधूताध्येषणाः, असङ्कसुकस्वभावाः, प्रणतप्रणयिनः, शमितसमस्तशाखान्तरसंशीतयः, उद्घाटितसमग्रग्रन्थार्थग्रन्थयः, कवयः, वाग्मिनः, विमत्सराः, सरसं[5]भाषितव्यसनिनः, विदग्धपरिहासवेदिनः, परिचयपेशलाः, नृत्यगीतवादित्रेष्वबाह्याः, ऐतिह्यस्याविवितृष्णाः, सानुक्रोशाः, सत्यशुचयः, साधुसंमताः, सर्वसत्त्वसौहार्दद्रवार्द्रहृदयाः, तथा सर्वगुणोपेता राजसेनानभिभूताः, क्षमाभाज आश्रितनन्दनाः, अनिस्त्रिंशा विद्याधराः, अजडाः कलावन्तः, अदोषास्तारकाः, अपरोपतापिनो भास्वन्तः, अनुष्माणो हुतभुजः, अकुसृतयो भोगिनः, अस्तम्भाः पुण्यालयाः, अलुप्तक्रतुक्रिया दक्षाः, अव्यालाः कामजितः, असाधारणा द्विजातयः ।

तेषु चैवमुत्पद्यमानेषु, संसरति संसारे, यात्सु युगेषु, अवतीर्णे कलौ, वहत्सु वत्सरेषु, व्रजत्सु वासरेषु, अतिक्रामति च काले, प्रसवपरम्पराभिरनवरतमापतति विकाशिनि वात्स्यायनकुले, क्रमेण कुबेरनामा वैनतेय इव गुरुपक्षपाती द्विजो जन्म लेभे । तस्याभवन्नच्युत ईशानो हरः पाशुपतश्चेति चत्वारो युगारम्भा इव ब्रह्मतेजोजन्यमानप्रजाविस्तारा नारायणबाहुदण्डा इव सचक्रनन्दकास्तनयाः । तत्र पाशुपतस्यैक एवाभवद्भूभार इवाचलकुलस्थितिश्चतुरुदधिगम्भीरोऽर्थपतिरिति नाम्ना समग्राग्रजन्मचक्रचूडामणिर्महात्मा सूनुः । सोऽजनयद्भृगुं हंसं शुचिं कविं महीदत्तं धर्मं जातवेदसं

१ 'वत्सात्प्र' ब. २ 'विमल:' ब. ३ 'कौर' क; 'कौर' ब. ४ '०धिषणा विधूताध्येषणा' ब. ५ 'परसुभाषित०' ब.

चित्रभानुं [1]त्र्यक्षमहिदत्तं विश्वरूपं चेत्येकादश रुद्रानिव सोमामृतरसशीकरच्छुरितमुखान्पवित्रान्पुत्रान् । अलभत च चित्रभानुस्तेषां मध्ये राजदेव्यभिधानायां ब्राह्मण्यां बाणमात्मजम् । स बाल एव विधेर्बलवतो वशादुपसम्पन्नया व्ययुज्यत जनन्या । जातस्नेहस्तु नितरां पितैवास्य मातृतामकरोत् । अवर्धत च तेनाधिकतरमे[2]धीयमानधृतिर्धाम्नि निजे ।

कृतोपनयनादिक्रियाकलापस्य समावृत्तस्य चतुर्दशवर्षदेशीयस्य पितापि श्रुतिस्मृतिविहितं कृत्वा द्विजजनोचितं निखिलं पुण्यजातं कालेनादशमीस्थ एवास्तमगात् । संस्थिते च पितरि महता शोकेनाभीलमनुप्राप्तो दिवानिशं दह्यमानहृदयः कथंकथमपि कतिपयान्दिवसानात्मगृह एवानैषीत् । गते च विरलतां शोके शनैः शनैरविनयनिदानतया स्वातन्त्र्यस्य, कुतूहलबहुलतया च बालभावस्य, धैर्यप्रतिपक्षतया च यौवनारम्भस्य, शैशवोचितान्यनेकानि चापलान्याचरन्नित्वरो बभूव । अभवंश्चास्य व[3]यसा समानाः सुहृदः सहायाश्च । तथा च । भ्रातरौ पारशवौ चन्द्रसेनमातृषेणौ, भा[4]षाकविरीशानः परं मित्रम्, प्रणयिनौ रुद्रनारायणौ, विद्वांसौ वारबाणवासबा[5]णौ, वर्णकविर्वेणीभारतः, प्राकृतकृत्कुलपुत्रो वायुविकारः, बन्दिनावनङ्गबाणसूचीबाणौ, कात्यायनिका चक्रवाकिका, जाङ्गुलिको [6]मयूरकः, ताम्बूलदायकश्चण्डकः, भिषक्पुत्रो मन्दारकः, पुस्तकवाचकः सुदृष्टिः, कलादश्चामीकरः, हैरिकः सिन्धुषे[7]णः, लेखको गोविन्दकः, चित्रकृद्वीरवर्मा, पुस्तकृत्कुमारदत्तः, मार्दङ्गिको जीमूतः, गायनौ सोमिलग्रहादित्यौ, सैरन्ध्री कुरङ्गिका, वांशिकौ मधुकरपारावतौ, गान्धर्वोपाध्यायो दर्दुरकः, संवाहिका केरलिका, लासकयुवा ताण्डविकः, आक्षिक आखण्डलः, कितवो भीमकः, शैलालियुवा शिखण्डकः, नर्तकी हरिणिका, पाराशरी सुमतिः, क्षपणको वीरदेवः, कथको जयसेनः, शैवो वक्रघोणः, मन्त्रसाधकः करालः, असुरविवरव्यसनी लोहिताक्षः, धातुवादविद्विहङ्गमः, [8]दार्दुरिको दामोदरः, ऐन्द्रजालिकश्चकोराक्षः, मस्करी ताम्रचूडः । स एतैश्चान्यैश्चानुगम्यमानो बालतया निघ्नतामुपगतो देशान्तरालोकनकौतुकाक्षिप्तहृदयः सत्स्वपि पितृपितामहोपात्तेषु ब्राह्मणजनोचितेषु विभवेषु सति चाविच्छिन्ने विद्याप्रसङ्गे गृहान्निरगात् । अगाच्च निरवग्रहो ग्रहवानिव नव[9]यौवनेन स्वैरिणा मनसा महतामुपहास्यताम् ।

अथ शनैः शनैरत्युदारव्यवहृतिर्मनोहृन्ति बृहन्ति राजकुलानि वीक्षमाणः, निरवद्यविद्याविद्योतितानि च गुरुकुलानि सेवमानः, महार्हालापगम्भीरगुणवद्गोष्ठीश्चोपतिष्ठमानः, स्वभावगम्भीर[10]धीधनानि विदग्धमण्ड-

---

१ 'त्र्यक्षं महिदत्तम्' ब. २ 'आधीयमान०' ब. ३ 'सवयसः समानाः' ब. ४ 'कविरीशानः' ब. ५ 'वासधारौ' ब. ६ 'मायूरकः' ब. ७ 'सिद्धसेनः' ब. ८ 'दार्दरिकः' ब. ९ 'यौवनस्वैरिणा' ब. १० '०धीर्धनानि' ब–अ.

क्लानि च गाहमानः, पुनरपि तामेव वैपश्चितीमात्मवंशोचितां प्रकृतिमभजत् । महतश्च कालात्तामेव भूयो वात्स्यायनवंशाश्रयामात्मनो जन्मभुवं ब्राह्मणाधिवासमगमत् । तत्र च चिरदर्शनादभिनवीभूतस्नेहसद्भावै ससंस्तव[1]प्रकटितज्ञातेयैराप्तैरुत्सवदिवस इवाभिनन्दितागमनो बालमित्रमण्डलस्य मध्यगतो मोक्षसुखमिवान्वभवदिति ।

इति श्रीबाणभट्ट[2]कृतौ हर्षचरिते वात्स्यायनवंशवर्णनं नाम प्रथम उच्छ्वासः ।

---

१ 'ससंभ्रम०' क; 'संस्तवप्रकटित' ख. २ 'इति श्रीमहाकविचक्रचूडामणिश्रीबाणभट्टविरचिते हर्षचरिते महाकाव्ये वात्स्यायनवंशवर्णनं नाम प्रथम उच्छ्वासः सम्पूर्णः' ख.

द्वितीय उच्छ्वासः ।

अतिगम्भीरे भूपे कूप इव जनस्य निरवतारस्य ।
दधति समीहितसिद्धिं गुणवन्तः पार्थिवा घटकाः ॥ १ ॥

रागिणि नलिने लक्ष्मीं दिवसो निदधाति दिनकरप्रभवाम् ।
अनपेक्षितगुणदोषः परोपकारः सतां व्यसनम् ॥ २ ॥

अथ तत्रानवरताध्ययनध्वनिमुखराणि, भस्मपुण्ड्रकपाण्डुरललाटैः कपिलशिखाजालजटिलैः कृशानुभिरिव ऋतुलोभागतैर्बटुभिरध्यास्यमानानि, सेकसुकुमारसोमकेदारिकाहरितायमानप्रघनानि, कृष्णाजिनविकीर्णशुष्यत्पुरोडाशीयश्यामाकतण्डुलानि, बालिकाविकीर्यमाणनीवारबलीनि, शुचिशिष्यशतानीयमानहरितकुशपूलीपलाशसमिन्धि, इन्धनगोमयपिण्डकूटसङ्कटानि, आमिक्षीयक्षीरक्षारिणीनामग्निहोत्रधेनूनां खुरवलयैर्विलिखिताजिरवितर्दिकानि, कमण्डलव्यमृत्पिण्डमर्दनव्यग्रयतिजनानि[1], वैतानवेदीशङ्कव्यामामौदुम्बरीणां शाखानां राशिभिः पवित्रितपर्यन्तानि, वैश्वदेवपिण्डपङ्क्तिपाण्डुरितप्रदेशानि[2], हविर्धूमधूसरिताङ्गनविटपिकिसलयानि, वत्सीयवत्सपालकलालिततरलतर्णकानि[3], क्रीडत्कृष्णशारच्छागशावकप्रकटितपशुबन्धप्रबन्धानि, शुकसारिकारब्धाध्ययनदीयमानोपाध्यायविश्रान्तिसुखानि, साक्षात्त्रयीतपोवनानीव चिरदृष्टानां बान्धवानां प्रीयमाणो भ्रमन्भवनानि सुखमतिष्ठत् ।

तत्रस्थस्य चास्य कदाचित्कुसुमसमययुगमुपसंहरन्नजृम्भत ग्रीष्माभिधानः सम्फुल्लमल्लिकाधवलाट्टहासो महाकालः । प्रत्यग्रनिर्जितस्यास्तमुपगतवतो वसन्तसामन्तस्य बालापत्येष्विव पयःपायिषु नवोद्यानेषु दर्शितस्नेहो मृदुरभूत् । अभिनवोदितश्च सर्वस्यां पृथिव्यां सकलकुसुमबन्धनमोक्षमकरोत्प्रतपत्तुष्णसमयः । स्वयमृतुराजस्याभिषेकार्द्रा[4]श्चामरकलापा इवागृह्यन्त कामिनीनां चिकुरचयाः कुसुमायुधेन । हिमदग्धसकलकमलिनीकोपेनेव हिमालयाभिमुखीं यात्रामदादंशुमाली ।

अथ ललाटन्तपे तपति तपने लिखित[5]ललाटिकापुण्ड्रकैरलक[6]चीरचीवरसंवीतैः स्वेदोदबिन्दुमुक्ताक्षवलयवाहिभिर्दिनकराराधननियमा इवागृह्यन्त ललनाललाटेन्दुभिः[7] । चन्दनधूसराभिरसूर्यम्पश्याभिः कुमुदिनीभिरिव दिवसमसुप्यत सुन्दरीभिः । निद्रालसा रत्नालोकमपि नासहन्त दृशः, किमुत जरठमातपम् । अशिशिरसमयेन चक्रवाकमिथुनाभिनन्दिताः सरित इव

---

१ 'कामण्डलव्य०' अ–क. २ '०पिण्डपाण्डुरित०' ब. ३ 'वत्सीयबालकलालित०' अ–क. ४ '०राजस्यागृह्यन्ताभिषेका०' ब. ५ 'चन्दनलिखित०' ब. ६ 'अलकचीवर०' ब. ७ '०ललाटेन्दुद्युतिभिः' ब.

तनिमानमानीयन्त सोडुपाः शर्वर्यः। अभिनवपट्टुपाटलामोदसुरभिपरिमलं न केवलं जलम्, जनस्य पवनमपि पातुमभूदभिलाषो दिवसकरसन्तापात्।

क्रमेण च खरखगमयूखे,[१] खण्डितशैशवे, शुष्यत्सरसि, सीदत्स्रोतसि, मन्दनिर्झरे, झिल्लिकाझाङ्कारिणि, कातरकपोतकूजितानुबन्धबधिरितविश्वे, विश्वसत्[२]पतत्रिणि, करीषङ्कषमरुति, विरलवीरुधि, रुधिरकुतूहलिकेसरिकिशोरकलिह्यमानकठोरधातकीस्तबके, ताम्यत्स्तम्बेरमयूथवमथुतिम्यन्महामहीधरनितम्बे, दिनकर[३]दूयमानद्विरददीन[४]वदनाश्यानदानश्यामिकालीनमूकमधुलिहि, लोहितायमानमन्दारसिन्दूरितसीम्नि, सलिलस्यन्दसन्दोह[५]सन्देहमुह्यन्महामहिषविषाणकोटिविलिख्यमानस्फुटत्स्फाटिकदृषदि, घर्मममर्रितगर्मुति, तप्तपांशु[६]कुकूलविकरणकातरविकिरे, विवरशरणश्वाविधे, तटार्जुनकुररकूजाज्वर[७]विवर्तमानोत्तानशफरशारपङ्कशेषपल्वलाम्भसि, दावजनितजगन्नीराजने, रजनीराजयक्ष्मणि, कठोरीभवति निदाघकाले, प्रतिदिशमाटीकमाना इवोषरेषु प्रपावार्ट[८]कुटीपटलप्रकटलुण्ठकाः, प्रपक्वकपिकच्छूगुच्छच्छटाच्छोटनचापलैरकाण्डकण्डूला इव कर्षन्तः शर्करिलाः कर्करस्थलीः, स्थूलदृषच्चूर्णमुचः, मुचुकुन्दकन्दलदलनदन्तुराः, समन्ततः[९] पतन्मुखरचीरीगणमुखशीकरशीक्यमानतनवः, तरुणतरतरणितापतरले तरन्त इव तरङ्गिणि मृगतृष्णिकातरङ्गिणीनामलीकवारिणि, शुष्यच्छमीमर्मरमारवमार्गलङ्घनलाघवजवजङ्घालाः, रैणवावर्तमण्डलीरेचकरासरसरभसारब्धनर्तनारम्भारभटीनटाः, दावदग्धस्थलीमषीमलनमलिनाः, शिक्षितक्षपणकवृत्तय इव वनमयूरपिच्छचयानुच्चिन्वन्तः, सप्रयाणगुञ्जा इव शिञ्जानजरत्करञ्जसञ्जरीबीजजालकैः, सप्ररोहा इवातपातुरवनमहिषनासानिकुञ्जस्थूलनिःश्वासैः, सापत्या इवोड्डीयमानजवनवातहरिणपरिपाटीपेटकैः, सभ्रुकुटय इव दह्यमानखलधानबुसकूटकुटिलधूमकोटिभिः, सावीचिवीचय इव महोष्ममुक्तिभिः, लोमशा इव शीर्यमाणशाल्मलिफलतूलतन्तुभिः, दद्रुणा[१०] इव शुष्कपत्रप्रकराकृष्टिभिः, सिराला इव तृणवेणीविकिरणैः,[११] उच्छ्मश्रव इव धूयमाननवयवशूकशकलशङ्कुभिः, दंष्ट्राला इव चलितशललसूचीशतैः, जिह्वाला इव वैश्वानरशिखाभिः, उत्सर्पत्सर्पकञ्चु[१२]कचूडालाः, ब्रह्मस्तम्भरसाभ्यवहरणाय कवलग्रहमिवोष्णैः कमलमधुभिरभ्यस्यन्तः, सकलसलिलोच्छोषणघर्मघोषणापटहै[१३]रिव शुष्कवेणुवनास्फोटनपटुरवैस्त्रिभुवनभीषिकामुद्भावयन्तः, च्युतचलचाषपक्षश्रेणीशारितसृतयः, त्विषिमन्मयूखलतालातप्लोषकल्माषवपुष इव स्फुटितगुञ्जाफलस्फुलिङ्गाङ्गाराङ्कि-

१ '०मयूखखण्डित०' ब. २ 'श्वसत्पत०' ब. ३ 'दिनकर'—इत्येतन्नास्ति अ-क-पुस्तकयोः. ४ 'दीनदानाश्यानश्यामिका०' अ-क. ५ 'सन्दोहमुह्य०' ब. ६ '०कुकूलकातर०' अ-क. ७ 'कूटाज्वर०' क; 'कूटज्वरनिवर्त०' अ. ८ 'प्रपाकट०' ब. ९ 'सन्तततपनतापमुखर०' ब. १० 'दद्रुला' क. ११ '०विकिरणैः' अ-क. १२ '०कश्चुकैश्चूडाला इव' ब. १३ 'घोषणाघोरपटलरिव' ब.

ताङ्गाः, गिरिगुहागम्भीरझाङ्कारभीषणभ्रान्तयः, भुवनभस्मीकरणाभिचारच-रुपचनचतुरा रुधिराहुतिभिरिव पारिभद्रद्रुमस्तबकवृष्टिभिस्तर्पयन्तस्तारवान्व-नविभावसून्, अशिशिरसिकतातारकितरंहसः, तप्तशैलविलीयमानशिलाजतु-रसलवलिप्तदिशः, दावदहनपच्यमानचटकाण्डखण्डखचिततरुकोटरकीटपटल-पुटपाकगन्धकटवः, प्रावर्तन्तोन्मत्ता मातरिश्वानः।

सर्वतश्च भूरिभस्त्रासहस्रसन्धुक्षणक्षुभिता इव जरठाजगरगम्भीरगलगु-हावाहिर्वायुभिः, क्वचित्स्वच्छन्दतृणचारिणो हरिणाः, क्वचित्तरुतलविवरविव-र्तिनो बभ्रवः, क्वचिज्जटावलम्बिनः कपिलाः, क्वचिच्छकुनिकुलकुलायपातिनः श्येनाः, क्वचिद्विलीनलाक्षारसलोहितच्छवयोऽधराः, क्वचिदासादितशकुनिप-क्षकृतपटुगतयो विशिखाः, क्वचिद्दग्धनिःशेषजन्महेतवो निर्वाणाः, क्वचित्कुसु-मवासिताम्बरसुरभयो रागिणः. क्वचित्सधूमोद्गारा मन्दरुचयः, क्वचित्सकल-जगद्ग्रासघस्मराः सभस्मकाः, क्वचिद्वेणुशिखरैलग्नमूर्तयोऽत्यन्तवृद्धाः, क्वचिद्-घलोपयुक्तशिलाजतवः क्षयिणः, क्वचित्सर्वरसभुजः पीवानः, क्वचिद्दग्धगुग्गु-लवो रौद्राः, क्वचिज्ज्वलितनेत्रदहनदग्धसकुसुमशरमदनाः कृतस्थाणुस्थितयः, चटुलशिखानर्तनारम्भारभटीनटाः, शुष्ककासारसृतिभिः स्फुटत्क्षीरसनीवार-बीजलाजवर्षिभिर्ज्वालाञ्जलिभिरचर्यन्त इव घर्मघृणिम्, अघृणा इव हठहूय-मानकठोरस्थलकमठवसाविस्रगन्धगृध्नवः, स्वमपि धूममम्भोदसमुद्भूतिभि-येव भक्षयन्तः, सतिलाहुतय इव स्फुटद्दहलबालकीटपटलाः कक्षेपु, श्विल्लिण इव प्लोषविचटद्धलकलधवलशम्बूकशुक्तयः शुष्केषु सरःसु, स्वेदिन इव विलीयमानमधुपटलगोलगलितमधूच्छिष्टवृष्टयः काननेषु, खलतय इव परिशीर्यमाणशिखासंहतयो महोषरेषु, गृहीतशिलाकवला इव ज्वलितसूर्यम-णिशकलेषु शिलोच्चयेषु, प्रत्यदृश्यन्त दारुणा दावाग्नयः।

तथाभूते च तस्मिन्नत्युग्रे ग्रीष्मसमये कदाचिदस्य स्वगृहावस्थितस्य भुक्तवतोऽपराह्णसमये भ्राता पारशवश्चन्द्रसेननामा प्रविश्याकथयत्—'एष खलु देवस्य चतुःसमुद्राधिपतेः सकलराजचक्रचूडामणिश्रेणीशाणकोणकषण-निर्मलीकृतचरणनखमणेः सर्वचक्रवर्तिनां धौरेयस्य महाराजाधिराजपरमेश्व-रश्रीहर्षदेवस्य भ्राता कृष्णनाम्ना भवतामन्तिकं प्रज्ञाततमो दीर्घाध्वगः प्रहितो द्वारमध्यास्ते' इति। सोऽब्रवीत्—'आयुष्मन्, अविलम्बितं प्रवेशयै-नम्' इति।

अथ तेनानीयमानम्, अतिदूरागमनगुरुजङ्घजङ्घम्, कार्दमिकचेलची-रिकानियमितोच्चण्डचण्डातकम्, पृष्ठप्रेङ्खत्पटच्चरकर्पटघटितर्गलितग्रन्थिम्, अतिनिबिडसूत्रबन्धनिम्नितान्तरालकृतव्यवच्छेदया लेखमालिकया परिकलि-

१ '०वायवः' अ—क. २ 'जटावल्कलावलम्बिनः' ब. ३ 'क्वचिदवलम्बितवेत्रयष्ट-योऽत्यन्त०' ब. ४ 'सृतिपु' ब. ५ 'कक्ष्येपु' अ—क. ६ 'शबल' ब. ७ 'पर्यन्तशी-र्यमाण०' ब. ८ 'गलग्रन्थिम्' ब. ९ 'निर्मित' ब.

तमूर्धानम्, प्रविशन्तं लेखहारकमद्राक्षीत् । अप्राक्षीच्च दूरादेव—'भद्र, भद्रमशेषभुवननिष्कारणबन्धोस्तत्रभवतः कृष्णस्य' इति । सः 'भद्रम्' इत्युक्त्वा प्रणम्य नातिदूरे समुपाविशत् । विश्रान्तश्चाब्रवीत्—'एष खलु स्वामिनो माननीयस्य लेखः प्रहितः' इति विमुच्य चार्पयत् । अथ बाणः सादरं गृहीत्वा स्वयमेवावाचयत्—'मेखलकात्सन्दिष्टमवधार्य फलप्रतिबन्धी धीमन्निरपहरणीयः कालातिपात इत्येतावदत्रार्थजातम् । इतरद्वार्तासंवादनमात्रकम्' । अवधृतलेखार्थश्च समुत्सारितपरिजनः सन्देशं पृष्टवान् । मेखलकस्त्ववादीत्—'एवमाह मेधाविनं स्वामी—जानात्येव मान्यो यथैकगोत्रता वा, समानजातिता वा, समं संवर्धनं वा, एकदेशनिवासो वा, दर्शनाभ्यासो वा, परस्परानुरागश्रवणं वा, परोक्षोपकारकरणं वा, समानशीलता वा, स्नेहस्य हेतवः । त्वयि तु विना कारणेनादृष्टेऽपि प्रत्यासन्ने बन्धाविव बद्धपक्षपातं किमपि स्निह्यति मे हृदयं दूरस्थेऽपीन्दोरिव कुमुदाकरे । भवन्तमन्तरेणान्यथा चान्यथा चायं चक्रवर्ती दुर्जनैर्ग्राहित आसीत् । न च तत्तथा । न सन्त्येव ते येषां सतामपि सतां न विद्यन्ते मित्रोदासीनशत्रवः । शिशुचापलपराचीनचेतोवृत्तितया च भवतः केनचिदसहिष्णुना यत्किञ्चिदसदृशमुदीरितमितरो लोकस्तथैव तद्गृह्णाति वक्ति च । सलिलानीव खलु गतानुगतिकानि लोलानि भवन्त्यविवेकिनां मनांसि बहुमुखश्रवणनिश्चलीकृतनिश्चयः किं करोतु पृथिवीपतिः । तत्त्वान्वेषिभिश्चास्माभिर्दूरस्थितोऽपि प्रत्यक्षीकृतोऽसि । विज्ञप्तश्चक्रवर्ती त्वदर्थं यथा—प्रायेण प्रथमे वयसि सर्वस्यैव चापलैः शैशवमपराध्यतीति । तथेति च प्रतिपन्नं स्वामिना । अतो भवता राजकुलमकृतकालक्षेपमागन्तव्यम् । अवकोशीवादृष्टपरमेश्वरो बन्धुमध्यमधिवसन्नासि मे बहुमतः । न च सेवावैषम्यविषादिना वा परमेश्वरोपसर्पणभीरुणा वा भवता भवितव्यम् । यतो यद्यपि—

स्वेच्छोपजातविषयोऽपि न याति वक्तुं
देहीति मार्गणशतैश्च ददाति दुःखम् ।
मोहात्समाक्षिपति जीवनमप्यकाण्डे
कष्टं मनोभव इवेश्वरदुर्विदग्धः ॥ ३ ॥

तथाप्यन्ये ते भूपतयः, अन्य एवायं न्यक्कृतनृगनलनिषधनहुषाम्बरीषदशरथदिलीपनाभागभरतभगीरथययातिरमृतमयः स्वामी । नास्याहङ्कारकालकूटविषदिग्धदुष्टा दृष्टयः, न गर्वगुरुगरगलग्रहगदगद्गदा गिरः, नातिस्मयोष्मापस्मारविस्मृतस्थैर्याणि स्थानकानि, नोद्दामदर्पदाहज्वरवेगविक्लवा विकाराः, नाभिमानमहासंनिपातनिर्मिताङ्गभङ्गानि गतानि, न मदार्दितवक्रीकृतौष्ठनिष्ठ्यूतनिष्ठुराक्षराणि जल्पितानि । तथा च, अस्य विमलेषु साधुषु रत्नबुद्धिः, न शिलाशकलेषु । मुक्ताधवलेषु प्रसाधनधीः, नाभरणभारेषु ।

१ 'समानज्ञानता वा' इत्येतदधिकं ब-पुस्तके. २ 'गतागतिकानि' अ-क.

दानवत्सु कर्मसु साधनश्रद्धा, न करिकीटेषु। सर्वाग्रेसरे[1] यशसि महाप्रीतिः, न जीवितजरत्तृणे। गृहीतकरास्वाशासु प्रसाधनैताभियोगः[2], न निजकलत्रचर्मपुत्रिकासु। गुणवति धनुषि सहायबुद्धिः, न पिण्डोपजीविनि सेवकजने। अपि च। अस्य मित्रोपकरणमात्मा, भृत्योपकरणं प्रभुत्वम्, पण्डितोपकरणं वैदग्ध्यम्, बान्धवोपकरणं लक्ष्मीः, कृपणोप्रकरणमैश्वर्यम्, द्विजोपकरणं सर्वस्वम्, सुकृतसंस्मरणोपकरणं हृदयम्, धर्मोपकरणमायुः[3], साहसोपकरणं शरीरम्, असिलतोपकरणं पृथिवी, विनोदोपकरणं राजकम्, प्रतापोपकरणं प्रतिपक्षः। नास्याल्पपुण्यैरवाप्येत सर्वातिशायिसुखरसप्रसूतिः पादपल्लवच्छाया' इति। श्रुत्वा च तमेव चन्द्रसेनं समादिशत्—'कृतकशिपुं विश्रान्तसुखिनमेनं कारय' इति।

अथ गते च तस्मिन्, पर्यस्ते च वासरे, सङ्घट्ट[4]मानरक्तपङ्कजसम्पुटपीयमान इव क्षयिणि क्षामतां व्रजति बालवायसास्यारुणेऽपराह्णातपे, शिथिलितनिजवाजिजवे जपापीडपाटले[5]ऽस्ताचलशिखरस्खलिते खञ्जतीव कमलिनीकण्टकक्षतपादपल्लवे पतङ्गे, पुरः परापतति प्रेङ्खदन्धकारले[6]शलम्बालके शशिविरहशोकश्याम इव श्यामामुखे, कृतसंध्योपासनः शयनीयमगात्। अचिन्तयच्चैकाकी—'किं करोमि। अन्यथा सम्भावितोऽस्मि राज्ञा। निर्निमित्तबन्धुना च सन्दिष्टमेवं कृष्णेन। कष्टा च सेवा। विषमं च भृत्यत्वम्। अतिगम्भीरं महद्राजकुलम्। न च तत्र मे पूर्वजप्रवर्तिता प्रीतिः, न कुलक्रमागता गतिः, नोपकारस्मरणानुरोधः, न बालसेवास्नेहः, न गोत्रगौ[7]रवम्, न पूर्वदर्शनदाक्षिण्यम्, न प्रज्ञासंविभागोपप्रलोभनम्, न विद्यातिशयकुतूहलम्, नाकारसौन्दर्यादरः, न सेवाकाकुकौशलम्, न विद्वद्गोष्ठीबन्धवैदग्ध्यम्, न वित्तव्ययवशीकरणम्, न राजवल्लभपरिचयः। अवश्यं गन्तव्यम्। सर्वथा भगवान्पुरारातिर्भुवनगुरुर्गतस्य[8] मे[9] सर्वं सांप्रतमाचरिष्यति' इत्यवधार्य गमनाय मतिमकरोत्।

अथान्यस्मिन्नहन्युत्थाय, प्रातरेव स्नात्वा, धृतधौतधवलदुकूलवासाः, गृहीताक्षमालः, प्रास्थानिकानि सूक्तानि मन्त्रपदानि च बहुशः समावर्त्य, देवदेवस्य विरूपाक्षस्य क्षीरस्नपनपुरःसरां सुरभिकुसुमधूपगन्धध्वजबलिविलेपनप्रदीपकबहुलां विधाय पूजां परमया भक्त्या, प्रथमहुततरलतिलत्वग्विघट्टन[10]चटुलमुखरशिखाशेखरं प्राज्याज्याहुतिप्रवर्धितदक्षिणार्चिषं भगवन्तमाशुशुक्षणिं हुत्वा, दत्वा द्युम्नं यथाविद्यमानं द्विजेभ्यः, प्रदक्षिणीकृत्य प्राङ्मुखीं नैचिकीम्, शुक्लाङ्गरागः, शुक्लमाल्यः, शुक्लवासाः, रोचनाचित्रदूर्वाग्रपल्लवग्रथितगिरिकर्णिकाकुसुमकृतकर्णपूरः, शिखासक्तसिद्धार्थकः, पितुः कनीयस्या

१ 'सर्वाशाग्रेसरे' ब. २ 'दिक्षु प्रसाधनाभियोगः' ब. ३ 'धर्म' ब. ४ 'संघटमान' ब. ५ 'पाटलिम्नि' ब. ६ 'लेखा' ब. ७ 'तन्त्रगौरवम्' ब. ८ 'भवानीपतिर्भुवनपतिः' ब. ९ 'मे शरणं सर्वं' ब. १० 'विघटन' अ—क.

स्वस्रा मात्रेव स्नेहार्द्रहृदयया श्वेतवाससा साक्षादिव भगवत्या महाश्वेतया मालत्याख्यया कृतसकलगमनमङ्गलः, दत्ताशीर्वादो बान्धववृद्धाभिः, अभिनन्दितः परिजनजरन्तीभिः, वन्दितचरणैरभ्यनुज्ञातो गुरुभिः, अभिवादितैराघ्रातः शिरसि कुलवृद्धैः, वर्धितगमनोत्साहः शकुनैः, मौहूर्तिकमतेन कृतनक्षत्रदोहदः, शोभने मुहूर्ते हरितगोमयोपलिप्ताजिरस्थण्डिलस्थापितमसितेतरकुसुममालापरिक्षिप्तकण्ठं पिष्ट¹पञ्चाङ्गुलपाण्डुरं मुखनिहितनवचूतपल्लवं पूर्णकलशमुदीक्षमाणः, प्रणम्य कुलदेवताभ्यः, कुसुमफलपाणिभिरप्रतिरथं जपद्भिर्निजद्विजैरनुगम्यमानः, प्रथमचलितदक्षिणचरणः, प्रीतिकूटान्निरगात् ।

प्रथमेऽहनि घर्मकालकष्टं निरुदकं निष्पत्रपादपविषमं पथिकजननमस्क्रियमाणप्रवेशपादपोत्कीर्णकात्यायनीप्रतियातनं शुष्कमपि पल्लवितमिव तृषितश्वापदकुललम्बितलोलजिह्वालतासहस्रैः पुलकितमिवाच्छभल्लगोलाङ्गूललिह्यमानमधुगोलचलितसरघासङ्घातैः रोमाञ्चितमिव दग्धस्थलीरूढस्थूलाभीरुकन्दलशतैः शनैश्चण्डिकाकाननमतिक्रम्य मल्लकूटनामानं ग्राममगात् । तत्र च हृदयनिर्विशेषेण भ्रात्रा सुहृदा च जगत्पतिनाम्ना सम्पादितसपर्यः सुखमवसत् । अथापरेद्युरुत्तीर्य भगवतीं भागीरथीं यष्टिग्रहकनाम्नि वनग्रामके निशामनयत् । अन्यस्मिन्दिवसे स्कन्धावारमुपमणितारमन्वजिरवति कृतसंनिवेशमाससाद । अतिष्ठच्च नातिदूरे राजभवनस्य ।

निर्वर्तितस्नानाशनव्यतिकरो विश्रान्तश्च मेखलकेन सह याममात्रावशेषे दिवसे भुक्तवति भूभुजि प्रख्यातानां क्षितिभुजां बहून्शिबिरसंनिवेशान्वीक्षमाणः शनैः शनैः पट्टबन्धार्थमुपस्थापितैश्च डिण्डिमाधिरोहणायाहूतैश्चाभिनवबद्धैश्च विक्षेपोपार्जितैश्च कौशलिकागतैश्च नागवीथीपालप्रेषितैश्च प्रथमदर्शनकुतूहलोपनीतैश्च दूतसंप्रेषणप्रेषितैश्च पल्लीपरिवृढढौकितैश्च स्वेच्छायुद्धक्रीडाकौतुकाकारितैश्च दीयमानैश्चाच्छिद्यमानैश्च मुच्यमानैश्च यामस्थापितैश्च सर्वद्वीपविजिगीषया गिरिभिरिव सागरसेतुबन्धार्थमेकीकृतैर्ध्वजपटपटुपटहशङ्खचामराङ्गरागरमणीयैः पुण्याभिषेकदिवसैरिव कल्पितैर्वारणेन्द्रैः श्यामायमानम्, अनवरतचलितखुरपुटप्रहतमृदङ्गैर्नर्तयद्भिरिव राजलक्ष्मीमुपहसद्भिरिव सृक्किपुटप्रसृतफेनाट्टहासेन जवजडजङ्घां हरिणजातिमाकारयद्भिरिव सङ्घट्टहेतोर्हर्षहेषितैनोच्चैःश्रवसमुत्पतद्भिरिव दिवसकररथतुरगरुषा पक्षायमाणमण्डनचामरमालैर्गगनतलं तुरङ्गैस्तरङ्गायमानम्, अन्यत्र प्रेषितैश्च प्रेष्यमाणैश्च प्रेषितप्रतिनिर्वृत्तैश्च बहुयोजनग-

१ 'दत्तपिष्ट०' ब. २ 'शुष्कगलगो०' ब. ३ 'चण्डिकायतनकानन०' ब. ४ 'यष्टिगृहक०' ब. ५ 'मणिपुरमन्व०' ब. ६ 'यामावस्थितैश्च' ब. ७ 'हेषितेनोच्चैरुच्चैःश्रवस०' ब. ८ 'प्रतीपनिवृत्तै०' अ-क.

मनगणनसंख्याक्षरावलीभिरिव वराटिकावलीभिर्घटितमुखमण्डनकैस्तारकितैरिव संध्यातपच्छेदैररुणचामरिकारचितकर्णपूरैः सरक्तोत्पलैरिव रक्तशालिशालेयैरनवरतझणझणायमानचारुचामीकरघुरुघुरुकमालिकैर्जरत्करञ्जवदनैरिव रणितशुष्कबीजकोशीशतैः श्रवणोपान्तप्रेङ्खत्पद्मरागवर्णोर्णाचित्रसूत्रजूटजटालैः कपिकपोलकपिलैः क्रमेलककुलैः कपिलायमानम्, अन्यत्र शरज्जलधरैरिव सद्यःसुतपयःपटलधवलतनुभिः कल्पपादपैरिव मुक्ताफलजालकजायमानालोकलुसच्छायामण्डलैर्नारायणनाभिपुण्डरीकैरिवाश्लिष्टगरुडपक्षैः क्षीरोदोद्देशैरिव द्योतमानविकटविद्रुमदण्डैः शेषफणाफलकैरिवोपरिस्फुरत्स्फीतमाणिक्यखण्डैः श्वेतगङ्गापुलिनैरिव राजहंसोपसेवितैरभिभवद्भिरिव निदाघसमयमुपहसद्भिरिव विवस्वतः प्रतापमापिबद्भिरिवातपं चन्द्रलोकमयमिव जीवलोकं जनयद्भिः कुमुदमयमिव कालं कुर्वद्भिर्ज्योत्स्नामयमिव वासरं विरचयद्भिः फेनमयीमिव दिवं दर्शयद्भिरकालकौमुदीसहस्राणीव सृजद्भिरुपहसद्भिरिव शातक्रतवीं श्रियं श्वेतायमानैरातपत्रखण्डैः श्वेतायमानम्[1], क्षणदृष्टनष्टाष्टदिङ्मुखं च मुष्णद्भिरिव भुवनमाक्षेपोत्क्षेपदोलायितं दिनं गतागतानीव कारयद्भिरिव कुनृपतिसम्पर्ककलङ्ककालीं कालेयीं स्थितिं विकचविशदकाशवनपाण्डुरदिशं शरत्समयमिवोपपादयद्भिर्बिसतन्तुमयमिवान्तरिक्षमाविर्भावयद्भिः शशिकरशुचीनां चलतां चामराणां सहस्रैर्दोलायमानम्, अपि च हंसयूथायमानं करिकर्णशङ्खैः, कल्पलतावनायमानं कदलिकाभिः, माणिक्यवृक्षकवनायमानं मायूरातपत्रैः, मन्दाकिनीप्रवाहायमानमंशुकैः, क्षीरोदायमानं क्षौमैः, कदलीवनायमानं मरकतमयूखैः, जन्यमानान्यदिवसमिव पद्मरागबालातपैः, उत्पद्यमाना[2]पराम्बरमिवेन्द्रनीलप्रभापटलैः, आरभ्यमाणापूर्वनिशमिव महानीलमयूखान्धकारैः, स्यन्दमानानेककालिन्दीसहस्रमिव गरुडमणिप्रभाप्रतानैः, अङ्गारकितमिव पुष्परागरश्मिभिः, कैश्चित्प्रवेशमलभमानैरधोमुखैश्चरणनखपतितवदनप्रतिबिम्बनिभेन लज्जया स्वाङ्गानीव विशद्भिः कैश्चिदङ्गुलीलिखितायाः क्षितेर्विकीर्यमाणकरनखकिरणकदम्बकव्याजेन सेवाचामराणीवार्पयद्भिः कैश्चिदुरःस्थलदोलायमानेन्द्रनीलतरलप्रभापट्टैः स्वामिप्रकोपप्रशमनाय कण्ठबद्धकृपाणपट्टैरिव, कैश्चिदुच्छ्वाससौरभभ्राम्यद्भ्रमरपटलान्धकारितमुखैरपहृतलक्ष्मीशोकधृतलम्बश्मश्रुभिरिवान्यैः शेखरोड्डीयमानमधुपमण्डलैः प्रणामविडम्बनाभयपलायमानमौलिभिरिव निर्जितैरपि संमानितैरिवानन्यशरणैरन्तरान्तरा निष्पततां प्रविशतां चान्तरप्रतीहाराणामनुमार्गप्रधावितानेकार्थिजनसहस्राणामनुयायिनः पुरुषानश्रान्तैः पुनः पुनः पृच्छद्भिः 'भद्र, अद्य भविष्यति भुक्ता[3]स्थानं दास्यति दर्शनं परमेश्वरः, निष्पतिष्यति वा बाह्यां कक्ष्याम्' इति दर्शनाशया दिवसं नयद्भिर्भुजनिर्जितैः शत्रुमहासामन्तैः समन्तादासेव्यमानम्, अन्यैश्च प्रतापानुरागागतै-

१ 'श्वेतद्वीपायमानम्' ब–क. २ 'उत्पाद्यमाना०' ब. ३ 'भुक्त्वा स्थाने' अ–क.

र्नानादेशजैर्महीपालैः प्रतिपालयद्भिर्नरपतिदर्शनकालमध्यास्यमानम्, एकान्तोपविष्टैश्च जैनैरार्हतैः पाशुपतैः पाराशरिभिर्वर्णिभिश्च सर्वदेशजन्मभिश्च जनपदैः सर्वाम्भोधिवेलावनवलयवासिभिश्च म्लेच्छजातिभिः सर्वद्वीपान्तरागतैश्च दूतमण्डलैरुपास्यमानम्, सर्वप्रजानिर्माणभूमिमिव प्रजापतीनां लोकत्रयसारोच्चयरचितं चतुर्थमिव लोकम्, महाभारतशतैरप्यकथनीयसमृद्धिसम्भारम्, कृतयुगसहस्रैरिव कल्पितसंनिवेशम्, स्वर्गार्बुदैरिव विहितरामणीयकम्, राजलक्ष्मीकोटिभिरिव कृतपरिग्रहं राजद्वारमगमत्।

अभवच्चास्य जातविस्मयस्य मनसि—'कथमिवेदमियत्प्रमाणं प्राणिजातं जनयतां प्रजासृजां नासीत्[1]परिश्रमो महाभूतानां वा परिक्षयः, परमाणूनां वा परि[2]च्छेदः, कालस्य वान्तः, आयुषो वा व्युपरमः, आकृतीनां वा परिसमाप्तिः' इति। मेखलकस्तु दूरादेव द्वारपाललोकेन प्रत्यभिज्ञायमानः 'तिष्ठतु तावत्क्षणमात्रमत्रैव पुण्यभागी' इति तमभिधायाप्रतिहतः पुरः प्राविशत्।

अथ स मुहूर्तादिव प्रांशुना, कर्णिकारगौरेण, वीध्रकञ्चुकच्छन्नवपुषा, समुन्मिषन्माणिक्यपदकबन्धबन्धुरशस्त्र[3]बन्धकृशावलग्नेन, हिमशैलशिलाविशालवक्षसा, हरवृषककुदकूटविकटांसतटेन, उरसा चपलहृषीकहरिणकुलसंयमनपाशमिव हारं बिभ्रता, 'कथयतं यदि सोमवंशसम्भवः सूर्यवंशसम्भवो वा भूपतिरभूदेवंविधः' इति प्रष्टुमानीताभ्यां सोमसूर्याभ्यामिव श्रवणगताभ्यां मणिकुण्डलाभ्यां समुद्भासमानेन, वह[4]द्वदनलावण्यविसरवेणिकाक्षिप्यमाणैरधिकारगौरवाद्दीयमानमार्गेणेव दिनकृतः किरणैः, प्रसादलब्धया विकचपुण्डरीकमुण्डमालिकयेव दीर्घया दृष्ट्या दूरादेवानन्दयता, नैष्ठुर्याधिष्ठानेऽपि प्रतिष्ठितेन पदे प्रश्रयमिवावनम्रेण मौलिना पाण्डुरमुष्णीषमुद्वहता, वामेन स्थूलमुक्ताफलच्छुरणदन्तुरत्सरुं करकिसलयेन कलयता कृपाणम्, इतरेणापनीततरलतां ताडितीमिव लतां शातकौम्भीं वेत्रयष्टिमुन्मृष्टां धारयता पुरुषेणानुगम्यमानो निर्गत्यावोचत्—'एष खलु महाप्रतीहाराणामनन्तरश्चक्षुष्यो देवस्य पारियात्रनामा दौवारिकः। समनुगृह्णात्वेनमनुरूपया प्रतिपत्त्या कल्याणाभिनिवेशी' इति। दौवारिकः समुपसृत्य कृतप्रणामो मधुरया गिरा सविनयमभाषत—'आगच्छत। प्रविशत दर्शनाय। कृतप्रसादो देवः' इति। बाणस्तु 'धन्योऽस्मि, यदेवमनुग्राह्यं मां देवो मन्यते' इत्युक्त्वा तेनोपदिश्यमानमार्गः प्राविशदभ्यन्तरम्।

अथ वनायुजैः, आरट्टजैः, काम्बोजैः, भारद्वाजैः, सिन्धुदेशजैः, पारसीकैश्च, शोणैश्च, श्यामैश्च, श्वेतैश्च, पिञ्जरैश्च, हरिद्भिश्च, तित्तिरिकल्माषैश्च, पञ्चभद्रैश्च, मल्लिकाक्षैश्च, कृत्तिकापिञ्जरैश्च, आयतनिर्मांसमुखैः, अनुत्कटक-

---

१ 'नासीन्महाभूतानां' अ—क. २ 'विच्छेदः' ब. ३ 'वस्तबन्धलुप्ताव०' ब.
४ 'बृहद्वदन०' अ.

र्णकोशैः, सुवृत्तश्लक्ष्णसुघटितघण्टिकाबन्धैः, यूपानुपूर्वीवक्रायतोदग्रग्रीवैः, उपचयश्वयत्स्कन्धसन्धिभिः, निर्भुग्नोरःस्थलैः, अस्थूलप्रगुणप्रसृतैर्लोहपीठकठिनखुरम-डलैः, अतिजवत्रुटनभयादनिर्मितान्त्राणीवोदराणि वृत्तानि धारयद्भिः, उद्यद्द्रोणीविभज्यमानपृथुजघनैः, जगतीदोलायमानबालपल्लवैः, कथमप्युभयतो निखातदृढभूरि[1]पाशसंयमननियन्त्रितैः, आयतैरपि पश्चात्पाशबन्धप्रसारितैकाङ्घ्रिभिरायततरैरिवोपलक्ष्यमाणैः, बहुगुणसूत्रग्रथितग्रीवागण्डकैरामीलितलोचनैः, दूर्वारसश्यामलफेनलवशबलान्दशनगृहीतमुक्तान्स्फरफरितत्वचः कण्डूजुषः प्रती[2]कान्प्रचालयद्भिः, सालसवलितवालधिभिः, एकशफविश्रान्तिस्रस्तशिथिलितजघनार्धैः, निद्रया प्रध्यायद्भिश्च, स्खलितहुङ्कारमन्दमन्दशब्दायमानैश्च ताडितखुरधरणीरणितमुखरशिखरखुरलिखितक्ष्मातलैर्घासमभिलषद्भिश्च, प्रकीर्यमाणयवसग्रासरसमत्सरोद्भूतक्षोभैश्च, प्रकुपितचण्डचण्डालहुङ्कारकातरतरतरलतारकैश्च, कुङ्कुमप्रमृष्टिपिञ्जराङ्गतया सततसंनिहितनीराज[3]नानलैरिव लक्ष्यमाणैरुपरिविततवितानैः, पुरः पूजिताभिमतदैवतैः, भूपालवल्लभैस्तुरङ्गैरारचितां मन्दुरां विलोकयन्, कुतूहलाक्षिप्तहृदयः किञ्चिदन्तरमतिक्रान्तो हस्तवामेनात्युच्चतया निरवकाशमिवाकाशं कुर्वाणम्, महता कदलीवनेन परिवृतपर्यन्तं सर्वतो मधुकरमयीभिर्मदस्रुतिभिर्नदीभिरिवापतन्तीभिरापूर्यमाणम्, आशामुखविसर्पिणा बकुलवनानामिव विकसतामामोदेन लिम्पन्तं घ्राणेन्द्रियं दूरादव्यक्तमिभधिष्ण्[4]यागारमपश्यत्। अपृच्छच्च—'अत्र देवः किं करोति' इति। असावकथयत्—'एष खलु देवस्यौपवाह्यो बाह्यं हृदयं जात्यन्तरित आत्मा बहिश्चराः प्राणा विक्रमक्रीडासुहृद्दर्पशात इति यथार्थनामा वारणपतिः। तस्यावस्थानमण्डपोऽयं महान्दृश्यते' इति। स तमवादीत्—'भद्र, श्रूयते दर्पशातः। यद्येवमदोषो वा पश्यामि तावद्वारणेन्द्रमेव। अतोऽर्हसि मामत्र प्रापयितुम्। अतिपरवानस्मि कुतूहलेन' इति। सोऽभाषत—'भवत्वेवम्। आगच्छतु भवान्। को दोषः। पश्यतु तावद्वारणेन्द्रम्' इति।

गत्वा च तं प्रदेशं दूरादेव गम्भीरगलगर्जितै[5]र्वियति चातककदम्बकैर्भुवि च भवननीलकण्ठकुलैः कलकेकाकलकलमुखरमुखैः क्रियमाण[6]कलकोलाहलम्, विकचकदम्बसंवादिमदसुरासौरभभरितभुवनम्, कायवन्तमिव[7]कालमेघकालम्, अविरलमधुबिन्दुपिङ्गलपक्ष्मजालकितां सरसीमिवाभ्यवगाढां दशां चतुर्थीमुत्सृजन्तम्, अनवरतमवतंसशङ्खैरामन्द्रकर्णतालदुन्दुभिध्वनिभिः पञ्चमीप्रवेशमङ्गलारम्भमिव गार्यन्तम्, अविरतचलनचित्रत्रिपदीललितलास्य-

---

१ 'भूमिपाश' ब. २ 'प्रदेशान्' ब. ३ '°नलरक्ष्यमाणैरिवो०' अ-क.
४ '०दव्यक्तमिव धिष्ण्याकार०' ब; 'धृष्ण्या०' अ. ५ 'गर्जितोर्जितैः' अ-क.
६ 'क्रियमाणाकाल०' ब. ७ 'कायवन्तमिव काल०' ब. ८ 'सूचयन्तम्' ब.

लघयन्तं दोलायमानदीर्घदेहाभोगतया[1] मेदिनीविदलनभयेन भारमिव लघयन्तं दिग्भित्तितटेषु कायमिव कण्डूयमानम्, आहवायोदस्तहस्ततया दिग्वारणानिवाह्वयमानम्, ब्रह्मस्तम्भमिव स्थूलनिशितदन्तेन करपत्रेण पाटयन्तम्, अमान्तं भुवनाभ्यन्तरे बहिरिव निर्गन्तुमीहमानम्, सर्वतः सरसकिशलयलतालासिभिर्लेशिकैश्चिरपरिचयोपचितैर्वनैरिव[2] विक्षिप्तसशैवलबिसविसरशबलसलिलैः सरोभिरिव चाधोरणैराधीयमाननिदाघसमयसमुचितोपचारानन्दम्, अपि च प्रतिगजदानपवनादानदूरोत्क्षिप्तेनानेकसमरविजयगणनालेखाभिरिव वलिवलयराजिभिस्तनीयसीभिस्तरङ्गितोदरेणातिस्थवीयसा हस्तार्गलदण्डेनार्गलयन्तमिव सकलं सकुलशैलसमुद्रद्वीपकाननं ककुभां चक्रवालम्, एकं करान्तरार्पितेनोत्पलाशेन कदलीदण्डेनान्तर्गतशीकरसिच्यमानमूलं मुक्तपल्लवमिवापरं लीलावलम्बिना मृणालजालकेन समररसोच्चरोमाञ्चकण्टकितमिव दन्तकाण्डं वहन्तम्, विसर्पन्त्या च दन्तकाण्डयुगलकस्य कान्त्या सरःक्रीडास्वादितानीव कुमुदवनानि बहुधा वमन्तं निजयशोराशिमिव दिशामपर्यन्तं कुकरिकीटपाटनदुर्ललितान्सिंहानिवोपहसन्तं कल्पद्रुमदुकूलमुखपटमिव चात्मनः कल्पयन्तम्[3], हस्तकाण्डदण्डोद्धरणलीलासु च लक्ष्यमाणेन रक्तांशुकसुकुमारतलेन[4] तालुना कवलितानि रक्तपद्मवनानीव वर्षन्तमभिनवकिसलयराशिमिवोद्गिरन्तम्, कमलकवलपीतं मधुरसमिव स्वभावपिङ्गलेन वमन्तं[5] चक्षुषा, चूतचम्पकलवलीलवङ्गकक्कोलवन्यैलालतामिश्रितानि ससहकाराणि कर्पूरपूरपूरितानि पारिजातकवनानीवोपभुक्तानि[6] पुनः पुनः करटाभ्यां बहलमदामोदव्याजेन विसृजन्तम्, अहर्निशं विभ्रमकृतहस्तस्थितिभिरर्धखण्डितपुण्ड्रेक्षुकाण्डकण्डूयनलिखितैरलिकुलवाचालितैर्दानपट्टकैर्विलभमानमिव सर्वकाननानि करिपतीनाम्, अविरलोदबिन्दुस्यन्दिना हिमशिलाशकलमयेन विभ्रमनक्षत्रमालागुणेन शिशिरीक्रियमाणम्, सकलवारणेन्द्राधिपत्यपट्टबन्धबन्धुरमिवोच्चैस्तरां शिरो दधानम्, मुहुर्मुहुः स्थगितापावृतदिङ्मुखाभ्यां कर्णतालवृन्ताभ्यां वीजयन्तमिव भर्तृभक्त्या दन्तपर्यङ्किकास्थितां राजलक्ष्मीम्, आयतवंशक्रमागतेन गजाधिपत्यचिह्नेन चामरेणेव चलता वालधिना विराजमानम्, स्वच्छशिशिरशीकरच्छलेन दिग्विजयपीताः सरित इव पुनः पुनर्मुखेन मुञ्चन्तम्, क्षणमवधानदाननिस्पन्दीकृतसकलावयवानामन्यद्विरदडिण्डिमाकर्णनाङ्गवलनानामन्ते दीर्घफूत्कारैः परिभवदुःखमिवावेदयन्तम्, अलब्धयुद्धमिवात्मानमनुशोचन्तम्, आरोहाधिरूढिपरिभवेन लज्जमानमिवाङ्गुलीलिखितमहीतलं मदं मुञ्चन्तम्, अवज्ञागृहीतमुक्तकवलकुपितारोहारटनानुरोधेन मदतन्द्रीनिमीलितनेत्रत्रिभागं कथं कथमपि मन्दमन्दमनादरादाददानं कवलान्, अवजग्धतमालपल्लवस्नुतश्यामलरसेन प्रभूततया मद-

---

१ '०भोगवत्तया' ब. २ '०चितैर्घनै०' अ–क. ३ 'कलयन्तम्' अ–क. ४ '०सुकुमारतरेण' ब. ५ 'गलन्तम्' ब. ६ '०भुक्तानि पुरः करटाभ्याम्' अ–क.

प्रवाहमिव मुखेनाप्युत्सृजन्तम्, दलन्तमिव दर्पेण, श्वसन्तमिव शौर्येण, मूर्च्छन्तमिव मदेन, शुष्यन्तमिव तारुण्येन, द्रवन्तमिव दानेन, वल्गन्तमिव बलेन, माद्यन्तमिव मानेन, उद्यन्तमिवोत्साहेन, ताम्यन्तमिव तेजसा, लिम्पन्तमिव लावण्येन, सिञ्चन्तमिव सौभाग्येन, स्निग्धं नखेषु, परुषं रोमविषये, गुरुं मुखे, सच्छिष्यं विनये, मृदुं शिरसि, दृढं परिचयेषु, ह्रस्वं स्कन्धबन्धे, दीर्घमायुषि, दरिद्रमुदरे, सततप्रवृत्तं दाने, बलभद्रं मदलीलासु, कुलकलत्रमायत्ततासु, जिनं क्षमासु, वह्निवर्षं क्रोधमोक्षेषु, गरुडं नागोद्धृतिषु, नारदं कलहकुतूहलेषु, शुष्काशनिपातमवस्कन्देषु, मकरं वाहिनीक्षोभेषु, आशीविषं दशनकर्मसु, वरुणं हस्तपाशाकृष्टिषु, यमवागुरामरातिसंवेष्टनेषु, कालं परिणतिषु, राहुं तीक्ष्णकरग्रहणेषु, लोहिताङ्गं वक्रचारेषु, अलातचक्रं मण्डलभ्रान्तिविज्ञानेषु, मनोरथसम्पादकं चिन्तामणिपर्वतं विक्रमस्य, दन्तमुक्ताशैलस्तम्भनिवासप्रासादमभिमानस्य, घण्टाचामरमण्डनमनोहरमिच्छासञ्चरणविमानं मनस्वितायाः, मदधारादुर्दिनान्धकारं गन्धोदकधारागृहं क्रोधस्य, सकाञ्चनप्रतिमं महानिकेतनमहङ्कारस्य, सगण्डशैलप्रस्रवणं क्रीडापर्वतमवलेपस्य, सदन्ततोरणं वज्रमन्दिरं दर्पस्य, उच्चकुम्भकूटाट्टालकविकटं सञ्चारि गिरिदुर्गं राज्यस्य, कृतानेकबाणविवरसहस्रं लोहप्राकारं पृथिव्याः, शिलीमुखशतझाङ्कारितं पारिजातपादपं भूनन्दनस्य, तथा च सङ्गीतगृहं[2] कर्णतालताण्डवानाम्, आपानमण्डपं मधुपमण्डलानाम्, अन्तःपुरं शृङ्गाराभरणानाम्, मदनोत्सवं मदलीलालास्यानाम्, अक्षुण्णप्रदोषं नक्षत्रमालामण्डलानाम्, अकाल[3]प्रावृट्कालं मदमहानदीपूरप्लवानाम्, अलीकशरत्समयं सप्तच्छदवनपरिमलानाम्, अपूर्वहिमागमं शीकरनीहाराणाम्, मिथ्याजलधरं गर्जिताडम्बराणाम्, दर्पशातमपश्यत् ।

आसीच्चास्य चेतसि—'नूनमस्य निर्माणे गिरयो ग्राहिताः परमाणुताम् । कुतोऽन्यथा गौरवमिदम् । आश्चर्यमेतत् । विन्ध्यस्य दन्तावादिवराहस्य करः' इति विस्मयमान[4]मेव तं दौवारिकोऽब्रवीत्—'पश्य ।

मिथ्यैवालिखितां मनोरथशतैर्निःशेषनष्टां श्रियं
चिन्तासाधनकल्पनाकुलधियां भूयो वने विद्विषाम् ।
आयातः कथमप्ययं स्मृतिपथं शून्यीभवच्चेतसां
नागेन्द्रः सहते न मानसगतानाशागजेन्द्रानपि ॥ ४ ॥

तदेहि । पुनरप्येनं द्रक्ष्यसि । पश्य तावद्देवम्' इत्यभिधीयमानश्च तेन मदजलपङ्किल[5]कपोलपट्टपतितां मत्तामिव मदपरिमलेन मुकुलितां कथमपि तस्माद्दृष्टिमाकृष्य तेनैव दौवारिकेणोपदिश्यमानवर्त्मा समतिक्रम्य भूपालसहस्रसङ्कुलानि त्रीणि कक्ष्यान्तराणि चतुर्थे भुक्तास्थानमण्डपस्य पुरस्तादजिरे

१ 'चलन्तमिव' अ. २ 'गृहकं' ब. ३ 'अकाण्ड' ब. ४ '०मानमेतं' अ—क. ५ '०जलकज्जलकालकपोल०' ब.

स्थितम्, दूरादूर्ध्वस्थितेन प्रांशुना कर्णिकारगौरेण व्यायामव्यायतवपुषा शस्त्रिणा मौलेन शरीरपरिचारकलोकेन पङ्क्तिस्थितेन कार्तस्वरस्तम्भमण्डलेनेव परिवृतम्, आसन्नोपविष्टविशिष्टेष्टलोकम्[1], हरिचन्दनरसप्रक्षालिते तुषारशीकरशीतलतले दन्तपाण्डुरपादे शशिमय इव मुक्ताशैलशिलापट्टशयने समुपविष्टम्, शयनीयपर्यन्तविन्यस्ते समर्पितसकलविग्रहभारं भुजे, दिङ्मुखविसर्पिणि देहप्रभावितानै विततमणिमयूखे घर्मसमयसुभगे सरसीव मृदुमृणालजालजटिलजले सराजकं रममाणम्, तेजसः परमाणुभिरिव केवलैर्निर्मितम्, अनिच्छन्तमपि[2] बलादारोपयितुमिव सिंहासनं सर्वावयवेषु सर्वलक्षणैर्गृहीतम्, गृहीतब्रह्मचर्यमालिङ्गितं राजलक्ष्म्या, प्रतिपन्नासिधाराधारणव्रतमविसंवादिनं राजर्षिम्, विषमराजमार्गविनिहितपदस्खलनभियेव सुलग्नं धर्मे, सकलभूपालपरित्यक्तेन भीतेनेव लब्धवाचा सर्वात्मना सत्येन सेव्यमानम्, आसन्नवारविलासिनीप्रतियातनाभिश्चरणनखपातिनीभिर्दिग्भिरिव दर्शभिः[3] प्रणम्यमानम्, दीर्घैर्दिगन्तपातिभिर्दृष्टिपातैर्लोकपालानां कृताकृतमिव प्रत्यवेक्षमाणम्, मणिपादपीठपृष्ठप्रतिष्ठितकरेणोपरिगमनाभ्यनुज्ञां मृग्यमाणमिव दिवसकरेण, भूषणप्रभासमुत्सारणबद्धपर्यन्तमण्डलेन प्रदक्षिणीक्रियमाणमिव[4] दिवसेन, अप्रणमद्भिर्गिरिभिरपि[5] दूयमानं शौर्योष्मणा, फेनायमानमिव चन्दनधवलं लावण्यजलधिमुद्वहन्तम्, एकराज्यैर्जितत्येन[6] निजप्रतिबिम्बान्यपि नृपचक्रचूडामणिधृतान्यसहमानमिव, दर्पदुःखासिकया चामरानिलनिभेन बहुधेव श्वसन्तीं राजलक्ष्मीं दधानम्, सकलमिव चतुःसमुद्रलावण्यमादायोत्थितया श्रिया समुपश्लिष्टम्, आभरणप्रभाजालजायमानानीन्द्रधनुःसहस्राणीन्द्रप्राभृतप्रहितानि विलभमानमिव राज्ञाम्, सम्भाषणेषु परित्यक्तमपि मधु वर्षन्तम्, काव्यकथास्वपीतमप्यमृतमुद्वमन्तम्, विस्रम्भभाषितेष्वनाकृष्टमपि हृदयं दर्शयन्तम्, प्रसादेषु निश्चलामपि श्रियं स्थाने स्थाने स्थापयन्तम्, वीरगोष्ठीषु पुलकितेन कपोलस्थलेनानुरागसन्देशमिवोपांशु रणश्रियः शृण्वन्तम्, अतिक्रान्तसुभटकलहालापेषु स्नेहवृष्टिमिव दृष्टिमिष्टे कृपाणे पातयन्तम्, परिहासस्मितेषु गुरुप्रतापभीतस्य राजकस्य स्वच्छमाशयमिव दशनांशुभिः कथयन्तम्, सकललोकहृदयस्थितमपि न्याये तिष्ठन्तम्, अगोचरे गुणानामभूमौ सौभाग्यानामविषये वरप्रदानानामशक्ये आशिषाममार्गे मनोरथानामतिदूरे दैवस्यादिश्युपमानानामसाध्ये धर्मस्यादृष्टपूर्वे लक्ष्म्या महत्त्वे स्थितम्, अरुणपादपल्लवेन सुगतमन्थरोरुणा वज्रायुधनिष्ठुरप्रकोष्ठपृष्ठेन वृषस्कन्धेन भास्वद्बिम्बाधरेण प्रसन्नावलोकितेन चन्द्रमुखेन कृष्णकेशेन वपुषा सर्वदेवतावतारमिवैकत्र दर्शयन्तम्, अपि च मांस-

---

१ '०विष्टविशिष्टलोकम्' ब. २ 'अनिच्छन्तं बला०' अ–क. ३ अस्मात्परं 'विग्रहावर्जिताभिः' इत्यधिकं ब–पुस्तके. ४ अस्मात्परं 'गलितोष्मणा' इत्यधिकं ब–पुस्तके. ५ 'गिरिभिरपि भूभृद्भिः' ब. ६ '०राज्योर्जितेन' ब.

लमयूखमालामलिनितमहीतले महति महार्हे माणिक्यमालामण्डितमेखले महानीलमये पादपीठे कलिकालशिरसीव सलीलं विन्यस्तवामचरणमाक्रान्तकालियफणाचक्रवालं बालमिव पुण्डरीकाक्षम्, क्षौमपाण्डुरेण चरणनखदीधितिप्रतानेन प्रसरता महीं महादेवीपट्टबन्धेनेव महिमानमारोपयन्तम्, अप्रणतलोकपालकोपेनेवातिलोहितौ सकलनृपतिमौलिमालास्वतिपीतं पद्मरागरत्नातपमिव वमन्तौ सर्वतेजस्विमण्डलास्तमयसंध्यामिव धारयन्तावशेषराजकशेखरकुसुममधुरसस्रोतांसीव स्रवन्तौ समस्तसामन्तसीमन्तोत्तंसस्रक्सौरभभ्रान्तैर्भ्रमरमण्डलैरमित्रोत्तमाङ्गैरिव मुहूर्तमप्यविरहितौ संवाहनतत्परायाः श्रियो विकचरक्तपङ्कजवनवासभवनानीव कल्पयन्तौ जलजशङ्खमीनमकरसनाथतलतया कथितचतुरम्भोधिभोगचिह्नाविव चरणौ दधानम्, दिङ्नागदन्तमुसलाभ्यामिव विकटमकरमुखप्रतिबन्धबन्धुराभ्यामुद्वेललावण्यपयोनिधिप्रवाहाभ्यामिव फेनाहितशोभाभ्यां च[1]न्दनद्रुमाभ्यामिव भोगिमण्डलशिरोरत्नरश्मिरज्यमानमूलाभ्यां हृदयारोपितभूभारधारणमाणिक्यस्तम्भाभ्यामूरुदण्डाभ्यां विराजमानम्, अमृतफेनपिण्डपाण्डुना मेखलामणिमयूखखचितेन नितम्बबिम्बव्यासङ्गिना विमलपयोधौतेन नेत्रसूत्रनिवेशशोभिनाधरवाससा वासुकिनिर्मोकेणेव मन्दरं द्योतमानम्, अघनेन सतारागणेनोपरिकृतेन द्वितीयाम्बरेण भुवनाभोगमिव भासमानम्, इभपतिदशनमुसलसहस्रोल्लेखकठिनमसृणेनापर्याप्ताम्बरप्रथिम्ना विविधवाहिनीसंक्षोभकलकलसंमर्दसहिष्णुना कैलासमिव महता स्फटिकतटेनोरुणोरःकवाटेन राजमानम्, श्रीसरस्वत्योरुरोवदनोपभोगविभागसूत्रेणेव पातितेन शेषेणेव च तद्भुजस्तम्भविन्यस्तसमस्तभूभारलब्धविश्रान्तिसुखप्रसुप्तेन हारदण्डेन प[2]रिवेष्टितकन्धरम्, जीविताविधिगृहीतसर्वस्वमहादानदीक्षाचीरेणेव हारमुक्ताफलानां किरणनिकरेण प्रावृतवक्षःस्थलम्, अजजिगीषया बालैर्भुजैरिवापरैः प्ररोहद्भिर्बाहूपधानशायिन्याः श्रियः कर्णोत्पलमधुरसधारासन्तानैरिव गलद्भिर्भुजजन्मनः प्रतापस्य निर्गमनमार्गैरिवाविर्भवद्भिररुणैः केयूररत्नकिरणदण्डैरुभयतः प्रसारितमणिमयपक्षवितानमिव माणिक्यमहीधरम्, सकललोकालोकमार्गार्गलेन चतुरुदधिपरिक्षेप[3]खातशिलाप्राकारेण सर्वराजहंसबन्धवज्रपञ्जरेण भुवनलक्ष्मीप्रवेशमङ्गलमहामणितोरणेनातिदीर्घदोर्दण्डयुगलेन दिशां दिक्पालानां च युगपदायतिमपहरन्तम्, सोदर्यल[4]क्ष्मीचुम्बनलोभेन कौस्तुभमणेरिव मुखावयवतां गतस्याधरस्य गलता रागेण पारिजातपल्लवरसेनेव सिञ्चन्तं दिङ्मुखानि, अन्तरान्तरा सुहृत्परिहासस्मितैः प्रकीर्यमाणविमलदशनशिखाप्रतानैः प्रकृतिमूढाया राजश्रियाः प्रज्ञालोकमिव दर्शयन्तम्, मुखजनितेन्दुसन्देहागतानि कुमुदिनीवनानीव प्रेषयन्तम्, स्फुटस्फटिकधवलदशन-

१ 'कल्पचन्दन०' ब. २ 'परिवलित०' अ. ३ 'खातशातकुम्भशिला' ब.
४ 'सौन्दर्य०' ब.

पङ्क्तिकृतकुमुदवनशङ्काप्रविष्टां शरज्ज्योत्स्नामिव विसर्जयन्तम्, मदिरामृतपारिजातगन्धगर्भेण भरितसकलककुभा मुखामोदेनामृतमथनदिवसमिव सृजन्तम्, विकचमुखकमलकर्णिकाकोशेनानवरतमापीयमानश्वाससौरभमिवाधोमुखेन नासावंशेन, चक्षुषः क्षीरस्निग्धस्य धवलिम्ना दिङ्मुखान्यपूर्ववदनचन्द्रोदयोद्वेलक्षीरोदप्लावितानीव कुर्वाणम्, विमलकपोलफलकप्रतिबिम्बितां चामरग्राहिणीं विग्रहिणीमिव मुखनिवासिनीं सरस्वतीं दधानम्, अरुणेन चूडामणिशोचिषा सरस्वतीर्ष्याकुपितलक्ष्मीप्रसादनलग्नेन चरणालक्तकेनेव लोहितायित[1]ललाटतटम्, आपाटलांशुतन्त्री[2]सन्तानवलयिनीं कुण्डलमणिकुटिलकोटिबालवीणामनवरतचलितचरणानां वादयतामुपवीणयतामिव स्वरव्याकरणविवेकविशारदं श्रवणावतंसमधुकरकुलानां कलक्वणितमाकर्णयन्तम्, उत्फुल्लमालतीमयेन राजलक्ष्म्याः कचग्रहलीलालग्नेन नखज्योत्स्नावलयेनेव मुखशशिपरिवेशमण्डलेन मुण्डमालागुणेन परिकलितकेशान्तम्, शिखण्डाभरणभुवा मुक्ताफलालोकेन मरकतमणिकिरणकलापेन चान्योन्यसंवलनवृजिनेन प्रयागप्रवाहवेणिकावारिणेवागत्य स्वयमभिषिच्यमानम्, श्रमजलविलीनबहलकृष्णागुरुपङ्कतिलककलङ्ककलिपतेन कालिम्ना प्रार्थनाचाटुचतुरचरणपतनशतश्यामिकाकिणेनेव नीलायमानललाटेन्दु[3]लेखाभिः क्षुभितमानसोद्गतैरुत्कलिकाकलापैरिव हारैरुल्लसद्भिरवष्टभ्यमानाभिर्विलासवल्गनचटुलैर्भ्रूलताकल्पैरीर्ष्ययया श्रियमिव तर्जयन्तीभिरायामिभिः श्वसितैरविरलपरिमलैर्मलयमारुतमयैः पाशैरिवाकर्षन्तीभिर्विकटबकुलावलीवराटकवेष्टितमुखैर्बृहद्भिः स्तनकलशैः स्वदारसन्तोषरसमिवाशेषमुद्धरन्तीभिः कुचोत्कम्पिकाविकारप्रेङ्खितानां हारतरलमणीनां रश्मिभिराकृष्य हृदयमिव हठात्प्रवेशयन्तीभिः प्रभामुचामाभरणमणीनां मयूखैः प्रसारितैर्बहुभिरिव बाहुभिरालिङ्गन्तीभिर्जृम्भानुबन्धबन्धुरवदनारविन्दावरणीकृतैरुत्तानैः करकिसलयैः सरभसप्रधावितानि मानसानीव निरुन्धतीभिर्मदान्धमधुकरकुलकीर्यमाणकर्णकुसुमरजःकणकूणितकोणानि कुसुमशरशरनिकरप्रहारमूर्च्छामुकुलितानीव लोचनानि चतुरं सञ्चारयन्तीभिरन्योन्यमत्सरादाविर्भवद्भ्रङ्गुरभ्रुकुटिविभ्रमक्षिप्तैः कटाक्षैः कर्णेन्दीवराणीव ताडयन्तीभिरनिमेषदर्शनसुखरसराशिं मन्थरितपक्ष्मणा चक्षुषा पीतमिव कोमलकपोलपालीप्रतिबिम्बितं वहन्तीभिरभिलाषलीलानिर्निमित्तस्मितैश्चन्द्रोदयानिव मदनसाहायकाय सम्पादयन्तीभिरङ्गभङ्गवलनान्योन्यघटितोत्तानकरवेणिकाभिः स्फुटनमुखराङ्गुलीकाण्डकुण्डलीक्रियमाणनखदीधितिनिवहनिभेनाकिञ्चित्करकामकार्मुकाणीव रुषा भञ्जतीभिर्वारविलासिनीभिर्विलुप्यमानसौभाग्यमिव सर्वतः, स्पर्शस्विन्नवेपमानकरकिसलयगलितचरणारविन्दां चरणग्राहिणीं विहस्य कोणेन लीलालसं शिरसि ताडयन्तम्, अनवरतकरकलितकोणतया चात्मनः प्रियां वीणामिव श्रिय-

---

१ 'लोहितायत' अ–क. २ 'तनुतन्त्री०' ब. ३ 'ललाटलेखाभिः' अ–क.

मपि शिक्षयन्तम्, निःस्नेह इति धनैरनाश्रयणीय इति दोषैर्निग्रहरुचिरितीन्द्रियैर्दुरुपसर्प इति कलिना नीरस इति व्यसनैर्भीरुरित्ययशसा दुर्ग्रहचित्तवृत्तिरिति चित्तभुवा स्त्रीपर इति सरस्वत्या पण्ढ इति परकलत्रैः काष्ठामुनिरिति यतिभिर्धूर्त इति वेश्याभिर्नेय इति सुहृद्भिः कर्मकर इति विप्रैः सुसहाय इति शत्रुयोधैरेकमप्यनेकधा गृह्यमाणम्, शन्तनोर्महावाहिनीपतिम्, भीष्माजितकाशिनम्, द्रोणाच्चापलालसम्, गुरुपुत्रादमोघमार्गणम्, कर्णान्मित्रप्रियम्, युधिष्ठिराद्बहु[1]क्षमम्, भीमादनेकनागायुतबलम्, धनञ्जयान्महाभारतरणयोग्यम्, कारणमिव कृतयुगस्य, बीजमिव विबुधसर्गस्य, उत्पत्तिद्वीपमिव दर्पस्य, एकागारमिव करुणायाः, प्रातिवेशिकमिव पुरुषोत्तमस्य, खनिपर्वतमिव पराक्रमस्य, सर्वविद्यासङ्गीतकगृहमिव सरस्वत्याः, द्वितीयामृतमथनदिवसमिव लक्ष्मीसमुत्थानस्य, बलदर्शनमिव वैदग्ध्यस्य, एकस्थानमिव स्थितीनाम्, सर्वस्वकथनमिव कान्तेः, अपवर्गमिव रूपपरमाणुसर्गस्य, सकलदुश्चरितप्रायश्चित्तमिव राज्यस्य, सर्वबलसन्दोहावस्कन्दमिव कन्दर्पस्य, उपायमिव पुरन्दरदर्शनस्य, आवर्तनमिव धर्मस्य, कन्यान्तःपुरमिव कलानाम्, परमप्रमाणमिव सौभाग्यस्य, राजसर्गसमाप्त्यवभृथस्नानदिवसमिव सर्वप्रजापतीनाम्, गम्भीरं च प्रसन्नं च त्रासजननं च रमणीयं च कौतुकजननं च पुण्यं च चक्रवर्तिनं हर्षमद्राक्षीत् ।

दृष्ट्वा चानुगृहीत इव निगृहीत इव साभिलाष इव[2] तृप्त इव रोमाञ्चमुचा मुखेन मुञ्चन्नानन्दबाष्पवारिबिन्दून्दूरादेव विस्मयस्मेरः समचिन्तयत्—'सोऽयं सुजन्मा सुगृहीतनामा तेजसां राशिः चतुरुदधिकेदारकुटुम्बी भोक्ता ब्रह्मस्तम्भफलस्य सकलादिराजचरितजयज्येष्ठमल्लो देवः परमेश्वरो हर्षः । एतेन च खलु राजन्वती पृथ्वी, नास्य हरेरिव वृषविरोधीनि बालचरितानि, न पशुपतेरिव दक्षोद्वेगकारीण्यैश्वर्यविलसितानि, न शतक्रतोरिव गोत्रविनाशपिशुनाः प्रवादाः, न यमस्येवातिवल्लभानि दण्डग्रहणानि, न वरुणस्येव निस्त्रिंशग्राहसहस्ररक्षिता रत्नालयाः, न धनदस्येव निष्फलाः सन्निधिलाभाः, न जिनस्येवार्थवादशून्यानि दर्शनानि[3], न चन्द्रमस इव बहुलदोषोपहताः श्रियः । चित्रमिदमत्यमरं राजत्वम् । अपि चास्य त्यागस्यार्थिनः, प्रज्ञायाः शास्त्राणि, कवित्वस्य वाचः, सत्त्वस्य साहसस्थानानि, उत्साहस्य व्यापाराः, कीर्तेर्दिङ्मुखानि, अनुरागस्य लोकहृदयानि, गुणगणस्य संख्या, कौशलस्य कला, न पर्याप्तो विषयः । [4]अस्मिंश्च राजनि यतीनां योगपट्टकाः, पुस्तकर्मणां पार्थिवविग्रहाः, षट्पदानां दानग्रहणकलहाः, वृत्तानां पादच्छेदाः, अष्टापदानां चतुरङ्गकल्पना, पन्नगानां द्विजगुरुद्वेषाः, वाक्यविदामधिकरणविचाराः' इति । समुपसृत्य चोपवीती स्वस्तिशब्दमकरोत् ।

---

१ 'बाहुक्षमम्' ब. २ 'इवातृप्त इव' ब. ३ 'विज्ञानदर्शनानि' ब. ४ 'यस्मिंश्च' ब.

अथोत्तरेण नातिदूरे राजधिष्ण्यस्य गजपरिचारको मधुरमपरवक्त्रमुच्चैरगायत्—

'करिकलभ विमुञ्च लोलतां चर विनयव्रतमानताननः।
मृगपतिनखकोटिभङ्गुरो गुरुरुपरि क्षमते न तेऽङ्कुशः' ॥ ५ ॥

राजा तु तच्छ्रुत्वा दृष्ट्वा च तं गिरिगुहागतसिंहबृंहितगम्भीरेण स्वरेण पूरयन्निव नभोभागमपृच्छत्—'एष स बाणः' इति। 'यथाज्ञापयति देवः। सोऽयम्' इति विज्ञापितो दौवारिकेण। 'न तावदेनमकृतप्रसादः पश्यामि' इति तिर्यङ्नीलधवलांशुकशारां तिरस्करिणीमिव भ्रमयन्नपाङ्गनीयमानतरलतारकस्यायामिनीं चक्षुषः प्रभां परिवृत्य प्रेष्ठस्य पृष्ठतो निषण्णस्य मालवराजसूनोरकथयत्—'महानयं भुजङ्गः' इति। तूष्णीम्भावेन त्वगमितनरेन्द्रवचसि तस्मिन्मूके च राजलोके मुहूर्तमिव तूष्णीं स्थित्वा बाणो व्यज्ञापयत्—'देव अविज्ञाततत्त्व इव, अश्रद्दधान इव, नेय इव, अविदितलोकवृत्तान्त इव च कस्मादेवमाज्ञापयसि। स्वैरिणो विचित्राश्च लोकस्य स्वभावाः प्रवादाश्च। महद्भिस्तु यथार्थदर्शिभिर्भवितव्यम्। नार्हसि मामन्यथा सम्भावयितुमविशिष्टमिव। ब्राह्मणोऽस्मि जातः सोमपायिनां वंशे वात्स्यायनानाम्। यथाकालमुपनयनादयः कृताः संस्काराः। सम्यक्पठितः साङ्गो वेदः। श्रुतानि यथाशक्ति शास्त्राणि। दारपरिग्रहादभ्यगारिकोऽस्मि। कामे भुजङ्गता। लोकद्वयाविरोधिभिस्तु चापलैः शैशवमशून्यमासीत्। अत्रानपलापोऽस्मि। अनेनैव च गृहीतविप्रतीसारमिव मे हृदयम्। इदानीं तु सुगत इव शान्तमनसि मनाविव कर्तरि वर्णाश्रमव्यवस्थानां समवर्तिनीव च साक्षाद्दण्डभृति देवे शासति ससाम्बुराशिरशनामशेषद्वीपमालिनीं महीं क इवाविशङ्कः सर्वव्यसनबन्धोरविनयस्य मनसाप्यभिनयं कल्पयिष्यति। आसतां तावन्मानुष्यकोपेताः। त्वत्प्रभावादलयोऽपि भीता इव मधु पिबन्ति, रथाङ्गनामानोऽपि लज्जन्त इवाभ्यनुवृत्तिव्यसनैः प्रियाणाम्, कपयोऽपि चकिता इव चपलायन्ते, शरारवोऽपि सानुक्रोशा इव श्वापदगणाः पिशितानि भुञ्जते। सर्वथा कालेन मां ज्ञास्यति स्वामी स्वयमेव। अनपाचीनचित्तवृत्तिग्राहिण्यो हि भवन्ति प्रज्ञावतां प्रकृतयः' इत्यभिधाय तूष्णीमभूत्।

भूपतिरपि 'एवमस्माभिः श्रुतम्' इत्यभिधाय तूष्णीमेवाभवत्। सम्भाषणासनदानादिना तु प्रसादेन नैनमन्वग्रहीत्। केवलममृतवृष्टिभिः स्नपयन्निव स्नेहगर्भेण दृष्टिपातमात्रेणान्तर्गतां प्रीतिमकथयत्। अस्ताभिलाषिणि च लम्बमाने सवितरि विसर्जितराजलोकोऽभ्यन्तरं प्राविशत्। बाणोपि निर्गत्य धौतारकूटकोमलातपत्विषि निर्वाति वासरे, अस्ताचलकूटकिरीटे निचुलमञ्जरीभांसि तेजांसि मुञ्चति वियन्मुचि मरीचिमति, रोमन्थमन्थरकुरङ्गकुटुम्बकाध्यास्यमानम्रदिष्ठगोष्ठीनपृष्ठास्वरण्यस्थलीषु, शोकाकुलकोककामिनीकूजितक-

१ 'अथोत्तरे' अ. २ '०प्रसादं' ब. ३ 'मरीचिमालिनि, अतिरोमन्थ०' अ.

रुणासु तरङ्गिणीतटीषु, वासविटपोपविष्टवाचाटचटकचक्रवालेष्वालवालावर्जितसेकजलकुटेषु निष्कुटेषु[1], दिवसविहृतिप्रत्यागतं प्रस्नुतस्तनं स्तनन्धये धयति धेनुवर्गमुद्गतक्षीरं क्षुधिततर्णकव्राते, क्रमेण चाधराधरधातुधुनीपूरप्लावित इव लोहितायमानमहसि मज्जति संध्यासिन्धुयानपात्रे[2] पातङ्गे मण्डले, कमण्डलुजलशुचिशयचरणेषु चैत्यप्रणतिपरेषु पाराशरिषु, यज्ञपात्रपवित्रपाणौ प्रकीर्णबर्हिष्युत्तेजसि जातवेदसि हवींषि वषट्कुर्वति यायजूकजने, निद्राविद्राणद्रोणकुलकलिलकुलायेषु कापेयविकलकपिकुलेष्वारामतरुषु, निर्जिगमिषति जरत्तरुकोटरकुटीकुटुम्बिनि कौशिककुले,मुनिकरसहस्रप्रकीर्णसंध्यावन्दनोदबिन्दुनिकर इव दन्तुरयति तारापथस्थलीं स्थवीयसि तारकानिकुरम्बे, अम्बराश्रयिणि शर्वरीशबरीशिखण्डे, खण्डपरशुकण्ठकाले कवलयति बाले ज्योतिःशेषं सांध्यमन्धकारावतारे, तिमिरतर्जननिर्गतासु दहनप्रविष्टदिनकरकरशाखास्विव स्फुरन्तीषु दीपलेखासु, अररसम्पुटसंक्रीडनकथितावृत्तिष्विव गोपुरेषु, शयनोपजोषजुषि जरतीकथितकथे शिशयिषमाणे शिशुजने, जरन्महिषमषीमलीमसतमसि जनितपुण्यजनप्रजागरे विजृम्भमाणे भीषणतमे तमीमुखे, मुखरितविततज्यधनुषि वर्षति शरनिकरमनवरतमशेषसंसारशेमुषीमुषि मकरध्वजे, रताकल्पारम्भशोभिनि शम्भलीभाषितभाजि[3] भजति भूषां भुजिष्याजने, सैरन्ध्रीबध्यमानरशनाजालजल्पाकजघनासु जनीषु, वशिकविशिखाविहारिणीष्वनन्यजानुप्लवासु प्रचलितास्वभिसारिकासु, विरलीभवति वरटानां वेशन्तशायिनीनां मञ्जुनि मञ्जीरशिञ्जितजडे जल्पिते, निद्राविद्राणद्राघीयसि द्रावयतीव च विरहिहृदयानि सारसरसिते, भाविवासरबीजाङ्कुरनिकर इव च विकीर्यमाणे जगति प्रदीपप्रकरे निवासस्थानमगात् । अकरोच्च चेतसि—'अतिदक्षिणः खलु देवो हर्षो यदेवमनेकबालचरितचापलोचित[4]कौलीनकोपितोऽपि मनसा स्निह्यत्येव मयि । यद्यहमक्षिगतः स्याम्, न मे दर्शनेन प्रसादं कुर्यात् । इच्छति तु मां गुणवन्तम् । उपदिशन्ति हि विनयमनुरूपप्रतिपत्त्युपपादनेन वाचा विनापि भर्तव्यानां स्वामिनः । अपि च धिङ्मां स्वदोषान्धमानसमनादरपीडितमेवमतिगुणवति राजन्यन्यथा चान्यथा च चिन्तयन्तम् । सर्वथा करोमि तथा, यथा यथावस्थितं जानाति मामयं कालेन' इत्येवमवधार्य चापरेद्युर्निष्क्रम्य कटकात्सुहृदां बान्धवानां च भवनेषु तावदतिष्ठत्, यावदस्य स्वयमेव गृहीतस्वभावः पृथिवीपतिः प्रसादवानभूत् । अविशच्च पुनरपि नरपतिभवनम् । स्वल्पैरेव चाहोभिः परमप्रीतेन प्रसादजन्मनो मानस्य प्रेम्णो विस्रम्भस्य द्रविणस्य नर्मणः प्रभावस्य च परां कोटिमानीयत नरेन्द्रेणेति ।

इति श्रीबाणभट्टकृते[5] हर्षचरिते राजदर्शनं नाम द्वितीय उच्छ्वासः ।

---

१ '०जलकूटेषु निष्कूटेषु' ब. २ 'पानपात्रे' अ–क. ३ 'शम्भलीसुभाषित०' ब. ४ 'चापलोपचित०' ब. ५ 'इति श्रीमहाकविचक्रचूडामणिश्रीबाणभट्टविरचिते हर्षचरिते महाकाव्ये राजदर्शनं नाम द्वितीय उच्छ्वासः सम्पूर्णः' ब.

तृतीय उच्छ्वासः ।

निजवर्षाहितस्नेहा बहुभक्तजनान्विताः ।
सुकाला इव जायन्ते प्रजापुण्येन[1] भूभुजः ॥ १ ॥

साधूनामुपकर्तुं लक्ष्मीं द्रष्टुं विहायसा गन्तुम् ।
न कुतूहलि कस्य मनश्चरितं च महात्मनां श्रोतुम् ॥ २ ॥

अथ कदाचिद्विरलितबलाहके, चातकातङ्ककारिणि, क्वणत्कादम्बे, दर्दुरद्विषि, मयूरमदमुषि, हंसपथिकसार्थसर्वातिथौ, धौतासिनिभनभसि, भास्वरभास्वति, शुचिशशिनि, तरुणतारागणे, गलत्सुनासीरशरासने, सीदत्सौदामनीदाम्नि, दामोदरनिद्राद्रुहि, द्रुतवैदूर्यवर्णार्णसि, घूर्णमानमिहिकालघुमेघमोघमघवति, निमीलन्नीपे, निष्कुसुमकुटजे, निर्मुकुलकन्दले, कोमलकमले, मधुस्यन्दीन्दीवरे, कह्लाराह्लादिनि, शेफालिकाशीतलीकृतनिशि, यूथिकामोदिनि, मोदमानकुमुदावदातदशदिशि, सप्तच्छदधूलिधूसरसमीरे, स्तबकितबन्धुरबन्धूकाबध्यमानाकाण्डसंध्ये, नीराजितवाजिनि, उद्दामदन्तिनि, दर्पक्षीबौक्षके, क्षीयमाणपङ्कचक्रवाले, बालपुलिनपल्लवितसिन्धुरोधसि, परिणामश्यानश्यामाके, जनितप्रियङ्गुमञ्जरीरजसि, कठोरत्रपुसत्वचि, कुसुमस्मेरशरे, शरत्समयारम्भे राज्ञः ससीपाद्बाणो बन्धून्द्रष्टुं पुनरपि तं ब्राह्मणाधिवासमगात् ।

समुपलब्धभूपालसंमानातिशयपरितुष्टास्तस्य ज्ञातयः श्लाघमाना निर्ययुः। क्रमेण च कांश्चिदभिवादयमानः, कैश्चिदभिवाद्यमानः, कैश्चिच्छिरसि चुम्ब्यमानः, कांश्चिन्मूर्ध्नि समाजिघ्रन्, कैश्चिदालिङ्ग्यमानः, कांश्चिदालिङ्गन्, अन्यैराशिषानुगृह्यमाणः, पराननुगृह्णन्, बहुबन्धुमध्यवर्ती परं मुमुदे। संभ्रान्तपरिजनोपनीतं चासनमासीनेषु गुरुषु भेजे। भजमानश्चार्चादिसत्कारं नितरां ननन्द। प्रीयमाणेन च मनसा सर्वांस्तान्पर्यपृच्छत्—'कच्चिदेतावतो दिवसान्सुखिनो यूयम् । अप्रत्यूहा वा सम्यक्करणपरितोषितद्विजचक्रा क्रातवी क्रियते क्रिया। यथावदविकलमन्त्रभाञ्जि भुञ्जते वा हवींषि हुतभुजः। यथाकालमधीयते वा बटवः। प्रतिदिनमविच्छिन्नो वा वेदाभ्यासः। कच्चित्स एव चिरन्तनो यज्ञविद्याकर्मण्यभियोगः, तान्येव व्याकरणे परस्परस्पर्धानुबन्धावन्ध्यदिवसदर्शितादराणि व्याख्यानमण्डलानि, सैव वा पुरातनी परित्यक्तान्यकर्तव्या प्रमाणगोष्ठी, स एव वा मन्दीकृतेतरशास्त्ररसो मीमांसायामतिरसः। कच्चित्त एव वाभिनवसुभाषितसुधावर्षिणः काव्यालापाः' इति ।

---

१ 'प्रजाः पुण्येन' ब.

अथ ते तमूचुः—'तात, सन्तोषजुषां सततसन्निहितविद्याविनोदानां वैतानवह्निमात्रसहायानां कियन्मात्रं नः कृत्यं सुखितया सकलभुवनभुजि भुजङ्गराजदेहदीर्घे रक्षति क्षितिं क्षितिभुजो[1] भुजे। सर्वथा[2] सुखिन एव वयम्, विशेषेण तु त्वयि विमुक्तकौसीद्ये परमेश्वरपार्श्ववर्तिनि वेत्रासनमधितिष्ठति। सर्वे च यथाशक्ति यथाविभवं यथाकालं च सम्पाद्यन्ते विप्रजनोचिताः क्रियाकलापाः' इति। एवमादिभिरालापैः स्कन्धावारवार्ताभिश्च शैशवातिक्रान्तक्रीडानुस्मरणैः पूर्वजकथाभिश्च विनोदितमनास्तैः सह सुचिरमतिष्ठत्। उत्थाय च मध्यन्दिने यथाक्रियमाणाः स्थितीरकरोत्। भुक्तवन्तं च तं सर्वे ज्ञातयः पर्यवारयन्।

अत्रान्तरे दुकूलपट्टप्रभवे शिखण्ड्यपाङ्गपाण्डुनी पौण्ड्रे वाससी वसानः, स्नानावसानसमये बन्दितया तीर्थमृदा गोरोचनया च रचिततिलकः, तैलामलकमसृणितमौलिः, अनुच्चचूडाचुम्बिना निबिडेन कुसुमापीडकेन समुद्भासमानः, [3]सकृदुपयुक्तताम्बूलविमलाधरकान्तिः, एकशलाकाञ्जनजनितलोचनरुचिः, अचिरभुक्तः, विनीतमार्यं च वेषं दधानः, पुस्तकवाचकः सुदृष्टिराजगाम। नातिदूरवर्तिन्यां चासन्द्यां निषसाद। स्थित्वा च मुहूर्तमिव तत्कालापनीतसूत्रवेष्टनमपि नखकिरणैर्मृदुमृणालसूत्रैरिव वेष्टितं पुस्तकं पुरोनिहितशरशलाकायन्त्रके निधाय, पृष्ठतः सनीडसन्निविष्टाभ्यां मधुकरपारावताभ्यां[4] दत्ते स्थानके, प्राभातिकप्रपाठकच्छेदचिह्नीकृतमन्तरपत्र[5]मुत्क्षिप्य, गृहीत्वा च कतिपयपत्रलघ्वीं कर्पाटिकाम्[6], क्षालयन्निव मषीमलिनान्यक्षराणि दन्तकान्तिभिः, अर्चयन्निव सितकुसुममुक्तिभिर्ग्रन्थम्, मुखसन्निहितसरस्वतीनूपुररवैरिव गमकैर्मधुरैराक्षिपन्मनांसि श्रोतृणां गीत्या पवमानप्रोक्तं पुराणं पपाठ।

तस्मिंश्च तथा श्रुतिसुभगगीतिगर्भं पठति सुदृष्टौ नातिदूरवर्ती बन्दी सूचीबाणस्तारमधुरेण गीतिध्वनिमनुवर्तमानः स्वरेणेदमार्यायुगलमपठत्[7]—

'तदपि मुनिगीतमतिपृथु तदपि जगद्व्यापि पावनं तदपि।
हर्षचरितादभिन्नं प्रतिभाति हि मे पुराणमिदम्॥ ३॥
वंशानुगमविवादि स्फुटकरणं भरतमार्गभजनगुरु।
श्रीकण्ठविनिर्यातं गीतमिदं हर्षराज्यमिव॥ ४॥'

तच्छ्रुत्वा बाणस्य चत्वारः पितामहमुखपद्मा इव वेदाभ्यासपवित्रितमूर्तयः, उपाया इव सामप्रयोगललितमुखाः, गणपतिरधिपतिस्तारापतिः श्यामल इति पितृव्यपुत्रा भ्रातरः, प्रसन्नवृत्तयो गृहीतवाक्याः कृतगुरुपदन्यासा न्यायवेदिनः[8] सुकृतसंग्रहाभ्यासगुरवो लब्धसाधुशब्दा लोक इव व्याकरणे-

---

१ 'क्षितिपो भुजे' ब. २ 'सर्वदा' ब. ३ 'असकृदुप०' अ–क. ४ असात्परं 'वांशिकाभ्याम्' इत्यधिकं ब–पुस्तके. ५ 'अन्तरं पत्रं' ब. ६ 'कापालिकाम्' ब. ७ 'अगायत्' ब. ८ 'न्यायवादिनः' अ–क.

ऽपि, सकलपुराणराजर्षिचरिताभिज्ञाः, महाभारतभावितात्मानः, विदितसकलेतिहासाः, महाविद्वांसः, महाकवयः, महापुरुषवृत्तान्तकुतूहलिनः, सुभाषितश्रवणरसरसायनावितृष्णाः[1], वयसि वचसि यशसि तपसि महसि वपुषि यजुषि च प्रथमाः, पूर्वमेव कृतसङ्गराः, विवक्षवः स्मितसुधाधवलितकपोलोदराः, परस्परस्य मुखानि व्यलोकयन् ।

अथ तेषां कनीयान्कमलदलदीर्घलोचनः श्यामलो नाम बाणस्य प्रेयान्प्राणानामपि वशयिता दत्तसंज्ञस्तैः सप्रणयं दशनज्योत्स्नास्नपितककुभा मुखेन्दुना बभाषे—'तात बाण, द्विजानां राजा गुरुदारग्रहणमकार्षीत् । पुरूरवा ब्राह्मणधनतृष्णया दयितेनायुषा व्ययुज्यत । नहुषः परकलत्राभिलाषी महाभुजङ्ग आसीत् । ययातिराहितब्राह्मणीपाणिग्रहणः पपात । सुद्युम्नः स्त्रीमय एवाभवत् । सोमकस्य प्रख्याता[2] जन्तुवधनिर्घृणता । मान्धाता मार्गणव्यसनेन सपुत्रपौत्रो रसातलमगात् । पुरुकुत्सः कुत्सितं कर्म तपस्यन्नपि मेकलकन्यकायामकरोत् । कुवलयाश्वो भुजङ्गलोकपरिग्रहादश्वतरकन्यामपि न परिजहार । पृथुः प्रथमपुरुषकः परिभूतवान्पृथिवीम् । नृगस्य कृकलासभावे[3] वर्णसङ्करः समदृश्यत । सौदासेन नरक्षिता पर्याकुलीकृता क्षितिः । नलमवशाक्षहृदयं कलिरभिभूतवान् । संवरणो मित्रदुहितरि विक्लवतामगात् । दशरथ इष्टरामोन्मादेन मृत्युमवाप । कार्तवीर्यो गोब्राह्मणातिपीडनेन निधनमयासीत्[4] । मरुत्त इष्टबहुसुवर्णकोऽपि देवद्विजबहुमतो न बभूव । शन्तनुरतिव्यसनादेकाकी वियुक्तो वाहिन्या विपिने विललाप । पाण्डुर्वनमध्यगतो मत्स्य इव मदनरसाविष्टः प्राणान्मुमोच । युधिष्ठिरो गुरुभयविषण्णहृदयः समरशिरसि सत्यमुत्सृष्टवान् । इत्थं नास्ति राजत्वमपकलङ्कमृते देवदेवादमुतः सर्वद्वीपभुजो हर्षात् । अस्य हि बहून्याश्चर्याणि श्रूयन्ते । तथा हि—अत्र बलजिता निश्चलीकृताश्चलन्तः कृतपक्षाः क्षितिभृतः । अत्र प्रजापतिना शेषभोगिमण्डलस्योपरि क्षमा कृता । अत्र पुरुषोत्तमेन सिन्धुराजं प्रमथ्य लक्ष्मीरात्मीकृता[5] । अत्र बलिना मोचितभूभृद्वेष्टनो मुक्तो महानागः । अत्र देवेनाभिषिक्तः कुमारः । अत्र स्वामिनैकप्रहारपातितारातिना प्रख्यापिता शक्तिः । अत्र नरसिंहेन स्वहस्तविशसितारातिना प्रकटीकृतो विक्रमः । अत्र परमेश्वरेण तुषारशैलभुवो दुर्गाया गृहीतः करः । अत्र लोकनाथेन दिशां मुखेषु परिकल्पिता लोकपालाः सकलभुवनकोशश्चाग्रजन्मनां विभक्त इति । एवमादयः प्रथमकृतयुगस्येव दृश्यन्ते महासमारम्भाः । अतोऽस्य[6] सुगृहीतनाम्नः पुण्यराशेः पूर्वपुरुषवंशानुक्रमेणादितः प्रभृति चरितमिच्छामः श्रोतुम् । सुमहान्कालो नः शुश्रूषमाणानाम् । अयस्कान्तमणय इव लोहानि नीरसनि-

१ '०रसायनाः, वितृष्णाः,' अ. २ अस्मात्परं 'जगति' इत्यधिकं ब-पुस्तके. ३ '०भावेऽपि' ब. ४ अस्मात्परं 'रामो मनोभवभ्रान्तहृदयो जनकतनयामपि न परिहृतवान्' इत्यधिकं ब-पुस्तके. ५ 'आत्मीया कृता' ब. ६ 'यतो यस्य' ब.

क्षुराणि क्षुल्लकानामप्याकर्षन्ति मनांसि महतां गुणाः, किमुत स्वभावसरसमृदूनीतरेषाम्। कस्य न द्वितीयमहाभारते भवेदस्य चरिते कुतूहलम्। आचष्टां भवान्। भवतु भार्गवोऽयं वंशः शुचिनानेन राजर्षिचरितश्रवणेन सुतरां शुचितरः' इत्येवमभिधाय तूष्णीमभूत्।

बाणस्तु विहस्याब्रवीत्—'आर्य, न युक्त्यनुरूपमभिहितम्। अघटमानमनोरथमिव भवतां कुतूहलमवकल्पयामि। शक्याशक्यपरिसंख्यानशून्याः प्रायेण स्वार्थतृषः। परगुणानुरागिणी प्रियजनकथाश्रवणरसरभसमोहिता च मन्ये महतामपि मतिरपहरति प्रविवेकम्। पश्यत्वार्यः क्व परमाणुपरिमाणं बटुहृदयम्, क्व समस्तब्रह्मस्तम्भव्यापि देवस्य चरितम्, क्व परिमितवर्णवृत्तयः कतिपये शब्दाः, क्व संख्यातिगास्तद्गुणाः। सर्वज्ञस्याप्ययमविषयः, वाचस्पतेरप्यगोचरः, सरस्वत्या अप्यतिभारः, किमुतास्मद्विधस्य। कः खलु पुरुषायुषशतेनापि शक्नुयादविकलमस्य चरितं वर्णयितुम्। एकदेशे तु यदि कुतूहलं वः, सज्जा वयम्। इयमधिगतकतिपयाक्षरलवलघीयसी जिह्वा क्वोपयोगं गमिष्यति। भवन्तः श्रोतारः। वर्ण्यते हर्षचरितम्। किमन्यत्। अद्य तु परिणतप्रायो दिवसः। पश्चाल्लम्बमानकपिलकिरणजटाभारभास्वरो भगवान्भार्गवो राम इव समन्तपञ्चकरुधिरमहाह्रदे निमज्जति संध्यारागपटले पूषा। श्वो निवेदयितास्मि' इति। सर्वे च ते 'तथा' इति प्रत्यपद्यन्त। नातिचिरादुत्थाय संध्यामुपासितुं शोणमयासीत्।

अथ मधुमदपल्लवितमालवीकपोलकोमलातपे मुकुलितेऽह्नि कमलिनीमीलनादिव लोहिततमे तमोलिहि रवौ लम्बमाने, रविरथतुरगमार्गानुसारेण यममहिष इव धावति नभसि तमसि, क्रमेण च गृहतापसकुटीरकपटलावलम्बिषु रक्तातपच्छेदैः सह संहृतेषु वल्कलेषु, कलिकल्मषमुषि पुण्[1]णति गगनमग्निहोत्रधामधूमे, सनियमे यजमानजने मौनव्रतिनि, विहारवेलाविलोले पर्यटति पल्लीजने, विकीर्यमाणहरितश्यामाकशालिपूलिकासु दुग्धासु होमकपिलासु, हूयमाने वैतानतनूनपाति, पूतविष्टरोपविष्टे कृष्णाजिनजटिले जटिनि, जपति बटुजने, ब्रह्मासनाध्यासिनि ध्यायति योगिगणे, तालध्वनिधावमानानन्तान्तेवासिनि अलसवृद्धश्रोत्रियानुमतेन गलद्ग्रन्थदण्डकोद्गारिणि संध्यां समवधार[2]यति वठरविटबटुसमाजे, समुन्मज्जति च ज्योतिषि तारकाख्ये खे, प्राप्ते प्रदोषारम्भे भवनमागत्योपविष्टः स्निग्धैर्बन्धुभिश्च सार्धं तयैव गोष्ठ्या तस्थौ। नीतप्रथमयामश्च गणपतेर्भवने परिकल्पितं शयनीयमसेवत। इतरेषां तु सर्वेषां निमीलितदृशामप्यनुपजातनिद्राणां कमलवनानामिव सूर्योदयं प्रतिपालयतां कुतूहलेन कथमपि सा क्षपा क्षयमगच्छत्।

अथ यामिन्यास्तुर्ये यामे प्रतिबुद्धः स एव बन्दी श्लोकद्वयमगायत्—

---

१ 'मुष्णाति' ब. २ 'समवधीरयति' ब.

'पश्चादङ्घ्रिं प्रसार्य त्रिकनतिविततं द्राघयित्वाङ्गमुच्चै-
रासज्याभुग्नकण्ठो मुखमुरसि सटां धूलिधूम्रां विधूय ।
घासग्रासाभिलाषादनवरतचलत्प्रोथतुण्डस्तुरङ्गो
मन्दं शब्दायमानो विलिखति शयनादुत्थितः क्ष्मां खुरेण ॥ ५ ॥
कुर्वन्नाभुग्नपृष्ठो मुखनिकटकटिः कन्धरामातिरश्चीं
लोलेनाहन्यमानं तुहिनकणमुचा चञ्चता केसरेण ।
निद्राकण्डूकषायं कषति निबिडितश्रोत्रशुक्तिस्तुरङ्ग-
स्त्वङ्गत्पक्ष्माग्रलग्नप्रतनुबुसकणं कोणमक्ष्णः खुरेण ॥ ६ ॥'

बाणस्तु तच्छ्रुत्वा समुत्सृज्य निद्रामुत्थाय प्रक्षाल्य वदनमुपास्य भगवतीं संध्यामुदिते भगवति सवितरि गृहीतताम्बूलस्तत्रैवातिष्ठत् । अत्रान्तरे सर्वेऽस्य ज्ञातयः समाजग्मुः परिवार्य चासाञ्चक्रुः । असावपि पूर्वोद्घातेन विदिताभिप्रायस्तेषां पुरो हर्षचरितं कथयितुमारेभे—

श्रूयताम्—अस्ति पुण्यकृतामधिवासो वासवावास इव वसुधामवतीर्णः, सततमसङ्कीर्णवर्णव्यवहारस्थितिः कृतयुगव्यवस्थः, स्थलकमलबहलतया पोत्रोन्मूल्यमानमृणालैरुद्गीतमेदिनीसारगुणैरिव कृतमधुकरकोलाहलैर्हलैरुल्लिख्यमानक्षेत्रः, क्षीरोदपयःपायिपयोदसिक्ताभिरिव पुण्ड्रेक्षुवाटसन्ततिभिर्निरन्तरः, प्रतिदिशमपूर्वपर्वतकैरिव खलधानधामभिर्विभज्यमानैः सस्यकूटैः सङ्कटसीमान्तः, समन्तादुद्घातघटीसिच्यमानैर्जीरकजूटैर्जटिलितभूमिः, उर्वरावरीयोभिः शा[1]लेयैरलङ्कृतः, पाकविशरारुराजमाषनिकरकिर्मीरितैश्च स्फुटितमुद्गफलकोशीकपिशितैर्गोधूमधामभिः स्थलीपृष्ठैरधिष्ठितः, महिषपृष्ठप्रतिष्ठितगायद्गोपालपालितैश्च कीटपटललम्पटचटकानुसृतैरवटुघटितघण्टाघटीरटितरमणीयैरटद्भिरटवीं हरवृषभपीतमामयाशङ्कया बहुधा विभक्तं क्षीरोदमिव क्षीरं क्षरद्भिर्बाष्पच्छेद्यतृणतृप्तैर्गोधनैर्धवलितविपिनः, विविधमखहोमधूमान्धशतमन्युमु[2]क्तैर्लोचनैरिव सहस्रसंख्यैः कृष्णशारैः शारीकृतोद्देशः, धवलधूलीमुचां केतकीवनानां रजोभिः पाण्डुरीकृतैः प्र[3]मथनाथोद्धूलनभस्मधूसरैः शिवपुरस्येव प्रवेशैः प्रदेशैरुपशोभितः, शाककन्दलश्यामलितग्रामोपकण्ठकाश्यपीपृष्ठः, पदे पदे करभपालीभिः पीलुपल्लवप्रस्फोटितैः करपुटपीडितमातुलुङ्गीदलरसोपलिप्तैः स्वेच्छाविचितकुङ्कुमकेसरकृतपुष्पप्रकरैः प्रत्यग्रफलरसपानसुखसुप्तपथिकैर्वनदेवतादीयमानामृतरसप्रपागृहैरिव द्राक्षामण्डपैः स्फुटि[4]तफलानां च बीजलग्नशुकचञ्चुरागाणामिव समारूढकपिकुलकपोलसन्दिह्यमानकुसुमानां दाडिमीनां वनैर्विलोभनीयोपनिर्गमः, वनपालपीयमाननारिकेलरसासवैश्च पथिकलोकलुप्यमानपिण्डखर्जूरैर्गोलाङ्गूललिह्यमानमधुरामोदपिण्डीरसैश्चकोरचञ्चुजर्जरितारुकैरुपवनैरभिरामः, तुङ्गार्जुनपालीपरिवृतैश्च गोकुलावतारकलु-

---

१ 'शालीयैः' अ–क. २ 'सक्तैः' ब. ३ 'प्रमथोद्धूलनधूसरैः' अ–क. ४ 'स्फुरत्फलानां' अ–क.

षितकूलकीलालैरध्वगशतशरण्यैररण्य[1]धराबन्धैरवन्ध्यत्रनरन्ध्रः, करभीयकुमारकपाल्यमानैरौष्ट्रकैरौरभ्रकैश्च कृतसम्बाधः, दिशि दिशि रविरथतुरगविलोभनायेव विलोठनमृदितकुङ्कुमस्थलीरससमालब्धानामुत्प्रोथपुटैरुन्मुखैरुदरशायिकिशोरकजवजननाय प्रभञ्जनमिव चापिबन्तीनां वातहरिणीनामिव स्वच्छन्दचारिणीनां वडवानां वृन्दैर्विचरद्भिराचितः, अनवरतक्रतुधूमान्धकारप्रवृत्तैर्हंसयूथैरिव [2]बाणैर्धवलितभुवनः, सङ्गीतगतमुरजरवमत्तैर्मयूरैरिव विभवैर्मुखरितजीवलोकः, शशिकरावदातवृत्तैर्मुक्ताफलैरिव गुणिभिः प्रसाधितः, पथिकशतविलुप्यमानस्फीतफलैर्महातरुभिरिव सर्वातिथिभिरभिगमनीयः, मृगमदपरिमलवाहिमृगरोमाच्छादितैर्हिमवत्पादैरिव महत्तरैः स्थिरीकृतः, प्रोद्दण्डसहस्रपत्रोपविष्टद्विजोत्तमैर्नारायणनाभिमण्डलैरिव तोयाशयैर्मण्डितः, मथितपयःप्रवाहप्रक्षालितक्षितिभिः क्षीरोदमथनारम्भैरिव महाघोषैः पूरिताशः श्रीकण्ठो नाम जनपदः।

यत्र त्रेताग्निधूमाश्रुपातजलक्षालिता इवाक्षीयन्त कुदृष्टयः। पच्यमानचयनेष्टकादहनदग्धानीव नादृश्यन्त दुरितानि। छिद्यमानयूपदारुपरशुपाटित इव व्यदीर्यताधर्मः। मखशिखिधूमजलधरधाराधौत इव ननाश वर्णसङ्करः। दीयमानानेकगोसहस्रश्रृङ्गखण्ड्यमान इवापलायत कलिः। सुरालयशिलाघट्टनटङ्कनिकरनिकृत्ता इव व्यदीर्यन्त विपदः। महादानविधानकलकलाभिद्रुता इव प्राद्रवन्नुपद्रवाः। दीप्यमानसत्रमहानससहस्रसन्तापिता इव व्यलीयन्त व्याधयः। वृषविवाहप्रहतपुण्यपटहपटुरवत्रासिता इव नोपासर्पन्नपमृत्यवः। सन्ततब्रह्मघोषबधिरीकृता इवापजग्मुरीतयः। धर्माधिकारपरिभूतमिव न प्राभवद्दुर्दैवम्।

तत्र चैवंविधे नानारामाभिरामकुसुमगन्धपरिमलसुभगो यौवनारम्भ इव भुवनस्य, कुङ्कुममलनपि[3]ञ्जरितबहुमहिषीसहस्रशोभितोऽन्तःपुरनिवेश इव धर्मस्य, मरुदुद्धूयमानचमरीबालव्यज[4]नशतधवलितप्रान्त एकदेश इव सुरराज्यस्य, ज्वलन्मखशिखिसहस्रदीप्यमानदशदिगन्तः शिबिरसन्निवेश इव कृतयुगस्य, पद्मासनस्थितब्रह्मर्षिध्यानाधीयमानसकलाकुशलप्रशमः प्रथमोऽवतार इव ब्रह्मलोकस्य, कलकलमुखरमहावाहिनीशतसङ्कुलो विप[5]क्ष इवोत्तरकुरूणाम्, ईश्वरमार्गणसन्तापानभिज्ञसकलजनो विजिगीषुरिव त्रिपुरस्य, सुधारससिक्तधवलगृहपङ्क्तिपाण्डुरः प्रतिनिधिरिव चन्द्रलोकस्य, मधुमत्त[6]मत्तकाशिनीभूषणरवभरितभुवनो नामाभिहार इव कुबेरनगरस्य, स्थाण्वीश्वराख्यो जनपदविशेषः।

यस्तपोवनमिति मुनिभिः, कामायतनमिति वेश्याभिः, सङ्गीतशालेति लासकैः; यमनगरमिति शत्रुभिः, चिन्तामणिभूमिरित्यर्थिभिः, वीरक्षेत्रमिति

---

१ 'अरण्यवरुणधरा०' ब. २ 'गुणैः' ब. ३ '०मलनापञ्जरित०' ब. ४ 'व्यजनधवलित०' अ–क. ५ 'विक्षेपः' ब–क. ६ 'मधुमदमत्तकासिनी' ब.

शस्त्रोपजीविभिः, गुरुकुलमिति विद्यार्थिभिः, गन्धर्वनगरमिति गायनैः, विश्वकर्ममन्दिरमिति विज्ञानिभिः, लाभभूमिरिति वैदेहकैः, द्यूतस्थानमिति बन्दिभिः, साधुसमागम इति सद्भिः, वज्रपञ्जरमिति शरणागतैः विटगोष्ठीति विदग्धैः, सुकृतपरिणाम इति पथिकैः, असुरविवरमिति वातिकैः, शाक्याश्रम इति शमिभिः, अप्सरःपुरमिति कामिभिः, महोत्सवसमाज इति चारणैः, वसुधारेति च विप्रैरगृह्यत।

यत्र च मातङ्गगामिन्यः शीलवत्यश्च, गौर्यो विभवरताश्च, श्यामाः पद्मरागिण्यश्च, धवलद्विजशुचिवदना मदिरामोदिश्वसनाश्च, चन्द्रकान्तवपुषः शिरीषकोमलाङ्ग्यश्च, अभुजङ्गगम्याः कञ्चुकिन्यश्च, पृथुकलत्रश्रियो दरिद्रमध्यकलिताश्च, लावण्यवत्यो मधुरभाषिण्यश्च, अप्रमत्ताः प्रसन्नोज्ज्वल[1]रागाश्च, अकौतुकाः प्रौढाश्च प्रमदाः।

यत्र च प्रमदानां चक्षुरेव सहजं मुण्डमालामण्डनं भारः कुवलयदलदामानि। अलकप्रतिबिम्बान्येव कपोलतलगतान्यक्लिष्टाः श्रवणावतंसाः पुनरुक्तानि तमालकिसलयानि। प्रियकथा एव सुभगाः कर्णालङ्कारा आडम्बरः कु[2]ण्डलानि। कपोला एव सततमालोककारका विभवो[3] निशासु मणिप्रदीपाः। निःश्वासाकृष्टमधुकरकुलान्येव रमणीयं मुखावरणं कुलस्त्रीजनाचारो जालिका। वाण्येव मधुरा वीणा बाह्यविज्ञानं तन्त्रीताडनम्। हासा एवातिंशयसुरभयः पटवासा निरर्थकाः कर्पूरपांसवः। अधरकान्तिविसर एवोज्ज्वलतरोऽङ्गरागो निर्गुणो लावण्यकलङ्कः कुङ्कुमपङ्कः। बाहव एव कोमलतमाः परिहासप्रहारवेत्रलता निष्प्रयोजनानि मृणालानि। यौवनोष्मस्वेदबिन्दव एव विदग्धाः कुचालङ्कृतयो हारास्तु भाराः। श्रोण्य एव विशालस्फाटिकशिलातलचतुरस्त्रा रागिणां विश्रमकारणमनिमित्तं भवनमणिवेदिकाः। कमललोभनिलीनान्यलिकुलान्येव मुखराणि पदाभरणकानि निष्फलानीन्द्रनीलनूपुराणि। नूपुररवा[4]हूता भवनकलहंसा एव समुचिताः सञ्चरणसहाया ऐश्वर्यप्रपञ्चाः परिजनाः।

तत्र च साक्षात्सहस्राक्ष इव सर्ववर्णधरं धनुर्दधानः, मेरुमय इव कल्याणप्रकृतित्वे, मन्दरमय इव लक्ष्मीसमाकर्षणे, जलनिधिमय इव मर्यादायाम्, आकाशमय इव शब्दप्रादुर्भावे, शशिमय इव कलासंग्रहे, वेदमय इवाकृत्रिमालापत्वे, धरणिमय इव लोकधृतिकरणे, पवनमय इव सर्वपार्थिवरजोविकारहरणे, गुरुर्वचसि, पृथुरुरसि, विशालो मनसि, जनकस्तपसि, सुयात्रस्तेजसि, सुमन्त्रो रहसि, बुधः सदसि, अर्जुनो यशसि, भीष्मो धनुषि, निषधो वपुषि, शत्रुघ्नः समरे, शूरः शूरसेनाक्रमणे, दक्षः प्रजाकर्मणि, सर्वादिराजतेजःपुञ्जनिर्मित इव राजा पुष्पभूतिरिति नाम्ना बभूव।

१ '०मुखरागाश्च' ब. २ 'कुण्डलादिः' अ–क. ३ 'विभवो निश्वासमणि०' ब. ४ 'रवोहृताः' ब.

पृथुमा गौरियं[1] कृतेति वः स्पर्धमान इव मर्ती महिषीं चकार । निसर्ग-स्वैरिणी स्वरुच्यनुरोधिनी च भवति हि महतां मतिः । यतस्तस्य केनचिद्नुपदिष्टा महजैव शैशवादारभ्यान्यदेवताविमुखी[2] भगवति भक्तिसुलभे भुवनभृति भूतभावने भवच्छिदि भवे भूयसी भक्तिरभूत् । अकृतवृषभध्वज-पूजाविधिर्न स्वप्नेऽप्याहारमकरोत् । अजम्, अजरम्, अमरगुरुम्, असुर-पुररिपुम्, अपरिमितगणपतिम्, अचलदुहितृपतिम्, अखिलभुवनकृतचरण-नतिम्, पशुपतिं प्रपन्नोऽन्यदेवताशून्यममन्यत त्रैलोक्यम् । भर्तृचित्तानुव-र्तिन्यश्चानुजीविनां प्रकृतयः । तथा हि । गृहे गृहे भगवानपूज्यत खण्डपर-शुः । ववुरस्य होमालवाल[3]विलीयमानबहलगुग्गुलुगन्धगर्भाः स्नपनक्षीरशीक-रक्षोदक्षारिणो बिल्वपल्लवदामदलोद्वाहिनः पुण्यविषयेषु[4] वायवः । शिवसप-र्यासमुचितैरुपायनैः प्राभृतैश्च पौराः पादोपजीविनः सचिवा भुजबलनिर्जि-ताश्च करदीकृता महासामन्तास्तं सिषेविरे । तथा हि । कैलासकूटधवलैः कनकपत्रलतालङ्कृतविषाणकोटिभिर्महाप्रमाणैः संध्याबलिवृषैः सौवर्णैश्च स्नपनकलशैरर्घभाजनैश्च धूपपात्रैश्च पुष्पपट्टैश्च मणियष्टिप्रदीपैश्च ब्रह्मसूत्रैश्च महार्हमाणिक्यखण्डखचितैश्च मुखकोषैः परितोषमस्य मनसि चक्रुः । अन्तः-पुराण्यपि स्वयमारब्धबालेयतण्डुलकण्डनानि[5] देवगृहोपलेपनलोहिततरकर-किसलयानि कुसुमग्रथनव्यग्रसमस्तपरिजनानि तस्याभिलषितमन्ववर्तन्त । तथा च । परममाहेश्वरः स भूपालो लोकतः शुश्राव भुवि भगवन्तमपरमिव साक्षाद्दक्षमखमथनं दाक्षिणात्यं बहुविधविद्याप्रभावप्रख्यातैर्गुणैः शिष्यैरिवा-नेकसहस्रसंख्यैर्व्याप्तमर्त्यलोकं भैरवाचार्यनामानं महाशैवम् । उपनयन्ति हि हृदयमदृष्टमपि जनं शीतलसंवादाः । यतः स राजा श्रवणसमकालमेव तस्मिन्भैरवाचार्ये भगवति द्वितीय इव कपर्दिनि दूरगतेऽपि गरीयसीं बबन्ध भक्तिम् । आचकाङ्क्ष च मनोरथैरप्यस्य सर्वथा दर्शनम् ।

अथ कदाचित्पर्यस्तेऽस्ताचलचुम्बिनि वासरेऽन्तःपुरवर्तिनं राजानमुपसृत्य प्रतीहारी विज्ञापितवती—'देव, द्वारि परिव्राडास्ते कथयति च भैरवाचार्य-वचनाद्देवमनुप्राप्तोऽस्मि' इति । राजा तु तच्छ्रुत्वा सादरम्—'क्वासौ आन-यात्रैव । प्रवेशयैनम्' इति चाब्रवीत् । तथा चाकरोत्प्रतीहारी । न चिराच्च प्रविशन्तं प्रांशुमाजानुभुजम्, भैक्षक्षाममपि स्थूलास्थिभिरवयवैः पीवरमि-वोपलक्ष्यमाणम्, पृथूत्तमाङ्ग[6]मुत्तुङ्गवलिभङ्गस्थपुटललाटम्, निर्मांसगण्डकूप-कम्, मधुबिन्दुपिङ्गलपरिमण्डलाक्षम्, ईषदावक्रघोणम्, अतिप्रलम्बैककर्ण-पाशम्, अलाबुबीजविकटोन्नतदन्तपङ्क्तिम्, तुरगानूकश्लथाधरलेखम्, लम्ब-चिबुकायततरलपनम्, अंसावलम्बिना काषायेण योगपट्टकेन विरचितवैक-क्षकम्, हृदयमध्यनिबद्धग्रन्थिना च रागेणेव खण्डशः कृतेन धातुरसारुणेन

---

१ 'गौरिवेयं' ब. २ 'अनन्यदेवता भगवति' ब. ३ 'होमालवालानलविलीय०' ब. ४ 'पुण्याविषयेषु' ब. ५ 'खण्डनानि' ब. ६ 'पृथुसमाङ्गम्' ब.

कर्पटेन कृतोत्तरासङ्गम्, पुनरुक्तवालप्रग्रहवेष्टननिश्चलमूलेन बद्धमृत्परिशोधनवंशत्वक्तितउना कौपीनसनाथशिखरेण खर्जूरपुटसंमुद्गकगर्भीकृतभिक्षाकपालकेन दारवफलकत्रयत्रिकोणत्रियष्टिनिविष्टकमण्डलुना बहिरुपपादितपादुकावस्थानेन स्थूलदशासूत्रनियन्त्रितपुस्तिकापूलिकेन वामकरधृतेन योगभारकेणाध्यासितस्कन्धम्, इतरकरगृहीतवेत्रासनं मस्करिणमद्राक्षीत्। क्षितिपतिरप्युपगतमुचितेन चैनमादरेणान्वग्रहीत्। आसीनं च पप्रच्छ—'क्व भैरवाचार्यः' इति। सादरनरपतिवचनमुदितमनास्तु परिव्राट् तमुपनगरं सरस्वतीतटवनावलम्बिनि शून्यायतने स्थितमाचचक्षे। भूयश्चाबभाषे—'अर्चयति हि महाभागं भगवानाशीर्वचसा' इत्युक्त्वा चोपनिन्ये योगभारकादाकृष्य भैरवाचार्यप्रहितानि रत्नवन्ति बहलालोकलिप्तान्तःपुराणि पञ्च राजतानि पुण्डरीकाणि।

नरपतिस्तु प्रियजनप्रणयभङ्गकातरो[1] दाक्षिण्यमनुरुध्यमानो ग्रहणलाघवं च लङ्घयितुमसमर्थो दोलायमानेन मनसा स्थित्वा कथं कथमप्यतिसौजन्यनिघ्नस्तानि जग्राह। जगाद च—'सर्वफलप्रसवहेतुः शिवभक्तिरियं नो मनोरथदुर्लभानि फलति फलानि। येनैवमस्मासु प्रीयते तत्रभगवान्भुवनगुरुर्भैरवाचार्यः। श्वो द्रष्टास्मि भगवन्तम्' इत्युक्त्वा च मस्करिणं व्यसर्जयत्। अनया च वार्तया परां मुदमवाप। अपरेद्युश्च प्रातरेवोत्थाय[2] वाजिनमधिरुह्य समुच्छ्रितश्वेतातपत्रः समुद्धूयमानधवलचामरयुगलः कतिपयैरेव राजपुत्रैः परिवृतो भैरवाचार्यं सवितारमिव शशी द्रष्टुं प्रतस्थे। गत्वा च किञ्चिदन्तरं तदीयमेवाभिमुखमापतन्तमन्यतमं शिष्यमद्राक्षीत्। अप्राक्षीच्च—'क्व भगवानास्ते' इति। सोऽकथयत्—'अस्य जीर्णमातृगृहस्योत्तरेण बिल्ववाटिकामध्यास्ते' इति। गत्वा च तं प्रदेशमवततार तुरगात्। प्रविवेश च बिल्ववाटिकाम्।

अथ महतः कार्पटिकवृन्दस्य मध्ये प्रातरेव स्नातम्, दत्ताष्टपुष्पिकम्, अनुष्ठिताग्निकार्यम्, कृतभस्मरेखापरिहारपरिकरे हरितगोमयोपलिप्तक्षितितलवितते व्याघ्रचर्मण्युपविष्टम्, कृष्णकम्बलप्रावरणनिभेनासुरविवरप्रवेशाशङ्कया पातालान्धकारावासमिवाभ्यस्यन्तम्, उन्मिषता विद्युत्कपिलेनात्मतेजसा महामांसविक्रयक्रीतेन मनःशिलापङ्केनेव शिष्यलोकं लिम्पन्तम्, जटीकृतैकदेशलम्बमानरुद्राक्षशङ्खगुटिकेनोर्ध्वबद्धेन शिखापाशेन बध्नन्तमिव विद्यावलेपदुर्विदग्धानुपरि सञ्चरतः सिद्धान्, धवलकतिपयशिरोरुहेण वयसा पञ्चपञ्चाशतं वर्षाण्यतिक्रामन्तम्, खालित्यक्षीयमाणशङ्खलोमलेखम्, लोमशकर्णशष्कुलीप्रदेशम्, पृथुललाटतटम्, तिरश्च्या भस्मललाटिकया बहुशः शिरोर्ध्वधृतदग्धगुग्गुलुसन्तापस्फुटितकपालास्थिपाण्डुरराजिशङ्कामिव जनयन्तम्, सहजललाटवलिभङ्गसङ्कोचितकूर्चभागां बभ्रुभासं भ्रूसङ्गत्या

1 'कातरम्' ब. 2 अस्मातपरं 'कृतकृत्यः' इत्यधिकं ब–पुस्तके.

निरन्तरामायामिनीमेकामिव भ्रूलेखां बिभ्राणम्, ईषत्काचकाचरकनीनिकेन रक्तापाङ्गनिर्गतांशुप्रतानेन मध्यधवलभासेन्द्रायुधेनेवातिदीर्घेण लोचनयुगलेन परितो महामण्डलमिवानेकवर्णरागमालिखन्तं सितपीतलोहितपताकावलीशबलं शिवबलिमिव दिक्षु विक्षिपन्तम्, तार्क्ष्यतुण्डकोटिकुब्जाग्रघोणम्, दूरविदीर्णसृक्किसंक्षिप्तकपोलम्, किञ्चिद्दन्तुरतया सदाहृदयसन्निहितहरमौलिचन्द्रातपेनेव निर्गच्छता दन्तालोकेन धवलयन्तं दिशां जालकम्, जिह्वाग्रस्थितसर्वशैवसंहितातिभारेणेव मनाक्प्रलम्बितौष्ठम्, प्रलम्बश्रवणपालीप्रेङ्खिताभ्यां स्फाटिककुण्डलाभ्यां शुक्रबृहस्पतिभ्यामिव सुरासुरविजयविद्यासिद्धिश्रद्धयानुबध्यमानम्, बद्धविविधौषधिमन्त्रसूत्रपङ्क्तिना सलोहवलयेनैकप्रकोष्ठेन शङ्खखण्डं पूष्णो दन्तमिव भगवता भवेन भग्नं भक्त्या भूषणीकृतं कलयन्तम्, अखिलरसकूपोदञ्चनघटीयन्त्रमालामिव रुद्राक्षमालां दक्षिणेन पाणिना भ्रमयन्तम्, उरसि दोलायमानेनापिङ्गलाग्रेण कूर्चकलापेन संमार्जयन्तमिवान्तर्गतं निजरजोनिकरम्, अतिनिबिडनीललोममण्डलनिचितं च ध्यानलब्धेन ज्योतिषा दग्धमिव हृदयदेशं दधानम्, ईषत्प्रशिथिलवलिवलयबध्यमानतुन्दम्, उपचीयमानस्फिञ्मांसपिण्डकम्, पाण्डुरपवित्रक्षौमावृतकौपीनम्, सावष्टम्भपर्यङ्कबन्धमण्डलितेनामृतफेनश्वेतरुचा योगपट्टकेन वासुकिनेवाप्रतिहतानेकमन्त्रप्रभावाविर्भूतेन प्रदक्षिणीक्रियमाणम्, अरुणतामरससुकुमारतलस्य पादयुगलस्य निर्मलैर्नखमयूखजालकैर्जर्जरयन्तमिव महानिधानोद्धरणरसेन रसातलम्, तोयक्षालितशुचिना धौतपादुकायुगलेन हंसमिथुनेनेव भागीरथीतीर्थयात्रापरिचयागतेनामुच्यमानचरणान्तिकम्, शिखरनिखातकुब्जकालायसकण्टकेन वैणवेन विशाखिकादण्डेन सर्वविद्यासिद्धिविघ्नविनायकापनयनाङ्कुशेनेव सततपार्श्ववर्तिना विराजमानम्, अबहुभाषिणम्, मन्दहासिनम्, सर्वोपकारिणम्, कुमारब्रह्मचारिणम्, अतितपस्विनम्, महामनस्विनम्, कृशक्रोधम्, अकृशानुरोधम्, महानगरमिवादीनप्रकृतिशोभितम्, मेरुमिव कल्पतरुपल्लवराशिसुकुमारच्छायम्, कैलासमिव पशुपतिचरणरजःपवित्रितशिरसम्, शिवलोकमिव माहेश्वरगणानुयातम्, जलनिधिमिवानेकनदनदीसहस्रप्रक्षालितशरीरम्, जाह्नवीप्रवाहमिव बहुपुण्यतीर्थस्थानशुचिम्, धाम धर्मस्य, तीर्थं तथ्यस्य, कोशं कुशलस्य, पत्तनं पूततायाः, शालां शीलस्य, क्षेत्रं क्षमायाः, शालेयं शालीनतायाः, स्थानं स्थितेः, आधारं धृतेः, आकरं करुणायाः, निकेतनं कौतुकस्य, आरामं रामणीयकस्य, प्रासादं प्रसादस्य, अगारं गौरवस्य, समाजं सौजन्यस्य, सम्भवं सद्भावस्य, कालं कलेः, भगवन्तं साक्षादिव विरूपाक्षं भैरवाचार्यं ददर्श। भैरवाचार्यस्तु दूरादेव राजानं दृष्ट्वा शशिनमिव जलनिधिश्चचाल। प्रथमतरोत्थितशिष्यलोकश्चोत्थाय प्रत्युज्जगाम

१ 'एकामेव' ब. २ 'ईषत्काचर०' ब.

समर्पितश्रीफलोपायनश्च जह्नुकर्णसमुद्गीर्यमाणगङ्गाप्रवाहह्रादगम्भीरया गिरा स्वस्तिशब्दमकरोत्।

नरपतिरपि प्रीतिविस्तार्यमाणधवलिम्ना चक्षुषा प्रत्यर्पयन्निव बहुतराणि पुण्डरीकवनानि ललाटपट्टपर्यस्तेन चोदंशुना शिखामणिना महेश्वरप्रसादमिव तृतीयनयनोद्गमेन प्रकाशयन्नावर्जितकर्णपल्लवपलायमानमधुकरः शिवसेवासमुन्मूलिताशेषपाप[1]लवमुच्यमान इव दूरावनतः प्रणाममभिनवं चकार। आचार्योऽपि—'आगच्छ। अत्रोपविश' इति शार्दूलचर्मात्मीयमदर्शयत्। उपदर्शितप्रश्रयस्तु राजा मत्तहंसकलगद्गदस्वरसुभगां मधुरसमयीं महानदीमिव प्रवर्तयन्वाचं व्याजहार—'भगवन्, नार्हसि मामन्यनृपस्खलितैः खलीकर्तुम्। अशेषराजकोपेक्षितताया हतलक्ष्म्याः खल्वयं शीलापराधो द्रविणदौरात्म्यं वा यदेवमाचरति मयि गुरुः। अभूमिरयमुपचाराणाम्। अलमतियन्त्रणया। दूरस्थितोऽपि मनोरथशिष्योऽयं जनो भवताम्। माननीयं च गुरुवत्नोल्लङ्घनमर्हति गुरोरासनम्। आसतां च भवन्त एवात्र' इति व्याहृत्य परिजनोपनीते वाससि निषसाद। भैरवाचार्योऽपि प्रीत्यानतिक्रमणीयं नृपवचनमनुवर्तमानः पूर्ववत्तदेव व्याघ्राजिनमभजत।

आसीने च सराजके परिजने शिष्यजने च समुचितमर्घ्योदिकं चक्रे। क्रमेण च नृपमाधुर्यहृतान्तःकरणः शशिकरनिकरविमला दशनदीधितीः स्फुरन्तीः शिवभक्तीरिव साक्षाद्दर्शयन्नुवाच—'तात, अतिनम्रतैव ते कथयति गुणानां गौरवम्। सकलसम्पत्पात्रमसि। विभवानुरूपास्तु प्रतिपत्तयः। जन्मनः प्रभृत्यदत्तदृष्टिरस्मि स्वापतेयेषु। यतः सकलदोषकलापानलेन्धनैर्धनैरविक्रीतं क्वचिच्छरीरकमस्ति। भैक्षरक्षिताः सन्ति प्राणाः। दुर्गृहीतानि कतिचिद्विद्यन्ते विद्याक्षराणि। भगवच्छिवभट्टारकपादसेवया समुपार्जिता[2] कियत्यपि सन्निहिता पुण्यकणिका। स्वीक्रियतां यदत्रोपयोगार्हम्। प्रतनुगुणग्राह्याणि कुसुमानीव हि भवन्ति सतां मनांसि। अपि च। विद्वत्संमताः श्रूयमाणा अपि सुखयन्ति[3] साधवः शब्दा इव, सुधीरेऽपि हि मनसि यशांसि कुर्वन्ति विवरं, विशतः कुतूहलस्य फेनधवलैः स्रोतोभिरिवापह्रियमाणो गुणगणैरानीतोऽस्मि कल्याणिना' इति।

राजा तु तं प्रत्यवादीत्—'भगवन्, अनुरक्तेष्वपि शरीरादिषु साधूनां स्वामिन एव प्रणयिनः। युष्मद्दर्शनादुपार्जितमेव चापरिमितं कुशलजातम्। अनेनैवागमनेन[4] स्पृहणीयं पदमारोपितोऽस्मि गुरुणा।' इति विविधाभिश्च कथाभिश्चिरं स्थित्वा गृहमगात्।

अन्यस्मिन्दिवसे भैरवाचार्योऽपि राजानं द्रष्टुं ययौ। तस्मै च राजा सान्तःपुरं सपरिजनं सकोषमात्मानं निवेदितवान्। स च विहस्योवाच—

---

१ 'पापमललव०' ब. २ 'समुपार्जिताः कियत्योपि सन्निहिताः पुण्यकणिकाः' ब
३ 'सुखयन्ति' इति नास्ति अ-क-पुस्तकयोः. ४ 'कृतमनेनैवानुगमनेन' ब.

'तात, क्व विभवः, क्व च वयं वनवर्धिताः । धनोष्मणा म्लायत्यलं लतेव मनस्विता । खद्योतानामिवास्माकमियमपरोपतापिनी राजते तेजस्विता । भवादृशा एव भाजनं भूतेः' इति स्थित्वा च कञ्चित्कालं जगाम ।

परिव्राट् तेनैव क्रमेण पञ्च पञ्च राजतानि पुण्डरीकाण्युपायनीचकार । एकदा तु श्वेतकर्पटावृतं किमप्यादाय प्राविशत् । उपविश्य च पूर्ववत्स्थित्वा मुहूर्तमब्रवीत्—'महाभाग, भवन्तमाह भगवान्यथास्मच्छिष्यः पातालस्वामिनामा ब्राह्मणः । तेन ब्रह्मराक्षसहस्तादपहृतो महासिरट्टहासनामा । सोऽयं भवद्भुजयोग्यो गृह्यताम्' । इत्यभिधायापहृतकर्पटावच्छादनात्परिवारादाचकर्ष शरद्गगनमिव पिण्डतां नीतम्, कालिन्दीप्रवाहमिव स्तम्भितजलम्, नन्दकजिगीषया कृष्णकोपितं कालियमिव कृपाणतां गतम्, लोकविनाशाय प्रकाशितधारासारं प्रलयकालमेघखण्डमिव नभस्तलात्पतितम्, दृश्यमानविकटदन्तमण्डलं हासमिव हिंसायाः, हरिबाहुदण्डमिव कृतदृढमुष्टिग्रहम्, सकलभुवनजीवितापहरणक्षमेण कालकूटेनेव निर्मितम्, कृतान्तकोपानलतप्तेनेवायसा घटितम्, अतितीक्ष्णतया पवनस्पर्शेनापि रुषेव क्वणन्तम्, मणिसभाकुट्टिमपतत्प्रतिबिम्बच्छद्मनात्मानमपि द्विधेव पाटयन्तम्, अरिशिरश्छेदलग्नैः कचैरिव किरणैः करालितधारम्, मुहुर्मुहुस्तडिदुन्मेषतरलैः प्रभाचक्रच्छुरितैर्जर्जरितातपम्, खण्डशश्छिन्दन्तमिव दिवसम्, कटाक्षमिव कालरात्रेः, कर्णोत्पलमिव कालस्य, ओङ्कारमिव क्रौर्यस्य, अलङ्कारमहङ्कारस्य, कुलमित्रं कोपस्य, देहं दर्पस्य, सुसहायं साहसस्य, अपत्यं मृत्योः, आगमनमार्गं लक्ष्म्याः, निर्गमनमार्गं कीर्तेः, कृपाणम् ।

भवनिपतिस्तु तं गृहीत्वा करेणायुधप्रीत्या प्रतिमानिभेनालिङ्गन्निव सुचिरं ददर्श । सन्दिदेश च—'वक्तव्यो भगवान्परद्रव्यग्रहणावज्ञादुर्विदग्धमपि हि मे मनो युष्मद्विषये न शक्नोति वचनव्यतिक्रमव्यभिचारमाचरितुम्' इति । परिव्राट् तु गृहीते तस्मिन्परितुष्टः 'स्वस्ति भवते, साधयामः' इत्युक्त्वा निरयासीत् । नृपश्च प्रकृत्या वीररसानुरागी तेन कृपाणेनामन्यत करतलवर्तिनीं मेदिनीम् ।

अथ व्रजत्सु दिवसेष्वेकदा भैरवाचार्यो राजानमुपह्वरे सोपग्रहमवादीत्—'तात, स्वार्थालसाः परोपकारदक्षाश्च प्रकृतयो भवन्ति भव्यानाम् । भवादृशां चार्थिदर्शनं महोत्सवः प्रणयनमाराधनमर्थग्रहणमुपकारः । भूमिरसि सर्वलोकमनोरथानां येनाभिधीयसे । श्रूयताम् । भगवतो महाकालहृदयनाम्नो महामन्त्रस्य कृष्णस्रगम्बरानुलेपेनाकल्पेन कल्पकथितेन महाश्मशाने जपकोट्या कृतपूर्वसेवोऽस्मि । तस्य वेतालसाधनावसाना सिद्धिः । असहायैश्च सा दुरवापा । त्वं चालमस्मै कर्मणे । त्वयि च गृहीतभरे भविष्यन्त्यपरे

१ 'स्वार्थलालसाः' ब.

सहायास्त्रयः । एकः स एवास्माकं टीटिभनामा बालमित्रं मस्करी यो भवन्तमुपतिष्ठते । द्वितीयः स पातालस्वामी । अपरो मच्छिष्य एव कर्णतालनामा द्राविडः । यदि साधु मन्यसे ततो नीयतामयं दिङ्नागहस्तदीर्घो गृहीताट्टहासो निशामेकामेकदिङ्मुखार्गलतां बाहुः' इति । कृतवचसि च तस्मिन्नन्धकारं प्रविष्ट इव दृष्टप्रकाशः प्राप्तोपकारावकाशः प्रमुदितेनान्तरात्मना नरेन्द्रः समभाषत—'भगवन्, परमनुगृहीतोऽस्म्यनेन शिष्यजनसामान्येन निदेशेन कृतपरिग्रहमिवात्मानमवैमि' इति । ननन्द च तेन नरेन्द्रव्याहृतेन भैरवाचार्यः । चकार च सङ्केतम्—'अस्यामेवागामिन्यामसितपक्षचतुर्दशीक्षपायामियत्यां वेलायाममुष्मिन्महाश्मशानसमीपभाजि शून्यायतने शस्त्रद्वितीयेनायुष्मता द्रष्टव्या वयम्' इति ।

अथातिक्रान्तेष्वहःसु प्राप्तायां च तस्यामेव कृष्णचतुर्दश्यां शैवेन विधिना दीक्षितः क्षितिपो नियमवानभूत् । कृताधिवासं च सम्पादितगन्धधूपमाल्यादिपूजं खड्गमट्टहासमकरोत् । ततः परिणते दिवसे केनापि कर्मसाधनाय कृतरुधिरबलिविधानास्विव लोहितायमानासु दिक्षु, रुधिरबलिलम्पटासु च वेतालजिह्वास्विव लम्बमानासु च रविदीधितिषु, नरेन्द्रानुरागेण गृहीतापरदिशि स्वयमिव दिक्पालतां चिकीर्षति सवितरि, यातुधानीष्विव वर्धमानासु तरुच्छायासु, पातालतलवासिषु विज्ञाय दानवेष्विवोत्तिष्ठत्सु तमोमण्डलेषु, नभसि पुञ्जीभवति रौद्रं कर्म दिदृक्षमाण इव नक्षत्रगणे, विगाढायां शर्वर्याम्, सुप्तजने[1] निःशब्दस्तिमिते निशीथे, राजा सान्तःपुरं परिजनं वञ्चयित्वा वामकरस्फुरत्त्सरुर्दक्षिणकरेणोत्खातं खड्गमट्टहासमादाय विसर्पता च खड्गप्रभापटलेन नीलांशुकपटेनेव दर्शनभयादवगुण्ठितनिखिलगात्रयष्टिरनादिष्टयाप्यनुगम्यमानो राजलक्ष्म्या पृष्ठतः परिमललग्नमधुकरवेणिव्याजेन केशेष्विव कर्मसिद्धिमाकर्षन्नेकाकी नगरान्निरगात् । अगाच्च तमुद्देशम् ।

अथ प्रत्युज्जग्मुस्ते त्रयो द्रौणिकृपकृतवर्माण इव सौप्तिके सन्नद्धाः, स्नाताः, स्रग्विणो गृहीतविकटवेशाः, कुसुमशेखरसञ्चारिभिः क्रियमाणमन्त्रशिखाबन्धा इव गुञ्जद्भिः षट्चरणैः, उष्णीषपट्टकाँल्ललाटमध्यघटितविकटस्वस्तिकाग्रन्थीन्महामुद्राबन्धानिव धारयन्तो मूर्धभिः, एकश्रवणविवरविततविमलदन्तपत्रप्रभालोकलेपधवलितकपोलैर्मुखैरापिबन्त इव निशाचरापचयचिकीर्षया शार्वरमन्धकारम्, इतरकर्णावलम्बिनां रत्नकुण्डलानामरुच्छाच्छया रुचा गोरोचनयेव मन्त्रपरिजप्तया समालब्धाः[2], स्वप्रतिबिम्बगर्भान्कर्मसिद्धये दत्तपुरुषोपहारानिवोल्लासयन्तो निशितान्निस्त्रिंशान्, निस्त्रिंशांशुसन्तानसीमन्तिततिमिरामात्मीयात्मीयदिग्भागसंरक्षणाय त्रिधेव त्रियामां पाटयन्तः, सार्धचन्द्रैः कलधौतबुद्बुदावलितरलतारागणैर्निशाया इव परुषासिधारानिकृत्तैः खड्गैर्गृहीतैश्चर्मफलकैरकाण्डशार्वरीमपरां घटयन्तः, काञ्चनशृङ्खलाकलापनियमित-

१ 'जननिःशब्द०' अ—क. २ '०लब्धाङ्गाः' ब.

निबिडनिष्प्रवाणयः, बद्धासिधेनवः, टीटिभकर्णतालपातालस्वामिनो निवेदितवन्तश्चात्मानम्। अवनिपतिस्तु—'कोऽत्र कः' इति त्रीनपृच्छत्। आचचक्षिरे च स्व स्वं नाम त्रयोऽपि ते। तैरेव चानुगम्यमानो जगाम तां बलिदीपालोकजर्जरितगुग्गुलुधूपधूमगृह्यमाणदिग्भागतया विक्षिप्यमाणरक्षासर्षपाधेदग्धान्धकारपलायमाननिशामिव समुपकल्पितसर्वोपकरणां निःशब्दां च गम्भीरां च भीषणां च साधनभूमिम्।

तस्यां च कुमुदधूलिधवलेन भस्मना लिखितस्य महतो मण्डलस्य मध्ये स्थितं दीप्ततरतेजःप्रसरम्, पृथुपरिवेशपरिक्षिप्तमिव शरत्सवितारम्, मध्यमानक्षीरोदावर्तवर्तिनमिव मन्दरम्, रक्तचन्दनानुलेपिनो रक्तस्रगम्बराभरणस्योत्तानशयस्य शवस्योरस्युपविश्य जातजातवेदसि मुखकुहरे प्रारब्धाग्निकार्यम्, कृष्णाङ्गरागम्, कृष्णप्रतिसरम्, कृष्णवाससम्, कृष्णतिलाहुतिनिभेन विद्याधरत्वतृष्णया मानुषनिर्माणकारणकालुष्यपरमाणूनिव क्षयमुपनयन्तम्, आहुतिदानपर्यस्ताभिः प्रेतमुखस्पर्शदूषितं प्रक्षालयन्तमिवाशुशुक्षणिं करनखदीधितिभिः, धूमालोहितेन चक्षुषा क्षतजाहुतिमिव हुतभुजि पातयन्तम्, ईषद्विवृताधरपुटप्रकटितसितदशनशिखरेण दृश्यमानमूर्तमन्त्राक्षरपङ्क्तिनेव मुखेन किमपि जपन्तम्, होमश्रमस्वेदसलिलप्रतिबिम्बिताभिरासन्नदीपिकाभिर्दहन्तमिव सिद्धये सर्वावयवान्, अंसावलम्बिना बहुगुणेन विद्याराजेनेव ब्रह्मसूत्रेण परिगृहीतं भैरवाचार्यमपश्यत्। उपसृत्य चाकरोन्नमस्कारम्। अभिनन्दितश्च तेन स्वव्यापारमन्वतिष्ठत्।

अत्रान्तरे पातालस्वामी शातक्रतवीमाशामङ्गीचकार। कर्णतालः कौबेरीम्। परिव्राट् प्राचेतसीम्। राजा तु त्रैशङ्कवेन ज्योतिषाङ्कितां ककुभमलङ्कृतवान्।

एवं चावस्थितेषु दिक्पालेषु दिक्पालभुजपञ्जरप्रविष्टे विस्रब्धं कर्म साधयति भैरवं भैरवाचार्येऽतिचिरं कृतकोलाहलेषु निष्फलप्रयत्नेषु प्रत्यूहकारिषु शान्तेषु कौणपेषु गलत्यर्धरात्रसमये मण्डलस्य नातिदवीयस्युत्तरेणाकस्मात्प्रलयमहावराहदंष्ट्राविवरमिव दर्शयन्ती क्षितिरदीर्यत। सहसैव च तस्माद्विवरादाशावारणोत्क्षिप्त इवालानलोहस्तम्भः, महावराहपीवरस्कन्धपीठो नरकासुर इव भुवो गर्भादुद्भूतः, बलिदानव इव भित्त्वोत्थितः पातालम्, इन्द्रनीलप्रासाद इवोपरिज्वलितरत्नप्रदीपः, स्निग्धनीलघननिबिडकुटिलकुन्तलकान्तमौलिरुन्मीलन्मालतीमुण्डमालः, गद्गदतया स्वरस्य स्वभावपाटलतया च चक्षुषः क्षीब इव यौवनमदेन, वल्गद्वलदामकः, करसम्पुटमृदितया मृदा दिङ्नागकुम्भाभावंसकूटौ पुनः पुनः परिपङ्कयन्, सान्द्रचन्दनकर्दमदत्तैरव्यवस्थास्थासकैरतिसितजलधरशकलशारित इव शारदाकाशैकदेशः, केतकीगर्भपत्रपाण्डुरस्य चण्डातकस्योपरि क्षामतरीकृतकुक्षिः कक्ष्याबन्धं विधाय

विलासविक्षिप्तेन धवलव्यायामफालीपटान्तेन धरणितलगेन धार्यमाण इव पृष्ठतः शेषेण, स्थिरस्थूलोरुदण्डः, भूमिभङ्गभयेनेव मन्थराणि स्थापयन्पदानि, निर्भरगर्वगुरु कथमपि शैलमिव गात्रमुद्वहन्दर्पेण, मुहुर्मुहुरुरसि द्विगुणिते दोष्णि वामे तिर्यगुत्क्षिप्ते च दक्षिणे जङ्घाकाण्डे कुण्डलिते चण्डस्फोटनटाङ्कारैः कर्मविघ्ननिर्घातानिव पातयन्नेकेन्द्रियविकलमिव जीवलोकं कुर्वन्कुवलयश्यामलः पुरुष उज्जगाम। जगाद च विहस्य नरसिंहनादनिर्घोषघोरया भारत्या—'भो विद्याधरीश्रद्धाकामुक किमयं विद्यालवावलेपः सहायमदो वा यदस्मै जनायाविधाय बलिं बालिश इव सिद्धिमभिलषसि। का ते दुर्बुद्धिरियम्। एतावता कालेन क्षेत्राधिपतिरस्य मन्नाम्नैव लब्धव्यपदेशस्य देशस्य नागतस्ते श्रोत्रोपकण्ठं श्रीकण्ठनामा नागोऽहम्। अनिच्छति मयि का शक्तिर्ग्रहगणस्यापि गन्तुं गगने। भूनाथोऽप्ययमनाथस्तपस्वी यस्त्वादृशैः शैवापसदैरुपकरणीक्रियते। सहस्वेदानीं सहामुना दुर्नरेन्द्रेण दुर्नरेन्द्रदुर्नयस्य फलम्' इत्यभिधाय च निष्ठुरैः प्रकोष्ठप्रहारैस्त्रीनपि टीटिभप्रभृतीनभिमुखं प्रधावितान्सशरीरावरणकृपाणानपातयत्।

अथापूर्वाधिक्षेपश्रवणादशस्त्रव्रणैरप्यमर्षस्वेदच्छलेनानेकसमरपीतमसितमसिधाराजलमिव वमद्भिरवयवैरपि रोमाञ्चनिभेन मुक्तशरशतशल्यनिकरभरलघुमिवात्मानं रणाय कुर्वद्भिरट्टहासेनापि प्रतिबिम्बिततारागणेन स्पष्टदृष्टधवलदन्तमालमवज्ञया हसतेव कथ्यमानसत्त्वावष्टम्भः परिकरबन्धविभ्रमभ्रमितकरनखकिरणचक्रवालेन व्यपगमनाशङ्कया नागदमनमन्त्रमण्डलबन्धेनेव रुन्धन्दश दिशो नरनाथः सावज्ञमवादीत्—'अरे काकोदर काक, मयि स्थिते राजहंसे न जिह्रेषि बलिं याचितुम्। अमीभिः किं वा परुषभाषितैः। भुजे वीर्यं निवसति सताम्[1], न वाचि। प्रतिपद्यस्व शस्त्रम्। अयं न भवसि। अगृहीतहेतिष्वशिक्षितो मे भुजः प्रहर्तुम्' इति। नागस्तु—'अनादृततरमेहि। किं शस्त्रेण। भुजाभ्यामेव भनज्मि भवतो दर्पम्' इत्यभिधायास्फोटयामास। नरपतिरपि निरायुधमायुधेन युधि लज्जमानो जेतुमुत्सृज्य सचर्मफलकमट्टहासमसिमर्धोरुकस्योपरि बबन्ध बाहुयुद्धाय कक्ष्याम्। युयुधाते च निर्दयास्फोटनस्फुटितभुजरुधिरशीकरसिच्यमानौ शिलास्तम्भैरिव पतद्भिर्बाहुदण्डैः शब्दमयमिव कुर्वाणौ भुवनं तौ। नचिराच्च पातयामास भूतले भुजङ्गं भूपतिः। जग्राह च केशेषु। उच्चखान च शिरश्छेत्तुमट्टहासम्। अपश्यच्च वैकक्षकमालान्तरेणास्य यज्ञोपवीतम्। उपसंहृतशस्त्रव्यापारश्चावादीत्—'दुर्विनीत, अस्ति ते दुर्नयनिर्वाहबीजमिदम्। यतो विश्रब्धमेवाचरसि चापलानि' इत्युक्त्वोत्ससर्ज तम्। अनन्तरं च सहसैवातिबहलां ज्योत्स्नां

---

१ 'दुर्नरेन्द्रेण दुर्नयस्य' अ–क. २ एतन्नास्ति अ–क–पुस्तकयोः.

ददर्श शरदि विकसतां कमलवनानामिव च घ्राणावलेपिनमामोदमजिघ्रत्। झटिति च नूपुरशब्दमश्रृणोत्। व्यापारयामास च शब्दानुसारेण दृष्टिम्।

अथ करतलस्थितस्या[1]ट्टहासस्य मध्ये तडितमिव नीलजलधरोदरे स्फुरन्तीम्, प्रभया पिबन्तीमिव त्रियामाम्, तामरसहस्ताम्, कोमलाङ्गुलिरागराजिजालकानि च चरणलग्नानि वेलाबालविद्रुमलतावनानीवाकर्षन्तीम्, करपङ्कजसङ्कोचाशङ्कया शशाङ्कमण्डलमिव खण्डशः कृतं निर्मलचरणनखनिवहनिभेन बिभ्रतीम्, गुल्फावलम्बिनूपुरपुटतया स्थितनिबिडकटकावलिबन्धनादिव परिभ्रश्यागताम्, बहुविधकुसुमशकुनिशतशोभितात्पवनचलिततनुतरङ्गादतिस्वच्छादंशुकादुदधिसलिलादिवोत्तरन्तीम्, उदधिजन्मप्रेम्णा त्रिवलिच्छलेन त्रिपथगयेव परिष्वक्तमध्याम्, अत्युन्नतस्तनमण्डलाम्, दृश्यमानदिङ्नागकुम्भामिव ककुभम्, मदे[2]लग्नैरावतकरशीकरनिकरमिव शरत्तारागणतारं हारमुरसा दधानाम्, धवलचामरैरिव च मन्दमन्दनिःश्वासदोलायितैर्हारकिरणैरुपवीज्यमानाम्, स्वभावलोहितेन मदान्धगन्धेभकुम्भास्फालनसंक्रान्तसिन्दूरेणेव करद्वयेन द्योतमानाम्, हरशिखण्डेन्दुद्वितीयखण्डेनेव कुण्डलीकृतेन ज्योत्स्नामुचा दन्तपत्रेण विभ्राजमानाम्, कौस्तुभगभस्तिस्तबकेनेव च श्रवणलग्नेनाशोककिसलयेनालङ्कृताम्, महता मातङ्गमदमयेन तिलकेनादृश्यच्छत्रच्छायामण्डलेनेवाविरहितललाटाम्, आपादतलादासीमन्ताच्च चन्द्रातपधवलेन चन्दनेनादिराजयशसेव धवलीकृताम्, धरणितलचुम्बिनीभिः कण्ठकुसुममालाभिः सरिद्भिरिव सागराधिष्ठाभि[3]रधिष्ठिताम्, मृणालकोमलैरवयवैः कमलसम्भवत्वमनक्षरमाचक्षाणां स्त्रियमपश्यत्। असंभ्रान्तश्च पप्रच्छ—'भद्रे, कासि क[4]स्यासि । किमर्थं वा दर्शनपथमागतासि' इति। सा तु स्त्रीजनविरुद्धेनावष्टम्भेनाभिभवन्तीवाभाषत तम्—'वीर, विद्धि मां नारायणोरःस्थलीलीलाविहारहरिणीम्, पृथुभरतभगीरथादि[5]राजवंशपताकाम्, सुभटभुजजयस्तम्भविलासशालभञ्जिकाम्, रणरुधिरतरङ्गिणीतरङ्गक्रीडादोहददुर्ललितराजहंसीम्, सितनृपच्छत्रषण्डशिखण्डिनीम्, अतिनिशितशस्त्रधारावनभ्रमणविभ्रमसिंहीम्, असिधाराजलकमलिनीं श्रियम्। अपहृतास्मि तवामुना शौर्यरसेन । याचस्व । ददामि ते वरमभिलषितम्' इति।

वीराणां त्वपुनरुक्ताः परोपकाराः। यतो राजा तां प्रणम्य स्वार्थविमुखो भैरवाचार्यस्य सिद्धिं ययाचे। लक्ष्मीस्तु देवी प्रीततरहृदया विस्तीर्यमाणेन चक्षुषा क्षीरोदेनेवोपरि पर्यस्तेनाभिषिञ्चन्ती भूपालम् 'एवमस्तु' इत्यब्रवीत्। अवादीच्च पुनः—'अनेन सत्त्वोत्कर्षेण भगवच्छिवभट्टारकभक्त्या चासाधार-

---

१ '०स्थितस्यैवाट्ट' ब. २ 'मध्यलग्नैरा०' ब. ३ 'सागरादृष्टाभिः' ब.
४ एतन्नास्ति अ-क-पुस्तकयोः. ५ '०राजपृथुवंश०' ब.

णया भवान्भुवि सूर्याचन्द्रमसोस्तृतीय इवाविच्छिन्नस्य प्रतिदिनमुपचीयमानवृद्धेः शुचिसुभगसत्यत्यागधैर्यशौण्डपुरुषप्रकाण्डप्रायस्य महतो राजवंशस्य कर्ता भविष्यति। यस्मिन्नुत्पत्स्यते सर्वद्वीपानां भोक्ता हरिश्चन्द्र इव हर्षनामा चक्रवर्ती त्रिभुवनविजिगीषुर्द्वितीयो मान्धातेव।यस्यायं करः स्वयमेव कमलमपहाय ग्रहीष्यति चामरम्' इति वचसोऽन्ते तिरोबभूव।

भूमिपालस्तु तदाकर्ण्य हृदयेनातिमात्रमप्रीयत। भैरवाचार्योऽपि तस्या देव्यास्तेन वचसा कर्मणा च सम्यगुपपादितेन सद्य एव कुन्तली किरीटी हारी केयूरी मेखली मुद्गरी खड्गी[2] च भूत्वावाप विद्याधरत्वम्। प्रोवाच च—'राजन्, अदूरव्यापिनः फल्गुचेतसामलसानां मनोरथाः। सतां तु भुवि विस्तारवत्यः स्वभावेनैवोपकृतयः। स्वप्नेऽप्यसम्भावितां दातुमिमां दक्षिणां क्षमः कोऽन्यो भवन्तमपहाय। सम्पत्कणिकामपि प्राप्य तुलेव लघुप्रकृतिरुन्नतिमायाति। त्वदीयैर्गुणैरुपकरणीकृतस्य त्वत्त एव च लब्धात्मलाभस्य निर्लज्जतेयमस्य मूढहृदयस्य यदिच्छामि[3] येन केनचित्कार्यलवोपपादनोपयोगेन स्मारयितुमात्मानम्' इति। प्रत्युपकारदुष्प्रवेशास्तु भवन्ति धीराणां हृदयावष्टम्भाः। यतस्तं राजा 'भवत्सिद्ध्यैव परिसमाप्तकृत्योऽस्मि। साधयतु मान्यो यथासमीहितं स्थानम्' इति प्रत्याचचक्षे।

तथोक्तश्च भूभुजा जिगमिषुः सुदृढं समालिङ्ग्य टीटिभादीन्कुवलयवनेनेवावश्यायशीकरस्राविणा सास्रेण चक्षुषा वीक्षमाणः क्षितिपतिं पुनरुवाच—'तात, ब्रवीमि—यामीति न स्नेहसदृशम्। त्वदीयाः प्राणा इति पुनरुक्तम्। गृह्यतामिदं शरीरकमिति व्यतिरेकेणार्थकरणम्। तिलशः क्रीता वयमिति नोपकारानुरूपम्। बान्धवोऽसीति दूरीकरणमिव। त्वयि स्थितं हृदयमित्यप्रत्यक्षम्। त्वद्विरहकारिणी[4] कारणेयं नः सिद्धिरित्यश्रद्धेयम्। निष्कारणस्तवोपकार इत्यनुवादः। स्मर्तव्या वयमित्याज्ञा। सर्वथा कृतघ्नालापेष्वसज्जनकथासु च चेतसि कर्तव्योऽयं स्वार्थनिष्ठुरो जनः' इत्यभिधाय वेगच्छिन्नहारोच्छलितमुक्ताफलनिकरताडिततारागणं गगनतलमुत्पपात। ययौ च सीमन्तितग्रहग्रामः सिद्धचुचितं धाम। श्रीकण्ठोऽपि—'राजन्, पराक्रमक्रीतः कर्तव्येषु नियोगेनानुग्राह्यो ग्राहितविनयोऽयं जनः[5]' इत्यभिधाय राजानुमोदितस्तदेव भूयो भूविवरं विवेश।

नरपतिस्तु क्षीणभूयिष्ठायां क्षपायां, प्रवातुमारब्धे प्रबुध्यमानकमलिनीनिःश्वाससुरभौ वनदेवताकुचांशुकापहरणपरिहासस्वेदिनीव सावश्यायशी-

---

१ '०सुभगमान्यसत्यत्यागशौर्यशौण्डि०' ब. २ अस्मात्परं 'कवची' इत्यधिकं ब-पुस्तके. ३ 'तदिच्छामि' अ-क. ४ '०रहानुकारिणी' ब. ५ 'परिजनः' ब.

करे परिमलाकृष्टमधुकृति कुमुदनिद्रावाहिनि निशापरिणतिजडे तुषारलेशिनि[1] वनानिले, विरहविधुरचक्रवाकचक्रनिःश्वसितसन्तापितायामिवापरजलनिधिमवतरन्त्यां त्रियामायां, साक्षादागतलक्ष्मीविलोकनकुतूहलिनीष्विव समुन्मीलन्तीषु नलिनीषु, उन्निद्रपक्षिणि क्षरति कुसुमविसरमिव तुहिनकणनिकरं मृदुपवनलासितलते कानने, कमललक्ष्मीप्रबोधमङ्गलशङ्खेष्विव रसत्स्वन्तर्बद्धध्वनन्मधुकरेषु मुकुलायमानेषु कुमुदेषु, उज्जिहानरविरथवाजिविसृष्टैः प्रोथपवनैः प्रोत्सार्यमाणास्विव वारुण्यां ककुभि पुञ्जीभवन्तीषु श्यामालताकलिकासु तारकासु, मन्दरशिखराश्रयिणि मन्दानिललुलितकल्पलतावनकुसुमधूलिविच्छुरित इव धूसरीभवति सप्तर्षिमण्डले, सुरवारणाङ्कुश इव च्युते गलति तारामये मृगे, त्रीनपि टीटिभादीन्गृहीत्वा नागयुद्धव्यतिकरमलीमसानि शुचिनि वनवापीपयसि प्रक्षाल्याङ्गानि नगरं विवेश । अन्यस्मिन्नहनि तेषामात्मशरीरानन्तरस्नान[2]भोजनाच्छादनादिना प्रीतिमकरोत् ।

कतिपयदिवसापगमे च परिव्राट् भूभुजा वार्यमाणोऽपि वनं ययौ । पातालस्वामिकर्णतालौ तु शौर्यानुरक्तो तमेव सिषेवाते । सम्पादितमनोरथातिरिक्तविभवौ च सुभटमण्डलमध्ये निष्कृष्टमण्डलाग्रौ समरमुखेषु प्रथममुपयुज्यमानौ कथान्तरेषु चान्तरान्तरा राज्ञा समादिष्टौ विचित्राणि भैरवाचार्यचरितानि शैशववृत्तान्तांश्च कथयन्तौ तेनैव सार्धं जरामाजग्मतुरिति ।

इति श्रीबाणभट्टकृते[3] हर्षचरिते राजवंशवर्णनं नाम
तृतीय उच्छ्वासः ।

---

१ 'तुषारलेखिनि' ब. २ 'शरीरानन्तरं स्नान' ब. ३ 'इति श्रीमहाकविचक्रचूडामणि–श्रीबाणभट्टविरचिते हर्षचरिते महाकाव्ये राजवंशवर्णनं नाम तृतीय उच्छ्वासः सम्पूर्णः' ब.

चतुर्थ उच्छ्वासः।

योगं स्वप्नेऽपि नेच्छन्ति कुर्वते न करग्रहम्।
महान्तो नाममात्रेण भवन्ति पतयो भुवः॥ १॥

सकलमहीभृत्कम्पकृदुत्पद्यत एक एव नृपवंशे।
विपुलेऽपि पृथुप्रतिमो दन्त इव गणाधिपस्य मुखे॥ २॥

अथ तस्मात्पुष्पभूते[1]र्द्विजवरस्वेच्छागृहीतकोषो नाभिपद्म इव पुण्डरीकेक्षणात्, लक्ष्मीपुरःसरो रत्नसञ्चय इव रत्नाकरात्, गुरुबुधकविकलावत्[2]तेजस्विभूनन्दनप्रायो ग्रहगण इवोदयस्थानात्, महाभारवाहनयोग्यः सागर इव सगरप्रभावात्, दुर्जयबलसनाथो हरिवंश इव शूरान्निर्जगाम राजवंशः। यस्मादविनष्टधर्मधवलाः प्रजासर्गा इव कृतमुखात्, प्रतापाक्रान्तभुवनाः किरणा इव तेजोनिधेः, विग्रहव्याप्तदिङ्मुखा गिरय इव भूभृत्प्रभ[3]वात्, धरणिधारणक्षमा दिग्गजा इव ब्रह्मकरात्, उदधीन्पातुमुद्यता जलधरा इव घनागमात्, इच्छाफलदायिनः कल्पतरव इव नन्दनात्, सर्वभूताश्रया विश्वरूपप्रकारा इव श्रीधरादजायन्त राजानः।

तेषु चैवमुत्पद्यमानेषु क्रमेणोदपादि हूण[4]हरिणकेसरी सिन्धुराजज्वरो गुर्जरप्रजागरो गान्धाराधिपगन्धद्विपकूट[5]पाकलो लाटपाटवपाट[6]च्चरो मालवलक्ष्मीलतापरशुः प्रतापशील इति प्रथितापरनामा प्रभाकरवर्धनो नाम राजाधिराजः। यो राज्याङ्गसङ्गीन्यभिषिच्यमान एव मलानीव मुमोच धनानि। यः परकीयेणापि कातरवल्लभेन रणमुखे तृणेनेव धृतेनालज्जत जीवितेन। यः करधृतधौतासिप्रतिबिम्बितेनात्मनाप्यदूयत समितिषु सहायेन रिपूणां पुरः प्रध्वनेषु धनुषापि नमता। यो मानी मानसेनाखिद्यत। यश्चान्तर्गतां[7]परिमितरिपुशल्यशङ्कुकीलितामिव निश्चलामुवाह राजलक्ष्मीम्। यश्च सर्वासु दिक्षु समीकृतसरित्तटावट[8]विटपाटवीतरु[9]तृणगुल्मवल्मीकगिरिगहनैर्दण्डयात्रापथैः पृथुभिर्भृत्योपयोगाय व्यभजतेव वसुधां बहुधा। यं चालब्धयुद्धदोहदमात्मीयोऽपि सकलरिपुसं[10]मुत्सारकः परकीय इव ततापः प्रतापः। यस्य च वह्निमयो हृदये-

१ 'पुष्यभूतेः' ब. २ 'कलाभृत्' ब. ३ 'भूभृत्प्रवरात्' ब. ४ 'हून॰' ब. ५ '॰कूटहस्तिज्वरः पाकलो' ब. ६ 'पाटज्वरः' ब. ७ 'अन्तर्गतामपरि॰' ब. ८ 'समीकृततटावट' अ. ९ 'तरुकण्टकतृण' ब. १० 'रिपुसमूहसमु॰' ब.

षु जलमयो लोचनपुटेषु मारुतमयो निःश्वसितेषु क्षमामयोऽङ्गेषु आकाशमयः शून्यतायां पञ्चमहाभूतमयो मूर्त इवादृश्यत निहतप्रतिसामन्तान्तःपुरेषु प्रतापः। यस्य चासन्नेषु भृत्यरत्नेषु प्रतिबिम्बितेव तुल्यरूपा समलक्ष्यत लक्ष्मीः। तथा च यस्य प्रतापाग्निना भूतिः शौर्योष्मणा सिद्धिरसिधाराजलेन वंशवृद्धिः शस्त्रव्रणमुखैः पुरुषकारोक्तिर्धनुर्गुणकिणेन करगृहीतिरभवत्। यश्च वैरमुपायनं विग्रहमनुग्रहं समरागमं महोत्सवं शत्रुं निधिदर्शनमरिबाहुल्यमभ्युदयमाहवाह्वानं वरप्रदानमवस्कन्दपातं दिष्टवृद्धिं शस्त्रप्रहारपतनं वसुधारा[1]ममन्यत। यस्मिंश्च राजनि निरन्तरैर्यूपनिकरैरङ्कुरितमिव कृतयुगेन, दिङ्मुखविसर्पिभिरध्वरधूमैः पलायितमिव कलिना, ससुधैः सुरालयैरवतीर्णमिव स्वर्गेण, सुरालयशिखरोद्धूयमानैर्धवलध्वजैः पल्लवितमिव धर्मेण, बहिरुपरचितविकटसभासत्रप्रपाप्राग्वंशमण्डपैः प्रसूत[2]मिव ग्रामैः, काञ्चनमयसर्वोपकरणैर्विभवैर्विशीर्णमिव मेरुणा, द्विजदीयमानैरर्थकलशैः फलितमिव भाग्यसम्पदा।

तस्य च जन्मान्तरेऽपि सती पार्वतीव शङ्करस्य, गृहीतपर[3]हृदया लक्ष्मीरिव लोकगुरोः, स्फुरत्तरलतारका रोहिणीव कलावतः, सर्वजनजननी बुद्धिरिव प्रजापतेः, महाभूभृत्कुलोद्गता गङ्गेव वाहिनीनायकस्य, मानसानुवर्तनचतुरा हंसीव राजहंसस्य, सकललोकार्चितचरणा त्रयीव धर्मस्य, दिवानिशममुक्तपार्श्वस्थितिररुन्धतीव महामुनेः, हंसमयीव गतिषु, परपुष्टमयीवालापेषु, चक्रवाकमयीव पतिप्रेम्णि, प्रावृण्मयीव पयोधरोन्नतौ, मदिरामयीव विलासेषु, निधिमयीवार्थसञ्चयेषु, वसुधारामयीव प्रसादेषु, कमलमयीव कोषसंग्रहेषु, कुसुममयीव फलदानेषु, संध्यामयीव वन्द्यत्वे, चन्द्रमयीव निरूष्मत्वे, दर्पणमयीव प्रतिप्राणिग्रहणेषु, सामुद्रमयीव परचित्तज्ञानेषु, परमात्ममयीव व्याप्तिषु, स्मृतिमयीव पुण्यवृत्तिषु, मधुमयीव सम्भाषणेषु, अमृतमयीव तृष्यत्सु, वृष्टिमयीव भृत्येषु, निर्वृतिमयीव सखीषु, वेतसमयीव गुरुषु, गोत्रवृद्धिरिव विलासानाम्, प्रायश्चित्तशुद्धिरिव स्त्रीत्वस्य, आज्ञासिद्धिरिव मकरध्वजस्य, व्युत्थानबुद्धिरिव रूपस्य, दिष्टवृद्धिरिव रतेः, मनोरथसिद्धिरिव रामणीयकस्य, दैवसम्पत्तिरिव लावण्यस्य, वंशोत्पत्तिरिवानुरागस्य, वरप्राप्तिरि[4]व कान्तेः, सर्गसमाप्तिरिव सौन्दर्यस्य, आयतिरिव यौवनस्य, अनभ्रवृष्टिरिव वैदग्ध्यस्य, अयशःप्रमृष्टिरिव लक्ष्म्याः, यशःपुष्टिरिव चारित्रस्य, हृदयतुष्टिरिव धर्मस्य, सौभाग्य[5]परमाणुसृष्टिरिव प्रजापतेः, शमस्यापि शान्तिरिव, विनयस्यापि विनीतिरिव, आभिजात्यस्याप्यभिजातिरिव, संयमस्यापि संयतिरिव, धैर्यस्यापि धृतिरिव, विभ्रमस्यापि विभ्रान्तिरिव यशोमती नाम महा-

---

१ '०धारारसममन्यत' अ. २ 'प्रसुतमिव' ब. ३ 'गृहीतहृदया' ब. ४ 'वरप्राप्तिरिव सौभाग्यस्य, उत्पत्तिभूमिरिव कान्तेः' ब. ५ 'सौहार्दम्य भाग्यरूपपरमाणु०' ब.

देवी प्राणानां प्रणयस्य विस्रम्भस्य धर्मस्य सुखस्य च भूमिरभूत्। यास्य वक्षसि नरकजितो लक्ष्मीरिव ललास।

निसर्गत एव च स नृपतिरादित्यभक्तो बभूव। प्रतिदिनमुदये दिनकृतः स्नातः सितदुकूलधारी धवलकर्पटप्रावृतशिराः प्राङ्मुखः क्षितौ जानुभ्यां स्थित्वा कुङ्कुमपङ्कानुलिप्ते मण्डलके पवित्रपद्मरागपात्रीनिहितेन स्वहृदयेनेव सूर्यानुरक्तेन रक्तकमलषण्डेनार्चां[1] ददौ। अजपच्च जप्यं सुचरितः प्रत्युषसि मध्यन्दिने दिनान्ते चापत्यहेतोः प्राध्वं प्रयतेन मनसा जञ्जपूको मन्त्रमादित्यहृदयम्।

भक्तजनानुरोधविधेयानि तु भवन्ति देवतानां मनांसि। यतः स राजा कदाचिद्ग्रीष्मसमये यदृच्छया सितकरकरसितसुधाधवलस्य हर्म्यस्य पृष्ठे सुष्वाप। पार्श्वे चास्य द्वितीयशयने देवी यशोमती शिश्ये। परिणतप्रायायां तु श्यामायाम्, आसन्नप्रभातवेलाविलुप्यमानलावण्ये लिलम्बिषमाणे सीदत्तेजसि तारकेश्वरे, कराग्रस्पृष्टकुमुदिनीप्रमोदजन्मनि शशधरस्वेद इव गलत्यतिशीतलेऽवश्यायपयसि, मधुमदमत्तप्रसुप्तसीमन्तिनीनिःश्वासाहतेषु संक्रान्तमदेष्विव घूर्णमानेष्वन्तःपुरप्रदीपेषु, राजनि च विमलनखप्रतिबिम्बिताभिः संवाह्यमानचरण इव तारकाभिर्विस्रब्धप्रसारितैर्दिगङ्गनानामिवार्पितैरङ्गैर्मधुसुगन्धिभिः स्वहस्तकमलतालवृन्तवातैरिव श्वसितैर्मुखश्रिया वीज्यमाने विमलकपोलस्थलस्थितेन सितकुसुमशेखरेणेव रतिकेलिकचग्रहलम्बितेन प्रतिमाशशिबिम्बेन विराजिते स्वपति देवी यशोमती सहसैव 'आर्यपुत्र, परित्रायस्व परित्रायस्व' इति भाषमाणा भूषणरवेण व्याहरन्तीव परिजनमुत्कम्पमानाङ्गयष्टिरुदतिष्ठत्।

अथ तेन सर्वस्यामपि पृथिव्यामश्रुतपूर्वेण किमुत देवीमुखे परित्रायस्वेति ध्वनिना दग्ध इव श्रवणयोरेकपद एव निद्रां तत्याज राजा। शिरोभागाच्च कोपकम्पमानदक्षिणकराकृष्टेन कर्णोत्पलेनेव निर्गच्छताच्छधारेण धौतासिना सीमन्तयन्निव निशामन्तरालव्यवधायकमाकाशमिवोत्तरीयांशुकं विक्षिपन्वामकरपल्लवेन करविक्षेपवेगगलितेन हृदयेनेव भयनिमित्तान्वेषिणा भ्रमता दिक्षु कनकवलयेन विराजमानः, सत्वरावतारितवामचरणाक्रान्तिकम्पितप्रासादः, पुरःपतितेनासिधारागोचरगतेन शशिमयूखखण्डेनेव खण्डितेन हारेण राजमानः, लक्ष्मीचुम्बनलग्नताम्बूलरसरञ्जिताभ्यामिव निद्रया कोपेन चातिलोहिताभ्यां लोचनाभ्यां पाटलयन्[2]पर्यन्तानाशानाम्, बद्धान्धकारया त्रिपताकया भ्रुकुट्या पुनरिव त्रियामां परिवर्तयन् 'देवि, न भेतव्यम्, न भेतव्यम्' इत्यभिदधानो वेगेनोत्पपात। सर्वासु च दिक्षु विक्षिप्तचक्षुर्यदा नाद्राक्षीत्किंचिदपि तदा पप्रच्छ तां भयकारणम्।

---

१ 'अर्घं' ब. २ 'पटलयन्' ब.

अथ गृहदेवतास्विव प्रधावितासु यामिकिनीषु, प्रबुद्धे च समीपशायिनि परिजने, शान्ते च हृदयोत्कम्पकारिणि साध्वसे सा समभाषत—'आर्यपुत्र, जानामि स्वप्ने भगवतः सवितुर्मण्डलान्निर्गत्य द्वौ कुमारकौ तेजोमयौ बालातपेनेव पूरयन्तौ दिग्भागान् वैद्युतमिव जीवलोकं कुर्वाणौ मुकुटिनौ कुण्डलिनौ अङ्गदिनौ कवचिनौ गृहीतशस्त्रौ इन्द्रगोपकरुचा रुधिरेण[1] स्नातौ उन्मुखेनोत्तमाङ्गघटमानाञ्जलिना जगता निखिलेन प्रणम्यमानौ कन्ययैकया च चन्द्रमूर्त्येव सुषुम्णरश्मिनिर्गतयानुगम्यमानौ क्षितितलमवतीर्णौ। तौ च मे विलपन्त्याः शस्त्रेणोदरं विदार्य प्रवेष्टुमारब्धौ। प्रतिबुद्धास्मि चार्यपुत्रं विक्रोशयन्ती वेपमानहृदया' इति।

एतस्मिन्नेव च कालक्रमे राजलक्ष्म्याः प्रथमालापः प्रथयन्निव स्वप्नफलमुपतोरणं रराण प्रभातशङ्खः। भाविनीं भूतिमिवाभिदधाना दध्वनुरमन्दं दुन्दुभयः। चकाण कोणाहतानन्दादिव[2] प्रत्यूषनान्दी। जय जयेति प्रबोधमङ्गलपाठकानामुच्चैर्वाचोऽश्रूयन्त। पुरुषश्च वल्लभतुरङ्गमन्दुरामन्दिरे मन्दमन्दं सुप्तोत्थितः सप्तीनां कृतमधुरहेषारवाणां पुरश्च्योतत्तुषारसलिलशीकरं किरन्मरकतहरितं यवसं वक्त्रापरवक्त्रे पपाठ—

'निधिस्तरुविकारेण सन्मणिः स्फुरता धाम्ना।
शुभागमो निमित्तेन स्पष्टमाख्यायते लोके॥ ३॥
अरुण इव पुरःसरो रविं पवन इवातिजवो जलागमम्।
शुभमशुभमथापि वा नृणां कथयति पूर्वनिदर्शनोदयः'॥ ४॥

नरपतिस्तु तच्छ्रुत्वा प्रीयमाणेनान्तःकरणेन तामवादीत्—'देवि, मुदोऽवसरे विषीदसि। समृद्धास्ते गुरुजनाशिषः पूर्णा नो मनोरथाः परिगृहीतासि कुलदेवताभिः प्रसन्नस्ते भगवानंशुमाली नचिरेणैवातिगुणवदपत्यत्रयलाभेनानन्दयिष्यति भवतीम्' इति। अवतीर्य च यथाक्रियमाणाः क्रियाश्चकार। यशोमत्यपि[3] तुतोष तेन पत्युर्भाषितेन।

ततः समतिक्रान्ते कस्मिंश्चित्कालांशे देव्यां च यशोमत्यां देवो राज्यवर्धनः प्रथममेव सम्बभूव गर्भे। गर्भस्थितस्यैव च यस्य यशसेव पाण्डुतामादत्त जननी। गुणगौरवक्रान्तेव गात्रमुद्वोढुं न शशाक। कान्तिविसरामृतरसतृप्तेवाहारं प्रति पराङ्मुखीबभूव। शनैः शनैरुपचीयमानगर्भभरालसा च गुरुभिर्वारितापि वन्दनाय कथमपि सखीभिर्हस्तावलम्बेनानीयत। विश्राम्यन्ती सालभञ्जिकेव समीपगतस्तम्भभित्तिष्वलक्ष्यत। कमललोभनिलीनैरलिभिरिव वृतावुद्धर्तुं नाशकच्चरणौ। मृणाललोभेन च चरणनखमयूखलग्नैर्भवनहंसैरिव सञ्चार्यमाणा मन्दमन्दं बभ्राम। मणिभित्तिपातिनीषु प्रतिमास्वपि हस्तावलम्बनलोभेन प्रसारयामास करकमलम्, किमुत सखीषु।

---

१ 'रुधिरेण धाम्ना स्नातौ' ब. २ 'कोणाभिहता०' ब. ३ 'यशोवत्यपि' अ.

माणिक्यस्तम्भदीधितीरप्यालम्बितुमाचकाङ्क्ष, किं पुनर्भवनलताः। समादेष्टुमप्यसमर्थासीद्गृहकार्याणि कैव कथा कर्तुम्। आस्तां नूपुरभारखेदितं चरणयुगलं मनसापि नोदसहत सौधमारोढुम्। अङ्गान्यपि नाशक्नोद्धारयितुं दूरे भूषणानि। चिन्तयित्वापि क्रीडापर्वताधिरोहणमुत्कम्पितस्तनी तस्तान। प्रत्युत्थानेषूभयजानुशिखरविनिहितकरकिसलयापि गर्वादिव गर्भेणाधार्यत। दिवसं चाधोमुखी स्तनपृष्ठसंक्रान्तेनापत्यदर्शनौत्सुक्यादन्तःप्रविष्टेनेव मुखकमलेनैवं प्रीयमाणा ददर्श गर्भम्। उदरे तनयेन हृदये च भर्त्रा तिष्ठता द्विगुणितामिव लक्ष्मीमुवाह। सख्युत्सङ्गमुक्तशरीरा च शरीरपरिचारिकाणामङ्केषु सपत्नीनां. तु शिरःसु पादौ चकार। अवतीर्णे च दशमे मासि सर्वोर्वीभृत्पक्षपाताय वज्रपरमाणुभिरिव निर्मितम्, त्रिभुवनभारधारणसमर्थं शेषफणामण्डलोपकरणैरिव कल्पितम्, सकलभूभृत्कम्पकारिणं दिग्गजावयवैरिव विहितमसूत देवं राज्यवर्धनम्। यस्मिञ्जाते जातप्रमोदा नृत्यमय्य इवाजायन्त प्रजाः। पूरितासंख्यशङ्खशब्दमुखरं प्रहतपटहशतपटुरवं गम्भीरभेरीनिनादनिर्भरभरितभुवनं प्रमोदोन्मत्तमर्त्यलोकमनोहरं मासमेकं दिवसमिव महोत्सवमकरोन्नरपतिः।

अथान्यस्मिन्नतिक्रान्ते कस्मिंश्चित्काले कन्दलिनि कुड्मलितकदम्बतरौ रूढतोक्मतृण[1]स्तम्बे स्तम्भिततामरसे विकसितचातकचेतसि मूकमानसौकसि नभसि मासि[2] देव्या देवक्या इव चक्रपाणिर्यशोमत्या हृदये गर्भे च सममेव सम्बभूव हर्षः। शनैः शनैश्चास्याः सर्वप्रजापुण्यैरिव परिगृहीता भूयोऽप्यापाण्डुतामङ्गयष्टिर्जगाम। गर्भारम्भेण श्यामायमानचारुचूचुकचूलिकौ चक्रवर्तिनः पातुं मुद्रिताविव[3] पयोधरकलशौ बभार[4]। स्तन्यार्थमाननिहिता दुग्धनदीव दीर्घस्निग्धधवला माधुर्यमधत्त दृष्टिः। सकलमङ्गलगणाधिष्ठितगात्रगरिम्णेव गतिरमन्दायत। मन्दं मन्दं सञ्चरन्त्या निर्मलमणिकुट्टिमनिमग्नप्रतिबिम्बनिभेन गृहीतपादपल्लवा पूर्वसेवामिवारेभे पृथिव्यस्याः। दिवसमधिशयानायाः शयनीयसपाश्रयपत्रभङ्गपुत्रिकाप्रतिमा विमलकपोलोदरगता प्रसवसमयं प्रतिपालयन्ती लक्ष्मीरिवालक्ष्यत। क्षपासु सौधशिखराग्रगताया गर्भोन्माथमुक्तांशुके स्तनमण्डले संक्रान्तमुडुपतिमण्डलमुपरि गर्भस्य श्वेतातपत्रमिव केनापि धार्यमाणमदृश्यत। सुप्ताया वासभवने चित्रभित्तिचामरग्राहिण्योऽपि चामराणि चालयांचक्रुः। स्वप्नेषु करविधृतकमलिनीपलाशपुटसलिलैश्चतुर्भिरपि दिक्करिभिरक्रियताभिषेकः। प्रतिबुध्यमानायाश्च चन्द्रशालिकासालभञ्जिकापरिजनोऽपि जयशब्दमसकृदजनयत्। परिजनाह्वानेष्वादिशेत्यशरीरा वाचो निश्चेरुः। क्रीडायामपि नासहताज्ञाभङ्गम्। अपि च चतुर्णामपि महार्णवानामेकीकृतेनाम्भसा स्नातुं वाञ्छा बभूव। वेला-

---

१ अ omits रूढ. २ अ omits मासि. ३ 'मुद्रिताविव जतुना' ब.
४ 'बभारोरुस्थलम्' ब.

वनलतागृहोदरपुलिनपरिसरेषु पर्यटितुं हृदयमभिललाष । आत्ययिकेष्वपि कार्येषु सविभ्रमं भ्रूलता चचाल । सन्निहितेष्वपि मणिदर्पणेषु मुखमुत्खाते खड्गपट्टे वीक्षितुं व्यसनमासीत् । उत्सारितवीणाः स्त्रीजनविरुद्धा 'ानुर्ध्वनयः श्रुतावसुखायन्त । पञ्जरकेसरिषु चक्षुररमत । गुरुप्रणामेष्वपि स्तम्भितमिव शिरः कथमपि ननाम । सख्यश्चास्याः प्रमोदविस्फारितैर्लोचनपुटैरासन्नप्रसवमहोत्सवधियेव धवलयन्त्यो भवनं विकचकुमुदकमलकुवलयपलाशवृष्टिमयं रक्षाबलिविधिमिवानवरतं विदधाना दिक्षु क्षणमपि न मुमुचुः पार्श्वम् । आत्मोचितस्थाननिषण्णाश्च महान्तो विविधौषधिधरा भिषजो भूधरा इव भुवो धृतिं चक्रुः । पयोनिधीनां हृदयानीव लक्ष्म्या सहागतानि ग्रीवासूत्रग्रन्थिषु प्रशस्तरत्नान्यबध्यन्त ।

ततश्च प्राप्ते ज्येष्ठामूलीये मासि बहुलासु बहुलपक्षद्वादश्यां व्यतीते प्रदोषसमये समारुरुक्षति क्षपायौवने सहसैवान्तःपुरे समुदपादि कोलाहलः स्त्रीजनस्य । निर्गत्य च ससंभ्रमं यशोमत्याः स्वयमेव हृदयनिर्विशेषा धात्र्याः सुता सुयात्रेति[१] नाम्ना राज्ञः पादयोर्निपत्य 'देव, दिष्ट्या वर्धसे द्वितीयसुतजन्मना' इति व्याहरन्ती पूर्णपात्रं जहार ।

अस्मिन्नेव च काले राज्ञः परमसंमतः शतशः संवादितातीन्द्रियादेशो दर्शितप्रभावः सङ्कलिती[२] ज्योतिषि सर्वासां ग्रहसंहितानां पारदृश्वा सकलगणकमध्ये महितो हितश्च त्रिकालज्ञानभाग्भोजकस्तारको नाम गणकः समुपसृत्य विज्ञापितवान्—'देव, श्रूयताम्[३] । मान्धाता किलैवंविधे व्यतीपातादिसर्वदोषाभिषङ्गरहितेऽहनि सर्वेषूच्चस्थानस्थितेष्वेवं ग्रहेष्वीदृशि लग्ने भेजे जन्म । अर्वाक्ततोऽस्मिन्नन्तराले पुनरेवंविधे योगे चक्रवर्तिजनने नाजनि जगति कश्चिदपरः । सप्तानां चक्रवर्तिनामग्रणीश्चक्रवर्तिचिह्नानां महारत्नानां च भाजनं सप्तानां सागराणां पालयिता सप्ततन्तूनां सर्वेषां प्रवर्तयिता सप्तसप्तिसमः सुतोऽयं देवस्य जातः' इति ।

अत्रान्तरे स्वयमेवानाध्माता अपि तारमधुरं शङ्खा विरेसुः । अताडितोऽपि क्षुभितजलनिधिजलध्वनिधीरं जुगुञ्जाभिषेकदुन्दुभिः । अनाहतान्यपि मङ्गलतूर्याणि रेणुः । सर्वभुवनाभयघोषणापटह इव दिगन्तरेषु बभ्राम तूर्यप्रतिशब्दः । विधुतकेसरसटाश्च साटोपगृहीतहरितदूर्वापल्लवकवलप्रशस्तैर्मुखपुटैः समहेषन्त हृष्टा वाजिनः । सलीलमुत्क्षिप्तैर्हस्तपल्लवैर्नृत्यन्त इव श्रवणसुभगं जगर्जुर्गजाः । ववौ चाचिराच्चक्रायुधमुत्सृजन्त्या लक्ष्म्या निःश्वास इव सुरामोदसुरभिर्दिव्यानिलः । यज्वनां मन्दिरेषु प्रदक्षिणशिखाकलापकथितकल्याणागमाः प्रजज्वलुरनिन्धना वैतानवह्नयः । भुवस्तलात्तपनीयशृङ्खलाबन्धबन्धुरकलशीकोशाः समुदगुर्महानिधयः । प्रहतमङ्गलतूर्यप्रतिशब्दनिभेन दिक्षु दिक्पालैरपि प्रमोदादक्रियतेव दिष्टवृद्धिकलकलः । तत्क्षण एव च शुक्लवाससो

१ 'सुपात्रेति' ब. २ 'सङ्कलितो' ब. ३ 'श्रूयते' ब.

ब्रह्ममुखाः कृतयुगप्रजापतय इव प्रजावृद्धये समुपतस्थिरे द्विजातयः । साक्षाद्धर्म इव शान्त्युदकफलहस्तस्तस्थौ पुरः पुरोधाः । पुरातन्यः स्थितय इवादृश्यन्नागता बान्धववृद्धाः । प्रलम्बश्मश्रुजालजटिलाननानि बहलमलपङ्ककलङ्ककालकायानि नश्यतः कलिकालस्य बान्धवकुलानीवाकुलान्यधावन्त मुक्तानि बन्धनवृन्दानि । तत्कालापक्रान्तस्याधर्मस्य शिबिरश्रेणय इवालक्ष्यन्त लोकविलुण्ठिता विपणिवीथ्यः । विलसदुन्मुखवामनकबधिरवृन्दवेष्टिताः साक्षाज्जातमातृदेवता इव बहुबालकव्याकुला ननृतुर्वृद्धधात्र्यः । प्रावर्तत च विगतराजकुलस्थितिरधःकृतप्रतीहाराकृतिरपनीतवेत्रिवेत्रो निर्दोषान्तःपुरप्रवेशः समस्वामिपरिजनो निर्विशेषबालवृद्धः समानशिष्टाशिष्टजनो दुर्ज्ञेयमत्तामत्तप्रविभागस्तुल्यकुलयुवतिवेश्यालापविलासः प्रनृत्तसकलकटकलोकः पुत्रजन्मोत्सवो महान् ।

अपरेद्युरारभ्य सर्वाभ्यो दिग्भ्यः स्त्रीराज्यानीवावर्जितानि, असुरविवराणीवापावृतानि, नारायणावरोधानीव प्रचलितानि, अप्सरसामिव महीमवतीर्णानि कुलानि, परिजनेन पृथुकरण्डपरिगृहीताः स्नानीयचूर्णावकीर्णकुसुमाः सुमनःस्रजः, स्फटिकशिलाशकलशुक्लकर्पूरखण्डपूरिताः पात्रीः, कुङ्कुमाधिवासभाञ्जि भाजनानि च मणिमयानि, सहकारतैलतिम्यत्तनुखदिरकेसरजालजटिलानि चन्दनधवलपूगफलफालीदन्तुरदन्तशफरुकाणि, गुञ्जन्मधुकरकुलपीयमानपारिजातपरिमलानि पाटलकानि[1] च, सिन्दूरपात्राणि च पिष्टातकपात्राणि च बाललतालम्बमानविटकवीटकांश्च ताम्बूलवृक्षकान्बिभ्राणेनानुगम्यमानानि चरण[2]निकुट्टनरणितमणिनूपुरमुखरितदिङ्मुखानि नृत्यन्ति राजकुलमागच्छन्ति समन्तात्सामन्तान्तःपुरसहस्राण्यदृश्यन्त ।

शनैः शनैर्व्यजृम्भत च क्वचिन्नृत्तानुचितचिरन्तनशालीनकुलपुत्रकलोकलास्यप्रथितपार्थिवानुरागः क्वचिदन्तःस्मितक्षितिपालापेक्षितक्षीबक्षुद्रदासीसमाकृष्यमाणराजवल्लभः क्वचिन्मत्तकटककुट्टनीकण्ठलग्नवृद्धार्यसामन्तनृत्तनिर्भरहसितनरपतिः क्वचित्क्षितिपाक्षिसंज्ञादिष्टदुष्टदासेरकगीतसूच्यमानसचिवचौर्यरतप्रपञ्चः क्वचिन्मदोत्कटकुटहारिकापरिष्वज्यमानजरत्प्रव्रजितजनितजनहासः क्वचिदन्योन्यनिर्भरस्पर्धोद्धुरविटचेट[3]कारब्धावाच्यवचनयुद्धः क्वचिन्नृपाबलाबलात्कारनर्त्यमाननृत्यानभिज्ञान्तःपुरपालभावितभुजिष्यः, सपर्वत इव कुसुमराशिभिः, सधारागृह इव सीधुप्रपाभिः, सनन्दनवन इव पारिजातकामोदैः, सनीहार इव कर्पूररेणुभिः, साट्टहास इव पटहरवैः, सामृतमथन इव कलकलैः, सावर्त इव रासकमण्डलैः, सरोमाञ्च इव भूषणमणिकिरणैः, सपट्टबन्ध इव चन्दनललाटिकाभिः, सप्रसव इव प्रतिशब्दकैः, सप्ररोह इव प्रसाददानैरुत्सवामोदः ।

---

१ 'पाटलानि पोटलकानि च सिन्दूर०' अ. २ 'चरणानि कुट्टन०' ब. ३ 'चेटकपेटकारब्ध०' ब.

स्कन्धावलम्बमानकेसरमालाः काम्बोजवाजिन इवास्कन्दन्तस्तरलतारका हरिणा इवोड्डीयमानाः सगरसुता इव खनित्रैर्निर्दयैश्चरणाभिघातैर्दारयन्तो भुवमनेकसहस्रसंख्याश्चिक्रीडुर्युवानः। कथमपि तालावचरचारणचरणक्षोभं चक्षमे क्षमा। क्षितिपालकुमारकाणां खेलतामन्योन्यास्फालैराभरणेषु मुक्ताफलानि फेलुः। सिन्दूररेणुना पुनरुत्पन्नहिरण्यगर्भगर्भशोणितशोणाशमिव ब्रह्माण्डकपालमभवत्। पटवासपांशुपटलेन प्रकटितमन्दाकिनीसैकतसहस्रमिव शुशुभे नभस्तलम्। विप्रकीर्यमाणपिष्टातकपरागपिञ्जरितातपा भुवनक्षोभविशीर्णपितामहकमलकिञ्जल्करजोराजिरञ्जिता इव रेजुर्दिवसाः। सङ्घट्टविघटितहारपतितमुक्ताफलपटलेषु चस्खाल लोकः।

स्थानस्थानेषु च मन्दमन्दमास्फाल्यमाना[1]लिङ्ग्यकेन शिञ्जानमञ्जुवेणुना झणझणायमानझल्लरीकेण ताड्यमानतन्त्रीपटहिकेन वाद्यमानानुत्तानाला[2]बुवीणेन कलकांस्यकोशीक्वणितकाहलेन समकालदीयमानानुत्तालताल[3]केनातोद्यवाद्येनानुगम्यमानाः, पदेपदे झणझणितभूषणरवैरपि सहृदयैरिवानु[4]वर्तमानताललयाः, कोकिला इव मदकलकाकलीकोमलालापिन्यो विटानां कर्णामृतान्यश्लीलरासकपदानि गायन्त्यः, समुण्डमालिकाः, सकर्णपल्लवाः, सचन्दनतिलकाः, समुच्छ्रिताभिर्वलयावलीवाचालाभिर्बाहुलतिकाभिः सवितारमिवालिङ्गयन्त्यः, कुङ्कुमप्रमृष्टिरुचिरकायाः काश्मीरकिशोर्य इव वल्गन्त्यः, नितम्बबिम्बलम्बिविकटकुरण्टकशेखराः प्रदीप्ता इव रागाग्निना, सिन्दूरच्छटाच्छुरितमुखमुद्राः शासनपट्टपङ्क्तय इवाप्रतिहतशासनस्य कन्दर्पस्य, मुष्टिप्रकीर्यमाणकर्पूरपटवासपांसुलमनोरथसञ्चरणरथ्या इव यौवनस्योद्दामकुसुमदामताडिततरुणजनाः प्रतीहार्य इव तरुणमहोत्सवस्य, प्रचलत्पत्त्रकुण्डला लसन्त्यो लता इव मदनचन्दनद्रुमस्य, ललितपदहंसकरवमुखराः समुल्लसन्त्यो वीचय इव शृङ्गार[5]रससागरस्य, वाच्यावाच्यविवेकशून्या बालक्रीडा इव सौभाग्यस्य, घनपटहरवोत्कण्टकितगात्रयष्टयः केतक्य इव कुसुमधूलिमुद्गिरन्त्यः, कमलिन्य इव दिवसमुत्फुल्लाननाः, कुमुदिन्य इव रात्रावनुपजातनिद्राः, आविष्टा इव नरेन्द्रवृन्दपरिवृताः, प्रीतय इव हृदयमपहरन्त्यः, गीतय इव रागमुद्दीपयन्त्यः, पुष्टय इवानन्दमुत्पादयन्त्यः, मदमपि मदयन्त्य इव, रागमपि रञ्जयन्त्य इव, आनन्दमपि आनन्दयन्त्य इव, नृत्यमपि नर्तयमाना इव, उत्सवमप्युत्सुक[6]यन्त्य इव, कटाक्षेक्षितेषु पिबन्त्य इवापाङ्गशुक्तिभिः, तर्जनेषु संयमयन्त्य इव नखमयूखपाशैः, कोपाभिनयेषु ताडयन्त्य इव भ्रूलताविभागैः, प्रणयसम्भाषणेषु वर्षन्त्य इव सर्वरसान्, चतुरचङ्क्रमणेषु विकिरन्त्य इव विकारान्, पण्यविलासिन्यः प्रानृत्यन्।

---

१ '०मानलिङ्गकेन' ब. २ 'अनुत्तालालाबु०' ब. ३ ०'तालिकेन' ब. ४ 'अनुवर्त्यमान०' ब. ५ 'शृङ्गाररसस्य' अ. ६ 'उत्सवयन्त्यः' ब.

अन्यत्र वेत्रिवेत्रवित्रासितजनदत्तान्तरालाः, ध्रियमाणधवलातपत्रवना वनदेवता इव कल्पतरुतलविचारिण्यः, काश्चित्स्कन्धोभयपालीलम्बमानलम्बोत्तरीय[1]ग्रहस्ता लीलादोलाधिरूढा इव प्रेङ्खन्त्यः, काश्चित्कनककेयूरकोटिपाट्यमानपट्टांशुकोत्तरङ्गास्तरङ्गिण्य इव तरच्चक्रवाकसीमन्त्यमानस्रोतसः, काश्चिदुद्धूयमानधवलचामरसटालग्नत्रिकण्टकवलितविकटकटाक्षाः सरस्य इव हंसाकृष्यमाणनीलोत्पलवनाः, काश्चिच्चलच्चरणच्युतालक्तकारुणस्वेदशीकरसिच्यमानभवनहंसाः संध्यारागरज्यमानेन्दुबिम्बा इव कौमुदीरजन्यः, काश्चित्कण्ठनिहितकाञ्चनकाञ्चीगुणाञ्चितकञ्चुकिविकारा[2]कुञ्चितभ्रुवः कामवागुरा इव प्रसारितबाहुपाशा राजमहिष्यः प्रारब्धनृत्या विलेसुः[3]।

सर्वतश्च नृत्यतः स्त्रैणस्य गलद्भिः पदालक्तकैररुणिता रागमयीव शुशोण क्षोणी। समुल्लसद्भिः स्तनमण्डलैर्मङ्गलकलशमय इव बभूव महोत्सवः। भुजलताविक्षेपैर्मृणालवलयमय इव रराज जीवलोकः। समुल्लसद्भिर्विलासस्मितैस्तडिन्मय इवाक्रियत कालः। चञ्चलानां चक्षुषामंशुभिः कृष्णसा[4]रमया इवासन्वासराः। समुल्लसद्भिः शिरीषकुसुमस्तबककर्णपूरैः शुकपिच्छमय इव हरितच्छायोऽभूदातपः। विस्रंसमानैर्धम्मिल्लतमालपल्लवैः कज्जलमयमिवालक्ष्यतान्तरिक्षम्। उत्क्षिप्तैर्हस्तकिशलयैः कमलिनीमय्य इव बभासिरे सृष्टयः। माणिक्येन्द्रायुधानामर्चिषा चाषपत्रमया इव चकाशिरे रविमरीचयः। रणतामाभरणगणानां प्रतिशब्दकैः किङ्किणीमय्य इव शिशिञ्जिरे दिशः। जरत्योऽप्युन्मादिन्य इव रमण्यो रेणुः। वर्षीयांसोऽपि ग्रहगृहीता इव नापत्रेपिरे। विद्वांसोऽपि मत्ता इवात्मानं विसस्मरुः। निर्नर्तिषया मुनीनामपि मनांसि विपुस्फुलुः। सर्वस्वं च ददौ नरपतिः। दिशि दिशि कुबेरकोषा इवालुप्यन्त लोकेन द्रविणराशयः।

एवं च वृत्ते तस्मिन्महोत्सवे शनैः शनैः पुनरप्यतिक्रामति काले, देवे चोत्तमाङ्गनिहितरक्षासर्षपे[5], समुन्मिषत्प्रतापाग्निस्फुलिङ्ग इव गोरोचनापिञ्जरितवपुषि, समभिव्यज्यमानसहजक्षात्रतेजसीव हाटकबद्धविकटव्याघ्रनखपङ्क्तिमण्डितग्रीवके, हृदयोद्भिद्यमानदर्पाङ्कुर इव प्रथमाव्यक्तजल्पितेन सत्यस्य शनैः शनैरोंकारमिव कुर्वाणे, मुग्धस्मितैः कुसुमैरिव मधुकरकुलानि बन्धुहृदयान्याकर्षति, जननीपयोधरकलशपयःशीकरसेकादिव जायमानैर्विलासहसिताङ्कुरैर्दशनकैरलंक्रियमाणमुखकमलके, चारित्र इवान्तःपुरस्त्रीकदम्बकेन पाल्यमाने, मन्त्र इव सचिवमण्डलेन रक्ष्यमाणे, वृत्त इव कुलपुत्रकलोकेनामुच्यमाने, यशसीवात्म[6]वंशेन संवर्ध्यमाने, मृगपतिपोत इव रक्षिपुरुषशस्त्रपञ्जरमध्यगते, धात्रीकराङ्गुलिलग्ने पञ्चषाणि पदानि प्रयच्छति हर्षे, षष्ठं

---

१ '०लग्ना लीला०' अ. २ 'विकारकुञ्चितभुवः' ब. ३ 'विरेसुः' ब. ४ 'कृष्णशार०' अ. ५ '०सर्षपकणे' ब. ६ 'आत्मवशेन' ब.

वर्षमवतरति च राज्यवर्धने देवी यशोमती गर्भेणाधत्त नारायणमूर्तिरिव वसुधा देवीं राज्यश्रियम् ।

पूर्णेषु च प्रसवदिवसेषु दीर्घरक्तनालनेत्रामुत्पलिनीमिव सरसी, हंसमधुरस्वरां शरदमिव प्रावृट्, कुसुमसुकुमारावयवां वनराजिमिव मधुश्रीः, महाकनकावदातां वसुधारामिव द्यौः, प्रभावर्षिणीं रत्नजातिमिव वेला, सकलजननयनानन्दकारिणीं चन्द्रलेखामिव प्रतिपत्, सहस्रनेत्रदर्शनयोग्यां जयन्तीमिव शची, सर्वभूभृदभ्यर्थितां गौरीमिव मेना, प्रसूतवती दुहितरम्। यया द्वयोः सुतयोरुपरि स्तनयोरिवैकावलीलतया नितरामराजत ।

अस्मिन्नेव तु काले देव्या यशोमत्या भ्राता सुतमष्टवर्षदेशीयमुद्धूयमानकुटिलकाकपक्षकशिखण्डं खण्डपरशुहुंकाराग्निधूमलेखानुबद्धमूर्धानं मकरध्वजमिव पुनर्जातम्, एकेनेन्द्रनीलकुण्डलांशुश्यामलितेन शरीरार्धेनेतरेण च त्रिकण्टकमुक्ताफलालोकधवलितेन संपृक्तावतारमिव हरिहरयोर्दर्शयन्तम्, पीनप्रकोष्ठप्रतिष्ठितपुष्पलोहवलयं परशुराममिव क्षत्रक्षपणक्षीणपरशुपाशचिह्नितं बालतां गतम्, कण्ठसूत्रग्रथितभङ्गुरप्रवालाङ्कुरं हिरण्यकशिपुमिवोरःकाठिन्यखण्डितनरसिंहनखरखण्डम्, गृहीतजन्मान्तरं शैशवेऽपि सावष्टम्भं बीजमिव वीर्यद्रुमस्य भण्डिनामानमनुचरं कुमारयोरर्पितवान् ।

अवनिपतेस्तु तस्योपरि पुत्रयोस्तृतीयस्य नेत्रयोरिवेश्वरस्य तुल्यं दर्शनमासीत् । राजपुत्रावपि सकलजीवलोकहृदयानन्ददायिनौ तेन प्रकृतिदक्षिणेन मधुमाधवाविव मलयमारुतेनोपेतौ नितरां रेजतुः । क्रमेण चापरेणेव भ्रात्रा प्रजानन्देन सह वर्धमानौ यौवनमवतेरतुः स्थिरोरुस्तम्भौ च पृथुप्रकोष्ठौ दीर्घभुजार्गलौ विकटोरःकपाटौ प्रांशुसालाभिरामौ महानगरसंनिवेशाविव सर्वलोकाश्रयक्षमौ बभूवतुः ।

अथ चन्द्रसूर्याविव स्फुरज्ज्योत्स्नायशःप्रतापाक्रान्तभुवनावभिरामदुर्निरीक्ष्यौ, अग्निमारुताविव समभिव्यक्ततेजोबलावेकीभूतौ, शिलाकठिनकायबन्धौ हिमवद्विन्ध्याविवाचलौ, महावृषाविव कृतयुगयोग्यौ, अरुणगरुडाविव हरिवाहनविभक्तशरीरौ, इन्द्रोपेन्द्राविव नागेन्द्रगतौ,कर्णार्जुनाविव कुण्डलकिरीटधरौ, पूर्वापरदिग्भागाविव सर्वतेजस्विनामुदयास्तमयसम्पादनसमर्थौ, अमान्ताविवातिमानेनासन्नवेलार्गलनिरोधसङ्कटे कुकुटीरके तेजःपराङ्मुखीं छायामपि जुगुप्समानौ, स्वात्मप्रतिबिम्बेनापि पादनखलग्नेन लज्जमानौ, शिरोरुहाणामपि भङ्गेन दुःखमवतिष्ठमानौ, चूडामणिसंक्रान्तेनापि द्वितीयेनातपत्रेणापत्रपमाणौ, भगवति षण्मुखेऽपि स्वामिशब्देनासुखायमानश्रवणौ, दर्पणदृष्टेनापि प्रतिपुरुषेण दूयमाननयनौ, संध्याञ्जलिघटनेष्वपि शूलायमानोत्तमाङ्गौ, जलधरधृतेनापि धनुषा दोदूयमानहृदयौ, आलेख्यक्षितिपतिभिरप्यप्रणमद्भिः सन्तप्यमानचरणौ, परिमितमण्डलसन्तुष्टं तेजः सवितुरप्यबहुमन्यमानौ,

१ 'अमान्ताविवाभिमानेन' ब. २ 'दोधूयमान०' ब.

भूभृदपहृतलक्ष्मीकं सागरमप्युपहसन्तौ, बलवन्तमकृतविग्रहं मारुतमपि निन्दन्तौ, हिमवतोऽपि चमरीबालव्यजनवीजितेन दह्यमानौ, जलधीनामपि शङ्खैः ह्रियमाणौ, चतुःसमुद्राधिपतिमपरं प्रचेतसमप्यसहमानौ, अनपहृतच्छत्रानपि विच्छायानवनिपालान्कुर्वाणौ, साधुष्वप्यसेवितप्रसन्नौ, मुखेन मधु क्षरन्तौ, दुष्टराजवंशानूष्मणा दूरस्थितानपि म्लानिमानयन्तौ, अनुदिवसं शास्त्राभ्यासश्यामिकाकलङ्कितमशेषराजकप्रतापाग्निनिर्वापणमलिनमिव करतलमुद्वहन्तौ, योग्याकालेषु धीरैर्धनुर्ध्वनिभिरभ्यर्णोपभोगाद्दिग्वधूभिरिवालपन्तौ, राज्यवर्धन इति हर्ष इति सर्वस्यामेव पृथिव्यामाविर्भूतशब्दप्रादुर्भावौ, स्वल्पीयसैव कालेन द्वीपान्तरेष्वपि प्रकाशतां जग्मतुः।

एकदा च तावाहूय भुक्तवानभ्यन्तरगतः पिता सस्नेहमवादीत्—'वत्सौ, प्रथमं राज्याङ्गं दुर्लभाः सद्भृत्याः। प्रायेण परमाणव इव समवायेष्वनुगुणीभूय द्रव्यं कुर्वन्ति पार्थिवं क्षुद्राः। क्रीडारसेन नर्तयन्तो मयूरतां नयन्ति बालिशाः। दर्पणमिवानुप्रविश्यात्मीयां प्रकृतिं संक्रामयन्ति पल्लविकाः[1]। स्वप्ना इव मिथ्यादर्शनैरसद्बुद्धिं जनयन्ति विप्रलम्भकाः। गीतनृत्यहसितैरुन्मत्ततामावहन्त्युपेक्षिता विकारा इव वातिकाः। चातका इव तृष्णावन्तो न शक्यन्ते ग्रहीतुमकुलीनाः। मानसे मीनमिव स्फुरन्तमेवाभिप्रायं गृह्णन्ति जालिकाः। यमपट्टिका इवाम्बरे चित्रमालिखन्त्युद्गीतकाः। शल्यं हृदये निक्षिपन्त्यतिमार्गणाः। यतः सर्वैर्दोषाभिष्वङ्गैरसङ्गतौ बहुधोपधाभिः परीक्षितौ शुची विनीतौ विक्रान्तावभिरूपौ मालवराजपुत्रौ भ्रातरौ भुजाविव मे शरीरादव्यतिरिक्तौ कुमारगुप्तमाधवगुप्तनामानावस्माभिर्भवतोरनुचरत्वार्थमिमौ निर्दिष्टौ, अनयोरुपरि भवद्भ्यामपि नान्यपरिजनसमवृत्तिभ्यां भवितव्यम्' इत्युक्त्वा तयोराह्वानाय प्रतीहारमादिदेश।

नचिराद्द्वारदेशनिहितलोचनौ राज्यवर्धनहर्षौ प्रतीहारेण सह प्रविशन्तम्, अग्रतो ज्येष्ठमष्टादशवर्षवयसं नात्युच्चं नातिखर्वमतिगुरुभिः पदन्यासैरनेकनरपतिसञ्चरणचलां निश्चलीकुर्वाणमिवोर्वीम्, अनवरताभ्यस्तलङ्घनघनोपचयकठिनमांसमेदुरादूरुद्वयान्निष्पततेवानुल्बणजानुग्रन्थिप्रसूतेन तनुतरजङ्घाकाण्डयुगलेन भासमानम्, उल्लिखितपार्श्वप्रकाशितकृशिम्ना मन्दरमिव सुरासुररभसभ्रमितवासुकिकषणक्षीणेन मध्येन लक्ष्यमाणम्, अतिविस्तीर्णेनोरसा स्वामिसम्भावनानामपरिमितानामवकाशमिव प्रयच्छन्तम्, प्रलम्बमानस्य भुजयुगलस्य निभृतललितैर्विक्षेपैरतिदुस्तरं तरन्तमिव यौवनोदधिम्, वामकरकटकमाणिक्यमरीचिमञ्जरीजालिन्या समुद्भिद्यमानप्रतापानलशिखापल्लवयेव चापगुणकिणलेखयाङ्कितपीवरप्रकोष्ठम्, आलोहिनीमुच्चांसतटावलम्बिनीमस्त्रग्रहणव्रतविधृतां रौरवीमिव त्वचं कर्णाभरणमणेः प्रभां बिभ्राणम्, उत्कोटिकेयूरप-

१ 'पल्लवकाः' ब.

त्रभङ्गपुत्रिकाप्रतिविम्बगर्भकपोलं मुखं चन्द्रमसमिव हृदयस्थितरोहिणीकमुद्वहन्तम्, अचपलस्तिमिततारकेणाधोमुखेन चक्षुषा शिक्षयन्तमिव लक्ष्मीलाभोत्तानितमुखानि पङ्कजवनानि विनयम्, स्वाम्यनुरागमिव म्लातकमुत्तंसीकृतं शिरसा धारयन्तम्, निर्दयया कङ्कणभङ्गभीतसकलकार्मुकार्पितामिव नम्रतां प्रकाशयन्तम्, शैशव एव निर्जितैरिन्द्रियैररिभिरिव संयतैः शोभमानम्, प्रणयिनीमिव विश्वासभूमिं कुलपुत्रतामनुवर्तमानम्, तेजस्विनमपि शीलेनाह्लादकेन सवितारमिव शशिनान्तर्गतेन विराजमानम्, अचलानामपि कायकार्कश्येन गन्धनमिवाचरन्तम्, दर्शनक्रीतमानन्दहस्ते विक्रीणानमिव जनं सौभाग्येन कुमारगुप्तम्, पृष्ठतस्तस्य कनीयांसमतिप्रांशुतया गौरतया च मनःशिलाशैलमिव सञ्चरन्तम्, अनुच्चणमालतीकुसुमशेखरनिभेन निर्जिगमिषता गुरुणा शिरसि चुम्बितमिव यशसा, परस्परविरुद्धयोर्विनययौवनयोश्चिरात्प्रथमसङ्गमचिह्नमिव भ्रूसङ्गतकेन कथयन्तम्, अतिधीरतया हृदयनिहितां स्वामिभक्तिमिव निश्चलां दृष्टिं धारयन्तम्, अच्छाच्छचन्दनरसानुलेपशीतलं सन्निहितहारोपधानं वक्षःस्थलमनन्तसामन्तसंक्रान्तिश्रान्तायाः श्रियो विशालं शशिमणिशिलापट्टशयनमिव बिभ्राणम्, चक्षुः कुरङ्गैर्घोणावंशं वराहैः स्कन्धपीठं महिषैः प्रकोष्ठबन्धं व्याघ्रैः पराक्रमं केसरिभिर्गमनं मतङ्गजैर्मृगयाक्षपितशेषैर्भीतैरुत्कोचमिव दत्तं दर्शयन्तं माधवगुप्तं ददृशतुः।

प्रविश्य च तौ दूरादेव चतुर्भिरङ्गैरुत्तमाङ्गेन च गां स्पृशन्तौ नमश्चक्रतुः। स्निग्धनरेन्द्रदृष्टिनिर्दिष्टामुचितां भूमिं भेजाते। मुहूर्तं च स्थित्वा भूपतिरादिदेश तौ—'अद्यप्रभृति भवद्भ्यां कुमारावनुवर्तनीयौ। अहर्निशमस्तापरव्यापाराभ्यां प्रतिबिम्बकाभ्यामिवाङ्गभूताभ्यामनयोः कुमारयोश्चरतोस्तिष्ठतोः स्वपतोर्जाग्रतोश्चान्तिकं क्षणमपि न मोक्तव्यम्। एवं वामचिरात्सकलाः सङ्कल्पाः कल्पतरव इवाभिमतफलसम्पदुत्कर्षविशेषप्रदा भविष्यन्ति' इत्याकर्ण्य 'यथाज्ञापयति देवः' इति मेदिनीदोलायमानमौलिभ्यां युगपदभिहिते ताभ्यामुत्थाय राज्यवर्धनहर्षौ पितरं प्रणेमतुः। आदाय च तौ निर्जग्मतुः। ततश्चारभ्य क्षणमपि निमेषोन्मेषाविव चक्षुर्गोचरादनपयान्तावुच्छ्वासनिःश्वासाविव नक्तन्दिवमभिमुखं स्थितौ भुजाविव सततं पार्श्ववर्तिनौ कुमारयोस्तौ बभूवतुः।

अथ राज्यश्रीरपि नृत्यगीतादिषु विदग्धासु सखीषु सकलासु कलासु च प्रतिदिवसमुपचीयमानपरिचया शनैः शनैरवर्धत परिमितैरेव च दिवसैर्यौवनमारुरोह। निपेतुरेकस्यां तस्यां शरा इव लक्ष्यभुवि भूभुजां सर्वेषां दृष्टयः। दूतप्रेषणादिभिश्च तां ययाचिरे राजानः। कदाचित्तु राजान्तःपुरप्रासादस्थितो बाह्यकक्ष्यावस्थितेन पुरुषेण स्वप्रस्तावागतां गीयमानामार्यामशृणोत—

---

१ 'अहर्निश...भविष्यन्ति' इति नास्ति अ-पुस्तके. २ 'मौलिभ्यामुत्थाय राज्यवर्धनहर्षौ प्रणेमतुः। तौ च पितरम्' अ.

'उद्वेगमहावर्ते पातयति पयोधरोन्नमनकाले[1]।
सरिदिव तटमनुवर्षं विवर्धमाना सुता पितरम् ॥ ५ ॥'

तां च श्रुत्वा पार्श्वस्थितां महादेवीमुत्सारितपरिजनो जगाद—

'देवि, तरुणीभूता वत्सा राज्यश्रीः। एतदीया गुणवत्तेव[2] क्षणमपि हृदयान्नापयाति मे चिन्ता। यौवनारम्भ एव च कन्यकानामिन्धनीभवन्ति पितरः सन्तापानलस्य। हृदयमन्धकारयति मे दिवसमिव पयोधरोन्नतिरस्याः। केनापि कृता धर्म्या नाभिमता मे स्थितिरियं यदङ्गसम्भूतान्यङ्कलालितान्यपरित्याज्यान्यपत्यकान्यकाण्ड एवागत्यासंस्तुतैर्नीयन्ते। एतानि तानि खल्वङ्कनस्थानानि संसारस्य। सेयं सर्वाभिभाविनी शोकाग्नेर्दाहशक्तिर्यदपत्यत्वे समानेऽपि जातायां दुहितरि दूयन्ते सन्तः। एतदर्थं जन्मकाल एव कन्यकाभ्यः प्रयच्छन्ति सलिलमश्रुभिः साधवः। एतद्भयादकृतदारपरिग्रहाः परिहृतगृहवसतयः शून्यान्यरण्यान्यधिशेरते मुनयः। को हि नाम संहेत[3] सचेतनो विरहमपत्यानाम्। यथा यथा समापतन्ति दूता वराणां वराकी लज्जमानेव चिन्ता तथा तथा नितरां प्रविशति मे हृदयम्। किं क्रियते। तथापि गृहगतैरनुगन्तव्या एव लोकवृत्तयः। प्रायेण च सत्स्वप्यन्येषु वरगुणेष्वभिजनमेवानुरुध्यन्ते धीमन्तः। धरणीधराणां च मूर्ध्नि स्थितो माहेश्वरः पादन्यास इव सकलभुवननमस्कृतो मौखरिवंशः[4]। तत्रापि तिलकभूतस्यावन्तिवर्मणः सूनुरग्रजो ग्रहवर्मा नाम ग्रहपतिरिव गां गतः पितुरन्यूनो गुणैरेनां प्रार्थयते। यदि भवत्या अपि मतिरनुमन्यते ततस्तस्मै दातुमिच्छामि' इत्युक्तवति भर्तरि दुहितृस्नेहकातरतरहृदया साश्रुलोचना महादेवी प्रत्युवाच—'आर्यपुत्र, संवर्धनमात्रोपयोगिन्यो धात्रीनिर्विशेषा भवन्ति खलु मातरः कन्यकानाम्। प्रदाने तु प्रमाणमासां पितरः। केवलं कृपाकृतविशेषः सुदूरेण तनयस्नेहादतिरिच्यते दुहितृस्नेहः। यथा[5] नेयं यावज्जीवमावयोरार्तिता प्रतिपद्यते तथार्यपुत्र एव जानाति' इति।

राजा तु जातनिश्चयो दुहितृदानं प्रति समाहूय सुतावपि विदितार्थावकार्षीत्। शोभने च दिवसे ग्रहवर्मणा कन्यां प्रार्थयितुं प्रेषितस्य पूर्वागतस्यैव प्रधानदूतपुरुषस्य करे सर्वराजकुलसमक्षं दुहितृदानजलमपातयत्। जातमुदि कृतार्थे गते च तस्मिन्नासन्नेषु च विवाहदिवसेषूद्दामदीयमानताम्बूलपटवासकुसुमप्रसाधितसर्वलोकम्, सकलदेशादिश्यमानशिल्पिसार्थागमनम्, अवनिपालपुरुषगृहीतसमग्रग्रामीणानीयमानोपकरणसम्भारम्, राजदौवारिकोपनीयमानानेकनृपोपायनम्, उपनिमन्त्रितागतबन्धुवर्गसंवर्गणव्यग्रराजवल्लभम्, लब्धमधुमदप्रचण्डचर्मकारकरपुटोल्लालितकोणपटुविघट्टनरणन्मङ्गलपटहम्, पिष्टपञ्चाङ्गुलमण्ड्यमानोलूखलमुसलशिलाद्युपकरणम्, अशेषाशा-

१ '०कालः' ब. २ 'गुणवृत्तेव' ब. ३ 'सहते विरह०' अ. ४ 'मौखरी' ब. ५ 'यथा यावज्जीव०' अ.

मुखाविर्भूतचारणपरम्परापूर्यमाण[1]प्रकोष्ठं प्रतिष्ठाप्यमानेन्द्राणीदैवतम्, सितकुसुमविलेपनवसनसत्कृतैः सूत्रधारैरारादीयमानविवाहवेदीसूत्रपातम्, उत्कूर्चककरैश्च सुधाकर्परस्कन्धैरधिरोहिणीसमारूढैर्धवलैर्धवलीक्रियमाणप्रासादप्रतोलीप्राकारशिखरम्, क्षुण्णक्षाल्यमानकुसुम्भकसम्भाराम्भःप्लवपूररज्यमानजनपादपल्लवम्, निरूप्यमाणयौतकयोग्यमातङ्गतुरङ्गतरङ्गिताङ्गनम्, गणनाभियुक्तगणकगणगृह्यमाणलग्नगुणम्, गन्धोदकवाहिमकरमुखप्रणालीपूर्यमाणक्रीडावापीसमूहम्, हेमकारचक्रप्रक्रान्तहाटकघटनटाङ्कारवाचालितालिन्दकम्, उत्थापिताभिनवभित्तिपात्यमानबहलवालुकाकण्ठकालेपाकुलालेपकलोकम्, चतुरचित्रकरचक्रवाललिख्यमानमङ्गल्यालेख्यम्, लेप्यकारकदम्बकक्रियमाणमृण्मयमीनकूर्ममकरनारिकेलकदलीपूगवृक्षकम्, क्षितिपालैश्च स्वयमाबद्धकक्ष्यैः स्वाम्यर्पितकर्मशोभासम्पादनाकुलैः सिन्दूरकुट्टिमभूमीश्च मसृणयद्भिर्विनिहितसरसातर्पणहस्तान्विन्यस्तालक्तकपाटलांश्च चूताशोकपल्लवलाञ्छितशिखरानुद्वाहवितर्दिकास्तम्भानुत्तम्भयद्भिः प्रारब्धविविधव्यापारम्, आसूर्योदयाच्च प्रविष्टाभिः सतीभिः सुभगाभिः सुरूपाभिः सुवेशाभिरविधवाभिः सिन्दूररजोराजिराजितललाटाभिर्वधूवरगोत्रग्रहणगर्भाणि श्रुतिसुभगानि मङ्गलानि गायन्तीभिर्बहुविधवर्णकादिग्धाङ्गुलीभिर्ग्रीवासूत्राणि च चित्रयन्तीभिश्चित्रपत्रलतालेख्यकुशलाभिः कलशांश्च धवलिताञ्शीतलशाराजिरश्रेणीश्च मण्डयन्तीभिरभिन्नपुटकर्पासतूलपल्लवांश्च वैवाहिककङ्कणोर्णासूत्रसंनाहांश्च रञ्जयन्तीभिर्बलाशनाघृतघनीकृतकुङ्कुमकल्कमिश्रितांश्चाङ्गरागांल्लावण्यविशेषकृन्ति च मुखालेपनानि कल्पयन्तीभिः कक्कोलमिश्राः सजातीफलाः स्फुरत्स्फीतस्फाटिककर्पूरशकलखचितान्तराला लवङ्गमाला रचयन्तीभिः समन्तात्सामन्तसीमन्तिनीभिर्व्याप्तम्, बहुविधभक्तिनिर्माणनिपुणपुराणपौरपुरंध्रिबध्यमानैर्बद्धैश्चाचारचतुरान्तःपुरजरतीजनितपूजाराजमानरजकरज्यमानै[2] रक्तैश्चोभयपटान्तलग्नपरिजनप्रेङ्खोलितैश्छायासु शोष्यमाणैः शुष्कैश्च कुटिलक्रमरूपक्रियमाणपल्लवपरभागैरपरैरारब्धकुङ्कुमपङ्कस्थासकच्छुरणैरपरैरुद्भुजभुजिष्याभज्यमानभङ्गुरोत्तरीयैः क्षौमैश्च बादरैश्च दुकूलैश्च लालातन्तुजैश्चांशुकैश्च नेत्रैश्च निर्मोकनिभैरकठोररम्भागर्भकोमलैर्निःश्वासहार्यैः स्पर्शानुमेयैर्वासोभिः सर्वतः स्फुरद्भिरिन्द्रायुधसहस्रैरिव सञ्छादितम्, उज्ज्वलनिचोलकावगुण्ठ्यमानहंसकुलैश्च शयनीयैस्तारामुक्ताफलोपचीयमानैश्च कञ्चुकैरनेकोपयोगपाट्यमानैश्चापरिमितैः पट्टपटीसहस्रैरभिनवरागकोमलै[3]र्दुकूलराजमानैश्च पटवितानैः स्तवरकनिवहनिरन्तरच्छाद्यमानसमस्तपटलैश्च मण्डपैरुच्छ्रिताग्रनेत्रपटवेष्ट्यमानैश्च स्तम्भैरुज्ज्वलं रमणीयं चौत्सुक्यदं च मङ्गल्यं चासीद्राजकुलम्।

१ 'प्रकोष्ठप्रतिष्ठाप्य०' अ. २ 'रजकमहादारजतरज्यमानैः' ब. ३ '०कोमलैर्दुकूल०' ब.

देवी तु यशोमती विवाहोत्सवपर्याकुलहृदया हृदयेन भर्तरि कुतूहलेन जामातरि स्नेहेन दुहितरि उपचारेण निमन्त्रितस्त्रीषु आदेशेन परिजने शरीरेण सञ्चरणे चक्षुषा कृताकृतप्रत्यवेक्षणेषु आनन्देन महोत्सवे एकापि बहुधा विभक्तेवाभवत्। भूपतिरप्युपर्युपरि विसर्जितोष्ट्रवामीजनितजामातृजोषः सत्यप्याज्ञासम्पादनदक्षे मुखेक्षणपरे परिजने समं पुत्राभ्यां दुहितृस्नेहविक्लवः सर्वं स्वयमकरोत्।

एवं च तस्मिन्नविधवामय[1] इव भवति राजकुले, मङ्गलमय इव जायमाने जीवलोके, चारणमयेष्विव लक्ष्यमाणेषु दिङ्मुखेषु, पटहमय इव कृतेऽन्तरिक्षे, भूषणमय इव भ्रमति परिजने, बान्धवमय इव दृश्यमाने सर्गे, निर्वृत्तिमय इवोपलक्ष्यमाणे काले, लक्ष्मीमय इव विजृम्भमाणे महोत्सवे, निधान इव सुखस्य फल इव जन्मनः परिणाम इव पुण्यस्य यौवन इव विभूतेर्यौवराज्य इव प्रीतेः सिद्धिकाल इव मनोरथस्य वर्तमाने, गण्यमान इव जनाङ्गुलीभिः, आलोक्यमान इव मार्गध्वजैः, प्रत्युद्गम्यमान इव मङ्गल्यवाद्यप्रतिशब्दकैः, आहूयमान इव मौहूर्तिकैः, आकृष्यमाण इव मनोरथैः, परिष्वज्यमान इव वधूसखीहृदयैराजगाम विवाहदिवसः। प्रातरेव प्रतीहारैः समुत्सारितनिखिलानिबद्धलोकं विविक्तमक्रियत राजकुलम्।

अथ महाप्रतीहारः प्रविश्य नृपसमीपम् 'देव, जामातुरन्तिकात्ताम्बूलदायकः पारिजातकनामा संप्राप्तः' इत्यभिधाय स्वाकारं युवानमदर्शयत्। राजा तु तं दूरादेव जामातृबहुमानाद्दर्शितादरः 'बालक, कच्चित्कुशली ग्रहवर्मा' इति पप्रच्छ। असौ तु समाकर्णितनराधिपध्वनिर्धावमानः कतिचित्पदान्युपसृत्य प्रसार्य च बाहू सेवाचतुरश्रिरं वसुन्धरायां निधाय मूर्धानमुत्थाय 'देव, कुशली यथाज्ञापयस्यर्चयति च देवं नमस्कारेण' इति व्यज्ञापयत्। आगतजामातृनिवेदनागतं च तं ज्ञात्वा कृतसत्कारं राजा 'यामिन्याः प्रथमे यामे विवाहकालात्ययकृतो यथा न भवति दोषः[2]' इति सन्दिश्य प्रतीपं प्राहिणोत्।

अथ सकलकमलवनलक्ष्मीं वधूमुख इव सञ्चार्य समवसिते वासरे, विवाहदिवसश्रियः पादपल्लव इव रज्यमाने सवितरि, वधूवरानुरागलघूकृतप्रेमलज्जितेष्विव विघटमानेषु चक्रवाकमिथुनेषु, सौभाग्यध्वज इव रक्तांशुकसुकुमारवपुषि नभसि स्फुरति संध्यारागे, कपोतकण्ठकर्बुरे वरयात्रागमनरजसीव कलुषयति दिङ्मुखानि तिमिरे, लग्नसम्पादनसज्ज इवोज्जिहाने ज्योतिर्गणे, विवाहमङ्गलकलश इवोदयशिखरिणा समुत्क्षिप्यमाणे वर्धमानधवलच्छाये ताराधिपमण्डले वधूवदनलावण्यज्योत्स्नापरिपीततमसि प्रदोषे वृथोदितमुपहसत्स्विव रजनिकरमुत्तानितमुखेषु कुमुदवनेष्वाजगाम मुहुर्मुहु-

१ 'अविधवाधत्ते' ब. २ 'दोषस्तथा विधीयतामिति' ब.

रुल्लासितस्फारस्फुरितारुणचामरैर्मनोरथैरिवोत्थितरागाग्रपल्लवैः पुरो धावमानैः पादातैरुत्कर्णकटकहयप्रतिहेषितदीयमानस्वागतैरिव वाजिनां वृन्दैश्चापूरितदिग्भागश्चलकर्णचामराणां चामीकरमयसर्वोपकरणानां वर्ण्कलम्बिनां बलिनां घण्टाटाङ्कारिणां करिणां घटाभिः घटयन्निव पुनरिन्दूदयविलीनमन्धकारं नक्षत्रमालामण्डितमुखीं करिणीं निशाकर इव पौरन्दरीं दिशमारूढः प्रकटितविविधविहगविरुतैस्तालावचरचारणैः पुरःसरैर्बालो वसन्त इवोपवनैः क्रियमाणकोलाहलो गन्धतैलावसेकसुगन्धिना दीपिकाचक्रवालस्यालोकेन कुङ्कुमपटवासधूलिपटलेनेव पिञ्जरीकुर्वन्सकलं लोकमुत्फुल्लमल्लिकामुण्डमालामध्याध्यासितकुसुमशेखरेण शिरसा हसन्निव सपरिवेशक्षपाकरं कौमुदीप्रदोषमात्मरूपनिर्जितमकरकेतुकरापहृतेन कार्मुकेणेव कौसुमेन दाम्ना विरचितवैकक्ष्यकविलासः कुसुमसौरभगर्वभ्रान्तभ्रमरकुलकलप्रलापसुभगः पारिजात इव जातः श्रिया सह पुनरवतारितो मेदिनीं नववधूवदनावलोकनकुतूहलेनेव कृष्यमाणहृदयः पतन्निव मुखेन प्रत्यासन्नलग्नो ग्रहवर्मा ।

राजा तु तमुपद्वारमागतं चरणाभ्यामेव राजचक्रानुगम्यमानः ससुतः प्रत्युज्जगाम । अवतीर्णं च तं कृतनमस्कारं मन्मथमिव माधवः प्रसारितभुजो गाढमालिलिङ्ग । यथाक्रमं परिष्वक्तराज्यवर्धनहर्षं च हस्ते गृहीत्वाभ्यन्तरं निन्ये । स्वनिर्विशेषासनदानादिना चैनमुपचारेणोपचचार ।

नचिराच्च गम्भीरनामा नृपतेः प्रणयी विद्वान्द्विजन्मा ग्रहवर्माणमुवाच—'तात, त्वां प्राप्य चिरात्खलु राज्यश्रिया घटितौ तेजोमयौ सकलजगद्गीयमानबुधकर्णानन्दकारिगुणगणौ सोमसूर्यवंशाविव पुष्पभूतिमुखरवंशौ । प्रथममेव कौस्तुभमणिरिव गुणैः स्थितोऽसि हृदये देवस्य । इदानीं तु शशीव शिरसा परमेश्वरेणासि वोढव्यो जातः' इति । एवं वदत्येव तस्मिन्नृपमुपसृत्य मौहूर्तिकाः 'देव, समासीदति लग्नवेला व्रजतु जामाता कौतुकगृहम्' इत्यूचुः । अथ नरेन्द्रेण 'उत्तिष्ठ गच्छ' इति गदितो ग्रहवर्मा प्रविश्यान्तःपुरं जामातृदर्शनकुतूहलिनीनां स्त्रीणां पतितानि लोचनसहस्राणि विकचनीलकुवलयवनानीव लङ्घयन्नाससाद कौतुकगृहद्वारम् । निवारितपरिजनश्च प्रविवेश ।

अथ तत्र कतिपयाप्तप्रियसखीस्वजनप्रमदाप्रायपरिवाराम्, अरुणांशुकावगुण्ठितमुखीं प्रभातसंध्यामिव स्वप्रभया निष्प्रभान्प्रदीपकान्कुर्वाणाम्, अतिसौकुमार्यशङ्कितेनेव यौवनेन नातिनिर्भरमुपगूढाम्, साध्वसनिरुध्यमानहृदयदेशदुःखमुक्तैर्निभृतायतैः श्वसितैरपयान्तं कुमारभावमिवानुशोचन्तीम्, अत्युत्कम्पिनीं पतनभियेव त्रपया निष्पन्दं धार्यमाणाम्, हस्तं तामरसप्रतिपक्षमासन्नग्रहणं शशिनमिव रोहिणीं भयवेपमानमानसामवलोकयन्तीम्,

चन्दनधवलतनुलतां ज्योत्स्नादानसञ्चितलावण्यात्कुमुदिनीगर्भादिव प्रसूताम्, कुसुमामोदनिर्हारिणीं वसन्तहृदयादिव निर्गताम्, निःश्वासपरिमलाकृष्टमधुकरकुलां मलयमारुतादिवोत्पन्नाम्, कृतकन्दर्पानुसरणां रतिमिव पुनर्जाताम्, प्रभालावण्यमदसौरभमाधुर्यैः कौस्तुभशशिमदिरापारिजातामृतप्रभवैः सर्वरत्नगुणैरपरामिव सुरासुररुषा रत्नाकरेण कल्पितां श्रियम्, स्निग्धेन बालिकालोकेन सितसिन्धुवारकुसुममञ्जरीमिरिव मुक्तादीधितिभिः कल्पितकर्णावतंसाम्, कर्णाभरणमरकतप्रभाहरितशाद्वलेन कपोलस्थलीतलेन विनोदयन्तीमिव हारिणीं लोचनच्छायाम्, अधोमुखीं वरकौतुकालोकनाकुलं मुहुर्मुहुः कृतमुखोन्नमनप्रयत्नं सखीजनं हृदयं च निर्भर्त्सयन्तीं वधूमपश्यत्।

प्रविशन्तमेव तं हृदयचौरं वध्वा समर्पितं जग्राह कन्दर्पः। परिहासस्मेरमुखीभिश्च नारीभिः कौतुकगृहे यद्यत्कार्यते जामाता तत्तत्सर्वमतिपेशलं चकार। कृतपरिणयानुरूपवेशपरिग्रहां गृहीत्वा करे वधूं निर्जगाम। जगाम च नवसुधाधवलां निमन्त्रितागतैस्तुषारशैलोपत्यकामिव त्र्यम्बकाम्बिकाविवाहाहूतैर्भूभृद्भिः परिवृताम्, सेकसुकुमारयवाङ्कुरदन्तुरैः पञ्चास्यैः कलशैः कोमलवर्णिकाविचित्रैरमित्रमुखैश्च मङ्गल्यफलहस्ताभिरञ्जलिकारिकाभिरुद्धासितपर्यन्ताम्, उपाध्यायोपश्रीयमानेन्धनधूमायमानाग्निसन्धुक्षणाक्षणिकोपद्रष्टृद्विजाम्, उपकुशानुनिहितानुपहतहरितकुशाम्, संनिहितदृषदजिनाज्यस्रुक्समित्पूलीनिवहाम्, नूतनशूर्पार्पितश्यामलशमीपलाशमिश्रलाजहासिनीं वेदीम्। आरुरोह च तां दिवमिव सज्योत्स्नः शशी। समुत्ससर्प च वेल्लितारुणशिखापल्लवस्य शिखिनः कुसुमायुध इव रतिद्वितीयो रक्ताशोकस्य समीपम्। हुते च हुतभुजि दक्षिणावर्तप्रवृत्ताभिर्वधूवदनविलोकनकुतूहलिनीभिरिव ज्वालाभिरेव सह प्रदक्षिणं बभ्राम। पात्यमाने च लाजाञ्जलौ नखमयूखधवलिततनुरदृष्टपूर्ववधूवररूपविस्मयस्मेर इवादृश्यत विभावसुः।

अत्रान्तरे स्वच्छकपोलोदरसंक्रान्तमनलप्रतिबिम्बमिव निर्वापयन्ती स्थूलमुक्ताफलविमलबाष्पबिन्दुसन्दोहदर्शितदुर्दिना निर्वेदनविकारं रुरोद वधूः। उदश्रुविलोचनानां च बान्धववधूनामुदपादि महानाक्रन्दः। परिसमापितवैवाहिकक्रियाकलापस्तु जामाता वध्वा समं प्रणनाम श्वशुरौ। प्रविवेश च द्वारपक्षलिखितरतिप्रीतिदैवतं प्रणयिभिरिव प्रथमप्रविष्टैरलिकुलैः कृतकोलाहलम्, अलिकुलपक्षपवनप्रेङ्खोलितैः कर्णोत्पलप्रहारभयप्रकम्पितैरिव मङ्गलप्रदीपैः प्रकाशितम्, एकदेशलिखितस्तबकितरक्ताशोकतरुतलभाजाधिज्यचापेन तिर्यक्कूणितनेत्रत्रिभागेण शरमृजूकुर्वता कामदेवेनाधिष्ठितम्, एकपार्श्वन्यस्तेन काञ्चनाचामरुकेणेतरपार्श्ववर्तिन्या च दान्तशफरुकधारिण्या कनकपुत्रिकया साक्षाल्लक्ष्म्येवोद्दण्डपुण्डरीकहस्तया सनाथेन सोपधानेन स्वास्तीर्णेन

१ 'प्रदक्षिणा०' ब. २ 'काञ्चनावामनकेन' ब.

शयनेन शोभमानम्, शयनशिरोभागस्थितेन च कृतकुमुदशोभेन कुसुमायुधसाहायकायागतेन शशिनेव निद्राकलशेन राजतेन विराजमानं वासगृहम्।

तत्र च ह्रीताया नववधूकायाः पराङ्मुखप्रसुप्ताया मणिभित्तिदर्पणेषु मुखप्रतिबिम्बानि प्रथमालापाकर्णनकौतुकागतगृहदेवताननानीव मणिगवाक्षकेषु वीक्षमाणः क्षणदां निन्ये। स्थित्वा च श्वशुरकुले शीलेनामृतमिव श्वश्रूहृदये वर्षन्नभिनवाभिनवोपचारैरपुनरुक्तान्यानन्दमयानि दश दिनानि स्थित्वा दत्त्वा राजदौवारिकमिव राजकुले रणरणकं यौतकनिवेदितानीव शम्बलान्यादाय हृदयानि सर्वलोकस्य कथं कथमपि विसर्जितो नृपेण वध्वा सह स्वदेशमगमदिति।

इति श्रीबाणभट्टकृतौ हर्षचरिते चक्रवर्तिजन्मवर्णनं नाम
चतुर्थ उच्छ्वासः।

पञ्चम उच्छ्वासः ।

नियतिर्विधाय पुंसां प्रथमं सुखमुपरि दारुणं दुःखम् ।
कृत्वालोकं तरला तडिदिव वज्रं निपातयति ॥ १ ॥

पातयति महापुरुषान्सममेव बहूननादरेणैव ।
परिवर्तमान एकः कालः शैलानिवानन्तः ॥ २ ॥

अथ कदाचिद्राजा राज्यवर्धनं कवचहरमाहूय हूणान्[1]हन्तुं हरिणानिव हरिर्हरिणेशकिशोरकमपरिमितबलानुयातं चिरन्तनैरमात्यैरनुरक्तैश्च महासामन्तैः कृत्वा साभिसरमुत्तरापथं प्राहिणोत्।

प्रयान्तं च तं देवो हर्षः कतिचित्प्रयाणकानि तुरङ्गमैरनुवव्राज। प्रविष्टे च कैलासप्रभाभासिनीं ककुभं भ्रातरि वर्तमानो[2] नवे वयसि विक्रमरसानुरोधिनि केसरिशरभशार्दूलवराहबहुलेषु तुषारशैलोपकण्ठेषूत्कण्ठमानवनदेवताकटाक्षांशुशारितशरीरकान्तिः क्रीडन्मृगयां मृगलोचनः कतिपयान्यहानि बहिरेव व्यलम्बत। चकार चाकर्णान्ताकृष्टकार्मुकनिर्गतभासुरभल्लवर्षी स्वल्पीयोभिरेव दिवसैर्निःश्वापदान्यरण्यानि[3]। एकदा तु वासतेय्यास्तुरीये यामे प्रत्युपस्येव स्वप्ने चटुलज्वालापुञ्जपिञ्जरीकृतसकलककुभा दुर्निवारेण दवहुतभुजा दह्यमानं केसरिणमद्राक्षीत्। तस्मिन्नेव च दावदहने समुत्सृज्य शावकानुत्प्लुत्य चात्मानं पातयन्तीं सिंहीमपश्यत्। आसीच्चास्य चेतसि—'लोके हि लोहेभ्यः कठिनतराः खलु स्नेहमया बन्धनपाशाः, यदाकृष्टास्तिर्यञ्चोऽप्येवमाचरन्ति' इति। प्रबुद्धस्य चास्य मुहुर्मुहुर्दक्षिणेतरमक्षि पस्पन्दे। गात्रेषु चाकस्मादेव वेपथुर्विपप्रथे। निर्निमित्तमेवान्तर्बन्धनस्थानाच्चचालेव हृदयम्। अकारणादेव चाजायत गरीयसी दुःखासिका। किमिदमिति च समुत्पन्नविविधविकल्पविमथितमतिरपगतधृतिश्चिन्तावनमितवदनः स्तिमिततारकेण चक्षुषा समुद्विग्यमानस्थलकमलिनीवनामिव चकार चकोरेक्षणः क्षणं क्षौणीम्। अह्नि च तस्मिञ्शून्येनैव च चेतसा चिक्रीड मृगयाम्। आरोहति च हरितहये मध्यमह्नो भवनमागत्योभयतो मन्दमन्दं संवाह्यमानतनुतालवृन्तः क्षितितलविततामतिशिशिरमलयजरसलवलुलितवपुषमिन्दुधवलोपधानधारिणीं वेत्रपट्टिकामधिशयानः साशङ्क एव तस्थौ।

अथ दूरादेव लेखगर्भया नीलीरागमेचकरुचा चैलचीरिकया[4] रचितमुण्डमालकम्, श्रमातपाभ्यामारोप्यमाणकायकालिमानमन्तर्गतेन शोकशिखिनाङ्गारतामिव नीयमानम्, अतित्वरागमनद्रुततरपदोद्धूयमानधूलिराजिव्याजेन राजवार्ताश्रवणकुतूहलिन्या मेदिन्येवानुगम्यमानम्, अभिमुखपवन-

१ 'हूनान्' ब. २ 'निवर्तमानो' ब. ३ 'निःश्वासप्रदानि' ब. ४ 'चीरचीरिकया' अ.

प्रेङ्खत्प्रविततोत्तरीयपटप्रान्तवीज्यमानोभयपार्श्वमतित्वरया कृतपक्षमिवाशु परापतन्तम्, प्रेर्यमाणमिव पृष्ठतः स्वाम्यादेशेन, कृष्यमाणमिव पुरस्तादायतैः श्रमश्वासमोक्षैः, स्विद्यल्ललाटतटघटमानप्रतिबिम्बकेन कार्यकौतुकाद्दपह्रियमाणलेखमिव भास्वता, संभ्रमभ्रष्टैरिवेन्द्रियैः शून्यीकृतशरीरम्, लेखार्पितप्रयोजनगौरवादिव समेऽपि वर्त्मनि शून्यहृदयतया स्खलन्तम्, कालमेघशकलमिव पतिष्यतो दुर्वार्तावज्रस्य, धूमपल्लवमिव ज्वलिष्यतः शोकज्वलनस्य, बीजमिव फलिष्यतो दुष्कृतशालेरनिमित्तभूतदीर्घाध्वगं कुरङ्गकनामानमायान्तमद्राक्षीत्।

दृष्ट्वा च पूर्वनिमित्तपरम्पराविर्भावितभीतिरभिद्यत हृदयेन। कुरङ्गकस्तु कृतप्रणामः समुपसृत्य प्रथममाननलग्नं विषादमुपनिन्ये, पश्चाल्लेखम्। तं च देवो हर्षः स्वयमेवादायावाचयत्। लेखार्थेनैव च समं गृहीत्वा हृदयेन सन्तापमवग्रहरूपोऽभ्यधात्—'कुरङ्गक, किं मान्द्यं तातस्य' इति। स चक्षुषा बाष्पजलबिन्दुभिर्मुखेन च खञ्जाक्षरैः क्षरद्भिर्युगपदाचचक्षे—'देव दाहज्वरो महान्' इति। तच्चाकर्ण्य सहसा सहस्रधेवास्य हृदयं पफाल। कृताचमनश्च जनयितुरायुष्कामोऽपरिमितमणिकनकरजतजातमात्मपरिबर्हमशेषं ब्राह्मणसादकरोत्। अभुक्त एवोच्चचाल। 'दापय वाजिनः पर्याणम्' इति च पुरःस्थितं शिरःकृपाणं बिभ्राणं बभाण युवानम्। वेपमानहृदयश्च संभ्रमप्रधावितपरिवर्धकोपनीतमारुह्य तुरङ्गमेकाक्येव प्रावर्तत।

अकाण्डप्रयाणसंज्ञाशङ्खक्षुभितं तु संभ्रमात्सज्जीभूतमुद्धूतमुखरखुररवभरितसकलभुवनविवरमागत्यागत्य सर्वाभ्यो दिग्भ्यो धावमानमश्वीयमढौकत। प्रस्थितस्य चास्य प्रदक्षिणेतरं प्रयान्तो विनाशमुपस्थितं राजसिंहस्य हरिणाः प्रकटयांबभूवुः। अशिशिररश्मिमण्डलाभिमुखश्च हृदयमवदारयन्निव दावशुष्के दारुणि दारुणं रराण वायसः। कज्जलमय इव बहुदिवससमुपचितबहलमलपटलमलिनिततनुरभिमुखमाजगाम शिखिपिच्छालाञ्छनो नग्नाटकः। दुर्निमित्तैरनभिनन्द्यमानगमनश्च नितरामशङ्कत हृदयेन पितृस्नेहाहितम्रदिम्ना च तत्तदुपेक्षमाणस्तुरङ्गमस्कन्धबद्धलक्ष्यं चक्षुरविचलं दधानो दुःसमवसितहसितसङ्कथस्तूर्णींभूतेन भूपाललोकेनानुगम्यमानो बहुयोजनसम्पिण्डितमध्वानमेकेनैवाह्ना समलङ्घयत्।

उपलब्धनरेन्द्रमान्द्यवार्ताविषण्ण इव नष्टतेजस्यधोमुखीभवति भगवति भानुमति भण्डिप्रमुखेन प्रणयिना राजपुत्रलोकेन बहुशो विज्ञाप्यमानोऽपि नाहारमकरोत्। पुरःप्रवृत्तप्रतीहारगृह्यमाणग्रामीणपरम्पराप्रकटितप्रगुणवर्त्मा च वहन्नेव निन्ये निशाम्।

अन्यस्मिन्नहनि मध्यन्दिने विगतजयशब्दम्, अस्तमिततूर्यनादम्, उपसंहृतगीतम्, उत्सारितोत्सवम्, अप्रगीतचारणम्, अप्रसारितापणपण्यम्,

१ 'उत्तरीयकर्पट' ब.

स्थानस्थानेषु पवनबलकुटिलाभिः कोटिहोमधूमलेखाभिरुल्लसन्तीभिर्यममहिषविषाणकोटिभिरिवोल्लिख्यमानम्, कृतान्तपाशवागुराभिरिवावेष्ट्यमानम्, उपरि कालमहिषालङ्कारकालायसकिङ्किणीभिरिव कटु क्वणन्तीभिर्दिवसं वायसमण्डलीभिर्भ्रमन्तीभिरावेद्यमानप्रत्यासन्नाशुभम्, क्वचित्प्रतिशायितस्निग्धबान्धवाराध्यमानाहिर्बुध्न्यम्, क्वचिद्दीपिकां[1]दह्यमानकुलपुत्रकप्रसाद्यमानमातृमण्डलम्, क्वचिन्मुण्डोपहाराहरणोद्यतद्रविडप्रार्थ्यमानामर्दकम्, क्वचिदान्ध्रोद्क्रियमाणबाहुवप्रोपयाच्यमानचण्डिकम्, अन्यत्र शिरोविधृतविलीयमानगु[2]ग्गुलुविकलनवसेवकानुनीयमानमहाकालम्, अपरत्र निशितशस्त्रीनिकृत्तात्ममांसहोमप्रसक्तासवर्गम्, अपरत्र प्रकाशनरपतिकुमारकक्रियमाणमहामांसविक्रयप्रक्रमम्, उपहतमिव श्मशानपांशुभिरमङ्गलैरिव परिगृहीतम्, यातुधानैरिव विध्वस्तम्, कलिकालेनेव कवलितम्, पापपटलैरिव सञ्छादितम्, अधर्मविक्षेपैरिव लुण्ठितम्, अनित्यताधिक्का[3]रैरिवाक्रान्तम्, नियतिविलासैरिवात्मीकृतम्, शून्यमिव सुप्तमिव मुषितमिव विलक्षितमिव छलितमिव मूर्छितमिव स्कन्धावारं समाससाद।

प्रविशन्नेव च विपणिवर्त्मनि कुतूहलाकुलबहलबालकपरिवृतमूर्ध्वयष्टिविष्कम्भवितते वामहस्तवर्तिनि भीषणमहिषाधिरूढप्रेतनाथसनाथे चित्रवति पटे परलोकव्यतिकरमितरकरकलितेन शरकाण्डेन कथयन्तं यमपट्टिकं ददर्श। तेनैव च गीयमानं श्लोकमशृणोत्—

'मातापितृसहस्राणि पुत्रदारशतानि च।
युगे युगे व्यतीतानि कस्य ते कस्य वा भवान्॥ ३॥' इति

तेन चाधिकतरमवदीर्यमाणहृदयः क्रमेण राजद्वारं प्रतिषिद्धसकललोकप्रवेशं ययौ। तुरगादवतीर्णश्चाभ्यन्तरान्निष्क्रामन्तमप्रसन्नमुखरागमुन्मुक्तमिवेन्द्रियैः सुषेणनामानं वैद्यकुमारकमद्राक्षीत्। कृतनमस्कारं चाप्राक्षीत्—'सुषेण, अस्ति तातस्य विशेषो न वा' इति। सोऽब्रवीत्—'नास्तीदानीं यदि भवेत्कुमारं दृष्ट्वा' इति। मन्दं मन्दं द्वारपालैः प्रणम्यमानश्च दीयमानसर्वस्वम्, पूज्यमानकुलदेवतम्, प्रारब्धामृतचरुपचनक्रियम्, क्रियमाणषडाहुतिहोमम्, हूयमानपृषदाज्यलवलिप्तप्रचलदूर्वापल्लवम्, पठ्यमानमहामायूरीप्रवर्त्यमानगृहशान्तिनिर्वर्त्यमानभूतरक्षाबलिविधानम्, प्रयतविप्रप्रस्तुतसंहिताजपम्, जप्यमानरुद्रैकादशीशब्दायमानशिवगृहम्, अतिशुचिशैवसम्पाद्यमानविरूपाक्षक्षीरकलशसहस्रस्नपनम्, अजिरोपविष्टैश्चानासादितस्वामिदर्शनदूयमानमानसैरभ्यन्तरनिष्पतितनिकटवर्तिपरिजननिवेद्यमानवा[4]र्तैर्वार्तीभूतस्नानभोजनशयनैरुज्झितात्मसंस्कारमलिनवेशैर्लिखितैरिव निश्चलैर्नरपतिभिर्नीयमाननक्तन्दिवं दुःखदीनवदनेन च प्रघनेषु बद्धमण्डलेनोपांशुव्याहृतैः

१ 'दीपिकादहनदह्यमान०' ब. २ 'विलीयमानबहलगलद्गुग्गुलु०' ब. ३ 'अनित्यताधिकारैः' ब. ४ '०वान्तैः' ब.

केनचिच्चिकित्सकदोषानुद्भावयता, केनचिदसाध्यव्याधिलक्षणपदानि पठता, केनचिद्दुःस्वप्नानावेदयता, केनचित्पिशाचवार्तां विवृण्वता, केनचित्कार्तान्तिकादेशान्प्रकाशयता, केनचिदुपलिङ्गानि गायता, अन्येनानित्यतां भावयता संसारं चापवदता कलिकालविलसितानि च निन्दता दैवं चोपालभमानेनापरेण धर्माय कुप्यता राजकुलदेवताश्चाधिक्षिपता, अपरेण क्लिष्टकुलपुत्रकभाग्यानि गर्हयता, बाह्यपरिजनेन कथ्यमानकष्टपार्थिवावस्थं राजकुलं विवेश।

अविरलबाष्पपयःपरिप्लुतलोचनेन पितृपरिजनेन वीक्ष्यमाणो त्रिविधौषधिद्रव्यद्रवगन्धगर्भमुत्क्वथतां क्वाथानां सर्पिषां तैलानां च पच्यमानानां गन्धमाजिघ्रन्नवाप तृतीयं कक्ष्यान्तरम्।

तत्र चातिनिःशब्दे गृहावग्रहणीग्राहिबहुवेत्रिणि, त्रिगुणतिरस्करिणीतिरोहितसुवीथीपथे, पिहितपक्षद्वारके, परिहृतकपाटरटिते, घटितगवाक्षरक्षितमरुति, दूयमानपरिचारके, चरणताडनस्वनत्सोपानप्रकुपितप्रतीहारे, निभृतसंज्ञानिर्दिश्यमानसकलकर्मणि, नातिनिकटोपविष्टकङ्कटिनि, कोणस्थिताह्वानचकिताचमनवाहिनि, चन्द्रशालिकालीनमूकमौललोके, महाधिविधुरबान्धवाङ्गनावर्गगृहीतप्रच्छन्नग्रग्रीवके, सञ्जवनपुञ्जितोद्विग्नपरिजने, प्रविष्टकतिपयप्रणयिनि, गम्भीरज्वरारम्भभीतभिषजि, दुर्मनायमानमन्त्रिणि, मन्दायमानपुरोधसि, सीदत्सुहृदि, विद्राणविपश्चिति, सन्तप्तासामन्ते, विचित्तचामरग्राहिणि, दुःखक्षामशिरोरक्षिणि, क्षीयमाणप्रसादवित्तमनोरथसम्पदि, स्वामिभक्तिपरित्यक्ताहारहीयमानबलविकलवल्लभभूभृति, क्षितितलपतितसकलरजनीजागरूकराजपुत्रकुमारके, कुलक्रमागतकुलपुत्रकनिवहोह्यमानशुचिशोकसङ्कुचितकञ्चुकिनि, निराजन्दवन्दिनि, निःश्वसन्निराशासन्नसेवके, निःसृतताम्बूलधूसराधरवारयोषिति, विलक्षवैद्योपदिश्यमानपथ्याहरणावहितपौरोगवे, अनुजीविपीयमानोच्चपकधारावारिविनोद्यमानास्यशोषरुजि, राजाभिलापभोज्यमानबहुभुजि, भेषजसामग्रीसम्पादनव्यग्रसमग्रव्यवहारिणि, मुहुर्मुहुराहूयमानतोयकर्मान्तिकानुमितघोरातुरतृषि, तुषारपरिकरितकरकशिशिरीक्रियमाणोदश्विति, श्वेतार्द्रकर्पटार्पितकर्पूरपरागशीतलीकृतशलाके, नाश्यानपङ्कलिप्यमाननवभाण्डगतगण्डूषग्रहणमस्तुनि, निम्यत्कोमलकमलिनीपलाशप्रावृतमृदुमृणालके, सनालनीलोत्पलपूलीसनाथसलिलपानभाजनभुवि, धारानिपातनिर्वाप्यमाणक्वथिताम्भसि, पटुपाटलशर्करामोदमुचि, मञ्चकाश्रितसिकतिलकर्करीविश्रान्तान्तरचक्षुषि, सरसशैवलवलयितगलद्गोलयन्त्रके, गल्वर्कशालाजिरोल्लासितलाजसक्तुनिपीतमसारपारीपरिगृहीतकर्कशर्करे, शिशिरौषधरसचूर्णावकीर्णस्फटिकशुक्तिशङ्खसञ्चये, सञ्चितप्रचुरप्राचीनामलकमातुलुङ्गद्राक्षादाडिमादिफले, प्रतिग्राहितविप्रविप्रकीर्यमाणशान्त्युदकविप्रुषि, प्रेष्यापेक्ष्यमाणल-

१ 'पीयमानोच्चचपक' ब. २ '°श्विनि' ब. ३ 'सरल' अ.

ललाटलेपोपदिग्धदृपदि धवलगृहे स्थितम्, परलोकविजयाय नीराज्यमानमिव ज्वरज्वलनेनानवरतपरिवर्तनैस्तरङ्गिणि शयनीये शेषमिव विषोष्मणा क्षीरोदन्वति विचेष्टमानम्, मुक्ताफलवालुकाधूलिधवलितं जलधिमिव क्षयकाले शुष्यन्तम्, कालेन कैलासमिव दशाननेनोद्ध्रियमाणम्, अविरतचन्दनचर्चापराणां परिचारकाणामत्युष्णावयवस्पर्शभस्मीभूतोदरैरिव धवलैः करैः स्पृश्यमानं लोकान्तरप्रस्थितम्, स्थाणुना स्वयशसैव चन्दनानुलेपनच्छलेनापृच्छ्यमानम्, अविच्छिन्नदीयमानकमलकुमुदेन्दीवरदलं कालकटाक्षपतनशबलमिव शरीरमुद्वहन्तम्, निबिडदुकूलपट्टनिपीडितकेशान्तकथ्यमानकष्टवेदनानुबन्धं मूर्धानं धारयन्तम्, दुर्धरवेदनोन्नमन्नीलशिराजालककरालेन च कालाङ्गुलिलिख्यमानलेखाख्यातमरणावधिदिवससंख्यानेनेव ललाटफलकेन भयमुपजनयन्तम्, आसन्नयमदर्शनोद्वेगादिव च किंचिदन्तःप्रविष्टतारकं चक्षुर्दधानम्, शुष्यद्दशनपङ्क्तिप्रसूतधूसरदीधितितरङ्गिणीं मृगतृष्णिकामिवोष्णां निश्वासपरम्परामुद्वहन्तम्, अत्युष्णनिश्वासदग्धयेव श्यामायमानया रसनया निवेद्यमानदारुणसन्निपातारम्भम्, उरःस्थलस्थापितमणिमौक्तिकहारचन्दनचन्द्रकान्तं कृतान्तदूतदर्शनयोग्यमिवात्मानं कुर्वाणम्, अङ्गभङ्गवलनोत्क्षिप्तभुजयुगलम्, पर्यस्तहस्तनखमयूखैर्धारागृहमिव तापशान्तये रचयन्तम्, नेदिष्ठसलिलमणिकुट्टिमादर्शोदरेषु निपतद्भिः प्रतिबिम्बैरपि सन्तापातिशयमिव कथयन्तम्, स्पृशन्तीं प्रणयिनीमिव विश्रामभूमिं मूर्छामपि बहु मन्यमानम्, अन्तकाह्वानाक्षरैरिव सभयभिषग्दृष्टैररिष्टैराविष्टम्, महाप्रस्थानकाले स्वसन्तापसन्तानमाप्तहृदयेषु सञ्चारयन्तम्, अरतिपरिगृहीतमीर्ष्ययेव छायया मुच्यमानम्, उद्योगमिवोपद्रवाणाम्, सर्वास्त्रमोक्षमिव क्षामतायाः, हस्तीकृतं विहस्ततया, विषयीकृतं वैषम्येण, क्षेत्रीकृतं क्षयेण, गोचरीकृतं ग्लान्या, दष्टं दुःखासिकया, आत्मीकृतमस्वास्थ्येन, विधेयीकृतं व्याधिना, क्रोडीकृतं कालेन, लक्ष्यीकृतं दक्षिणाशया, पीतमिव पीडाभिः, जग्धमिव जागरेण, निगीर्णमिव वैवर्ण्येन, ग्रासीकृतं गात्रभङ्गेन, ह्रियमाणमिव विपद्भिः, वण्ठ्यमानमिव वेदनाभिः, लुण्ठ्यमानमिव दुःखैः, आदिष्टं दैवेन, निरूपितं नियत्या, घ्रातमनित्यत्वेन, अभिभूयमानमभावेन, परिकलितं परासुतया, दत्तावकाशं क्लेशस्य, निवासं वैमनस्यस्य, समीपे कालस्य, अन्तिकेऽन्त्योच्छ्वासस्य, मुखे महाप्रवासस्य[2], द्वारि दीर्घनिद्रायाः, जिह्वाग्रे जीवितेशस्य वर्तमानम्, विरलं वाचि, चलितं चेतसि, विह्वलं वपुषि, क्षीणमायुषि, प्रचुरं प्रलापे, सन्ततं श्वसिते[1], जितं जृम्भिकाभिः, पराधीनमाधिभिः, अनुबद्धमनुबन्धिकाभिः, पार्श्वोपविष्टयानवरतरोदनोच्छूननयनया गृहीतचामरिकयापि निश्वसितैरेव वीजयन्त्या विविधौषधिधूलिधूसरितशरीरया मुहुर्मुहुः 'आर्यपुत्र स्वपिषि' इति व्याहरन्त्या देव्या यशोमत्या शिरसि वक्षसि च स्पृश्यमानं पितरमद्राक्षीत्।

---

१ 'विश्वास०' अ. २ '०प्रयासस्य' अ.

दृष्ट्वा च प्रथमदुःखसम्पातमथ्यमानमतिराशङ्कित इव भागधेयेभ्यः समभवत्। अन्तकपुरवर्तिनमेव च पितरममन्यत। निराकृत इव चान्तःकरणेन क्षणमासीत्। अवधूतश्च धैर्येण, क्षेत्रीकृतः क्षोभेण, रिक्तीकृतो रत्या, विषयीकृतो विषादेन, पावकमयमिव हृदयमुद्वहन्, विषमविषदूषितानीव मुह्यन्तीन्द्रियाणि बिभ्राणः, तमसा रसातलमपि विशेषयन्, शून्यत्वेनाकाशमप्यतिशयानो नाविन्दत कर्तव्यम्। पस्पर्श च हृदयेन भियमुत्तमाङ्गेन च गाम्।

अवनिपतिस्तु दूरादेव दृष्ट्वातिदयितं तनयं तदवस्थोऽपि निर्भरस्नेहावर्जितः प्रधावमानो मनसा प्रसार्य भुजौ 'एह्येहि' इत्याह्वयञ्शरीरार्धेन शयनादुदगात्। ससंभ्रममुपसृतं चैनं विनयावनम्रमुन्नमय्य बलादुरसि निवेश्य विशन्निव प्रेम्णा निशाकरमण्डलमध्यम्, मज्जन्निवामृतमये महासरसि, स्नापयन्निव[1] महति हरिचन्दनरसप्रस्रवणे, अभिषिच्यमान इव तुषाराद्रिद्रवेण, पीडयन्नङ्गैरङ्गानि, कपोलेन कपोलमवघट्टयन्, निमीलयन्पक्ष्माग्रग्रथिताजस्रास्रविस्राविणी विलोचने विस्मृतज्वरसंज्वरः सुचिरमालिलिङ्ग कथं कथमपि चिराद्विमुक्तमपसृत्य[2] कृतनमस्कारं प्रणतजननीकमुपागतमासीनं च शयनान्तिके पिबन्निव विगतनिमेषनिश्चलेन चक्षुषा व्यलोकयत्। पस्पर्श च पुनः पुनर्वेपथुमता पाणितलेन क्षयक्षामकण्ठश्च कृच्छ्रादिवावादीत्—'वत्स, कृशोऽसि' इति। भण्डिस्त्वकथयत्—'देव, तृतीयमहः कृताहारस्यास्याद्य' इति।

तच्छ्रुत्वा बाष्पवेगगृह्यमाणाक्षरं कथं कथमप्यायतं निःश्वस्योवाच—'वत्स, जानामि त्वां पितृप्रियमतिमृदुहृदयम्। ईदृशेषु विधुरयति धीमतोऽपि धियमतिदुर्धरो बान्धवस्नेहः सर्वप्रमाथी यतो[3] नार्हस्यतिमात्रमात्मानं शुचे दातुम्। उद्दामदाहज्वरदग्धोऽपि दह्ये खल्वहमधिकतरमनेनायुष्मदाधिना। निशितमिव शस्त्रं तक्ष्णोति मां त्वदीयस्तनिमा। सुखं च राज्यं च वंशश्च प्राणाश्च परलोकश्च[4] त्वयि मे स्थिताः। यथा मम तथा सर्वासां प्रजानाम्। त्वद्विधानां पीडाः पीडयन्ति सकलमेव भुवनतलम्। न ह्यल्पपुण्यभाजां वंशमलङ्कुर्वन्ति भवादृशाः। फलमस्यनेकजन्मान्तरोपार्जितस्याकलुषस्य कर्मणः। करतलगतमिव कथयन्ति चतुर्णामप्यर्णवानामाधिपत्यं ते लक्षणानि। त्वज्जन्मनैव कृतार्थोऽस्मि। निरभिलाषोऽस्मि जीवितव्ये। भिषगनुरोधः पाययति मामौषधम्। अपि च सर्वप्रजापुण्यैः सकलभुवनतलपरिपालनार्थमुत्पत्स्यमानानां भवादृशां जन्मग्रहणोपायः पितरौ। प्रजाभिस्तु बन्धुमन्तो राजानः, न ज्ञातिभिः। तदुत्तिष्ठ। कुरु पुनरेव सर्वाः क्रियाः। कृताहारे च त्वय्यहनपि स्वयमुपयोक्ष्ये पथ्यम्' इत्येवमभिहितस्य चास्य धक्ष्यन्निव हृदयमतितरां शोकानलः सन्दुधुक्षे। क्षणमात्रं च स्थित्वा पित्रा पुनराहारार्थमादिश्यमानो धवलगृहादवततार। चकार च चेतसि—'अकाण्डे खल्वयं समु-

१ 'स्नानिव' अ. २ 'उपसृत्य' अ. ३ 'अतो नार्हस्यात्मानम्' अ. ४ A omits this.

पस्थितो महाप्रलयो व्यभ्र इव वज्रपातः। सामान्योऽपि तावच्छोकः सोच्छ्वासं मरणम्, अनुपदिष्टौषधो महाव्याधिः, अभस्मीकरणोऽग्निप्रवेशः, अनुपरतरौव नरकवासः, निर्ज्योतिरङ्गारवर्षम्, अशकलीकरणं क्रकचदारणम्, अव्रणो वज्रसूचीपातः। किमुत विशेषाश्रितः। किमत्र करवाणि' इति।

राजपुरुषेणाधिष्ठितश्च गत्वा स्वधाम धूममयानिव कृताश्रुपातान्, अग्निमयानिव जनितहृदयदाहान्, विषमयानिव दत्तमूर्छावेगान्, महापातकमयानिवोत्पादितघृणान्, क्षारमयानिवानीतवेदनान्, कतिचित्कवलानगृह्णात्। आचामंश्च चामरग्राहिणमादिदेश—'विज्ञायागच्छ कथमास्ते तातः' इति। गत्वा च प्रतिनिवृत्य च 'देव तथैव' इति विज्ञापितस्तेनागृहीतताम्बूल एवोत्ताम्यता मनसास्ताभिलाषिणि सवितरि सर्वानाहूयोपह्वरे वैद्याः किमस्मिन्नेवंविधे विधेयमधुनेति विषण्णहृदयः पप्रच्छ। ते तु व्यज्ञापयन्—'देव, धैर्यमवलम्बस्व। कतिपयैरेव वासरैः पुनः स्वां प्रकृतिमापन्नं श्रोष्यसि पितरम्' इति।

तेषां तु भिषजां मध्ये पौनर्वसवो युवाष्टादशवर्षदेशीयस्तस्मिन्नेव राजकुले कुलक्रमागतो गतः पारमष्टाङ्गस्यायुर्वेदस्य भूभुजा सुतनिर्विशेषं लालितः प्रकृत्यैवातिपटीयस्या प्रज्ञया यथावद्विज्ञाता व्याधिस्वरूपाणां रसायनो नाम वैद्यकुमारकः साश्रुस्तूष्णीमधोमुखोऽभूत्। पृष्टश्च राजसूनुना—'सखे रसायन, कथय तथ्यं यद्यसाध्विव पश्यसि' इति। सोऽब्रवीत्—'देव, श्वः प्रभाते यथावस्थितमावेदयितास्मि' इति।

अत्रैव चान्तरे भवनकमलिनीपालः कोकमाश्वासयन्नपरवक्त्रमुच्चैरपठत्—

'विहग कुरु दृढं मनः स्वयं त्यज शुचमास्स्व विवेकवर्त्मनि।
सह कमलसरोजिनीश्रिया श्रयति सुमेरुशिरो विरोचनः ॥ ४ ॥'

तच्चाकर्ण्य, वाङ्गिमित्तज्ञः पितरि सुतरां जीविताशां शिथिलीचकार। गतेषु च भिषक्षु क्षतधृतिः क्षपामुखे क्षितिपालसमीपमेव पुनराररोह। तत्र च—'दाहो महान्। आहर हारान्हरिणि, मणिदर्पणान्मे देहे देहि वैदेहि, हिमलवैर्लिम्प ललाटं लीलावति, घनसारक्षोदधूलीर्निधेहि धवलाक्षि, निक्षिप चक्षुषि चन्द्रकान्तं कान्तिमति, कपोले कलय कुवलयं कलावति, चन्दनचर्चां रचय चारुमति, पाटय पटमारुतं पाटलिके, मन्दय दाहमिन्दुमति, अरविन्दैर्जनय जलार्द्रया मुदं मदिरावति, समुपनय मृणालानि मालति, तरलय तालवृन्तमावन्तिके, मूर्धानं धावमानं बधान बन्धुमति, कन्धरां धारय धारणिके, उरसि सशीकरं करं कुरु कुरङ्गवति, संवाहय बाहू बलाहिके, पीडय पादौ पद्मावति, गृहाण गाढमनङ्गसेने, का वेला विलासवति नैति निद्रा, कथय कुमुद्वति' इत्येवंप्रायान्पितुरालापाननवरतमाकर्णयन्दूयमानहृदयो दुःखदीर्घां जाग्रदेव निशामनैषीत्।

उषसि चावतीर्य राजद्वारदेशोपसर्पिणा परिवर्धकेनोपस्थापितेऽपि तुरङ्गे चरणाभ्यामेवाजगाम स्वमन्दिरम्। तत्र च त्वरमाणो भ्रातुरागमनार्थमुपर्युपरि क्षिप्रपातिनो दीर्घाध्वगान्प्रजविनश्चोष्ट्रपालान्प्राहिणोत्। प्रक्षालितवदनश्च परिजनोपनीतमपि प्रतिकर्म नाग्रहीत्। अग्रतः स्थितानां राजपुत्रयूनां विमनसां 'रसायनो रसायनः' इति जल्पितमव्यक्तमश्रौषीत्। पर्यपृच्छच्च तान्—'भद्राः, कथयत किं रसायनः' इति। पृष्टाश्च ते सर्वे सममेव तूष्णींबभूवुर्भूयोभूयश्चानुबध्यमाना दुःखेन कथंकथमप्याचचक्षिरे—'देव, पावकं प्रविष्टः' इति। तच्च श्रुत्वा प्लुष्ट इवान्तस्तापेन सद्यो विवर्णतामगात्। उत्पाट्यमानमिव च न शशाक शोकान्धं धारयितुं हृदयम्। आसीच्चास्य चेतसि 'कामं स्वयं न भवति न तु श्रावयत्यप्रियं वचनमरतिकरमितर इवाभिजातो जनः। कृच्छ्रे च यथानेनानुष्ठितमुज्ज्वलीकृतमधिकतरं ज्वलनप्रवेशेन कल्याणप्रकृति कार्तस्वरमिव कौलपुत्रमस्य' इति। पुनश्चाचिन्तयत्—'समुचितमेवाथवा स्नेहस्येदम्। किमस्य तातो न तातः, किं वाम्बा न जननी, वयं न भ्रातरः। अन्यस्मिन्नपि तावत्स्वामिनि दुर्लभीभवति भवन्त्यसवो ध्रियमाणा ह्रीहेतवो लोके किमुतामृतमयेऽनुजीविनां निर्व्याजबान्धवेऽवन्ध्यप्रसादे सुगृहीतनाम्नि ताते। संप्रति सांप्रतमाचरितमनेनात्मानं दहता किं वास्याकल्पमवस्थितस्य स्थेयसो यशोमयस्य दह्यते। पतितः स केवलं दहने। दग्धास्तु वयम्। धन्यः खल्वसावग्रणीः पुण्यभाजाम्। अपुण्यभाक्त्विदमेव राजकुलं कुलपुत्रेण यत्तादृशा वियुक्तम्। अपि च ममापि कः खल्वेतेषां प्राणानां कार्यातिभारः कृतशेषो वा, का वा व्यापृतता, येन नाद्यापि निष्ठुराः प्राणाः प्रतिष्ठन्ते, को वान्तरायो हृदयस्य येन सहस्रधा न दलति' इति। दुःखार्तश्च न जगाम राजसद्म। समुत्ससर्ज च सर्वकार्याणि। शयनीये निपत्य उत्तरीयवाससा सोत्तमाङ्गमात्मानमवगुण्ठ्यातिष्ठत्।

इत्थंभूते च देवे हर्षे राजनि च तदवस्थे सर्वस्य लोकस्य कपोलेषु कीलिता इव कराः, लोचनेषु लेप्यमय्य इवाश्रुस्रुतयः, नासाग्रेषु ग्रथिता[1] इव दृष्टयः, कर्णेषूत्कीर्णा इव रुदितध्वनयः, जिह्वासु सहजानीव हाकष्टानि, लपनेषु पल्लवितानीव श्वसितानि, अधरेषु लिखितानीव परिदेवितपदानि, हृदयेषु निधानीकृतानीव दुःखान्यभवन्। उष्णाश्रुदाहभीतेव नाभजत नेत्रोदराणि निद्रा। निःश्वासवातविधुता इव व्यलीयन्त हासाः। निरवशेषदग्धेव च सन्तापेन न प्रावर्तत वाणी। कथास्वपि नाश्रूयन्त परिहासाः। क्वागमन्निति नाज्ञायन्त गीतगोष्ठ्यः। जन्मान्तरातीतानीव नास्मर्यन्त लास्यानि। स्वप्नेऽपि नागृह्यन्त प्रसाधनानि। वार्तापि नालभ्यतोपभोगानाम्। नामापि नाकीर्त्यताहारस्य। खपुष्पप्रतिमान्यासन्नापानमण्डलानि। लोकान्तरमिवानीयन्त बन्दिवाचः। युगान्तर इवावर्तन्त निर्वृतयः[2]। पुनरिवादह्यत शोकाग्निना मकरकेतुः।

१ 'प्रथिताः' ब. २ 'निवृत्तयः' ब.

दिवापि नामुच्यन्त शयनानि । शनैः शनैश्च महापुरुषविनिपातपिशुनाः समं समन्तात्समुदभवन्भुवने भूयांसो भूपतेरभावाय भयमुत्पादयन्तो भूतानां महोत्पाताः ।

तथा हि । दोलायमानसकलकुलाचलचक्रवाला पत्या सार्धं गन्तुकामेव प्रथममचलद्धरित्री । धन्वन्तरेरिवान्तरे तस्मिन्स्मरन्तः परस्परास्फालनवाचालवीचयो विजुघूर्णिरेऽर्णवाः । भूभृदभावभीतानां विततशिखा[1]कलापविकटकुटिलाः केशपाशा इवोर्ध्वीबभूवुर्धूमकेतवः ककुभाम् । धूमकेतुकरालितदिङ्मुखं दिक्पालारब्धायुष्कामहोमधूमधूम्रमिवाभवद्भुवनम् । भ्रष्टभासि तप्तकालायसकुम्भबभ्रुणि भानुमण्डले भयङ्करक[2]बन्धकायव्याजेन कोऽपि पार्थिवप्राणितार्थी पुरुषोपहारमिवोपजहार । ज्वलितपरिवेशमण्डलाभोगभास्वरो जिघृक्षाजृम्भमाणस्वर्भानुभयादुपरचिताग्निप्राकार इव प्रत्यदृश्यत श्वेतभानुः । अवनिपतिप्रतापप्रसाधिताः प्रथमतरकृतपावकप्रवेशा इवादह्यन्तानुरक्ता दिशः । स्रुतशोणितशीकरासारारुणिततनुरनुमरणाय प्रावृतपाटलांशुकपटेवादृश्यत वसुधावधूः । नराधिपविनाशसंभ्रमभीतैर्लोकपालैरिव कालायसकवाटपुटैरकालकालमेघपटलैररुध्यन्त दिग्द्वाराणि । प्रेतपतिप्रयाणप्रहताः पटवः पटहा इवारटन्तो हृदयस्फोटनाः प[3]स्फायिरे निर्घातानां घोरा निर्घोषाः । निकटीभवद्यममहिषखुरपुटोद्धूता इव द्युमणिधाम धूसरीचक्रुः क्रमेलककचकपिलाः पांशुवृष्टयः । वि[4]रसविराविणीनामुन्मुखीनां शिखिनो ज्वालाः प्रतीच्छन्त्य इव पतन्तीरुल्का नभसो ववाशिरे शिवानां राजयः । राजधामनि धूमायमानकबरीविभागविभावितविकाराः प्रकीर्णकेशपाशप्रकाशितशोका इव प्राकाशन्त प्रतिमाः कुलदेवतानाम् । उपसिंहासनमाकुलं कालरात्रिविदूयमानवृजिनवेणीबन्धविभ्रमं विभ्राणं बभ्राम भ्रामरं पटलम् । अटतामन्तःपुरस्योपरि क्षणमपि न शशाम व्याक्रोशी वायसानाम् । श्वेतातपत्रमण्डलमध्याजीवितमिव राज्यस्य सरसपिशितपिण्डलोहितं चञ्चञ्चञ्चुरुच्चैरुच्चखान खण्डं माणिक्यस्य कूजञ्जरद्गृध्रः । महोत्पातदूयमानश्च कथमपि निनाय निशाम् ।

अन्यस्मिन्नहनि समीपमस्य राजकुलाद्द्रुतगतिवशविशीर्यमाणालङ्कारझांकारिणी विजयघोषणेव विषादस्याकुलचरणचलत्तुलाकोटिक्वणितवाचालिताभिरुद्ग्रीवाभिः किं किमिति पृच्छ्यमानेव दूरादेव भवनहंसीभिः, स्खलितविशालश्रोणिशिञ्जानरशनानुराविणीभिश्च बाष्पान्धा समुपदिश्यमानमार्गेव गृहसारसीभिः, अदृष्टकवाटपट्टसङ्घट्टस्फुटितललाटपट्टरुधिरपटलेन [5]पटान्तेनेव रक्तांशुकस्य मुखमाच्छाद्य प्ररुदती, सन्तापबलविलीनकनकवलयरसधारामिव वेत्रलतामुत्सृजन्ती, मुखमरुत्तरङ्गितामुत्तरीयांशुकपटीं स्फुरन्तीं फणिनीव

१ 'विततशिखी०' अ. २ 'भयङ्करं कबन्ध०' ब. ३ 'पस्फायिरे निपततां' ब. ४ 'विसर०' अ. ५ 'पदान्तेनेव' ब.

निर्मोकमञ्जरीमाकर्षन्ती, नम्रांसस्रंसिनानिलविलोलेन नीलतमेन तमालपल्लवचीरचीवरेणेव शोकोचितेन धम्मिल्लरचनारहितेन शिरोरुहसञ्चयेन चञ्चता प्रावृतकुचा, कुचताडनपीडया समुच्छूनाताम्रश्यामतलं मुहुर्मुहुरत्युष्णाश्रुप्रमार्जनप्रदग्धमिव करकिशलयं धुनाना, चक्षुर्निर्झरे शीर्यति स्नपयन्तीव शोकाग्निप्रवेशाय स्वकपोलतलप्रतिबिम्बितमासन्नलोकं, लोललोचनप्रवृत्तैस्तरलैस्तारकांशुभिः श्यामायमानमात्मदुःखेन दिवसमपि दहन्तीव 'क्व कुमारः, क्व कुमारः' इति प्रतिपुरुषं पृच्छन्ती वेलेति नाम्ना यशोमत्याः प्रतीहार्याजगाम । विषण्णलोकलोचनप्रत्युद्गता चोपसृत्य कुट्टिमन्यस्तहस्तयुगला गलन्तीभिः सिञ्चतीव शुष्यन्तं दशनदीधितिधाराभिराधूसरमधरमधोमुखी विज्ञापितवती—'देव, परित्रायस्व परित्रायस्व । जीवत्येव भर्तरि किमप्यध्यवसितं देव्या' इति ।

ततस्तदपरमाकर्ण्य च्युत इव सत्त्वेन, द्रुत इव दुःखेन, आचान्त इव चिन्तया, तुलित इव तापेन, अङ्गीकृत इवातङ्केनाप्रतिपत्तिरासीत् । आसीच्चास्य चेतसि—'प्रतिपन्नसंज्ञस्य बहुशोऽपि हृदये दुःखाभिषङ्गो निपतन्नश्मनीव लोहप्रहारः कठिने हुतभुजमुत्थापयति न तु भस्मसात्करोति मे निरनुक्रोशस्य कायम्' इति । उत्थाय च त्वरमाणोऽन्तःपुरमगात् । तत्र च मर्तुमुद्यतानां राजमहिषीणामश्रृणोद्दूरादेव 'तात चूत, चिन्तयात्मानं प्रवसति ते जननी । वत्स जातीगुच्छ, गच्छाम्यापृच्छस्व माम् । मया विनाद्यानाथा भवसि भगिनि भवनदाडिमलते । रक्ताशोक, मर्षणीयाः पादप्रहाराः कर्णपूरपल्लवभङ्गापराधाश्च । पुन्नक अन्तःपुरबालबकुलक वारुणीगण्डूषग्रहणदुर्ललित, दृष्टोऽसि । वत्से प्रियङ्गुलतिके, गाढमालिङ्ग मां दुर्लभा भवामि ते । भद्र भवनद्वारसहकारक, दातव्यो निवापतोयाञ्जलिरपत्यमसि । भ्रातः पञ्जरशुक, यथा न विस्मरसि माम्, किं व्याहरसि दूरीभूतास्मि ते । शारिके, स्वप्ने नः समागमः पुनर्भूयात् । मातः, मार्गलग्नं कस्य समर्पयामि गृहमयूरकम् । अम्ब, सुतवल्लालनीयमिदं हंसमिथुनं मन्दपुण्यया मया न सम्भावितोऽस्य चक्रवाकयुगलस्य विवाहोत्सवः । मातृवत्सले, निवर्तस्व गृहहरिणिके । समुपनय सौविदल्ल वल्लभवल्लकीं परिष्वजे तावदेनाम् । चन्द्रसेने, सुदृष्टः क्रियतामयं जनः । बिन्दुमति, इयं तेऽन्त्या वन्दना । चेटि, मुञ्च चरणौ । आर्ये कात्यायनिके, किं रोदिषि नीतास्मि दैवेन । तात कञ्चुकिन्, किं मामलक्षणां प्रदक्षिणीकरोषि । धात्रेयि, धारयात्मानं किं पादयोः पतसि । भगिनि, गृहाण मामपश्चिमां कण्ठे । कष्टं न दृष्टा प्रियसखी मलयवती । कुरङ्गवति, अयमामन्त्रणाञ्जलिः । सानुमति, अयमन्त्यः प्रणामः । कुवलयवति, एष तेऽवसानपरिष्वङ्गः । सख्यः, क्षन्तव्याः प्रणयकलहाः' इत्येवंप्रायानालापान् ।

दह्यमानश्रवणश्च तैः प्रविशन्नेव निर्यान्तीं दत्तसर्वस्वापतेयां गृहीतमरणप्रसाधनाम्, जानकीमिव जातवेदसं पत्युः पुरः प्रवेक्ष्यन्तीम्, प्रत्यप्रस्ना-

नार्द्रदेहतया श्रियमिव भगवतीं सद्यः समुद्रादुत्थिताम्, कुसुम्भबभ्रुणी वाससी दिवमिव तेजसी सांध्ये दधानाम्, ताम्बूलदिग्धरागान्धकाराधरप्रभापटलपाटलं पट्टांशुकमिव विधवामरणचिह्नमङ्गलग्नमुद्वहन्तीम्, रक्तकण्ठसूत्रेण कुचान्तरावलम्बिना स्फुटितहृदयविगलितरुधिरधाराशङ्कां कुर्वतीम्, तिर्यक्कुटिलकुण्डलकोटिकण्टकाकृष्टतन्तुना हारेण वलितेन सितांशुकपाशेनेव कण्ठमुत्पीडयन्तीम्, सरसकुङ्कुमाङ्गरागतया कवलितामिव दिधक्षता चितार्चिष्मता, चितानलार्चनकुसुमैरिव धवलधवलैरश्रुविन्दुभिरंशुकोत्सङ्गमापूरयन्तीम्, गृहदेवतामन्त्रणबलिमिव वलयैर्विगलद्भिः पदे पदे विकिरन्तीम्, आप्रपदीनां कण्ठे गुणकुसुममालां यमदोलामिवारूढाम्, अन्तर्गुञ्जन्मधुकरमुखरेणामन्त्र्यमाणलोचनोत्पलामिव कर्णोत्पलेन, प्रदक्षिणीक्रियमाणामिव मणिनूपुरबन्धुभिर्बद्धमण्डलं भ्रमद्भिर्भवनहंसैः, संनिहितप्राणसमं मरणाय चित्तमिव चित्रफलकमविचलं धारयन्तीम्, अर्चाबद्धोद्धूयमानधवलपुष्पदामकाम्, पतिव्रतापताकामिव पतिप्रासयष्टिमिष्टामुपगूहमानाम्, बन्धोरिव निजचारित्रधवलस्य नृपातपत्रस्य पुरो नेत्रोदकमुत्सृजन्तीम्, पत्युः पादपतनसमुद्गमदभ्यधिकबाष्पाम्भःप्रवाहप्रतिरुद्धदृशः कथमपि प्रतिपन्नादेशान्सचिवान्सन्दिशन्तीम्, अनुनयनिवर्तितविधुरवृद्धबन्धुवर्गवर्धमानध्वनिभिर्गृहाक्रन्दैराकृष्यमाणश्रवणाम्, भर्तृभाषितनिभैः पञ्जरसिंहबृंहितैर्ह्रियमाणहृदयाम्, धात्र्या भर्तृभक्त्या च निजया प्रसाधिताम्, जरत्या मूर्च्छया च संस्तुतया धार्यमाणाम्, सख्या पीडया च व्यसनसङ्गतया समालिङ्गिताम्, परिजनेन सन्तापेन च गृहीतसर्वावयवेन परीताम्, कुलपुत्रैरुच्छ्वसितैश्च[१] महत्तरैरधिष्ठिताम्, कञ्चुकिभिर्दुःखैश्चातिवृद्धैरनुगताम्, भूपालवल्लभान्कौलेयकानपि सास्रमालोकयन्तीम्, सपत्नीनामपि पादयोः पतन्तीम्, चित्रपुत्रिका अप्यामन्त्र्यमाणाम्, गृहपतत्त्रिणामप्यञ्जलिं पुरस्तादुपरचयन्तीम्, पशूनप्यापृच्छ्यमानाम्, भवनपादपानपि परिष्वजमानां मातरं ददर्श।

दूरादेव च बाष्पायमाणदृष्टिरभ्यधात्—'अम्ब, त्वमपि मां मन्दपुण्यं त्यजसि। प्रसीद। निवर्तस्व' इत्यभिदधान एव च सस्नेहमिव नूपुरमणिमरीचिभिश्चुम्ब्यमानचूडश्चरणयोर्न्यपतत्। देवी तु यशोमती तथा तिष्ठति पादनिहितशिरसि विमनसि कनीयसि प्रेयसि तनये गुरुणा गिरिणेवोद्वेगावेगेनावष्टभ्यमाना, मूर्च्छान्धतमसं रसातलमिव प्रविशन्ती, बाष्पप्रवाहेणेव चिरनिरोधसम्पिण्डितेन स्नेहसम्भारेण निर्भराविर्भूतेनाभिभूयमाना, कृतप्रयत्नापि निवारयितुं न शशाक बाष्पोत्पतनम्। उत्कटकुचोत्कम्पप्रकटितासह्यशोकाकूता च गद्गदिकागृह्यमाणगलविकला निःसामान्यमन्युतरलीक्रियमाणाधरोद्देशा पुनरुक्तस्फुरणनिबिडितनासापुटा निमील्य नयने नयनाम्भःसेकप्लवेन प्लावयन्ती विमलौ कपोलौ सम्छाद्य करनखमयूखमालाखचिततनुना

१ 'कुलपुत्रोच्छ्वसितैश्च' ब.

तन्वन्तरनिर्गच्छदच्छास्रस्रोतसेवांशुकपटान्तेन किंचिदुत्तानितं वदनेन्दुं दूयमानमानसा स्मरन्ती प्रस्नुतस्तनी प्रसवदिवसादारभ्य सकलमङ्कशायिनः शैशवमस्य ज्ञातिगृहगतहृदया 'अम्ब, तात, न पश्यतं पापां परलोकप्रस्थितां मामेवमतिदुःखिताम्' इति मुहुर्मुहुराक्रन्दन्ती पितरौ, 'हा वत्स, विश्रान्तभागधेयया न दृष्टोऽसि' इति प्रेष्ठं ज्येष्ठं तनयमसंनिहितं क्रोशन्ती, 'अनाथा जाता' इति श्वशुरकुलवर्तिनीं दुहितरमनुशोचन्ती, 'निष्करुण, किमपराद्धं तवामुना जनेन' इति दैवमुपालभमाना, 'नास्ति मत्समा सीमन्तिनी दुःखभागिनी' इति निन्दन्ती बहुविधमात्मानम्, 'मुषितास्मि नृशंस त्वया' इत्यकाण्डे कृतान्तं गर्हमाणा मुक्तकण्ठमतिचिरं प्राकृतप्रमदेव प्रारोदीत्।

प्रशान्ते च मन्युवेगे सस्नेहमुत्थापयामास सुतम्। हस्तेन चास्य प्ररुदितस्य पक्ष्मपालीपुञ्ज्यमाननखकिरणनिवहां द्रुतामिवाधिकतरं क्षरन्तीं दृष्टिमुन्ममार्ज। स्वयमपि कठोररागपरिपीयमानेन धवलिम्ना मुच्यमानोदरे क्वथदस्रश्वयत्पर्यन्ते शुक्लशीकरतारतारकितपक्ष्मणी सूक्ष्मतराश्रुबिन्दुपरिपाटीपतनानुबन्धविधुरे लोचने पुनः पुनरापूर्यमाणे प्रमृज्य बाष्पार्द्रगण्डगृहीतां च श्रवणशिखरमारोप्य शोकलम्बामलकलतामधःस्रस्तविलोलबालिकाव्याकुलितां च समुत्सार्य तिरश्चीं चिकुरसटामश्रुप्रवाहपूरितमार्द्रं च किंचिच्च्युतमुत्क्षिप्य हस्तेन स्तनोत्तरीयं तरङ्गितमिव[1] मग्नांशुकपटान्ततनुताम्रलेखालाञ्छितलावण्यकुञ्जिका[2]वर्जितराजतराजहंसास्यसमुद्गीर्णेन पयसा प्रक्षाल्य मुखकमलं कलमूकलोकविधृते वासःशकले शुचिनि समुन्मृज्य पाणी सुतवदनविनिहितनिभृतनयनयुगला चिरं स्थित्वा पुनः पुनरायतं निश्वस्यावादीत्— 'वत्स, नासि न प्रियो निर्गुणो वा परित्यागार्हो वा। स्तन्येनैव सह त्वया पीतं मे हृदयम्। अस्मिंश्च समये प्रभूतप्रभुप्रसादान्तरिता त्वां न पश्यति दृष्टिः। अपि च पुत्रक, पुरुषान्तरविलोकनव्यसनिनी राज्योपकरणमकरुणा वा नास्मि लक्ष्मीः क्षमा वा। कुलकलत्रमस्मि चारित्रमात्रधना धर्मधवले कुले जाता। किं विस्मृतोऽसि मां समरशतशौण्डस्य पुरुषप्रकाण्डस्य केशरिण इव केशरिणीं गृहिणीम्। वीरजा वीरजाया वीरजननी च मादृशी पराक्रमक्रीता कथमन्यथा कुर्यात्। एवंविधेन पित्रा ते भरतभगीरथनाभागनिभेन नरेन्द्रवृन्दारकेण गृहीतः पाणिः। आसेवितः सेवासंभ्रान्तानन्तसामन्तसीमन्तिनीसमावर्जितजाम्बूनदघटाभिषेकः शिरसा। लब्धो मनोरथदुर्लभो महादेवीपट्टबन्धसत्कारलाभो ललाटेन। आपीतौ युष्मद्विधैः पुत्रैरमित्रकलत्रबन्दीवृन्दविधूयमानचामरमरुच्चलचीनांशुकधरौ पयोधरौ। सपत्नीनां शिरःसु निहितं नमन्निखिलकटककुटुम्बिनीकिरीटमाणिक्यमालार्चितं चरणयुगलकम्। एवं कृतार्थसर्वावयवा किमपरमपेक्षे क्षीणपुण्या। मर्तुमविधवैव

१ 'तरङ्गितमिव नखांशुपटलेन' ब. २ 'कुब्जिका' ब.

वाञ्छामि । न च शक्नोमि दग्धस्य भर्तुरार्यपुत्रविरहिता रतिरिव निरर्थकान्प्रलापान्कर्तुम् । पितुश्च ते पादधूलिरिव प्रथमं गगनगमनमावेदयन्ती बहुमता भविष्यामि शूरानुरागिणीनां सुराङ्गनानाम् । प्रत्यग्रदृष्टदारुणदुःखदग्धायाश्च मे किं धक्ष्यति धूमध्वजः । मरणाच्च मे जीवितमेवास्मिन्समये साहसम् । अतिशीतलः पतिशोकानलादक्षयस्नेहेन्धनादस्मादनलः । कैलासकल्पे प्रवसति जीवेश्वरे जरत्तृणकणिकालघीयसि जीविते लोभ इति क्व घटते । अपि च जीवन्तीमपि मां नरपतिमरणावधीरणमहापातकिनीं न स्प्रक्ष्यन्ति पुत्र पुत्रराज्यसुखानि । दुःखदग्धानां च भूतिरमङ्गला चाप्रशस्ता च निरुपयोगा च भवति । वत्स, विश्वस्तानां यशसा स्थातुमिच्छामि लोके न वपुषा । तदहमेव त्वां तावत्तात प्रसादयामि न पुनर्मनोरथप्रातिकूल्येन कदर्थनीयास्मि ।' इत्युक्त्वा पादयोरपतत् ।

स तु ससंभ्रममपनीय चरणयुगलमवनमिततनुरुभयकरविधृतवपुषमवनितलगतशिरसमुदनमयन्मातरम् । दुर्निवारतां च शुचः समवधार्य कुलयोषिदुचितां च तामेव श्रेयसीं मन्यमानः क्रियां कृतनिश्चयां च तां ज्ञात्वा तूष्णीमधोमुखोऽभवत् ।

अभिनन्दति हि स्नेहकातरापि कुलीनता देशकालानुरूपम् । देव्यपि यशोमती परिष्वज्य समाघ्राय च शिरसि निर्गत्य चरणाभ्यामेव चान्तःपुरात्पौराक्रन्द[1]प्रतिशब्दनिर्भराभिरुपरुध्यमानेव दिग्भिः सरस्वतीतीरं ययौ । तत्र च स्त्रीस्वभावकातरैर्दृष्टिपातैः प्रविकसितरक्तपङ्कजपुञ्जैरिवार्चयित्वा भगवन्तं भानुमन्तमिव मूर्तिरैन्दवी चित्रभानुं प्राविशत् । इतरोऽपि मातृमरणविह्वलो बन्धुवर्गपरिवृतः पितुः पार्श्वं प्रायात् । अपश्यच्च स्वल्पावशेषप्राणवृत्तिं परिवर्त्यमानतारकं तारकराजमिवास्तमभिलषन्तं जनयितारम् । असह्यशोकोद्रेकाभिद्रुतश्च त्याजितः स्नेहेन धैर्यम् । आश्लिष्यास्य सकलदुर्मदमहीपालमौलिमालालालितौ पादपद्मावन्तस्तापान्मुखचन्द्रमिव द्रवीभवन्तं दशनज्योत्स्नाजालमिव जलतामापद्यमानं लोचनलावण्यमिव विलीयमानं मुखसुधारसमिव स्यन्दमानमच्छाच्छमश्रुस्रोतसां सन्तानं महामेघमयविलोचन इव वर्षन्नितरवद्विमुक्तारावश्चिरं रुरोद ।

राजा तु तमुपरुध्यमानदृष्टिरविरतरुदितशब्दाश्रितश्रवणः प्रत्यभिज्ञाय शनैः शनैरवादीत्—'पुत्र, नार्हस्येवं भवितुम् । भवद्विधा न ह्यमहासत्त्वाः । महासत्त्वता हि प्रथममवलम्बनं लोकस्य पश्चाद्राजबीजिता । सत्त्ववतां चाग्रणीः सर्वातिशयाश्रितः क्व भवान्, क्व वैक्लव्यम् । 'कुलप्रदीपोऽसि' इति दिवसकरसदृशतेजसस्ते लघूकरणमिव । 'पुरुषसिंहोऽसि' इति शौर्यपटुप्रज्ञोपबृंहितपराक्रमस्य निन्देव । 'क्षितिरियं तव' इति लक्षणाख्यातचक्रवर्तिपदस्य पुनरुक्तमिव । 'गृह्यतां श्रीः' इति स्वयमेव श्रिया गृहीतस्य विपरीतमिव ।

---

[1] 'पौराक्रन्दनिर्भराभिः' अ-

'अध्यास्यतामयं लोकः' इत्युभयलोकविजिगीषोरपुष्कलमिव। 'स्वीक्रियतां कोषः' इति शशिकरनिकरनिर्मलयशःसञ्चयैकाभिनिवेशिनो निरुपयोगमिव। 'आत्मीक्रियतां राजकम्' इति गुणगणात्मीकृतंजगतो[1] गतार्थमिव। 'उह्यतां राज्यभारः' इति भुवनत्रयभारोचितस्यानुचितनियोग इव। 'प्रजाः परिरक्ष्यन्ताम्' इति दीर्घदोर्दण्डार्गलितदिङ्मुखस्यानुवाद इव। 'परिजनः परिपाल्यताम्' इति लोकपालोपमस्यानुषङ्गिकमिव। 'शस्त्राभ्यासः कार्यः' इति धनुर्गुणकिणकलङ्ककालीकृतप्रकोष्ठस्य किमादिश्यते। 'निगृह्यतां चापलम्' इति नूतनतरवयसि निगृहीतेन्द्रियस्य निरवकाशेव मे वाणी। 'निरवशेषतां शत्रवो नेयाः' इति सहजस्य तेजस एवेयं चिन्ता।' इत्येवं वदन्नेवापुनरुन्मीलनाय निमिमील राजसिंहो लोचने[2]।

अस्मिन्नेवान्तरे पूषाप्यायुषेव तेजसा व्ययुज्यत। ततश्च लज्जमान इव नरपतिजीवितापहरणजनितादात्मापराधादधोमुखः समभवत्। भूपालाभावशोकशिखिनेव चान्तस्ताप्यमानस्ताम्रतां प्रपेदे। मन्दं मन्दमप्रियप्रश्नार्थमिव स्थितिमनुवर्तमानो लौकिकीमवातरद्दिवः। दित्सुरिव जनेशाय जलाञ्जलिमपरजलनिधिसमीपमुपससर्प। सद्योदत्त[3]नृपजलाञ्जलिर्दुःखदहनदग्धमिव करसहस्रमालोहितमधत्त।

एवं च महानराधिपनिधननिधीयमानविपुलवैराग्य इव शान्तवपुषि विशति गिरिगुहागह्वरं गभस्तिमालिनि, समुपोह्यमानमहाजनाश्रुदुर्दिनार्द्रीकृत इव निर्वात्यातपे, रोदनताम्रसकललोकलोचनरुचेव लोहितायति जगति, उष्णायमानानेकनरनिश्वाससन्तापप्लुष्ट इव च नीलायमाने दिवसे, नृपानुगमनप्रचलितयेव लक्ष्म्या मुच्यमानासु कमलिनीषु, पतिशुचेव परिवृतच्छायायां श्यामायमानायां भुवि, कुलपुत्रेष्विव परित्यक्तकलत्रेषु कृतकरुणप्रलापेषु वनान्तानाश्रयत्सु दुःखितेषु चक्रवाकेषु, छत्रभङ्गभीतेष्विव निगूढकोशेषु कुशेशयेषु, स्फुटितदिग्वधूहृदयरुधिरप्लव इव गलिते रक्तातपे, क्रमेण च लोकान्तरमुपगतवत्यनुरागशेषे जाते तेजसामधीशे, गगनतलवितन्यमानबहलरायपाटलायां[4] प्रेतपताकायामिव प्रवृत्तायां संध्यायाम्, शवशिबिकालङ्काकृष्णचामरमालास्विव स्फुरन्तीषु दर्शनप्रतिकूलासु तिमिरलेखासु, असितागुरुकालकाष्ठायां केनापि चितायामिव रचितायां रजन्याम्, दन्तामलपत्त्रप्रसाधितकर्णिकासु केसरमालाकल्पितमुण्डमालिकासु अनुमर्तुमिवोद्यतासु प्रहसितमुखीषु कुमुदलक्ष्मीषु, अवतरत्त्रिदशविमानकिङ्किणीक्वणित इव श्रूयमाणे शाखिशिखरकुलायलीयमानशकुनिकुलकूजिते, नाकपथप्रस्थितपार्थिवप्रत्युद्गतपुरुहूतातपत्र इव पूर्वस्यां दिशि दृश्यमाने चन्द्रमसि, नरेन्द्रः स्वयं समर्पितस्कन्धैर्गृहीत्वा शवशिबिकां शिबिसमः सामन्तैः पौरैश्च पुरोहितपुरःसरैः सरितं

१ '०गणात्मीकृतं जगतो' ब. २ 'प्रत्यपद्यत च पूषात्मजः' इत्यधिकं ब-पुस्तके. ३ '०दत्तजला०' अ. ४ '०पटलायाम्' अ.

सरस्वतीं नीत्वा नरपतिसमुचितायां चितायां हुताशसत्क्रियया यशः-शेषतामनीयत।

देवोऽपि हर्षः पुञ्जीभूतेन सकलेनेव जीवलोकेन लोकेन राजकुलसम्बद्धेनाशेषेण शोकमूकेन परिवृतोऽन्तर्वर्तिनापि शोकानलतप्तेन स्नेहद्रवेण बहिरिव सिच्यमानो निर्व्यवधानायां धरण्यामुपविष्ट एव तां निशीथिनीं भीमरथीभीमामखिलां सराजको जजागार। अजनि चास्य चेतसि। 'ताते दूरीभूते संप्रत्येतावान्खलु जीवलोकः, लोकस्य भग्नाः पन्थानः, मनोरथानां खिलीभूतानि भूतिस्थानानि, स्थगितान्यानन्दस्य द्वाराणि, सुप्ता सत्यवादिता, लुप्ता लोकयात्रा, विलीना बाहुशालिता, प्रलीना प्रियालापिता, प्रोषिताः पुरुषकारविहारविकाराः, समाप्ता समरशौण्डता, ध्वस्ता परगुणप्रीतिः, विश्रान्ता विश्वासभूमयः, अपदान्यपदानानि, निरुपयोगानि शास्त्राणि, निरवलम्बना विक्रमैकरसता, कथावशेषा विशेषज्ञता, ददातु जनो जलाञ्जलिमौर्जित्याय, प्रतिपद्यतां प्रव्रज्यां प्रजापालता, बध्नातु वैधव्यवेणीं वरमनुष्यता, समाश्रयतु राजश्रीराश्रमपदम्, परिधत्तां धवले वाससी वसुमती, वहतु वल्कले विलासिता, तपस्यतु तपोवनेषु तेजस्विता, प्रावृणोतु चीवरे वीरता, क्व गम्यतां पुनस्तस्य कृते कृतज्ञतया, क्व पुनः प्राप्स्यति तादृशान्महापुरुषनिर्माणपरमाणून्परमेष्ठी, शून्याः संवृत्ता दश दिशो गुणानाम्, जगज्जातमन्धकारं धर्मस्य, निष्फलमधुना जन्म शस्त्रोपजीविनाम्। तातेन विना कुतस्त्यास्तादृश्यो दिवसमसमसमररससमारब्धकलहकथाकण्टकितसुभटकपोलभित्तयो वीरगोष्ठ्यः। अपि नाम स्वप्नेऽपि दृश्येत दीर्घरक्तनयनं पुनस्तन्मुखसरोजम्, जन्मान्तरेऽपि पुनः परिष्वज्येत तल्लोहस्तम्भाभ्यधिकगरिमगर्भं भुजयुगलम्। लोकान्तरेऽपि पुत्रेत्यालपतः श्रूयेत सा सुधारसमुद्गिरन्ती मथ्यमानक्षीरसागरोद्गारगम्भीरा भारती' इति। एतानि चान्यानि च चिन्तयत एवास्य कथमपि सा क्षयमियाय यामिनी।

ततः शुचेव मुक्तकण्ठमारटत्सु कृकवाकुकुलेषु, गृहगिरितरुशिखरेभ्यः पातयत्स्वात्मानं मन्दिरमयूरेषु परित्यक्तनिवासेषु च वनाय प्रस्थितेषु पत्ररथेषु, सद्यस्तनूभूते ताम्यति तमसि, मन्दीभूतात्मस्नेहेष्वभावमभिलषत्सु प्रदीपेषु, स्फुरदरुणकिरणवल्कलप्रावृतवपुषि प्रव्रज्यामिव प्रतिपन्ने नभसि, प्रभातसमयेन समुत्तीर्यमाणासु पार्थिवास्थिशकलकलास्विव कलविङ्ककन्धराधूसरासु तारकासु, भूभृद्धातुगर्भकुम्भधारिषु विविधसरःसरित्तीर्थाभिमुखेषु प्रस्थितेषु वनकरिकुलेषु, शावशुचिसिक्थपटलपाण्डुरे पिण्ड इवापरपयोनिधिपुलिनपरिसरे पात्यमाने शशिनि, क्रमेण नृपचितानलधूमविसरधूसरीकृततेजसीव नरपतिशोकपावकदाहकिणकलङ्ककालीकृतचेतसीव प्रोषितसमस्तान्तःपुरपुरंध्रिमुखचन्द्रवृन्दोद्वेगविद्राणवपुषीव प्रथमास्तमितरोहिणीरणरणकविमनसीव चास्तमुपगते रजनिकरे, राजतीव देवे दिवमारूढे सवितरि, परिवृत्ते

राज्य इव रजनीप्रबन्धे प्रबुद्धराजहंसमण्डलप्रबोध्यमानः पङ्कजाकर इव चचाल[1] चोपस्नानाय देवो हर्षः। ततश्च नूपुररवविराममूकमन्दमन्दिरहंसेषु, शोकाकुलकतिपयकञ्चुकिमात्रावशेषेषु शुद्धान्तेषु, पतितयूथप इव वनगजयूथे कक्ष्यान्तरवर्तिनि पितृपरिजने, विषादिन्युपरिरुदन्निषादिनि च स्तम्भनिषण्णे निष्पन्दमन्दे राजकुञ्जरे, मन्दुरापालकाक्रन्दकथिते चाजिरभाजि राजवाजिनि, विश्रान्तजयशब्दकलकले च शून्ये च महास्थानमण्डपे दह्यमानदृष्टिर्निर्जगाम राजकुलात्। अगाच्च सरस्वतीतीरं तस्यां स्नात्वा पित्रे ददावुदकम्। अपस्नातश्चानिष्पीडितमौलिरेव परिधायोद्गमनीयदुकूलवाससी निश्वासपरो निरातपत्रो निरुत्सारणः समुपनीतेऽपि सप्तौ चरणाभ्यामेव नासाग्रासक्तेन रक्ततामरसताम्रेण चक्षुषा हृदयावशेषस्यापि पितुर्दाहशङ्कया शोकाग्निमिव उद्गिरन्नताम्बूलस्यापि सुचिरप्रक्षालितस्य कल्पतरुकिसलयस्येव[2] स्वभावपाटलस्याधरपल्लवस्य प्रभया मांसरुधिरकवलानिव हृदयाभिघातादुद्वमन्नुष्णनिश्वासमोक्षैर्भवनमाजगाम।

राजवल्लभास्तु भृत्याः सुहृदः सचिवाश्च तस्मिन्नेवाहनि निर्गत्य प्रियं पुत्रदारमुत्सृज्योद्वाष्पैर्बन्धुभिर्वार्यमाणा अपि बहुनृपगुणगणहृतहृदयाः केचिदात्मानं भृगुषु बबन्धुः, केचित्तत्रैव तीर्थेषु तस्थुः, केचिदनशनैरास्तीर्णतृणकुशा व्यथमानमानसाः शुचमसमामर्शमयन्, केचिच्छलभा इव वैश्वानरं शोकावेगविवशा विविशुः, केचिद्दारुणदुःखदहनदह्यमानहृदया गृहीतवाचस्तुषारशिखरिणं शरणमुपययुः, केचिद्विन्ध्योपत्यकासु वनकरिकुलकरशीकरासारसिच्यमानतनवः पल्लवशयनशयिनः सन्तापमशमयन्, केचित्संनिहितानपि विषयानुत्सृज्य सेवाविमुखाः परिच्छिन्नैः पिण्डकैरटवीभुवः शून्या जगृहुः, केचित्पवनाशना धर्मधना धमद्धमनयो मुनयो बभूवुः, केचिद्गृहीतकाषायाः कापिलं मतमधिजगिरे गिरिषु, केचिदाचोटितचूडामणिषु शिरःसु शरणीकृतधूर्जटयो जटा जघटिरे। अपरे परिपाटलप्रलम्बचीवराम्बरसंवीताः स्वाम्यनुरागमुज्वलं चक्रुः। अन्ये तपोवनहरिणजिह्वाञ्चलोल्लिह्यमानमूर्तयो जरां ययुः। अपरे पुनः पाणिपल्लवप्रमृष्टैराताम्ररागैर्नयनपुटैः कमण्डलुभिश्च वारि वहन्तो गृहीतव्रता मुण्डा विचेरुः।

देवमपि हर्षं तदवस्थं पितृशोकविह्वलीकृतम्, श्रियं शाप इति महीं महापातकमिति राज्यं रोग इति भोगान्भुजङ्गा इति निलयं निरय इति बन्धुं बन्धनमिति जीवितमयश इति देहं द्रोह इति कल्यतां कलङ्क इति आयुरपुण्यफलमिति आहारं विषमिति विषममृतमिति चन्दनं दहन इति कामं क्रकच इति हृदयस्फोटनमभ्युदय इति च मन्यमानम्, सर्वासु क्रियासु विमुखम्, पितृपितामहपरिग्रहागताश्चिरन्तनाः कुलपुत्राः वंशक्रमाहितगौरवाश्च ग्राह्यगिरो गुरवः श्रुतिस्मृतीतिहासविशारदाश्च जरद्द्विजातयः श्रुताभि-

---

१ 'चचाल देवो हर्षः' अ. २ 'किसलयकोमलस्येव' ब.

जनशीलशालिनो मूर्धाभिषिक्ताश्चामात्या राजानो यथावदधिगतात्मतत्त्वाश्च संस्तुता मस्करिणः समदुःखसुखाश्च[1] समाश्रिताः सनाभयश्चित्तज्ञाश्च प्रधाना सचिवाः निष्कारणबान्धवाश्च मुनयः संसारासारत्वकथनकुशला ब्रह्मवादिनः शोकापनयननिपुणाश्च पौराणिकाः पर्यवारयन्।

अस्वतन्त्रीकृतश्च तैर्मनसापि नालभत शोकानुप्रवणमाचरितुम्। अनुनीयमानश्च कथं कथमप्याहारादिकासु क्रियास्वाभिमुख्यमभजत। भ्रातृगतहृदयश्चाचिन्तयत्–अपि नाम तातस्य मरणं महाप्रलयसदृशमिदमुपश्रुत्य आर्यो बाष्पजलस्नातो न गृह्णीयाद्वल्कले, नाश्रयेद्वा राजर्षिराश्रमपदम्, न विशेद्वा पुरुषसिंहो गिरिगुहाम्, अस्रसलिलनिर्भरभरितनयननलिनयुगलो वा पश्येदनाथां पृथिवीम्, प्रथमव्यसनविषमविषविह्वलः स्मरेदात्मानं वा पुरुषोत्तमः, अनित्यतया जनितवैराग्यो वा न निराकुर्यादुपसर्पन्तीं राज्यलक्ष्मीम्, दारुणदुःखदहनप्रज्वलितदेहो वा प्रतिपद्येताभिषेकम्, इहागतो वा राजभिरभिधीयमानो न पराचीनतामाचरेत्। अतिपितृपक्षपाती खल्वार्यः। सर्वदा तातश्लाघया[2] मामभिधत्ते—'तात हर्ष, कस्यचिद्भूद्भविष्यति वा पुनः काञ्चनतालतरुप्रांशु कायप्रमाण[3]मिदम्। ईदृक्च दिवसकरप्रीत्या दिवसमुन्मुखविकसितं मुखमहाकमलम्। एतौ च वज्रस्तम्भभास्वरौ भुजकाण्डौ। एते च हसितमदालसहलधरविभ्रमा विलासाः। कोऽन्यो मानी विक्रान्तो वदान्यो वा' इति। एतानि चान्यानि च चिन्तयन्दर्शनोत्सुकहृदयो भ्रातुरागमनमुदीक्षमाणः कथं कथमप्यतिष्ठदिति।

इति श्रीबाणभट्टकृतौ हर्षचरिते महाराजमरणवर्णनं
नाम पञ्चम उच्छ्वासः।

---

१ '०सुखाश्च मुनयः' अ. २ 'तातश्लाघायाम्' ब. ३ '०प्रांशु प्रमाण०' ब.

षष्ठ उच्छ्वासः ।

उत्क्षिप्योत्क्षिप्य भुवि प्रहितनिगूढात्मदूतनीतानाम् ।
विजिगीषुरिव कृतान्तः शूराणां संग्रहं कुरुते ॥ १ ॥

विस्रब्धघातदोषः स्ववधाय खलस्य वीरकोपकरः ।
नवतरुभङ्गध्वनिरिव हरिनिद्रातस्करः करिणः ॥ २ ॥

अथ प्रथमप्रेतपिण्डभुजि भुक्ते द्विजन्मनि, गतेषूद्वेजनीयेष्वशौचदिवसेषु, चक्षुर्दाहदायिनि दीयमाने द्विजेभ्यः शयनासनचामरातपत्रामत्रपत्रशस्त्रादिके नृपनिकटोपकरणकलापे, नीतेषु तीर्थस्थानानि सह जनहृदयैः कीकसेषु, कल्पितशोकशल्ये सुधानिचयचिते चिताचैत्यचिह्ने, वनाय विसर्जिते महाजिजिति राजगजेन्द्रे, क्रमेण च मन्देष्वाक्रन्देषु, विरलीभवत्सु च विलापेषु, विश्राम्यत्यश्रुणि, शिथिलीभवत्सु श्वसितेषु, अविस्पष्टेषु हाकष्टाक्षरेषु, उत्सार्यमाणासु च व्यसनशय्यासु, उपदेशश्रवणक्षमेषु श्रोत्रेषु, अनुरोधावधानयोग्येषु हृदयेषु, गणनीयेषु नृपगुणेषु, प्रदेशवृत्तितामाश्रयति शोके, कृतेषु कविरुदितकेषु, जाते च स्वप्नावशेषदर्शने हृदयावशेषावस्थाने, चित्रावशेषाकृतौ काव्यावशेषनाम्नि नरनाथे देवो हर्षः कदाचिदुत्सृष्टव्यापारः पुञ्जीभूतवृद्धबन्धुवर्गाग्रेसरेणावनतमूकमुखेन महाजनेन मौलेनाकाल आत्मानं वेष्ट्यमानमद्राक्षीत् । दृष्ट्वा चाकरोन्मनसि—'किमन्यदार्यमागतमावेदयत्ययं शोकपराभूतो लोकाकरः' इति । वेपमानहृदयश्च पप्रच्छ प्रविशन्तमधिकतरप्रचारमन्यतमं पुरुषम् 'अङ्ग, कथय किमार्यः प्राप्तः' इति । स मन्दमब्रवीत्—'देव, यथादिशसि द्वारि' इति श्रुत्वा च सोदर्यस्नेहनिहितनिरतिशयमन्युमृदूकृतमनाः कथमपि न ववाम बाष्पवारिप्रवाहोत्पीडेन सह जीवितम् ।

अनन्तरं च द्वारपालमुक्तेन प्रथमप्रविष्टेन परिजनेनेवाक्रन्देन कथ्यमानम्, दूरद्रुतागमनमुषितबाहुल्येन विच्छिन्नच्छत्रधारेण लम्बिताम्बरवाहिना भ्रष्टभृङ्गारग्राहिणा च्युताचमनधारिणा ताम्यत्ताम्बूलिकेन खञ्जत्खड्गग्राहिणा कतिपयप्रकाशदासेरकप्रायेण बहुवासरान्तरितस्नानभोजनशयनश्यामक्षामवपुषा परिजनेन परिवृतम्, अविरलमार्गधूलिधूसरितशरीरतया शरणीकृतमिवाशरणया क्रमागतया वसुन्धरया, हूणनिर्जयसमरशरव्रणबद्धपट्टकैर्दीर्घधवलैः समासन्नराज्यलक्ष्मीकटाक्षपातैरिव शबलीकृतकायम्, अवनिपतिप्राणपरित्राणार्थमिव च शोकहुतभुजि हुतमांसैरतिकृशैरवयवैरावेद्यमानदुःखभारम्, अपगतचूडामणिनि मलिनाकुलकुन्तले शेखरशून्ये शिरसि शुचमारूढां मूर्तिमतीमिव दधानम्, आतपगलितस्वेदराजिना रुदतेव पितृपादपतनोत्कण्ठितेन ललाटपट्टेन लक्ष्यमाणम्, प्रथीयसा बाष्पपयःप्रवाहेनामिमतपतिमरणमूर्च्छि-

तामिव महीमनवरतं सिञ्चन्तम्, अनन्तसन्तताश्रुप्रवाहनिपतननिम्नीकृताविव दुःखक्षामौ कपोलावुद्वहन्तम्, अत्युष्णमुखमारुतमार्गगतेन द्रवतेव गलितताम्बूलरागेणाधरबिम्बेनोपलक्षितम्, पवित्रिकामात्रावशेषेन्द्रनीलिकांशुश्यामायमानमचिरश्रुतपितृमरणमहाशोकाग्निदग्धमिव श्रवणप्रदेशमुद्वहन्तम्, अस्फुटाभिव्यक्तव्यञ्जनेनाप्यधोमुखस्तिमितनयननीलतारकामयूखमालाखचितेन शोकप्ररूढश्मश्रुश्यामलेनेव मुखशशिना लक्ष्यमाणम्, केशरिणमिव महाभूभृद्विनिपातविह्वलं निरवलम्बनम्, दिवसमिव तेजःपतिपतनपरिम्लानश्रियं श्यामीभूतम्, नन्दनमिव भग्नकल्पपादपं विच्छायम्, दिग्भावमिव प्रोषितदिक्कुञ्जरं शून्यम्, गिरिमिव गुरुवज्रपातदारितं कम्पमानम्, क्रीतमिव ऋशिम्ना, किङ्करीकृतमिव कारुण्येन, दासीकृतमिव दौर्मनस्येन, शिष्यीकृतमिव शोचितव्येन, आत्मीकृतमिवाधिना[1], मूकीकृतमिव मौनेन, पिष्टमिव पीडया, स्विन्नमिव सन्तापेन, उच्चितमिव चिन्तया, लुप्तमिव विलापेन, धृतमिव वैराग्येण, प्रत्याख्यातमिव प्रतिसंख्यानेन, अवज्ञातमिव प्रज्ञया, दूरीकृतमिव दुरभिभवत्वेन, अबोध्येन वृद्धबुद्धीनाम्, असाध्येन साधुभाषितानाम्, अगम्येन गुरुगिराम्, अशक्येन शास्त्रशक्तीनाम्, अपथेन प्रज्ञाप्रयत्नानाम्, अगोचरेण सुहृदनुरोधानाम्, अविषयेण विषयोपभोगानाम्, अभूमिभूतेन कालक्रमोपचयानां शोकेन कवलीकृतं ज्येष्ठं भ्रातरमपश्यत्। आवेगोद्गतकृत्स्नस्नेहोत्कलिकाकलापोत्क्षिप्यमाणकाय इव च परवशः समुदगात्।

अथ तं दूरादेव दृष्ट्वा देवो राज्यवर्धनश्चिरकालकलितं बाष्पवेगं मुमुक्षुः सुदूरप्रसारितेन सङ्कलयन्निव सर्वदुःखानि दीर्घेण दोर्दण्डद्वयेन गृहीत्वा कण्ठे मुक्तकण्ठं पुनः पतितक्षौमे क्षामे वक्षसि पुनः कण्ठे पुनः स्कन्धभागे पुनः कपोलोदरे निधाय तथा तथा रुरोद यथा सबन्धनानीवोदपाट्यन्त हृदयानि । अश्रुस्रोतः शिरा इव अमुच्यत लोचनेषु लोकेन[2]। स्मृतनृपतिना राजवल्लभेनापि प्रतिशब्दनिभेन निर्भरमिवारुद्यत। सुचिराच्च कथं कथमपि निर्वृष्टनयनजलः पर्जन्य इव शरदि स्वयमेवोपशशाम। उपविष्टश्च परिजनोपनीतेन तोयेन तत्कर[3]नखमयूखपुञ्जतया महाजलप्लवजायमानफेनलेखमिव पुनः पुनः प्रमृष्टमपि पक्ष्माग्रसङ्गलद्बिन्दुवृन्दमन्दोन्मेषमुषितदर्शनं कथं कथमपि चक्षुरक्षालयत्। ताम्बूलिकोपस्थापितेन च वाससा चन्द्रातपशकलेनेवोष्णोष्णबाष्पदग्धं वदनमुन्ममार्ज। तूष्णीमेव च चिरं स्थित्वोत्थाय स्नानभूमिमगात्। तस्यां च स्थित्वा विभूषं विलस्तव्यस्तकुन्तलं मौलिमनादरान्निष्पीड्य सावशेषमन्युस्फुरितेन जिजीविषतेव जलधौतसुभगमात्मानमपि चुचुम्बिषतेवाधरेण क्षालितस्य चक्षुषः श्वेतिम्ना च शारदशशिकरविकसित-

---

१ 'अन्धीकृत०' ब. २ एतद्वाक्यं नास्ति अ-पुस्तके. ३ 'तरत्कर०' ब.

विशदकुमुदवनदलावलिबलिविक्षेपैरिव दिग्देवतार्चनकर्म कुर्वाणश्चतुःशालवितर्दिकायां नीचापाश्रयविनिहितैकोपबर्हायां पर्यङ्किकायां निपत्य जोषमस्थात्।

देवोऽपि हर्षस्तथैव स्नात्वा धरणितलनिहितकुथाप्रसारितमूर्तिरदूर एवास्य तूष्णीमेव समवातिष्ठत। दृष्ट्वा दृष्ट्वा दूयमानमानसमग्रजन्मानं समस्फुटदिवास्य सहस्रधा हृदयम्। औरसदर्शनं हि यौवनं शोकस्य। लोकस्य तु नरपतिमरणदिवसादपि दारुणः स बभूव दिवसः। सर्वस्मिन्नेव नगरे न केनचिदपाचि न केनचिदस्नायि नाभोजि सर्वत्र सर्वेणारोदि। केवलमनेन क्रमेणातिचक्राम दिवसः। स च प्रत्यग्रत्वष्टृटङ्कतष्टतनुरिव वहद्बहलरुधिररसमांसच्छविरपरपारावारपयसि ममज्ज मञ्जिष्ठारुणोऽरुणसारथिः। मुकुलायमानकमलिनीकोषविकलं चकाण चञ्चरीककुलं कमलसरसि। सविधविरहव्याधिविधुरवधूवाध्यमानं बबन्ध बन्धाविव विबुद्धबन्धूकभासि भास्वति सास्रां दृशं चक्रवाकचक्रवालम्। सञ्चरन्त्याः समधुकररवं कैरवाकरं कलहंसरमणीरमणीयं माणिक्यकाञ्चीकिङ्किणीजालमिवा[2]ण श्रियः। प्रकटकलङ्कमुदयमानं विशङ्कटविषाणोत्कीर्णपङ्कसङ्करशङ्करशङ्कु[3]रशक्करककुदकूटसङ्काशमकाशताकाशे शशाङ्कमण्डलम्।

अस्यां च वेलायामनतिक्रमणवचनैरुपसृत्य प्रधानसामन्तैर्विज्ञाप्यमानः कथं कथमप्यभुक्त। प्रभातायां च शर्वर्यां सर्वेषु प्रविष्टेषु राजसु समीपस्थितं हर्षदेवमुवाच—'तात, भूमिरसि गुरुनियोगानाम्। शैशव एवाग्राहि गुणवत्पताकेव भवता तातस्य चित्तवृत्तिः। यतो भवन्तमेवंविधं विधेयं विधिविधानोपनतनैर्घृण्यमिदं किमपि विभणिषति मे हृदयम्। नावलम्बनीया बालभावसुलभा प्रेमविलोपा वामता। वैधेय इव मा कृथाः प्रत्यूहमीहितेऽस्मिन्। शृणु। न खलु न जानासि लोकवृत्तम्। लोकत्रयत्रातरि मान्धातरि मृते किं कृतं पुरुकुत्सेन भ्रूलतादिष्टाष्टादशद्वीपे दिलीपे वा रघुणा महासुरसमरमध्याध्यासितत्रिदशरथे दशरथे वा रामेण गोष्पदीकृतचतुरुदन्वदन्ते दुष्यन्ते वा भरतेन। तिष्ठन्तु तावदेते तातेनैव शतसमधिकाध्वरधूमविसरधूसरितवासववयसि सुगृहीतनाम्नि तत्रभवति परासुतां गते पितरि किं नाकारि राज्यम्। यं च किल शोकः समभिभवति तं कापुरुषमाचक्षते शास्त्रविदः। स्त्रियो हि विषयः शुचाम्। तथापि किं करोमि। स्वभावस्य सेयं कापुरुषता वा स्त्रैणं वा यदेवमोऽस्पदं[4] पितृशोकहुतभुजो जातोस्मि। मम हि भूभृति पर्यस्ते निरवशेषतः प्रस्रवणानीव स्रुतान्यश्रूण्यस्तमिते महति तेजस्यन्धकारीभूतदशाशस्य प्रणष्टः प्रज्ञालोकः[5] प्रज्वलितं हृदयम्, आत्मदाहभीत इव स्वप्नेऽपि नोपसर्पति विवेकः, बली-

---

१ 'वितर्दिकाविनिवेशितायामप्रतिपादिकायां चापाश्रय०' ब. २ 'जालमिवाचकाण' अ. ३ 'बर्कुरशक्कर' ब. ४ 'यदेवमसादपि' ब. ५ 'प्रज्ञानलोकः' अ.

यसा सन्तापेन जातुषमिव विलीनमखिलं धैर्यम्, पदे पदे दिग्धरोपाहतेव हरिणी मुह्यति मतिः, पुरुषद्वेषिणीव [1]दूरेण भ्रमति परिहरन्ती स्मृतिः, अम्बेव तातेनैव सह गता धृतिः, वार्द्धुषिकप्रयुक्तानीव वित्तानि प्रतिदिवसं वर्धन्ते दुःखानि, शोकानलधूमसम्भारसम्भूताम्भोधरभरितमिव वर्षति नयनवारिधाराविसरं शरीरम्। सर्वः पञ्चजनः प[2]ञ्चत्वमुपरतः प्रयाति वितथमेतद्वदति बालो लोकः। तातो हुताशनतामेव केवला[3]मापन्नो येनैवं दहति माम्। इदमसाम्परायिकमिव हृदयमवष्टभ्य व्युत्थितः शोको दुर्निवारः वाडव इव वारिराशिम्, पविरिव पर्वतम्, क्षय इव क्षपाकरम्, राहुरिव रविम्, दहति दारयति तनूकरोति कवलयति च माम्। न शक्नोति मे हृदयं तादृशस्य सुमेरुकल्पस्य कल्पमहापुरुषस्य विनिपातमश्रुभिरेव केवलैरतिवाहयितुम्। राज्ये विष इव चकोरस्य मे विरक्तं चक्षुः। बहुमृतपटावगुण्ठनां रञ्जितरङ्कां जनङ्गमानामिव वंशबाह्यामनार्यां श्रियं त्यक्तुमभिलषति मे मनः। क्षणमपि दग्धगृहे शकुलिरिव न पारयामि स्थातुम्। सोऽहमिच्छामि मनसि वाससीव सुलग्नं स्नेहमलमिदममलैः शिखरिशिखरप्रस्रवणस्वच्छस्रोतोऽम्बुभिः क्षालयितुमाश्रमपदे। यतस्त्वमन्तरितयौवनसुखामनभिमतामपि जरामिव पूरुराज्ञया गुरोर्गृहाण मे राज्यचिन्ताम्। त्यक्तसकलबालक्रीडेन हरिणेव दीयतामुरो लक्ष्म्यै। परित्यक्तं मया शस्त्रम्।' इत्येवमभिधाय खड्गग्राहिणो हस्तादादाय निजं निस्त्रिंशमुत्ससर्ज धरण्याम्।

अथ तच्छ्रुत्वा निशितशिखेन शूलेनेवाहतः प्रविदीर्णहृदयो देवो हर्षः समचिन्तयत्—किं नु खलु मामन्तरेणार्यः केनचिदसहिष्णुना किंचिद्व्याहितः कुपितः स्यात्। उतानया दिशा परीक्षितुकामो माम्। उत शोकजन्मा चेतसः समाक्षेपोऽयमस्य। आहोस्विदार्य एवायं न भवति। किं वार्येणान्यदेवाभिहितमन्यदेवाश्रावि मया शोकशून्येन श्रवणेन्द्रियेण। आर्यस्य वान्यदेव विवक्षितमन्यदेवापतितं मुखेन। अथवा सकलवंशविनाशाय निपातनोपायोऽयं विधेः, मम वा निखिलपुण्यपरिक्षयोपक्षेपः कर्मणामननुकूलसमग्रग्रहचक्रवालविलसितं वा, अथवा तातविनाशनिःशङ्ककलिकालक्रीडितं येनायं यः कश्चिदिव यत्किंचनकारिणं मामपुष्पभूतिवंशसम्भूतमिव, अताततनयमिव, अनात्मानुजमिव, अभक्तमिव, अ[4]दृष्टदोषमपि श्रोत्रियमिव सुरापाने सद्भृत्यमिव स्वामिद्रोहे सज्जनमिव नीचोपसर्पणे सुकलत्रमिव व्यभिचारे, अतिदुष्करे कर्मणि समादिष्टवान्। तदेतत्तावदनुरूपं यच्छौर्योन्मादमदिरोन्मत्तसमस्तसामन्तमण्डलसमुद्रमथनम[5]न्दरे तादृशि पितरि मृते तपोवनं वा गम्यते वल्कलानि वा गृह्यन्ते तपांसि वा सेव्यन्ते। या तु मयि राज्याज्ञा सा दग्धेऽपि दाहकारिणी मय्यवग्रहग्लपिते धन्वनीवाङ्गार-

---

१ 'दूरत एव भ्रमन्ती परिहरति' अ. २ 'उपरतः' इति नास्ति ब-पुस्तके. ३ 'आपन्नोऽपि नैवं मां दहति.' ब. ४ 'दृष्टदोषमिव' अ. ५ 'मन्दिरे' ब.

वृष्टिः। तदसदृशमिदमार्यस्य। यद्यपि च विभुरनभिमानः, द्विजातिरनेषणः, मुनिररोषणः, कपिरचपलः, कविरमत्सरः, वणिगतस्करः, प्रियजानिरकुहनः, साधुरदरिद्रः, द्रविणवानखलः, कीनाशोऽनक्षिगतः, मृगयुरहिंस्रः, पाराशरी ब्राह्मण्यः, सेवकः सुखी, कितवः कृतज्ञः[1], गोप्यः प्रियवाक्, अमात्यः सत्यवादी, राजसूनुरदुर्विनीतश्च जगति दुर्लभः, तथापि ममार्य एवाचार्यः। को हि नाम तद्विधे निपतिते राजगन्धकुञ्जरे जनयितरि ईदृशे च विफलीकृतविशालशिलास्तम्भोरुभुजे भूपजिति भ्रातरि त्यक्तराज्ये ज्यायसि नववयसि तपोवनं गच्छति सकललोकलोचनजलपातापवित्रं मृद्वोलकं वसुधाभिधानं धनमदखेलनिखिलखलमुखविकारलक्षणाख्यायमाननीचाचरणां श्रीसंज्ञिकां सुभटकुटुम्बकर्मकुम्भदासीं चण्डालोऽपि कामयेत। कथमिव सम्भावितमत्यन्तमनुचितमिदमार्येण। किमुपलक्षितमनवदातमिदं मयि। किं वास्य चेतसश्च्युतः सौमित्रिर्विस्मृता वा वृकोदरप्रभृतयः। अनपेक्षितभक्तजना स्वार्थैकनिष्पादननिष्ठुरा नासीदियमार्यस्येदृशी प्रभविष्णुता। अपि चार्ये तपोवनं गते जिजीविषुः को हि नाम महीं मनसापि ध्यायेत्। कुलिशशिखरखरनखरप्रचयप्रचण्डचपेटापाटितमत्तमातङ्गोत्तमाङ्गमदच्छटाच्छुरितचारुकेसरभारभास्वरमुखे केसरिणि वनविहाराय विनिर्गते निवासं गिरिगुहां कः पाति पृष्ठतः। प्रतापसहाया हि सत्त्ववन्तः। कश्चपलां लक्ष्मीं प्रत्यनुरोधोऽयमार्यस्य यदीयमपि न चीवरान्तरितकुचा कुशकुसुमसमित्पलाशपूलिकां वहन्ती तत्रैव तपोवने वनमृगीव नीयते जराजालिनी। किं वा ममानेन वृथा बहुधा विकल्पितेन। तूष्णीमेवार्यमनुगमिष्यामि। गुरुवचनातिक्रमकृतं च किल्बिषमेतत्तपोवने तप एवापास्यति। इत्यवधार्य मनसा प्रथमतरं गतस्तपोवनमधोमुखस्तूष्णीमवातिष्ठत।

अत्रान्तरे पूर्वादिष्टेनैव रुदता वस्त्रकर्मान्तिकेन समुपस्थापितेषु वल्कलेषु निर्दयकरतलताडनमिव क्वापि गते हृदये रटति राजस्त्रैणे तारमब्रह्मण्यमूर्ध्वदोष्णि विरुदति विप्रजने, पादप्रणतिपरे फूत्कुर्वति पौरवृन्दे, विद्राति विद्रुतचेतसि चिरन्तने परिजने, परिजनावलम्बिते[2] वेपमानवपुषि पर्याकुलवाससि शोकगद्गदवचसि गलितनयनपयसि निवारणोद्यतमनसि[3] वर्षीयसि विशति बन्धुवर्गे, निराशेषु नखलिखितमणिकुट्टिमेष्ववाङ्मुखेषु निश्वसत्सु सामन्तेषु, सबालवृद्धासु तपोवनाय प्रस्थितासु सर्वासु प्रजासु सहसैव प्रविश्य शोकविक्लवः प्रक्षरितनयनसलिलो राज्यश्रियः परिचारकः संवादको नाम प्रज्ञाततमो विमुक्ताक्रन्दः सदस्यात्मानमपातयत्।

अथ संभ्रान्तो भ्रात्रा सह स्वयं देवो राज्यवर्धनस्तं पर्यपृच्छत्—'भद्र, भण भण किमसद्व्यसनव्यवसायवर्धनबद्धधृतिः[4], अवनिपतिमरणमुदित-

१ 'कृतज्ञः, परिव्राडबुभुक्षुः, नृशंसः प्रियवाक्' अ. २ '०लम्बिते गते वर्षीयसि' ब. ३ '०मनसि विशति' ब. ४ '०व्यसनमव्यवसाय' अ.

मतिः, अधृतिकरमपरमधिकतरमितः दुःखातिशयं समुपनयति विधिः' इति। स कथं कथमप्यकथयत्—'देव, पिशाचानामिव नीचात्मनां चरितानि छिद्रप्रहारीणि प्रायशो भवन्ति। यतो यस्मिन्नहन्यवनिपतिरुपरत इत्यभूद्वार्ता तस्मिन्नेव देवो ग्रहवर्मा दुरात्मना मालवराजेन जीवलोकमात्मनः सुकृतेन सह त्याजितः। भर्तृदारिकापि राज्यश्रीः कालायसनिगडयुगलचुम्बितचरणा चौराङ्गनेव संयता कान्यकुब्जे कारायां निक्षिप्ता। किंवदन्ती च यथा किलानायकं साधनं मत्वा जिघृक्षुः सुदुर्मतिरेतामपि भुवमाजिगमिषतीति विज्ञापिते प्रभुः प्रभवति' इति।

ततश्च तादृशमनुपेक्षणीयमसम्भावितमाकस्मिकमपरं व्यतिकरमाकर्ण्याश्रुतपूर्वत्वात्परिभवस्य, परपरिभवासहिष्णुतया च स्वभावस्य, दर्पबहुलतया च नवयौवनस्य, वीरक्षेत्रसम्भवत्वाच्च जन्मनः, कृपाभूमिभूतायाश्च स्वसुः स्नेहात्स तादृशोऽपि बद्धमूलोऽप्यत्यन्तगुरुरेकपद एवास्य ननाश शोकावेगः। विवेश च सहसा केसरीव गिरिगुहागृहं गम्भीरं हृदयं भयङ्करः कोपावेगः। केशिनिषूदनशङ्काकुलकालियकुलभङ्गुरभ्रूभङ्गतरङ्गिणी श्यामायमाना यमस्वसेव प्रथीयसि ललाटपट्टे भीषणा भ्रुकुटिरुदभिद्यत। दर्पात्परामृशन्नखकिरणसलिलनिर्झरैः समरभारसम्भावनाभिषेकमिव चकार दिङ्नागकुम्भकूटविकटस्य बाहुशिखरकोषस्य वामः पाणिपल्लवः। सङ्गलत्स्वेदसलिलपूरितोदरो निर्मूलं मालवोन्मूलनाय गृहीतकेश इव दुर्मदश्रीकचग्रहोत्कण्ठयेव च कम्पमानः पुनरपि समुत्ससर्प भीषणं कृपाणं पाणिरपरः। शस्त्रग्रहणमुदितराजलक्ष्मीक्रियमाणदिष्टवृद्धिविधुतसिन्दूरधूलिरिव कपिलः कपोलयोरदृश्यत रोषरागः। समासन्नसकलमहीपालचूडामणिचक्राक्रमणजाताहङ्कार इव च समारुरोह वाममूरुदण्डमुत्तानितश्चरणो दक्षिणः। निष्ठुराङ्गुष्ठकषणनिष्ठ्यूतधूमलेखो निर्वीरोर्वीकरणाय विमुक्तशिख इव लिलेख मणिकुट्टिममितरः पादपद्मः। दर्पस्फुटितसरसव्रणोच्छलितरुधिरच्छटावसेकैः शोकविषप्रसुप्तं प्रबोधयन्निव पराक्रममनुजमवादीत्—'आयुष्मन्, इदं राजकुलम्, अमी बान्धवाः, परिजनोऽयम्, इयं भूमिः, भूपतिभुजपरिघपालिताश्चैताः प्रजाः गतोऽहमद्यैव मालवराजकुलप्रलयाय। इदमेव तावद्वल्कलग्रहणमिदमेव तपः शोकापगमोपायश्चायमेव यदत्यन्ताविनीतारिनिग्रहः। सोऽयं कुरङ्गकैः कचग्रहः केशरिणः, भेकैः करपातः कालसर्पस्य, वत्सकैर्बन्दिग्रहो व्याघ्रस्य, अलगर्दैर्गलग्रहो गरुडस्य, दारुभिर्दाहादेशो दहनस्य, तिमिरैस्तिरस्कारो रवेः, [2]यो मौखराणां मालवैः परिभवः पुष्पभूतिवंशस्य च। अन्तरितस्तापो मे महीयसा मन्युना। तिष्ठन्तु सर्व एव राजानः करिणश्च त्वयैव सार्धम्। अयमेको भण्डिरयुतमात्रेण तुरङ्गमाणामनुयातु माम्।' इत्यभिधाय चानन्तरमेव प्रयाणपटहमादिदेश।

---

१ 'इतः समुपनयति' अ. २ 'यो मालवैः' अ.

तं च तथा समादिशन्तमाकर्ण्य जामिजामातृवृत्तान्तविज्ञानप्रकोपाधानदूयमाने मनसि निवर्तनापदेशेन[1] दूरप्ररूढप्रणयपीड इव प्रोवाच देवो हर्षः—'कमिव दोषं पश्यत्यार्यो ममानुगमनेन । यदि बाल इति नितरां तर्हि न परित्याज्योऽस्मि, रक्षणीय इति भवद्भुजपञ्जरं रक्षास्थानम्, अशक्त इति क्व परीक्षितोऽस्मि, संवर्धनीय इति वियोगस्तनूकरोति, अक्लेशसह इति स्त्रीपक्षे निक्षिप्तोऽस्मि, सुखमनुभवत्विति त्वयैव सह तत्प्रयाति, महानध्वनः क्लेश इति विरहोऽविषह्यतरः, कलत्रं रक्षत्विति श्रीस्ते निस्त्रिंशेऽधिवसति, पृष्ठतस्तिष्ठत्विति[2] तिष्ठत्येव ते प्रतापः, राजकमनधिष्ठितमिति तत्सुबद्धमार्यगुणैः, न बाह्यः सहायो महत इति व्यतिरिक्तमेव मां गणयसि, प्रलघुपरिकरः प्रयामीति पादरजसि कोऽतिभारः, द्वयोर्गमनमसांप्रतमिति मामनुगृहाण गमनाज्ञया, कातरो भ्रातृस्नेह इति सदृशो दोषः । का चेयमात्मम्भरिता भुजस्य ते यदेकाकी क्षीरोदफेनपटलपाण्डुरममृतमिव यशः पिपासति । अवञ्चितपूर्वोऽस्मि प्रसादेषु[3] । तत्प्रसीदत्वार्यो नयतु मामपि' इत्यभिधाय क्षितितलविनिहितमौलिः पादयोरपतत् ।

तमुत्थाप्य पुनरग्रजो जगाद—'तात किमेवमतिमहारम्भपरिग्रहणेन गरिमाणमारोप्यते बलादतिलघीयानप्यहितः । हरिणार्थमतिह्रेपणः सिंहसम्भारः । तृणानामुपरि कति कवचयन्त्याशुशुक्षणयः । अपि च तवाष्टादशद्वीपाष्टमङ्गलकमालिनी मेदिन्यस्त्येव विक्रमस्य विषयः । नहि कुलशैलनिवहवाहिनो वायवः संनह्यन्त्यतितरले तूलराशौ । न सुमेरुवप्रप्रणयप्रगल्भा वा दिक्करिणः परिणमन्त्यणीयसि वल्मीके । ग्रहीष्यसि सकलपृथ्वीपतिप्रलयोत्पातमहाधूमकेतुं मान्धातेव चारुचामीकरपत्रलतालङ्काराङ्ककायं कार्मुकं ककुभां विजये । मम तु दुर्निवारायामस्यां विपक्षक्षपणक्षुधि क्षुभितायां क्षम्यतामयमेकाकिनः कोपकवल एकः । तिष्ठतु भवान् ।' इत्यभिधाय च तस्मिन्नेव वासरे निर्जगामाभ्यमित्रम् ।

अथ तथागते भ्रातरि, उपरते च पितरि, प्रोषितजीविते च जामातरि, मृतायां च मातरि, संयतायां च स्वसरि, स्वयूथभ्रष्ट इव वन्यः करी देवो हर्षः कथं कथमप्येकाकी कालं तमनैषीत् । अतिक्रान्तेषु बहुषु वासरेषु कदाचित्तयैव भ्रातृगमनदुःखासिकया दत्तप्रजागरस्त्रिभागशेषायां त्रियामायां यामिकेन गीयमानामिमामार्यां शुश्राव—

'द्वीपोपगीतगुणमपि समुपार्जितरत्नराशिसारमपि ।
पोतं पवन इव विधिः पुरुषमकाण्डे निपातयति ॥ ३ ॥'

तां च श्रुत्वा सुतरामनित्यताभावनया दूयमानहृदयः प्रक्षीणभूयिष्ठायां क्षपायां क्षणमिव निद्रामलभत स्वप्ने चाभ्रंलिहं लोहस्तम्भं भज्यमानमपश्यत् । उत्कम्पमानहृदयश्च पुनः प्रत्यबुध्यत । अचिन्तयच्च—'किं नु खलु

---

१ 'निवर्तनादेशेन' अ. २ 'पृष्ठतः शून्य'-ब. ३ 'विप्रप्रसादेषु' ब.

मामेवममी सततमनुबध्नन्ति दुःस्वप्नाः। स्फुरति च दिवानिशमकल्याणाख्यानविचक्षणमदक्षिणमक्षि। सुदारुणाश्चाक्षुद्रक्षितिपक्षयमाचक्षाणाः क्षणमपि न शाम्यन्ति पुनरुत्पाताः। प्रत्यहं राहुरविकलकायबन्ध इव कबन्धवति ब्रध्नबिम्बे घटमानो विभाव्यते। तपःकरणकालकवलितानिव धूसरितसमग्रग्रहानुद्गिरन्ति धूमोद्गारान्सप्तर्षयः। दिने दिने दारुणा दिशां दाहा दृश्यन्ते। दिग्दाहभस्मकणनिकर इव निपतति नभस्तलात्तारागणः। तारापातशुचेव निष्प्रभः शशी। निशि निशि इतस्ततः प्रज्वलिताभिरुल्काभिरुग्रं ग्रहयुद्धमिव वियति विलोकयन्ति विलोलतारकाः ककुभः। राज्यसञ्चारसूचकः सञ्चारयतीव क्ष्मां क्वापि वहद्बहलरजःपटलकलिलशर्कराशकलसूत्कारी मारुतः। न कुशलमिव पश्यामि लग्नस्य। अस्मिन्नस्मद्वंशे करिण इव करीरं कोमलमपि कलयतः कृतान्तस्य कः परिपन्थी। सर्वथा स्वस्ति भवत्वार्याय।' इति चिन्तयित्वा च अन्तर्भिन्नं भ्रातृस्नेहकातरं द्रवदिव हृदयं कथं कथमपि संस्तभ्योत्थाय यथाक्रियमाणं क्रियाकलापमकरोत्।

आस्थानगतश्च सहसैव प्रविशन्तम्, अनुप्रविशता विषण्णवदनेन लोकेनानुगम्यमानम्, असह्यदुःखोष्णनिश्वासधूमरक्ततन्तुनेव मलिनेन पटेन प्रावृतवपुषम्, जीवितधारणलज्जयेवावनतमुखम्, नासावंशस्याग्रे ग्रथितदृष्टिम्, दुःखदूरप्ररूढरोम्णा मूकेनापि मुखेन स्वामिव्यसनमविच्छिन्नैरश्रुबिन्दुभिर्विज्ञापयन्तं कुन्तलं नाम बृहदश्ववारम्, राज्यवर्धनस्य प्रसादभूमिमभिजाततमं[1] ददर्श। दृष्ट्वा च जाताशङ्कश्चक्षुषि सलिलेन, मुखशशिनि श्वसितेन, हृदये हुताशेन, उत्सङ्गे भुवा, दारुणाप्रियश्रवणसमये सममिव सर्वैष्वङ्गेष्वगृह्यत लोकपालैः। तस्माच्च हेलानिर्जितमालवानीकमपि गौडाधिपेन मिथ्योपचारोपचितविश्वासं मुक्तशस्त्रमेकाकिनं विश्रब्धं स्वभवन एव भ्रातरं व्यापादितमश्रौषीत्।

श्रुत्वा च महातेजस्वी प्रचण्डकोपपावकप्रसरपरिचीयमानशोकावेगः सहसैव प्रजज्वाल। ततश्चामर्षविधुतशिरःशीर्यमाणशिखामणिशकलाङ्गारकिर्तमिव[2] रोषाग्निमुद्वमन्, अनवरतस्फुरितेन पिबन्निव सर्वतेजस्विनामायूंषि रोषनिर्भुग्नेन दशनच्छदेन, लोहितायमानलोचनालोकविक्षेपैर्दिग्दाहानिव दर्शयन्, रोषानलेनाप्यसह्यसहजशौर्योष्मदहनदह्यमानेनेव वितन्यमानस्वेदसलिलशीकरासारदुर्दिनः, स्वावयवैरप्यदृष्टपूर्वप्रकोपभीतैरिव कम्पमानैरुपेतः, हर इव कृतभैरवाकारः, हरिरिव प्रकटितनरसिंहरूपः, सूर्यकान्तशैल इवापरतेजःप्रसरदर्शनप्रज्वलितः, क्षयदिवस इवोदितद्वादशदिनकरदुर्निरीक्ष्यमूर्तिः, महोत्पातमारुत इव सकलभूभृत्कम्पकारी, विन्ध्य इव विवर्धमानविग्रहोत्सेधः, महाशीविष इव दुर्नरेन्द्राभिभवरोषितः, पारीक्षित इव सर्वभोगिदहनोद्यतः, वृकोदर इव रिपुरुधिरतृषितः, सुरगज इव प्रतिपक्षवारणप्र-

---

१ 'अभिज्ञात०' ब. २ 'शकलाङ्गारकिताङ्गमिव' ब.

धावितः, पूर्वागम इव पौरुषस्य, उन्माद इव मदस्य, आवेग इवावलेपस्य, तारुण्यावतार इव तेजसः, सर्वोद्योग इव दर्पस्य, युगागम इव यौवनोष्मणः, राज्याभिषेक इव रणरसस्य, नीराजनदिवस इवासहिष्णुतायाः, परां भीषणतामयासीत्।

अवादीच्च। 'गौडाधिपाधममपहाय कस्तादृशं महापुरुषं तत्क्षण एव निर्व्याजभुजवीर्यनिर्जितसमस्तराजकं मुक्तशस्त्रं कलशयोनिमिव कृष्णवर्त्मप्रसूतिरीदृशेन सर्ववीरलोकविगर्हितेन मृत्युना शमयेदार्यम्। अनार्यं च तं मुक्त्वा भागीरथीफेनपटलपाण्डुराः केषां मनःसु सरःसु राजहंसा इव परशुरामपराक्रमस्मृतिकृतो न कुर्युरार्यशौर्यगुणाः पक्षपातम्। कथमिवात्युग्रस्यास्यार्यजीवितहरणे निदाघरवेरिव कमलाकरसलिलशोषणेऽनपेक्षितप्रीतयः प्रसृताः कराः। कां नु गतिं गमिष्यति, कां वा योनिं प्रवेक्ष्यति, कस्मिन्वा नरके निपतिष्यति। श्वपाकोऽपि क इदमाचरेत्। नामापि गृह्णतोऽस्य पापकारिणः पापमलेन लिप्यत इव मे जिह्वा। किं वाङ्गीकृत्य कार्यमार्यस्तेन क्षुद्रेणानुप्रविश्य विगतघृणेन घुणेनेव सकलभुवनाह्लादनचतुरश्चन्दनस्तम्भः क्षयमुपनीतः। नूनं नानेन मूढेन मधुरसास्वादलुब्धेन मध्विवार्यजीवितमाकर्षता भावी दृष्टः[1] कष्टशिलीमुखसम्पातोपद्रवः। निजगृहदूषणं जालमार्गप्रदीपकेन कज्जलमिवातिमलिनं केवलमयशः सञ्चितं[2] गौडाधमेन। न त्वाश्वेवास्तमुपगतवत्यपि त्रिभुवनचूडामणौ सवितरि वेधसादिष्टः[3] सत्पथशत्रोरन्धकारस्य निग्रहाय ग्रहषण्डविहारैकहरिणाधिपः शशी। विनयविधायिनि भग्नेऽपि चाङ्कुशे विद्यत एव व्यालवारणस्य विनयाय सकलमत्तमातङ्गकुम्भस्थलस्थिरशिरोभागभिदुरः खरतरः केसरिनखरः। तादृशाः कुवैकटिका इव तेजस्विरत्नविनाशकाः कस्य न वध्याः। क्वेदानीं यास्यति दुर्बुद्धिः।' इत्येतदभिदधत एवास्य पितुरपि मित्रं सेनापतिः समग्रविग्रहप्राग्रहरो हरितालशैलावदातदेहः, परिणतप्रगुणसालप्रकाण्डप्रकाशः, प्रांशुरतिशौर्योष्मणेव परिपाकमागतो गतभूयिष्ठे वयसि वर्तमानः, बहुशरशयनसुप्तोत्थितोऽपि हसन्निव शान्तनवमतिदीर्घेणायुषा, दुरभिभवशरीरतया जरयापि भीतभीतयेव प्रकटितप्रकम्पया परामृष्टः कथमपि सारमयेषु शिरोरुहेषु, शशिकरनिकरसितसरलशिरोरुहसटालः[4] सैंहीमिव निष्कपटपराक्रमरसरचितां संक्रान्तो जीवन्नेव जातिम्, अपरस्वामिमुखदर्शनमहापातकपरिजिहीर्षयेव भ्रूयुगलेन वलिन[5]शिथिलप्रलम्बचर्मणा स्थगितदृष्टिः, धवलस्थूलगुञ्जापिच्छप्रच्छादितकपोलभागभास्वरेण वमन्निव विक्रमकालमकालेऽपि विकाशिकाशकाननविशदं शरदारम्भं भीमेन मुखेन, मृतमपि हृदयस्थितं स्वामिनमिव सितचामरेण वीजयन्नाभिलम्बेन कूर्चकलापेन, परिणामेऽपि धौतासिधाराजलपानतृषितैरिव विवृतवदनैर्बृहद्भिर्व्रणविदारैर्विषमितविशालवक्षाः, निशितशस्त्रटङ्ककोटि-

१ 'दृष्टः शिली'-अ. २ 'सञ्चितं नत्वाश्वेवास्त' ब. ३ 'वेधसादिसृष्टः' ब.
४ 'सटालाम्' अ. ५ 'वलित' अ.

कुट्टितबहुबृहद्व्रणाक्षरपङ्क्तिनिरन्तरतया च सकलसमरविजयपर्वगणनामिव कुर्वन्पूर्वपर्वत इव[1] पादचारी, विविधवीररसवृत्तान्तरामणीयकेन महाभारतमपि लघयन्निव, प्रतिपक्षक्षपणातिनिर्बन्धेन परशुराममपि शिक्षयन्निव, अब्भ्रमणेनानादरश्रीसमाकर्षणविभ्रमेण मन्दरमपि मन्दयन्निव, वाहिनीनायकमर्यादानुवर्तनेनाम्भोधिमप्यभिभवन्निव, स्थैर्यकार्कश्योन्नतिभिरचलानपि ह्रेपयन्निव, सहजप्रचण्डतेजःप्रसरपरिस्फुरणेन सवितारमपि तृणीकुर्वन्निव, ईश्वरभारोद्वहनघृष्टपृष्ठतया हरवृषभमपि हसन्निव, अरणिरमर्षाग्नेः, ऐश्वर्यं शौर्यस्य, मदो मदस्य, विसर्पो दर्पस्य, हृदयं हठस्य, जीवितं जिगीषुतायाः, उच्छ्वसितमुत्साहस्य, अङ्कुशो दुर्मदानाम्, नागदमनो दुष्टभोगिनाम्, विरामो वरमनुष्यतायाः, कुलगुरुर्वीरगोष्ठीनाम्, तुला शौर्यशालिनाम्, सीमान्तदृश्वा शस्त्रग्रामस्य, निर्वोढा प्रौढवादानाम्, संस्तम्भयिता भग्नानाम्, पारगः प्रतिज्ञायाः, मर्मज्ञो महाविग्रहाणाम्, आघोषणापटहः समरार्थिनाम्, सन्निधावेव समुपविष्टः सिंहनादनामा स्वरेणैव दुन्दुभिनिर्घोषगम्भीरेण सुभटानां समररसमानयन्विज्ञापितवान्—'देव, न क्वचित्कृताश्रयया मलिनया मलिनतराः कोकिलया काका इव कापुरुषा हतलक्ष्म्या विप्रलभ्यमानमात्मानं न चेतयन्ते। श्रियो हि दोषान्धतादयः कामला विकाराः। छत्रच्छायान्तरितरवयो विस्मरन्त्यन्यं तेजस्विनं जडधियः। किं वा करोतु वराकः येनातिभीरुतया नित्यपराङ्मुखेन न तु दृष्टान्येव सर्वातिशायिशौर्यातिशयश्वयथुकपिलकपोलपुलकपल्लवितकोपानलानि कुपितानां तेजस्विनां मुखानि। नासौ तपस्वी जानात्येवं यथाभिचारा इव विप्रकृताः सद्यः सकलकुलप्रलयमुपाहरन्ति मनस्विनः। जलेऽपि ज्वलन्ति ताडितास्तेजस्विनः। सकलवीरगोष्ठीबाह्यस्य तस्यैवेदमुचितमनुत्तारनिरयनिपातनिपुणं कर्म। मनस्विनां हि प्रधनप्रधानधने धनुषि ध्रियमाणे सति च कमलाकलहंसीकेलिकुवलयकानने कृपाणे कृपणोपायाः पयोधिमथनप्रभृतयोऽपि श्रीसमुत्थानस्य किं पुनरीदृशाः। येषां च धात्रा धरित्रीं त्रातुं नियुक्ताः स्वयमसमर्था इव कुलिशकर्कशभुजपरिघप्रहरणहेतोरुद्गिरन्ति गिरयोऽपि लोहानि ते कथमिव बाहुशालिनो मनसापि विमलयशोबान्धवा ध्यायेयुरकार्यम्। सर्वग्रहाभिभवभास्वराणां हि सुभटकराणामग्रतो दिग्ग्रहणे पङ्गवः पतङ्गकराः। महामहिषशृङ्गतरङ्गभङ्गभङ्गुर[2]भीषणान्तराला लोकप्रवादमात्रेण दक्षिणाशा परमार्थतो भटभ्रुकुटिरधिवासो यमस्य। चित्रं च यदुन्मुक्तसिंहनादानां सहसासाहसरसरोमाञ्चकण्टकनिकरेण सह न निर्यान्ति सटाः शूराणां रणेषु। द्वयमेव च चतुःसागरसम्भूत[3]स्य भूतिसम्भारस्य भाजनं प्रतिपक्षदाहि दारुणं वडवामुखं वा महापुरुषहृदयं वा। तेजस्विनः सकलाननवाप्य पयोराशीन्सहजस्य कुतो निवृत्तिरूष्मणः। वृथाविततविपुलफणाभारो भुजङ्गानां भर्ता

१ 'पर्वपूर्वपर्वत इव' ब. २ 'भङ्गुरभङ्गिभीषणा—' ब. ३ 'सम्भूतस्य' ब.

बिभर्ति यो भोगीन मृत्पिण्डमेव केवलम् । अप्रतिहतशासनाक्रान्त्युपभोगसुखरसं तु रसाया दिक्कुञ्जरकरभारभास्वरप्रकोष्ठा वीरबाहव एव जानन्ति । रविरिवोन्मुखपद्माकरगृहीतपादपल्लवः सुखेनाखण्डिततेजा दिवसान्नयति शूरः । कातरस्य तु शशिन इव हरिणहृदयस्य पाण्डुरपृष्ठस्य कुतो द्विरात्रमपि निश्चला लक्ष्मीः । अपरिमितयशःप्रकरवर्षी विकासी वीररसः । पुरःप्रवृत्तप्रतापप्रहताः पन्थानः पौरुषस्य । शब्दविद्रुतद्विषन्ति भवन्ति द्वाराणि दर्पस्य । शस्त्रालोकप्रकाशिताः शून्या दिशः शौर्यस्य । रिपुरुधिरशीकरासारेण भूरिव श्रीरप्यनुरज्यते । बहुनरपतिमुकुटमणिशिलाशाणकोणकषणेन चरणनखराजिरिव राजताप्युज्वलीभवति । अनवरतशस्त्राभ्यासेन करतलानीव रिपुमुखानि श्यामीभवन्ति । विविधव्रणबद्ध[१]पट्टकशतैः शरीरमिव यशोऽपि धवलीभवति । कवचिषु रिपूरःकपाटेषु पात्यमानाः पावकशिखामिव श्रियमपि वमन्ति निष्ठुरा निस्त्रिंशप्रहाराः । यश्चाहितहतस्वजनो मनस्विजनो द्विषद्योषिदुरस्ताडनेन कथयति हृदयदुःखम् । परुषा[२]सिलतानिपातपर्वणे[३]नोच्छ्वसिति निरुच्छ्वसितशत्रुशरीराश्रुधारापातेन रोदिति विपक्षवनिताचक्षुषा ददाति जलं स श्रेयान्नेतरः । न च स्वप्नदृष्टनष्टेष्विव क्षणिकेषु शरीरेषु निबध्नन्ति बन्धुबुद्धिं प्रबुद्धाः । स्थायिनि यशसि शरीरधीर्वीराणाम् । अनवरतप्रज्वलिततेजःप्रसरभास्वरस्वभावं च मणिप्रदीपमिव कलुषः कज्जलमलो न स्पृशत्येव तेजस्विनं शोकः । स त्वं सत्त्ववतामग्रणीः प्राग्रहरः प्राज्ञानां प्रथमः समर्थानां प्रष्ठोऽभिजातानामग्रेसरस्तेजस्विनामादिरसहिष्णूनाम् । एताश्च सततसन्निहितधूमायमानकोपाग्नयः सुलभासिधारातोयतृसयो विकटबाहुवनच्छायोपगूढा धीरताया निवासशिशिरभूमयः स्वायत्ताः सुभटानामुरःकवाटभित्तयः । यतः किं गौडाधिपाधमेनैकेन । तथा कुरु यथा नान्योऽपि कश्चिदाचरत्येवं भूयः । सर्वोर्वीश्रद्धाकामुकानामलीकविजिगीषूणां सञ्चारय चामराण्यन्तःपुरपुरंध्रिनिश्वसितैः । उच्छिन्धि रुधिरगन्धान्धगृध्रमण्डलाच्छादनैश्छत्रच्छायाव्यसनानि । अपाकुरु कदुष्णशोणितोदकस्वेदैः कुलक्ष्मीकुलटाकटाक्षचक्षूरागरोगान् । उपशमय निशितशरशिरावेधै[४]र्वैरकार्यशौर्यश्वयथून् । उन्मूलय लोहनिगडापीडमालामलै[५]र्महौषधैः पादपीठदोहददुर्ललितपादपद्मान्यानि । क्षपय तीक्ष्णाज्ञाक्षरक्षारपातैर्जयशब्दश्रवणकर्णकण्डूः । अपनय चरणनखमरीचिचन्दनचर्चाललाटलेपैरनमितस्तिमितमस्तकस्तम्भविकारान् । उद्धर करदानसन्देशसन्दंशैर्द्रविणदर्पोष्मायमाणदुःशीललीलाशल्यानि । भिन्धि मणिपादपीठदीधितिप्रदीपिकाभिः शुष्कसुभटाटोपभ्रुकुटिबन्धान्धकारान् । जय चरणलङ्घनलाघवगलितशिरोगौरवारोग्यैर्मिथ्याभिमानमहासन्निपातान् । श्रदय सततसेवाञ्जलिमुकुलितकरसम्पुटोष्मभिरिष्वसनगुणकिण-

१ 'बन्ध' ब. २ 'परुषानसि' ब. ३ 'निपातवनेन' अ. ४ 'वेधैर्वीरकार्य'- ब. ५ 'मालामलयमहौषधैः' ब.

कार्कश्यानि। येनैव ते गतः पिता पितामहः प्रपितामहो वा तमेव मा हासीस्त्रिभुवनस्पृहणीयं पन्थानम्। अपहाय कुपुरुषोचितां शुचं प्रतिपद्यस्व कुलक्रमागतां केसरीव कुरङ्गीं राजलक्ष्मीम्। देव, देवभूयं गते नरेन्द्रे दुष्टगौडभुजङ्गजग्धजीविते च राज्यवर्धने वृत्तेऽस्मिन्महाप्रलये धरणीधारणायाधुना त्वं शेषः। समाश्वासय अशरणाः प्रजाः क्षमापतीनां शिरःसु शरत्सवितेव ललाटंतपान्प्रयच्छ पादन्यासान्। अहितानामभिनवसेवादीक्षादुःखसन्तप्तश्वासधूममण्डलैर्नखरम्पचैः प्रचलितचूडामणिचक्रवालबालातपैश्चायाहि कल्माषपादताम्। अपि च हते पितर्येकाकी तपस्वी मृगैः सह संवर्धितः सहजब्राह्मण्यमार्दवसुकुमारमनाः कृतनिश्चयश्चण्डचापवनाटनिटांकारनादनिर्मदीकृतदिग्गजं गुञ्जज्ज्याजालजनितजगज्ज्वरं समग्रमुद्यतमेकविंशतिकृत्वः कृत्तवंश[1]मुत्खातवान्राजन्यकं परशुरामः। किं पुनर्नैसर्गिककायकार्कश्यकुलिशायमानमानसो मानिनां मूर्धन्यो देवः। तदद्यैव कृतप्रतिज्ञो गृहाण गौडाधमजीवितध्वस्तये जीवितसङ्कलनाकुलकालाकाण्डयात्राचिह्नध्वजं धनुः। न ह्ययमरातिरक्तचन्दनचर्चाशिशिरोपचारमन्तरेण शाम्यति परिभवानलपच्यमानदेहस्य देवस्य दुःखदाहज्वरः सुदारुणः। निकारसन्तापशान्त्युपायपरिक्षये हि हिडिम्बाचुम्बनास्वादितमिव रिपुरुधिरामृतममन्दरोपायमपायि पवनात्मजेन। जामदग्न्येन च शाम्यन्मन्युशिखिशिखासंज्वरसुखायमानस्पर्शशीतलेपु क्षत्रियक्षतजह्रदेष्वस्नायि।' इत्युक्त्वा व्यरंसीत्।

देवस्तु हर्षस्तं प्रत्यवादीत्—'करणीयमेवेदमभिहितं मान्येन। इतरथा हि मे गृहीतभुवि भोगिनाथेऽपि दायादद्दष्टिरीर्ष्यालोर्भुजस्य। उपरि गच्छतीच्छति निग्रहाय ग्रहगणेऽपि भ्रूलता चलितुम्। अनमत्सु शैलेष्वपि कचग्रहमभिलषति दातुं करः। तेजोदुर्विदग्धानर्ककरानपि चामराणि ग्राहयितुमीहते हृदयम्। राजशब्दरुषा मृगराजानामपि शिरांसि वाञ्छति पादः पादपीठीकर्तुम्। स्वच्छन्दलोकपालस्वेच्छागृहीतानामाक्षेपादेशाय दिशामपि स्फुरत्यधरः। किं पुनरीदृशे दुर्जाते जाते जातामर्षनिर्भरे च मनसि नास्त्येवावकाशः शोकक्रियाकरणस्य। अपि च हृदयविषमशल्ये मुसल्ये जीवति जाल्मे जगद्विगर्हिते गौडाधिपाधमचण्डाले जिह्रेमि शुष्काधरपुटः पोटेव प्रतिकारशून्यं शुचा सूत्कर्तुम्। अकृतरिपुबलाबलाविलोललोचनोदकदुर्दिनस्य मे कुतः करयुगलस्य जलाञ्जलिदानम्। अदृष्टगौडाधमचिताधूममण्डलस्य वा चक्षुषः स्वल्पमप्यश्रुसलिलम्। श्रूयतां मे प्रतिज्ञा। शपाम्यार्यस्यैव पादपांशुस्पर्शेन यदि परिगणितैरेव वासरैः सकलचापचापलदुर्ललितनरपतिचरणरणरणायमाननिगडां निर्गौडां न करोमि मेदिनीं ततस्तनूनपाति पीतसर्पिषि पतङ्ग इव पातकी पातयाम्यात्मानम्।' इत्युक्त्वा च महासन्धिविग्रहाधिकृतमवन्तिमन्तिकस्थमादिदेश—'लिख्यताम्। आ रविरथच-

---

१ 'कृतवंशं' ब.

ऋचीत्कारचकितचारणमिथुनमुक्तसानोरुदयाचलात्, आ त्रिकूटकटककुट्टाक-टङ्कलिखितकाकुत्स्थलङ्कालुण्ठनव्यतिकरात्सुवेलात्, आ वारुणीमदस्खलितव-रुणवरनारीनूपुररवमुखरकुहरकुक्षेरस्तगिरेः, आ गुह्यकगेहिनीपरिमलसुगन्धि-गन्धपाषाणवासितगुहागृहाच्च गन्धमादनात्, सर्वेषां राज्ञां सज्जीक्रियन्तां कराः करदानाय शस्त्रग्रहणाय वा, गृह्यन्तां दिशश्चामराणि वा, नमन्तु शिरांसि धनूंषि वा, कर्णपूरीक्रियन्तामाज्ञा मौर्व्यो वा, शेखरीभवन्तु पादर-जांसि शिरस्त्राणि वा, घटन्तामञ्जलयः करिघटाबन्धा वा, मुच्यन्तां भूमय इषवो वा, समालम्ब्यन्तां वेत्रयष्टयः कुन्तयष्टयो वा, सुदृष्टः क्रियतामात्मा मच्चरणनखेषु कृपाण[1]दर्पणेषु वा परागतोऽहमिति। पङ्गोरिव मे कुतो निवृ-त्तिस्तावद्यावन्न कृतः सर्वद्वीपान्तरसञ्चारी सकलनरपतिमुकुटमणिशिलालोक-मयः पादलेपः।' इति कृतनिश्चयश्च मुक्तास्थानो विसर्जितराजलोकः स्नाना-रम्भाकाङ्क्षी सभामत्याक्षीत्। उत्थाय च स्वस्थवन्निःशेषमाह्निकमकार्षीत्। अगलच्च दर्पप्रसर इव श्रुतप्रतिज्ञस्य शाम्यदूष्मा दिवसस्त्रिभुवनस्य।

ततश्च निजाधिकारापहारभीत इव भगवत्यपि क्वापि गते गततेजस्यहिम-तामरसवनेष्वपि निगूढशिलीमुखालापेषु त्रासादिव सङ्कुचत्सु, विहगगणेष्वपि समुपसंहृतनिजपक्षविक्षेपनिश्चलेषु भियेवाप्रकटीभवत्सु, भुवनव्यापिनीं संध्यां प्रतिज्ञामिव मानयति नतशिरसि घटिताञ्जलिवने जने सकले, स्वपदच्युतिचकितदिक्पालदीयमानाभ्रंलिहलोहप्राकारवल[2]यास्विव बहलति-मिरमालातिरोधीयमानासु दिक्षु प्रदोषास्थाने नातिचिरं तस्थौ। नमन्नृप-लोकलोलांशुकपवनकम्पितशिखैर्दीपिकाचक्रवालैरपि प्रणम्यमान इव प्राहि-णोल्लोकं प्रतिषिद्धपरिजनप्रवेशश्च शयनगृहं प्राविशत्। उत्तानश्च मुमोचा-ङ्गानि शयनतले। दीपद्वितीयं च तमभिसर इव लब्धावसरस्तरसा भ्रातृशोको जग्राह। जीवन्तमिव हृदये निमीलितलोचनो ददर्शाग्रजम्। उपर्युपरि भ्रातृजीवितान्वेषिण इव प्रसस्रुः श्वासाः। धवलांशुकपटान्तेनेव चाश्रुजलप्लवेन मुखमाच्छाद्य निःशब्दमतिचिरं रुरोद। चकार च चेतसि। कथं नामाकृ-तेस्तादृश्या युक्तः परिणामोऽयमीदृशः। पृथुशिलासङ्घातकर्कशकायबन्धात्ता-तादचलादिव लोहधातुः कठिनतर आसीदार्यः। कथं चास्य मे हतहृदयस्या-र्यविरहे सकृदपि युक्तमुच्छ्वसितुम्। इयं सा प्रीतिर्भक्तिरनुवृत्तिर्वा। बालि-शोऽपि कः सम्भावयेदार्यमरणे मज्जीवितम्। तत्तादृशमैक्यमेकपद एव क्वापि गतम्। अयत्नेनैव हतविधिना पृथक्कृतोऽस्मि। दग्धरोषान्तरितशुचा सुचिरं रुदितमपि न मुक्तकण्ठं गतघृणेन मया। सर्वथा लूतातन्तुच्छटाच्छिदुरास्तु-च्छाः प्रीतयः प्राणिनाम्। लोकयात्रामात्रनिबन्धना बान्धवता यतोऽहमपि नाम पर इवार्ये स्वर्गस्थे स्वस्थ इवासे। किं च दैवहतकेन फलमासादितमी-दृशि परस्परप्रीतिबन्धनिर्वृतहृदये सुखभाजि भ्रातृमिथुने विघटिते। तथा

---

१ 'मणिदर्पणेषु' ब. २ 'वलयकलितास्विव' ब.

चन्द्रमया इव जगदाह्लादिनो लोकान्तरीभूतस्य लग्नचिताग्नय इवार्यस्य त एव दहन्ति गुणाः। इत्येतानि चान्यानि च हृदयेन पर्यदेवत। प्रभातायां च शर्वर्यां प्रातरेव प्रतीहारमादिदेशाशेषगजसाधनाधिकृतं स्कन्दगुप्तं द्रष्टुमिच्छामीति।

अथ युगपत्प्रधावितबहुपुरुषपरम्पराहूयमानः, स्वमन्दिरादप्रतिपालितकरेणुश्चरणाभ्यामेव संभ्रान्तः, ससंभ्रमैर्दण्डिभिरुत्सार्यमाणजनपदः, पदे पदे प्रणमतः प्रतिदिशमिभभिषग्वरान्वरवारणानां विभावरीवार्ताः पृच्छन् उच्छ्रितशिखिपिच्छलाञ्छितवंशलतावनगहनगृहीतदिगायामैर्विन्ध्यवनैरिव वारणबन्धविमर्दोद्योगागतैः पुरःप्रधावद्भिरनायतमण्डलैराधोरणगणैश्च मरकतहरितघासमुष्टीश्च दर्शयद्भिर्नवग्रहगजपतींश्च प्रार्थयमानैश्च लब्धाभिमतमत्तमातङ्गमुदितमानसैश्च सुदूरमुपसृत्य नमस्यद्भिरात्मीयमातङ्गमदागमांश्च निवेदयद्भिः, डिण्डिमाधिरोहणाय च विज्ञापयद्भिः, प्रमादपतितापराधापहृतद्विरददुःखधृतदीर्घश्मश्रुभिरग्रतो गच्छद्भिः, अभिनवोपसृतैश्च कर्पटिभिर्वारणाप्तिसुखप्रत्याशया धावमानैः, गणिकाधिकारिगणैश्चिरलब्धान्तरैरुच्छ्रितकरैः, कर्मण्यकरेणुकासङ्कथनाकुलैरुल्लासितपल्लवचिह्नाभिररण्यपालपङ्क्तिभिश्च, निष्पादितनवग्रहनागनिवहनिवेदनोद्यताभिरुत्तम्भिततुङ्गतोत्रवनाभिर्महामात्रपेटकैश्च प्रकटितकरिकर्मचर्मपुटैः, अभिनवगजसाधनसञ्चरणवार्तानिवेदनविसर्जितैश्च नागवनवीथीपालदूतवृन्दैः, प्रतिक्षणप्रत्यवेक्षितकरिकवलकूटैः, कटभङ्गसंग्रहं ग्रामनगरनिगमेषु निवेदयमानैः, कटककदम्बकैः क्रियमाणकोलाहलः, स्वामिप्रसादसम्भृतेन महाधिकाराविष्कारेण स्वाभाविकेन चावष्टम्भाभोगेनोदासीनोऽप्यादिशन्निव, असंख्यकरिकर्णशङ्खसम्पत्सम्पादनाय समुद्रानाज्ञापयन्निव, शृङ्गारगैरिकपङ्काङ्गरागसंग्रहाय गिरीन्मुष्णन्निव, दिग्गजाधिकारं ककुभामैरावतमिवापहरन्हरेर्हरपदभारनमितकैलासगिरिगुरुभिः पादन्यासैर्गुरुभारग्रहणगर्वमुर्व्याः संहरन्निव, गतिवशविलोलस्य चाजानुलम्बस्य बाहुदण्डद्वयस्य विक्षेपैरालानशिलास्तम्भमालामिवोभयतो निखनन्, ईषदुत्तुङ्गलम्बेनाधरबिम्बेनामृतरसस्वादुना नवपल्लवकोमलेन कवलेनेव श्रीकरेणुकां विलोभयन्, निजनृपवंशदीर्घं नासावंशं दधानः, अतिस्निग्धमधुरधवलविशालतया पीतक्षीरोदेनेव पिबन्नीक्षणयुग्मायामेन दिशामायामम्, मेरुतटादपि विकटविपुलालिकः, सततमविच्छिन्नच्छत्रच्छायाप्ररूढिवशादिव नितान्तायतनीलकोमलच्छविसुभगेन स्वभावभङ्गुरेण कुन्तलबालवल्लरीवेल्लितविलासिना लुनन्निव लुप्तालोकानर्ककरान्बर्बरकेण, अरिपक्षपरिक्षयपरित्यक्तकार्मुककर्मापि सकलदिगन्तश्रूयमाणगुरुगुणध्वनिः, आत्मस्थसमस्तमत्तमातङ्गसाधनोऽप्यस्पृष्टो मदेन, भूतिमानपि स्नेहमयः, पार्थिवोऽपि गुणमयः, करिणामिव दानवतामुपरि स्थितः, स्वामितामिव स्पृहणीयां भृत्यतामप्यपरिभूतामुद्वहन्नेकभर्तृभक्तिनिश्चलां कुलाङ्गनामिवान-

१ 'प्रमादापतित' ब.

न्यगम्यां प्रभुप्रसादभूमिमारूढः, निष्कारणबान्धवो विदग्धानाम्, अभृतभृत्यो भजताम्, अक्रीतदासो विदुषाम्, स्कन्दगुप्तो विवेश राजकुलम्। दूरादेव चोभयकरकमलावलम्बितं स्पृशन्मौलिना महीतलं नमस्कारमकरोत्।

उपविष्टं नतिनिकटे तं तदा जगाद देवो हर्षः—'श्रुतो विस्तर एवास्यार्थव्यतिकरस्यास्मच्चिकीर्षितस्य च। अतः शीघ्रं प्रवेश्यन्तां प्रचारनिर्गतानि गजसाधनानि। न क्षाम्यत्यतिस्वल्पमप्यार्यपरिभवपीडापावकः प्रयाणविलम्बम्[1]।' इत्येवमभिहितश्च प्रणम्य व्यज्ञापयत्—'कृतमवधारयतु स्वामी समादिष्टं किंतु स्वल्पं विज्ञाप्यमस्ति भर्तृभक्तेः। तदाकर्णयतु देवः। देवेन हि पुष्पभूतिवंशसम्भूतस्याभिजनस्याभिजात्यस्य[2] सहजस्य तेजसो दिक्करिकरप्रलम्बस्य बाहुयुगलस्यासाधारणस्य च सोदरस्नेहस्य सर्वं सदृशमुपक्रान्तम्। काकोदराभिधानाः कृपणाः कृमयोऽपि न मृष्यन्ति निकारं[3] किमुत भवादृशास्तेजसां राशयः। केवलं देवराज्यवर्धनोदन्तेन कियदपि दृष्टमेव देवेन दुर्जनदौरात्म्यम्। ईदृशाः खलु लोकस्वभावाः प्रतिग्रामं प्रतिनगरं प्रतिविषयं प्रतिदेशं प्रतिद्वीपं प्रतिदिशं च भिन्ना वेशाश्चाकाराश्चाहाराश्च व्याहाराश्च व्यवहाराश्च जनपदानाम्। तदियमात्मदेशाचारोचिता स्वभावसरलहृदयजा त्यज्यतां सर्वविश्वासिता। प्रमाददोषाभिषङ्गेषु श्रुतबहुवार्त एव प्रतिदिनं देवः। यथा नागकुलजन्मनः सारिकाश्रावितमन्त्रस्यासीन्नाशो[4] नागसेनस्य पद्मावत्याम्। शुकश्रुतरहस्यस्य च श्रीरशीर्यत श्रुतवर्मणः श्रावस्त्याम्। स्वप्नायमानस्य च मन्त्रभेदोऽभून्मृत्यवे मृत्तिकावत्यां सुवर्णचूडस्य। चूडामणिलग्नलेखप्रतिबिम्बवाचिताक्षरा च चारुचामीकरचामरग्राहिणी यमतां ययौ यवनेश्वरस्य। लोभबहुलं च बहुलनिशि निधानमुत्खनन्तमुत्खातखड्गप्रमाथिनी ममन्थ माथुरं बृहद्रथं विदूरथवरूथिनी। नागवनविहारशीलं च मायामातङ्गाङ्गान्निर्गता महासेनसैनिका वत्सपतिं न्ययंसिषुः। अतिदयितलास्यस्य च शैलूषमध्यमध्यास्य मूर्धानमसिलतया मृणालमिवालुनादग्निमित्रात्मजस्य सुमित्रस्य मित्रदेवः। प्रियतन्त्रीवाद्यस्यालाबूवीणाभ्यन्तरशुषिरनिहितनिशिततरवारयो गान्धर्वच्छात्रच्छद्मानः चिच्छिदुरश्मकेश्वरस्य शरभस्य शिरो रिपुपुरुषाः। प्रज्ञादुर्बलं च बलदर्शनव्यपदेशदर्शिताशेषसैन्यः सेनानीरनार्यो मौर्यं बृहद्रथं पिपेष पुष्यमित्रः स्वामिनम्। आश्चर्यकुतूहली च चण्डीपतिर्दण्डोपनतयवननिर्मितेन नभस्तलयायिना यन्त्रयानेनानीयत क्वापि। काकवर्णः शैशुनागिश्च नगरोपकण्ठे कण्ठे निचकृते निस्त्रिंशेन। अतिस्त्रीसङ्गरतमनङ्गपरवशं शुङ्गममात्यो वसुदेवो देवभूतिदासीदुहित्रा देवीव्यञ्जनया वीतजीवितमकारयत्। असुरविवरव्यसनिनं चापजहुरपरिमितरमणीमणिनूपुरक्षणक्षणाह्लादरम्यया मागधं गोधनगिरिसुरुङ्गया स्वविषयं मेकलाधिपमन्त्रिणः। महाकालमहे च महा-

१ 'प्रणयविलम्बम्' ब. २ 'सम्भूतस्याजात्यस्य' अ-क. ३ 'विकारम्' अ-क.
४ 'प्लावितमन्त्रस्य' ब.

मांसविक्रयवादवातूलं वेतालस्तालजङ्घो जघान जघन्यजं प्रद्योतस्य पौणर्किं कुमारं कुमारसेनम्। रसायनरसाभिनिवेशिनश्च वैद्यव्यञ्जनाः सुबहुपुरुषान्तरप्रकाशितौषधगुणा गणपतेर्विदेहराजसुतस्य राजयक्ष्माणमजनयन्। स्त्रीविश्वासिनश्च महादेवीगृहगूढभित्तिभागभ्राता भद्रसेनस्याभवन्मृत्यवे कालिङ्गस्य वीरसेनः। मातृशयनीयतूलिकातलनिषण्णश्च तनयोन्यं तनयमभिषेक्तुकामस्य दध्रस्य करूषाधिपतेरभवन्मृत्यवे। उत्सारकरुचिं च रहसि ससचिवमेव दूरीचकार चकोरनाथं शूद्रकदूतश्चन्द्रकेतुं जीवितात्। मृगयासक्तस्य च मञ्चतो गण्डकानुद्दण्डनड्वलनलवननिलीनाश्च चम्पाधिपचमूचरभटाश्चामुण्डीपतेराचेमुः प्राणान्पुष्करस्य। बन्दिरागपरं च परप्रयुक्ता जयशब्दमुखरमुखा मङ्खा मौखरिं मूर्खं क्षत्रवर्माणमुदखनन्। अरिपुरे च परकलत्रकामुकं कामिनीवेशगुप्तश्च चन्द्रगुप्तः शकपतिमशातयदिति। प्रमत्तानां प्रमदाकृताः प्रमादाः श्रुतिविषयमागता एव देवस्य। यथा मधुमोदितं मधुरकसंलिप्तैर्लाजैः सुप्रभा पुत्रराज्यार्थं महासेनं काशिराजं जघान। व्याजजनितकन्दर्पदर्पा च दर्पणेन क्षुरधारापर्यन्तेनायोध्याधिपतिं परन्तपं रत्नवती जारूथम्, विषचूर्णचुम्बितमकरन्देन च कर्णेन्दीवरेण देवकी देवरानुरक्ता देवसेनं सौह्मयम्, योगपरागविसरवर्षिणा च मणिनूपुरेण वल्लभा सपत्नीरुषा वैरन्त्यं[1] रन्तिदेवम्, वेणीनिगूढेन च शस्त्रेण बिन्दुमती वृष्णिं विदूरथम्, रसदिग्धमध्येन च मेखलामणिना हंसवती सौवीरं वीरसेनम्, अदृश्यागदलिप्तवदना च विषवारुणीगण्डूषपायनेन पौरवी पौरवेश्वरं सोमकम्।' इत्युक्त्वा विरराम स्वाम्यादेशसम्पादनाय च निर्जगाम।

देवोऽपि हर्षः सकलराज्यस्थितीश्चकार। ततश्च तथा कृतप्रतिज्ञे प्रयाणं विजयाय दिशां समादिशति[2] देवे हर्षे गतायुषां प्रतिसामन्तानामुदवसितेषु बहुरूपाण्युपलिङ्गानि वितेनिरे। तथा ह्यविप्रकृष्टाः[3] कालदूतदृष्टय इवेतस्ततश्चेरुश्चटुलाः कृष्णशारश्रेणयः। प्रचलितलक्ष्मीनूपुरप्रणादप्रतिमा मधुसरघासंघातझंकारा जह्रादिरेऽजिरे[4]। विवृतविकृतवदनविवरविसृतवह्निविसरा वासरेऽपि विरसं विरेसुश्चिरमशिवार्थमशिवाः[5] शिवाः। शवपिशितप्ररूढप्रसरा[6] इव कपिपोतकपोलकपिलपक्षतयः काननकपोताः पेतुः। आमन्त्रयमाणा इव दधुरकालकुसुमानि सममुपवनतरवः। तरलकरतलप्रहारप्रहतपयोधरा रुरुदुः प्रसभं सभाशालभञ्जिकाः। ददृशुरासन्नकचग्रहभयोत्क्रान्तोत्तमाङ्गमिवात्मानं कबन्धमादर्शोदरेषु योधाः। चूडामणिषु चक्रशङ्खकमललक्ष्माणः प्रादुरभवन्पादन्यासा राजमहिषीणाम्। चेटीचामराण्यकस्मादधावन्त पाणिपल्लवात्। प्रणयकलहेऽपि दत्तपृष्ठाश्चिरमभवन्भटाः पराङ्मुखा मानिनीनाम्। करिकपोलेषु[7] व्यघटन्त मधुलिहां मधुमदिरापानगोष्ठ्यः। समाघ्रातयममहिषगन्धा

---

१ 'वैरन्त्या' ब. २ 'दित्सति' ब. ३ 'प्रविष्टकाल०' ब. ४ 'जह्रादिरे। चिरम्' ब. ५ 'विरेसुरुपशिबिरं शवार्थम्' ब. ६ 'प्ररूढप्रणयेव' अ-क. ७ '०करिणीकपोलेषु' ब.

इव ताम्यन्तः स्तम्बकरिमपि हरयो हरितं नवयवसं न चेरुः। चलवलयावलीवाचालबालिकातालिकातोद्यलालिता अपि न ननृतुर्मन्दा मन्दिरमयूराः। निशि निशि रजनिकरहरिणनिहितनयन इवोन्मुखस्तारमुपतोरणमकारणमकाणीत्कौलेयकगणः। गणयन्तीव गतायुषस्तर्जनतरलया तर्जन्या दिवसमाट वाटकेषु कोटवी। कुट्टिमेषु कुटिलहरिणखुरवेणीतरङ्गिण्यः शष्पराजयोऽजायन्त। जनितवेणीबन्धानि निरञ्जनरोचनारोचींषि चषकमधुनि मुखकमलप्रतिबिम्बान्यदृश्यन्त भटीनाम्। समासन्नात्मापहारचकिता इव चकम्पिरे भूमयः। वध्यालङ्काररक्तचन्दनरसच्छटा इवालक्ष्यन्त शूराणां पतिताः शरीरेषु विकसितबन्धूककुसुमशोणितशोचिषः शोणितवृष्टयः। पर्यन्नीकुर्वाणा इव विनश्वरीं श्रियमविरलस्फुरत्स्फुलिङ्गाङ्गारोद्गारदग्धतारागणा गणशः पतन्तः प्रज्वलन्तो न व्यरंसिषुरुल्कादण्डाः। प्रथममेव प्रतीहारीवापहरन्ती प्रतिभवनं चामरातपत्रव्यजनानि परुषा बभ्राम वात्येति।

इति श्रीबाणभट्टकृतौ हर्षचरिते राजप्रतिज्ञावर्णनं नाम षष्ठ उच्छ्वासः।

---

१ '०कृते हर्षचरिते षष्ठ' क; 'इति श्रीमहाकविचक्रचूडामणिश्रीबाणभट्टविरचिते हर्षचरिते महाकाव्ये राजप्रतिष्ठा नाम षष्ठ उच्छ्वासः सम्पूर्णः' ब.

सप्तम उच्छ्वासः ।

अङ्गनवेदी वसुधा कुल्या जलधिः स्थली च पातालम् ।
वल्मीकश्च सुमेरुः कृतप्रतिज्ञस्य वीरस्य ॥ १ ॥

धृतधनुषि बाहुशालिनि शैला न नमन्ति यत्तदाश्चर्यम् ।
रिपुसंज्ञकेषु गणना कैव वराकेषु काकेषु ॥ २ ॥

अथ व्यतीतेषु च केषुचिद्दिवसेषु मौहूर्तिकमण्डलेन शतशः सुगणिते सुप्रशस्तेऽहनि दत्ते चतसृणामपि दिशां विजययोग्ये दण्डयात्रालग्ने सलिलमोक्षविशारदैः शारदैरिवाम्भोधरैः कालधौतैः शातकौम्भैश्च[1] कुम्भैः स्नात्वा विरचय्य परमया भक्त्या भगवतो नीललोहितस्यार्चामुदर्चिषं हुत्वा प्रदक्षिणावर्तशिखाकलापमाशुशुक्षणिं दत्त्वा द्विजेभ्यो रत्नवन्ति राजतानि जातरूपमयानि च सहस्रशस्तिलपात्राणि कनकपत्रलतालङ्कृतशफशृङ्गशिखरा गाश्चार्बुदशः समुपविश्य विततव्याघ्रचर्मणि भद्रासने विलिप्य प्रथमविलिप्तायुधो निजयशोधवलेनाचरणतश्चन्दनेन शरीरं परिधाय राजहंसमिथुनलक्ष्मणी सदृशे दुकूले परमेश्वरचिह्नभूतां शशिकलामिव कल्पयित्वा सितकुसुममुण्डमालिकां शिरसि नीत्वा कर्णाभरणमरकतमयूखमिव कर्णगोचरतां[2] गोरोचनाच्छुरितमभिनवं दूर्वापल्लवं विन्यस्य सह शासनवलयेन गमनमङ्गलप्रतिसरं प्रकोष्ठे परिपूजितप्रहृष्टपुरोहितकरप्रकीर्यमाणशान्तिसलिलसीकरनिकराभ्युक्षितशिराः संप्रेष्य महार्हाणि वाहनानि बहलरत्नालोकलिप्तककुम्भि च भूषणानि भूभुजां संविभज्य क्लिष्टकार्पटिककुलपुत्रलोकमोचितैः प्रसाददानैश्च विमुच्य बन्धनानि नियुज्य तत्कालस्मरणस्फुरणेन कथितात्मानमिव चाष्टादशद्वीपजेतव्याधिकारे दक्षिणं भुजस्तम्भमहमहमिकया सेवकैरिव सुनिमित्तैरपि समग्रैरग्रतो भवद्भिः प्रमुदितप्रजाजन्यमानजयशब्दकोलाहलो हिरण्यगर्भ इव ब्रह्माण्डात्कृतयुगकरणाय भवनान्निर्जगाम ।

नातिदूरे च नगरादुपसरस्वति निर्मिते महति तृणमये, समुत्तम्भिततुङ्गतोरणे, वेदीविनिहितपल्लवललामहेमकलशे, बद्धवनमालादाम्नि[3], धवलध्वजमालिनि, भ्रमच्छुक्लवाससि, पठद्द्विजन्मनि, मन्दिरे प्रस्थानमकरोत् । तत्रस्थस्य चास्य ग्रामाक्षपटलिकः सकलकरणिपरिकरः 'करोतु देवो दिवसग्रहणमद्यैवावन्ध्यशासनः शासनानाम्' इत्यभिधाय वृषाङ्कामभिनवघटितां हाटकमयीं मुद्रामुपनिन्ये । जग्राह च तां राजा । समुपस्थापिते च प्रथमत एव मृत्पिण्डे परिभ्रश्य करकमलादधोमुखी महीतले पपात मुद्रा । मन्दाश्यानपङ्कपटले मृदुमृदि सरस्वतीतीरे स्फुटं व्यराजन्त राजयो वर्णानाम् ।

१ 'शातकुम्भैश्च' क. २ 'कर्णपूरगोचरताम्' ब. ३ 'धाम्नि' ब.

अमङ्गलाशङ्किनि च विषीदति परिजने नरपतिरकरोन्मनस्येतत्—'अतत्त्वं[१]दर्शिन्यो हि भवन्त्यविदग्धानां धियः। तथाहि एकशासनमुद्राङ्का भूर्भवतो भविष्यतीति निवेदितमपि निमित्तेनान्यथा गृह्णन्ति ग्राम्याः।' इत्यभिनन्द्य मनसा महानिमित्तं तत्सीरसहस्रसंमितसीम्नां ग्रामाणां शतमदाद्द्विजेभ्यः। निनाय च तत्र तं दिवसम्। प्रतिपन्नायां शर्वर्यां संमानितसर्वराजलोकः सुष्वाप।

अथ गलति तृतीये यामे सुप्तसमस्तसत्त्वनिःशब्दे दिक्कुञ्जरजृम्भमाणगम्भीरध्वनिरताड्यत प्रयाणपटहः। अग्रतः स्थित्वा च मुहूर्तमिव पुनः प्रयाणक्रोशसंख्यापकाः स्पष्टमष्टावदीयन्त प्रहाराः पटहे पटीयांसः।

ततो रटत्पटहे, नन्दन्नान्दीके, गुञ्जत्कुञ्जे, कूजत्काहले, शब्दायमानशङ्खे, क्रमोपचीयमानकटककलकले, परिजनोत्थापनव्यापृतव्यवहारिणि, द्रुतद्रुघनघातघट्यमानकोणिकाकीलकोलाहलकलितककुभि, बलाधिकृतबध्यमानपाटीपतिपेटके, जनज्वलितोल्कासहस्रालोकलुप्यमानत्रियामातमसि, यामचेटीचरणचलनोत्थाप्यमानकामिमिथुने, कटुकं[२]टुकनिर्देशनश्यन्निद्रोन्मिषन्निषादिनि, प्रबुद्धहास्तिकशून्यीक्रियमाणशय्यागृहे, सुप्तोत्थिताश्वीयविधूयमानसटे, रटत्कटकमुखरखनित्रखन्यमानक्षोणीपाशे, समुत्कील्यमानकीलशिञ्जानहिञ्जीरे, उप[३]नीयमाननिगडतालककलरवोत्तालतुरङ्गतरङ्ग्यमाणखुरपुटे, लेशिकमुच्यमानमदस्यन्दिदन्तिसन्दानश्रृङ्खलाखनखननिनादनिर्भरभरितदशदिशि, घासपूलक[४]प्रहारप्रमृष्टपांसुलकरिपृष्ठप्रसार्यमाणप्रस्फोटित[५]प्रमृष्टचर्मणि, गृहचिन्तकचेटकसंवेष्ट्यमानपटकुटीकाण्डपटमण्डपपरिवस्त्रावितानके, कीलककलापापूर्यमाणचिपिटचर्मपुटे, सम्भाण्डायमानभाण्डागारिणि, भाण्डागारवहनवाह्यमानबहुनालीवाहिके, निषादिनिश्चलानेकानीकर्पा[६]रोप्यमाणकोशकलशपीडापीडसङ्कटायमानसामन्तौकसि, दूरगतदक्षदासेरकक्षिप्रप्रक्षिप्यमाणोपकरणसम्भारभ्रियमाणदुष्टदन्तिनि, तिर्यगानमज्जाघ[७]निककरकृच्छ्राकृष्टलम्बमानपरतन्त्रतुन्दिलचुन्दीजनजनितजनहासे, पीड्यमानशारशारिवरत्रागुणग्राहितगात्रविहारबृंहद्बहुबृहदुन्मदकरिणि, करिघटाघटमानघण्टाटांकारक्रियमाणकर्णज्वरे, पृष्ठप्रतिष्ठाप्यमानकण्ठालककदर्थितकूजत्करभे, अभिजातराजपुत्रप्रेष्यमाणकुप्रयुक्ताकुलकुलीनकुलपुत्रकलत्रवाहने, गमनवेलाविप्रलब्धवारणाधोरणान्विष्यमाणनवसेवके, प्रसादवित्तपत्तिनीयमाननरपतिवल्लभवारवाजिनि, चारुचारभटसैन्यन्यस्यमाननासीरमण्डलाडम्बरस्थूलस्थासके, स्थानपालपर्याणलम्बमानलवणकला[८]यीकिङ्किणीनालीसनाथसङ्कलितत्तलसारके, कुण्डलीकृतावरक्षणीजालजटिलवल्लभपालाश्वघटानिवेश्यमानशाखामृगे, परिव-

---

१ 'तत्त्व–' अ. २ 'कटुककटुक–' अ–क. ३ 'पनीयमान' ब. ४ 'पूलिक' ब. ५ 'प्रस्फोटितचर्मणि' अ–क. ६ 'अनेकानेकपा–' अ–क. ७ 'घनिकर' अ. ८ 'कलापि' क.

ध्वंकाकृष्यमाणार्धजग्धप्राभातिकयोग्याशनप्रारोहके, व्याक्रोशीविजृम्भमाणघासिकाघोषे, गमनसंभ्रमभ्रष्टभ्रमदुत्तुण्डतरुणतुरङ्गमतन्यमानानेकमन्दुराविमर्दे, सज्जीकृतकरेणुकारोहाह्वानसत्वरसुन्दरीदीयमानमुखालेपने, चलितमातङ्गतुरङ्गप्रधावितप्राकृतप्रातिवेश्यकलोकलुण्ठ्यमाननिर्घास[1]सस्यसञ्चये, सञ्चरच्चेलचक्राक्रान्तचक्रीवति, चक्रचीत्कारिगन्त्रीगणगृह्यमाणप्रहतवर्त्मनि, अकाण्डदीयमान[2]भाण्डभरितानडुहि, निकटघासलाभलुभ्यल्लम्बमानप्रथमप्रसार्यमाणसारसौरभेये, प्रमुखप्रवर्त्यमानमहासामन्तमहानसे, पुरःप्रधावद्ध्वजवाहिनि, प्रियशतोपलभ्यमानासङ्कटकुटीरकान्तरालनिःसरणे, करिचरण[3]चलितमठिकोत्थितलोकलोष्टहन्यमानमेण्ठक्रियमाणासन्नसाक्षिणि, सङ्घट्टविघट्टमानव्याघ्रपल्लीपलायमानक्षुद्रकुटुम्बके, कलकलोपद्रवद्द्रवद्द्रविणबलीवर्दविद्राणवणिजि, पुरःसरदीपिकालोकविरलायमानलोकोत्पीड[4]प्रस्थितान्तःपुरकरिणीकदम्बके, हयारोहाहूयमानलम्बितशुनि, सरभसचरणनिपतननिश्चलगमनसुखायमानखक्खट[5]स्तूयमानतुङ्गतुङ्गण[6]गुणे, त्रस्तवेसरविसंवादिसीदद्दाक्षिणात्यसादिनि, रजोजग्धजगति प्रयाणसमये, प्रतिदिशमागच्छद्भिर्गजवधूसमारूढैराधोरणैरूर्ध्वध्रियमाणहेमपत्रभङ्गशारशार्ङ्गैः, अन्तरासनासीनान्तरङ्गगृहीतासिभिः, ताम्बूलिकविधूयमानचामरपल्लवैः, पश्चिमासनिकार्पितभस्त्राभरणभिन्दिपालपूलिकैः, पत्रलताकुटिलकलधौतनलकपल्लवितपर्याणैः, पर्याणपक्षकपरिक्षेपपट्टिकाबन्धनिश्चलपट्टोपधानस्थिरावधानैः, प्रचलपादफलिकास्फालनस्फायमानपदबन्धमणिशिलाशब्दैः, उच्चित्रनेत्रसुकुमारस्वस्थान[7]स्थगितजङ्घाकाण्डैश्च कार्दमिकपटकल्माषितपिशङ्गपिङ्गैः, अलिनीलमसृणसतुलासमुत्पादितसितसमायोगपरभागैश्चावदातदेहवर्णविराजमानराजावर्तमेचकैः, कञ्चुकै[8]श्चापचितचीनचोलकैश्च तारमुक्तास्तबकितस्तवरकवारबाणैश्च नानाकषायकर्बुरकूर्पासकैश्च शुकपिच्छच्छायाच्छादनकैश्च व्यायामोल्लुप्तपार्श्वप्रदेशप्रविष्टचारुश[9]स्त्रैश्च गतिवशवेल्लितहारलतागलल्लोलकुण्डलोन्मोचनप्रधावितपरिजनैश्च चामीकरपत्राङ्कुरकर्णपूरकविघट्टमानवाचालबालपाशैश्चोष्णीषपट्टविष्ट[10]ब्धकर्णोत्पलनालैश्च कुङ्कुमरागकोमलोत्तरीयान्तरितोत्तमाङ्गैश्च चूडामणिखण्डखचितक्षौमखोलै[11]श्च मायूरा[12]तपत्रायमाणशेखरषट्पदपटलैश्च मार्गागतशारिक[13]शारिवाहवेगदण्डैः, पुरश्चञ्चच्चामरकिर्मीरकार्दरङ्गचर्ममण्डलमण्डनोड्डीयमानचटुलडामरचारभटभरितभुवनान्तरैः, आस्कन्दत्काम्बोजवाजिशतशिञ्जानजातरूपायानरवमुखरितदिङ्मुखैश्च निर्दयप्रहतलम्बापटहशतपटुरवबधिरीकृतश्रवणविवरैः, उ-

---

१ 'निघाससञ्चये' ब. २ 'अकाण्डोड्डीयमान-' ब. ३ 'चरणदलित' अ-क. ४ 'लोकोत्पीडा' ब. ५ 'खक्खटक्षत्रियस्तूय०' ब. ६ 'तङ्गण' ब. ७ 'स्वस्थगनस्थगित' अ-क. ८ 'कञ्चुकैश्चोप' अ-क. ९ '०शस्तैश्च' ब. १० 'पट्टावष्टब्ध' अ-क. ११ 'चोलैश्च' अ-क. १२ 'मायूरपत्राय'-अ-क. १३ 'शारीरिकशारिवाह' ब.

द्घोष्यमाणनामभिः, उन्मुखपादातप्रतिपाल्यमानाज्ञापातै राजभिरापुपूरे राजद्वारम् ।

उदिते च भगवति दिनकृति राज्ञः समायोगग्रहणसमयशंसी सस्वान संज्ञाशङ्खो मुहुर्मुहुः । अथ नचिरादिव प्रथमप्रयाण एव दिग्विजयाय दिग्गजसमागममिव गमनविलोलकर्णतालदोलाविलासैः कुर्वाणया करेणुकया सिद्धयात्रयोह्यमानः, वैदूर्यदण्डविकटेनोपरि प्रत्युप्तपद्मरागखण्डखचिततया सूर्योदयदर्शनकोपादिव लोहितायतया ध्रियमाणेन मङ्गलातपत्रेण, कदलीगर्भाभ्यधिकम्रदिम्ना नवनेत्रनिर्मितेन द्वितीय इव भोगिनामधिपतिरङ्गलग्नेन कञ्चुकेन, अमृतमथनदिवस इव क्षीरोदफेनपटलधवलाम्बरवाही, बाल एव पारिजातपादप इवाखण्डलभूमिमारूढः, विधूयमानचामरमरुद्विधूतकर्णपूरकुसुममञ्जरीरजसा सकलभुवनवशीकरणचूर्णेनेव दिशश्छुरयन्, अभिमुखचूडामणिघटमानपाटलप्रतिबिम्बमुदयमानं सवितारमपि पिबन्निव तेजसा, बहलताम्बूलसिन्दूरच्छुरितया विलभमान इव द्वीपान्तराण्योष्ठमुद्रयानुरागस्य स्फुरन्महाहारमरीचिचक्रवालानि चामराणीव दिशोऽपि ग्राहयन्, राजकेक्षणोत्क्षिप्तत्रिभागया त्रीनपि लोकान्करदानायाज्ञापयन्निव सविभ्रमं भ्रूलतया, द्राघीयसा बाहुप्राकारेण परिक्षिपन्निव रिरक्षया सप्तापि सागरमहाखातान्, अखिलमिव क्षीरोदमाधुर्यमादायोद्गतया लक्ष्म्या समुपगूढः, गाढममृतमय इव पीयमानः कुतूहलोत्तानकटकलोकलोचनसहस्रैः, स्नेहार्द्रेषु राज्ञां हृदयेषु गुणगौरवेण मज्जन्निव, मज्जामपि[2] लिम्पन्निव सौभाग्यद्रवेण द्रष्टॄणाम्, अमरपतिरिवाग्रजवधकलङ्कप्रक्षालनाकुलः, पृथुरिव पृथिवीपरिशोधनावधानसङ्कलितसकलमहीभृत्समुत्सारणः, पुरःसैरालोककारकैः सहस्रसंख्यैरर्क इव किरणैरधिकारचातुर्यचञ्चलचरणैर्व्यवस्थास्थापननिष्ठुरैः भयपलायमानलोकोत्पीडान्तरिता दशापि दिशो ग्राहयद्भिरिव चलितकदलिकासम्पातपीतप्रचारं पवनमपि विनये स्थापयद्भिरिव द्रुतचरणोद्धूतधूलिपटलावधूतान्दिनकरकिरणानप्युत्सारयद्भिरिव कनकवेत्रलतालोकविक्षिप्यमाणं दिनमपि दूरीकुर्वद्भिरिव दण्डिभिरितस्ततः समुत्सार्यमाणजनसमूहो निर्जगाम नरपतिः ।

अवनमति च विनयनमितवपुषि भयचकितमनसि चलनशिथिलमणिकनकमुकुटकिरणनिकररुचिरशिरसि विलुलितकुसुमशेखररजसि राजचक्रे, प्रभामुचां चूडामणीनामवाञ्चस्तिर्यञ्च उदञ्चश्च चञ्चन्तो मरीचयश्चाषराशय इव सुशकुनसम्पादनाय चेलुः । मेघायमानरेणुमेदुरं मन्दिरशिखण्डिन इव खमुड्डीयमानाः कोमलकल्पपादपपल्लववन्[3]दनमालाकलापा इवाबध्यन्त दिग्द्वारेषु

१ 'करेणुकयोह्य०' अ-क. २ 'मज्जामपि' इति नास्ति अ-क- पुस्तकयोः.
३ 'चन्दनमाला' अ-क.

दिक्पालैः प्रणम्यमानश्च नेत्रत्रिभागैश्च कटाक्षैश्च समप्रेक्षितैर्भूवञ्चितैश्चार्धस्मितैश्च परिहासैश्च छेकालापैश्च कुशलप्रश्नैश्च प्रतिप्रणामैश्चोन्मत्तभ्रूवीक्षितैश्चाज्ञादानैश्चाक्रीणन्निव[1] मानमयान्प्राणान्प्रणयदानैः प्रवीराणां वीरो यथानुरूपं विबभाज राजकम् ।

अथ प्रस्थिते राजनि कलकलत्रस्तदिङ्नागशूत्काररव इवेतस्ततस्तस्तार तारतरस्तूर्याणां प्रतिध्वनिराशातटेषु । दिग्गजेभ्यः प्रकुपितानां त्रिप्रस्रुतानां करिणां मदप्रस्रवणवीथीभिरलिकुलकालीभिः कालिन्दीवेणिकासहस्राणीव सस्यन्दिरे । सिन्दूररेणुराशिभिररुणायमानबिम्बे रवावस्तमयसमयं शशङ्किरे शकुनयः । करिणां षट्पदकोलाहलमांसलैः कर्णतालनिस्वनैस्तिरोदधिरे दुन्दुभिध्वनयः । दोधूयमानश्च सचराचरमाचचाम चामरसङ्घातो विश्वम् । अश्वीयश्वासनिक्षिप्तैः शिश्विन्दे सिन्धुवारदामशुचिभिर्निरन्तरमन्तरिक्षं फेनपिण्डैः । पिण्डीभूततगरस्तबकपाण्डुराणि पपुरिव परस्परसङ्घट्टनष्टाष्टदिशं[2] दिवसमुच्चचामीकरदण्डान्यातपत्रवनानि । रजोरजनीनिमीलितोपि मुकुटमणिशिलावलीबालातपेन विचकास वासरः । राजतैर्हिरण्मयैश्च मण्डनकभाण्डमण्डलैर्ह्रादमानैर्हरितीकृताः[3] परिह्रादा हरितो बधिरतां दधुः । अरिप्रतापानलनिर्मूलनायेव मदोष्मशीकरैः शिशीकिरे[4] करिणः ककुभां चक्रम् । चक्षुषामुन्मेषं मुमुषुस्तडिच्चञ्चलानि चूडामणीनामर्चींषि । स्वयमपि विसिष्मिये बलानां भूपालः सर्वतो विक्षिप्तचक्षुश्चाद्राक्षीदावासस्थानसकाशात्प्रतिष्ठमानं स्कन्धावारम्, अघोक्षजकुक्षेरिव युगादौ निष्पतन्तं जीवलोकम्, अम्भोनिधिमिव कुम्भभुवो वदनात्प्लावितभुवनमुद्भवन्तम्, अर्जुनबाहुदण्डसहस्रसंपिण्डितोन्मुक्तमिव सहस्रधा प्रवर्तमानं प्रवाहं नर्मदायाः । 'प्रसर तात । भाव, किं विलम्बसे । त्वङ्गति[5] तुरङ्गमः । भद्र, भग्नचरण इव सञ्चरसि यावदमी पुरःसराः सरभसमुपरि पतन्ति । वाहयसि किमुष्ट्रम् । न पश्यसि निर्दय निःशूकशिशुं शयानम् । वत्स रामिल, रजसि यथा न नश्यसि[6] तथा समीपे भव । किं न पश्यसि गलति सक्तुप्रसेवकः । किमेवमित्वर त्वरसे । सौरभेयसरणिमपहाय हयमध्यं धावसि धीवरि । विशसि गन्तुकामा मातङ्गि मातङ्गमार्गम् । भङ्ग, गलति तिरश्चीना चणकगोणी गणयसि न मामारटन्तम्[7] । अवटमेवटेनावतरसि । सुखमास्स्व स्वैरिणि सौवीरककुम्भो भग्नः । मन्थरक, खादिष्यसि गतः सक्षिक्षुम् । उक्षाणं प्रसारय[8] । कियच्चिरं चिनोषि चेट बदराणि दूरं गन्तव्यम् । किमद्यैव विद्रासि द्रोणक द्राघीयसी दण्डयात्रा । विनैकेन निष्ठुरकेण निष्क्रेयमस्माकम् । अग्रतः पन्थाः स्थपुटकः[9] । स्थावरक, यथा न भनक्षि फाणितस्थालीम् । गरीयान्गण्डकतण्डुलभारको न निर्वहति दम्यः । दासक, मौषीणा[10]-

---

१ '०क्रीडन्निव' अ. २ 'दिशि' ब. ३ '०कृतापराह्लादा' ब. ४ 'शिशेकिरे' अ-क. ५ 'लङ्घति' ब. ६ 'नश्यसि न पश्यसि' अ; 'नश्यसि नो पयसि' क. ७ 'अतटेन' अ-क. ८ 'प्रसादय' अ-क. ९ 'स्थपुटक' अ-क. १० 'माषीणाममुतो' अ.

दमुतो द्राग्दात्रेण मुखघासपूलकं लुनीहि। को जानाति यवसगतं गतानाम्। धव, वारय बलीवर्दान्, वाहीकरक्षितं क्षेत्रमिदम्। लम्बिता शकटी, शाक्करं धुरन्धरं धुरि धवलं नियुङ्क्ष्व। यक्षपालित, प्रमदाः पिनक्षि। अक्षिणी किं ते स्फुटिते। हत हस्तिपक[1] रे, दीव्यसि करिकरदण्डे। समद, संमर्दकर्दमे स्खलसि। भ्रातर्भाव विधुरबन्धो[2], उद्धर पङ्कादनड्वाहम्। इत एहि माणवक, घनेभघटासङ्कटसङ्कटे नास्ति निस्सरणसरणिः[3]।' इत्येवमादिप्रवर्तमानानेकसंलापं क्वचित्स्वेच्छामृदितोद्दामसस्यघासविघससुखसम्पन्नान्नपुष्टैः केलिकलैः किलकिलायमानैर्मेण्ठवण्ठवठरलम्बनलेशिकलुण्ठकचेटचाटचण्डालमण्डलैराण्डीरैः स्तूयमानम्, क्वचिदसहायैः क्लेशार्जितकुग्रामककुटुम्बिसम्पादितसीदत्सौरभेयशम्बलसंवाहनायासावेगागतसंयोगैः स्वयंगृहीतगृहोपस्करणैः 'इयमेका कथंचिद्दण्डयात्रा यातु। यातु पातालतलं तृष्णाभूतेरभवनिः। भवतु शिवम्। सेवा करोतु। स्वस्ति सर्वदुःखकूटाय कटकाय' इति दुर्विधकुलपुत्रकैर्निन्द्यमानम्, क्वचिदतितीक्ष्णसलिलस्रोतःपातिनौगतैरिव ग्रथितैरिव पङ्क्तिभूतैर्जनैरतिद्रुतं द्रवद्भिः कृष्णकठिनस्कन्धगुरुलगुडैर्गृहीतसौवर्णपादपीठीपर्यङ्ककरङ्ककलशपतद्ग्रहावग्राहैः[5][6] प्रत्यासन्नपार्थिवोपकरणग्रहणगर्वदुर्वारैः सर्वमेव बहिः कारयद्भिर्भूपतिभृतकभारिकैर्महानसोपकरणवाहिमिश्र बद्धवराहवध्रवाध्रीणसैर्लम्बमानहरिणचटुकचटकजूटजटिलैः शिशुशशकशाकपत्रवेत्राग्रसंग्रहसंग्राहिभिः शुक्लकर्पटप्रावृतमुखैकदेशदत्तार्द्रमुद्रागुप्तगोरसभाण्डैस्तलकतापकतापिकाहस्तकताम्रचरुककटाहसङ्कटपिटकभारिकैः समुत्सार्यमाणपुरोवर्तिजनम्, क्वचित् 'क्लेशोऽस्माकम्। फलकालेऽन्य एव विटाः समुपस्थास्यन्ते' इति मुखरैः पदे पदे पततां दुर्बलबलीवर्दानां नियुक्तैः[7] स्खलने खलचेटकैः खेद्यमानासंविभक्तकुलपुत्रलोकम्, क्वचिन्नरपतिदर्शनकुतूहलादुभयतः प्रजवितप्रधावितग्रामेयकजनपदम्, मार्गग्रामनिर्गतैराग्रहारिकजाल्मैः पुरःसरजरन्महत्तरोत्तम्भिताम्भःकुम्भैरुपायनीकृतदधिगुडखण्डकुसुमकरण्डैर्धनघटितपेटकैः सरभसं समुत्सर्पद्भिः प्रकुपितप्रचण्डदण्डिवित्रासनविद्रुतैर्दूरगतैरपि स्खलद्भिरपि पतद्भिरपि नरेन्द्रनिहितदृष्टिभिरसतोऽपि पूर्वभोगपतिदोषानुद्भावयद्भिरतिक्रान्तयुक्तकशतानि च शंसद्भिश्चिरन्तनचाटापराधांश्चामिदधानैरुद्धूयमानधूलिपटलम्, क्वचिदेकान्तप्रवृत्ताश्ववारचक्रैश्चर्व्यमाणागामिगौडविमृग्यमाणसस्यसंरक्षणम्[8], अपरैरादिष्टपरिपालकपुरुषपरितुष्टैः 'धर्मः प्रत्यक्षो देवः' इति स्तुतीरातन्वद्भिरपरैर्लूयमाननिष्पन्नसस्यप्रकटितविषादैः क्षेत्रशुचा सकुटुम्बैरेव निर्गतैः प्ररूढप्राणच्छेदैः परितापत्याजितभयैः 'क्व राजा कुतो राजा कीदृशो वा राजा' इति प्रारब्धनरनाथनिन्दम्, शशकैश्च पदे पदे प्रजविप्र-

१ 'हस्तिपको नेदीयसि करीकरदण्डे समदः' ब. २ 'विधुरे बन्धुरुद्धर' ब. ३ 'निस्तरणम्' अ–क. ४ 'शाट' ब. ५ 'पीठीकरङ्क' अ–क. ६ 'पतद्ग्राहावगाहैः' अ–क. ७ 'नियुक्तैः खेटने खेटचेटकैः' अ–क. ८ 'चर्व्यमाण' ब.

चण्डदण्डपाणिपेटकानुबद्धैर्गिरिगुडकैरिव हन्यमानैरितस्ततः सञ्चरद्भिरपरैर्युग-पत्परापतितमहाजनग्रस्तैस्तिलशो विलुप्यमानैरनेकजन्तुजङ्घान्तरालनिःसरण-कुशलिभिः कुटिलिकाव्यंसितसादिबहुश्वभिः पतल्लोष्टलगुडकोणकुठारकीलकु-द्दालखनित्रदात्रयष्टिभिरपि[1] निःसरद्भिरायुषो बलात्कृतकलकलम्, अन्यत्र स-ङ्घशो घासिकैर्बुसधूलीधूसरितघासजालजालकितजघनैश्च पुराणपर्याणैकदेश-दोलायमानदात्रैश्च शीर्णोर्णाशकलशिथिलमलिनमलकुथैश्च प्रभुप्रसादीकृतपाटि-तपटच्चरचलच्चोलकधारिभिश्च धावमानैरुद्धूयमानधूलिपटलम्, क्वचिदेकान्त-प्रवृत्ताश्ववारचक्रचर्व्यमाणागामिगौडविग्रहम्, क्वचित्पङ्किलप्रदेशपूरणादेशाकु-लसकललोकलूयमानतृणपूलकम्, क्वचित्तलवर्तिवेत्रिवेत्रवित्रास्यमानशाखिशि-खरगतविक्रोशद्विवादिब्राह्मणम्, क्वचित्कुलुण्ठकपाशविवेष्ट्यमानग्रासीणकग्रा[2]-माकृष्टकौलेयकम्, क्वचिदन्योन्यविभवस्पर्धोद्धुरराजपुत्रवाह्यमानवाजिसङ्घट्टम[3]-ण्डितम्, अनेकवृत्तान्ततया कौतुकजननम्, प्रलयजलधिमिव जगद्ग्रासग्रह-णाय प्रवृत्तम्, पातालमिव महाभोगिनां गुप्तये समुत्पादितम्, कैलासमिव परमेश्वरवसतये सृष्टम्, दृश्यमानसकलप्राणिपर्यायं चतुर्युगसर्गकोशमिव प्र-जापतीनाम्, क्लेशबहुलमपि तपःकरणमिव क्रमकारणं[4] कल्याणानाम्, एवं च वीक्षमाणः कटकं जगाम।

आसन्नवर्तिनां च तत्रभवताम्, 'मान्धात्रा प्रवर्तिताः पन्थानो दिग्विज-याय। अप्रतिहतरथरंहसा रघुणा लघुनैव कालेनाकारि ककुभां प्रसादनम्। शरासनद्वितीयः करदीचकार चक्रं क्रमागतभुजबलाभिजनधनमदावलिप्तानां भूभुजां पाण्डुः। पाण्डवः सव्यसाची चीनविषयमतिक्रम्य राजसूयसम्पदे क्रुध्यद्गन्धर्वधनुष्कोटिटांकारकूजितकुञ्जं हेमकूटपर्वतं पराजैष्ट। सङ्कलपान्तरि-तो विजयस्तरस्विनाम्। सहिमहिमवद्व्यवहितोऽप्युवाह बाहुबलव्यतिकरका-तरः करं कौरवेश्वरस्य किङ्कर इवाकृती द्रुमः। नातिजिगीषवः खलु पूर्वे ये-नाल्प एव भूभागे भूयांसो भगदत्तदन्तवक्रक्राथकर्णकौरवशिशुपालसाल्वज-रासन्धसिन्धुराजप्रभृतयोऽभवन्भूपतयः। सन्तुष्टो राजा युधिष्ठिरो यो ह्यसहत समीप एव धनञ्जयजयजनितजगत्कम्पः किंपुरुषाणां राज्यम्। अलसश्चण्ड-कोशो यो न प्राविक्षत्क्ष्मां जित्वा स्त्रीराज्यम्। हसीय एवान्तरं तुषारगिरिगन्ध-मादनयोः उत्साहिनः किष्कुस्तुरुष्कविषयः, पारसीकदेशः प्रादेशः, शशपदं श-कस्थानम्, अदृश्यमानप्रतिप्रहारे पारियात्रे यात्रैव शिथिला, शौर्यशुल्कः सुल-भो दक्षिणापथः, दक्षिणार्णवकल्लोलानिलचलितचन्दनलतासौरभसुन्दरीकृत-दरीमन्दिराद्दर्दुरादद्रेर्नेदीयसि मलयो मलयलग्न एव च महेन्द्रः।' इत्येवंप्रा-यानुद्योगद्योतकानामालापान्पार्थिवकुमाराणां बाहुशालिनां शृण्वन्नेवाससा-दावासम्। मन्दिरद्वारि चोभयतः सबहुमानं भ्रूलताभ्यां विसर्जितराजलोकः

१ 'यष्टिवृष्टिभिरपि' ब. २ 'कुलुण्डकपाशविवेच' क. ३ 'विभाव' ब. ४ 'कारिणम्' क.

प्रविश्य चावततार बाह्यास्थानमण्डपस्थापितमासनमाचक्राम। प्रास्तसमायोगश्च क्षणमासिष्ट।

अथ तत्र प्रतीहारः पृथ्वीपृष्ठप्रतिष्ठापितपाणिपल्लवो विज्ञापितवान्—'देव, प्राग्ज्योतिषेश्वरेण कुमारेण प्रहितो हंसवेगनामा दूतोऽन्तरङ्गस्तोरणमध्यास्ते' इति। राजा तु 'तमाशु प्रवेशय' इति सादरमादिदेश। अथ दक्षतया क्षितिपालादराच्च प्रतीहारः स्वयमेव निरगात्। अनन्तरं च हंसवेगः सविनयमाकृत्यैव नयनानन्दसम्पादनसुभगाभोगभद्रया समुल्लङ्घ्यमानगुणगरिमा प्रभूतप्राभृतभृतां पुरुषाणां समूहेन महतानुगम्यमानः प्रविवेश राजमन्दिरम्। आरादेव पञ्चाङ्गालिङ्गिताङ्गनः प्रणाममकरोत्। 'एह्येहि' इति सबहुमानमाहूतश्च प्रधावितोऽपसृतः पादपीठलुठितललाटलेखो न्यस्तहस्तः पृष्ठे पार्थिवेनोपसृत्य भूयो नमश्चक्रे। स्निग्धनरेन्द्रदृष्ट्या निर्दिष्टमविप्रकृष्टं स प्रदेशमध्यास्त। ततो राजा तिरश्चीं तनुमीषदिव दधानश्चामरग्राहिणीमन्तरालवर्तिनीं समुत्सार्य संमुखीनस्तं सप्रश्रयं पप्रच्छ—'हंसवेग, श्रीमान्कच्चित्कुशली कुमारः' इति। स तमन्ववादीत्—'अद्य कुशली येनैवं स्नेहस्नपितया सौहार्दद्रवार्द्रया सगौरवं गिरा पृच्छति देवः' इति।

स्थित्वा च मुहूर्तमिव पुनः स चतुरम्भोधिभोगभूतिभाजनभूतस्य देवस्य सद्भावगर्भमपहाय हृदयमेकमन्यदनुरूपं प्राभृतमेव दुर्लभं लोके तथाप्यस्मत्स्वामिना सन्देशमशून्यतां नयता पूर्वजोपार्जितं वारुणातपत्रमाभोगाख्यमनुरूपस्थानन्यासेन कृतार्थीकृतमेतत्। अस्य च कुतूहलकृन्ति बहूनि आश्चर्याणि दृश्यन्ते। तथाहि प्रतिदिवसं प्रविशति शैत्यहेतोश्छायायाः किरणसहस्रादेकैकः सोमस्य रश्मिरस्मिन्। यस्मिन्प्रविष्टे प्रध्यानानन्तरं स्वादवो दन्तवीणोपदेशाचार्याश्च्योतन्ति चन्द्रभासामम्भसां मणिशलाकाभ्यो यावदिच्छमच्छा धाराः। प्रचेता इव यश्चतुर्णामर्णवानामधिपतिर्भूतो भावी वा तमिदमनुगृह्णाति च्छायया नेतरम्। इदं च न सप्तार्चिर्दहति, न पृषदश्वो हरति, नोदकमार्द्रयति, न रजांसि मलिनयन्ति, न जरा जर्जरयति। एतत्तावदनुगृह्णातु दृशा देवः सन्देशमपि विस्रब्धं श्रोष्यति।' इत्येवमभिधाय विवृत्यात्मीयं पुरुषमभ्यधात्—'उत्तिष्ठ दर्शय देवस्य' इति।

स वचनानन्तरमुत्थाय पुमानूर्ध्वीचकार तद्धौतदुकूलकल्पिताच्च निचोलकादकोषीत्। आकृष्यमाण एव च यस्मिन्नतिसितमहसि सरभसमहासीव हरेण, रसातलादुदलासीव शेषफणिफणाफलकमण्डलेन, अस्थायीव चक्रीभूयान्तरिक्षे क्षीरोदेन, अघटीव गगनाङ्गने गोष्ठीबन्धः शारदेन बलाहकव्यूहेन, विश्रान्तमिव विततपक्षतिना वियति पितामहविमानहंसयूथेन, अत्रिनेत्रनिर्गतस्य धवलधाममण्डलमनोहरो दृष्ट इव जनेन जन्मदिवसः कुमुदबन्धोः, प्रत्यक्षीकृत इवोद्गमनक्षणो नारायणनाभिपुण्डरीकस्य, आहितेव कौमुदीप्रदोषदर्शनानन्दतृप्तिरक्षणाम्, उदमाङ्क्षीदिव मन्दाकिनीपुलिनमण्डलं

महदम्बरोदरे, परिवर्तित इव दिवसः पौर्णमासीनिशया, मन्दमन्दमिन्दूदयसन्देहदूयमानमानसैर्विघटितं विघटमानचञ्चुच्युतमृणालकोटिभिरासन्नकमलिनीचक्रवाकमिथुनैः, शरज्जलधरपटलाशङ्कासङ्कोचितकेकारवमूकमुखपुटैः पराङ्मुखीभूतं भवनशिखण्डिमण्डलैः, प्रबुद्धमाबद्धचन्द्रानन्दोद्दामोद्दलद्दलपुटाट्टहासविशदं कुमुदषण्डैः ।

चित्रीयमाणचेताश्च सराजको राजा दण्डानुसाराधिरोहिण्या दृष्ट्या सादरमैक्षिष्ट तत्तिलकमिव त्रिभुवनस्य, शैशवमिव श्वेतद्वीपस्य, अंशावतारमिव शरदिन्दोः, हृदयमिव धर्मस्य, निवेशमिव शशिलोकस्य, दन्तमण्डलकद्युतिधवलं मुखमिव चक्रवर्तित्वस्य, मौक्तिकजालपरिकरासितं सीमन्तचक्रमिव दिवः, बहलज्योत्स्नाशुक्लोदरमैन्दवमिव परिवेशवलयम्, शौक्ल्यापहसितशङ्खश्रीकं श्रवणमण्डलमिव निश्चलतां गतमैरावतस्य, श्वेतगङ्गावर्तपाण्डुरं पदमिव त्रिभुवनवन्दनीयं त्रिविक्रमस्य, प्रचेतसश्चूडामणिमरीचिशिखाभिरिव श्लिष्टाभिर्मानसबिसतन्तुमयीभिश्चामरिकावलीभिर्विरचितपरिवेशम्, उपरि चक्रवर्तिलक्ष्मीनूपुरस्वनश्रवणदोहदनिश्चलेनेव लक्ष्मणा विततपत्रेण हंसेन सनाथीकृतशिखरम्, स्पर्शवता च प्रभावस्तम्भितेन मन्दाकिनीमृणालेन मुकुलितफणेन वासुकिनेव नीतेन दण्डतां द्योतमानम्, धवलिम्ना क्षालयदिव नक्षत्रपथम्, प्रभाप्रवाहप्रथिम्ना प्रावृण्वदिव दिवसम्, समुच्छ्रायेणाधःकुर्वदिव दिवम्, उपरिस्थितमिव सर्वमङ्गलानाम्, श्वेतमण्डपमिव श्रियः, स्तबकमिव ब्रह्मस्तम्भस्य, नाभिमण्डलमिव ज्योत्स्नायाः, विशदहासमिव कीर्तेः, फेनराशिमिव खड्गधाराजलानाम्, यशःपटलमिव शौर्यशालितायाः, त्रैलोक्याद्भुतं महच्छत्रम् ।

दृष्टे च तस्मिन्राज्ञा प्रथमं शेषमपि प्राभृतं प्रकाशयांचक्रुः क्रमेण कार्मिकाः । तद्यथा परार्घ्यरत्नांशुशोणीकृतदिग्भागान्, भगदत्तप्रभृतिख्यातपार्थिवपरागतानाहतलक्षणानलङ्कारान्, प्रभालेपिनां च चूडामणीनां समुत्कर्षान्, क्षीरोदधेर्धवलताहेतूनिव हारान्, अनेकरागरुचिरवेत्रकरण्डकुण्डलीकृतानि शरच्चन्द्रमरीचिरुञ्चि शौचक्षमाणि क्षौमाणि कुशलशिल्पिलोकोल्लिखितानां च शुक्तिशङ्खगल्वर्कप्रमुखानां पानभाजनानां निचयान्, निचोलकरक्षितरुचां च रुचिरकाञ्चनपत्त्रभङ्गभङ्गुराणामतिबन्धुरपरिवेशानां कार्दरङ्गचर्मणां सम्भारान्, भूर्जत्वक्कोमलाः स्पर्शवतीः जातीपट्टिकाः, चित्रपटानां च म्रदीयसां समूरुकोपधानादीन्विकारान्, प्रियङ्गुप्रसवपिङ्गलत्वञ्चि चासनानि वेत्रमयान्यगुरुवल्कलकल्पितसञ्चयानि च सुभाषितभाञ्जि पुस्तकानि, परिणतपाटलपटोलत्विषि च तरुणहारीतहरिन्ति क्षीरक्षारीणि च पूगानां पल्लवलम्बीनि सरसानि फलानि, सहकारलतारसानां च कृष्णागुरुतैलस्य च कुपितकपिकपोलकपिलकापोतिकापलाशकोशीकवचिताङ्गीः स्थवीयसीर्वैणवीर्नाडीश्च, पट्टसूत्रप्रसेव-

१ 'दूयमान' अ-क. २ 'मण्डलधवलं' अ-क. ३ '०तैलस्य च कपोतकपिल०' ब.

कार्पितांश्च भिन्नाञ्जनकृष्णस्य[1] कृष्णागुरुणो गुरुपरितापमुषश्च गोशीर्षचन्दनस्य तुषारशिलाशकलशिशिरस्वच्छसितस्य च कर्पूरस्य कस्तूरिकाकोशकानां च पक्क-फलजूटजटिलानां च कक्कोलपल्लवानां लवङ्गपुष्पमञ्जरीणां जातीफलस्तबकानां च राशीन्, अतिमधुरमधुरसामोदनिर्हारिणीश्चोल्लककलशीः सितासितस्य च चामरजातस्य निचयान्, अवलम्बमानतूलिकालाबुकांश्च लिखितानालेख्यफल-[2]कसम्पुटान्, कुतूहलकृन्ति कनकश्रृङ्खलानियमितग्रीवाणां किंनराणां च वन-मानुषीणां च जीवञ्जीवकानां च जलमानुषाणां च मिथुनानि, परिमलामो-दितककुभश्च कस्तूरिकाकुरङ्गान्, गेहपरिसरणपरिचिताश्च चमरीः, चामीकर-रसचित्रवेत्रपञ्जरान्तर्गतांश्च बहुसुभाषितजल्पाकजिह्वांश्च[3] शुकशारिकाप्रभृती-न्पक्षिणः प्रवालपञ्जरगतांश्च चकोरान्, जलहस्तिनामुदग्रकुम्भमुक्ताफलदाम-दन्तुराणि च दन्तकाण्डकुण्डलानि।

राजा तु छत्रदर्शनात्प्रहृष्टहृदयः प्रथमप्रयाणे शोभननिमित्तमिति मनसा जग्राह। हंसवेगं च प्रीयमाणो बभाषे—'भद्र, सकलरत्नधाम्नः परमेश्वरशि-रोधारणार्हस्यास्य महातपत्रस्य महार्णवादिव कुमुदबान्धवस्य कुमाराल्लाभो न विस्मयाय। बालविद्याः खलु महतामुपकृतयः' इति। अपनीते च तस्मात्प्र-देशात्प्राभृतसम्भारे क्षणमिव स्थित्वा 'हंसवेग, विश्रम्यताम्' इति प्रतीहार-भवनं विसर्जयांबभूव। स्वयमप्युत्थाय स्नात्वा मङ्गलाकाङ्क्षी प्राङ्मुखः प्रावि-शदाभोगस्य छायाम्।

अथ विशत एवास्य छायाजन्मना जडिम्ना चूडामणितामनीयतेव शशि-बिम्बमम्बुबिन्दुमुचश्चुचुम्बुरिव चन्द्रकान्तमणयो ललाटतटं कर्पूररेणव इव व्यलीयन्त लोचनयुगले गलत्तुहिनकणनिकरकृतनीहारा हारा इवाबध्यन्त हरिचन्दनरसासारेणेवापाति सन्ततमुरसि कुमुदमयमिव हृदयमभवदतिशिशि-रमन्तर्हितहिमशिलेव विलीयमाना व्यलिम्पदङ्गानि। जातविस्मयश्चाकरोन्म-नसि एकमजर्यं[4] सङ्गतमपहाय कास्त्यन्या प्रतिकौशलिकेति। आहारकाले च हंसवेगाय धवलकर्पटप्रावृतधौतनालिकेरपरिगृहीतं विलिप्तशेषं चन्दनमङ्ग-स्पृष्टे च वाससी शरत्तारकाकारतारमुक्तास्तबकितपदं परिवेशं नाम कटिसूत्र-मतिमहार्हपद्मरागालोकलोहितीकृतदिवसं च तरङ्गकं नाम कर्णाभरणं प्रभूतं च भोज्यजातं प्राहिणोत्। एवंप्रायेण च क्रमेण जगाम दिवसः।

ततः कटकस्थबलबहलधूलिधूसरितवपुरंशुमाली मलीमसमङ्गमिव क्षाल-यितुमपरजलनिधिमवातरत्। आभोगातपत्रप्रदानवार्तामिव निवेदयितुं वरु-णाय वारुणीं दिशमयासीत्। मुकुलायमानसकलकमलवना प्रमुख एव बद्धसेवाञ्जलिपुटेव सद्वीपा भूरभूद्भूपतेः। नृपानुरागमय[5] इव निखिलजीव-लोकलोकाञ्जलिर्बन्धबन्धुर्जगज्जग्राह[6] संध्यारागः। गौडापराधशङ्किनीव श्या-

१ 'वर्णस्य' ब. २ 'लिखितानेकलेख्य०' ब. ३ '०जिह्वांश्च जातीः कौशिकशुक०' ब. ४ 'अजर्ये' ब. ५ 'भूपालानुरागराशिमय' ब. ६ 'बद्ध' ब.

मतां प्रपेदे दिक्प्राची। प्रचिततिमिरनिर्वहा निर्वाणान्यनृपप्रतापानलकलापेव कालिमानमतानीन्मेदिनी। मेदिनीशप्रदोषास्थानपुष्पनिकरमिव विकचतगैररुचिरमवचककरुरुडुनिकरमविरलं ककुभः। स्कन्धावारगन्धगजमदामोदधाविकलस्येव मार्गो वियति विरराज रजःपाण्डुरैरावतस्य। कुपितनृपव्याघ्राघ्रातामुपसृष्टामिव पौरुष्टुर्ती विहाय विहायस्तलमारुरोह रोहिणीरमणः। प्रयाणवार्ता इव मानिनीनां हृदयभेदिन्यो ययुरिन्दुदीधितयो दश दिशः। नवनृपदण्डयात्राप्रासातुरा इव तरलितसत्त्ववृत्तयश्चक्षुभुः पतयो वाहिनीनाम्। चिन्तेव भूभृतां हृदयानि विवेश गुहाविवराणि विमुक्तसर्वाशा तिमिरसन्ततिः। प्रतिसामन्तचक्षुषामिव ननाश निद्रा कुमुदवनानाम्।

अस्यां च वेलायां विततवितानतलवर्ती नरेन्द्रो 'यात तावत्' इति विसर्ज्यानुजीविनो हंसवेगमादिष्टवान्--'कथय सन्देशम्' इति। प्रणम्य स कथयितुं प्रास्तावीत्—'देव, पुरा महावराहसम्पर्कसम्भृतगर्भया भगवत्या भुवा नरको नाम सूनुरसावि रसातले। वीरस्य यस्याभवन्बाल्य एव पादप्रणामप्रणयिनश्चूडामणयो लोकपालानाम्। यस्य च त्रिभुवनभुजो भुजशौण्डस्य भवनकमलिनीचक्रवाकीकोपकुटिलकटाक्षेक्षितोऽपि भयचकितारुणपरिवर्तितरथो नाज्ञया विना रविरस्तमव्राजीत्। यश्च वरुणस्य बहिर्वृत्ति हृदयमिदमातपत्रमहार्षीत्। महात्मनस्तस्यान्वये भगदत्तपुष्पदत्तवज्रदत्तप्रभृतिषु व्यतीतेषु बहुषु मेरूपमेषु महत्सु महीपालेषु प्रपौत्रो महाराजभूतिवर्मणः पौत्रश्चन्द्रमुखवर्मणः पुत्रो देवस्य कैलासस्थिरस्थितेः स्थितिवर्मणः सुस्थिरवर्मा नाम महाराजाधिराजो जज्ञे तेजसां राशिर्मृगाङ्क इति [3]यं जना जगुः। योऽयमर्[4]जेनेवाजायत सहैवाहंकारेण। यश्च बाल एव प्रीत्या द्विजातीनप्रीत्या चारातीन्समग्रान्प्रतिग्रहानग्राहयत्। यत्र चातिदुर्लभं लवणालयसम्भूतायाः परं माधुर्यमभूल्लक्ष्म्याः। तथा च यो वाहिनीनाथानां शङ्खानहार न रत्नानि, पृथिव्याः स्थैर्यं जग्राह न करम्, अवनिभृतां गौरवमादत्त न नैष्ठुर्यम्। तस्य च सुगृहीतनाम्नो देवस्य देव्यां श्यामादेव्यां भास्करद्युतिर्भास्करवर्मापरनामा तनयः शन्तनोर्भागीरथ्यां भीष्म इव कुमारः समभवत्। अयमस्य च शैशवादारभ्य सङ्कल्पः स्थेयान्स्थाणुपादारविन्दद्वयादृते नाहमन्यं नमस्कुर्यामिति। ईदृशश्चायं मनोरथस्त्रिभुवनदुर्लभस्त्रयाणामन्यतमेन सम्पद्यते सकलभुवनविजयेन वा मृत्युना वा यदि वा प्रचण्डप्रतापज्वलन[5]जनितदिग्दाहेन जगत्येकवीरेण देवोपमेन मित्रेण। मैत्री च प्रायः कार्यव्यपेक्षिणी क्षोणीभृताम्। कार्यं च कीदृशं नाम तद्भवेद्यदुपन्यस्यमानमुपनयेन्मित्रतां देवम्। देवस्य हि यशांसि सञ्चिचीषतो बहिरङ्गभूतानि धनानि। बाहावेव च केवले निषण्णस्य शेषावयवानामपि साहायकसम्पादनमनोरथो निरवकाशः किमुत बाह्यजन-

१ 'निर्वाहा' ब. २ 'तवर' ब. ३ 'प्रियं जना' ब. ४ 'योऽयमजेनेवा०' अ-क. ५ 'ज्वलनदिग्दाहेन' अ-क.

स्य। चतुःसागरग्रामग्रहणघस्मरस्य पृथिव्येकदेशदानोपन्यासेनापि का तुष्टिः। अभिरूपकन्याविश्राणनविलोभनमपि लक्ष्मीमुखारविन्ददर्शनदुर्ललितदृष्टेरकिंचित्करम्। एवमघटमानसकलोपायसम्पादितपदार्थेऽस्मिन्प्रार्थनामात्रकमेव केवलमनुरुध्यमानः शृणोतु देवः। प्राग्ज्योतिषेश्वरो हि देवेनैकपिङ्ग इवानङ्गद्विषा, दशरथ इव गोत्रभिदा, धनञ्जय इव पुष्कराक्षेण, वैकर्तन इव दुर्योधनेन, मलयानिल इव माधवेन, अजर्यं सङ्गतमिच्छति। यदि च देवस्यापि मैत्रीयति हृदयमवगच्छति च पर्यायान्तरितं दास्यमनुतिष्ठन्ति सुहृद इति ततः किमास्यते समाज्ञाप्यतामनुभवतु विष्णोर्मन्दरगिरिरिव विकटकेयूरकोटिमणिविघट्टनक्वणितकटकमणिशिलाशकलानि गाढोपगूढानि देवस्य कामरूपाधिपतिः। अस्मिन्नातृसेरनवरतविमललावण्यसौभाग्यसुधानिर्झरिणि मुखशशिनि चिराच्चक्षुषी लालयतु प्राग्ज्योतिषेश्वरश्रीः। नाभिनन्दति चेद्देवः प्रणयमाज्ञापयतु किं कथनीयं मया स्वामिनः' इति।

विरतवचसि तस्मिन्भूपालः पूर्वोपलब्धैरेव गुरुभिर्गुणैरारोपितबहुमानः कुमारे सुदूरमाभोगातपत्रव्यतिकरेण तु परां कोटिमारोपिते प्रेम्णि लज्जमान इव सादरं जगाद—'हंसवेग, कथमिव तादृशि महात्मनि महाभिजने पुण्यराशौ गुणिनां प्राग्रहरे परोक्षसुहृदि स्निह्यति मद्विधस्यान्यथा स्वप्नेऽपि प्रवर्तेत मनः। सकलजगदुत्तापनपटवोऽपि शिशिरायन्ते त्रिभुवननयनानन्दकरे कमलाकरे करास्तिग्मतेजसः। सुबहुगुणगणक्रीताश्च के वयं सख्यस्य। सज्जनमाधुर्याणामभूतदास्यो दश दिशः। एकान्तावदातोत्तानस्वभावसम्भृतसादृश्यस्य कुमुदस्य कृते केनाभिहितः शिशिररश्मिः। श्रेयांश्च सङ्कल्पः कुमारस्य। स्वयं बाहुशाली मयि च समालम्बितशरासने सुहृदि हराद्दते कमन्यं नमस्यति। संवर्धिता मे प्रीतिरमुना सङ्कल्पेन। अवलेपिनि पशावपि केसरिणि बहुमानो हृदयस्य किं पुनः सुहृदि। तत्तथा यतेथा यथा न चिरमियमस्मान्क्लेशयति कुमारदर्शनोत्कण्ठा' इति।

हंसवेगस्तु विज्ञापयाम्बभूव—'देव, किमपरमिदानीं क्लेशयत्यभिजातमभिहितं देवेन। सेवाभीरवो हि सन्तः, तत्रापि विशेषेणायमहङ्कारधनो वैष्णवो वंशः। आस्तां तावदस्मत्स्वामिवंशः। पश्यतु देवः पुरुषस्य हि सेवां प्रति दुर्जनन्येवातिवृद्धया दुर्गत्या वाभिमुखीक्रियमाणस्य, कुटुम्बिन्येवासन्तुष्टया तृष्णया वा प्रेर्यमाणस्य, दुरपत्यैरिव यौवनजनितैर्नानाभिलाषिभिरसत्सङ्कल्पैर्वाकुलीक्रियमाणस्य, जरत्कुमारीमिव परमार्गणयोग्यामतिमहतीं वा अवस्थां पश्यतः, स्वगृहे दुर्बन्धुभिरिव दुःस्थितैः समग्रैर्ग्रहैर्वा ग्राह्यमाणस्याभियोगं, पुरातनैरतिदुस्त्यजैर्भृत्यैरिव मलिनैः कर्मभिर्वानुवर्त्यमानस्य, सकलशरीरसन्तापकरं कारीषाग्निमिव दुष्कृतिनः कृतचित्तस्य संप्रवेष्टुं राजकुलम्, उपहतसकलेन्द्रियशक्तेरिव मिथ्यैव हृदयगतविषयग्रामग्रहणाभिलाषस्य, प्रथममेव तोरणतले वन्दनमालाकिशलयस्येव शुष्यतो द्वाररक्षिभिर्निरुद्धस्य, पीडितस्य

प्रविशतो द्वारे हरिणस्येवापरैर्हन्यमानस्य, करिकर्मचर्मपुटस्येव मुहुर्मुहुः प्रतिहारमण्डलकरप्रहारैर्निरस्यमानस्य, निधिपादपप्ररोहस्येव[1] द्रविणाभिलाषादधोमुखीभवतः, दूरममार्गणस्याप्यतिविप्रकृष्टविवृत्त[2]विसर्जितस्योद्वेगं व्रजतः, अकण्टकस्यापि चरणतललग्नस्याकृष्य क्षेपीयः क्षिप्यमाणस्य, अमकरकेतोरप्यकालोपसर्पणप्रकुपितेश्वरदृष्टिदग्धस्य प्रलयमुपगच्छतः, कपेरिव कोपनिर्भर्त्सितस्याप्यभिन्नमुखरागस्य, ब्रह्मघ्न इव प्रतिदिवसवन्दनोद्घृष्टशिरःकपालस्य, स्पर्शरहितस्याशुभकर्माणि निर्वहतः, त्रिशङ्कोरिवोभयलोकभ्रष्टस्य नक्तन्दिनमर्वाक्शिरसस्तिष्ठतः, वाजिन इव कवलवशेन सुखवाह्यमात्मानं विदधानस्य, अनशनशायिन इव हृदयस्थापितजीवनाशस्य शरीरं क्षपयतः, शुन इव निजदारपराङ्मुखस्य जघन्यकर्मलग्नमात्मानं ताडयतः, प्रेतस्येवानुचितभूमिदीयमानान्नपिण्डस्य, बलिभुज इव जिह्वालौल्योपयुक्तपुरुषवर्चसो वृथा विहितायुषो जीवतः, श्मशानपादपानिव पिशाचस्य दग्धभूत्या परुषीकृताम्राजवल्लभानुपसर्पतः, विपरीतजिह्वाजनितमाधुर्यैरोष्ठमात्रप्रकटितरागै राजशुकालापैः शिशोरिव मुग्धविलोभ्यमानस्य, वेतालस्येव नरेन्द्रप्रभावाविष्टस्य न किंचिन्नाचरतः, चित्रधनुष इवालीकगुणाध्यारोपणैकक्रियानित्यनम्रस्य निर्वाणतेजसः, संमार्जनीसमुपार्जितरजसोऽवकरकूटस्येव निर्माल्यवाहिनः, कफविकारिण इव दिने दिने कटुकैरुद्वेज्यमानस्य, सौगतस्येवार्थशून्यविज्ञप्तिजनितवैराग्यस्य काषायाण्यभिलषतः, निशास्वपि मातृबलिपिण्डस्येव दिक्षु विक्षिप्यमाणस्य, अशौचगतस्येव कुशयनजनितसमधिकतरदुःखवृत्तेः, तुलायन्त्रस्येव पश्चात्कृतगौरवस्य तोयार्थमपि नमतः, अतिकृपणस्य शिरसा केवलेनासन्तुष्टस्य वचसापि पादौ स्पृशतः, निर्दयवेत्रिवेत्रताडनत्रस्तयेव त्रपया त्यक्तस्य, दैन्यसङ्कोचितहृदयहृतावकाशयेवाहोपुरुषिकया परिवर्जितस्य, कुत्सितकर्माङ्गीकरणकुपितयेवोन्नत्या वियुक्तस्य, धनश्रद्धया क्लेशानुपार्जयतः, स्ववृद्धिबुद्ध्यावमानं वर्धयतो मूढस्य, सत्यपि विविधकुसुमाधिवाससुरभिणि वने तृष्णाञ्जलिमुपरचयतः, कुलपुत्रस्यापि कृतागस इव भीतभीतस्य समीपमुपसर्पतः, दर्शनीयस्याप्यालेख्यकुसुमस्येव निष्फलजन्मनः, विदुषोऽपि वैधेयस्येवापशब्दमुखस्य, शक्तिमतोऽपि श्वित्रिण इव सङ्कोचितकरयुगलस्य, समसमुत्कर्षेषु निरग्निपच्यमानस्य, नीचसमीकरणेषु निरुच्छ्वासं म्रियमाणस्य, परिभवैस्तृणीकृतस्य, दुःखानिलेनानिर्वृतेः, ज्वलतो भक्तस्याप्यभक्तस्य, निरूष्मणः सन्तापयतो बन्धून्विमानस्याप्यगतिकस्य, च्युतगौरवस्याप्यधस्ताद्गच्छतः, निःसत्त्वस्यापि महामांसविक्रयं कुर्वतः, निर्मदस्याप्यस्वतन्त्रवृत्तेरयोगिनोऽपि ध्यानवशीकृतात्मनः शय्योत्थायं प्रणमतो दग्धमुण्डस्य गोत्रविदूषकस्य नक्तंदिनं नृत्यतो मनस्विजनं हासयतः, कुलाङ्गारस्य वंशं दहतः, नृपशोः तृणेऽपि लब्धे कन्धरामवनमयतः, जठरपरिपूरणमात्रप्रयोजनजन्मनो मांसपिण्डस्य गर्भरोगस्य

---

१ '०प्ररोठदारुमयदेहस्येव द्रविणा-' ब. २ 'विवृत' ब.

मातुः,अपुण्यानां कर्मणामाचरणाद्भृतकस्य किं प्रायश्चित्तम्, का प्रतिपत्तिक्रिया, क्व गतस्य शान्तिः, कीदृशं जीवितम्, कः पुरुषाभिमानः, किंनामानो विलासाः, कीदृशी भोगश्रद्धा, प्रबलपङ्क इव सर्वमधस्तान्नयति दारुणो दासशब्दः। धिक्तदुच्छ्वसितमुपयातु[1] तद्धनं निधनमभवनिर्भूतेरस्तु तस्याः नमो भगवद्भ्यस्तेभ्यः सुखेभ्यस्तस्यायमञ्जलिरैश्वर्यस्य तिष्ठतु दूर एव सा श्रीः शिवं स परिच्छदः करोतु यदर्थमुत्तमाङ्गं गां गमिष्यति[2] सुखप्रियरतः क्लीबः पूतिमांसमयः कृमिरगण्यमानो नरकः, पादरजोधूसरोत्तमाङ्गो जङ्गमः पादपीठः, पुंस्कोकिलः काकुक्वणितेषु, शिखी सुखकरकेकासु, स्थूलकूर्मः क्रोडकषणेषु, श्वा नीचचाटुकरणेषु, वेणुर्मूर्च्छनासु, वेश्याकायः करणबन्धक्लेशेषु, पलालं सत्त्वशालिषु, कृकलासः[3] शिरोविडम्बनासु, जाहक आत्मसङ्कोचनेषु, प्रतिपादकः पादसंवाहनासु, कन्दुकः करतलताडनेषु, वीणादण्डः कोणाभिघातेषु, वराकः सेवकोऽपि मर्त्यमध्ये राजिलोऽपि वा भोगी पुलाकोऽपि वा कलमः वरं क्षणमपि कृता मानवता[4] मानवता न मतो नमतस्त्रैलोक्याधिराज्योपभोगोऽपि मनस्विनः। तदेवमभिनन्दितास्मदीयप्रणयो देवोऽपि दिवसैः कतिपयैरेव परागतः प्राग्ज्योतिषेश्वर इति करोतु चेतसि' इत्युक्त्वा तूष्णीमभूदचिराच्च नमस्कृत्य निर्जगाम।

राजापि रजनीं तां कुमारदर्शनौत्सुक्यस्वीकृतहृदयः समनैषीत्। आत्मार्पणं हि महताममूलमन्त्रमयं वशीकरणम्। प्रभाते च प्रभूतं प्रतिप्राभृतं प्रधानप्रतिदूताधिष्ठितं दत्त्वा हंसवेगं प्राहिणोत्। आत्मनापि ततः प्रभृति प्रयाणकैरनवरतैरभ्यमित्रं प्रावर्तत। कदाचित्तु राज्यवर्धनभुजबलोपार्जितमशेषं मालवराजसाधनमादायागतं समीप एवावासितं लेखहारकाद्भण्डिमश्रृणोत्। श्रुत्वा चाभिनवीभूतभ्रातृशोकहुताशनः कातरहृदयो बभूव मूर्च्छान्धकारमिव विवेशातिष्ठच्च समुत्सृष्टसकलव्यापारः प्रतीहारनिवारणनिभृतनिःशब्दपरिजने निजमन्दिरे सराजकपरिवारस्तदागमनमुदीक्षमाणो मुहूर्तम्।

अथ भण्डिरेकेनैव वाजिना कतिपयकुलपुत्रपरिवृतो मलिनवासा रिपुशरशल्यपूरितेन निखातबहुलोहकीलकपरिकररक्षितस्फुटनेनेव हृदयेन, हृदयलग्नैः स्वामिसत्कैरिव श्मश्रुभिः शुचं समुपदर्शयन्, दूरीकृतव्यायामशिथिलभुजदण्डदोलायमानमङ्गलवलयैकशेषालङ्कृतिः, अनादरोपयुक्तताम्बूलविरलरागेण शोकदहनदह्यमानस्य हृदयस्याङ्गारेणेव दीर्घनिश्वासवेगनिर्गतेनाधरेण शुष्यता, स्वामिविरहविधृतजीवितापराधवैलक्ष्यादिव बाष्पवारिपटलेन पटेनेव प्रावृतवदनः, विशन्निव दुर्बलीभूतैः स्वाङ्गमपत्रपयाङ्गैः, वमन्निव च व्यर्थीभूतभुजोष्माणमायतैर्निश्वसितैः, पातकीव, अपराधीव, द्रोहीव, मुषित

१ 'उपयातु निधनं धनम्' ब.
२ 'गमिष्यत्यशापानुग्रहक्षमस्तपस्वी मुख–' ब.
३ 'कृकलासः····सङ्कोचनेषु' इत्येतत् 'नीचचाटुकरणेषु' इत्यस्यानन्तरं ब–पुस्तके.
४ 'मानवताम्' ब.

इव, छलित इव, यूथपतिपतनविषण्ण इव वेगदण्डवारणः, सूर्यास्तमयनिःश्रीक इव कमलाकरः, दुर्योधननिधनदुर्मना इव द्रौणिः, अपहृतरत्न इव सागरो राजद्वारमाजगाम। अवतीर्य च तुरङ्गमादवनतमुखो विवेश राजमन्दिरम्। दूरादेव च विमुक्ताक्रन्दः पपात पादयोः।

अवनिपतिरपि दृष्ट्वा तमुत्थाय विरलैः पदैः प्रत्युद्गम्योत्थाप्य च गाढमुपगुह्य कण्ठे करुणमतिचिरं रुरोद। शिथिलीभूतमन्युवेगश्च पुरेव पुनरागत्य निजासने निषसाद। प्रथमप्रक्षालितमुखे च भण्डौ मुखमक्षालयत्। समतिक्रान्ते च कियत्यपि काले भ्रातृमरणवृत्तान्तमप्राक्षीत्। अथाकथयच्च यथावृत्तमखिलं भण्डिः। अथ नरपतिस्तमुवाच—'राज्यश्रीव्यतिकरः कः' इति। स पुनरवादीत्—'देव, देवभूयं गते देवे राज्यवर्धने गुप्तनाम्ना च गृहीते कुशस्थले देवी राज्यश्रीः परिभ्रश्य बन्धनाद्विन्ध्याटवीं सपरिवारा प्रविष्टेति लोकतो वार्तामश्रृणवम्। अन्वेष्टारस्तु तां प्रति प्रभूताः प्रहिता जना नाद्यापि निवर्तन्ते' इति। तच्चाकर्ण्य भूपतिरब्रवीत्—'किमन्यैरनुपदिभिः यत्र सा तत्र परित्यक्तान्यकृत्यः स्वयमहं यास्यामि। भवानपि कटकमादाय प्रवर्ततां गौडाभिमुखम्।' इत्युक्त्वा चोत्थाय स्नानभुवमगात्। कारितशोकश्मश्रुवपनकर्मणा च महाप्रतीहारभवनस्नातेन शारीरिकवसनकुसुमाङ्गरागालङ्कारप्रेषणप्रकटितप्रसादेन भण्डिना सार्धमभुक्त निनाय च तेनैव सह वासरम्।

अथापरेद्युरुषस्येव भण्डिर्भूपालमुपसृत्य व्यज्ञापयत्—'पश्यतु देवः श्रीराज्यवर्धनभुजबलार्जितं साधनं सपरिबर्हं मालवराजस्य' इति। नरपतिना स 'एवं क्रियताम्' इत्यभ्यनुज्ञातो दर्शयाम्बभूव। तद्यथा—अनवरतगलितमदमदिरामोदमुखरमधुकरजूटजटिलकरटपट्टपङ्किलगण्डान् गण्डशैलानिव जङ्गमान् गम्भीरगर्जितरवाञ्जलधरानिव महीमवतीर्णानुत्फुल्लसप्तच्छदवनामोदमुचः शरद्दिवसानिव पुञ्जीभूताननेकसहस्रसंख्यान्करिणः, चारुचामीकरचित्रचामरमण्डलमनोहरांश्च हरिणरंहसो हरीन्, बालातपविसरवर्षिणां च किरणैरनेकेन्द्रायुधीकृतदशदिशामलङ्काराणां विशेषान्, विस्मयकृतः स्मरोन्मादितमालवीकुचपरिमलदुर्ललितांश्च निजज्योत्स्नापूरप्लावितदिगन्तानपि तारान्हारान्, उडुपतिपादसञ्चयशुचीनि निजयशांसीव बालव्यजनानि, जातरूपमयनालं च निवासपुण्डरीकमिव श्रियः श्वेतातपत्रम्, अप्सरस इव बहुसमररससाहसानुरागावतीर्णा वारविलासिनीः, सिंहासनशयनासन्दीप्रभृतीनि राज्योपकरणानि, कालायसनिगडनिश्चलीकृतचरणयुगलं च सकलं[1] मालवराजलोकमशेषांश्च ससंख्यालेख्यपत्रान् सालङ्कारापीडैपीडान्[2] कोषकलशान्। अथालोच्य तत्सर्वमवनिपालः स्वीकर्तुं यथाधिकारमादिक्षदध्यक्षान्। अन्यस्मिंश्चाहनि हयैः स्वसारमन्वेष्टुमुच्चचाल विन्ध्याटवीमवाप च परिमितैरेव प्रयाणकैस्ताम्।

---

१ 'कालकलाकलापे' ब. २ सालङ्कारपेडापीडान्' ब.

अथ प्रविशन्दूरादेव दह्यमानषष्टिकबुसविसरविसारिविभावसूनां वन्यधान्यबीजधानीनां धूमेन धूसरिमाणमादधानैः, शुष्कशाखासञ्चयरचितगोवाटवेष्टितविकटवटैः, व्यापादितवत्सरूपकरोषरचितै[1]र्व्याघ्रयन्त्रैः, [2]अयन्त्रितवनपालहठह्रियमाणपरग्रामीणकाष्ठिककुठारैः, गहनतरुषण्डनिर्मितचामुण्डामण्डपैर्वनप्रदेशैः प्रकाश्यमानम्, अटवीप्रायप्रान्ततया कुटुम्बभरणाकुलैः कुद्दालप्रायकृषिभिः कृषीवलैरबलीवर्दैरवलम्बिरुच्चभागभाषितेन भज्यमानभूरि[3]शालिखलक्षेत्रखण्डलकम्, अल्पावकाशैश्च [4]कांशिलैः कालायसैरिव कृष्णमृत्तिकाकठिनैः स्थानस्थानस्थापितस्थाणूत्थितस्थूलपल्लवैः दुरुपगमश्यामाकप्ररूढिभिरलम्बुसबहुलैरविरहितकोकिलाक्षक्षुपैर्विरलविरलैः केदारैः कृच्छ्रकृष्यमाणैर्नातिप्रभूतप्रवृत्तगतागताप्रहतभुवमुपक्षेत्रमुपरचितैरुच्चैर्मञ्चैश्च सूच्यमानश्वापदोपद्रवम्, दिशि दिशि च प्रतिमार्गद्रुमकृतानां पथिकपादप्रस्फोटनधूलिधूसरैर्नव[5]पल्लवैर्लाञ्छितच्छायानाम्, अटवीसुलभसालकुसुमस्तबकाञ्चितनवखातकूपिकोपकण्ठप्रतिष्ठितनागस्फुटानामच्छिद्रकटकल्पितकुटीरकाणाम्, कुटिलकीटवेणीवेष्ट्यमानशक्तुशारशरावश्रेणीश्रितानामध्वगजनजग्धजम्बूफलास्थिशबलसमीपभुवामुद्धूलितधूलीकदम्बस्तबकप्रकरपुलकिनीनाम्, कण्टकितकर्करीचक्राक्रान्तकाष्ठमञ्चिकामुषिततृषाम्, तिम्यत्तलशीतलसिकतिलकलशीशमितश्रमाणामाश्यानशैवलश्यामलितालिञ्जरजायमानजलजडिम्नामुदकुम्भाकृष्टपाटलशर्कराशकलशिशिरीकृतदिशाम्, घटमुखघटितकटहारपाटलापुष्पपुटानाम्, शीकरपुलकितपल्लवपूलीपाल्यमानशोष्यसरसशिशुसहकारफलजूटीजटिल[6]स्थाणूनाम्, विश्राम्यत्कार्पटिकपेटकपरिपाटीपीयमानपयसामटवीप्रवेशप्रपाणां शैत्येन त्याजयन्तमिव ग्रैष्ममुष्माणं क्वचिदन्यत्र ग्राहयन्तमिवाङ्गारीयदारुसंग्रहदाहिभिः न्योकारैः, सर्वतश्च प्रातिवेश्यविषयवासिनां समासन्नग्रामै[7]र्गृहस्थापितस्थविरपरिपाल्यमानपाथेयस्थगितेन कृतदारुणदारुव्यायामयोग्याङ्गाभ्यङ्गेन स्कन्धाध्यासितकठोरकुठारकण्ठलम्बमानप्रातराशपुटेन पाटच्चरप्रत्यवायप्रतिपन्नपटच्चरेण कालवेत्रकत्रिगुणव्रततिवलयपाशग्रथितग्रीवाग्रथितैः पत्रवीटावृतमुखैः पीतकूटैरूढवारिणा पुरःसरवलद्बलीवर्दयुगसरेण नैकटिककुटुम्बिकलोकेन काष्ठसंग्रहार्थमटवीं प्रविशता, श्वापदव्यधनव्यवधानबहलीसमारोपितकुटीकृतकूटपाशैश्च गृहीतमृगतन्तुतन्त्रीजालवलयवागुरैः बहिर्व्याधैर्विचरद्भिः, अंसावसक्तवीतंसव्यालम्बमानबालपाशिकैश्च संगृहीतग्राहकक्कङ्करकपिञ्जलादिपञ्जरकैः शाकुनिकैः सञ्चरद्भिः, च्युत[8]लासकलेशलिप्तलतावधूलट्वालम्पटानां च पेटकैः पाशिकशिशूनामटद्भिः, तृणस्तम्बान्तरिततित्तिरितरलायमानकौलेयककुलचाटुकारैश्च विहगमृगयां मृगयुयुवभिः क्रीडद्भिः, परिणतचक्रवाककण्ठकषायरुचां शीधव्यानां वल्कलानां

१ 'रोषाविष्टगोपालकल्पितव्याघ्र-' ब. २ 'यन्त्रित' अ-क. ३ 'भूरिखिलक्षेत्र०' ब.
४ 'कापिलैः' अ. ५ 'वनपल्लवैः' ब. ६ 'स्थूणानाम्' ब. ७ 'ग्रामगृहस्थगृह०' ब.
८ 'संचरद्भिश्च्युतच्युत' ब.

कलापान्, नातिचिरोद्धृतानां च धातुत्विषां धातकीकुसुमानां गोणीरगणिताः पिचव्यानां चातसीगणपट्टमूलकानां पुष्कलान्सम्भारान्, भारांश्च मधुनो माक्षिकस्य मयूराङ्गजस्याक्लिष्टमधूच्छिष्टचक्रमालानां लम्बमानलामज्जकं[1]जूटजटानामपत्वचां खदिरकाष्ठानां कुष्ठस्य कठोरकेशरिसटाभारबभ्रुणश्च रोध्रस्य भूयसो भारकान् लोकेनादाय व्रजता प्रविचितविविधवनफलपूरितपिटकमस्तकाभिश्चाभ्यर्णग्रामगत्वरीभिस्त्वरमाणाभिर्विक्रयचिन्ताव्यग्राभिर्ग्रामेयिकाभिर्व्याप्तदिगन्तरम्, इतस्ततश्च युक्तशूरशकुरशाक्कराणां पुराणपांसूत्किरकरीषकूटवाहिनीनां धूर्गतधूलिधूसरसैरिकें[2]सरोषस्वरसार्यमाणानां संक्रीडच्चटुलचक्रचीत्कारिणीनां शकटश्रेणीनां सम्पातैः सम्पाद्यमानदुर्बलोर्वीविरूक्षक्षेत्रसंस्कारम्, आरक्षक्षिप्तक्षिप्रदान्तवाहकदण्डोड्डीयमानहरिणहेलालङ्घिततुङ्गवैणववृतिभिश्च निखातगौरकरङ्कशङ्कुशङ्कितशशकशकलिततुङ्गशुङ्गैः प्रयत्नप्रभृतविशङ्कटविटपैर्वाटैरैक्षवैर्बहुभिः श्यामायमानोपकण्ठम्, अतिविप्रकृष्टान्तरैर्मरकतस्निग्धस्नुहावाटवेष्टितैः कार्मुककर्मण्यवंशविटपसङ्कटैः कण्टकितकरञ्जराजिदुष्प्रवेश्यैः उरुबूकवचावङ्ककसुरससूरणशिग्रुग्रन्थिपर्णगवेधुकागर्मुद्गुल्मगहनगृहवाटिकैः, निखातोच्चकाष्ठारोपितकाष्ठालुकलताप्रतानविहितच्छायैः, परिमण्डलबदरीमण्डपकतलनिखातखादिरकीलबद्धवत्सरूपैः; कथमपि कुक्कुटरटितानुमीयमानसंनिवेशैरङ्गनाग[3]स्तिस्तम्बतलविरचितक्षिप्रपक्षिपूपिकावापिकैर्विकीर्णबदरपाटलपटलैः, वेणु[4]पोटदलनलशरमयवृतिविहितभित्तिभिः, किंशुकरोचनारचितमण्डलमण्डपबल्वजबद्धाङ्गारराशिभिः, शाल्मलिफलतूलसञ्चयबहुलैः, संनिहितनलशालिशालूकखण्डकुमुदबीजवेणुतण्डुलैः, सङ्गृहीतमालबीजैः, भस्ममलिनम्लानकाश्मर्यकूटव्याध्तकटैराश्यानराजादनमदनफलस्फीतैर्मधूकासवमद्यप्रायैः, कुसुम्भकुम्भगण्डकुसूलैरविरहितराजमाषत्रपुषकर्कटिकाकूष्माण्डालाबुबीजैः, पोष्यमाणवनविडालमालुधाननकुलशालिजातजातकादिभिरटवीकुटुम्बिनां गृहैरुपेतं वनग्रामकं ददर्श तत्रैवं[5] चावसदिति ।

इति श्रीबाणभट्टकृतौ हर्ष[6]चरिते छत्रलब्धिर्नाम

सप्तम उच्छ्वासः ।

---

१ 'लामज्जकमुञ्जजूटक' ब. २ 'सैरिभ' अ-क. ३ 'अङ्गनाशस्तिस्तम्भ... क्षिप्रपूपिका अ-क. ४ 'पोटपटलनलकलितशरमय' ब. ५ 'तत्रैव च तं दिवसमत्यवाहयत्' ब. ६ '०कृते हर्षचरिते सप्तम' क; 'इति श्रीमहाकविचक्रचूडामणिश्रीबाणभट्टविरचिते श्रीहर्षचरिते महाकाव्ये छत्रलब्धिर्नाम सप्तम उच्छ्वासः सम्पूर्णः' ब.

अष्टम उच्छ्वासः।

सहसा सम्पादयता मनोरथप्रार्थितानि वस्तूनि।
दैवेनापि क्रियते भव्यानां पूर्वसेवेव ॥ १ ॥
विद्वज्जनसम्पर्को नष्टेष्टज्ञातिदर्शनाभ्युदयः।
कस्य न सुखाय भवने भवति महारत्नलाभश्च ॥ २ ॥

अथापरेद्युरुत्थाय पार्थिवस्तस्माद्ग्रामकान्निर्गत्य विवेश विन्ध्याटवीम्। आट च तस्यामितश्चेतश्च सुबहून्दिवसान्। एकदा तु भूपतेर्भ्रमत एवाटविकसामन्तशरभकेतोः सूनुर्व्याघ्रकेतुर्नाम कुतोऽपि कज्जलश्यामलश्यामलतावलयेनाधिललाटमुच्चैः कृतमौलिबन्धम्, अन्धकारिणीमकारणभुवा भ्रुकुटिभङ्गेन त्रिशाखेन त्रियामामिव साहससहचारिणीं ललाटस्थलीं सदा समुद्वहन्तम्, अवतंसितैकशुकपक्षकप्रभाहरितायमानेन पिनद्धकाचरकाचमणिकर्णिकेन श्रवणेन शोभमानम्, किंचिच्चुलस्य प्रविरलपक्ष्मणश्चक्षुषः सहजेन रागरोचिषा रसायनरसोपयुक्तं तारक्षवं क्षतजमिव क्षरन्तम्, अवनाटनासिकम्, चिपिटाधरम्, चिकिनचिबुकम्, अहीनहनूत्कटकपोलकूटास्थिपर्यन्तमीषदवाग्रग्रीवाबन्धम्, स्कन्नस्कन्धार्धभागम्, अनवरतकोदण्डकुण्डलीकरणकर्कशव्यायामविस्तारितेनांसलेनोरसा हसन्तमिव तटशिलाप्रथिमानं विन्ध्यगिरेः, अजगरगरीयसा च भुजयुगलेन लघयन्तं तुहिनशैलशालद्रुमाणां द्राघिमाणम्, वराहबालवलितबन्धनाभिर्नागदमनजूटिकावाटिकाभिर्जटिलीकृतपृष्ठे प्रकोष्ठे प्रतिष्ठां गतं गोदन्तमणिचित्रं त्रापुषं वलयं बिभ्राणम्, अतुन्दिलमपि तुण्डिभम्, अहीरमणीचर्मनिर्मितपट्टिकयोश्चित्रचित्रकत्वक्त्सारकितपरिवारया सङ्कुब्जाजिनजालकितया शृङ्गमयमसृणमुष्टिभागभास्वरया पारदरसलेशलिप्तसमस्तमस्तकया कृपाण्या करालितविसङ्कटकटिप्रदेशम्, प्रथमयौवनोल्लिख्यमानमध्यभागभ्रष्टमांसभरिताविव स्थवीयसावूरुदण्डौ दधतम्, अच्छभल्लचर्ममयेन भल्लीप्रायप्रभूतशरभृता शबलशार्दूलचर्मपट्टपीडितेनालिकुलकालकम्बललोम्ना पृष्ठभागभाजा भस्त्राभरणेन पल्लवितमिव कार्श्यमुपदर्शयन्तम्, उत्तरत्रिभागोत्तंसितचाषपिच्छचारुशिखरे खदिरजटानिर्माणे खरप्राणे प्रचुरमयूरपित्तपत्रलताचित्रितत्वचि त्वचिसारगुरुणि वामस्कन्धाध्यासितधनुषि दोषि लम्बमानेनावाक्शिरसा शितशरकृत्तैकनलकविवरप्रवेशितेतरजङ्घाजनितस्वस्तिकबन्धेन बन्धूकलोहितरुधिरराजिरञ्जितघ्राणवर्त्मना वपुर्विततिव्यक्तविभाव्यमानकोमलक्रोडरोमशुक्लिम्ना शशेन शिताटनीशिखाग्रग्रथितग्रीवेण चापावृतचञ्चूत्तानताम्रतालुना तित्तिरिणा वर्णकमुष्टिमिव मृगयाया दर्शयन्तम्, विषमविषदूषितवदनेन च विकर्णेन कृष्णाहिनेव मूलगृहीतेन व्यग्रदक्षिणकराग्रम्, जङ्गममिव

१ 'पूर्वसेवैव' ब. २ 'अहीरणि०' क. ३ 'अच्छवलचर्मयेन (?)' ब. ४ 'विवर्णेन' अ.

गिरितटतमालपादपम्, यन्त्रोल्लिखितमश्मसारस्तम्भमिव भ्रमन्तम्, अञ्जनशिलाच्छेदमिव चलन्तम्, अयःसारमिव गिरेर्विन्ध्यस्य गलन्तम्, पाकलं करिकुलानाम्, कालपाशं कुरङ्गयूथानाम्, धूमकेतुं मृगराजचक्राणाम्, महानवमीमहं महिषमण्डलानाम्, हृदयमिव हिंसायाः, फलमिव पापस्य, कारणमिव कलिकालस्य, कामुकमिव कालरात्रेः, शबरयुवानमादायाजगाम। दूरे च स्थापयित्वा विज्ञापयांबभूव—'देव, सर्वस्यास्य विन्ध्यस्य स्वामी सर्वपल्लीपतीनां प्राग्रहरः शबरसेनापतिर्भूकम्पो नाम। तस्यायं निर्घातनामा स्वस्रीयः सकलस्यास्य विन्ध्यकान्तारारण्यस्य पर्णानामप्यभिज्ञः किमुत प्रदेशानाम्। एनं पृच्छतु देवः योग्योऽयमाज्ञां कर्तुम्।' इति कथिते च निर्घातस्तु क्षितितलनिहितमौलिः प्रणाममकरोदुपनिन्ये च तित्तिरिणा सह शशोपायनम्। अवनिपतिस्तु संमानयन्स्वयमेव तमप्राक्षीत्—अङ्ग, अभिज्ञा यूयमस्य सर्वस्योद्देशस्य। विहारशीलाश्च दिवसेष्वेतेषु भवन्तः। सेनापतेर्वान्यस्य वा तदनुजीविनः कस्यचिदुदाररूपा नार्यागता भवेद्दर्शनगोचरम्' इति।

निर्घातस्तु भूपालालापनप्रसादेनात्मानं बहुमन्यमानः प्रणनाम दर्शितादरं च व्यज्ञापयत्—'देव प्रायेणात्र हरिण्योऽपि नापरिगताः सञ्चरन्ति सेनापतेः कुत एव नार्यो नाप्येवंरूपा काचिदबला। तथापि देवादेशादिदानीमन्वेषणं प्रति प्रतिदिनमनन्यकृत्यैः क्रियते यत्नः। इतश्चार्धगव्यूतिमात्र एव मुनिमहिते महति महीधरमालामूलरुहि महीरुहां षण्डे पिण्डपाती प्रभूतान्तेवासिपरिवृतः पाराशरी दिवाकरमित्रनामा गिरिनदीमाश्रित्य प्रतिवसति स यदि विन्देद्वार्ताम्' इति। तच्छ्रुत्वा नरपतिरचिन्तयत्—'श्रूयते हि तत्रभवतः सुगृहीतनाम्नः स्वर्गतस्य ग्रहवर्मणो बालमित्रं मैत्रायणीयस्त्रयीं विहाय ब्राह्मणायनो विद्वानुत्पन्नसमाधिः सौगते मते युवैव काषायाणि गृहीतवानिति। प्रायशश्च जनस्य जनयति सुहृदपि दृष्टो भृशमाश्वासम्। अभिगमनीयाश्च गुणाः सर्वस्य। कस्य न प्रतीक्ष्यो मुनिभावः। भगवती वैधेयेऽपि धर्मगृहिणी गरिमाणमापादयति प्रव्रज्या किं पुनः सकलजनमनोमुषि विदुषि जने। यतो नः कुतूहलि हृदयमभूत्सततमस्य दर्शनं प्रति प्रासङ्गिकमेवेदमापतितमतिकल्याणं पश्यामः प्रयत्नप्रार्थितदर्शनं जनम्' इति। प्रकाशं चाब्रवीत्—'अङ्ग, समुपदिश तमुद्देशं यत्रास्ते स पिण्डपाती' इति। एवमुक्त्वा च तेनैवोपदिश्यमानवर्त्मा प्रावर्तत गन्तुम्।

अथ क्रमेण गच्छत एव तस्य अनवकेशिनः, कुड्मलितकर्णिकाराः, प्रचुरचम्पकाः, स्फीतफलेग्रहयः, फलभरभरितनमेरवः, नीलदलनलदनारिकेलनिकराः, हरिकेसरसरलपरिकराः, कोरकनिकुरुम्बरोमाञ्चितकुरबकराजयः, रक्ताशोकपल्लवलावण्यलिप्यमानदशदिशः, प्रविकसितकेसररजोविसरब²ध्यमानवासरधूसरिमाणः, स्वरजःसिकतिलतिलकतलाः, प्रविचलितहिङ्गवः,

१ 'पालकम्' ब. २ 'बध्यमानचारुधू०' अ-क.

प्रचुरपूगफलाः, प्रसवपूगपिङ्गलप्रियङ्गवः, परागपिञ्जरितमञ्जरीपुञ्ज्यमानमधुपमञ्जुशिञ्जाजनितजनमुदः, मदमलमेचकितमुचुकुन्दस्कन्धकाण्डकण्ड्यमाननिःशङ्ककरिकरटकण्डूतयः, उड्डीयमाननिःशङ्कचटुलकृष्णशारशावसकलशाद्वलसुभगभूमयः, तमःकालतमतमालमालामीलितातपाः, स्तबकदन्तुरितदेवदारवः, तरलताम्बूलीस्तम्बजालकितजम्बूजम्बीरवीथयः, कुसुमरजोधवलधूलीकदम्बचक्रचुम्बितव्योमानः, बहलमधुमोक्षोक्षितक्षितयः, परिमलघटितघ्राणतृप्तयः, कतिपयदिवसप्रसूतकुक्कुटीकुटीकृतकुटजकोटराः, चटकासञ्चार्यमाणवाचाटचाटकेरक्रियमाणचाटवः, सहचरीचारणचञ्चुरचकोरचञ्चवः, निर्भयभूरिभुरुण्डभुज्यमानपाककपिलपीलवः, सदाफलकदम्बफलफलविशसननिःशूकशुकशकुन्तशातितशलाटवः, शैलेयसुकुमारशिलातलसुखशयितशशशिशवः, शेफालिकाशिफाविवरविस्रब्धविवर्तमानगौधेरराशयः, निरातङ्करङ्कवः, निराकुलनकुलकुलकेलयः, कलकोकिलकुलकवलितकलिकोद्गमाः, सहकारारामरोमन्थायमानचमूरयूथाः, यथासुखनिषण्णनीलाण्डजमण्डलाः, निर्विकारवृकविलोक्यमानपोतपीतगवयधेनवः, श्रवणहारिसनीडगिरिनितम्बनिर्झरनिनादनिद्रानन्दमन्दायमानकरिकुलकर्णतालदुन्दुभयः, समासन्नकिन्नरीगीतरवरसमानरुरवः, प्रमुदिततरतरक्षवः क्षतहरितहरिद्राद्रवरज्यमाननववराहपोतपोत्रवलयः, गुञ्जाकुञ्जगुञ्जाहकाः, जातीफलकसुप्तशालिजातकवलयः, दशनकुपितकपिपोतपेटकपाटितपाटलमुखकीटपुटकाः, लकुचलम्पटगोलाङ्गूललङ्घ्यमानलवलयः, बद्धवालुकालवालवलयाः, कुटिलकुटावलिवलितवेगगिरिनदिकास्रोतसः, निबिडशाखाकाण्डलम्बमानकमण्डलवः, सूत्रशिक्यासक्तरिक्तभिक्षाकपालपल्लवितलतामण्डपाः, निकटकुटीकृतपाटलमुद्राचैत्यकमूर्तयः, चीवराम्बररागकषायोदकदूषितोद्देशाः, मेघमया इव कृतशिखण्डिकुलकोलाहलाः, वेदमया इवापरिमितशाखाभेदगहनाः, माणिक्यमया इव महानीलतनवः, तिमिरमया इव सकलजननयनमुषः, यामुना इवोर्ध्वीकृतमहाह्रदाः, मरकतमणिश्यामलाः क्रीडापर्वतका इव वसन्तस्य, अञ्जनाचला[1] इव पल्लविताः, तनया इवाटवीजाता विन्ध्यस्य, पातालान्धकारराशय इव भित्त्वा भुवमुत्थिताः, प्रतिप्रवेशका[2] इव वर्षावासराणाम्, अंशावतारा इव कृष्णरा[3]त्रीणाम्, इन्द्रनीलमयाः प्रासादा इव वनदेवतानाम्, पुरस्ताद्दर्शनपथमवतेरुस्तरवः।

ततो नरपतेरभवन्मनस्यदूरवर्तिना खलु भवितव्यं भदन्तेनेति। अवतीर्य च गिरिसरिति समुपस्पृश्य युगपद्विश्रामसमयसमुन्मुक्तहेषाघोषबधिरीकृताटवीगहनामस्मिन्नेव प्रदेशे स्थापयित्वा वाजिसेनामवलम्ब्य च तपस्विजनदर्शनोचितं विनयं हृदयेन दक्षिणेन च हस्तेन माधवगुप्तमंसे विरलैरेव राजभिरनुगम्यमानश्चरणाभ्यामेव प्रावर्तत गन्तुम्।

---

१ 'अञ्जनाचलमया इव' ब. २ 'प्रतिवेशिका' अ. ३ 'कृष्णार्धरात्रीणाम्' ब.

अथ तेषां तरूणां मध्ये नानादेशीयैः स्थानस्थानेषु स्थाणूनाश्रितैः शिलातलेषूपविष्टैर्लताभवनान्यध्यावसद्भिररण्यानीनिकुञ्जेषु निलीनैर्विटपच्छायासु निषण्णैस्तरुमूलानि निषेवमाणैर्वीतरागैरार्हतैर्मस्करिभिः श्वेतपटैः पाण्डुरभिक्षुभिर्भागवतैर्वर्णिभिः केशलुञ्चनैः कापिलैर्जैनैर्लौकायतिकैः काणादैरौपनिषदैरैश्वरकारणिकैः कारन्धमिभिर्धर्मशास्त्रिभिः पौराणिकैः साप्ततन्तवैः शैवैः शाब्दैः पाञ्चरात्रिकैरन्यैश्च स्वान्स्वान्सिद्धान्ताञ्शृण्वद्भिरभियुक्तैश्चिन्तयद्भिश्च प्रत्युच्चरद्भिश्च संशयानैश्च निश्चिन्वद्भिश्च व्युत्पादयद्भिश्च विवदमानैश्चाभ्यस्यद्भिश्च व्याचक्षाणैश्च शिष्यतां प्रतिपन्नैर्दूरादेवावेद्यमानम्, अतिविनीतैः कपिभिरपि चैत्यकर्म कुर्वाणैस्त्रिसरणपरैः परमोपासकैः शुकैरपि शाक्यशासनकुशलैः कोशं समुपदिशद्भिः शिक्षापदोपदेशदोषोपशमशालिनीभिः शारिकाभिरपि धर्मदेशनां दर्शयन्तीभिरनवरतश्रवणगृहीतालोकैः कौशिकैरपि बोधिसत्त्वजातकानि जपद्भिर्जातसौगतशीलशीतलस्वभावैः शार्दूलैरप्यमांसाशिभिरुपास्यमानम्, आसनोपान्तोपविष्टविस्रब्धानेककेसरिशावकतया मुनिपरमेश्वरमकृत्रिम इव सिंहासने निषण्णम्, उपशममिव पिबद्भिर्वनहरिणैर्जिह्वालताभिरुपलिह्यमानपादपल्लवम्, वामकरतलनिविष्टेन नीवारमश्नता पारावतपोतेन कर्णोत्पलेनेव प्रियां मैत्रीं प्रसादयन्तम्, इतरकरकिसलयनखमयूखलेखाभिर्जनितजनव्यामोहम्, उद्ग्रीवं मयूरं मरकतमणिकरकमिव वारिधाराभिः पूरयन्तम्, इतस्ततः पिपीलकश्रेणीनां श्यामाकतण्डुलकणान्स्वयमेव किरन्तम्, अरुणेन चीवरपटलेन म्रदीयसा संवीतम्, बहलबालातपानुलिप्तमिव पौरन्दरं दिग्भागमुल्लिखितपद्मरागप्रभाप्रतिमया रक्तावदातया देहप्रभया पाटलीकृतानां काषायग्रहणमिव दिशामप्युपदिशन्तम्, अनौद्धत्यादधोमुखेन मन्दमुकुलितकुमुदाकारेण स्निग्धधवलप्रसन्नेन चक्षुषा जनक्षुण्णक्षुद्रजन्तुजीवनार्थममृतमिव वर्षन्तम्, सर्वशास्त्राक्षरपरमाणुभिरिव निर्मितं परमसौगतमप्यवलोकितेश्वरम्, अस्खलितमपि तपसि लग्नम्, आलोकमिव यथावस्थितसकलपदार्थप्रकाशकं दर्शनार्थिनाम्, सुगतस्याप्यभिगमनीयमिव, धर्मस्याप्याराधनीयमिव, प्रसादस्यापि प्रसादनीयमिव, मानस्यापि माननीयमिव, वन्द्यत्वस्यापि वन्दनीयमिव, [1]आत्मनोऽपि स्पृहणीयमिव, ध्यानस्यापि ध्येयमिव, ज्ञानस्यापि ज्ञेयमिव, जन्म[2] जपस्य, नेमिं नियमस्य, तत्त्वं तपसः, शरीरं शौचस्य, कोशं कुशलस्य, वेश्म विश्वासस्य, [3]सर्वस्वं सद्वृत्तताया[4]ः, दाक्ष्यं दाक्षिण्यस्य, पारं परानुकम्पायाः, निर्वृतिं सुखस्य, मध्यमे वयसि वर्तमानं दिवाकरमित्रमद्राक्षीत्। अतिप्रशान्तगम्भीराकारारोपितबहुमानश्च सादरं दूरादेव समं शिरसा मनसा वचसा च ववन्दे।

दिवाकरमित्रस्तु मैत्रीमयः प्रकृत्या विशेषतस्तेनापरेणादृष्टपूर्वेणामानुष-

१ 'आत्मनोऽपि...ज्ञेयमिव' इत्येतन्नास्ति अ-क पुस्तकयोः. २ 'जन्म यमस्य' अ-क. ३ 'सद्वृत्तम्' अ-क. ४ 'सद्वृत्ततायाः, सर्वस्वं सर्वज्ञतायाः' अ-क.

लोकोचितेन'सर्वाभिभाविना महानुभावाभोगभाजा भ्राजिष्णुना भूपतेरप्राकृतेनाकारविशेषेण तेन चाभिजात्यप्रकाशकेन गरीयसा प्रश्रयेण चाह्लादितश्चक्षुषि च चेतसि च युगपदग्रहीत् । वीरस्वभावोऽपि च सम्पादितससंभ्रमाभ्युत्थानः सङ्कलय्य किंचिदुद्गमनकेन विलोलं विलम्बमानं वामांसाच्चीवरपटान्तमुत्क्षिप्यानेकाभयदानदीक्षादक्षिणो दक्षिणं महापुरुषलक्षणलेखाप्रशस्तं हस्तं स्निग्धमधुरया वाचा सगौरवमारोग्यदानेन राजानमन्वग्रहीत् । अभ्यनन्दच्च स्वागतगिरा गुरुमिवाभ्यागतं बहु मन्यमानः स्वेनासनेनाध्वमत्रेति निमन्त्रयांचक्रे । पार्श्वे स्थितं च शिष्यमब्रवीत्—'आयुष्मन्, उपानय कमण्डलुना पादोदकम्' इति । राजा त्वचिन्तयत्—'अलोहः खलु संयमनपाशः सौजन्यमभिजातानाम् । स्थाने खलु तत्रभवान्गुणानुरागी ग्रहवर्मा बहुशो वर्णितवानस्य गुणान्' इति । प्रकाशं चाबभाषे—'भगवन्, दर्शनपुण्यानुगृहीतस्य मम पुनरुक्त इवायमार्यप्रयुक्तः प्रतिभात्यनुग्रहः । चक्षुष्प्रमाणप्रसादस्वीकृतस्य च परकरणमिवासनादिदानोपचारचेष्टितम् । अतिभूमि[१]र्भूमिरेवासनं भवादृशां पुरः सम्भाषणामृताभिषेकप्रक्षालितसकलवपुषश्च मे प्रदेशवृत्तिः । पाद्यमप्यपार्थकम् । आसतां भवन्तो यथासुखम् । आसीनोऽहम्' इत्यभिधाय क्षिताववोपाविशत् ।

'अलंकारो हि परमार्थतः प्रभवतां प्रश्रयातिशयः, रत्नादिकस्तु शिलाभारः' इत्याकलय्य पुनः पुनरभ्यर्थ्यमानोऽपि यदा न प्रत्यपद्यत पार्थिवो वचनं तदा स्वमेवासनं पुनरपि भेजे भदन्तः । भूपतिमुखनलिननिहितनिभृतनयनयुगलनिगडनिश्चलीकृतहृदयश्च स्थित्वा कांचित्कालकलां[२] कलिकालकल्मषकालुष्यमिव क्षालयन्नमलाभिर्दन्तमयूखमालाभिर्मूलफलाभ्यवहारसम्भवमुद्वमन्निव च परिमलसुभगं विकचकुसुमपटलपाण्डुरं लतावनमवादीत्—'अद्यप्रभृति न केवलमयमनिन्द्यो वन्द्योऽपि प्रकाशितसत्सारः संसारः । किं नाम नालोक्यते जीवद्भिरद्भुतं येन रूपमचिन्तितोपनतमिदं दृक्पथमुपगतम् । एवंविधैरनुमीयन्ते जन्मान्तरावस्थितसुकृतानि हृदयोत्सवैः । इहापि जन्मनि दत्तमेवास्माकममुना तपःक्लेशेन फलमसुलभदर्शनं दर्शयता देवानां प्रियम् । आ तृप्तेः पीतममृतमीक्षणाभ्याम् । जातं निरुत्कण्ठं मानसं निवृत्तिसुखस्य । महद्भिः पुण्यैर्विना न विश्राम्यन्ति सज्जने त्वादृशि दृशः । सुदिवसः स यस्मिञ्जातोऽसि । सा सुजाता जननी या सकलजीवलोकजीवितजनकमजनयदायुष्मन्तम् । पुण्यवन्ति पुण्यान्यपि तानि येषामसि परिणामः । सुकृततपसस्ते परमाणवो ये तव परिगृहीतसर्वावयवाः । तत्सुभगं सौभाग्यमाश्रितोऽसि येन । भव्यः स पुरुषभावो भवत्यवस्थितो यः । यत्सत्यं मुमुक्षोरपि मे पुण्यभाजमालोक्य पुनः श्रद्धा जाता मनुजजन्मनि । नेच्छद्भिरप्यस्माभिर्दृष्टः कुसुमायुधः । कृतार्थमद्य चक्षुर्वनदेव-

---

१ 'अतिभूमिरेव भवादृशाम्' अ-क. २ 'कालकक्ष्याम्' ब.

तानाम् । अद्य सफलं जन्म वनपादपानां येषामसि गतो गोचरम् । अमृतमयस्य भवतो वचसां माधुर्यं कार्यमेव । अस्य त्वीदृशे शैशवे विनयस्योपाध्यायं ध्यायन्नपि न सम्भावयामि । भुवि सर्वथा शून्य आसीदजाते दीर्घायुषि गुणग्रामः । धन्यः स भूभृद्यस्य वंशे मणिरिव मुक्तामयः सम्भूतोऽसि । एवंविधस्य च पुण्यवतः कथंचित्प्राप्तस्य केन प्रियं समाचराम इति पारिप्लवं चेतो नः । सकलवनचरसार्थ[1]साधारणस्य कन्दमूलफलस्य गिरिसरिदम्भसो वा के वयम् । अपरोपकरणीकृतस्तु कायकलिरयमस्माकम् । सर्वस्वमवशिष्टमिष्टातिथ्याय । स्वायत्ताश्च विद्यन्ते विद्याबिन्दवः कतिचित् । उपयोगं तु न प्रीतिर्विचारयति । यदि च नोपरुणद्धि कश्चित्कार्यलवमरक्षणीयाक्षरं वा कथनीयं तत्कथयतु भवाञ्श्रोतुमभिलषति हृदयं सर्वमिदं नः । केन कृत्यातिभारेण भव्यो भूषितवान्भूमिमेतामभ्रमणयोग्याम् । कियदवधिर्वायं शून्याटवीपर्यटनक्लेशः कल्याणराशेः । कस्माच्च सन्तप्तरूपेव ते तनुरियमसन्तापार्हा विभाव्यते' इति ।

राजा तु सादरतरमब्रवीत्—'आर्य, दर्शितसंभ्रमेणानेन मधुरसविसरम[2]मृतमिव हृदयधृतिकरमनवरतं वर्षता वचसैव ते सर्वमनुष्ठितम् । धन्योऽस्मि यदेवमभ्यर्हितमनुपचरणीयमपि मान्यो मन्यते माम् । अस्य च महावनभ्रमणपरिक्लेशस्य कारणमवधारयतु मतिमान् । मम हि विनष्टनिखिलेष्टबन्धोर्जीवितानुबन्धस्य निबन्धनमेकैव यवीयसी स्वसावशेषा[3] । सापि भर्तुर्वियोगाद्वैरिपरिभवभयाक्रमन्ती कथमपि विन्ध्यवनमिदम्, अशुभशबरबलबहुलम्, अगणितगजकुलकलिलम्, अपरिमितमृगपतिशरभभयम्, उरुमहिषमुषितपथिकगमनम्, अतिनिशितशरकुशपरुषम्, अवटशतविषममविशत् । अत[4]स्तामन्वेष्टुं वयमनिशं निशिनिशि च सततमिमामटवीमटामः । न चैनामासादयामः । कथयतु च गुरुरपि यदि कदाचित्कुतश्चिद्वने चरतः श्रुतिपथमुपगता तद्वार्ता' इति ।

अथ तच्छ्रुत्वा जातोद्वेग इव भदन्तः पुनरभ्यधात्—'धीमन्, न खलु कश्चिदेवंरूपो वृत्तान्तोऽस्मानभ्युपगतवान् । अभाजनं हि वयमीदृशानां प्रियाख्यानोपायनानां [5]भवताम् ।' इत्येवं भाषमाण एव तस्मिन्नकस्मादागत्यापरः शमिनि वयसि वर्तमानः संभ्रान्तरूप इव पुरस्तादुपरचिताञ्जलिर्जातकरुणः प्रक्षरितचक्षुर्भिक्षुरभाषत—'भगवन्भदन्त, महत्करुणं वर्तते । बालैव बलवद्व्यसनाभिभूता भूतपूर्वापि कल्याणरूपा स्त्री शोकवेगविवशा वैश्वानरं विशति । सम्भावयतु तामप्रोषितप्राणां भगवान् । अभ्युपपद्यतां समुचितैः समाश्वासनैः । अनुपरतपूर्वं कृमिकीटमपि दुःखितं दयाराशेरार्यस्य गोचरगतम्' इति ।

---

१ 'सार्थासाधारणस्य' ब. २ 'विसरं धृतमिव हृदय-' ब. ३ 'अवशेषात्' ब. ४ 'अयोगादतस्ताम्' ब. ५ 'भवतम्' ब.

राजा तु जातानुजाशङ्कः सोदर्यास्नेहाक्रान्तद्रुत इव दुःखेन दोदूयमान-हृदयः कथमपि गद्गदिकागृहीतकण्ठो विकलवाग्बाष्पायमाणदृष्टिः पप्रच्छ—"पाराशरिन्, कियद्दूरे सा योषिदेवंजातीया जीवेद्वा कालमेतावन्तमिति। पृष्टा वा त्वया 'कासि, कस्यासि, कुतोऽसि, किमर्थं वनमिदमभ्युपगतासि, विशसि च किंनिमित्तमनलम्' इत्यादितः प्रभृति कार्त्स्न्येन कथ्यमानमिच्छामि श्रोतुं कथमार्यस्य गता गोचरमाकारतो वा कीदृशी" इति।

तथाभिहितस्तु भूभुजा भिक्षुराचचक्षे—'महाभाग, श्रूयताम्। अहं हि प्रत्यूषस्येवाद्य वन्दित्वा भगवन्तमनेनैव गिरिनदीरोधसा सैकतसुकुमारेण यदृच्छया विहृतवानतिदूरम्। एकस्मिंश्च वनलतागहने गिरिनदीसमीपभाजि भ्रमरीणामिव हिमहतकमलाकरकातराणां रसितं सार्यमाणानामतितारतानवर्तिनीनां वीणातन्त्रीणामिव[1] झांकारमेकतानं नारीणां रुदितमधृतिकरमतिकरुणमाकर्णितवानस्मि। समुपजातकृपश्च गतोऽस्मि तं प्रदेशम्। दृष्टवानस्मि च दृषत्खण्डखण्डिताङ्गुलिगलल्लोहितेन च पार्ष्णिप्रविष्टशरशलाकाशल्यशूलसङ्कोचितचक्षुषा चाध्वनीनश्रमश्वयथुनिश्चलचरणेन च स्थाणवव्रणव्यथितगुल्फबद्धभूर्जत्वचा च वातखुडखेदखञ्जजङ्घाजातज्वरेण च पांसुपाण्डुरपिण्डिकेन च खर्जूरजूटजटाजर्जरितजानुना च शतावरीविदारितोरुणा च विदारीदारिततनुदुकूलपल्लवेन चोत्कटवंशविटपकण्टककोटिपाटितकञ्चुककर्पटेन च फललोभालम्बितानम्रबदरीलताजालकैरुत्कण्टकैरुल्लिखितसुकुमारकरोदरेण च कुरङ्गशृङ्गोत्खातैः कन्दमूलफलैः कदर्थितबाहुना च ताम्बूलविरहविरसमुखखण्डितकोमलामलकीफलेन च कुशकुसुमाहतिलोहितानां श्वयतां[2]मक्ष्णां लेपीकृतमनःशिलेन च कण्टकिलतालूनालकलेशेन च केनचित्किसलयोपपादितातपत्रकृत्येन केनचित्कदलीदलव्यजनवाहिना केनचित्कमलिनीपलाशपुटगृहीताम्भसा केनचित्पाथेयीकृतमृणालपूलिकेन केनचिच्चीनांशुकदशाशिक्यनिहितनालिकेरकोशकलशीकलितरसालतैलेन[3], कतिपयावशेषशोकविक्लव[4]कलमूककुब्जवामनबधिरबर्बराविरलेनाबलानां चक्रवालेन परिवृताम्, आपत्कालेऽपि कुलोद्गतेनेवामुच्यमानां प्रभालेपिना लावण्येन, प्रतिबिम्बितैरासन्नवनलताकिसलयैः सरसैर्दुःखक्षतैरिवान्तःपटलीक्रियमाणकायाम्, कठोरदर्भाङ्कुरक्षतक्षारिणा क्षतजेनानुसरणालक्तकेनेव रक्तचरणाम्, उष्मालेनान्यतरनारीधृतेनारविन्दिनीदलेन कृतच्छायमपि विच्छायं मुखमुद्वहन्तीम्, आकाशमपि शून्यतयातिशयानाम्, मृण्मयीमिव निश्चेतनतया, मरुन्मयीमिव निश्वाससम्पदा, पावकमयीमिव सन्तापसन्तानेन, सलिलमयीमिवास्रप्रस्रवणेन, वियन्मयीमिव निरवलम्बनतया, तडिन्मयीमिव पारिप्लवतया, शब्दमयीमिव

१ 'वर्णातन्त्रीणाम्' ब. २ 'श्वयथ्युमता-' ब. ३ 'कलितसरलतैलेन' ब. ४ 'विकलमूक' अ-क.

परिदेवितवाणीबाहुल्येन, मुक्तमुक्तांशुकरत्नकुसुमकनकपत्राभरणां कल्पलतामिव महावने पतिताम्, परमेश्वरोत्तमाङ्गपातदुर्ललिताङ्गां गङ्गामिव गां गताम्, वनकुसुमधूलिधूसरितपादपल्लवाम्, प्रभातचन्द्रमूर्तिमिव लोकान्तरमभिलषन्तीम्, निजजलमोक्षकदर्थितदर्शितधवला¹यतनेत्रशोभाम्, मन्दाकिनीमृणालिनीमिव परिम्लायमानाम्, दुःसहरविकिरणसंस्पर्शखेदनिमीलितां कुमुदिनीमिव दुःखेन दिवसं नयन्तीम्, दग्धदशाविसंवादितां प्रत्यूषप्रदीपशिखामिव क्षामक्षामां पाण्डुवपुषम्, पार्श्ववर्तिवारणाभियोगरक्ष्यमाणां वनकरिणीमिव महाह्रदे निमग्नाम्, प्रविष्टां वनगह²ने ध्याने च, स्थितां तरुतले मरणे च, पतितां धात्र्युत्सङ्गे महानर्थे च, दूरीकृतां भर्त्रा सुखेन च, विरेचितां श्रमणेनायुषा च, आकुलां केशकलापेन मरणोपायेन च, विवर्णितामध्वधूलिभिरङ्गवेदनाभिश्च, दग्धां चण्डातपेन वैधव्येन च, धृतमुखीं पाणिना मौनेन च, गृहीतां प्रियसखीजनेन मन्युना च, तथा च भ्रष्टैर्बन्धुभिर्विलासैश्च, मुक्तेन श्रवणयुगलेनात्मना च, परित्यक्तैर्भूषणैः सर्वारम्भैश्च, भग्नैर्वलयैर्मनोरथैश्च, चरणलग्नाभिः परिचारिकाभिर्दर्भाङ्कुरसूचीभिश्च, हृदयविनिहितेन चक्षुषा प्रियेण च, दीर्घैः शोकश्वसितैः केशैश्च, क्षीणेन वपुषा पुण्येन च, पादयोः पतन्तीभिर्वृद्धाभिरश्रुधाराभिश्च, स्वल्पावशेषेण परिजनेन जीवितेन च, अलसामुन्मेषे, दक्षामश्रुमोक्षे, सन्ततां चिन्तासु, विच्छिन्नामाशासु, कृशां काये, स्थूलां श्वसिते, पूरितां दुःखेन, रिक्तां सत्त्वेन, अध्यासितामायासेन, शून्यां हृदयेन, निश्चलां निश्चयेन, चलितां धैर्यात्, अपि च वसतिं व्यसनानाम्, आधानमाधीनाम्, अवस्थानमनवस्थानाम्, आधारमधृतीनाम्, आवासमवसादानाम्, आस्पदमापदाम्, अभियोगमभाग्यानाम्, उद्वेगमुद्वेगानाम्, कारणं करुणायाः, पा³रं परायत्तताया योषितम्। चिन्तितवानस्मि च चित्रमीदृशीमप्याकृतिमुपतापाः स्पृशन्तीति। सा तु समीपगते मयि तदवस्थापि सबहुमानमानतमौलिः प्रणतवती। अहं तु प्रबलकरुणाप्रेर्यमाणस्तामालपितुकामः पुनः कृतवान्मनसि—कथमिव महानुभावामेनामामन्त्रये। 'वत्से' इत्यतिप्रणयः, 'मातः' इति चाटु, 'भगिनि' इत्यात्मसम्भावना, 'देवि' इति परिजनालापः, 'राजपुत्रि' इत्यस्फुटम्, 'उपासिके' इति मनोरथः, 'स्वामिनि' इति भृत्यभावाभ्युपगमः, 'भद्रे' इतीतरस्त्रीसमुचितम्, 'आयुष्मति' इत्यवस्थायामप्रियम्, 'कल्याणिनि' इति दशायां विरुद्धम्, 'चन्द्रमुखि' इत्यमुनिमतम्, 'बाले' इत्यगौरवोपेतम्, 'आर्ये' इति जरारोपणम्, 'पुण्यवति' इति फलविपरीतम्, 'भवति' इति सर्वसाधारणम्। अपि च 'कासि' इत्यनभिजातम्, 'किमर्थं रोदिषि' इति दुःखकारणस्मरणकारि, 'मा रोदीः' इति शोकहेतुमनपनीय न शोभते, 'समाश्वसिहि' इति किमाश्रित्य, 'स्वागतम्' इति यातयामम्, 'सुखमास्यते' इति मिथ्या। इत्येवं

१ '०धवलायित०' ब. २ 'गहनं ध्यानं च' अ-क. ३ 'पदं परायत्तयतताया' ब.

चिन्तयत्येव मयि तस्मात्क्षणादुत्थायान्यतरा योषिदार्यरूपेव शोकविक्लवा समुपसृत्य कतिपयपलितशारं शिरो नीत्वा महीतलमतुलहृदयसन्तापसूचकैरश्रुबिन्दुभिश्चरणयुगलं दहन्ती ममातिकृपणैरक्षरैश्च हृदयमभिहितवती—'भगवन्, सर्वसत्त्वानुकम्पिनी प्रायः प्रव्रज्या। प्रतिपन्नपरदुःखक्षपणदीक्षादक्षाश्च भवन्ति सौगताः। करुणाकुलगृहं च भगवतः शाक्यमुनेः शासनम्। सकलजनोपकारसज्जा सज्जनता जैनी। परलोकसाधनं च धर्मो मुनीनाम्। प्राणरक्षणाच्च न परं पुण्यजातं जगति गीयते जनेन। अनुकम्पाभूमयः प्रकृत्यैव युवतयः किं पुनर्विपदभिभूताः। साधुजनश्च सिद्धक्षेत्रमार्तवचसाम्[1]। यत इयं नः स्वामिनी मरणेन[2] पितुरभावेन भर्तुः प्रवासेन च भ्रातुः भ्रंशेन च शेषस्य बान्धववर्गस्यातिमृदुहृदयतयानपत्यतया च निरवलम्बना, परिभवेन च नीचारातिकृतेन प्रकृतिमनस्विनी, अमुना च महाटवीपर्यटनक्लेशेन कदर्थितसौकुमार्या, दग्धदैवदत्तैरेवंविधैर्बहुभिरुपर्युपरि व्यसनैर्विक्लवीकृतहृदया, दारुणं दुःखमपारयन्ती सोढुं निवारयन्तमनतिक्रान्तपूर्वं स्वप्नेऽप्यवगणय्य गुरुजनमनुनयन्तीरखण्डितप्रणया नर्मस्वपि समवधीर्य प्रियसखीर्विज्ञापयन्तमशरणमश्रुव्याकुलनयनमपरिभूतपूर्वं मनसापि परिभूय भृत्यवर्गमग्निं प्रविशति। परित्रायताम्। आर्योऽपि तावदसह्यशोकापनयनोपायोपदेशनिपुणां व्यापारयतु वाणीमस्याम्' इति चातिकृपणं व्याहरन्तीमहमुत्थाप्योद्विग्नतरः शनैरभिहितवान्—'आर्ये, यथा कथयसि तथा अस्मद्गिरामगोचरोऽयमस्याः पुण्याशयायाः शोकः। शक्यते चेन्मुहूर्तमात्रमपि त्रातुमुपरिष्टान्न व्यर्थेयमभ्यर्थना भविष्यति। मम हि गुरुरपर इव भगवान्सुगतः समीपगत एव। कथिते मयास्मिन्नुदन्ते नियतमागमिष्यति परमदयालुः। दुःखान्धकारपटलभिदुरैश्च सौगतैः सुभाषितैः स्वकैश्च दर्शितनिदर्शनैर्नानागमगुरुभिर्गिरां कौशलैः कुशलशीलामेनां प्रबोधपदवीमारोपयिष्यति' इति। तच्च श्रुत्वा 'त्वरतामार्यः' इत्यभिदधाना सा पुनरपि पादयोः पतितवती। सोऽहमुपगत्य त्वरमाणो व्यतिकरमिममधतिकरमशरण[3]कृपणबहुयुवतिमरणमतिकरुणमत्रभवते गुरवे निवेदितवान्' इति।

अथ भूभृद्भैक्षवं समवधार्य तद्भाषितमश्रुमिश्रितमश्रुतेऽपि स्वसुर्नाम्नि निम्नीकृतमना मन्युना सर्वाकारसंवादिन्या दशयैव दूरीकृतसन्देहो दग्ध इव सोदर्यावस्थाश्रवणेन श्रवणयोः श्रमणाचार्यमुवाच—'आर्य, नियतं सैवेयमनार्यस्यास्य जनस्यातिकठिनहृदयस्यातिनृशंसस्य मन्दभाग्यस्य भगिनी भागधेयैरेतामवस्थां नीता निष्कारणवैरिभिर्वराकी विदीर्यमाणं मे हृदयमेवं निवेदयति' इत्युक्त्वा तमपि श्रमणमभ्यधात्—'आर्य, उत्तिष्ठ। दर्शय क्वासौ।

---

१ 'आर्यवचसाम्' ब. २ 'मरणेन च मातुः प्रवसनेन च पितुरभावेन च भर्तुः परलोकगमनेन च भ्रातुर्भ्रंशेन च' ब. ३ 'अशरणम्' ब.

यतस्व प्रभूतप्राणिपरित्राणपुण्योपार्जनाय[1] । यामः । यदि कथंचिज्जीवन्तीं सम्भावयामः' इति भाषमाण एवोत्तस्थौ ।

अथ समग्रशिष्यवर्गानुगतेनाचार्येण तुरगेभ्यश्चावतीर्य समस्तेन सामन्तलोकेन पश्चादाकृष्यमाणाश्वीयेनानुगम्यमानः पुरस्ताच्च तेन शाक्यपुत्रीयेण प्रदिश्यमानवर्त्मा पद्भ्यामेव तं प्रदेशमविरलैः पदैः पिबन्निव प्रावर्तत । क्रमेण च समुपगतः शुश्राव लतावनान्तरितस्य मुमूर्षोर्महतः स्त्रैणस्य तत्कालोचितानेकप्रकारानालापान्—'भगवन्धर्म, धाव शीघ्रम् । क्वासि कुलदेवते । देवि धरणि, धीरयसि न दुःखितां दुहितरम् । क्व नु खलु प्रोषिता पुष्पभूतिकुटुम्बिनी लक्ष्मीः । अनाथां नाथ मुखरवंश्य विविधाधिविधुरां वधूं विधवां विबोधयसि किमिति नेमाम् । भगवन्, भक्तजने संज्वरिणि सुगत सुप्तोऽसि । राजधर्म पुष्पभूतिभवनपक्षपातिन्, उदासीनीभूतोऽसि कथम् । त्वय्यपि विपद्बान्धव विन्ध्य वन्ध्योऽयमञ्जलिबन्धः । मातर्महाटवि, रटन्तीं न शृणोषीमां[2] मापत्पतिताम् । पतङ्ग, प्रसीद पाहि पतिव्रतामशरणाम् । प्रयत्नरक्षित कृतघ्न चारित्रचण्डाल, न रक्षसि राजपुत्रीम् । किमवधृतं लक्षणैः । हा देवि दुहितृस्नेहमयि यशोमति, मुषितासि दग्धदैवदस्युना । देव, दुहितरि दह्यमानायां नापतसि प्रतापशील, शिथिलीभूतमपत्यप्रेम । महाराज राज्यवर्धन, न धावसि मन्दीभूता भगिनीप्रीतिः । अहो निष्ठुरः प्रेतभावः । व्यपेहि पाप पावक स्त्रीघातनिर्घृण, ज्वलन्न लज्जसे । भ्रातर्वात, दासी तवास्मि । संवादय द्रुतं देवीदाहं देवाय दुःखितजनार्तिहराय हर्षाय । नितान्तनिःशूक शोकश्वपाक, सकामोऽसि । दुःखदायिन्वियोगराक्षस, तुष्टोसि । विजने वने कमाक्रन्दामि, कस्मै कथयामि, कमुपयामि शरणम्, कां दिशं प्रतिपद्ये, करोमि किमभागधेया । गान्धारि, गृहीतोऽयं लतापाशः । पिशाचि मोचनिके, मुञ्च शाखाग्रहणकलहम् । कलहंसि, हंसि किमतः[3]परमुत्तमाङ्गम् । मङ्गलिके, मुक्तगलं किमद्यापि रुद्यते । सुन्दरि, दूरीभवति सखीसार्थः । स्थास्यसि कथमिवाशिवे शवशिबिरे शबरिके । सुतनु, तनूनपाति पतिष्यसि त्वमपि । मृणालकोमले मालावति, म्लानासि । मातर्मातङ्गिके, अङ्गीकृतस्त्वयापि मृत्युः । वत्से वत्सिके, वत्स्यसि [4]कथमनभिप्रेते प्रेतनगरे । नागरिके, गरिमाणमागतास्यनया स्वामिभक्त्या । विराजिके, विराजितासि राजपुत्रीविपदि जीवितव्ययव्यवसायेन । भृगुपतनाभ्युद्यमभागाभिज्ञे भृङ्गारधारिणि, धन्यासि । केतकि, कुतः पुनरीदृशी [5]सुस्वामिनी । मेनके, जन्मनि जन्मनि देवीदास्यमेव ददातु देवो देहं दहन्दहनः । विजये वीजय कृशानुम् । सानुमति, नमतीन्दीवरिका दिवं गन्तुकामा । कामदासि, देहि दहनप्रदक्षिणावकाशम् । विचरिके, विरचय वह्निम् । विकिर किरातिके कुसुमप्रकरम् । कुररिके, कुरु

---

१ 'यतः सुप्रभूतप्राण०' अ–क. २ 'शृणोषि मामापत्०' ब. ३ 'किमपरमुत्त०' ब. ४ 'कथनमभि–' अ–ब. ५ 'स्वस्वामिनी' ब.

कुरुबककोरकाञ्चितां चिताम्। चामरं चामरग्राहिणि गृहाण। पुनरपि कण्ठे मर्षयितव्यानि नर्मदे नर्मनिर्मितानि निर्मर्यादहसितानि। भद्रे सुभद्रे, भद्रमस्तु ते परलोकगमनम्। अग्रामीणगुणानुरागिणि ग्रामेयिके, गच्छ सुगतिम्। वसन्तिके, अन्तरं प्रयच्छ। आपृच्छते छत्रधारी देवि देहि दृष्टिम्। दृष्टा तव जहाति जीवितं विजयसेना। सेयं मुक्तिका मुक्तकण्ठमारटति निकटे नाटकसूत्रधारी। पादयोः पतति ते ताम्बूलवाहिनी बहुमता राजपुत्रि पत्रलता। कलिङ्गसेने, अयं पश्चिमः परिष्वङ्गः पीडय निर्भरमुरसा माम्। असवः प्रवसन्ति वसन्तसेने। मञ्जुलिके, मार्जयसि कतिकृत्वः सुदुःसहदुःखसहस्रास्रदिग्धं दग्धचक्षुरिदं रोदिषि कियदाश्लिष्य च माम्। निर्माणमीदृशं प्रायशो यशोधने। धीरयस्यद्यापि किं मां माधविके। केयमवस्था संस्थापनानाम्। गतः कालः कालिन्दि सखीजनानुनयाञ्जलीनाम्। उन्मत्तिके मत्तपालिके, कृताः पृष्ठतः प्रणयिनीप्रणिपातानुरोधाः। शिथिलय चकोरवति चरणग्रहणं ग्रहिणि। कमलिनि, किमनेन पुनः पुनर्दैवोपालम्भेन। न प्राप्तं चिरं सखीजनसङ्गमसुखम्। आर्ये महत्तरिके तरङ्गसेने नमस्कारः। सखि सौदामिनि, दृष्टासि। समुपनय हव्यवाहनार्चनकुसुमानि कुमुदिके। देहि चितारोहणाय रोहिणि हस्तावलम्बनम्। अम्ब धात्रि, धीरा भव। भवन्त्येवंविधा एव कर्मणां विपाकाः पापकारिणीनाम्। आर्यचरणानामयमञ्जलिः। परः परलोकप्रयाणप्रणामोऽयं मातः। मरणसमये कस्माल्लवलिके हलहलको बलीयानानन्दमयो हृदयस्य मे। हृष्यन्त्युच्चरोमाञ्चमुच्चि किमङ्गीकृत्याङ्गानि। वामनिके, वामेन मे स्फुरितमक्ष्णां। वृथा विरमसि वयस्य वायस वृक्षे[1] क्षीरिणि क्षणे क्षणे क्षीणपुण्यायाः पुरः। हरिणि, हेषितमिव हयानामुत्तरतः। कस्येदमातपत्रमुच्चमत्र पादपान्तरेण प्रभावति विभाव्यते। कुरङ्गिके, केन सुगृहीतनाम्नो नाम गृहीतममृतमयमार्यस्य। देवि, दिष्ट्या वर्धसे देवस्य हर्षस्यागमनमहोत्सवेन।' इत्येतच्च श्रुत्वा सत्वरमुपससर्प। ददर्श च मुह्यन्तीमग्निप्रवेशायोद्यतां राजा राज्यश्रियम्। आललम्बे च मूर्च्छामीलितलोचनाया ललाटं हस्तेन तस्याः ससंभ्रमम्।

अथ तेन भ्रातुः प्रेयसः प्रकोष्ठबद्धानामोषधीनां रसविसरमिव प्रत्युज्जीवनक्षमं क्षरता वमतेव पारिहार्यमणीनामचिन्त्यं प्रभावममृतमिव नखचन्द्ररश्मिभिरुद्गिरता बध्नतेव चन्द्रोदयच्युतशिशिरशीकरं चन्द्रकान्तचूडामणिं मूर्धनि मृणालमयाङ्गुलिनेवातिशीतलेन निर्वापयता दह्यमानं हृदयं प्रत्यानयतेव कुतोऽपि जीवितमाह्लादकेन हस्तसंस्पर्शेन सहसैव समुन्मिमील राज्यश्रीः। तथा चासम्भावितागमनस्याचिन्तितदर्शनस्य सहसा प्राप्तस्य भ्रातुः स्वप्नदृष्टदर्शनस्येव कण्ठे समाश्लिष्य तत्कालाविर्भावनिर्भरेणाभिभूतसर्वात्मना दुःखसम्भारेण निर्दयं नदीमुखप्रणालाभ्यामिव मुक्ताभ्यां स्थूलप्रवाहमुत्सृजन्ती

१ 'प्लक्षवृक्षे' ब.

बाष्पवारि विलोचनाभ्याम् 'हा तात, हा अम्ब, हा सख्यः' इति व्याहरन्ती मुहुर्मुहुरुच्चैस्तरां च, समुद्भूतभगिनीस्नेहसद्भावभारभावितमन्युना मुक्तकण्ठमतिचिरं विक्रुश्य 'वत्से, स्थिरा भव त्वम्' इति भ्रात्रा करस्थगितमुखी समाश्वास्यमानापि, 'कल्याणिनि, कुरु वचनमग्रजस्य गुरोः' इत्याचार्येण याच्यमानापि, 'देवि, न पश्यसि देवस्यावस्थाम् । अलमतिरुदितेन' इति राजलोकेनाभ्यर्थ्यमानापि, 'स्वामिनि, भ्रातरमवेक्षस्व' इति परिजनेन विज्ञाप्यमानापि, 'दुहितर्, विश्रम्य पुनरारटितव्यम्' इति निवार्यमाणापि बान्धववृद्धाभिः, 'प्रियसखि, कियद्रोदिषि । तूष्णीमास्स्व । दृढं दूयते देवः' इति सखीभिरनुनीयमानापि, चिरसम्भावितानेकदुःखनिवहनिर्वहणबाष्पोत्पीडपीड्यमानकण्ठभागा, प्रभूतमन्युभारभरितान्तःकरणा करुणं[1] काहलेन स्वरेण कालमतिदीर्घं रुरोद । विगते च मन्युवेगे वह्नेः समीपादाक्षिप्य भ्रात्रा नीता निकटवर्तिनि तरुतले निषसाद ।

शनैराचार्यस्तु तथा हर्ष इति विज्ञाय विवर्धितादरः सुतरां मुहूर्तमिवातिवाह्य निभृतसंज्ञाज्ञापितेन शिष्येणोपनीतं नलिनीदलैः स्वयमादाय नप्त्रो मुखप्रक्षालनायोदकमुपनिन्ये । नरेन्द्रोऽपि सादरं गृहीत्वा प्रथममनवरतरोदनाताम्रं चिरप्रवृत्ताश्रुजलजालं रक्तपङ्कजमिव स्वसुश्चक्षुरक्षालयत्पश्चादात्मनः । प्रक्षालितमुखशशिनि च महीपाले सर्वतो निःशब्दः सम्बभूव सकलो लिखित इव लोकः । ततो नरेन्द्रो मन्दमन्दमब्रवीत्स्वसारम्—'वत्से, वन्दस्वात्रभवन्तं भदन्तम् । एष ते भर्तुर्हृदयं द्वितीयमस्माकं च गुरुः' इति । राजवचनात्तु राजदुहितरि पतिपरिचयश्रवणोद्घातेन पुनरानीतनेत्राम्भसि नमन्त्यामाचार्यः प्रयत्नरक्षितागतबाष्पाम्भःसम्भारभज्यमानधैर्यार्द्रलोचनः किंचित्परावृत्तनयनो दीर्घं निशश्वास । स्थित्वा च क्षणमेकं प्रदर्शितप्रश्रयो मृदुवादी मधुरया वाचा व्याजहार—'कल्याणराशे, अलं रुदित्वातिचिरम् । राजलोको नाद्यापि रोदनान्निवर्तते । क्रियतामवश्यकरणीयः स्नानविधिः । स्नात्वा च गम्यतां तामेव भूयो भुवम्' इति ।

अथ भूपतिरनुवर्तमानो लौकिकमाचारमाचार्यवचनं चोत्थाय स्नात्वा गिरिसरिति सह स्वस्रा तामेव भूमिमयासीत् । तस्यां च सपरिजनां प्रथममाहितावधानः पार्श्ववर्ती परवतीं शुचा पतिपिण्डप्रदर्शितप्रयत्नप्रतिपन्नाभ्यवहारकरणां[2] भगिनीमभोजयत् । अनन्तरं च स्वयमाहारस्थितिमकरोत् । भुक्तवांश्च बन्धनात्प्रभृति विस्तरतः स्वसुः कान्यकुब्जाद्गौडसंभ्रमं गुप्तितो गुप्तनाम्ना कुलपुत्रेण निष्कासनं निर्गतायाश्च राज्यवर्धनमरणश्रवणं श्रुत्वा चाहारनिराकरणमनाहारपराहतायाश्च विन्ध्याटवीपर्यटनखेदं जातनिर्वेदायाः पावकप्रवेशोपक्रमणं यावत्सर्वमश्रृणोद्व्यतिकरं परिजनतः । ततः सुखासीनमेकत्र तरुतले विविक्तभुवि भगिनीद्वितीयं दूरस्थितानुजीविजनं राजान-

१ 'करुणकाहलेन' अ-क. २ '०हारकारणाम्' ब.

माचार्यः समुपसृत्य शनैरासांचक्रे। स्थित्वा च कंचित्कालांशं लेशतो वक्तुमुपचक्रमे—'श्रीमन्, आकर्ण्यताम्। आख्येयमस्ति नः किंचित्—

अयं हि यौवनोन्मादात्परिभूय भूयसीर्भार्या यौवनावतारतरलतरास्तारा-राजो रजनीकर्णपूरः पुरुहूतपुरोधसो धिषणस्य पुरंध्रीं धर्मपत्नीं पत्नीयन्नतिततरलस्तारां नामापजहार। नाकतश्च पलायांचक्रे। चकितचकोरलोचनया तया सहातिकामया सर्वाकाराभिरामया रममाणो रमणीयेषु देशेषु चचार। चिराच्च कथंचित्सर्वगीर्वाणवाणीगौरवाद्गिरां पत्युः पुनरपि प्रत्यर्पयामास ताम्। हृदये त्वनिन्धनमदह्यत विरहाद्वरारोहायास्तस्याः सततम्।

एकदा तु शैलादुदयादुदयमानो विमले वारिणि वारुणालयस्य संक्रान्तमात्मनः प्रतिबिम्बं विलोकितवान्। दृष्ट्वा च तदा सस्मार सस्मरः स्मेरगण्डस्थलस्य ताराया मुखस्य। मुमोच च मन्मथोन्मादमथ्यमानमानसः स्वःस्थोऽप्यस्वस्थः स्थवीयसः पीतसकलकुमुदवनप्रभाप्रवाहधवलताराभ्यामिव लोचनाभ्यां बाष्पवारिबिन्दून्। अथ पततस्तानुदन्वति समस्तानेवाचेमुर्मुक्ताशुक्तयः। तासां च कुक्षिकोषेषु मुक्ताफलीभूतानवाप तान्कथमपि रसातलनिवासी वासुकिर्नाम विषमुचामीशः। स च तैर्मुक्ताफलैः पातालतलेऽपि तारागणमिव दर्शयद्भिरेकावलीमकल्पयत्। चकार च मन्दाकिनीति नाम तस्याः। सा च भगवतः सोमस्य सर्वासामोषधीनामधिपतेः प्रभावादत्यन्तविषघ्नी हिमामृतसम्भवत्वाच्च स्पर्शेन सर्वसत्त्वसन्तापहारिणी बभूव। यतः स तां सर्वदा विषोष्मशान्तये वासुकिः पर्यधत्त।

समतिक्रामति च कियत्यपि काले कदाचित्तामेकावलीं तस्मान्नागराजान्नागार्जुनो नाम नागैरेवानीतः पातालतलं भिक्षुरभिक्षत लेभे च। निर्गत्य रसातलात्त्रिसमुद्राधिपतये सातवाहननाम्ने नरेन्द्राय सुहृदे स ददौ ताम्। सा चास्माकं कालेन शिष्यपरम्परया कथमपि हस्तमुपगता। यद्यपि च परिभव इव भवति भवादृशां दत्त्रिम उपचारस्तथाप्योषधिबुद्ध्या बुद्धिमता सर्वसत्त्वराशिरक्षाप्रवृत्तेन रक्षणीयशरीरेणायुष्मता विषरक्षापेक्षया गृह्यताम्। इत्यभिधाय भिक्षोरभ्याशवर्तिनश्चीवरपटान्तसंयतां मुमोच तामेकावलीं मन्दाकिनीम्।

उन्मुच्यमानाया एव यस्याः प्रभालेपिनि लब्धावकाशे विशदमहसि[1] महीयसि विसर्पति रश्मिमण्डले युगपद्धवलायमानेषु दिङ्मुखेषु मुकुलितलतावधूत्कण्ठितैरामूलाद्विकसितमिव तरुभिः, अभिनवमृणाललुब्धैर्धावितमिव धुतपक्षपुटपटलधवलितगगनं वनसरसीहंसयूथैः, स्फुटितमिव भरवशविशीर्यमाणधूलिधवलैर्गर्भभेदसूचितसूचीसञ्चयशुचिभिः केतकीवाटैः, उद्दलितदलदन्तुराभिः[2] प्रबुद्धमिव कुमुदिनीभिः, विधुतासितसटाभारभरितदिक्चक्रैश्च-

---

१ 'विषद' अ–क. २ 'उद्दलित–' ब.

लितमिव केसरिकुलैः, प्रहसितमिव सितदशनांशुमालालोकलिप्यमानवनं वनदेवताभिः, विकसितमिव शिथिलितकुसुमकोशकेसराट्टहासनिरङ्कुशं काशकाननैः, भ्रान्तमिव संभ्रमभ्रमितबालपल्लवपरिवेशश्वेतायमानैश्चमरीकदम्बकैः, प्रसृतमिव स्फायमानफेनिलतरलतरतरङ्गोद्गारिणा गिरिनदीपूरेण, अपरतारागणलाभमुदितेनोदितमिव विकचमरीचिचक्राक्रान्तककुभा पूर्णचन्द्रेण, प्रक्षालित इव दावानलधूलिधूसरितदिगन्तो दिवसः, पुनरिव धौतान्यश्रुजलक्लिष्टानि नारीणां मुखानि ।

राजा तु मांसलैस्तस्याः संमुखैर्मयूखैराकुलीक्रियमाणं मुहुर्मुहुरुन्मीलयन्निमीलयंश्च चक्षुः कथमपि प्रयत्नेन ददर्श सर्वाशापूरणीं पङ्क्तीकृतामिव दिङ्नागकरशीकरसंहतिम्, घनमुक्तां शारदीमिव लेखीकृतां ज्योत्स्नाम्, प्रकटपदकचिह्नां सञ्चारणवीथीमिव बालेन्दोर्निश्चलीभूतां सप्तर्षिमालामिव हस्तमुक्ताम्, अभिभूतसकलभुवनभूषणभूतिप्रभावा[२]मैशानीमिव शशिकलाम्, धवलतागुणपरिगृहीतां कान्तिमिव निर्गतां क्षीरराशेः, अनेकमहामहीभृत्परम्परागतां गङ्गामिव दुर्गतिहराम्, अनवरतस्फुरिततरलांशुकां पुरःसरपताकामिव महेश्वरभावागमस्य, घनसारशुक्लां दन्तपङ्क्तिमिवाभिमुखस्येश्वरस्य, वरमनोरथपूरणसमर्थां स्वयंवरस्रजमिव भुवनश्रियः, निजकरपल्लवावरणदुर्लक्ष्यां चक्षूरागविहसतिकामिव वसुधायाः, मन्त्रकोषसाधनप्रवृत्तस्याक्षमालामिव राजधर्मस्य, समुद्रालङ्कारभूतां संख्यालेख्यपट्टिकामिव कुबेरकोशस्य । पश्यंश्चैतां विस्मयमाजगाम मनसा सुचिरम् । आचार्यस्तु तामुद्धृत्य बबन्ध बन्धुरे स्कन्धभागे भूपतेः । अथ नरपतिरपि प्रीतिमुपदर्शयन्प्रत्यवादीत्—'आर्य, रत्नानामीदृशानामनर्हाः प्रायेण पुरुषाः । तपःसिद्धिरियमार्यस्य देवताप्रसादो वा । के च वयमिदानीमात्मनोऽपि किमुत ग्रहणस्य प्रत्याख्यानस्य वा । दर्शनात्प्रभृति प्रभूतगुरुगुणगणहृतेन हृदयेन परवन्तो वयम् । सङ्कल्पितमिदमा मरणादार्योपयोगाय शरीरम् । अत्र कामचारो वः कर्तव्यानाम्' इति ।

समतिक्रान्ते च कियत्यपि काले गते चैकावलीवर्णनालापे लोकस्यानन्तरं लब्धविश्रम्भा राज्यश्रीस्ताम्बूलवाहिनीं पत्रलतामाहूयोपांशु किमपि कर्णमूले शनैरादिदेश । दर्शितविनया च पत्रलता पार्थिवं व्यज्ञापयत्—देव, देवी विज्ञापयति न स्मराम्यार्यस्य पुरः कदाचिदुच्चैर्वचनमपि । कुतो विज्ञापनम् । इयं हि शुचामसह्यता[३] व्यापारयन्ती हतदैव[४]दत्तादेशा शिथिलयति विनयम् । अबलानां हि पतिरपत्यं वावलम्बनम् । उभयविकलानां तु दुःखानलेन्धनायमानं प्राणितमशालीनत्वमेव केवलम् । आर्यागमनेन च

---

१ 'लोभ' ब. २ 'प्रभावामिवैशानीम्' ब. ३ 'असह्यतां...हतदैवदत्ता च दशा' ब. ४ 'देव०' अ.

कृतोऽपि प्रतिहतो मरणप्रयत्नः । अतः काषायग्रहणाभ्यनुज्ञयानुगृह्यतामयमपुण्यभाजनं जनः' इति । जनाधिपस्तु तदाकर्ण्य तूष्णीमेवावातिष्ठत ।

अथाचार्यः सुधीरमभ्यधात्—'आयुष्मति, शोको हि नाम पर्यायः पिशाचस्य रूपान्तरमाक्षेपस्य तारुण्यं तमसो विशेषणं विषस्यानन्तकः प्रेतनगरनायकः । अयमनिर्वृतिधर्मा दहनः । अयमक्षयो राजयक्ष्मा । अयमलक्ष्मीनिवासो जनार्दनः । अयमपुण्यप्रवृत्तः क्षपणकः । अयमप्रतिबोधो निद्राप्रकारः । अयमनलसधर्मा सन्निपातः । अयमशिवसहचरो विनायकः । अयमबुधसेवितो ग्रहवर्गः । अयमयोगसमुत्थो ज्योतिःप्रकारः । अयं स्नेहाद्वायुप्रकोपः, मानसादग्निसम्भवः, आर्द्रभावाद्रजःक्षोभः, रसादभि[1]शोषः, रागात्कालपरिणामः । तदस्याजस्रस्राविणो हृदयमहाव्रणस्य बहुलदोषान्धकारलब्धप्रवेशप्रसरस्य प्राणतस्करस्य शून्यताहेतोर्महाभूतग्रामघातकस्य सकलविग्रहक्षपणदक्षस्य दोषचक्रवर्तिनः कार्श्यश्वासप्रलापोपद्रवबहलस्य दीर्घरोगस्यासह्यस्य सकललोकक्षयधूमकेतोर्जीवितापहारदक्षस्याक्षणरुचेरनभ्रवज्रपातस्य स्फुरदनवद्यविद्याविद्युदुद्द्योतमानानि गहनग्रन्थग्रन्थिगूढगर्भग्रहणगम्भीराणि भूरिकाव्यकथाकठोराणि बहुशास्त्रोद्वहनबृहन्ति विदुषामपि हृदयानि नालं सोढुमापातं किमुत नवनवमालिकाकुसुमकोमलानां सरसबिसतन्तुदुर्बलकमबलानां हृदयम् ।

एवं सति सत्यव्रते, वद किमत्र क्रियते, कतम उपालभ्यते, कस्य पुर उच्चैराक्रन्द्यते, हृदयदाहि दुःखं वा ख्याप्यते । सर्वमक्षिणी निमील्य सोढव्यममूढेन मर्त्यधर्मणा । पुण्यवति, पुरातन्यः स्थितय एताः केन शक्यन्तेऽन्यथाकर्तुम् । संसरन्त्यो नक्तंदिवं द्राघीयस्यो जन्मजरामरणघटनघटीयन्त्रराजिरजवः पञ्चजनानाम् । पञ्चमहाभूतपञ्चकुलाधिष्ठितान्तःकरणव्यवहारदर्शननिपुणाः सर्वंकषा विषमा धर्मराजस्थितयः । क्षणमपि क्षममाणा गलन्त्यायुष्कलाकलनकुशला निलये निलये कालनालिकाः । जगति सर्वजन्तुजीवितोपहारपातिनी सञ्चरति झटिति चण्डिका यमाज्ञा । रटन्त्यनवरतमखिलप्राणिप्रयाणप्रकटनपटवः प्रेतपतिपटहाः । प्रतिदिशं पर्यटन्ति पेटकैः प्रतिपुरं प्रतप्तलोहलोहिताक्षाः कालकूटकान्तिकालकायाः कालपाशपाणयः कालपुरुषाः । प्रतिभवनं भ्रमन्ति भीषणकिङ्करकरघट्टितयमघण्टापुटपटुटांकारभयङ्कराः सर्वसत्त्वसङ्घसंहरणाय घोराघातघोषणाः । दिशि दिशि वहन्ति बहुचिताधूमधूसरितप्रेतपतिपताकापटुपतितगृध्रदृष्टयः शोककृतकोलाहलाकुलकुटुम्बिनीविकीर्णकेशकलापशबलशवशिबिकासहस्रसङ्कुलाः किलकिलायमानश्मशानशिबिरशिवाशावकाः परलोकावसथपथिकसार्थप्रस्थानविशिखावीथयः । सकललोककवलावलेहलम्पटा बहला वहंलिहा लेढि लोहिताचिता चिताङ्गारकाली कालरात्रीजिह्वा जीवितानि जीविनाम् । तृप्तिमशिक्षिता च

१ 'अतिशोषः' ब.

भगवतः सर्वभूतभुजो बुभुक्षा मृत्योः । अतिद्रुतवाहिनी चानित्यतानदी । क्षणिकाश्च महाभूतग्रामगोष्ठ्यः । रात्रिषु भङ्गुराणि गात्रयन्त्रपञ्जरदारूणि देहिनाम् । अशुभशुभावेशविवशा विशरारवः शरीरनिर्माणपरमाणवः । छिदुरा जीवबन्धनपाशतन्त्रीतन्तवः । सर्वमात्मनोऽनीश्वरं विश्वं नश्वरम् । एवमवधृत्य नात्यर्थमेवार्हसि मेधाविनि मृदुनि मनसि तमसः प्रसरं दातुम् । एको हि प्रतिसंख्यानक्षण आधारीभवति धृतेः । अपि च दूरगतेऽपि हि शोके नन्विदानीमपेक्षणीय एवाय ज्येष्ठः पितृकल्पो भ्राता भवत्या गुरुः । इतरथा को न बहु मन्येत कल्याणरूपमीदृशं सङ्कल्पमत्रभवत्याः काषायग्रहणकृतम् । अखिलमनोज्वरप्रशमनकारणं हि भगवती प्रव्रज्या । ज्यायः खल्विदं पदमात्मवताम् । महाभागस्तु भिनत्ति मनोरथमधुना । यदयमादिशति तदेवानुष्ठेयम् । यदि भ्रातेति यदि ज्येष्ठ इति यदि वत्सल इति यदि गुणवानिति यदि राजेति सर्वथा स्थातव्यमस्य नियोगे ।' इत्युक्त्वा व्यरंसीत् ।

उपरतवचसि च तस्मिन्निजगाद नरपतिः—'आर्यमपहाय कोऽन्य एवमभिदध्यात् । अनभ्यर्थितदैवनिर्मिता हि विषमविपदवलम्बनस्तम्भा भवन्तो लोकस्य । स्नेहार्द्रमूर्तयो मोहान्धकारध्वंसिनश्च धर्मप्रदीपाः । किंतु प्रणयप्रदानदुर्ललिता दुर्लभमपि मनोरथमतिप्रीतिरभिलषति । धीरस्यापि धाष्ट्र्यमारोपयति हृदयलघिमलङ्घितमतिवल्लभत्वम् । युक्तायुक्तविचारशून्यत्वाच्च शालीनमपि शिक्षयन्ति स्वार्थतृष्णाः प्रागल्भ्यम् । अभ्यर्थनाया रक्षन्ति च जलनिधय इव मर्यादामार्याः । दत्तमेव च शरीरमिदमनभ्यर्थितेन प्रथममेवातिथ्याय माननीयेन भवता मह्यम् । अतः किंचिदर्थये भदन्तम्-इयं नः स्वसा बाला च बहुदुःखखेदिता च सर्वकार्यावधीरणोपरोधेनापि यावल्लालनीया नित्यम् । अस्माभिश्च भ्रातृवधापकारिरिपुकुलप्रलयकरणोद्यतस्य बाहोर्विधेयैर्भूत्वा सकललोकप्रत्यक्षं प्रतिज्ञा कृता । पूर्वावमाननाभिभवमसहमानैरर्पित आत्मा कोपस्य । अतो नियुञ्ज्महे कियन्तमपि कालमात्मानमार्योऽपि कार्ये मदीये । दीयतामतिथये शरीरमिदम् । अद्यप्रभृति यावदयं जनो लवयति प्रतिज्ञाभारमाश्वासयति च तातविनाशदुःखविक्लवाः प्रजाः, तावदिमामत्रभवतः कथाभिश्च धर्म्याभिः, कुशलप्रतिबोधविधायिभिरुपदेशैश्चारजोभिः, शीलोपशमदायिनीभिश्च देशनाभिः, क्लेशप्रहाणहेतुभूतैश्च तथागतैर्दर्शनैः, अस्मत्पार्श्वोपयायिनीमेव प्रतिबोध्यमानामिच्छामि । इयं तु ग्रहीष्यति मयैव समं समाप्तकृत्येन काषायाणि । अर्थिजने च किमिव नातिसृजन्ति महान्तः । सुरनाथमात्मास्थिभिरपि यावत्कृतार्थमकरोद्धैर्योदधिर्दधीचः । मुनिनाथोऽप्यनपेक्षितात्मस्थितिरनुकम्पेति कृत्वा कृपावानात्मानं वठरसत्त्वेभ्यः कतिकृत्वो न दत्तवान् । अतः परं भवन्त एव बहुतरं जानन्ति ।' इत्युक्त्वा तूष्णींबभूव भूपतिः ।

१ 'पात्र' अ-क. २ '०विधायिनीभिरुपदेशैश्च दूरापसारितरजोभिः' ब.

भूयस्तु बभाषे भदन्तः—'भव्या न द्विरुच्चारयन्ति वाचम्। चेतसा प्रथममेव प्रतिग्राहिता गुणास्तावकाः कायबलिमिमाम्। अमुना जनेनोपयोगस्तु निरुपयोगस्यास्य लघुनि गुरुणि वा कृत्ये गुणवदायत्तः' इति। अथ तथा तस्मिन्नभिनन्दितप्रणये प्रीयमाणः पार्थिवस्तत्र तामुषित्वा विभावरीमुषसि वसनालङ्कारादिप्रदानपरितोषितं विसर्ज्य निर्घातमाचार्येण सह स्वसारमादाय प्रयाणकैः कतिपयैरेव कटकमनुजाह्नवि निविष्टं प्रत्याजगाम।

तत्र च राज्यश्रीप्राप्तिव्यतिकरकथां कथयत एव प्रणयिभ्यो रविरपि ततार गगनतलम्। बहलमधुपङ्कपिङ्गलः पङ्कजाकर इव सञ्चुकोच चक्रवाकवल्लभो वासरः। प्रकीर्णानि नवरुधिररसारुणवर्णानि लोकालोकजूंषि यजूंषीव कुपितयाज्ञवल्क्यवक्त्रवान्तानि निजवपुषि पूषा पापमूंषि पुनरपि सञ्जहार जालकानि रोचिषाम्। क्रमेण च समुपोह्यमानमांसलरागरोचिष्णुरुष्णांशुः, उष्णीषबन्धसहजचूडामणिरिव वृकोदरकरपुटोत्पाटितः प्रत्यग्रशोणितशोणाङ्गरागरौद्रो द्रौणायनस्य, रुद्रभिक्षादानशौण्डपुरमथनमुक्तमुण्डशिरानाडिरुधिरपूरणशोणितकपिलः[1] कपालकर्पर इव च पैतामहः, पितृवधरुषितरामरागरचितः पृथुविकटकार्तवीर्यांसकूटकुट्टाककुठारतुण्डतष्टदुष्टक्षत्रियकण्ठकुहररुधिरकुल्याप्रणालसहस्रपूरितो ह्रद इव दूररोधी रौधिरः, भयनिगूढकरचरणमुण्डमण्डलाकृतिर्गुल्लारुडनखपञ्जराक्षेपपक्षपणक्षिप्तक्षतजोक्षितो व्यसुर्विभावसुः[2], कमठ इव च लोठ्यमानो नभसि, अरुणगर्भमांसपिण्डाण्ड इव च खण्डिमानमानीतो नियतकालातिपातदूयमानदाक्षायणीक्षिप्तः, धातुतट इव च सुमेरोरसुरवधाभिचारचरुपचनपिशुनः, शोणितक्वाथकषायितकुक्षिरतिविसङ्कटः कटाह इव च बार्हस्पत्यः, सद्योगलितगजदानवदेहलोहितोपलेपभीषणो मुखमण्डलाभोग इव महाभैरवस्य मुहूर्तमदृश्यत। जलनिधिजलप्रतिबिम्बितरविबिम्बराजिभास्वराश्रावलम्बिनी गृहीतार्द्रमांसभारेव चाबभासे वासरावसानवेला वेतालनिभा। ज्वलत्संध्यारागरज्यमानजलप्रवाहः पुनरिव पुराणपुरुषपीवरोरुसम्पुटपिष्टमधुकैटभरुधिरपटलपाटलवपुरभवदधिपतिरर्णसाम्। अवसिते संध्यासमये समनन्तरमपरिमितयशःपानतृषिताय मुक्ताशैलशिलाचषक इव निजकुलकीर्त्या, कृतयुगकरणोद्यतायादिराजराजतशासनमुद्रानिवेश इव राज्यश्रिया, सकलद्वीपजिगीषाचलिताय श्वेतद्वीपदूत इव चायत्या, श्वेतभानुरुपानीयत निशया नरेन्द्रायेति॥

इति श्रीबाणभट्टकृतौ[3] हर्षचरितेऽष्टम उच्छ्वासः।

---

१ 'पूरणकपिलः' अ-क. २ 'विभावसुकमट इव' ब. ३ '०कृते' ब; 'श्रीचित्रभानुसुनुमहाकविचक्रचूडामणिश्रीबाणभट्टकृतौ श्रीहर्षचरिते महाकाव्ये विन्ध्याद्रिनिवेशनं नामाष्टम उच्छ्वासः सम्पूर्णः। समाप्तमिदं श्रीहर्षचरितमहाकाव्यम्' ब.

NOTES

Uchchhvāsa I

हर्षस्य चरितमधिकृत्य कृतो ग्रन्थः हर्षचरितम्. The affixes अण् (अ) and छ (ईय) are added to words to denote works, according to the Sûtra 'अधिकृत्य कृते ग्रन्थे' पा. IV. 3. 87. But, according to the Vārtika 'लुबाख्यायिकाभ्यो बहुलम्', these affixes are generally omitted in the case of works called आख्यायिकाs. The हर्षचरित is an आख्यायिका, for a definition of which see Intro. p. XX. उच्छ्वासः means 'a chapter of a book.' It is a division peculiarly associated with works of the आख्यायिका class. Note verse 10 below.

In some Mss. the first verse is इच्छादि०, which contains a salutation to सरस्वती. इच्छादि...प्रभावा the power of which, in presenting the whole (world) by the successive working (प्रसरः) of the several faculties beginning with volition, is well-known. निचयः collection. Ideas are conveyed by words over which सरस्वती presides. Words are made up of letters (sounds) the production of which is explained by the following from the शिक्षा 'आत्मा बुद्ध्या समेत्यार्थान् मनो युङ्क्ते विवक्षया । मनः कायाग्निमाहन्ति स प्रेरयति मारुतम् । मारुतस्तूरसि चरन् मन्द्रं जनयति स्वरम् ।... सोदीर्णो मूर्ध्न्यभिहतो वक्त्रमापद्य मारुतः । वर्णाञ्जनयते &c.' It will be noticed that according to this quotation it is the *desire* to speak (विवक्षा = वक्तुमिच्छा) that is the first step in the evolution of वर्णs. Separate या (सरस्वती) आध्यायिनाम् (of those who reflect). आध्यायिनां may be connected with हृदय in the compound हृदय० or with रूप. The poet perhaps intends both. हृदयमेव कोकनदं तस्मिन् प्रतिष्ठा यस्याः which is installed in the lotus of the heart (of reflecting men). The heart is fitly compared to कोकनद which is a red lotus. 'रक्तोत्पलं कोकनदम्' इत्यमरः. In the Upanishads the heart is often spoken of as a lotus in which the supreme soul dwells. 'अथ यदिदमस्मिन् ब्रह्मपुरे दहरं पुण्डरीकं वेश्म दहरोऽस्मिन्नन्तराकाशस्तस्मिन्यदन्तस्तदन्वेष्टव्यम्' छान्दोग्य 8.1.1. सरस्वती is but a शक्ति of the Supreme Soul. रूपं प्रकाशयति—It is speech that manifests (conveys) objects (रूपं) to the mind. The meaning may also be 'that manifests her real nature (to those who are contemplative).' वाक् is said to be fourfold, परा, पश्यन्ती, मध्यमा and वैखरी. This is a description of परा वाक्. The metre is वसन्ततिलका. We may also read या ध्यायिनां or separate as वा अध्यायिनां (from इ with अधि).

Verse 1. Connect नमः with शम्भवे. It is usual for Sanskrit authors to begin their works with an invocation to some deity. तुङ्गं शिरः चुम्बते इति ०चुम्बी चन्द्रः एव चामरं तेन चारुः तस्मै. The head of शिव never bows down to any one else; hence it is तुङ्ग. Both the moon and चामर are white. त्रैलोक्यमेव नगरं तस्य आरम्भे मूलस्तम्भः तस्मै—who is the first pillar in constructing the city in the form of the three worlds. The author looks upon शिव as the supreme deity, the cause of the creation, maintenance and absorption of the Universe. It is well-known that in constructing a house the first pillar (whether of wood or stone) is erected on an auspicious day and with great ceremony. चामरs may be tied on to it for the sake of beauty and auspiciousness. 'नगरारम्भे हि मूलस्तम्भो भवति। तत्र च पट्टबन्धादिवदुत्क्षेपणानन्तरमुन्नते पृष्ठदेशे चन्द्रतुल्यं श्वेतं चामरं क्रियते इति स्थितिः' सं. शङ्कर notes that other commentators construe the word शम्भु as referring also to विष्णु and ब्रह्मा. " 'स्वयम्भूः शम्भुरादित्यः' इति नामसहस्रे दृष्टत्वाद्धरेः, 'शम्भू ब्रह्मत्रिलोचनौ' इत्यभिधाकोशदर्शनाच्च ब्रह्मणोऽपि नमस्कारोऽयमित्यन्ये वदन्ति। व्याकुर्वते च हरिपक्षे त्रैलोक्याक्रमणकाले यद्वा 'यस्याग्निरास्यं द्यौर्मूर्धा खं नाभिश्चरणौ मही' इत्यभिप्रायेण तुङ्गमुच्छ्रितं शुलक्षणं यच्छिरस्तच्चुम्बि चन्द्र एव चामरं तेन चारवे। ब्रह्मपक्षे चन्द्रः स्वर्णं तन्मयं चामरमिव चामरं केशकलापः। हिरण्यकेशो हि ब्रह्मा त्रैलोक्यादीनि सर्वत्र तुल्यमिति." From this verse and from indications in the 2nd उच्छ्वास (देवदेवस्य विरूपाक्षस्य...विधाय पूजां परमया भक्त्या) we can say that Bāṇa was specially devoted to शिव. C and T note that this verse occurs entire in an inscription (vide Indian Antiquary vol. XIII. p. 92) of the western चालुक्य king त्रिभुवनमल्ल II dated S'ake 1006.

Verse 2. हरस्य कण्ठः तस्य ग्रहः तेन आनन्दः तेन मीलिते (closed) अक्षिणी यस्याः—Whose eyes were closed by the joy of clasping the neck of S'iva. कालकूटविषस्य स्पर्शेन जातः मूर्च्छायाः आगमः (advent, beginning) यस्याः. When the gods and demons churned the ocean for jewels, the first thing that came out was the poison हालाहल. शिव drank it to save the universe from destruction. The poison showed its strength by making S'iva's throat dark. See रामायण I. 45 (निर्णयसागर ed.) and भागवतपुराण VIII. Compare 'अमृतमथनसमयमिव तीरावस्थितशितिकण्ठपीयमानविषम्' कादम्बरी (p. 123 of P). Umā (पार्वती) clasped the neck of S'iva and closed her eyes in the ecstasy of love. The poet fancies that the closing of the eyes was due to the fainting fit caused by touching the poison in the throat of शिव. It is well-known that poison causes fainting. For the derivation of उमा see कुमार० I. 26. 'उ मेति मात्रा तपसो निषिद्धा पश्चादुमाख्यां सुमुखी जगाम.'

Verse 3. The poet in this verse after invoking deities salutes Vyāsa the author of the महाभारत and thereby shows his great reverence for him. सर्वं वेत्तीति सर्वविद् तस्मै. कविवेधसे—who is Brahmā among poets. Brahmā is called सुरज्येष्ठ; so व्यास is the best of poets. The word may also mean 'who is the creator of (the effusions of) poets.' The idea is that later poets derive their inspiration from his work. The महाभारत itself gives expression to this idea. 'इतिहासोत्तमादस्माज्जायन्ते कविबुद्धयः' आदिपर्व 2. 385; 'इदं कविवरैः सर्वैराख्यानमुपजीव्यते' आदि० 2. 389; 'यदिहास्ति तदन्यत्र यन्नेहास्ति न तत्क्वचित्'. यः सरस्वत्याः वर्षमिव पुण्यं भारतं चक्रे who composed the sacred (work called) Bhārata which is as it were a shower of speech. The भारत contains the choicest speech in abundance. The poet conveys another idea. यः सरस्वत्या (वाचा) भारतं पुण्यं चक्रे सरस्वत्या (नद्या) भारतं वर्षमिव. Vyāsa by his holy words sanctified भारतवर्ष (India) as the sacred river सरस्वती sanctifies भारतवर्ष. According to ancient ideas of Geography, the earth was divided into seven द्वीपs (जम्बु, प्लक्ष, शाल्मल, कुश, क्रौञ्च, शाक and पुष्कर). Each of these द्वीपs was subdivided into 9 वर्षs, had its own mountains and was surrounded by a sea. जम्बुद्वीप had 9 वर्षs (कुरु, हिरण्मय, रम्यक, इलावृत, हरि, केतुमाल, भद्राश्व, किन्नर and भारत). Vide विष्णुपुराण II. 1-3 and मार्कण्डेय chap. 54 ff. भारतवर्ष is defined as 'उत्तरं यत्समुद्रस्य हिमाद्रेश्चैव दक्षिणम् । वर्षं तद्भारतं नाम भारती यत्र सन्ततिः ॥'. सरस्वती was a sacred river in the Panjab now lost in the sands of the great desert of India. We may also interpret 'who sanctified the line descended from भरत by his speech.' The महाभारत narrates the story of the Kauravas and Pāṇḍavas who were descendants of भरत, son of दुष्यन्त and शकुन्तला. Vide आदिपर्व chap. 74. 'भरताद्भारती कीर्तिर्येनेदं भारतं कुलम् ॥' verse 131. The word कविवेधसे may also mean 'who is a creator in the form of a poet.' A poet is often spoken of as a creator (of high thoughts and aspirations). Compare the first verse of काव्यप्रकाश and 'अपारे काव्यसंसारे **कविरेव प्रजापतिः** । यथास्मै रोचते विश्वं तथेदं परिवर्तते' ॥ ध्वन्यालोक III. p. 222 and also अग्निपुराण chap. 339. 10.

Verse 4. कुकवयः bad poets, poetasters. रागेण अधिष्ठिता दृष्टिः येषाम्—whose vision (intellect) is dominated by (evil) passions (with कुकवयः); whose eye is dominated by redness (with कोकिलाः). Poetasters are not inspired by noble ideals and thoughts; but their effusions are due to the envy of good poets and such other evil tendencies. The three words रागा०,

वाचालाः and °कारिणः apply equally to bad poets and cuckoos and so the author compares bad poets with cuckoos. वाचालाः loquacious (with poets); making a noise (with cuckoos). कामकारिणः doing just as they please; that excite passion (with कोकिलाः). Poetasters compose poems throwing to the winds all canons of good taste and sound criticism. The notes of the cuckoo are an excitant of love. According to the terminology of Sanskrit rhetoricians रति is the स्थायिभाव of शृङ्गाररस; the नायक and नायिका are the आलम्बनविभाव; वसन्त, the moon, the notes of the cuckoo are the उद्दीपनविभाव; external indications such as स्वेद are the अनुभावs and चिन्ता, जडता &c. are व्यभिचारिभावs. Bāṇa in this verse finds fault with poetasters and says that the voice of a true poet is very rarely heard amidst the din of poetasters. The com. suggests another meaning; 'such is the natural charm of poetry; even bad poets give pleasure; how much more will those who are specially gifted ?' But this is rather strained and not in keeping with the next verse. सं० gives another sense of कुकवयः 'कुकन्ति गृह्णन्ति चेतांसि इति कुकाः ते च वयो मयूरप्रवराः पक्षिणः'.

Verse 5. This verse is full of puns. The plain meaning is 'Innumerable are the poets to be found in each house that can write only plain and matter of fact descriptions, like dogs (that are also numberless). Poets that possess creative genius are not many, like शरभs'. जाति is another name for स्वभावोक्ति. It consists in describing objects (particularly the doings of children, lower animals &c.) as they are in their various positions. 'नानावस्थं पदार्थानां रूपं साक्षाद्विवृण्वती । स्वभावोक्तिश्च जातिश्चेत्याद्या सालङ्कृतिर्यथा ॥' काव्यादर्श II. 8. See also भोज's सरस्वतीकण्ठाभरण III and रुद्रट's काव्यालंकार 7. 30–31. जाति (or स्वभावोक्ति) is opposed to वक्रोक्ति, which latter was often looked upon as the soul of poetry and as something which a poet should strive for. Note 'सैषा सर्वत्र वक्रोक्तिरनयार्थो विभाव्यते । यत्नोऽस्यां कविना कार्यः कोऽलङ्कारोऽनया विना ॥' भामह II. जातिभाजः also means 'possessed of the common characteristic' (श्वत्व or कवित्व). The idea is:—the most wretched cur and the best hound are both dogs *i. e.* they possess the जाति (species) श्वत्व in common; but there is great disparity in their worth; so poetasters (कुकवयः) possess the जाति कवित्व in common with poets of genius. असंख्याः also means 'of no account, useless (with poets); that do not fight' (with dogs). 'मृधमास्कन्दनं संख्यं समीकं सांपरायिकम्' इत्यमरः. उत्पादकाः उद्गताः पादकाः (पादाः)

येषां that have feet upwards (growing on their backs). शरभाः—शरभ is a fabulous animal with eight legs and stronger than a lion. See वनपर्व chap. 119 for the story of a dog that was successively turned into a leopard, a tiger, an elephant, a lion and lastly into a शरभ 'अष्टपादूर्ध्वनयनः शरभो वनगोचरः। स सिंहं हन्तुमागच्छन्मुनेस्तस्य निवेशनम् ॥' verse 13.

Verse 6. In this verse Bāṇa speaks of so-called poets that are merely plagiarists. अन्य—वृत्त्या by (merely) changing the words of other (poets). बन्ध...गूहनैः by concealing the distinctive marks of their compositions. अना...भाव्यते a poet without being (expressly) declared (to be so) is revealed to be a thief (a plagiarist) in the midst of the good. The idea is:—the composition of a plagiarist is seen in its true light by the good, though there is no express declaration that it is merely a patchwork. The words अना...मध्ये may also mean 'who is not esteemed among the good.' This meaning also suits the word चौरः. We can also separate as अ-ना आख्यातः 'he (the plagiarist or the thief) is not counted a man'. ना is the nom. sing. of नृ. बन्ध...गूहनैः—the idea (according to the com.) is:—great poets compose works containing particular words like श्री, लक्ष्मी in particular verses or in some particular order. The plagiarist in copying suppresses such indications. बन्धः also means the arrangements of the letters of a stanza in a particular way, such as खड्गबन्ध, शृङ्खलाबन्ध, सर्वतोभद्र. Or बन्धचिह्न may be used in a general sense *viz.* 'the characteristic style of a good composition.' 'बन्धः पदरचना' वामन's काव्यालंकारसूत्रवृत्ति 3. 1. 4. A thief also changes colour *i. e.* his face becomes pale (when challenged in the midst of the good). He also tries to conceal the marks left (in his flesh) by the chains (with which he was bound when caught). Although a thief conceals these marks and so is not declared to be a thief (अनाख्यात), yet by the pallor that comes over his face when challenged he is revealed in his true light.

Verse 7. The author in this verse points out that the poets of particular countries exhibit only a few poetic excellences in their works and not all. श्लेष...च्येषु Among the northern (poets), a work most exhibits puns. श्लेष is of two kinds, शब्दश्लेष and अर्थश्लेष. In the first a particular word when used gives rise to different senses; but if that word be omitted and a synonym substituted, then the double meaning vanishes *e. g.* बालेवोद्यानमालेयं **सालकाननशोभिनी.** Here take the word साल० as meaning सालकं (अलकैः सह) आननं तेन शोभिनी (with बाला) and सालानां काननं तेन शोभिनी (with उद्यानमाला). If for सालक we substitute सकुन्तल then the श्लेष vanishes. In अर्थश्लेष, even if we change the words, there are two meanings; *e. g.* 'उदयमयते दिङ्मालिन्यं निराकुरुतेतरां नयति निधनं निद्रामुद्रां प्रवर्तयति क्रियाः। रचयतितरां स्वैराचारप्रवर्तनकर्तनं बत बत लसत्तेजःपुञ्जो विभाति विभाकरः॥' काव्यप्रकाश X. (Here a king called विभाकर and the Sun are both praised). अर्थमात्रकम्—The poets of the west care only for the meaning (they do not exhibit charm of style or figures of speech). उत्प्रेक्षा is a figure of speech. To explain it briefly, it consists in representing (poetically, not through mistake) one thing as another thing or in representing a particular effect as due to some cause other than the real one or representing something done with one motive as due to another. It is generally introduced by such words as मन्ये, शङ्के, ध्रुवं or इव (as it were). Bāṇa's works bristle at every step with this figure. The verse 'हरकण्ठ' is a good example of उत्प्रेक्षा. गौडे...डम्बरः among Gauda poets there is only show of words (high-flown language). Their works do not contain charming thoughts or such qualities as perspicuity &c. Daṇḍin, who was at least a contemporary of Bāṇa, if he was not earlier still, speaks of two literary styles. (रीति), *viz.*, वैदर्भी and गौडी. He says that ten Guṇas (such as प्रसाद, माधुर्य and ओजः) are the essence of the Vaidarbhî style, while the Gauḍî style is the reverse of the Vaidarbhî (काव्यादर्श I. 41–42). He tells us that the Gauḍas were very fond of अनुप्रास (काव्यादर्श I. 54) and that even in verse they employed long compounds (काव्यादर्श I. 80). वामन says in his काव्यालङ्कारसूत्रवृत्ति (I. 2. 12.) 'समस्तात्युद्भटपदामोजःकान्तिगुणान्विताम्। गौडीयामपि गायन्ति रीतिं रीतिविचक्षणाः॥'. गौड is the district of Gaur, central part of Bengal; formerly it extended from वङ्ग to the borders of Orissa.

Verse 8. नवोर्थः—a new topic (*i. e.* a subject not dealt with by former writers) or a striking subject or meaning. This refers to the imaginative side of a poet's mind, called प्रतिभा by Sanskrit rhetoricians. 'प्रज्ञा नवनवोन्मेषशालिनी प्रतिभा मता'. जातिरग्राम्या description of nature or objects that is not vulgar. For जाति, see above p. 4. दण्डी gives the following as examples of ग्राम्य and अग्राम्य ways of description respectively, although the meaning is the same. 'कन्ये कामयमानं मां न त्वं कामयसे कथम्। इति ग्राम्योऽप्रमर्थोऽस्मा वैरस्याय प्रकल्पते ॥ कामं कन्दर्पचाण्डालो मयि वामाक्षि निर्दयः। त्वयि निर्मत्सरो दिष्ट्येत्यग्राम्योऽर्थो रसावहः ॥' (काव्या॰ I. 63-64). जाति also means a particular class of metres regulated by Mātrās, such as आर्या. Compare 'पद्यं चतुष्पदी तच्च वृत्तं जातिरिति द्विधा' काव्या॰ I. 11. जाति also means 'a composition or verse in which the same words represent Sanskrit or Prakrit.' Both these meanings are not suitable here. श्लेषः—for explanation, see the preceding verse. अक्लिष्टः not laboured. 'व्यवहितार्थप्रत्ययं क्लिष्टम्' काव्यालङ्कारसूत्र II. 1. 21. स्फुटो रसः A sentiment (which is the subject matter of a poem) that is easily understood. रस is the soul of Kāvya. It is that sentiment which rules a composition and which is the object of the poem to present to the mind of the reader. Rasas are eight शृङ्गार, वीर, करुण, हास्य, रौद्र, भयानक, बीभत्स, अद्भुत. Some add a ninth रस *viz.* शान्त. विक...बन्धः—The Com. says 'उदारतालक्षणबन्धगुणयुक्तः यत्र सति नृत्यन्तीव पदानि प्रतिभासन्ते.' In this he follows वामन's काव्यालङ्कारसूत्र III. 1. 22 'विकटत्वमुदारता'—वृत्ति "बन्धस्य विकटत्वं यदसौ उदारता। यस्मिन्सति नृत्यन्तीव पदानीति जनस्य वर्णभावना भवति तत् विकटत्वं लीलायमानत्वमित्यर्थः। यथा 'स्वचरणविनिविष्टैर्नूपुरैर्नर्तकीनां झणिति रणितमासीत्तत्र चित्रं कलं च'। न पुनः 'चरणकमलकलग्नैर्नूपुरैर्नर्तकीनां झटिति रणितमासीन्मञ्जु चित्रं च तत्र.'" This means that in विकटत्व the sound must be an echo to the sense. C and T translate 'language rich in sonorous words.' The author in our opinion rather refers to ओजोगुण about which दण्डी says 'ओजः समासभूयस्त्वमेतद्गद्यस्य जीवितम्। पद्येऽप्यदाक्षिणात्यानामिदमेकं परायणम् ॥' काव्या. I. 80. कृत्स्न...ष्करम् all this it is difficult to find in one composition.

Verse 9. किं...काव्येन what is the use of the poetry of that poet? C and T translate 'what has that poet to do with poetry?' This does not yield a good sense. Construe यस्य सर्ववृत्तान्तगामिनी भारती जगत्त्रयं न व्याप्नोति सर्ववृत्तान्तगामिनी भारती कथेव (सा यथा जगत्त्रयं व्याप्नोति)—whose Muse comprehending the furthest limit of metrics does not cover the three worlds (*i. e.* does not become well-known in the world) like the Bhārata story. सर्वेषां वृत्तानां (metres) अन्तं गच्छति इति (with Muse); सर्वान् वृत्तान्तान् (इतिहासान्) गमयतीति that conveys all sorts of narratives (with भारती कथा). The Mahābhārata contains numerous episodes.

Verse 10. Here Bāṇa offers his meed of praise to the authors of आख्यायिकाs that preceded him. आख्यायिकाs were composed from very ancient times. Vide Introduction p. XIII.

For a definition of आख्यायिका given by भामह, see Introduction p. XX. The salient points are that it is in prose, has a high topic, is divided into sections called उच्छ्वासs, contains verses in the वक्त्र and अपरवक्त्र metres which suggest coming events. The साहित्यदर्पण (परिच्छेद VI) calls the sections आश्वासs. कथ...श्वराः how are those princes among poets, *viz.* the authors of आख्यायिकाs, not to be praised? (*i. e.* they deserve the highest praise). उच्छ्वा...न्नाः unwearied even at the end of an उच्छ्वास *i. e.* who are able to compose another उच्छ्वास equal in merit to its predecessor. येषां...स्वती in whose verses (in the वक्त्र metre) the goddess of speech dwells. In the वक्त्र metre, there are eight syllables in each पाद as in अनुष्टुभ्. It is defined as 'नाद्यान्नसौ स्यातामब्धेर्योऽनुष्टुभि ख्यातम्'. After the first letter in each पाद there should be no नगण nor सगण and after the first four letters there should be a यगण. उच्छ्वा...खिन्नाः—conveys another idea. A man who is tired heaves out a deep breath. There is an apparent विरोध in saying that they are not exhausted even when they are breathing hard. कवीश्वराः may also mean 'the omniscient gods' *i. e.* the creator (the plural being used for श्लेष or to show respect). The supreme spirit is often called कवि in the Upanishads and the Gîtā. 'कविं पुराणमनुशासितारं' &c. गीता 8. 9; 'कविर्मनीषी परिभूः स्वयम्भूः' ईशावास्योपनिषद् 8. उच्छ्वा...खिन्नाः would mean 'not exhausted or afflicted even at the end of the Universe.' In the Upanishads the Universe containing the Vedas, the Heavens, the earth &c. is said to be the निःश्वसित of the Supreme. 'अस्य महतो भूतस्य निःश्वसितमेतद्यदृग्वेदो... अस्यैवैतानि निःश्वसितानि' बृहदारण्यकोपनिषद् II. 4. 10. वक्त्रे...सरस्वती The goddess of speech is often poetically described as dwelling in the mouth of Brahmā. Compare 'चतुर्मुखमुखाम्भोजवनहंसवधूर्मम । मानसे रमतां नित्यं सर्वशुक्ला सरस्वती ॥' काव्यादर्श I. 1.

Verse 11. Construe कर्णगोचरं गतया वासवदत्तया नूनं कवीनां दर्पः अगलत् कर्णगोचरं गतया पाण्डुपुत्राणां शक्त्या इव कवीनां (दर्पः अगलत्). The pride of poets indeed melted away on account of वासवदत्ता when it reached their ears, just as the pride of Droṇa vanished when the missile of the sons of Pāṇḍu given by Vāsava (Indra) came near Karṇa. वासवदत्ता—This seems to be the work of Subandhu. It is a कथा technically so called. Vide Introduction p. XX. It cannot be the आख्यायिका वासवदत्ता mentioned by Patañjali (Introduction p. XIII). The authors of आख्यायिकाs came in for high praise in the preceding verse. We naturally expect that in this verse the author should refer to another class of works. In this Introduction Bāṇa assigns only one verse to each of the poets or works mentioned below. There is no reason why he should depart from that rule in the case of आख्यायिका. A कथा is very much like an आख्यायिका and so it is but proper that the वासवदत्ता of सुबन्धु (being a कथा) should receive encomiums after the authors of आख्यायिकाs, if सुबन्धु preceded Bāṇa, as we hold. कवि also means द्रोण. The plural कवीनां may be explained as due to the exigencies of श्लेष or as expressing respect. द्रोण was the son of भरद्वाज 'भरद्वाजस्य च स्कन्नं द्रोण्यां शुक्रमवर्धत । महर्षेरुग्रतपसस्तस्माद् द्रोणो व्यजायत ॥' आदिपर्व 63. 6. कवि is a name for शुक्र and so indicates द्रोण. The story of कर्ण, the son of कुन्ती, is well-known. The reference seems to be to the defeat of कर्ण by भीम (vide द्रोणपर्व chap 129, 131, 133). We may also construe कवीनां पाण्डुपुत्राणां (दर्पः) कर्णगोचरं गतया वासवदत्तया शक्त्या इव (अगलत्) 'as the pride of the wise sons of Pâṇḍu melted away through the javelin that was given by इन्द्र and that came to the hands of Karṇa. Karṇa was a generous man. Once Indra who was interested in Arjuna came to Karṇa as a Brāhmaṇa and begged of him his divine armour and ear-rings. Karṇa true to his word gave Indra what he wanted. Indra being pleased with Karṇa gave him a शक्ति that would kill one महारथी whoever he might be. See आदिपर्व chap. 111. 'ददौ शक्तिं सुरपतिर्वाक्यं चेदमुवाच ह ॥ देवासुरमनुष्याणां गन्धर्वोरगरक्षसाम् । यमेकं जेतुमिच्छेथाः सोऽनया न भविष्यति ॥' verses 29–30.

Verse 12. भट्टार...यते the prose composition of the revered हरिचन्द्र acts like a king *i. e.* is pre-eminent like a king. भट्टारः or भट्टारकः is a term of respect applied to kings in dramas and inscriptions. 'राजा भट्टारको देवः' इत्यमरः. It was also applied by Jain writers to those who abandoned the worldly life. नृप इव आचरति नृपायते according to 'कर्तुः क्यङ् सलोपश्च' पा. 3. 1. 11. पद... ज्ज्वलः charming or brilliant on account of the arrangement of words (with गद्यबन्ध); splendid on account of the firmness of his position (with नृप). पदानां शब्दानां बन्धेन (रचनया) उज्ज्वलः; पदस्य बन्धेन &c. हारी charming (with गद्यबन्ध); wearing a necklace (with नृप). We may also separate as ०ज्ज्वलो अहारी (with गद्यबन्ध). अहारी not stealing (from the works of others). कृत...स्थितिः—कृता वर्णानां क्रमेण (अलङ्कारशास्त्रानुसारेण) स्थितिः यस्मिन्; कृता वर्णानां ब्राह्मणादीनां क्रमेण (शास्त्रक्रमेण) स्थितिः येन—In which letters are employed in accordance with the rules of poetics (with गद्यबन्ध); who makes the four Varṇas follow the rules prescribed for each (with नृप). It was the canon of rhetoricians that माधुर्यगुण was most appropriate in शृङ्गार and करुण, and ओजः in वीररस. माधुर्य consists in employing letters from क् to म्, except टवर्ग, preceded by the nasals of their class, and that in ओजः one should employ conjunct consonants joining the first and second or third and fourth letters of each class, टवर्ग, श् and ष्. 'टवर्गवर्जिताः स्पर्शाः स्वस्ववर्गान्तशेखराः। लघुरेफलकारौ च कोमलाः परिकीर्तिताः॥ रेफेन यस्य कस्यापि योग आद्यतृतीययोः। स्वोत्तराभ्यां तुल्ययोर्वा परुषाष्टगणः शषौ॥' रत्नापण on प्रतापरुद्र. भट्टारहरिचन्द्र is no more than a mere name to us. His prose composition has not yet been discovered. There is a *poem* called धर्मशर्माभ्युदय written by a Jain writer हरिचन्द्र. A verse of the Gauḍavaho (Vide Intro. p. XII) speaks of a हारियन्द (Prakrit for हारिचन्द्र) बन्ध. Is this a reference to this हरिचन्द्र?

Verse 13. The principal sentence is सातवाहनः सुभाषितैः रत्नैरिव कोशमकरोत्—सातवाहन made a treasure with fine sayings as with jewels. अविनाशिनम् Immortal (as applied to the collection of सुभाषितs); inexhaustible (with the treasure of jewels). अग्राम्यम्—not vulgar or indecent *i. e.* refined (with सुभाषितकोश); not produced in villages (with रत्नकोश). Jewels are found in the sea or in mines (not in villages). विशुद्धा जातिः स्वभावोक्तिः येषु (with सुभाषितैः); विशुद्धा जातिः येषां (with रत्नैः) of purest character. विशुद्धजातिभिः means the same thing as 'जातिरग्राम्या' above. कोशं- a collection of verses that are unconnected with one another *i. e.* the same subject does not run through them all. It also means 'a treasure.' 'कोशः श्लोकसमूहस्तु स्यादन्योन्यानपेक्षकः' साहित्यदर्पण VI. See also काव्यादर्श I. 13. "मुक्तकं कुलकं **कोशः** सङ्घात इति तादृशः। सर्गबन्धाङ्गरूपत्वादनुक्तः पद्यविस्तरः॥'. In this verse the author seems to praise the गाथासप्तशती of हाल. That work consists of 700 Prakrit verses. It is a collection of verses composed by हाल (सप्तशती I. 3) in the Āryā metre (which is a subdivision of जाति for which see p. 7). 'मात्राभिर्गणना यत्र सा जातिरिति काश्यप।' अग्निपुराण chap. 337. 22. सातवाहन (Prakrit सालाहण) is identified by हेमचन्द्र with हालं 'सालाहणम्मि हालो' देशीनाममाला VIII. 66. In the अभिधानचिन्तामणि we have 'हालः स्यात्सातवाहनः'. हाल seems to us to be an abbreviated form of the Prakrit सालाहण (स् and ह् being often interchanged even in modern vernaculars like the Gujarati). क्षीरस्वामी quotes several verses enumerating the names of famous emperors of old among whom occurs हाल 'हालः स्याच्छालिवाहनः'. A king सातवाहन is connected with गुणाढ्य the author of the बृहत्कथा, for which see verse 17. सुभाषित is defined as 'पुराणेष्वितिहासेषु तथा रामायणादिषु । वचनं सारभूतं यत्तत्सुभाषितमुच्यते ॥'.

Verse 14. प्रवरसेनस्य कुमुदोज्ज्वला (कुमुदवत् उज्ज्वला) कीर्तिः सेतुना सागरस्य परं पारं प्रयाता कुमुदोज्ज्वला (कुमुदेन तदाख्येन वानरसेनापतिना) उज्ज्वला कपिसेना सेतुना सागरस्य परं पारमिव प्रयाता. The author here praises the Prakrit poem called सेतुबन्ध or रावणवध. Bāṇa is engaged in this Introduction in celebrating the names of *authors* and their works. Hence it follows that प्रवरसेन was the author of सेतुबन्ध. There is a tradition that the सेतुबन्ध was composed by कालिदास and that प्रवरसेन was only the patron of that great poet. Bāṇa's words at least do not lend any support to this tradition. The Rājatarangiṇī speaks of several kings of Kashmir that bore the name प्रवरसेन. At the command of हर्ष-विक्रमादित्य of उज्जयिनी the kingdom of काश्मीर was offered to a poet मातृगुप्त who is often identified with कालिदास without any reason beyond the fact that both names mean the same thing. When at Harsha's death मातृगुप्त abdicated the throne, प्रवरसेन (II) ascended it and generously treated मातृगुप्त; vide राजतरङ्गिणी III. 125–323. Daṇḍin says that the language of the country of Mahārāshṭra is Prakrit *par excellence* and that the सेतुबन्ध is composed in (महाराष्ट्री) प्राकृत. 'महाराष्ट्राश्रयां भाषां प्रकृष्टं प्राकृतं विदुः । सागरः सूक्तिरत्नानां सेतुबन्धादि यन्मयम् ॥' काव्यादर्श I. 34. If, as tradition says, the author of the सेतुबन्ध was a king, may we hazard a conjecture that he may have been one of the Vākāṭaka kings? In the Chammak and Sivani copperplate grants (C. I. I. III pp. 235, 243) we have two प्रवरसेनs of the Vakāṭaka family. In the army of the monkeys कुमुद was a commander. 'शरभः कुमुदो वह्निर्वानरो रम्भ एव च ॥ एते चान्ये च बहवो वानराः कामरूपिणः ।' रामायण किष्किन्धा 39. 37–38. The monkeys under the supervision of their leader नल, son of विश्वकर्मा, constructed the bridge by means of which they crossed over to लङ्का. See युद्धकाण्ड chapter 22. 74–75 'तानि कोटिसहस्राणि वानराणां महौजसाम् ॥ बध्नन्तः सागरे सेतुं जग्मुः पारं महोदधेः ।'. The Com. construes प्रवरसेनस्य also with कपिसेना 'प्रवे प्लुते रसो येषां ते प्रवरसाः वानरास्तेषामिनः स्वामी, प्रवरा च सेना यस्य स सुग्रीवश्च'. According to this प्रवरसेन is सुग्रीव (प्रव-रस-इन), because he was the master of monkeys who have a liking for leaping or because he had an excellent army. कुमुद is a white lotus and कीर्ति is poetically represented as white.

Verse 15. Bāṇa here eulogises the dramatist Bhāsa. Kālidāsa speaks of him in his मालविकाग्निमित्र as very famous. For a reference to him in the Gauḍavaho see p. XII of the Introduction. The सरस्वतीकण्ठाभरण quotes the verse 'भासश्चल्यपि भासादी कविवर्गे जगत्त्रयीम् । के न यान्ति निबन्धारः कालिदासस्य दासताम् ॥'. The सूक्तिमुक्तावलि quotes a verse of राजशेखर about भास 'भासनाटकचक्रेऽपि छेकैः क्षिप्ते परीक्षितुम् । स्वप्नवासवदत्तस्य दाहकोऽभून्न पावकः ॥' Peterson's Intro. to सुभाषितावलि pp. 80-81. Until very recently it was believed by all that Bhāsa's dramas were lost. Mr. T. Ganapatisastri of Trivandrum has published about thirteen plays the authorship of which he ascribes to Bhāsa on several grounds. We have our own doubts as to whether the plays now put forward are the genuine works of Bhāsa. But obvious considerations prevent us from entering into that question here. The principal sentence is भासः नाटकैः देवकुलैरिव यशो लेभे. सूत्र...रम्भैः—सूत्रधारेण कृतः आरम्भः येषाम्—that had an introduction spoken by the manager of the stage (with नाटकैः); that were constructed by architects (with देवकुलैः). बह्व्यो भूमिकाः येषु; बहवः भूमयः येषु—in which there are numerous characters (with नाटकैः); in which there are several stories. The affix क is optionally added to all बहुव्रीहि compounds. सपताकैः containing पताकाs (with नाटकैः); possessed of banners (with देवकुलैः). पताका is a term in dramaturgy. There are five अर्थप्रकृतिs (the leading sources of the principal object in a drama) *viz.*, बीज, बिन्दु, पताका, प्रकरी and कार्य. पताका is defined by भरत 'यद्वृत्तं हि परार्थं स्यात्प्रधानस्योपकारकम् । प्रधानवच्च कल्प्येत सा पताकेति कीर्तिता ॥' नाट्यशास्त्र. 19. 23. It is an episode which has no purpose in itself, but is put in by the author for serving as a foil to the principal theme; *e. g.* the representation of the career of सुग्रीव when the principal theme is रामचरित. The दशरूप says 'प्रासङ्गिकं परार्थस्य स्वार्थो यस्य प्रसङ्गतः। सानुबन्धं पताकाख्यं प्रकरी च प्रदेशभाक् ॥' I. 13. On this धनिक's comment is 'दूरं यदनुवर्तते प्रासङ्गिकं सा पताका । सुग्रीवादिवृत्तान्तवत् । पताकेवासाधारणनायकचिह्नवत्तदुपकारित्वात् । यदल्पं सा प्रकरी श्रवणादिवृत्तान्तवत्.' The साहित्यदर्पण defines पताका as 'व्यापि प्रासङ्गिकं वृत्तं पताकेत्यभिधीयते.' This is quite different from पताकास्थानक, which is of four kinds. See साहित्यदर्पण VI. for it. It is not to be supposed that Bhāsa alone among the dramatists before Bāṇa wrote plays that were commenced by सूत्रधारs or that contained varied dramatis personae or पताकाs. Bāṇa's only object is to show, by taking three paronomastic clauses, similarity between temples and dramas.

Verse 16. In this verse Bāṇa offers a very glowing tribute of praise to the prince of Sanskrit poets. Translate 'who indeed does not feel delight the moment the fine sayings of Kālidāsa are uttered, sayings which are sweet and agreeable (सान्द्र) like sprays of flowers ?' The idea is that even men of ordinary intelligence are delighted with Kālidāsa's sayings, much more therefore will those possessed of high critical faculty find delight in them. वा does not mean 'or' here. It is to be connected with कस्य (कस्य वा न प्रीतिर्जायते), the meaning being 'I should like to know who is not &c.' Compare for this use of वा 'परिवर्तिनि संसारे मृतः को वा न जायते.' Note also the use of इव in a similar way 'परैस्त्वदन्यः क इवापहारयेन्मनोरमामात्मवधूमिव श्रियम् ॥' किरातार्जुनीय I. 31. निर्गतासु when uttered by anyone (with सूक्तिषु); come out (मञ्जरीषु). The मञ्जरी also is fragrant and thick or glossy (सान्द्र). The reading मधुरसार्द्रासु (wet with sweet juice) is not so good, as it cannot be well construed with सूक्तिषु. This verse indicates, in our humble opinion, that Kālidāsa was an household word in the days of Bāṇa and that therefore the former preceded the latter by a long interval of time.

Verse 17. The principal sentence here is–बृहत्कथा हरलीला इव कस्य विस्मयाय नो (भवेत्)—In whom would the बृहत्कथा not cause marvel, as the sportive action of S'iva does ? The बृहत्कथा here spoken of is a work in a Prakrit dialect called पैशाची ascribed to गुणाढ्य. The original work in पैशाची is not now extant. But it is certain that in the 11th and 12th centuries of the Christian era it was available. We have abridgments of the work in Sanskrit compiled by two Kashmirian Pandits, Kshemendra (11th century) and Somadeva (12th century). सोमदेव tells us in the कथासरित्सागर 'यथामूलं तथैवैतन्न मनागप्यतिक्रमः । ग्रन्थविस्तरसंक्षेपमात्रं भाषा च भिद्यते ॥' I. 1. 10. A third redaction of the ancient बृहत्कथा was issued by a French Scholar M. Lacôte. See J. R. A. S. for 1906 p. 689 for a Tamil work based upon the बृहत्कथा. Why the book was written in पैशाची is explained in the 6th and 7th chapters (तरङ्ग) of the first लम्बक of the कथासरित्सागर. The story resembles that of the sibylline books. गुणाढ्य was originally a minister of शातवाहन king of the Deccan. Being defeated in a wager he went to the विन्ध्य forest, learnt पैशाची, wrote a work in his own blood containing seven lakhs of verses. When the king would not receive a strange work like that, गुणाढ्य read each page and burnt it. Ultimately the king sent for गुणाढ्य when only a lakh of verses remained. For references to गुणाढ्य and his बृहत्कथा see Introduction p. XXII (footnote). According to the कथासरित्सागर, गुणाढ्य had to forego संस्कृत, प्राकृत and देशभाषाs. We hazard the conjecture that पैशाची was the name given to Pâli or some dialect similar to it by गुणाढ्य to prove true to his word or by others before him in derision as the language of the Buddhistic heretics (who would be no better than पिशाचs to orthodox Indians). The बृहत्कथा excites wonder on account of the marvellous stories it contains. समुद्दीपितः कन्दर्पः यया by which passion is excited (with बृहत्कथा). The बृहत्कथा, to judge from its abridgments, contained numerous stories of love and intrigue. The Com. explains in another way also 'समुद्दीपितः प्रकाशितः ख्यातिं नीतः कन्दर्पो नरवाहनदत्तो यस्यामिति । स हि कामांश इति आगमः'. नरवाहनदत्त was the son of वत्सराज and वासवदत्ता and was crowned king of the विद्याधरs. 'गगनादुच्चचारैव काले तस्मिन्सरस्वती ॥ कामदेवावतारोऽयं राजञ्जातस्तवात्मजः । नरवाहनदत्तं च जानीह्येनमिहाख्यया ॥' कथासरित्सागर 4th लम्बक 3rd तरङ्ग verses 72-73. समुद्दीपितः कन्दर्पः यस्याम् or यया (with हरलीला) by which Cupid was burnt up. Or we may separate समुत् and दीपितकन्दर्पा. समुद् (मुदा सह) = सहर्षा full of joy. मदन wanted to help the gods against the demon तारक who was destined to be killed by the son of शिव. In order to induce शिव to marry पार्वती Cupid was about to shoot his flowery arrow, when S'iva, coming to know his intention, burnt him to ashes in wrath with the fire from his third eye. कृतं गौर्याः प्रसाधनं (*lit.* accomplishment *i. e.* propitiating) यस्याम्. The Com. explains in two ways. गौरी was a goddess presiding over some विद्या which was propitiated by नरवाहनदत्त. The other is a strained explanation 'गौरीं प्राति पूरयति गौरीप्रः । साधनं परिकरबन्धो यथाप्रस्तावो यस्याम् । गौरीप्रेरितेन हि हरेण तथा तस्यां परिकरबन्धः कृतो यथा साऽतीव पिप्रिये'. The story narrated in the बृहत्कथा was first given to पार्वती by शिव. *Vide* बृहत्कथामञ्जरी I. 1. There is no necessity to divide the words in an unusual way (as गौरीप्र and साधन). The simple meaning is:—शिव propitiated गौरी by telling her the original story of the बृहत्कथा. प्रसाधन also means 'decoration' (with हरलीला).

Verse 18. This is a very hard verse. Various interpretations have been proposed. The Com. takes आढ्यराज to be some poet and explains उत्साह as 'beating time in dancing' and then quotes the explanations of others. 'उत्साहो नृत्ते तालवि-

श्लेषः । उदीर्यमाणगीत्याधारभूतपदोपचारात्काव्यमप्युत्साह इति केचित् । यत्र पूर्वं श्लोकेनार्थ उपक्षिप्यते पश्चात्स एव गद्येन वितन्यते मध्ये वृत्तनिबन्धश्च भवति स परिसमाप्तार्थ उत्साह उच्यते इत्यन्ये'. In construing this verse we have to remember two things. Firstly, in the preceding verses Bâṇa eulogises eminent poets and their works; so it is not unnatural to expect that आढ्यराज is the name of a poet. Secondly, in the following verse the author in a strain of humility says that he is taking a bold step in writing an Âkhyâyikâ about his patron Harsha. He intimates that he has no intention to rival the works of the great poets of old, but that his sole motive is to give expression to his admiration for his patron The plain meaning is 'my tongue, as if drawn inwards by the Utsâhas composed by Âḍhyarâja, does not set about to write a poem'. The idea is that the Utsâhas of आढ्यराज are such works of genius that I (बाण) cannot embark on making an effort in the same direction for fear of being ridiculed when my puny gifts are compared by people with the giant intellect of आढ्यराज. The idea conveyed by हृदयस्थैः स्मृतैरपि is this—Bâṇa had studied the उत्साहs of आढ्यराज and so they were हृदयस्थ. As they were हृदयस्थ (and so inside the body) they may be fancied as able to draw his tongue in. But the works of आढ्यराज were not bodily present in Bâṇa's heart. They were only remembered. In order to draw anything, the presence of the person drawing is necessary. But in the case of the उत्साहs their very memory (the mere memory of their worth and greatness) is sufficient to draw his tongue in (*i. e.* to prevent Bāṇa from writing any poetic work). This is the force of the word अपि in स्मृतैरपि.

Who आढ्यराज was and what were the उत्साहs he composed it is difficult to say. The alternative explanations given by the com. convey some idea of what they may have been. According to the commentator रत्नेश्वर on the सरस्वतीकण्ठाभरण, आढ्यराज is another name of शालिवाहन who encouraged the study of Prakrit (*vide* Intro. p. X footnote). Against accepting this interpretation the only objection is that Bâṇa has already praised सातवाहन (who is the same as शालिवाहन) in verse 13. Peterson thinks that it is a mistake to take आढ्यराज as a proper noun (Intro. to Kâdambarî p. 96). He regards आढ्यराज as almost the same as आद्यराज. He takes उत्साह to mean 'brave deeds'. Some MSS. read आद्यराज but that seems to be an emendation due to the difficulty of explaining आढ्यराज. One edition reads 'कृतोच्छ्वासैः' which also seems to be an unauthorised emendation. Pischel held that आढ्यराज was Harsha himself (J. R. A. S. for 1903 p. 830). But it is not clear why Harsha should be called आढ्यराज. Some take the verse in a sarcastic sense. If आढ्यराज is शालिवाहन (or सातवाहन), we know how he discouraged (the opposite of उत्साह) गुणाढ्य when the latter brought his strange work of seven lakhs of verses. But several objections can be urged against this way of explaining the verses. There is no reason why Bâṇa should indulge in sarcasm against a famous king that died several centuries before him. Besides this sense does not fall in well with the next verse. Mr. F. W. Thomas is troubled by the word अपि in स्मृतैरपि and thinks that the reference may be to some psychological doctrine according to which memory does not reside in the heart (J. R. A. S. 1903 p. 830).

Verse 19. तथापि although I am afraid of the ridicule that may be poured upon me in striving to reach the position of a poet of the eminence of आढ्यराज. नृपते... चापलम् through my devotion to my king (Harsha), I, being undismayed and eager to carry out (my undertaking), make bold to plunge with my tongue in the ocean of Ákhyâyikâ. He means that he is going to write an आख्यायिका about हर्ष and sing his praises with his tongue. That is a rash undertaking (चापलं) for one like him. Separate भक्त्या अभीतः. अभीतः may also mean 'being surrounded *i. e.* protected all round' (अभि + इतः). प्लवनं Swimming. प्लवनं एव चापलम्. It is a rash act to plunge in the deep ocean. निर्वहणे आकुलः would also mean 'anxious to go across to the other side' (with one who plunges into the ocean).

Verse 20. Here आख्यायिका is compared to a bed (शय्या). सुख...लिता (सुखेन प्रबोधः ज्ञानं तेन ललिता) charming on account of conveying knowledge with ease or charming on account of its being easy to understand. The Vedas and S'āstras contain injunctions laying down how one should act. Poetry like a bitter pill coated with sugar inculcates good conduct and abstinence from sin in a sweet persuasive manner. Compare 'स्वादुकाव्यरसोन्मिश्रं शास्त्रार्थमपि भुञ्जते। प्रथमालीढमधवः पिबन्ति कटु भेषजम् ॥'; compare also 'कटुकौषधवच्छास्त्रमविद्याव्याधिनाशनम् । आह्लाद्यमृतवत्काव्यमविवेकगदापहम् ॥' काव्यालङ्कारकामधेनु. सुख...ललिता that is agreeable because one rises from it in a happy mood (with शय्या). सुखः प्रबोधः (waking up from sleep) तेन ललिता. शोभनानां वर्णानां घटना (arrangement) तेन उज्ज्वलैः (शब्दैः). See above p. 10 as to the employment of particular letters for a particular purpose. सुवर्ण...ज्ज्वलैः brilliant on account of being overlaid with gold or on account of the combination of agreeable colours (with प्रतिपादकैः). प्रतिपादकैः that convey sense (with शब्दैः); with the feet (of the bed). शय्या is used in another sense also. It means 'such a collocation of words in a poem that no word can be substituted by another without marring the beauty of the poem. 'या पदानां परान्योन्यमैत्री शय्येति कथ्यते ।' प्रतापरुद्र (वृत्ति—पदविनिमयासहिष्णुत्वाद्बन्धस्य पदानुगुण्यरूपा शय्या). बाण employs the word in this sense in the कादम्बरी 'स्फुरत्कलालापविलासकोमला करोति रागं हृदि कौतुकाधिकम् । रसेन **शय्यां** स्वयमभ्युपागता कथा जनस्याभिनवा वधूरिव ॥' (Intro. 8th verse). The words सुख०, सुवर्ण० and प्रति० mean the same thing with शय्या in this sense as with आख्यायिका. The अग्निपुराण says that शय्या is the same as मुद्रा 'अभिप्रायविशेषेण कविशक्ति विवृण्वती । मुत्प्रदायिनीति सा मुद्रा सैव शय्यापि नो मते ॥' 342.26.

Verse 21. ज्वलन् प्रतापज्वलनः एव प्राकारः तेन कृता जगतः रक्षा येन who protects the world by the rampart-wall (प्राकारः) of the fire of his glorious valour. सकलानां प्रणयिनां मनोरथाः तेषां सिद्धौ श्रीपर्वतः Who is a श्रीपर्वत in fulfilling the desires of all suppliants. प्रणयिन् a friend, or one who comes with a request. श्रीपर्वत is a mountain in Telingana sacred to शिव. 'श्रीपर्वते महादेवो देव्या सह महाद्युतिः । न्यवसत्परमप्रीतो ब्रह्मा च त्रिदशैः सह ॥' वनपर्व 85. 19-20. The story runs that लक्ष्मी practised penance there and secured the boon of always reclining on the chest of Vishṇu. Compare 'श्रीपर्वताश्चर्यवार्तासहस्राभिज्ञेन जरद्द्रविडधार्मिकेण (p. 227 of कादम्बरी Peterson's ed.).

P. 2 ll. 20—28 **एव... प्रादुरभवन्.** अनुश्रूयते *lit.* it is heard *i. e.* it is handed down by tradition. किल indicates 'as the story goes.' '**वार्ता**सम्भाव्ययोः **किल**' इत्यमरः. स्व...तिष्ठन् presiding over (or dwelling in) his world (*i. e.* ब्रह्मलोक or सत्यलोक). परमेष्ठी = ब्रह्मा (परमे पदे तिष्ठतीति). It is the subject of आसाञ्चक्रे. विका... विष्टः occupying his lotus seat that was fully expanded. इन् (in विकासिन्) is affixed in the sense of नित्ययोग (the lotus on which ब्रह्मा reclines is always expanded). 'भूमनिन्दाप्रशंसासु **नित्ययोगे**ऽतिशायने । सम्बन्धेस्तिविवक्षायां च भवन्ति मतुबादयः ॥'. पद्मं एव विष्टरः (विस्तीर्यते इति). '**विष्टरो** विटपी दर्भमुष्टिः **पीठाद्यमासनम्**' इत्यमरः. ब्रह्मा is called कमलासन. सुनासीरः (इन्द्रः) प्रमुखः येषाम्. The word is also written as शुनासीर; क्षीरस्वामी derives as 'शोभना नासीरा अग्रेसरा अस्य शुनासीरयोरपत्यमित्येके'. गीर्वाणैः = देवैः. गीः (वाक्) एव वाणः (बवयोरभेदात्) बाणः येषाम्. सं. also explains as 'गिरः स्तुतिरूपा वणन्ति भजन्तीति'. ब्रह्मो...कुर्वन् engaged in philosophical discussion about ब्रह्म. ब्रह्मोद्यं = ब्रह्मणः वदनं उक्तिः. ब्रह्मोद्य is generally used as a noun in the neuter, but here it is an adjective of कथाः. ब्रह्म means either Veda or the supreme all-pervading apirit which is the subject–matter of the Upanishads. 'वदः सुपि क्यप् च' पा. 3.1.106 (वदेर्भावे क्यप् स्यात् चात् यत् अनुपसर्गे सुपि उपपदे । ब्रह्मोद्यम् । ब्रह्मवद्यम् । सि. कौ.). सं० explains 'ब्रह्मोद्या सा कथा यस्यामुच्यते ब्रह्म शाश्वतम्.' See मनुस्मृति 3.231 'यद्यद्रोचेत विप्रेभ्यस्तत्तद्दद्यादमत्सरः । ब्रह्मोद्याश्च कथाः कुर्यात्पितॄणामेतदीप्सितम् ॥'. मेधातिथि on मनु० explains 'ब्रह्मोद्या ब्रह्मणि वेदे या उद्यन्ते कथ्यन्ते ता ब्रह्मोद्याः देवासुरयुद्धं वृत्रवधः सरमादूत्यमित्याद्याः । अथवा कः स्विदेकाकी चरतीत्यादि'. अन्याश्च...भावयन् engaged in (*lit.* causing to be, putting forward) other blameless (निरवद्य) discussions on various lores. विद्याs were either four or fourteen. The four are आन्वीक्षिकी (metaphysics), त्रयी (the three Vedas), वार्ता (agriculture and trade), दण्डनीति (science of Government). See चाणक्य's अर्थशास्त्र p. 6. 'पुराणन्यायमीमांसाधर्मशास्त्राङ्गमिश्रिताः । वेदाः स्थानानि विद्यानां धर्मस्य च चतुर्दश ॥' याज्ञ० I. 3 (*i. e.* four Vedas, six वेदाङ्गs, पुराण, न्याय, मीमांसा and धर्मशास्त्र). These are the fourteen Vidyâs. गोष्ठी an assembly or discourse. In ancient times गोष्ठी was somewhat like a modern club. 'समानविद्यावित्तशीलबुद्धिवयसामनुरूपैरालापैरेकत्रासनबन्धो गोष्ठी' सं. If we read निरवद्याविद्या as one word, then we shall have to separate as निरवद्य अविद्या०, which does not yield a good sense. If we read निरवद्यविद्या० the meaning will be the same or we may interpret as 'discussion about the knowledge of the Blameless One' (*i. e.* ब्रह्म). निरवद्य is an epithet of ब्रह्म. Compare 'निष्कलं निष्क्रियं शान्तं निरवद्यं निरञ्जनम्' श्वेताश्वतरोपनिषद् 6.19. Note the words 'निरवद्यविद्याविद्योतितानि' in the last para. of the first उच्छ्वास (p. 19 text). Separate तथा आसीनं (sitting). त्रिभुवनेन प्रतीक्ष्यं पूज्यम् (from ईक्ष् with प्रति). प्रजापतयः—In the मनुस्मृति the ten प्रजापतिs enumerated do not include मनु, दक्ष and चाक्षुष. 'पतीन्प्रजानामसृजं महर्षीनादितो दश ॥ मरीचिमत्र्यङ्गिरसौ पुलस्त्यं पुलहं क्रतुम् । प्रचेतसं वसिष्ठं च भृगुं नारदमेव च ॥' मनु० I. 34-35. In the मनुस्मृति (I. 36) we are told that these ten प्रजापतिs created seven Manus of whom चाक्षुष is the sixth (मनु० I. 62). The रामायण gives a slightly different list (अरण्यकाण्ड 14.7-9). दक्ष is a well-known प्रजापति. He was born from the right अङ्गुष्ठ of ब्रह्मा (*vide* आदिपर्व 66.10). Probably the author uses the word प्रजापति not in a technical sense, but in a general sense 'progenitors.' सप्तर्षयः पुरःसराः (मुख्याः) येषाम्. The seven sages are मरीचि, अत्रि, अङ्गिरस्, पुलस्त्य, पुलह, क्रतु, वसिष्ठ. के...चारयन् some uttered with proper accents hymns from the Rigveda that are appropriate for praising (God). The Rigveda mostly consists of verses praising various deities, describing their wondrous works and soliciting the gods for various boons. केचि... पठन् some recited the Yajus formula containing worship. 'क्षयार्चयोरपचितिः' इत्यमरः. अपचितिं पूजां भजन्ते इति. प्रशंसासामानि Sāman hymns containing praise. साम verses are to be sung. Almost the whole of the सामवेद is taken from the Rigveda. A Yajus is in prose, while a ऋक् is in a metrical form. Bāṇa uses appropriate verbs and descriptive words with reference to the ऋग्वेद, the यजुर्वेद and the सामवेद. विवृतं क्रतुक्रियातन्त्रं यैः that explained (*lit.* laid bare) the doctrines (or dogmas) of the performance of sacrifice. 'तन्त्रं प्रधाने सिद्धान्ते' इत्यमरः. व्याचचक्षिरे expounded (3rd plu. Perfect of चक्ष् with वि and आ). विद्यानां विसंवादः (difference) तेन कृताः due to the difference of the lores they had studied. It is better to read with B 'अन्योन्यस्य विवादाः.' प्रादुरभवन्—(naturally or spontaneously) arose. What the author means is:—The sages had each of them made a profound study of some particular विद्या and so disputes arose among them not out of envy or pride, but because each was specially devoted to a particular विद्या and so gave expression to his views without meaning any offence to other personages present.

P. 2 l. 29–p. 3 l. 15 अथाति...जहास. अति...प्रकृत्या by nature extremely irritable. अत्रेस्तनयः–अत्रि's wife was अनसूया a daughter of दक्ष. अत्रि had three sons सोम, दुर्वासस् and दत्तात्रेय. See विष्णुपुराण I. 10. तारापतेः (चन्द्रमसः) भ्राता. The moon is said to have sprung from the lustre of Atri's eye. See हरिवंश 25 'नेत्राभ्यां वारि सुस्राव दशधा द्योतयद्दिशः। तं गर्भं विधिना हृष्टा दश देव्यो दधुस्तदा॥ समेत्य धारयामासुर्न च ताः समशक्नुवन्॥ स ताभ्यः सहसैवाथ दिग्भ्यो गर्भः प्रभान्वितः। पपात भासयँल्लोकाञ्शीतांशुः सर्वभावनः॥' verses 6–8. Note 'अत्रिनेत्रनिर्गतस्य... दृष्ट इव जनेन जन्मदिवसः कुमुदबन्धोः' हर्षचरित 7th उच्छ्वास. मन्दपालः नाम यस्य सः मन्दपालनामा तेन. कलहं करोति इति कलहायते according to 'शब्दवैरकलहाभ्रकण्वमेघेभ्यः करणे' पा. 3.1.17 (एभ्यः कर्मभ्यः करोत्यर्थे क्यङ् स्यात्। सि. कौ.). विस्वरमकरोत् he struck a discordant note. विस्वरम् may be taken as an adjective of साम or as an adverb. सर्वेषु goes with मुनिषु. शापभयात् प्रतिपन्नं मौनं यैः that took to silence through fear of a curse. दुर्वासस् was well-known for cursing persons at the slightest offence. अन्या...सम्भवे while Brahmâ paid no heed (to the lapse of दुर्वासस्) being engaged in conversing with some one else. ब्रह्मा is supposed to have sprung from the lotus in the navel of Vishṇu. Compare first para of the 4th उच्छ्वास 'द्विजवरस्वेच्छागृहीतकोषो नाभिपद्म इव पुण्डरीकेक्षणात्.' भगवती कुमारी—connect these with देवी सरस्वती below. The principal sentence is भगवती कुमारी देवी सरस्वती श्रुत्वा जहास. किञ्चित् उन्मुक्तः बालभावः यस्मिन् or येन (*adj.* of वयसि) which had just cast aside childhood *i. e.* which had just passed the stage of being a mere girl. भूषितं नवयौवनं येन—The idea is:—she was so charming at that age that youth itself had its charms heightened by claiming her as one of its owners. गृहीतचामरा प्रचलन्ती भुजलता यस्याः whose creeperlike hand held a chowrie and was waving. पितामहं = ब्रह्माणम्. उपवीजयन्ती fanning. निर्भर्त्सनार्थं ताडनं तेन जातः रागः (रक्तवर्णः) ययोः. निर्भर्त्सन... समाना brilliant with her spray-like feet naturally red, that as if seemed to have grown red by stamping (on the ground) for censuring (दुर्वासस्). Her feet were naturally red; the poet fancies that they grew red because she stamped with her feet on the ground by way of finding fault with दुर्वासस् who had committed a mistake in singing a साम verse. शिष्य... चरणा whose feet were musical with two anklets that jingled in accordance with the movements (क्रमः) of her steps, as if they (नूपुरयुगल) were two pupils. वाचालितौ चरणौ यस्याः. As she moved about, the anklets on the feet jingled. The words पद० and वाचा० yield another sense with शिष्यद्वय. The पदपाठ of the Rigveda is ascribed to शाकल्य in the निरुक्त. क्रम, जटा and घन are certain arrangements of the verses of the Rigveda intended to preserve the purity of the text. The क्रमपाठ is ascribed to पाञ्चाल बाभ्रव्य. See शान्तिपर्व 343.103. The अनुशासनपर्व (85.90) mentions both पद and क्रम. The क्रमपाठ of the verse 'इदं विष्णुर्विचक्रमे त्रेधा निदधे पदम्' would be 'इदं विष्णुः । विष्णुर्वि । वि चक्रमे । चक्रमे त्रेधा । त्रेधा नि । नि दधे । दधे पदम् । पदमिति पदम् ।'. शिष्यs would be noisy (मुखर) by repeating the पदपाठ and the क्रमपाठ. The words चरण and शाखा are sometimes used as synonyms; चरण means 'शाखाध्येतृ' *i. e.* 'those who study a particular शाखा of the Veda, an ideal succession of teachers and pupils.' This latter sense is required here (with शिष्य०). मदन... द्वितयम् who (सरस्वती) had legs appearing like the pillars of the arched portal of the city of love. मदननगरस्य तोरणं तस्य स्तम्भयोः इव विभ्रमः यस्य (*adj.* of °द्वितयम्). Her legs were straight and delicately proportioned. Therefore they as if supported (*i. e.* excited) love, as pillars support the portal of a city. This is not a very elegant way of describing सरस्वती. The reading धर्मनगर० would make सरस्वती the support of धर्म. This is somewhat better. सलीलं is to be connected with विन्यस्त०. उत्काः कलहंसाः तेषां कुलं तस्य कलः आलापः तद्वत् प्रलपति इति °प्रलापिनि. सलील...किसलया who had sportively placed her sprout-like left hand on the string of her girdle that jingled like the sweet murmur of the swarms of love-sick कलहंसs. उत्कः = उत्कण्ठितः. 'उत्क उन्मनाः' पा. 5.2.80. Small bells were attached to girdles. विन्यस्तं वामहस्त एव किसलयं यया. विद्व... काया whose body was rendered pure by the Brahmanical thread hanging down from her shoulder, as if it (ब्रह्मसूत्र) were a coil of virtues that stuck to her on account of dwelling in the heart of the wise. ब्रह्मसूत्रं = यज्ञोपवीतम् (ब्रह्मणि वेदग्रहणकाले धृतं सूत्रम्). सरस्वती dwells in the mind of the wise; गुणs (virtues) also occupy the heart of the wise. The मानस lake was created by ब्रह्मा whose daughter was सरस्वती; so she may be said to be dwelling on the मानस lake. ब्रह्मसूत्र is a coil of गुणs (threads). 'कैलासशिखरे राम मनसा निर्मितं सरः । ब्रह्मणा प्रागिदं यस्मात्तदभून्मानसं सरः ॥' रामायण. Compare the description of महाश्वेता 'मण्डलीकृतेन ब्रह्मसूत्रेण पवित्रीकृतकायाम्' कादम्बरी p. 130 of P. भास्वान् मध्यनायकः (मध्यरत्नं) यस्य—the central gem of which is brilliant. अने... यातं inlaid with many pearls (अनेकमुक्ताभिः अनुयातम्). अपवर्गमार्गम् = मोक्षमार्गम्. हार is fancied to be मोक्षमार्ग because the two epithets भास्व० and अनेक० apply to both. भास्वतः सूर्यस्य मध्यं नयतीति ०नायकः—the path of final beatitude leads through the sun. The Upanishads speak of two paths, देवयान and पितृयाण. Those who follow the doctrine of works, reach by various stages the moon and after enjoying the fruits of their good works there, they have to be born again. Those who follow the path of knowledge were supposed to reach by various stages the sun and thence to attain to मोक्ष. When there is मोक्ष, the cycle of births and deaths ceases. 'ते य एवमेतद्विदुर्ये चामी अरण्ये श्रद्धां सत्यमुपासते तेऽर्चिरभिसम्भवन्ति, अर्चिषोऽहः, अह्न आपूर्यमाणपक्षमापूर्यमाणपक्षाद्यान्षण्मासानुदङ्ङादित्य एति मासेभ्यो देवलोकं देवलोकादादित्यमादित्याद्वैद्युतं तान्वैद्युतान्पुरुषोऽमानव एत्य ब्रह्मलोकान् गमयति तेषु ब्रह्मलोकेषु पराः परावतो वसन्ति तेषां न पुनरावृत्तिः' बृहदारण्यकोपनिषद् XI. 2. 14. In the गीता, they are called शुक्लगति and कृष्णगति. 'शुक्लकृष्णे गती ह्येते जगतः शाश्वते मते । एकया यात्यनावृत्तिमन्ययावर्तते पुनः ॥' VIII. 26. The com. quotes the verse 'परिव्राड् योगयुक्तश्च शूरश्चाभिमुखं हतः । द्वाविमौ पुरुषौ लोके सूर्यमण्डलभेदिनौ ॥' which is महा० उद्योगपर्व

33. 61 with slight variations. वदन...राजमाना resplendent with her quivering lip that was red as if with the Alaktaka dye from the feet of all the Vidyās that had entered her mouth. Alaktaka dye was applied to the feet by young ladies. Her lip was naturally red. The poet fancies that the redness was due to the fact that Vidyâs (ladies) in entering her mouth left some lac sticking to her lip. A very learned person is often spoken of as one on the tip of whose tongue dance Vidyâs. Compare 'अमुष्य विद्या रसनाग्रनर्तकी.' सरस्वती, as presiding over all Vidyâs, would naturally have them at the tip of her tongue. 'ओष्ठाधरौ तु रदनच्छदौ दशनवाससी' इत्यमरः. सं... प्रतिमाम् (her cheek) on which was reflected (संक्रान्त) an image of the black antelope skin of Brahmâ. साम... हरिणामिव as if the deer in the moon had got down on it for listening to her singing sweet with Sâman (hymns). सामभिः or साम्नां मधुरं गीतं तस्य आकर्णनाय अवतीर्णः शशिहरणः यस्याम् (*adj.* of कपोलस्थलीम्). Deer are very found of music. The spots on the moon were supposed to be either a deer or hare. Compare the verse 'अङ्कं केऽपि शशङ्किरे जलनिधेः पङ्कं परे मेनिरे सारङ्गं कतिचिच्च सञ्जगदिरे भूच्छायमैच्छन्परे ॥ इन्दौ यद्दलितेन्द्रनीलशकलश्यामं दरीदृश्यते तत्सान्द्रं निशि पीतमन्धतमसं कुक्षिस्थमाचक्ष्महे ॥.' The reflection of the deerskin of Brahmâ on her bright cheek is fancied as being the deer in the moon. The bright cheek was like the moon. As the goddess was in heaven, it is appropriate that the deer in the moon is spoken of (and not an ordinary one). ति... लता One of whose creeper—like eyebrows was raised in a curve (तिर्यक्) and with contempt (सावज्ञम्). अवज्ञया सह यथा स्यात्तथा. She felt contempt for दुर्वासस् when the latter committed a mistake through wrath. श्रोत्र... प्रवाहेण as if washing one ear that was soiled by hearing the discordant note (of दुर्वासस्) with a stream of tears issuing out of the corner (अपाङ्गः) of her eye. The poet fancies that, her ear being soiled, she wanted to wash it clean with water. The curved eyebrow looked like a stream of water issuing from the corner of the eye and proceeding towards its neighbour the ear to free it of its taint. It is not to be supposed that she had tears in her eyes. इतर... मदा who, with the other ear that had on it a white full-blown सिन्धुवार bunch and that looked as if it were smiling, manifested her pride of knowledge. Smiles are poetically represented as white. The सिन्धुवार flower on her ear is fancied as the smile of सरस्वती. We smile at the fall

of others. सरस्वती under the garb of the white flower smiled at the lapse of दुर्वासस्. श्रुति...स्यमाना who was attended upon by swarms of bees in the flowers of her ear-ornament that (bees) besought her ear, as if they (bees) were Oṃkâras. The bees hovering round the flowers on her ear seemed to be making requests (प्रणय) to her ear. प्रणव (*i. e.* the syllable Om) also is श्रुतिप्रणयि (*i. e.* the friend or constant attendant of Veda). The mystic syllable ओम् precedes the study of the Veda or a Vedic text. Compare 'ओङ्कारः स्वर्गद्वारं तस्माद् ब्रह्म अध्येष्यमाणः एतदादि प्रतिपद्येत' आपस्तम्बधर्मसूत्र I. 13.6; 'आसीत्महीक्षितामाद्यः प्रणवश्छन्दसामिव' रघु. I. 11. श्रुतिं वेदं प्रणयन्ति that lead forth *i. e.* introduce Veda. सूक्ष्म...शरीरा whose figure was covered with a spotless silken robe of fine texture (सूक्ष्म) as if with a flash of intellect. प्रतानः shoot or tendril. सूक्ष्म subtle (with प्रज्ञा). विमल pure (and not wicked or sinful), with प्रज्ञा. Her fine robe was like the subtle flashes of intellect. वाङ्मयं...किरन्ती spreading in all directions the pure moon-light of her teeth, as if it were literature. ज्योत्स्नायाः आलोकः तम्. The bright teeth of सरस्वती gleamed forth when she laughed at दुर्वासस्. The teeth, as they belonged to सरस्वती, were really वाङ्मय (वाचः सरस्वत्याः विकारः). वाङ्मयं also means 'literature.' Pure literature spreads enlightenment in the world.

P. 3 ll. 16-25 **दृष्ट्वा...जग्राह.** The principal sentence is दृष्ट्वा च तां तथा हसन्तीं स मुनिः...वारिणा समुपस्पृश्य शापजलं जग्राह. दुर्गृहीतः विद्यालवः तेन अवलेपः तेन दुर्विदग्धे (vocative) that are puffed up with vanity at the (acquisition of) particle of ill-understood knowledge. शिरः...शरारोः (*adj.* of ०कलापस्य) that fell dishevelled as the knot was unloosened when he shook his head. शिरःकम्पेन शीर्यमाणः बन्धः तेन विशरारुः (from शॄ with वि) तस्य. 'शॄवन्द्योरारुः' पा. 3.2.173 (शरारुः, वन्दारुः). उन्मिषन् पिङ्गलिमा यस्य the yellow colour of which flashed forth. पिङ्गलिमन् *m.* from पिङ्गल with affix इमन्. 'पृथ्वादिभ्य इमनिज्वा' पा. 5.1.122. रोचिषा = तेजसा कान्त्या वा. सिञ्च...दिशः as if sprinkling the ten quarters with the fluid of the fire of his wrath. The reddish—yellow gleam of his matted hair is fancied to be a fluid spreading over the world. Fire has a reddish flame. The reddish जटा is like a flame of fire (here identified with wrath). कृत...बध्नन्—This clause contains a complicated pun. The plain sense is that Durvāsas knit his eyebrow into a terrific curve whereby his broad forehead was contracted into wrinkles. These wrinkles looked like the lines on a chessboard (अष्टापदम्). अन्धकारितं ललाटपट्टमेव अष्टापदं यया (*adj.* of भ्रुकुटिम्). This is one of the earliest allusions to the game of chess, which was invented in India. 'अष्टापदं शारिफलम्' इत्यमरः (अष्टौ पदान्यस्य). It is a board divided into eight rows, each row having eight squares. It is a question with some whether अष्टापद is a chess board or only a draught board (Marathi सोंगट्यांचा पट). We incline to the former view. Bâṇa at all events associates it with the game of chess. Compare 'अष्टापदानां चतुरङ्गकल्पना' हर्षचरित 2nd उच्छ्वास. चतुरङ्ग refers to the four arms of the ancient Indian army *viz.* infantry, cavalry, elephant riders and chariots. Pâṇini was aware of the word अष्टापद being used in a technical sense 'अष्टनः संज्ञायाम्' पा. 6.3.125 (उत्तरपदे दीर्घः। अष्टापदम्। सि. कौ.). Moreover Pâṇini refers to a particular position of S'āras (chessmen) in 'अनुपद-सर्वान्न-अयानयं बद्धा-भक्षयति-नेयेषु' पा. 5.2.9 (अयानयः स्थलविशेषः तं नेयः आयानयीनः शारः। सि. कौ.). पतञ्जलि comments on this सूत्र and explains the technical meaning of अय and अनय (see Kielhorn's महाभाष्य vol. II. p. 373). In कादम्बरी we have 'अष्टापदपरिचयचतुराभिः' (p. 196 of P.). कृत...धानाम् has three senses· (1) कृतं कालस्य कृष्णवर्णस्य सन्निधानं यया that had blackness near it (with भ्रुकुटि, which was dark); (2) कृतं कालस्य कृष्णवर्णशारस्य सन्निधानं येन (with अष्टापद)—That had black chessmen on it. Chessmen were grouped into black and white or red to mark the opposing sides. कृतं कालस्य यमस्य सन्निधानं यया (with अन्तःपुर... मकरिका) that was near यम or that took persons in the presence of यम. दुर्वासस् by his curses made people perish and so brought them before यम. So his भ्रुकुटि is properly spoken of as driving people into the presence of यम. अन्तः...मकरिकाम् that (frowning eyebrow) was the crocodile ornament painted on the (faces of the) wives (of यम). पत्रभङ्ग–drawings of ornamental figures on the face, bosom etc. The knit brow resembled the figure of a crocodile drawn on the cheeks of Yama's wives. A crocodile is an emblem of death and so is an appropriate decoration for Yama's wives. अति... प्रयच्छन् with his extremely red eye offering as it were the oblation (उपहारः) of his own blood to the goddess of wrath (अमर्षः). His eyes were suffused red with wrath and seemed to drop down blood. So the poet fancies that he was going to offer an oblation of blood to अमर्षदेवता. निर्दयं दष्टः दशनच्छदः तस्मात् भयं तेन पलायमानाम्. निर्दय...च्छलेन under the guise of the rays of his teeth, confining his speech that was as if fleeing through fear at the merciless biting of his lip. The idea is:-दुर्वासस् being enraged bit his lips and when he did so his bright teeth gleamed forth. The poet fancies that his speech was afraid of being mercilessly dealt with as his lip was and so wanted to run away, but was confined inside by the rays of his gleaming teeth. अंसा...जिनस्य tying in another way the knot of his deerskin that slipped from his shoulder, as if it were an edict (giving him authority) for cursing. As the skin slipped from his shoulder he tied it in another way so as not to allow it to drop down. The deerskin had a brownish surface with dark spots. A शासनपट्ट is a grant (generally on copperplate or silk cloth) of land or it is a proclamation announcing the orders of a king. The brown deerskin resembled a copperplate or silken charter and the dark spots resembled the letters. In the case of दुर्वासस् it is fancied to be a charter giving him the authority to curse others. स्वेद...यव: held in all limbs by gods, demons and sages that were reflected in the drops of perspiration (on his body) and that had as if come in refuge to him out of fear of the curse (that he might pronounce). प्रतिपन्नाः सर्वे अवयवाः यस्य. दुर्वासस् perspired on account of his intense rage and the assembly of gods was reflected in the bright drops. The poet fancies that they out of fear of a curse came beseeching him to be merciful. कोपात् कम्पः तेन तरलिताः (tremulous) अङ्गुलयः यस्य (*adj.* of करेण). करेण... क्षिप्य tossing aside his rosary (अक्षमाला) as if it were a string of letters that stuck (to his hand) for propitiating (प्रसादनं) him. He had his rosary in his hand, but, when he began to shake with wrath, he threw it away. The poet fancies that it was not the अक्षमाला that was thrown away, but the letters of the alphabet. The letters of the alphabet are here represented as the partisans of सरस्वती and as interceding with दुर्वासस् for सरस्वती (who presides over all learning and therefore also over letters). The sage as if intimated that he would listen to no intercession. अक्षरमाला suggests अक्षमाला for two reasons. Letters constitute a string as beads do. Besides अक्ष may be used as an abbreviated way of indicating all the letters from अ to क्ष. कामण्डलव (from कमण्डलु with the affix अण्) contained in his water pot. समुपस्पृश्य having sipped water and ejected it. A curse was generally pronounced with the pouring of water.

P. 3 l. 26—**P. 4**. l. 10 **अत्रान्तरे...समुत्तस्थौ**. The principal sentence is अत्रान्तरे स्वयम्भुवोऽभ्याशे समुपविष्टा देवी सावित्री चतुर्भिर्वेदैः सह समुत्तस्थौ. स्वयम्भुवः ब्रह्मणः अभ्याशे समीपे. मूर्तिमती in a corporeal form. पीयूष...वसाना wearing a fine bark robe of the tree of paradise that (robe) was as white as the mass of the foam of nectar. This and the following clauses in the nominative qualify सावित्री. बिस...ग्रन्थिः that had tied between her high breasts a knot with an upper garment (a shawl) made of lotus filaments. उन्नतस्तनयोर्मध्ये बद्धा गात्रिक ग्रन्थिः यया. सं० remarks 'गात्रिकाग्रन्थिर्ग्रन्थिविशेषः स्वस्तिकाकारः स्त्रीणामुत्तरीयस्य स्तनोद्देशे भवति.' She had tied the knot of her shawl in the form of a स्वस्तिक on her bosom. तपोबलेन निर्जितं त्रिभुवनं तस्य जयः तस्य पताकाभिः. भस्म...राजिभिः with lines of the marks of ashes. पुण्ड्रकः a mark on the forehead made with sandal &c., showing the particular sect to which the votary belongs. विराजितं ललाटाजिरं (ललाटं अजिरमिव) यस्याः Her forehead being broad is compared to a court-yard. The three lines of ashes on her forehead are compared to banners indicating her conquest of the worlds by the power of her austere penance. The worlds are three and पताकाs may be fluttering on an open space (अजिरं). 'वक्रा ललाटगास्तिस्रो भस्मरेखास्त्रिपुण्ड्रकम् ॥' हारावली. 'ऊर्ध्वपुण्ड्रं मृदा कुर्यात् त्रिपुण्ड्रं भस्मना सदा । तिलकं वै द्विजः कुर्याच्चन्दनेन यदृच्छया ॥'. योग...कक्ष्यका whose वैकक्ष्यक scarf was made up of an ascetic's wrap. वैकक्ष्यकम् or वैकक्षकम् (विकक्षायां भवं) is primaring a garland (and secondarily an ornamental robe) worn over one shoulder and under the other like a यज्ञोपवीत. 'वैकक्षकं तु तत् । यत्तिर्यक् क्षिप्तमुरसि' इत्यमरः. योगपट्टकं a cloth thrown over the back and knees of an ascetic during contemplation. 'पृष्ठजान्वोः समायोगे वस्त्रं वलयवद् दृढम् । परिवेष्टय यदूर्ध्वं जुस्तिष्ठेत्तद्योगपट्टकम् ॥'. स्कन्धा ... ना hanging down from her shoulder (with पट्टकेन); that supports itself on a section of the wind (with ०स्रोतसा). The wind (वायु) is believed to be divided in-to seven स्कन्धs, one of which called परिवह supports the Ganges. Compare शाकुन्तल VII **'त्रिस्रोतसं** वहति यो गगनप्रतिष्ठां...वायोरिमं परिवहस्य वदन्ति मार्गम् ॥'. See विष्णुपु. II. 12. 28 also. सुधाफेनवत् धवलेन (with both पट्टकेन and स्रोतसा). तपः...स्रोतसेव—The idea is :—The white योगपट्टक passing over her shoulder and underneath is fancied to be the stream of the Ganges (both being white and both being ०लम्बिन्) that had been coiled round her body by the power of her austerities. सव्येन goes with करेण. कलयन्ती holding. **ब्रह्मो... कमण्डलुं**—the crystal vessel resembled the white lotus bud from which Brahmā was supposed to spring. दक्षिणं goes with **करं**

(p. 4 l. 2) which is the object of उत्क्षिपन्ती. अक्षमालया कृतः परिक्षेपः यस्य—that (कर) was encircled by a rosary. कम्बुनिर्मिताः (made of conch-shell) ऊर्मिकाः (rings) ताभिः दन्तुरितं (bristling). On her right hand she had bright rings of conch-shell (instead of glass bangles as at present). 'कम्बुर्ना वलये शङ्खे' इति, 'अङ्गुलीयकमूर्मिका' इति चामरः. तर्जने तरङ्गिता तर्जनी यस्य the fore-finger of which was waved in chiding (दुर्वासस्). For क see above p. 12. उत्क्षिपन्ती raising or tossing up. क्रोधोपहत overwhelmed by wrath. अनात्मज्ञ not knowing thyself. ब्रह्मबन्धु is a term of reproach meaning 'a ब्राह्मण only by caste or in name and not in deeds.' 'ब्रह्मबन्धुरधिक्षेपः' इत्यमरः (ब्राह्मणस्य बन्धुः परमनुष्ठानाभावाज्जातिब्राह्मणः—क्षीरस्वामी). मुनिखेट miserable or villainous sage. खेट added to words gives the sense of 'अधम.' अपसदः = नीचः. निराकृत an abandoned wretch (lit. expelled). The com. explains 'निराकृतोऽस्वाध्यायः' *i. e.* one who does not study the Vedas. आत्मनः स्खलितेन (mistake) विलक्षः (dismayed or ashamed). 'विलक्षो विस्मयान्विते' इत्यमरः. रोषात् विमुक्तं वेत्रासनं यैः. This and the following words in the instrumental qualify वेदैः (l. 9). ओङ्कारेण मुखरितं (noisy) मुखं येषाम्. The Vedas are represented as repeating loudly the sacred syllable ओम्. उत्क्षेपेण (by their rapid rising up) दोलायमानः (waving to and fro) जटाभारः तेन भरिताः दिशः यैः. The reading आक्षेप॰ (snatching) does not yield a good sense. परिकरबन्धे भ्रमितं कृष्णाजिनं तस्य आटोपः (expanse) तस्या छाया तया श्यामायमानः दिवसः येषाम् who made the day look dark with the colour of their expanded deer skins that were flung round (their body) in girding up their loins. They girt up their loins out of impatience at Durvāsas' conduct. The reading कृष्णाजिनपटच्छाया॰ is not bad. It means 'the colour of their deer skin garments.' अमर्षात् क्रोधात् निःश्वासाः एव दोलाः (swings) तासु प्रेङ्खोलितः (tossed, swung) ब्रह्मलोकः यैः—the whole ब्रह्मलोक vibrated with their rapid breaths. सोम...स्रवद्भिः—They perspired through wrath. The poet fancies that it was सोमरस that oozed from their body and not perspiration. विसरः = समूहः. अग्निहोत्रस्य पवित्रं भस्म तेन स्मेरं ललाटं येषाम् whose forehead was bright with the holy ashes of oblations offered into fire. कुश...वरिभिः—कुशतन्तूनां चारु चामरं चीरचीवरं च ते ॰चीवरे स्तः एषां—who had a charming chowrie of Kus'a threads (*i. e.* slender कुश grass) and were clad in bark garments. The affix इन् is added to the द्वन्द्व compound ॰चीवरे. आषाढिभिः bearing a staff of the पलाश wood. 'पालाशो दण्ड आषाढः' इत्यमरः (आषाढासु जातः—क्षीर॰). 'विशाखाषाढादण् मन्थदण्डयोः' पा. 5. 1. 110 (वैशाखो मन्थः, आषाढो दण्डः). A ब्रह्मचारी of each of the three Varṇas was to carry a staff of a particular tree 'ब्राह्मणो बैल्वपालाशौ क्षत्रियो वाटखादिरौ । पैलवौदुम्बरौ वैश्यो दण्डानर्हन्ति धर्मतः ॥' मनुस्मृति II. 45. प्रहरणीकृतं कमण्डलुमण्डलं यैः. They seized their water vessels in their hands as their weapons. मूर्तैः in a corporeal form. वृषीमपहाय abandoning their seats. बृषी or वृषी ('व्रतिनामासनं वृषी' इत्यमरः) a seat of कुश grass for ascetics.

P. 4 ll. 11–17 **ततो...न्यवारयत्.** मर्षय forgive. अभू...शापस्य she is not a fit person for a curse. अनु...बुधैः though besought by the gods. नाथ् 1 P to solicit, but A when it means 'to bless'. बद्धं अञ्जलिपुटं यैः that folded their hands. मा...इम् Do not cause loss to your austerities. **'विघ्नोऽन्तरायः प्रत्यूहः'** इत्यमरः. It was supposed that by pronouncing a curse a person lost his merit. रोषस्य आवेशेन विवशः beside himself with the emotion of wrath. दुर्विनीत impudent, ill-mannered. व्यपनयामि I shall remove. उन्नतिम्—is used in two senses; (1) going up, (2) exalted or proud position. The first meaning contrasts well with the words 'अधस्ताद्गच्छ.' प्रति...द्यतं who was ready to give a curse in return. सावित्रीम्—is the object of न्यवारयत्. असं...माननीयाः Brāhmaṇas, though their minds are not well disciplined, deserve respect solely for their very birth (caste). Compare वनपर्व 200. 89 'यथा श्मशाने दीप्तौजाः पावको न प्रदुष्यति । एवं विद्वानविद्वान्वा ब्राह्मणो दैवतं महत् ॥'.

P. 4 l. 18—**P. 5** l. 16 **अथ तां...मगात्.** पितामहः is the subject of उवाच (l. 23). कम...द्वहन् having a body wearing a white sacrificial thread as if lotus fibres stuck to it when it (body) sprang from the lotus. कमलात् उत्पत्तौ लग्नानि मृणालसूत्राणि यस्याः. For the birth of ब्रह्मा from the lotus in the navel of Vishṇu, see above p. 20. The fibres and यज्ञोपवीत are both white. The poet fancies that lotus fibres stuck to the body of Brahmā when he sprang from a lotus. उद्ग...कलम् having stopped the tumult consequent upon the curse with his right hand, from which shot up a pencil of the rays of the clear emerald on his ring and which therefore seemed to hold a bundle of Kus'a grass for warding off the calamity of the three worlds. उद्गच्छन् अच्छस्य अङ्गुलीयकमरकतस्य मयूखलताकलापः यस्मिन्. त्रिभुवनस्य उपप्लवः (calamity, injury) तस्य प्रशमाय कुशानां आपीडः समूहः तं धारयतीति. The rays of the emerald resemble green blades of कुश grass. कुश grass was supposed to ward off evil. It was a calamity for the three worlds that सरस्वती was cursed. C and T refer to अथर्ववेद 19. 30. 4 and 6. 43. 1 (where दर्भ is called मन्युशमन) for showing that कुश grass originated from a world convulsion and that कुश had power to allay passion. अति... किरणैः with the pure and far-reaching rays of his teeth he as if let fall in all directions lines for constructing the coming कृतयुग. In constructing a building a carpenter takes measurements with plumblines that are also long (दीर्घ) and white (with chalk). The rays of Brahmā's teeth resembled such lines. The poet fancies that ब्रह्मा measured with lines the directions for constructing the future कृतयुग. कृतयुग is the first of the four Yugas (कृत, त्रेता, द्वापर and कलि). At the time about which बाण spoke, it was कलियुग and hence he uses the word भावि. सर...पटहेनेव—his voice resembled the sound of an auspicious drum beaten at the time of starting on a journey. सरस्वती, being cursed, was to start on her journey to the world of mortals. निह...स्तात् It will ruin you hereafter. उद्दामं प्रसृताः इन्द्रियाण्येव अश्वाः तैः समुत्थापितं raised by the steeds of senses that rush unchecked. रजः (1) dust (with अश्व); passion (with इन्द्रिय). रज...जिताम्—Rajas clouds the vision of those that have not conquered the अक्षs (senses, axles). Dust raised by horses when the charioteer cannot control the chariot (the axle) enters the eye and obscures the vision. If proper control be not exercised over the senses, passion clouds the intellect. Compare 'यस्त्वविज्ञानवान्भवत्ययुक्तेन मनसा सदा। तस्येन्द्रियाण्यवश्यानि दुष्टाश्वा इव सारथेः॥' कठोपनिषद् I. 3. 5. अक्षः axle, cart. अक्षं = इन्द्रियं. कि...क्षते How far indeed can the (physical) eye see? The idea is that it has only a limited scope. For the use of वा, see verse 16 above. कृतबुद्धयः whose minds are perfect or educated. असतः सतो वा good or bad; or the meaning is 'actually existent before the eye or not so existent' (*i. e.* absent). निसर्गविरोधिनी opposed by nature. धर्म means 'performance of one's duties enjoined by the S'āstras'. एकत्र वृत्तिः = एकत्र अवस्थानम्. आलोकः (1) light, (2) enlightenment. तमसि (1) in darkness, (2) in ignorance, delusion. पर...दक्षा clever in detecting the defects of others (applies to both दृष्टि and बुद्धि). दृष्टि... पश्यति your angry mind, like the inflamed eye, does not observe your own sin *viz.* your flying into passion. दुर्वासस् saw the fault of सरस्वती *viz.* laughing at him, but his mind did not dwell upon the mistake he had committed nor did he observe that he was swayed by passion (राग). When the eye is inflamed (कुपित) it cannot see its own redness (राग). The word कुपित in medicine means 'suffering from a deranged state of the three humours वात, पित्त and कफ.' क...क—two कs denote great incongruity or inconsistency between two things. वैवधिक one who carries loads on a pole. 'विभाषा विवधात्' पा. 4. 4. 17. (विवधेन हरति विवधिकः, पक्षे ठक् । वैवधिकः । विवधवीवधशब्दौ उभयतो बद्धशिक्ये स्कन्धवाह्ये काष्ठे वर्तेते । सि. कौ.). पुरोभागित्वम्—finding only the faults of others, censoriousness. 'दोषैकदृक् पुरोभागी' इत्यमरः. चक्षुष्मा...जनः that man though possessed of eye-sight is really blind. नहि...कर्तव्यं वा obscured by rage, the mind does not discriminate between what should and should not be done. कुपितस्य...भ्रुकुटिः of the man flying into a passion, wisdom first becomes clouded and then his eye-brow. In this and the three following sentences, the verbs अन्धकारीभवति and others are used in a literal physical sense and also in a secondary sense. When a man is angered his brow becomes dark (threatening) and his wisdom forsakes him for the moment. रागः passion; redness. समास्कन्दति overwhelms; attacks. चरमं चक्षुः lastly (redness attacks) the eye *i. e.* the eye becomes red when a man is angry. तपो गलति the austerities (performed by the angry man) are dissolved *i. e.* have to give way before the wave of passion. पश्चा...लिलम्—the angry man perspires. पूर्व...धरः—If a person becomes angry, that gives rise to an evil reputation; the angry man's lips quiver. ०नाशाय—the dative shows the effect wrought by दुर्वासस्. A poisonous tree also kills people and has fibrous roots (जटा) and bark. मूले लग्नकचे जटा' इत्यमरः (वृक्षादिमूलं जटा). अनुचिता...वृत्तिः this tendency of your mind is not in keeping with this garb of a sage (that you wear) as a necklace of pearls (is not appropriate to मुनिवेश). वृत्तमुक्ता (वृत्तेन मुक्ता) devoid of good conduct (with ०वृत्तिः); (वृत्ताः मुक्ताः यस्याः) the pearls of which are round (with ०यष्टिः). शैलूषः इव like an actor. 'शिलूषस्य ऋषेः अपत्यं शैलूषः' क्षीरस्वामी. कृत्रिमम् not natural, counterfeit. उपशमशून्येन—the actor dressed as an ascetic has no restraint over his senses (उपशम) nor had दुर्वासस्. आकल्पः dress. अल्प...जातम् I do not see even the slightest virtue in you. The words may also mean 'I don't see the slightest happiness in you (*i. e.* proceeding from you to others)'. अतिलघिम्ना (1) by great levity; (2) by extreme lightness (in weight). उपर्येव...प्लवतः you are floating only on the surface of the ocean of knowledge (*i. e.* you have not penetrated deep into the mysteries of knowledge). What is light floats on the sea. अनेलमूकाः deaf and dumb. 'जडोऽज्ञेऽनेडमूकस्तु वक्तुं श्रोतुमशिक्षिते' इत्यमरः. ड and ल are often interchanged. एडाः deaf. The meaning is:—All these sages are not deaf and dumb nor are they fools. They also understand the mistake you committed. So you should rather feel ashamed in their presence than select सरस्वती for cursing. The reading षण्ढाः means 'eunuch'. The idea would be 'these sages are not impotent, they also can curse you in return, but they have restrained themselves.' रोषः एव दोषः तेन निषद्ये that is fit to be inhabited by the sin of wrath; or रोषदोषस्य निषद्या (market) यस्मिन्. 'आपणस्तु निषद्यायाम्' इत्यमरः. स्व...ग्राह्ये when your own heart should have been checked. अनागस् *adj.* innocent. आत्मनः प्रमादः तेन स्खलितं तस्मात् वैलक्ष्याणि (विलक्षस्य भावः) occasions of shame arising from mistakes due to one's own carelessness (प्रमादः). यै...जनः whereby a person not properly educated incurs blame. The reading याप्यतां conveys the same sense. याप्य = गर्ह्य. विनोदयिष्यति will divert or comfort. आत्मजस्य मुखकमलं तस्य अवलोकनं अवधिः यस्य—that will end at the sight &c. विसर्जितं (dismissed, dissolved) ०मण्डलं येन. ससंभ्रमं (hastily) उपगतः नारदः तस्य स्कन्धे विन्यस्तः हस्तः येन (*adj.* of पितामहः above). देवर्षि नारद was one of the ten mind-born sons of ब्रह्मा. See मनु० I. 35 quoted above p. 18. समु...तिष्ठत् got up for the performance of his usual daily rites. 'आह्निकं स्यात्पुनरहर्निर्वर्त्ये नित्यकर्मणि' हेमचन्द्र. सरस्वत्यपि–connect this with गृहमगात् (l. 16). धवल...पातयन्ती who let fall on her bosom her glance that was white, dark and variegated, as if it (दृष्टि) were a strip of deer-skin. The white of the eye and the dark pupil together make the glance variegated and make it resemble a deer-skin with dark spots thereon. The word धवलः further suggests a bold contradiction. धवलः कृष्णशारः (spotted antelope) यस्मिन्. A कृष्णशार cannot be धवल. षट्...माणा The dark bees are fancied to be the incarnate letters of the curse. A curse being an evil thing would be dark. शापशोकेन शिथिलितौ (without energy) हस्तौ यस्याः. उपदिश्यमानः मर्त्यलोकावतरणमार्गः यस्यै. अधो...जालकेन—the idea is:—The rays of her nails naturally spread downwards; the poet fancies that in spreading downwards from heaven they pointed out to her the way to descend to the world of mortals. अधोमुखीभूतेन—one who tells another unpleasant news hangs down his face. नूपुराणां व्याहारः (utterance, noise) तेन आहूतैः. Domestic हंसs are always represented as following the tinkling of the anklets of ladies. Compare 'प्रदक्षिणीक्रियमाणामिव मणिनूपुरबन्धुभिर्बद्धमण्डलं भ्रमद्भिर्भवनहंसैः' हर्षचरित 5th उच्छ्वास. The कलहंसs are compared to the hearts of the inhabitants of ब्रह्मलोक who, out of their affection for सरस्वती, followed her mentally.

P. 5 l. 17—p. 7 l. 10 **अत्रान्तरे...इति.** मध्यमं लोकम्—the earth (which is between the Heavens and the पाताल). अंशुमाली = सूर्यः. सरस्वती...माली—the idea is:—the sun descended from his position in mid heavens to the western horizon (the earth) in the evening. This is fancied to be due to the fact that the sun wanted to announce that सरस्वती was coming down to the earth. मुकुलितानां बिसिनीनां (कमलिनीनां) विसरः समूहः तस्य व्यसनं (calamity) तेन विषण्णानि (dejected) सरांसि यस्मिन्. Lotuses close their petals in the evening. The day looked gloomy when they did so. मन्दायमाने वासरे when the day waned. This and the following clauses up to स्पष्टे प्रदोषसमये (p. 6 l. 18) are locatives absolute, the principal sentence being सावित्री सरस्वतीमवादीत् (p. 6 l. 19). मधुमद...भगवति when the holy (sun), the sole eye of the world, as red as the face (लपनं) of a very young monkey, quickly (क्षेपीयः) descended on to the peak of (the western) mountain, as if he (the sun) was tossed down by the angrily bent glances of loving women exhilarated by the intoxication of wine. The beauties flushed with wine were eager for the night. The natural descent of the sun to the western horizon is fancied as being due to his being thrown by the angry glances of the beauties. क्षेपीयः (comparative of क्षिप्र) is here used as an adverb. सं० explains the propriety of some words 'सम्भोगान्तरायकारी कथमयमद्यापि नास्तमेतीत्यतः कोपः। क्षिप्यमाणश्चातित्वरितं पतति...लोकेत्यादिना सम्भोगविघ्नकारित्वमेव प्रकाश्यते'. प्रस्नुतानि मुखानि (nipples of udders) यासां ताः ०मुखाः माहेय्यः तासां यूथस्य क्षरन्त्यः क्षीरधाराः ताभिः धवलितेषु that were white with the flowing streams of milk of the herds of cows the udders of which began to drip. 'माहेयी सौरभेयी गौः' इत्यमरः (मह्यते पूज्यते मह्या तस्या अपत्यं माहेयी—क्षीरस्वामी). आसन्नेन चन्द्रोदयेन उद्दामः (tumultuous) क्षीरोदः (क्षीरसागरः) तस्य लहरीभिः क्षालितेषु. उपशल्य out-skirts. 'ग्रामान्त उपशल्यं स्यात्' इत्यमरः. It is well-known that the waters of the ocean rise up at moon-rise. The oceans are said to be seven surrounding the seven द्वीपs. 'एते द्वीपाः समुद्रैस्तु सप्त सप्तभिरावृताः। लवणेक्षुसुरासर्पिर्दधिदुग्धजलैः समम्॥' विष्णुपुराण II. 2. 6. The reading प्रस्तुतमखमाहेयी० would mean 'cows that are useful for the sacrifices that were begun'. अपरा...रावते when ऐरावत starting on his afternoon stroll (प्रचारः) and having a chowric (on his head) was rending at his will (स्वैरं) the banks of the river (स्रवन्ती) of the gods, his tusks being reddened by striking against the golden sides (of the river). चामरिणि—chowries were placed on the heads of elephants and horses. चामीकरतटे (सुवर्णतटे) ताडनेन अरुणिताः रदनाः (दन्ताः) यस्य. रदति pr. p. of रद् 1 P to split. सुरस्रवन्ती the Ganges. ऐरावत is the elephant of Indra. His tusks became red because some of the gold stuck to them after the impact. Elephants are represented as fond of butting against banks and mounds. The reading ०ताडनरणितरदने would mean 'whose tusks resounded by striking etc.' प्रसृ...पाटलताम् when the sky (तारापथः) presented a rosy colour, as if it (sky) were besmeared (अनुलिप्त) with the Alaktaka dye of the feet of the several thousands of विद्याधर damsels that were moving about (towards their rendezvous). The sky was suffused red in the evening; the poet fancies that the rosy colour was due to the अलक्तक etc. विद्याधर is a class of semi-divine beings. अभिसारिका a young woman who goes out to meet her lover or keeps on appointment made by him. 'कान्तार्थिनी तु या याति सङ्केतं साऽभिसारिका' इत्यमरः. तारापथ...द्रवे when red sandal juice, poured out (आवर्जित) in the sun-set worship offered by the Siddhas journeying in the sky, flowed colouring the quarters and possessing the hue of safflower (कुसुम्भं) as though it (juice) were the perspiration of the Evening delighted at her obeisance to S'iva. तारापथे प्रस्थिताः सिद्धाः (semidivine beings) तैः दत्तं दिनकरस्य अस्तमये अर्घ्यं तस्मिन् आवर्जिते (*adj.* of द्रवे). अर्घ्यम्--materials of worship, such as water, sandal &c. रञ्जिताः ककुभः (दिशः) येन (*adj.* of ०द्रवे). कुसुम्भस्य इव भाः यस्य. Connect स्रवति (pr.p. loc. sing.) with ०द्रवे. पिनाकिने प्रणतिः तया मुदिता &c. As सन्ध्या is red, her perspiration also would look red. The red sandal juice is fancied to be the perspiration of Evening. वन्दारु...लोके when the world of ब्रह्मा, where crowds of the best of worshipping sages folded their hands in evening adoration, seemed as though all the lotus beds had come to wait upon that from which Brahmā sprang. For वन्दारु see शरारु above p. 23. वन्दारूणां (bowing) मुनीनां वृन्दारकाः (श्रेष्ठाः) तेषां वृन्दं तेन बध्यमानं सन्ध्याञ्जलिवनं यस्मिन्. ब्रह्मणः उत्पत्तिः यस्मात् तत् ब्रह्मोत्पत्ति कमलं तस्य सेवार्थे आगतः सकलानां कमलानां आकरः यस्मिन्. The hands folded in सन्ध्या adoration look like lotus buds; hence the उत्प्रेक्षा in ब्रह्मोत्पत्ति०. समुच्चा...ब्रह्मणि when Brahmā had uttered the Vedic hymns of the third Savana. समुच्चारितं तृतीयसवनस्य ब्रह्म (वेदः) येन. There were three सवनs (sacrifices at which libations of सोम were offered) प्रातःसवन, माध्यन्दिनसवन and तृतीयसवन. The meaning may also be 'when Brāhmaṇas had uttered &c.' Here the singular ब्रह्मणि is used for the whole class. Some taken सवन in the sense of स्नान.

ज्वलित...मन्दिरेषु when the houses of the seven sages had their courts full (जटाल) of the flames of blazing sacrificial (वैतान) fires, as if in them (houses) was begun the lustration of the camp that was a means of securing the performance of one's duties. ज्वलिताः वैतानाः ज्वलनाः तेषां ज्वालाः ताभिः जटालानि अजिराणि येषाम्. आरब्धं धर्मसाधनस्य शिबिरस्य नीराजनं येषु or आरब्धं धर्मसाधनाय शिबिरस्य &c. नीराजन was a religious and military ceremony, performed by kings and generals before they took the field; it consisted in waving lights before the components of an army. As sacrificial fires blazed in the houses, the poet fancies that नीराजन was being performed over the houses (which looked like camps), the object for which the houses were erected being धर्मसाधन and not जयसाधन or अर्थसाधन. Another sense also is suggested. साधन means 'army'. An army is housed in a camp (शिबिरं) over which नीराजन may be performed. For सप्तर्षि see above p. 19. C and T translate 'as though a camp lustration had commenced in an army devoted to Dharma'. This is not correct and does not bring out the उत्प्रेक्षा properly. अघमर्षणेन मुषितः किल्बिषविषगदः (किल्बिषं पापं एव विषगदः) येषां ते ०गदाः उल्लाघाः लघवश्च. अघ...यतिषु when the hermits had light hearts, being free from the poison disease of sin that was removed by the अघमर्षण hymn. उल्लाघ convalescent. 'उल्लाघो निर्गतो गदात्' इत्यमरः. A person who has been taking medicines against poison becomes convalescent and light—hearted. अघमर्षण is a term applied to the hymn (of three verses) beginning with 'ऋतं च सत्यं चाभीद्धात्तपसोऽध्यजायत' (ऋग्वेद X. 190). 'सर्वैनसामपध्वंसि जप्यं त्रिष्वघमर्षणम्' इत्यमरः. सन्ध्योपासनाय आसीनानां तपस्विनां पङ्क्त्या (row, line) पूतं पुलिनं (sandy bed) यस्य (*adj.* of ०जले). प्लवमानाः नलिनयोनियानहंसाः एव हासः तेन दन्तुरिताः ऊर्मयः यस्य the waves of which were furrowed by the smile-like हंसs, the vehicles of ब्रह्मा, floating thereon. हंस is the वाहन of ब्रह्मा. हंसs are white and so resemble हास which is poetically described as white. One who smiles shows his teeth. The हंसs sailing on the waves divide them into crests that look like teeth. जल...वने when the beds of कुमुदs (night-lotuses) were about to expand, causing delight to bees and sweetly perfumed with their own honey, that (beds) were the umbrellas of water nymphs and were the private mansions of the wives of the tribes of birds. Water nymphs dwelt under the shelter of कुमुदs and birds also made them their haunts. कृता मधुपानां मुत् येन. There is another sense also. When Kumudas open (*i. e.* at night) those who drink wine (मधुप) are exhilarated. मुमुदिषमाणे *pr. p.* of the desiderative of मुद् to delight or expand with joy. दिवसा...यूथे when the crowds of flamingoes, delighted by their drinking bout on the sweet honey of the day-lotuses that were going to languish as the day closed, were about to sleep, fanning the blue-lotus (राजीवं) lakes with rows of their flapping (धुत) wings and turning their necks into coils in order to be scratched by the soft lotus stalks. दिवसस्य अवसाने ताम्यतां तामरसानां मधुरं मधु तस्य सपीतिः (सहपानं) तया प्रीते. 'सपीतिः स्त्री तुल्यपानम्' इत्यमरः. सुषुप्सति *pr. p.* loc. sing. of the desiderative base of स्वप्. ०काण्डेन कण्डूयनं तदर्थं कुण्डलिता कन्धरा येन. The flamingoes bent their neck in a circle round the lotus stalks in order to get it scratched. धुतानां पक्षाणां राज्या वीजितं राजीवसरः येन. तट...नभस्वति when a slight (तनीयस्) evening breeze, resembling the sigh of Night, began to blow, making the river grey with the pollen of the flowers of creepers growing on the bank, and bearing the perfume of the jasmine flowers in the braids (धम्मिल्लः) of the matrous (पुरन्ध्रि) of the city of Siddhas. ०धूलिभिः धूसरिता सरित् येन (qualifies नभस्वति). सरति *pr. p.* *loc. sing.* of सृ. ०पुरन्ध्रीणां धम्मिल्लेषु मल्लिकाः तासां गन्धं गृह्णन्ति इति. मल्लिका is a flower that opens in the evening. सङ्कोचेन उदञ्चन्तः (erected) उच्चाः (stiff) केसराः तेषां कोटिभिः सङ्कटः कुशेशयानां कमलानां कोशः तस्य कोटरः एव कुटी तस्यां शेते इति—that lay in the hut in the form of the cavity of the lotuses that were full of the tips of filaments high and stiff by the closing (of the petals). As the lotuses contracted at sunset, their filaments that were loose became straightened up and barred the way of escape out of the lotuses, the bees being confined inside as in a hut. नृत्तो...गणे the constellations of stars, presenting the appearance of the bunches of कुटज buds in the forest of the matted hair of S'iva tossed up in dance, were scattered in clusters in the sky. स्तबकयति a denominative verb from स्तबक. The clusters of stars looked like कुटज buds, which are white. कुटज is a wild flower and hence the word अटवी is put in. The stars appeared scattered about. शिव is represented as fond of dancing. When शिव danced, the flowers in his hair would be scattered about. सन्ध्या...तमसि darkness, that was not yet full grown, that was reddish with the continuance of twilight, that had the colour of the skin of a ripe Tāla fruit and that was thick (मेदुर) like a dark cloud, closed round the earth. सन्ध्यायाः अनुबन्धः तेन ताम्रे—twilight had not yet completely vanished and so a slight rosy hue still persisted and was mixed up with the darkness. परिणमत् तालफलं तस्य त्वचः इव त्विट् (कान्तिः) यस्य. कालमेघ also means 'the clouds at the end of the world.' नवं वयः यस्य. तरुण...प्रकरे when numerous lamps, capable of piercing (पाटनं) the veil of fresh (not yet fullgrown *i. e.* not deep or pitchy) darkness, began to blaze forth, being a cluster of champaka buds serving as the ear-ornaments of the lady of Night. The flame of a lamp is like a चम्पक bud. Therefore the lamps lit at night are said to be the कर्णपूरs of the lady (Night). प्रतनु...मुखे when the region of Indra (*i. e.* the east), pale with the lovely light of the few rays of the moon and appearing like the sandy islet of the Jumna slightly dry and free from its blue waters, reduced the darkness. In the east the moon was about to rise. The first rays of the moon lessened the darkness and the east lookd grey (white-dark). The east therefore resembled the sandy bed of the Jumna from which the waters had just receded, the sand being white, but the remnants of water being dark. The water of the Jumna is dark as compared with the Ganges. प्रतनु (slight) तुहिनकिरणस्य शीतरश्मेः किरणाः तेषां लावण्यं तस्य आलोकेन पाण्डुनि. आश्यानं (partially dried) नीलनीरेण मुक्तं कालिन्दीकूलं तस्य वालुकायुक्तं पुलिनं, पुलिनं इव आचरति पुलिनायते. The reading बालपुलिनायमाने for वालुका° is better, as in कूलवालुका° there are too many words. बालपुलिनं would mean 'a sandy spot just raised out of water.' शतक्रतोः (इन्द्रस्य) इदं शातक्रतवम्. कृशयति *pr. p. loc.* sing. of कृशयति denominative verb from कृश. खमुञ्चि...तमसि when darkness that had blackened (मेचकित) the lake of expanded blue lotuses, that (तमः) was a veritable cluster of the tresses of the S'abarî in the form of the night, that (तमः) had the colour of the wings of a jay (चाषः), was leaving the sky and was being dissolved, being disturbed by having its hair seized by the rays of the moon, like the mind of a proud beauty. खं आकाशं मुञ्चति इति ख°. At the approaching rise of the moon darkness left the sky and was massed on the earth. मेचकितं °सरः येन. शश...विले and विलीयमाने apply both to तमसि and °मनसि. शशधरस्य कराणां (किरणानां) निकरेण कचग्रहः तेन आविले. When a person is seized by the hair, he is harshly and forcibly dealt with. The moon's rays forcibly drove away darkness. आविल turbid, muddy. शशधर...मनसि—the idea here is:—a proud young lady, being offended with her husband, resolved upon accepting no reconciliation. When the moon caressed her hair with its rays, her resolve began to waver and at last her proud mind gave way (विलीयमान) and she was quickly reconciled. The word कर also means 'hand' and the clause suggests 'when her tresses were stroked by the gentle hand of her husband by way of reconciliation, she wavered'. शर्वरी (निशा) एवं शबरी तस्याः चिकुरचयः कुन्तलभारः. शबरी is a woman of an aboriginal tribe, such as the Bhils. Both शर्वरी and शबरी are dark and further the two words are almost the same in sound. चाषपक्षस्य इव त्विट् यस्य. उदिते...श्वेतभानौ when the moon (श्वेतभानुः), now risen, assumed a red form (वपुः) as though covered (निचित) with the mass of blood dropping from his own deer slain by the weapon (हेति) of the sharp paw of the lion (हरिः) in the cave of the slopes (कटकं) of the peaks of the Rising Mountain, a red form that was as though the lower lip of the damsel of Night possessed of glow at the rise (of the moon). The disc of the moon was red when it rose. There are two उत्प्रेक्षाs in this clause. The first up to निचितमिव is concerned with redness and the second (in उदय...धरमिव) is concerned with the red orb of the moon. The poet fancies that the natural redness of the disc at moon-rise is due to the blood &c. For the deer in the moon see notes p. 22. उदयगिरि a fabulous mountain in the east from behind which the sun and the moon were supposed to come up. The red and round orb of the moon appears like the red and full lip of a young lady. So the poet fancies it to be the lip of the lady of Night. The word उदयरागधरम् conveys two ideas. The lip of a fair woman possesses the same redness (रागः) as is seen (in the moon) at moon-rise. The night also possesses rosy hue (राग) at moon-rise (on the eastern horizon). C and T translate 'the form of the Lord of white splendour... assumed the glow of the Udaya mountain, resembling the lip of the nymph of night'. This does not appear to us to be correct. वपुः is the object of धारयति and ०धरमधरम् is in apposition to वपुः. अचलात् (पर्वतात् अर्थात् उदयगिरेः) च्युताः चन्द्रकान्तस्य जलधाराः ताभिः धौते. From the चन्द्रकान्त stone water oozes at the rise of the moon. ध्वान्ते = तमसि. गो...मण्डले when the orb of the moon had begun to fill the ocean, as though it (orb) were a great ivory conduit with the shape of a crocodile's mouth bearing a stream of milk dropping from the world of cows. The bright rays of the moon fell on the ocean which rose in a high tide. The streaming rays of the moon looked like a stream of milk. The pale white moon looked like ivory (hence दन्तमय). The orb of the moon presented the appearance of the end of a conduit pipe (प्रणालः) as large as the mouth of a crocodile. गो also means 'rays'. दन्तमयः मकरमुखः (मकरस्य इव मुखं यस्य) महाप्रणालः तस्मिन्. स्पष्टे... समये when the evening time was clear *i. e.* when the night had advanced beyond the stage of dusk or twilight. त्रि...जल्पन्ती my tongue prattling to thee feels shame before thee that are clever enough to instruct the three worlds. यादृश्यः—connect with दैवस्य वामाः वृत्तयः. जानास्येव...वृत्तयः thou knowest already what the crooked actions (वृत्तयः, ways) of Fate are, actions that are unsteady (विसंस्थुल), that are unkind like the wicked even to worthy men, changing in a moment, not to be resisted and unpleasant. The word वामाः also means 'handsome women, or women in general'. Women also, according to the estimation of many people, are unsteady, changeful to a degree, heartless hard to be resisted (when once they set their heart on achieving an object). Compare '**विमुक्तधर्माश्चपलास्तीक्ष्णा** भेदकराः स्त्रियः॥' अरण्यकाण्ड 45.30. '**पौंश्चल्याच्चलचित्ताच्च नैःस्नेह्याच्च** स्वभावतः ।' मनुस्मृति 9.15. न रमणीयाः does not well apply to women. Hence the words should have been omitted in the text (as B does). निष्कारणा...पतन्ती even the slightest insult, when without cause, coming from an inferior person, disturbs the mind even of a high-souled person. निकारः insult or wrong. कणिका a particle. Here सरस्वती is the high-souled person and दुर्वासस the inferior man. मानस means also 'the मानस lake.' It may become turbid by a particle (of dust) falling in it. अन...सिच्यमानः—sprinkled with ceaseless tears (with शोकः); अनवरतं नयनं यस्य एतादृशं जलं तेन सिच्यमानः sprinkled with water that is carried incessantly (with तरुः). विपल्लवः—विपदः (of adversity) लवः यस्मिन् in which there is a slight misfortune *i. e.* caused by slight misfortune (with शोकः); विपल्लवः void of foliage (with तरुः). प्ररोहति increases (with शोकः); puts forth shoots. The more one dwells on one's misfortune and sheds tears, the greater the pangs of it. अतिसुकुमारं applies both to जनं and ०कुसुमम्. सन्तापपरमाणवः atoms of affliction *i. e.* slight affliction (with जनम्); atoms of heat *i. e.* slight heat (with ०कुसुमम्). महतां on the great; of large size (elephants). अणुः small (with क्लेशः); with a fine edge (with सृणिः). अणुरपि...लम् even a slight affliction is sufficient to torment them (the great) as the piercing goad is sufficient to humble (the big elephants). कदर्थनम् is a noun from the denominative verb कदर्थयति, which is formed from कदर्थ.

'कोः कत्तत्पुरुषेऽचि' पा. 6. 3. 101 (कु when followed in a तत्पुरुष by a word beginning with a vowel becomes कत्). कुत्सितः अर्थः कदर्थः. अलम् in the sense of 'sufficient or able' governs the dative. सहजः स्नेहपाशः (स्नेहः पाशः इव) तस्य ग्रन्थिना बन्धनं येषां or यासाम्. सहज...भूमयः our native home, which is linked to us like a kinsman by fast (*lit.* knotted) ties of natural affection, is hard to give up. जन्मभूमिः also means 'mother'. दारुणः terrible (with ०विरहः); of wood (with ०पातः). Construe दारुणः ०विरहः हृदयं दारयति ०पातः दारुणः हृदयं (central part) इव. क्रकचपातः the stroke of a saw. संस्तुत familiar, dear. अभूमि...सवानाम् you are not the soil for the shoots of the poison plant of sorrow. The idea is that sorrow should not take a footing in you. 'क्ष्वेडस्तु गरलं विषम्' इत्यमरः. अपि च...शुचाम् what occasion have the wise for grief, when in front of and behind us stand our powerful deeds, whether good or bad, that rule us and yield fruit to us? It is our own actions, good or bad, that produce the vicissitudes of our lives. If adversities assail us, that is due to the bad actions of our former lives. If we were put into trouble without any fault on our part, then there would be room for sorrow. But we know that under the inexorable law of *Karma* there is no such thing as chance. The idea of तिष्ठ...पृष्ठतश्च is:—It is our own *Karma* that determines the rewards that we are to enjoy and *Karma* encompasses us on all sides. शुचाम् is genitive plural of शुच्. प्रष्ठ=पुरःसर. 'प्रष्ठोऽग्रगामिनि' पा. 8. 3. 92 (प्रतिष्ठते इति प्रष्ठो गौः। अग्रतो गच्छतीत्यर्थः। सि.कौ.). Compare for the idea 'यादृशं कुरुते कर्म तादृशं फलमश्नुते' रामायण उत्तरकाण्ड 15. 23. त्रिभुवनस्य मङ्गलं तदर्थं एकं (केवलं) कमलम्. अपवित्रं कुर्वन्ति अपवित्रयन्ति. तदलम् therefore enough (of this weeping). अवतितीर्षति desires to descend. पुण्यभाजि—that will be blest (by your descent thereon). तपोवनधामसु=तपोवनस्थानेषु. तपस्यन्ती performing austerities. अयं सखीजनः means सावित्री herself. उप...पेशलः skilful in serving you and agreeable (पेशल) on account of familiarity with you (commencing from) playing in the dust together. The idea is they were intimate playmates since early childhood. न अन्यत् शरणं (रक्षितृ) यस्याः सा ०शरणा who seeks no other refuge (than S'iva). प्रतिपद्यस्व resort to (the object being त्र्यम्बकम्). सर्व...तारम् the author of all lores. धातारम् the supporter of all. स्वश्रेयसे for your own welfare. Connect this with प्रतिपद्यस्व. स्वचरणरजसा पवित्रिताः त्रिदशाः असुराश्च येन (adj. of त्र्यम्बकम्). सुधासूतिः (सुधायाः अमृतस्य सूतिः यस्मात्) चन्द्रः एव कलिका तया कल्पितः कर्णावतंसः यस्य (adj. of त्र्यम्बकम्)—whose ear-ornament is formed by the crescent (*lit.* bud) of the moon. त्रिभुवनगुरुम् to be honoured by the three worlds. त्र्यम्बकं=शिवम्. The reading of A and C दातारं श्वःश्रेयसस्य means 'who bestowes future happiness'. श्वः tomorrow *i. e.* future. From Bāṇa's usual style we can infer that he wrote as in the text (repeating धातारम्). श्वःश्रेयसस्य is rather an unusual combination and ungrammatical. ते=तुभ्यम्. शापेन शोकः तस्य विरतिम् (cessation). वितरिष्यति दास्यति. ब्रह्मा had already declared (text p. 5 l. 9) that the curse would end with the birth of a son. By S'iva's favour that happy event would follow in a very short time.

P. 7 ll. 11–27 **एवमुक्त्वा...निर्जगाम.** मुक्ताः मुक्ताफलवत् धवलाः लोचनजललवाः यया that shed tears bright like pearls. केवलं...हृदयम् it is only the happiness of serving Brahmā (to which I shall be a stranger till the curse lasts) that makes my heart soft (*i. e.* makes my heart wistful and sad). भुवि...धामानि the places on the earth where Dharma can be performed. समाधिसाधनानि means of abstract meditation; or the word may be taken as in apposition to स्थानानि, meaning 'places that will help in abstract meditation'. समाधि is the eighth and last अङ्ग of योग. 'यमनियमासनप्राणायामप्रत्याहारधारणाध्यानसमाधयोऽष्टावङ्गानि' योगसूत्र II. 29. योग is defined as 'योगश्चित्तवृत्तिनिरोधः' योगसूत्र. I. 2. रणरणकेन उपनीतः प्रजागरः यस्यै who was kept awake by agitation. अनिमीलिते (not closed) लोचने यस्याः. त्रिभुवनशेखरे head jewel of the three worlds. खर...वपुषि whose form was red, as though with the blood (क्षतजम्) scattered from the mouths of his (the sun's) own horses pierced by the rough (खर) and clanking bit (खलीनः-नम्). The redness of the morning sun is fancied to be due to the blood &c. Vide a similar conceit above in the case of the moon (text p. 6 l. 15). उद...मणौ—the resplendent sun appeared like a crest jewel of the eastern mountain. जरन् कृकवाकुः (कुक्कुटः) तस्य चूडा तद्वत् अरुणः अरुणः पुरःसरः यस्य who is ushered by Aruṇa rosy like an old cook's comb. Aruṇa is a personification of the ruddy sky before sunrise. He is the charioteer of the sun. 'कृकवाकुस्ताम्रचूडः कुक्कुटश्चरणायुधः' इत्यमरः (कृकेण शीरोग्रीवेण वक्ति—क्षीर०). विरोचने=सूर्ये. नाति...र्ती not being far away (from the place where सरस्वती passed a sleepless night). विविच्य having reflected. पिता...पालः the keeper of the tribe of Haṁsas that are the conveyances (विमानः-नम्) of Brahmā. अपरवक्त्र is a metre defined as 'अयुजि ननरला गुरुः समे तदपर-

वक्त्रमिदं नजौ जरौ' (in the first and third pādas there are eleven letters *i. e.* two तगण, a रगण, one लघु letter and one गुरु letter and in the 2nd and 4th पाद्s there are twelve letters, the गणs being न, ज, ज, र). An आख्यायिका must contain verses in the वक्त्र and अपरवक्त्र metres. Vide Intro. XX. तर...त्सुकाम् why do you make thy anxious eye tremulous? अक...लालिते (vocative) you that are fondled by dwelling with Brahmā whose mind is pure (with सरस्वती); that are fondled by dwelling in the pure मानस lake (with कलहंसी). अकलुषं मानसं यस्य स ०मानसः ब्रह्मा तेन वासः &c. अकलुषं मानसं (सरः) तस्मिन् वासः &c. अवतर वापिकाम् descend into the well (with कलहंसी). The word वापिका suggests the world of mortals where we have to reap as we sow (वप्). The कलहंसी finds it hard to descend into a pond after being long familiar with the pure मानस lake; so सरस्वती found it hard to descend to earth after enjoying the pure atmosphere of Heaven. पङ्कजालयम् the abode of lotuses *i. e.* the lake (with ०हंसी); Brahmā (with सरस्वती). पङ्कजं आलयः यस्य. Brahmā sprang from a lotus. अह...युक्ता it was as if I that was asked by him (or censured by him). कृतः महीतलावतरणस्य सङ्कल्पः (resolve) यया. वियोगेन विक्लवम् (distressed). परित्यज्य—the object is ०परिजनम्. ज्ञाति...गणय्य not minding her kindred. अवगणा (*adj.* of सरस्वती) separated from her companions (अवयुक्ता गणात्). कथमपि with great difficulty. अनुनयेन निवर्तितः अनुयायिव्रतिव्रातः यया—who sent back with courteous words the crowd of devotees that followed her.

P. 7 l. 28—**P. 8** l. 30 **ततः क्रमेण...वाहयत्.** The first sentence is ततः क्रमेण...मन्दाकिनीमनुसरन्ती मर्त्यलोकमवततार (P. 8 l. 12). ध्रुव...धराम्—this and the following clauses qualify मन्दाकिनीम् below. ध्रुवप्रवृत्ताम् (1) that springs from Vishṇu or that flows from the firmament or from the ध्रुव constellation; that starts from a post. The Ganges is said to have sprung from the toe of Vishṇu. See 'श्वेतगङ्गावर्तपाण्डुरं पदमिव त्रिविक्रमस्य' हर्ष० 7th उच्छ्वास. Compare 'वामपादाम्बुजाङ्गुष्ठे नखस्रोतोविनिर्गता । विष्णोर्बिभर्ति यां भक्त्या शिरसाहर्निशं ध्रुवः ॥' विष्णुपु० II. 8. 10; see also मार्कण्डेयपु० 56. 1. ध्रुव is a name of विष्णु. Vide विष्णुसहस्रनाम in अनुशासनपर्व 149. 'स्थविष्ठः स्थविरो ध्रुवः' verse 19. विष्णु's third step is ध्रुव (constellation) and as the Ganges springs from the foot of विष्णु, it may be said to be ध्रुवप्रवृत्त. 'ऊर्ध्वोत्तरमृषिभ्यस्तु ध्रुवो यत्र व्यवस्थितः । एतद्विष्णुपदं दिव्यं तृतीयं व्योम्नि भास्वरम् ॥' विष्णुपुराण 2. 8. 99. आकाश is ध्रुव (*i. e.* नित्य) according to the नैयायिकs. A cow also starts from a post (ध्रुवः) to which it is tied. 'स्थाणुर्वा ना ध्रुवः शङ्कुः' इत्यमरः. अधो धावमानाः

धवलाः पयोधराः (मेघाः यस्याः) the clouds from which (celestial Ganges) are white and stream downwards (towards the earth). The water of the Ganges being white, the clouds are supposed to be white. अधो...धराम् (with धेनु) the white udders of which stream downwards. The Ganges is called धर्मधेनु because it enables one to secure holiness and merit. उद्धुरः (unchecked, loud) ध्वनिः यस्याः. अन्धकमथनः शिवः तस्य मौलिः (शिरः) तस्मिन् मालती-मालिकाम्. The celestial Ganges fell on the head of शिव in its descent to the earth to purify the sons of सगर reduced to ashes by Kapila. Both the Ganges and a wreath of Mālatī are white. The demon अन्धक was slain by S'iva when the former attempted to carry off पारिजात from heaven. See रामायण III. 30. 27 'रुद्रेणेव विनिर्दग्धः श्वेतारण्ये यथान्धकः.' आलीयमानैः वालखिल्यैः रुद्धं रोधः यस्याः the banks of which were covered (or obstructed) by the वालखिल्यs that settled down upon it. The वालखिल्यs were 60000 diminutive sages born of the प्रजापति क्रतु and his wife सन्नति as large as a man's thumb. 'षष्टियानि सहस्राणि मुनीनामूर्ध्वरेतसाम् । अङ्गुष्ठपर्वमात्राणां ज्वलद्भास्करतेजसाम् ॥' विष्णुपुराण I. 10. 12. Vide मार्कण्डेयपुराण 52. 24-25. Compare 'अनेकशो वालखिल्यकदम्बककृतसन्ध्योपासनं (सरः)' कादम्बरी p. 123 (of P.). अरुन्धत्या धौता तारवी (तरोः इयं) त्वक् यस्याम्. तारवत्वक् bark of a tree (used as a garment). अरुन्धती, the wife of वसिष्ठ, is a type of holiness and conjugal fidelity. Note the high praise of her in the उत्तररामचरित IV. 10. 'यया पूतंमन्यो निधिरपि पवित्रस्य महसः &c'. Read त्वङ्गत्तुङ्ग for त्वङ्गत्तङ्ग. त्वङ्गन्तः तुङ्गाः तरङ्गाः तेषु तरन्तः तरलतराः ताराः तारकाः यस्याम्—that had the tremulous bright (तार) stars crossing over high surging (त्वङ्गत्) waves. It should be remembered that it is the celestial Ganges that is being described. तापसैः विकीर्णं (scattered) विरलं तिलोदकं तेन पुलकितानि (bristling) पुलिनानि यस्याः. तिलाश्च उदकं च तिलोदकं तेषां समाहारः (समाहारद्वन्द्व). पुलकित—from पुलक (=रोमाञ्च) with the affix इत according to 'तदस्य सञ्जातं तारकादिभ्य इतच्' पा. 5. 2. 36. Sesame and water were offered to the dead. वितीर्ण (given) is also a good reading. Note मनुस्मृति III 207 and 210. 'अवकाशेषु चोक्षेषु **नदीतीरेषु** चैव हि । विविक्तेषु च तुष्यन्ति दत्तेन **पितरः** सदा ॥ तेषा**मुदक**मानीय सपवित्रांस्तिलानपि । अग्नौ कुर्यादनुज्ञातो ब्राह्मणो ब्राह्मणैः सह ॥'. आप्लवनेन (स्नानेन) पूतः पितामहः (ब्रह्मा) तेन पातिताः पितृपिण्डाः (पितृभ्यो दत्ताः पिण्डाः) तैः पाण्डुरितः पारः यस्याः. पितृ here must be taken in the sense of 'a particular class of divine beings' and not in the sense of 'father' or 'dead ancestors'. There is some incongruity in ascribing to Brahmā human actions such as पितृपिण्डदान. The balls of rice are white and hence the word पाण्डुरित is used. 'अक्रोधनाः शौचपराः सततं ब्रह्मचारिणः । न्यस्तशस्त्रा महाभागाः पितरः **पूर्वदेवताः** ॥' मनु० III. 192. See the following verses for various classes of Pitṛis. पर्यन्ते सुप्ताः सप्तर्षयः तेषां कुशशयनेन सूचितः सूर्यग्रहसूतके उपवासः यस्याम्—on which the fast due to the impurity (सूतकं) caused by a solar eclipse was indicated by the Kus'a bed of the seven sages sleeping nearby. An eclipse causes impurity and people observe a fast before it and on the day of eclipse. Compare धर्मसिन्धु (परिच्छेद I) 'त्रिरात्रमेकरात्रं वा समुपोष्य ग्रहणे स्नानदानाद्यनुष्ठाने महाफलम्, एकरात्रपक्षे ग्रहणदिनात्पूर्वदिने उपवास इति केचित् ग्रहणसम्बन्धाहोरात्र उपवास इत्यपरे'. So निर्णयसिन्धु (परिच्छेद I) says 'सर्वेषामेव वर्णानां **सूतकं** राहुदर्शने । स्नात्वा कर्माणि कुर्वीत शृतमन्नं विवर्जयेदिति हेमाद्रौ षट्त्रिंशन्मतात्'. A person in impurity was to sleep on a spare bed of mats, grass &c. Note धर्मसिन्धु (परिच्छेद III) 'तृणकटास्तीर्णभूमौ पृथक्शयीरन्कम्बलाद्यास्तीर्णभूमौ.' आचमनेन शुचिः शचीपतिः (इन्द्रः) तेन मुच्यमानः अर्चनकुसुमानां निकरः (समूहः) तेन शाराम्. The flowers being of various colours, the river looked variegated. The voluptuous Indra did not care to bathe, as Brahmā did. शिवपुरात् आपतितं निर्माल्यमन्दारदाम यस्याम् in which was dropped from the city of S'iva a garland of मन्दार flowers that had been already offered in worship. For क, see above p. 12. निर्माल्यं remains of flowers and other things offered to deities, flowers that are used and cast off. मन्दार is one of the five trees of Paradise. 'पञ्चैते देवतरवो **मन्दारः** पारिजातकः । सन्तानः कल्पवृक्षश्च पुंसि वा हरिचन्दनम् ॥' इत्यमरः. अना...दृषदम् that cleft with ease the stones in the caves of Mandara. The celestial Ganges had such a powerful stream that it cleft stones. मन्दर is a mountain to the east of Meru. Compare मार्क० 56. 3-5 'मेरुकूटतटान्तेभ्यो निपतन्ती विवर्तिता ॥ विकीर्यमाणसलिला निरालम्बा पपात सा । **मन्दराद्येषु पादेषु** प्रविभक्तोदका समम् ॥ चतुर्ष्वपि **पपाताम्बुविभिन्नाद्रिशिलोच्चया** ॥.' अनेकनाकनायकानां निकायाः तेषां कामिन्यः तासां कुचकलशैः विलुलितः विग्रहः (शरीरं) यस्याः which was tremulous with the jar-like bosoms of the beautiful wives of the hosts (निकायः) of the chief leaders of heaven. The beauties bathed in the Ganges and caused ripples. ग्राहाणां ग्राव्णां च ग्रामः (समूहः) तस्मिन् स्खलनं तेन मुखरितं स्रोतः यस्याः the stream of which resounded as it stumbled over numerous crocodiles and stones. सुषुम्णास्रुता शशिनः सुधा तस्याः शीकराणां स्तबकेन तारकितं तीरं यस्याः—the banks of which were spotted with clusters of the spray of the nectar of the moon flowing from the सुषुम्णा ray. It was believed that the waxing of the moon was due to a ray of the sun called सुषुम्ण. We should read सुषुम्ण०,

as the quotations below require. 'सूर्यरश्मिः सुषुम्नो यस्तर्पितस्तेन चन्द्रमाः । कृष्णपक्षेऽमरैः शश्वत्पीयते वै सुधामयः ॥' विष्णुपु० II. 11. 22. यास्क has an interesting note on this ray "अथाप्यस्यैको रश्मिश्चन्द्रमसं प्रति दीप्यते तदेतेनोपेक्षितव्यमादित्यतोऽस्य दीप्तिर्भवतीति । 'सुषुम्णः सूर्यरश्मिश्चन्द्रमा गन्धर्वः' इत्यपि निगमो भवति ।" (निरुक्त II. 2. 2.). बाण frequently refers to सुषुम्ण 'कन्यया एकया च चन्द्रमूर्त्येव सुषुम्णरश्मिनिर्गतयानुगम्यमानौ' हर्ष० 4th उच्छ्वास; 'अलीकं चेदं यथा किल सकलाः कलाः कलावतो बहुलपक्षे क्षीयमाणस्य सुषुम्णनाम्ना रश्मिना रविरापिबतीति' कादम्बरी p. 141 of P. धिषणस्य (बृहस्पतेः) अग्निकार्य (offering oblations to fire) तस्य धूमः तेन धूसरितं सैकतं यस्याः. सैकत *adj.* 'sandy,' according to 'सिकताशर्कराभ्यां च' पा. 5. 2. 104 (सैकतो घटः). But in the sense of 'a sandy tract,' we have सिकता, सिकतिल, सैकत and सिकतावत् 'देशे लुबिलचौ च' पा. 5. 2. 105 (चात् अण् मतुप् च। सिकताः सन्त्यस्मिन् देशे इति सिकताः सिकतिलः &c.). सिद्ध...धराम् where the विद्याधरs ran away in fear (त्रासः) of crossing over (or treading upon) the sandy *lingas* made by *Siddhas*. To cross over or tread upon a sacred object is sinful. विद्याधरs were afraid of unwarily crossing over the लिङ्गs and thus incurring sin and the wrath of शिव. निर्मो...रगस्य as though it (Ganges) were the cast-off slough of the sky serpent. It is the celestial Ganges that is described; hence the word गगनोरगस्य (गगनमेव उरगः). Both the slough and the Ganges are white. गगन which is blue resembles a dark serpent. त्रिविष्टपः (सुरलोकः) एव विटः. ललाटिका a mark of sandal or other fragrant powder on the forehead. 'कर्णललाटात्कनलङ्कारे' पा. 4. 3. 65. Both the Ganges and sandal are white. A विट is a voluptury, a companion of a prince or dissolute young man in dramas. He decks himself with sandal marks on the forehead. विक्रय...पण्यस्य as if it (Ganges) were a stall for the sale of the merchandise of merit. पुण्यमेव पण्यं तस्य. As wares are exhibited in a row of shops, so the Ganges flowed, on both banks of which पुण्य could be acquired. दन्ता...द्वारस्य the ivory bolt against the gate of the city of Hell. The current of the white Ganges looked like an ivory bolt. The Ganges prevents people from falling into Hell for their sins, just as a bolt fastening the gate prevents entrance into a city. All the clauses indicate either the whiteness or holiness of the Ganges. अंशु...नृपस्य as if it were the silken turban fold of the king—Meru. 'मेरुः सुमेरुर्हेमाद्री रत्नसानुः सुरालयः' इत्यमरः. सुमेरुः एव नृपः तस्य. The celestial Ganges flows from the slopes of Meru. See above p. 43. A king's head may be wrapped in a white silken turban. सुमेरुनृप may also mean 'the lord of Meru *i. e.* S'iva.' The Ganges is placed on the head of S'iva and looks like a white turban fold. दुकूल...कुञ्जरस्य as if it were the fine-textured banner (कदलिका) of the elephant—the Kailāsa range. पद्धति...वर्गस्य as if it were the beaten road to *Moksha*. नेमि...चक्रस्य as if it were the ring of the wheel of the Kṛita age. कृतयुगमेव चक्रं तस्य. A wheel has a rim (which is its centre). The Ganges is the centre of कृतयुग (*i. e.* of holiness and righteousness). The कृतयुग is an era of unmixed holiness and righteousness. 'चतुष्पात्सकलो धर्मः सत्यं चैव कृते युगे । नाधर्मेणागमः कश्चिन्मनुष्यान्प्रति वर्तते ॥' मनु० I. 81. सप्त...महिषीं the queen of the lord of seven oceans *i. e.* of क्षीरसमुद्र. All rivers are poetically represented as the wives of the ocean. क्षीरसागर being the last and best of the seven may be called the king of oceans. For the seven oceans, see above p. 32. The com. says 'सप्तसागरराजः क्षीरसमुद्रः । चन्द्राख्यपर्वत इति केचित्'. अपश्यत्—the object is महानदम् (l. 16). हारमिव—this and the following clauses are intended to convey the crystal-like pellucid waters of the शोण. वरुण is the lord of the ocean, in which pearls are found. चन्द्रः एव अचलः (पर्वतः). The moon is supposed to be full of अमृत. From a mountain springs (निर्झरः) proceed. शशिमणि = चन्द्रकान्तमणि. विन्ध्यस्य—the शोण springs in the Vindhya range. कर्पूर...रण्यस्य as if it were a flood of the sap of camphor trees from the Daṇḍakā forest. Camphor is white. This clause shows that the शोण flowed through the दण्डका forest. The precise extent of the दण्डकारण्य is far from certain. It seems to have been a general name comprising all forests from the Jumna to the Krishṇā. गुह who helped भरत to cross the Ganges is described as well-acquainted with दण्डकारण्य. So it seems that दण्डकारण्य stretched right up to the Ganges. 'एष ज्ञातिसहस्रेण स्थपतिः परिवारितः । कुशलो दण्डकारण्ये वृद्धो भ्रातुश्च ते सखा ॥ तस्मात्पश्यतु काकुत्स्थ त्वां निषादाधिपो गुहः ।' अयोध्याकाण्ड 84. 12-13. हेमाद्रि in his व्रतखण्ड says that देवगिरि (modern Daulatabad) was in सेउणदेश which was on the confines of दण्डकारण्य (*Vide* Bombay Gazetteer part II p. 231). लावण्यं bright complexion. स्फाटिक...श्रियाः as if it were the crystal couch of the Beauty of the sky. A beauty reclines on a couch white like crystal. The sky was reflected in the pellucid waters of the शोण. रामणीयकेन (loveliness) हृतं हृदयं यस्याः. मधुराः मयूराणां विरुतयः (केकाः) यासु (*adj.* of ०भूमयः, l. 20). ०पटलेन सिकतिलानि (sandy) तरुतलानि यासु. For सिकतिल, see सैकत above p. 44. परिमलेन मत्तानां मधुपानां वेणी (string, line) एव वीणा तस्याः रणितेन रमणीयाः. The humming of the rows of bees was like the music of a lute. मन्दीकृता मन्दाकिनीद्युतिः येन that obscured the lustre of the Ganges. उपकण्ठभूमयः places in the neighbourhood. पक्ष...मे my heart has taken a liking to stay here. अभिनन्दितं (approved) वचनं यस्याः (*adj.* of सरस्वती). तथेति is to be connected with अभिनन्दित. सावित्री approved of सरस्वती's choice. तया = सावित्र्या (सह). ०मण्डपे...बबन्ध she fixed upon a bower as her house. उच्चितानि (gathered) अर्चनाय कुसुमानि यया. पुलिनपृष्ठे प्रतिष्ठापितं सैकतं शिवलिङ्गं यया. पञ्चब्रह्माणि पुरःसराणि यस्याः (*adj.* of पुष्पिकाम्) that was preceded by the पञ्चब्रह्म prayer. This is a prayer recited by the Brahmaṇas at the time of smearing the body with sacred ashes. The prayer is addressed to सद्योजात, वामदेव, तत्पुरुष, अघोर and ईशान. See ऋग्वेदिब्रह्मकर्म (भस्मधारणविधि). Compare शिवस्तुति 3rd verse '**महेश** महितोसि **तत्पुरुष** पूरुषाग्र्यो भवान**घोर** रिपुघोर तेऽनवम **वामदेवा**ञ्जलिः। नमः **सपदिजात** ते त्वमिति **पञ्चरूपो**चित प्रपञ्चचयपञ्चवृन्मम मनस्तमस्ताडय॥'. सम्यङ् मुद्राबन्धः तेन विहितः परिकरः यस्याः (*adj.* of ०पुष्पिकाम्) which was preceded by the ceremony of properly intertwining the fingers and hands in worship. परिकरः 'beginning'. On मुद्राबन्ध note 'मुद्राविमुक्तहस्तेन क्रियते कर्म दैविकम्। यदि तन्निष्फलं तस्मात्कर्म मुद्रान्वितश्चरेत्॥'. ध्रुवा गीतिः गर्भे यस्याः (*adj.* of ०पुष्पिकाम्) between the intervals of which she sang the ध्रुवा song. 'गीतिस्रुग्भेदयोर्ध्रुवा' शाश्वतः 4. The song was probably in the ध्रुवताल. अवनि...ध्यायन्ती contemplating all the eight forms *viz.* the earth, the wind, water (वनं), the sky, the fire, the sun (तपनः), the moon and the sacrificer. These are said to be the eight forms of शिव. Vide the first verse of the शाकुन्तल. अष्टपुष्पिका a bunch of eight flowers (with referene to the eight forms). Compare कादम्बरी 'अतिरोषणतया कदाचिद्दुर्न्यस्ताष्टपुष्पिकापातोत्पादितक्रोधेन' p. 227 of P. The commentators on the कादम्बरी say 'बकं द्रोणं च दुर्धूरं सुमना पाटला तथा। पद्ममुत्पलगोसूर्यमष्टौ पुष्पाणि शङ्करे॥'. सं० also explains that अष्टपुष्पिका refers to the eight acts of worship each of which may be metaphorically called पुष्प. They are:—पार्थिवपुष्प *i. e.* smearing the deity with some fragrant substance, because गन्ध is the special quality of पृथ्वी; आप्यपुष्प *i.e.* bathing with water or milk, as रस is the special quality of अप्; तैजस० *i. e.* waving lights; वायवीय *i. e.* applying cooling unguents, as स्पर्श is the special quality of वायु; आकाशीय *i. e.* playing on musical instruments and singing, as शब्द is the special गुण of आकाश; मानस *i. e.* contemplation of the god S'iva; बौद्ध *i. e.* a firm idea that S'iva is all pervading, as the विषय of बुद्धि is निश्चय; आहङ्कारिक *i. e.* the knowledge of the non-difference of the soul from the Supreme, expressed by the Upanishads in the words

'अहं ब्रह्मास्मि'. अय...तेन that was obtained without effort. अमृत... स्वादिम्ना that tended (*lit.* desired) to surpass even nectar by its sweetness. अति...माणेन *pr. p.* of the desiderative base of शी with अति. स्वादिम्ना *Instru. sing.* of स्वादिमन् which is formed like पिङ्गलिमन् (notes p. 23). शरीर...रोत् she sustained her body. अतिवाहितः (passed) दिवसः यया. कल्पितं पल्लवानां शयनं यया.

P. 8 l. 31—**P. 9** l. 12 **एव...सन्ददर्श**. याम ... रवौ when the sun had gone up (in the sky) only for one watch. यामः means a period of three hours. 'द्वौ यामप्रहरौ समौ' इत्यमरः. ककुभि = दिशि. प्रतिशब्दैः (by the echoes) पूरितं वनगह्वरं (वनगुहा) येन. तुरङ्ग... ह्रादम् the sound (ह्रादः) of the neighing of horses. विकच...सङ्घातं mass of dust grey like the inner leaves of the blossoming Ketakî. नातिदवीयसि (*loc. sing.* of दवीयस् which is the comparative form of दूर) not very far from her. क्रमेण च—the principal sentence is क्रमेण च...पदातिबलेन सनाथमश्ववृन्दं सन्ददर्श. सामीप्येन उपजायमाना अभिव्यक्तिः यस्य that became distinctly visible the nearer it came. This qualifies अश्ववृन्दम्. शफरो...प्लवमानं floating in the dust grey like the belly of a fish, as though it were a school of crocodiles floating in water. शफ...सरे (with पयसि) means 'grey with the bellies of fishes'. प्लवमानं goes with ०वृन्दं below. पुरः प्रधावमानेन—this and the following clauses in the instrumental qualify ०बलेन below. प्रलम्बैः कुटिलैः कचपल्लवैः घटितं ललाटे जूटकं येन that had on their foreheads a mass of long curling hair. सं० says 'घटितललाटजूटा दाक्षिणात्येषु वेशः.' धवल...भित्तिना whose ample cheeks were smiling (*i. e.* bright) with the lustre of the white ear-ornaments (दन्तपत्रिका). पिनद्धाः कृष्णागुरुपङ्ककल्कस्य च्छुरणेन कृष्णशबलकषायाः कञ्चुकाः येन that had girt themselves in jackets dark, variegated and fragrant (कषाय) by being smeared with the paste (कल्कः-म्) of black aloe-wood. पिनद्ध is *past p. p.* of नह् with अपि, अ being elided in accordance with 'वष्टि भागुरिरल्लोपमवाप्योरुपसर्गयोः'. उत्तरीयेण कृतं शिरोवेष्टनं यस्य that had made their upper garments into turbans. वाम...कटकेन that had bright (स्पष्ट) golden bracelets (कटकः-कम्) placed on their left fore-arms (प्रकोष्ठः). Even now rich men sometimes wear golden bracelets on their left forearms. द्वि...धेनुना whose daggers (असिधेनुः) were fastened in firm knots of their sashes (पट्टिका) of double folded cloth. 'छुरिका चासिधेनुका' इत्यमरः. The daggers were fixed fast by having their handles wrapped in bandages of fine cloth which were doubled. अनवरतः व्यायामः (physical exercise) तेन कृशं कर्कशं (hard) शरीरं यस्य. वात...मानेन that leapt high again and again as if they were a herd of swift deer. वातहरिण is a very swift deer (called also वातप्रमी). लङ्घित...विटपेन that jumped over even and uneven ground, pits (अवटः) and bushes (विटपः). कोणः a stick, club. सेवायै (for worship) गृहीतानि विविधानि वन...पर्णानि येन. अनवरतं कृतः कलकलः येन. युवप्रायेण consisting mostly of young men. सनाथम् accompanied by.

P. 9 l. 13—**P. 10** l. 33 **मध्ये च...पुरुषम्.** The sentence is मध्ये च तस्य (अश्ववृन्दस्य) अष्टादशवर्षदेशीयं युवानमद्राक्षीत् (p. 10 l. 27). ०चन्द्रेण, ०मालिना, ०खचितेन and ०पाण्डुरेण qualify both क्षीरोदेन and आतपत्रेण. सार्धचन्द्रेण—the umbrella had the figure of a crescent-shaped moon on it; the sea is सार्धचन्द्र, as the moon sprang from it at the time of the churning. मुक्ता...मालिना that (umbrella) was encircled by a heap of pearls. अर्धचन्द्र also means 'the semi-circular marks on a peacock's tail.' The umbrella might have such marks by way of ornament. The sea also has in it heaps of pearls. रत्न...खचितेन—the umbrella was inlaid with precious stones; the sea also is called रत्नाकर. शङ्ख...पाण्डुरेण white like a conch, milk and foam (with umbrella); white with conches, milk and foam (with क्षीरोदेन). क्षीरोदेनेव—The umbrella being सार्धचन्द्र, मुक्ता...मालिन् &c., the poet fancies it to be क्षीरसागर. स्वयं...तेन—the umbrella lent a charm (लक्ष्मी) to the youth over whom it was held. The force of स्वयं in the case of क्षीरोद is this:—when the three worlds became devoid of श्री by the curse of दुर्वासस् pronounced against Indra, the gods had to churn the ocean to find out the jewels including लक्ष्मी. The ocean did not of his own accord yield up लक्ष्मी. But the umbrella fancied to be क्षीरोद lent a लक्ष्मी (charm) to the young man without the latter making any effort to acquire it. गगनगतेन raised high in the air. आतपत्रेण—an umbrella is among the insignia of royalty. कृता छाया यस्य. कृतच्छायम्—this and the following clauses in the accusative qualify युवानं below (p. 10 l. 27). अच्छाच्छेन...गम्यमानम्—the idea is:—the youth was surrounded by a bright circle of the rays of the brilliant ornaments he wore. The poet fancies that it was a ring (चक्रवालं) of the quarters that stuck very close round him, because the quarters were very fond of seeing him (who was so young and handsome). Ordinarily चक्रवाल (horizon) is far from a person. आनितम्ब...राजमानम् who was decked with a wreath of Mālatī flowers on his head that hung down to his hips, as if it (wreath) were the banner of his beauty won by the conquest of the whole world. He surpassed by his beauty everyone in the world. A conqueror triumphantly carries away the banner from his vanquished rivals. The long wreath looked like a waving pennon. उत्सर्पिभिः...वपुषम् whose body rendered dirty by the dust on the road was being rubbed by the red up-shooting (उत्सर्पिभिः) rays of the ruby in his crest, as if with tender leaves held by invisible nymphs of the forest. 'शिखण्डखण्डिका चूडाभरणम्' com. The red rays resemble slender and reddish fresh leaves. प्रमृज्यमानं मार्गरेणुना परुषं वपुः यस्य. Dust may be rubbed off with पल्लवs. The reading रूषित would mean 'covered or soiled'. बकुल...दिवसम् with his head lovely by being decked with a wreath (मुण्डमाला) of Bakula buds and having a profusion of curling hair, he seemed as though drinking the day, the light of which was contracted. मीलितः आतपः यस्य (*adj.* of दिवसम्). The brilliance of the day is lessened by the approach of night. The white Bakula is like the light of day and his dark hair in contact with the white Bakula buds is like night. With his dark hair he as though lessened the light of day, which remained only in a scattered form in the shape of Bakula buds. पशु रिक्षम् with the brilliance, yellowish red like arsenic paste, of his broad forehead that was possessed of natural (सहज) loveliness (लक्ष्मी), he as though smeared the sky as if it (the forehead) were composed of the second portion of the moon that is the crown of the matted hair of S'iva. He had a bright and naturally lovely forehead. It was bright like the moon and so the poet fancies that it was made of the moon. The propriety of द्वितीय॰ is this:—शिव placed the crescent of the moon on his head. So if his ललाट was made of the moon, it could not have been that (part of the) moon that was placed by शिव on his head and so the forehead must have been made of the remaining portion of the moon (the second piece). The forehead being thus fancied to be मृगाङ्कघटित, it would be naturally embraced by लक्ष्मी that was born of the ocean along with the moon (सहज). For the churning of the ocean, see विष्णुपुराण I. 9 and रामायण I. 44. अभिनवं यौवनं तस्य आरम्भेण अवष्टम्भः (pride) तेन प्रगल्भाः दृष्टिपाताः तैः तृणीकृतं त्रिभुवनं येन. He was proud and his eye seemed to look upon the world as of no account. Compare 'दृष्टिस्तृणीकृतजगत्त्रयसत्त्वसारा' उत्तररामचरित VI. 19. प्रथिम्ना (instru. sing. of प्रथिमन् from पृथु)—vide notes on पिङ्गलिमा p. 23. ॰सहस्रैः सञ्छादिताः दश दिशः यया (*adj.* of शरदम्). In शरद् lotuses of various sorts abound. कुमुद is a white lotus, while कुवलय is dark and कमल is red. When he cast glances from his large eyes, the white of his eyes looked like कुमुदs and the dark pupils like कुवलयs and the red corners looked like कमलs. शर...तैयन्तम् who as though caused the season of autumn. आयत...शोभमानम्—the idea is:—his long nose is deemed to be a dam (सेतुबन्धः) over the borders (सीमान्त) of the two rivers *viz.*, the two eyes. His nose separated the two eyes, as a dam would separate a river in two. Further the nose is fancied to be a stream of the water of beauty dropping from the slab of moonstone in the form of the forehead. His bright forehead resembled चन्द्रकान्त, from which water oozes when the moon rises. The nose also rises up after there is a depression from the forehead. His nose was charming and so is fancied to be the stream of the water of loveliness. अति...वमन्तम् with his mouth emitting the perfume of very fragrant mango, camphor, *kakkola*, cloves and Pârijātaka and resounding with the hum of the swarms of intoxicated bees, he vomited as if the season of spring together with the Nandana garden. Even now camphor, कक्कोल (Marathi कंकोळ) and cloves are taken with ताम्बूल. सहकार and पारिजातक are explained by the com. as certain fragrant substances, 'सहकारः सुगन्धद्रव्यभेदः सहकारफलेनैव क्रियते पारिजातकोऽनेकद्रव्यसंस्कृतो मुखवासविशेषः'. The youth had partaken of कर्पूर, कक्कोल &c. with his ताम्बूल and emitted their fragrance with his breath. In वसन्त also, there is the fragrance of mango blossoms and of other flowers and the humming of bees. नन्दन is the garden of Indra. पारिजातक is one of the five trees of Paradise. *Vide* notes p. 43. Hence the poet says 'सनन्दनवनं'. The reading अवतारयन्तम् is more striking than वमन्तम्, but is probably an emendation. It means 'he made वसन्त descend to the earth together with नन्दनवन'. The critics had laid down that the use of words like वान्त (*past p. p.* of वम्) and उद्गीर्ण in their literal sense was against good taste (ग्राम्य) and so the copyists thinking that the word वमन्तं was so used here probably changed it to अवतारयन्तम्. But it is to be noted that Bāna uses it only in a figurative sense. 'निष्ठ्यूतोद्गीर्णवान्तादि गौणवृत्तिव्यपाश्रयम् । अतिसुन्दरमन्यत्र ग्राम्यकक्षां विगाहते ॥' काव्या० I. 95. आसन्नाः सुहृदः तेषां परिहासाः (jests) तेषां भावनया (appreciation, understanding) उत्तानितं मुखं तस्य मुग्धैः हसितैः. दशनज्योत्स्नया स्नपितानि दिङ्मुखानि यैः that bathed the quarters in the moonlight of his teeth. Whenever he smiled at the jests of his friends, his bright teeth gleamed forth and cast their lustre all round. That lustre resembled moonlight. पुनः पुनः...कल्पयन्तम् who again and again created the light of the moon moving about in the sky. As he smiled now and then (and not continuously), he seemed to create moonlight at different times and so the poet uses the word पुनःपुनः. There is a pun on the word नभसि (in the sky; in the month of श्रावण). In श्रावण, the moon is seen now and then on account of the clouds and not continuously (just like his bright smiles). कदम्बमुकुलवत् स्थूलं मुक्ताफलयुगलं तस्य मध्ये अध्यासितं (placed) मरकतं यस्मिन् (*adj.* of ०भरणस्य). त्रि... भरणस्य three-pointed ear-ornament. His ear-ornament was made of two big pearls between which was inserted an emerald. This ornament seems to be somewhat like the भिकबाळी worn by men in Mahārāshṭra. त्रिकण्टक 'त्रिकण्टकस्तु त्र्यश्रः स्यात्त्रिभी रत्नैश्च भूषणम्'. Compare 'काश्चिदुद्धूयमानधवलचामरसटालग्नत्रिकण्टकवलितविकटकटाक्षाः' हर्ष० 4th उच्छ्वास. प्रेङ्खतः (*adj.* of ०भरणस्य) dangling. प्रभया... लक्ष्यमाणम् by the up-spreading lustre (of the ear-ornament) it seemed as though he had an ear-ornament made of green *Kunda* leaves together with their flowers. *Kunda* flowers, being white, are like pearls and the leaves are green like emerald. कृतः सकुसुमेन हरितकुन्दपल्लवेन कर्णावतंसः यस्य. आमोदितः (आमोदः सञ्जातः अस्य) मृगमदपङ्कः तेन लिखितः पत्रभङ्गः तेन भास्वरम् adorned with ornamental lines drawn with very fragrant musk paste. 'मृगनाभिर्मृगमदः कस्तूरी च' इत्यमरः. For पत्रभङ्ग see notes p. 24. भुजयुगलम्—object of दधानम्. उद्दाम...दधानम् possessing (arms) that seemed to be the two poles of the banner of Cupid (मकरकेतुः), that (poles) had on their tops (the figure of) a formidable crocodile. उद्दामेन मकरेण आक्रान्तं शिखरं यस्य. This may apply to भुजयुगलं also, meaning '(arms) the tops of which had on them a loose (or formidable) crocodile-shaped ornament'. Long arms are a sign of good fortune and high position. As he was handsome like Cupid and had long arms, they (arms) are said to be poles. The marks of the black musk on the arms looked like the dark crocodile, which is the emblem on the banner of Cupid. सीमन्तितं parted (*adj.* of देहम्). सीमन्त is the parting line of the hair of women. It is white. His ब्रह्मसूत्र also was white and was placed across his body like a line. He had a formidable body which was encircled by the white यज्ञोपवीत. The white यज्ञोपवीत is like the fair Ganges. So the poet fancies that his body was the मन्दर mountain chained (encircled) by the stream of the Ganges indignant at the churning of the ocean. When the ocean was churned for jewels, मन्दर was made the churning handle. The ocean is poetically spoken of as the husband of the Ganges (and also of all other rivers). The Ganges (ब्रह्मसूत्र) was as if angry at the harassment of her husband and bound down मन्दर (his body) in order to stay the churning. **'मन्थानं मन्दरं** कृत्वा नेत्रं कृत्वा तु वासुकिम् । मथ्यताममृतं देवाः साहाय्ये मय्यवस्थिते ॥' विष्णुपु० I. 9. 76. 'बद्धे सन्दानितम्' इत्यमरः. कर्पूर... पांशुलेन rendered dusty, being smeared with a handful of camphor powder (क्षोदः). कान्तायाः उच्चौ कुचौ एव चक्रवाकौ तयोः युगलं तस्य विपुलं पुलिनं तेन. His broad chest was like a vast sandy beach for the चक्रवाकs—*viz.*, the high breasts of his (future) wife. His wife would rest on his broad chest, as the चक्रवाक does on a पुलिन. A beach also is dusty (पांशुल) with white sand (resembling camphor). उरःस्थलेन...क्रम्—the idea is:—He had a very broad chest and stout long arms. The poet fancies that by his long arms he embraced the distant quarters and brought them together in a heap (पुञ्जित). The heaped up quarters were allowed expansion on his broad chest. आयामः length. पुरस्ता...भागम्—the author describes here the under-garment (something like modern मांडचोळणा) of the youth. पुरस्ता...कमनीयेन that was charming because one end (कोणः) of it was set in front a little below his navel. पृष्ठत...पल्लवेन the hem of which hung behind over his girdle (कक्ष्या). पल्लव (Marathi गोंडा) the hem of the strings with which the garment was made fast. उभय...भागेन that was so wound on both sides as to display a third part of his thighs. हारीत...वाससा by his lower garment that was green like the हारीत (pigeon) bird and that tightly (निबिड) pressed (his waist). विभ...भागम् whose very slender waist was divided (from the upper part of his body). अनवरतव्यायामेन उपचितमांसे कठिने विकटे मकरमुखसंलग्ने जानुनी ययोः *(adj.* of ऊरुदण्डाभ्याम्) the knees of which had flesh accumulated by incessant exercise, were hard, formidable and firmly knit to the parts above them. 'मकरमुखं जानुनोरुपरिभागः' सं०. We may also explain मकरमुखसंलग्न as 'knees that had a crocodile shape and that were thick-set (and not loose or flabby)'. विशाल... स्तम्भाभ्याम् (thighs) that were stone pillars for supporting (उत्तम्भन) the stone platform of his broad chest. The image here is taken from architecture. His long and tapering thighs were like stone columns. His broad chest was like the entablature (constituting the architrave, frieze and cornice) resting on slender pillars. चारु...कान्तिभ्याम् the beauty of which was rendered patent by the lovely marks of sandal thereon. Sandal paste had been applied to that part of the thighs that was not covered. स्थासकः perfuming the body with unguents. 'चर्चा तु चार्चिक्यं स्थासकः' इत्यमरः. ऊरु...यामम् with his long thighs, he as if laughed in scorn at the length of the trunk of ऐरावत. The trunk of an elephant is long and tapering downwards like the thigh. ऐरावत is white and the youth's thigh also was besmeared with white sandal paste. अति...काण्डम् his shanks (जङ्घा) were very slender, as though through the fatigue (खेदः) caused by bearing the burden of his very stout (भरित) thighs (ऊरु). One who carries burdens is slim (and not fat). कल्प...पाटलस्य—his feet were red like the fresh shoots of the tree of Paradise. The shoots of a tree are red; much more of a कल्पवृक्ष. उभय...लम्बिनः His feet hung on both sides (of the horse he was riding). दोला...रचयन्तम्—the idea is:—the motion of the horse caused the rays from his toe-nails to move about. The bright rays of the nails resemble a white chowrie. As he was riding the nails appeared to be a chowrie placed on the horse. Chowries were placed on horses and elephants. Compare शाकुन्तल I 'निष्कम्पचामरशिखा निभृतोर्ध्वकर्णाः। ...धावन्त्यमी मृगजवाक्षमयेव रथ्याः॥'. अभि...भुवि that (horse) tore the earth with its hoofs that were raised (उदञ्चत्) aloft in front, that seemed as though to rest long in the air and that fell forcibly on account of their curvetting (वलितं). The high spirited steed pranced, remained standing on its hind legs for a long time as if it wanted to give them rest and then came down on the earth with force with its front legs, thereby raising dust from the earth. वलितेन विकटं यथा स्यात्तथा (अव्ययीभाव)—to be taken with पतद्भिः. ०भुवि and the following locatives qualify वाजिनि (l. 15). प्रतिक्षणं दशनैः (आदौ) ग्रहः (पश्चात्) मुक्तिश्च ताभ्यां खणखणायितं खरं खलीनं (खे तालुनि लीनम्) येन. The hard bridle-bit made a sound when the horse bit it between its teeth and then let it off. The reading दशनविमुक्त conveys almost the same sense. दीर्घघ्राणे लीना लालिका यस्य सः ०लालिकः स चासौ ललाट...चक्रकश्च. ललाटे लुलितानि (tossed, waving) चारूणि चामीकरस्य (सुवर्णस्य) चक्रकाणि (rings) यस्य. लालिका is explained by सं० as 'the end of the bit'. It is better to read with B 'दीर्घ...लालिके ललाट०,' as then it is easier to dissolve the compounds. शिञ्जान...शोभिनि

adorned with tinkling (शिञ्जान) golden trappings. 'तपनीयं शातकौम्भम्' इत्यमरः ('शतकुम्भे गिरौ भवं शातकौम्भम्, अनुशतिकादित्वादुभयपदवृद्धिः, शातकुम्भमित्येके' क्षीर॰). शातकौम्भम् (or—कुम्भम् according to some) gold. 'जयनं हयमण्डनमाला' सं॰. 'अश्वादीनां च सन्नाहे जये च जयनं मतम्' शाश्वत 515. मनसः इव रंहः (वेगः) यस्य. गोलाङ्गूलस्य कपोलवत् कालानि (dark) कायलोमानि यस्य. गोलाङ्गूलः an ape with a dark face and a tail like a cow's. 'कृष्णमुखो गोलाङ्गूलः' क्षीर॰. उभय...हस्ताभ्याम् whose hands gripped the saddle (पर्याणं) cloth on both sides. आसन्नपरिचारकः body-guard. दोधूयमानं (*pr. p.* of the frequentative base of धू to shake) चामरिकायुगलं यस्य. बन्दिनः of the bard. 'बन्दिनः स्तुतिपाठकाः' इत्यमरः. सुभाषितम्—object of भावयन्तम्. उत्कण्टकितः (रोमाञ्चितः) कपोलफलकः यस्य. लग्न...कलेनेव—the idea is:—his cheek had hair standing on end on account of emotion roused by the song of the bard; the poet fancies the रोमाञ्च to be pieces of the fine hairy growth (पक्ष्म) on the filaments (केसरम्) of the lotus on his ear. भावयन्तम् reflecting over, appreciating. अनङ्ग...दर्शयन्तम् who as if showed (in his person) the advent of the *yuga* (the era) of Cupid. He was charming like Cupid. सं॰ says 'अनङ्गजन्मना यदुपलक्षितं युगं कालविशेषः, तस्य नूतनमदनसादृश्यात्, यद्वा अनङ्गयोर्युगं तदवतारमिव । द्वित्वसंख्यापूर्वकत्वात्'. This and the following clauses lay stress on the extreme loveliness of the youth in various ways and the effects he produced on others. चन्द्र...यन्तम् who as though created a world full of moonlight. He was bright like the moon and shed his lustre over the whole world. विलासप्रायम्—his youthful smiles and gestures were to be seen everywhere. अन्यः सर्गः (सृष्टिः) सर्गान्तरम्. अनु...रचयन्तम्—this world is full of love and hatred; but he was the centre of the affection of all; no one hated him. So he brought about another world as it were, where there was nothing but affection. The student will note Bāṇa's command over language. He uses different words like उत्पादयन्तं, जनयन्तं &c., to convey the same sense. शृङ्गारमयम्—full of love. He was the cynosure of all eyes the whole day. राग...यन्तम् inaugurating a reign of affection. आक...चक्षुषोः he was to the eyes as though the infatuating collyrium. It was supposed that some magical collyrium when applied to the eye by a person made that person attractive to every spectator. He by his beauty fascinated the eyes of all. वशी॰—certain incantations were supposed to have the power of subduing the will of others. Note the following मन्त्र credited with great power. 'ॐ

गणपतये स्वाहेति। अयं गणपतेर्मन्त्रो धनविद्याप्रदायकः। इममष्टसहस्रं च जप्त्वा बद्ध्वा शिखां ततः। व्यवहारे जयः स्याच्च शतजाप्यान्नृणां प्रियः॥.' स्वस्था...णाम् he was as though a powder that influences the senses to be comfortable. The idea is:—in his presence, the senses of the spectators were lulled into pleasure. C and T translate to the senses a powder able to affect the healthiest'. This is not so good as the meaning we suggest. अस...कस्य—the curiosity to see him is never satiated. सिद्ध...ग्यस्य he was as though the never-failing remedy of blessedness. The moment he was seen, everyone felt blessed. पुनर्जं०—Cupid was once burnt by S'iva; but on seeing that handsome youth, hearts fell under the sway of Love (*i. e.* love was born again). रसायनमिव यौवनस्य—रसायनम् (रसः mercury + अयनम्) a medical preparation containing mercury. In ancient India, it was believed, as in many other countries, that mercury, if properly prepared, would make men immortal and free from old age. Note the passages 'संसारस्य परं पारं दत्तेऽसौ पारदः स्मृतः'; 'एकोऽसौ रसराजः शरीरमजरामरं कुरुते'. The सर्वदर्शनसंग्रह devotes a chapter to रसेश्वरदर्शन 'the philosophy of Mercury' (रस being identified with शिव). As रसायन produces perfect health, so youth attained perfection in the young man. एक...रामणीयकस्य—रामणीयक shared the youth with nothing else *i. e.* loveliness reigned supreme in him. कीर्ति...रूपस्य.—He was so charming that he seemed to be a pillar set up for all time to commemorate the triumph of beauty. मूल...लावण्यस्य as the principal amount of loveliness. The loveliness in others is like interest *i. e.* it is subsidiary (inferior) to the principal (the youth's charms). पुण्य...संसारस्य—the good deeds of the world bore fruit in the splendid form of the youth. कान्तिः (beauty) एव लता तस्याः प्रथमाङ्कुरम्—none as handsome as the youth had preceded him. सर्गा...पतेः—Brahmā had created the world several times. By practice one acquires great skill and perfection. So the beauty of the youth was the result of the skill acquired by Brahmā. प्रतापः glory, greatness. विभ्रमः amorous or sportive movements. यशः...ग्ध्यस्य—learning had attained the highest pitch of excellence in him. अष्टा...देशीयम् about 18 years old. The affixes कल्प, देश्य and देशीय are added in the sense of 'a little less than, about'. 'ईषदसमाप्तौ कल्पब्देश्यदेशीयरः' पा. 5. 3. 67. (ईषदूनो विद्वान् विद्वत्कल्पः विद्वद्देशीयः। सि. कौ.). द्वितीयम्—This and the following clauses in the accusative qualify पुरुषम् (l. 33). अपर...तुरङ्गम्—न परेण संश्लिष्टः तुरङ्गः यस्य whose horse was not touched by another. This may mean that his saddle was not held by any attendants as that of the youth was or that his horse was not closely followed by another *i. e.* other riders kept at a respectful distance. We prefer the former meaning. From the fact that the young man was cracking jokes with his companions, it seems that they were close to him (and so to the old man also). उत्तप्त...कारम् whose form was like a pillar of heated (molten) gold (तपनीयं) *i. e.* he was bright and red in complexion. परिणतं वयः यस्य—old. नीच...कचम् who had short nails, beard and hair. He did not allow these to grow. शुक्तिखलतिम् bald-headed as a shell. His head had no hair and the skin was white and glossy like mother-o'-pearl. रोमशं उरःस्थलं यस्य. 'लोमादि-पामादि—पिच्छादिभ्यः श-न-इलचः' पा. 5. 2. 100 (लोमादिभ्यः शः। लोमशः। रोमवान्। पामादिभ्यो नः। पामनः। सि. कौ.). र् and ल् are often interchanged as in रोमन् and लोमन्. अनु...शिक्षयन्तम् who, being dressed elegantly but not gaudily, seemed as though to teach even old age decorousness. It is old age that makes men decorous. He was old and such an embodiment of decorum that old age might have taken lessons from him. उल्बण showy, gaudy. गुणा...नयन्तम् who seemed as though lending weight (importance or greatness) even to virtues. He was so virtuous that he seemed to heighten the worth of the virtues themselves. गरिमा—from गुरु. Vide notes on पिङ्गलिमा p. 23. महानुभावता dignity or nobility. He was so noble or dignified that even Dignity may have something to learn from him. आचारः correct deportment. आचार्यकम् teaching, instruction. आचार्यस्य भावः कर्म वा—according to 'योपधाद्गुरूपोत्तमाद्वुञ्' पा. V. 1. 132 (रामणीयकम्। आभिधानीयकम्। सि. कौ.). वारबाणः or-वाणः a coat of mail, jacket. 'कञ्चुको वारवाणोऽस्त्री' इत्यमरः (वारं आच्छादकं वानमस्य इति वारवाणः—क्षीर०). ०पट्टिकया परिवेष्टितः मौलिः यस्य. पुरुषम्—is to be connected with अद्राक्षीत् (l. 27) above.

P. 11 l. 1—**P. 12** l. 32 **अथ स...दृशम्.** पुरोयायिनाम् soldiers that had gone ahead, vanguard. यथा...कथयताम् who, having come back, narrated all as they saw with astonished minds. The vanguard was deep in wonder at the superhuman beauty of the two maidens. The reading प्रतीत्य may mean प्रतिनिवृत्य and also 'having approached'. उपलभ्य having learnt. दिव्या आकृतिः यस्य (*adj.* of ०युगलम्). ०युगलम्—object of उपलभ्य. प्रतूर्णतुरगः whose horse began to gallop (*i. e.* he urged his horse to greater speed). निवारितः परिजनः येन who prohibited his servants (to follow him).

तेन—refers to the old companion of the youth described above. कृतं उपसङ्ग्रहणं याभ्याम् who made a respectful salutation. तौ—object of उपजग्राह. किस...जग्राह received them according to their precedence with hospitality usual in forest life beginning with the offering of a seat of tender foliage and ending with the present of fruit and flowers. सकुसुमैः फलैः अर्धः (पूजाविधिः) अवसानं (अन्तः) यस्य (*adj.* of आतिथ्येन). आसीनयोश्च तयोः when they sat. प्रवयस् an old man. प्रगतं वयः यस्य. 'प्रवयाः स्थविरो वृद्धः' इत्यमरः. सहजा (inborn) लज्जा धनं यस्य. सहज...जनस्य to address (another man) first (*i. e.* before he addresses) is (seems) an immodest act in the case of young women to whom innate bashfulness is all-in-all, particularly in the case of highborn maidens that are simple like the does of the forest. शालीन—bashful, shy–from शाला with the affix ख (ईन). 'शालीनकौपीने अधृष्टाकार्ययोः' पा. 5. 2. 20 (शालाप्रवेशमर्हति शालीनः अधृष्टः। सि. कौ.। अप्रागल्भ्यादन्यत्र गन्तुमशक्तः शालामेव प्रवेष्टुमर्हतीत्यर्थः। तत्त्वबोधिनी). The propriety of the word वन is this. A doe, by contact with human beings, may become bold; but one brought up in the forest far from human habitation will retain its original shyness and innocence. केवल...वृत्तिः But this (my) sense of hearing, envious of (my) eye that is blest (कृतार्थ) by seeing you, urges me, being eager to hear the news (of you). What सावित्री means is:—on seeing this extremely handsome young man, our eyes have been rewarded and gratified; but our ears have not yet heard anything concerning him and are therefore envious of the eye. चक्षुषे स्पृहयन्ती (०वृत्तिः)—स्पृह् governs the dative of the object of desire or envy. 'स्पृहेरीप्सितः' पा. 1. 4. 36. 'वार्ता प्रवृत्तिर्वृत्तान्त उदन्तः स्यात्' इत्यमरः. प्रथम...प्रणयम् a good man at first sight offers his affection (प्रणयः) as though it were a present. She means that both the men, being good, have given their good will to the two maidens even at the first meeting. अप्र...वाचालयति *lit.* the heart offered by the great (प्रभवत्) with courtesy (प्रश्रयः) makes even a timid person talkative, as wine does. She means:—we are timid. You are great and courteously offered your heart (*i. e.* your regard) to us. This your regard for us makes us bold enough to address you. Wine also makes even a timid person garrulous, when he gets drunk. प्रभ...र्पितं (with मधु) means 'proffered with over-powering courtesy' or 'proffered by a great man with courtesy'. अति...विस्रम्भः confidence easily reaches its highest pitch in the case of a very yielding good man, as the bowstring on the bow. She means:—you are very good and yielding. So we treat you with the greatest confidence. The words नम्र and कोटि are श्लिष्ट. The bow-string easily reaches the furthest tip (कोटि) when the bow is extremely bent (नम्र). It is better to read आरोहति with B. With आरोपयति (causal of रुह् with आ) we naturally expect one more noun in the accusative (besides कोटिम्). आरोपयति will yield a very good sense, if we could read विस्रम्भम् and in that case गुणः (virtue, string) will be श्लिष्ट and will be construed with both साधौ and धनुषि. अति... धियाम् in those whose minds are steady or who are very wise. स्रष्टुः...शयाः master-pieces of creation from the Creator's hands. त्रि...भावि surpassing (everything) in the three worlds. अस्य— refers to the young man. सौजन्य...तरलता it is not fickleness that is natural to young women that causes me to speak, but it is the great beauty of this one dear to the gods, which (भद्रता) is under the control of kindness (that makes me talk). She means:—this young man is extremely handsome and yet very considerate (and not capricious in the vanity of his charms). It is this that urges me to know something more about him. सावित्री very much desired that सरस्वती should be married to such a young man if otherwise eligible. सह उत्तिष्ठति इति सहोत्था. The word देवानां प्रिय is used by Bâṇa in a good sense *i. e.* as meaning 'worthy, honourable'. Compare 'इहापि जन्मनि दत्तमेवास्माकममुना तपःक्लेशेन फलमसुलभदर्शनं दर्शयता देवानां प्रियम्' हर्षचरित 8th उच्छ्वास. As'oka in his edicts calls himself देवानां प्रिय. The महाभाष्य uses it in a good sense 'के पुनर्भवदादयः । भवान् दीर्घायुः देवानां प्रियः आयुष्मानिति' on पा. 5. 3. 14 (Kielhorn vol. II. p. 405). But later Sanskrit grammarians assign the meaning of 'fool' to this Aluk compound. Mr. R. R. Kale takes देवानां प्रिय in this sense and applies it to सावित्री, but that is not correct. Besides the sense becomes involved. We may also take देवानां प्रियस्य as referring to the old courtier. आगमनेन—connect with शून्यतां नीतः. अपुण्यभाक् unhappy. विजृम्भिता विरहव्यथा यस्य in which the pain of separation is growing. अपहृतः हरस्य हुङ्काराहङ्कारः येन who humbles the pride of the defiant roar of S'iva. A wrathful man makes the sound हुम्. शिव in wrath burnt मदन by the fire from his third eye. Vide p. 14 (notes). But the youth, who was as handsome as Cupid, humbled S'iva's pride by his very existence. This passage is reminiscent of the verse 'असह्यहुङ्कारनिवर्तितः पुरा पुरारिमप्राप्तमुखः शिलीमुखः । इमां हृदि व्यायतपातमक्षिणोद्विशीर्णमूर्तेरपि पुष्पधन्वनः ॥

कुमारसम्भव V. 54. अनन्यजः—न अन्यसात् जायते इति—Love is mind-born and has no physical birth. So Cupid is called अनन्यज or अनन्यजन्मा. किं नाम यस्य सः किंनामा तस्य. समृद्धं तपः यस्य—her idea is that none who does not possess a store of merit or austerities can be blest with such a son. अमृतवर्षी showering nectar *i. e.* great delight (with the youth); कौस्तुभ sprang from the ocean along with अमृत. कौस्तुभ...ह्लादयति—The कौस्तुभ jewel churned from the ocean was placed on his chest by Vishṇu. 'कौस्तुभाख्यमभूद्रत्नं पद्मरागो महोदधेः । तस्मिन्हरिः स्पृहां चक्रे वक्षोऽलङ्करणे मणौ ॥' भागवतपुराण VIII. 8. 5. The word is derived as 'कुं भुवं स्तुभ्नाति व्याप्नोति कुस्तुभः सागरः तत्र भवः'. त्रि.. स्या deserving to be worshipped by the three worlds. महतस्तेजसः of this very brilliant man. प्रभातसन्ध्येव—The morning twilight gives birth to the sun, the great luminary, and people perform their adoration in the morning. कानि...क्षराणि what fortunate letters come to be his name (अभिख्या)? 'अभिख्या नामशोभयोः' इत्यमरः. The student will notice how politely सावित्री asks for information concerning the young man's country of birth, his destination, his parentage and his name. आर्य...हृदयस्य in seeking to know your honour, the same order is followed by my heart that acts as curiosity dictates. She wants to know the same four things (country of birth &c.) about the old man. प्रकटितः प्रश्रयः (courtesy) येन. सतां...विद्या to speak what is agreeable is a hereditary art with the good (*i. e.* they are past masters in that). न...वचोभिः—handsome women are described as चन्द्रानना. सावित्री had not only a moon-like face, but her words also were चन्द्रमय, were such as gladdened the heart of the listener by their ambrosial sweetness. चन्द्रमय—made of the moon. सुधा०—The moon is said to shower down nectar with his rays, being called सुधांशु. सौजन्य...जायन्ते women like you, who are the birthplace of goodness, come into the world as the arts for moulding good men after a great deal of merit (शुभ *i. e.* पुण्य). He means:—It is due to the accumulation of the good deeds of the world that noble women like you are born. Such noble women fashion men into good men, as the study of the arts enables a person to fashion from raw materials finished articles. दूरे...पयन्ति let alone mutual conversation, even the interchange of glances with the noble (अभिजात) raises a man to the highest pitch (of goodness or glory). भूषणं goes with दधीचः. भार्गववंशस्य—च्यवन the father of दधीच belonged to the भृगुगोत्र. The story of च्यवन and his wife सुकन्या is alluded to in विष्णुपुराण IV.1. In रामायण सुन्दरकाण्ड chap. 24 she is mentioned in a list of पतिव्रताs (verse 1.). The story is given in great detail in पद्मपुराण 4th खण्ड (पातालखण्ड) chap. 14 ff. च्यवन was the son of भृगु. He performed such severe austerities that an ant-hill grew upon him. The daughter of king शर्याति in play thrust a pin in the anthill and put out च्यवन's eye. In order to propitiate the sage he gave that daughter to him in marriage. भू...लकस्य who is an ornament of the three worlds भूः, भुवः and स्वः. These are the first three out of the seven worlds (भूः, भुवः, स्वः, महः, जनः, तपः, सत्यम्). अदभ्रेण (प्रचुरेण) प्रभावेण स्तम्भितः (paralysed) जम्भारेः (इन्द्रस्य) भुजस्तम्भः येन. The As'vins cured च्यवन of old age and blindness. च्यवन gave सोम at a sacrifice to the As vins who were never before allowed that honour. Indra becoming angry at this raised his hand to strike the sage with his वज्र. च्यवन paralysed the hand of Indra. Vide पद्मपुराण 4th खण्ड chap. 16. 'शक्रं वज्रधरं दृष्ट्वा मुनिः स्वहननोद्यतम् ॥ हुङ्कारमकरोद्धीमान् स्तम्भयामास तद्भुजम् ॥' verses 15-16. ०शिलासु शयनं तेन दुर्ललितं पादपङ्केरुहं यस्य—Gods and demons bowed their crowned heads at his feet, which were thus over-fondled (दुर्ललित) by treading on the jewels in their crowns. निजतेजःप्रसरेण (by the spreading of his own lustre) प्लुष्टः (scorched) पुलोमा येन. When भृगु went out leaving his pregnant wife alone, the demon पुलोमा made bold to lay hands on her, when her foetus slipped from her womb. On seeing that foetus so fallen, the demon was burnt to ashes. See आदिपर्व chap. 5-6. बहिर्वृत्ति जीवितं *lit.* his life existing outside *i. e.* the son was dear to his father as his own life. Separate जननी अस्य. जितं जगत् येन. शर्यातस्य—In विष्णुपुराण (IV. 1) king शर्याति is said to be the son of मनु. अन्तर्वत्नीं pregnant ('अन्तर्वत्नी च गर्भिणी' इत्यमरः) from अन्तर् with the affix वत्. 'अन्तर्वत्पतिवतोर्नुक्' पा. 4. 1. 32 (एतयोः स्त्रियां नुक् स्यात् । अन्तरस्त्यस्यां गर्भ इति...अन्तर्वत्नी । पतिवत्नी । सि. कौ.). वैजनने मासि in the month in which the child was expected 'सूतिमासो वैजननः' इत्यमरः. विजनने भवः or विजननस्य अयं वैजननः. पिता...नाययत्—Even now a woman is brought to her father's house particularly when it is the first delivery. Separate अनेहसा (by time, in course of time) अवर्धत. अनेहस् *m.* time. तत्रैव—in the palace of king शर्यात. बालः young (applies to the child दधीच as well as to the moon). The young moon gives delight to all. राजीवलोचनः lotus-eyed. भर्तृ...दुहितरि even when his daughter (सुकन्या) returned to her husband's house. आसेचनकदर्शनम्

(आसेचनकं दर्शनं यस्य) whose sight never satiated him *i. e.* though he saw him continuously, he wanted to see him more still. 'तदासेचनकं तृप्तेर्नास्त्यन्तो यस्य दर्शनात्' इत्यमरः (आसिच्यते आप्यायते दृगनेन आसेचनकं यस्य दर्शनात् दृग्न तृप्यति—क्षीर०). मातामहः—refers to शर्यात. मनोविनोदनम् that diverted or gave solace to his mind. विद्याः—see above p. 18. कलाः—The Kalās were said to be 64, such as नृत्त, गीत, आलेख्य. They are enumerated in वात्स्यायन's कामसूत्र (I. 3.). उपारूढं यौवनं यस्मिन्. अहमिव refers to शर्यात and असौ to च्यवन. सुगृहीतं नाम यस्य whose name is auspicious. भृत्यपरमाणुम् an atom of a servant *i. e.* an insignificant servant. अवधारयतु understand. आयान्तम्—refers to दधीच. मया...स्वामी my master made me his attendant. अभिसारः companion. अभिसारेण सह साभि० (बहुव्रीहि). Compare 'महासामन्तैः कृत्वा साभिसारम्' first para 5th उच्छ्वास. तद्धि... कुलम् that (of शर्यात) is a royal family to which we (*i. e.* I) have been hereditarily attached. C and T translate 'our royal house follows the rule of heredity'. This inverts the sequence of ideas. उत्तमानां...मन्दाक्षम् length (of service) produces in the good (in good masters) a certain amount of kindly (or partial) feeling even towards dependents. मन्दाक्षम्—partiality, connivance. मन्दं अक्षि इव यत्र मन्दाक्षम्, according to 'अक्ष्णोऽदर्शनात्' पा. 5. 4. 76. (अचक्षुःपर्यायादक्ष्णोऽच् स्यात्समासान्तः। गवामक्षीव गवाक्षः। सि. कौ.). He puts down this and the following sentences for showing that, though he is unworthy to be the confidential companion of the noble prince, yet his master favoured him for his long and faithful service. अ...महताम् inexhaustible indeed is the treasure of kindness in the great. इत...मात्रमिव only at the distance of about two kros'as from this place. This is accusative of distance. 'गव्यूतिः स्त्री क्रोशयुगम्' इत्यमरः (from गो+यूति according to the Vārtikas 'गोर्यूतौ छन्दस्युपसंख्यानम्' and 'अध्वपरिमाणे च' on 'वान्तो यि प्रत्यये' पा. 6. 1. 79.). पारेशोणम्—beyond the S'oṇa. शोणस्य पारे पारे०, according to 'पारे मध्ये षष्ठ्या वा' (पारमध्यशब्दौ षष्ठ्यन्तेन सह वा समस्येते। एदन्तत्वं चानयोर्निपात्यते। पक्षे षष्ठीतत्पुरुषः। पारेगङ्गादानय। गङ्गापारात्।...सि. कौ.). स्व...देशम् the appellation of which was derived from his own name. निर्मितः व्यपदेशः यस्य. चैत्र...कल्पम् almost like चैत्ररथ. For the affix कल्प, *vide* notes on अष्टादशवर्षदेशीय above p. 55. चैत्ररथम् name of the garden of कुबेर, the lord of riches. 'अलकायाः बहिश्चान्यद्वनं चैत्ररथं प्रिये। योजनायुतविस्तीर्णं सर्वं कल्पद्रुमाकुलम् ॥'. तत् (काननं) अवधिः यस्याः. तद...यात्रा this our journey is to end there. यदि...परि if your courteousness accepts or seizes this moment (to do us a favour) or your heart enter-

6

tains regard for us. गृहीतः क्षणः येन. अविद्यमाना अवहेला (disdain or contempt) यस्मिन्. भूमि...र्हो वा or if this person (*i. e.* I) is an object of favour (with you) or worthy of being listened to (by you). प्रथमः...हलस्य first request of curiosity (*i. e.* due to or out of curiosity). शुश्रूषवः desirous to hear. शुश्रूषु—from the desiderative base of श्रु with the affix उ, according to सन्-आशंस-भिक्ष उः' पा 3. 2. 168. ने...चरति this your (noble) form cannot fail to be (*i. e.* must be) divine. The idea is that there is an invariable concomitance between such nobility of form and दिव्यता. गोत्रनामनी family and name. स्पृहणीयतां नीतः was made an object of envy. सम...र्थानाम् who is a combination of mutually conflicting things. तथा हि for instance, to explain. It will be noticed that in the following four lines, the विरोध is only verbal, the words being श्लिष्ट and that in each case the incongruity is explained away by taking different senses of the same words. सन्नि...र्तिश्च-(1) सन्निहितः बालः अन्धकारः यस्याम् in whom fresh darkness was present; (2) सन्निहितः बालेषु अन्धकारः यस्याम् who had darkness (*i. e.* dark colour) present in her locks. (1) भास्वतः (सूर्यस्य) मूर्तिः यस्याम् in whom the sun was present; (2) भास्वती मूर्तिः यस्याः whose form was brilliant. Here if the first sense of the two words be taken, there is विरोध, but there is none if the second sense of each clause be taken. पुण्ड...मुखी (1) with a tiger in her face (पुण्डरीकः व्याघ्रः मुखे यस्याः); (2) with a face resembling a lotus. हरिणलोचना (1) having deer in her eye; (2) who had the eyes of a deer. 'व्याघ्रेऽपि पुण्डरीको ना' इत्यमरः. C and T following the com. take पुण्डरीक as 'lion'. बाला...धरा (1) possessing the lustre of the young sun; (2) bright like the lustre of the morning sun or having a lower lip lustrous like the morning sun. बालातपप्रभः अधरः यस्याः. कु...सिनी (1) possessing laughing night-lotuses; (2) whose smile is bright like कुमुद्s. कुमुद्s are white lotuses that open by night. There is विरोध in saying that she possessed the morning sunlight and also opening कुमुद्s. But the विरोध vanishes if we say that her complexion was rosy like fresh morn and her smile was bright like कुमुद्s. Smiles are poetically said to be white. कल...स्वना (1) that possessed the cackling of कलहंसs (कलहंसानां स्वनः यस्याम्); (2) whose voice was like that of a कलहंस (कलहंसस्य इव स्वनः यस्याः). स...धरा (1) that had clouds rising (समुन्नताः पयोधराः मेघाः यस्याम्); (2) whose bosom was high-swelling (समुन्नतौ पयोधरौ यस्याः). When there are clouds, the sound of कलहंसs cannot be heard, because at the approach of the rains हंसs were supposed to migrate to the मानस lake. Or the विरोध may be this:—if there is thunder in her, how can she have the low cackling of कलहंसs? कमल...करा (1) possessing the delicate lustre of lotuses; (2) whose hand is delicate like a lotus. हिम...तम्बा (1) whose hips are broad with slabs of the Himālaya mountain; (2) whose hips are broad like &c. Lotuses and slabs of snow cannot exist together, as snow blights lotuses. Compare 'हिमसेकविपत्तिरत्र मे नलिनी पूर्वनिदर्शनं मता' रघु० VIII. 45. करभोरुः (1) having the thigh of a camel; (2) having a thigh round and tapering like the trunk of an elephant. करभः a young camel; also 'the back portion of the hand from the wrist to the root of the fingers.' वि...मना (1) whose gait is slow; (2) whose gait is languidly sportive. A camel is well-known to be a fast animal. One who has the camel's thigh cannot be slow. अमु...भावा (1) who has not given up devotion to Kumāra *i. e.* कार्तिकेय; (2) who has not yet passed the stage of girlhood. अमुक्तः कुमारे स्कन्दे भावः भक्तिः यया. अमुक्तः कुमारभावः यया. स्निग्धः (affectionate) तारकः (तदाख्यः असुरः) यस्याम्. स्निग्धा (charming) तारका (pupil of the eye) यस्याः. The demon तारक was killed by स्कन्द. One who is devoted to स्कन्द cannot secure the affection of तारक. अध्वा the road *i. e.* the distance. परि...रिष्यति Familiarity (with us) will surely make (everything) clear. अनुषङ्गे दृष्टः seen by chance. अनुषङ्गः incidental connection. नवः अम्भसां भरः (burden) तेन गम्भीरः अम्भोधराणां (मेघानां) ध्वानः (ध्वनिः) तन्निभया तत्सदृश्या. भारत्या in a voice. नर्तयन् भुजगभुजः making the peacocks dance. Peacocks subsist on reptiles and dance when clouds thunder. The voice of दधीच was mistaken by the peacocks to be the thunder of clouds. भुजगभुजः (with दधीच) would mean 'whose arms were (long and lithe) like snakes.' Separate प्रसादम् आर्या आराध्य०. कृता नमस्कृतिः येन. उच्चचाल started away. उत्तम्भितं पक्ष्म यस्य the eyelashes of which were raised up. निश्चला तारका यस्य. लिखितेनेव चक्षुषा with an eye that was as though drawn in a picture (*i. e.* that was quite motionless). कृच्छ्रा...दृशम् with difficulty she withdrew her eye (from that direction).

P. 12 l. 33—**P. 13** l. 10. **अथ...सुष्वाप.** तस्य = दधीचस्य. रूपसम्पदम् perfection of beauty. अवशेव as though helpless. अप्रहितमपि though not sent. कुतोऽपि (1) from some indescribable cause; (2) from the earth. The creeper with its shoots springs from the earth. सालस्या इव—आलस्येन सह (बहुव्रीहि). शून्या vacant in mind.

सनिद्रा sleepy, dreamy. अस्तमुपयाति—connect with तेजसि. प्रत्यक् पर्यस्तं मण्डलं यस्य whose orb was thrown westward. लाङ्ग...त्विषि the brilliance of which was rosy like a bunch of लाङ्गलिका. कमलिनीकामुक the lover of lotuses plants. कमलिनी plants bloom at the advent of the sun. कठोर...शोचिषि the lustre (शोचिः) of which was red like the head of a fully developed (कठोर) crane. सावित्रं सवितुः इदं सावित्रम्. त्रयीमये—त्रयीमय is an appellation of the sun. त्रयी means 'the three Vedas'. As the sun is worshipped with the Veda or as the most sacred verse of the Rigveda, the गायत्री, is addressed to the sun, the latter is called त्रयीमय or त्रयीतनु. Compare भागवतपुराण 5. 20. 4. '**त्रय्या विद्यया** भगवन्तं **त्रयीमयं** सूर्यमात्मानं यजन्ते'. तमाल is a tree the leaves of which are dark. मलिनयति *loc. sing.* of the *pr. p.* of the denominative verb मलिनयति from मलिन. व्योम is the object of मलिनयति. सञ्च...तलम् when the moon very slowly crept up the sky, like a swan of the Ganges following the tinkling of the anklets of the roaming Siddha damsels. For सिद्ध, see above (text p. 5 l. 25). सिद्ध does not mean 'saint' here as C and T think. A हंस is white and hence the moon is compared to हंस. The moon sailed in the Milky Way, which is white and resembles the मन्दाकिनी. कृतः सन्ध्यायै प्रणामः यया. निशामुखे at the very beginning of night. She was languid and tired and so took the first opportunity to lie down. This contrasts with उचिते शयनकाले below. विमुक्तानि अङ्गानि यस्याः whose limbs were drooping or languid. कृत्वा...कलापम् having gone through her evening ritual as it was being usually performed by her. कलापः = समूहः. This shows that she was unaffected, while सरस्वती was perturbed by the wave of passion.

P. 13 ll. 11—28 इतरा...कुलैः. अङ्ग...तला whose bed of tender leaves was disarranged (विलुलित) by the tossing of her limbs. निमीलित closed. मर्त्य...परि the world of mortals is surely above (*i. e.* superior to) all worlds. एवंविधानि—refers to दधीच. सक...गुरूणि (1) worthy of respect on account of (the possession of) all virtues (with दधीच); (2) heavy even to the collection of all threads (with रत्नानि). Even numerous threads may not bear the burden of a big jewel; what of a single thread? ग्रामः = समूहः. She explains in the following clauses how he possesses all the qualities and is an ornament to त्रिभुवन. तस्य...न्दुः—the moon is but a drop oozing from the stream of the beauty of his face. The moon is round and bright like a drop. His face is so much more charming than the moon, that the latter seems but a drop as compared with the stream of his beauty. Explain the following clauses similarly. विक्षेपाः glances. For विकच...कराः, compare above 'चक्षुषः प्रथिम्ना विकचकुमुदकुवलयकमलसरःसहस्रसञ्छादितदशदिशं' (text p. 9. ll. 23–24 and notes p. 50). आकरः = समूहः. अधरमणेः of. his jewel-like lip. His red lip is like a red jewel. दीधितयः = किरणाः. बन्धूकम् is a red flower. The word विकसित is put in to indicate deep red. तस्य...नङ्गः The disembodied one (Cupid) is only a means (उपकरणं) of enhancing the beauty of his body. There is a picturesque effect in saying that his अङ्ग has its beauty enhanced by अनङ्ग (one who is without body). 'परभागो गुणोत्कर्षः' क्षीरस्वामी. बाण is fond of this word. Compare 'उपहितकान्तिपतिपरभागा लक्ष्मच्छायेव चन्द्रमसः' कादम्बरी p. 267 of P; "कुटिलक्रमरूपक्रियमाणपल्लवपरभागैरपरैः' हर्षचरित 1st उच्छ्वास. Connect स्त्रैणानि with the three, चक्षूंषि, चेतांसि and यौवनानि. स्त्रैणानि of women (from स्त्री). 'स्त्रीपुंसाभ्यां नञ्स्नञौ भवनात्' पा. 4. 1. 87. येषा...दर्शनस्य within whose vision be comes. The reading अविषयः is explicable. The meaning then would be 'the eyes, minds and youths of those women are blessed who do not see him', the idea perhaps being that it is better that he be not seen at all rather than suffer for his sake an insatiable longing. क्षणं...धर्मेण in showing him to me only for a moment, my evil deeds of former lives have as though borne their fruit. She means that if he could be seen continuously, there would then be no distress, but only bliss. This sentence has been explained differently. 'My misconduct (in laughing at दुर्वासस्), though done in this very life, has borne fruit, as though it were done in a previous life, by showing that rare young man to me, though for a moment'. It is generally the actions of past lives that bear fruit in this life. But this is not a very happy explanation. We think that the mere fact of laughing at a mistake would hardly be called an अधर्म even by सरस्वती. It will be noticed that from the words अजायत च नवपल्लव &c. (p. 13 l. 1 ff), Bāṇa describes the various stages of Love in strict accordance with writers on Rhetoric. 'अभिलाषश्चिन्ता–स्मृति–गुणकथनोद्वेगसम्प्रलापश्च । उन्मादोऽथ व्याधिर्जडता मृतिरिति दशाऽत्र कामदशाः ॥' साहित्यदर्पण III. 190. The sentence अजायत॰ shows अभिलाष; the next shows चिन्ता. The sentence 'कृतसन्ध्याप्रणामा...तस्थौ' indicates स्मृति and in 'मर्त्यलोकः खलु' we have the fourth अवस्था 'गुणकथन.' In the sentence 'मदनशर॰' (l. 21) we have the 5th stage of उद्वेग. प्रतिपत्तिः course of action; means. का...दानीम् what should I do now ? स्वप्ने आसादितं द्वितीयं दर्शनं यया. आकर्णं आकृष्ट

कार्मुकं (धनुः) येन. Cupid smote her with all his power. प्रतिबुद्धा when she awoke. At his very first sight she fell in love with him. But when she saw him again in her dreams, she was hopelessly smitten by love. मदन...जगाम unrest came to her who was struck by the arrows of Cupid, as though to learn the news (of her state). The plain meaning is:—being smitten by love, she became restless. When a person falls ill or is beaten or meets with an accident, people call on him to express their sympathy or regard. So here अरति is fancied to have made a call on her. अरतिः—'स्वाभीष्टवस्त्वलाभेन चेतसो याऽनवस्थितिः। अरतिः सा'. Another sense also is hinted. रति is the wife of मदन. As मदन struck her (सरस्वती), अरति (one who is opposed to रति, the wife of the offending मदन) made a call on her. The meanings of नञ् (अ) are six 'तत्सादृश्यमभावश्च तदन्यत्वं तदल्पता। अप्राशस्त्यं विरोधश्च नञर्थाः षट् प्रकीर्तिताः॥'. कुसुम...धत्त—one who is beaten feels pain. But she felt pain though not beaten. The cause of pain was really her love-sick condition. In this and the following five sentences Bāṇa describes her condition by employing the figure of speech called विभावना. It consists in stating that an effect follows though its cause is non—existent. 'क्रियायाः प्रतिषेधेऽपि फलव्यक्तिर्विभावना' काव्यप्रकाश X. In such cases only the well-known cause is absent; while some other cause works to bring about the effect. Compare for this and the last clause 'कुसुमितलताभिरहताप्यधत्त रुजमलिकुलैरदष्टाऽपि।' परिवर्तते स नलिनीलहरीभिरलोलिताप्यघूर्णत सा॥'. मन्द... मुमोच when dust (रजः) enters one's eyes, tears fall. She shed tears through love-pangs, though the pollen (रजः) of flowers did not soil her eyes. हंसपक्षाः एव तालवृन्तानि (fans) तै वान्ताः (emitted) वाताः तैः विततः (spread) तैः. शोणशीकरैः the spray of the S'oṇa river. आर्द्रता (1) becoming wet; (2) becoming full of soft feeling. प्रेङ्ख...दोलाभिः though not borne on the pairs of roving (प्रेङ्खत्) Kādambas she rolled on the swinging waves of the sylvan lotus ponds. 'कादम्बः कलहंसः स्यात्' इत्यमरः. कमलिनी—a place abounding in कमलs. 'पुष्करादिभ्यो देशे' पा. 5. 2. 135 (पुष्करिणी। पद्मिनी। सि. कौ.). The ripples of the pond wafting the scent of lotuses excited her and made her roll on her bed. विघटमानानि (separating) चक्रवाकयुगलानि तैः विसृष्टैः (*adj.* of धूमैः). श्यामतामाससाद she became dark (*i. e.* lost the colour of her complexion as she was love-sick). One is darkened by smoke. The sighs heaved by the separated चक्रवाकs are like धूम. The चक्रवाक male was poetically supposed to become separated from its mate at the approach of night. व्यचेष्टत she wriggled. A man stung by bees would fling his body about.

P. 13 l. 29—**P. 14** l. 11 **अथ...यासीत्.** गण...गमे after the lapse of many nights. 'गणरात्रं निशा बह्वयः' इत्यमरः. निवर्तमानः—विकुक्षि returned after accompanying दधीच to his father's place. तथैव—as before (when दधीच left his attendants behind). छत्रधारः (umbrella-bearer) द्वितीयः यस्य. डुढौके Perfect of ढौकृ 1 A to approach. वन...द्ग्रीवा stretching her neck like a woodland doe. मार्ग...दृशा she as though bathed him who was tired by the journey with her glance that whitened the ten quarters. One's fatigue is lessened by a bath. She steadfastly looked at him. The glances of her bright eye were like water. कृतः आसनपरिग्रहः येन. कच्चि...कुमारः is the prince well? कच्चित् *(ind.)* indicates 'I hope'. स्मरति भवत्योः—the genitive is used in accordance with 'अधीगर्थदयेशां कर्मणि' पा. 2. 3. 52 (words having the sense of इ with अधि 'to remember' and दय् and ईश् govern the genitive of the object). केव...बिभर्ति only he is somewhat emaciated in body in these days. अवि...धत्ते he has a certain vacantness (of mind) which is inexplicable and without any (apparent) cause. अन्वक्षम् *adv.* immediately, forthwith. अक्षस्य (रथस्य इन्द्रियस्य वा) पश्चात् अन्वक्षम् (अव्ययीभाव). The reading अन्वक् means the same thing. 'अन्वगन्वक्षमनुगेऽनुपदं क्लीबमव्ययम्' इत्यमरः. The meaning प्रत्यक्षं assigned by the com. does not suit the context. वाणिनी = दूती. 'वाणिन्यौ नर्तकीदूत्यौ' इत्यमरः. उच्छ्वसितं—the breath or life *(i. e.* she is a great confidante of the prince). महानुभावः magnanimous, noble. यदे...बध्नाति that he thus keeps up familiarity with a person not known to him and seen only for a moment. तस्य...मासीत् his mind was somehow by chance fixed on us (caught by us) while he passed (on his way), as a shawl may be caught by wayside creepers (in the case of a traveller). अशून्यं...सूनोः the nobility of your prince is not devoid of high birth *i. e.* in the prince high birth and nobility of character are combined. अशून्यम् not devoid of, full. स्वामिसूनु must mean prince here. विकुक्षि was the servant of शर्यात, whose *grandson* (and not son) दधीच was. Or सूनु may be used in the sense of 'off-spring in general'. A daughter's son was in ancient times like a son of the body. 'औरसो धर्मपत्नीजस्तत्समः पुत्रिकासुतः ।' याज्ञ० II. 128. अलसः...मनांसि people are indeed lazy that they do not make their own *(lit.* buy) the hearts of the great that are easily befriended by offering something or other. सुलभं सौहार्दं (मैत्री) येषाम्. She means:—she and her friend did very little for the prince; but he being great and noble offered his affection to them in return for what little they did. If the world will also offer something ever so little to the great, the latter will befriend them. सो... भुवनम् it is this excess of magnanimity in the great, not found in ordinary people, that makes the three worlds the instruments (of the great). The three worlds come under the control (are willing to abide by the orders) of the great on account of the latter's औदार्य. उच्चावचैः high and low, various. 'उच्चावचैः प्रकृतवस्त्वसंस्पर्शिभिः, विचित्रैरिति वा' सं०. 'उदक् च अवाक् च उच्चावचं उन्नतं चावनतं च वा' क्षीरस्वामी. It is a compound of the मयूरव्यंसकादि class (पा. II. 1. 72.).

P. 14 l. 12—**P. 15** l. 25. **अपरे...र्मनसी.** The first sentence is अपरेद्युः मालती समदृश्यत (p. 15. l. 17). उद्यति loc. sing. of *pr. p.* of इ with उद्. द्युमणौ—the jewel of the heavens. उद्दामा द्युतिः यस्य. अभिद्रुताः (attacked) तारकाः येन. तामरसानां व्यासः (विकासः) तस्य व्यसनं (intent application) अस्ति अस्य इति व्यसनिन् तस्मिन्. Red lotuses open at sunrise. आयान्ती this and the following adjectives (in the *nom. sing. f.*) qualify मालती (p. 15. l. 17). तरल...नयन्ती under the guise (छलं) of the covering of the sparkling (तरल) complexion of her body, she seemed to bring all the very clear water of the S'oṇa. The poet fancies that her sparkling complexion was really the transparent water of the शोण which she brought with her when crossing it. वितानः—म् canopy. Here the figure is अपह्नुति, which consists in the poetic denial of the real character of a thing and establishing in its place something else resembling it. 'प्रकृतं यन्निषिध्यान्यत्साध्यते सा त्वपह्नुतिः' काव्यप्रकाश X. स्फुटितानां (opened, expanded) अतिमुक्तककुसुमानां स्तबकेन समा त्विट् (कान्तिः) यस्य—*adj.* of तुरङ्गमे and मृगपतौ. सटाल having a mane (*adj.* of both मृगपतौ and तुरङ्गमे). मृगपतौ इव गौरी as पार्वती rides a lion. गौरी also means 'fair' (as applied to मालती). सिंह is the वाहन of दुर्गा. सली...तस्य (*adj.* of ०युगलस्य) that were gracefully placed on the girth of the horse. उरोबन्धम्—the leathern strap passing round the horse's chest. तिर्य...रणितस्य (*adj.* of ०युगलस्य) the sharp jingle (रणितं) of the anklets on which was listened to by the horse with slantingly upraised ears. अति... वितस्य that were decked with very thick Alaktaka dye. 'पिण्डालक्तकः कथितोऽलक्तकरसः' सं०. पल्लवितस्य—पल्लवाः सञ्जाताः अस्य सः पल्लवितः—the soles of the feet were so dyed with Alaktaka as to look like the new leaves (which are reddish) of trees. कु...पृष्ठस्य the upper surface of which (feet) was reddened with saffron. उभयतः—as she rode astride, her feet were on both sides of the horse. ताडन...गतानि come out of their craving for her kicks. It was a convention among Sanskrit poets that the red As'oka tree put forth blossoms when kicked by handsome young ladies. Such conventions are summarised in the following verse 'स्त्रीणां स्पर्शात् प्रियङ्गुर्विकसति बकुलः सीधुगण्डूषसेकात् पादाघातादशोकस्तिलककुरबकौ वीक्षणालिङ्गनाभ्याम् । मन्दारो नर्मवाक्यात्पटुमृदुहसनाच्चम्पको वक्त्रवाताच्चूतो गीतान्नमेरुर्विकसति च पुरो नर्तनात्कर्णिकारः ॥' quoted by मल्लिनाथ on मेघदूत' II. 17. 'रक्ताशोकश्चलकिसलयः'. दोहदम् longing. 'अथ दोहदम् । इच्छाकाङ्क्षा स्पृहेहा तृट्' इत्यमरः. Her feet being dyed red both beneath and above and being on both sides of the horse, the poet fancies that she as if drew along with her forests of red As'oka trees that had put forth foliage (किसलयित) and that accompanied her in the desire of being kicked by her. The lines (पल्लवs) of अलक्तक dye on her soles correspond to the किसलयs of the रक्ताशोक. सकल...स्थला on whose hips jingled a girdle as though it were a proclamation (आघोषणा) for forcibly seizing the hearts of the whole mortal world. She was so handsome that she forcibly captivated the hearts of all. The jingling रशना was the proclamation announcing this pillage of the hearts. C and T translate 'a proclamation devoting to murder and rapine the hearts'. It is difficult to see how 'murder' comes in here. धौत...लता whose creeper-like form was covered by a gown (कञ्चुकः) made of washed and white silk and reaching up to her toes and lighter than even serpent's slough (निर्मोकः). नेत्रम्—silk cloth. 'स्याज्जटांशुकयोर्नेत्रम्' इत्यमरः. निर्मोकात् लघुतरेण. आप्रपदीन—from आप्रपद with the affix ख (ईन), according to 'आप्रपदं प्राप्नोति' पा. 5. 2. 8. (पादस्याग्रं प्रपदं तन्मर्यादीकृत्य आप्रपदम्). छात...सरसी who, with her limbs white with slightly dried (आश्यान) sandal and visible through the fine (छात) gown, seemed as though she were a lotus plant, the stalks of which were clearly visible (विभाव्यमान) in the transparent water. 'अमांसो दुर्बलश्छातः' इत्यमरः. छात lean, thin (from छो to cut). अवयवैः—understand उपलक्षिता after it. The instrumental is used in accordance with 'इत्थम्भूतलक्षणे' पा. 2. 3. 21 (जटाभिस्तापसः । सि. कौ.). कुसुम्भ...दधाना wearing a petticoat (चण्डातकं) red with safflower dye, variegated with spots (पुलकः) of different colours and gleaming inside (the gown), as thoush she were a crystal spot bearing a treasure (निधानं) of jewels. Her gown was white and glossy like crystal. Inside it was the red चण्डातक as inside the crystal ground red gems may be found. Jewels are red like safflower dye (कुसुम्भरागवत् पाटलं). The spots of various colours on the petticoat looked like precious stones called पुलक. पुलक also means 'yellow orpiment.' "नानावर्णबिन्दुविन्यासः पुलकबन्धः, मणिविशेषाश्च पुलकाः' सं०. 'कृमिप्रभेदे रोमाञ्चे पुलकं प्रस्तरे विदुः' शाश्वत 373. चण्डातकं—a petticoat reaching to the middle of the thighs. 'अर्धोरुकं वरस्त्रीणां स्याच्चण्डातकमंशुकम्' इत्यमरः. हारेणा...द्यौः with a necklace having pearls round like Āmalakī fruit, she seemed to be the autumnal sky variegated (शार) with bright (स्फुरित) and large clusters of stars and overcast with a veil of thin white clouds. She was like the autumnal sky; her white silken कञ्चुक like the white thin clouds of शरद् and the large and round pearls like the stars in the sky. आमलकीफलवत् निस्तलानि (without a bottom *i. e.* round) मुक्ताफलानि यस्य. The reading निस्तुल (incomparable) is not good. कुच...धारयन्ती over her breasts resembling full jars, she had tied a jewelled necklace shooting forth red and green rays, as though it (necklace) were a garland of wild flowers (indicating) the entrance into her heart of some (indescribable) happy man. कुचौ पूर्णकलशौ इव. प्रालम्बमालिका is a garland or necklace reaching from the neck to the chest. 'प्रालम्बमृजुलम्बि स्यात्कण्ठात्' इत्यमरः. The jewels were red and green (emerald) and so resembled red and green leaves (किसलय). Jars full of water were placed at the entrance of houses as auspicious. पल्लवs were placed on the tops of such jars and garlands were tied round the necks of jars and on gates. Hence the poet fancies that her breasts on which rolled a necklace were jars with leaves and flowers indicating the auspicious entrance of some one in her heart. He whoever swayed her heart with love must be called blessed (पुण्यवत्). 'वनमाला विधातव्या पल्लवैः कुसुमैः फलैः' विष्णुरहस्य. Compare for the ideas 'उभयपार्श्वस्थापितोत्पल्लवमुखपूर्णहेमकलशं (कायमानं)' कादम्बरी p. 281 of P; 'वेदीविनिहितपल्लवललामहेमकलशे बद्धवनमालादाम्नि ...मन्दिरे' हर्षचरित 7th उच्छ्वास (2nd para); 'समुल्लसद्भिः स्तनमण्डलैर्मङ्गलकलशमय इव बभूव लोकः' हर्षचरित IV. एकैकस्य of each one (out of the many she wore). हाटककटकस्य of the golden bracelet. मर...नाथस्य—the golden bracelets were inlaid with emerald stones cut into the shape of a crocodile. वेदिका—level ground (on which the stone was set). स्थल...माना who was as though followed by land lotus plants under the belief that she was लक्ष्मी. The emeralds on her bracelets emitted pencils (सन्तति) of green rays in all directions, which (pencils) the poet fancies to be स्थलकमलिनीs that are also green (with leaves). Lotus plants are ordinarily in water. As she moved on land the मयूखसन्तति is fancied to be स्थलकमलिनी. लक्ष्मी dwells in lotus beds. मालती resembled लक्ष्मी in her beauty. बहल...वमन्ती from her lips darkened by the dark streak (कृष्णिका) of plenty of betel, she as though emitted darkness mixed with the glow of evening that was drunk by the moon of her face. The moon swallows darkness. Her face was like the moon. The dark-red tint of ताम्बूल taken by her in abundance resembled darkness mingled with evening radiance. मुखमेव शशी तेन पीतम्. विकचं नयनकुवलयं तस्मिन् कुतूहलेन आलीनया (settling or sitting upon). संहत्या = समूहेन. निरुद्धं अर्धवदनं यस्याः. Bees followed her dark eyes, thinking them to be lotuses and covered the upper part of her face, as though with a veil (जालिका) of blue silk. नीलीरागेण निहितः नीलिमा यस्मिन् (*adj.* of दन्तपत्रेण) which was made blue with indigo-colour. नीलिमा is formed from नील like पिङ्गलिमा (p. 23). शिखि...शितिना as blue as the throat of a peacock. The reading शितिगल° would mean 'as blue as (the throat of) शिव.' शिव is called शितिकण्ठ, as his throat grew dark when he drank कालकूट. See notes p. 2. दन्तपत्रं an ear-ornament. काल...माना—she was fair and bright like lightning and the dark दन्तपत्र was like a streak of dark (काल) cloud. पल्लवs also are placed on the ear as ornament. कल्पितेन made. बालिका—an ear-ornament dangling from the lobe of the ear. '**बालिका** । बालायां वालुकापत्रकाहला-**कर्णभूषणे** ॥' मेदिनी (कान्तवर्ग 130). आलोकः (light) एव जलं or जलमिव तत् वर्षतीति. The bright light of the pearl pendants hanging downwards (अधोमुख) fell on her creeperlike arms. Tender creepers may be watered by two girls (बालिकायुगल) bending down. The bright light resembles clear water. दक्षिण...तला with the inner leaf of Ketakī flower placed on her right ear as an ear-ornament, she seemed to have her cheek licked through greed for beauty by the creeperlike tongue of the moon. The long and white केतकी leaf dangling on her cheek is fancied to be the tongue of the moon. The moon desired more grace and licked her cheek, which was very bright and fair. मृग...ष्यन्दिना that emitted the perfume of musk. तिलक...दहन्ती with the round mark on her forehead she bore a face which seemed to be the all-in-all of Cupid kept under a seal. The dark round तिलक of कस्तूरी resembled the mark of a seal.

One keeps one's treasure under seal. Her beautiful face was the सर्वस्व of Cupid *i. e.* she was calculated to inspire love in anyone. लला...चुम्बिनः dancing on her forehead and touching the parting line of her hair. The com. reads 'चटुलातिलक' and explains 'सुवर्णशृङ्खलाबद्धो नानारत्नौघमण्डितः। ललाटलम्ब्यलङ्कारश्चटुलातिलको मतः॥'. चटुलतिलकमणि may mean 'a jewel dangling on the forehead' (where the तिलक mark is made). उदञ्चता shooting up. कृतं शिरोऽवगुण्ठनं यस्याः. The red rays of the jewel on the forehead shooting round her head are fancied to be a red veil of silk. पृष्ठे प्रेङ्खन् अनादरसंयमनेन शिथिलश्च जूटिकाबन्धः यस्याः—whose thick hair dangled on her back, being loose as she tied it carelessly. नील... पताका as though she, who had a crocodile-like crest jewel (in her hair), was the banner of Cupid, with the ornament of a blue chowrie. Her loose and dangling hai was like a dark chowrie, which is placed as an ornament on banners; chowries are generally white, but her hair being dark, we have नीलचामर here. On the banner of Cupid (who is called मकरकेतु) there would be figures of crocodiles. Her चूडामणि was of the shape of a crocodile. A banner indicates the approach of a conquering general. She would help Cupid to subdue anybody by her charms. 'अवचूलं चिह्नम्' सं०. अवचूलः—a pendant tuft or garland, an ornament hanging from the top of a banner. मल्लिनाथ on शिशुपालवध 5. 13. says '"अस्योच्चूडावचूडाख्यावूर्ध्वाधोमुखचूडकौ' इति ध्वजाङ्गेषु हलायुधः'. बाण is very fond of this word. Compare 'दिवसकरवारणस्यावचूलचामरकलाप इवोपलक्ष्यमाणे...किरणजाले' का० p. 26; 'समदगजघटावचूलसहस्रसंरुद्धम्' p. 114. 'बहलरजोधूसरितमशिशिरकिरणबिम्बमवचूलचामरमिव निष्प्रभमभवत्' का० p. 116; केशकलापकान्तिना च कृष्णचामरावचूलेन... उपरचितदण्डं (ध्वजम्)' का० p. 224. कुल...मसः—As one worships one's कुलदेवता everyday and on every important undertaking, so the moon, by honouring her, would obtain her charms (in which the moon falls far short of her). पुनः०—Cupid was once burnt by S'iva; but she would revive him again (*i. e.* she inspires love in anyone). सञ्जीवनौषधि brings a person back to life. 'पुष्पधन्वा रतिपतिः' इत्यमरः. वेले...गरस्य As the ocean cannot go beyond the shore, so love reaches its high water-mark in her. Or the meaning is 'As the ocean beats with the greatest fury on the shore, so she creates the most furious passion by her charm.' ज्योत्स्ने...दयस्य as at moonrise, moonlight covers everything, so her charming youth brings under its sway everything. रतिरसः एव अमृतं तस्य—A great river has plenty of water

('पयः कीलालममृतम्' इत्यमरः). She was full of ambrosial (*i. e.* delightful) love. कु...तरोः a tree reaches its perfection by putting forth flowers. बाल...ग्ध्यस्य what one learns in boyhood, one hardly forgets. So she was never left by cleverness. कौमुदीव कान्तेः—even Grace may derive charms from her, as the mellow moonlight lends beauty to everything. धृ...र्यस्य she was the strength of firmness *i. e.* she was so firm of resolve that even Firmness may draw upon her to add to itself. सं० gives another curious explanation 'यद्वा धृतिः प्रवेशरक्षणम् । यथा प्रविशन्कश्चिद्राजनिकटं ध्रियते केनचित्तथा धैर्यं तावत्प्रसरति यावदेषा न दृष्टा । एतस्यां दृष्टायां सर्वे धैर्यशून्या इति.' गुरु...वस्य she is as though the teacher's hall for reverence. Even Reverence would respect her or even reverence would learn from her as one learns in a teacher's house. बीज...नयस्य modesty would be nursed in her *i. e.* she would be the source of all modesty. गोष्ठी०—all virtues met in her, as persons meet at an assembly or in a club. मन...भावतायाः—Those who are noble are always spirited and yet they would have to take lessons from her in मनस्विता. मनस्विता high-spirited nature. तृप्ति...ण्यस्य—तारुण्य after reaching her was satisfied *i. e.* did not find another, who could surpass her in charms. ०दामवत् दीर्घे लोचने यस्याः. This and the following words in the instru. qualify ०करङ्कवाहिन्या. पाटलः (red) अधरः यस्याः. पाटल is also a kind of flower. कुन्दकुड्मलवत् स्फुटाः (bright) दशनाः यस्याः. कुन्द buds are white. शिरीष is one of the most delicate of flowers. चम्पकवत् अवदातया who was bright and fair (in complexion) like the *champaka*. 'अवदातः सिते पीते' इत्यमरः. कुसुममय्या इव—It will be noticed that her limbs, body and breath are compared to various flowers and hence the poet fancies that she was made of flowers. ताम्बूलकरङ्कवाहिनी the bearer of betel-box. महाप्रमाणः अश्वतरः (mule) तमारूढया. कतिपये परिचारकाः (attendants) परिकरः (retinue) यस्याः. दधीचप्रेम्णा on account of the love she bore for दधीच (whose confidante मालती was). This is to be connected with the words लुण्ठिता, आकृष्टा &c. लुण्ठि...रथैः she (मालती) was plundered by सरस्वती with her desires. Although मालती was far away, from her face सरस्वती's longing and loving heart understood what मालती had to say. So the poet says that मनोरथs of सरस्वती looted from मालती what she came to convey. प्रत्युद्ग...काभिः she (मालती) was received with welcome by her (सरस्वती's) longings. 'उत्कण्ठोत्कलिके समे' इत्यमरः. Though she was far off, on seeing her सरस्वती became eager to know her message and her eager heart went forward to meet मालती, though she herself sat where she was. विलुप्तेव स्मितेन she (मालती) was as though seized by her (सरस्वती's) smile. Her bright smile reached (was seen by मालती) and brought her hurriedly. The reading विलिप्ता adopted by C and T is much better. Her bright smile resembled sandal with which a person is anointed. आच्छा...पुण्डरीकेण—she cast continuous glances at her (मालती) and her face was fixed on her When one's friend comes to one's house, one welcomes him, embraces him, fans him, honours him &c. The poet represents that all these actions were done by सरस्वती, though मालती was yet far off. स...शया—मालती appeared to her a friend, as she (सरस्वती) hoped that मालती was the harbinger of good news from दधीच. सविधम् = समीपम्. अगृह्णा...तया she captured (their hearts) by her polish (in all things) beginning with her (majestic) form. पेशलैः clever or soft.

P. 15 l. 26—**P. 16** l. 25 **क्रमेण...मभूत्.** शोण...स्नातुम् when Sâvitrī had gone to the S'oṇa to bathe. साकूता with feeling. प्रस्तरः couch. वि...रहसि I have to make you a request in private. किं वक्ष्यति what would she (मालती) say? स्तने विनिहितः वामकरः तस्य नखानां किरणैः दन्तुरितं (bristling). To calm down the turmoil of her bosom she placed her hand on it. उद्भिद्यमानाः कुतूहलस्य अङ्कुरनिकराः यस्मात्. Her heart was curious to know what she would say. The poet fancies that the rays of her nails were the shoots of curiosity bursting out of her heart. गलता...धावमानेन—(understand उपलक्षिता after ०पल्लवेन) the tender leaves on her ear used as an ornament dropped down (in her flurry), as though it were her ear running to hear (what मालती was going to say). अनव...लम्बमाना supporting herself on a neighbouring creeper, as though it were the hope of her life that was made to sway by her incessant sighs. ०सन्दोहेन (समूहेन) दोलायिता. दोलायिता placed in a swing *i. e.* moved to and fro. The creeper swayed to and fro on account of her incessant sighs. दोलायित also means 'held in suspense' (with जीविताशा). The hope for her life was also in suspense *i. e.* her life was in suspense on account of the incessant sighs. It seemed that life would depart from her body which was so much agitated. समु...लोकम्—her moon-like face became bright at the sight of a messenger from her lover and bathed the world in its brilliance. That brilliance being due to love, the poet fancies that she flooded the world with शृङ्गाररस (the sentiment of love; the fluid of love). ०लग्नैः

sticking or attracted by. कदम्बकैः = समूहैः. मदना...प्यमाणा—the idea is:—she got up from her flowery bed, on which bees clustered. The poet fancies that the dark bees were her longings (for union with दधीच) that came out of her in a visible form and lifted her up, being scorched by the fire of love (in her) and so being rendered dark. What is scorched becomes black. कुसुम...गात् she very slowly got up from her flowery bed, being in a high fever due to the darts of love. One who is laid up with fever rises slowly from his bed. Flowers are the darts of Cupid and as she slept on them they tormented her. 'अरविन्दमशोकं च चूतं च नवमल्लिका। नीलोत्पलं च पञ्चैते पञ्चबाणस्य सायकाः॥'. 'सन्तापः सञ्ज्वरः समौ' इत्यमरः. उपांशु *adv.* in a whisper, secretly. कपोल...वेशयन्ती—In her bright cheek Mālatī was reflected. The poet fancies that she placed मालती (reflected in her cheek) near her ear that she (मालती) may deliver her message in a whisper. She would have felt ashamed (लज्जयेव) if people had heard what मालती would have said loudly. काह...प्राणानां वा who am I as to paying attention or as to the body or life? मालती requested her above to pay attention (text p. 15, l. 28). सरस्वती says that she has no control over her attention or body or even life and that all of them are at the disposal of Mālatī and her prince. C and T take शरीरस्य प्राणानां वा with the next sentence; but in that case we expect that वा should follow सर्वस्य. सर्वे...जनः even without a request, an extremely handsome man is master of everything. अविद्यमानं प्रार्थितं (प्रार्थना) यस्य—A handsome man has not to make a request for anything; he gets it without a request. The reading अप्रार्थितेऽपि would convey the same sense. अतिवेलम् = अत्यर्थम्. अतिक्रान्तं वेलां यथा स्यात्तथा. The reading अतिपेशलः means 'very fine or graceful'. चक्षुष्यः (चक्षुषि साधुः) = प्रियदर्शनः. सा...समा च There is nothing that you are not to me, a sister, a loving (प्रणयिनी) friend, a second self. She says:—you are to me in place of whatever relationship I may think of. Then she specifies some of these *viz.* स्वसा, सखी, प्राणसमा. नियुज्य...मिदम् Appoint this my frail body to (do) whatever task, great or small, it is capable (क्षम) of. क्षोदीयस् and गरीयस् are respectively the comparative forms of क्षुद्र and गुरु. क is added to शरीर in the sense of अनुकम्पा or कुत्सा (contempt). 'कुत्सिते' पा. 5. 3. 74. (कुत्सितं शरीरं शरीरकम्); 'अनुकम्पायाम्' पा. 5. 3. 76. अविद्यमानः अवस्करः (गुह्यं) यस्य—that has no secrets. आश्रव *adj.* obedient. 'वचने स्थित आश्रवः' इत्यमरः (आशृणोति वाक्यमिति). प्रतिसर dependent.

'प्रतिसरश्चमूपृष्ठे नियोज्यकरसूत्रयोः' हेमचन्द्रः. विधेय controlled by, at the disposal of. प्रीत्या...ते Through my affection I am dependent on you and at your disposal. व्या...क्षितम् lay open, fair lady, what you desire to say. विवक्षित *past p. p.* of the desiderative base of वच्. वरः वर्णः (complexion) अस्याः इति वर०. That word also suggests another sense 'one who describes the bridegroom I have chosen'. लोलु...ग्रामस्य (you know well) that the array of senses ardently hankers (after gratification). पारिप्लवता = चञ्चलता. अतो...मर्हसि hence you will please not blame me (*lit.* wait upon me with censure). न च...कारणम् my talkativeness is not due to my foolishness or fickleness or trickery. A चारण is a wandering actor, who has to change his appearance as occasion demands. Hence चारणता means धूर्तता. न...भक्तिः there is nothing that great devotion to one's master would not induce a person to do (*i. e.* a devoted servant would do anything for his master). अस्य कामो गुरुः Cupid is his teacher (*i. e.* he is learning the lore of Love). अस्य (दधीचस्य) is to be connected with each of the following clauses. Another sense is 'his Love (for you) is great (गुरु).' चन्द्र...शः the moon is the lord of his life (*i. e.* cools down his torment by its ambrosial rays). जीवितेशः also means 'Death'. The moon increases the excitement of those who are love-sick and thus may cause their death. Compare शाकुन्तल III. 'तव कुसुमशरत्वं शीतरश्मित्वमिन्दोर्द्वयमिदमयथार्थं दृश्यते मद्विधेषु।'. The com. gives a third sense. As दधीच is called देव (king) above, he requires a पुरोहित. जीवितेश means पुरोहित. पुरोहित was the first of the ten ministers that constituted a king's council according to the S'ukranīti (See Sacred Books of the Hindus vol. 13 p. 68). So the meaning would be 'the moon is his first councillor.' मलय...हेतुः the wind from the मलय mountain (in the south) is support to him. उच्छ्वासहेतु means 'a source of consolation *i. e.* a friend'. It also means 'a cause of sighs.' The southern wind is an excitant of love and causes a love-sick person to heave deep sighs (उच्छ्वास). Compare 'तस्याश्चन्दनपरिमल इव दक्षिणानिलेन सह समागच्छति मोहः' का० p. 255 of P. मलय is one of the seven principal mountains of India 'महेन्द्रो मलयः सह्यः शुक्तिमानृक्षपर्वतः। विन्ध्यश्च पारियात्रश्च सप्तैते कुलपर्वताः॥' वायुपुराण 45. 88. आध...स्थानेषु mental torments are in place of (*i. e.* occupy the position of) confidential persons. Another meaning is 'mental distress pervades his inside parts (*i. e.* his heart).' स...हृत् pain is his great friend. Another meaning is 'pain greatly harasses his life' (separate परम् + असु + हृत्) Or we may take 'परम् + अ—सुहृत्' (pre-eminently an enemy). प्र...प्तः wakefulness is his relative or friend. आप्त also means 'obtained,' the idea being 'he has secured wakefulness.' मनो...गताः yearnings are his spies. Another meaning is 'desires (for union with you) pervade him all round.' निः...सराः sighs are his vanguard (also 'sighs go in front of his body'). विग्रहः battle, body. मृत्यु...वर्ती Death is his personal attendant; also 'death stands near him' *i. e.* he will die if he be not united with you. He, being a prince, has death attending him (*i. e.* he condemns offenders to death). Compare 'यस्य प्रसादे पद्मा श्रीर्विजयश्च पराक्रमे। मृत्युश्च वसति क्रोधे सर्वतेजोमयो हि सः ॥' मनु० VII. 11. रण...रकः Disquiet is his emissary; also 'his unrest makes him wander about.' सं० says 'द्विविधा हि चाराः संस्थाः सञ्चारकाश्च' (*i. e.* spies are of two kinds, those who stay in one place and those who move about from place to place). In सर्वगताः above we had the first kind of spies. सङ्क...वृद्धाः his fancies are the elders that instruct his intellect; also 'his fancies have increased, being incited by his intellect.' The idea is he listens to his fancies, as one would listen to the advice of elders. अनु.. वना If I were to say 'he is a good match for your ladyship', then it would be highly honouring oneself. In this and the following sentences, she puts forward several sentiments and finds fault with each as not being suited to adequately express her master's feeling towards सरस्वती. In saying 'अनुरूपो' &c., she would be regarded as only honouring her master, as being partial to him. That must be said by others and by सरस्वती. The words आत्म० also mean 'that is purely my own supposition' (not necessarily shared by सरस्वती and others). Bâṇa is very fond of passages in this strain. Compare हर्षचरित 3rd उच्छ्वास 'यामीति न स्नेहसदृशम् &c.' (text p. 54); 'अतिप्रियोऽसीति पौनरुक्त्यम् &c.' कादम्बरी p. 237 of P. शील...रुद्धम् If I were to say 'he is possessed of a noble character,' that would be in conflict with what he has now begun. A man of high character would not be over head and ears in love with a maiden seen only casually and would not send a दूती to her. धीर...रीतम् If I say 'he is firm or wise,' that would be inconsistent with his state (described by me already). सु...यत्तम् If I say 'he is blessed', that is in your hands. It is in your hands to make him happy by accepting him as your husband. सुभग means 'a person fortunate in securing the love of the woman he loves.' स्थिर...क्षेप: If I say 'he is constant in his affection,' that would be a clever hint or statement. Those words would insinuate that other handsome young men are not constant in their affections. जानाति...चितम् If I say 'he knows how to serve (his fiancee),' that would not be appropriate to his position as a prince. A prince does not ordinarily know how to serve; he only knows how to command. इच्छति...लाप: to say 'he desires to be your slave till death' would be the words of a rogue (*i. e.* all false). Being a prince, he cannot be a *slave*. भवन...लोभनम् 'you would be the mistress of his home' would be offering an allurement. A noble lady like you would not be tempted by the allurements of pomp and wealth and palaces. You would accept him only for his intrinsic worth. पुण्य...पात: 'blessed is she who secures such a husband' would be (sheer) partiality for one's master. त्वं...प्रियम् 'you are his death' is unpleasant (speech). अगु...क्षेप: 'you do not know his worth' would be a censure (of you). स्वप्ने...क्षिकम् 'you have often shown him favours in his dreams' would be without a witness. She means:—he is so deep in love with you, that he often sees you in his dreams. But that statement cannot be corroborated by producing any witness, as no one saw him dreaming of you. अविद्यमानः साक्षी यस्य. For क, see above p. 12. प्राण...तरता 'he solicits you for his life' would be cowardliness. A prince like him should not beg even for his life. She intimates by this how deep his love is. तत्रा...ज्ञा 'come there' would be a command. She means she has no authority nor right to command her (सरस्वती). वारि...भव: 'even though forbidden (by you), he will perforce come' would be an insult to you. तदे...मसि you are thus beyond the range of words. She means that she (मालती) has not words that would appropriately describe what दधीच feels for her and what she (सरस्वती) should do for him. The words she may employ are defective in some way or other.

P. 16 l. 26—**P. 17** l. 11 **अथ सरस्वती**...**इति.** विस्फारित wide, expanded. सितेन वदतीति ०वादिनी. ०वादिनि O lady of smiling speech. यदा...साद: what you order is a great favour (*i. e.* even your orders are &c.). प्र...वशा beside herself with joy. विदितः वृत्तान्तः यया. उत्कण्ठायाः भारं बिभर्ति इति ०भृत् तेन—that laboured under the burden of longing. ताम्यता languishing. One carrying a burden feels fatigue. कल्पायितम्—*past p. p.* of कल्पायते

denominative verb from कल्प (कल्प इव आचरति). The rest of the day seemed to her as long as a कल्प on account of her longing. कल्प is a day of Brahmā, and is a period of 1000 महायुगs (कृत, त्रेता, द्वापर and कलि being one महायुग). Each महायुग has 4320000 human years. गभस्तिमति = रवौ. The sentence here is सरस्वती (p. 17 l. 1) प्रतिपालयामास (l. 8). स्तिमिततरम् noiselessly. प्रहसि... चन्द्रमसि when the moon came up from the eastern quarter that was now bright as if smiling, as a lion comes out of a cave. The east gleamed with moonlight and hence is said to be प्रहसिता (smiles being described as white). पुरन्दरः इन्द्रः तस्य इयं पौरन्दरी. इन्द्र is the lord of the East. *Vide p.* 36. above. The words शुचिनि...कोमले may apply to both शयने and ०सैकते. But there would be repetition in ची...मारे and ०कोमले. So it is better to take the first three words with सैकते and ०कोमले alone with शयने as the com. does. शुचिनि white; pure. ची...मारे (1) soft with china silk; (2) soft like &c. तरङ्गिणि (1) that has waves *i. e.* is crumpled up or has a shining coverlet; (2) that has ripples (marks left by receding ripples). स्वप्न...दधाना having an ornamental mark on her forehead that (mark) seemed to be the lustre (चन्द्रिका) of the toe-nails of दधीच, that (चन्द्रिका) stuck (to her forehead) when she in her dream fell at his feet in supplication. स्वप्ने कृता प्रार्थना तस्यां पादपतनं तस्मिन् लग्नाम्. The white mark of sandal on her forehead is fancied to be the light of दधीच's toes sticking to her forehead &c. गण्डस्थलमेवादर्शः तस्मिन् प्रति० (*adj.* of इन्दुना). अय...जनः Here have I brought the person (दधीच) dear to you. निवेद्यमानः मदनसन्देशः यस्यै—The moon was reflected in her bright cheek. The poet fancies that that moon as if whispered in her ear this message of Love 'अयमसौ &c.' विकीर्य...पट्टम् fanning her perspiring bright (स्पष्ट) cheek with her hand that scattered pencils (चक्रवालं) of the rays of her nails, as though it (hand) had turned into a yak-tail fan the digits of the moon. She had no fan; therefore she fanned her cheek with her hand. Her cheek perspired on account of the deep emotion agitating her heart. स्वेद is one of the eight सात्त्विकभावs that are indicative of deep feeling. 'स्तम्भः स्वेदोऽथ रोमाञ्चः स्वरभङ्गोऽथ वेपथुः । वैवर्ण्यमश्रु प्रलय इत्यष्टौ सात्त्विकाः स्मृताः ॥'. When she moved her hand to and fro, the rays of her bright nails were tossed about. Those rays resemble the digits of the moon. A yak's tail is also white. बालव्यजनीकृतः चन्द्रकलाकलापः येन. Connect ०मृणालिकां with वहन्ती. She had placed across her breasts a fresh lotus-stalk to allay the fever of love. She placed the stalk across the breasts as they were plump and not between them. सं० explains 'स्तनमध्ये प्रवेशाभावात्तिरश्चीनमित्युक्तम्.' स्तनयोरधि अधिस्तनम् (अव्ययीभाव). The white lotus-stalk resembled a cane. The poet fancies that the lotus-stalk was a cane sportively let fall on her bosom by Cupid (चित्तभू) intimating that no one but दधीच was to enter her heart (*i. e.* only दधीच was to be her lover). A doorkeeper also uses his cane and prevents people from entering the royal gate. स्तनयन्ती murmuring (to herself). If we read स्तनयन्तीम्, the meaning is 'the lotus-stalk on her bosom made a sound'. मनोजन्मना=कामेन. जघन्या इव like a low woman. 'जघन्योन्त्येऽधमेपि च' इत्यमरः. का...तरुणीषु of what account are other poor (तपस्विनी) extremely excitable young women?

P. 17 ll. 12—23 **आजगाम...धिकम्.** The sentence is आजगाम च...मालतीद्वितीयो दधीचः (l. 18.). मधुमासः—the month of चैत्र, the first month of वसन्त. **'स्याच्चैत्रे** चैत्रिको **मधुः'** इत्यमरः. In this and the following clauses, the poet compares दधीच, who was accompanied by मालती, to several things by paronomastic words. मधुमास is an excitant of love. The poet hints by reference to मधुमास, मलयानिल &c., that the love of both दधीच and सरस्वती had reached the highest pitch through exciting surroundings. सु...वहः which has sweet breezes (with मधुमासः); who bore (on his body) sweet perfumes (with दधीच). Spring is the season of flowers and hence the breezes are charged with fragrance. सुरभिः गन्धवहः (वायुः) यस्मिन्; सुरभिं गन्धं वहतीति. कृता मृणालानां धृतिः (धारणं) येन— who bore lotus-stalks; कृता मृणालैः धृतिः (प्राणधारणं) येन that subsists on lotus-stalks. दधीच bore lotus-stalks to alleviate the burning torment of love. Haṁsas subsist on lotus-stalks. Compare 'मृणाललोभेन च चरणनखमयूखलग्नैर्भवनहंसैरिव सञ्चार्यमाणा मन्दमन्दं बभ्राम' हर्षचरित 4 उच्छ्वास. शिखण्डी peacock. घनप्रीत्या उन्मुखः—that uplifts its face in joy at (seeing) a cloud (with शिखण्डी); whose face was upturned (in expectation) on account of his deep (घन) love (with दधीच). आहितः सरसायाः चन्दनस्य धवलायाः तनुलतायाः उत्कम्पः येन that shakes a juicy tender white creeper (growing) on a sandal tree (with मलयानिल). Or we may explain as the com. does. 'सरसान् चन्दनान् धवांश्च लान्ति इति सरस...लाः तनुलताः' *i. e.* tender creepers that hang upon juicy sandal and धव trees. आहितः सरसेन चन्दनेन धवलायाः तनुलतायाः उत्कम्पः यस्मिन् whose delicate body white with viscous sandal had a tremor (with दधीच). We may also dissolve as आहितः...उत्कम्पः येन who caused the delicate body (of

सरस्वती) to shake (through love for him). But this is rather far-fetched. The poet is describing the personal appearance of दधीच and not of सरस्वती. दधीच's body shook with the emotion of love. कम्प is one of the eight सात्त्विकभावs, for which see above p. 79. कृष्य...पतिना as if drawn forward by the lord of planets (the moon) that as though seized his hair by his करs (rays, hands). When we want to drag a man, we may do so by seizing his hair with our hands. The moon's rays fell on his head. The moon is an excitant of love and urged him forward. कृतः करैः (रश्मिभिः) करेण (हस्तेन) वा कचग्रहः येन. कन्दर्पस्य उद्दीपने (exciting) दक्षेण. उह्यमान...रसेन as though he was borne by the रस (sentiment, water *i. e.* flood) of love abounding in उत्कलिकाs (agitation, waves). The student will notice the appropriate words कृष्यमाण, प्रेर्यमाण, उह्यमान used by the author in each clause. परि...यष्टिः whose body was covered with a swarm of bees that crowded (over him) on account of the perfumes (his body bore), as though it (swarm) was a blue piece of cloth. अन्तः...दरः one of whose cheeks was whitened by the reflection of the moon gleaming inside it, which (reflected moon) appeared like the temporal bone over the ear of the intoxicated cupid—elephant, as though by the graceful embarrassed smile of the first union (of a loving couple). 'शङ्खो निधौ ललाटास्थ्नि' इत्यमरः. मत्तः मदनकरी (मदनः एव करी) तस्य कर्णशङ्खवत् आचरति ०शङ्खायते तेन. His bright cheek had a reflection of the moon. The bright image of the moon on his cheek looked like the temporal bone over the ears of an elephant. Bones are white. An intoxicated elephant, from whose temples मद flows, might expose the temporal bone to view. The moon is a friend and excitant of Love. Hence the poet says मत्तमदनकरी. Or we may explain in another way. The reflection of the moon was like the temporal bone and her broad cheek was like the broad ear of an elephant. Smiles are bright and so resemble the image of the moon. The poet probably puts in the word एक in एककपोलोदरः by way of a picturesque contrast to मालतीद्वितीयः. Or perhaps the idea is that only one of his cheeks was turned towards the rising moon. हृदय...गिरा in a voice broken like that of Haṁsas, as though mingled with the tinkling of the anklets of his beloved enshrined in his heart. His voice was broken by emotion. The poet fancies that it was interrupted by the tinkling &c. कृतं सम्भाषणं येन. यथा...ज्ञापयति—connect this and the following clauses with तथा तां...रामाम् अरमयत्. उपजातः विस्रम्भः (confidence) यस्याम्. आत्मानमकथयत्—she declared to him who she really was (*i. e.* she told him that she was सरस्वती). संवत्सरमधिकम् a year or more. It will be noticed how Bāṇa very appropriately draws the veil of silence over the amorous sports of the meeting of सरस्वती and दधीच. It is a canon of rhetoricians that the love sports of divinities are not to be dwelt upon in a poem. In this respect Bāṇa offers a pleasing contrast to Kālidāsa who could not resist the temptation of describing the S'ṛingāra of S'iva and Pārvatī in the कुमारसम्भव (VIII). Vide ध्वन्यालोक (उद्द्योत III under verse 14) 'तस्मादभिनेयार्थे च काव्ये यदुत्तमप्रकृते राजादेरुत्तमप्रकृतिभिर्नायिकाभिः सह ग्राम्यसम्भोगवर्णनं तत्पित्रोः सम्भोगवर्णनमिव सुतरामसभ्यम्। तथैवोत्तमदेवताविषयम्। **न च सम्भोगशृङ्गारस्य सुरतलक्षण एवैकः प्रकारः**, यावदन्येऽपि प्रभेदाः परस्परप्रेमदर्शनादयः सम्भवन्ति। ते कस्मादुत्तमप्रकृतिविषये न वर्ण्यन्ते।...**यत्त्वेवंविधे विषये महाकवीनामप्यसमीक्ष्यकारिता लक्ष्ये दृश्यते स दोष एव।**'.

P. 17 l. 24—**P. 18** l. 8 **अथ दैव...मान्तिकम्.** सर्व...रामम् lovely on account of possessing all (auspicious) characteristics. The following verse summarises most of them 'त्रिषु विपुलो गम्भीरस्त्रिष्वेव षडुन्नतश्चतुर्ह्रस्वः। सप्तसु रक्तो राजा पञ्चसु दीर्घश्च सूक्ष्मश्च॥' बृहत्संहिता 68. 84. जातमात्रायैव the moment he was born. सरहस्याः together with the esoteric or mystical meaning. Or सरहस्याः may mean 'together with the esoteric portion *viz.* the Upanishads.' वेद is often defined as 'मन्त्रब्राह्मणात्मकः'. Compare 'वेदः कृत्स्नोऽधिगन्तव्यः सरहस्यो द्विजन्मना॥' मनु II. 165, where मेधातिथि says 'रहस्यमुपनिषदः'. स्वय...ष्यन्ति will spontaneously manifest themselves. सद्भर्तृ...दधीचम् The idea is:—when सरस्वती left the mortal world at the bidding of ब्रह्मा, she started, enshrining her husband दधीच in her heart. The poet fancies that she carried him in her heart for the purpose of boastfully displaying to the heavenly assembly that she had secured an ideal husband. श्लाघा boast. पिता...देशात्—her curse was to end, according to Brahmā, when she bore a son. Vide text p. 5. l. 9. हृदये...हतः struck in the heart as though by a thunderbolt or by a lightning flash. 'ह्रादिन्यौ वज्रतडितौ' इत्यमरः. भ्रातुः of his cousin (as दधीच had no brother). C and T think that भ्रातृ was a proper name, as it would be unnecessary to describe दधीच's brother or cousin as a Brāhmaṇa. In our opinion ब्राह्मणस्य is purposely put in. दधीच was the son of च्यवन and सुकन्या (the daughter of a क्षत्रिय) and so was only ब्राह्मणसदृश. Vide मनु० 10. 6 'स्त्रीष्वनन्तरजातासु द्विजैरुत्पादितान्सुतान्। सदृशानेव तानाहुर्मातृदोषविगर्हितान्॥'. बाण wants to intimate that

दधीच's cousin was the offspring of Brâhmaṇa parents. अक्षमाला अभिधानं यस्याः. निर्विशेषम् *adv.* without making any difference (connect with समवर्धयत्). सामान्यं स्तन्यं ययोः who were fed alike with the same milk. सारस्वतः (सरस्वत्याः अपत्यं पुमान्) आख्या यस्य. सोदर्ययोरिव like that of brothers. समानोदरे शयितः सोदर्यः according to 'विभाषोदरे' पा. 6. 3. 88 and 'सोदराद्यः' पा. 4. 4. 109. आविर्भूतः अशेषाणां (सकलानां) विद्यानां सम्भारः (समूहः) यस्मिन्. सवयसि—of the same age. समानं वयः अस्य सवयाः. वाङ्मयं...यामास imparted the whole literature. प्राचुर्येण प्रस्तुता वाक् अत्र इति वाङ्मयम् according to 'तत्प्रकृतवचने मयट्' पा. 5. 4. 21. कृतः दाराणां परिग्रहः येन who took a wife. अस्य...वासम् he out of affection made for him in that very place a dwelling named प्रीतिकूट. प्रीतिकूट seems to be the name given to the house of Bāṇa's ancestors. It was so called because सारस्वत built it out of love (प्रीति) for his cousin. आत्मनाऽपि as for himself. आषाढी—see above p. 27. कृष्णाजिनं अस्ति अस्य. These and the following words show that he remained a ब्रह्मचारी. मेखला is a girdle made of grass (मुञ्ज &c). तपस्यतः—*geni. sing.* of the *pr. p.* of तपस्यति denominative verb from तपस् (तपः आचरति).

P. 18 ll. 9--25 **अथ तस्मात्...द्विजातयः.** The first sentence is अथ तस्मात् (वत्सात्)...प्रावर्तत विपुलो वंशः. All the adjectives apply to भागीरथीप्रवाह and वंश. The reading वत्सात् is good. प्रवर्धमानः आदिपुरुषैः (भार्गवादिभिः) जनिता या आत्मचरणस्य उन्नतिः तया निर्गतः प्रघोषः यस्य whose noisy fame went on increasing on account of the eminence of the school (चरणः) established by the first founders (with वंश). वत्स belonged to भार्गवगोत्र. For चरण see above p. 20. Or प्रवर्धमान may be connected with आदिपुरुष, meaning 'who increased *i. e.* had progeny'. प्रवर्धमानः आदिपुरुषः (विष्णुः) तेन जनिता आत्मचरणात् उन्नतिः यस्य ०न्नतिः स चासौ निर्गतप्रघोषश्च (with ०प्रवाहः)—that emitted a loud uproar, issuing from the foot of Vishṇu. The com. sees here (in प्रवर्धमान) a reference to the वामनावतार, when विष्णु, first coming to बलि as a dwarf, assumed a huge form and covered the worlds. 'किल त्रैलोक्याक्रान्तिकाले ब्रह्मलोकप्राप्ताद्विष्णुपदाद् ब्रह्मणा कमण्डलुजलक्षालितात् गङ्गा समभवदिति वार्ता'. For the Ganges rising from the foot of विष्णु, see above p. 41. परमेश्वरेण (शिवेन) शिरसि धृतः (०प्रवाहः); परमेश्वरैः (नृपैः) शिरसि धृतः honoured by kings (with वंश). The Ganges in her descent at भगीरथ's request to purify his ancestors fell on S'iva's head. सकलकलः (कलकलेन सह) आगमः (आगमनं) तेन गम्भीरः—deep (in stream) on account of its coming (from heaven) with an uproar (with ०प्रवाहः); सकलानां कलानां (नृत्यादीनां) आगमेन (by the acquisition) गम्भीरः deep *i. e.* well versed (with

वंशः). महा...मान्यः applies in the same sense to both. Or महामुनि may refer to जह्नु, whose daughter the Ganges became by being let off from his ear. Note रामायण I. 43. 'ततो हि यजमानस्य जह्नोरद्भुतकर्मणः । गङ्गा संप्लावयामास यज्ञवाटं महात्मनः ॥ 35 तस्यावलेपनं ज्ञात्वा क्रुद्धो जह्नुश्च राघव । अपिबत्तु जलं सर्वं गङ्गायाः परमाद्भुतम् ॥ 36...गङ्गां चापि नयन्ति स्म दुहितृत्वे महात्मनः । ततस्तुष्टो महातेजाः श्रोत्राभ्यामसृजत्प्रभुः ॥ 38.' विपक्षाणां शत्रूणां क्षोभः तस्य क्षमः (with वंशः); विपक्षाणां (विगताः पक्षाः येषां ते विपक्षाः पर्वताः तेषां) क्षोभः &c. The Ganges wears out mountains by its flood. Mountains had once wings and harassed the earth by flying anywhere. Indra cut off their wings. Compare 'उदधिमिव भयान्तःप्रविष्टसपक्षभूमिभृत्सहस्रसङ्कुलम्' काम्दबरी p. 90 of P; also रघु० 13. 7. क्षितितले लब्धा आयतिः (दैर्घ्यं प्रभावश्च) येन. The Ganges stretches for a long distance over the earth. The family attained dignity (आयति). अस्ख...त्तः that proceeded without stumbling *i. e.* without minding any obstacle (with गङ्गा); that conducted itself without deviating (from the path of right). The sentence is यस्माद् अजायन्त वात्स्यायना नाम...द्विजातयः. गृहमुनयः who were sages dwelling in houses (and not in forests). A मुनि is a sage or a recluse, who has given up worldly life. The ancestors of Bāṇa were householders but their conduct was so pure that they might be as well styled *munis.* Compare भगवद्गीता 2. 56 for a description of a मुनि. आश्रितं श्रौतं यैः that had recourse to ritual prescribed by the Vedas. अनालम्बिता अलीका बककाकुः यैः (1) that did not resort to the crane-like disagreeable (अलीक) tones; (2) that did not assume false hypocritical tones. There is an apparent contradiction between आश्रितश्रौताः and अना...काकवः in the first sense. Those who studiously perform the ritual of the Vedas have to recite in disagreeable tones the Vedic texts. This विरोध is got over by taking the second sense of अना०. A बक is a symbol of hypocrisy, as it stands on one leg as though deep in meditation and then pounces down upon a fish. काकुः is a change of voice due to fear, sorrow &c. 'काकुः स्त्रियां विकारो यः शोकभीत्यादिभिर्ध्वनेः' इत्यमरः. For बकवृत्ति, note मनु० 'बकवच्चिन्तयेदर्थान्' VII. 106. Explain the विरोध in the following clauses similarly. Read ०व्रता for ०वृता. कृतं कुक्कुटव्रतं यैः (1) that observed the vow of fasting called कुक्कुटव्रत; (2) that devoured cocks. अबैडाला वृत्तिः येषाम् (1) whose conduct was not ferocious, (2) whose conduct was not cat-like. Cats (बिडाल) pounce upon cocks. There is विरोध in the second senses of both compounds; but none if the first sense of each be taken. In कुक्कुटव्रत, one is to subsist on a lump of food not bigger than the egg of a hen. विवर्जिता जनपङ्क्तिः यैः (1) that avoided the cooking of (ordinary or low) people *i. e.* who did not take food cooked by common people; (2) that avoided the company of their castemen at dinner (*i. e.* that avoided a life of bustle and luxury). C and T translate 'averse to worldly pretence.' We cannot understand how this sense is arrived at. परि...कूताः that were free from thoughts (आकूतं) of fraud, bragging and hypocrisy (कूर्च). It is difficult to say what the words कीर and कुची mean. कीर means a parrot and so might stand for 'uttering words without understanding the meaning, bragging.' अगृहीतं गह्वरं यैः (1) that did not resort to caves (*i. e.* remained householders and did not become recluses); (2) that were not hypocrites. 'गुहादम्भौ गह्वरे द्वे' इत्यमरः. न्यक्कृता निकृतिः (शाठ्यं) यैः that disdained dishonesty. प्रसन्ना (tranquil) प्रकृतिः (स्वभावः) येषाम्. We may also dissolve प्रसन्नाः प्रकृतयः (राजामात्याः) येषु. 'अमात्याद्याश्च पौराश्च सद्भिः प्रकृतयः स्मृताः' क्षीर० quoting कात्य. विगताः विकृतयः (changes of mind) येभ्यः. परेषां परिवादः (निन्दा) तस्मात् पराचीनं (पराङ्मुखं) चेतः येषाम्. वर्णत्रयस्य व्यावृत्त्या विशुद्धं अन्धः (अन्नं) येषाम् whose food was pure, the three Varnas being excluded *i. e.* they did not take food with people of the three Varṇas other than that to which they belonged. व्यावृत्तिः exclusion. C and T suggest another sense. 'Whose darkness *i.e.* delusion was corrected by sublating the three colours'. In the श्वेताश्वतरोपनिषद्, (IV. 5. अजामेकां लोहितशुक्लकृष्णां &c.) the three colours शुक्ल, लोहित and कृष्ण represent सत्त्व, रजः and तमः and stand for the material world as opposed to the spirit. Having excluded the material world, their error was at an end and they properly understood the Reality underlying the material world. धीरया धिषणया (बुद्ध्या) अवधूताः अध्येषणाः यैः—who disregarded desires by their firm intellect. 'सनिस्त्वध्येषणा याच्ञा' इत्यमरः. The reference is probably to बृहदारण्यकोपनिषद् 4. 4. 22 'ते ह स्म पुत्रैषणायाश्च वित्तैषणायाश्च लोकैषणायाश्च व्युत्थायाथ भिक्षाचर्यं चरन्ति' or to desires in general. असङ्कसुकः—स्थिरः. 'सङ्कसुकोऽस्थिरे' इत्यमरः (from कस् 10 'to move' with सम्). प्रणत०—who befriended those that came seeking their help (*lit.* that bowed to them). शमिताः समस्तानां शाखान्तराणां संशीतयः (संशयाः) यैः that removed (explained) all the doubts of other schools. शाखा is a traditional recension of a particular Veda, as शाकल of the ऋग्वेद. Here it seems to be used in the sense of शाखाध्येतृ. उद्घाटिताः (opened *i. e.* expounded) समग्राः

ग्रन्थार्थानां ग्रन्थयः (knotty or difficult points) यैः. वाग्मिनः eloquent. वाग्मिन् is used in a good sense, while वाचाल and वाचाट (derived from the same word वाच्) are used in a bad sense. स...निनः fond of clever speech. If we read परसुभा० then the meaning is 'fond of the good sayings of others'. विद...वेदिनः appreciating clever jokes. They did not *themselves crack* jokes, but could appreciate them; they, though वेदाभ्यासरत, were not devoid of a sense of wit and humour. परि...बाह्याः they were charming in their intercourse (with others) and not strangers to dancing, singing and music. They knew a little of नृत्य and other arts, but were not solely devoted to them. ऐति...तृष्णाः who were never surfeited with traditional tales. 'पारम्पर्योपदेशे स्यादैतिह्यमितिहाव्ययम्' इत्यमरः. ऐतिह्यम् from इतिह with the affix ञ्य (य), according to 'अनन्तावसथेतिहभेषजाञ्ञ्यः' पा. 5. 4.23. (आनन्त्यम्, ऐतिह्यम्). सानुक्रोशाः = सदयाः. सत्येन शुचयः pure on account of truthfulness. सर्वसत्त्वेषु सौहार्दं (good will, friendship) एव द्रवः तेन आर्द्रं हृदयं येषाम्. तथा सर्व० the clauses from this downwards are to be taken singly and also in pairs. Taken singly each is construable by itself; if they are taken in pairs, there is an apparent विरोध. सर्व...पेताः possessed of all virtues. सर्व...भूताः possessed of all Guṇas (सत्त्व, रजः and तमः) and (yet) not overwhelmed by the quality of रजस्. राजसेन (गुणेन) अनभिभूताः. राजस is from रजस्. राज...भूताः is construable by itself; but in avoiding the विरोधे with सर्व...पेताः, we may explain it as राजसेनया अनभिभूताः—not treated with dishonour by the royal army (०सेना अनभि०). Explain the following clauses similarly. क्षमाभाजः who are forbearing. क्षमा...नन्दनाः who resort to the earth and have recourse to the Nandana garden. नन्दन is the garden of Indra. Those who resort to it cannot be on the earth. आ...नन्दनाः also means 'who delight their dependents'. अनिस्त्रिंशाः = अक्रूराः. विद्याधराः—those that possess Vidyās. अनि...धराः—that are without swords and (yet) विद्याधरs. निस्त्रिंशः a sword. निष्क्रान्तस्त्रिंशतोऽङ्गुलिभ्यः—that which is longer than 30 finger-breadths. विद्याधरs are semi-divine beings that are always armed with swords. 'मालाखड्गगुलिकाञ्जनादिना भेदेन भिन्नानामपि विद्याधराणां खड्गहस्तत्वं न व्यभिचरति' सं०. अज...वन्तः not dull and well-versed in the arts. अज...वन्तः not cold and (yet) moons. 'शिशिरो जडः' इत्यमरः. अदो...काः free from faults (sins) and helping others (against difficulties or sins). तारयन्तीति तारकाः. अदो...काः without nights (दोषा) and yet constellations. Stars cannot be seen without night. अप...

स्वन्तः not causing distress to others and brilliant (in appearance); not heating others and yet suns. अनु...भुजः without pride (ऊष्मन् *m.*) and sacrificers; without heat and (yet) fires. हुतं भुञ्जते those who enjoy (the fruit of) what they offer as an oblation. अकु...गिनः who had no deceit and were not addicted to pleasure; who did not creep on the earth and (yet) were serpents. अविद्यमाना कुसृतिः शाठ्यं येषाम्. 'कुसृतिर्निकृतिः शाठ्यम्' इत्यमरः. अविद्यमाना कौ (पृथिव्यां) सृतिः (सरणं) येषाम्. भोगिन् *m.* 'a serpent' (from भोगः hood + इन्). अस्त...लयाः who were free from stiffness (arrogance) and were abodes of good deeds; without pillars and (yet) holy places (temples &c.) A house cannot be without a pillar. अलुप्त...दक्षाः who never ceased in the performance of sacrifices and were skilful; the performance of their sacrifice was not disturbed and (yet) they were दक्षs. दक्ष was a famous प्रजापति. He once celebrated a sacrifice at which he did not invite his own daughter सती and her husband शिव. She went uninvited, was insulted and threw herself into fire. S'iva destroyed the sacrifice of दक्ष, pursued the latter and killed him. Compare 'न पशुपतेरिव दक्षोद्वेगकारीण्यैश्वर्यविलसितानि' हर्षचरित II;'दक्षाध्वरक्रियामिवोद्धतगणकचग्रहभयोपसेवितत्र्यम्बकाम्' कादम्बरी p. 128 of P. and कुमारसम्भव I. 21. अ...जितः who were not deceitful and had restrained desires; without serpents and vanquishers of Cupid (*i. e.* S'ivas). S'iva has serpents encircling his body. कामान् जयन्तीति or कामं कन्दर्पं जयन्तीति. 'भेद्यलिङ्गे शठे व्यालः पुंसि श्वापदसर्पयोः' इत्यमरः. असा...जातयः who were pre-eminent and Brāhmaṇas; who had nothing in common (with others) and (yet) had two jātis. A जाति (genus) is defined as 'नित्यमेकमनेकानुगतम्'. A जाति like गोत्व is common to all cows. So if they had two जातिs they must have certain characteristics in common with others and so could not be असाधारण.

P. 18 l. 26–**P. 19** l. 5 तेषु...निजे. संसरति संसारे the world went on or revolved. वहत्सु वत्सरेषु as years rolled. प्रसवः... कुले as the वात्स्यायन family incessantly went on growing in an unbroken chain of progeny. वैनतेयः = गरुडः. गुरु...पाती (1) who was devoted to (had a liking for) his teachers or parents (with कुबेरनामा); that flies on his big wings (with गरुड). द्विजः (1) a Brāhmaṇa; a bird. गरुड was the son of विनता one of the wives of कश्यप. विनता lost a wager with her co-wife कद्रू and had to be the latter's slave. She was released from slavery by Garuda who gave nectar as a ransom after vanquishing Indra. युगा...विस्तारः (1) whose progeny expanded by their Brāhmanical lustre (*i. e.* by their knowledge of the Vedas); (2) which have a vast creation of beings produced from Brahmā's lustre (with युगारम्भाः.). In the beginning of the कृतयुग, ब्रह्मा was alone and from him sprang the creation. चत्वारः may be connected also with युगारम्भाः as there are four Yugas. स...नन्दकाः— (1) that delighted the assembly of the good (with sons); that have the discuss and the नन्दक sword (with नारायणबाहु०). सतां (साधूनां) चक्रं नन्दयन्तीति; सतौ चक्रनन्दकौ येषाम्. चक्र is one of the weapons of नारायण, who also has four arms. नन्दक is the sword of विष्णु. भूभारः इव like the heavy earth. अचल...स्थितिः (1) who never swerved from the usages of his family (with सूनुः); (2) that obtained steadiness by the group of mountains. अचला कुलस्थितिः यस्य; अचलकुले (पर्वतसमूहे) स्थितिः यस्य. It was believed that the earth, which was at first unsteady, was made steady by the mountains. Compare 'भिषजो भूधरा इव भुवो धृतिं चक्रुः' हर्षचरित IV; 'अनुजीविभूभृच्छतसहस्रकल्पिताबष्टम्भं सञ्चारिणं द्वितीयमिव मेदिनीसंनिवेशम्' कादम्बरी. Each वर्ष has its कुलपर्वतs; for the seven कुलपर्वतs of भरतवर्ष, see above p. 76. In अचलकुल, the author refers to the कुलपर्वतs. चतुरुदधिवत् गम्भीरः (सूनुः), चतुरुदधिभिः गम्भीरः (भूभारः). समग्राणां अग्रजन्मनां (ब्राह्मणानां) चक्रं समूहः तस्य चूडामणिः. एकादश—the eleven sons are compared to the Rudras that are also eleven. They are manifestations of शिव. सोमा...मुखान् (1) whose mouths were full of the spray of the nectar-like Soma juice (with पुत्रान्); whose faces are covered with the spray of the nectar from the moon (with रुद्रान्). सोम juice was drunk in sacrifices. सोमः अमृतरस इव तस्य शीकरैः च्छुरितानि मुखानि येषाम्; सोमस्य (चन्द्रमसः) अमृतरसः तस्य शीकरः तेन &c. शिव has the moon on his head and, as the moon was full of nectar, शिव's face would be covered with nectar spray. राजदेवी अभिधानं यस्याः. उपसम्पन्नया who died (connect with विधेर्वशात्). एधीयमाना (increasing) धृतिः (energy, steadiness) यस्य. धाम्नि = गृहे.

P. 19 ll. 6–28 **कृतोप...हास्यताम्.** कृतः उपनयनादिक्रियाकलापः यस्य. समावृत्त *lit.* 'returned' *i. e.* one who returns from his teacher's house to his home after finishing his study. Compare मनु० III. 4. 'गुरुणानुमतः स्नात्वा समावृत्तो यथाविधि। उद्वहेत द्विजो भार्यां सवर्णां लक्षणान्विताम्॥.' समावर्तन is what is now symbolised in सोडमुंज (in Marathi). For देशीय, see above (notes p. 55). चतुर्दश०–fourteen was rather an early age for समावर्तन, but it contrasts most favourably with the unseemly haste with which समावर्तन is now performed. श्रुति means the Vedas and Smṛitis are woks like the मनुस्मृति, which contain the traditional laws and usages of the Âryas. 'श्रुतिस्तु वेदो विज्ञेयो धर्मशास्त्रं तु वै स्मृतिः' मनु० 2. 10. पुण्यजातम्—is the object of कृत्वा. अदशमीस्थ एव *lit.* 'without reaching the tenth decade of life' *i. e.* not in ripe old age. The full period of human life is 100 years, as expressed in the Vedic words 'शतायुर्वै पुरुषः.' This was divided into ten decades. दशमीस्थ would be one between 90 and 100 years of age. 'दशमीस्थौ क्षीणरागवृद्धौ' इत्यमरः—दशम्यां वयोवस्थायां तिष्ठतीति. संस्थिते = मृते. आ...प्राप्तः overwhelmed with great distress. 'स्यात्कष्टं कृच्छ्रमाभीलम्' इत्यमरः—आ समन्तात् भियं लातीति (क्षीरस्वामी). अवि... तन्त्र्यस्य as independence is the prime source (निदानं) of misconduct. Bāṇa became his own master at the tender age of fourteen. 'निदानं त्वादिकारणम्' इत्यमरः. This and the following clauses assign reasons as to why he became इत्वर. कुतू...भावस्य as adolescence is a period when curiosity predominates. 'बाल आ षोडशाद्वर्षात्'. Bāṇa wanted to gratify the curiosity he felt as to various things in the world. धैर्य...रम्भस्य as the first stage of youth is opposed to steadiness. शैश... चरन् doing many rash acts in keeping with his youth. इत्वरः—from इ to go, according to 'इण्-नश्-जि-सर्तिभ्यः करप्' पा. 3. 2. 163 (इत्वरः, नश्वरः, जित्वरः)—a wanderer, a wild man. वयसा...याश्च friends and companions of the same age (as himself). The list shows that Bāṇa must have been in very affluent circumstances and must have led a life of ease and luxury. पारशवौ—they were the sons of his uncles from wives of the S'ūdra caste. Note मनु० 9. 178. 'यं ब्राह्मणस्तु शूद्रायां कामादुत्पादयेत्सुतम्। स पारयन्नेव शवस्तस्मात्पारशवः स्मृतः ॥'. पारयन्नेव (जीवन्नेव) शवः (a corpse) पारशवः—this kind of son was so called because he was no better than a corpse for conferring the spiritual benefits which a son was expected to confer. भाषाकविः a vernacular poet. The word भाषा was often applied to the spoken vernaculars as opposed to संस्कृत, when the latter ceased to be spoken by the masses. The com. also explains as 'a composer of songs.' 'भाषा गेयवस्तुवाचः तेषु (?) कविः' सं०. प्रणयिनौ loving (dependents). विद्वांसौ = पण्डितौ. वर्णकविः probably means 'a poet celebrating the renown of others, a bard or panegyrist.' But we have 'बन्दिनौ' a little later on. The com. takes the word to mean 'a poet of Gāthās or versifier in the अपभ्रंश dialects.' 'वर्णकविर्गाथादिषु गीतिदः। अपभ्रष्टगीतविद्यः' सं०. प्रा...पुत्रः a young noble composing Prâkrit poems. महाराष्ट्री was the Prākrit *par excellence*, the other important प्राकृत dialects being शौरसेनी, मागधी and पैशाची. प्राकृत is derived as 'प्रकृतिः संस्कृतं तत्र भवं तत आगतं वा;' while some take it as meaning the language of the masses as opposed to संस्कृत, the speech of polished society. कात्यायनिका—'कात्यायन्यर्धवृद्धा या काषायवसनाधवा' इत्यमरः—an elderly widow dressed in the ascetic's red robes. जाङ्गुलिकः = विषवैद्यः—a dealer in antidotes or a snake-doctor. भिषक्पुत्रः a young physician. 'कलादो रुक्मकारके' इत्यमरः. कलादः a goldsmith. 'कलामादत्ते, कलं सुवर्णकालिकामाद्यति आखण्डयति वा' क्षीर०. हैरिकः supervisor (of goldsmiths), according to सं०. लेखकः scribe. चित्रकृत् a painter. पुस्तकृत् a model-maker, a manufacturer of dolls 'पुस्तकृल्लेप्यकारः.' 'मृदा वा दारुणा वाथ वस्त्रेणाप्यथ चर्मणा । लोहरत्नैः कृतं चापि पुस्तमित्यभिधीयते ॥'. मार्दङ्गिकः versed in playing on a drum (मृदङ्ग). 'मृदङ्गवादनं शिल्पमस्य मार्दङ्गिकः' according to 'शिल्पम्' पा. 4. 4. 55. गायनौ singers. सैरन्ध्री—a female who, not being a regular servant, is employed in others' houses for doing things requiring skill, such as decoration of the hair &c. 'सैरन्ध्री परवेश्मस्था स्ववशा शिल्पकारिका' इत्यमरः. वांशिकौ—a flute-player, piper. गान्धर्वम् music. संवाहिका shampooer. लासकयुवा a young dancer. ताण्डविक—It will be noticed that many of the names of Bāna's associates such as सुदृष्टि, चामीकर, जीमूत are very appropriate to the art they cultivated or the profession they followed. This is rather suspicious. आक्षिकः one who plays at dice. अक्षैर्दीव्यति or जयति इति आक्षिकः, according to 'तेन दीव्यति खनति जयति जितम्' पा. 4. 4. 2. कितवः a gambler. 'धूर्तोऽक्षदेवी कितवोऽक्षधूर्तो द्यूतकृत्समाः' इत्यमरः. शैलालियुवा a young actor. 'पाराशर्यशिलालिभ्यां भिक्षुनटसूत्रयोः' पा. 4. 3. 110 (शिलालिना प्रोक्तं नटसूत्रमधीयते शैलालिनो नटाः). पाराशरी—an ascetic that has studied the Sûtra of Parās'ara. पाराशर्येण प्रोक्तं भिक्षुसूत्रं अधीयते पाराशरिणो भिक्षवः. See Pāṇini's sūtra quoted above. क्षपणकः—a Jain monk. कथकः a narrator or story—teller; one who publicly reads and expounds the Purāṇas. मन्त्रसाधकः a magician, one who is an adept in incantations. असुर... सनी-treasure—seeker. Bāṇa very frequently uses this word; but it is not easy to give the exact sense. On considering all the passages where the word occurs, we think that असुरविवर was a term applied to shafts of mines that had already been worked up in bygone days. They were believed to be the work of Asuras and to lead to the treasures of पाताल, in hopes of reaching which many people must have endangered their lives. Note 'यः (जनपदविशेषः) असुरविवरमिति वातिकैः (अगृह्यत)' हर्ष० 3rd उच्छ्वास; 'असुरविवराणीवापावृतानि' हर्ष० 4th उच्छ्वास; '**असुरविवरव्यसनिनं** चापजहुः... मागधं **गोधनगिरिसुरङ्गया** स्वविषयं मेकलाधिपमन्त्रिणः;' हर्ष० 6th उच्छ्वास; 'लग्नासुरविवरप्रवेशपिशाचेन' कादम्बरी p. 227 of P. धातु...वित् who knew the धातुवाद *i. e.* the transmutation of metals into gold, an alchemist. Vide notes above p. 55 as to mercury. दार्दुरिकः a potter, according to 'शब्ददर्दुरं करोति' पा. 4.4.34 (शब्दं करोति शाब्दिकः। दर्दुरं करोति दार्दुरिकः कुलालः). दर्दुर was a musical instrument like a drum. The word probably means 'a player on दर्दुर' like मार्दङ्गिक above. ऐन्द्रजालिकः juggler, illusionist. मस्करी = परिव्राजकः A Sannyāsin. 'भिक्षुः परिव्राट् कर्मन्दी पाराशर्यपि मस्करी' इत्यमरः. पतञ्जलि derives the word from मा and कृ. 'मा कृत मा कृत कर्माणि शान्तिर्वः श्रेयसीति आहातो मस्करी परिव्राजकः' महाभाष्य (Kielhorn Vol. III. p. 96). The word occurs in the 5th उच्छ्वास also. बाल...गतः being easily guided (led away) on account of his youth. निघ्न dependent, in the hands of others. 'अधीनो निघ्न आयत्तः' इत्यमरः. ०कौतुकेन आक्षिप्तं (drawn) हृदयं यस्य. उपात्त obtained. सति...सङ्गे in spite of the fact that his attachment to learning was unbroken. His self-willed action in wasting his valuable youth in wanderings made him a butt of ridicule to the great. अगाच्च—connect with उपहास्यताम्. निरवग्रहः being without any check. 'स्वच्छन्दो निरवग्रहः' इत्यमरः. ग्रह...यौवनेन as if possessed by his fresh youth. One possessed by a ghost does strange things. स्वैरिन् doing just as it pleases.

P. 19 l. 29–**P. 20** l. 5. **अथ...भवदिति**. अत्युदारा व्यवहृतिः यस्य whose conduct or dealing was very charming or noble. This would be an adjective of बाण. Some MSS. read ०हृतिमनोहन्ति 'charming on account of noble practices.' राजकुलानि courts. निर...द्योतितानि made illustrious by blameless lores. Vide notes p. 18 on निरवद्यविद्या. गुरुकुलानि schools. Mark the contrast between वीक्षमाणः and सेवमानः. महार्हैः आलापैः गम्भीराः (deep *i. e.* full) गुणवतां गोष्ठ्यः. महा...मानः attending the meetings of the meritorious that were full of valuable discussions. स्वभावेन गम्भीरा धीः धनं येषाम्. पुनर...भाजन् he again recovered that same scholarly attitude of mind which was appropriate to his family. विपश्चितः इयं वैपश्चिती. 'विद्वान् विपश्चिद्दोषज्ञः' इत्यमरः. ब्राह्मणाधिवास may be the name of Bāṇa's village, as प्रीतिकूट was the name of his home. ब्राह्मणाधिवास would also mean 'the resort of Brāhmaṇas.' अभिनवीभूतौ स्नेहसद्भावौ येषाम् whose affection and amiability were renewed. संस्तवेन प्रकटितं ज्ञातेयं (बन्धुता) यैः that manifested their relationship by being very intimate with him. 'संस्तवः स्यात्परिचयः' इत्यमरः. ज्ञातेय—from ज्ञाति, according to 'कपिज्ञात्योर्ढक्' पा० 5. 1. 127 (कापेयम्, ज्ञातेयम्)—ज्ञातेर्भावः कर्म वा ज्ञातेयम्. अभिनन्दितं अभिगमनं यस्य. आप्तैः relatives; those whose words are always true (Seers).

बाल...गतः being in the midst of the friends of his boyhood. The words may also mean 'going through the midst of the disc of the sun (मित्र) that has become mild.' The liberated soul was supposed to proceed through the sun on the path of liberation. Vide notes p. 21 on देवयान. The com. says that the sun's lustre is reduced at sight of a Yogin. "उक्तं च—'तपस्यन्तं रविं दृष्ट्वा निस्तेजा जायते रविः । मोक्षमार्गप्रयत्ने तु तेजो नैवास्य विद्यते ॥.'" इति—This is added to show that the chapter has come to an end.

Uchchhvāsa II

Verse 1. The verse contains many श्लिष्ट words. The sentence is अतिगम्भीरे भूपे निरवतारस्य जनस्य समीहितसिद्धिं गुणवन्तः घटकाः पार्थिवाः दधति कूपे इव--with a very profound king it is the virtuous and energetic princes that bring about the fulfilment of what is desired by people who have no entrance (to the king), as with a well. The idea is that good princes that are about the person of an emperor intercede with the latter for bestowing favours on people. This and the next verse suggest how कृष्ण the cousin of हर्ष introduced बाण to the favour of हर्ष. गम्भीर means one whose feelings of anger &c. are not indicated by his gestures or appearance. अवतारः entrance or access. घटकाः those that accomplish. अतिगम्भीरे कूपे निरवतारस्य जनस्य गुणवन्तः पार्थिवाः घटकाः ०सिद्धिं दधति in the case of a deep well, small earthen (पार्थिव) jars to which strings (गुण) are attached bring about the fulfilment of the desires of people who have no means of descending (into the well). अवतारः a flight of steps. The metre is Âryā. From the definition of आख्यायिका (Intro. p. XX) it will be seen that the verses occurring therein were to suggest future events.

Verse 2. रागि...भवाम्—the day plants in the red lotus beauty that is due to the sun. रागिन् also means 'affectionate, devoted.' लक्ष्मी wealth. This suggests how कृष्ण (who was like दिवस) planted wealth in Bāṇa who was devoted to the king हर्ष (who corresponds to the sun), the wealth being the gift of हर्ष and he (कृष्ण) being only the intercessor. अनपेक्षिताः गुणदोषाः यस्मिन् in which no regard is paid to merits or faults. The good are passionately devoted to the task of helping others, irrespective of their merits or faults. Here there is a veiled reference to the चापल्य of Bāṇa's youth.

P. 21 ll. 5–16 **अथ...तिष्ठत्.** The principal sentence is अथ तत्र...बान्धवानां भवनानि भ्रमन् सुखमतिष्ठत्. भस्मपुण्ड्रकैः पाण्डुराणि ललाटानि येषाम् (*adj.* of बटुभिः). For पुण्ड्क, see notes p. 26. कपि...टिलैः that had tawny hair (with बटुभिः); that were full of tawny flames (with कृशानुभिः). कृशानुभिः = अग्निभिः. क्रतु०—The boys had come to see the sacrifices and partake of the दक्षिणा. They are fancied to be fires coming with the desire that sacrifices may be offered to them. अध्यास्यमानानि inhabited. This and the following nouns in the accusative qualify भवनानि below. सेकेन सुकुमारा सोमकेदारिका तया हरितायमानाः प्रघनाः येषाम् the porches in front of the doors of which were green with the small beds of Soma plants that looked fine (fresh) on account of being (recently) watered. केदारिका small field. 'प्रघाणप्रघणालिन्दा बहिर्द्वारप्रकोष्ठके' इत्यमरः. The juice of Soma plants was required in sacrifices. कृष्णाजिनेषु विकीर्यमाणाः (spread) शुष्यन्तः पुरोडाशीयाः श्यामाकतण्डुलाः येषु. पुरोडाशीय (from पुरोडाश with the affix छ *i. e.* ईय) useful for पुरोडाश, which means 'a sacrificial oblation made of ground rice and offered in vessels.' 'विभाषा हविरपूपादिभ्यः' पा. 5. 1. 4. (पुरोडाश्याः तण्डुलाः, पुरोडाशीयाः वा). श्यामाकः a kind of grain (called सांवे in Marathi). बालिकाभिः विकीर्यमाणाः नीवार— बलयः येषु. नीवार is a kind of wild rice growing without cultivation. The girls offered the grain to the birds and their pets. ०शतैः आनीयमानाः ०समिधः येषु. पूली a bundle. पलाशम् a leaf. समिध् *f.* fuel. They brought green Kus'a grass, leaves and fuel. Or we make take पलाशसमिधः as meaning 'small twigs of the पलाश tree' that were required for being thrown into the fire. इन्ध... कूटानि full of heaps (कूटः) of fuel (इन्धनं) and cowdung cakes. आमिक्षा a mixture of curds and boiled milk, offered in the वैश्वदेव oblation. 'पक्के पयसि दध्यानयति सा वैश्वदेव्यामिक्षा' quoted by क्षीर० as a श्रुति. For आमिक्षीय (आमिक्षायै हित) see पुरोडाशीय above. खुर...र्दिकानि the covered platforms (वितर्दिः) in the court-yards of which were rubbed by the round hoofs. 'स्याद्वितर्दिस्तु वेदिका' इत्यमरः (दारुपरिष्कृता चतुरस्रा विश्रान्तिभूः' क्षीर०). कमण्डलव्य useful or fit for making pots (कमण्डलु). 'उ—गवादिभ्यो यत्' पा. 5. 1. 2. मर्दनम् pounding. वै...व्यानाम् useful for making pegs for measuring the sacrificial (वैतान) altar. शङ्कव्य from शङ्कु with affix यत्, according to 'तस्मै हितम्' पा. 5. 1. 5. (शङ्कवे हितं शङ्कव्यम्). Pegs of the branches of उदुम्बर trees were used in measuring altars. पवित्रिताः पर्यन्ताः (borders, outskirts) येषाम्. वैश्वदेवपिण्ड—the offerings of boiled rice made to all the deities (विश्वेदेवाः) before taking one's dinner. हवि...लयानि the tender leaves of the trees (विटपिन् *m.*) in the courts of which were darkened with the smoke of the oblations. वत्सीय...तर्णकानि where the newly born calves, being caressed (लालित) by the cowherds (वत्सपालकः) that were fond of them, frisked about. वत्सीयः (वत्सेभ्यो हितः) is formed like शङ्कव्य. From the numerous words formed with the affixes छ (ईय) and यत् it seems as though बाण wanted to illustrate the first Pāda of the 5th अध्याय of the अष्टाध्यायी. 'सद्यो-जातस्तु तर्णकः' इत्यमरः. ०पालकैः लालिताः ललन्तः (sportive) तरलाः (चञ्चलाः) तर्णकाः येषु. क्रीडद्भिः कृष्णशारच्छागशावकैः प्रकटितः पशुबन्धानां (यज्ञानां) प्रबन्धः (सन्ततिः) येषु where the continuous performance of animal sacrifices was indicated by the young goats, dark and variegated (शार), playing about. This shows that in Bāṇa's day animal sacrifices were frequently performed. शुक...सुखानि where the teachers were given rest by the fact that parrots and *mainas* (सारिका) commenced to repeat (the Vedas). The idea is:—the parrots and सारिकाs, having repeatedly heard the teachers reciting the Vedas, themselves correctly repeated them and the students could take lessons from them, instead of from the teachers, who thus got rest. Compare 'स्वतःप्रमाणं परतः प्रमाणं कीराङ्गना यत्र गिरं गिरन्ति । द्वारस्थनीडान्तरसंनिरुद्धा जानीहि तन्मण्डनपण्डितौकः ॥' माधवाचार्य's शङ्करदिग्विजय VIII. 6. सा...नीव as though they were the penance groves of the three Vedas incarnate. भवनानि—is the object of भ्रमन्.

P. 27 ll. 17–23 **तत्र...माली.** Bāṇa now describes the advent of summer in highly paronomastic sentences, the season (कालः) being identified with शिव in his terrific form (महाकाल). तत्रस्थस्य while staying in the houses of his kinsmen. कुसुमसमयः (वसन्तः) एव युगम्. उपसंहरन् bringing to an end. ग्रीष्म brings to an end the season of spring. शिव when destroying the world brings the युग to an end. अजृम्भत *lit.* yawned *i. e.* increased. ग्रीष्मः अभिधानं यस्य. सम्फुल्लमल्लिकाभिः धवलाः अट्टाः (market stalls) एव हासाः यस्य where the stalls smiled with white full blown jasmine flowers. The मल्लिका is a flower of the hot season. ०मल्लिकावत् धवलः अट्टहासः यस्य. The loud laugh of शिव is called अट्टहास. महाकालः the great season (of summer); S'iva. प्रत्य...तस्य recently conquered. The poet now changes the metaphor. ग्रीष्म is a conqueror that subdues the prince वसन्त, but at first treats kindly the children of his vanquished rival. वसन्तः एव सामन्तः तस्य. पयः पायिषु that drink milk (with बालपल्लेषु); that drink water *i. e.* are thirsty (with नवोद्यानेषु). दर्शितः स्नेहः येन. स्नेहः affection; moisture. नवोद्यानेषु (with ०पल्लेषु) would also mean 'who have just begun to walk.' मृदुरभूत्—summer did not at once scorch the gardens, but was mild at first. सकल...रोत् made the stalks of all flowers loose *i. e.* summer scorched the flowers of spring which easily dropped down from the stem.

A king at his accession (अभिनवोदित:) lets loose prisoners from his jails. It was usual to set prisoners free on the accession of a king or at the birth of a prince or on other great occasions. Compare हर्ष० 4th उच्छ्वास 'अधावन्त मुक्तानि बन्धनवृन्दानि' and notes thereon. प्रतपन् showing his valour; very hot. ऋतुः एव राजा तस्य. अभिषेकार्द्राः wet after a bath (with कामिनीनां ०चयाः); wet at the time of the coronation (with चामरकलापाः). At a king's coronation, holy water is poured over him. Chowries are a symbol of royalty; they may become wet at a coronation. In ग्रीष्म, young women bathe their heads with water; their hair looks very charming after the bath and excites love. In वसन्त, love is excited spontaneously, but in the scorching heat of ग्रीष्म, such extraneous aids as charming tresses are required. This is spoken of as कामिनीनां ०चयाः कुसुमायुधेन स्वयमगृह्यन्त. The hair of the women is fancied to be the chowrie of the king–summer, that is held in his own hand by Cupid. Bāṇa seems to follow the रघुवंश in this description as suggested by the com. Compare 'स्नानार्द्रमुक्तेष्वनुधूपवासं विन्यस्तसायन्तनमल्लिकेषु । कामो वसन्तात्ययमन्दवीर्यः केशेषु लेभे रतिमङ्गनानाम् ॥' रघु० 16. 50. हिमा...माली the sun made his expedition towards the Himālaya (*i. e.* towards the north). यात्रा journey, expedition. It is in ग्रीष्म that the sun reaches the northernmost point in his apparent yearly motion. This natural phenomenon is fancied to be due to the wrath which the sun feels at the fact that the lotuses (that open by daylight) are blighted by snow. For the effect of हिम on कमलिनी, see notes p. 63.

P. 21 l. 24—**P. 22** l. 2 **अथ...सन्तापात्**. ललाटं तपतीति ललाटन्तपः scorching the brow (*lit.* forehead), according to 'असूर्यललाटयोर्दृशितपोः' पा. 3. 2. 36 (असूर्यपश्या राजदाराः, ललाटन्तपः सूर्यः । सि. कौ.), a nasal being inserted after ललाट in accordance with 'अरुर्द्विषदजन्तस्य मुम्' पा. 6. 3. 67. तपने = सूर्ये. लिखितः ललाटिका एव पुण्ड्रकः यैः. For ललाटिका, see p. 44 and for पुण्ड्रक, see p. 26. अलकाः (curls) एव चीरचीवरं (ragged dress of a mendicant) तेन संवीतैः (covered). दिन...न्दुभिः the foreheads of ladies as though undertook vows (नियमाः) for propitiating the sun. One who observes a व्रत has a पुण्ड्रक on his forehead, wears ragged garments and a rosary; ladies (on account of the fierce heat) had sandal mark on their foreheads, allowed their curls to play about their foreheads and had drops of perspiration (resembling pearls in their brightness). चन्दनेन धूसराभिः (with सुन्दरीभिः); चन्दनवत् धू० (with कुमुदिनीभिः). असूर्यम्पश्या—see notes above on ललाटन्तप. The women did not come out in the sun; the कुमुद plants close their buds in the day. कुमुदs are white and so the plants are called चन्दनधू०. दिवसमसुप्यत—the ladies slept the whole day; the कुमुद plants closed their petals in the day. निद्रा...तपम् the eyes, heavy with sleep, could not bear even the light of the jewels; what of the fully grown heat? अशि...शर्वर्यः In the season of summer the moonlit nights became shorter and shorter, being esteemed by pairs of चक्रवाकs, like rivers. चक्रवाक is separated from its mate at night and so they welcome the shortness of the nights. सोडुपाः possessed of the moon (with शर्वर्यः); with rafts (with सरितः). There are boats on rivers, which are welcomed by चक्रवाकs, as they live near them. उडुपः lord of stars (उडु *f. n.*) *i. e.* the moon. उडुपः–पम् raft. अभिनवः पटुः (strong) पाटलानां आमोदः तेन सुरभिः परिमलः यस्य (*adj.*of जलं and पवनं also). पाटल (trumpet flower) is a kind of fragrant summer flower. Compare शाकुन्तल I 'सुलभसलिलावगाहाः पाटलसंसर्गसुरभिवनवाताः ।'.

P. 22 l. 3–**P. 23** l. 5. **क्रमेण......मातरिश्वानः.** The sentence is क्रमेण च ...प्रावर्तन्त...मातरिश्वानः. खराः (fierce) खगस्य (सूर्यस्य) मयूखाः यस्मिन्. 'शरार्कविहगाः खगाः' इत्यमरः. This and the following clauses in the locative qualify निदाघकाले (l. 12). खण्डितं शैशवं यस्य whose childhood was gone *i. e.* when the season had far advanced. सीदन्ति स्रोतांसि यस्मिन् when the streams sank low *i. e.* had hardly any water left in them. झिल्लि...रिणि resounding with the cries of crickets. कातर...विश्वे when the world was deafened by the continued cooing of the distressed doves. वि...त्रिणि when the birds breathed very heavily. करीषङ्कषः मरुत् यस्मिन् when the wind swept dried cowdung. 'सर्वकूलाभ्रकरीषेषु कषः' पा. 3-2-42. (सर्वङ्कषः खलः । कूलङ्कषा नदी । करीषङ्कषा वात्या । सि. कौ). 'गोविड् **गोमय**मस्त्रियाम् । तत्तु **शुष्कं करीषो**ऽस्त्री' इत्यमरः. विरलाः वीरुधः (लताः) यस्मिन्. As the leaves fell off through heat, the creepers grew less dense. रुधिर...स्तबके when the bunches of fullgrown (कठोर) धातकी flowers were licked by the young of lions in their greed for blood. धातकी flowers are very red. ताम्यत् स्तम्बेरमानां यूथं तस्य वमथुः तेन तिम्यन्तः महामहीधराणां नितम्बाः यस्मिन् where the slopes (नितम्बः) of large mountains became wet with the spray spouted from the trunks of languid elephants. स्तम्बेरमः हस्ती

स्तम्बे (तृणे) रमते इति (अलुक्समास) according to 'स्तम्बकर्णयो रमिजपोः' पा. 3-2-13. (स्तम्बेरमः कर्णेजपः). 'वमथुः करशीकरः' इत्यमरः. दिनकरेण दूयमानाः द्विरदाः तेषां दीनेषु (distressed) वदनेषु आश्याना (partially dried) दानस्य (ichor) श्यामिका (dark streak) तस्यां आलीनाः मूकाः मधुलिहः (bees) यस्मिन्. The thirsty bees stuck to whatever was left of the ichor. लोहितायमानाः मन्दारैः सिन्दूरिताः सीमानः यस्मिन् when the boundaries (of villages) looked red, being as though smeared with vermilion by the मन्दार flowers. मन्दार trees were planted on the boundaries. Their red flowers looked like सिन्दूर. Even now boundary stones are smeared with सिन्दूर. स्यन्दः stream, trickling line. सन्दोहः mass. ०सन्दोहस्य सन्देहेन मुञ्चन्तः महामहिषाः तेषां विषाणकोटिभिः विलिख्यमानाः (scratched) स्फुटन्त्यः स्फाटिकदृषदः यस्मिन्—The crystal slabs looked like trickling water; so the buffaloes in hopes of getting more water vehemently struck them with their horns. घर्मेण (by heat) मर्मरिताः (rustled) गर्मुतः (creepers) यस्मिन्. The leaves being dry, the creepers produced a rustle. त...किरे when the scratching cocks were afraid of scratching (for food) in husk-fire due to the heated dust. कुकूलः-लम् fire burning in chaff. Cocks ordinarily scratch for food in chaff, which is heaped up in dust. The dust being heated set fire to a portion of the chaff and so cocks became afraid to scratch near it. विकिरः a bird, particularly, a cock (from कॄ with वि). 'विष्किरः शकुनिर्विकिरो वा' पा. 6. 1. 150. विवरशरणाः (विवरं शरणं येषां) श्वाविधाः (porcupines) यस्मिन्. Generally the word is श्वाविध्, but Bāṇa uses the form श्वाविध. तटा...म्भसि when the waters of the ponds (being dried up) left only mud and were coloured by the fish rolling (विवर्तमान) on their backs, the fish being distressed by the cries (कूजा) of the ospreys (कुरराः) on the Arjuna trees on the banks of the ponds. The com. reads कूटज्वर० and explains 'कूटः शब्द एव सन्तापकारित्वात् ज्वरः.' ०वर्तमानाः उत्तानाः शफराः तै शारं पङ्कशेषं (पङ्कः शेषः यस्य) पल्वलाम्भः यस्मिन्. On the connection between the cries of ospreys and the distress of fishes, the com. remarks 'कुररास्तटस्था यदा कूजन्ति तदा मत्स्याः पीडिताः सन्तः उत्प्लवन्तीति वस्तुधर्मोऽयम्.' दावेन जनितं जगन्नीराजनं यस्मिन्. The forest conflagration as though performed the नीराजन rite of the world. For नीराजन, see above p. 34. रज...यक्ष्मणि which was the (cause of) the consumption of night. In summer night slowly dwindles, as a man gradually becomes emaciated in consumption. Compare 'घर्मवृद्धिरपां प्रस्थः क्षपाह्रास उदग्गतौ' वेदाङ्गज्योतिष. कठो...काले when the season of summer was far advanced. प्रति...लुण्ठका: that openly carried off in desert places the roofs (पटलं) of water-sheds (प्रपा), garden enclosures (वाट:) and huts, as though they were leaping in all directions. This and the following nouns in the nominative qualify उन्मत्ता मातरिश्वान: below. A mad man (उन्मत्त) also wanders (आटीकमान) everywhere. ऊषर: a desert. प्रपा is Marathi पाणपोई. लुण्ठक: robber. प्रपक्व...स्थली: rubbing against sandy (शर्करिल) hard (कर्कर) places, as though they (the winds) were all of a sudden itching on account of their rashness in cracking (आच्छोटनं) the lines of the bushes of ripe कपिकच्छू. A person whose skin is itching rubs it against a hard substance. The wind broke the bushes of the prickly कपिकच्छू plant (that causes itch) and also dragged the sand off hard stony places. 'स्त्री शर्करा **शर्करिल:** शार्कर: शर्करावति । देश एवादिमौ' इत्यमर:. Vide notes on सैकत above p. 44. A mad man also may break the bush of the prickly कपिकच्छू, have itch thereby and rub his hands against stones. कपीनामपि कच्छू: यस्या: सा कपिकच्छू:. स्थूल...मुच:—The strong winds carried off gravel of comparatively large size. मुचु...दन्तुरा: bristling with the shoots (कन्दल:-लम्) of मुचुकुन्द broken by them. दलनं breaking. The broken shoots looked like teeth. A mad man also shows his teeth. In most of the following clauses reference is made to a mad man's appearance and actions. We shall not explain all of them, as almost all can be easily understood. समन्त...तनव: that were moistened by the spray from the mouths of the noisy tribes of crickets (चीरी) flying all round. 'भृङ्गारी चीरुका **चीरी झिल्लिका** च स्त्रियामिमा:' इत्यमर:. ०शीकरे शीक्यमाना तनु: येषाम्. शीक् 10th *conj.* to moisten. तरुणतर: तरणि: (सूर्य:) तस्य तापेन तरले चञ्चले (*adj.* of ०वारिणि). तरुण...वारिणि as though floating on the illusory and tremulous waters of the mirage, as they (waters) trembled with the heat of the fierce (*lit.* young) sun. The heat of the sun produced the appearance of a mirage on sandy deserts. The air being set in motion by the heat produced the appearance of waves. As the winds swept over the desert while the mirage lasted, they are fancied to be floating in the false water &c. तरङ्गिणी a stream. A mad man also may lie on a sandy bank and pretend to be swimming though there be no water. शुष्य...जङ्घाला: (winds) that blew with velocity easily crossing the desert tracks rustling (मर्मर) with dry S'amī trees. The winds swept with violence over deserts. मारव from मरु with the affix अ. मरो: अयं मारव: मार्ग: तस्य लङ्घने लाघवं (नैपुणं) तेन

जवः तेन जङ्घालाः (rapid). A mad man also runs rapidly. 'जङ्घालोऽरिजवस्तुल्यौ' इत्यमरः. रैणवः (रेणूनां अयं) आवर्तः (circular motion, eddy) तेषां मण्डली (समूहः) तस्याः रेचकं रासे रसेन रभसारब्धं नर्तनं तस्य आरम्भे आरभटीनटाः (winds) that were wild actors in beginning a dance commenced with violence through liking (रसः) for the circular dance (रासः), that (नर्तनं) purged (swept away) whirling columns of dust. The idea is that whirl-winds arose, raised moving columns of dust and carried the dust columns from place to place. This clause contains several technical words pertaining to the science of dramaturgy. आरभटी is one of the four styles (वृत्ति) in dramatic compositions, the other three being भारती, सात्वती and कैशिकी. It is defined in Bharata's नाट्यशास्त्र as follows:—'आरभटप्रायगुणा तथैव बहुकपटवञ्चनोपेता। दम्भानृतवचनवती त्वारभटी नाम विज्ञेया॥ प्रस्तावपातप्लुतलङ्घितानि छेद्यानि मायाकृतमिन्द्रजालम्। चित्राणि युद्धानि च यत्र नित्यं तां तादृशीमारभटीं वदन्ति॥' chap 20. 25–26. The साहित्यदर्पण (VI. 132–133) says 'मायेन्द्रजालसंग्रामक्रोधोद्भ्रान्तादिचेष्टितैः॥ संयुक्ता वधबन्धाद्यैरुद्धतारभटी मता।' This style consists in representing intrigues, deceits, falsehoods, illusions, fight, imprisonments &c. The com. derives as 'इरयन्तीति (*v. l.* इयरतीति) अरा अराश्च ते भटाश्च अरभटास्तेषामियमारभटी.' रास is a dance in a circle in which men and women join, holding one another's hands. It is frequently mentioned in connection with कृष्ण and the Gopis. See भागवतपुराण X. 33. 'तत्रारभत गोविन्दो रासक्रीडामनुव्रतैः। स्त्रीरत्नैरन्वितः प्रीतैरन्योन्याबद्धबाहुभिः॥' 2. The com. quotes 'अष्टौ षोडश द्वात्रिंशद्यत्र नृत्यन्ति नायकाः। पिण्डीबन्धानुसारेण तन्नृत्तं रासकं स्मृतम्॥' In a रास, there is आवर्तमण्डली *i. e.* a ring of dancers that moves round and round. Compare 'सावर्त इव रासकमण्डलैः' हर्ष० 4th उच्छ्वास. रेचक means 'movements of the eye, brows &c. which indicate love'. 'तत्राक्षिभ्रूविकाराश्च शृङ्गाराकारसूचकाः। सग्रीवा रेचका ज्ञेयो हावश्चित्तसमुत्थितः॥' नाट्यशास्त्र chap. 22. 10. As to रेचक, the com. says that they are three कटीरेचक, हस्तरेचक and ग्रीवारेचक. Mad men also dance. मलनं crushing. Mad men also are मलिन. We may connect this clause with the next. A क्षपणक remained as मलिन as soot. Compare 'कज्जलमय इव बहुदिवससमुपचितबहलमलपटलमलिनिततनुरभिमुखमाजगाम शिखिपिच्छालाञ्छनो नग्नाटकः' हर्ष० 5th उच्छ्वास. Note the आचाराङ्गसूत्र (Sacred Books of the East Vol. XXII. p. 124) II. 2. 2. 1. 'Some householders are of clean habits and the mendicants, because they never bathe, are covered with uncleanliness.' शिक्षित...चिन्वतः that (winds) gathered up the feathers of the forest peacocks, as though they had learnt the ways of Jain ascetics. Jain ascetics (Digambara) carry peacock's feathers to sweep insects from their path. 'लुञ्चिताः पिच्छिकाहस्ताः पाणिपात्रा दिगम्बराः' सर्वदर्शनसंग्रह (आर्हतदर्शन). सप्र...जालकैः—करञ्ज is a wild tree so called even in Marathi. The dried seeds in its pods (मञ्जरी) rattle when the wind violently blows against them. That rattling resembles the noise of drums (गुञ्जा) beaten to announce the march of a prince &c. 'गुञ्जा तु काकचिञ्चायां पटहे च कलध्वनौ' मेदिनी. See भट्टिकाव्य XIV. 2. 'वेणून् पुपूरिरे गुञ्जा जुगुञ्जुः करघट्टिताः.' आतपेन आतुराः (distressed) वनमहिषाः तेषां नासाः निकुञ्जाः (bowers) इव तेषां स्थूलनिश्वासैः—the buffaloes heavily snorted. Their noses being compared to bowers, their deep breaths are properly fancied to be shoots (प्ररोहः). वातहरिण very swift deer. परिपाटी row, line. पेटकैः = समूहैः. The very swift deer springing up in the air seemed to be the children of the winds, as they equalled the wind in velocity. सभ्रु...कोटिभिः with the curling (कुटिल) lines of the smoke of the burning heaps of chaff (बुसं) on the threshing floor (खलधानं), they (winds) as though seemed to knit their brows. The curved lines of smoke resemble dark and curved eyebrows. सा...मुक्तिभिः by the emission of great heat, they (winds) seemed as though possessed of the waves of the अवीचि hell. Hell is a place of torments. अवीचि is one of the numerous hells mentioned in the Purāṇas. 'स्यान्नारकस्तु नरको... । तद्भेदास्तपनावीचिमहारौरवरौरवाः' इत्यमरः. अवीचिवीचिभिः सह सावीचि० (*adj.* of मातरिश्वानः). The waves are of fire burning in them. मनुस्मृति (IV. 87-90) enumerates 21 hells of which महावीचि is one. लोम...तन्तुभिः with the threads of the cotton of the silk-cotton pods that were cleft (by the heat), they (winds) seemed as though they were shaggy. Mad men do not shave and so are लोमश. दद्रुणा...ष्टिभिः by the carrying of the heaps of dried leaves, they seemed as though suffering from leprosy or cutaneous eruptions. The dry leaves present the appearance of दद्रू. Or we may explain that those who suffer from दद्रू cover the skin with leaves to ward off flies. दद्रुण is formed from दद्रू with the affix न like पामन from पामन्, according to 'रोमादिपामादिपिच्छादिभ्यः शनेलचः' पा. 5. 2. 100. दद्रू is one of the eleven क्षुद्रकुष्ठकs. It is a name for skin diseases such as Eczema, Erysipelas. 'सकण्डुरागपिटिकं दद्रुमण्डलमुद्गतम्.' सिरा...करणैः by scattering the long lines of grass, they seemed to have exposed their veins. वेणी and veins are both dark. Mad men, being underfed, may expose their veins. उच्छ्म...शङ्कुभिः with the shaking points (शङ्कुः) of the pieces of barley awns (शूकः—

कम्), they seemed to have long beards. उद्गतं श्मश्रु येषाम्. दंष्ट्रा... शतैः—The pointed quills (शललं) of porcupines resemble teeth. जिह्वा...खाभिः—the flames of fire resemble tongues. उत्स...लाः possessed of crests in the serpents' sloughs that were whirled up by them. ब्रह्म...स्यन्तः that, with the hot honey of lotuses, practised the taking of mouthfuls for the purpose of swallowing up the moisture in the whole universe. The winds carried away the hot honey of lotuses. They made a mouthful of it. The poet fancies that the winds were only practising in order to be able to swallow the fluid (*i. e.* to dry up) of the whole universe. अभ्यवहरणं भोजनम्. Another sense is suggested. There are six *rasas* मधुर, अम्ल, लवण, कटु, कषाय and तिक्त. The winds took the sweet (मधुर) honey, the first रस, in order gradually to be able to taste all the six. ब्रह्मस्तम्भः the universe. The word is usually written as °स्तम्ब. 'स्तम्बशब्देनोर्ध्वत्वादिसादृश्याद्गौण्या भुवनाण्डान्युच्यन्ते' वीरराघव on महावीरचरित 3. 48. For ब्रह्मस्तम्भ, see text p. 30 l. 3. सकल... यन्तः producing an alarm (विभीषिका) for the three worlds by the sharp sounds of the cracking of dried bamboo forests, as though they (sounds) were drums announcing the (might) of heat (घर्मः) that dries up all water. °च्छोषणः घर्मः तस्य घोषणा तदर्थं पटहैः. Read त्रिभुवनविभीषिका°. च्युत...सृतयः that made the roads (सृतिः) variegated by the rows of the falling feathers of moving jays. The feathers of चाष are dark. त्विषि...ताङ्गाः that (winds) were marked with sparks (स्फुलिङ्गः) and cold cinders in the bursting Gunjā berries, as though their bodies were dark-red by being scorched with the firebrand of the rays of the sun. Small round Gunjā berries are red with a patch of black. The red represents sparks and the dark stands for charcoal (अङ्गारः). A firebrand (अलातं) is red and the scorched skin is dark. त्विषिमान् सूर्यः तस्य मयूखलता एव अलातं तेन प्लोषः (burning) तेन कल्माषं (variegated) वपुः येषाम्. By the sun's rays the Gunjā berries were split up. The bursting berries look like patches of skin scorched by contact with firebrands. गिरिगुहासु गम्भीराः झाङ्काराः तैः भीषणा भ्रान्तिः (भ्रमणं) येषाम् the movements of which were terrible as they roused echoes in the mountain caves (by their fierce velocity). Mad men also wander among mountains. भुवनभस्मीकरणार्थं अभिचारः तस्य चरुः तस्य पचने चतुराः. अभिचारः a magical spell for securing some malevolent purpose. चरुः an oblation of rice. One who wants to effect some evil object offers a चरु with red powder sprinkled thereon or offers even blood. The bunches of the पारिभद्र flowers, being red, resemble oblations of blood. तारवः—तरोः अयम्. तर्पय... वसून् propitiating the forest fires (feeding) on trees. Oblations are thrown into fire. The winds carried the red पारिभद्र flowers and there were forest fires also. The poet fancies that the winds propitiated fires with oblations of blood. पारिभद्र is निम्बतरु. Compare हर्ष० 8th उच्छ्वास last para. 'असुरवधाभिचारचरुपिशुनः शोणितक्वाथकषायितकुक्षिः...कटाह इव च बार्हस्पत्यः.' अशि...रंहसः the velocity (the path) of which was bestarred with hot sand. शिलाजतुः bitumen. It is used as a medicine. ०रसलवैः लिप्ताः दिशः यैः. दावदहनेन पच्यमानानि चटकाण्डानि तेषां खण्डैः खचितानि तरुकोटरकीटपटलानि तेषां पुटपाकः तेन गन्धः तेन कटवः. The forest fires made the sparrow's eggs burst open. The shells of the eggs fell all round the insects in the hollows of trees and covered them as in a vessel of leaves. Inside them the insects were baked. That produced a strong smell. पुटपाक is a particular method of preparing drugs. The ingredients are wrapped up in leaves and then plastered over with clay. The whole is then roasted in the fire of cowdung cakes. मातरिश्वानः =वायवः. मातरि आकाशे श्वयति or श्वसिति or मातरि शु (आशु) अनिति.

P. 23 ll. 6–22. **सर्वतश्च...दावाग्नयः.** The sentence is सर्वतश्च... प्रत्यदृश्यन्त दावाग्नयः. भूरि...वायुभिः with the breaths blowing from the deep cavern-like jaws of old huge serpents, they (forest fires) seemed to be as though kindled by being fanned with thousands of bellows (भस्त्रा). क्वचि...हरिणाः—fires are yellowish (हरिण) and burn grass. Deer (हरिणाः) also subsist on grass. 'हरिणः पाण्डुरः पाण्डुः' इत्यमरः. In this and the following clauses up to ०स्थितयः (l. 14) there are pairs of words that serve to qualify दावाग्नयः and also serve another purpose. The latter in each pair of words is a noun with which the former can be construed as an adjective. क्वचित्—क्वचित् in some places—in other places. ०विवर्तिनः rolling. बभ्रवः yellowish-red; ichneumons. 'विपुले नकुले विष्णौ बभ्रुः स्यात्पिङ्गले त्रिषु' इत्यमरः जटा...कपिलाः resting on fibrous roots and tawny. जटा also means 'matted hair.' कपिलाः the sage Kapila, the founder of the सांख्य system, the plural being used to show respect. Or कपिलाः may stand for 'followers of कपिल'. शकु...श्येनाः that make the nests (कुलायः) of birds fall and are white (श्येन). Hawks (श्येनाः) bring down the nests of smaller birds. विलीनलाक्षारसवत् लोहिता छविः (कान्तिः) येषाम्. अधराः that could not be controlled. The lips of ladies are red like melting lac and also red with lac. आसा...

शिखाः the motion of which became greater by the wings of the birds that were overtaken (by the fires) and that (fires) had flames blazing up. The oily wings of the birds added to the strength of the conflagration. विगताः शिखाः (flames) येषाम्. विशिखाः also 'arrows.' आसा...गतयः (with arrows) 'the velocity of which was increased by obtaining the feathers of birds.' Arrows have feathers attached to them. दग्धाः निःशेषाः जन्महेतवः यैः, दग्ध...र्वाणाः—The fires burnt up the woods, leaves &c., from which they were produced and then became extinguished. निर्वाण from वा with निर्. निर्वाणम् also means 'मोक्ष' and निर्वाणाः would mean 'those that are liberated from संसार, the cycle of births and deaths.' दग्ध...हेतवः (with 'liberated') 'that have completely burnt up the causes of birth, *viz.* all actions.' Actions done for gratifying this or that desire produce their results for enjoying which one has to go through the cycle of births and deaths. When correct knowledge of the nature of the soul and the Supreme is acquired, then the ज्ञानी does not desire the fruits of his actions. No man can be free from actions; but what he can be free from and what he is advised to be free from is the desire to obtain for himself the fruits of his actions. Compare the following from the भगवद्गीता 'ज्ञानाग्निः सर्वकर्माणि भस्मसात्कुरुते तथा ॥' chap. 4. 37; अनाश्रितः कर्मफलं कार्यं कर्म करोति यः । स संन्यासी च योगी च न निरग्निर्न चाक्रियः ॥ chap. 6. 1; त्यक्त्वा कर्मफलासङ्गं नित्यतृप्तो निराश्रयः । कर्मण्यभिप्रवृत्तोऽपि नैव किञ्चित्करोति सः ॥ chap. 4. 20. कुसुम...रागिणः that are charged with the fragrance of the sky (अम्बरं) perfumed with flowers and are of rosy hue (रागिणः); also 'lovers, that give out the perfume of garments (अम्बरं) scented with flowers'. The com. takes कुसुम to mean 'smoke' in the first case (with fires). स...रुचयः that emit smoke and have a faint lustre (रुचिः); those that have no taste for food (suffering from indigestion) emit smoky (foul) eructations. धूमस्य उद्गारः तेन सह स० (बहुव्रीहि) with दावाग्नयः; सधूमः उद्गारः (eructation) येषाम् (with मन्दरुचयः). सकल...सकाः that swallow the whole world as a morsel and have ashes; those that suffer from the disease called भस्मकरोग are prepared to devour the food in the whole world. घस्मर = भक्षक. ग्रासः mouthful, food. 'कट्वादिरूक्षान्नभुजो नराणां क्षीणे कफे मारुतपित्तवृद्धौ । अतिप्रवृद्धः पवनान्वितोऽग्निः क्षणाद्रसं शोषयति प्रसह्य ॥ भुक्तं क्षणाद्भस्म करोति यस्मात्तस्मादयं भस्मकसंज्ञकोऽभूत् ।' योगरत्नाकर. वेणु...वृद्धाः that were seen (blazing) on the tops of bamboos and had assumed large proportions; very old persons rest their bodies on the tops of bamboo sticks (*i. e.* they cannot walk without the support of a stick). अचलो...क्षयिणः that consumed (उपयुक्त) bitumen on mountains and wrought destruction; consumptives (क्षयिणः) consume bitumen continuously. शिलाजतु was supposed to cure consumption. 'शिलाजतु रसायनं कटुकतिक्तमुष्णं कृमिक्षयोदरभिदश्मरीश्वयथुपाण्डुकण्डूहरम्।' योगरत्नाकर. Compare com. 'शिलाधातुप्रयोगाद्वा प्रसादाद्वाथ शाङ्करात् अजामूत्रप्रयोगाद्वा क्षयः क्षीयेत नान्यथा॥.' सर्व...पीवानः destroyed all fluidity and had assumed vast proportions; those that eat all kinds of food become plump and fat. पीवत् fat. For the six *Rasas* see above p. 102. रौद्राः terrible; worshippers of Rudra (शिव). गुग्गुलु (Marathi गुग्गुळ) is a kind of fragrant gum, burnt in the temples of शिव. Compare 'शिरोविधृतविलीयमानगुग्गुलुविकलनवसेवकानुनीयमानमहाकालम्' हर्ष० 5th उ०. ज्वलित...स्थितयः (fires) that burnt the reeds and Madana trees together with flowers by the fire of the blazing roots and stood (blazing) on the stumps of trees. ज्वलितानि नेत्राणि (मूलानि) तेषां दहनेन दग्धाः सकुसुमाः शराः मदनाश्च येषु. कृता स्थाणुषु स्थितिः यैः. ज्वलित...स्थितयः that behaved like S'iva, who burnt up Cupid together with his flowery arrows by the blazing fire from his eye. ज्वलितेन नेत्रदहनेन दग्धः सकुसुमशरः मदनः यैः. कृता स्थाणोः शिवस्य स्थितिः व्यवहारो यैः. For the burning of मदन, *vide* p. 14. Separate ०शिखा नर्तनारम्भ०. चटुल...नटाः the flames of which quivered and which (therefore) looked like wild dancers at the beginning of their dance. चटुल०—The dancers in the आरभटी style have their hair waving when they begin to dance. For आरभटी see above p. 100. शुष्केषु कासारेषु सृतिः (सरणं येषाम्) that pass over dried up tanks. The com. connects this with the preceding clause. "कासाराणि नड्वलास्तेषु याः सृतयः क्वचित् स्मृतय इति पाठः। इतरत्र तु शुष्ककं शुष्कगीतं झण्टुमादि। आसार्यन्ते इति आसाराः। आसारितानि यद्यपि गीयन्त एव तथापि 'वर्धमानमथापीह ताण्डवं यत्र योज्यते' इति ताण्डवं हि आरभटीप्रधानम्' सं०. स्फुट...घृणिम् with their flames—hands, that showered the bursting dry grains of wild rice, they seemed as though worshipping the sun. One may make an offering of parched grain (लाज) to the sun. When the fires made their way over dried up tanks, they parched up the seeds of नीवार rice growing there. घर्मघृणिः means 'one whose rays (घृणिः) are very hot' *i. e.* the sun. अघृणाः without disgust. 'जुगुप्साकरुणे घृणे' इत्यमरः. हठ...गृध्नवः greedy (गृध्नु) for the stinking smell of the fat (वसा) of the full—grown (कठोर) land tortoises that were forcibly offered (in the fires). One would be disgusted with the smell of fat and would avoid sacrificing the tortoises. 'विस्रं स्यादामगन्धि यत्' इत्यमरः. अघृणाः also means 'pitiless.' स्व...भक्षयन्तः that swallowed up their own smoke as though through the fear of the rise of clouds. Clouds are dark like smoke. The poet fancies that the fires thought that smoke might form into clouds which bring rain and extinguish them. So the fires consumed their own smoke. Or we may explain differently. Smoke itself was supposed to form clouds. Compare 'धूमज्योतिःसलिलमरुतां सन्निपातः क्व मेघः' मेघदूत. सति...कक्षेषु—The fires burnt up the small insects on grass and thereby produced a crackling sound. Sesame also are small and produce a crackling sound when thrown into fire. 'कक्षौ च तृणवीरुधौ' इत्यमरः. प्लोषेण विचटन्तः वल्कलवत् धवलाः शम्बूकशुक्तयः येषु. श्वित्रिण...सरःसु that made the bi-valvular shells white like barks burst open by heat in dried-up lakes, like leprous persons. 'शम्बूका जलशुक्तयः' इत्यमरः. The shells in the beds of lakes were split by the heat and made a crackling noise. श्वित्रिणः persons suffering from white leprosy (श्वित्रम्). The skin (वल्कलं) of lepers is white like shells and cracks up owing to the burning sensation (प्लोषः) they feel. स्वेदि...काननेषु in forests they had showers of bees'-wax dropping from bee-hives that began to melt, as though they had perspiration. The drops of wax look like drops of perspiration. विलीयमानः मधुपटलगोलः तस्मात् गलितं मधूच्छिष्टं तस्य वृष्टिः येषां ते ०वृष्टयः. खल...षरेषु. ऊषरः-रम् barren saline soil. As nothing grew on the barren soil, the flames (शिखा) of the fires lost their thickness *i. e.* became gradually extinguished. A bald man (खलतिः) also has very scanty hair (शिखा) on his head. ज्वलितानि सूर्यमणिशकलानि येषु (*adj.* of शिलोच्चयेषु). गृहीत...च्चयेषु—The सूर्यकान्त emits fire when the sun blazes forth. In summer these stones began to blaze forth and their blaze mingled with the forest fires, which thus seemed to be devouring pieces of stones.

P. 23 ll. 23–29 **तथाभूते...इति.** अपराह्णसमये—connect with प्रविश्य and not with भुक्तवतः as C and T do. For पारशव, see above p. 89. चतुः...पतेः—this was a title applied to universal kings that ruled over the whole (known) world. Vide Intro. p. XV (last footnote). The earth was often spoken of as bounded by four oceans in the (principal) directions. Compare 'चतुरम्भोधिभोगभूतिभाजनस्य देवस्य' हर्ष० 7th उच्छ्वास. सकलं राजचक्रं

(राजसमूहः) तस्य चूडामणीनां श्रेणी (row) सा एव शाणः (touch-stone) तस्य कोणैः (corners) कषणं तेन निर्मलीकृताः चरणनखमणयः यस्य सः ०मणिः तस्य. Diamonds are made bright by being rubbed against शाणs. हर्ष's toe-nails were bright like jewels. When the feudatory kings bowed their crowned heads at the feet of हर्ष, the jewels in their crowns rubbed his toes and made his nails look brighter. धौरेयस्य = मुख्यस्य. 'धुरो यड्ढकौ' पा. 4. 4. 77. धुरं वहतीति धुर्यः धौरेयः. महा...श्वर०—these were the titles assumed by paramount kings. Compare the inscription of Harsha, Intro. p. XXVIII. and the 2nd footnote on p. XXXVI. of the Intro. भ्रात्रा—must mean here 'cousin.' प्रज्ञाततमः most famous. दीर्घाध्वगः *lit.* that goes a long distance *i. e.* a messenger.

P. 23 l. 30—**P. 25** l. 10 **अथ तेना...इति.** The first sentence is अथ तेन (भ्रात्रा) आनीयमानं...लेखहारकमद्राक्षीत् (p. 24. l. 1). अतिदूरागमनेन गुर्वी (heavy) जडा (slow) जङ्घा (leg) यस्य. कार्दमिकं चेलं (वस्त्रं) तस्य चीरिका (strip) तया नियमितं (bound, girt) उच्चण्डं (gaudy) चण्डातकं (tunic) यस्य. For चण्डातक, see above p. 69. कर्दमेन रक्तं कार्दमिकं (stained with mud). पृष्ठे प्रेङ्खन् (rolling) पटच्चरकर्पटघटितः गलितः ग्रन्थिः यस्य—who had a loose knot made of a strip (कर्पटः-टम्) of ragged cloth rolling on his back. The knot contained probably some coin. It was loose by long travel. 'पटच्चरं जीर्णवस्त्रम्' इत्यमरः. If we read गलग्रन्थिम्, then the meaning is:—he had round his throat a portion of a ragged garment, the rest being allowed to roll on his back. अतिनिबिडसूत्रबन्धे निम्नितं अन्तरालं तेन कृतः व्यवच्छेदः यस्याः. The letters he carried were tied in the middle by a thick thread. Thereby the middle part was much depressed (निम्नित) and the bundle of letters was thus divided into two distinct portions. व्यवच्छेदः division. लेखमालिकया—there were many letters, sent with him by other people also. Or it is possible that because the letter was placed on the head, the author compares it to a chaplet. परिकलितः (occupied) मूर्धा यस्य. तत्रभवतः पूज्यस्य. 'पूज्ये तत्रभवानत्र भवांश्च भगवानपि.' तत्रभवत् is applied to a person who is not present. विमुच्य having unloosened it. मेखलक was the name of the messenger. सन्दिष्टमवधार्य having understood the message. फल...पातः loss of time should be avoided by the wise, as it hinders the (desired) object. धीमद्भिः—refers to Bāṇa. एता...मात्रकम् this is the only substantial thing in this letter; all else is merely communication of (ordinary) news. मेखलक was to deliver the real message orally. The letter contained only one important sentence *viz.* that Bāṇa should start at once. All else in the letter was of a complimentary character. अवधृतः (understood) लेखार्थः येन. समुत्सारितः (sent away) परिजनः येन. मेधाविनं refers to बाण. स्वामी refers to कृष्ण. एकगोत्रता belonging to the same family. In this sentence are collected most of the circumstances that give rise to friendship and affection. समानजातिता belonging to the same caste. The words समानज्ञानता in B would mean 'pursuing the same subject of study'. दर्शनाभ्यासः repeatedly seeing each other. परो...करणं conferring benefits in one's absence. प्रत्यासन्न near. बद्धः पक्षपातः (liking) येन. किमपि in an indescribable way. कुमुदानाम् आकरे. भवन्त...आसीत् with reference to you, this (our) emperor had been informed by bad men in various ways *i. e.* he had been prejudiced by them against you. न...था but that is not so *i. e.* there is no truth in what the wicked said about you. न...शत्रवः there exist no persons who, even though they may be good, will not have friends, neutrals and enemies. सतामपि सताम्—this has a picturesque effect. The first सताम् means 'साधूनाम्.' शिशु...भवतः as your mind was not averse to boyish follies. Read चापलपराचीन. ०चापलेभ्यो अपराचीना चित्तवृत्तिः यस्य सः ०वृत्तिः तस्य भावः ०वृत्तिता तया. 'पराङ्मुखः पराचीनः' इत्यमरः. असदृशम् not worthy of or deserved by you. इतरो...वक्ति च other people take it up and repeat it. सलि...मनांसि the minds of the unreflecting (public) are blind and fickle, like water. गतस्य अनुगतिर्यस्य. The unreflecting people blindly follow what others say. Water also rushes in a continuous stream. Put a vertical line after मनांसि. बहु...श्चयः who arrives at a firm conclusion after listening to many people. A king has to form his opinion as best as he can after listening to the various opinions of other people about things and individuals. पृथिवीपतिः refers to हर्ष. तत्त्वान्वेषिभिः who seek to know the truth. दूर...कृतोऽसि though you are far off, I know you as well as if you were before me. सर्व...राधि the youth of every one is guilty of follies. It is unfortunate that Bāṇa nowhere specifies clearly the follies he was guilty of. He merely makes a vague reference to 'चापल.' In the penultimate paragraph of the first उच्छ्वास also, he vaguely alludes to 'चापलानि'. Again in the last para of this chapter, he speaks of 'बालचरितचापल'. Later on हर्ष accuses him of being a भुजङ्ग (a gallant, a dissolute person) but he repudiates that charge. तथे...मिना and the king accepted it to be so *i. e.* he accepted that proposition or excuse (about बाण). अकृतः कालस्य क्षेपः यथा स्यात्तथा

(अव्ययीभाव) without loss of time. Read अवकेशी &c. अवके...मतः I do not approve of your dwelling in the midst of your kindred without seeing the great king (हर्ष), like a tree without fruit. अवकेशी इव. 'वन्ध्योऽफलोऽवकेशी च' इत्यमरः (अवके शून्ये ईष्टे इति—क्षीर०). A tree without fruits is not liked by anybody. अदृष्टः परमेश्वरः येन that does not see the god (sun). बन्धु...वसन् being in the midst of (*i. e.* in the shade of) other trees. न च...भवितव्यम् you should not be despondent (विषादिन्) by the difficulties of attendance in court nor should you be afraid of waiting upon the lord. यतो०–There is one sentence from यतो to स्वामी (including the verse). The words in the verse are capable of three meanings, one applying to Cupid (मनोभव), the second to a vain master and the third to S'iva (ईश्वर). The first and second are those principally intended. स्वस्य इच्छया सङ्कल्पेन उपजातः उत्पन्नः विषयः यस्य the realm of which (Cupid) springs from one's own fancy. काम is called सङ्कल्पज. Compare दशकुमारचरित 'कः कामः सङ्कल्पः'. स्वेच्छोपजाताः विषयाः यस्य (with a bad king) that has under his rule as many countries as he desires. स्वेच्छायाः उपजाताः विषयाः यस्य from whose mere will, this world of objects springs up (with शिव). न...देहीति who cannot be described as possessing a body (with काम). काम is अनङ्ग and so he cannot be called देही. न...देहि इति who cannot be addressed with the words 'give' (with a bad king). A bad king, though possessed of vast territory, cannot be thus addressed for fear of his punishing the suppliant. शिव cannot be described as देही, because thereby one would detract from his all-pervading nature. मार्ग...दुःखम् he causes pain with numerous darts (with काम). मार्गणाः बाणाः. मार्गण also means याचक (with bad king). मार्गण will mean 'search for truth' or begging (with शिव). One has to pray to शिव with hundreds of requests; or one has to search for truth about God in various ways. This causes trouble. मोहा...काण्डे all of a sudden he snatches life (of lovers) by producing infatuation (with काम). मोहा...काण्डे (a bad king) takes away livelihood (such as grants of villages &c.) through his folly. मोहात्...काण्डे—शिव, who typifies the principle of destruction, takes away the lives of all, when मोह (*i. e.* तमोगुण) predominates. कष्टं alas. ईश्वरदुर्विदग्धः (with काम) badly burnt by शिव. ईश्वरश्चासौ दुर्विदग्धश्च a conceited king. C and T understand the verse differently. They take ईश्वर...ग्ध as 'one who is unskilled in waiting upon a king' (ईश्वरे दुर्विदग्धः). This sense may possibly be extracted from the words, but to regard that sense as the principal one (as C and T do) is wrong. The subject matter of discussion is the conduct of kings and not the want of skill of courtiers. न्यकृता:... ०ययातय: येन who humbles, puts into the shade Yayāti &c. Here is a long list of famous ancient emperors. The story of नृग who was cursed for making delay in deciding a disputed claim is narrated in रामायण उत्तरकाण्ड chap. 53. नल is well-known. नल was king of निषध. What king is meant by निषध is not clear. It is probably निषध the great-grandson of राम. Vide रघु० 18. 1 and हरिवंश 15. 26. नहुष son of आयु: and father of ययाति. He was cursed to be अजगर. See विष्णुपुराण IV. 10. अम्बरीष is referred to in कौटिल्य's अर्थशास्त्र as a king that had conquered the six enemies (काम &c.). दिलीप was an ancestor of Rāma. नाभाग—See विष्णुपु० IV. 1. and मार्कण्डेय chap. 113. ff. भरत—the son of दुष्यन्त and शकुन्तला. भगीरथ who brought down the Ganges is well-known. ययाति, son of नहुष, transferred his old age to पूरु. अहङ्कार: एव कालकूटविषं तेन दिग्धा: अत एव दुष्टा:. ना...दृष्टय:. his eyes are not polluted and stained with the deadly poison of conceit. As he is called अमृतमय, कालकूट, which is the opposite of अमृत, is naturally suggested and अहङ्कार is compared to it. न...गिर: his speech is not choked by the disease of the throat due to the terrible poison (गर:) of pride *i. e.* he does not speak proudly. गर्व: गुरुगर: तेन गलग्रहगद: तेन गद्गदा:. गलग्रह: inflammation of the throat due to various causes. अतिस्मयेन ऊष्मा एव अपस्मार: तेन विस्मृतं स्थैर्यं येषु. नाति...स्थानकानि his postures are not such that he will forget his serenity by the epilepsy of puffed up pride. स्मय: pride. ऊष्मा stiffness. In epilepsy there is loss of consciousness (विस्मृतं) and the body becomes stiff (*i. e.* the man falls down in a fit). उद्दाम: (overbearing) दर्प: एव दाहज्वर: (burning fever) तस्य वेगेन (operation) विक्लवा: (distressed, overwhelmed). अभिमानं: एव महासन्निपात: तेन निर्मित: अङ्गभङ्ग: यस्मिन्. गतानि movements. सन्निपात is a fatal fever in which there is a combined derangement of the three humours वात, पित्त and कफ. The योगरत्नाकर (आनन्दाश्रम ed. p. 98) gives the general symptoms. In it there is अङ्गभङ्ग (the limbs become stiff and painful). मद: एव अर्दितं तेन वक्रीकृत: ओष्ठ: तस्मात् निष्ठ्यूतानि (emitted) निष्ठुराणि अक्षराणि येषु. A haughty man may curl up his lips and utter harsh words. अर्दित is a वातव्याधि, which may affect the lips. 'उच्चैर्व्याहरतोत्यर्थं खादत: कठिनानि च । हसतो जृम्भतो भाराद्विषमाच्छयनासनात् ॥ शिरोनासौष्ठचिबुकललाटेक्षणसन्धिषु । अर्दयत्यनिलो वक्त्रमर्दितं जनयेत्तत: ॥'. अस्य...

शकलेषु he looks upon good men of unblemished character as jewels and not on pieces of stone. He cares for नररत्नs and not for ordinary jewels. In this and the following clauses बाण employs the figure of speech called परिसंख्या, of which he is very fond. It occurs where an express specification of one thing, either made in answer to a question or not, tends to exclude either expressly or impliedly other similar things; *i. e.* किं भूषणं सुदृढमत्र यशो न रत्नं किं कार्यमार्यचरितं सुकृतं न दोषाः।. In the text, the figure occurs without a preceding question. 'किंचित्पृष्टमपृष्टं वा कथितं यत्प्रकल्पते। तादृगन्यव्यपोहाय परिसंख्या तु सा स्मृता॥' काव्यप्रकाश X. Read ०धवलेषु गुणेषु. मुक्ता...भारेषु He looks upon virtues pure like pearls as decorations and not on loads of ornaments white with pearls. दान...कीटेषु he believes in deeds of liberality as साधन and not in the worms of elephants that are दानवत्. दानवत् endowed with gifts; possessed of ichor. 'मदो दानम्' इत्यमरः. साधनम् a means of accomplishing one's object; army. Elephants were one of the four component parts of the ancient Indian army. सर्वाग्रेसरे that is the foremost of all. He wanted such fame as would make him the most pre-eminent man. जीवितं एव जरत्तृणम्—to him life was like rotten grass; glory was everything. Life (with ordinary men) is the foremost of all (things). If we read सर्वाशा० then आशा means 'quarters, hopes'. It is a good reading. गृहीतः करः (tribute) याभ्यः; गृहीतः करः (पाणिः) यासाम् (with ०पुत्रिकासु). गृहीत...योगः he exerts himself to subdue (*lit.* to accomplish) the quarters from which he levies tribute. अभियोगः exertion, perseverance. He makes no प्रसा...योगः (effort to adorn) the dolls *viz.* his wives whose hand he took (in marriage). चर्मपुत्रिका dolls of leather. गुणवति strung (with धनुषि); possessed of good qualities (with ०जने). पिण्डो० that live on the crumbs that he gives. अस्य...मात्मा His soul is for serving his friends *i. e.* he is devoted heart and soul to his friends. उपकरणम् what helps; an instrument, means *i. e.* something subservient or subsidiary. भृत्यो...भुत्वम् his sovereignty is for helping his servants. पण्डित...गध्यम्—his learning enables him to understand the worth of learned men and to help them. कृपण wretched. सु...हृदयम् his heart is to him a means to remember the good deeds of others or to gratefully remember the benefits received from others. साह...शरीरम्—the one use that he makes of his body is to plunge in bold undertakings. असि...थिवी the earth enables him to show his skill in sword-play *i. e.* he vanquishes everyone in the world with his sword. वि...जकम् he requires the circle of kings (attending on him) for amusing himself (he does not require their help in battle). 'अथ राजकम् । राजन्यकं च नृपतिक्षत्रियाणां गणे क्रमात् ॥' इत्यमरः. प्र...पक्षः his enemies only serve to show his valour (or glory). सर्वम् अतिशेते ०शायि सुखमेव रसः तस्य प्रसूतिः यस्याः from which flows happiness that excels other pleasures. As his feet are compared to पल्लव, the happiness of serving him is compared to रस. पल्लवs give shade. His feet afford protection. पाद...च्छाया may also mean the brilliance of his sprout-like (*i. e.* red) feet. कृतं कशिपु (food and clothing) यस्य. 'कशिपु त्वन्नमाच्छादनं द्वयम्' इत्यमरः. विश्रान्तश्चासौ सुखी च that has taken rest and feels refreshed.

P. 25 ll. 11-24. **अथ गते...मकरोत्.** पर्यस्ते वासरे when the day was scattered about (was drawing to a close). सङ्घट्ट...तपे when the afternoon sunlight, red like a young crow's mouth, was growing fainter and fainter (क्षाम *lit.* emaciated), as though drunk by the cavities (सम्पुटः) of the closing red lotuses. सङ्घट्ट् or सङ्घट् 1 A to unite or join. क्षयिणि decreasing; consumptive. A consumptive also becomes emaciated. Red lotuses close their cups in the evening. The poet fancies that the sunlight grew faint because it was drunk the whole day by the red lotuses that were fully expanded. One may drink water with हस्तसम्पुट. शिथिलितः (lessened) निजवाजिजवः येन (*adj.* of पतङ्ग) The sun is represented as drawn by seven horses. जपा...ले as rosy as a bunch (आपीडः) of china roses. अस्ता...पतङ्गे when the sun stumbled (स्खलित) on to the top of the setting mountain, as though he was limping, having tender feet pierced by the thorns of lotus plants. The hairy growth on the stems of lotus plants is like thorns. One whose feet are pierced by thorns limps and may stumble if he has to ascend to the tops of mountains. ०कण्टकैः क्षतः पादपल्लवः यस्य. पुरः...मुखे when the first part (मुखं) of the night (श्यामा) came hurrying in the east (पुरः), having her long tresses of slight darkness dangling about, and being dark through grief at the absence of the moon. अन्धकारलेशः एव लम्बालकाः, प्रेङ्खन्तः ०लकाः यस्मिन्. The idea is that it was a moonless night and the east began to look dark. श्यामा also 'a handsome young woman.' खञ्जति *loc. sing.* of *pr. p.* of खञ्ज् 1 P to limp. A lady's face (मुखं) also may lose its brightness through separation and she might have her hair rolling on her back, because not tied up. A woman, whose husband had gone on a journey, was not to decorate her body &c. 'हास्यं परगृहे यानं समाजोत्सवदर्शनम् । क्रीडां शरीरसंस्कारं त्यजेत्प्रोषितभर्तृका ॥.' कृतं सन्ध्योपासनं येन. अन्य...राज्ञा I have been misunderstood by the king. निर्निमित्त = निष्कारण. कष्टा distressing. विषमम् full of difficulties. तत्र = राजकुले. न...गतिः I cannot claim to have affection for the royal family first started by my ancestors, nor have I access to it from their time. In these and the following clauses he intimates that neither his ancestors nor himself had ever before visited the court and so he is diffident as to how he might acquit himself when once there. नो...रोधः nor do I possess that regard (of the king) which comes of remembering (former) benefits. अनुरोधः consideration. बाल...स्नेहः affection that springs from serving (the king) from one's childhood. गोत्रगौरवम् family position or importance. पूर्व...ण्यम् the courtesy due to old acquaintance. न प्रज्ञा...लोभनम् nor can I offer the allurement of the exchange of thoughts. विद्या...हलम् nor can I claim the admiration due to vast learning. आ...दरः—regard paid to fine appearance. सेवा...लम् skill in the changes of tones necessary in service. A servant has to assume tones of humility even when exasperated. For काकु, see above p. 84. वि...ग्ध्यम् the cleverness requisite in the meeting of the learned. वित्तव्ययेन वशीकरणम् winning over (people about the court) by expenditure of money. अवश्यं गन्तव्यम्—In spite of all these drawbacks I must go. पुरारातिः 'enemy of the cities' *i. e.* शिव. He was so called because he burnt down the three cities of gold, silver and iron built by Maya for demons in the sky, air and earth. 'असुराणां पुराण्यासंस्त्रीणि वीर्यवतां दिवि । आयसं राजतं चैव सौवर्णं परमं महत् ॥' द्रोणपर्व chap. 202. 64. भुवनगुरुः the object of worship to the world. गतस्य...ष्यति will do everything that is proper (सांप्रत) when I go there.

P. 25 l. 25—**P. 26** l. 9 **अथान्य...रगात्.** The sentence is अथ अन्यस्मिन्नहनि...प्रीतिकूटात् निरगात्. In this paragraph we have a very interesting and instructive account of how an orthodox Brāhmaṇa left his home on an important undertaking. धृतं धौतं धवलं दुकूलवासः येन. गृहीता अक्षमाला (rosary) येन. प्रास्था...वर्त्य having many times recited the Vedic hymns and portions of *mantras* suited to one starting on a journey. प्रस्थाने भवं or प्रस्थानं प्रयोजनमस्य इति प्रास्थानिकम्, according to 'प्रयोजनम्' पा. 5. 1. 109. विरूपाक्षः शिवः. He is so called because he has three eyes. क्षीरस्नपनं पुरःसरं यस्याः

(*adj.* of पूजा) preceded by a bath of milk. The image of शिव was washed with milk by Bāṇa. क्षीराभिषेक is even now resorted to to propitiate Rudra. Compare 'अतिशुचिशैवसम्पाद्यमानविरूपाक्षक्षीरकलश-सहस्रस्नपनं (राजकुलं)' हर्ष० 5th उच्छ्वास. सुर...बहुलां mostly consisting of or abounding in sweet flowers &c. विलेपनं sandal ointment. प्रथमहुताः तरलाः तिलाः तेषां त्वचः विघटनं तेन चटुलाः मुखराः शिखा एव शेखरः यस्य—whose crest was formed by the rolling and crackling flames that split open the husks of the sesame that were offered first of all and hurled about (being heated by the fire). प्राज्यं (plentiful) आज्यं (ghee) तस्य आहुत्या प्रवर्धिता दक्षिणार्चिः यस्य whose right flame was kindled &c. Flames of fire curving to the right were regarded as indicating good luck. Compare 'तस्मै सम्यग्घुतो वह्निर्वाजिनीराजनाविधौ । प्रदक्षिणार्चिर्व्याजेन हस्तेनेव जयं ददौ ॥' रघु० IV. 25; 'प्रदक्षिणार्चिर्हविरग्निराददे । बभूव सर्वं शुभशंसि तत्क्षणं' रघु० III. 14; 'उदर्चिषं हुत्वा प्रदक्षिणावर्तशिखाकलापमाशुशुक्षणिं' हर्ष० 7th उ० 1st para. आशुशुक्षणिं = अग्निम्. This is a Vedic word rarely used in classcial literature. It is variously derived from शुच् or शुष्. द्युम्नं = धनम् This is again a word very frequently used in the Vedas. यथाविद्यमानं according to his means. प्राङ्मुखीं facing the east. नैचिकी an excellent cow or a sacrificial cow. 'उत्तमा गोषु नैचिकी' इत्यमरः. शुक्लः अङ्गरागः (ointment) यस्य. शुक्लं माल्यं (garland) यस्य. रोचनया चित्राः दूर्वाग्रपल्लवाः तैः ग्रथितानि ०कुसुमानि तैः कृतः कर्णपूरः यस्य whose ear was adorned with गिरिकर्णिका flowers that were interwoven with the tips of दूर्वा grass that was smeared with रोचना. रोचना—bright yellow pigment prepared from the urine or bile of a cow or found in its head. All the three रोचना, दूर्वा and गिरिकर्णिका (a kind of white flower) are auspicious. रोचना was used to ward off evil spirits and the evil eye. शिखायां आसक्ताः सिद्धार्थकाः (white mustard) येन. The white mustard was believed to protect against evil spirits. सिद्धः अर्थः यस्मात्. मात्रे...यया whose heart overflowed with affection, as if she were his mother. श्वेतं वासः यस्याः. कनीयस्या स्वस्रा this is a personal matter mentioned only casually by the author. महाश्वेतया—it is difficult to say what goddess is alluded to. Both दुर्गा and सरस्वती are fair and may be called महाश्वेता. We believe it is दुर्गा that is meant. दुर्गा is also named गौरी and सर्वमङ्गला. Here the chief point is the auspicious rites performed when Bāṇa started. The देवीभागवत says 'श्वेतं शुक्लं शिवस्थानं यस्माच्चेह समागता । महाभावसमुत्पन्ना महाश्वेता ततः स्मृता ॥'. सं० says 'महाश्वेता देवताविशेषः रविस्थदेवतेत्यन्ये'. महाश्वेतया would also mean 'who (मालती) was very fair'. अभि...जरन्तीभिः congratulated or applauded by the old female servants. वन्दितौ चरणौ येषाम्. अभि... वृद्धैः kissed on the head by the elders in the family at whose feet he fell. वर्धितः गमनोत्साहः यस्य. मौहू...हृदः having made, in accordance with the opinions of astrologers, offerings to the lunar mansions to satisfy their desires *i. e.* he offered such things as were calculated to propitiate the नक्षत्र on which he started. मुहूर्तं वेद मौहूर्तिकः (with affix ठक्), according to 'तदधीते तद्वेद' पा. 4. 2. 59. कृतं नक्षत्रदोहदं येन. हरितगोमयेन उपलिप्तं (plastered) अजिरं तस्मिन् स्थण्डिलं (a raised plot for sacrifice) तस्मिन् स्थापितम् *(adj.* of ०कलशं). असितेतराणां (धवलानां) कुसुमानां मालया परिक्षिप्तः (encircled) कण्ठः यस्य *(adj.* of ०कलशं). पिष्ट...पाण्डुरं white with five finger marks of flour. The five fingers were dipped in some powder (or flour) mixed with milk and the jar was smeared with the finger—marks by way of मङ्गल. Compare 'पिष्टपञ्चाङ्गुल--मण्ड्यमानोलूखलमुसलशिलाद्युपकरणम्' हर्ष० 4th उ० below. मुख...पल्लवम् even now आम्रपल्लवs are placed in the mouth of jars as auspicious. For पूर्णकलश as being auspicious, *vide* notes above p. 70. कुसुमानि फलानि च पाणिषु येषाम्. अप्र...पद्भिः that recited the *apratiratha* hymn. It is ऋग्वेद X. 103. अप्रतिरथ is the name of the sage who composed the hymn. निजद्विजैः by the Brāhmaṇas that were his dependents. प्रथम...चरणः putting forward his right foot first. The right foot, eye, hand in the case of males and the left foot, eye, hand in the case of females are auspicious.

P. 26 ll 10–18 **प्रथमे...भवनस्य.** घर्म...कष्टं very distressing owing to summer. This and the clauses up to रोमाञ्चितमिव qualify ०काननम् (l. 14). निष्प...षमं terrible on account of the leafless trees. पथिकजनेन नमस्क्रियमाणाः प्रवेशपादपे उत्कीर्णाः कात्यायनीप्रतियातनाः यस्मिन् in which the images of Durgā carved under (or on) the trees at the entrance (of the forest) were paid homage by travellers. **'प्रतिमा प्रतियातना** प्रतिच्छाया' इत्यमरः. शुष्क...सहस्रैः though dried up, it (forest) seemed as though full of sprouts with thousands of tremulous long tongues that hung from (the mouths of) thirsty beasts. The red and tremulous tongues resemble red and restless पल्लवs. पुलकित...सङ्घातैः seemed to be spotted with the swarms of bees (सरघा) flying from the honey combs (मधुगोलः) that were licked by bears and monkeys. अच्छाः निर्मलाः भल्लाः शस्त्राणि नखानि यस्य. For पुलक in the sense of 'spots,' see above notes pp. 69–70. As रोमाञ्चित follows immediately afterwards, we cannot take पुलकित in the sense of रोमाञ्चित. For गोलाङ्गूल see p. 54. 'सरघा मधुमक्षिका' इत्यमरः.

रोमा... शतैः bristling with horripilation with the hundreds of the stout shouts of asparagus (अभीरु) that grew on the soil burnt (by forest fires). दग्धस्थलीषु रूढा अभीरुः तस्याः कन्दलशतैः. अभीरु is a plant called शतावरी or नारायणी. When soil is burnt, it becomes more fertile; hence the word स्थूल. Seeds that are lying deep down in the debris spring up vigorously after the burning of forest trees by conflagration. हृदयनिर्विशेषेण not different from (*i. e.* as dear as) his own heart. The com. takes भ्रात्रा to refer to चन्द्रसेन. सुहृदा is to be connected with जगत्पतिनाम्ना. We may possibly take भ्रात्रा (cousin) also with जगत्पति. We are not told anywhere that चन्द्रसेन accompanied Bāṇa. सम्पादिता सपर्या (पूजा) यस्य. स्कन्धावारम् (object of आससाद) army. मणितारस्य समीपे उप० (अव्ययीभाव). मणितार was a town. अजिरवतीमन्वायतम् अन्व० (अव्ययीभाव) along the river अजिरवती. कृतः सन्निवेशः येन encamped.

P. 26 l. 19—**P. 28** l. 7. **निर्वर्तित...गमत्.** The principal sentence is निर्वर्तित...करः मेखलकेन सह...राजद्वारमगमत्. निर्वर्तितः ०करः येन who carried out the usual incidents of bathing and taking his meals. याममात्रं अवशेषः यस्य when only one watch (of three hours) remained. पट्ट...पितैः that were brought (near the royal gate) for tying on their heads the fillets of honour. This and the following nouns in the instrumental qualify वारणेन्द्रैः (p. 26. l. 27). A पट्टबन्ध was a mark of great honour. Compare 'लब्धो मनोरथदुर्लभो महादेवीपट्टबन्धसत्कारलाभो ललाटेन' हर्ष० 5th उ०. डिण्डि...हृतैश्च (some) brought for mounting drums (डिण्डिमः) on their backs. विक्षे...प्रेषितैः some acquired by way of tribute, some received as presents and some sent by the rangers of the elephant depots. सं० says 'विक्षेपः करः;' we may translate 'वि०...र्जितैः' as 'collected for being despatched to various places'. कौशलिकं or–का a present (from कुशलम्). नागवीथी rows of elephants or place where elephants were caught and trained. प्रथम...ढौकितैः that were brought near for being seen with curiosity (or admiration) for the first time, that were sent at the time of despatching an envoy, and that were presented (ढौकित) by the chiefs of small villages (in forests). पल्ली a small village or settlement. परिवृढः Head. 'प्रभुः परिवृढोऽधिपः' इत्यमरः. स्वेच्छा...कारितैः that were called for the pleasure. (कौतुक) of a mimic fight at will. दीय...मानैश्च that were given (*i. e.* put together for a sham fight), that were separated (when they had faught for some time) and were led off. यामस्थापितैः that were placed at the watch (at the place where the hours of the watch were marked). सर्व...कृतैः that were collected together, as though they were mountains, for constructing a dam across the ocean in order to conquer all continents. The elephants were dark and big like mountains. The king wanted to conquer the continents beyond the sea. He would cast the hills of elephants into the sea and would thereby cross over to the other side. In the Purāṇas, the द्वीपs are seven (जम्बु, प्लक्ष, शाल्मल, कुश, क्रौञ्च, शाक and पुष्कर). See विष्णुपु. II. 1. 11. *ff.* Sometimes they are spoken of as eighteen. 'अष्टादशद्वीपनिखातयूपः' रघु० 6. 38; 'भ्रूलतादिष्टाष्टादशद्वीपे दिलीपे' and 'अष्टादशद्वीपाष्टमङ्गलकमालिनी मेदिनी' हर्ष० 6th उ०. ध्वज...कल्पितैः that were made like so many festive days of पुष्याभिषेक, charming with banner-cloths, sharp drums, conches, chowries and unguents. पुष्याभिषेक is the day when the king takes a ceremonial bath, the moon being in the Pushya asterism. On these days the king is accompanied by ध्वज &c., which are the insignia of royalty. The elephants also had these on their body. श्यामायमानम्—this qualifies राजद्वारम् (p. 28. l. 7). The dark elephants made the gate look dark. There is another sense suggested. 'The day looked like night on account of the dark elephants.' अनवरतचलितैः खुरपुटैः प्रहतं मृदः (पृथिव्याः) अङ्गं यैः—that struck the earth with their hoofs that pranced ceaselessly. ०पुटैः प्रहतः मृदङ्गः यैः the sound of the hoofs resembled the beating of a tabor to the accompaniment of dancing. Hence the poet says 'न...लक्ष्मीम्'—that made Royal Glory to dance (while they themselves beat the drum). उप...जातिम् with the laugh-like foam spreading over the the corners of their lips, they seemed as though mocking the tribe of deer that (compared with the horses) had slow legs. The idea is that the horses were swifter than deer. Both फेन and हास are white. सृक्किन् *n.* corner of the lip. आका...श्रवसम् that challenged with their joyous neighing the horse of Indra to a combat (सङ्घट्टः). उच्चैःश्रवस् is the horse of Indra, one of the 14 jewels churned from the ocean. उत्पत...तलं that as though flew up into the sky in anger against the horses of the sun, their ornamental chowries serving them as wings. पक्षायमाणा मण्डनचामरमाला येषाम्. पक्षः इव आचरति पक्षायते. तुरङ्गै...मानम् (राजद्वारम्) that was as though in waves with horses. प्रे...वृत्तैः returning after being sent. From प्रेषितैश्च to ०कपिलैः (p. 27 l. 5) we have words qualifying क्रमेलककुलैः. बहु...मण्डनकैः their mouths were ornamented with rows of cowries (वराटिका) as though they (cowries) were rows of numerical figures in counting the distance of many *yojanas* they had travelled. तार...च्छेदैः that looked as though they were patches (छेद) of evening light marked with stars. The white cowries on the mouths of the camels looked like stars and their tawny skins like the yellow glow of sunlight in the evening. अरुण...लेयैः that, having their ears ornamented with red chowries, looked as though they were fields of red rice covered with red lotuses. The अरुण-चामरिका looked like red chowrie and the tawny skin like a field of red rice. 'क्षेत्रं व्रैहेयशालेयं व्रीहिशाल्युद्भवोचितम्' इत्यमरः. 'व्रीहिशाल्योर्ढक्' पा. 5. 2. 2. (शालीनां भवनं क्षेत्रम् । ढक्). अनव...शतैः having strings of charming golden bells tinkling incessantly, they seemed to be groves of old *karanja* trees with hundreds of dry pods of seed rattling on them. घुरुघुरुक a small bell (Marathi घुंगुर). For करञ्जबीज see text p. 22 l. 20. श्रव...जटालैः that were full of beautiful (चित्र) tufts of woollen threads of five colours, dangling near their ears. The next clause is अन्यत्र...आतपत्रखण्डैः श्वेतायमानम् (l. 13). शर...तनुभिः (umbrellas) that were white like milk freshly flowing, as though they were autumnal clouds. Autumnal clouds are white when a mass of water (पयःपटल) drops from them. कल्प...मण्डलैः the circular shadow of which was annihilated by the light (आलोकः) due to a mass of pearls (which encircled the umbrellas), as though they were trees of paradise. A कल्पपादप yields whatever one desires and so it may yield pearls. नारा...पक्षैः had jewels (emeralds) sticking to them, as though they (आतपत्र) were the lotuses in the navel of Vishṇu. पुण्डरीकs and the umbrellas are white. The lotus in Vishṇu's navel may touch the wings of गरुड who is the वाहन of विष्णु. आश्लिष्टाः गरुडपक्षाः येषु. गरुडपक्ष is a kind of gem, otherwise called गारुत्मत. 'गारुत्मतं मरकतम्' इत्यमरः. क्षीरो...दण्डैः that had brilliant and large rods of coral, as though they were regions (उद्देशः) of the milky ocean. The umbrellas were white like milk. Coral is found in the sea. शेष...खण्डैः that had large (स्फीत) rubies sparkling on them, as though they were the board-like (*i. e.* broad) hoods of शेष. It was supposed that serpents had red gems in their hoods. शेष has a 1000 hoods and is as white as the umbrellas. श्वेत...सेवितैः that were resorted to by swanlike kings, as though they were the islands of the heavenly Ganges.

Swans (राजहंस) resort to the celestial Ganges. अभि...तपम् overpowering the season of summer, laughing at the splendour (or heat) of the sun, and drinking up the light of the sun. The umbrellas did not allow the heat to be felt. चन्द्र...जनयद्भिः in the shade of the umbrellas people felt as cool as in moonlight. There is an apparent विरोध *viz.* how can जीवलोक be turned into चन्द्रलोक? कुमुद...कुर्वद्भिः the (white) umbrellas made the season full of white lotuses. The umbrellas look like कुमुदs. There is विरोध in saying that umbrellas turned the season (it was ग्रीष्म then) into कुमुदमयकाल (*i. e.* the season of शरद्). There is another विरोध. काल means 'dark.' What is कुमुदमय (and so white) cannot be dark. There is विरोध between ज्योत्स्ना and वासर, फेन and sky (there can be no foam in the sky). अकाल...सृजद्भिः—the white umbrellas in the day looked like moonlight. कौमुदी means 'the full-moon day in आश्विन.' It was ग्रीष्म then and so the poet uses the word अकाल. उप...श्रियम् laughing at the glory of Indra. शतक्रतोः इयं शातक्रतवी. खण्डः-म् Mass. श्वेतायमानैः resembling conch-shell. The reading श्वेतद्वीपायमानम् is better than श्वेतायमानम्. The royal gate seemed on account of the numerous white umbrellas to be like श्वेतद्वीप (where everything is white). For a description of it see शान्तिपर्व chap. 336. 'क्षीरोदधेर्योत्तरतो हि द्वीपः श्वेतः स नाम्ना प्रथितो विशालः ॥ 8...श्वेताः पुमांसो गतसर्वपापाः' 10. The next clause is क्षण...दोलायमानम् (l. 17). क्षण...भुवनम् that (chowries) as though seemed to steal away the world, the eight regions of which were seen for a moment and then lost to view. क्षणदृष्टनष्टानि (क्षणदृष्टानि पश्चान्नष्टानि) अष्टदिङ्मुखानि यस्य. The idea is:—thousands of chowries were waved to and fro. So the people could see the regions beyond where they were standing between one waving of the chowries and another. That interval being very short, the author says that the worlds disappeared from view after being seen for a moment. आक्षे...कारयद्भिः—the idea is:—when the chowries were uplifted (उत्क्षेप) they shaded the sun from view and so caused darkness (*i. e.* the day went away); when the were lowered down (आक्षेप), the sun again came into view (*i. e.* the day came). The poet fancies that the day was as if placed on a swing by the chowries and was made to come near and then go away as a person sitting on a swing does. Mark they two accusatives दिनं and ०गतानि. दिनं गतागतानि करोति (primitive sense of कृ); दिनेन दिनं वा ०गतानि कारयन्ति चामराणि (causal). 'हृक्रो-

रन्यतरस्याम्' पा. 1. 4. 53 (the subject of हृ and कृ in the primitive sense is put in the instrumental or accusative in the causal). उत्सारयद्भिः has been omitted by oversight after कारयद्भिः. उत्सा... स्थितिम् that as though drove away the rule of *Kali* rendered dark (काली) by the stain of the contact of bad kings. *Kaliyuga* had set in long before हर्ष began to rule. Bad kings ruled in Kali. Everything that is evil and sinful is represented as dark. Kali's rule must be dark with the misdeeds of bad kings. The white चामरs as though removed this darkness. कालेय is derived from कलि with the affix ढक्. विकचैः विशदैः (bright) काशवनैः पाण्डुराः दिशः यस्मिन् (*adj.* of ॰समयम्). विकच...पादयद्भिः— The white काश flowers are seen in शरद्. The white chowries resemble काशs and so are fancied as bringing about autumn. बिस...र्भावयद्भिः—chowries are white like lotus fibres and are waved in the air. So the poet fancies that chowries made the sky बिसमय. शशिकरवत् शुचीनां (pure, bright). हंस...शङ्खैः that (राजद्वार) seemed like a flock of Haṁsas with the conchshells in the ears of elephants. Both हंसs and शङ्ख are white. Rings of conchshell were suspended from the ears of elephants for ornamentation or as auspicious. This explanation of करिकर्णशङ्ख will do in 'अन्तःस्फुरता मत्तमदनकरिकर्णशङ्खायमानेन प्रतिमेन्दुना' (text p. 17 ll. 16-17). See below अनवरतमवतंसशङ्खैः &c. (text p. 29 l. 30). कल्प...काभिः—the कदलिकाs (banners; plantain trees) were so many that there seemed to be a forest of कल्पलताs. माणिक्य...पत्रैः—the umbrellas of peacock's feathers looked like a forest of ruby trees (on account of the reddish tinge of the eyes). मन्दा...क्षौमैः—the white and flowing silken dresses looked like the stream of the Ganges and the white linen dresses like the milky ocean. कद...यूखैः—emeralds are green like plantain trees. जन्य...तपैः that seemed to create as though a second day by the (rosy) morning hues of rubies. It was afternoon when बाण saw the राजद्वार. The red light shed by the rubies there was like बालातप and hence there seemed to be morning in the afternoon. जन्यमानः अन्यदिवसः यस्मिन्. उत्पद्यमानं अपरं अम्बरं (आकाशं) यस्मिन्. उत्पद्य...पटलैः—Sapphires are blue like the sky. आरभ्यमाणा अपूर्वा निशा यस्मिन्. The dark महानील stones produced the appearance of night in the day; hence the author uses the word अपूर्व. स्यन्दमानं अनेककालिन्दीसहस्रं यस्मिन्. The Jumna is dark like गरुडमणि. See गरुडपक्ष above (text p. 27, l. 7). अङ्गा... रश्मिभिः with the rays of topaz it seemed to be full of charcoal.

The blue topaz would look like charcoal. If it was reddish, then it would look like a live piece of coal or like Mars (अङ्गारक). The next sentence is कैश्चि...शत्रुमहासामन्तैः समन्तादासेव्यमानम् (l. 34). कैश्चि...विशद्भिः some did not get admission, hung down their heads (on that account) and seemed, under the guise (निभः) of the image of faces reflected in the nails of their feet, to enter their own bodies through shame. 'निभस्तु कथितो व्याजे पुलिङ्गः सदृशे त्रिषु' मेदिनी. As they hung down their faces, the latter were reflected in the bright toe-nails. The poet fancies that through shame they entered their own bodies in the shape of reflections. कैश्चि...र्पयद्भिः under the guise (व्याजः) of the pencil of the rays of the nails of their hands that were scattered about, some (kings) seemed to hand over chowries for service to the earth which they scratched with their fingers. To scratch the earth is inauspicious. The vanquished kings, being deeply engrossed in sad thoughts and having nothing to do, drew lines on the ground with their nails. The rays of the bright nails resemble chowries. The poet fancies that chowries were handed over to the earth (poetically represented as the queen of a king) that the latter might thereafter serve king Harsha with the chowrie. 'रेखानिर्माणमुर्व्यां च्छदतृणलवनं पादयोश्चाप्यपूजा दन्तानामप्यशौचं वसनमलिनता रूक्षता मूर्धजानाम् । सन्ध्यायुग्मे च निद्रा विवसनशयनं ग्रासहास्यातिरेकः स्वाङ्गे वाद्यं च पुंसां निधनमुपनयेत्केशवस्यापि लक्ष्मीम् ॥'. उरःस्थले दोलायमानः इन्द्रनीलतरलप्रभापट्टः येषाम्. तरल is the central gem in a necklace. 'तरलो हारमध्यगः' इत्यमरः. कैश्चि...पट्टैः—the rays of the blue sapphire resemble a sword blade. The poet fancies that the kings had suspended from their necks swords (instead of carrying them in their hands) in order to propitiate their lord (हर्ष). तरल (=चञ्चल) suggests that the swords flashed like sapphires. कैश्चि...श्मश्रुभिरिव—the bees hovering round their faces are fancied to be the beard allowed to grow through grief at the loss of their kingdoms. One who is in mourning for the death of a relative does not shave himself. शेखरे (chaplet) उड्डीयमानं मधुपमण्डलं येषाम्. ०भयेन पलायमानः मौलिः (crown of the head) येषाम्. The bees on the white chaplet are fancied to be their heads (with the dark hair growing on them) running away for fear of having to submit to the humiliation of bowing at Harsha's feet. अविद्यमानं (हर्षात्) अन्यत् शरणं येषाम् that have no protector other than हर्ष. Another sense is (अविद्यमानं अन्यस्मात् शरणं रक्षणं येषाम्) 'who are not protected by any one else'; with this latter sense we have to construe संमानितैरिव—they were as though honoured because they did not require another to protect them. 'शरणं रक्षणे गेहे वधरक्षकयोरपि' हेमचन्द्रः. अन्तरान्तरा from time to time. निष्पतताम् coming out. आन्तर...पृच्छद्भिः that ceaselessly (अश्रान्त) asked again and again the servants that accompanied inner doorkeepers after whose track ran thousands of suppliants. अद्य भविष्यति will it be to-day ? भुक्तं आस्थानं यस्मिन्. भुक्ता...कक्ष्याम् will the emperor grant an interview after sitting in the audience-hall ? Will he come out into the outer court ? भुक्तं आस्थानं यथा स्यात्तथा or भुक्तं आस्थानं यस्मिन्. We may take 'अद्य...स्थानं' as one sentence and translate 'will there be an audience hall (*i. e.* will he hold his court) after taking his dinner ?' If we read भुक्त्वास्थाने, the meaning is 'will he, after taking his dinner, grant an interview in the audience-hall ?' The king was to enter the hall of justice after taking his dinner. 'भुक्तवान् विहरेच्चैव स्त्रीभिरन्तः-पुरे सह । विहृत्य तु यथाकालं पुनः कार्याणि चिन्तयेत् ॥' मनु० VII. 221. आसेव्यमानम्—qualifies राजद्वारम्. Connect महीपालैः with अध्यास्यमानम् (occupied). प्रति...कालम् that waited for the time when the emperor would be seen. एका...विष्टैः sitting in a spot by themselves. जैनैः आर्हतैः—we must understand the Bauddhas by जैनैः as आर्हतैः follows. जिन and अर्हत् are epithets that are applied to the founders of both Jainism and Buddhism by their followers. But in the usage of Brahmanical writers आर्हत stands for the system of महावीर (as in आर्हतदर्शन in the सर्वदर्शनसंग्रह). So जैनैः is equal to बौद्धैः. Compare 'न जिनस्येवार्थवादशून्यानि दर्शनानि' below (text p. 35. ll. 25-26). पाशुपतैः—The पाशुपतs are a sect of माहेश्वरs. For a brief statement and refutation of the पाशुपत system see शारीरकभाष्य on वेदान्तसूत्र II. 2. 37. *ff.* According to them शिव is called पशुपति (the lord of पशुs *viz.* the जीवs) and is only the निमित्तकारण of the world. पाराशरिभिः—for the meaning, see above p. 90. वर्णिभिः—वर्णिन् means 'ब्रह्मचारिन्' (from वर्ण + इन्) 'वर्णिनो ब्रह्मचारिणः'-according to 'वर्णाद्ब्रह्मचारिणि' पा. 5. 2. 134. For a longer list of the followers of various sects, see हर्ष० 8th उ० 5th para. सर्वदेशेषु जन्म येषाम्. सर्व...दूतमण्डलैः we know that ambassadors used to be sent to Indian courts by kings of Persia, Greece, Rome &c. In the frescoes in the caves of Ajanta there is a representation of a Persian embassy. सर्व...पतीनाम्—there were so many people of various tribes and nations that it seemed as though it was the place where the primeval sages created beings of various kinds. For प्रजापतिs, see above p. 18. It was these ten

प्रजापतिs that created everything. *Vide* मनु I. 36-41. लोक...रचितं made by gathering together the essence of the three worlds. अकथनीयः समृद्धिसम्भारः यस्य. The महाभारत is the biggest work in the Sanskrit language and yet a work of that vast extent would have fallen far short of adequately describing the glory of Harsha's gate. कृत...वेशम् the position of which was effected by a thousand कृतयुगs. Various meanings are possible. The royal gate was so gorgeous that it would seem to an observer to have been the work of long ages. Or the royal gate conveyed an atmosphere of so much purity and righteousness that as though a thousand कृतयुगs had combined to form it. For कृतयुग as an era of unmixed virtue, *vide* p. 45. स्वर्गाणां अर्बुदैः. अर्बुद is equal to 10 कोटिs. 'लक्षं च नियुतं चैव कोटिरर्बुदमेव च। वृन्दः खर्वो निखर्वश्च शङ्खपद्मौ च सागरः। अन्त्यं मध्यं परार्धं च दशवृद्ध्या यथाक्रमम्॥'. विहितं रामणीयकं यस्य. राज...ग्रहं that was surrounded or resorted to (*lit.* accepted) by crores of royal glories.

P. 28 ll. 8-13 **अभव...प्राविशत्.** जातः विस्मयः यस्मिन्. इयत् प्रमाणं यस्य (*adj.* of ०जातं) of this (vast) extent. प्रजासृजां of those (प्रजापतिs) that created beings. महा...क्षयः how is it that the great elements were not exhausted (in creating these numerous beings)? महाभूतs are the five gross elements *viz.* पृथिवी, अप्, तेजः, वायु and आकाश, from which the bodies of all beings are created. परिच्छेदः limit. The idea is that in creating so many beings, the furthest limit of the number of atoms must have been reached and exhausted. विच्छेदः is a better reading, but is probably an emendation. परमाणूनां परिच्छेदः is more in accordance with the style of Bāṇa who cares for अनुप्रास more than for anything else. व्युपरमः cessation, end. आकृ...प्तिः the exhaustion of all forms. पुण्यभागी (refers to बाण)—because he was soon to be ushered into the presence of the glorious हर्ष. तम् = बाणम्. अप्रतिहतः without being obstructed.

P. 28 ll. 14-30 **अथ स...भ्यन्तरम्.** The first sentence is अथ स मुहूर्तादिव...पुरुषेणानुगम्यमानः निर्गत्य अवोचत्. सः = मेखलकः. The instrumentals from प्रांशुना qualify पुरुषेण. कर्णिकारवत् गौरेण. वीध्रकेन (विमलेन) कञ्चुकेन छन्नं वपुः यस्य. समु...लग्नेन whose waist (अवलग्नं) was small, being bound by a belt (शस्तं) that was studded (बन्धुर) with ornaments of flashing rubies. पदकं metal plate studded with stones. ०पदकबन्धेन बन्धुरं शस्तं तस्य बन्धेन कृशं अवलग्नं यस्य. In the lexicons the meaning assigned to शस्त is 'finger-guard'

'अङ्गुलित्रं शस्तकं च तथा चाङ्गुष्ठरक्षकम्'. But that meaning will not do here. If we read वस्तबन्ध, the meaning is 'by a strap of goat-skin.' ०शिलावत् विशालं वक्षः यस्य. हरस्य (शिवस्य) वृषः तस्य ककुदं (hump) तस्य कूटो (राशिः) तद्वत् विकटः (formidable) अंसतटः. He was fair and formidable like हरवृष. उरसा...बिभ्रता wearing on his chest a necklace as though it (हार) were a rope to restrain the tribe of deer in the form of restless organs of sense. हृषीकं = इन्द्रियम्. इति... समानेन—the jewelled rings in his ear are fancied to be the sun and the moon brought there to inquire of them whether there existed any one in their families equal to हर्ष. वह...किरणैः for whom room was as though made by the rays of the sun out of regard for his (पुरुष's) position, the rays being eclipsed (*lit.* pulled away) by the flowing (वहत्) stream (वेणिका) of the beauty of his face. विसरः = समूहः. When there is a crowd and a way has to be made for a great man, people have to be dragged out (आक्षिप्यमाण). The bright lustre of his face surpassed the sun's rays. प्रसादेन लब्धया obtained through the favour of his master (with ०मालिकया); serene (with दृष्टया). लब्धः प्रसादः (serenity) यया सा लब्धप्रसादा or प्रसादलब्धा, according to 'वाहिताग्न्यादिषु' पा. 2. 2. 37 (आहिताग्निः । अग्न्याहितः). आहिताग्नि is an आकृतिगण (illustrative list only and not exhaustive). मुण्डमालिका a chaplet. नैष्ठु...हता bearing on his bent head a white turban as if it (turban) were courtesy itself, though he occupied a position that was the centre (अधिष्ठानं) of sternness. As the chief of all doorkeepers his position required him to be stern in keeping discipline; yet he was courteous and had bent his head when approaching Bāṇa. C and T translate 'lifting his white turban as a token of respect'. This is quite wrong. No one in India would lift his turban *as a token of respect.* The learned authors are misled by western notions. वामेन goes with ०लयेन and ०त्सरुं with कृपाणम्, which latter is the object of कलयता. स्थूलमुक्ताफलानां छुरणेन (inlaying) दन्तुरः (uneven, jagged) त्सरुः (handle) यस्य. कलयता (goes with पुरुषेण) holding. 'त्सरुः खड्गादिमुष्टौ स्यात्' इत्यमरः. इतरे...धारयता holding in the other (*i. e.* right) hand a polished (उन्मृष्टां) golden staff, as though it (staff) were a streak of lightning without its unsteadiness. अपनीता तरलता यस्याः. For शातकौम्भ see above p. 54. ताडिती is from तडित्. अप...रलतां (with वेत्रयष्टिम्) also means 'that prevents wanton actions' (of the crowd at the door). अपनीता तरलता यया. अनन्तरः = मुख्यः. चक्षुष्यः = प्रियः. See above p. 75. द्वारे नियुक्तः

दौवारिकः. सम...वेशी let your honour (Bāṇa) who is intent on welfare treat him with befitting behaviour. प्रतिपत्तिः respectful behaviour, course of conduct. कल्याणे अभिनिवेशः अस्य ०शिन्. The word means the same thing as कल्याणिन्. Compare 'आलोकयतु तावत्कल्याणाभिनिवेशी लक्ष्मीमेव प्रथमाम्' का० p. 104 of P; 'एतत्प्रायेण कल्याणाभिनिवेशिनः श्रुतिविषयमापतितमेव' का० p. 136 (P). आगच्छत—the plural shows the respect he paid to बाण. एव...ग्राह्यं worthy to be thus favoured.

P. 28 l. 31—**P. 29** l. 25. **अथ...इति.** The first sentence is अथ...तुरङ्गैः आरचितां मन्दुरां विलोकयन् (l. 14)...अव्यक्तं इभधिष्ण्यागारमपश्यत् (l. 19). वनायुजैः born in the country of वनायु. The words in the instrumental from वनायुजैः qualify तुरङ्गैः below (l. 14). From वनायुजैः to पारसीकैः we have the breeds of horses from various countries. हलायुध and विश्व give वनायुज and पारसीक as synonyms. But that will not do here as पारसीक follows. आरट्ट—'पञ्च नद्यो वहन्त्येता यत्र निःसृत्य पर्वतात्। आरट्टा नाम वाहीका न तेष्वार्यो द्व्यहं वसेत् ॥'. The country of कम्बोज was beyond the Hindookush mountains (probably eastern Persia) and was known in very ancient times. It produced one of the best breeds of horses. See रघु० IV. 69-70. यास्क refers to the country 'शवतिर्गतिकर्मा कम्बोजेष्वेव भाष्यते विकारमस्यार्येषु भाषन्ते शव इति' निरुक्त. See पाणिनि IV. 1. 75. पारसीक is Persia. From शोणैः, we have horses of various colours. ति...षैः dappled like partridges. In this para, the author shows his familiarity with शालिहोत्र, the science of horses. पञ्चभद्रः-horse having on the head and four hoofs five auspicious marks. According to सं०, it is a horse whose face together with the head and four hoofs is white.' 'सिताश्च यस्य वाजिनः शफाः समस्तकं मुखं स पञ्चभद्रनामको नृपस्य राज्यसौख्यदः ।' 'पञ्चभद्रस्तु हृत्पृष्ठमुखपार्श्वेषु पुष्पितः' हेमचन्द्र. On मल्लिकाक्षैः, सं० says "शुक्लपर्यन्ते असिततारके नयने येषां ते मल्लिकाक्षाः। उक्तं च 'पृथुस्निग्धाः समा चैव मल्लिकाकुसुमप्रभा । राजी यस्य तु पर्यन्ते परिक्षिप्ये तु लोचने । स हयो मल्लिकाक्षस्तु दृष्टिपर्यन्ततारकः ॥' इति." They are horses on the corners of whose eyes there are spots of white hair. कृत्तिकापिञ्जरैः—सं० 'तारकाकदम्बककल्पानेकबिन्दुकल्माषितत्वचः'—horses the coat of which is marked with numerous starlike spots. कृत्तिका is a cluster of six stars. आयतं (long) निर्मांसं मुखं येषाम्. अनुत्कटः (ह्रस्वः) कर्णकोशः येषाम्. सुवृत्तः (well rounded) श्लक्ष्णः (soft or delicate) सुघटितः (well proportioned) घण्टिकाबन्धः येषाम्. घण्टिकाबन्ध-that part of the neck where bells are tied. The com. says "शिरसो ग्रीवायाश्च यन्मध्यं स घण्टिकाबन्धः यो निगाल इत्युच्यते। तस्य सुवृत्तादि शस्यते। यदाह 'ग्रीवाशिरोन्तर-

श्लिष्टो दीर्घवृत्तः समाहितः । नोद्वर्तो नार्धितो नातिदुर्नाह्योऽतिविधानतः । सुदिग्धोनुपदिग्धश्च निगालो गदितः शुभः ॥' इति". यूपानुपूर्व्या वक्रा आयता उदग्रा ग्रीवा येषाम् with curved, long and up-turned necks resembling a sacrificial post in their contour. आनुपूर्वी order, regular succession of parts. पूर्वानुक्रमेण अनुपूर्वं तस्य भावः आनुपूर्वी or ०पूर्व्यम्. उपचयेन श्वयन्तः स्कन्धसन्धयः येषाम् whose shoulder joints were stout (swelling) on account of the accumulation (of flesh). निर्भुग्नं (projecting, convex) उरःस्थलं येषाम्. The com. says 'स्थूलास्थि महदच्छिद्रं पृथुलं यच्च निर्वलि । उर ईदृक्प्रशंसन्ति स्थूलक्रोड़ं महत्तरम् ॥'. अस्थूलाः (not thick) slender प्रगुणाः (straight) प्रसृताः (legs) येषाम्. लोहपीठवत् कठिनं खुरमण्डलं येषाम्. अति...धारयद्भिः that had bellies round and as though without entrails through fear of their being broken through great speed. अनिर्मिताणि अन्त्राणि येषु. अन्त्राणि suggests the idea of interstices or ups and downs. What is वृत्त (well rounded) cannot have ups and downs. उद्यन्त्या (large) द्रोण्या विभज्यमानं पृथुजघनं येषाम् whose broad flanks were divided by a large depression. द्रोणी is a feature of beauty in a horse. It is a depression on the chest, back and flanks of a horse. The com. quotes 'पृष्ठोरःकटिपार्श्वस्य मांसोत्कर्षणनिर्मिता । द्रोणिकेति प्रशंसन्ति शोभा वाजिनि पञ्चमी ॥'. जगती...पल्लवैः whose leaf-like tails rolled on the ground (जगती). C and T translate 'with the hairs like new shoots swaying about in the wind'. कथ...यन्त्रितैः that were restrained with difficulty by the numerous firm ropes fixed (in the earth) on both sides. The ropes held their necks. If we read भूमिपाश०, then the meaning is 'ropes in the ground firmly fixed &c'. We then expect the order to be भूमिनिरवात &c. आय...माणैः although already long enough, they (horses) seemed to be longer still as one of their hinder legs was stretched because it was tied with a rope. पाशबन्ध is Marathi पायबन्द. बहुगुणेन सूत्रेण ग्रथितः ग्रीवागण्डकः येषाम् the neck-ornament of which was suspended with a cord of many strings. आमीलिते (closed) लोचने येषाम्. दूर्वा...चालयद्भिः that kept moving their limbs that were itching, the skin of which twitched, that were held between the teeth and then let go, that were spotted with bits of foam darkened by Dūrvā juice. दशनैः आदौ गृहीताः पश्चात् मुक्ताः. फरफरिता पुनः पुनः ईषत्कम्पिता त्वक् येषाम्. When their limbs had itch, the skin twitched and they held the itching skin between their teeth to ease the itching sensation. This caused the foam and the juice of the Dūrvās they were grazing upon to stick to their bodies. 'प्रतीकोऽवयवेऽपि स्यात्' मेदिनी.

C and T take the word as meaning 'mouths'. But we cannot then construe ०मुक्तान् with प्रतीकान्, as mouths cannot be bitten by teeth. सालसं वलितः वालधिः (पुच्छं) यैः that lazily moved their tails. बाला धीयन्ते अस्मिन् इति बालधिः (वालधिः also). एक...घनार्धैः half of whose flanks was drooping (स्रस्त) and relaxed as they rested on one hoof. निद्र...यद्भिः that seemed to ponder when they slept. स्खलित...यमानैः that emitted low rumbling neighing when they stumbled. ताडिता खुरधरणी तस्याः रणितेन मुखरं शिखरं येषां ते ०शिखराः खुराः तैः लिखितं क्ष्मातलं यैः. खुरधरणी is a wooden foot-rest. The object may be to allow the urine to pass through a hole in the foot-rest into a gutter underneath over which the plank is placed. प्रकीर्यमाणाः यवसग्रासाः तेषु रसः (liking) तेन or तस्मात् मत्सरः तेन उद्भूतः क्षोभः येषाम्. When fodder was scattered before other horses, they became enraged and jealous. प्रकुपिताः चण्डाः चण्डालाः (अश्वपालाः) तेषां हुङ्कारैः (threatening words) कातरतराः तरलाः तारकाः (pupils) येषाम्. कुङ्कुम...लक्ष्यमाणैः As their bodies were yellowish red because saffron was rubbed over them, they seemed to have always near them the lustration-fires. Both कुङ्कुम and fire are red. For नीराजन, see above p. 34. उपरिविततं वितानं (canopy) येषाम्. पुरः पूजितं अभिमतदैवतं येषाम्. The अभिमतदैवत according to the com. is गोविन्द. आरचितां filled. मन्दुरा stable. 'वाजिशाला तु मन्दुरा' इत्यमरः. हस्तवामेन to the left of his hand. अत्युच्च...कुर्वाणम्—this and the following clauses qualify ०गारम्. अत्युच्च०—which, on account of its great height, as though left the sky no room. The elephant stable was very high and crowded the whole sky. कदली plantain tree; banner. परिवृताः पर्यन्ताः यस्य the outskirts of which were surrounded. सर्व...पूर्यमाणम् that was filled on all sides with streams (स्रुति) of ichor full of bees, as though with rivers. आशा...न्द्रियं that filled the nostrils with the odour, as though of blooming Bakula trees, spreading in all directions. The odour of the ichor of the best elephants was said to be like that of Bakula. Separate विकसताम् + आमोदेन. The com. says "तदुक्तम् । 'मालतीमुक्तपुन्नागबकुलोपमसौरभम् । दानं पि(मि?)ष्टाम्बुसदृशं मुञ्चच्छ्वेतं तु शीतलम् ॥.' दूरादव्यक्तम् not quite distinct owing to distance. इभ...गारम् a stable where elephants were housed. 'धिष्ण्यं स्थाने गृहे' इत्यमरः. अत्र...करोति—the elephant—stable looked from a distance like a palace. So बाण asked this question. औपवाह्यः—'राजवाह्यस्त्वौपवाह्यः सन्नाह्यः समरोचितः' क्षीरस्वामी—a king's elephant meant for riding only (and not for fighting). जात्यन्तरितः आत्मा his very soul separated from him by another species. The king's soul was in a human body, while in दर्पशात it was in an elephantine body. दर्पशातः—literally means 'one who destroys the pride' (of other elephants). दर्पं शातयति इति. C and T strangely enough explain it as 'keen (or perhaps attenuated and lacking) in pride'. श्रूयते—I have only *heard*, but never seen. यद्ये...न्द्रमेव If it be so (*i. e.* if दर्पशात is housed here) and if there be no objection (in seeing it), then I shall first of all see the great elephant. अतिपरवान् overcome.

P. 29 l. 26—**P. 31** l. 22. **गत्वा च...पश्यत्.** The principal sentence is गत्वा च दूरादेव...दर्पशातमपश्यत्. गम्भीर...गर्जितैः—by the deep sounds issuing from his throat. कल low, sweet. गम्भीर...हलम्—the idea is:—The big elephant trumpeted in deep grunts (as is usual with these animals); that sound resembled the rumbling of a cloud. So the चातक and the peacock welcomed the sound (thinking that a cloud was near) with vociferous notes. A चातक was supposed not to be able to drink the water flowing on the earth; it had to rest content with a few drops from the cloud falling direct into its mouth. Hence the word वियति with चातककदम्बकैः and भुवि with peacocks (नीलकण्ठ). Compare 'चातका इव तृष्णावन्तो न शक्यन्ते ग्रहीतुमकुलीनाः' हर्ष० 4th उ०. See for peacocks dancing when it thunders, p. 63. क्रियमाणः कलः कोलाहलः यस्य. This and the following words in the accusative singular qualify दर्पशातं below. विकचानि कदम्बानि संवदति (resembling) इति ०संवादी मदः सुरा इव तस्याः सौरभेण भरितं भुवनं येन. काय...कालम् that seemed as though he were the premature season of clouds wearing an embodied form. Both the elephant and clouds are dark. In the season of clouds (rains) one sees चातकs, peacocks dancing and the कदम्ब tree putting forth buds. Therefore the elephant (whose ichor resembled the odour of *Kadamba* buds) is fancied to be the season of clouds incarnate. It was then the middle of ग्रीष्म and not वर्षा. So the word अकाल is put in. अविरल...त्सृजन्तम् leaving (about to leave) the fourth stage of life that had reached its perfection by his skin being marked with spots brown like thick drops of honey as though it were a lake. अभ्यवगाढाम् full developed (with दशाम्); deep (with सरसीम्). अविरलमधुबिन्दुवत् पिङ्गलानि पद्मजालकानि सञ्जातानि अस्याः इति ०जालकिताम् (with दशाम्). *Vide* notes on तारकित p. 42. पद्मजालकम्—marks of reddish spots on the elephant's skin. 'पद्मकं बिन्दुजालकम्' इत्यमरः (पद्मप्रतिकृति

रक्तत्वात्पद्मकम् तारुण्ये हि हस्तिनां देहे रक्तबिन्दवः स्युः । क्षीर०). 'चतुर्थ्यामवगाढायां लेखाबिन्दुभिराचितः' सं०. ०बिन्दुभिः पिङ्गलानि पद्मानि (कमलानि) तैः जालकिताम् (with सरसीम्). There is brown honey in lotuses. सरसीम्—'दक्षिणापथे हि महान्ति सरांसि सरस्य इत्युच्यन्ते' महाभाष्य (Kielhorn Vol I. p. 73.). चतुर्थीदशा means 'the age between 30 and 40'; compare कौटिल्य's अर्थशास्त्र 'That which is seven अरत्नि‍s in height, nine in length, ten in circumference and is 40 years old is the best' (translation p. 207). आमन्द्रः कर्णताल एव दुन्दुभिध्वनिः येषु (*adj.* of शंखैः). अन...गायन्तम् that chanted (the tune suited to) the beginning of his auspicious entrance into the fifth stage with the conch-shell ornaments on his ears that were blended with the low drum-like rumbling of the flapping of his ears. For शङ्खs on elephant's ears, see above text p. 27 l. 18. At an auspicious ceremony such as the first entrance in a new house, there is the music of drums (दुन्दुभि) and conches may be blown. पञ्चमी stands for पञ्चमीदशा. अविरतचलने चित्रा (charming) त्रिपदी एव ललितं (fine) लास्यं (dancing) तस्य लयैः (harmony). त्रिपदी standing on three legs, while one is lifted up. This is a characteristic action with the elephant. 'गानगेययोरन्यूनाधिक्ये श्लिष्टता लयो द्रुतादिः वाद्यादीनामन्योन्यं समत्वमिति यावत्' क्षीरस्वामी. The elephant moved incessantly and he rested his body on three legs. So he seemed to be engaged in dancing and there was a certain rhythmical method in his movements. दोलायमानः दीर्घदेहस्य आभोगः (expanse) यस्य सः ०भोगः तस्य भावः ०भोगता तया. मेदिनी...यमानम्—the idea is:—by his incessantly standing on three legs, he seemed to be lessoning his weight on the earth for fear of (otherwise) breaking it (विदलन). His incessant movements to and fro looked like rubbing the itching body against the quarters. Buffaloes and elephants may rub their bodies against walls. लघयन्तम् *pr. p.* of लघयति denominative verb from लघु. आहवः fight. उदस्तहस्ततया because he threw up his trunk (into space). उदस्त *past p. p.* of अस् to throw with उद्. There are eight guardian elephants of the eight quarters. 'ऐरावतः पुण्डरीको वामनः कुमुदोऽञ्जनः । पुष्पदन्तः सार्वभौमः सुप्रतीकश्च दिग्गजाः ॥' इत्यमरः. ह्वे with आ in the sense of 'to challenge to a fight' takes the आत्मनेपद only. 'स्पर्धायामाङः' पा. 1. 3. 31. (कृष्णश्चाणूरमाह्वयते). करपत्रम् saw (Marathi करवत); saw-like trunk (करः पत्रमिव). स्थूलाः निशिताः दन्ताः यस्य. A saw has teeth and cleaves pillars (स्तम्भः). स्थूलौ निशितौ दन्तौ बस्मिन् (with trunk). He moved his trunk armed with sharp tusks and seemed to cleave the world (ब्रह्मस्तम्भः). See above

p. 102 for ब्रह्मस्तम्भ. अमा...मानम् he seemed to desire to go out, as though the world could not contain him. His incessant movements and large body give rise to this conceit. The next clause is सर्वतः...नन्दम्, the chief portion of which is सर्वतः लेशिकैः आधोरणैः च आधीय...नन्दम्—to whom delight was caused by riders (लेशिक) and keepers (आधोरण) who treated him with remedies (उपचारः) appropriate to summer. आधीयमानः ०समयसमुपचितोपचारैः आनन्दः यस्मिन्. 'आधोरणा हस्तिपकाः' इत्यमरः. सरस...वनैरिव by riders who tossed (over the elephants) creepers full of juice and sprouts and who seemed as though they were forests gathered together through long familiarity. In forests also there are dancing creepers full of juice &c. The elephant roamed in forests which as though came there in crowds (उपचित) to alleviate his torment. If we read घनैः, the words चिर...चितैः cannot be well-explained; clouds also cause creepers to dance when they pour water over them. विक्षिप्त...धोरणैः keepers that threw water mixed with juicy moss and bundles (विसरः) of lotus stalks (on them) looked like lakes. In lakes also there are waters, moss and lotus stalks. The chief words in the next clause are अपि च अतिस्थवीयसा ०दण्डेन अर्गलयन्तमिव सकलं ककुभां चक्रवालम्–and who seemed to chain the circle of the quarters by his very stout bolt-like trunk. स्थवीयस् comparative of स्थूल. प्रति...क्षिप्तेन (*adj.* of ०दण्डेन) that was tossed aloft as though he smelt (*lit.* took the wind) the ichor of some rival elephants. प्रतिगजदानपवनस्य आदानेन दूरक्षिप्तः तेन. अनेक...दरेण which was wavy with small lines of wrinkles (वलिः) round it as though with marks (lines) to reckon his victories in many battles. Ignorant persons reckon by drawing lines on the earth or wall &c. The wrinkles on the trunk are fancied to be such lines. Compare 'बहुयोजनगमनगणनसंख्याक्षरावलीभिरिव' &c. (text p. 27 l. 1). कुलशैलाः समुद्राः द्वीपाः काननानि च तैः सह (बहुव्रीहि)—*adj.* of चक्रवालम्. For the कुलपर्वतs, see above p. 76, for the seven seas p. 32 and the seven continents p. 3. एकं and अपरं qualify दन्तकाण्डम्. करा...पल्लवमिव—When a plant is watered it puts forth पल्लवs. The leaves of the कदली held in the trunk seemed to be the पल्लवs of his tusk, the tusk being watered by the juice oozing from the कदली stem. करान्तरे अर्पितेन. उद्गतानि पलाशानि यस्य. मुक्ताः पल्लवाः येन. It is not correct to understand मुक्तपल्लव as 'a shooting twig of pearls.' In that case मुक्तपल्लव cannot be properly dissolved and the उत्प्रेक्षा is not properly worked out. अपर...दन्तकाण्डे—From the other tusk hung down lotus fibres, which resembled रोमाञ्च due to his great zest for fighting. 'विसर्पन्त्या...कान्त्या'-these words are to be connected with वमन्तं, अर्पयन्तं, ०हसन्तं and कल्पयन्तम्. सर...वमन्तम्—His tusks were very white. कुमुद्s also are white. When the brilliance of the tusks spread all round, the poet fancies that he vomitted the कुमुद् bed that he had eaten when he sported in the lakes. On the use of वान्त in poetry, *vide* p. 50. निज... र्पयन्तम्—the brilliance of tusks spreading in the world is fancied to be his fame (which is white) spreading in all directions. कु...हसन्तम्—he seemed to laugh at lions that were naughty (दुर्ललित) because they had broken down some wretched worms of elephants. हास is white. कल्प...कल्पयन्तम् he seemed to make for himself a silken veil manufactured from the heavenly tree. The brilliance of his tusks spreading round his face looked like a fine white silken veil. हस्त...लक्ष्यमाणेन which (palate) was seen when he gracefully lifted up his trunk. रक्ता...वर्षन्तम् when he showed his red palate, be seemed to vomit the red lotuses he had devoured. His तालु was red like रक्तांशुक and fresh किसलय. A red तालु showed an excellent elephant and so did a brown (पिङ्गल) eye. Compare बृहत्संहिता 'ताम्रोष्ठतालुवदनाः' 67. 6. चूत...विसृजन्तम्—the plain idea is that the ichor flowing from his cheeks (करटः) was as fragrant as चूत, पारिजातक &c. 'काकेभगण्डौ करटौ' इत्यमरः. अहर्निशं... पतीनाम् that seemed to bestow on the elephants all the forests by दानपट्टकs, on which he gracefully placed his trunk, that were rubbed with a half-cut sugarcane reed, and that resounded with a swarm of bees. विभ्रमेण (लीलया) कृता हस्तस्य शुण्डायाः स्थितिः येषु. अर्धखण्डितं पुण्ड्रेक्षुकाण्डं तेन कण्डूयनं तस्मिन् लिखितैः. पुण्ड्र is a kind of very sweet red sugarcane. करिपतीनाम्—the genitive is used in the sense of the dative. दानपट्टकैः is used in two senses; (1) streams of ichor; (2) royal grants declaring a gift. All the clauses have an application to royal grants. विभ्रम...स्थितिभिः on which (royal copperplates or other edicts) the hand (royal signature) is gracefully (or hastily) made. Mark the use of the word हस्त in inscriptions as in 'स्वहस्तो मम &c'. Intro. p. XXIX footnote. लिखितैः suggests that royal orders are written with a pen (लेखनी) of reed (resembling इक्षुकाण्ड). वाचालितैः— royal grants are loudly read by the donees (who resemble bees that seek the दान). Take away the comma after क्रियमाणम्. शिशिरी० qualifies शिरः. अविरल...दधानम्—the idea is:—As the heat was intense, his high head was cooled with a garland made of pieces of ice. His head on which the white pieces of ice were placed seemed to be covered with a पट्टबन्ध (fillet) studded with bright jewels. The jewels resemble stars, as do the pieces of ice. A पट्टबन्ध indicated authority. *Vide* notes p. 116. 'बन्धुरं तून्नतानतम्' इत्यमरः. 'सैव नक्षत्रमाला स्यात्सप्तविंशतिमौक्तिकैः' इत्यमरः. As there were no pearls, but only icy pieces, the author says विभ्रमन॰ &c. आदौ स्थगितानि (covered, concealed) पश्चात् अपावृतानि (opened, laid bare) दिङ्मुखानि याम्यां. कर्णौ तालवृन्ते (fans) इव. As he flapped his large ears, he screened from view for sometime the worlds and then again allowed them to be seen. Compare for a similar conceit 'क्षणदृष्टनष्टाष्टदिङ्मुखं' &c. (text p. 27 l. 13). कर्ण...क्ष्मीम् out of devotion to his master, he, as though fanned Royal glory resting on the couch of his tusks. A lady resting on a couch of ivory (in summer) may be fanned by a servant. The elephant is a symbol of लक्ष्मी. Further the elephant helped the king to secure राजलक्ष्मी. The flapping ears would fan his tusks. आ...गतेन (1) that descended in a well-proportioned shape from the backbone (with बालधिना); that was handed down through a long family in succession (with चामरेण). A chowrie was one of the signs of royalty (आधिपत्यचिह्न) and may be handed down from father to son. चलता waving (applies to both चामर and बालधि). वंशः family; back-bone. आयत long. On आयतवंश॰, सं॰ remarks "आयतवंशः, वक्रवंशः, शरवंशः, बालवंशश्चेति चत्वारो वंशाः। तेषु बालवंश आयत एव शास्त्रकृतामभिप्रेतः। तथा च 'यावत्पूरितपाशश्च वंशश्चापलताकृतिः। शुभो ज्ञेयो गजेन्द्राणामायतः कुरुते सुखम् ॥' इति तैरुक्तम्। आयताद्वंशात्तत्क्रमेण गोपुच्छवदायत इति विग्रहः। समानार्हो हि बालधिः शोकं करोति। यदुक्तम् 'वक्रं स्थूलं च ह्रस्वं च पुच्छं कचविवर्जितम्। समानार्हं हि नागस्य भर्तुः शोककरं स्मृतम् ॥.' शीकर the spray from the elephant's trunk. दिग्विजयपीताः—he had drunk the waters of several rivers when he accompanied his master Harsha on the latter's दिग्विजय. अवधानदानेन निस्पन्दीकृताः (made motionless) सकलावयवाः येषु (*adj.* of वलनानां). अन्य...वलनानाम् of the twistings of his body when he heard the sound of the drum borne by other elephants. क्षण...शोचन्तम्–the idea is:—When he heard the sound of drums on other elephants, he attentively listened for a moment and then again became restless and trumpeted. A person, when insulted, heaves deep sighs. The author fancies that the elephant trumpeted because it wanted to convey that it was insulted by there being other elephants carrying drums and that it bewailed its own lot that it could not fight with those elephants. आरो...मुञ्चन्तम्—the elephant scratched the ground and dropped ichor (मद). The poet fancies that the elephant did these actions through shame at the humiliation of having to bear on his back the riders (आरोहाः). A person who feels ashamed scratches the ground and gives up pride (मद). अवज्ञया (आदौ) गृहीताः (पश्चात्) मुक्ताः कवलाः तैः कुपिताः आरोहाः तेषां आरटनस्य अनुरोधेन in obedience to the shouts of the riders &c. The riders shouted angrily when the elephant took up mouthfuls and then dropped them. मदस्य तन्द्रा (drowsiness) निमीलितः नेत्रत्रिभागः यथा स्यात्तथा. अनादरात् unwillingly. अवजग्धेभ्यः (eaten) तमालपल्लवेभ्यः स्रुतः श्यामलः रसः यस्मिन् (*adj.* of मुखेन). As the juice of तमाल leaves was dark, it resembled मद. मुखेनापि—it is from the temples that ichor flows. दल...र्पेण he seemed as though splitting with pride. It will be noticed that from these words up to सिञ्चन्तमिव सौभाग्येन, there are pairs of words, each of which begins with the same letter. So the reading दलन्तं is better than चलन्तम्. श्व...मदेन who breathed heavily as though through bravery (that finds no outlet), who swelled as though through pride. मूर्च्छन्तम् also means 'fainting.' मदेन through intoxication. स्त्रु...दानेन breaking through youth, flowing with ichor. He was so full of youthful energy that it, not being contained within him, as though split him up. वल्गन्तम् prancing. माद्य...त्साहेन he was as though intoxicated through arrogance and seemed to rise aloft through his energy. ताम्य...सौभाग्येन he gasped on account of his own brilliance, he smeared (everything) with his grace, he sprinkled (the world) with his loveliness. Heat (तेजस्) makes one languid (ताम्यत्). स्निग्धं smooth; affectionate. Smooth nails in elephants were highly thought of. "उक्तं च 'नखाः स्निग्धाः सिताः शस्ताः' इति" सं०. परुष rough; unkind. It will be noticed that the first words in each pair of clauses are contradictory as in स्निग्धं परुषं and गुरुं सच्छिष्यम्. गुरुम् large; teacher. सच्छिष्यं विनये a good disciple in modesty or discipline. मृदुं soft; affectionate. दृढं hard; firm (in friendship). ह्रस्वं...बन्धे short of neck. दरिद्रं slender; poverty-stricken. सत...दाने ceaselessly flowing with ichor; ceaselessly giving gifts. बलभद्र is बलराम, the elder brother of कृष्ण. मदलीलासु in pranks due to being in rut; pranks due to drink. भद्र is an elephant of the best type. *Vide* चाणक्य's अर्थशास्त्र II. chap. 31 for भद्र and मन्द्र elephants and बृहत्सं.

हिता 67. 1. 'भद्रो मन्द्रो मृगश्चेति विज्ञेया त्रिविधा गजाः.' बलराम was notorious for drinking. See विष्णुपु॰ V. 25. कुल...तासु who was like a high-born wife in his obedient nature. आयत्तता obedience, docility. जिनं क्षमासु a Jina in patience जिन may stand for Buddha or Mahāvīra, the founder of Jainism, both of whom laid emphasis on क्षमा. वह्नि...मोक्षेषु he was a very shower of fire, when he let loose his wrath. ना...षु (1) pulling out or lifting serpents; (2) in destroying elephants. Garuḍa is the implacable foe of serpents. दर्पशात destroyed his rivals in battle. कलहकुतूहलेषु in his eagerness for quarrels (or fights). नारद–*vide* p. 18. नारद is represented as always proceeding from heaven to earth and *vice versa* with some mission or news and as fond of quarrels. Note the Marathi expression 'कळीचा नारद'. He is therefore styled कलिप्रिय. शुष्का...स्कन्देषु—In the rains one expects अशनिपात. But a thunderbolt when there is no rain (no cloud) is unexpected. So दर्पशात made sudden (and hence terrific) attacks (अवस्कन्दः). वाहिनीक्षोभेषु (1) in agitating rivers; (2) in terrifying armies. आश्यां विषं यस्य सः आशीविषः सर्पः. दशनकर्मसु (1) in biting; (2) in using his tusks. पाश...ष्विषु (1) in drawing (sinners) with the noose in his hand; (2) in drawing with his charming trunk. The word पाश at the end of compounds conveys the idea of 'beauty' as in केशपाश. प्रशस्तः हस्तः हस्तपाशः. The god Varuṇa, who in the Rigveda is represented as ruling over the moral laws of the world, has a पाश as his weapon. Compare 'उदुत्तमं मुमुग्धि नो वि पाशं मध्यमं चृत । अवाधमानि जीवसे' ऋग्वेद I. 25. 21. यम...वेष्टनेषु he is the net of Yama in entangling his enemies. 'वागुरा मृगबन्धनी' इत्यमरः. यम is represented as drawing the soul of a dying man with his पाश. Compare सावित्र्युपाख्यान (वनपर्व 297. 17) 'ततः सत्यवतः कायात्पाशबद्धं वशङ्गतम् । अङ्गुष्ठमात्रं पुरुषं निश्चकर्ष यमो बलात् ॥.' कालम् (1) dark; (2) time. परिणतिषु (1) in butting with his tusks; (2) in maturity or old age. Time makes one old or time brings to maturity one's actions. The elephant was dark and butted with his tusks or the elephant meant death (destruction) when परिणत as he butted against anything. परिणत when applied to an elephant has a technical sense. 'तिर्यग्दन्तप्रहारस्तु गजः परिणतो मतः' हलायुध quoted by मल्लिनाथ on शिशुपालवध 4. 29. तीक्ष्णकरः सूर्यः तस्य ग्रहेषु in eclipsing the Sun; तीक्ष्णं करेण ग्रहणं तेषु in seizing forcibly with his trunk. लोहिताङ्ग the planet Mars (that is red in appearance). वक्रचारेषु (1) in crooked movements; (2) in retrograde motion. The movements of the earth and the other planets round the sun give rise at times to an apparent retrograde motion. This occurs very often in the case of Mars and therefore वक्र itself means 'Mars.' When Mars is retrograde, it is an evil sign. अलातचक्रं a firebrand. मण्डल...ज्ञानेषु (1) in the knowledge of moving in a circle; (2) in the false knowledge of a circle of fire. If a firebrand is quickly revolved round, it produces the appearance of a circle of fire. The elephant knew how to move in a circle. The com. sees here a reference to difficult combinations of letters in a verse that were indulged in by certain poets like भारवि and माघ and were called चित्रबन्धs such as गोमूत्रिका. 'गोमूत्रिकामण्डले त्रिविधा हि गतिः । तत्रालातचक्रमुल्मुकचक्रं भ्रमणं करोति'. मनो...क्रमस्य—The elephant was big like a hill and he was very heroic, the result being that the king succeeded in whatever he desired. A चिन्तामणि was a fabulous jewel supposed to yield whatever one desired. दन्त...मानस्य the elephant is now called a palace of pride or high-mindedness. A palace may have columns of ivory and pearls. The elephant had tusks resembling (in whiteness) pillars of pearl stones. दन्तानां मुक्ताशैलानां च स्तम्भाः यस्मिन् स °स्तम्भः निवासप्रासादः; दन्तौ मुक्ताशैलस्य स्तम्भौ इव तयोः निवासप्रासादः. घण्टा...हरम् charming with bells, chowries and ornaments. Both the elephant and the celestial car are so adorned. इच्छा...स्विताया: the heavenly car of nobility or high spirits moving at will. The elephant conveys his master where he wishes. मद...क्रोधस्य to irritability he is a shower-bath of scented water, dark with a cloud of ichor-stream. मदधारा एव दुर्दिनं (rainy day) तस्य अन्धकारः यस्मिन्. 'मेघच्छन्नेऽह्नि दुर्दिनम्' इत्यमरः. धारागृह is comparatively dark and has scented water. The ichor is dark and has odour. सकाञ्चना प्रतिमा (image) यस्मिन्. A big temple is स...प्रतिम (has a golden image). The elephant also was स...प्रतिम; he had a head marked with gold. प्रतिमा is the part of an elephant's head between the tusks. Compare 'विपुलेऽपि पृथुप्रतिमो दन्त इव गणाधिपस्य मुखे' हर्ष० 4th उच्छ्वास, 2nd verse. निकेतनम् a house, (here) temple. क्रीडापर्वत has प्रस्रवणs (streams) and गण्डशैलs (boulders). The elephant also had प्रस्रवण (the flow of ichor) from his hill-like cheeks. गण्डौ शैलौ इव तौ च प्रस्रवणं (दानं) च तैः सह (with दर्पशातं); गण्डशैलाश्च प्रस्रवणानि (वारिप्रवाहाः) च तैः सह. 'गण्डशैलास्तु च्युताः स्थूलोपला गिरेः' इत्यमरः ('च्युताः भूकम्पादिना' क्षीर०). The elephant was hard like adamant (वज्र) and had tusks and neck (तोरणम्). A मन्दिर has an arched gate of ivory. सदन्तः तोरणः यस्य. 'तोरणोऽस्त्री बहिर्द्वारम्' इत्यमरः. दन्तौ च तोरणं च तैः सह. A गिरिदुर्ग (hill-fort) is stationary. The elephant is like a difficult (दुर्ग) hill or affords protection like a hill-fort, but is moving (सञ्चारि). उच्चौ कुम्भकूटौ अट्टालकौ इव ताभ्यां विकटम् formidable with his tower-like high temple bones (कुम्भकूट) (with दर्पशात); a hill fort is formidable with कूटs and towers. 'अट्टालकः प्राकाराग्रे रणगृहमिति कौटिल्यः' क्षीर०. 'कूटं पूर्द्वारि यद्धस्तिनखस्तस्मिन्' इत्यमरः ('दुर्गद्वारावतरणार्थः क्रमनिम्नो हस्तिनखाभो मृत्कूटः' क्षीर०) *i. e.* it is a sloping earthen mound at the gate of a fort. The elephant was dark and strong like an iron rampart (प्राकारः) and served to protect the earth as a rampart does. कृतानि अनेकबाणैः विवरसहस्राणि यस्मिन्—the elephant was pierced in battle by arrows. कृतानि अनेकबाणविवरसहस्राणि यस्मिन् in the fort-wall, there were loopholes for discharging arrows. The com. says this is called इन्द्रकोश in चाणक्य's work. 'Between the tower and the broad street there shall be constructed an Indrakosha which is made up of covering pieces of wooden planks affording seats for three archers' अर्थशास्त्र (English Translation) p. 58. दर्पशात is called पारिजातपादप for two reasons. He belonged to the king (भूनन्दनः) and had bees humming (over his ichor). नन्दन, the garden of इन्द्र, has पारिजात which is pursued by bees (शिलीमुखः). भूः एव नन्दनं or भुवः नन्दनः. For भूनन्दन (prince), see 4th उच्छ्वास first para. In a music hall, there is dancing. The loud flapping of दर्पशात's ears resembled ताण्डव. आपा...ण्डलानाम् a drinking saloon for the swarms of bees. मधुप also means 'drunkards.' Amorous sports (शृङ्गार) and ornaments are seen in the ladies of the harem. दर्पशात also had ornaments and शृङ्गार (marks with vermilion on the head and trunk). 'शृङ्गारं चूर्णसिन्दूरलवङ्गकुसुमेषु च' विश्वः. In the festival of Cupid (which is now celebrated in फाल्गुन) there is dancing through intoxication of youth (or drink). दर्पशात was full of graceful movements (लीलालास्य) due to being in ichor. अक्षुण्णप्रदोषम्—on a clear (*lit.* untrodden) night, the stars are visible. दर्पशात had the नक्षत्रमाला ornament, for which see text p. 30 l. 23. मदः एव महानदीपूरः तेन प्लवः (flooding). दर्पशात emitted floods of ichor even without the proper season of rain. सप्तच्छद—The tree सप्तच्छद (Marathi सातवीण) blossoms in शरद् and ichor has an odour resembling its flowers. *Vide.* रघु० IV. 23. 'प्रसवैः सप्तपर्णानां मदगन्धिभिराहताः। असूययेव तन्नागाः सप्तधैव प्रसुस्रुवुः ॥' Dew (नीहारः) is found only in the cold season; but dewy spray (from the trunk) was emitted by him at all times. A cloud thunders. The elephant produced thunder-like trumpetings. 'आडम्बरस्तूर्यरवे गजेन्द्राणां च गर्जिते' इत्यमरः.

P. 31 l. 23—**P. 35** l. 17 **आसी...द्राक्षीत्.** नून...णुताम् surely in creating this elephant, hills were used as atoms. Ordinarily the size of atoms from which all things are produced is atomic. But the elephant was so vast that it seemed impossible that atoms could make his huge body. So hills must have been taken as the smallest constituents which went to make up his body. विन्ध्य...करः—this is a hyperbolical description. The idea is:—बाण saw the firm and stout tusks and the formidable trunk. The elephant was massive and strong like the विन्ध्य mountain. The strikingness consists in assigning tusks to a mountain. दन्त suggests 'peak'. दर्पशात was powerful like the primeval Boar. The Boar had no कर (hand); but दर्पशात had a कर (trunk). **Verse 4**. Read 'लिखतां' for लिखिताम्. This verse is full of puns and is applicable to दर्पशात (the best of elephants) and also to the king. The principal portion is विद्विषां कथमपि स्मृतिपथं आयातः नागेन्द्रः मान...नपि न सहते—When this big elephant is somehow remembered by the enemies (of the king हर्ष), he (दर्पशात) does not brook even the hope-elephants in their minds *i. e.* the high hopes (of regaining their kingdoms) crumble to nothing the moment they remember the prowess of दर्पशात. The words मान... गजेन्द्रानपि also mean 'he does not brook the (presence of) दि-ग्गज residing on the मानस lake'. आशा = दिशा. शून्यीभवत् चेतः येषाम्—whose minds are vacant and who therefore are totally at a loss what to do. आलिखताम् (*adj.* of विद्विषाम्). मि...श्रियम् who vainly paint in their desires their royalty which is totally lost to them. They build high hopes of regaining what they have lost. चिन्ता... धियाम् (1) whose intellect is distracted by thoughts that are simply a source of anxiety; (2) whose minds are overwhelmed with thoughts (चिन्ता) and imaginings as to the means (of regaining their lost kingdoms). वने that were banished in the forests. King Harsha also does not brook the hopes they entertain, the moment he is remembered. The metre is शार्दूलविक्रीडित. तेन = दौवारिकेण. ०जलेन पङ्किलः (dirty, soiled) कपोलपट्टः तस्मिन् पतिताम् (*adj.* of दृष्टिम्). दृष्टिमाकृष्य—बाण took away his eyes with difficulty from the elephant. One who is मत्त may fall in dirt and has half-closed (मुकुलित) eyes, and has to be dragged out of mire by his friends. सङ्कुलानि crowded. क-

क्ष्यान्तराणि courts (object of समतिक्रम्य). भुक्ते आस्थानमण्डपः तस्य पुरस्तात् in front of an audience-pavilion after he had taken his meal. For भुक्तास्थान, see above text p. 27. l. 32. स्थितम्—the principal sentence is स्थितं...चक्रवर्तिनं हर्षमद्राक्षीत् (p. 35. l. 17). The next clause is दूरा...वृतम्. दूरात् (surrounded) at a distance. ऊर्ध्व-स्थितेन standing erect. All the adjectives qualify ०लोकेन ard ०स्तम्भमण्डलेन. प्रांशुना tall; the rays of which spread all round. प्रकृष्टाः or प्रसृताः अंशवः यस्य. व्यायामेन व्यायतं (firm, powerful) वपुः यस्य (with ०लोकेन); व्यायामव्यायतं वपुः यस्य that were as long (व्यायत) as the distance between the outstretched hands (about six feet). शस्त्रिणा armed; on which weapons were tied or that were shaped with instruments (with स्तम्भमण्डलेन). व्यायाम is the same as व्याम (Marathi वांव). 'व्यामो बाह्वोः सकरयोस्ततयोर्तिर्यगन्तरम्' इत्यमरः. मौलेन hereditary (मूलं वेत्ति मूलादागतो मूले भवो वा); placed on a base or pedestal. As the attendants were of ruddy complexion they are compared to golden pillars. आ...लोकम् near whom were sitting his distinguished (विशिष्ट) favourites. हरिचन्दन is a kind of very fragrant sandal. तुषारः ice. दन्त...पादे the feet of which (bedstead) were white being made of ivory; the rays of which are white like ivory. The words ०तले and ०पादे furnish the reason why the bedstead of pearl-stone is fancied to be made of the moon. शय...भुजे who rested the whole weight of his body on his arm that was placed on the end of the bedstead. दिङ्मुख...रममाणम्—the idea is:—The lustre of his body spread all round like a canopy (वितानं), being blended with the rays of jewels. As the Emperor with his vassal kings was bathed in the brilliance, he seemed to be bathing in a lake, the lustre being the water and the rays of jewels lotus fibres. A bath is very agreeable (सुभग) in summer. विततः मणिमयूखाः यस्मिन् (*adj.* of ०विताने). राजकेन सह. For राजक, see p. 112. तेजसः... र्मितम्—Ordinarily every being is पञ्चमहाभूतात्मक. But he, being all brilliance, seemed to be created from the atoms of तेजस् alone. अनि...गृहीतम् he was seized by all auspicious marks in all limbs as though in order to place him on the throne, though he was unwilling to occupy it. The idea is—all his limbs had the auspicious signs as required by the सामुद्रिकशास्त्र. One who has such signs becomes a king. If a person be unwilling to sit in a place, he has to be made to occupy the place by being seized. The word गृहीत has two senses 'seized, accepted.' C and T think that in this clause there is probably a reference to the facts underlying Hiuen Tsang's story that Harsha at the advice of a Bodhisattva refrained from mounting the '*siṃhāsana.*' We do not think there is any such reference. The author indulges in an उत्प्रेक्षा on seeing the king occupying the throne and his great brilliance. Compare 'लक्षणैरपि रागाविष्टैरिवाधिष्ठितसर्वाङ्गाम्' (कादम्बरीम्) का० p. 186 of P. गृहीतं ब्रह्मचर्यं येन who was observing the vow of celibacy. There is विरोध between गृही...चर्यम् and आ...क्ष्म्या. Compare 'द्यूतं च जनवादं च परिवादं तथानृतम् । स्त्रीणां च प्रेक्षणालम्भमुपघातं परस्य च ॥' मनु० 2. 179 (ब्रह्मचारी वर्जयेत्). The विरोध can be got over by taking आ...क्ष्म्या as meaning 'who was possessed of royal glory.' गृ० may be explained in this way. According to Manu, a householder who was devoted solely to his wife and observed certain rules about cohabitation was as good as a ब्रह्मचारी. 'ऋतुकालाभिगामी स्यात्स्वदारनिरतः सदा । पर्ववर्जं व्रजेच्चैनां तद्व्रतो रतिकाम्यया ॥ निन्द्यास्वष्टासु चान्यासु स्त्रियो रात्रिषु वर्जयन् । ब्रह्मचार्येव भवति यत्र तत्राश्रमे वसन् ॥' मनु० III. 45 and 50. The com. refers to a curious tradition "था त्वेवमनुश्रूयते 'यावन्मया न सकला जिता भूमिस्तावन्मे ब्रह्मचर्यम्' इति श्रीहर्षः प्रतिज्ञातवान् । द्वादशभिश्च वर्षैर्जित्वा तां महिषीमब्रवीत् 'प्रतिज्ञा मे निर्व्यूढा' इति । ततो रोषात् 'अहमपि द्वादशवर्षं ब्रह्मचर्यं चरामि' इति सा प्रतिज्ञामकरोत् । इति ब्रह्मचर्येणाशाकालोऽतिवाहितः." We may expllain गृहीत० as गृहीता ब्रह्मणः वेदस्य चर्या येन 'who practised the study of the Veda.' In the next clause also there is an apparent विरोध. प्रतिपन्नं (accepted) असिधाराधारणव्रतं येन. A ऋषि has nothing to do with wielding a sword. So he could not be called a consistent (अविसंवादिन्) ऋषि, as he wielded a sword. But there is no inconsistency in his wielding the sword for protecting the good and the distressed and in being a saintly king (राजर्षि). प्रति० suggests another sense 'who wields the sword against those that come to him for protection'. प्रतिपन्नेषु असिधाराधारणं व्रतं यस्य. If he does so, how can he be called a राजर्षि (whose first duty is to protect)? Compare मनु I. 89 and 10. 80. प्रति० also means 'who observes the vow called असिधाराव्रत.' A ऋषि would observe such a व्रत. It is explained as 'यत्रैकशयनस्थापि प्रमदा नोपभुज्यते । असिधाराव्रतं नाम वदन्ति मुनिपुङ्गवाः ॥.' *Vide* मल्लिनाथ on रघु 13. 67. विषम...धर्मे who firmly clung to धर्म as though through fear of stumbling in his steps placed on the uneven path of kings. विषमः (uneven, difficult to carry out) राजमार्गः (royal road, the duties of kings) तस्मिन् विनिहितं पदं (foot, position) तस्य स्खलनं (stumbling, deviating)

त्रस्य भिया (भीत्या). One who is afraid of stumbling on a public road supports himself (सुलग्न) on a stick. भीते...सेव्यमानम् who was attended whole-heartedly by Truth that had obtained his word, as though it (truth) were afraid. The idea is:– all kings had given up truth; हर्षे alone stuck to it whole-heartedly. One who is abandoned by others becomes afraid and goes to another who would promise to protect him. लब्धा वाक् (रक्षणरूपा येन). Truth resorts to speech *i. e.* it is word that must be kept. वारविलासिनी nautch girl. प्रतियातना reflection. In the ten toe-nails of his feet the girls were reflected. The poet fancies that the ten quarters (the ten reflections) were bowing to him. दीर्घै...वीक्षमाणम् with his long glances that reached the ends of the quarters he seemed as though to examine what the regents of the worlds had done or left undone. Bāṇa seems to use the word लोकपाल in the sense of दिक्पाल. The दिक्पालs and लोकपालs are eight, but slightly differ. 'इन्द्रो वह्निः पितृपतिर्नैर्ऋतो वरुणो मरुत् । कुबेर ईशः पतयः पूर्वादीनां दिशां क्रमात् ॥' इत्यमरः. 'सोमाग्न्यर्कानिलेन्द्राणां वित्ताप्पत्योर्यमस्य च । अष्टानां लोकपालानां वपुर्धारयते नृपः ॥' मनु 5. 96. मणि...करेण—मणि...पृष्ठे प्रतिष्ठिताः कराः (किरणाः, हस्ताः) यस्य. The sun's rays were reflected in his footstool (पादपीठ). One who makes a request may fold his hands at the feet of the king. भूषणप्रभया समुत्सारणं (driving away) तेन बद्धं पर्यन्ते मण्डलं (circle, ring) येन. The idea is:—daylight was eclipsed by the brilliance of his ornaments up to a certain distance from the king on all sides; beyond that he was surrounded by daylight as in a circle. So the poet fancies that daylight performed प्रदक्षिणा round him. The reading गलितोष्मणा would mean 'whose pride (or heat) was gone.' शौर्यमेव ऊष्मा तेन. He was so brave that he could not endure that the mountains should remain stiff before him. Heat (ऊष्मा) causes distress. फेना...हन्तम्—his personal grace being compared to the ocean, the white sandal-wood paste applied to his body to alleviate heat is compared to the foam of the ocean. The reading भूभृद्भिः would mean 'that support the earth; kings.' The com. connects शौर्योष्मणा with फेनायमानम् 'जलं सन्तापेन सफेनं भवति'. This is not bad. एक...र्जित्येन on account of his greatness in wielding the sole sovereignty of the world. ऊर्जितस्य भावः और्जित्यम्. When the vassal kings fell at his feet, his image was reflected in their crest jewels. He could not endure that the kings should honour anyone else (even though his own reflection). Compare 'यः करधृतधौतासिप्रतिबिम्बितेनात्मनाप्यदूयत समितिषु सहायेन' हर्ष० 4th उ० 2nd para. दर्प...दधानम् who bore royal glory that, under the guise of the breezes of chowries, as though heaved many sighs through the pain of pride. He had snatched the राजलक्ष्मी of other kings. This rankled in her heart and she heaved deep sighs—the breezes set in motion by chowries. दुःखमासते अस्यामिति or दुःखं असिका इव poignant pain or grief. सकल...श्लिष्टम्—At the time of the churning, लक्ष्मी (the wife of विष्णु) rose from the *single ocean;* but he was embraced by लक्ष्मी that came to him bringing the *entire* लावण्य (beauty, salt) of the *four* oceans. This shows his superiority over विष्णु. In the case of विष्णु, लक्ष्मी did not bring all लावण्य (as the sea is still very salt). लवणस्य भावः लावण्यम्. In his case, लक्ष्मी brought all the लावण्य (beauty). आभरण...राज्ञाम् he as though distributed among the vassal kings thousands of rainbows produced from the radiance of his ornaments, as though they were sent by Indra as a present to him (हर्ष). The rays of his jewels presented rainbow colours and spread over his vassals. The poet insinuates that even Indra sent presents (इन्द्रधनुः) to हर्ष. प्राभृतम् present. 'प्रकर्षेण आराधनार्थं आभ्रियते ढौक्यते स प्राभृतम्' क्षीर०. For वि...राज्ञाम् compare above 'विलम्बमानमिव सर्वकाननानि करिपतीनाम्' text p. 30 ll. 21–22. मधु honey, wine. सम्भा...वर्षन्तम्—There is विरोध in his showering मधु when he had given it up. But he had given up (drinking) wine and he was very sweet in conversation. परित्यक्तमपि (as an *adj.* of the king) would mean 'though he was so poor, (still he showered मधु)'. The words अमृतं, हृदयं and श्रियम् in the three following clauses are similarly श्लिष्ट. काव्य...मन्तम्—One vomits what one has eaten or drunk. In discussion about poetry he poured out sweet words that were all his own (which he had not copied from anyone else). He had not drunk अमृत (only the gods did so) and yet he poured it out. विश्रम्भ०—In confidential conversations, he exhibited his हृदय though he did not draw it out (of his body). What is meant is he showed his real thoughts, though the persons speaking with him did not draw him out. प्रसादेषु...पयन्तम्—लक्ष्मी is निश्चल in him (and not चञ्चल as in other kings) and yet in showing favours he distributed it in various places (that is made लक्ष्मी leave himself). What is meant is that he distributed श्री (wealth) among worthy objects (स्थाने). वीरगोष्ठीषु in meetings of heroes. When he heard about the heroic deeds of his soldiers that had secured a victory his cheek became thrilled. The poet fancies that the thrill (रोमाञ्च) was due to the message of love whispered in his ear by रणश्री (victory). Love causes रोमाञ्च, which is one of the eight सात्त्विकभावs. *Vide* p. 79. उपांशु *adv.* secretly. अति...पातयन्तम् in talking about his past fights with warriors, he cast his glance at his favourite sword, as though it (दृष्टि) were a shower of स्नेह (affection, oil). He lovingly looked at his sword as his trusty companion in battles. When fighting is over (अतिक्रान्त) oil is applied to swords in order that they may not get rusty. परिहास...यन्तम्—when he smiled at jests, the rays of his teeth spread round the kings. The pure rays of teeth are fancied to be his good will (pure meaning) towards them. One who is afraid of great heat (प्रताप) will gain confidence, if a clear reservoir (of water) be shown to him. सकल...तिष्ठन्तम्—there is विरोध in saying that he was सकल० and yet stood in न्याय alone. न्याये तिष्ठन्तम् means (in a secondary sense) 'he held fast to the path of right'. The words अगोचरे, अभूमौ, अविषये, अमार्गे, अतिदूरे, अदिशि all mean the same thing and all the clauses are to be explained similarly, connecting स्थितम् with each. अगोचरे गुणानाम् (स्थितम्) who stood beyond the reach of गुणs. The idea is:—he was perfect in virtues; he was wanting in none and so there was no scope for any गुण to come to him and make him perfect. अवि...नाम् boons could not make him more prosperous than he already was. अदि...धर्मस्य he was beyond all comparison and there was nothing which धर्म could accomplish for him. अदृष्ट...स्थितम् he had an unprecedented vastness of glory (or wealth). All the words from अरुण to कृष्णकेशेन have two meanings, one referring to his body and the other to some देवता. अरुणाः (red) पादपल्लवाः यस्य. All the instrumentals qualify वपुषा. अरुणः (the charioteer of the sun) पादपल्लवे यस्य. सुगतौ (of graceful gait) मन्थरौ (slow) ऊरू (thighs) यस्य; सुगतः (बुद्धः) मन्थरयोः ऊर्वोः यस्य. वज्रायुधवत् (like the weapon thunderbolt) निष्ठुरं (hard) प्रकोष्ठस्य (forearm) पृष्ठं यस्य; वज्रायुधः इन्द्रः (वज्रं आयुधं यस्य) निष्ठुरे प्रकोष्ठपृष्ठे यस्य. वृषस्य इव स्कन्धः यस्य whose shoulder was stout like that of a bull; वृषः (धर्मः) स्कन्धे यस्य. 'वृषो हि भगवान्धर्मः' मनु० VIII. 16. भास्वान् (bright) बिम्बवत् अधरः (lip resembling the ripe *bimba* fruit) यस्य. भास्वान् (रविः) तस्य बिम्बं अधरे यस्य. प्रसन्नं (mild, gracious) अवलोकितं (glance) यस्य; प्रसन्नः अवलोकितः (अवलोकितेश्वरः) यस्य. अवलोकितेश्वर is a बोधिसत्त्व specially worshipped in northern Buddhism. Compare 'परमसौगतमप्यवलोकितेश्वरम्' हर्ष० 8th उ० 4th para. There is another possible explanation. प्रसन्ना अवलोकिते यस्य. This explanation keeps the symmetry of the passage. The first word in each clause is a देवता. That will be departed from if we take अवलोकित as the देवता. प्रसन्ना means 'wine', which is generally personified as वारुणी देवता. 'बभूव वारुणी देवी मदाघूर्णितलोचना ।' विष्णुपु० I. 9, 92. 'गन्धोत्तमा प्रसन्नेरा' इत्यमरः. The only objection is that वारुणी is not a देवता to which any honour would be paid by बाण and who would hardly be enumerated along with धर्म, कृष्ण &c. कृष्णाः केशाः यस्य; कृष्णः केशेषु यस्य. **P. 33.** मांसलाभिः (thick) मयूखमालाभिः मलिनितं (darkened) महीतलं येन (*adj.* of ०पीठे). माणिक्यमालया मण्डिता मेखला (girdle, centre) यस्य. महानील was a kind of blue gem. कलि...चरणम्—to plant one's left foot on another's head is symbolical of utterly humiliating him. कलि, being an age of sin, is dark. The poet fancies that the blue footstool on which the king's foot rested was the head of कलि, the idea being that Harsha's reign ousted the evil age of sin. आक्रान्त...क्षम्—who looked like the child Krishna (पुण्डरीकाक्ष) that trod on the line of the hoods of कालिय. The foot-stool of blue gems looked like the dark hoods of कालिय. हर्ष was lotus-eyed (पुण्डरीकाक्ष). The serpent कालिय was in the waters of the Jumna and rendered it poisonous. No tree except a कदम्ब grew on its banks. कृष्ण threw himself from the कदम्ब into the river and trampled upon the hoods of the serpent. The serpent and its wives begged कृष्ण to be merciful. कृष्ण said 'नात्र स्थेयं त्वया सर्प कदाचिद्यमुनाजले । सभृत्यपरिवारस्त्वं समुद्रसलिलं व्रज ॥ मत्पदानि च ते सर्प दृष्ट्वा मूर्धनि सागरे । गरुडः पन्नगरिपुस्त्वयि न प्रहरिष्यति ॥' विष्णुपु० V. 7. 75-76. क्षौमवत् पाण्डुरेण pale like fine linen (with प्रतानेन); क्षौमेण पाण्डुरः तेन pale-white with fine linen (with ०बन्धेन). ०प्रतानेन...यन्तम्—The bright rays of the toenails spread over the earth; the poet fancies that they were the पट्टबन्ध, which he conferred on the earth and thus raised her to high rank. The earth is often spoken of as the wife of a king. A crowned queen wears a पट्टबन्ध (tiara) of fine silk or linen. *Vide* notes on पट्टबन्ध p.116. All the words from ०लोहितौ to ०चिह्नौ qualify चरणौ. अप्र...लोहितौ–his feet were naturally red. The poet fancies that they became red because the लोकपालs did not bow to them. For लोकपाल see above p. 140. सकल...धारयन्तौ—the idea is:—when the vassal chiefs bowed their heads at his feet, the yellowish (अतिपीत) brilliance of his feet resembling the पद्मराग (rubies) spread over them; the rosy light of his feet resembled the rosy hues of evening, when the disc of the luminary (the sun) sets. His feet also deprived all powerful persons (तेजस्विन्) of their might. His feet as though drank (पीत) the light of rubies अशेष...स्रवन्तौ—the hue of his feet was like that of the honey in the flowers of the chaplets on the heads of kings (which heads were placed on his feet). समस्त...रहितौ—his feet were never left by bees because they were attracted by the fragrance of the chaplets (उत्तंस) of the chieftains who bowed their heads. The dark bees looked like the heads of his enemies covered with hair (their crowns being wrested from them). पुंस्युत्तंसावतंसौ द्वौ कर्णपूरेऽपि शेखरे' इत्यमरः. संवाहनं shampooing. श्रियो...कल्पयन्तौ—his red feet resembled red lotuses and were charming (*i. e.* लक्ष्मी waited on them to shampoo them). लक्ष्मी is represented as dwelling in a red lotus. Mark the name पद्मालया given to लक्ष्मी. Compare 'अधोमुखेन चक्षुषा शिक्षयन्तमिव लक्ष्मीलाभोत्तानितमुखानि पङ्कजवनानि विनयम्' हर्ष० 4th उ०. जलजशङ्खमीनमकराः तैः सनाथं तलं ययोः तयोः भावः ०तलता तया. जलजं कमलम्. The soles of his feet were marked with lines that resembled a lotus, conch &c. These are looked upon as very auspicious signs and as indicative of greatness. कथित... चिह्नौ इव that had marks announcing his sovereignty of the four oceans. There were four marks जलज, शङ्ख, मीन and मकर and these four indicated that he would rule over the four oceans (*i. e.* the whole world). ०मुसलाभ्याम् and the following instrumentals are to be connected with ऊरुदण्डाभ्याम्. ०मुसलाभ्याम् his thighs were like huge (pestle-like) tusks of दिग्गज. विकट... बन्धुराभ्याम् that were uneven (or charming) on account of the obstruction caused by the block of flesh over the knees. For मकरमुख see notes p. 52. The evenness of his thigh was broken by the protuberant (fleshy) part above the knee. उद्वेलः (going beyond the usual water line) लावण्यपयोनिधिः. फेनेन आहिता शोभा ययोः. His thighs that were charming looked more beautiful by being rubbed over with the polishing powder of white cuttle-fish bone (फेनः). The ocean also looks charming with foam. चन्दन...मूलाभ्याम्—at the foot of sandal trees, serpents (भोगिन्) dwell, in whose hoods jewels were supposed to exist. The roots of his thighs were coloured by the head jewels of kings (भोगिन्) that bowed ot his feet. ०रश्मिभिः रज्यमानं मूलं ययोः. 'भोगी भुजङ्गमेऽपि स्यादाममात्रे नृपे पुमान्' मेदिनी. हृदये आरोपितः भूभारः तस्य धारणाय माणिक्यस्तम्भौ. His fair thighs were like ruby pillars. Pillars support weight. His thighs supported his broad chest (हृदय) on which rested the earth. His mind cared for the government of his kingdom. Compare for a similar conceit 'विशालवक्षःस्थलोपलवेदिकोत्तम्भन-शिलास्तम्भाभ्यां...ऊरुदण्डाभ्याम्' (text p. 10 ll. 7–8). The words from अमृत...पाण्डुना to ०शोभिना qualify both अधरवाससा (lower garment) and ०निर्मोकेण (slough of the serpent वासुकि). For mountain मन्दर as the churning handle and the serpent वासुकि as the rope (नेत्रम्), see notes p. 52. The king looked like मन्दर and his lower garment like slough. ०पिण्डवत् पाण्डुना (०वाससा); ०पिण्डेन पाण्डुना (with ०निर्मोकेण). As अमृत was churned out of the ocean, its foam might have stuck to मन्दर. मेखला girdle; the central part of a mountain. The garment was covered with the jewels of the girdle she wore. The slough had the rays of the jewels on the centre of मन्दर. नितम्बः hips; slopes. व्यासङ्गिन् in contact with, clinging. पयः water, milk. It was the क्षीरसागर that was churned. नेत्र...शोभिना charming by the texture of the silken (नेत्रं) threads; charming on account of being placed on the rope. 'स्याज्जटांशुकयोर्नेत्रम्' इत्यमरः, 'नेत्रं मन्थगुणे वस्त्रभेदे मूले द्रुमस्य च' मेदिनी. अघनेन...मानम्—the king looked like the expanse (आभोगः) of the world. He had a second garment (upper one). The world also has अम्बर (the sky). अघनेन not thick (*i. e.* fine); without clouds. स...गणेन spotted with stars of various colours; full of stars (sky). उपरिकृतेन that he wore on the upper part of his body; that is overhead. इभ...राजमानम्—his broad (उरु) chest (उरः-कवाटं panel-like chest) is compared to स्फटिकतट and he himself is compared to कैलास. इभ...मसृणेन (applies both to ०कवाटेन and ०तटेन in the same sense) glossy though hardened by being struck with the tusks of elephants. The king was struck in battles and elephants are found in the कैलास range. अपर्याप्तः अम्बरप्रथिमा यस्य which was not contained within the limits of his dress (coat); which was not contained within the limits of the sky. वाहिनी army; river. संक्षोभः shock; agitation. कैलास is white and very high and so is chosen for comparison. श्री...पातितेन (हारदण्डेन)—his long neklace looked like a dividing line for separating the respective realms of glory and learning. The proper sphere of सरस्वती is the mouth and of राज्यश्री the chest (on which it is represented as resting). So the necklace at the neck serves to separate these two. शेषेणेव—the necklace resembled in colour the शेष serpent. तस्य (हर्षस्य) भुजस्तम्भे विन्यस्तः समस्तः भूभारः तेन लब्धं विश्रान्तिसुखं तेन प्रसुप्तेन. शेष is supposed to support the earth. Compare 'त्रिभुवन-भारधारणसमर्थं शेषफणामण्डलोपकरणैरिव कल्पितम्' हर्ष० 4th उ० and notes thereon. The poet fancies that the necklace lying on his chest is the serpent शेष gone to sleep because it has no longer to support the earth. परिवेष्टिता कन्धरा यस्य. जीविता...स्थलम्—His chest was covered with the pure rays of the pearls of the necklace. They looked like a bark garment (चीरं) which is worn when a person carries out the vow (दीक्षा) of making a gift of all he possessed as long as he lived. In this one may see a reference to the practice of Harsha, as narrated by Hiouen Tsang, of giving everything in charity once every five years. *Vide* Intro. XL. In the विश्वजित् sacrifice, everything was given away. **'स विश्वजितमाजह्रे यज्ञं सर्वस्वदक्षिणम् ।'** रघु० IV. 86. अज...महीधरम्—In this clause, the principal part is अरुणैः...धरम्—with the reddish rays of the jewels of the armlets (he wore on the upper arms) he seemed to be a mountain of rubies having as though outstretched canopy-like wings of jewels. Formerly Mountains had wings; *vide* p. 84. प्रसारितं मणिमयं पक्षवितानं यस्मिन्. In अज...र्भवद्भिः there are three उत्प्रेक्षाs suggested by the spreading rays of the jewels on the armlets. अज...रोहद्भिः as if they (rays) were other arms freshly growing with the desire of vanquishing Vishṇu. Vishṇu has four arms; so the king in order to rival him had as if growing on his arms others in the form of the rays. **'अजा विष्णुहरच्छागाः'** इत्यमरः. बाहुरेव उपधानं (pillow) तस्मिन् शेते इति ०शायिनी. बाहू...गलद्भिः-लक्ष्मी is poetically represented as resting on the arm of a king. Women used to place a lotus as an ornament on the ear. The rays of the jewels resembled the honey in a lotus (which is yellowish red). भुज...र्भवद्भिः—the pencils of rays looked like long avenues that served as the outlets for the प्रताप (prowess; bright light) of his arms. भुजात् जन्म यस्य. In the next clause the principal part is अति...हरन्तम्—with his very long arms he simultaneously deprived the regions and their guardians of their आयति (length; might or greatness). 'स्यात्प्रभावेऽपि **चायतिः**' इत्यमरः. Long arms were looked upon as a sign of greatness. For दिक्पाल, see above p. 140. सकल...र्गलेन which (arms) were the bolts to all the paths of लोकालोक. A bolt blockades the path leading to a destination beyond the door. लोकालोक is a mythical mountain in पुष्करद्वीप, the last of the seven द्वीपs. On the other side of the mountain there was complete darkness and on this side, the sun and light. See विष्णु पु० II. 4. 'लोकालोकस्ततः शैलो योजनायुतविस्तृतः । ततस्तमः समावृत्य तं शैलं सर्वतः स्थितम् । तमश्चाण्डकटाहेन समन्तात् परिवेष्टितम् ॥' 95-96. Note 'लोकालोकजूषि...पूषा पुनरपि

सञ्जहार जालकानि रोचिषाम्' हर्ष० 8th उ० last para. His arms protected the world up to लोकालोक. सकल...र्गलेन also means 'that were the bolts to the vision of all people *i. e.* that arrested the sight of all people by their prowess'. चतु...कारेण that were the stone wall to the ditch (खातं) of the circle of the four oceans. He ruled over (*i. e.* protected the earth girt by) the four oceans. Ordinarily it is the ditch that surrounds the wall. But his wall-like arms protected (surrounded) the ditch-like oceans. सर्वे...पञ्जरेण—He had vanquished all great kings by the adamantine power of his arms. A राजहंस (swan) may be confined in a cage (पञ्जरं). भुवन...तोरणेन—The लक्ष्मी (*i. e.* the dominion) of the worlds came to him (*lit.* entered him) by the power of his arms. A person makes an entrance under an auspicious तोरण (arch). His arms were decked with jewels and so are said to be मणितोरण. सोदर्य...दिङ्मुखानि—the idea is:—his red lip cast its red lustre in all directions. The poet fancies that the red lip was कौस्तुभमणि that had become a part of his mouth with the desire of kissing लक्ष्मी, its sister, (that dwelt with the king). Both लक्ष्मी and कौस्तुभ were born of the ocean, when the fourteen jewels were churned out and so are here said to be सोदर्य. दिङ्मुखानि is the object of सिञ्चन्तम्, which qualifies हर्षम् below. The redness (राग) of the lips spreading all round is fancied to be the exudation of the पल्लवs (that are red) of पारिजात. अन्तरान्तरा at intervals. प्रकीर्यमाणः विमलानां दशनशिखानां प्रतानः येषु (*adj.* of स्मितैः). शिखा ray of light. अन्तरा...दर्शयन्तम्—the idea is:—when he smiled at the jests of his friends, bright rays from his white teeth shot forth. The poet fancies that the king displayed the light of intelligence to लक्ष्मी that is by nature dull. The two clauses ending with प्रेषयन्तम् and विसर्जयन्तम् are to be connected with सुहृ...स्मितैः. मुखेन जनितः इन्दुसन्देहः तेन आगतानि. His face was like the moon. कुमुदs are white like स्मित and open at night. The poet fancies that कुमुद lotus plants in the form of smiles had come mistaking his face to be the moon. He sent them away in the form of the spreading rays of his teeth. स्फटिकवत् धवलाः दशनाः तेषां पङ्क्तिः तया कृता कुमुदवनशङ्का तया प्रविष्टाम्. His smile was like autumnal moonlight, which rests on कुमुदs blooming at night. मदिरा...जातानां गन्धः गर्भे यस्य. भरिताः सकलाः ककुभः दिशः येन. His mouth (that had partaken of ताम्बूल) emitted a fragrance like that of wine, अमृत and पारिजात. मदिरा, अमृत and पारिजात were among the jewels churned out of the ocean, when their combined fragrance must have spread over the world. मदिरा...गर्भेण may also mean '(his mouth) that had the fragrance of ambrosial wine and पारिजात (a fragrant powder).' For पारिजात in this sense, see text p. 9. l. 27 'अतिसुरभि...पारिजातकपरिमलमुचा...मुखेन... वसन्तमिव वमन्तम्.' विकच...वंशेन—the fragrance of his breath was as though continuously inhaled by his high overhanging nose which was the pericarp cup of his lotus-like face. चक्षुषः... कुर्वाणम्—the brilliance of the white of his eye spread all round. It seemed as though the world was flooded by the Milky Ocean rising high (उद्वेल) at the rise of the moon of his unsurpassed face. अपूर्वः वदनमेव चन्द्रः तस्य उदयेन उद्वेलः क्षीरोदः तेन प्लावितानि. विग्रहिणी = शरीरिणी. The female chowrie-bearer was reflected in his bright cheek. The poet fancies that in the form of reflection he bore the embodied सरस्वती in his mouth. सरस्वती is described as मुखनिवासिनी or रसनाग्रनर्तकी. °शोचिषा = कान्त्या. लोहितायितः ललाटतटः यस्य. लोहितायित *past p. p.* of लोहितायति (or -ते) denominative verb from लोहित, according to 'लोहितादि-डाजभ्यः क्यष्' पा. 3. 1. 13 and 'वा क्यषः' पा. 1. 3. 90. सरस्वतीर्ष्याकुपिता लक्ष्मीः तस्याः प्रसादने लग्नेन. The idea is:—The red rays of his crest jewel rendered his forehead red. The poet fancies that the redness of the forehead was due to the अलक्तक dye of the feet of लक्ष्मी sticking to his forehead when he bowed at her feet to appease her. लक्ष्मी was angry because he showed preference to सरस्वती. Sanskrit poets delight in dwelling upon the feud between लक्ष्मी and सरस्वती. आ...यन्तम् the principal idea is 'he was listening to the sweet (कल) song of bees that served as an ornament (अवतंसः) to his ear.' The author indulges in a metaphor derived from playing on a lute. आपाट...वादयताम् (of bees) that played on the small lute made up by the curved ends (कोटिः) of the jewel in his ear-ring and which (lute) was surrounded (वलयिनी) by a web of strings (तन्त्री) in the form of slightly red rays (of the jewels). The reddish rays resemble the copper strings of a वीणा. अन...चरणानाम् the bees constantly moved their feet (*i. e.* they hovered round the कुण्डलमणि). One playing on a lute has constantly to move his fingers. उप...मिव—as if they worshipped him by playing on a lute. It is from उपवीणयति a denominative verb. स्वर...शारदं (may be construed both with the king and with कणित) who was proficient in the understanding of the analysis of notes (with हर्ष); that (कणित) was emineut by its judicious evolution of the notes. The musical notes are seven. 'निषादर्षभगान्धारषड्ज-मध्यमधैवताः । पञ्चमश्चेत्यमी सप्त तन्त्रीकण्ठोत्थिताः स्वराः ॥' इत्यमरः. The next clause 'उत्फुल्ल...केशान्तम्' describes a wreath of full-blown मालती flowers that was placed on his locks. परिकलितः केशान्तः यस्य. For मुण्डमाला, see text p. 9. l. 19. राज...वलयेनेव—the wreath of white मालती flowers was like moonlight and bright rays of nails. The poet fancies that it (मालती wreath) was the moonlight of the nails of राजलक्ष्मी when the latter took hold of his hair in playful dalliance. मुख...मण्डलेन—the मालती wreath was like the halo (परिवेशः) of the moon, *viz.* his face. शि...भुवा proceeding from the ornament in his top-knot. शिखण्डः = चूडा. शिखण्ड...मानम् The blending of the bright light of pearls and of the rays of dark-green emerald in his top-knot presented the appearance of the braidlike stream of the Ganges and the Jumna at Prayāga (Allahabad). The poet fancies that the confluence of the holy rivers came of its own accord for anointing him as king. At a king's coronation (अभिषेक) the water of holy rivers is used. The water of the Ganges is white and of the Jumna dark. अन्यो...वृजिनेन turbid by being mixed with each other (with ०वारिणा and ०कलापेन). वृजिन also means 'curved' (with वारिणा). In the next clause 'श्रमजल...सर्वतः' (l. 32), the chief part is 'वार...सर्वतः'—whose loveliness was being eclipsed on all sides by dancing girls. All the words in the instrumental plural (feminine) are to be connected with ०विलासिनीभिः. श्रम...लेखाभिः whose crescent-like foreheads were blackened by the darkness (कालिमन् *m.*) produced through the mark of thick black agallochum *tilaka* that melted by the drops of perspiration, as though it (darkness) were a dark callosity (किणः) due to their repeated prostrations at his feet that were agreeable on account of their coaxing requests. If one's forehead is rubbed repeatedly in prostrations, a dark mark (किण) may be produced. चाटु *m. n.* endearing words. क्षुभित...मानाभिः enveloped by their flashing necklaces (or garlands) that rose up from their agitated hearts, as if they were masses of उत्कलिकाs. The word मानस has three senses here. The हारs rolled (through dancing) on their swelling bosoms (मानस). उत्कलिका longing; wave. Their minds were agitated with longings. The मानस lake is tossed by waves. विलास...जैयन्तीभिः that as though rebuked Lakshmî herself in jealousy with their charming creeper-like eyebrows that were tremulous (चटुल) with their playful movements (वल्गनं). भ्रूः एव लता तस्याः आकल्पैः (ornamentation). The eyebrow becomes curved in threatening a person. The reading भ्रूलताकम्पैः of B is more easy. आ...कर्षन्तीभिः drawing (captivating) him (हर्ष) by their long (deep) sighs thick with perfume as though they (sighs) were bonds made of the *malaya* breeze. अविरलः परिमलः येषाम् (goes with श्वसितैः and पाशैः). They breathed hard through the effort of dancing. For मलयमारुत, see p. 76. मलयमारुत is redolent with the perfume of sandal and excites love. विकट...द्धरन्तीभिः. विकट large. वराटकः rope '**वराटकः पद्मबीजकोशे रज्जौ कपर्दके**' मेदिनी. ०लावली एव वराटकः तेन वेष्टितं मुखं येषाम्. स्तनौ एव कलशौ. रसः feeling; water. Water is taken out by means of jars to which ropes are attached. On their breasts rolled garlands of *Bakula* flowers which resembled ropes. कुचो... शयन्तीभिः forcibly (हठात्) making him enter their hearts after dragging him with the rays of the central gems of their necklaces which shook to and fro on account of the trembling of their bosoms. 'तरलो हारमध्यगः' इत्यमरः. प्रभां मुञ्चन्तीति तेषां प्रभामुचाम्. The spreading rays of their jewels looked like out-stretched arms. जृम्भानां अनुबन्धेन बन्धुरं वदनं एव अरविन्दं तस्य आवरणीकृतैः that covered their lotus-like mouths that looked charming.(बन्धुर) by continuous yawning (जृम्भा). They yawned on account of the heat and the fatigue of dancing. उत्तानैः open. सर...रुन्धतीभिः— the idea is:- They closed their yawning mouths with their open hands. The poet fancies that they did so because they wanted to confine their hearts that started hastily in order to come out of their mouths. The heart is inside the body and as though wanted to come out of the opening mouth. Their minds were impetuous in their love for the king. A lotus flower also opens (जृम्भा) and is covered with the rays (कर) of the sun. मानस means also the मानस lake in which there are lotuses. मदनेन अन्धं ०कुलं तेन कीर्यमाणाः कर्णकुसुमस्य (of the flower placed on the ear as ornament) रजःकणाः तैः कूणितः (contracted) कोणः (corner) येषाम्. कुसुमशरः मदनः तस्य शरैः प्रहारः तेन मूर्छा तया मुकुलितानि (closed). One who receives a terrific blow faints and closes his eyes. Their eyes were contracted because pollen entered them; the poet fancies that they were closed by the swoon due to their being struck by the arrows of Cupid. चतु...न्तीभिः that skilfully cast (their eyes at the king). अन्योन्य...डयन्तीभिः that struck the blue lotuses on their ears with their glances playfully shot u with knit brows through mutual jealousy. The dark pupils of their eyes resembled the इन्दीवर on the ears and so grew jealous of them and shot glances at them. अनिमेषं दर्शनं तस्य सुखरसः तस्य राशिम् (हर्षम्). मन्थरितं (made motionless) पक्ष्म यस्य. अनिमेष... वहन्तीभिः-the idea is:—they looked with a steadfast eye at him, whereby they derived immense pleasure. He was also reflected in their bright cheeks. The poet fancies that his reflection on the cheeks was due to his being drunk by them with their eyes. A रसराशि (mass of water) may be reflected in a bright-surface like that of a jewel. If we read ०राशिमन्थरित०, that yields a good sense. ०सुखराशिना मन्थरितं पक्ष्म यस्य. We need not in this case take ०राशि as referring to हर्ष. अभि...स्मितैः with their causeless (*i. e.* spontaneous, natural) smiles in their playful longings. Smiles are bright like moonlight. The moon is a friend (an excitant) of Love. *Vide* p. 81. साहायकं (from सहायः) assistance. So far the author described the various charms of the dancing girls and the various tricks they employed to captivate the king's mind. But they failed in their object. अङ्गभङ्गवलने अन्योन्यघटिताः उत्तानाः करवेणिकाः ताभिः—they bent their limbs in various modes (while dancing); in doing so they intertwined the fingers of their hands and opened them towards the king. Their fingers cracked. When we want to crack our finger-joints, we intertwine our fingers and push the palms out. The intertwined hands look like वेणिका (braid). स्फुटनेन मुखराणि अङ्गुलीकाण्डानि तेषु कुण्डलीक्रियमाणः नखदीधितिनिवहः तस्य निभेन (under the guise). अकिञ्चित्कर of no use. The idea is:—When their fingers cracked the rays of the bright nails formed a curve over them. That curve looked like a bent bow. The poet says that it was not their fingers that they cracked, but that it was the bow of Cupid that was snapped by them in anger, as it was of no avail against हर्ष. वार...सर्वतः—If his सौभाग्य was eclipsed by them, they must have been very handsome indeed. स्पर्शेन स्विन्नं (perspiring) वेपमानं करकिसलयं तस्मात् गलितं चरणारविन्दं यस्याः. चरणग्राहिणी the woman that shampooed his feet. The woman on touching his feet became thrilled with emotion and perspired and his feet slipped from her hands. स्वेद and वेपथु are among the eight सात्त्विकभावs. Vide p. 79. कोणेन with the bow (of a lute) or fiddle-stick. 'कोणो वीणादिवादनम्' इत्यमरः. विहस्य he laughed because he understood why she let slip his foot fpom her hand and struck her with the कोण by way of a mild chastisement. लीलया अलसं (slowly) यथा स्यात्तथा. अनवरतं करे कलितः (held) कोणः येन सः ०कोणः तस्य भावः ०कोणता तया. प्रियां—both the lute and श्री were dear to him. शिक्षयन्तम् teaching. कोण also means 'a point of the compass' *i. e.* a region. The meaning (with श्री) is 'who held all the regions and thus taught the राजश्री of the whole world (to attend on him).' निःस्नेह...गृह्यमाणम्—the idea in this clause is that though हर्ष was good and virtuous, yet various persons and things found fault with him, as he could not make them his own. Though one he looked different to different eyes. Understand गृह्यमाणम् after each sub-clause. निःस्नेह...धनैः Riches took him to be wanting in affection *i. e.* he had no regard for lucre. अना...दोषैः—sins found him inaccessible. निग्रहे रुचिः (liking) यस्य who was bent upon curbing (the senses). निग्रहः also means 'punishment or imprisonment'. दुरु...कलिना—the age of sin and discord found him difficult to approach. नीरस...व्यसनैः vices found him to be नीरस (dry, passionless) *i. e.* he had no vice in him. भीरु...शसा *i. e.* he was afraid of infamy. दुर्ग्रहा चित्तवृत्तिः यस्य—whose mind was difficult to seize or understand. चित्तभुवा = मदनेन. Cupid could not sway his mind. स्त्रीपर...सरस्वत्या—To be स्त्रीपर (*i. e.* स्त्रीलम्पट) is ordinarily a blemish. सरस्वती found that he was solely devoted to woman, *viz.* herself *i. e.* he was a single-minded votary of learning. C and T suggest that स्त्री refers to लक्ष्मी but that is not good. षण्ढः impotent. काष्ठ...यतिभिः the ascetics found him to be a काष्ठामुनि. We see that all the words in this clause convey some apparent defect, which, on being properly understood, turns out to be a merit. So काष्ठामुनि should be taken to mean 'an ascetic only for a moment'. काष्ठा is $\frac{1}{30}$ th of a कला. 'अष्टादशनिमेषास्तु काष्ठा त्रिंशत्तु ताः कलाः' इत्यमरः. काष्ठा also means दिशा. So काष्ठामुनि would mean the same thing as राजर्षि. The com. assigns another meaning 'काष्ठा परा धारा (highest limit) तत्प्रधानो मुनिः काष्ठामुनिरतिशयवांस्तपस्वी'. धूर्तः clever, gambler. He does not fall a victim to the wiles of वेश्याs. नेयः easily led (*i. e.* misled); doing as his friends desire. कर्मकरः a mere servant; who performs the proper rites. Read शत्रुयोधैः. सु...योधैः the warriors opposed to him found that he was सुसहाय. शोभनाः सहायाः यस्य who has good allies or councillors. This is good; but the apparent defect that is suggested is 'he has no intrinsic worth; he has only good allies'. शन्त...पतिम्—he was more truly a महावाहिनीपति than शन्तनु. महावाहिनी great army; the great river *i. e.* the Ganges. In this and the following clauses, the poet establishes by श्लिष्ट words that Harsha deserved certain epithets far better than many heroes of old to whom they were applied. शन्तनु married the Ganges. Their son was भीष्म. Vide महाभारत आदिपर्व chap. 98-99. गङ्गा married for the sake of the eight Vasus who were cursed by वसिष्ठ. She plunged in water each son as he was born. When the 8th was born, she spared him at the pressing request of शन्तनु and left him. The ablative शन्तनोः is used in accordance with 'पञ्चमी विभक्ते' पा. 2. 3. 42 (विभागो विभक्तम् । निर्धार्यमाणस्य यत्र भेद एव तत्र पञ्चमी स्यात् । माथुराः पाटलिपुत्रकेभ्य आढ्यतराः । सि. कौ.). जितकाशिनम्—has several senses. भीष्म vanquished काशिराज and married his daughters अम्बिका and अम्बालिका to विचित्रवीर्य, son of शन्तनु and सत्यवती. See आदिपर्व chap 102. जितः काशी (काशिराजः) येन. जितकाशी also means 'जितेन्द्रिय.' शन्तनु fell in love with सत्यवती, the daughter of a fisherman. Out of fear of Bhīshma, he would not allow शन्तनु to marry her. भीष्म promised to resign the kingdom in favour of the son of सत्यवती. Then the fisherman said that he feared that भीष्म's sons would contest the claims of सत्यवती's son. Thereupon भीष्म promised to remain a celibate all his life and carried out the promise. See महाभारत आदिपर्व chap 103. जितकाशी also means 'proud of victories' (जितेन जयेन काशते शोभते इति जययुक्तः). द्रोण was the teacher of the कौरव and पाण्डव princes in धनुर्वेद. See p. 9 for the story of his birth. चापे लालसम् fond of the bow. We may also explain चापले अलसम् (with the king) 'who was averse to follies'. We may separate as च अपलालसम् (अपगता लालसा यस्मात्) 'who was free from desires'. गुरुपुत्र is a term applied to अश्वत्थामा, the son of द्रोण, who was the गुरु of the कौरवs and पाण्डवs. अमोघाः (unerring, reaching the mark) मार्गणाः बाणाः यस्य. अमोघं मार्गणं (याचनं) यस्मिन् requests made to whom were never fruitless. The point of the allusion in the case of अश्वत्थामा is this:-When भीमसेन ran after अश्वत्थामा to kill the latter for his night attack, he discharged a terrible missile called ब्रह्मशिरः for the destruction of all the पाण्डवs. अर्जुन discharged an equally terrible अस्त्र, but only for the purpose of nullifying the effect of अश्वत्थामा's missile and not for killing अश्वत्थामा. Later on अर्जुन withdrew his अस्त्र, but अश्वत्थामा could not do so. The अस्त्र, being अमोघ, deprived अश्वत्थामा of his jewel on the head and killed the गर्भ of उत्तरा by way of a compromise at the desire of Vyāsa. *Vide* सौप्तिकपर्व chap. 13-15. 'गर्भेषु पाण्डवेयानाममोघं चैतदुत्तमम् । न च शक्तोऽसि भगवन्संहर्तुं पुनरुद्यतम् ॥'

chap. 15. 32. कर्ण was the son of कुन्ती, born mysteriously from repeating a Mantra sacred to the Sun. See आदिपर्व chap. 111. So he is represented as the son of the Sun who took special interest in him. मित्रप्रियम् dear to his friends (with the king). कर्ण also was dear to his friend दुर्योधन. बह्वी क्षमा (forbearance, patience) यस्य (with युधिष्ठिर). बहुक्षमम् who ruled over plenty of land (with हर्ष). क्षमा earth. युधिष्ठिर was very patient even under the gravest of provocations (*viz.* द्रौपदीवस्त्रहरण). अनेकनागायुतानां बलं यस्य who had the strength of several thousands of Nāgas (with भीम); who had an army consisting of several thousands of elephants (with हर्ष). अयुतम् ten thousand. भीम was poisoned by दुर्योधन and thrown into water. He was taken to नागलोक, where through the favour of वासुकि he became endowed with the strength of thousands of नागs. *Vide* आदिपर्व chap. 128–129. 'यत्ते पीतो महाबाहो रसोऽयं वीर्यसम्भृतः । तस्मान्नागायुतबलो रणेऽधृष्यो भविष्यसि ॥' chap. 129. 22. धनञ्जय is अर्जुन, the greatest warrior in the great Bhārata war. महाभारत-रण-योग्यम् fit to figure in the great war of the महाभारत. महा-भार-तरण-योग्यम् worthy of wielding (*lit.* crossing) great responsibility (of governing the world). कारण...युगस्य—कृतयुग is an age of complete virtue and righteousness. Under Harsha also these reigned supreme. विबुधसर्गस्य (1) of the creation of gods (विबुधः); of the creation of wise men. He encouraged learned men. उत्पत्ति... दर्पस्य he was the first among the proud or confident. एकागारम् the only house. प्रातिवेशिकः a next door neighbour *i. e.* a very intimate friend; also 'closely resembling.' पुरुषोत्तमस्य of the best of men; of विष्णु. हर्ष befriended good men and resembled विष्णु. खनिपर्वत—a mountain where mines are opened (for jewels &c). सर्व...त्याः the music hall where all lores meet for सरस्वती. सरस्वती was delighted with him as one is delighted in a सङ्गीतगृह. He was the meeting place of all विद्याs. लक्ष्मीसमुत्थान (1) the rising of लक्ष्मी (out of the ocean); increase of royal glory. As there was already one लक्ष्मीसमुत्थान at the time of churning, the author uses the word द्वितीया०. बल...ग्ध्यस्य it was in him that cleverness exhibited its utmost strength. एक... तीनाम् in him all rules of good conduct were to be found in one place. सर्व...कान्तेः Beauty announced in his person her all-in-all *i. e.* he was the *beau ideal*, the *ne plus ultra* of loveliness. अप... सर्गस्य who was the perfection of the creation of the atoms of beauty. अपवर्गः completion, highest point. 'स्यादपवर्गस्त्यागे मोक्षे

कार्यावसानसाफल्ये' मेदिनी. There is another sense hinted at. Where there is अपवर्ग (*i. e.* मोक्ष), सर्ग (birth) comes to an end (अपवर्ग). सकल...राज्यस्य—the idea is:—he was so holy and pure that all the misdeeds of the kings (of all ages in securing kingdoms) were altogether got rid of by expiation. It is not proper to explain that his merit was sufficient to expiate all the sins of subjects put together (as Mr Kale does). सर्वे...पैस्य he was as though the surprise attack of Cupid with all his forces *i. e.* he was irresistible in his charms. उपा...र्शनस्य he was a means of seeing पुरन्दर *i. e.* in him one saw पुरन्दर. पुरन्दर—Indra; one who storms cities. आवर्तनम् fusing together; practising. धर्म was as though put into a crucible and moulded into his form. He practised धर्म incessantly. कन्या...लानाम् as women confined in the अन्तःपुर move about freely there, so the कलाs were to be found only in him and to the fullest extent. परमप्रमाणं highest authority. राज...पतीनाम्—For प्रजापतिs, see above p. 18. When a sacrifice was finished, the sacrificer took a ceremonial bath called अवभृथस्नान. The प्रजापतिs, to whom was entrusted the task of creation, produced Harsha as the highest point (समाप्ति) of perfection in the creation of kings. गम्भीरं च प्रसन्नं च. There are three pairs of adjectives in each of which there is an apparent विरोध. गम्भीरम् (deep; serene). प्रसन्न transparent; gracious. When water is deep, we cannot see the bottom (it is not transparent). त्रासजननं—he produced fear in the irreverent or sinful. The com. refers to रघु I. 16. 'भीमकान्तैर्नृपगुणैः स बभूवोपजीविनाम् । अधृष्यश्चाभिगम्यश्च यादोरत्नैरिवार्णवः ॥'. कौतुकम् curiosity; admiration. What rouses one's curiosity may be sinful.

P. 35 ll. 18—33 **दृष्ट्वा...करोत्.** अनुगृहीत इव as though blessed (by the sight of such a holy king). निगृहीत इव as though checked (by the august appearance of the king). साभि...तृप्त इव eager (to see him more) and yet satisfied (by feeling blessed on seeing him). रोमाञ्चं मुञ्चतीति ०मुच् तेन. विस्मयेन स्मेरः (smiling). शोभनं जन्म यस्य. सुगृहीतं नाम यस्य whose name is honoured. चत्वारः उदधयः एव केदारं तेन कुटुम्बी who is a house-holder of the field in the form of the four oceans *i. e.* who looks upon the whole world as his family. Compare 'उदारचरितानां तु वसुधैव कुटुम्बकम् ।'. For ब्रह्मस्तम्भ, see above p. 102. हर्ष enjoyed the best the universe could yield. A केदारकुटुम्बी (*i. e.* an humble farmer) enjoys the standing crops. सकलानां आदिराजानां चरितं तस्य जये ज्येष्ठः (प्रधानः) मल्लः the foremost protagonist in vanquishing (*i. e.*

eclipsing) the deeds of the primeval kings (like मनु, पृथु). राजन्वती ruled by a good king. राजवती ruled by a king. 'सुराज्ञि देशे राजन्वान् स्यात्ततोऽन्यत्र राजवान्' इत्यमरः. 'राजन्वान् सौराज्ये' पा. 8. 2. 14. नास्य...चरितानि his youthful actions are not opposed to वृष (धर्म), as those of Kṛishṇa were. Even as a boy he did not do any rash act. कृष्ण killed a demon अरिष्ट that had assumed the form of a bull (वृष). *Vide* विष्णुपु० V. 14. In these and the following clauses up to न...श्रियः, the author shows by श्लिष्ट words the superiority of हर्ष to various deities. न...लसितानि the manifestations of his ऐश्वर्य (greatness, prosperity) do not cause sorrow to दक्ष (clever men), as those of शिव did. The king, though prosperous, does not offend the clever. ऐश्वर्य also means 'ईश्वरस्य शिवस्य भावः'. For दक्ष whose sacrifice was destroyed by शिव, *vide* p. 87. There is an emphasis on the word पशुपति. शिव acted very brutally in destroying his own father-in-law. न...वादाः There are no प्रवाद्s (rumours) about him indicating (पिशुन) the ruin of his गोत्र (family), as in the case of Indra. प्रवादाः also 'myths.' गोत्राः mountains (गां पृथ्वीं त्रायन्ते इति). There are myths relating that Indra destroyed the wings of mountains. Indra is therefore called गोत्रभिद्. *Vide* p. 84. 'पिशुनौ खलसूचकौ' इत्यमरः. दण्डग्रहणानि (1) taking of fines (as punishment); (2) holding the rod. दण्डधर is one of the names of यम. The king did not like to be too severe in exacting fines. नि...रक्षिताः guarded by thousands of pitiless (निस्त्रिंश)sea-monsters (ग्राहः). रत्नालयाः treasure-houses; the seas. In the sea we have cruel ग्राह्s. वरुण is the lord of the sea. निस्त्रिंशग्राह would mean 'swordsman.' धनदः=कुबेरः. न निष्फला...लाभाः obtaining his presence (*i. e.* an interview with him) is never fruitless *i. e.* he bestows gifts on those who come near him. In the case of कुबेर, the excellent निधिs (treasures) that he has secured are lying idle (he does not make a gift of anything). कुबेर is the lord of the nine निधिs. 'महापद्मश्च पद्मश्च शङ्खो मकरकच्छपौ । मुकुन्दकुन्दनीलाश्च खर्वश्च निधयो नव ॥'. न अर्थ...दर्शनानि the sight of him (हर्ष) is never bereft of solid gain *i. e.* when anyone sees him, one gets अर्थ (wealth) and people talk (वाद) about it. जिन must mean here बुद्ध. दर्शनानि means 'systems of philosophy'. अर्थ...शून्यानि not recognising the doctrine of the existence of (material) objects. There are four Buddhistic schools, सौत्रान्तिक, वैभाषिक (both of which maintained that thoughts as well objects are real), योगाचार and माध्यमिक (that maintained the unreality of thoughts, as well as objects). What is common to all these schools is the idea of क्षणिकत्व. The author here refers to the योगाचार school. That school holds that the only reality is विज्ञान (thought); there are no real entities (अर्थ or बाह्यार्थ) in the external world corresponding to the thoughts that a person is conscious of. This theory is called विज्ञानवाद. *Vide* वेदान्तसूत्र II. 2. 28 and S'aṁkara's Bhāshya thereon. Compare 'बौद्धबुद्धिमिव निरालम्बनाम्' कादम्बरी p. 131 of P. बहुलैः दोषैः उपहताः marred by many sins. श्रियः = लक्ष्म्यः. बहुलस्य कृष्णपक्षस्य दोषा (रात्रिः) तस्यां उपहताः (reduced). श्रियः—beauty. चित्रम् wonderful. अत्यमरम् surpassing the gods. अमरान् अतिक्रान्तं अत्यमरम्. 'अत्यादयः क्रान्ताद्यर्थे द्वितीयया' वार्तिक on पा. I. 4. 79. अपि...र्थिनः (न पर्याप्तो विषयः) and moreover suppliants do not afford a sufficient (पर्याप्त) scope for his liberality *i. e.* there is not a sufficient number of suppliants to enable him to exercise his liberality to the fullest. Understand 'न पर्याप्तो विषयः' in each of the following clauses and explain similarly. प्रज्ञायाः शास्त्राणि all the शास्त्रs do not give sufficient employment to his intellect. कवित्वस्य वाचः language fails to give adequate expression to his poetic gifts. सत्त्वं spirit, courage. उत्साह (energy) is one of the three शक्तिs of a king *viz.* प्रभुशक्ति, उत्साहशक्ति and मन्त्रशक्ति. व्यापाराः undertakings. कीर्तेर्दिङ्मुखानि the ten regions are not sufficient to contain his fame. गुण...संख्या—*i. e.* his virtues were beyond enumeration. कौशलस्य कला the 64 *kalās* did not exhaust his skill. अस्मिंश्च राजनि while this king rules. यती...ट्टकाः—योगपट्टक was to be seen only with यतिs and nowhere else (in another sense). For the योगपट्टक of ascetics, see p. 26 above. योगपट्टकाः—योगेन कूटकर्मणा युक्ताः पट्टकाः false or forged grants. For योग in the sense of 'deceit', *vide* the first verse of the 4th उच्छ्वास. There are numerous examples of परिसंख्यालङ्कार here. पुस्त...ग्रहाः—पार्थिवविग्रहs (earthen bodies; fights among princes) were to be seen in पुस्तकर्म only (in the manufacture of dolls). *Vide* notes on पुस्तकृत् above p. 90. षट्पदः = भ्रमरः. दान...लहाः the quarrels over receiving ichor; quarrels about the recovery of debts. As nobody incurred debts there were no quarrels about the recovery of money lent. वृत्तानां of metres. पादच्छेदाः division into four parts; the cutting off of feet. अष्टापदानाम्—*Vide* notes p. 24. चतु...ल्पना arrangement of the four members (*i. e.* chess); the cutting off of the four limbs (hands and feet). No one committed grave offences for which hacking of limbs was prescribed by the Smṛitis. द्विज...द्वेषाः hatred of the chief of birds (*i. e.* गरुड); hatred of Brāhmaṇas and teachers. वाक्यविदाम् those who know the rules of the interpretation of Vedic sentences *i. e.* मीमांसकs. अधिकरणविचाराः examination of अधिकरणs (cases for discussion); considerations in a court of justice. No one resorted to the courts of justice, as there were no disputes. Or we may separate as अधिक-रण-विचाराः (thoughts of great fights). The पूर्वमीमांसा of जैमिनि and the उत्तरमीमांसा of बादरायण are divided into अध्यायs, each अध्याय into पादs and each पाद into अधिकरणs, each अधिकरण containing one or more सूत्रs and completely treating of one topic. अधिकरण has five members. 'विषयो विशयश्चैव पूर्वपक्षस्तथोत्तरम् । निर्णयश्चेति सिद्धान्तः शास्त्रेऽधिकरणं स्मृतम् ॥'. According to others the five members are विषय, सन्देह (or विशय), सङ्गति, पूर्वपक्ष and सिद्धान्त. उपवीती—'प्रोद्धृते दक्षिणे पाणावुपवीत्युच्यते द्विजः'—क्षीरस्वामी quoting from मनु–wearing the sacred cord in the usual manner (over the left shoulder and under the right arm). 'उपवीतं यज्ञसूत्रं प्रोद्धृते दक्षिणे करे' इत्यमरः.

P. 36 ll. 1–27. **अथोत्तरेण...मभूत्.** उत्तरेण...धिष्ण्यस्य not far to the north of the royal seat. Words ending in एन like दक्षिणेन and उत्तरेण govern the accusative or genitive. अपरवक्त्रम्—*Vide* notes p. 40. **Verse 5.** करिकलभ (vocative) young elephant ! लोलता = चञ्चलता. चर...व्रतम् observe the vow of discipline (humility). आनतं आननं यस्य whose head is bent (not held high in pride). मृगपतिनखवत् भङ्गुरः (curved). गुरुः formidable. उपरि held above (the elephant's head). क्षमते...शः the hook would not tolerate your लोलता. The अङ्कुश brought round the elephant when it became restless and disobedient. This verse contains a veiled rebuke of Bāṇa for his लोलता in his youth, when he was like करिकलभ. The words मृगपति and गुरुः (who teaches or chastises) refer to the king. The verse reminds the king of the presence of बाण, about whose चापल he had heard reports. Mr. R. R. Kale sees a veiled allusion to the king even in the words करिकलभ &c., but that does not seem to us to be proper. He takes गुरु as referring to the preceptor of the king. तं = बाणम्. गिरि...गम्भीरेण as deep as the roar (बृंहितं) of a lion in a mountain cave. एष...बाणः is he that बाण ? न...पश्यामि I shall not see him without showing him favour. Bāṇa conveys that the very way in which the king addressed him (महानयं भुजङ्गः) showed that the king had favoured him. The king spoke the words to the मालव

prince and then looked बाण in the face. The reading अकृतप्रसादम् (अकृतः प्रसादः यस्मिन्) would convey the same sense. नीलैः धवलैः अंशुकैः (किरणैः, वस्त्रैः) शाराम् (variegated) *adj.* of प्रभाम् and तिरस्करिणीम्. भ्रमयन्—the object is प्रभाम्. अपाङ्गे नीयमाना तरला तारका (pupil) यस्य. आयामिनीं long *i. e.* spreading. परिवृत्य having turned (his body). In order to look at the मालव prince, he turned his eye sideways (तिर्यक्). The rays of the dark pupil became mixed with the lustre of the white eye and so the lustre of the whole eye looked शार. The rays of the eye resembled a curtain made of white and dark silk. His pupil was moved towards the corner of the eye. A curtain may have stars on the borders (अपाङ्ग). प्रेष्ठ superlative of प्रिय. मालवराजसूनोः—(*Vid.* Intro. p. XXXII) this seems to have been माधवगुप्त the younger of the two princes that were the companions of Harsha and his elder brother. भुजङ्गः a gallant, a man of dissolute habits. 'भुजङ्गः सर्पषिङ्गयोः' हेमचन्द्रः. तूष्णी...तस्मिन् when that (मालव prince) showed by his silence that he had not understood the king's words. अगमितं नरेन्द्रवचः येन. अविज्ञातं तत्त्वं येन who does not know the truth. अश्रद्दधान इव as if you do not believe me (in my real character). नेय इव like one led (by others). आज्ञापयसि—this and the correlative विज्ञापयामि or विज्ञापयति are employed by ordinary persons in addressing a person very much superior in the sense of वदसि, कथयामि &c. स्वैरिणः capricious, unrestrained. विचित्राः various, strange. प्रवादाः rumours. महद्भिः...तव्यम् but the great ought to see things as they are. नार्हे...शिष्टमिव you will please not misunderstand me, as if I were an ordinary man. अविशिष्टम् without anything to distinguish him. सोमपायिनाम् that drink सोम *i. e.* that performed the सोमयागs. संस्काराः the purificatory ceremonies performed in the case of a द्विज from conception to death, such as जातकर्म, नामकरण, उपनयन &c. साङ्गः—the अङ्गs (auxiliary branches of study) of the वेद are six, *viz.* शिक्षा (phonetics), कल्प (ritual of sacrifices), व्याकरण (grammar), निरुक्त (etymology and exegesis), छन्दः (metrics) and ज्योतिष (astronomy). In these three sentences बाण seems to have in view the well-known verse 'जन्मना ब्राह्मणो ज्ञेयः संस्कारैर्द्विज उच्यते । विद्यया याति विप्रत्वं त्रिभिः श्रोत्रिय उच्यते ॥'. शास्त्राणि—such as अलङ्कार, न्याय, वेदान्त &c. दार...रिकोऽस्मि since my marriage I have been a diligent householder. 'कुटुम्बव्यापृतस्तु यः । स्यादभ्यागारिकः' इत्यमरः. 'अभितोऽगारे भवः अभ्यागारिकः' क्षीर०. कामे भुजङ्गता—this sentence is capable of three senses, two of which are principally intended. (1) Wherein consists my भुजङ्गता (being a lewd person)? What is there in all my life which deserves to be referred to in the words 'महानयं भुजङ्गः?' (2) भुजङ्गता is to be found only in काम (Cupid) and not in me. (3) What woman was embraced by me? (का मे भुजं गता). लोक... मासीत् but (I must admit) that my youth was not without those follies which are not inconsistent with the two worlds (*i. e.* this world and the next). He says he was guilty of trifling follies that would not be very much censured in this world or would not come in the way of his attaining heaven. अविद्यमानः अपलापः (concealment, denial) यस्य. अत्रा...स्मि I do not deny this much. अनेनै...हृदयम् my heart does feel repentance (विप्रतीसारः) for this. सुगतः = बुद्धः. शान्तमनसि—this, कर्तरि and दण्डभृति are to be connected with देवे. मना...श्रमाणाम् who carries out all the rules of the (four) Varṇas and the (four) *ās'ramas*, like Manu. Bāṇa refers probably to the मनुस्मृति wherein are laid down the rules of वर्णs and आश्रमs that were supposed to have been promulgated by Manu. *Vide* मनुस्मृति I. 2 and 107. सम...भृति when you wield the rod of punishment like यम. 'धर्मराजः पितृपतिः समवर्ती परेतराट्' इत्यमरः. Death deals equally with all; यम is also called दण्डधर. The king also is दण्डधर (he punishes wrongdoers). सप्ता...रशनाम् whose girdle is formed of the seven oceans. For the seven oceans, see p. 32. For the द्वीपs, see p. 3. अविशङ्कः without fear. क इव सर्व...कल्पयिष्यति what man possibly will act the part of improper conduct even in his mind, improper conduct which is closely related to all calamities. From अविनय spring all calamities. Even the *acting* of improper conduct is impossible; much more actual performance. आसतां...पेताः let alone human beings. मनुष्यस्य भावः मनुष्याणां समूहो वा मानुष्यकम्. त्वत्प्र...पिबन्ति In consequence of your power, even bees drink honey in fear. To drink मधु (wine) was a महापातक. So the bees are as though afraid of the punishment that may be meted out to them. 'ब्रह्महत्या सुरापानं स्तेयं गुर्वङ्गनागमः । महान्ति पातकान्याहुः संसर्गश्चापि तैः सह ॥' मनु० 11. 54. रथाङ्गं (चक्रं) नाम येषाम् (चक्रवाकाः). लज्जन्ते...प्रियाणाम् are ashamed of their great attachment to their mates. अभ्यनुवृत्तिः (pleasing, following) एव व्यसनं (vice; attachment). A चक्रवाक is a type of love. चपलायन्ते play their tricks. शरारवः destructive, ferocious. For शरारु see p. 23. सानुक्रोशा इव as though compassionate. पिशितानि = मांसानि. अन...ग्राहिण्यः understanding the minds of others as they are. अनपाचीन not opposite (to the real state of things).

P. 36 l. 28—**P. 37.** l. 32. **भूपति...णेति.** **केवल...कथयत्** he only revealed his inward pleasure by merely casting at him an affectionate glance which seemed to bathe him in a shower of nectar. The king did not show him any *outward* marks of favour such as सम्भाषण; but बाण understood from the king's look that *inwardly* the king was pleased with him. लम्बमाने hanging (on the western horizon). The next sentence is बाणोऽपि... निवासस्थानमगात् (l. 21). धौतः (washed, polished) आरकूटः (brass) तस्य इव कोमला आतपत्विट् यस्मिन् (*adj.* of वासरे). The light of the sun in the evening (on trees and mountains) looked like polished brass. निर्वाति *loc. sing.* of *pr. p.* of वा with निर्—to be extinguished. अस्ता...मति when the sun (मरीचिमत्), leaving the sky, the diadem (किरीटं) of the crest of the setting mountain, let fall his rays like the sprays of *Nichula* trees. 'कूटोऽस्त्री शिखरं शृङ्गं' इत्यमरः. निचुलमञ्जरीणामिव भाः येषाम्. निचुल is a tree with scarlet flowers. 'निचुलो हिज्जलोऽम्बुजः' इत्यमरः. रोमन्थेन मन्थराणि कुरङ्गकुटुम्बकानि तैः अध्यास्यमानं म्रदिष्ठं गोष्ठीनपृष्ठं यासु. रोमन्थ... स्थलीषु when the soft surfaces of deserted cowpens in the forests had families of deer sitting on them lazily ruminating. म्रदिष्ठ—superlative of मृदु. We must read गौष्ठीन. गोष्ठः भूतपूर्वः (that was formerly a cow-pen) गौष्ठीनं, according to 'गोष्ठात् खञ् भूतपूर्वे' पा. 5. 2. 18. शोका...तटीषु when the banks of rivers were plaintive with the cries (कूजितं) of the female चक्रवाक birds overwhelmed with sorrow. At the approach of night the चक्रवाकs were supposed to be separated from their mates. वासविटपेषु (on branches where they had made their nests) उपविष्टानि वाचाटानि चटकानां चक्रवालानि येषु. आलवालेषु (basins round trees) आवर्जिताः (emptied) सेकार्थं जलकुटाः (water pots) येषु—*adj.* of निष्कुटेषु (pleasure groves). 'घटः कुटनिपावस्त्री' इत्यमरः. 'गृहारामास्तु निष्कुटाः' इत्यमरः (कुटात् गृहात् निष्क्रान्ताः निष्कुटाः). दिवस...व्राते when herds of hungry calves (तर्णकः) began to suck the flowing udders of cows that returned after wandering (विहृतिः) the whole day. प्रस्नुताः स्तनाः यस्य (*adj.* of वर्गम्). स्तनन्धय—from स्तन and the root धे 1 P. to suck (स्तनं धयतीति), a nasal being inserted according to 'नासिकास्तनयोर्ध्माधेटोः' पा 3. 2. 29. उद्धृतं क्षीरं यस्मात्. Read चास्तधराधर०. अस्त...मण्डले when the disc of the sun, the boat in the ocean of evening (twilight), with red hue, sank (below the horizon), as though it were plunged into the flood of the stream (धुनी) of the minerals (धातुः) on the western mountain. गैरिक (red chalk) is particularly known as धातु (in the case of mountains). 'धातुर्मनःशिलाद्यद्रेर्गैरिकं तु विशेषतः' इत्यमरः. पतङ्गस्य इदं पातङ्गम्. The sun's disc became extremely red when about to dip into the ocean. The poet fancies that it was swept into the stream of red chalk. The disc resembles a small boat and the rosy hues of the evening sky resemble the sea. पानपात्रे is not so good as यानपात्रे. It will mean 'the disc of the sun looked like a goblet for drinking the ocean of evening.' The evening being red, the goblet containing it would also look red. °जलेन शुचयः शयचरणाः येषाम्. 'पञ्चशाखः शयः पाणिः' इत्यमरः. Brāhmanical ascetics washed their hands and feet before worshipping in the shrine. चैत्यः a sanctuary; a temple; a holy tree (growing by the side of a road). 'चैत्यमायतनं तुल्ये' इत्यमरः ('चित्यायामिदं चैत्यं देवकुलमहावृक्षाद्युपाश्रयः' क्षीर°). पाराशरिषु—see above p. 90. यज्ञपात्रैः पवित्राः पाणयः येषाम् (*adj.* of °जने). प्रकीर्णाः (spread round) बर्हिषः (कुशाः) यस्य (*adj.* of °वेदसि). उद्गतं तेजः यस्य the flames of which leapt up (when oblations were thrown into it). वषट्कृ to offer (an oblation) with the cry वषट्. वषट् is an exclamation on offering an oblation (the name of the deity being put in the dative) *e. g.* इन्द्राय वषट्. यायजूकः—one who frequently performs sacrifices—from यज् with affix ऊक, according to 'यजजपदशां यङः' पा. 3. 2. 166 (यायजूकः, जञ्जपूकः, दन्दशूकः). निद्राविद्राणानि द्रोणकुलानि तैः कलिलाः (full of) कुलायाः येषु. द्रोणाः काकाः. The com. explains निद्राविद्राण as 'dull with sleep'. But elsewhere विद्राण is used in the sense of 'awake'. Compare 'विद्राणविपश्चिति' हर्ष° 5th उ° 11th para. So we take 'निद्राविद्राण' as 'not yet gone to sleep' (though crowding in their nests). Or we may separate as निद्रा-अविद्राण meaning 'not awake through sleep'. कापेयविकलानि (free from their pranks) कपिकुलानि येषु. At night the monkeys desist from their pranks. 'कापेयं चापलादिकम्' क्षीर° (कपेः भावः कर्म वा). आरामतरुषु on the trees in the gardens. निर्जि...कुले when the swarms of owls (कौशिकः), settled (*lit.* householders) in their huts *viz.* the hollows of old trees, were about to go out. मुनि...रम्बे—The clusters of bright stars looked like the bright drops of water scattered about in सन्ध्यावन्दन by the sages. दन्तुरयति *loc. sing.* of *pr. p.* of दन्तुरयति (make indented or serrated) denominative verb from दन्तुर. The clusters also looked like the bright teeth (of a lady *viz.* the sky). As drops are scattered on the ground (स्थली), so the stars were scattered in the sky. स्थवीयस्—comparative of स्थूल. 'निकुरम्बं कदम्बकम्' इत्यमरः. अम्बरा...शिखण्डे when the topknot of the S'abarī of night rose in the sky *i. e.* when the sky was overcast with darkness. For शर्वरीशबरी compare 'शर्वरीशबरीचिकुरचये...तमसि' text p. 6. l. 13. अम्बरा०—The topknot of a शबरी may be dangling on her garment (अम्बरं). खण्डपरशुः (शिवः) तस्य कण्ठवत् काले (dark)-goes with ०तारे. For S'iva's dark throat, see notes p. 2. कव...तारे when the young (fresh, recent) *avatara* (advent) of darkness swallowed all that remained of the evening light. सान्ध्यम्–सन्ध्यायाः अयं सान्ध्यः (०शेषः) तम्. तिमिर... र्गतासु (०तर्जनाय निर्गतासु) that came forth as if to chide darkness. दहनं प्रविष्टः दिनकरः तस्य करशाखासु (fingers; branch-like rays). The blazing lamps are fancied to be the fingers of the sun. Fingers start from the hand and one of them (called तर्जनी) is employed in threatening or chiding a person. Flames are tapering like fingers. It was believed that the sun, when setting, entered fire. Compare रघु० IV. 1. 'स राज्यं गुरुणा दत्तं प्रतिपद्याधिकं बभौ। दिनान्ते निहितं तेजः सवित्रेव हुताशनः॥'. अररसम्पुटसंक्रीडनेन कथिता आवृत्तिः यैः. अररं panel. 'कवाटमररं तुल्ये' इत्यमरः. 'पुरद्वारं तु गोपुरम्' इत्यमरः. अरर...पुरेषु when the city gates as though announced their clo sing (आवृत्ति) by the creaking of their folding panels. It would be better if we could read ०वृतिषु. आवृति means 'shutting', while आवृत्ति usually means 'revolving.' शय...जुषि enjoying the pleasure (उपजोषः) of lying on their beds. They first lay on their beds for some time and then went to sleep. जरतीभिः कथिताः कथाः यस्मै. शिशयिषमाणे (*pr. p.* of the desiderative of शी) was about to sleep. जरन् महिषः मषी (lamp-black, ink) च तद्वत् मलीमसं (dark) तमः यस्य. जनितः पुण्यजनानां (goblins) प्रजागरः येन. 'यातुधानाः पुण्यजनाः' अमरः. Goblins stalk abroad at night. पुण्यजन also means 'यक्ष'. They are guardians of कुबेर's treasures and as such must be awake at night. विजृम्भमाणे (growing, yawning). तमीमुखे the mouth (or first part) of Night. 'रजनी यामिनी तमी' अमरः मुखरितं (twanging) विततज्यं (वितता ज्या यस्य) धनुः यस्य (*adj.* of ०ध्वजे). अशेषस्य संसारस्य शेमुषीं (मतिं) मुष्णाति इति ०मुष् तस्मिन्—Cupid blinds the intellect of every one in the world. रतस्य आकल्पः (dress) तस्य आरम्भेण शोभते इति. शम्भलीनां (procuress) भाषितं भजते इति. 'कुट्टनी शम्भली समे' अमरः. भूषा ornaments, decoration. भुजिष्या a maid harlot. सैरन्ध्या बध्यमानं रशनाजालं तेन जल्पाकं (noisy, jingling) जघनं (loins) यासाम्. 'स्याज्जल्पाकस्तु वाचालः' अमरः. For सैरन्ध्री, see notes p. 90. जनीषु young ladies. 'समाः स्नुषा जनी वध्वः' अमरः. वशिकासु (empty) विशिखासु (roads) विहरन्तीति विहारिण्यः (wandering) तासु. 'वशिकं तुच्छरिक्तके' अमरः. 'रथ्या प्रतोली विशिखा' अमरः (विगतशिखा मुण्डितेव, समन्ताद्विशीर्यते जनसंमर्देन वा' क्षीर०). अनन्यजः (कामः) अनुप्लवः

यासाम्. 'अनुप्लवः सहायश्च' अमरः. They went alone, with hearts aflame. अभिसारिकासु—see notes p. 33. विरली...जल्पिते when the sweet (मञ्जु) chatter of the females of *Haṁsas* lying in the ponds, as dull (low) as the jingling of anklets (मञ्जीरः-रम्), gradually ceased. 'हंसस्य योषिद्वरटा' अमरः; 'वेशन्तः पल्वलं चाल्पसरः' अमरः. For निद्राविद्राण, see notes above p. 162. निद्रा...रसिते when the notes of cranes, appearing to grow longer to those that were kept awake, as though melted the hearts of separated lovers. In the stillness of night, the notes appeared longer. भावि...निकरे इव—the lamps scattered about were like the shoots of the seeds of the coming day. From shoots large trees grow. The flickering lamps contained in them the potential day that was to dawn. अनेकानि बालचरितचापलानि तस्य उचितं (appropriate to) कौलीनं (evil report) तेन कोपितः. 'कौलीनं पशुभिर्युद्धे कुलीनत्वापवादयोः' इति धरणिः. कौलीन (कुलीनस्य कर्म भावो वा) according to 'हायनान्तयुवादिभ्योऽण्' पा. 5. 1. 130. If we read 'चापलोपचित' the meaning is 'the scandals that grew on account of my follies'. मनसा—there is emphasis on this word. *Vide* notes p. 161. यद्य...स्याम् if I were an eye-sore to him, if he were displeased with me. इच्छति...वन्तम् but he wishes me to be virtuous. उप...स्वामिनः for masters teach their dependents proper conduct even without words by granting them an honour (प्रतिपत्तिः) suited to them. स्वदोषेण अन्धं मानसं यस्य. अनादरपीडितम् who am pained by the absence of (outward) respect (shown by the king). अति...चिन्तयन्तम् who entertain various fancies about this most virtuous king. यथा...स्थितम् as I really am. कटकात्—It will be remembered that Harsha was encamped on the अजिरवती (text p. 26. l. 17). गृहीतः (understood) स्वभावः येन. परमप्रीतेन—qualifies नरेन्द्रेण. प्रसादात् जन्म यस्य springing from the favour (of the king). This qualifies all the words from मानस्य to प्रभावस्य. नर्मन् *n.* amusement, merriment.

Uchchhvāsa III

Verse 1. The principal sentence is सु...भूभुजः—kings (of the character described in the first half of the verse) are born like fine seasons (prosperous times) through the merit of the subjects (of the people). निज...स्नेहाः (निजे वर्षे देशे आहितः स्नेहः यैः) that plant their affection in their kingdom *i. e.* that love their kingdoms; (निजेन वर्षेण वृष्ट्या आहितः स्नेहः रसः घृतं वा यैः) that produce moisture (or ghee) by rain. वर्ष is a subdivision of द्वीप (as in भरतवर्ष). बहु...न्विताः (बहुभिः भक्तजनैः अन्विताः) followed by many devoted persons; (बहूनां भक्तानां अन्नानां ओदनानां वा जनेन समूहेन अन्विताः) that are marked by plenty of rice-crops or plenty of food. 'भक्तमन्धोऽन्नमोदनोऽस्त्री स दीदिविः' अमरः. This verse foreshadows the greatness of पुष्पभूति, the founder of Harsha's family, the treatment he gave to his subjects and the prosperity of his kingdom. The metre is अनुष्टुभ्.

Verse 2. लक्ष्मीं द्रष्टुम् to see लक्ष्मी; to obtain wealth. विहायसा गन्तुम् to sail in the sky; to rise high. न...मनः whose mind is not eager ? This verse shadows forth the four principal topics of this उच्छ्वास. Here also the king पुष्पभूति conferred an obligation on भैरवाचार्य; the king had a vision of लक्ष्मी in flesh and blood; भैरवाचार्य assumed a semi-divine form and the cousins of बाण became eager to hear the story of Harsha's life. The metre is आर्या.

P. 38 ll. 2–16 **अथ...समगात्.** The principal sentence is अथ...शरत्समयारम्भे वाणः बन्धून् द्रष्टुं पुनरपि तं ब्राह्मणाधिवासमगात्. Here we have a description of autumn. All the words in the locative (singular) qualify शरत्समयारम्भे. विरलिताः बलाहकाः (मेघाः) यस्मिन्. चातकस्य आतङ्कं करोतीति. 'रुक्तापशङ्कास्वातङ्कः' अमरः. For चातक, see above p. 128. When the clouds disappeared the चातक would not get even a drop of water. क्वणन्तः कादम्बाः (कलहंसाः) यस्मिन्. कलहंसs are at ease in the rainy season. दर्दुरद्विषि—which is an enemy to frogs. मयूरस्य मदं मुष्णाति इति. The peacock dances at the appearance of clouds and so in शरद् when clouds become rare it pines away. हंसा एव पथिकसार्थः सर्वः अतिथिः यस्य whose only guest is the swarm of travellers–the swans. At the approach of the rains, हंसs were supposed to leave the plains and run to the मानस lake, whence they returned after the rains were over. शरद् welcomes the tribe of हंसs as guests by offering them clear water. धौतासिनिभं (॰सदृशं) नभः यस्मिन्. In शरद् the sky is blue and clear. भास्वरः भास्वान् (सूर्यः) यस्मिन्. शुचिः शशी यस्मिन्. In the rains the moon is obscured by clouds. तरुणः (young, bright) तारागणः यस्मिन्. गलत् (disappearing) सुनासीरस्य (इन्द्रस्य) शरासनं (धनुः) यस्मिन्. Rain-bows are seen when there are clouds. For सुनासीर, see pp. 17–18. सीदत् (vanishing, sinking) सौदामन्याः (विद्युतः) दाम (streak, girdle) यस्मिन्. दामोदरनिद्रायै दुह्यति इति that (शरद्) was an enemy to the sleep of विष्णु. दाम उदरे यस्य (दाम्ना उदरे बद्धः). *Vide* विष्णुपु॰ V. 6.20 for derivation. विष्णु was supposed to fall asleep in आषाढ for the four months of the rainy season and to get up in कार्तिक. Compare 'शापान्तो मे भुजगशयनादुत्थिते शार्ङ्गपाणौ' मेघदूत; 'जलधरसमयमिव वनगहनमध्यसुखसुप्तहरिम्' कादम्बरी p. 40 of P; 'न खलु सांप्रतमाचरति जलशयनदोहदं देवो रथाङ्गपाणिः' कादम्बरी p. 124 of P. द्रुतं (running, flowing) वैदूर्यवर्णं (of the colour of *lapis lazuli*) अर्णः (water) यस्मिन्. घूर्णमानाः (rolling about) मिहिकावत् लघवः मेघाः तैः मोघः (idle) मघवा (इन्द्रः) यस्मिन् मिहिका fog, dew. The clouds, if at all seen, are very light in autumn and hardly any rain falls. So इन्द्र, the lord of rain, is then idle. निमीलन्तः (closing) नीपाः यस्मिन्. नीप is कदम्ब. A कदम्ब tree puts forth buds in the rainy season. Compare 'मरुन्नवाम्भःप्रविधूतसिक्ता कदम्बयष्टिः स्फुटकोरकेव ॥' उत्तररामचरित III. 42; 'कुड्मलितकदम्बतरौ...नभसि मासि' हर्ष॰ 4th उ॰, 11th para. नि...कुटजे—कुटज trees blossom in the rains. निर्मु...कन्दले when the plantain puts forth no buds. मधुस्यन्दि इन्दीवरं (blue lotus) यस्मिन्. कह्लारैः (water-lilies) आह्लादिनि. शेफालिकया शीतलीकृता निट् (रात्रिः) यस्मिन्. यूथिकाभिः (jasmine) आमोदिनि. मोदमानैः कुमुदैः (white night lotuses) अवदाताः (सिताः) दश दिशः यस्मिन्. सप्तच्छदानां धूलिभिः (pollen) धूसरः समीरः (wind) यस्मिन्. For सप्तच्छद, see above p. 136. स्तबकितैः (formed into bunches) बन्धुरैः (lovely) बन्धूकैः आबध्यमाना अकाण्डसन्ध्या (sudden evening hues) यस्मिन्. बन्धूक is a red flower. नीराजिताः वाजिनः यस्मिन्. The नीराजन ceremony was performed in शरद्. For नीराजन, see p. 34. *Vide.* रघु॰ IV. 24–25. उद्दामाः (wild, unchecked) दन्तिनः यस्मिन्. दर्पेण क्षीबं (intoxicated) औक्षकं यस्मिन्. औक्षकम् multitude of oxen. 'उक्ष्णां संहतिरौक्षकम्' अमरः. It is derived from उक्षन् *(m)* with affix वुञ् according to 'गोत्रोक्षोष्ट्रोरभ्रराजराजन्यराजपुत्रवत्समनुष्याद्वुञ्' पा. 4. 2. 39. (एभ्यः समूहे वुञ् स्यात्). क्षीयमाणं पङ्कस्य (mud) चक्रवालं (समूहः) यस्मिन्. बालपुलिनैः (small islands) पल्लवितानि सिन्धूनां (नदीनां) रोधांसि (banks) यस्मिन्. The waters having receded, small islands are formed in the rivers in शरद्. परिणामेन (by being ripe) आश्यानाः (partially dry)

श्यामाकाः यस्मिन्. जनितं प्रियङ्गुमञ्जरीषु रजः (pollen) यस्मिन्. कठोरा त्रपुसत्वक् यस्मिन्. त्रपुसं cucumber. कुसुमैः स्मेराः शराः (reeds) यस्मिन्.

P. 38 ll. 17—30 **समुप...इति.** समुपलब्धः भूपालात् (हर्षात्) संमानातिशयः तेन परितुष्टाः. ज्ञातयः kinsmen. श्लाघमानाः applauding. कांश्चि...मानः—he bowed to those that were older than himself and was saluted by those that were younger. Explain each of the following pairs similarly. सम्भ्रान्तेन (excited, flurried) परिजनेन उपनीतं (brought). आसनं...भेजे he took his seat after his elders had taken theirs. भज...त्कारं accepting the hospitality consisting of flower offerings &c. कच्चि...यूयम् have you been happy all these days? (I hope you have &c.). अप्रत्यूहा = अविघ्ना. सम्यक्करणेन परितोषितं द्विजचक्रं यस्याम्. अप्र...क्रिया does the performance of sacrifice proceed without obstacles, gratifying the groups of Brāhmaṇas by its proper procedure? क्रतोः इयं क्रातवी. यथा...भुजः do the fires consume the oblations accompanied by faultless mantras as prescribed (in works on ritual)? अविकलान् मन्त्रान् भजन्ते इति भाञ्जि (हवींषि). A मन्त्र is अविकल (perfect, entire) when it is recited with correct accent and without slurring over any letter. Compare '**मन्त्रो हीनः स्वरतो वर्णतो** वा मिथ्याप्रयुक्तो न तमर्थमाह। स वाग्वज्रो यजमानं हिनस्ति यथेन्द्रशत्रुः स्वरतोऽपराधात्॥' शिक्षा. अविच्छिन्नः unbroken, continuous. कच्चि...योगः. Is there (I hope there is) the same intent application as in years long past to the practice of यज्ञविद्या (the lore of sacrifice)? अभियोगः—'आभिमुख्येन उद्यमः' क्षीर०. परस्परस्पर्धानुबन्धेन अवन्ध्यः (not useless, fruitful) दिवसः तेन दर्शितः आदरः येषु. The words सः, तानि, सा are used in the sense of प्रसिद्ध. तान्येव...मण्डलानि are there the same assemblies for the exposition of grammar, showing their regard (to the study of व्याकरण) by days rendered fruitful by continuous emulation of each other? Each one of the assembly tried to excel the others in the exposition of knotty points of grammar. On व्याख्यान, the महाभाष्य says 'न केवलं चर्चापदानि व्याख्यानं वृद्धिः आत् ऐजिति। किं तर्हि। उदाहरणं प्रत्युदाहरणं वाक्याध्याहार इत्येतत्समुदितं व्याख्यानं भवति' (Kielhorn Vol. I. p. 11). परित्यक्तं अन्यकर्तव्यं यस्याम् which disregarded all other occupations. प्रमाणगोष्ठी assembly or society for the discussion of the means of knowledge. This refers to logic. The very first topic for treatment mentioned in the first Sūtra of the न्यायसूत्र is प्रमाण. Generally four प्रमाण्s are mentioned *viz.* प्रत्यक्ष, अनुमान, उपमान and शब्द. मन्दीकृतः इतरशास्त्रेषु रसः (liking) येन. मीमांसा—refers to the पूर्वमीमांसा of जैमिनि and to the उत्तरमीमांसा of बादरायण. In these three clauses बाण suggests that his cousins were पदवाक्यप्रमाणज्ञ, पद standing for grammar, वाक्य for मीमांसा and प्रमाण for न्यायशास्त्र. अभिनवं सुभाषितं एव सुधा तां वर्षन्तीति. For सुभाषित see p. 11.

P. 39 ll. 1-9 **अथ...वारयन्.** तात a term of endearment applied even by elders to youngsters and by friends to friends. Compare 'नहि कल्याणकृत्कश्चिदुर्गतिं तात गच्छति' गीता. 6. 40. सन्तोषजुषां who are contented (*adj.* of नः). सततं सन्निहितः विद्याविनोदः (intellectual diversion) येषाम्. वैतानः वह्निः एव ०वह्निमात्रं सहायः येषाम्. किय...तया what have we to do with being happy (we have but little concern with being happy)? It should be noticed that the first question asked by बाण was 'कच्चित्...सुखिनो यूयम्.' They reply by saying that they have all those things that make for happiness *viz.* friends (वैतानवह्नि), amusements and contentment and that they need not bother themselves further, as king हर्ष will look to the rest (to their protection &c.). सकलभुवनानि भुनक्ति (protects). भुजङ्गराजः शेषः तस्य देहवत् दीर्घे. शेष also supports (protects) the earth. क्षितिभुजः = हर्षस्य. विमुक्तं कौसीद्यं येन. कौसीद्य—from कुसीद (कुत्सितं सीदति अस्मिन्) with affix ष्यञ्. The kinsmen of बाण administer him a delicate rebuke. यथाविभवं as our wealth permits. शैश...कथाभिः remembrances of past boyish sports and stories of their ancestors. यथा...करोत् he performed the usual observances.

P. 39 ll. 10—22 **अत्रान्तरे...पपाठ.** दुकू...वसानः wearing a pair of silken Pauṇḍra garments, as white as the corner of the peacock's eye, and cut off from a long piece of silk cloth. पट्ट here stands for what is called तागा in Marathi. He had cut off two pieces from a long roll of silk cloth. पौण्ड्र–Manufactured in the Puṇḍra country. पुण्ड्र would correspond to modern Bengal and Bihar. शिखण्डिनः अपाङ्गवत् पाण्डुनी. अवसानं end. बन्दितया because he was a bard. The bards formed a distinct class, sprung from क्षत्रिय father and S'ūdra mother. तीर्थ...तिलकः whose *tilaka* (on the forehead) was made of *gorochanā* and clay from a sacred spot (river &c.). Various substances were prescribed as affording fit material for making a तिलक. 'तीर्थमृद्यज्ञकाष्ठं च बिल्वो मलयसम्भवम् । जाह्नवीमृन्महानिम्बतुलसीकाष्ठमेव च । ...गोरोचना गन्धकुष्ठं जलं चागुरुगोमयम् ।...स्नानान्ते सर्ववर्णानामाश्रमाणां तथैव च । एतानि तिलकान्याहुः सन्ध्यादिसर्वकर्मसु ॥.' तैलामलकाभ्या मसृणितः (made smooth and glossy) मौलिः (केशाः) यस्य. अनु...चुम्बिना kissing his short topknot. निबिडेन dense with flowers. सकृ...कान्तिः the colour of his lip was bright because he had chewed betel only once. If he had taken betel very often, his lip would have been dark-red and not विमल. So the reading असकृदुपयुक्त is not good. एक...रुचिः the lustre of whose eye was heightened by the application of an eye-salve with a pin. विनी...दधानः wearing a simple (not gaudy) and respectable dress. आसन्दी = पीठिका—a chair. तत्कालं अपनीतं सूत्रवेष्टनं यस्य (*adj.* of पुस्तकं). तत्काल...निधाय having laid, on a stand (यश्रकं) made of reedstalks placed in front, his book which seemed as if bound with soft lotus fibres on account of the rays of his nails, although its band was removed at that very moment. His nails were bright and the rays from them resembled lotus-fibres. When he passed his hand round the book in unloosening the string in which it was wrapped, he as though seemed to be tying it up again. पृष्ठतः... स्थानके when a place was assigned behind him to मधुकर and पारावत that sat near (सनीड). The two seem to have been persons that played upon flutes by way of accompaniment. So the reading of B 'वांशिकाभ्यां' is good. C and T translate मधुकर and पारावत as bee and dove. What purpose these served is not clear. Perhaps they were pets. वांशिक-वंशवादनं शिल्पमस्य (from वंश + ठक्) according to 'शिल्पम्' पा. 4. 4. 55. It would mean 'that served as flute-players.' प्राभातिक...त्क्षिप्य having taken out the leaf inserted inside as a mark to indicate the portion read in the morning. प्राभातिकः प्रपाठकः (section) तस्य छेदः (end) तस्य चिह्नीकृतम्. प्रपाठक also means 'reader', the meaning being 'made as a mark to denote the portion read by the morning reader.' गृहीत्वा...पाटिकां he took a small block (*lit.* panel) light (not heavy) because there were a few leaves only. क्षालय...ग्रंन्थम्—the idea is:—the bright rays of his teeth when he recited the verses looked like bright water and like white flowers. मुख...श्रोतृणाम् captivating the hearts of his hearers by the sweet intonations of his voice, as though they were the jinglings of the anklets of सरस्वती residing in his mouth (tongue). सरस्वती is spoken of as dwelling in the mouth of a learned man. On गमक the com. says 'गमयन्ति रागस्वरूपमिति गमकाः असाधारणानि स्वराणां निमीलनानि यानि लक्ष्येष्वान्तरमार्गे इति प्रसिद्धास्तैर्गमकैः स्वरयतिविशेषैः.' गमक is thus defined 'गमकः स्वश्रुतिस्थानच्छायां श्रुत्यन्तराश्रयाम्। स्वरो यो मूर्छनामेति गमकः स इहोच्यते ॥ कम्पितः स्फुरितो नीलो भिन्नः स्थविर एव च। आहतान्दोलितौ चेति गमकाः सप्त कीर्तिताः ॥.' According to the सङ्गीतरत्नाकर, गमक

is a certain कम्प of the voice; it enumerates 15 kinds of it 'स्वरस्य कम्पो गमकः श्रोतृचित्तसुखावहः ।' 3rd chap. 45. गीत्या पपाठ he sang or chanted. पवमानप्रोक्तं पुराणं the Purāṇa promulgated by Vāyu *i. e.* the वायुपुराण. सूत says in the वायुपुराण I. 47–48. 'पुराणं संप्रवक्ष्यामि यदुक्तं मातरिश्वना ॥ पृष्टेन मुनिभिः पूर्वं नैमिषीयैर्महात्मभिः ।'. सूत had learnt it from व्यास (verse 46). The वायुपुराण is one of the most ancient of Purāṇas. The topics generally treated of in a पुराण are summarised in the following verse 'सर्गश्च प्रतिसर्गश्च वंशो मन्वन्तराणि च । वंशानुचरितं चैव पुराणं पंचलक्षणम् ॥'.

P. 39 l. 23—**P. 40** l. 5 **तस्मिंश्च...लोकयन्.** श्रुतिभिः सुभगा गीतिः गर्भे यथा स्यात् तथा. श्रुति is a technical term in music. It means 'a particular division of the octave, a quarter tone or interval.' They are 22 in number. श्रुतिs are those elementary नादs from which the seven स्वरs (सरिगमपधनि) are evolved. 'हृद्यूर्ध्वनाडिकास्य-द्वाविंशत्यणुतिरोजनाडीषु । तावन्तः श्रुतिसंज्ञाः स्युर्नादाः परपरोच्चोच्चाः ॥ एवं गले च शीर्षे ताभ्यः सप्त स्वराः श्रुतिभ्यः स्युः ।' रागविबोध verses 13–14. तार...स्वरेण accompanying the note of the chant in a voice loud (तार) and sweet. **Verse 3.** The first half contains words that apply both to हर्षचरित and पुराण. तदपि that also. मुनिगीतम् sung by sages. अतिपृथु very large. The वायुपुराण contains several thousand verses. अतिपृथु surpassing पृथु, the first king (पृथुमतिक्रान्तं). For पृथु vide notes on the 2nd verse in the 4th उ०. पावनं holy (applies to both). पावनं also means 'composed by पवन *i. e.* by वायु'. हर्ष...मिदम् this Purāṇa does not seem to me to differ from the career of Harsha. **Verse 4.** The four adjectives qualify both गीत and हर्षराज्य. वंशा...वादि that is chanted in notes that are in harmony with the flute (with गीत); where disputants follow their family *i. e.* where there are no disputes among members of the same family. वंशस्य (flute) अनुगमः ययोः तौ ०गमौ विवादिनौ (स्वरौ) यत्र; वंशस्य (family) अनुगमः येषां ते ०गमाः विवादिनः यस्मिन्. The seven स्वरs are gruped into four classes in भरत's नाट्यशास्त्र (Chap. 28. 23.) 'चतुर्विधत्वमेतेषां विज्ञेयं श्रुतियोगतः । वादी चैवाथ संवादी ह्यनुवादी विवाद्यपि ॥'. Then he says 'विवादिनस्तु ये तेषां स्याद्विंशतिकमन्तरम् । तद्यथा ऋषभगान्धारौ धैवतनिषादौ'. Those are विवादिस्वरs (*viz.* ऋषभ and गान्धार, धैवत and निषध) between which there is a difference of 20 श्रुतिs. The रागविबोध (verse 38) puts the matter differently 'एकश्रुत्यन्तरितौ विवादिनौ वैरिणौ मिथो भवतः ।'. Those are विवादिs that are separated by one श्रुति (*i. e.* ultimately 20 श्रुतिs, as there are only 22 श्रुतिs) and are destructive of the harmony of each other. स्फुटकरणं which is clearly pronounced or the rhythmie pauses of which are clear

(with गीत). स्फुटं करणं (pronunciation) यस्मिन् or स्फुटानि करणानि यस्मिन्. करणं means 'the beating of the hands to indicate the proper ताल'. मल्लिनाथ on कुमारसम्भव 6. 40 says "करणैस्तालव्यवस्थापकैस्ताडनविशेषैः । तदुक्तं राजकन्दर्पेण 'नृत्यवादित्रगीतानां प्रयोगवशभेदिनाम् । संस्थानं ताडनं रोधः करणानि प्रचक्षते ॥' इति". स्फुटानि करणानि यस्मिन् (with ०राज्यम्) in which the documents (of sale &c.) were clear (and not ambiguous). For this meaning of करण see मनु० VIII. 145. भरत... गुरु weighty (important) because of its conforming to the path of Bharata (with गीत). भरत is the reputed author of the science of dancing and music. The extant नाट्यशास्त्र claims to be his work. The chant of सुदृष्टि conformed to the rules laid down by भरत. भरत...गुरु (with राज्यं) 'that was wide because it embraced the path (the region) of Bharata.' Here there is a reference to भरतवर्ष (India) which was so named according to the वायुपुराण (chap. 33. 50–52) and the भागवतपुराण (V. 4. 9. and XI. 2. 15–17) after भरत, son of ऋषभ. According to ब्रह्मपुराण (13. 57) भरतवर्ष was named after भरत son of दुष्यन्त and शकुन्तला. श्री... र्यातम्—(1) issuing from a sweet throat (with गीत); issuing from श्रीकण्ठ. श्रीकण्ठ was the name of the country where हर्ष's ancestors ruled. श्रीयुक्तः कण्ठः श्रीकण्ठः. Or श्रीकण्ठ means शिव. Then गीत would refer to the वायुपुराण and not the chanting of it by सुदृष्टि. As all learning springs from शिव, the पुराण may also be called श्री०. हर्षराज्यम् (with गीतम्) would mean 'which is the realm of joy'. These verses serve to introduce the request made by Bāṇa's cousins. चत्वारः qualifies ०पद्माः and भ्रातरः. पितामहमुखानि एव पद्माः. Brahmā has four mouths. वेदाभ्यासेन पवित्रिताः मूर्तयः येषाम् (applies to both ०पद्माः and भ्रातरः). Each of the four Vedas was promulgated by a special mouth of Brahmā. *Vide* विष्णुपुराण I. 5. ऋग्वेद, यजुर्वेद, सामवेद and अथर्ववेद were respectively created from his four mouths beginning with the eastern. उपायाः—these are the four methods of policy in politics *viz.* साम (reconciliation), दान (bribery), भेद (internal dissensions) and दण्ड (open attack). साम...मुखाः whose mouths are charming by the repeating of the सामवेद or by adopting the policy of conciliation (with भ्रातरः); the commencement of which is charming by the employment of reconciliation (with उपायाः). साम is the first उपाय. गणपति—These are the names of बाण's cousins. भ्रातरः—connect this with परस्परस्य मुखानि व्यलोकयन्. प्रसन्न...व्याकरणेऽपि—In the world as well as in grammar they were प्रसन्नवृत्तयः &c. The words in this clause have two meanings throughout. प्रसन्ना वृत्तिः येषाम् whose conduct is gracious or mild (with लोके); whose exposition (of पाणिनि's सूत्रs) is clear (with व्याकरणे). It is not posssible to suppose that the काशिकावृत्ति of वामन and जयादित्य is referred to here. According to Itsing's statement, the काशिकावृत्ति was composed about 660 A. D. But Itsing's statements are rather confused and in our humble opinion not entitled to the weight given to them by western scholars. *Vide* Dr. Takakusu's translation of Itsing's work (Oxford 1896 pp. 175-176 for what is called वृत्तिसूत्र there). गृहीतं वाक्यं (गुरुवाक्यं आप्तवाक्यं वा) यैः that listened to the words of relatives or elders (with लोके); that had understood the Vārtikas of कात्यायन (according to the com.). वाक्य may refer also to the वाक्यपदीय of भर्तृहरि. कृतः गुरुपदे न्यासः यैः that followed in the foot-steps of their teachers or that had planted their feet on (*i. e.* had attained) an eminent position (with लोके); कृतः (अभ्यस्तः) गुरुपदेषु न्यासः यैः that studied the न्यास on difficult words (in the Sūtras of पाणिनि). न्यास is a name applied to the commentary of जिनेन्द्रबुद्धि on the काशिकावृत्ति. But it is hardly possible that Bāṇa refers to it. न्यास was a name given to several grammatical works. Bhāmaha (8th century A. D.) mentions a न्यास, which seems to be जिनेन्द्रबुद्धि's work. 'शिष्टप्रयोगमात्रेण न्यासकारमतेन वा। तृचा समस्तषष्ठीकं न कथञ्चिदुदाहरेत् ॥'. माघ in शिशु० II. 112. refers to a न्यास, वृत्ति and निबन्धन (*i. e.* महाभाष्य). न्यायवेदिनः who knew what was proper; who knew the maxims of grammar. The महाभाष्य mentions many न्यायs like the कूपखानकन्याय (vol I. p. 11), कुम्भीधान्यन्याय (vol I p. 265), अर्धजरतीयन्याय (vol II p. 231), अविरविकन्याय (vol. III. p. 124). Or न्याय means 'rules for the interpretation of the Sūtras', such as 'असिद्धं बहिरङ्गमन्तरङ्गे' (vol I. p. 26) or 'छंदोवत्सूत्राणि भवन्ति' (vol I. p. 37). सु...गुरवः (सुकृतं पुण्यं तस्य संग्रहः (सञ्चयः) तस्य अभ्यासे गुरवः) that were great in the repeated accumulation of merit; सुकृतः संग्रहस्य अभ्यासः तेन गुरवः who became teachers (of grammar) because they had well studied the संग्रह (a work of व्याडि). In the महाभाष्य, the work called संग्रह is frequently referred to 'संग्रहे एतत्प्राधान्येन परीक्षितं नित्यो वा स्यात्कार्यो वेति' (vol I. p. 6). In the days of भर्तृहरि, author of the वाक्यपदीय, the work was lost. 'प्रायेण संक्षेपरुचीनल्पविद्यापरिग्रहान्। सम्प्राप्य वैयाकरणान् संग्रहेऽस्तमुपागते ॥' वाक्यपदीय II. 484. Therefore it seems unlikely that बाण is serious when he says that his cousins had studied the संग्रह. His sole aim is to bring out similarity between लोक and व्याकरण by puns. लब्ध...शब्दाः that were called 'good' by the people; that employed only grammatically correct words. महाभारतेन भाविताः (purified) आत्मानः येषाम्. 'आर्षादिबहुधाख्यानं देवर्षिचरिताश्रयम् । इतिहासमिति प्रोक्तं भविष्यद्भूतधर्मयुक् ॥.' महा...इलिनः eager to know the stories of heroes. सुभाषितश्रवणे रसः एव रसायनं तस्मिन् अवितृष्णाः not free from desire as to the elixir *viz.* pleasure of listening to सुभाषितs. For रसायन, see p. 55. They had no desires except this. वयसि प्रथमाः foremost in years. वचसि in eloquence. महसि in (Brahmanical) lustre. यजुषि in sacrificial prayers, or in the (study of) the यजुर्वेद. पूर्व...ङ्कराः who had already made an agreement (सङ्करः) (to request बाण to tell the story of Harsha's life). विवक्षवः = वक्तुम् इच्छवः. स्मितं एव सुधा तया धवलितं कपोलोदरं येषाम्

P. 40 l. 6–**P. 41** l. 4. **अथ...मभूत्.** कमलदलवत् दीर्घे लोचने यस्य. दत्ता संज्ञा यस्मै to whom a signal was given. दशनानां ज्योत्स्नया स्नपिताः ककुभः येन. The rays of his white teeth resembled moonlight. द्विजानां...कार्षीत् The moon, lord of *dvijas*, carried off the wife of his preceptor. In this and the following sentences, the author finds various faults in the kings and heroes of old to show that only Harsha is spotless. Some of the blemishes, however, are merely verbal. 'द्विजराजः शशधरः नक्षत्रेशः क्षपाकरः' इत्यमरः. गुरुदारग्रहण is a महापातक. *Vide* notes p. 160. It is to be noted that this passage up to युधिष्ठिरः &c. corresponds almost *verbatim* with a passage in the वासवदत्ता of सुबन्धु, where however there is no reference to मान्धाता, सौदास, मरुत्त, पाण्डु and पृथु. Our humble opinion is that examples had already been collected in works that preceded सुबन्धु and बाण and that both derived their inspiration from them. If there is any borrowing between the two, then it is बाण that borrows. बाण adds to the list and also to the phraseology employed in the वासवदत्ता, as we shall show later on. *Vide* Hall's Vāsavadattā pp. 273-276 and pp. 337–340 of the Srīrangam edition. सोम performed राजसूय and became conceited. He carried away तारा, the wife of बृहस्पति, and did not give her back though asked by Brahmā to do so. He had a son from her named बुध. *Vide* विष्णुपु॰ IV. 6. See 'सकलजगद्गीयमानबुधकर्णानन्दकारिणौ सोमसूर्यवंशाविव' हर्ष॰ 4th उ॰ and notes thereon. दयिते...त was separated from Āyus, dear to him. आयुस् means 'life' also. आयुस् was the son of पुरूरवस् and उर्वशी. The com. gives the story alluded to here as follows:—'पुरूरवाः पूर्वां दिशं जेतुं गच्छन्केनाप्याहृतप्रभूतधनेन विप्रेण यज्ञे निमन्त्रितो लोभाक्षिप्तस्तद्धनं जिहीर्षुस्तच्छापान्नष्टः । तस्मिन्मृते स विप्रो नृपं विना प्रजा

निवर्तेते इति ज्ञात्वा तदायुषा राजर्षिमायुर्नामानमजीजनदिति'. In the वासवदत्ता we have 'पुरूरवा ब्राह्मणधनतृष्णया विननाश.' नहुष...आसीत्—नहुष, desiring another's wife, became a great serpent. Note that भुजङ्ग also means 'a lewd or dissolute person'. नहुष was the eldest son of आयुः. When Indra ran away through fear of the sin of ब्रह्महत्या in killing वृत्र, नहुष, who had performed numerous sacrifices, was appointed इन्द्र by the gods. In his vanity he cast lustful eyes on शची, the wife of इन्द्र. At the advice of बृहस्पति, she agreed to yield to his wishes if he would come to her in a palanquin carried by sages. While coming in that way, he struck अगस्त्य, who was slow, with his foot urging him to greater speed with the words 'सर्प सर्प'. Then अगस्त्य cursed him to be a सर्प. *Vide* महाभारत वनपर्व Chapter 181. Compare रघु० 13. 36. 'भ्रूभेदमात्रेण पदान्मघोनः प्रभ्रंशयां यो नहुषं चकार ।'. ययाति was the second son of नहुष and married देवयानी, the daughter of शुक्र, who was a ब्राह्मण. आहितं ब्राह्मण्याः पाणिग्रहणं येन—Who took the hand of a Brāhmaṇa girl (*i. e.* married her); who held a ब्राह्मणी (देवयानी) in his hand (when rescuing her from a well). पपात fell off from caste usages; perished (*i. e.* became prematurely old). A male belonging to any one of the four Varṇas could marry a girl of the same Varṇa as himself or of a lower Varṇa; but was forbidden to marry one of a higher वर्ण. Compare what ययाति himself says 'अविवाह्या हि राजानो देवयानि पितुस्तव ।' आदि० 81. 18. ययाति being a क्षत्रिय, there could be no marriage between him and देवयानी, who was a ब्राह्मणी, according to caste usages. Therefore he incurred sin. शुक्र was the preceptor of वृषपर्वा, king of the असुरs. The latter's daughter शर्मिष्ठा quarrelled with देवयानी and threw her in a well. ययाति, while hunting, found her there and took her out with his hand. वृषपर्वा, afraid of शुक्र's curse, wanted to please her. She demanded that his daughter शर्मिष्ठा should be her slave. शुक्र, seeing that his daughter loved ययाति, consented to their marriage. Seeing शर्मिष्ठा in her service, he secretly married her also. When देवयानी complained to her father of ययाति's faithlessness he cursed him to be prematurely old. It will be seen from the above that marrying a ब्राह्मणी was not the *cause* of ययाति's premature old age; but that the latter was only an incident that occurred later on. बाण of course presses it in his service to find fault with ययाति. *Vide* महाभारत आदिपर्व chap. 78–83. Note 'तामथो ब्राह्मणीं राजा विज्ञाय नहुषा-

त्मजः । गृहीत्वा दक्षिणे पाणावुज्जहार ततोऽवटात् ॥ chap. 78. 22. स्त्रीमय एवाभवत्—there are three senses; (1) he was born a woman; (2) he became a woman; (3) he could think of nothing but women *i. e.* he was extremely lascivious. The last is the fault found in him. The first two are matters of mythology. See the following from विष्णुपुराण IV. 1. 8. *ff.* 'इष्टिं च मित्रावरुणयोर्मनुः पुत्रकामश्चकार । तत्रापहृते होतुरपचारादिला नाम कन्या बभूव ॥ सैव मित्रावरुणप्रसादात्सुद्युम्नो नाम मनोः पुत्रो मैत्रेयासीत्पुनश्चेश्वरकोपात् स्त्री सती सोमसूनोर्बुधस्याश्रमसमीपे बभ्राम ।.' *Vide* also मार्कण्डेयपु० chap. 111. सुद्युम्न, when hunting, trespassed upon a grove sacred to पार्वती who was promised by शिव that whoever trespassed on the spot where it was would become a female. सुद्युम्न then again became a female. See भागवत पुराण 9.1. जन्तु...निर्घृणता cruelty of killing living beings; cruelty in killing (his own son) जन्तु. सोमक had 100 wives and only one son in old age. The son जन्तु was once bitten by an ant and the whole royal family was very much distressed and therefore he wanted a hundred sons. 'धिगस्त्विहैकपुत्रत्वमपुत्रत्वं वरं भवेत् ।' वनपर्व chap. 127. 12. He sacrificed his only son and after smelling the smoke of his fat his queens gave birth to a 100 sons. The com. gives the story "सोमकस्य राज्ञो जन्तुर्नाम एकः पुत्रोऽभूत् । स च एकपुत्रत्वादपुत्रत्वं वरमिति जानन्नुद्विग्नः पुरोधसा अभ्यधायि 'बहून्पुत्रांश्चेदिच्छसि तदस्य सुतस्य वपया होमः क्रियताम् । ततो यावत्यो धूममाजिघ्रन्ति ताः पुत्रैर्युज्यन्ते' इति । स चापि घृणामपहाय तथा कारितवानिति ।." See वनपर्व chap. 127–128. मार्गणव्यसनेन—by his great liking for arrows (*i. e.* for fighting); by his vice of begging. रसातलमगात्—went to पाताल; perished. रसातल is one of the seven पातालs, अतल, वितल, सुतल, महीतल, रसातल, तलातल and पाताल. मान्धाता, son of युवनाश्व, conquered the earth and wanted to vanquish इन्द्र. Indra offered to hand over his kingdom when he would conquer the demon लवण. So मान्धाता attacked लवण, who had secured a शूल of miraculous powers from शिव. मान्धाता perished with all his army in the fight against लवण. *Vide* रामायण उत्तरकाण्ड chap. 67. The रामायण does not mention that the son and grandson of मान्धाता accompanied him in the fight. पुरुकुत्सः...करोत्—पुरुकुत्स, though practising penance, committed a bad deed on the daughter of मेकल (the suggestion being that he had intercourse with a कन्यका a maiden). मेकलकन्यका means the river नर्मदा. पुरुकुत्स was guilty of bad conduct while practising penance on the Narmadâ. The com. says 'पुरुकुत्सः पुरा तपश्चरन्नर्मदायां स्नानं कुर्वन्काम्यप्यङ्गनामालोक्य कामाविष्टो नीतिमुत्ससर्ज'. The वासदत्ता has 'पुरुकुत्सः

कुत्सित एवाभवत्.' कुवलयाश्वः—According to the मार्कण्डेयपुराण (chap. 20 ff.) the king ऋतध्वज had secured a horse named कुवलय. He pursued a demon that had disturbed the sage गालव in his austerities and went to पाताल. After various incidents which need not be detailed here, he married मदालसा, daughter of a नाग अश्वतर. भुज...ग्रहात् by resorting to the world of नागs (*viz.* पाताल); by associating with भुजङ्गs (rakes). अश्वतरकन्या means 'the daughter of a mule'. न परिजहार did not omit. The com. gives the story differently 'कुवलयाश्वो राजा मृगयाक्रीडनप्रसङ्गेन घर्मातुरो मज्जनरभसेन सरसीमवतीर्णो रसातलं प्राप्तोऽश्वतराभिधां नागकन्यामूढवानिति'. The वासदत्ता has 'कुवलयाश्वो अश्वतरकन्यामपि जगाम.' प्रथमपुरुषकः the first man; foremost of bad men. क is added according to 'कुत्सिते' पा. 5. 3. 74. कुत्सितः पुरुषः पुरुषकः. परि... पृथिवीम् violated पृथिवी; humbled the earth. पृथु was the first king. During his reign, on account of a draught, people were dying of hunger and the earth yielded nothing. People came to him. He took his bow, when the earth assumed the form of a cow and ran away. Then पृथु pursued her and got from her whatever he desired. *Vide* विष्णुपु० I. 13. कृकलासभावे in being a chameleon (Marathi सरडा). वर्णसङ्करः—a combination of colours; confusion of castes (by intermarriage). It is well-known that the chameleon changes the colours of its skin. वर्णसङ्कर was looked upon as sinful. Compare गीता I. 42. 'सङ्करो नरकायैव.' नृग gave by mistake the cow belonging to one ब्राह्मण to another. The real owner and the donee had a dispute and came to the king's palace to get it settled. नृग, being absorbed in pleasures, did not see them for many days. They cursed him. 'अर्थिनां कार्यसिद्ध्यर्थं यस्मात्त्वं नैषि दर्शनम्। अदृश्यः सर्वभूतानां कृकलासो भविष्यसि ॥' रामायण उत्तरकाण्ड Chap. 53. 18. The वासदत्ता says 'नृगः कृकलासतामगमत्.' सौदा...क्षितिः by सौदास the earth was not protected but (only) disturbed or agitated. न रक्षिता (goes with क्षितिः). नरक्षिता (instru. sing. of नरक्षित्) will also mean 'who killed human beings' (with सौदासेन). To protect the earth is the first duty of a king. 'क्षत्रियस्य परो धर्मः प्रजानामेव पालनम्' मनु० 7. 144. King सौदास also called कल्माषपाद, when tired by hunting, asked a sage named शक्ति the eldest son of वसिष्ठ to make way for him on a road. When he did not move the king whipped him, whereupon the sage cursed him to be a राक्षस subsisting on human flesh. नरान् क्षिणोति इति नरक्षित्. See महाभारत आदिपर्व chap. 176. नलम्—the story of नल is well-known. अवशं अक्षहृदयं यस्य who was not master of the secret of managing dice. गृहीत्वा चाश्वहृदयं राजन्भाङ्गासुरिर्नृपः ॥ निषधाधिपतेश्चापि दत्वाक्षहृदयं नृपः ।' वनपर्व Chap. 77. 18–19. अवशानि अक्षाणि हृदयं च यस्य whose heart and senses were not under his control. This is the fault found in him and also that कलि overcame him (while हर्ष had controlled his senses and his reign was an era of righteousness). दमयन्ती chose नल, though even gods like इन्द्र had attended the स्वयंवर. कलि enraged at this entered the body of नल. नल became addicted to gambling, lost his kingdom in favour of his brother who was an expert in gambling, and had to leave his country. After various vicissitudes, he learnt अक्षहृदय from ऋतुपर्ण and regained his wife, kingdom &c. *Vide* वनपर्व Chap. 53–77. The वासवदत्ता has 'नलः कलिनाभिभूतः.' मित्र ...गात् had his mind disturbed in regard to the daughter of मित्र; had a weakness for his friend's daughter. The last is the fault found in him. One's friend's daughter should be like one's own daughter. संवरण—सूर्य had a daughter named तपती, who was married by king संवरण who was a devotee of the sun. *Vide* आदिपर्व Chap. 171–173. इष्टः (प्रियः) रामः तस्य उन्मादेन (intense love); इष्टा रामा (a handsome woman) तस्याः उन्मादेन (by his mad love for). The latter is the fault found in दशरथ. दशरथ died when राम left for the forest to keep his father's promise given to कैकेयी. कार्तवीर्यः refers to सहस्रार्जुन. A king, according to ancient ideas, should be गोब्राह्मणप्रतिपालक and not ०पीडक. गो...पीडनेन also means 'by troubling a ब्राह्मण for a cow'. कार्तवीर्य, a king of माहिष्मती on the नर्मदा, took away the calf of the कामधेनु of जमदग्नि, father of परशुराम. परशुराम killed him. His sons killed जमदग्नि when परशुराम in revenge took the vow of destroying the क्षत्रिय race. *Vide* वनपर्व chap. 115–117. इष्टं बहु सुवर्णं यस्य to whom plenty of gold was dear. इष्टः बहुसुवर्णकः येन who performed a sacrifice called बहुसुवर्णक (in which there was gold and nothing else. *i. e.* in which the utensils were of gold and gold was distributed like water). देवानां द्विजः बृहस्पतिः तस्य बहुमतः (liked); देवानां द्विजानां च बहुमतः. The fault found in him is that he was not देव...मतः (while हर्ष was देवद्विजबहुमत). *Vide* विष्णुपु० IV. 1. 'मरुत्तस्य यथा यज्ञस्तथा कस्याभवद्भुवि । सर्वं हिरण्मयं यस्य यज्ञवस्त्वतिशोभितम् ॥ अमाद्यदिन्द्रः सोमेन दक्षिणाभिर्द्विजातयः । मरुतः परिवेष्टारः सदस्याश्च दिवौकसः ॥ 18–19. The verse मरुतः परिवेष्टारो मरुत्तस्या &c. is well-known to every Brāhmaṇa. मरुत्त desiring to rival इन्द्र asked बृहस्पति to officiate at his sacrifice, but the latter refused. So he had it performed by बृहस्पति's brother संवर्त. बृहस्पति was very much pained at the prosperity of मरुत्त. *Vide* chap. 8. 36. *Vide* महाभारत आश्वमेधिकपर्व chap. 6–10. For शन्तनु see above p. 153. अतिव्यसनात् through extreme attachment. वियुक्तो वाहिन्या separated from the river (Ganges); separated from his army. One who is separated from an army is left all alone (एकाकी). To cry because he was left alone does not become a great king. The वासवदत्ता has 'शन्तनुरतिव्यसनाद्वने विललाप.' वन—means 'forest' (with पाण्डु) and 'water' (with मत्स्य). मदनरसेन आविष्टः overwhelmed by the passion of love; that has tasted the fruit of the मदन tree. For this story see आदिपर्व chap. 125. He had been cursed by sage किन्दम that he would die when he had intercourse with his wife. गुरु...हृदयः whose heart was despondent through fear (of the prowess) of his teacher (द्रोणाचार्य). गुरुभय also means 'great fear'. It does behove a king to give up truth through fear, however great it may be. When द्रोण made a terrible havoc in the Pāṇḍava hosts, a rumour spread that अश्वत्थामा (son of द्रोण) was killed. द्रोण who believed implicitly in the truthfulness of युधिष्ठिर asked him what the truth was. यु०, who knew that it was only an elephant named अश्वत्थामा that was killed, said 'हतः कुञ्जरः,' the latter word being uttered in a very low tone. The old man heard only the first word, laid aside his weapon in grief, when धृष्टद्युम्न killed him. *Vide* द्रोणपर्व chap. 190. Compare 'मुक्तशस्त्रं कलशयोनिमिव कृष्णवर्त्मप्रसूतिः' हर्ष० 6thउ०. The वासवदत्ता omits 'गुरु...हृदयः'. इत्थ...कलङ्कम् thus there has been no king without (some) stain. अपगतः कलङ्कः यस्मात्. ऋते except (governs the ablative). तथाहि—Here follow several sentences in which बाण shows by श्लिष्ट words how हर्ष emulates the deeds of gods and heroes of old. बल...भृतः (1) by Indra, the moving mountains possessed of wings (पक्षः) were made steady; by Harsha who subdues armies, fickle kings, that had formed coalitions, were paralysed. In this sentence the king is shown as doing what इन्द्र did. For the cutting off of the wings of mountains, see p. 84. अत्र...कृता (1) By Brahmā (प्रजापति) the earth (क्ष्मा) was placed over the hoods of the serpent (भोगिन्) शेष; by (हर्ष) the lord of the people, forgiveness was shown to the circle of the remaining kings. For शेष, see above p. 145. अत्र पुरु...कृता (1) Vishṇu, having churned the ocean-king (*viz.* क्षीरसागर), made लक्ष्मी his own (wife); by (हर्ष) the best of men, glory was made his by vanquishing the king of सिन्धु. सिन्धु—country on the Sindhu river. There is a reference to the conquests of हर्ष

in this and some of the following sentences. बलिना...नागः By Bali (king of असुरs) the great serpent (वासुकि) was let loose, who (वासुकि) had unloosened up his coils round the mountain (मन्दर); by the powerful Harsha, the great elephant (दर्पशात) was abandoned (in the forest), having loosened a king from the coils (of the trunk). वासुकि was the rope in the सागरमथन, while मन्दर mountain (भूभृत्) was the churniug handle, which must have had round it the coils of वासुकि. The churning was done both by gods and demons. Compare 'मन्दरमिव सुरासुररभसभ्रमितवासुकिकषणक्षीणेन' हर्ष० 4th उ०. मोचितं भूभृतः वेष्टनं येन. As to the reference to हर्ष the com. says 'श्रीकुमारो नाम राजा किल दर्पशातेनोपजातमदेन हस्तिना वेष्टितः ततः श्रीहर्षेणाकृष्य खङ्गं तस्मान्मोचितोऽसौ दन्ती च रोषाद्वने परित्यक्त इति वार्ता.' देवे...कुमारः—by God, कार्तिकेय was crowned (as the commander-in-chief of the gods against the demon तारक); by the Lord (हर्ष), कुमार was crowned. This may refer to the fact that हर्ष crowned his own son in his life-time. We think, however, that the reference is rather to some other prince. It may be कुमारगुप्त, the elder of the two princes of Mālava, that were the companions of Harsha in his boyhood. Or कुमार may be the king of प्राग्ज्योतिष referred to in the 7th उच्छ्वास. स्वामि... शक्तिः by कार्तिकेय who felled the enemy with one stroke, his weapon (called शक्ति) was made famous; by the lord (हर्ष) who destroyed his enemies at one stroke, his prowess was made known. स्वामी is a name of कार्तिकेय. He wielded a weapon called शक्ति and killed the demon तारक. कार्तिकेय is also called शक्तिधर. नरसिंहेन...क्रमः—नरसिंह (Vishṇu in his man-lion *avatara*) that killed his foe (हिरण्यकशिपु) with his own hand (not with weapons) manifested his valour; the best of men (हर्ष), who destroyed his enemies in person (not with the help of an army), showed his might. Perhaps the word विक्रम (which means 'a footstep') contains an allusion to the वामनावतार. परमेश्व... कर:—the great शिव took the hand of (*i. e.* married) Durgā the daughter of Himālaya; by the great Lord (हर्ष) tribute (करः) was levied from the inaccessible (दुर्ग) Himālaya regions. According to Buhler this passage refers to Harsha's conquest of Nepal. लोक... विभक्तः by Brahmā guardians of the world were appointed in the quarters and the treasures of the world were divided among the first-born (kings). 'हिरण्यगर्भो लोकेशः स्वयम्भूश्चतुराननः' इत्यमरः. For लोकपाल, see above p 140. भुवनकोश means the whole universe or world. अग्रजन्मनाम् the kings like मनु and पृथु that were first born. लोक...विभक्तः by the lord of the world (हर्ष), guardians of the people (great officers) were appointed in the regions and the treasure collected (by taxation) from the whole world was distributed among Brāhmaṇas. For this distribution, vide Intro. XL and notes p. 146. There is a third meaning suggested. लोकनाथ means बुद्ध. कोश is the Buddhist dictionary of वसुबन्धु. Compare 'शुकैरपि शाक्यशासनकुशलैः कोशं समुपदिशद्भिः' हर्ष० 8th उ० 5th para. महासमारम्भाः Great beginnings (with कृतयुग); great undertakings or efforts (with हर्ष). The propriety of प्रथम is this. According to Pauranic accounts, the present is the 7th Manu called वैवस्वत. Fourteen Manus are equal to a day of ब्रह्मा, which latter again is equal to 1000 महायुगs (constituted by the four युगs, कृत, त्रेता, द्वापर and कलि). A day of ब्रह्मा is called कल्प. It will be seen therefore that numerous कृतयुगs have passed away since the world began. In the first कृतयुग, however, very great beginnings had to be made as everything was new; the earth had to be made steady &c.; in the succeeding ones there were no such great beginnings. पूर्व...क्रमेण in the order of the lineage of his ancestors. सु...माणानाम् It is long since we entertained the desire to hear. अयस्कान्तमणयः magnets. नीरस-निष्ठुराणि—dry and hard (with लोहानि); without taste (apprecia-tion) and harsh (with मनांसि). क्षुल्लकानाम् of insignificant (or mean) persons. स्वभावेन सरसानि (affectionate, appreciative) मृदूनि च. These two words are the opposite of नीरस and निष्ठुर. इतरेषाम् of those who are not क्षुल्लक. भार्गवो वंशः—we saw above (text p. 17 l. 29) that Bāṇa's ancestor वत्स belonged to the भार्गववंश.

P. 41 ll. 5—18 बाणस्तु...यासीत्. न...हितम् you did not say what would be reasonable (or fit). The idea is that it does not stand to reason that a puny narrator like बाण could narrate the wondrous tale of Harsha's life. अघटमानः मनोरथः यस्मिन्. अघट...कल्प-यामि I am of opinion that your curiosity cannot secure its object. शक्या...तृषः those who are eager to secure their object are generally wanting in the proper estimate as to what is possible and what is not possible. स्वार्थे तृट् येषां ते ०तृषः or स्वार्थाय तृष्यन्ति ते ०तृषः or तृषः may mean simply 'desires'. प्रियजनकथायाः श्रवणे रसः (passion, liking) तस्य रभसेन (excess) मोहिता. प्रविवेक—judgment. क्व-क्व Two क्वs show great disparity or incongruity between two things. परमाणोरिव परिमाणं यस्य the capacity of which is as small as that of an atom. बटुहृदयम्—refers to Bāṇa. For ब्रह्मस्तम्भ, see above p. 102. परिमितेषु वर्णेषु वृत्तिः (वर्तनं, जीवनं) येषाम् that are produced by a small number of letters; that subsist upon &c. The letters of the alphabet which go to make up words are very few. संख्यामतिगच्छन्ति numberless. वाचस्पतेः = बृहस्पतेः. अगोचरः = अविषयः. सरस्व...भारः even the goddess of speech will find this (narration of हर्षचरित) a very heavy burden. अविकलम् entire. एक...वयम् if your curiosity will be satisfied with a part, then I am ready. अधिगताः कतिपयाक्षरलवाः तैः लघीयसी which is light by having acquired a few drops of letters. जिह्वा was originally जड (when बाण was a child), but later on it acquired agility. What is nimble can turn in any direction. किमन्यत्—what more (can be desired)? This is the best combination to induce a person to wax eloquent. परि...दिवसः the day is almost ended. पश्चाल्लम्बमानाः कपिलकिरणाः एव जटाभारः तेन भास्वरः—(1) brilliant with the tawny rays, resembling matted hair, that hang down in the west (with पूषा); brilliant with matted hair hanging behind resembling the tawny rays of the evening sun (with रामः). भगवान् goes with रामः and पूषा. भार्गवो रामः—Rāma of the भृगु race *viz.* परशुराम. महाह्रदे in the great lake. निमज्जति sinks; bathes. पूषा the sun. समन्त...ह्रदे—As to the extirpation of the क्षत्रियs by परशुराम, see 'परशुराममिव क्षत्रक्षपणक्षीणपरशुपाशचिह्नितं' हर्ष०4th उ० and notes thereon. परशुराम accumulated the blood of the slaughtered क्षत्रियs in five lakes. 'त्रिःसप्तकृत्वा पृथिवीं कृत्वा निःक्षत्रियां प्रभुः। समन्तपञ्चके पञ्च चकार रुधिरह्रदान्॥ स तेषु तर्पयामास भृगून् भृगुकुलोद्वहः।' वनपर्व 117. 9–10; see also आदिपर्व 2. 3–5. Bāṇa very frequently refers to the story of परशुराम. समन्तपञ्चक was in कुरुक्षेत्र. Compare 'जामदग्न्येन च शाम्यन्मन्युशिखिशिखासङ्वरसुखायमानस्पर्शशीतलेषु क्षत्रियक्षतजह्रदेष्वस्नायि' हर्ष० 6th उ०. तथा...पद्यन्त they assented with the words 'let it be so'.

P. 41 ll. 19—32 **अथ...गच्छत्.** The first sentence is 'अथ... प्रदोषारम्भे...बन्धुमिश्र सार्धं तयैव गोष्ठ्या तस्थौ (बाणः). मधुमदेन (by the intoxication of wine) पल्लविताः (reddish) मालवीकपोलाः तद्वत् कोमलः आतपः (glow) यस्य. मालवी a lady from Malva. मुकुलितेऽह्नि when the day had closed (*lit.* folded itself like a bud). कम...लम्बमाने when the sun hung down kissing darkness, being very red as though through the closing of the lotus plants. The idea is:—when the sun was about to set, the day lotuses closed their petals. The poet fancies that the sun, on finding that the कमलिनीs did not respond to his feelings, became angry (red) and began to kiss darkness instead (in revenge against the कमलिनीs). रवि...तमसि when darkness came hurrying on in the sky following the track of the horses of the Sun, as though it (तमः) were Yama's buffalo. The simple idea is that the east first became dark and that darkness gradually spread over the whole sky up to the western horizon. A buffalo is dark and Yama's buffalo must be particularly so. गृह...वल्कलेषु when the bark garments hanging from the roofs (पटलं) of the huts (कुटीरकः) of house ascetics were removed along with the patches (च्छेदः) of the red sunglow. Ascetics may wander from place to place or may have a fixed abode. They had exposed the garments for drying and removed them at nightfall. The lingering red glow also vanished. कलेः कल्मषं (पापं) मुष्णाति इति °मुष् तस्मिन्. पुष्णति *loc. sing* of *pr. p.* of पुष् 9th con. गगनं object of पुष्णति. कलि...धूमे when the smoke issuing from the places where the sacred fire was kindled filled *(lit.* nourished) the sky, the smoke that removed the sins of the Kali age. सनियमे that had undertaken the performance of some vow. 'नियमस्तु स यत्कर्मानित्यमागन्तुसाधनम्' इत्यमरः. मौनव्रतं अस्ति अस्य इति °व्रतिन्. वि...लोले restless because it was the time for amusing themselves (by moving about here and there). Just when the sun went down, the house-wives had some time which they spent in strolling about. विकीर्यमाणाः हरिताः श्यामाकशालिपूलिकाः यासाम् before whom were spread green bundles of the hay of श्यामाक corn. दुग्धासु that had been milked. कपिला a cow (from its tawny colour). वैतान sacrificial (from वितान). 'क्रतुविस्तारयोरस्त्री वितानम्' इत्यमरः. तनूनपात् = अग्निः (तनूं देहं न पातयति इति). पूते विष्टरे (आसने) उपविष्टे. कृष्णाजिनेन जटिले looking hairy with antelope skin. जटिन् ascetic wearing matted hair. ब्रह्मासनं अध्यास्ते इति °सिन्. ब्रह्मासन means a posture of the body for profound meditation. It seems that ब्रह्मासन was a generic name applicable to any आसन, such as पद्मासन. 'ध्यानयोगासने ब्रह्मासनम्' अमरः (ब्रह्मणः सम्बन्धि आसनं ब्रह्मासनम्; ध्यानस्य योगः उपायः ध्यानमेव योगः इति वा तस्यासनम्). Some define it as 'एकपादमुरौ दत्त्वा तिष्ठेद्दण्डाकृतिर्भवेत्'. तालध्वनिभिः धावमानाः अन्तेवासिनः शिष्याः यस्मिन्. The meaning is that the disciples came running and clapping their hands (as boys would do) or that the disciples came running, being called by the clapping of their preceptors' hands. अलस...मतेन under the supervision *(lit.* with the permission) of languid and old teachers of the Veda. गलन्तः ग्रन्थदण्डकाः तान् उद्गिरति इति or गलन्तः ग्रन्थदण्डकाः यथा

स्युः तथा उद्गिरति इति that recited (*lit.* emitted) disconnected lines (दण्डकः) of the text or that recited the texts in such a way that many lines were dropped (in the effort to recite). The idea seems to be this:—naughty and dull boys were called upon by their wearied old teachers to perform सन्ध्यावन्दन either by repeating what the teacher would himself first pronounce or by repeating what they had been taught before. In this process the careless boys omitted certain portions and loudly repeated the rest. The old and wearied preceptors did not seem to notice the lapses of the students. सन्ध्यां...यति that listened to the evening prayer. The reading समवधीरयति is in one way better, meaning 'that treated with contempt the evening prayer.' वठरः dullard; compare 'मुनिनाथोऽपि...कृपावानात्मानं वठरसत्त्वेभ्यः कतिकृत्वो न दत्तवान्' हर्ष० 8th उ०. विटः sensualist, dandy. तारका आख्या (name) यस्य (*adj.* of ज्योतिषि). समुन्म...खे (*lit.*) when in the sky (खं) emerged the lights called stars *i. e.* when the stars began to twinkle. तथै...तस्थौ he stood in the same company (as before). नीतः प्रथमः यामः (प्रहरः) येन who passed the first part of the night. गणपतेः—गणपति was one of the four cousins of बाण mentioned above (text p. 39 l. 30). निमीलिता (closed) दृक् (eye) येषां. अनुपजाता निद्रा येषाम्—They could not sleep (through expectant curiosity) though they closed their eyes. सूर्यो...लयताम् that waited for the rise of the sun. कमलs also close their buds at night and wait for सूर्योदय when they bloom.

P. 41 l. 33—**P. 42** l. 12 **अथ...रेभे.** तुर्ये चतुर्थे. प्रतिबुद्धः waking up. **Verse 5**. This is cited by the काव्यप्रकाश as an instance of the figure स्वभावोक्ति. For जाति or स्वभावोक्ति *vide* notes p. 4. The principal sentence is तुरङ्गः क्ष्मां (पृथ्वीं) खुरेण विलिखति (paws, scratches). पश्चा...सार्य having stretched his foot behind. त्रिक...मुच्चैः having lengthened out upwards his body that was stretched (to full length) by bending the lower part of the spine. 'पृष्ठवंशाधरे त्रिकम्' अमरः (पृष्ठास्थ्नोऽध ऊर्वोः सन्धौ त्रिसङ्घट्टस्त्रिकम्—क्षीर०). विततं *adj.* of अङ्गम् or we may take it as an अव्ययीभाव. त्रिकस्य नत्या विततं यथा स्यात्तथा. द्राघयति is a denominative verb from दीर्घ. आस...रसि with bent (आभुग्न) neck having rested his mouth on his chest. सटां...धूय having tossed his mane grey with dust. घासः fodder. अनवरतं चलत् प्रोथं यस्य तत् अ...प्रोथं ०प्रोथं तुण्डं यस्य सः ०तुण्डः (nostril). 'घोणा तु प्रोथमस्त्रियाम्' अमरः. मन्दं शब्दायमानः gently neighing. शब्दं करोति इति शब्दायते, according to 'शब्दवैरकलहाभ्रकण्वमेघेभ्यः करणे' पा. 3. 1. 17. The metre is स्रग्धरा. **Verse 6**.

कुर्वन् (तुरङ्गः)—the object is कन्धराम् (neck). आभुग्नं पृष्ठं यस्य. मुख...कटिः bringing his loins near his mouth. आतिरश्चीम् curved sideways. लोलेना...केसरेण that (कोण) was struck with his restless and waving mane that dropped down particles of dew (तुहिनं). केसर is that part of the mane which is on the forehead. निद्रा...कषायम् that was reddish through the itch after sleep (or through sleep and itch). कषति—the subject is तुरङ्गः and the object is कोणम्. निबिडिता श्रोत्रशुक्तिः येन that closed his shell-like ears (with his mane). त्वङ्गन्ति पक्ष्माग्राणि तेषु लग्नाः प्रतनुबुसकणाः यस्मिन् (the corner of the eye) on the restless lashes of which stuck small particles of chaff. खुरेण—is to be connected with कषति. The metre is स्रग्धरा. ज्ञातयः=बान्धवाः. पूर्वो...प्रायः who understood their intention by the discussion that had already taken place. उद्घातः allusion, reference.

P. 42 l. 13—**P. 43** l. 12. श्रूयताम्...जनपदः. The principal sentence is अस्ति...श्रीकण्ठो नाम जनपदः. पुण्य...तीर्णः which was inhabited by the meritorious, as though it were the abode (आवासः) of Indra descended upon the earth. पुण्यकृत् also means 'gods'. It was believed that those who accumulated merit by the performance of sacrifices went to Indra's heaven and returned to the earth when their merit was exhausted. Compare 'त्रैविद्या मां सोमपाः पूतपापा यज्ञैरिष्ट्वा स्वर्गतिं प्रार्थयन्ते। ते पुण्यमासाद्य सुरेन्द्रलोकमश्नन्ति दिव्यान्दिवि देवभोगान्॥ ते तं भुक्त्वा स्वर्गलोकं विशालं क्षीणे पुण्ये मर्त्यलोकं विशन्ति।' भगवद्गीता Chap. IX. 20-21. असङ्कीर्णे वर्णानां व्यवहारस्थिती (व्यवहारः स्थितिश्च) यस्मिन् where the practices and usages of the (four) Varṇas were not confused. कृतयुगस्येव व्यवस्था यस्मिन्. In कृतयुग there was no वर्णसङ्कर, nor was there any in the country of श्रीकण्ठ. If we read कृतकृत॰, then we dissolve as कृता कृतयुगस्य व्यवस्था यस्मिन्. स्थल...क्षेत्रः abounding as it did in land lotuses, its fields were broken by ploughs (हलम्) the points (पोत्रं) of which uprooted lotus fibres and which caused a humming of bees, as though they (हल) sang the excellent (सार) qualities of the soil. स्थलकमल—distinguish them from water-lotuses, that are simply कमलs. पोत्रैः उन्मूल्यमानानि मृणालानि येषाम्. 'मुखाग्रे क्रोडहलयोः पोत्रम्' अमरः. उद्गीताः मेदिन्याः साराः गुणाः यैः. There is a श्लेष on the word गुण (quality, string). The मृणालs are गुणs. The poet fancies that the hum of bees on the lotuses that were uprooted is a song declaring the fertility of the soil. उल्लिख्यमानानि क्षेत्राणि यस्य. क्षीरो...न्तरः that was dense with rows of plantations (वाटः-टम्) of Puṇḍra sugarcane, as though they

(rows) were watered by clouds that had drunk the waters of the milky ocean. पुण्ड्र is a very sweet variety of sugar-cane. The poet fancies that the sweetness must be due to their being watered by clouds from क्षीरसागर (and not from the salt ocean). It is a general rule that the qualities of effects arise from similar qualities in their causes. Compare 'कारणगुणपूर्वकः कार्यगुणो दृष्टः' वैशेषिकसूत्र II. 1. 24 or the न्याय 'कारणगुणा हि कार्यगुणानारभन्ते.' प्रति...सीमान्तः the borders of which were in every direction crowded (सङ्कट) with heaps of corn, as though they were strange hills, separated (from each other) by threshing floors. खलधानं threshing floor. धामन् *n.* place. The heaps were big like hills. The com. says 'खलधानधामभिः खलपालैः' *i. e.* it takes it to mean 'by the owners or watchmen of the threshing floors.' (खलधानं धाम येषाम्). This is not good. सम...भूमिः the ground of which was thickly covered (जटिलित) with beds of cumin seed (जीरकः) being watered by the pots of the water-wheel. क्षीर० says that, according to कौटिल्य, उद्घातन means 'घटीयन्त्र.' We must ascribe the same sense to उद्घात. 'उद्घाटनं घटीयन्त्रम्' अमरः. उर्वरा...कृतः adorned with rice fields extending (beyond their proper limits) on account of the very fertile soil. 'उर्वरा सर्वसस्याढ्या' अमरः. For शालेय see p. 118. वरीयः is the comparative of उरु. The idea is:—the land surrounding the rice fields also was fertile and so beyond the fields proper grew ricecrops due to the fact that some grains were carried away by the birds or by the ants and grew luxuriantly there. पाक...छितः that had stretches of wheat fields (गोधूमधामन्) variegated (किर्मीरित) by heaps of *Rājamāsha* beans bursting as they were ripe and rendered brown (कपिशित) by the split pods of *mudga.* मुद्ग is Marathi मूग. पाकेन विशरारवः राजमाषाः तेषां निकरैः किर्मीरितानि तैः. The next clause is महिष...विपिनः. महिषपृष्ठे प्रतिष्ठिताः (mounted) गायन्तः गोपालाः तैः पालितानि तैः *(adj.* of गोधनैः). कीट...सृतैः (गोधनैः) that were followed by sparrows greedy (लम्पट) for the swarms of insects. The insects (probably flies) pursued the cows (as they had ulcers on their backs or feet &c.) and were in their turn pursued by चटकाs. अवटुः (ग्रीवा) तस्यां घटिताः घण्टाः एव घट्यः तासां रटितेन रमणीयैः charming with the tinkling of jar-like bells bound round their necks. 'कम्बुग्रीवा त्रिरेखा सावटुर्घाटा कृकाटिका' अमरः. अटद्भिरटवीं that wandered over the forest. हर...क्षरद्भिः that dropped milk (from their udders), as though it (milk) were the milky ocean drunk by the bull of S'iva and then distributed in many places (*viz.* the cows) for fear of disease (*i. e.* indigestion). बाष्प...तृणैः that were fed on very tender grass. बाष्प...तृण means 'grass that can be cut with tears' *i. e.* very soft and tender. Note 'कृत्यैरधिकार्थवचने' पा. 2. 1. 33. (स्तुतिनिन्दाफलकमर्थवादवचनमधिकार्थवचनं तत्र कर्तरि करणे च तृतीया कृत्यैः सह प्राग्वत्। वातच्छेद्यं तृणम्। काकपेया नदी। सि. कौ.). कृत्य means potential participles. 'गोधनं स्याद्गवां व्रजे' अमरः. धवलितानि विपिनानि यस्य. The cows were white. विविध...देशः the districts (उद्देशः) of which were variegated with black antelopes in thousands, as though they were the eyes let fall (from heaven on earth) by Indra (शतमन्युः) blinded by the smoke of the offerings of various sacrifices. शतं मन्यवः क्रतवः अस्य इति शतमन्युः. Indra also has a 1000 eyes; eyes are कृष्णशार (dark and variegated). The pupil is dark, while the corners of the eye are reddish and the other part is white; hence the word कृष्णशार. For the 1000 eyes of इन्द्र *vide* 'सहस्रनेत्रदर्शनयोग्यां जयन्तीमिव शची' हर्ष० 4th उ० and notes thereon. धवल...शोभितः adorned with regions whitened with the pollen of *Ketakī* groves that scattered about white dust, as though they (regions) were the entrances of the city of S'iva grey with the ashes sprinkled over the lord of प्रमथs. प्रमथs are the attendants of शिव. उद्धूलनम् smearing the body with ashes. शिव is represented as fond of this. शाककन्दलैः श्यामलितानि ग्रामाणां उपकण्ठे (समीपे) काश्यपीपृष्ठानि यस्मिन्. शाककन्दलैः with the shoots of vegetables; or 'with vegetables and plantains.' काश्यपी—the earth, so called because परशुराम, after vanquishing the क्षत्रियs, made a gift of it to कश्यप. 'क्षोणी ज्या काश्यपी क्षितिः' अमरः. करभपालीभिः with rows of young camels. Understand उपलक्षितः after this, in accordance with the Sūtra 'इत्थम्भूतलक्षणे' पा. 2. 3. 21. For करभ, mark the Sūtra 'शृङ्खलमस्य बन्धनं करभे' पा. 5. 2. 79. (शृङ्खलकः करभः). The instrumentals from ०प्रस्फोटितैः to ०पथिकैः qualify द्राक्षामण्डपैः. पीलुपल्लवैः प्रस्फोटितं येषु—where (the dust on the feet of travellers) was rubbed off with the tender leaves of the Pīlu tree. For this use of प्रस्फोटित compare 'पथिकपादप्रस्फोटनधूलिधूसरैर्नवपल्लवैर्लाञ्छितच्छायानाम् (अटवीप्रवेशप्रपाणां)' हर्ष० 7th उ० last para; 'विश्रान्तकार्पटिकप्रस्फोटितचरणधूलिधूसरकिसलयलाञ्छितोपकण्ठैः' कादम्बरी p. 223 of P. प्रस्फोटित may also mean 'pierced.' The com. says 'प्रस्फोटितैर्नीराजनीकृतैः.' करपुटैः पीडितानि (squeezed) मातुलुङ्गीदलानि (citron leaves) तेषां रसेन उपलिप्तैः besmeared. मातुलुङ्गी is Marathi महाळुंग. स्वेच्छया विचिताः कुङ्कुमकेसराः तैः कृतः पुष्पप्रकरः येषु—where the saffron filaments gathered at their pleasure (by the travellers) served as the offering of flowers. प्रत्यग्राणां (fresh) फलानां रसः तस्य पानेन सुखसुप्ताः पथिकाः येषु. वन...गृहैरिव—the poet fancies that the vine arbours under which the travellers rested were as though the water-hostels where nectar was given by wood nymphs. The juice of the sweet grapes that the travellers eat is like nectar. The words from ०प्रस्फोटितैः to ०पथिकैः suggest certain characteristics of a प्रपागृह (Marathi पाणपोई). The dust in a प्रपा may be cleared away with पल्लवs; it may be उपलिप्त with cowdung as green as मातुलुङ्गीदलरस. Offerings of flowers (पुष्पप्रकरः) are made on the floor of प्रपाs. Travellers take rest after drinking water (रसपान) there. द्राक्षामण्डपैः—is to be connected with विलो... र्गमः. स्फुटन्ति (bursting open) फलानि यासाम्—*adj.* of दाडिमीनां. बीजलग्नः शुकचञ्चुरागः यासाम्. The reddish grains of the pomegranate look like the red beaks of parrots. The poet fancies that the redness of beaks stuck to the seeds, when parrots pecked the फलs. समारूढं कपिकुलं तस्य कपोलैः सन्दिह्यमानानि कुसुमानि यासाम्. The flowers of the pomegranate trees looked like the cheeks of the monkeys that had climbed them, so that one had difficulty in distinguishing them. विलोभनीयाः उपनिर्गमाः यस्य the approaches to which (country of श्रीकण्ठ) were fascinating. वनपालैः पीयमानः नारिकेलरसासवः (the wine of cocoanut juice) येषु—*adj.* of उपवनैः. पथिकलोकेन लुप्यमानाः (pillaged) पिण्डखर्जूराः (datetrees) येषु *adj.* of उपवनैः. गोलाङ्गूलैर्लिह्यमानः मधुरामोदः (मधुरः आमोदः यस्य) पिण्डीरसः येषु. पिण्डी is a kind of palm tree. For गोलाङ्गूल, see p. 54. ०चञ्चुभिः जर्जरिताः आरुकाः येषु. आरुकः a plant growing in the हिमालय with cooling properties. ०वृतैः—*adj.* of ०बन्धैः. अर्जुन is a kind of tree. गोकुलानां अवतारेण कलुषितं कूलकीलालं येषाम्—the water on the edges of which was rendered turbid by the descent of herds of kine. अध्वगः a traveller. शरण्य that afforded refuge. शरणे साधुः शरण्यः, according to 'तत्र साधुः' पा. 4. 4. 98. अरण्यधराबन्धैः forest pools. अवन्ध्यानि वनरन्ध्राणि यस्मिन् the hollows (or valleys) in the forests of which are not barren (on account of pools). करभेभ्यो हितः करभीयः; *vide* notes on शङ्कव्य and वत्सीय p. 94. उष्ट्राणां (camels) समूहः औष्ट्रकम्, उरभ्राणां (rams) समूहः औरभ्रकम्, according to 'गोत्रोक्षोष्ट्रोरभ्रराजराजन्यराजपुत्रवत्समनुष्याजाद्वुञ्' पा. 4. 2. 39 (एभ्यः समूहे वुञ् स्यात्). *Vide* औक्षक p. 166. कृतः सम्बाधः (crowd) यस्मिन्. In the next clause दिशि...चितः, the principal part is वडवानां...चितः full of the wandering droves of mares (वडवा). विलो...लब्धानाम् that were smeared with the juice of saffron plots that were crushed

(मृदित) by their rolling (विलोठनं) on them. समालब्ध 'smeared with unguents'. For the rolling of horses on saffron spots, compare रघु. 4. 67. विनीताध्वश्रमास्तस्य सिन्धुतीरविचेष्टनैः। दुधुवुर्वाजिनः स्कन्धाँल्लग्नकुङ्कुमकेसरान् ॥.' The poet fancies that the mares were smeared with saffron and wandered about (as अभिसारिकाs would do) for seducing the horses (seven) of the Sun. उत्प्रोथपुटैः and उन्मुखैः are equivalent to उद्गतप्रोथ° and उद्गतमुखैः—with their up-turned nostrils and mouths. उदर...पिबन्तीनाम्—the poet fancies that the mares turned up their noses because they wanted to take in the wind (प्रभञ्जनः) for the purpose of producing speed in the young lying in their wombs. वातहरिणीनामिव–This word has several senses. वातहरिण is a very swift kind of deer. The wind-gods (Maruts) are supposed to be drawn by deer. पृषदश्व is a synonym of वात. The word may also suggest the sense 'that surpass the wind (in speed)'. अनवरतानां क्रतूनां धूमः तेन अन्धकारः तस्मिन् प्रवृत्तैः that were produced (kindled) in the darkness of the smoke of &c. बाणैः—fires. हंसs have white wings and hence the fires are fancied to be हंसयूथs. हंसs move about in the dark (अन्धकार) resembling the smoke &c. There is an apparent विरोध between अन्धकारप्रवृत्तैः and धवलितभुवनः. What springs from darkness cannot whiten the world. If we read गुणैः for बाणैः, then the meaning is similar. By the performance of क्रतुs, merit is produced. पुण्य and यशः are poetically said to be white. सङ्गीत...लोकः with the vast resources (prosperity) of which the mortal world resounded, as though with peacocks intoxicated by the sound of drums. °मुरजः a drum beaten in a concert. Peacocks are overjoyed when it thunders. They mistook मुरजरव for thunder. Another sense is suggested by सङ्गीत...मत्तैः—the wealth of the people was so vast that they were mad after singing &c. शशि...वृत्तैः whose conduct was as pure (अवदात) as the rays of the moon (with virtuous men); that were round (वृत्त) and bright like the rays of the moon (with pearls). गुणिभिः (with pearls) would also mean 'that were strung together.' प्रसाधितः adorned. पथिकशतैः विलुप्यमानानि (pillaged) स्फीतानि (abundant) फलानि येषाम् (with trees); °विलुप्यमानं स्फीतं फलं (ऐश्वर्यं येषाम्)—the guests obtained plenty of money in that country, which (money) was distributed by them among other travellers. अभिगमनीयः sought for (by all guests); inviting (with big trees). मृग...कृतः that was steadied (protected) by the headmen of villages (महत्तरः) clad in garments of deer-skin bearing the fragrance of musk, as though they were the hills at the foot of the हिमालय. For मृगमद, see p. 51. मृग...दितैः (with ०पादैः) means 'covered with the hair of the deer scented with' &c. The musk-deer is found in the Himālaya range. महत्तरैः with ०पादैः means 'very large.' 'पादाः प्रत्यन्तपर्वताः' अमरः. महत्तर as the name of an officer occurs in numerous grants (compare I. A. vol. VIII p. 20 and vol. XII p. 25). The word occurs in the 7th उच्छ्वास also. प्रोद्दण्ड...त्तमैः on the lotuses of which with upraised stalks were seatd the best of birds (with reservoirs of water); on the lotus of which with upraised stalk was seated Brahmā (with the navel of Vishṇu). 'सहस्रपत्रं कमलम्' इत्यमरः. For नारायणनाभि, see notes pp. 20 and 28 above. For द्विजोत्तम as meaning ब्रह्मा, see 'द्विजवरस्वेच्छागृहीतकोषो नाभिपद्म इव' हर्ष० 4th उ० first para. प्रोद्दण्ड...मण्डितः also conveys another sense. The best of Brāhmanas in thousands sat on thousands of leaves near the lakes in that country for perfoming सन्ध्यावन्दन &c. मथितः...क्षितिभिः where the ground (or earth) was washed with streams of churned milk (with महाघोषैः aud ०रम्भैः). मथितं also means 'buttermilk.' 'तक्रं ह्युदश्विन्मथितं पादाम्ब्वर्धाम्बु निर्जलम्' अमरः. महाघोषः a big hamlet of cowherds. महान् घोषः (uproar) येषु (*adj.* of रम्भैः). At the time when the gods and demons began to churn there must have been a great uproar. पूरिताशः the regions of which were filled (with जनपदः). The directions were filled with great uproar at the time of churning or the effort of churning satisfied the hopes (of the gods and demons). जनपदः a country.

P. 43 ll. 13—21. **यत्र...दैवम्.** यत्र...दृष्टयः where wrong doctrines faded away, as though washed by the water of the tears due to the smoke of the three fires. 'दक्षिणाग्निर्गार्हपत्याहवनीयौ त्रयोऽग्नयः । अग्नित्रयमिदं त्रेता' अमरः. As the people stuck to Vedic rites, heresies departing from the Veda ceased to exist. कुदृष्टयः also 'weak eyesight.' Weak eyesight may be cured by medicines applied to the eye, which cause the eye to drop tears. पच्य...दुरितानि sins were not seen (*i. e.* vanished) as though burnt by the fire of the bricks (इष्टका) that were being baked for construoting altars. As the people were virtuous, no sins were committed. The poet fancies that sins vanished because they were consumed &c. Explain the following उत्प्रेक्षाs similarly. छिद्यमानं यूपाय दारु येन सः ०दारुः परशुः तेन पाटितः cleft. मख...धौत इव as though washed by the streams of the clouds made up of the smoke of sacrificial fires (शिखिन् *m.*). For clouds being formed of smoke, see notes p. 106. वर्णसङ्करः (a combination of colours) may be washed with water and then no colour would remain. सुरा...इव as though cut up by numerous chisels (टङ्कः) for shaping (घट्टनं) the stones of the temples. 'टङ्कः पाषाणदारणः' अमरः. महा...द्रवाः calamities ran away, as though routed by the tumult of the making of महादानs. महादान is a name of certain very munificent gifts (16 in number), the first being तुलापुरुषदान. उपद्रवः a misfortune or national calamity (such as a famine). दीप्य...पिता इव as though heated by thousands of blazing kitchens in the great sacrifices. 'सत्रमाच्छादने यज्ञे' अमरः. वृष...त्रासिताः इव as though frightened by the sharp sound of the holy drums beaten at the marriages of bulls. On the eleventh day after the death of a person, a bull is let loose along with cows, which is called वृषोत्सर्ग or वृषविवाह. 'एकादशाहे प्रेतस्य यस्य चोत्सृज्यते वृषः। प्रेतलोकं परित्यज्य स्वर्गलोकं स गच्छति॥.' अपमृत्यवः untimely deaths. ब्रह्मघोष = वेदघोष. 'वेदस्तत्त्वं तपो ब्रह्म' अमरः. ईतयः—Distress or calamity. ईतिs are usually said to be six. 'अतिवृष्टिरनावृष्टिर्मूषिकाः शलभाः शुकाः। अत्यासन्नाश्च राजानः षडेता ईतयः स्मृताः॥.' क्षीर०. शलभाः locusts. अत्यासन्नाः राजानः extreme proximity of kings (*i. e.* encampment of soldiers, whether hostile or friendly). धर्मा... दैवम् As the sole अधिकार (power) rested with धर्म, दुर्दैव could not become a प्रभु (lord) in that country.

P. 43 ll. 22—31. तत्र...विशेषः. The principal sentence is तत्र च एवंविधे...स्थाण्वीश्वराख्यो जनपदविशेषः. नाना आरामाः (gardens) तेषां अभिरामः ०परिमलः तेन सुभगः (with ०विशेषः). नाना रामाः (beautiful women) अभिरामाः ०परिमलाश्च तैः सुभगः (with यौवनारम्भः). As youth is the most charming period of one's life, so the country was the most charming in the world. कुङ्कुम...शोभितः decked with many thousands of buffaloes reddened (पिञ्जरित) by crushing (*i. e.* rolling in) saffron (with country); decked with many thousands of crowned queens (महिषी) reddened with saffron unguents (with अन्तःपुरनिवेशः). अन्तः...धर्मस्य—As the अन्तःपुर is a spot loved by a king, where he moves about freely and confidently, so in that country धर्म reached its highest pitch. मरुता (वातेन) उद्धूयमानानि ०व्यजनानि तेषां शतैः धवलिताः प्रान्ताः यस्य (with the country); मरुत्सु (देवेषु) उद्धूयमानानि (being waved) ०व्यजनानि &c. In the country roamed चमरी deer the tails of which were shaken by the wind. In heaven (सुरराज्य) chowries are waved before gods. ज्वलन्तः मखशिखिनः तेषां सहस्रैः दीप्यमानाः दश दिगन्ताः

यस्मिन्. As thousands of sacrifices were performed, a vast store of merit was accumulated. In कृतयुग also there was vast merit. So the country is fancied to be an encampment. In a camp also fires blaze forth at night. Or the reference may be to the fires in the नीराजन ceremony of the camp. *Vide* p. 34. The com. shows that कृतयुग also means 'king'. 'कृतं प्रतिसमाहितं युगं द्वयं स्वपक्षपरपक्षरूपं येन स राजोच्यते.' पद्ममेव आसनं तस्मिन् स्थितः ब्रह्मर्षिः(ब्रह्मा चासौ ऋषिश्च) तस्य ध्यानेन आधीयमानः (brought about) सकलस्य अकुशलस्य (evil, calamity) प्रशमः यस्मिन् (with अवतारः); पद्मासनं आसनभेदः तस्मिन् स्थिताः ब्रह्मर्षयः तेषां ध्यानेन &c. Brahmā sits on the lotus in the navel of विष्णु. For ब्रह्मा warding off evil, compare 'त्रिभुवनोपप्लवप्रशमकुशापीडधारिणेव दक्षिणेन करेण' (text) p. 4. l. 20. In the country there were ब्रह्मर्षिs (saintly Brāhmaṇas) sitting in the *yogic* posture called पद्मासन. In this आसन the right foot is placed on the left thigh and the left foot on the right thigh; the toes are to be firmly held by the hands; the chin is to be on the heart and one has to look at the tip of the nose. 'वामोरूपरि दक्षिणं च चरणं संस्थाप्य वामं तथा दक्षोरूपरि पश्चिमेन विधिना धृत्वा कराभ्यां दृढम् । अङ्गुष्ठौ हृदये निधाय चिबुकं नासाग्रमालोकयेदेतद्व्याधिविनाशकारि यमिनां पद्मासनं प्रोच्यते ॥ हठयोगप्रदीपिका. महावाहिनी great river; great army. विपक्ष...कुरूणाम् that was as though the enemy *(i. e.* the rival) of the country of उत्तरकुरु. An enemy (विपक्ष) has large armies. In the country described there were both large armies and large rivers. उत्तरकुरु is one of the four द्वीपs near मेरु (भीष्मपर्व 6. 13). The great river there is the Ganges. 'दक्षिणेन तु नीलस्य मेरोः पार्श्वे तथोत्तरे । उत्तराः कुरवो राजन् पुण्याः सिद्धनिषेविताः॥' भीष्मपर्व 7. 2. If we read विक्षेपः the meaning is 'that throws off (into the background) *i. e.* surpasses.' वि...पुरस्य like the conqueror of the three cities *i. e.* like S'iva; that desired to conquer *(i. e.* that equalled in splendour) the three cities of the Asuras (with the country). For त्रिपुरदाह, see p. 113 above. ईश्वरः शिवः तस्य मार्गणाः बाणाः तैः सन्तापः तस्य अनभिज्ञाः सकलजनाः यस्मिन्; ईश्वरस्य नृपस्य मार्गणं तस्य &c. The idea in the latter case is either that the people of that country did not know the harassment due to the exacting demands of the king or that they did not know how to solicit favours from the king. सुधारसेन (by *chunam* or whitewash) सिक्तानि धवलगृहाणि तेषां पङ्क्त्या पाण्डुरः. The country had whitewashed houses and so resembled moonlight. In चन्द्रलोक there must be houses sprinkled with nectar (as the moon is full of सुधा). मधुमत्ताः (intoxicated by drink) मत्तकाशिन्यः (handsome and fascinating women) तेषां भूषणरवेण भरितं भुवनं यस्मिन्. मत्तकाशिनी—मत्ता क्षीबा इव काशते भाति इति मत्तकाशिनी. The com. says that मत्तकाशिनी also means 'यक्षिणी'. यक्षs are the servants of कुबेर. नामाभिहार: carrying away the name (and depositing it in another place) *i. e.* a synonym. As there was the jingling of the ornaments of मत्तकाशिनीs, the country was a synonym of कुबेरनगर. स्थाण्वीश्वरः—the modern Thanesar. जन...शेषः—श्रीकण्ठ was a large country of which स्थाण्वीश्वर was a part.

P. 43 l. 32—**P. 44** l. 6. **यस्तपो...गृह्यत.** The principal sentence is यः...अगृह्यत. We have to supply अगृह्यत in each clause. कामायतनम् abode of Cupid or the temple of Cupid. लासकैः = नटैः. यम...श्रुभिः—the country was so well guarded that enemies were as much afraid of it as of Death. For चिन्तामणि, see above p. 135. वीरक्षेत्रम् It was the home of heroes. गन्धर्वनगरम्-गन्धर्वs are the musicians of the gods. गायनैः by singers. विश्वकर्मा—is the architect of the gods and presides over all arts. विज्ञानिभिः by artisans, by those skilled in the 64 arts. 'मोक्षे धीर्ज्ञानमन्यत्र **विज्ञानं शिल्पशास्त्रयोः**' अमरः. वैदेहकैः = वणिग्भिः. '**वैदेहकः सार्थवाहो** नैगमो वाणिजो वणिक्' अमरः. द्यूत...बन्दिभिः—bards looked upon it as a gambling house. In a gambling house fortunes are made (and also lost) in a day. Bards were richly rewarded in that country. विट...दग्धैः by sharpwitted men (or crafty) it was looked upon as a club of clever voluptuaries. सुकृतपरिणामः as the fulfilment (ripening) of their good deeds. Travellers got there everything they desired. It is only through one's good deeds in former lives that one is so fortunate as to secure whatever one desires. असुरविवरम्—*vide* notes p. 90. वातिकैः—com. paraphrases as 'विवरव्यसनिभिराचार्यैः.' Probably there is a pun on the word वातिक which means 'mad' and 'those whose heads are turned by the thought of amassing money.' Mad men are confined in dark places. That country gave as much money to fortune-hunters as असुरविवर was supposed to yield. शा...भिः it was looked upon as a Buddhist monastery by those who wanted tranquility of mind. महोत्सवसमाजः concourse of people on a great festival. चारणैः wandering actors (देशान्तरभ्रमणाज्जीवति इति चारणः). वसुधारा stream of wealth. Munificent gifts were made to Brāhmaṇas in that country.

P. 44 ll. 7—11 **यत्र च...प्रमदाः.** In this paragraph, each adjective independently qualifies प्रमदाः. Further in each pair of adjectives there is an apparent contradiction due to श्लेष. मातङ्गगामिन्यः possessing the gait of elephants; having sexual intercourse with chaṇḍālas. 'चण्डालप्लवमातङ्गदिवाकीर्तिजनङ्गमाः।' अमरः. If they were मातङ्ग° (in the 2nd sense), they could not be शीलवत्यः (of pure conduct). गौर्यः fair; Gaurîs (पार्वती). विभवरताः attached to pomp and luxury; attached to a place where no शिव existed. विगतः भवः यस्मात् तस्मिन् रताः. If they were पार्वती, they must be भवरत (and not विभवरत). श्यामाः handsome; dark. श्यामा is a handsome lady described as 'शीते सुखोष्णसर्वाङ्गी ग्रीष्मे या सुखशीतला। तप्तकाञ्चनवर्णाभा सा स्त्री श्यामेति कथ्यते॥'. पद्म° decked with rubies; having the colour of (red) lotus. What is dark cannot be red. श्यामाः also means 'nights' and पद्मरागिण्यः would mean 'loving lotuses.' Nights cannot love day lotuses. धवल... वदनाः whose faces are bright with white teeth; whose mouths are pure like those of pure Brāhmaṇas. मदि...सनाः whose breath is fragrant like wine; whose breath...with wine. If they drank wine, their mouths could not be pure. Wine-drinking was forbidden to all, particularly to Brāhmaṇas. *Vide* notes above p. 160. चन्द्र...वपुषः whose bodies are charming like the moon; whose bodies are (hard) like the चन्द्रकान्त stone. शिरीष is a very delicate flower. अ...गम्याः not to be approched by gallants; not to be approached by serpents. कञ्चुकिन्यः wearing a bodice; female serpents (*lit.* possessed of slough). कञ्चुकिन्यः also means 'libidinous.' पृथु...श्रियः whose glory as wives spread far and wide (also 'whose beautiful hips are broad'); whose retinue of women is large. 'कलत्रं श्रोणिभार्ययोः' अमरः. दरिद्र...लिताः possessed of a slender waist; counted among the poor. लावण्यवत्यः possessed of beauty; possessed of salt. अप्रमत्ताः not rash or careless; not intoxicated. प्रसन्नः (clear) उज्ज्वलः रागः (colour) यासाम्; प्रसन्नावत् उज्ज्वलः रागः येषाम्. प्रसन्ना means 'wine.' *Vide* notes p. 143 on प्रसन्ना. अकौतुकाः that did not wear the marriage thread; that were free from (girlish) curiosity. For the meaning of कौतुक compare रघु° 8. 1 'अथ तस्य विवाहकौतुकं ललितं बिभ्रत एव पार्थिवः'. Being grown up (प्रौढ) they must once have worn the marriage thread.

P. 44 l. 12—24 **यत्र च...परिजनाः**. In this passage the poet describes that the women possessed naturally those things which they had added by way of decoration and so the latter were really superfluous. चक्षु...दामानि their very eyes are a natural wreath for the head, the garlands of lotus petals are a mere burden. Their eyes were darker than the blue कुवलयs. अलक...किसलयानि the images of their tresses reflected in their (bright) cheeks were ear-ornaments unimpaired (in beauty); the tender leaves of the *Tamāla* (placed on the ear as ornament) were superfluous. Their tresses were darker and more glossy than तमाल leaves. प्रियकथाः talk about their husbands. आडम्बरः show, external appendage. कपोला...दीपाः their (bright) cheeks alone caused continuous light (आलोकः); the jewelled lamps at night were merely (for the sake of) pomp. कुल...जालिका the veil (जालिका) was merely an appendage worn because it was the custom of high-born ladies to wear one. बाह्य...ताडनम् playing on the lute was an external accomplishment (*i. e.* an accomplishment for display). पटवासः perfumed powder. Their smile was bright like camphor and when they smiled their breath was also fragrant like camphor. 'पिष्टातः पटवासकः' अमरः (पटो वास्यतेऽनेन). अधर०—The redness of their lips surpassed that of saffron. निर्गुणः useless. लावण्यकलङ्कः a stain on their beauty. The paste of saffron only marred the beauty of their complexion. परि...लताः canes for striking in joke. Their arms were fair and slender like cane. यौ...बिन्दवः drops of perspiration due to the warmth of youth. विदग्धाः fine, artful. विशाल...स्रा square like broad crystal slabs. रागिणाम् of their lovers. Construe श्रोण्यः विश्रमकारणम्. अनि...वेदिकाः the jewelled couches in their houses were useless (for giving rest to their lovers). कमल...भरणकानि—bees hovered round their feet (that resembled red lotuses) mistaking them to be lotuses and so looked like sapphire anklets. समुचि...सहायाः the proper (or usual) companions of their strolls. For Haṁsas following the tinkling anklets of ladies, see p. 31 above. ऐ...जनाः attendants were but the details of their prosperity.

P. 44 ll. 25—32 **तत्र च...बभूव.** The principal sentence is तत्र च...राजा पुष्पभूतिरिति नाम्ना बभूव. सह...दधानः—इन्द्रधनुः possesses all colours. The king supported all (the four) castes. As to Indra's 1000 eyes, see above notes p. 186. कल्याणप्रकृतित्वे in being by nature well disposed to all (with पुष्पभूति); in being the source (प्रकृतिः) of gold (with मेरु). Meru is a mountain of gold. 'मेरुः सुमेरुर्हेमाद्रिः रत्नसानुः सुरालयः' अमरः. लक्ष्मीसमाकर्षणे in drawing Glory or prosperity towards himself; in drawing out लक्ष्मी (with मन्दर). For मन्दर see p. 52. मर्यादायाम् in propriety of conduct; in the boundary or shore. The sea does not pass beyond the shore. The king never transgressed the rules of decorum. शब्दप्रादुर्भावे in the diffusion of his fame or in the knowledge of grammar; in manifesting sound (with आकाश). According to the writers on Sanskrit logic, गन्ध, रस, रूप, स्पर्श and शब्द are respectively the special qualities of पृथिवी, अप्, तेजः, वायु and आकाश. आकाश is defined by them as 'शब्दगुणमाकाशम्'. कलासंग्रहे in the comprehension of the (64) arts; in the accumulation of the (16) digits (with शशी). अकृत्रिमालापत्वे in employing speech that is not false; in having its words not created (composed) by anyone. According to the मीमांसकs वेद is self-existent and eternal. It is अपौरुषेय. धरणिः the earth. लोक...करणे in steadying or supporting the people; in supporting (on its surface) the people (with धरणिः). सर्व...हरणे in removing the effects of *Rajas* in the case of all kings; in carrying away all the dust of the earth. The wind carries off the dust. रजः is one of the three Guṇas of the सांख्य system, *viz.* सत्त्व, रजः and तमः. Its effects are काम, क्रोध &c. Compare 'काम एष क्रोध एष रजोगुणसमुद्भवः' गीता 3. 37. पुष्पभूति subdued all kings (पार्थिव) and their passions. गुरुर्वचसि weighty or great in speech; Bṛihaspati in speech. It should be noted that the words from गुरु up to दक्ष are adjectives as well as proper nouns. पृथुरुरसि wide in the chest. पृथु also was a famous king. Note the 2nd verse of the 4th उच्छ्वास and *vide* the notes thereon. विशालो मनसि comprehensive in intellect. The com. says that विशाल was also the name of a बोधिसत्त्व. विशाल was also a son of इक्ष्वाकु and founder of the city विशाला. जनकस्तपसि—he performed various austerities. जनक, king of मिथिला, was famous for his holiness and spiritual knowledge. सुयात्रः whose expedition (or invasion) is grand. सुयात्र seems to be the name of a king. सुमन्त्रः whose policy is good; सुमन्त्र was the charioteer of दशरथ. शोभनः मन्त्रः यस्य. Works on politics lay down that a king should keep his line of policy secret till it bears fruit. Compare 'मन्त्र इव सचिवमण्डलेन रक्ष्यमाणे' हर्ष० 4th उ० and notes thereon. बुधः wise; Mercury (the son of the Moon). अर्जुनः white; the hero अर्जुन. भीष्मः terrific; the great warrior भीष्म. निषधः is the name of a mountain and also of a king, who was father of नल. निषधः hard, solid. शत्रुघ्नः who killed his enemies; the brother of Rāma. शूरः brave; a king of the यादवs, who was grand-father of कृष्ण. शूर...क्रमणे in vanquishing brave armies; in occupying the country of शूरसेन (*i. e.* मथुरा). दक्ष...मणि vigilant or clever in discharging his duty to his subjects. दक्ष is a well-known

प्रजापति. *Vide* notes p. 18. The प्रजापतिs were entrusted with the task of creating all sorts of beings. सर्वादि०—It will be noticed that in this passage famous primeval kings like पृथु are associated with the limbs and qualities of the king पुष्पभूति.

P. 45 ll. 1–23 **पृथुना...दर्शनम्.** पृथुना...कृता—for this legend, *vide* notes p. 176. इति therefore. स्पर्धमान इव as if vying with (पृथु). महिषी crowned queen; she-buffalo. निसर्ग...मतिः the minds of the great are by nature unrestrained and follow their own likings. अनुपदिष्टा (*adj.* of भक्तिः) untaught. भुवनभृति (*adj.* of भवे) who upholds the worlds. भूतभावने who creates all beings. भवच्छिदि that destroys the cycle of births and deaths. भवे = शिवे. 'जन्महरौ भवौ' अमरः. अकृतः वृषभध्वजस्य (शिवस्य) पूजाविधिः येन. अजरम् free from old age, never aging. अमरगुरुम् venerated by the gods. अपरिमितानां गणानां पतिम् the lord of innumerable attendants called गणs. अचलदुहितृ = पार्वती. ०नैः कृता चरणयोः नतिः यस्य. The student will notice that all the letters from अजम् to ०नतिम् are short, when the सन्धि rules are observed. पशुपतिं = शिवम्. प्रपन्नः devoted. भर्तृ...प्रकृतयः the dispositions of dependents follow the mind of their master. खण्डपरशुः = शिवः. बवुः अस्य... पुण्यविषयेषु वायवः in his holy country winds blew. ०गर्भः and the two following words qualify वायवः. होमालवाले (अग्निकुण्डे) विलीयमानः (melting) बहलः गुग्गुलुः तस्य गन्धः गर्भे येषाम्. For गुग्गुलु being burnt in the temples of शिव, *vide* notes p. 105. स्नपन... क्षारिणः that dropped particles (क्षोदः) of the spray of the milk for bathing (the images of शिव). For क्षीरस्नपन, *vide* notes p. 114. बिल्व...हिनः that carried along petals from the wreaths of *Bilva* leaves. शिव...चितैः proper in the worship of शिव. उपायनं a present (made personally). प्राभृतम् a present (sent with a messenger or servant). प्रकर्षेण आराधनार्थं आभ्रियते ढौक्यते स. पादोपजीविनः his dependents. करदीकृताः that were made to pay tribute (from करद one who pays tribute). तथाहि for instance. कैलास...वृषैः with huge bulls that were to be let loose in the evening worship (of शिव), white like the peaks of कैलास, the tips of whose horns were decked with golden figure-work. For पत्रलता, see notes on पत्रभङ्ग p. 24. Mr. R. R. Kale takes ०वृषैः to be stone or clay images of the bull of शिव; but there is very little warrant for this supposition. सन्ध्याबलिवृषैः bulls that were intended to be let loose as offerings in the evening worship of शिव. स्नपनकलश pitchers (for holding milk) for bathing (the image of शिव). अर्घभाजन vessels useful in worship. 'मूल्ये

पूजाविधावर्घः' अमरः. पुष्पपट्टैः cloths on which there were ornamental flowers woven in (with threads). मणि...प्रदीपैः lamps on jewelled sticks (stands). ब्रह्मसूत्रं = यज्ञोपवीतम्. महा... कोषैः cases (for covering शिवलिङ्ग) inlaid with pieces of very costly gems. 'मुखयुक्ताः कोषाः मुखकोषाः ये लिङ्गोपरि दीयन्ते' सं०. अन्तःपुराण्यपि...तस्य अभिलषितमन्ववर्तन्त his queens also complied with his desire. स्वयमारब्धं बालेयतण्डुलकण्डनं यैः that themselves threshed the rice used for making oblations (to शिव). बलये हिताः बालेयाः तण्डुलाः, according to 'छदिरुपधिबलेर्ढञ्' पा. 5. 1. 13. देवगृहस्य उपलेपनं (plastering with cowdung) तेन लोहिततराणि करकिसलयानि येषाम्. Their hands were already red; but the manual labour, to which the queens were not accustomed, made their palms redder. कुसुमग्रथने (in making wreaths) व्यग्रः समस्तः परिजनः येषाम्. परममाहेश्वरः a great devotee of शिव. हर्ष himself is called परममाहेश्वर; *vide* Intro. p. XXIX footnote. शुश्राव—the object is महाशैवम्. अपर... मथनम्—For the destruction of दक्ष's sacrifice *vide* notes p. 87. According to the भागवतपुराण (4th स्कन्ध 5th chap.) शिव produced from his जटा a terrific being called वीरभद्र that destroyed दक्ष's sacrifice. भैरव was the name of the S'aiva ascetic and भैरव is also one of the terrific forms of शिव. So the author says 'अपरमिव...मथनम्'. दाक्षिणात्य (from दक्षिणा with the affix त्यक्), according to 'दक्षिणापश्चात्पुरसस्त्यक्' पा. 4. 2. 98 (दक्षिणेत्याजन्तमव्ययम्). बहु...लोकम् who covered the world with thousands of good qualities, as though with pupils, that became far-famed by the mastery of various sciences. Read शीलसंवादाः. उप...वादाः Resemblance in character draws a person, though unseen, to one's heart (*i. e.* affection for him springs up even without seeing him). कपर्दिन्—कपर्दः जटाजूटः विद्यते अस्य इति कपर्दी शिवः. आचं...दर्शनम् he desired even in his wishes to see him by all means. The emphasis lies on the word मनोरथैः. If we want to see a person, we may use a chariot (रथ) for that purpose. He employed even मनोरथ for that purpose.

P. 45 l. 24—**P. 46** l. 11. **अथ...पुण्डरीकाणि.** पर्यस्ते scattered about, fading. वासरे the day, the sun. नचिराच्च—the sentence here is नचिराच्च...मस्करिणमद्राक्षीत् (p. 46. l. 5). All the words in the accusative singular from प्रविशन्तं qualify मस्करिणम्. आजानुभुजम् whose arms reached his knees. Arms reaching the knees were looked upon as a sign of greatness. भैक्ष...लक्ष्यमाणम् though emaciated (क्षाम) by living on alms, he appeared to be fat (पीवर) on account of his limbs having stout bones. भैक्षम्—भिक्षाणां समूहो भैक्षम्, according to 'भिक्षादिभ्योऽण्' पा. 4. 2. 38. पृथु

उत्तमाङ्गं (शिरः) यस्य. If we read पृथुतमाङ्गम्, then dissolve as पृथुतमं अङ्गं (शरीरं) यस्य. उत्तुङ्गेन वलिभङ्गेन स्थपुटं ललाटं यस्य—whose forehead was undulating with prominent folds of wrinkles. 'स्थपुटं तु नतोन्नतम्' क्षीरस्वामी. निर्मांसः गण्डकूपकः यस्य. गण्डकूपक is the hollow beneath the eye and above the cheek. मधु...क्षम् whose eyes were round and brown like drops of honey. ई...घोणम whose nose (घोणा) was slightly curved. अतिप्रलम्बः एकः कर्णपाशः (प्रशस्तः कर्णः) यस्य one of whose ears hung down very much. अलाबु... पङ्क्तिम् the row of whose teeth was prominent and formidable (विकट) like the seeds of bottle-gourd. These seeds are white and long. तुरगानूकवत् श्लथा अधरलेखा यस्य whose lip was loose like the अनूक of a horse. According to the com. अनूक is the lower lip of a horse. अनूकः-कम् means 'backbone or spine.' लम्बेन चिबुकेन आयततरं लपनं (मुखं) यस्य whose mouth looked elongated on account of a hanging chin. काषाय red. For योगपट्टक, see p. 26 above. विरचितः वैकक्षकः यस्य. For वैकक्षक see p. 26. हृदयमध्ये निबद्धः ग्रन्थिः (knot) यस्य. धातुरसारुणेन red because dyed with red chalk. *Vide* notes p. 161 for धातु. रागेणेव...कृतेन—the poet fancies that the red piece of cloth was राग (passion, redness) which he had cut into pieces. The ascetic had uprooted passions (राग) which sway the human heart (हृदय) and had as though tied into a knot on the chest the pieces of passion as red garment. कर्पटः a ragged garment. कृतः उत्तरासङ्गः यस्य. उत्तरासङ्गः upper garment (उत्तरे ऊर्ध्वाङ्गे आसज्यते उत्तरासङ्गः). पुन...मूलेन—this and the following instrumentals qualify योगभारकेण. What a योगभारक means is not quite clear. It seems to have been something like an 'hold-all,' a bag tied to a pole. C and T render it as 'yoke pole'. पुनरुक्तं ०वेष्टनं तेन निश्चलं मूलं यस्य the root of which was made firm with fastenings (प्रग्रहः) of hair tied over and over again. The bag was tied to the pole by hair ropes. दद्धः मृत्परिशोधनाय वंशत्वचः तितउः यस्मिन् on which was tied a sieve (तितउः) of bamboo bark for straining earth. 'चालनी तितउः पुमान्' अमरः. कौपीनेन सनाथं शिखरं यस्य. कौपीनम्—loin-cloth (from कूप) according to 'शालीनकौपीने अधृष्टाकार्ययोः' पा. 5. 2. 20 (कूपपतनमर्हति कौपीनं पापं तत्साधनत्वात्तद्गोप्यत्वात्पुरुषलिङ्गमपि । तत्सम्बन्धात्तदाच्छादनमपि । सि. कौ.). खर्जूर...कपालके whose alms bowl was placed inside a box (समुद्गकः) made of date leaves. दारव...कमण्डलुना that had his water pot placed on a stool of three sticks inserted into the corners of three wooden planks. दारव-from दारु. Three planks were joined together to make a triangular base. In their corners a stick was fixed.

दहिरुपपादितं ०स्थानं यस्मिन् outside which a place was found for his slippers (of wood). स्थूलेन दशासूत्रेण नियन्त्रिता पुस्तिकापूलिका यस्मिन्— that had his bundle of manuscripts tied by a stout rope made of the hems of garments. अध्यासितः स्कन्धः यस्य. इतरकरेण (दक्षिणेन करेण) गृहीतं वेत्रासनं (caneseat) येन. मस्करिणम्—*vide* notes p. 91. This clause gives a vivid and picturesque description of an ascetic and reminds us of modern *Gosavis* and *Sādhus.* उपगतम् when he came near. नगरस्य समीपे उपनगरम् (अव्ययीभाव). शून्यायतने in a deserted house or temple. उपनिन्ये presented. बहलेन आलोकेन लिप्तं अन्तःपुरं यैः. राजतानि made of silver.

P. 46 ll. 12—23 **नरपति…वाटिकाम्.** प्रिय…कातरः afraid to go contrary to the request or love of a person dear to him. दाक्षिण्यमनुरुध्यमानः following the dictates of courtesy. ग्रहण…समर्थः not able to get free from the (charge of) mean-mindedness if he accepted them. दोलायमानेन—vacillating. The king was afraid that if he refused the present, he would offend the ascetic for whom he had high regard; but the king also felt that if he being a king accepted from a poor mendicant a gift, that would be an act deserving to be censured by the people. अति…निघ्नः yielding to his own extreme goodness. सर्व…हेतुः the cause of the production of all rewards (goes with ०भक्तिः).शिव… फलानि It is our devotion to शिव that yields rewards that could not (otherwise) have been secured even in desires. येन since. समुच्छ्रितं श्वेतातपत्रं यस्य whose white umbrella was held high over him. समुद्धूयमानं (being waved) धवलं चामरयुगलं यस्य. The white umbrella and two chowries were indispensable insignia of royalty in ancient India. Compare 'अदेयमासीत् त्रयमेव भूपतेः **शशिप्रभं छत्रमुभे च चामरे**' रघु० 3. 16. राजपुत्रैः nobles. अन्तरं distance. अभि…शिष्यं another pupil coming towards (the king). He was other than the one that had come before with the five silver lotuses. अस्य…त्तरेण to the north of this dilapidated temple of the Mātṛis. The Mātris are eight (or seven, according to others) divinities said to be the attendants of शिव. 'ब्राह्मी माहेश्वरी चैन्द्री वाराही वैष्णवी तथा। कौमारी चर्ममुण्डा च कालसङ्कर्षणीति च ॥'. *Vide* 'साक्षाज्जातमातृदेवता इव बहुबालकव्याकुला ननृतुर्वृद्धधात्र्यः' हर्ष० 4th उ० and notes thereon. For उत्तरेण, *vide* notes p. 158.

P. 46 l. 24—**P. 48** l. 2 **अथ महतः…मकरोत्.** The first sentence is अथ…भगवन्तं…भैरवाचार्यं ददर्श (p. 47 l. 32). महत…मध्ये in the midst of a large crowd of pilgrims. कार्पटिक is derived from कर्पट with the affix ठक् (कर्पटेन चरति). स्नातम्—this and the following adjectives in the accusative singular qualify भैरवाचार्यं below. दत्ता अष्टपुष्पिका येन. For अष्टपुष्पिका, *vide* notes p. 46. पुष्पाणामष्टकमष्टपुष्पिका. अनुष्ठितं अग्निकार्यं येन. कृतः भस्मरेखापरिहारेण परिकरः यस्य that was surrounded by a circle of ashes. परिहारः a tract of common land round a village; hence, here 'a tract or circle'. Compare 'धनुःशतं **परीहारो** ग्रामस्य स्यात्समन्ततः ।' मनु० 8. 237. The com. says 'परिहारोऽत्र मर्यादा'. हरितेन गोमयेन उपलिप्तं ०तलं तस्मिन् वितते (spread). कृष्ण...भ्यस्यन्तम् under the guise (निभः) of wrapping himself in a dark woollen blanket, he as though was practising residence (आवासः) in the darkness of *pātāla* in the apprehension that he might have to enter into an *Asura* cavern. For असुरविवर, *vide* notes p. 90. Pātāla as the haunt of demons and sinners is supposed to be dark. An असुरविवर must also be very dark, if our explanation of it be correct. He did not want to enter असुरविवर; but the poet fancies that he was familiarising himself with darkness because he feared that he might one day have do so. उन्मिषता...लिम्पन्तम् who covered his disciples with the flashing lustre of his body as tawny as lightning, as though with red arsenic paste purchased by the sale of human flesh. मनःशिला is red and therefore would be like the glow of his body. मनःशिला costs money and so the question arises how the poor ascetic got it. The words महा...क्रीतेन explain this. They suggest that भैरवाचार्य was a शाक्त, had offered human flesh to शक्ति and the पिशाचs and thereby secured super-human powers. Compare 'अपरत्र प्रकाशनरपतिकुमारकक्रियमाणमहामांसविक्रयप्रक्रमम्' हर्ष० 4th उ० 7th para. The शाक्तs say 'अष्टम्यां रुधिरैर्मांसैर्महामांसैः सुगन्धिभिः । पूजयेद्बहुजातीयैर्बलिभिर्भोजनैः शिवाम् ॥.' जटी...सिद्धान् with his hair tied in a lump so as to peep upwards from a portion of which that was matted hung down the round globes of conch-shell and his rosary beads, he seemed to be imprisoning the Siddhas conceited by the pride of knowledge and roaming overhead (in the sky). जटीकृतः एकदेशः तस्मात् लम्बमानाः रुद्राक्षाणां शंखानां च गुटिकाः यस्मिन्. प्रशस्ता शिखा शिखापाशः. The शिखा was long (like a cord) and ऊर्ध्वबद्ध hence the उत्प्रेक्षा 'बध्नन्तमिव &c.' For सिद्धs, see above p. 83. The poet wants to suggest that he had secured superhuman powers (सिद्धिs) which enabled him even to imprison the सिद्धs. धवलाः कतिपये शिरोरुहाः (hair) यस्मिन् (*adj* of वयसा). वयसा...क्रामन्तम् in age he had passed beyond 55 years. खालित्येन क्षीयमाणा शङ्खलोम्नां लेखा यस्य the line of the hair on the front part of his head was faint owing to baldness. We expect खालत्य (from खलति) for खालित्य. 'शङ्को निधौ ललाटास्थि' अमरः. लोमशः (hairy) कर्णशष्कुलिप्रदेशः (the outer part of the ear) यस्य. तिरश्च्या...जनयन्तम् with his slanting forehead mark made with ashes, he led one to think that it was the white line of his skull-bone burst by the heat of the burnt *guggulu* repeatedly held over his head. It is better to read शिरोविधृत with some MSS. For ललाटिका, see p. 44. For the burning of गुग्गुलु in the temple of शिव and on the head, *vide* notes p. 105. Bones are white. The line of white ashes on the forehead is fancied to be the skull bone split up by heat. सहज...बिभ्राणम् who had as though a single, long (आयामिनी) and unbroken (निरन्तरा) brow by the meeting together of his brows, as the part between the brows was contracted by the natural folds of the wrinkles on his forehead, the brow being tawny in colour. ०भङ्गैः सङ्कोचितः कूर्चभागः यस्याः. 'कूर्चमस्त्री भ्रुवोर्मध्यम्' अमरः. बभ्रुः भाः यस्याः. Between the brows there is ordinarily a part of the head. But as his forehead was deeply wrinkled, the two brows presented a continuous line. निरन्तराम् leaving no intervening space. ईषत् काचवत् काचरा कनीनिका यस्य the pupil of which was greenish like glass. रक्तापाङ्गाभ्यां निर्गतः अंशुप्रतानः यस्य from the red corners of which shot forth rays. मध्ये धवला भाः यस्य तेन ०भासा. These three qualify ०युगलेन. इन्द्रायुधेनेव—The rainbow also presents red and green colours and so his eyes are fancied to be इन्द्रायुध. Then there are two more उत्प्रेक्षाs. लोचन...लिखन्तम्—the idea is:—when he cast glances all round from his eyes that were white, red (in the corners) and greenish-yellow (in the pupil), he seemed to draw all round a large circle tinged with various colours. A मण्डल is drawn on the ground in worshipping a deity. Compare 'कुङ्कुमपङ्कानुलिप्ते मण्डलके...रक्तकमलषण्डेनार्चां ददौ' हर्ष० 4th उ०, 4th para. सित...क्षिपन्तम् he seemed to scatter in all directions an oblation to शिव variegated with rows of white, yellow and red flags (or marks). That flags were used in the worship of शिव we see from the 2nd उ० 'सुरभिकुसुमधूपगन्धध्वजबलिविलेपनप्रदीपकबहुलां विधाय पूजाम्' (text p. 25). If we take पताका as meaning 'mark' (in a secondary sense), then there is a reference to an oblation of rice (which is white) smeared with red powder and yellow turmeric. Such oblations are even now placed where four roads meet. तार्क्ष्यतुण्डकोटिवत् कुब्जा अग्रघोणा (घोणायाः अग्रं or rather अग्रं चासौ घोणा च) यस्य the tip of whose nose was curved like the end of Garuḍa's beak. 'गरुत्मान्गरुडस्तार्क्ष्यः' अमरः. For the form अग्रघोणा, mark वामन's काव्यालङ्कारसूत्र 5. 2. 20 'हस्ताग्राग्रहस्तादयो गुणगुणिनोर्भेदाभेदात्'. दूर...कपोलम् whose cheeks looked narrow on account of the corners of his mouth being very far gashed. दूरविदीर्णे सृक्किणी ताभ्यां संक्षिप्तौ कपोलौ यस्य. किञ्चिदन्तुरतया because he had slightly prominent teeth. सदा हृदये सन्निहितः हरः तस्य मौलौ चन्द्रः तस्य आतपेन इव. He had white and prominent teeth, the brilliance of which brightened the circle of the quarters. The poet fancies that it was the light of S'iva's crescent issuing out of his mouth, शिव being always present in his heart. जिह्वाग्र...तौष्ठम्—his lip naturally hung down a little. He knew by heart (जिह्वाग्रस्थित) all the canonical works (संहिता) of the S'aivite sect. The poet fancies that his lip hung down as though on account of the weight of the संहिताs that were on the tip of the tongue. प्रलम्ब...बध्यमानम् with his crystal ear-rings dangling from his pendulous (प्रलम्ब) ear-lobes, he seemed as though pursued by Venus and Jupiter in the belief of acquiring (from him) a lore which would enable them to conquer the gods and demons (respectively). शुक्र and गुरु were respectively the preceptors of the असुरs and देवs. Venus and Jupiter, with which the two are identified, are the brightest of the planets. So the crystal ear-rings are fancied to be शुक्र and गुरु. बद्ध... कलयन्तम् wearing, on one of his forearms (प्रकोष्ठः) that had an iron bracelet and on which was tied a bundle of magic threads with various herbs, a piece of conchshell, as though it were the tooth of Pūshan broken by S'iva and turned by him (भैरवाचार्य) into an ornament out of devotion to शिव. The piece of शङ्ख was white like teeth. विविधौषधिभिः मन्त्रैः च युक्ता सूत्रपङ्क्तिः, बद्धा ०पङ्क्तिः यस्मिन्. Even now people wear dark thread on their forearms supposed to have magical properties. पूष्णो दन्तमिव— When वीरभद्र produced from S'iva's matted hair destroyed the sacrifice of दक्ष, some of the gods were severely dealt with. भग lost his eye, while one of the teeth of पूषन् was broken. *Vide* for the story भागवतपुराण 4. 5. 'भगस्य नेत्रं भगवान्पातितस्य रुषा भुवि। उज्जहार सदःस्थोऽक्ष्णो यः शपन्तमसूसुचत् ॥ पूष्णश्चापातयद्दन्तान् कालिङ्गस्य यथा बलः। शप्यमाने गरिमणि योऽहसद्दर्शयन्दतः ॥' verses 20–21. As the दन्त became holy by the touch of वीरभद्र, the ascetic is fancied as wearing it with भक्ति. There seems to be some faint reference even in the Rigveda to the story about the loss of the tooth of पूषन्. Compare 'वामं पूषा वामं भगो वामं देवः करूळती' (which last is explained as कृत्तदन्त) Rigveda IV. 30. 24. अखिल...मालामिव—The beads of the rosary looked like the pots for throwing up (उदञ्चन) the water (रस) in a well and the string of the rosary like the rope on which the pots are placed at intervals. He revolved the rosary in his right hand. A water-wheel also is turned with the right hand. अखिलस्य रसस्य कूपात् उदञ्चनं तदर्थं घटीयन्त्रमाला. The रुद्राक्षमाला also threw out all pleasures (रस) from his heart (which was concentrated solely on शिव). आ (ईषत्) पिङ्गलानि अग्राणि यस्य. कूर्चकलापेन by his thick beard. संमार्जे...निकरम्—the idea is:—a कूर्च (brush, peacock's feathers) is used in sweeping off a heap (निकर:) of dust (रज:); his beard that rubbed his chest. is fancied as sweeping off रज: (passion) contained in the heart. रज: is one of the three Guṇas according to the सांख्यs. It is रजोगुण that gives rise to काम and क्रोध and leads a person into sin. 'सत्त्वं लघु प्रकाशकमिष्टमुपष्टम्भकं चलं च रजः। गुरु वरणकमेव तमः' सांख्यकारिका; 'अथ केन प्रयुक्तोऽयं पापं चरति पूरुषः। अनिच्छन्नपि वार्ष्णेय बलादिव नियोजितः ॥ काम एष क्रोध एष रजोगुणसमुद्भवः।' गीता chap. 3. 36–37. निचितं full of (*adj.* of ०देशं). ध्यान...दधानम्—the idea is:—By meditation he had acquired the illumination (ज्योतिः) of knowledge. Light (ज्योतिः) such as that of fire or the sun burns; what is burnt up becomes dark. The dark hair on his chest is fancied to be the effect of ज्योतिः which illumines his heart. ईषत्प्रशिथिलेन वलिवलयेन बध्यमानं तुन्दं (उदरं) यस्य. उपचीयमानः (protuberant) स्फिङ्मांसपिण्डकः यस्य. स्फिच् *f.* buttocks, hips. 'स्त्रियां स्फिचौ कटिप्रोथौ' अमरः. पाण्डुरेण पवित्रेण क्षौमेण (linen cloth) आवृतं कौपीनं (private parts) यस्य. For कौपीन see above notes p. 198. सा...मण्डलितेन that was passed round (his body) while he sat in a dignified पर्यङ्क posture. When a person sits on his hams with legs cross-wise and a piece of cloth is firmly tied round his knees, loins and back, it is called पर्यङ्कबन्ध (Marathi जेठा मारून बसणें). बाण's description leaves no doubt about the meaning of पर्यङ्कबन्ध. But मल्लिनाथ commenting on the words 'पर्यङ्कबन्धस्थिरपूर्वकायम्' (कुमारसम्भव 3. 45) explains it as वीरासन and quotes two definitions of the latter, which do not agree with our explanation. *Vide* मल्लिनाथ's comment. अमृतफेनवत् श्वेता रुक् (कान्तिः) यस्य (with योगपट्टकेन); ०फेनेन श्वेता रुक् यस्य (with वासुकिना). For योगपट्टक, see p. 26. For वासुकि being the rope in churning, *vide* p. 52. वासुकि must have been sprinkled with the foam of अमृत as it came out of the churned ocean. अप्रतिहतः (irresistible) अनेकमन्त्राणां प्रभावः तेन आविर्भूतः तेन. The poet fancies that the योगपट्टक encircling his body was वासुकि manifesting itself through the irresistible might of the ascetic's incantations and then performing a प्रदक्षिणा round him. Even now it is believed that a मान्त्रिक can call out a serpent from its hiding place by the power of मन्त्रs. The suggested meaning is that, as वासुकि is the king of serpents, the ascetic must have been a great magician indeed. Compare for the conceit 'सुधाफेनधवलेन तप.-प्रभावकुण्डलीकृतेन गङ्गास्रोतसेव योगपट्टकेन विरचितवैकक्ष्यका' (text p. 3 ll. 29–30 above). अरुणतामरसवत् सुकुमारं तलं यस्य. जर्जरयन्त...तलम्—the idea is:—the bright rays of his reddish soles spread on the surface (तल) of the earth (रसा). The poet fancies that he crushed the earth (with the rays) in his passion or zeal (रसः) for bringing out the great treasures (supposed to be lying in the earth). The person who is believed to be able to see treasures hidden in the earth is called (in Marathi) पायाळु. तोयेन क्षालितं अत एव शुचि तेन (applies to both युगलेन and ०मिथुनेन). हंस...गतेन as though they were two हंसs that had come there in order to become familiar with the pilgrimage to holy places on the Ganges. He had often been to the holy Ganges and would again go there. Therefore हंसs (in the form of the wooden slippers) never left his feet. In the next clause the principal part is वैणवेन विशाखिकादण्डेन सततपार्श्ववर्तिना विराजमानम्—who had constantly at his side a bamboo विशाखिका staff. What विशाखिका means is not quite clear. Probably it is a staff the upper part of which branches off into two and forms a loop. Compare **'विशाखिका**शिखरनिबद्धनालिकेरीफलवल्कलमयधौतोपानद्युगोपेताम्' कादम्बरी p. 133 of P. The commentators of the कादम्बरी explain it variously as **'विशाखिका** भूमिशुद्ध्यर्थमाद्रियमाणा लोहयष्टिरूपा शिक्यभेदो वा;' **'विशाखिका** रुद्राङ्कुशः; **विशाखिका** विशाखा सा तरोरवयवान्तरम्'. शिखरे निखाताः (imbedded) कुब्जाः (curved) कालायसकण्टकाः (iron hooks) यस्य. Even now people in the Konkan use a staff that has a few iron hooks fixed at the top, which rattle when a man walks and frighten away reptiles. ०कण्टकेन applies to ०ङ्कुशेन also. An अङ्कुश (goad) also has an iron barb imbedded in it. सर्व...ङ्कुशेनेव as though it were a goad for driving away Ganes'a who causes obstacles in the mastery of all the lores. It should be remembered that an elephant is controlled by a goad and that गणेश has the head of an elephant. विनायक is called विघ्नराज (he controls as well as causes obstacles). विनायक also presides over learning. The suggestion is:—the ascetic had mastered all विद्याs; he had the goad-like staff always with him by way of a threat to गणेश if the latter wanted to cause any obstacle. बाण often uses विनायक for श्लेष. Compare 'अयमशिवसहचरो विनायकः' हर्ष० 8th उ०; 'अशिवमूर्तयो महाविनायकाधिष्ठिताः' कादम्बरी p. 287 of P. The words सर्व० would also mean 'with a goad that drives away the chief (विनायक) obstacles &c.' or 'with a goad that subdues (विनायक) and drives away the obstacles &c.' कुमारब्रह्मचारिणम् who had observed the vow of celibacy all his life from boyhood (*i. e.* he was a नैष्ठिकब्रह्मचारी 'a perpetual student' and not उपकुर्वाण). कृशः (thin *i. e.* restrained) क्रोधः यस्य. अकृशः (not thin *i. e.* great) अनुरोधः (complying with another's request, kindness) यस्य. 'अनुरोधोऽनुवर्तनम्' अमरः. अदीना (not wretched *i. e.* noble) प्रकृतिः (nature) तया शोभितम्. अदीन...शोभितम् (with महानगर 'capital') means 'adorned by noble ministers &c. or rich guilds'. प्रकृति means 'the constituent elements of a kingdom' or 'guilds of citizens.' 'स्वाम्यमात्यसुहृत्कोशराष्ट्रदुर्गबलानि च । राज्याङ्गानि प्रकृतयः पौराणां श्रेणयोऽपि च ॥' अमरः. क्षीर० quotes कात्य as "यत्कात्यः 'अमात्याद्याश्च पौराश्च सद्भिः प्रकृतयः स्मृताः.'" There is another sense possible. प्रकृति means 'the base' or 'the original accent of a word.' Each word (whether single or compounded with another word) has generally only one उदात्त accent. If a word be compounded with another, it may lose its accent and take the accent for the whole compound as determined by the rules. There is a rule that 'when नगर is the second member of a समास, the first letter of the first member has the उदात्त accent, except when the first word is महत् or नवन्.' 'अमहन्नवन्नगरेऽनुदीचाम्' पा. 6. 2. 89. In महानगर, the first word is महत्; therefore नगर retains its original accent (प्रकृतिस्वर) and the first letter has not the उदात्त accent. Thus in महानगर the प्रकृति (स्वर) is अदीन (not low-pitched; but is high-pitched, as उदात्त is). 'उच्चैरुदात्तः' and 'नीचैरनुदात्तः' पा. 1. 2. 29-30. कल्प...च्छायम्—०राशिवत् सुकुमारा छाया (कान्तिः) यस्य (with भैरवाचार्य); ०राशिभिः सुकुमारा छाया (shade) यस्य (with मेरु). मेरु is shaded with the delicate leaves of the trees of paradise. ०रजसा पवित्रितं शिरः (head, top) यस्य. On the top of कैलास dwells शिव. He had bowed his head at the feet of the image of शिव. मा...यातम् followed by a crowd (गणः) of Saivas (with भैरवाचार्य); peopled with the attendants (गणाः) of शिव. महेश्वरस्य इमे माहेश्वराः गणाः (प्रमथाः). 'सङ्घाते प्रमथे गणः' अमरः. ०सहस्रे प्रक्षालितं शरीरं येन; ०स्रेण प्रक्षालितं शरीरं यस्य (with जलनिधि). The ascetic had bathed in numerous rivers. Numerous rivers fall into the ocean. बहु...शुचिम् pure by residing in many holy spots (with भैरवाचार्य); pure with many holy तीर्थs situated on it (with ०प्रवाहम्). धाम place, dwelling. तीर्थं तथ्यस्य the sacred place of truth. कुशलस्य of welfare or prosperity. पूतता holiness. शालेयं शालीनतायाः the ricefield of modesty. For शालेय, see p. 118 and for शालीन p. 57. स्थानं स्थितेः abode of all propriety or decorum. आधारं धृतेः support of steadiness. आकरः mine. निकेतनं कौतुकस्य the house of admiration. All admired him. आरामं रामणीयकस्य the garden of loveliness. प्रासादं प्रसादस्य the palace of good-will (towards all). अगारं गौरवस्य house of respect. All respected him. समाजं सौजन्यस्य the conference of goodness. सम्भवं सद्भावस्य the source of amiability. कालं कलेः the death of Kali. He nullified the effects of Kali, the age of sin and discord. विरूपाक्षम् = शिवम्. शशि...चाल he got up, as the ocean rises up on seeing the moon. At moonrise, the waters of the ocean begin to rise in a tide. प्रथमतरं उत्थितः शिष्यलोकः यस्य. प्रत्युज्जगाम went forward to receive. समर्पितं श्रीफलोपायनं येन who gave him the present of Bilva fruit. **'बिल्वे** शाण्डिल्यशैलूषौ मालूर**श्री-फलावपि'** अमरः. The बिल्व tree is sacred to शिव. जह्नुकर्णात् समुद्गीर्यमाणः (emitted) गङ्गाप्रवाहः तस्य ह्रादः (roar) तद्वत् गम्भीरया. For Jahnu, see p. 84.

P. 48 ll. 3-15 **नरपति···भजत**· प्रीत्या विस्तार्यमाणः धवलिमा यस्य the whiteness of which increased through the joy he felt. प्रत्यर्प...वनानि—When he bowed, he cast glances from the whites of his eyes. These resembled the silver lotuses that भैरवाचार्य had sent. The poet fancies that he returned in the form of his glances the lotuses that he had received. The only difference was that he returned many (as he cast many glances), while he had received only five. ललाट...प्रकाशयन् with his crest-jewel dangling about on his forehead and having its rays shooting up he as though manifested the favour of S'iva by the appearance of a third eye. उद्गताः अंशवः यस्य. शिव has a third eye on the forehead. The red jewel dangling on the forehead of the king, when he bowed to भैरव, is fancied to be the third eye that appeared (उद्गमः) just at that moment. शिव favoured the king so much that he made him त्रिनेत्र like himself. आवर्जितः (bent down) कर्णपल्लवः तस्मात् पलायमानाः मधुकराः यस्य. When he bent down to bow, the bees ran away from his ear-ornament of flowers. शिवसेवया समुन्मूलिताः अशेषपापलवाः तैः मुच्यमानः. The dark bees look like sins (which are supposed to be dark). दूरावनतः bending very low. अभिनवम्—his bow is called अभिनव (a new or unique one), because it is accompanied by all the wonderful results described above. शार्दूल...दर्शयत्—the ascetic desired the king to be seated on his own tiger skin. To seat a person on one's आसन is a mark of great respect and friendship. It shows that the person so treated is at least the equal, if not the superior, of the person so treating. उपदर्शितः प्रश्रयः (humility) येन. मत्तहंसस्य कलः गद्गदः स्वरः तेन सुभगां (with नदीम्); तद्वत् सुभगां (with वाचम्). मधुरसमयीम् full of sweetness (with वाचम्); full of sweet water (with नदीम्). प्रवर्तयन् making flow; uttering. नार्हसि...कर्तुम् you will please not ill-treat me on account of the misdeeds of other kings. His meaning is:—Other kings might not have reverence for holy ascetics like you and might sit on the seat occupied by you. But I cannot occupy that seat honouring you as I do; and I do not like such formal treatment from you. अशेष...गुरुः that the teacher (your reverence) so deals with me is the fault of the character of that wretched Lakshmî (royalty) that is looked up to by all kings or is the ill-natured-ness of lucre. All kings care too much for लक्ष्मी and become wicked through wealth. You think that I am also one of those kings and would take umbrage if you did not offer me your own seat. The usual meaning of उपेक्षित is 'neglected, slighted.' But that meaning does not suit the context. अभूमि...चाराणाम् this person (*i. e.* I) is not a fit subject for ceremonious behaviour (उपचारः). अल...णया enough of great restraint (*i. e.* formality). मनोरथशिष्यः a pupil in wishes (*i. e.* I desired to be your disciple). नोल्लङ्घनमर्हति does not deserve to be trodden. परिजनेन उपनीते (brought). वाससि on a garment. अनतिक्रमणीय irresistible. अनुवर्तमानः acceding to, complying with.

P. 48 ll. 16—31 **आसीने...मगात्.** राजकेन सह सराजके (*adj.* of परिजने). अर्घ्यम् respectful offering of flowers, water &c. अर्घः पूजाविधिः तदर्थं द्रव्यं अर्घ्यम्. 'पादार्घाभ्यां च' पा. 5. 4. 25 (यत्). नृपमाधुर्येण हृतं (captivated) अन्तःकरणं यस्य. शशि...मलाः pure like the rays of the moon (with दशनदीधितीः); pure with the rays of the moon (with ॰भक्तीः). शिवभक्तीः (*accu. plu.* of ॰भक्ति)—if one were to worship शिव, then one's devotion would be illumined by the light of the moon that is on the head of शिव. अति...गौरवम् your very modesty declares the greatness (vast extent) of your qualities. The more the virtues that a man possesses, the more modest does he become, as he comes to know of his defects. It is only those that are shallow that become puffed up. गौरव also means 'weight'. What is heavy makes the carrier bend down. सकल...मसि you are a fit receptacle for all prosperity. विभ...पत्तयः your conduct (or undertakings) is quite in keeping with your greatness. जन्मनः...तेयेषु since my birth I never cast my eyes on wealth (*i. e.* I never paid any regard to it). स्वापतेयं wealth, from स्वपति, according to 'पथ्यतिथिवसतिस्वपतेर्ढञ्' पा. 4. 4. 104 (पथि साधु पाथेयम्।...स्वापतेयं धनम्। सि. कौ.). यतः...मस्ति since I possess this poor body not sold for money that is the fuel to the fire of all sins. He says that he is master of his own body, poor though it be. All persons sell their bodies to others for amassing money. As fuel feeds fire, so money feeds sins. So he never cared for money. क is added to शरीर to indicate that he does not care much even for that body. कुत्सितं शरीरं शरीरकम्. दुर्गृ... क्षराणि I have a few ill-understood syllables of knowledge. This he speaks in great humility. भट्टारक *adj.* venerable; *m.* god. पुण्यकणिका particle of merit. अत्र—out of the things enumerated (by him) *viz.* body, प्राणाः, विद्या and पुण्य. प्र...ग्राह्याणि to be captivated by a few virtues (with मनांसि); to be bound by a fine (प्रतनु) thread (with कुसुमानि). The comparison shows that the minds of the good are tender like flowers. विद्वत्संमताः highly thought of by the learned (with साधवः); approved by the learned (with शब्दाः). श्रूयमाणा अपि even when merely heard (though not actually seen). साधवः the good; grammatically pure (with words). सुधीरे...विवरम् fame makes a hole (*i. e.* an impression) in a mind even though it be very steady. A hole (विवर) cannot be easily made on what is firm. विशतः... कल्याणिना I, who was being borne away by the currents, white with foam, of curiosity that entered my heart, am now brought back by your auspicious self with your virtues. The idea is:—so long, not having seen you, my heart overflowed with curiosity to see you; but now that I see you, *you* occupy my heart and not *mere curiosity* about you. A stream becomes white with foam. गुणगण is white like foam. A person who is borne away by a flood is brought back by ropes (गुणगण). If we omit सुखयन्ति, then this passage becomes involved and difficult to explain. Then we must stop at कुर्वन्ति and take विवरं with विशतः. अनु...प्रणयिनः In the case of the bodies &c. of the good, though they be dear to them, friends are the masters *i. e.* friends can dispose of the bodies of the good just as they like, though the good may love their bodies. Here अनुरक्त has to be taken in an unusual sense. It is not शरीर that is अनुरक्त. It is the good that are अनुरक्त so far as their शरीर is concerned. So अनुरक्त means 'प्रिय' here. The com. seems to read 'अनुक्तेष्वपि.' This is a better reading. The meaning then is 'friends are the masters of the bodies &c. of the good, even though it be not declared in so many words.' अने...गुरुणा on this my coming here I am placed in an enviable position by the teacher. He means:—the mere fact that on my arrival here I was treated so well by you has given me great pleasure and has raised me to an exalted position.

P. 48 l. 32—**P. 49** l. 20 **अन्य...कृपाणम्.** तस्मै...वेदितवान् the king placed himself, his harem, his servants, and his treasury at his disposal. Mark this use of the word निवेदितवान्. निवेदय् to offer, to present. आत्मनिवेदन is the last stage in नवविधा भक्ति. 'श्रवणं कीर्तनं विष्णोः स्मरणं पादसेवनम्। अर्चनं वन्दनं दास्यं सख्यमात्मनिवेदनम् ॥ इति पुंसार्पिता विष्णौ भक्तिश्चेन्नवलक्षणा ॥' भागवतपु० 7. 5. 23-24. For two क्त्s, see above notes p. 180. धनो...स्विता high-mindedness surely withers away, like a creeper, by the heat of wealth. अलं is used here in the sense of 'excessively' or 'surely.' खद्यो...तेजस्विता The brilliance that we possess is like that of fire-flies, scorching no one else. अ...तापिन् not causing harm to others (with भैर०); not setting on fire any other thing (with खद्योत). Fireflies have a centre of light in their bodies, but it does not burn anyone. भैरवाचार्य says he prefers to have the तेजस्विता of moneyless asceticism, which has no power to hurt others and which is purely spiritual; while the तेजस्विता of wealth has great potentialities for evil. भाजनं=पात्रं. भूतेः=ऐश्वर्यस्य. तेनैव क्रमेण as before, as was his wont. श्वेत...वृतं wrapped in a white piece of cloth. ब्रह्मराक्षसः the ghost of a wicked ब्राह्मण, who, when living, used to commit sins such as carrying away the wives of others and the property of Brāhmaṇas. 'परस्य योषितं हृत्वा ब्रह्मस्वमपहृत्य च। अरण्ये निर्जले देशे भवति ब्रह्मराक्षसः ॥' याज्ञ० 3. 212. अपहृतं कर्पटावच्छादनं यस्य (*adj.* of परिवारात्) from which the covering of cloth was removed. परिवारः sheath. आचकर्ष—the object is कृपाणम् (l. 20). शर...नीतम् as though it were the autumnal sky turned into a solid mass. The author indulges here into many उत्प्रेक्षाs to convey the clearness, brightness and formidableness of the sword. पिण्डं also means 'steel.' 'लोहोऽस्त्री शस्त्रकं

तीक्ष्णं **पिण्डं** कालायसायसी' अमरः. The com. explains 'पिण्डं' as 'शस्त्रम्' (weapon) and quotes the above words of Amara in support. The sky is clear and bright like a sword in autumn. कालिन्दी... जलम् as though it were the stream of the Jumna with the water benumbed (*i. e.* not allowed to flow). The waters of the Jumna are dark and hence the उत्प्रेक्षा. नन्दक...गतम् as though Kāliya, irritated by Kṛishṇa, had assumed the form of a sword for conquering (*i. e.* surpassing) Nandaka (the sword of Vishṇu). For नन्दक, see p. 88 and for कालिय p. 143. The serpent कालिय was dark. लोक...तितम् as though it were a piece of cloud at the time of *pralaya* fallen from the sky, manifesting a heavy down-pour of water for the destruction of the world. प्रकाशितः धाराणां आसारः येन. 'धारासम्पात आसारः' अमरः. प्रकाशितः धारायाः सारः (बलं) येन that manifests the strength of its edge (with the sword). Or we may dissolve as प्रकटितः धारा एव आसारः येन. We speak of the 'water' of the edge of a sword. काल time; dark. A कल्प is a period of 1000 महायुगs and equal to 4320000000 human years. It is equal to a day of ब्रह्मा, the night being also of the same duration. At the end of one कल्प the whole universe is dissolved and merges in the supreme spirit and remains there for one कल्प and is then again produced. Note भगवद्गीता 8. 17–18. At the time of कल्पान्त or प्रलय, it was believed that the 49 winds began to blow, the twelve suns rose and dark clouds called पुष्कर and आवर्तक enveloped the sky. Compare 'महाप्रलयेषु प्रलयपयोदाः प्रलयदुर्दिनान्धकारितदशदिशः प्लावयन्ति भुवनान्तराणि' कादम्बरी p. 125 of P. The sword also manifests its धारासार for destroying people. दृश्यमानं विकटं दन्तमण्डलं यस्मिन्. दृश्य...हिंसायाः as though it were the laugh of destruction showing a terrible circle of teeth. In laughing one shows one's teeth. हिंसा (killing beings), if personified, must have terrible teeth. The sword was bright like a laugh (but of हिंसा, because it killed). The sword also had terrible दन्तs (indentations). हरि...ग्रहम् as though it were the stout arm of Hari, holding fast मुष्टि. कृतः दृढः मुष्टिग्रहः येन that tightly clinched the fist (with बाहुदण्ड); कृतः दृढः मुष्टिग्रहः यस्य the hilt of which was firmly held (with कृपाणम्); also 'that firmly seized the demon मुष्टि'. मुष्टिक was a demon killed by बलराम who is supposed to be an incarnation of Vishṇu. Compare 'केशव धृतहलधररूप जय जगदीश हरे' गीतगोविन्द. For मुष्टिक see भागवतपु० 10. 44. 24. सकल...क्षमेण capable of destroying the lives of all the worlds. This applies both to the sword and to कालकूट. कालकूट

is dark. *Vide* p. 2. कृतान्त...घटितम् as though manufactured of steel heated by the fire of the wrath of Yama. It was not ordinary fire that heated the steel going to make up the sword. In order to make it most destructive, it was heated in the fire of Yama's wrath. अति...कणन्तम्—A very irritable (तीक्ष्ण) man may fly into a rage even when merely touched by the wind. A very irritable person is popularly said to be one who quarrels with the wind. The sword having a very fine blade sounded when the wind blew upon it. मणि...पाटयन्तम् under the guise of its reflection falling on the jewelled pavement (कुट्टिमः-मम्) of the hall, it (sword) as though cleft itself in two. 'कुट्टिमोऽस्त्री निबद्धा भूः.' अरि...धारम् the edge of which looked indented (करालित) with the rays (shooting from it) as though they (rays) were hair sticking to it at the time of cutting off enemies' heads. कराल means दन्तुर. The rays look like so many दन्तs of the sword. 'करालो दन्तुरे तुङ्गे' अमरः. करालिता (uneven, jagged) धारा यस्य. मुहु...दिवसम् that as if cut into pieces daylight that was crushed by overspreading (छुरित) it with the circle of its radiance flickering again and again like flashes (उन्मेषः) of lightning. जर्जरितः आतपः यस्य (*adj.* of दिवसम्). The flashing light of the sword blade spread through and through over daylight and thus seemed to cleave it asunder into portions. Remove the comma after ०तपम्. कटा...रात्रेः a glance as though of the night of destruction. रात्रि is dark and so the sword is said to be its कटाक्ष. काल also means 'dark'. This and the following clauses are intended to convey the terrific aspect of the sword. उत्पल is a blue lotus. Hence the sword is said to be the ear lotus of Death. ओङ्कारमिव०—The syllable *om* precedes the study of the Veda. It is a mystic syllable credited with supernatural powers and is symbolical of Brahma itself. So the sword was the essence or centre of cruelty. Compare 'सत्यस्य शनैः शनैरोङ्कारमिव कुर्वाणे' हर्ष० 4th उ० and the notes thereon. Note 'एकाक्षरं परं ब्रह्म' मनु० 2.83. अलङ्का...कारस्य—It was an ornament to arrogance *i. e.* whoever had the sword could afford to be arrogant. कुलमित्रं family friend *i. e.* friend of long standing. देहं दर्पस्य—it was pride incarnate. अपत्यं मृत्योः—it possessed the qualities of Death, as a child is endowed with the qualities of its parent. आग...लक्ष्म्याः it was the way by which लक्ष्मी came *i. e.* it helped in securing wealth (and kingdom). निर्ग...कीर्तेः—it was the way by which fame went out into the world *i. e.* the sword would enable one to do heroic deeds whereby one's fame would spread in the world.

P. 49 ll. 21—26 **अवनि...मेदिनीम्.** आयुध...लिङ्गन्निव he seemed, under the guise of his reflection, as though embracing it out of affection for it (or out of his love for weapons of all kinds). The king was reflected in the bright sword-blade. The poet fancies that the king embraced it out of love for it. पर...विदग्धमपि though it is ill-mannered (or proud) enough to scorn accepting another's property. The words may also mean 'ignorant of the humiliation *viz.* accepting another's property.' But as here the emphasis is laid upon the word व्यतिक्रम, so अवज्ञा also must be understood in the sense of 'disregarding.' युष्मद्विषये in your case. वचन...रितुम् to commit (to be guilty of) the crime of disregarding your words (request). The words referred to are 'भवद्भुजयोग्यो गृह्यताम्'. साधयामः is used in the sense of 'गच्छामः,' which latter is not used, as it was believed to be an inauspicious word indicating 'perishing.' प्रकृत्या...रागी by nature loving the heroic temper.

P. 49 l. 27—**P. 50** l. 10 **अथ...इति.** उपह्वरे in secret. उपह्वरः a lonely place. उपग्रहेण यथा स्यात्तथा सोपग्रहम् in a conciliatory tone; with a request. स्वार्थ...भव्यानाम् The dispositions of the good are careless of their own interests but vigilant in obliging others. For भव्य, compare the first verse of the 8th उच्छ्वास 'दैवेनापि क्रियते **भव्यानां** पूर्वसेवेव.' भवादृशां...कारः to such as you the sight of suppliants is a great festival, requests (preferred by the needy) are a means of giving pleasure, acceptance of gifts (by others) is an obligation. The idea is that great persons like पुष्पभूति are pleased (आराधन) when requests are made to them; great persons feel obliged when the gifts they offer are accepted by others. भैरवाचार्य wants the king's help in a perilous undertaking and so makes this highly flattering introduction. भूमि-...धीयसे you are the centre of all men's hopes; therefore you are addressed (by me). He means that all men hope to fulfil their desires through your help. महाकालहृदयं नाम यस्य. महाकाल is शिव. As to the wonderful power ascribed to *mantras*, *vide* pp. 54–55. कृष्णाः स्रगम्बरानुलेपाः यस्मिन् (*adj* of आकल्पेन)—in which the garland, garment and unguents were all dark. आकल्पः decoration, equipment. कल्पकथितेन as declared in the ritualistic works (of the S'aiva sect). 'इतिकर्तव्यकलापोपदेशको ग्रन्थः कल्पः' सं०. जपकोट्या by muttering (the *mantra*) a crore of times. पूर्वं कृता कृतपूर्वा, कृतपूर्वा सेवा येन सः ०सेवः. वेतालसाधनं अवसाने (अन्ते) यस्य. तस्य...सिद्धिः complete attainment of that *mantra* ends with the subduing of a goblin. वेताल: ghost occupying a dead body. त्वं...कर्मणे you are quite a match for that deed (*i. e.* you will be able to achieve this). अलं in the sense of 'being sufficient for a thing or able to do a thing' governs the dative. 'नमः—स्वस्तिस्वाहास्वधाऽलंवषड्योगाच्च' पा. 2. 3. 16 (अलमिति पर्याप्त्यर्थग्रहणम् । दैत्येभ्यो हरिरलम् । सि. कौ.). गृहीतः भरः येन. त्वयि...भरे when you undertake the responsibility. भवन्तमुपतिष्ठते who waits upon you (who brought the silver lotuses). The Ātmanepada is in accordance with the वार्तिक 'उपाद्देवपूजासङ्गतिकरणमित्रकरणपथिष्विति वाच्यम्' (on 'उपान्मन्त्रकरणे' पा. 1. 3. 25). द्राविडः inhabitant of the द्रविड country. द्रविड was roughly between the कृष्णा and the कावेरी. Its capital was काञ्ची. यदि...मन्यसे If you approve. दिङ्नागः दिग्गजः तस्य हस्तवत् दीर्घः. गृहीतः अट्टहासः येन. नीयतामयं निशा...बाहुः let this arm (of yours) be made a bolt of one of the quarters for one night *i. e.* you must guard one of the (four) quarters on one night (that I shall appoint). The student will find that the king and the three others mentioned here guarded the four quarters while भैरवाचार्य was engaged in grim rites. कृतं वचः येन—when he had finished his words. अन्ध...प्रकाशः (delighted) like one in darkness that sees a light. प्राप्तः उपकारस्य अवकाशः (opportunity) येन—The king had been obliged by the ascetic who had made him a present of the sword called अट्टहास and of several silver lotuses. The king desired to oblige the ascetic in return. And this was the first opportunity he found to do so. अनेन...वैमि I look upon myself as accepted by you (as yours) by this task (निदेशः) which is shared by me in common with your pupils. कृतः परिग्रहः (स्वीकारः) यस्य. निदेशः order ; appointed task. व्याहृतं utterance. सङ्केतः an appointment; a place of meeting. असितपक्ष dark fortnight. The 14th day of the dark fortnight (particularly of माघ) is sacred to शिव. इयत्यां वेलायां at this hour or at such an hour.

P. 50 ll. 11–23. **अथाति...तमुद्देशम्.** शैवेन...दीक्षितः being initiated into the S'aiva ritual. नियमवान्—observing a fast (or other rules of a दीक्षा). कृतः अधिवासः यस्य—on which purificatory ceremonies were performed. अधिवासः or अधिवासनम् application of scents and perfumes 'संस्कारो गन्धमाल्याद्यैर्यः स्यात्तदधिवासनम्' अमरः. But बाण immediately afterwards says 'समाहित...पूजम्.' So अधिवास must be taken in the sense of 'preliminary consecration of an object of worship with suitable *mantras* before the commencement of a sacrifice.' 'अधिवासो नियमदिवसादाद्येऽहनि यथाशास्त्रं विधिना

मन्त्रन्यासादिः' सं०. सम्पादिता गन्ध...माल्यादिना पूजा यस्य. The next sentence is ततः परिणते दिवसे...एकाकी नगरान्निरगात्. परिणते दिवसे when the day came to a close. केनापि...दिक्षु when the regions put on a rosy hue as though someone had made offerings of blood for the purpose of securing success in his undertaking. कृतं रुधिरबलिविधानं यासु. The natural redness of the regions in the evening is fancied to be due to the offerings of blood. रुधिर... दीधितिषु when the rays of the sun hung down as though they were the tongues of goblins greedy (लम्पट) for the offering of blood. Blood is scattered about to propitiate वेतालs. लम्बमानासु applies to 'tongues' also, as they also loll out when greedy. रुधिर...लम्पटासु may apply to the rays of the sun. 'That are greedy (*i.e.* that fall upon) for red offerings' (smeared with red powder). Such offerings are placed on roads in the evening. नरेन्द्रा... सवितरि when the sun, that resorted to the west, as though himself desired to do duty as a guardian of the quarters out of affection for the king. The king had been asked to guard one direction. The sun set in the west. The poet fancies that the sun, seeing that his friend (the king) was to be दिक्पाल, himself wanted to be दिक्पाल and so resorted to the west. गृहीता अपरदिक् (west) येन; गृहीता अपरा (another, other than the one the king would accept) दिक् येन. यातुधानी = राक्षसी. The long and dark shadows of trees looked like demons. पाताल...मण्डलेषु—It was believed that demons infested पाताल, stalked abroad at night and caused obstacles to यज्ञ. पाताल is also supposed to be a region of darkness. पाताल०—this applies both to दानवेषु and ०मण्डलेषु. नभसि...गणे when the clusters of stars formed groups in the sky, as though they desired to witness the terrible rite. On कृष्णचतुर्दशी the night is very dark and so the clusters of stars appear very clear. Sight-seers gather together in small groups. रौद्रं कर्म may also mean 'rite of which the देवता is रुद्र (*i. e.* शिव).' विगाढा dense, deep. विगाढायां शर्वर्याम् in the depth of night *i. e.* when the night had advanced a great deal. सुप्ताः जनाः यस्मिन् (*adj.* of निशीथे). निःशब्दस्तिमिते noiseless and motionless. निशीथे at midnight. 'अर्धरात्रनिशीथौ द्वौ' अमरः. वञ्चयित्वा deceiving *i. e.* eluding. वामकरे स्फुरन् त्सरुः (hilt) यस्य (*adj.* of राजा). उत्खात drawn. विसर्पता...यष्टिः by the spreading radiance of the sword, his whole body was concealed as in a blue silken robe for fear that he might be seen. The king wanted to go unobserved. The dark hue of his sword surrounded his body as in a dark robe and effected his object. अनादिष्टया अपि although not ordered by him. पृष्ठतः...कर्षन् in the shape of the rows (*lit.* braids) of bees pursuing him on account of the fragrance (of his body) he dragged behind him by the hair success in the rite. The dark bees resemble the dark braid of a woman. The bees came behind him. The poet fancies that he seized by the hair कर्मसिद्धि and dragged her behind him (made her follow him), the suggestion being that it was a foregone conclusion that the undertaking was to be successful. उद्देशः spot.

P. 50 l. 24—**P. 51** l. 6. **अथ...भूमिम्.** The first sentence is अथ प्रत्युज्जग्मुस्ते त्रयः...टीटिभ...स्वामिनः (p. 51 l. 1) निवेदितवन्तश्चात्मानम्. द्रौणि...सौप्तिके like the son of द्रोण (*i. e.* अश्वत्थामा), कृप and कृतवर्मन् in the night attack. सुप्तेषु भवं सौप्तिकम्. The reference is to the सौप्तिकपर्व of the महाभारत. While कृप and कृतवर्मा lay under a न्यग्रोध tree at night towards the close of the great war, अश्वत्थामा saw an owl killing crows at night when they were asleep in their nests. This suggested to him a night attack on the Pāṇḍava camp. कृप and कृतवर्मा followed him. अश्वत्थामा entered into the camp and stationed the other two at the door. He killed almost all and those that ran towards the door were killed by कृप and कृतवर्मा. सन्नद्धाः wearing armour. गृहीतः विकटः (frightful, gaudy) वेशः यैः. क्रियमाणः मन्त्रैः शिखाबन्धः येषाम्. कुसुम... चरणैः—bees hovered over the flowers they wore in their top-knot and hummed. The poet fancies that the humming was the reciting of *mantras* and the dark bees were themselves the knot of their hair that was being tied to the accompaniment of mystic *mantras* (in order that they may come unscathed out of the perilous undertaking). उष्णीष...मूर्धभिः on their heads they wore turban wraps that were tied in a knot in the form of a large *svastika* on the middle part of their forehead, as though they were sectarial marks (on the forehead). ललाटमध्ये घटितः (formed) विकटः स्वस्तिकाग्रन्थिः यैः. We rather expect स्वस्तिकग्रन्थीन्. स्वस्तिक is a mystical figure and so the author indulges in the उत्प्रेक्षा 'महामुद्राबन्धानिव.' The *svastika*-like knot of the turban on the forehead seemed to be some mystic मुद्रा on the forehead. For another meaning of मुद्रा (which also may be applicable here) see p. 46. The figure of स्वस्तिक due to wrapping of the turban looks like the intertwining of the hands and figures practised in worship. 'अन्योन्यग्रथिताङ्गुष्ठा प्रसारितपराङ्गुली । **महामुद्रेयमुदिता** परमीकरणे बुधैः ॥'. एकश्रवणविवरे विततं

(spread, stretching) विमलं दन्तपत्रं (ear-ring) तस्य प्रभालोकलेपेन धवलितः कपोलः येषाम् (*adj.* of मुखैः). आपिबन्तः—governs अन्धकारम् as its object. निशा...र्षया from the desire to thin the (numbers of) goblins. निशाचराणां अपचयः (reducing) शर्वर्याः इदं शार्वरम्. If they swallowed up the darkness of night, the goblins would vanish. अच्छाच्छया रुचा by the very clear brilliance. गो...लब्धाः anointed as though with *gorochanā* (yellow pigment) over which *mantras* were muttered. For गोरोचना *vide* notes on रोचना p. 114. स्व...स्त्रिंशान् brandishing sharp swords in which their images were reflected, they seemed to make offerings of human beings for the success of their undertaking. The images reflected in the bright sword-blade are fancied to be human beings killed by the sword-blade for ensuring success. निस्त्रिंशस्य अंशवः तेषां सन्तानेन सीमन्तितं तिमिरं यस्याः (*adj.* of त्रियामाम्). निस्त्रिंशांशु...पाटयन्तः—the idea is:—by the rays of their swords they (being three) parted (सीमन्तित) the darkness of night into three parts. The poet fancies that they cut up the night into three parts in order to guard their several regions. Read खण्डैः for खड्गैः. सार्ध...घटयन्तः with their shields that had crescents on them and had flashing on them star-like silver knobs, which (shields) looked like pieces of night sheared (निकृत्त) by the sharp edge of their swords, they seemed to create another night all of a sudden. In a night there is generally the moon; on that particular night there could be no moon as it was कृष्णचतुर्दशी. Their shields had bright crescent-shaped figures. कलधौतं gold or silver 'कलधौतं रूप्यहेम्नोः' अमरः. ०वलिः एव तरलः तारागणः येषाम्. Stars twinkle in the night; on the shields there were star-like silver patches. The shields were dark. For these three reasons the poet fancies them to be pieces of night. They walked in a line holding their dark shields; and so the author fancies that they created another night. For बुद्बुद (a sphere or knob) compare 'परिणतवराटकघटितबुद्बुदार्धचन्द्रखण्डखचितं (ध्वजं)' काद० p. 224. काञ्चनशृङ्खलाकलापेन नियमितं (fastened) निबिडं (thick or close-fitting) निष्प्रवाणि (new unbleached cloth) येषाम्. 'अनाहतं निष्प्रवाणि' अमरः (छेदः क्षालनं भोगश्च आहननं तद्रहितमनाहतम्-क्षीर०). 'निष्प्रवाणिश्च' पा. 2. 2. 160 (कबभावोऽत्र निपात्यते । प्रवाणी तन्तुवायशलाका । निर्गता प्रवाणी अस्य निष्प्रवाणिः पटः । समाप्तवानः नवः इत्यर्थः । सि.कौ.). बद्धा असिधेनुः यैः that had daggers fixed (in their waist-belt). निवे...दमानम् they announced themselves. ताम्—this and the following adjectives in the accu. sing. *(f.)* qualify ०भूमिम्. बलि...

दिग्भागतया the regions being filled with the smoke of *guggulu* and incense that was overspread with the light of the lamps (that were lit in worship). विक्षिप्य...निशामिव—the idea is:—white mustard was being scattered in all directions for protection from evil spirits. The poet fancies that the smoke of गुग्गुलु and धूप looking glossy on account of बलिदीप was really the night running away, having its darkness half burnt by the mustard seeds. One whose limbs are half burnt runs away (not one who is completely burnt). For white mustard, see p. 114. समुपकल्पितानि (got ready) सर्वाणि उपकरणानि यस्याम्. साधनभूमिः place of accomplishing an object by magic *i. e.* cemetery.

P. 51 ll. 7—22 **तस्यां च...कृतवान्.** The first sentence is तस्यां च...भैरवाचार्यमपश्यत् (l. 18). कुमु...धवलेन as white as the pollen of कुमुद्s (white night lotus). दीप्ततरः तेजःप्रसरः यस्य whose radiance was very much aglow. Remove the comma after ०प्रसरम्. पृथु...सवितारम् like the sun in autumn surrounded by a broad halo (परिवेशः). In शरद्, the sun's disc is clear and not clouded (as it often is in summer). भैरवाचार्य looked like the sun and the circle of ashes like the halo. मध्य...मन्दरम्—भैरवाचार्य looked like the मन्दर mountain and the circle of ashes like the whirlpool of the milky ocean. For मन्दर as the churning handle, *vide* p. 52. रक्तानि स्रक् अम्बरं आभरणानि च यस्य (*adj.* of शवस्य). उत्तानशयस्य lying on its back. जातः जातवेदाः अग्निः यस्मिन् (*adj.* of मुखकुहरे). प्रारब्धं अग्निकार्यं येन. भैरवाचार्य sat on the chest of a corpse and offered oblations to fire kindled (by magic power) in the mouth of the corpse. कृष्णः अङ्गरागः (unguents) यस्य. कृष्णः प्रतिसरः (amulet) यस्य. 'भवेत्**प्रतिसरो** मन्त्रभेदे माल्ये च कङ्कणे।...**आरक्षे करसूत्रे** च' मेदिनी. कृष्ण...नयन्तम् under the guise of the oblation of black sesame, he seemed as though annihilating the defiled atoms that were the cause of his being born a man, with the desire of becoming a विद्याधर. The black sesame are fancied to be the atoms that go to make up the human body. They are supposed to be कलुषित (defiled) as compared with the constituents of the body of विद्याधरs. The तिलs being कृष्ण, the atoms are said to be कालुष्यपरमाणुs. आहुति...दीधितिभिः with the rays of his nails that were scattered about when he offered the oblations, he seemed to cleanse the fire that was polluted by contact with the mouth of a corpse. The bright rays resemble water used for cleansing. धूमेन आलोहितः (slightly red) तेन. क्षतजं blood.

The glances of his red eyes are fancied to be offerings of blood. ईषत् विवृतं (open) अधरपुटं तेन प्रकटितानि सितानि दशनशिखराणि यस्मिन् (*adj.* of मुखेन). दृश्य...पङ्क्तिना इव–the white tips of his teeth are fancied to be the lines of the syllables of the *mantras* he was muttering. होम...यवान्—the lamps that were lighted near him were reflected in the perspiration due to his efforts in offering oblations. The poet fancies that he burnt his body with those lamps to ensure success. बहुगुणेन consisting of many threads (with ब्रह्मसूत्रेण); of great efficacy (with विद्याराजेन). विद्याराज is a particular *mantra*. बहुगुणेन may also mean 'repeated many times' (with विद्याराजेन). There is another sense suggested. ब्रह्मसूत्र is the work of बादरायण dealing with the Vedānta philosophy. ब्रह्मविद्या is the king of विद्याs (विद्याराज). Compare गीता 9. 2 '**राजविद्या** राजगुह्यं पवित्रमिदमुत्तमम्'. शातक्रतवीमाशाम् the quarter of Indra (*i. e.* the east). For the guardians of the eight quarters, see p. 140. कौबेरीम् the north presided over by कुबेर. प्राचेतसीम् west presided over by प्रचेतस् (*i. e.* वरुण). त्रै...ककुभम् the quarter marked with the constellation of त्रिशङ्कु *i. e.* the south. त्रिशङ्कु was father of हरिश्चन्द्र. He wished to go to heaven with his mortal body. He went to his family priest वसिष्ठ who declared it to be impossible. He then went to वसिष्ठ's sons who also rejected his proposal. त्रिशङ्कु then went to विश्वामित्र who raised him towards heaven, when Indra refused to admit him and made him fall headlong. Then विश्वामित्र called upon him to stay where he was and created new worlds, नक्षत्रs &c. The gods intervened and made विश्वामित्र's creations as eternal as those of ब्रह्मा and त्रिशङ्कु blazed forth as a constellation. *Vide* रामायण बालकाण्ड 57–60. Compare 'त्रिशङ्कोरिवोभयलोकभ्रष्टस्य नक्तन्दिवमर्वाक्शिरसस्तिष्ठतः' हर्ष० 7th उ०; 'सुरलोकमारोहतस्त्रिशङ्कोरिव कुपितशतमखहुङ्कारनिपतिता राजलक्ष्मीः' कादम्बरी p. 8 of P. The author avoids the use of the words दक्षिणां दिशम्, as they are inauspicious.

P. 51 l. 23—**P. 52** l. 14. **एवं...पातयत्.** दिक्पाल...चार्ये while भैर० fearlessly performed his terrific work, being inside the cage of the arms of the four guardians of the quarters (*viz.* the king and the three others). अति...कौणपेषु when the demons causing obstacles, after making much noise for a long time and after having found that their efforts (to frighten the guardians and cause obstacles) proved futile, became quiet (*i. e.* vanished). '**राक्षसः कौणपः** क्रव्यात्' अमरः (कुणपमत्ति कौणपः). गल...समये when midnight had just passed. मण्डल...रेण not far to the north of the circle (of ashes in which भैर० was sitting). प्रलय...दीर्यंत the earth was rent open, as though exhibiting a chasm of the jaws of the Great Boar at the time of *pralaya*. For प्रलय see above p. 210. The demon हिरण्याक्ष, on the strength of a boon from Bramhā, became insolent and carried the earth into the ocean. Vishṇu assumed the form of a boar and brought it up. See भागवतपुराण 3rd स्कन्ध chap. 13–19. Compare 'येन **प्रलयवराह**घोणाभिघातभीता भूतधात्री... सागरमवतीर्णा' कादम्बरी p. 124 of P; 'वसति दशनशिखरे धरणी तव लग्ना। शशिनि कलङ्ककलेव निमग्ना। केशव धृतसूकररूप जय जगदीश हरे॥' गीतगोविन्द. The next sentence is सहसैव...तस्मात् विवरात्...कुवलयश्यामलः पुरुष उज्जगाम (p. 52 l. 6). आशावारणैः (दिग्गजैः) उत्क्षिप्तः (tossed up, uprooted). आ...स्तम्भः इव as though he were the iron post for tying elephants. 'आलानं बन्धस्तम्भे' अमरः. The post is fixed in the earth. As the पुरुष was dark-coloured, formidable and suddenly rose up from the earth, he is fancied to be आ...स्तम्भ. महावराहस्य इव पीवरं स्कन्धपीठं यस्य (*adj.* of पुरुषः) whose square shoulders were stout like those of the Great Boar. नर...द्धृतः—By the contact of महावराह with the earth at the time of raising it up out of the ocean, a demon was born of the earth, named नरक. He was very powerful and deprived वरुण of his umbrella, took away the ear-rings of अदिति. 'यदाहमुद्धृता नाथ त्वया सूकरमूर्तिना। त्वत्स्पर्शसम्भवः पुत्रस्तदायं मय्यजायत॥' विष्णुपुराण 5. 59. 23. The पुरुष also rose from the bowels (गर्भात्) of the earth. Compare 'पुरा महावराहसम्पर्कसम्भृतगर्भया भगवत्या भुवा नरको नाम सूनुरसावि रसातले' हर्ष० 7th उ०. बलि...पातालम् he seemed to be the demon Bali rising up after cleaving asunder *Pātāla*. When Bali became very powerful, Vishṇu assumed the form of a Brāhmaṇa boy and begged of him land measuring his three steps. Then Vishṇu assumed a universal form, covered heaven and earth in two steps and placed the third on Bali's head and sent him down to पाताल where he is supposed to reign even now, as he is one of the seven चिरजीविन्s. *Vide* भागवतपुराण 8th स्कन्ध chap. 20–23. Note 'तावत्सु**तल**मध्यास्तां विश्वकर्मविनिर्मितम्।' chap. 22. 32. उपरि ज्वलितः रत्नप्रदीप यस्य. Remove the comma after ०प्रदीपः. As his body and hair were dark, he is said to be a mansion of sapphire. As he had a brilliant मालती wreath on his head we have the words उपरि...दीपः. Jewelled lamps are lighted in palaces. स्निग्ध...मौलिः the top (मौलिः) of whose head was charming with glossy, dark, thick and curling hair. उन्मीलन्ती (gleaming) मालतीमुण्डमाला यस्य. गद्गद...मदेन by his gurgling (faltering) voice and his naturally red eye, he seemed as though drunk by the pride (or 'intoxication') of youth. One who has drunk wine has a red eye and hoarse voice. **'मत्ते शौण्डोत्कटक्षीबाः'** अमरः. वल्गत् गलदाम यस्य whose necklace dangled about his throat. For क added to बहुव्रीहि compounds, *vide* p. 12. कर...पङ्कयन् with the mud crushed in his clenched hands he again and again smeared his big shoulders resembling the foreheads of the elephants of the quarters. ०कुम्भस्य इव आभा ययोः. कुम्भः frontal globe on the temple of an elephant. This action is characteristic of our wrestlers even now. सान्द्र... देशः with the irregularly made marks of moist-(सान्द्र) sandal paste, he seemed to be a part of the autumnal sky variegated (शारित) with pieces of very white clouds. 'अविद्यमाना व्यवस्था येषु ते अव्यवस्थाः स्थासकाः तैः. For स्थासक, see p. 53 above. He had applied white sandal paste to his body in various places without any order. His body was dark like the clear blue sky of शरद्. In the sky also irregular patches of clouds are seen in शरद्. शारदं (शरदः इदं) आकाशं तस्य एकदेशः. For चण्डातक, see above p. 69. क्षामतरीकृतः कुक्षिः यस्य whose flanks looked small (by his waist being tightly bound). कक्ष्या...शेषेण after having tightly girt his waist, he gracefully let loose on the ground the fringe of his white cotton cloth used at exercise time and thereby he appeared as though supported from behind by शेष. The idea is:—over his चण्डातक, he had firmly tied his waist with the coils of a long white piece of cotton cloth which he used at the time of taking exercise. A portion of that cloth remained, which he allowed to reach the ground behind him. Being white, it resembled the serpent शेष that is also white. शेष also is धरणितलग *i. e.* it supports the earth. 'फाली कक्ष्याबन्धः' सं०. **'फालः** पुंसि महादेवे कालिन्दीभेदनेपि च। क्लीबं सीरोपकरणे **त्रिषु कार्पासवाससि** ॥' मेदिनी. स्थिरौ स्थूलौ ऊरुदण्डौ यस्य. भूमि...पदानि he planted his steps slowly as though he feared that the earth would break (if he walked faster). निर्भर...गुरु heavy with great pride. A शैल (mountain) also is heavy (गुरु). मुहुर्मुहुः... टाङ्कारैः by the terrible and twanging slapping (with his hand) of his left arm that was doubled (द्विगुणित) on his chest and of his right thigh, put forward slantingly and thus appearing to be coiled up. टाङ्कार is an onomatopoetic word. It is better to read चण्डास्फोटन. The पुरुष smote loudly his left arm doubled on his chest and his right thigh with his hand. This is a characteristic action for wrestless and is a sort of challenge. कर्म...कुर्वन्—The noise made by the slapping was so terrific that it seemed as though the पुरुष sent down निर्घातs for hindering the rite on which भै० was embarked and as though depriving the mortal world of one organ (*i. e.* of the sense of hearing). The noise of the आस्फोटन was deafening. निर्घात: 'noise of contending winds in the sky; a whirlwind.' 'पवनः पवनाभिहतो गगनादवनौ यदा समापतति । भवति तदा निर्घातः स च पापो दीप्तविहगरुतः ॥' बृहत्संहिता 39. 1. कुवलय is a blue lotus. नर...भारत्या in a voice as terrific as the echo (निर्घोषः) of the roar of the Man-lion. This is a reference to the 5th incarnation of Vishṇu when the latter tore off with his nails the chest of हिरण्यकशिपु विद्या...कामुक confident lover of विद्याधरीs. This is said in derision भैर० wanted to be a विद्याधर and believed that he would become one by the successful performance of the rite he was engaged in The emphasis is on the word श्रद्धा, the idea being 'you are sure that you would be a विद्याधर, but I shall show that your belief is worthless.' किम...लषसि Is this pride due to (the possession of) a little knowledge or the arrogance due to being helped by friends that without making an offering to this person (*i. e.* myself) you desire success (in this rite) like a fool ? एतावता कालेन during all this time. क्षेत्राधिपतिः lord or tutelary deity of a place. अस्य... देशस्य (to be connected with ०पतिः) of this country that is styled (श्रीकण्ठ) after me. लब्धः व्यपदेशः (नाम) येन. नागोहम्—even now the belief in the existence of guardian नागs presiding over various places is very common. अनि...गगने what power have the planets to move in the sky against my will ? Even the planets cannot act against his wishes. What of भै० who wanted to go to heaven as विद्याधर ? भूनाथो...क्रियते Though a king, he is no king and is wretched since he is made a tool by vile S'aivas like you. 'निहीनोऽपसदो जाल्मः' अमरः. The word अपसद is generally used at the end of compounds as a term of abuse. The contrast is between भूनाथः and अनाथः (no king; helpless in the hands of भै०). सहस्वे...फलम् now receive along with this bad king the fruit of the bad conduct of a bad snake-charmer. नरेन्द्र means 'a snake-doctor.' भैरवाचार्य was a bad नरेन्द्र in that he did not propitiate the नाग. A and C read दुर्नरेन्द्रेण दुर्नयस्य, but the reading in the text is preferable, as it is more in keeping with Bāṇa's style. नरेन्द्र—compare 'आविष्टा इव नरेन्द्रवृन्दपरिवृताः' हर्ष० 4th उ० and notes thereon; compare also 'महाशीविष इव दुर्नरेन्द्राभिभवरोषितः' हर्ष० 6th उ०. प्रकोष्ठप्रहारैः by the strokes of his forearms. स... कृपाणान् together with their armours and swords.

P. 52 l. 15—**P. 53** l. 2 **अथापूर्व...दृष्टिम्.** अपू...श्रवणात् on hearing the unprecedented insult. This was the first time that the king heard such insulting language. अविद्यमानः शस्त्रव्रणः येषाम् (*adj.* of अवयवैः). अशस्त्र...वमद्भिः that (limbs), though unwounded (then), as though vomitted, under the guise of the sweat due to wrath, the dark water of sword-edges drunk in many battles. The idea is:—He was sorely pained at heart by the insulting words of the नाग, though he was not physically wounded. Sweat due to fury appeared on his body. The poet fancies that the sweat was the 'water' of the sword edges (of his enemies) which had struck him in former battles. अवय...कुर्वद्भिः with his limbs, that under the guise of horripilation, made him light for battle by shooting out an array of arrow-points. His body had रोमाञ्च due to rage. The hair looked like arrow-points. The poet fancies that the hair were arrowheads, planted in his body in former battles but now taken out in order to make his body fit for combat. प्रतिबिम्बितः तारागणः यस्मिन् (*adj.* of अट्टहासेन). स्पष्टं दृष्टा धवला दन्तमाला यथा स्यात्तथा. अवज्ञया in contempt. हसता इव— The stars reflected in the blade looked like white teeth seen when one laughs. कथ्यमानः सत्त्वस्य (courage, spirit) अवष्टम्भः (pride, majesty) यस्य. The three clauses ०वमद्भिः, ०कुर्वद्भिः and ०हसता इव are to be connected with कथ्यमान. These three indicated the greatness of his courage, in spite of the fact that his three companions had been brought to the ground in no time. परिकरबन्धे विभ्रमेण भ्रमितः करः तस्य नखानां किरणचक्रवालेन. व्यप...दिशः— the idea is:—the king girded up his loins as a preparation for the impending fight. The rays of his hand gracefully girding up spread round. The poet fancies that the circle of rays was a charmed circle which the king drew for imprisoning the नाग and preventing it from running in the ten directions (which the king thought the नाग would do). For परिकरबन्ध, see text p. 4. l. 6 and notes thereon. नागदमनाय मन्त्रैः मण्डलबन्धः तेन. The com. says 'मण्डलं गारुडशास्त्रप्रसिद्धमैन्द्रादिकम्.' 'कुण्डली गूढपाच्चक्षुःश्रवाः **काकोदरः फणी'** अमरः (काकस्येव उदरमस्य). The king addressed the नाग as काक out of contempt. It is only a crow that asks for a बलि (as the नाग did above). Further the word is in contrast with the word राजहंस below. राजहंसे swan-like king; a राजहंस. A crow is a nonentity before राजहंसs. अमी...भाषितैः what is the use of these harsh words? अयं न भवसि you will be no more *i. e.* I shall kill you. अगृहीता हेतिः (weapon) यैः. अगृही...हर्तुम्

my arm has not been taught to strike the unarmed. It is better to take अनादृततरं outside the quotation marks. Connect अनादृततरम् (with great unconcern or disdain) with अभिधाय. आस्फोटयामास he slapped (his arm and thigh). निरायुधम्—object of जेतुम्. चर्मफलकेन सह स...फलकम् (*adj.* of असिम्) together with the shield. अर्धो...कक्ष्याम् above his cloak he girt up his loins for a fight with fists. अर्धोरुक is the same as चण्डातक. 'अर्धोरुकं वरस्त्रीणां स्याच्चण्डातकमंशुकम्' अमरः (ऊर्वोरर्धाच्छादकमंशुकमर्धोरुकं—क्षीर०). कक्ष्या girdle, waist. निर्दयेन आस्फोटनेन स्फुटितौ भुजौ तयोः रुधिरं तस्य शीकरेण सिच्यमानौ. The furious slapping of their arms caused blood to come out of them. शब्द...भुवनम्—the incessant slapping of their arms filled the world with the sound. उच्चखान drew out (of the sheath). अपश्य...वीतम् the king saw inside the wreath his sacred thread. For वैकक्षक, see p. 26. It is worn like the यज्ञोपवीत and hence the king did not notice it before. उपसंहृतः (stopped) शस्त्रव्यापारः येन. दुर्विनीत impudent. अस्ति...मिदम् you possess this seed (*i. e.* means) which (safely) carries you over your bad deeds. विश्रब्धम् *adv.* confidently. The यज्ञोपवीत showed that the नाग was a ब्राह्मण. A ब्राह्मण was never to be killed, however great his offence might be. ब्रह्महत्या was a महापातक; *vide* p. 160 above. Hence the king laid aside his weapon. घ्राणावलेपिनम् smearing his nose (*i. e.* overpowering it).

P. 53 ll. 3-28. **अथ...इति.** The first sentence is अथ... अट्टहासस्य मध्ये...स्फुरन्तीं...स्त्रियमपश्यत् (l. 20). तडि...स्फुरन्तीम्—the lady was fair like a flash of lightning and the sword was like a dark cloud. प्रभया...यामाम् that as though swallowed up the night by her radiance. तामरसं (red lotus) हस्ते यस्याः. The woman of whom the king had a vision was लक्ष्मी. So she was तामरसहस्ता. कोमला...कर्षन्तीम् that drew the webs of the glow of her delicate toes, as though they were the coral creepers on the seaside sticking to her feet. Her toes were red like coral. कर...बिभ्रतीम्—पद्म closes its petals in moonlight. Her toe-nails were bright like moonlight. Therefore the poet fancies that लक्ष्मी desiring to have the lotus in her hand always blooming carried the moon cut into pieces (*viz.* her toe-nails). To explain (as C and T and Mr. Kale do) that it was a night lotus and that therefore she carried the pieces of the moon is not happy. गुल्फा...गताम् as her anklets lay about her ankles (गुल्फः) she appeared to have escaped from fetters (or imprisonment) in which there were many thick links. कटकं a link. स्थिता निबिडा

कटकावलिः यस्मिन् तत् ०वलि बन्धनं तस्मात्. The anklet appeared to be the single link remaining on her ankle after she had burst asunder the chain with which she was imprisoned. बहु...शोभितात् ornamented with various flowers and birds (painted on or woven into the texture of the garment). On the waters of the ocean also are birds and flowers (offered by people in worship). पव... तरङ्गात् over which there were slight folds worked up by the breeze (with अंशुकात्); that had slight ripples caused by the wind (with ०सलिलात्). अंशु...रन्तीम् coming out (into view) from under her garment, as though from the water of the ocean. The garment was fine and bright like sea-water. उदधि... मध्याम् under the disguise of the three folds of skin (on her waist), her waist was as though embraced by the Ganges out of love for her because she was born of the ocean. The Ganges is represented as the queen of the ocean. It is called त्रिपथगा because it flows in heaven, on the earth and in पाताल. Three folds of skin are a sign of beauty among women. लक्ष्मी sprang out of the ocean at the time of churning. The poet fancies that the three folds of लक्ष्मी are the Ganges clasping her waist because she was the daughter of her husband, the ocean. Remove the comma after ०मण्डलाम्. दृश्यमानौ दिङ्नागकुम्भौ यस्याम् (*adj.* of ककुभम्). She with her swelling bosom looked like the quarter with the prominent frontal bones of its guardian elephant. मदलग्नः (समदः) ऐरावतः &c. The pearls of the necklace she wore appeared like the spray from the trunk of ऐरावत when in rut. ऐरावत is white and her bosom also was fair. The necklace was brilliant (तार) like the stars in autumn. धवल...वीज्यमानाम्— the rays of the necklace as it heaved up and down with her soft breathing resembled white chowries. मदान्धः गन्धेभः (गन्धगजः) तस्य कुम्भस्य आस्फालनेन संक्रान्तं सिन्दूरं यस्य. It is to be noted that the woman described here is लक्ष्मी. In India an elephant was the symbol of prosperity (लक्ष्मी). So लक्ष्मी is represented as riding an elephant. Red lead is applied to the temples of elephants by way of decoration. The poet fancies that the hands of लक्ष्मी (that were naturally red) became red because red lead was transferred to them when she rubbed the temple of her elephant. For गन्धेभ, compare 'गान्धाराधिपगन्धद्विपकूटपाकलः' हर्ष० 4th उ० 2nd para and notes thereon. The com. says 'श्रीर्हस्तिपृष्ठेन यातीति मदान्धेत्याद्युक्तम् । हस्तिवाहित्वाल्लक्ष्म्या एवमुक्तम्.' हरशिखण्डे इन्दुः तस्य द्वितीयखण्डेन इव. हर...भ्राजमानम्--the idea is:—her brilliant (*lit.* shedding moonlight) ear-ornament looked like the second piece of the moon on the top-knot of शिव turned into a ring. शिव has the crescent of the moon on his head. The remaining portion (the other half) of the moon was as though bent into a ring and made her ear-ornament. For a similar conceit, *vide* text p. 9 l. 21. कौस्तुभ...ङ्कृताम्—the shoots of अशोक on her ear resembled the cluster of the rays of the कौस्तुभ gem. महता...ललाटाम् on whose forehead was present a large *tilaka* of elephant's ichor, as thought it were the round shadow of an invisible umbrella. Her तिलक was large, round and dark (as ichor is dark). The shadow of an umbrella would be round and dark. An umbrella is a sign of sovereignty (राजलक्ष्मी). So लक्ष्मी must be accompanied by it, though it may not be actually visible. आपाद...सीमन्ताच्च from the soles of her feet to the parting line of her hair. यशस् is white. धरणि...नीभिः kissing (*i. e.* touching) the ground (with ०मालाभिः); flowing over the earth (with सरिद्भिः). सागराधिष्ठाभिः (सागरमधितिष्ठन्तीति ताभिः) that repose in the ocean. Rivers fall into the ocean. The long wreaths she wore were rivers that wafted her into the ocean from which she sprang at the time of churning. मृणाल...चक्षाणाम् with her limbs delicate like lotus fibres she declared her birth in a lotus without words. अनक्षरम्—अविद्यमानानि अक्षराणि यथा स्युः (अव्ययीभाव). लक्ष्मी is represented as rising from an expanded lotus. Compare 'चक्षुषा शिक्षयन्तमिव लक्ष्मीलाभोत्तानितमुखानि पङ्कजवनानि विनयम्' हर्ष० 4th उ०. असंभ्रान्तः not agitated. कस्यासि whose (wife) art thou? स्त्री...भवन्तीव as though overpowering him with a boldness (or dignity) at variance with her sex. नारायणस्य उरः एव स्थली तस्यां लीलया विहारे हरिणीम्—लक्ष्मी is represented as reclining on the chest of Vishṇu. Compare 'यास्य वक्षसि नरकजितो लक्ष्मीरिव ललास' हर्ष० 4th उ० 3rd para. A female deer also wanders at will on sylvan spots. पृथु...पताकाम् the banner of the families of the kings of old such as पृथु, भरत and भगीरथ. As a पताका is very prominent, so लक्ष्मी was very prominent in the families of these kings. A पताका (pennon) flutters from a वंश (bamboo pole). सुभटानां भुजाः एव जयस्तम्भाः तेषु विलासशालभञ्जिका—the idea is:—लक्ष्मी loves great heroes. In ancient India triumphal columns were often erected to proclaim the victories won by great kings. C and T call attention to the Mandasor stone pillar which has an inscription of Yas'odharman (*vide C. I. I.* Vol III p. 142). A शालभञ्जिका (doll, female figure) is carved on stone pillars. रण...हंसीम् the female flamingo spoilt (दुर्ललित) by the yearning (दोहदं) for playing on the ripples of the rivers of blood in battles. लक्ष्मी cannot be had without bloodshed. A राजहंसी plays on the ripples of rivers. सित...ण्डिनीम् the female peacock in the forest (षण्डः-ण्डम्) of white umbrellas of kings. A peacock dwells in thickets. White umbrellas are insignia of royalty. So लक्ष्मी may be said to dwell in them. 'अब्जादिकदम्बे **षण्ड**मस्त्रियाम्' अमरः. अति...सिंहीम् the lioness that sportively wanders in the forest of the edges of very sharp weapons. असि...कमलिनीम्—the idea is:—A lotus plant grows in water, so लक्ष्मी grows on the 'water' of swords' edges (*i. e.* it is the sharpest sword that wins लक्ष्मी). अप...रसेन I am captivated by this your love (रसः) for bravery. A fluid or stream (रसः) may carry away a person.

P. 53 l. 29—**P. 54** l. 5 **वीराणां...बभूव.** वीराणां...काराः In the case of heroes conferring of obligations on others is never wearisome *i. e.* heroes love to confer numerous obligations on others. पुनरुक्त repeated, superfluous; hence 'wearisome.' प्रीततरं हृदयं यस्याः. She was pleased to see that the king cared more for the success of भैरवाचार्य's undertaking than for any personal gain. विस्तीर्य...भूपालम्—the idea is—with an eye dilated through pleasure she looked at the king. The white of her eye was like the waters of क्षीरसागर. The poet fancies that the king was bathed in क्षीरसागर poured (पर्यस्त) over his head. At the time of coronation (अभिषेक), a king's head is bathed with holy water. सत्त्वोत्कर्षेण by the excess of courage or spirit. सूर्याचन्द्रमसोः—for the lengthening of सूर्य in this द्वन्द्व compound, note the Sūtra 'देवताद्वन्द्वे च' पा. 6. 3. 26 (इद्दोत्तरपदे परे आनङ् । मित्रावरुणौ । सि. कौ.). Two वंशs, that of the sun and the moon, were already well-known. लक्ष्मी promises him that he would be the founder of a third वंश as famous as the other two. अविच्छिन्नस्य unbroken. उपचीयमाना (growing) वृद्धिः यस्य. शुचीनि सुभगानि (handsome) सत्यत्यागधैर्यशौण्डानि पुरुषप्रकाण्डानि तत्प्रायस्य—mostly consisting of eminent men fond of truthfulness, liberality and courage. प्रकाण्ड at the end of compounds means 'pre-eminent.' 'मतल्लिकामचर्चिका**प्रकाण्ड**मुद्धतल्लजौ । प्रशस्तवाचकान्यमूनि' अमरः. हरिश्चन्द्रः— the story of हरिश्चन्द्र and his persecution by विश्वामित्र are well-known. *Vide* मार्कण्डेपु० chap. 7-8 for details. हरिश्चन्द्र was lord of all the earth except काशी, which was under the protection of शिव himself. Hence the words सर्वद्वीपानां भोक्ता.

मान्धाता was a great चक्रवर्ती and was desirous of conquering heaven after he had conquered the earth. Compare 'मान्धाता किलैवंविधे...हनि भेजे जन्म । अर्वाक्ततोऽस्मिन्नन्तराले पुनरेवंविधे योगे चक्रवर्तिजनने नाजनि जगति कश्चिदपरः' हर्ष० 4th उ० and *vide* notes thereon. यस्यायं... चामरम् over whom this hand (of mine) will itself wave the chowrie, abandoning the lotus. लक्ष्मी says she will throw away the lotus in her hand and hold a chowrie in it for waving it over that gret king. तिरोबभूव became invisible.

P. 54 ll. 6–16. **भूमि...चचक्षे.** देव्या...वचसा—लक्ष्मी had said 'एवमस्तु' when the king solicited her to crown the undertaking of भै० with success. कर्मणा...पादितेन because the rite was properly performed (to its finish). सद्य एव at once. केयूरी wearing an armlet. मेखली with a girdle. मुद्गरी with a mallet or club. खड्गी—with a sword. विद्याधरs always carry swords. Compare 'अनिस्त्रिंशा विद्याधराः' above (text p. 18. l. 22). अदूर...रथाः the ambitions of indolent and weak-minded people never soar high. फल्गु चेतः येषाम्. 'असारं फल्गु' अमरः. फल्गु unsubstantial, worthless, feeble. सतां...कृतयः but the favours of the good are naturally far-reaching. स्वप्नेऽप्यसम्भावितां not imagined even in dreams. दक्षिणाम् gift. सम्प...याति a man light by nature goes up (becomes puffed up) like a balance even after obtaining a particle of prosperity. In the case of a delicate balance, the equilibrium is disturbed even by a particle. त्वदीयैः...कृतस्य that is already made an instrument by your qualities. He says:—my heart is already captivated by your qualities. There is also another sense suggested. Threads (गुणs) are employed in binding a thing. लब्धः आत्मलाभः येन. त्वत्त...लाभस्य that has obtained its present position through you. He says that he owes his विद्याधरत्व to the king and to no one else. भै० wanted to do some good turn to the king out of gratitude. निर्ल...त्मानम् this my foolish heart is shameless in that I desire to keep myself in your memory by serving you in accomplishing some small affair of yours. प्रत्युप...ष्टम्भाः the dignity of the hearts of the wise is inaccessible to (the receiving of a) favour in return *i. e.* the wise never receive something in return for what they have done for others. प्रत्याचचक्षे he refused (the offer of भै०).

P. 54 ll. 17—28 **तथोक्त...विवेश.** कुवलय...स्राविणा as though it were a grove of blue lotuses dropping the spray of dew (अवश्यायः). The pupil of his eye resembled कुवलय and the bright tears dew-drops. ब्रवीमि...सदृशम् if I say 'I am going', that would not be suitable to the affection I bear to you. The roots या and गम् were inauspicious and would not be used by a person parting from his friend. In these and the following clauses, भैरवाचार्य puts forward various sentences and dismisses each of them as not suited to adequately express his sentiments when parting from his friend, the king. त्वदीयाः...सक्तम् If I say 'my life is at thy disposal,' that is merely superfluous. His meaning is 'without my saying so, my life is already at your service; so those words need not be uttered.' गृह्यता...करणम् 'take this wretched body' would be to keep things distinct (which are not so). You and I are one. Therefore what is mine is already yours. To ask you to receive my body would be to make a distinction (व्यतिरेकः) between you and me which does not exist. तिल...रूपम् 'I am purchased by you bit by bit' would not be appropriate to your obligations. Your obligations are so many and so great, that even if I were cut up into small particles the number of those particles would be too small as compared with them. बान्ध...करणमिव 'you are my kinsman' would be placing you at a distance. One is not necessarily very friendly and affectionate to one's kinsman. त्वयि...प्रत्यक्षम् 'my heart remains with you' cannot be directly perceived. I cannot show by प्रत्यक्षप्रमाण (by the testimony of the eye) that my heart is bound to yours. त्व...श्रद्धेयम् 'this my success (or attainment of superhuman power) that causes separation from you is a veritable torment (कारणा)' cannot be believed. As I aspired to be विद्याधर and worked hard to secure my object, no one will believe me if I say that my सिद्धि is a torment to me. **'कारणा तु यातना** तीव्रवेदना' अमरः. निष्का...वादः 'your kindness was disinterested' is a mere repetition (or praise). निष्कारणः would also mean 'without any merit in me (to deserve such kindness).' He means:—if I say 'निष्का...कारः,' I do not say anything new; it is your nature to do kind deeds without any merit in those whom you so benefit. So my words will repeat what already exists and I may be looked upon as simply praising you. Vedic sentences are divided into विधि and अर्थवाद. A विधि is that which lays down a rule or injunction or a religious commandment such as स्वर्गकामो ज्योतिष्टोमेन यजेत. An अर्थवाद is a sentence which recommends a विधि, which illustrates it, praises those that followed the विधि and points out the evils of not following a विधि. अनुवाद is one of the three kinds of अर्थवादs. अनुवाद is explained as 'सिद्धस्य उपन्यासः' or as 'विधिविहितस्य अनुवचनमनुवादः.' स्मर्तव्या...ज्ञा 'I should be remembered' sounds as a command. He says—'you are so great that it would be presumptuous on my part to command you.' सर्वथा...जनः At all events this person (*i. e.* I), remorseless in pursuing his own selfish purpose, should be kept in mind in talking about ungrateful persons and in narrating the accounts of bad men. He requests the king to remember him at least among ungrateful and bad men. वेगेन छिन्नः हारः तस्मात् उच्छलितः (shaken, tossed about) मुक्ताफलनिकरः तेन ताडितः तारागणः यस्मिन् (*adj.* of ०तलम्) or we may take it as an adverb (ताडितः तारागणः यथा स्यात्तथा). As he rose up with violent speed, his necklace was rent asunder and he struck the stars with the falling pearls. सीमन्तितः (parted) ग्रहग्रामः ग्रहसमूहः येन. As the white line parts the hair of women so he parted the planets while going through them. ग्राहितः विनयः येन who was taught modesty. श्रीकण्ठ had been humbled by the king. कर्तव्येषु...ग्राह्यः अयं जनः I should be favoured with a command whenever necessary.

P. 54 l. 29—**P. 55** l. 12 **नरपति...करोत्.** The principal sentence is नरपतिः...नगरं विवेश. क्षीण...क्षपायाम् when the night had almost run out. प्रवातुमारब्धे (connect with वनानिले) began to blow. प्रबुध्य...सुरभौ fragrant with the exhalations of the opening lotus plants; fragrant like the breaths of waking handsome women. कमलिनी = पद्मिनी. Writers on erotics divide women into four classes पद्मिनी, चित्रिणी, हस्तिनी and शङ्खिनी, the first being the best. ०परिहासेन स्वेदिनि इव. अवश्यायशीकरेण सह साव० (बहुव्रीहि). वन...शीकरे—the idea is:—the wind was charged with the dew of dawn; the poet fancies that the wind was a lover who was covered with sweat (in the form of dew drops) at the joke of removing the shawls from the bosoms of forest nymphs. परिमलेन आकृष्टाः मधुकृतः (मधुकराः) येन. कुमुद...वाहिनि that brought sleep to moon-lotuses. At the advent of morn कुमुदs close their petals. निशा...जडे chilled by the end of night; void of the warmth (of love) on account of the old age of Night. तुषारलेशिनि having particles of frost or snow. विरहेण विधुरं (helpless) चक्रवाकचक्रं तस्य निःश्वसितैः सन्तापितायाम् इव. विरह...त्रियामायाम्—the idea is:—चक्रवाक pairs are separated at night. Throughout the night they heaved hot sighs. The poet fancies that the night was corched by those hot sighs and entered the western ocean to allay the heat. One that is heated enters into water. As a matter of fact there is a glow of light in the east at dawn, while the west is still dark. Hence the words 'अपरजल०.' For चक्रवाक, *vide* notes pp. 67, 97. साक्षा... नलिनीषु when the lotus plants began to open (their eyes) as though curious to see Lakshmī that was bodily present. लक्ष्मी had showed herself to the king. As night was drawing to a close, the lotuses began to open. The poet fancies that they were curious to see the bodily presence of लक्ष्मी. उन्निद्राः पक्षिणः यस्मिन् (*adj.* of कानने) the birds in which awoke from sleep. क्षरति...कानने when the forests, the creepers in which were made to dance by a soft breeze, dropped down a mass of particles of frost as though it were a heap of flowers. Both flowers and particles of frost are bright. मृदुपवनेन लासिताः लताः यस्मिन्. कमल...कुमुदेषु when the closing *kumudas* (night lotuses) inside which were imprisoned buzzing bees hummed forth, as though they were auspicious conches (blown) to awaken the glory of day lotuses. Kings and great persons are aroused from sleep in the morning by the blowing of conches, by the lays of bards &c. अन्तर्बद्धाः ध्वनन्तः मधुकराः येषु. कुमुदs began to close in the morning and the bees were confined in them and made a noise inside. This noise is fancied to be the blowing of a conch. उज्जिहानाः (getting up from their beds) रविरथवाजिनः तैः विसृष्टैः. प्रोथपवनैः the breaths of their nostrils. प्रोत्सार्य...तारकासु when the stars, the buds of the creeper of Night, clustered together in the west, as though they were driven away (by the breaths of the sun's horses). श्यामा (रात्रिः) एव लता तस्याः कलिकासु or श्यामालता प्रियङ्गुलता तस्याः कलिकासु. The stars were like buds. In the east no stars were visible on account of the glow of day-break. The poet fancies that on the breaths of the sun's horses, stars were wafted towards the west and there clustered together. वारुण्यां ककुभि—वरुण is the lord of the west. मन्दानिलेन लुलितानि (shaken) ०कुसुमानि तेषां धूल्या विच्छुरिते (inlaid, covered). मन्दानिल... मण्डले—the constellation of the Great Bear looked grey in the light of morn. The poet fancies that it looked grey being covered with pollen &c. मन्दर...श्रयिणि—मन्दर is a mountain to the east of Meru. *Vide* notes above p. 43. The Sun, the Moon and the stars were supposed to revolve round Meru. Compare भागवतपुराण 5. 22. 'यथा कुलालचक्रेण भ्रमता सह भ्रमतां तदाश्रयाणां पिपीलिकादीनां गतिरन्यैव प्रदेशान्तरेष्वप्युपलभ्यमानत्वादेवं **नक्षत्रराशिभिरुपलक्षितेन कालचक्रेण ध्रुवं मेरुं च प्रदक्षिणेन** परिधावता सह &c.' सुर...मृगे when the starry deer sank (towards the west) as though it were the fallen goad of the elephant of the gods (*i. e.* of ऐरावत). The reference is to the constellation of मृगशीर्ष, particularly to the three stars (constituting the belt of Orion) that look like a dart. Those dart-like stars seemed to be the goad of ऐरावत fallen from the rider's hand. नाग...मलीमसानि (*adj.* of अङ्गानि) soiled by the incident (व्यतिकरः) of the fight with the Nāga. शुचिनि *adj.* of ०पयसि. आत्म...करोत् pleased all the three with bath, food and clothing that did not differ from his own. आत्मशरीरात् अनन्तरं (अविद्यमानं अन्तरं विशेषः यस्य) स्नान...च्छादनादि तेन. He gave them the same food that he partook of, the same rich clothing that he wore &c. The com. explains differently. The king made them bathe, take food &c. before himself and then took his bath, food &c. 'आत्मशरीरमनन्तरं यस्य तादृशेन स्नानभोजनाच्छादिना। तेषु कृत्वा पश्चादात्मनः करोतीत्यर्थः' सं०. C and T translate 'with unguents, food and clothing immediately after his own person.'

P. 55 ll. 13-17 **कतिपय...जग्मतुरिति.** परिव्राट् refers to टीटिभ. शौर्यानुरक्तौ devoted to the king on account of his bravery. सम्पादितः मनोरथात् अतिरिक्तः विभवः ययोः on whom was bestowed wealth exceeding even their desires. सुभ...मण्डलाग्रौ who drew out their swords in the midst of the guard of warriors. They were allowed, on account of their rank and devotion to the king, to walk with drawn swords in the midst of the king's guard or in the midst of the king's warlike courtiers. 'कौक्षेयको मण्डलाग्रः करवालः कृपाणवत्' अमरः (मण्डलाकृति अग्रमस्य). समर... युज्यमानौ they occupied the foremost rank in battle. अन्तरान्तरा now and then. राज्ञा समादिष्टौ when ordered by the king. शैशववृत्तान्तान् the incidents of their boyhood.

Uchchhvāsa IV

For a brief analysis of the contents of the first three Uchchhvāsas, see Appendix A. In the third Uchchhvāsa Bāṇa narrated how Pushpabhûti, king of Sthāṇvîs'vara (modern Thanesar) and the ancestor of Emperor Harsha, made the friendship of a S'aiva ascetic Bhairavāchārya, how the latter presented a miraculous sword to the king, and how the king helped the ascetic in the practice of magic for attaining a divine form.

P. 56 Verse 1 The words योग and करग्रह have two meanings. The great even in dreams do not desire to employ deceitful tricks (योग) nor do they take कर (tribute). In these two respects they are distinguishable from others who become *Pati*. Husbands desire union with their wives and take the hand of their wives (at the time of marriage). Without these two (योग and करग्रहण) the great become the masters (पति) of the world by their mere name *i. e.* their very name is sufficient to bring to them the devoted allegiance of the world.

Verse 2 Construe विपुलेऽपि नृपवंशे सकल...कृत् पृथुप्रतिमः एक एव उत्पद्यते विपुलेऽपि गणाधिपस्य मुखे पृथुप्रतिमः एक एव दन्त इव. सकल...कृत् One who strikes terror in (the heart of) all kings. पृथुप्रतिमः—resembling the (ancient king) Pṛithu. Pṛithu was the son of वेन. Formerly the mountains were rebellious and covered the earth just as they pleased. As no corn grew, people became famished and prayed to Pṛithu for deliverance. He levelled the earth by casting away the mountains with his bow and made it fertile. So पृथु also was सकल...कृत् (as महीभृत् means 'mountain' also). See विष्णुपुराण I. 13 'तत उत्सारयामास शैलान् शतसहस्रशः। धनुष्कोट्या तदा वैन्यस्तेन शैलविवर्धिताः' ॥ 82. Compare कादम्बरी (p. 5 of P) 'वैन्य इव चापकोटिसमुत्सारितसकलारातिकुलाचलः'. गणाधिप is the god गणेश, one of whose names is एकदन्त. 'सुमुखश्चैकदन्तश्च कपिलो गजकर्णकः। लम्बोदरश्च विकटो विघ्ननाशो गणाधिपः ॥ धूम्रकेतुर्गणाध्यक्षो भालचंद्रो गजाननः ॥' गणेशपुराण I chap. 92. पृथुः प्रतिमा यस्य (with दन्त) the size of which is great. प्रतिमा also means 'the part of an elephant's head between the tusks'. How Ganes'a became

एकदन्त is explained by the ब्रह्मवैवर्तपुराण. The story is:—एकदा रहसि स्थितयोः पार्वतीपरमेश्वरयोर्द्वारपालत्वमङ्गीकृतं गजाननेन । एतस्मिन्नन्तरे परशुरामः शिवं द्रष्टुमागतः । शिवदर्शनोत्सुकस्यान्तर्जिगमिषोर्द्वाररोधे कृते गणपतिना सह तस्य तुमुलं युद्धमभवत् । परशुरामक्षिप्तेन परशुना च गजाननस्य एको दन्तो भग्नः'.

In these two verses the poet suggests the greatness of Harsha whose birth forms the principal topic of the fourth Uchchhvāsa.

अथ...राजवंशः The principal sentence is अथ तस्मात् पुष्पभूतेः राजवंशः निर्जगाम. There are five dependent clauses containing comparisons. It is to be noted that all the words in these five clauses except the उपमानपदs apply also to राजवंश and पुष्पभूति (according to their respective cases). द्विज...क्षणात् as the navel lotus, the calix of which was resorted to of his own will by Brahmā, (springs) from विष्णु (पुण्डरीकेक्षण). द्विजवरेण ब्रह्मणा स्वेच्छया गृहीतः कोषः (कर्णिका) यस्य (स नाभिपद्मः). 'वा पुंसि पद्मं नलिनम्' इत्यमरः. In the Purāṇas Brahmā is represented as being born in a lotus which springs from the navel of विष्णु. Being स्वयम्भू, his birth must be said to be due to his own will. राजवंश also was द्विज... कोषः (द्विजवरैः ब्राह्मणश्रेष्ठैः स्वेच्छया गृहीतः कोषः यस्य). The kings of पुष्पभूति's line allowed learned Brahmins to take from their treasury as much as they liked. पुष्पभूति was पुण्डरीकेक्षण (कमलनयन). Dr. Buhler (E. I. I. p. 68) says that पुष्यभूति must have been the name of the king (after the constellation of पुष्य) and that the Mss. make little distinction between य and प. लक्ष्मी...रत्नाकरात् as the series of (14) jewels, chief of which was लक्ष्मी, (sprang) from the ocean. लक्ष्मीः पुरःसरा यस्य. This refers to the churning of the ocean, for which see विष्णुपुराण I. 9 and रामायण I. 44. राजवंश was favoured by लक्ष्मी (prosperity) and पुष्पभूति was रत्नाकर (रत्नानां आकरः mine of jewels, *i. e.* possessed all the best things in the world). गुरु...स्थानात् as the assembly of planets mostly consisting of Jupiter (गुरु), mercury (बुध), Venus (कवि), the moon (कलावत्), the sun (तेजस्विन्) and Mars (भूनन्दन) comes up from the mount in the east. गुरु...प्रायः (with राजवंशः) means 'mostly consisting of teachers, wise men, poets,artists (कलावत्), brave men and princes' (भूनन्दन). According to ancient Hindu astronomy there were nine ग्रहs (including the sun). उदयस्थानात् the sun, the moon and the planets were supposed to rise from a mountain in the east, more often called उदयगिरि. But for श्लेष, the word उदयस्थान is used here. कला 'digits of the moon'; 'the 64 arts, such as painting, dancing &c.' पुष्पभूति was the source of prosperity (उदयस्थान) to गुरुबुध०. महा...प्रभावात् as the ocean fit for bearing the great burden sprang from the might of the Sagaras (sons of सगर). By महाभार may be meant विष्णु who sleeps on the ocean or the reference may be to the ocean's keeping the earth inviolate. When the sacrificial horse of सगर was stolen away by इन्द्र, his sixty thousand sons dug the whole earth. The void thus created was filled by the rush of the Ganges brought from heaven by भगीरथ, descendant of सगर. राजवंश was महा...योग्यः (fit to bear the great responsibility of protecting the world). पुष्पभूति was सगरप्रभाव (सगरस्य इव प्रभावः यस्य). दुर्जय...शूरात् as the हरिवंश which comprises Vishṇu (दुर्जय) and Balarāma (sprang) from शूर. दुर्जयः बलश्च ताभ्यां सनाथः. दुर्जय is given as one of the thousand names of विष्णु in the अनुशासनपर्व (महाभारत 13.149.96 समावर्तो निवृत्तात्मा दुर्जयो दुरतिक्रमः). शूर was a descendant of यदु and grandfather of कृष्ण. राजवंशः दुर्जयेन बलेन सैन्येन सनाथः. पुष्पभूति was brave (शूर).

P. 56 यस्मा...राजानः The principal sentence is यस्मात् अजायन्त राजानः. Syntax requires that यस्मात् must be taken with राजवंशः. But it would be better to take it with पुष्पभूतेः, if the sense of what follows be carefully considered. Here again there are numerous dependent clauses containing comparisons. अविनष्ट...मुखात् As the creations of beings, rendered glorious by (the existence of) धर्म in its unimpaired state, are produced in the beginning of the Kṛita age. अविनष्टः (सकलः) धर्मः तेन धवलाः. According to ancient Hindu ideas, in the कृतयुग धर्म existed in its fullest splendour and there was not a trace of अधर्म. In each of the other three युगs (त्रेता, द्वापर and कलि) धर्म decreased by one quarter, and अधर्म increased by one quarter in an ascending scale. 'चतुष्पात्सकलो धर्मः सत्यं चैव कृते युगे। नाधर्मेणागमः कश्चिन्मनुष्यान्प्रति वर्तते॥ इतरेष्वागमाद्धर्मः पादशस्त्ववरोपितः। चौरिकानृतमायाभिर्धर्मश्चापैति पादशः॥' मनु० I. 81–82. The kings (राजानः) were also rendered glorious by the fact that in their regime धर्म was never on the wane. कृतं संस्कृतं मुखं यस्य (goes with यस्मात्). प्रतापेन (by light; by valour) आक्रान्तं भुवनं यैः. तेजोनिधेः (from the sun; from the राजवंश that is the centre of bravery). विग्रहेण व्याप्तानि दिङ्मुखानि यैः that covered the quarters with their bodies (with गिरयः); that filled the world with their battles (with राजानः). भूभृत्प्रभवात् from ब्रह्मा who is the creator of mountains (with गिरयः); from that which is the source of kings. Mountains had at first wings and they went where they pleased. The reading भूभृत्प्रवरात् would mean 'from the best of mountains (हिमकर); from the best of kings'. The latter meaning is unsuitable if we take यस्मात् as referring to राजवंश. धर...क्षमा capable of bearing the earth (applies to both दिग्गजाः and राजानः). There are eight guardian elephants of the quarters. They are supposed to support the earth. 'कमठकुलाचलदिग्गजफणिपतिविधृतापि चलति वसुधेयम्' भर्तृहरि. On the birth of the दिग्गजs from ब्रह्मकर, the हस्त्यायुर्वेद of पालकाप्य tells us 'सूर्यस्याण्डकपाले द्वे समानीय प्रजापतिः । हस्ताभ्यां परिगृह्यादौ सप्त सामान्यगायत ॥ गायतो ब्रह्मणस्तस्य समुत्पन्ना मतङ्गजाः । chap I. 218–219 (Anand. ed). ब्रह्मकरात् from that which produces ब्रह्म *i. e.* learning (with यस्मात्). 'वेदस्तत्त्वं तपो ब्रह्म' इत्यमरः. पातुम् to drink (with जलधराः); to protect (with राजानः). घनागमः वर्षाकालः तस्मात्. घनः (दृढः) आगमः (sacred knowledge) यस्य or यस्मिन् (with यस्मात्). इच्छा...यिनः applies to both तरवः and राजानः. कल्पतरु was one of the five trees of Paradise. 'पञ्चैते देवतरवो मन्दारः पारिजातकः । सन्तानः कल्पवृक्षश्च पुंसि वा हरिचन्दनम् ॥'. नन्दनात् from the garden of Indra; from that which gladdened. सर्व...धरात् as the various forms in the universe having for their substrata all the beings spring from Hari. सर्वभूतानि आश्रयाः येषाम् (with प्रकाराः); सर्वभूतानामाश्रयाः that gave shelter to all beings (with राजानः). विश्वस्य रूपाणि तेषां प्रकाराः. श्रीधरात् (with यस्मात्) that was possessed of prosperity.

P. 56 l. 16—**P. 2** l. 13 **तेषु...सम्पदा.** तेषु—supply राजसु. उदपादि 3rd sing. Aorist of पद् with उद्. हूण...केसरी a very lion to the deer in the form of the Hûṇas. हूणाः एव हरिणाः तेषां केसरी. Huns—This is a name given to several peoples:—(1) the Huns who invaded the Roman Empire between 372–453 A. D. and were most formidable under Attila; (2) the White Huns or Ephthalites who troubled Persia from 420 to 557 A. D.; they are probably the सितहूणs mentioned by वराहमिहिर (बृहत्संहिता 11.61); (3) the Hûṇas who invaded India about the same period. See the Mandasor stone inscription of यशोधर्मन् (C. I. III p. 146) and the Bhitari stone pillar inscription of स्कन्दगुप्त (C. I. III p. 54) of whom it is said, 'हूणैर्यस्य समागतस्य समरे दोर्भ्यां धरा कम्पिता'. गुर्जरप्रजागरः—who caused loss of sleep (through fear) to the Gurjara king (*i. e.* king of Bhinmal in Rajputana). गान्धाराधिपः एव गन्धद्विपः तस्य कूटपाकलः. गान्धार was the country round modern Kandahar. गन्धद्विपः an elephant of the best type. यस्य गन्धं समाघ्राय न तिष्ठन्ति प्रतिद्विपाः । स वै गन्धगजो नाम नृपतेर्विजयावहः ॥. कूटपाकलः

is a fever which attacks elephants. The reading in the text is better than 'कूटहस्तिज्वरः पाकलः'. The हस्त्यायुर्वेद of पालकाप्य tells us that all the fevers of elephants are called पाकल and that there are ten varieties of them. See अध्याय 9, which is styled पाकलाध्याय. कूट is one of the varieties and it is the deadliest of all. पालकाप्य says that it is called कूट because it kills elephants at once. 'तत्र गजस्याभीक्ष्णशो रूक्षान्नयवसकवलकुवलतिक्तकटुकषायलघुविषमरूक्षबहन्नभोजनात्, अथवातिगुरुभारहरणतरणविलङ्घनात्कुप्यति अनिलः । तदात्मकश्च कूटः । कूटो नामाशुघातनम् आशुघातनाद् द्विरदानाम् । तस्मात्कूटपाकलमाचक्ष्महे । तत्र श्लोकः । यथा हि हन्यात्कूटेन मृगशावं वनेचरः । तथा वातात्मको नागं हन्ति वै कूटपाकलः ॥'. The other reading would mean 'who was पाकल, that is a fever of elephants, working secretly'. This does not bring out the force and terror of the king's attack upon his enemies. Every fever (पाकल) is not equally dangerous to elephants. Compare 'अचिरेण वैकृतविवर्तदारुणः कलभं कठोर इव कूटपाकलः ॥' (मालतीमाधव I). लाट...चरः who steals (*i. e.* removes, renders nugatory) the skill of the king of Lāṭa (country about Broach *i. e.* Southern Gujerat). C and T translate 'a looter to the lawlessness of the Lāts.' This does not seem to be correct. मालवलक्ष्मीः एव लता तस्याः परशुः. मालव is modern Malva. प्रथितं (well-known) अपरनाम यस्य. The author means to say that प्रभाकरवर्धन had conquered the Huns, the Gurjaras &c. See Introduction. यो... धनानि who, the moment he was crowned, gave up wealth that sticks to the राज्याङ्गs (constituent elements of a state), as if it were dirt. One who bathes removes the dirt (मल m. n.) from his body (अङ्ग). In a coronation a king is bathed with the waters of sacred rivers and in commemoration of it money is distributed among Brahmins. राज्याङ्गानि सप्त 'स्वाम्यमात्यसुहृत्कोशराष्ट्रदुर्गबलानि च । राज्याङ्गानि' इत्यमरः. यः...जीवितेन who felt ashamed even when others clung to life in the first rush of battle, life which is dear to the cowardly, as if it were grass held in the mouth. To hold grass in the mouth is a sign of defeat and abject submission. Note the Marathi proverb 'दांतीं तृण धरून'. It is only the chickenhearted that will cling to life and save it at the cost of self-respect. When the king's enemies submitted to him in battle, he felt ashamed at *their* abject submission to save life, which to the brave is as तृण. कातरवल्लभेन goes with both तृणेन and जीवितेन. करे धृतः धौतः असिः तस्मिन् प्रतिबिम्बितेन. समितिषु सहायेन that (reflection of self) was his (only) companion in battles. प्रधनेषु in battles. The idea is this:—When the king fought with his enemies, he bent his bow for discharging arrows. In his bright sword-blade appeared the reflection of the king bending his bow. It appeared as if the king was helped by his reflection and even this made him uneasy (with the thought of having to receive another's help in battle). Further he was pained by the fact that his bow bent before his foes (though only for killing them). यो...खिद्यत there seems to be a pun, giving two opposite senses. यो मानी (proud) मानसेन अखिद्यत (was troubled by mind *i. e.* by the high soaring desires of his mind); यो मानी मानसे न अखिद्यत—who, proud as he was, was never troubled in mind (by difficulties). अन्तर्गताः अपरिमिताः रिपवः एव शल्यानि शङ्कवश्च तैः कीलिताम् nailed with the inserted (अन्तर्गत) points of darts in the form of numberless enemies in his empire. लक्ष्मी is said to be चंचल. But in his case it was निश्चल *i. e.* never left him. What is nailed becomes fixed. His sovereignty extended over many kings—his enemies whom he had subdued; so though they were like so many thorns in his side, yet they served the purpose of nails and made his sovereignty निश्चल. The reading in the text seems better than अन्तर्गताम्. Nails are inside ; so the subdued kings were inside his empire. C and T take अन्तर्गत to mean 'dead' (with foes). यश्च...बहुधा who, by the numerous (पृथु) roads for the march (यात्रा) of his troops (दण्डः) as it were cut up the earth in many parts in all directions for the benefit of his servants, (roads) by which (*i. e.* in making which) the river-banks, pits, trees with luxuriant branches, clumps of grass, anthills and forests were levelled up. समीकृतानि सरित्तटाः अवटाः, विटपानामटवी (समूहः) तया युक्ताः तरवः, तृणानां गुल्माः (समूहाः), वल्मीकगिरयः, गहनानि (वनानि) च—यैः (०पथैः). The king's victorious armies marched in various directions and so roads had to be prepared for them or were made by the very fact of marching in large numbers. Rivers, banks, clumps of trees and grass, and hills and forests-these serve as boundaries to demarcate one province from another. But these were all removed by his armies. It was only the broad roads that separated the several provinces which the king apportioned among his own servants. See मनु० 8. 246—47 '**सीमावृक्षांश्च** कुर्वीत न्यग्रोधाश्वत्थकिंशुकान् । गुल्मान्वेणूंश्च विविधान्छमीवल्लीस्थलानि च । शरान् कुब्जकगुल्मांश्च तथा सीमा न नश्यति ॥.' याज्ञवल्क्य II. 151 '**नयेयुरेते सीमानं स्थला—ङ्गारतुषद्रुमैः । सेतुवल्मीक**निम्नास्थिचैत्याद्यैरुपलक्षिताम् ॥'. अलब्धं युद्धस्य दोहदं येन whose longing or thirst for battle was not gratified. यं चा...

प्रतापः the idea is—his prowess was so great that nobody dared oppose him; the result was that his desire to fight was never gratified and his own prowess in this way caused him uneasiness, as if it were the prowess of another. If anyone else had great prowess that would have been a source of trouble to him. **P. 57** यस्य च...प्रतापः—the principal sentence is यस्य प्रतापः निहत... पुरेषु पञ्च...मयो मूर्त इवादृश्यत—whose prowess appeared as if it had an embodied existence made up of the five great elements in the wives of the chieftains that were slain in opposing him. निहताः प्रतिसामन्ताः तेषां अन्तःपुराणि तेषु. By his prowess the princes that opposed him were killed and their wives' hearts burnt through anguish, their eyes shed tears, they waved deep sighs, they had earth on their bodies because they rolled on the ground through grief, they felt the world a void (शून्य), as their husbands were dead. The author fancies that प्रताप was identical with the effects it produced on the widows of the princes that were killed. As these effects were perceptible, he says प्रताप was मूर्त. The word क्ष्मा means 'the earth'. All visible bodies are made up of the five elements पृथ्वी (here the word क्ष्मा is used for a pun), अप्, तेजः, वायु and आकाश. क्ष्मा also means 'patience'. The women had to suffer. यस्य...लक्ष्मीः—The idea is:—The best of his servants that were near him (*i. e.* high officers of state) were endowed by him with so much wealth and splendour that they appeared like him. A reflection is generally seen in objects that are near (आसन्न) and bright like jewels &c. 'जातौ जातौ यदुत्कृष्टं तद्रत्नमभिधीयते.' यस्य...भवत् Here the words भूति, सिद्धि, वंश, उक्ति, कर have double meanings. प्रतापः अग्निरिव तेन; also प्रतापसदृशः अग्निः तेन. Dissolve शौर्योष्मणा and असिधाराजलेन similarly. यस्य प्रता...भूतिः अभवत् who had भूति (prosperity, ashes) by the fire of his prowess. He became prosperous by his prowess; fire produces भूति (ashes). Explain the following similarly. शौर्योष्मणा सिद्धिः he attained his objects by the heat of his bravery. सिद्धि also means 'cooking', which is effected by ऊष्मन् (heat). असि...वृद्धिः his family (वंश) prospered by the water of his sword—blade. वंश (bamboo) when watered grows. शस्त्र...रोक्तिः his manliness (पुरुषकारः) was proclaimed by the mouths of the wounds received by him from weapons. उक्ति (utterance) can be made only by the mouth (मुख). धनु...गृहीतिः—he levied tribute by the scar made by the string of his bow *i. e.* fought his enemies with the bow, vanquished them and took tribute from them. By constantly wielding the bow his hands (कर) became hard and had scars, *i. e.* किण (corn) seized his hand. यश्च...मन्यत who looked upon enmity as a present, fight (विग्रह) as a blessing, the advent (आगम) of battle as a great festival. शत्रुं निधिदर्शनम् he regarded an enemy as the discovery of a treasure (because by conquering him, he would secure booty and tribute). अवस्क...वृद्धिम् a sudden attack as an auspicious event. वसुधारा—a stream of wealth. निरन्तरै...कृतयुगेन On account of the multitude of sacrificial posts that were erected close to each other it seemed as if the कृत age had put forth sprouts. The king performed numerous sacrifices, in each of which a यूप was required. There was thus a thick row of यूपs. In the कृतयुग also, people performed many sacrifices. Therefore it seemed as though कृतयुग, that had vanished (the present being कलियुग), had again come to life. दिक्षु...कलिना On account of the clouds of sacrificial smoke that spread in all directions, it seemed as if Kali had run away. Kali (being the age of sin and vice) is contemplated as dark; smoke is also dark. As the clouds of smoke were wafted hither and thither by the breeze, the poet fancies that it was Kali that was flying the country. ससुधैः plastered with chunam; possessed of सुधा (nectar). स्वर्ग which is the abode of the gods has सुधा. सुरालयशिखरेषु उद्धूयमानैः (that were being tossed to and fro). The fluttering banners on the spires of temples resemble the leaves पल्लव) of trees shaken by the wind. धर्म is contemplated as white. बहि...ग्रामैः—the idea is :—the king erected, when he performed sacrifices, outside the villages, large (विकट) सभामण्डपs, सत्रमण्डपs, प्रपाम० and प्राग्वंशमण्डपs. It seemed as if the ग्रामs had given birth to them. We take मण्डप with each of the four. सभा is the hall where the sacrificer, the priests and other learned men meet. सत्र is the room where food is distributed to all. प्रपा (Marathi पाणपोई) where water is given to travellers &c. प्राग्वंश is a room to the east of the अग्निशाला to be occupied by the wife and the household of the sacrificer. 'प्राग्वंशो प्राग्धविर्गेहात्' on which क्षीरस्वामी remarks 'प्राग्वंशः पत्नीशालाख्योऽग्निशालायाः प्राग्यो भागः.' काञ्चनमयानि सर्वाणि उपकरणानि (materials, utensils) येषु. विशीर्णमिव मेरुणा as if मेरु had been shattered into pieces. The golden utensils were so many that it seemed as if मेरु had been broken up into pieces which were turned into utensils. मेरु is said to be the mountain of gold. 'मेरुः सुमेरुर्हेमाद्री रत्नसानुः सुरालयः' इत्यमरः. द्विजेभ्यो दीयमानैः.

P. 57 l. 14—P. 58 l. 2 तस्य च ... ललास. The principal sentence is तस्य च यशोमती नाम महादेवी प्राणानां...भूमिरभूत्. All the genitives from शङ्करस्य (l. 14) to महामुनेः (l. 18) apply to the king also and all the nominatives in those clauses apply to यशोमती also. जन्मा...शङ्करस्य as पार्वती, who was called सती in her former life, was to S'iva. The queen was सती (पतिव्रता) and the king was शङ्कर (one who caused happiness). The word सती may also suggest (as the com. points out) that यशोमती was fair while पार्वती was श्यामा. दक्ष once celebrated a great sacrifice at which he did not invite his daughter सती nor her husband शिव. She went uninvited, but being greatly insulted, threw herself into the fire and perished. S'iva when he heard of this destroyed Daksha's sacrifice. सती was afterwards born as पार्वती. Compare कुमारसंभव I. 21. 'अथावमानेन पितुः प्रयुक्ता दक्षस्य कन्या भवपूर्वपत्नी । सती सती योगविसृष्टदेहा तां जन्मने शैलवधूं प्रपेदे ॥'. बाण refers often to the story of दक्ष. See कादम्बरी 'दक्षाध्वरक्रियामिवोद्धतगणकचग्रहभयोपसेवितत्र्यम्बकाम्' (महाश्वेताम्). गृहीतं परस्य (विष्णोः) हृदयं वक्षः यया—who rests on the bosom of विष्णु. Compare कादम्बरी 'उरःस्थलनिवाससंक्रान्तनारायणदेहप्रभाश्यामलितामिव श्रियम्' (p. 10–11 of P). The king was लोकगुरु (*i. e.* to be honoured by the world) and the queen was गृ...या (who had captivated the heart of the king). हृदय here means अन्तःकरण and पर means 'the last.' There are four अन्तःकरणs of which चित्त is the last. गृहीतं परं हृदयं (चित्तं) यया. 'मनोबुद्धिरहङ्कारश्चित्तं करणमान्तरम्.' The reading गृहीतहृदया seems to be due to an effort to make good sense. बाण perhaps intended to suggest another sense also (by putting the word पर) *viz.* Lakshmî transfers her affections to many kings. स्फुरन्ती तरला तारका यस्याः the star of which is brilliant and twinkling (with रोहिणी); the pupil (तारका) of whose eye was bright and unsteady (with यशोमती). रोहिणी is said in mythology to be the special favourite of the moon out of his 27 wives (the नक्षत्रs). The king also was कलावत् (well-versed in the arts). सर्वलोक...प्रजापतेः—ब्रह्मा desired to create all the beings and then they were produced. So the बुद्धि (thought) of ब्रह्मा is सर्वलोकजननी. The king was the lord of his subjects and the queen was like a mother to all her people. महा...नायकस्य—The Ganges springs from tha great mountain (हिमालय) and is looked upon as the queen of the ocean (the lord of rivers). The king was the lord of वाहिनी (an army) and यशोमती was born in the family of great kings. मान...तुरा clever in follow ing (the राजहंस) to the मानस lake. The मानस lake is said to be the native place of swans, where they are said to flock at the beginning of the monsoon. The king was a राजहंस (a swan among kings *i. e.* the best), while यशोमती was clever in acting according to the wishes of the king. सकल... धर्मस्य—त्रयी means वेदत्रयी (ऋग्वेद, यजुर्वेद and सामवेद). सकललोकैः अर्चिताः चरणाः यस्याः—(the three Vedas) the various schools of which are honoured by the people. The words चरण and शाखा are sometimes used as synonyms; sometimes चरण means 'शाखाध्येतृ' *i. e.* those who study a particular शाखा of the Veda, an ideal succession of teachers and pupils. This latter is the sense here. The king was धर्म incarnate and यशोमती was सकल ... चरणा (सकललोकेन वन्दितौ चरणौ यस्याः). दिवा ... महामुनेः—The great sage is वसिष्ठ here whose wife is अरुन्धती. अमुक्ता पार्श्वे स्थितिः यया—who always remains by his side. The star of अरुन्धती is always seen by the side of वसिष्ठ in the constellation of the Great Bear. अरुन्धती is regarded by the Indians as the type of conjugal fidelity and constancy and is pointed out to the bride by the bridegroom in marriage ceremonies. Note the high praise put by भवभूति in the mouth of जनक as regards अरुन्धती 'यया पूतंमन्यो निधिरपि पवित्रस्य महसः' (उत्तररामo IV). The king was महामुनि (a राजर्षि) and the queen never left his side day and night. हंसमयी...प्रेम्णि (literally) in her gait she was mostly a swan, in her tones a cuckoo, in love for her husband a ruddy goose (चक्रवाक) *i. e.* she had the gait of a हंस, the sweet high—pitched tone of a cuckoo &c. परपुष्ट=कोकिल (also called परभृत). It was believed that cuckoos place their eggs in the nest of crows and thus have their young ones looked after by others. 'प्रागन्तरिक्षगमनात्स्वमपत्यजातमन्यैर्द्विजैः परभृताः खलु पोषयन्ति ॥' शाकुन्तल V. The चक्रवाक bird is supposed to be separated from its mate at the advent of night and is a type of abiding love. Even though separated merely by a lotus leaf it cries for its mate. मय is affixed in the sense of प्राचुर्य or विकार. 'तत्प्रकृतवचने मयट्' पा. 5. 4. 21 and 'मयड्वैतयोर्भाषामभक्ष्याच्छादनयोः' पा. 4. 3. 143. प्रावृण्म...विलासेषु In the fulness of पयोधर (breast, cloud) she was as if the rainy season, in playfulness she was as if wine. निधि...प्रसादेषु in the collection of wealth, she was a treasure, in (bestowing) favours she was a stream of wealth. कोषसंग्रह (1) amassing a rich treasure (2) having a calix (with कमल). फलदानेषु—the queen gave what was desired by suppliants; flowers give rise to fruits. सन्ध्या०—people perform adoration (called सन्ध्यावन्दन) in the morning and evening; the queen was honoured by all people. चन्द्र...ष्मत्वे the moon and the queen had no ऊष्मन् (heat, pride of wealth). दर्पण...ग्रहणेषु a mirror takes in (*i. e.* reflects) every being; she drew (*i. e.* influenced by her goodness) all beings. सामुद्र...ज्ञानेषु In the knowledge of the character of others, she was the science of palmistry. समुद्र is supposed to be the author of the सामुद्रिकशास्त्र. परमा...व्याप्तिषु—The supreme spirit pervades everything; the queen could comprehend everything. According to the Vedānta, परमात्मन् (ब्रह्म) is everywhere and everything. Compare भगवद्गीता 'मया ततमिदं सर्वं जगदव्यक्तमूर्तिना.' स्मृति...वृत्तिषु Smṛitis, like that of मनु, lay down what is pure conduct (वृत्ति); her thoughts (वृत्ति) were pure or holy. अमृत...तृष्यत्सु she was full of अमृत (nectar, water) to the thirsty. निर्वृतिः bliss, happiness. वेतस...गुरुषु towards her elders, she was a वेतस (*i. e.* she was humble). वेतस is a symbol of humility. It bends when a flood sweeps down upon it. गोत्र...विलासानाम् she was the prosperity of the family of elegant gestures *i. e.* in her one could find the acme of fine gestures and dalliances. प्राय...स्त्रीत्वस्य she was as if the penance purity of womanhood. Penance purifies a sinful person. She had inherently the purity that comes of प्रायश्चित्त. आज्ञा...ध्वजस्य she was as if the fruition of the mandate of काम. She could have bewitched any one by her charms. व्युत्थान...रूपस्य she was as if the post-concentration consciousness of beauty. The idea is:—रूप had as if been in a समाधि (*i. e.* had given up moving about in the world); then रूप gave up its state of समाधि as a Yogin does and became conscious in the person of the queen. व्युत्थान means समाधिनिवृत्ति (cessation of the state of Yogic trance). For the meaning of व्युत्थान, note योगसूत्र III. 36 'ते समाधावुपसर्गा व्युत्थाने सिद्धयः' on which व्यासभाष्य says 'ते प्रतिभादयः समाहितचित्तस्योत्पद्यमाना उपसर्गास्तद्दर्शनप्रत्यनीकत्वात् । व्युत्थितचित्तस्योत्पद्यमानाः सिद्धयः'. C and T render the words as 'the Eureka of loveliness.' दिष्ट...रतेः she was as if the ovation of passion. दिष्टम् means 'fortune' (good or bad); here, good fortune. वृद्धि means congratulation; compare the use of the root वृध् in 'दिष्ट्या पुत्रमुखदर्शनेन भवान् वर्धते'. मनो...णीयकस्य she was the attainment of the desires of beauty. Beauty had been longing for a proper person to represent her and found the fulfilment of that longing in the person of the queen. वंशो...रागस्य she was the root of the ancestry of love. As a family traces its ancestry back to some founder, so true love started with her and was then propagated through succeeding generations of loving women. The readings of B also make good sense. सर्ग...सौन्दर्यस्य she was the utmost limit of the creation of loveliness. In her loveliness found its perfection. आयति...यौवनस्य she was as if the majesty of youth. 'प्रभावेपि चायतिः' इत्यमरः. अनभ्र...वैदग्ध्यस्य she was the cloudless rain of intelligence. Rainfall requires clouds; hence rain without clouds is looked upon as an extraordinary thing, a wonder. Her intelligence was wonderful. अयशः...लक्ष्म्याः. लक्ष्मी is said to be चञ्चल. This bad name that लक्ष्मी had acquired was wiped off by the queen, in whom लक्ष्मी was स्थिर. Compare 'येन श्रियः संश्रयदोषरूढं स्वभावलोलेत्ययशः प्रमृष्टम्' रघु० VI. 41. यशः... चारित्रस्य she was the fulness of the fame of chastity. C and T translate 'goodness' bloom of beauty', which is not correct. सौभाग्य...पतेः she was Brahmā's creation of the atoms of beauty. The idea seems to be this:—By creating her, Brahmā created the परमाणुs of beauty; whenever he wants to create another lovely form he would draw upon her beauty (the परमाणुs). According to the Vais'eshika philosophy, from atoms the whole world is produced. शम...शान्तिरिव the quietude of quiescence. शमः is restraint of passions or of the mind. The idea is that even शम would derive शान्ति from her. Explain the remaining clauses similarly. आभिजात्यम् (अभिजातस्य भावः) high birth. संयमः restraint. धैर्यम्—steadiness (of mind). विभ्रमः sportive or amorous action. यशोमती—From the Sonpat seal we see that the name of हर्ष's mother was यशोमती and not यशोवती. See Introduction. प्राणानां भूमिः she was the centre of the life of the king, she was the very life of the king. विश्रामस्य भूमिः—the king confided everything to her. धर्मस्य भूमिः she was the source of the righteousness of the king. A wife is the source of धर्माचरण, as said by आपस्तम्ब 'धर्मप्रजासम्पत्तिः प्रयोजनं दारसंग्रहस्य.' No यज्ञ could be performed without her. See तैत्तिरीय ब्राह्मण III. 3. 3. 1 'अयज्ञो वा एष योऽपत्नीकः'. The महाभारत says that the wife is the source of त्रिवर्ग (धर्म, अर्थ and काम) 'अर्धं भार्या मनुष्यस्य भार्या श्रेष्ठतमः सखा । भार्या मूलं त्रिवर्गस्य भार्या मूलं तरिष्यतः ॥' आदिपर्व 74.40. C and T render 'the centre of all creatures' love, confidence, duty and felicity'. This is not correct. अस्य = राज्ञः प्रभाकरवर्धनस्य. नरकजितः (1) of the conqueror of the demon नरक (*i. e.* of

विष्णु); (2) of the vanquisher of Hell. The king by his धर्माचरण had removed the possibility of going to Hell. लक्ष्मी is represented as resting on the bosom of Vishṇu. कृष्ण killed नरक who was the son of भूमि (the earth) and was king of प्राग्ज्योतिष; see विष्णुपुराण V. 29.

P. 58 ll. 3–8 निसर्गत...हृदयम्. उदये...कृत: at the rise of the sun (दिनकृत्). धवलेन कर्पटेन (piece of cloth) प्रावृतं शिरः यस्य. प्राङ्मुखः with his face towards the east. कुङ्कुममण्डलके in a circle that was smeared with saffron paste. C and T translate 'kneeling eastward upon the ground in a circle.' This is wrong. The king did not *kneel in a circle.* He had drawn up a circle with saffron paste on to which he put his offerings. पद्मराग—ruby (which is red in colour). स्व...ददौ he offered worship (अर्घ) with a bunch (षण्ड *m. n.*) of red lotuses that were reddened (अनुरक्त) by the sun, as if it (bunch) were his own heart devoted to the sun. सूर्ये अनुरक्तम् (हृदयम्); सूर्येण अनुरक्तम् (षण्डम्). The heart and the bunch of lotuses are both red and ०नुरक्त. जप्यम्—muttered prayer. शोभनं चरितं यस्य स सुचरितः अपत्यहेतोः for the purpose of (securing) issue. प्राध्वम् *ind.* favourably, suitably. 'आनुकूल्यार्थके प्राध्वम्' इत्यमरः. Here it may be taken as an adjective of मन्त्रम् meaning 'favourable.' प्रयत restrained, devout. जञ्जपूकः one who mutters prayers. 'यजजपदशां यङः' पा. 3. 2. 166 (The affix ऊक is applied to the frequentative base of यज्, जप् and दश्. यायजूक, दन्दशूक, जञ्जपूक). मन्त्रमादित्यहृदयम्—आदित्यः हृदयं (रहस्यं) यस्य. The आदित्यहृदय is a well-known स्तोत्र declared by कृष्ण to अर्जुन (see बृहत्स्तोत्ररत्नाकर Nir. ed.). For some of the details given in the text, note the following from the स्तोत्र. 'वृत्तं वा चतुरस्रं वा लिप्तभूमौ न्यसेच्छुचिः। त्रिधा तत्र लिखेत्पद्ममष्टपत्रं सकर्णिकम् ॥ 99...सकेसराणि पद्मानि करवीराणि चार्जुन। रक्तचन्दनमिश्राणि कृत्वा वै ताम्रभाजने। धृत्वा शिरसि तत्पात्रं जानुभ्यां धरणीं स्पृशेत् ॥ 104–5.

P. 58 ll. 9–21 भक्त...तिष्ठत्. भक्तजनानां अनुरोधः (entreaty) तेन विधेयानि—influenced by the entreaties of their devotees. सितकरस्य (चन्द्रमसः) कराः तद्वत् सिता (शुभ्रा) सुधा (*chunam*) तया धवलस्य. द्वितीयशयने on a second couch. On the propriety of this, see the com. 'द्वितीयेत्यादिनास्य सदाचारनिष्ठोक्ता। उक्तं हि नाश्नीयाद्भार्यया सार्कं न च सुप्यात्तया समम् ॥'. See मनु० 'समानशयने चैव न शयीत तया सह ॥' IV. 40. शिश्ये—Perfect 3rd sing. of शी. परिणत...तिष्ठत्—the principal sentence is देवी यशोमती सहसैव 'आर्यपुत्र परित्रायस्व' इति भाषमाणा उदतिष्ठत्. परिण...श्यामायाम् when the night had reached its close. आसन्ना

(approaching) प्रभातवेला तया विलुप्यमानं लावण्यं यस्य. लिलम्बिषमाणे (*loc. pr. p.* of the desiderative of लम्ब्) when (the moon) was declining (*lit.* about to hang down). सीदत् (sinking, waning) तेजः यस्य. तारकाणां ईश्वरः चन्द्रः. कराग्रैः स्पृष्टा कुमुदिनी तया प्रमोदः तस्मात् जन्म यस्य (with ०स्वेदे). कराग्र...पयसि when very cool drops of dew (अवश्यायः) were falling as if they were the perspiration of the moon (शशधरः) evoked by the joy of touching the night lotuses with the tips of his करs (rays, hands). The poets represent that when a young person intensely in love touches his sweetheart, he perspires. स्वेद is one of the eight सात्त्विकभावs. मधु... प्रदीपेषु when the lamps in the harem, being smitten (आहत *lit.* struck) by the breath of the sleeping beauties that were intoxicated by wine, flickered as if intoxication had been transferred to them. The lamps flickered owing to the breaths of sleeping women. The author represents this flickering as the staggering of intoxication. The lamps caught intoxication from the breath of women wafting the smell of wine. संक्रान्तः मदः येषु. राजनि—construe this with स्वपिति below. विमल...तारकाभिः whose feet were as if shampooed by the stars that were reflected in his white nails. संवाह्यमानौ चरणौ यस्य तस्मिन् (राजनि). It should be remembered that the king is represented as sleeping on the roof of his palace in the summer. Hence the stars were reflected in his nails. विस्रब्ध...अङ्गैः he had his limbs spread carelessly as if they were consigned to the women in the form of the quarters. Understand लक्षिते after अङ्गैः, the instrumental being used in accordance with the Sûtra 'इत्थंभूतलक्षणे' पा. 2. 3. 21. (जटाभिस्तापसः). दिश एव अङ्गनाः. मधु...वीज्यमाने who was fanned by the beauty (श्री) of his face with breath that was scented with मधु (wine, honey), as if the (breaths) were the breezes of the fan *viz.* the lotus in her hand. The king had drunk wine and his breath was charged with its odour. The poet fancies that he was fanned by the लक्ष्मी of his face with the breath. लक्ष्मी is represented as having a lotus in her hand. कमल would have मधु (honey in it). If the lotus were used as a fan the breeze would be charged with the scent of honey. ०गन्धिभिः goes with ०वातैः as well as श्वसितैः. स्वहस्ते यत्कमलं तदेव तालवृन्तं तस्य वातैः. विमल...विराजिते who was adorned by the image of the moon's disc reflected on his bright (विमल) cheek which (image) looked like a chaplet (शेखरः) of white flowers displaced by the seizing of hair in amorous sports. The reflection of the white moon looked like a white garland. A शेखर (which is worn on the head) may be displaced and dangle on the cheek when seized in रतिकेलि. रतिकेल्यां कचग्रहः तेन लम्बितः तेन. भूषण...जनम् as if calling on her attendants by the tinkling of her ornaments. उत्कम्पमाना (trembling) अङ्गयष्टिः यस्याः.

P. 58 ll. 22–33 अथ तेन...कारणम्. तेन—connect this with ध्वनिना. सर्वस्या...मुखे which (cry) was never heard before even in the whole world, much less in the queen's mouth. The king protected the world so well that not even the meanest had ever to cry 'help.' एकपदे *ind.* at once. शिरो...निशाम् who as if drew a parting line in the night with his bright (धौत) sword having a glittering edge, which (sword) was snatched from that part of his bed on which his head rested with his right hand that quivered with wrath, as if it (sword) were the white lotus in his ear coming out. सीमन्त the parting line in the hair on the head of women. सीमन्तयन् is the *pr. p.* of the denominative verb from सीमन्त. Night is dark as hair. The flash of the bright sword made a सीमन्त in the hair of the woman (night) *i. e.* darkness was parted by the white streak. The sword was kept below his pillow to be taken out in case of necessity. Being taken from under his head, the bright sword resembled a white lotus which is often placed on the ear as an ornament. अच्छा धारा यस्य. C and T translate 'whose glittering edge drew a line like a prolongation of his ear-wreath across the night.' This is obscure and does not bring out the sense. अन्तराल... पल्लवेन tossing aside with his left hand his upper garment, as if it were the ether that intervened in space. The garment was very fine and thin and hence is compared to आकाश. The fine garment screened his limbs. आकाश also screens from our view the things in space (अन्तराल). कर...राजमानः—his golden bracelet (worn on the left hand with which he tossed aside his upper garment) dropped down (from his hand) by the violent tossing of his hand and went rolling in all directions on the ground. The poet fancies that the वलय was his heart which wandered about in search of the cause of the alarm (of the queen). Some rich men even now wear golden वलयs on their left hand. सत्वरं अवतारितः (brought down) वामचरणः तस्य आक्रान्तिः (placing) तया कम्पितः प्रासादः येन. पुरः...मानः—his necklace was torn asunder by his violent movements, fell down before him and was reflected in the edge of his sword and looked like a piece of the rays of the moon. लक्ष्मी...आशानाम् he made the ends (पर्यन्त *m.*) of the quarters ruddy with his eyes that were red owing to sleep and rage, as if they (eyes) were coloured with betel juice when kissed by Lakshmî. The poet fancies that लक्ष्मी (sovereignty) had chewed betel and then out of love kissed his eyes. पाटलयन् is *pr. p.* of the denonimative verb from पाटल (red). The reading पटलयन् means 'veiling or covering' and does not yield a good sense. बद्धा...वर्तयन् as if again bringing back the night (त्रियामा) by his frowning brow that was trident—shaped and that caused darkness. बद्धः अन्धकारः यया. तिस्रः पताकाः (रेखा) यस्याः. His forehead was wrinkled into three lines by rage and his brows were dark. The author lays emphasis on त्रि in त्रिपताकया and त्रियामां. विक्षिप्तं चक्षुः येन.

P. 59 ll. 1–9 **अथ...इति.** यामिकिनी—a woman of the night watch (from यामिका meaning night). 'साध्वसं भयम्' इत्यमरः. बाला ...भागान् filling the different quarters as if with the glory of morn. कुण्डलिनौ...कवचिनौ wearing earrings, armlets and coat of mail. इन्द्र...स्नातौ bathed in saffron (juice) of the hue of the इन्द्रगोपक insect. The इन्द्रगोपकs are red insects that are seen at the beginning of the rainy season. इन्द्रगोपकस्येव रुक् (कान्तिः) यस्य. Saffron is auspicious and women used to apply saffron तिलक on their forehead as a mark of auspiciousness. C and T translate 'bathed in blood cochineal red'. This is bad. To see in a dream a person bathed in blood is not a good omen. The author intends the whole description to indicate good fortune. 'अथ कुङ्कुमम् ॥...रक्तसङ्कोचपिशुनं वीरलोहितचन्दनम् ॥' इत्यमरः (on which क्षीरस्वामी says 'रञ्जनाद्रक्तम् । अत एवासृक्संज्ञम्'). On the two meanings of रुधिर, note रघु 11. 20 'राममन्मथशरेण ताडिता दुःसहेन हृदये निशाचरी । गन्धवद्रुधिरचन्दनोक्षिता जीवितेशवसतिं जगाम सा ॥'. उत्तमाङ्गे (शिरसि) घटमानः अञ्जलिः यस्य that folded their hands on their heads (in token of submission and adoration). चन्द्रं...निर्गतया as if she were the moon issuing out from the सुषुम्ण ray. It was believed that the waxing of the moon was due to a ray of the sun called सुषुम्ण and that the waning was due to the digits of the moon being drunk by the gods. 'सूर्यरश्मिः सुषुम्नो यस्तर्पितस्तेन चन्द्रमाः । कृष्णपक्षेऽमरैः शश्वत्पीयते वै सुधामयः॥' विष्णु० II. 11. 22. यास्क has a very interesting note on this "अथाप्यस्यैको रश्मिश्चन्द्रमसं प्रति दीप्यते तदेतेनोपेक्षितव्यमादित्यतोऽस्य दीप्तिर्भवतीति । 'सुषुम्णः सूर्यरश्मिश्चन्द्रमा गन्धर्वः' इत्यपि निगमो भवति ।" निरुक्त II. 2. 2. Bāṇa frequently refers to this belief. See कादम्बरीं 'अलीकं चेदं यथा किल सकलाः कलाः कलावतो बहुलपक्षे क्षीयमाणस्य

सुषुम्णनाम्ना रश्मिना रविरापिबतीति;' हर्षचरित 'सुषुम्णास्रुतिशशिसुधाशीकरस्तबकतारकिततीराम्' (मन्दाकिनीम्). It should be noted that in the passage from कादम्बरी Bāṇa attributes the waning of the moon to सुषुम्णरश्मि. मे विलपन्त्याः In spite of the fact that I was weeping.

P. 59 ll. 10–24 **एतस्मिन्नेव...पत्युर्भाषितेन.** तोरणस्य समीपे उपतोरणम् (अव्ययीभाव)—near the royal porch. रराण *perfect 3rd. p. sing.* of रण् to sound. राज...फलम् as if it were the first utterance of royal splendour (personified) proclaiming the result of (*i. e.* indicated by) the dream. भाविनीं भूतिम् future prosperity. अमन्दम् violently. चकाण *perfect* of कण् *1. P.* to sound. कोणेन (drum-stick) आहता. Separate हता आनन्दात्. नान्दी—This has been explained as 'the symphony of twelve drums beaten simultaneously' ('एकदा द्वादशमृदङ्गघोषो नान्दी' रङ्गराज on उत्तररामचरित). प्रबोध...पाठकानाम् of (minstrels) that recited auspicious (verses or words) that rouse from sleep. वल्लभाः तुरङ्गाः तेषां मन्दुरामन्दिरम् (stables). आदौ सुप्तः पश्चादुत्थितः सुप्तोत्थितः. सप्ति...पुरः in front of the horses (सप्ति *m*) that neighed sweetly (कृतः मधुरहेषारवः यैः). च्योतन्तः तुषारसलिलस्य शीकराः यस्मात् (*adj.* of यवसम्) from which oozed out the spray of frost—water. किरन् *nom. sing. m.* of *pr. parti.* of कॄ (qualifies पुरुषः and has यवसं for its object). वक्त्रा ...वक्त्रे two verses in the वक्त्र and अपरवक्त्र metres respectively. According to some writers the species of composition called आख्यायिका (the हर्षचरित is one) should be divided into sections called उच्छ्वासs and should contain verses in the वक्त्र and अपरवक्त्र metres foreshadowing coming events. See the quotation from भामह in the Introduction. अपरवक्त्र is an अर्धसमवृत्त having eleven letters (न, न, र, ल, ग) in the 1st and 3rd Pāda and twelve letters (न, ज, ज, र) in the 2nd and 4th. 'अयुजि ननरला गुरुः समे तदपरवक्त्रमिदं नजौ जरौ ॥'. It is also called वैतालीय, as said by the वृत्तरत्नाकर 'वदन्त्यपरवक्त्राख्यं वैतालीयं विपश्चितः'. वक्त्र is defined as 'नाद्यान्नसौ स्यातामब्धेर्योऽनुष्टुभि ख्यातम्.' Like the अनुष्टुभ् it has eight letters in a पाद. After the first four letters in each पाद there is a यगण. C and T take वक्त्रा and अपरवक्त्रा to be the names of the metres. निधिस्तरुविकारेण स्पष्टमाख्यायते a hidden treasure is clearly indicated by the change in a tree (*i. e.* by some singular or remarkable thing about a tree). The com. says 'यत्राधो निधिस्तत्र परिणाहोद्गताधोमुखशाखामूलादिभाजो वृक्षा भवन्ति.' शुभस्य आगमः the advent of luck. अरुण is the charioteer of the sun in mythology and is a personification of the radiant sky at daybreak; compare 'यावत्प्रतापनिधिराक्रमते न भानुरह्नाय तावदरुणेन तमो निरस्तम्.' अतिजवः very rapid. पूर्व...दयः the previous appearance of an omen. मुदो...षीदसि you feel dejected when it is a time of joy. परिगृहीतासि thou art accepted (*i. e.* favoured). अंशुमाली = सूर्यः. अवतीर्य descending (from the roof where the king had slept).

P. 59 l. 25—**P. 60** l. 15 **ततः समति...पतिः.** गर्भ...जननी his mother took upon herself pallor as if on account of his glory though he was only in the womb yet. Being pregnant, she became pale. यशः is represented by poets as white. The poet fancies that her pallor (really) due to pregnency was due to the glory the son in the womb was to attain in future. गुण...क्लान्तेव as if exhausted by the weight of his virtues. कान्ति...बभूव she became averse to food as if she were satiated with the nectar of the expanding brilliance. On account of pregnancy, she became more brilliant in complexion and lovely. This the poet compares to अमृत. One who has taken अमृत would have no appetite for ordinary food. उपचीयमानः (increasing) गर्भः तस्य भरः तेन अलसा. गुरुभिर्वारितापि although dissuaded by her elders. C and T translate गुरु as parents. This is not necessary. She would have to bow to all elderly persons including her parents. Further it seems questionable whether her parents would be at her husband's palace ordinarily. वन्दनाय...अनीयत she was taken by her friends for saluting (her elders) with difficulty by supporting her with their hands. सालभञ्जिकेव The queen would support herself against walls and pillars and would look like a doll. कमल...रणौ she could not lift up her feet as if they were surrounded by bees that had sat upon them out of their greed for a lotus. Her feet were radiant like lotuses. She could not walk swiftly because she was गर्भभरालस. The poet represents that this was due to the weight of bees. The rays from her bright toenails resembled the delicate fibres of lotus plants. हंसs subsist upon मृणालs. मणि...कमलम्—the idea is that she was so eager for support that she would stretch out her hand expecting support even from her own images reflected in the jewelled walls. समा...कर्तुम् she was unable even to issue commands for the performance of household duties, much less to do them herself. आस्तां...रोढुम्—The idea is:—she could not bear to mount to the roof of the palace even in thought, much less with her feet that were oppressed by the weight of the anklets. उत्कम्पितौ स्तनौ यस्याः (on account of hard breathing). तस्तान (perfect of स्तन्) she groaned, breathed hard. प्रत्युत्थानेषु at times of rising to receive (some person worthy of honour). उभयजानुशिखरविनिहितौ करकिसलयौ यस्याः. गर्वा...र्येत she was held up by the child in the womb as if through pride. The idea is:—she wanted to rise to receive and tried to get up by placing her hands upon her knees. But she did not after all get up. The poet fancies that the child in the womb, being proud, did not like to bow to any body, as it would have to do if its mother bowed and so prevented her from rising. दिवसं all day long (accu. of time). The sentence is दिवसं अधोमुखी ददर्श गर्भम्. Her face was reflected in her bright bosom. The poet fancies that her face had entered inside her body (in the form of the reflection) because it was anxious to see the child. सखीनामुत्सङ्गेषु मुक्तं शरीरं यया. निर्मितं, कल्पितं and विहितं qualify राज्यवर्धनम्. सर्वोर्वी...मितम् composed as if with the atoms of वज्र for destroying the alliances of all kings. सर्वेषां उर्वीभृतां (राज्ञां) पक्षः (समूहः) तस्य पाताय (with राज्यवर्धन); सर्वेषां उर्वीभृतां पर्वतानां पक्षाः (wings) तेषां पाताय (with इन्द्र understood). The mountains had once wings and troubled the earth by flying anywhere. Indra cut off their wings with his वज्र. बाण refers to this story very often. कादम्बरी 'अशनिभयपुञ्जितकुलशैलमध्यगतमिव कनकशिखरिणम्'; 'मैनाकेनेवाविदितपक्षपातेन'. शेष...कल्पितम् as if made with the means, *viz.* the numerous hoods of शेष. It is supposed that the earth is borne by the serpent शेष on its hoods. Compare 'किं शेषस्य भरव्यथा न वपुषि क्ष्मां न क्षिपत्येष यत्' भर्तृहरि. राज्यवर्धन also would be able to bear the responsibility of the world. सकल...विहितम् (she gave birth to रा०) who caused tremor to all भूभृत्s (kings, mountains) and who was as if made with the limbs of the elephants of the quarters. ०मुखरं, ०रवं, ०भुवनं and मनोहरं qualify महोत्सवम्. पूरिताः असंख्याः शङ्खाः तेषां शब्दैः मुखरम् (resounding). प्रहतानि पटहशतानि तैः पटुः रवः यस्मिन्. गम्भीरेण भेरीनिनादेन निर्भरं भरितं भुवनं यस्मिन्. प्रमोदेन उन्मत्तः मर्त्यलोकः तेन मनोहरम्. मास...दिवसमिव for one month as if it were a single day.

P. 60 l. 16—**P. 61** l. 10 अथान्य...बध्यन्त. The locatives from कन्दलिनि to ०कसि qualify नभसि (*i. e.* the month of श्रावण). कन्दलिनि abounding in plantain trees. Wild plantain plants grow up spontaneously in the rainy season. कुड्मलिताः कदम्बतरवः यस्मिन् in which the *Kadamba* trees have put forth buds. The कदम्ब tree is said to put forth buds at the advent of thunder and rain;

compare 'मरुन्नवाम्भःप्रविधूतसिक्ता कदम्बयष्टिः स्फुटकोरकेव' उत्तरराम० III. कुड्मलाः सञ्जाताः अस्य इति कुड्मलितः according to 'तदस्य सञ्जातं तारकादिभ्य इतच्' पा. 5. 2. 36. रूढाः तोक्मतृणस्तम्बाः यस्मिन् in which the clusters (स्तम्बः) of barley blades had taken firm root. 'शितशूकयवौ समौ ॥ तोक्मस्तु तत्र हरिते' इत्यमरः. स्तम्भितानि तामरसानि यस्मिन् in which the red lotuses were supported (*i. e.* stood firm and erect, being nourished with plenty of water). विकसितं (delighted) चातकचेतः यस्मिन्. It was believed that the चातक could not drink water on the earth, but subsisted on a few drops from the clouds. मूकाः मानसौकसः (हंसाः, मानसे ओकः सद्म येषां) यस्मिन्. हंसs are said to migrate to the मानस lake at the commencement of the rainy season and so on the plains the cackling of हंसs was not heard. नभसि मासि—कृष्ण was born in श्रावण; while the poet says that हर्ष was conceived in श्रावण. चक्रं पाणौ यस्य = विष्णु (*i. e.* कृष्ण). हर्ष also was चक्रपाणि *i. e.* on his hand there were lines resembling a चक्र, which was looked upon as one of the चक्रवर्तिलक्षणs. See बृहत्संहिता 67. 47 'चक्रासिपरशुतोमरशक्तिधनुःकुन्तसन्निभा रेखाः। कुर्वन्ति चमूनाथं' &c. सममेव at the same time. हृदये हर्षः—यशोमती was delighted at heart and conceived the future हर्ष. सर्व...गृहीता as if accepted (*i. e.* endowed with) by all the merits of her subjects. पुण्य is represented as white. The queen's body became slightly pallid (आपाण्डु) on account of pregnancy; the poet fancies that it was the पुण्य of the subjects that had assumed shape and come to her in the form of her गर्भ, the idea being that the birth of a good Emperor like हर्ष is due to the पुण्य of the subjects. गर्भारम्भेण as pregnancy came on. श्मामायमाने चारुचूचुकचूलिके ययोः (also श्यामायमाना चारुचूचुकसदृशी चूलिका ययोः) चूचुक nipple. चूलिका crest. पयोधरौ कलशौ इव (also पयोधरसदृशौ कलशौ or पयसः धरौ पयोधरौ कलशौ). The queen's breasts had nipples growing dark on account of pregnancy. They would be sucked by an emperor (चक्रवर्तिन् *i. e.* हर्ष). Drinking *water* was brought for emperors in sealed (मुद्रित) jars in order to prevent poisoning. The dark crest of the seal resembled the crest of the nipple. स्तन्यार्थ...दृष्टिः her eye, long, glossy (स्निग्ध) and white became sweeter as if it were a stream of milk placed in her face for (supplying) milk (to her breast). दुग्धनदी also would be दीर्घ, स्निग्ध (viscous) and धवल. See for the same simile 'स्नपयति हृदयेशं स्नेहनिष्यन्दिनी ते धवलमधुरमुग्धा दुग्धकुल्येव दृष्टिः ॥' उत्तरराम III. 23. सकलमङ्गलानां गणेन अधिष्ठितं (occupied) गात्रं (body) तस्य गरिम्णा (by the weight). अमन्दायत became slow (from the denominative verb मन्दायते). Her gait became slow owing to pregnancy. The poet fancies that the slowness was due to the weight of the numerous auspicious signs due to the conception of a चक्रवर्तिन्. निर्मलं मणिकुट्टिमं (floor inlaid with gems) तस्मिन् निमग्नं प्रतिबिम्बं (reflection of the queen) तस्य निभेन (under the guise). गृहीतौ पादपल्लवौ यया. पूर्वं ... पृथिवी अस्याः (यशोमत्याः)—The queen was reflected in the brilliant pavement. The poet fancies that the earth was worshipping her feet by way of a prelude to what would follow when her son became the emperor of the world. दिवसम् *accu.* of time. शयनीयं is the object of अधिशयानायाः (यशोमत्याः). अपाश्रयः awning. पत्रभङ्गः drawing of lines or figures. ०प्रतिमा image of a figure drawn on the awning. विमलकपोलोदरे गता reflected in the bright cheek (of the queen). गर्भो...संक्रान्तम् reflected in her round bosom from which the garment had been taken away on account of the agitation (उन्माथः) of pregnancy. गर्भस्य उन्माथेन मुक्तं अंशुकं यस्मात्. उडुपतिः the moon. The reflection of the moon in the bosom appeared like a white umbrella held over the गर्भ. A white umbrella is an emblem of चक्रवर्तित्व; compare रघुवंश 3. 16. 'अदेयमासीत्त्रयमेव भूपतेः शशिप्रभं छत्रमुभे च चामरे.' चित्र...ग्राहिण्योपि even the women holding chowries on the painted walls (*i. e.* even pictures moved chowries). चामरs are among the insignia of royalty. करे (by the trunk) विधृतं कमलिन्याः पलाशानां (पत्राणां) पुटं तस्मिन् सलिलानि तैः. She dreamt that the four दिग्गजs bathed her with water. This was a precursor of the future sovereignty of her son. प्रतिबुध्यमानायाश्च and when she woke up. चन्द्रशालिका—a chamber on the roof. 'चन्द्रशाला शिरोगृहम्' क्षीरस्वामी. Even the puppets cried 'victory.' परिज...निश्चेरुः When she called out to her attendants, incorporeal voices issued forth saying 'command.' क्रीडा...भङ्गम्—This sentence and the following give expression to the popular notion that the mother's mind is influenced by the potential thoughts of the child in the womb, as said by the com. 'गर्भस्थजनचित्तवृत्त्यनुसारेण गर्भिण्या अपि चित्तवृत्तिर्भवति'. चतुर्णामपि—This indicates that हर्ष's empire would extend up to the four oceans. The oceans are sometimes spoken of as four or as seven. वेला...सरेषु in the vicinity (परिसरः) of sandy banks (पुलिनं, 'तोयोत्थितं तत्पुलिनम्' इत्यमरः) inside the bowers of creepers on the seashore. आत्य...चचाल Even as regards business of extreme importance, her eyebrow moved playfully. The idea is that she felt no concern or anxiety even as regards serious matters; so calm and collected she was. आत्ययिक—अत्ययः प्रयोजनं अस्य 'प्रयोजनम्' पा. 5. 1. 109 (प्रयोजनं फलं कारणं च). सन्नि...सीत though jewelled mirrors were near her, she had a strong liking (व्यसनम्) for seeing her face in a drawn (उत्खात) sword blade. उत्सारिता वीणा यैः. श्रुतौ असुखायन्त gave pleasure to her ear. स्तम्भितम् stiffened. सख्यश्चास्याः &c.—construe सख्यश्च अस्याः पार्श्वं क्षणमपि न मुमुचुः. विस्फारित stretched wide. आसन्न...भवनम् brightening the house as if with the idea of celebrating the festival of her delivery that was approaching. At जन्ममहोत्सव houses are washed with chunam. The friends whitened the house with their eyes expanded wide. विकच...विदधाना—The friends cast glances in all directions from their widely expanded eyes (that were white). The author fancies that the glances were so many white and blue flowers of various kinds of lotuses, offered in worship to protect the queen from evil. कुमुद is a white night lotus. कुवलय is a blue lotus. कमल is pale red. The white of the eye was mixed with the blue of the pupil and the white—red of the corners. आत्मो...चक्रुः eminent physicians holding various drugs and sitting in their proper places supported the queen like high mountains (occupying their proper places and having various plants growing on them and that made the earth steady). It was believed that the earth, which was formerly unsteady, was made steady by the mountains. Compare कादम्बरी 'अनुजीविभूभृच्छतसहस्रकल्पितावष्टम्भं सञ्चारिणं द्वितीयमिव मेदिनीसंनिवेशम्.' ग्रीवा...बध्यन्त in the knots of her necklace cord were tied excellent jewells. लक्ष्म्या...गतानि that had come with लक्ष्मी (*i. e.* royal splendour). She being a queen could command jewels. There is a pun on these words. Jewels were also produced from the oceans (पयोनिधि) at the time of the churning along with लक्ष्मी who was one of them. See above for सागरमन्थन.

P. 61 ll. 11–15 **ततश्च...जहार.** ज्येष्ठामूलीये मासि in the month of ज्येष्ठ. ज्येष्ठा मूलं च ज्येष्ठामूले. 'द्वन्द्वाच्छः' पा. 4. 2. 6 नक्षत्रद्वन्द्वाद्युक्ते काले छः स्यात्. बहुलासु = कृत्तिकासु—when the moon was in the कृत्तिका constellation. बहुलपक्ष = कृष्णपक्ष. समा...यौवने when the youth of the night was about to climb up (*i. e.* when night was just beginning). समारुरुक्षति *loc. sing.* of the *desiderative part.* of रुह् with सम् and आ. हृदयनिर्विशेषा not different from her own heart *i. e.* who was as dear to यशोमती as her own self. दिष्ट्या... जन्मना you are to be congratulated on the birth of a second son.

पूर्णपात्रम् a present given to or taken by one who brings some happy news. The com. defines पूर्णपात्र as 'आनन्ददो हि सौहार्दादेत्य वस्त्रादिकं बलात् । अजानतो हरत्येव पूर्णपात्रं तु तत्स्मृतम् ॥.' Another definition given in the शब्दकल्पद्रुम is 'हर्षादुत्सवकाले यदलंकारांशुकादिकम् । आकृष्य गृह्यते पूर्णपात्रं पूर्णालकं च तत् ॥'.

P. 61 ll. 16–24 **अस्मिन्नेव...जातः इति.** संवादिताः अतीन्द्रियादेशाः यस्य whose extraordinary predictions had come true. अतीन्द्रिय beyond the reach of the senses. दर्शितः प्रभावः येन. सङ्कलिती ज्योतिषी—who had grasped the science of astronomy. सङ्कलितमनेन इति सङ्कलितिन्—Words like अधीतिन् take the *loc.* of the object of study, according to वार्तिक 'सप्तमीविधाने क्तस्येन्विषयस्य कर्मण्युपसंख्यानम्' on 'सप्तम्यधिकरणे च' पा. 2. 3. 36 (अधीती व्याकरणे आम्नाती छन्दसि । महाभाष्य). सर्वासां...दृश्वा who had mastered all the treatises on planets. महितः = पूजितः. The बृहत्संहिता of वराहमिहिर refers to three branches of ज्योतिष *viz.* ग्रहगणित, संहिता and होराशास्त्र and remarks 'संहितापारगश्च दैवचिन्तको भवति'. It then gives a long list of the topics of संहिता (2nd chap.). हितः who was favourable to (the royal family). भोजकः—The com. says 'रविमर्चयित्वा पूजका हि भूयसा गणका भवन्ति । ये मगा इति प्रसिद्धाः भागवता इत्यन्ये.' This means that the astrologer was a Maga, a worshipper of the sun. The बृहत्संहिता tells us that in a temple of the sun, a मग should be placed in charge of the worship 'विष्णोर्भागवतान्मगांश्च सवितुः शम्भोः सभस्मद्विजान् &c.' (60. 19). C and T refer to Wilson's Vishṇu—purāṇa (Hall's ed) vol. V. p. 382 where an analysis of the last 12 chapters of the भविष्यपुराण is given concerning the मगs. साम्ब son of कृष्ण became a leper by the curse of दुर्वासस् and was cured by worshipping the sun. He gratefully built a temple of the sun and brought 18 families of मगs from शकद्वीप as priests and induced the भोजs of द्वारका, a branch of the यादवs, to give their daughters in marriage to the मगs. Hence the मगs were styled भोजकs. मान्धाता—He was a king of the solar race. युवनाश्व had no son and therefore the sages performed a sacrifice for him and placed a jar full of holy water on a *Vedī* and slept. युवनाश्व being thirsty drank the water and then a son was born from his side. The विष्णुपु० (IV. 2.) gives the origin of the name मान्धातृ as follows "गर्भश्च युवनाश्वोदरेऽभवत् । ...दक्षिणकुक्षिमवनिपतेर्निर्भिद्य निश्चक्राम नासौ ममार । जातो नामैष कं धास्यतीति ते मुनयः प्रोचुः ॥ 17 अथागत्य देवराजोऽब्रवीन्मामयं धास्यतीति ततो मान्धाता नामतोऽभवत् ।". About मान्धाता the रामायण says 'अयोध्यायां पुरा राज्ञा युवनाश्वसुतो बली । मान्धाता इति विख्यातस्त्रिषु लोकेषु वीर्यवान् ॥ स कृत्वा पृथिवीं कृत्स्नां शासने पृथिवीपतिः । सुरलो-

क्रमितो जेतुमुद्योगमकरोन्नृपः ।' उत्तरकाण्ड 67. 5–6. व्यती...रहिते free from the contact (अभिषङ्गः) of all evil positions such as व्यतीपात. व्यतीपात is the 17th योग out of the 27, beginning with विष्कम्भ. The धर्मसिन्धु says 'कुमारजन्मकाले तु व्यतिपातश्च वैधृतिः । संक्रमश्च रवेस्तत्र जातो दारिद्र्यकारकः ॥ अश्रियं मृत्युमाप्नोति नात्र कार्या विचारणा ॥'. उच्चस्थानस्थितेषु ग्रहेषु when the planets were in their places of exaltation. It is said that मेष, वृषभ, मकर, कन्या, कर्क, मीन and तुला are the उच्चs respectively of रवि, चंद्र, भौम, बुध, गुरु, शुक्र and शनि. See बृहज्जातक 'अजवृषभमृगाङ्गनाकुलीरा झषवणिजौ च दिवाकरादितुङ्गाः ।'. लग्नम् is that sign of the zodiac that is on the eastern horizon at the time of birth. अर्वाक् ततः after that *i. e.* since that time. योगः conjunction (in astrology). It seems to us impossible from an astrological point of view that all the planets were in their exaltation at the time of Harsha's birth. The day being the 12th of the dark half of ज्येष्ठ, the sun could not have been in मेष (which is the उच्च of the sun). सप्तानां चक्रवर्तिनाम्—the seven चक्रवर्तिs are 'भरतार्जुनमान्धातृभगीरथयुधिष्ठिराः । सगरो नहुषश्चैव सप्तैते चक्रवर्तिनः ॥'. अर्जुन must be सहस्रार्जुनकार्तवीर्य. चक्रवर्तिचिह्नानाम्—such as चक्र on the hand, जालग्रथितांगुलिकरत्व (mentioned in the 7th Act of शाकुन्तल). The great रत्नs are said to be fourteen in the विष्णुपुराण IV. 12. The शब्दकल्पद्रुम gives them as follows 'चक्रं रथो मणिः खड्गश्चर्म रत्नं च पञ्चमम् । केतुर्निधिश्च सप्तैवमप्राणानि प्रचक्ष्यते ॥ भार्या पुरोहितश्चैव सेनानी रथकृच्च यः । पत्त्यश्वौ कलभश्चेति प्राणिनः सप्त कीर्तिताः ॥ चतुर्दशैतानि रत्नानि सर्वेषां चक्रवर्तिनाम् ॥'. The great रत्नs according to the com. are six. 'मण्यश्वकरिचक्राणि वरा स्त्री परिनायकः । षडेतानि तु रत्नानि कीर्तितानि मनीषिभिः ॥'. The seven oceans are 'एते द्वीपा समुद्रैस्तु सप्त सप्तभिरावृताः । लवणेक्षुसुरासर्पिर्दधिदुग्धजलैः समम् ॥' विष्णुपु० II. 2. 6. सप्ततन्तुः means a 'sacrifice.' सप्तसप्तिः = सूर्यः (सप्त सप्तयः अश्वाः यस्य).

P. 61 l. 25—**P. 62** l. 11 **अत्रान्तरे...महान्.** अनाध्माताः—though not blown or filled with wind from the mouth. तारमधुरम् loudly and sweetly. विरेसुः perfect of रस् with वि. क्षुभितं जलनिधिजलं तस्य ध्वनिः तद्वत् धीरम् (deep). अभिषेकदुन्दुभिः—the drum that is beaten at the time of crowning a king. The author wants to indicate that the whole world, animate and inanimate, rejoiced at the birth of हर्ष who was destined to be a great emperor and vied in spontaneously manifesting its joy. सर्वभुवनस्य अभयं तस्य आघोषणा तस्याः पटहः—The echo of the tabors spread in all directions. The poet fancies that it was the kettledrum (पटहः) that proclaimed immunity from danger to the whole world. The idea is that हर्ष would give security against danger to the whole world. Even now proclamations are made known to the people by beat of drum. विधुताः केसरसटाः यैः that tossed the hair of their manes. Both केसर and सटा mean 'mane'. साटोपं (in a stately manner) गृहीतः हरितानां (green) दूर्वापल्लवानां कवलः (mouthful) तेन प्रशस्तैः (graced). हस्तपल्लवैः—has two senses. Those who dance make graceful movements with their hands (हस्त). The elephants tossed about their trunks (हस्त) in a graceful manner. सुरायाः आमोदः तद्वत् सुरभिः (with दिव्यानिलः); सुरायाः आमोदः तेन सुरभिः (निःश्वासः). Breezes redolent of the perfume of wine blew at the birth of हर्ष. This is fancied to be the sigh of लक्ष्मी leaving विष्णु. The idea suggested is—at the birth of हर्ष, लक्ष्मी left विष्णु and came to हर्ष. When leaving her husband विष्णु she sighed. चक्रं आयुधं यस्य. Compare for दिव्यानिल 'दिशः प्रसेदुर्मरुतो ववुः सुखाः प्रदक्षिणार्चिर्हविरग्निराददे । बभूव सर्वं शुभशंसि तत्क्षणं भवो हि लोकाभ्युदयाय तादृशाम् ॥' रघु० III. 14. प्रदक्षिणशिखानां कलापः तेन कथितः कल्याणागमः यैः that told of the forthcoming good luck by the mass of their flames curving to the right. अविद्यमानं इन्धनं (fuel) येषाम्. वैतानवह्नयः sacrificial fires. तपनीयस्य (सुवर्णस्य) शृङ्खला तया बन्धः तेन बन्धुरः (charming) कलशीकोशः येषाम्. कलशी a jar. कोश means 'the cuplike head or upper part of a jar'. Round the neck of the jar were tied chains of gold. समुदगुः aorist of इ with सम् and उद्. प्रहत...निभेन under the guise of the echo of the auspicious tabors that were beaten. दिक्पाल—these are eight 'इन्द्रो वह्निः पितृपतिर्नैर्ऋतो वरुणो मरुत् । कुबेर ईशः पतयः पूर्वादीनां दिशां क्रमात् ॥' इत्यमरः. दिष्टवृद्धिकलकलः—clamour of congratulation. The idea is—दिक्पालs were overjoyed at the birth of हर्ष. The echo of the tabors is fancied to be the clamour of congratulations from the दिक्पालs. शुक्लं वासः येषाम् (*adj.* of द्विजातयः). ब्रह्म वेदः मुखे येषाम् (with द्विजातयः); ब्रह्मा (the god ब्रह्मा) मुखं येषाम्—who had ब्रह्मा at their head (०पतयः). The Vedas being eternal, it may be said that the primeval प्रजापतिs also had the Veda on their lips. प्रजावृद्धये (1) for the well-being of the child (with ०जातयः); (2) for the propagation of the human race (with ०पतयः). कृतयुगप्रजापतयः—see मनुस्मृति I. 34-35 'अहं प्रजाः सिसृक्षुस्तु तपस्तप्त्वा सुदुश्चरम् । पतीन्प्रजानामसृजं महर्षीनादितो दश ॥ मरीचिमत्र्यङ्गिरसौ पुलस्त्यं पुलहं क्रतुम् । प्रचेतसं वसिष्ठं च भृगुं नारदमेव च ॥'. शान्त्युदकं फलं च हस्ते यस्य. पुरोधाः =पुरोहितः. पुरातन्यः स्थितयः as if they were the ancient rules (of conduct). प्रलम्बं (long) श्मश्रुजालं (beards) तेन जटिलानि आननानि येषाम्. It was usual to set prisoners free on the birth of a son or other great occasions. Note the अर्थशास्त्र of कौटिल्य 'बन्धनागारे च बालवृद्धव्याधितानाथानां च जातनक्षत्रपौर्णमासीषु विसर्गः' p. 146. बहलः मलपङ्ककलङ्कः तेन कालः (dark)

कायः (शरीरं) येषाम्. नश्यतः...कुलानीव as if they were the kindred of the Kali age that was vanishing. कलि (the age of sin) is fancied as dark. By the advent of हर्ष, an era of धर्म would be started and अधर्म would have to run away. The prisoners besmeared with dirt (and so dark) and running disorderly (आकुल) when freed are represented as the kindred of कलिकाल. बन्धनवृन्दानि crowds of prisoners. तत्कालापक्रान्तस्य that ran away at that moment (*viz.* at हर्ष's birth). शिबिरश्रेणयः rows of camps or tents. लोक...वीथ्यः the rows of stalls (विपणिः) that were plundered by the people. It seems that the stalls were looted by the permission of the king who compensated the traders for their loss. The stalls that were looted (and were therefore empty) looked like the camp lines from which अधर्म had run away, leaving them empty. विलसन्तः (making graceful movements) उन्मुखाः वामनकाः (dwarfs) बधिराश्च तेषां वृन्दं तेन वेष्टिताः (*adj.* of ०धात्र्यः). Dwarfs are often spoken of as the attendants of the harem 'निषेवितो वर्षवरैः कञ्चुकोष्णीषधारिभिः । अन्तःपुरेषु विचरेत् कुब्जकैरातवामनैः ॥' काम० 7. 41. जात...व्याकुलाः—the com. explains that 'in the lying-in-chamber a figure with a cat's face and surrounded by a crowd of children is set up' (probably to ward off evil). 'जातमातृदेवता मार्जारानना बहुपुत्रपरिवारा सूतिकागृहे स्थाप्यते.' Or we may take साक्षा...देवताः in another sense 'as if they were the divine Mātṛis become visible.' The Mātṛis, divine mothers, are said to attend on शिव and are seven or eight. 'ब्राह्मी माहेश्वरी चैन्द्री वाराही वैष्णवी तथा । कौबेरीत्यपि कौमारी सप्तैव मातरः स्मृताः ॥' हलायुधः. प्रावर्तत—the subject is पुत्रजन्मोत्सवः. The lines that follow contain clauses qualifying ०त्सवः. विगता राजकुलस्य स्थितिः यस्मिन् in which the rules of etiquette to be observed in the palace were (for the moment) gone. अधःकृता प्रतीहारस्य आकृतिः यस्मिन् in which the figure of the doorkeeper was disregarded *i. e.* anybody entered without minding the प्रतीहार. अपनीतः वेत्रिणां वेत्रः यस्मिन् in which the cane of the warders was taken away. निर्दोषः अन्तःपुरे प्रवेशः यस्मिन्. Ordinarily no one could have entered the seraglio. समौ स्वामिपरिजनौ यस्मिन् in which master and servant were brought to the same level. निर्विशेषौ बालवृद्धौ यस्मिन् in which there was no distinction between young and old. दुर्ज्ञेयः मत्तामत्तयोः प्रविभागः यस्मिन् in which no distinction was perceptible between drunk and sober persons (*i. e.* both acted in the same way). तुल्यौ कुलयुवतिवेश्ययोः आलापविलासौ यस्मिन् in which the words and gestures of noble ladies and harlots were the same. प्रनृत्तः सकलकटकलोकः यस्मिन्. कटकं—capital.

P. 62 ll. 12–21 **अपरेद्यु...दृश्यन्त.** The principal sentence is अपरेद्युः...बिभ्राणेन परिजनेन अनुगम्यमानानि...समन्तात् सामन्तान्तःपुरसहस्राणि अदृश्यन्त. अपरेद्युरारभ्य beginning from the next day. स्त्रीरा...तानि as if they (*i. e.* the wives of the सामन्तs) were the kingdoms of amazons brought together or poured forth (आवर्जित). The idea is that the women were so many. In the महाभारत, we read of प्रमीला, who fought with Arjuna, as being at the head of a स्त्रीराज्य. असुर...वृतानि as if they were the mines opened wide. For असुरविवर, see the description of स्थाण्वीश्वर in the 3rd उच्छ्वास, where we have 'असुरविवरमिति वार्तिकैः.' नारा...लितानि as if they were the wives of Vishṇu (*i. e.* Kṛishṇa) moving onwards. अवरोध is m., while अवरोधन is *n;* we should therefore read०रोधनानि. In the विष्णुपुराण, कृष्ण is said to have had 16101 wives 'षोडशसहस्राण्येकोत्तरशताधिकानि स्त्रीणामभवन्' विष्णु० 4. 15; 'षोडशात्र सहस्राणि स्त्रीणामन्यानि चक्रिणः ।...निशासु जगतः स्रष्टा तासां गेहेषु केशवः । उवास विप्र सर्वासां विश्वरूपधरो हरिः ॥' विष्णु० 5. 28. 5 and 18. Besides these, रुक्मिणी and seven others were his chief wives. The भागवतपु० gives the number of 16000 in various places (see X. 59. 33; X. 69. 8 and 44). अप्स...कुलानि—The Apsarases are the damsels of heaven and have fourteen कुलs as described by बाण himself in कादम्बरी 'एतत्प्रायेण कल्याणाभिनिवेशिनः श्रुतिविषयमापतितमेव यथा विबुधसद्मन्यप्सरसो नाम कन्यकाः सन्ति । तासां चतुर्दश कुलानि.' This clause shows that the wives of सामन्तs were very handsome. परिजनेन—this word is to be read with बिभ्राणेन below. स्रजः, पात्रीः and others are the objects of बिभ्राणेन. पृथु...स्रजः (carrying garlands of flowers (सुमनस् *f n*) contained in a large bamboo box (करण्डः) and which were sprinkled over (अवकीर्ण) with bath powder. स्नानीयं (स्नानाय हितं चूर्णं) तेन अवकीर्णानि कुसुमानि यासाम्. स्फटिकशिलायाः शकलवत् शुक्लं कर्पूरखण्डं तेन पूरिताः. पात्रीः dishes. कुङ्कुमा...मयानि jewelled pots containing the fragrant powder (अधिवासः) of saffron. सह...रुकाणि ivory boxes (दन्तशफरुकम्) jagged (दन्तुर) with rows (फाली) of arecanuts white like sandalwood and tufted (जटिल) with masses of small खदिर fibres wet (तिम्यत्) with mango-oil. सहकारतैलेन तिम्यत् तनुखदिरकेसरजालं तेन जटिलानि चन्दनवत् धवलानि पूगफलानि (the dry areca nut with the upper coating peeled off is white) तेषां फाली तेन दन्तुराणि दन्तशफरुकाणि. तिम् 4th P. to become wet. The solid extract of खदिर called खदिरसार (catechu) is now used for ताम्बूल. It seems that tender and small fibres of खदिर were so used in Bāṇa's time. गुञ्जन्तः मधुकराः तेषां कुलं तेन पीयमानः पारिजातपरिमलः येषाम्. पाटलकानि च—take away the comma after this. पाटलकानि pink red (*adj.* of ०पात्राणि). सिन्दूर...पात्राणि boxes of vermilion and fragrant powder (for perfuming garments). 'पिष्टातः पटवासकः' इत्यमरः. The reading of B, पोटलकानि, does not make much sense. पोटलक means 'bundle, packet.' बाल...बिभ्राणेन carrying betel trees with bundles of rolls of betel leaves hanging from young creepers. We must read वीटिकावीटकांश्च as suggested by C and T. विटक makes no sense. वीटिका is the same as Marathi विडा. बाललताभ्यः लम्बमानाः वीटिकावीटकाः येषु. The com. remarks 'विटकवीटकं पञ्चाशत्ताम्बूलपत्रैः क्रियते.' चरणनिकुट्टनेन रणिताः मणिनूपुराः तैः मुखरितानि दिङ्मुखानि यैः—that made the quarters to resound with the jewelled anklets that jingled when they stamped the earth with their feet (in dancing). The reading of B makes no sense.

P. 62 ll. 22–33 शनैः...मोदः. The principal sentence is शनैः शनैः व्यजृम्भत...उत्सवामोदः. क्वचित्—क्वचित् in one place, in another place. नृत्तस्य अनुचितः (not accustomed) चिरन्तनः (of ancient families) शालीनः (high born) कुलपुत्रकलोकः तस्य लास्यं तेन प्रथितः (shown) पार्थिवे अनुरागः यस्मिन्. This and the following nominatives qualify ०मोदः. शालीन not bold, bashful (usually applied to high born ladies) 'स्यादधृष्टे तु शालीनः' इत्यमरः. शालीन formed from शाला with the affix ख (ईन) according to 'शालीनकौपीने अधृष्टाकार्ययोः' पा. 5. 2. 20 (शालाप्रवेशमर्हति शालीनः अधृष्टः। सि. कौ.। अप्रागल्भ्यादन्यत्र गन्तुमशक्तः शालामेव प्रवेष्टुमर्हतीत्यर्थः। तत्वबोधिनी). कुलपुत्रकः a nobly born young man. लास्यम् is a peculiar kind of dance 'ललिताङ्गहाराभिनयं कैशिकीवृत्तिप्रधानं वासकसज्जादिनायिकाचरितं डोम्बिल्लिकादिनिबद्धं श्लिष्टत्वाल्लास्यम्। नृत्तं त्वङ्गविक्षेपमात्रं विवाहाभ्युदयादौ' क्षीरस्वामी. अन्तः स्मितं यस्य तेन क्षितिपालेन (प्रभाकरवर्धनेन) अपेक्षिताः क्षीबाभिः (drunk) क्षुद्रदासीभिः समाकृष्यमाणाः राजवल्लभाः यस्मिन्. The king smiled to himself when the drunken maids caught hold of his favourites. We expect अवेक्षिताः for अपेक्षिताः. The reading of two MSS. of B, उपेक्षित, would be also good. मत्ता कटककुट्टनी (bawd of the capital) तस्याः कण्ठे लग्नः वृद्धः आर्यः (noble, respectable) सामन्तः (chieftain, feudatory) तस्य नृत्तेन निर्भरं (much, loudly) हसितः नरपतिः यस्मिन्. क्षितिपस्य (प्रभाकरवर्धनस्य) अक्षिसंज्ञा (sign or hint given by the eye or glance) तया आदिष्टाः (ordered, instigated) दुष्टाः दासेरकाः (भृत्याः) तेषां गीतैः सूच्यमानः सचिवानां चौर्यरतप्रपञ्चः (numerous secret amours) यस्मिन्. दासेरक son of a दासी. दासेर is formed from दासी according to 'क्षुद्राभ्यो वा' पा. 4. 1. 131 (अङ्गहीनाः शीलहीनाश्च क्षुद्रास्ताभ्यो वा ढ्रक्। पक्षे ढक्। दासेरः दासेयः। सि. कौ.). मदोत्कटा कुटहारिका (water-girl) तया परिष्वज्यमानः जरन् (old) प्रव्रजितः (ascetic, संन्यासिन्) तेन जनितः जन-

हासः यस्मिन्. कुटः—टम् a water-jar + हारिका carrier. 'घटः कुटनिपावस्त्री' इत्यमरः. अन्योन्यस्य निर्भरा (excessive) स्पर्धा तया उद्धुराः (unrestrained, उद्गता धूः येभ्यः) विटचेटकाः तैः आरब्धं अवाच्यवचनयुद्धं यस्मिन्. विटः is a voluptuary and companion of a dissolute young man or courtezan. See the मृच्छकटिक for a specimen. चेटकः a servant. अवाच्यं वचनम् words that should not be uttered *i. e.* foul words. The servants engaged in a war of choice Billingsgate. नृपाबलाभिः (royal ladies) बलात्कारेण (by force) नर्त्यमानाः (made to dance) नृत्ये अनभिज्ञाः अन्तःपुरपालाः (chamberlains) तैः भाविताः (enlivened, entertained) भुजिष्याः परिचारिकाः यस्मिन्. 'नियोज्यकिङ्करप्रैष्यभुजिष्यपरिचारकाः' इत्यमरः ('भुङ्क्ते स्वाम्युच्छिष्टं भुजिष्यः' क्षीरस्वामी). स...राशिभिः with heaps of flowers it looked as if it were a mountain. Mountains have trees full of flowers. In the festival also heaps of flowers were used. स...प्रपाभिः with rum-booths it looked as if it had a showerbath. धारागृहम् is a showerbath or house furnished with jets of water. सीधुः rum. प्रपा lit. a place where water is distributed to travellers. In the festival rum flowed like water. पारि...मोदैः with the fragrance of पारिजातक. The पारिजातक is one of the five trees of Indra's garden (नन्दनवन). नीहारः frost. The dust of camphor spread in the उत्सव looked like frost. अट्टहासः the laugh of शिव in his ताण्डव dance. The sounds of drums beaten in the birth festival resembled the अट्टहास of शिव. अमृतमथनेन सह सा० (बहुव्रीहि). The uproar was so great that it resembled the noise made by the gods and demons at the time of the churning of the ocean as the रत्नs came out of the ocean. रास or—क is a dance (in a ring) practised by कृष्ण and गोपीs. See भागवतपुराण X. 33 'तत्रारभत गोविन्दो रासक्रीडामनुव्रतैः। स्त्रीरत्नैरन्वितः प्रीतैरन्योन्याबद्धबाहुभिः ॥ 2'. आवर्तः a whirlpool 'स्यादावर्तोऽम्भसां भ्रमः' इत्यमरः. The ring of dancers resembled a vortex. सरो...किरणैः—the rays shooting from the jewelled ornaments resembled hair standing on end. पट्टबन्धः tying of a piece of cloth on the head (a tiara, turban &c.). चन्दनललाटिका sandal marks on the forehead. Sandal is white and is compared to white cloth tied round the head. 'कर्णललाटात्कनलङ्कारे' पा. 4. 3. 65 (कर्णिका, ललाटिका). प्रसवः progeny, offspring. The echoes were as if the progeny of the original sounds. प्ररोहः sprout, leaf. The gifts of favour were given and appeared to spring forth like so many sprouts shooting forward in all directions.

P. 63 ll. 1-9 **स्कन्धा...लोकः** स्कन्धा...मालाः—स्कन्धे अवलम्बमानाः केसरमालाः (बकुलपुष्पमालाः) येषाम् (युवानः); स्कन्धे अवलम्बमानाः केसरमालाः

(केसराः माला इव) येषाम् (with ॰वाजिनः). The manes of the horses are compared to garlands. काम्बोजवाजिनः horses from the country of Kamboja. This country was looked upon as producing one of the best breeds of horses. See रघुवंश IV. 69–70 **'काम्बोजाः** समरे सोढुं तस्य वीर्यमनीश्वराः।...तेषां **सदश्वभूयिष्ठास्तुङ्गा** द्रविणराशयः।'. 'वनायुजाः पारसीकाः काम्बोजा वाह्लिका हयाः।' इत्यमरः. The country of कम्बोज was beyond the Hindookush mountain (probably eastern Persia) and it was known from very ancient times. See पाणिनि IV. 1. 75. Yāska refers to it 'शवतिर्गतिकर्मा कम्बोजेष्वेव भाष्यते... विकारमस्यार्येषु भाषन्ते शव इति' (निरुक्त II). आस्कन्दन्तः—treading the ground (with youths); leaping (with horses). तरलाः (unsteady) तारकाः (pupil of the eye) येषाम्—applies to both the youths and deer. सगर...भुवम्—who rent the earth with the violent stamping (अभिघातः) of their feet, as the sons of सगर did with spades. See p. 3 for the story of the sons of सगर. See विष्णुपुराण IV. 4 and रामायण I. 38–44. अनेक...संख्याः may apply also to the sons of सगर (who were 60000). कथमपि...क्षमा the earth bore with difficulty the agitation caused by the feet of the bards (चारणाः) dancing to time. तालः keeping time (in music) + अवचरः one who moves. अन्योन्यास्फालैः striking each other (in play). आभ... फेलुः the pearls in the ornaments were cleft asunder. फेलुः *perfect* of फल् 1 P. ब्रह्माण्डकपालम्—the world. पुनः उत्पन्नः हिरण्यगर्भस्य गर्भः तस्य शोणितेन शोणाः (रक्ताः) आशाः (दिशः) यस्मिन्. स्वयम्भू first of all produced waters and cast the seed in them. That seed became an egg and in it हिरण्यगर्भ remained for a year and then the egg was split into two parts. See मनुस्मृति 'सोभिध्याय शरीरात्स्वात्सिसृक्षुर्विविधाः प्रजाः। अप एव ससर्जादौ तासु बीजमवासृजत्॥ तदण्डमभवद्धैमं सहस्रांशुसमप्रभम्। तस्मिञ्जज्ञे स्वयं ब्रह्मा सर्वलोकपितामहः॥ तस्मिन्नण्डे स भगवानुषित्वा परिवत्सरम्। स्वयमेवात्मनो ध्यानात्तदण्डमकरोद्द्विधा॥' मनुस्मृति I. 8–9, 12. The world was reddened by the vermilion powder. Blood is red. The poet fancies that हिरण्यगर्भ was again being born in ब्रह्माण्डकपाल. पट...पटलेन by the cloud of the fragrant powder (used in perfuming garments). The fragrant powder resembled the sandy banks of the celestial Ganges. प्रकटितं मन्दाकिन्याः (वियद्गङ्गायाः) सैकतसहस्रं यस्मिन्. सैकतम् (from सिकता) according to 'सिकताशर्कराभ्यां च' and 'देशे लुबिलचौ च' पा. 5. 2. 104–5 (सिकताः सन्त्यस्मिन् देशे इति सिकताः। सिकतिलः। सैकतिलः। सि. कौ.). विप्रकीर्यमाणः पिष्टातकः (पटवासकः) तस्य परागः (pollen) तेन पिञ्जरितः (rendered yellow) आतपः (light) येषाम् (with दिवसाः). भुवनस्य क्षोभः तेन विशीर्णे पितामहस्य (ब्रह्मणः) कमलं तस्य किञ्जल्काः (filaments) तेषां रजोराजिः तया रञ्जिताः

इव. The world was disturbed by the riotous festival days. The poet fancies that the lotus on which ब्रह्मा sits was shattered by the भुवनs being shaken by the birth festivities. सङ्घट्ट...लोकः people tripped over masses of pearls that had fallen from necklaces rent asunder (विघटित) in collision (when people running in haste jostled against each other).

P. 63 ll. 10–33 **स्थान...प्रानृत्यन्.** The principal sentence is स्थानस्थानेषु च...वाद्येन अनुगम्यमानाः...पण्यविलासिन्यः प्रानृत्यन्. The instrumentals from ०लिङ्गयकेन to तानकेन qualify ०वाद्येन. मन्द... लिङ्गयकेन in which tambourines were struck gently. आलिङ्ग्यकः a drum having the shape of a barley-corn. According to the अमरकोश, it is a kind of मृदङ्ग 'मृदङ्गा मुरजा भेदास्त्वङ्क्यालिङ्ग्योर्ध्वकास्त्रयः'. 'चतुरङ्गुलहीनोऽङ्क्यान्मुखे चैकाङ्गुलेन यः। यवाकृतिः स आलिङ्ग्य आलिङ्ग्य स हि वाद्यते॥' शब्दार्णवः. शिञ्जानः (jingling) मञ्जुः (sweet) वेणुः (flute) यस्मिन्. झणझणायमाना झल्लरी यस्मिन् in which cymbals tinkled. झणझणायमाना pr. p. of the onomatopoetic verb ०णायते. क (in ०झल्लरीक) is affixed to बहुव्रीहि compounds having as the last member a feminine noun ending ई, ऊ, ॠ or a noun ending in ऋ. 'नद्यृतश्च' पा. 5. 4. 153. ताड्यमाना तन्त्रीपटहिका यस्मिन्—in which a stringed drum was played upon. वाद्यमाना अनुत्ताना अलाबुवीणा यस्मिन् in which the gourd lute that had its mouth turned downwards (अनुत्तान) was being played. This seems to have been some instrument like the बीन of these days. The reading of B 'अनुत्ताला०' makes a good sense. अनुत्ताल means 'low-pitched.' कलकांस्यकोश्या क्वणिताः काहलाः (बृहड्ढक्काः) यस्मिन् in which there were kāhalas booming sweetly and indistinctly on account of the sounding boxes of bell-metal. समकाले दीयमानः अनुत्तालः तानकः यस्मिन् in which a protracted tone was indulged in at the interval called सम. The reading of B is better and should have been kept in the text. ०दीयमाना अनुत्ताला तालिका यस्मिन् in which the hands were clapped gently at the interval called सम. सम is the principal interval in a ताल. C and T translate 'while all the time a subdued clapping proceeded.' आतोद्यवाद्येन by instrumental music. 'ततं चैवावनद्धं च घनं सुषिरमेव। चतुर्विधं तु विज्ञेयमातोद्यं लक्षणान्वितम्॥' नाट्यशास्त्र 28. 1. According to अमरकोश, आतोद्य and वाद्य are synonyms. अनुगम्यमानाः adj. of पण्यविलासिन्यः (harlots). अनुवर्तमानौ ताललयौ यासाम्. तालः keeping time. लयः harmony. Even the ornaments of the *naikins* kept time and jingled in harmony with their singing and thus looked as if they were intelligent beings (सहृदय).

There is another idea. Those who are masters in singing (सहृदय = मार्मिक) will unconsciously keep time when another person is singing. मदेन कला काकली तया कोमलः आलापः अस्ति आसां इति० लापिन्यः—who sang delicate tunes in a voice sweet but low on account of passion. 'काकली तु कले सूक्ष्मे ध्वनौ तु मधुरास्फुटे' इत्यमरः. विटानां...गायन्त्यः who sang the vulgar words of रासकs that were the nectar of the ear of dissolute young men. रासक here means either (1) a particular kind of dance (for which see above p. 29); or (2) a species of dramatic composition. See for a definition of the latter the साहित्यदर्पण VI. It has only five characters, it is in various dialects; there is no सूत्रधार; there is a single Act; the hero is a fool, while the heroine is famous. स... मालिकाः they had wreaths on their heads. समुच्छ्रित raised up (past p. p. of श्रि with सम् and उद्). कुङ्कुम...वल्गन्त्यः like Kashmir fillies they pranced, having bodies radiant with the stains of saffron. कुङ्कुमेन प्रमृष्टिः (rubbing the body) तया रुचिरः कायः येषाम् (with ०विलासिन्यः); कुङ्कुमे प्रमृष्टिः (rolling in) तया &c. (with किशोर्यः). नितम्बबिम्बे लम्बमानाः विकटाः (large) कुरण्टकशेखराः यासाम्. कुरण्टकः Amaranth. The glow cast on their bodies by the flowers is fancied to be due to the fire of राग (passion). सिन्दूरस्य छटाभिः (streaks) छुरिता (overspread) मुखमुद्रा (colour of their face) यासाम्. The women had marked their faces with vermilion streaks. These are fancied to be the lines of the plates (पट्टः) of the edict (शासन) of cupid. The plates were smeared with सिन्दूर in order that the letters of the seal might look prominent. सिन्दू...छुरिता मुखे मुद्रा (seal) यासाम् (with ०पङ्क्तयः). अप्रतिहतं शासनं यस्य whose command is irresistible. मुष्ट्या प्रकीर्यमाणौ कर्पूरपटवासौ ताभ्यां पांसुलाः. Read ०पांसुला मनो०. मनो...यौवनस्य they were as if the roads for the wandering of the desires of youth *i. e.* the desires of young men converged in them. There is a pun. A रथ (in मनोरथ) requires a road for सञ्चरण and the road may be पांसुल (dusty.) प्रतीहार्य इव—It is the business of door-keepers in any festival to use their canes when people make a rush. The women are fancied to be प्रतीहारीs of तरुणमहोत्सव. All young men would flock to them. Hence the propriety of the word तरुण. C and T translate तरुण० as 'of a children's festival'. This is wrong. प्रचलन्ति पत्रसदृशानि कुण्डलानि यासां—whose ear-rings resembling leaves dangled about (when they danced); प्रचलन्ति पत्राणि कुण्डलानीव यासाम् (with लताः) whose leaves resembling ear-rings tossed about. लसन्त्यः dancing;

moving (with लताः). मदनः चन्दनद्रुम इव; मदनसदृशः चन्दनद्रुमः. The harlots danced out of passion. The creeper clinging to a sandal tree would also move about when tossed by the wind. ललिते पदे हंसकः (पादकटकः anklet) तस्य रवेण मुखराः (with ०विलासिन्यः); ललितं पदं (gait) येषां ते ललितपदाः हंसकाः (हंसाः) तेषां रवेण मुखराः (with वीचयः). शृङ्गाररसः सागर इव. The harlots were the ripples of the ocean of passion. हंसs may be cackling near the waves of a lake. वाच्या...शून्याः void of discrimination as to what was to be said or not said (applies to both ०विलासिन्यः and ०क्रीडाः). घनः (deep) पटहरवः तेन उत्कण्टकिताः (thrilled) गात्रयष्टयः यासाम् (with ०विलासिन्यः); घनः मेघः पटहः इव तस्य रवः तेन उत्कण्टकिताः (सञ्जातकण्टकाः) गात्रयष्टयः यासाम् (with केतक्यः). The pollen from the flowers worn by the women was carried about. The केतकी flower also has pollen. The केतक blossoms forth when the cloud thunders (in the rainy season (and there are कण्टकs on the केतक petals). दिवसम् (acc. of time) the whole day. उत्फुल्लं आननं यासाम्. The कविसमय is that the कमल expands in the day and the कुमुद at night. अनुपजाता निद्रा यासाम्. The women had no sleep at night. The कुमुद plants open their buds at night. आविष्टाः इव like persons possessed. नरेन्द्र...वृताः surrounded by a host of princes; surrounded by a host of magicians. नरेन्द्रः means generally a विषवैद्य and not one who exorcises evil spirits. See शिशुपालवध II. 88. 'सुनिग्रहा नरेन्द्रेण फणीन्द्रा इव शत्रवः' (where also there is a pun). रागमुद्दीपयन्त्यः kindling passion (with women); heightening the melody. The principal रागs are six. पुष्ट्यः fatness. मदमपि मदयन्त्य इव who as if intoxicated intoxication itself. Even मद could draw upon them for adding to itself. The reading उत्सवयन्त्यः would be more in keeping with what precedes. कटाक्षे...शुक्तिभिः in casting sidelong eyes, they seemed to be drinking with the shells (शुक्ति) of the corners of their eyes. The idea is:—when they cast glances, they took the pupil of the eye far away and exposed only the white portion of the eye. The white of the eye resembles mother-o'-pearl which is used in drinking (particularly milk &c.). तर्जनेषु in frightening a person they seemed as if to fetter him with the chains of the rays of their nails. They used the forefinger (तर्जनी) in chiding people. Naturally their nails flashed. The rays are fancied to be पाशs with which to bind the person chid. कोपाभिनयेषु—when a person is angry or wants to convey that he is angry, he knits his brows. चतुर...विकारान् in their clever movements they seemed to scatter about emotions. Their various movements caused the spectators to be roused to various emotions.

P. 64 ll. 1–9 **अन्यत्र…विलेसुः.** The principal sentence is अन्यत्र…राजमहिष्यः…विलेसुः. वेत्रिणां वेत्रेण वित्रासिताः जनाः तैः दत्तं अन्तरालं यासाम् for whom room was made by people that had been terrified away by the cane of the warders or chamberlains. A cane is the symbol of the authority of a कञ्चुकिन्. Note 'आचार इत्यवहितेन मया गृहीता या वेत्रयष्टिरवरोधगृहेषु राज्ञः' शाकुन्तल II. This and the following adjectival clauses qualify राजमहिष्यः. ध्रियमाणं धवलातपत्राणां वनं (समूहः) यासु over whom was held a forest of white parasols. कल्प…रिण्यः wandering under the tree of paradise. The queens resembled the nymphs of the woods. स्कन्धयोः उभयपालीभ्यां लम्बमानं लम्बं उत्तरीयं तस्मिन् लग्नौ हस्तौ यासाम् whose hands clung to the waving upper garment hanging down from both sides of their shoulders. लीला…प्रेङ्खन्त्यः who swung as if mounted on a swing in play. The shawls of the queens when they danced fluttered on their shoulders and they tried to hold them with both their hands. This looked as if they held the ropes of a swing with their hands. कनककेयूरकोट्या पाट्यमानं पट्टांशुकं तेन उत्तरङ्गाः that were waving because the fine cloth they wore was torn by the ends of the golden armlets. तरन्तः चक्रवाकाः तैः सीमन्त्यमानं स्रोतः यासाम् (rivers) the water of which was separated into two by the चक्रवाक birds that floated in them. सीमन्त्यमान (from the noun सीमन्तः) *pr. p.* of the passive of the denominative verb सीमन्तयति. The golden armlet was like चक्रवाक, the fine cloth was like the stream and the queens therefore resembled rivers. उद्धूयमाना (being waved) धवला चामरसटा तस्यां लग्नः त्रिकण्टकः तस्मिन् वलिताः (turned) विकटाः कटाक्षाः यासाम्. हंसैः आकृष्यमाणं नीलोत्पलवनं यासु. सरस्यः lakes. त्रिकण्टकः an ear-ornament containing three gems 'त्रिकण्टकस्तु त्र्यश्रः स्यात्रिभी रत्नैश्च भूषणम्' quoted by the com. Their chowries stuck to their ear-ornament. When this happened they looked at the ornament to disentangle them. Their dark eyes resembled blue lotuses and the ornament with three gems resembled हंसs with their two feet and long beak; and the white chowries resembled the white body of the swans. The resemblance may also be due to the red colour of the gems and the redness of the feet and beak of राजहंसs. 'राजहंसास्तु ते चञ्चुचरणैर्लोहितैः सिताः' इत्यमरः. चलन्तौ चरणौ ताभ्यां च्युतः अलक्तकः तेन अरुणाः स्वेदशीकराः तैः सिच्यमानाः भवनहंसाः याभिः. सन्ध्यारागेण रज्यमानमिन्दुबिम्बं यासु. कौमुदीरजन्यः nights of the full moon in कार्तिक (which is in शरदृतु). In शरदृतु moonlight is at its best. The fair queens are like कौमुदी nights, the white हंसs like the moon's disc and the sweat reddened by lac-dye like the glow of evening. कण्ठे निहितः काञ्चनकाञ्चीगुणः तेन अञ्चितः (bent) कञ्चुकी तस्य विकाराः तै आकुञ्चिताः भ्रुवः यासाम्. The queens put their golden girdles round the neck of the chamberlain and bent him. The कञ्चुकिन् made contortions when so treated, at which the women knit their brows (in derision). वागुरा net. प्रसारितौ बाहुपाशौ याभिः. The out-stretched arms resemble the cords of the net (of love).

P. 64 ll. 10–22 **सर्वतश्च…राशयः.** स्त्रैणम् bevy of women. 'स्त्रीपुंसाभ्यां नञ्स्नञौ भवनात्' पा. 4. 1. 87. रागमयी full of राग (redness, love). शुशोण perfect of शोण् I P to become red. मङ्गलकलशमयः—jars full of water are looked upon as a good omen. विक्षेपः tossing. Their tender arms resembled the filaments of lotuses. विलासस्मितैः—Their flashing smiles appeared like the flashes of lightning. The word कालः means 'time (such as day &c.) or dark.' With the last meaning there is a विरोध in saying that काल became तडिन्मय (bright). Both smiles and lightning are bright. अंशुभिः = किरणैः. कृष्ण…वासराः the days seemed as if dappled. कृष्णसारः (1) spotted antelope; (2) dark and variegated. शिरीष…पुरैः by the bunches of शिरीष flowers used as ornaments of the ear. The शिरीष is a very delicate flower and used as ear-ornament. See शाकुन्तल I 'अवतंसयन्ति प्रमदा दयमानाः शिरीषकुसुमानि'. हरिता (green) छाया (कान्तिः) यस्य. आतपः daylight. विस्रंस…रिक्षम् the sky seemed as if full of collyrium by the sprays of तमाल in the braided hair becoming loose (by dancing). The तमाल leaf is dark and was used as decoration for the hair. 'धम्मिल्लः संयताः कचाः' इत्यमरः. हस्तकिशलयैः—their hands were delicate like tender leaves. माणिक्ये…षा by the radiance of the rain-bow in the gems. चाषपत्रमयाः full of the wings of चाष (blue jay). The sun's rays falling upon the gems of the women gave rise to rain-bow colours. ग्रहगृहीताः seized by a ghost. निनर्तिषया with the desire to dance (निनर्तिषा noun from the desiderative base of नृत्). विपुस्फुलुः *perfect* of स्फुल् 6 P with वि to throb, to vibrate. कुवेरकोषाः the treasures of कुबेर. कुबेर is the lord of riches and treasures. अलुप्यन्त were plundered.

P. 64 l. 23—**P. 65** l. 2 **एवं च…श्रियम्.** The principal sentence is देवी यशोमती गर्भेणाधत्त…राज्यश्रियम्. वृत्ते concluded. देवे—

this is to be connected with हर्षे below (last line of p. 9). उत्तमाङ्गे निहिताः रक्षासर्षपाः यस्य on whose head were placed mustard seeds to ward off (evil). This and the following words in the locative qualify हर्षे. समुन्मिषन्तः प्रतापः एव अग्निः तस्य स्फुलिङ्गाः यस्मिन् In whom the sparks of the fire of prowess were as if bursting forth. The idea is that the सर्षपs on the head were so many sparks of fire &c. The punctuation in the text is wrong. Take away the comma after सर्षपे, वपुषि and ग्रीवके and put it after स्फुलिङ्ग इव, तेजसीव, दर्पाङ्कुर इव. The सर्षपs employed were probably red. The white सर्षप is usually called सिद्धार्थ and is used as a protection against evil spirits. गोरोचनया पिञ्जरितं वपुः यस्य whose body was rendered yellow with गोरोचना. गोरोचना is a bright yellow pigment prepared from the urine or bile of a cow or found in the head of a cow; it is used as a medicine and to ward off the evil eye and evil spirits. समभिव्यज्यमानं सहजं क्षात्रतेजः यस्य. The yellow गोरोचना resembles तेजः. हाटके (सुवर्णे) बद्धा विकटा (large) व्याघ्रनखपङ्क्तिः तया मण्डिता ग्रीवा यस्य स °ग्रीवकः तस्मिन्. Even now the same ornament is tied round the necks of children. When क is added at the end of बहुव्रीहि compounds, the preceding vowel, if long, is shortened. 'केऽणः' पा. 7. 4. 13. (के परे अणो ह्रस्वः स्यात्). हृदयात् उद्भिद्यमानाः दर्पाङ्कुराः यस्मिन्. The poet fancies that the tiger's claws worn on the chest were the buds of pride bursting out of his heart. प्रथ...कुर्वाणे by his first indistinct prattle he seemed to make a beginning of truth. ओंकारं कृ (lit.) to utter Om *i. e.* to make a beginning. The syllables ओम् and अथ are very auspicious and are therefore uttered at the beginning of many things. A child even now is first taught the words 'ओं नमः सिद्धम्'. प्रणव or ओंकार precedes the study of the Veda. 'ओङ्कारः स्वर्गद्वारं तस्माद् ब्रह्माध्येष्यमाण एतदादि प्रतिपद्येत' आपस्तम्ब I. 13. 6. Compare रघु० I. 11 'आसीन्महीक्षितामाद्यः प्रणवश्छन्दसामिव'. Connect मुग्धस्मितैः with आकर्षति, which qualifies हर्षे. Smiles and flowers are both white. जनन्याः पयोधरौ कलशौ इव तयोः पयः दुग्धं तस्य शीकरः तस्य सेकः. वदन is compared to कमल, small teeth to अङ्कुर. पयोधर also means मेघ and पयः means ' water.' The child smiled a happy smile when nursed at the breast and showed its teeth, which looked like buds. चारित्र...पाल्यमाने—he was as much guarded by the women in the seraglio as their own chastity. मन्त्रः state policy determined upon by a king in consultation with his ministers. 'मन्त्रो विजयमूलं हि राज्ञो भवति राघव' अयोध्याकाण्ड 100. 16; 'विजयो मन्त्रमूलो हि राज्ञो भवति भारत' सभापर्व 5. 27. The मनुस्मृति says

'यस्य मन्त्रं न जानन्ति समागम्य पृथग्जनाः । स कृत्स्नां पृथ्वीं भुङ्क्ते कोशहीनोऽपि पार्थिवः ॥' VII. 148. 'मन्त्रमूलं यतो राज्यं तस्मान्मन्त्रं सुरक्षितम् । कुर्याद्यथास्य न विदुः कर्मणामा फलोदयात् ॥ याज्ञ० I. 344. वृत्तम् good conduct. यश...वर्ध्यमाने who was cherished by his kindred like their own good name. पञ्च वा षड् वा पञ्चषाणि (बहुव्रीहि). गर्भेणाधत्त राज्यश्रियम् became pregnant with राज्यश्री. Read वसुधां for वसुधा. गर्भे...वसुधाम् as the form of नारायण produced the earth through गर्भ (*i. e.* हिरण्यगर्भ). We have seen above (p. 30) that स्वयम्भू cast seed in the water, which became an egg in which हिरण्यगर्भ was produced. This हिरण्यगर्भ in his turn created heaven and earth. 'ताभ्यां स शकलाभ्यां च दिवं भूमिं च निर्ममे ।' मनु० I. 13. नारायण is identified in the मनुस्मृति with ब्रह्मा (see I. 10). If we take गर्भेणाधत्त in its ordinary sense (*viz.* 'conceived') it is difficult to point out the particular story to which Bāṇa alludes. We may explain thus:—the whole universe at the time of प्रलय lies in नारायणोदर and comes out of it at the time of creation; so पृथिवी is in the गर्भ (उदर) of नारायण.

P 65 ll. 3–8 **पूर्णेषु...राजत.** The principal sentence is (देवी यशोमती) प्रसूतवती दुहितरम्. दीर्घ...सरसी as the lake gives birth to a lotus plant that has long and red stalks and roots. दीर्घाणि रक्तानि नालानि नेत्राणि (मूलानि) च यस्याः (with उत्पलिनी). This and the adjectives in the following clauses apply to दुहितरं also. दीर्घरक्ते नालवत् नेत्रे यस्याः whose eyes are red and long like a lotus-stalk. Redness of the corner of the eye was looked upon as a sign of beauty. हंसैः मधुरः स्वरः यस्याम् (with शरदम्); हंसवत् मधुरः स्वरः यस्याः (with दुहितरम्). कुसुमैः सुकुमाराः अवयवाः भागाः यस्याः (वनराजिम्); कुसुमवत् सुकुमाराः अवयवाः हस्तादयः यस्याः (दुहितरम्). मधुश्रीः vernal beauty. महाकनकेन (grains of gold) अवदाता (resplendent); महाकनकवत् अवदाता. The com. says 'महाकनकं तिलसुवर्णं वसुधारा धनवृष्टिः । इयं च महाभ्युदयसूचनाय दिवा पतति ।'. वेला the shore of the sea. The sea is called रत्नाकर. सहस्रनेत्रः इन्द्रः तेन दर्शनं तस्य योग्याम्; सहस्रनेत्रैः दर्शनस्य योग्याम्. शची is the wife of इन्द्र. अहल्या the wife of the sage गौतम was seduced by इन्द्र who assumed the form of the sage. For this the sage cursed अहल्या to be a stone and इन्द्र had a thousand marks on his body, which were afterwards turned into eyes. See रामायण I. 48 and VII. 30 for the story. The कथासरित्सागर contains the story 'वराङ्गलुब्धस्याङ्गे ते तत्सहस्रं भविष्यति । दिव्यस्त्रीं विश्वकर्मा यां निर्मास्यति तिलोत्तमाम् ॥ तां विलोक्य तदैवाक्ष्णां सहस्रं भविता च ते ।' III. 3. 144–145. कुमारिलभट्ट in his तन्त्रवार्तिक explains this story along with others in a rationalistic manner. सर्वैः भूभृद्भिः

(पर्वतैः, राजभिः) अभ्यर्थिताम् solicited, wooed. गौरी=पार्वती. मेना the wife of हिमालय. See above p. 9 (notes) as to the birth of पार्वती. एकावली a single string of pearls. 'एकावल्येकयष्टिका' इत्यमरः.

P 65 ll. 9–16 अस्मिन्नेव...र्पितवान्. The principal sentence is अस्मिन्नेव तु काले...यशोमत्या भ्राता सुतम्...भण्डिनामानमनुचरं कुमारयोरर्पितवान्. अष्ट...देशीयम् about eight years old. The affixes कल्प, देश्य and देशीय are added in the sense of 'a little less than.' 'ईषदसमाप्तौ कल्पब्देश्यदेशीयरः' पा. 5. 3. 67. उद्धूयमानः कुटिलः काकपक्षकशिखण्डः यस्य. The अमरकोश gives काकपक्ष and शिखण्डक as synonyms. Therefore we may take शिखण्ड as meaning 'tuft of hair' and काकपक्षक as 'the side-locks of hair on the temples.' खण्डपरशोः (शिवस्य) हुंकारेणाग्निः तस्य धूमलेखा तया अनुबद्धः मूर्धा यस्य. खण्ड...जातम् who looked like cupid born again with his head encircled (अनुबद्ध) by the streak of smoke of the fire of S'iva's wrath. The boy was handsome and had dark curling hair. The poet fancies him to be मदन with धूम on his head. धूम is dark and waving. मदन wanted to help the gods against the demon तारक who was to be killed by the son of शिव. In order to induce शिव to marry पार्वती, Cupid was about to shoot his flowery arrow, when S'iva came to know Cupid's intention and in wrath burnt him to ashes by the fire from his third eye. Compare कुमारसम्भव III 'क्रोधं प्रभो संहर संहरेति यावद्गिरः खे मरुतां चरन्ति । तावत्स वह्निर्भवनेत्रजन्मा भस्मावशेषं मदनं चकार ॥'. त्रिकण्टके मुक्ताफलं तस्य आलोकः (light) तेन धवलितं तेन. संपृ...दर्शयन्तम् who exhibited as it were the compound *Avatara* of Vishṇu and S'iva. For त्रिकण्टक as an ear-ornment, see above p. 34. This refers to the mythological story that विष्णु is dark in colour and शिव bright. पीने प्रकोष्ठे (fore-arm) प्रतिष्ठितं पुष्पलोहस्य वलयं यस्य. The com. says 'पुष्पलोहं मणिभेदः'. क्षत्रस्य क्षपणे क्षीणः परशुः तस्य पाशः तेन चिह्नितं marked with the ring of the axe that had been worn away in destroying the क्षत्रियs. The idea is that in killing the क्षत्रियs the blade became worn out and what remained was the iron ring behind the blade. The वलय resembled the ring of the परशु thus worn away. बाण very frequently refers to the story of the slaughter of the क्षत्रियs by परशुराम. See pp. 44, 47 of the text. परशुराम killed कार्तवीर्य for carrying away the cow of his father जमदग्नि. The sons of कार्तवीर्य killed जमदग्नि in the absence of परशुराम. परशुराम on knowing this took the vow of exterminating the क्षत्रियs and fulfilled it 21 times. कण्ठसूत्रे ग्रथिताः भङ्गुराः (कुटिलाः) प्रवालाङ्कुराः (coral) यस्य. उरःकाठिन्येन खण्डितानि नरसिंहनखरस्य खण्डानि येन. The corals were red and curved. They are fancied to be the pieces of the nails of नरसिंह which stuck to the chest of हिरण्यकशिपु. प्रवाल is worn as an auspicious thing. Put the comma after ०न्तरं and not after ०खण्डम्. गृहीतं जन्मान्तरं येन. The boy looked like हिरण्यकशिपु born again. For persecuting his son प्रह्लाद who was a devotee of विष्णु, the latter assumed the man-lion form and killed हिरण्यकशिपु. The story is given in the भागवतपुराण (VII). शैश...ष्टम्भम् even in boyhood he bore himself proudly. बीज...द्रुमस्य—being a boy yet, he is styled 'the seed of the tree of valour'. अनुचरं कुमारयोः as an attendant of the two princes (राज्यवर्धन and हर्ष).

P. 65 ll. 17–22 अवनि...बभूवतुः. तस्य refers to भण्डि. ईश्वरस्य =शिवस्य. तुल्यं...सीत् he looked upon (his two sons and the third Bhaṇḍi) equally *i. e.* he bestowed equal care on all the three. दर्शन means also 'sight'. शिव saw with the third eye as well as with the other two. ईश्वरस्य applies to the king also. सकल... दायिनौ applies to राजपुत्रौ and मधुमाधवौ. तेन=भण्डिना. प्रकृतिदक्षिणेन courteous by nature (with तेन); blowing from the south by nature (with ०मारुतेन). मधुमाधवौ—चैत्र and वैशाख, the months of spring. 'मधुश्च माधवश्च वासन्तिकावृतू' तै. सं. 4. 4. 11. 1. मलय is one of the seven principal mountains of India. It is to be identified with the southern portion of the ghauts running from the south of Mysore and forming the eastern boundary of Travancore. मधुमास and मलयमारुत are both excitants of Love. The seven कुलपर्वतs are 'महेन्द्रो मलयः सह्यः शुक्तिमानृक्षपर्वतः । विन्ध्यश्च पारियात्रश्च सप्तैते कुलपर्वताः ॥' वायु० 45. 88. Compare for the श्लेष on दक्षिण and the idea also 'उत्पादयति लोकस्य प्रीतिं मलयमारुतः । ननु दाक्षिण्यसम्पन्नः सर्वस्य भवति प्रियः ॥' काव्यादर्श II. 174. अपरे...सह वर्धमानौ growing together with the joy of the subjects, as if it (joy) were another brother (of the two princes हर्ष and राज्यवर्धन). The idea is that as the princes became endowed with youth and all the esteemed qualities of young princes, the joy of the people also grew *pari passu*. The adjectives from ०स्तम्भौ to क्षमौ apply to the princes and to ०संनिवेश. स्थिरौ ऊरुस्तम्भौ (ऊरू स्तम्भौ इव) ययोः whose pillar-like thighs were firm (with princes); स्थिराः उरवः स्तम्भाः ययोः whose pillars are firm and big (with ०सन्निवेशौ). पृथुः प्रकोष्ठः ययोः (applies to both). प्रकोष्ठः the forearm; the room near the gate or a quadrangle. दीर्घौ भुजार्गलौ ययोः that had long bar-like arms. A city-gate has large bars to fasten it. विकटं उरःकपाटं ययोः whose chest was broad like the panel of a gate. The word is कपाट; but is also written कवाट. 'कं शिरः पाटयति प्रविशताम्' क्षीरस्वामी.

प्रांशुः (tall) सालः (rampart) तद्वत् अभिरामौ (charming); प्रांशुसालेन अभिरामौ (with संनिवेशौ). 'प्राकारो वरणः सालः' इत्यमरः. साल is also a tree. महा...वेशः the site of a large city. सर्व...क्षमौ capable of giving shelter to all people (applies to both).

P 65 l. 23--**P. 66** l. 9 **अथ चन्द्र...जग्मतुः.** The principal sentence is अथ...राज्यवर्धन इति हर्ष इति सर्वस्यामेव पृथिव्यां...द्वीपान्तरेष्वपि प्रकाशतां जग्मतुः. चन्द्र...र्निरीक्ष्यौ—they (the princes) were charming and not to be gazed at. They overpowered the world by their valour and their fame resembling flashing moonlight and therefore were like the sun and the moon. स्फुरन्ती ज्योत्स्ना तत्सदृशं यशः (द्वयोरपि धवलत्वात्) प्रतापश्च ताभ्यां आक्रान्तं भुवनं याभ्याम्. The moon is अभिराम, while the sun is दुर्निरीक्ष्य. स्फुरन्ती ज्योत्स्ना यशः इव प्रतापश्च (heat) ताभ्यां &c. The भुवन्s are either three or fourteen. अग्नि...भूतौ the princes were like fire and wind acting in unison and manifesting there effulgence and force. If fire and wind combined, the devastation wrought by them would be appalling. शिलाभिः कठिनः कायबन्धः ययोः (with हिमवत् and विन्ध्य); शिलावत् कठिनः (with princes). अचलौ—never wavering; mountains. महा...योग्यौ like two big bulls, they were fit for कृतयुग. The two princes were so righteous that they were fit to live in कृतयुग (the age of virtue, see above p. 3 notes). Bulls are fit to carry the yoke (युगं). There is another suggestion. वृष also means 'धर्म.' 'शुक्रले मूषिके श्रेष्ठे सुकृते वृषभे वृषः' इत्यमरः. धर्म is fit to live in its entirety in कृतयुग only. हरिः (अश्वः) वाहनं ययोः तौ हरिवाहनौ; विभक्तं शरीरं ययोः तौ ०शरीरौ—who rode horses and had well-proportioned bodies. हरि means सूर्य and विष्णु also. Mark the numerous senses of हरि 'यमानिलेन्द्रचन्द्रार्कविष्णुसिंहांशुवाजिषु। शुकाहिकपिभेकेषु हरिर्ना कपिले त्रिषु' इत्यमरः. हरिवाहने विभक्तं शरीरं ययोः (अरुणगरुडौ) whose bodies are assigned for carrying the sun and Vishṇu. अरुण is the charioteer of the sun and गरुड is the vehicle of विष्णु. उपेन्द्रः विष्णुः. नागेन्द्रगतौ—the princes rode the best of elephants. Or their gait was like that of the best of elephants (नागेन्द्रस्य इव गतं ययोः). Both इन्द्र and विष्णु are नागेन्द्रगत. इन्द्र rides the best of elephants (ऐरावत); विष्णु sleeps on शेष (the best of serpents). 'गजेऽपि नागमातङ्गौ' इत्यमरः. कुण्डल...धरौ the princes wore ear-rings and diadem. कर्ण, who had a कुण्डल and कवच given to him by the sun from his very birth, is a type of charity. Indra (who was careful to guard his son अर्जुन) came to Karṇa disguised as a ब्राह्मण and begged of him his कुण्डल and कवच and got them. इन्द्र being pleased with his liberality gave him a शक्ति. See वनपर्व Chap. 310–311

(Kumbakonam ed.). अर्जुन was called किरीटिन्. See विराटपर्व 43 'किरीटं सूर्यसंकाशं भ्राजते मे शिरोगतं 129...इन्द्रदत्तमनाहार्यं तेनाहुर्मां किरीटिनम्।' 130. सर्वतेजस्विनाम् of all luminaries; of all spirited persons. उदयास्तमयौ rising and setting; prosperity and decline. अमान्ता...कुटीरके who on account of their great pride could not contain themselves in the hut of the earth hemmed in (सङ्कट) by the restraint of tne bolt in the shape of the shores that are near it. अमान्तौ *pr. p.* of मा with the negative particle. आसन्ना वेला एव अर्गलः तेन निरोधः तेन सङ्कटः. कुः पृथ्वी एव कुटीरकः. The earth is bounded by the shores of the sea; and therefore it fell short of their ambitions. मान also means 'size.' कुकुटीरक also means 'wretched hut.' In a wretched hut even an ordinary man cannot contain himself. तेजः...मानौ who disliked even their shadow falling away from light. The shadow of an object naturally falls in the direction opposite to that from which a light comes. They being तेजस्विन् desired that everything that was theirs (even a shadow) should be तेजःसंमुख and not ०पराङ्मुख. जुगुप्समानौ—*pr. p.* of the desirative base of गुप् (though there is no sense of desire). 'गुप्तिज्किद्भ्यः सन्' पा० 3. 1. 5. (गुपेर्निन्दायाम् । जुगुप्सते). स्वात्म...लज्जमानौ. The idea is that they could not bear even this that their image should be reflected in the toe-nails of others (and thus it might appear that they were bowing at the feet of others). The idea is similar to 'यः करधौतासिप्रतिबिम्बितेनात्मनापि &c.' (p. 1 text). भङ्गेन (1) by the curling; (2) defeat or running away. चूडा...माणौ—the idea is:—when the umbrella (one of the insignia of sovereignty) was held over them it was reflected in their crest jewel and thus a second umbrella seemed to exist. They could not tolerate the existence of a second umbrella (a rival emperor) and therefore felt ashamed even when a second umbrella existed in reflection only. षण्मुखः कार्तिकेयः the son of शिव. स्वामिन् is one of the names of कार्तिकेय. असुखायमानौ श्रवणौ ययोः. The idea is that they wanted the term स्वामि (lord) to be applied to themselves alone and could not bear that any one else (even the God स्कन्द) should be so called. कार्तिकेय or स्कन्द is the Mars or god of war of Indian mythology. Most of his epithets have reference to the circumstances of his birth. शिव cast his seed in Agni, who unable to bear it, cast it into the Ganges. It was then transferred to the six कृत्तिकाs, each of whom bore a son. The six sons were then mysteriously combined into one with six mouths. He was the commander of the gods against the demon तारक whom he slew. See रामायण बालकाण्ड 36 and 37, कथासरित्सागर III. 6. and बृहत्कथामञ्जरी III. 1. 142. ff. प्रतिपुरुष (1) reflection; (2) rival. सन्ध्या...माङ्गौ Even in folding their hands at the morning and evening adoration, their heads ached. शूलायमानं उत्तमाङ्गं (शिरः) येषाम्. To fold the hands is a sign of humility and submission. They had to fold hands in सन्ध्यावन्दन. Even this caused them मस्तकशूल. जल...हृदयौ their hearts were pained even by the bow borne by the cloud. They could not tolerate any one wielding a bow and hence were distressed when they saw the rain-bow in the cloud. दोदूयमान *pr. p.* of the intensive base of दू. The reading दोधूयमान is not so good as दोदूयमान. It would mean 'whose hearts were shaken.' आले...पतिभिः by the kings painted in pictures. They were accustomed to the fact that ordinary rulers bowed at their feet. परिमितं मण्डलं (disc) तेन सन्तुष्टम्. The sun has only a limited मण्डल (disc); they wanted an unlimited मण्डल (sphere of influence extending over numerous neighbouring and distant kings). The कामन्दकीयनीतिसार (in the 8th Sarga) gives the views of several authors on the number of kings constituting a मण्डल. Ordinarily मण्डल comprises twelve near and distant kings. 'इतिप्रकारं बहुधा मण्डलं परिचक्षते। सर्वलोकप्रतीतं हि स्फुटं द्वादशराजकम्॥' का. 8. 41. See the मिताक्षरा on याज्ञवल्क्य॰ I. 345 'अरिर्मित्रमुदासीनोऽनन्तरस्तत्परः परः। क्रमशो मण्डलं चिन्त्यं सामादिभिरुपक्रमैः॥'. भूभृता (पर्वतेन मन्दरेण) अपहृता लक्ष्मीः यस्य. In churning the ocean the gods made मन्दर the churning handle. 'मन्थानं मन्दरं कृत्वा नेत्रं कृत्वा तु वासुकिम्। मथ्यतामममृतं देवाः साहाय्ये मय्यवस्थिते॥' विष्णु॰ I. 9. 76. लक्ष्मी was one of the 14 jewels churned out. The princes (हर्ष and राज्य॰) never allowed any भूभृत् (king) to carry off their लक्ष्मी (glory) and therefore laughed at the ocean that allowed its लक्ष्मी (the goddess) to be carried off by a भूभृत् (mountain). For क in ॰लक्ष्मीकं see above p. 31. अकृतः विग्रहः (शरीरं) येन. A powerful person would offer विग्रह (battle); the wind though powerful offered no विग्रह (it had no body). चमरीणां बालव्यजनेन वीजितं तेन. चमरी deer, of the tails of which chowries are made, are to be found in the Himālayas. The चामर is an emblem of sovereignty. Therefore they could not bear that the mountain should be fanned by the tails of चमरीs. जल...खिद्यमानौ—conches are found on the seashore. Conches were blown by great warriors only. There is perhaps another idea. शङ्ख is one of the nine निधिs. They could not allow शङ्ख (treasure) to remain with जलधि. The author perhaps intends also a picturesque effect. शङ्ख and जलधि are words meaning enormous numbers. 'लक्षं च नियुतं चैव कोटिरर्बुदमेव च। वृन्दः खर्वो निखर्वश्च शङ्खपद्मौ च सागरः। अन्त्यं मध्यं परार्धं च दशवृद्ध्या यथाक्रमम् ॥'. चतु...सहमानौ. वरुण (प्रचेतस्) is the lord of the ocean in mythology. हर्ष's sovereignty extended over the earth bounded by the four oceans. अनपहृतानि छत्राणि येषाम्. विगता छाया (shade; splendour) येषाम्. Parasols shade one from the sun. Though they did not carry away the parasols of kings whom they vanquished, they made them विच्छाय (*i. e.* void of splendour; void of shade against the sun). There is an apparent contradiction which is removed by taking the other sense of छाया. साधु...क्षरन्तौ they were pleased with (*i. e.* they bestowed favours upon) the good, though not courted by them (the good), and poured nectar (sweet words) with their lips on them. There is another meaning due to श्लेष, which gives rise to विरोधाभास. प्रसन्न means 'transparent, clear' (as applied to wine). मधु means 'wine'. 'Even on good (*i. e.* teetotallers) people they poured wine with their lips, they being प्रसन्न without having taken (wine)'. Remove the comma after ०प्रसन्नौ. वंशः (1) family; (2) bamboo. ऊष्मणा (1) by their pride; (2) by heat. म्लानि (1) decline; (2) withering. दूरस्थितानपि. The force of अपि lies in this—if bamboos were to be destroyed fire would have to be brought near them; but the two princes brought about the decline of even *distant* kings. दिवसे दिवसे अनुदिवसं (अव्ययीभाव). Read शस्त्राभ्यास० for शास्त्राभ्यास०. शस्त्राभ्यासेन श्यामिका (darkness) तया कलङ्कितम्. अशेषं राजकं (राज्ञां समूहः) तस्य प्रतापः एव अग्निः तस्य निर्वापणं तेन मलिनम्. 'अथ राजकम् ॥ राजन्यकं च नृपतिक्षत्त्रियाणां गणे क्रमात्।' इत्यमरः. Their hands were darkened by the practice of sword play. That darkness is fancied to be due to the extinguishing of the fire of the prowess of kings. योग्याकालेषु at the times of (martial) exercise. धीर deep. अभ्यर्णोपभोगात् after enjoyment that was near (*i. e.* that occurred a short while before). दिग्...लपन्तौ—the twang of their bows spread in all directions. The author fancies that the twang was the talk of the princes with the damsels (the quarters). आविर्भूतः शब्दस्य प्रादुर्भावः ययोः—whose names became known. द्वीपान्तरेषु—The द्वीपs are either spoken of as seven (जम्बु, प्लक्ष, शाल्मल, कुश, क्रौञ्च, शाक and पुष्कर) or eighteen. See विष्णुपुराण II. 1. 11 ff. and व्यासभाष्य on योगसूत्र III. 25 (for सप्तद्वीपा वसुमती) and रघुवंश for 'अष्टादशद्वीपनिखातयूपः' 6. 38.

P. 66 ll. 10–22 **एकदा...दिदेश.** भुक्तवान् that had taken his dinner. प्रथमं...भृत्याः good servants, the first essential of sovereignty, are difficult to obtain. For the seven Angas of राज्य see above p. 5. प्रायेण...क्षुद्रा: generally mean persons, being agreeable in company, make the king their wealth, like atoms. The idea is that mean persons are agreeable to whatever the king says when they are in his company and thus by flattery make him the source of wealth to themselves. There are double meanings. It is the atoms that produce the पार्थिव द्रव्य (earthy substance). द्रव्य and समवाय are technical words in the न्यायवैशेषिक philosophy. The द्रव्यs are 'पृथिव्यप्तेजोवाय्वाकाशकालदिगात्ममनांसि नवैव.' समवाय is one of the seven categories of the न्यायवैशेषिक system 'द्रव्यगुणकर्मसामान्यविशेषसमवायाभावाः सप्त पदार्थाः'. समवाय is defined as 'नित्यसम्बन्धः समवायोऽयुतसिद्धवृत्तिः' *i. e.* it is an inseparable connection of such things as the whole and its parts, qualities and actions and their abode &c. Action is produced in the atoms by the will of God; two परमाणुs give rise to a द्व्यणुक and three द्व्यणुकs to a चतुरणुक and so on, when the earthy and other substances are ultimately evolved. The परमाणुs are the causes of द्व्यणुक &c. and between these latter and the परमाणुs there is समवाय. So सम...भूय means (in the case of atoms) 'being favourable to समवाय (*i. e.* entering into समवाय relation with their effects, the द्व्यणुक &c.). क्रीडारसेन on account of their liking for play. नर्तयन्तः making to dance. बालिशाः (1) children (2) triflers. Children in play make the peacock dance. Rogues, in whose hands the king becomes a puppet, make him dance (act) as they please. The com. gives another sense of मयूर 'धूर्तजनयोग्यो हासः'. But this is not absolutely necessary. दर्पण...पल्लविकाः rogues having entered into the heart (*i. e.* having secured influence over the prince's mind) transfer their disposition to him, as in a mirror. In a mirror also tendrils transfer bodies (*i. e.* the forms of tendrils are reflected). 'पल्लविको विटः' क्षीरस्वामी. The शब्दकल्पद्रुम gives वेश्यापति as the meaning of पल्लवक and कामुक as the meaning of पल्लविक. विप्रलम्भकाः deceivers, impostors. मिथ्यादर्शनैः (1) by false sights; (2) by false doctrines. असद्बुद्धि (1) ideas about things that have no existence (असतः अविद्यमानस्य बुद्धिः, with स्वप्नः); (2) false notions. Impostors warp the mind of the prince with false doctrines; dreams delude us by presenting things to our vision that do not exist. गीत...वातिकाः rogues, not being watched, bring about intoxication by singing, dancing and laughter. उपेक्षिताः वातिकाः विकाराः—as diseases of wind when neglected bring on madness. वात is one of the three humours of the body (वात, पित्त and कफ).

A mad man sings, dances and laughs. तृष्णावन्तः (1) thirsty; (2) greedy (for wealth). अकुलीनाः (1) not lying on the earth; (2) low-born. न शक्यन्ते ग्रहीतुम्—(1) cannot be seized; (2) cannot be reconciled. The चातक bird always feels thirst because it cannot drink the water on the earth, but subsists on a few drops from the cloud. Sailing as it does through the sky (कौ पृथिव्यां लीनो न भवति इति अकुलीनः) it cannot be seized. मानसे (1) in the मानस lake; (2) in the mind. स्फुरन्तम् (1) moving about; (2) appearing. जालिकाः (1) fishermen; (2) cheats. जालेन चरतीति जालिकः. Fishermen catch fish in the मानस lake. Cheats are so clever that they grasp the thought (of the prince) the moment it rises in his mind. Ordinarily one's thoughts are understood by their effects. यमपट्टिकाः—those who exhibit canvas on which are drawn the torments of Hell inflicted by Yama on sinners. See मुद्राराक्षस Act I where we have a person showing यमपट. अम्बरे (1) on canvas ; (2) in the sky. उद्गीतकाः who sing loudly. Rogues draw paintings in the sky *i. e.* build castles in the air, represent to the king as possible what is impossible. शल्यम् (1) the point of an arrow, barb ; (2) pain. अतिमार्गणाः (1) very keen arrows; (2) importunate in their demands. Read अभिषङ्गैः for ०ष्वङ्गैः. अभिषङ्गः contact. उपधाभिः परीक्षितौ tested by trials of honesty. 'उपधा धर्माद्यैर्यत्परीक्षणम्' इत्यमरः. The अर्थशास्त्र of कौटिल्य contains a chapter styled 'उपधाभिः शौचाशौचज्ञानममात्यानाम्' (I. 6.) and details four kinds of उपधा called धर्मोपधा, अर्थो०, कामो० and भयोपधा. विक्रान्तौ valiant. अभिरूपौ handsome or learned. मालव...पुत्रौ sons of the king of Malva, or Rajputs from Malva. भुजा...रिक्तौ not separable from my body like my two arms (*i. e.* I regard them as my own body). कुमारगुप्त०—for these see Introduction. भव ... भवितव्यम्—You two should not behave towards them on the same footing as other attendants.

P 66 l. 22—**P. 67** l. 17 नचिरात्...ददृशतुः. The principal sentence is नचिरात्...राज्यवर्धनहर्षौ प्रतीहारेण सह प्रविशन्तं अग्रतो ज्येष्ठं...कुमारगुप्तं (p. 12 l. 9) पृष्ठतस्तस्य कनीयांसं ... माधवगुप्तं ददृशतुः. प्रविशन्तम्—this and the following adjectives in the accusative qualify कुमारगुप्तं below. अग्रतो ज्येष्ठम्—the eldest of the two brothers was in front, as was proper. अष्टादशवर्षाणि वयः यस्य. अतिखर्वम् very low in stature. अति...वीम् who, with very heavy steps, as if steadied the earth that was unsteady on account of being transferred to numerous kings. The earth has passed through the hands of several kings and so is चञ्चल like लक्ष्मी. ०नृपतिषु सञ्चरणं तेन चला. C and T translate 'which trembled with the movements of numerous kings.' This is not so striking as the sense given by us. अनवरताभ्यस्तं लङ्घनं (leaping) तेन घनः उपचयः (growth or mass) यस्य एतादृशं मांसं तेन मेदुरात् (fat). अन... भासमानम् endowed with a pair of very thin shanks (जङ्घा) issuing from the knee joints that were not prominent and that (therefore) appeared as if to fall down from a pair of thighs that were plump with hard flesh of tough growth due to leaping constantly practised. His thighs were muscular and round, while the knee bones were not prominent (as they would be n the case of one who was not muscular) and his legs were thin. The shanks therefore appeared to jump out of his rounded thighs. उल्लिखिताभ्यां पार्श्वाभ्यां (sides) प्रकाशितः कृशिमा यस्य तेन (with मध्येन). सुरासुरैः रभसेन (with force) भ्रमितः वासुकिः तेन कषणं (rubbing) तेन क्षीणेन. कुमारगुप्त had a waist the smallness of which was laid bare by his sides that were hollowed (being void of fatty layers). At the time of churning the ocean for the 14 jewels, मन्दर became the handle and वासुकि was the rope. See above (notes) p. 42. The sides of मन्दर were scratched off by the violent rubbing of the rope Vāsuki and so its मध्य became slight. स्वामि...यच्छन्तम् giving room to innumerable (tokens of) regard received from his master. Even now it is usual to wear on the chest medals awarded to a person for excelling in anything. C and T render 'offered room for unbounded feelings of respect for his master.' This is not good. The poet is giving the good points in the physique of कुमारगुप्त and not the largeness of his heart. The plural सम्भावनानाम् is also against the latter interpretation. निभृत...क्षेपैः by the quiet and graceful movements. One who swims has to move his arms backwards and forwards as in walking. Youth is a period that can scarcely be crossed without pit-falls. वामकरे कटकं (वलयं) तस्य माणिक्यं तस्य. मरीचीनां मञ्जरी तस्याः जालमस्याः अस्तीति ०जालिन्या (with ०लेखया). समुद्भिद्यमानः प्रतापानलस्य शिखापल्लवः यस्याः (with ०लेखया). अङ्कितः पीवरः प्रकोष्ठः यस्य वामकर...प्रकोष्ठम् whose round fore-arm was marked by the line of the scar of the bow-string, the scar that had a pencil of rays from the ruby in the bracelet of the left hand and from which (therefore) the budlike flame of the fire of valour seemed to shoot forward. As to the wearing of वलय on the left forearm, see notes above p. 15. His forearm had a scar made by the bowstring and on the scar rays from the jewelled bracelet fell, which appeared like flames of fire. आलोहिनीम् slightly red. उच्चं अंसतटं अवलम्बते इति that hung down from his high shoulder. On his shoulder fell the reddish light of the jewel in his ear-ornament. It resembled the skin of the Ruru deer, which is worn across the chest and shoulder by a क्षत्रियब्रह्मचारिन्. Hence the word असग्रहणव्रतविधृताम्. See बौधायनस्मृति I. 2. 14 'कृष्णरुरुबस्ताजिनान्यजिनानि.' For a graphic description of the equipment of a क्षत्रियब्रह्मचारिन्, see उत्तररामचरित IV. 20. उद्गता कोटिः यस्य सः उत्कोटिः केयूरः तस्य पत्रभङ्गे पुत्रिका तस्याः प्रतिबिम्बं गर्भे यस्य सः ०गर्भः, ०गर्भः कपोलः यस्य. हृदये स्थिता रोहिणी यस्य. ०कपोलं मुखं—a face on the cheeks of which there was a reflection of a female figure drawn in lines on the armlets that had projecting points. His face was like the moon. रोहिणी is said to be the special favourite of the moon. On his cheek there was the reflection of a पुत्रिका. The moon's heart thinks of रोहिणी. The star रोहिणी has flashing light, as the points of the केयूर flash light. For क at the end of बहुव्रीहि compounds, see above. p. 31. अचपला स्तिमिता च तारका (pupil) यस्य. लक्ष्म्याः लाभः तदर्थं उत्तानितानि मुखानि येषाम्. He had a downcast eye (by way of showing his humility) and therefore taught humility to lotus beds. लक्ष्मी is represented as standing in an expanded lotus. He, though desirous of लक्ष्मी (glory), had a downcast look and not an uplifted face like the lotuses. उत्तंसः crest, ornament worn on the crown of the head. अम्लातक is a kind of red flower. स्वाम्यनुरागः loyalty. रागः means 'redness' also. नम्रता (1) humility; (2) capacity to bend, flexibility. कङ्कणभङ्गात् भीतानि सकलानि कार्मुकाणि तैः अर्पिताम्—presented by all the bows that were afraid of being broken in their rings (*i. e.* their crests). Connect निर्दयया with भङ्ग. But to connect separate words with part of a समास is rather unusual. The reading of some of the MSS of B 'निर्दयाकर्षणभङ्ग' is much better, but seems to be a conscious improvement. Bows have नम्रता (they bend) and transferred it to him. संयतैः confined, restrained. प्रण...वर्तमानम् who acted according to the status of a nobly born youth, that (status) is the seat of trust, as if it were his sweet-heart. तेजस्विन् (1) brilliant; (2) high-spirited. आह्लादक applies to both शीलेन and शशिना. He was high-spirited and had a winning disposition and therefore resembled the sun, having a moon inside it. गन्धनम्—hurting, rubbing. दर्शन...सौभाग्येन who by the charm of his person purchased the people at sight and sold them into the hands of joy. The moment the people saw him, they gave their allegiance to him and were further delighted. What one buys, one may sell to another. कुमारगुप्तम्—connect with ददृशतुः. प्रांशु tall. गौर fair, white-red. मनःशिला (Mar. मनशीळ) red arsenic. अनुल्बण...निभेन under the guise of a crest of मालती flowers, that (crest) was not very prominent. This shows his विनय. निर्जिगमिषता = गन्तुमिच्छता. The white मालती crest resembled his great (गुरु) यशः which is poetically represented to be white. His यशः wanted to go out (*i. e.* spread in the world) and therefore kissed him on the head (as मालती flower) as a father (गुरु) when leaving the house on a journey may kiss his son on the head. भ्रूसङ्गतकेन by the meeting of his eyebrows. विनय and यौवन were united in him for the first time after a long interval. यौवन and विनय are rarely found together. His eyebrows that met were as it were the first sign of this union. हृदयनिहिता (1) placed in the heart (with °भक्ति); (2) fixed on his chest (with °दृष्टि). अच्छाच्छस्य अतिशुभ्रस्य चन्दनरसस्य अनुलेपेन शीतलम् (वक्षःस्थलं, which is the object of बिभ्राणम्). संनिहितं हारः एव उपधानं (pillow) यस्य. अनन्त...श्रान्तायाः tired by passing to innumerable chieftains. शशि...शयनम् a bed of the slabs of चन्द्रकान्त stones. His chest was smeared with cool चन्दन paste and therefore resembled the चन्द्रकान्त stone, which is also white and शीतल. His chest had a necklace of pearls which resembled a white pillow. His chest was broad like a slab. लक्ष्मी rested on his chest after being tired &c. चक्षुः and the other words in the accusative up to गमनं are governed by दर्शयन्तम्. चक्षुः कुरङ्गकैः भीतैरुत्कोचमिव दत्तं—eye which was given to him as a bribe (उत्कोचः) by the terrified deer. The same words are to be understood after वराहैः &c. The idea is that his eye was beautiful like that of the deer; the rest to be construed similarly. घोणावंशं bamboo-like (*i. e.* high) nose. स्कन्धपीठं broad shoulders. मृगया...शेषैः that remained out of those that were left after being hunt down in chase.

P. 67 ll. 18–28 **प्रविश्य...बभूवतुः.** चतुर्भिः अङ्गैः with four limbs *i. e.* hands and knees. गाम् the earth. स्निग्धा (affectionate) नरेन्द्रस्य दृष्टिः तया निर्दिष्टाम् (indicated). अस्तः (cast aside) अपरः व्यापारः याभ्याम्. सङ्कल्पाः...भविष्यन्ति your desires will give you this special distinction that the result will follow in all its fulness, like the trees of Paradise. मेदिन्यां दोलायमानः मौलिः ययोः whose head hung on the earth *i. e.* who prostrated themselves. युगपत् at the same time. ताभ्याम् by कुमारगुप्त and माधवगुप्त. उत्थाय—रा० and हर्ष got up. The reading of A 'उत्थाय राज्यवर्धनहर्षौ प्रणेमतुः तौ च पितरम्' means they (कुमारगुप्त and माधवगुप्त) got up and bowed to रा० and हर्ष and these two latter bowed to their father. It is better to suppose that राज्यवर्धन and हर्ष did not allow the young men any time to bow to themselves. निमेषो...यान्तौ not going away from the range of the (prince's) eye, like the opening and shutting of the eye. निमेष and उन्मेष are always present in the eye. The two princes always stood before हर्ष and राज्यवर्धन. उच्छ्वास (exhalation) and निश्वास (inhalation) are also अभिमुख (done through the mouth). भुजाविव पार्श्ववर्तिनौ our hands are constantly at our side.

P. 67 l. 29—**P. 68** l. 24 **अथ राज्यश्री...जानातीति.** विदग्धासु (applies to both सखीषु and कलासु)—clever; fine. कलासु—The कामसूत्र of वात्स्यायन (I. 3.) enumerates the 64 arts such as गीत, वाद्य, नृत्य, आलेख्य &c. उपचीयमानः परिचयः यस्याः whose familiarity (with सखीs and कलाs) was on the increase. शरा...भुवि as arrows on the target. बाह्य...स्थितेन occupying the outer court. स्व...गताम् that came (*i. e.* occurred to him) in its own context. The man was thinking on some topic or story and in connection with it he remembered a verse which he sang loudly. आर्या—'यस्याः प्रथमे पादे द्वादश मात्रास्तथा तृतीयेऽपि । अष्टादश द्वितीये चतुर्थके पञ्चदश साऽऽर्या ॥'. *Verse 5.* The sentence is विवर्धमाना सुता पितरं उद्वेगमहावर्ते पातयति सरित् तटमिव—a growing daughter casts her father in the whirlpool of gloom, as a rising river casts its bank in a whirlpool. उद्वेगः महावर्तः इव (with सुता); उद्वेगसदृशः महावर्तः (with सरित्). पयोधराणां (मेघानां) उन्नमनं तस्य काले at the time of the impending clouds ; पयोधरयोः स्तनयोः उन्नमनं (elevation) तस्य काले. अनुवर्षम्—(वर्षे वर्षे इति अव्ययीभाव) each year (with सुता). वर्षमनु after rainfall. अनु as a कर्मप्रवचनीय governs वर्ष in the accusative. Or we may also take अनुवर्षम् in the sense of 'at each rainy season.' It should be noted that the verse fits in with the topic of the youth of राज्यश्री and the seeking of her hand by various kings. उत्सारितः परिजनः येन. गुणवत्ता possession of good qualities. चिन्ता—anxiety (as to finding a proper husband for her) never left his heart, just as her गुणवत्ता never left him (*i. e.* he was always dwelling upon her good qualities). The reading गुणवृत्तेव makes no sense. C and T say in the appendix that गुणवृत्ता is an easier reading. We fail to see how. They render गुणवृत्ता as 'as if become an attribute' and therefore take it as an adjective of चिन्ता इन्धनीभवन्ति become the fuel (of the fire of torment). अस्याः पयोधरोन्नतिः (पयोधरयोः स्तनयोः उन्नतिः) मे हृदयमन्धकारयति. पयोधराणां मेघानां उन्नतिः दिवसमन्धकारयति. केना...रियं this rule of conduct (regarded as) right, by whomsoever it may have been made, is not approved of by me. धर्म्या—धर्मादनपेता—according to 'धर्मपथ्यर्थ—न्यायादनपेते' पा. 4. 4. 92. अङ्कलालितानि fondled on our knees. अकाण्ड एव...नीयन्ते are taken away by strangers (असंस्तुत) who come all of a sudden. एतानि...संसारस्य these indeed are the branded spots of this worldly existence *i. e.* these are the most painful of the events of this संसार. सर्वाभिभाविनी overwhelming all. अपत्य... सन्तः good men are grieved at the birth of a daughter though both (son and daughter) are equally (their) offspring. जन्मकाल...साधवः good men offer water by their tears to their daughters even at the time of their birth. Emphasis is laid on the word जन्मकाले, because water is offered to the dead. Good men shed tears when a daughter is born. अकृतः दाराणां परिग्रहः (acceptance) यैः. परिहृता (avoided) गृहे वसतिः यैः. अरण्यानि is the object of अधिशेरते. The roots शी, स्था, and आस्, when preceded by अधि, govern the accusative of the abode (आधार). 'अधिशीङ्—स्थासां कर्म' पा. 1. 4. 46. यथा...हृदयम् the more do the envoys of the suitors come in, the more does wretched anxiety enter deep into my heart, like a woman abashed. लज्जमानेव—a woman that feels abashed will run inside the house. गृहगतैः=गृहस्थैः. लोकवृत्तयः–the ways of the world. वरगुणेषु qualities in a bridegroom (or 'excellent qualities'). अभि...धीमन्तः the wise follow (*i. e.* pay great regard to) noble birth alone. Mark the verse 'कन्या वरयते रूपं माता वित्तं पिता श्रुतम् । बान्धवाः कुलमिच्छन्ति मृष्टान्नमितरे जनाः ॥' quoted by commentators on कुमारसम्भव V. 72. धर...स्थितः standing at the head of all kings. धरणीधराणां= पर्वतानाम्. माहेश्वरः पादन्यासः the foot-print of महेश्वर (शिव). शिव is said to reside on the top (मूर्धन्) of the कैलास mountain. माहेश्वरः with मौखरिवंशः would mean 'that was devoted to महेश्वर (*i. e.* शिव)'. मौखरिवंशः—for the Maukharis, see Introduction. From the inscriptions it appears that the correct form is either मौखरि or मौखर. The reading of A 'मौखरीवंशः' is therefore bad. Bāṇa in his introduction to the कादम्बरी has 'नमामि भर्वोश्चरणाम्बुजद्वयं सशेखरैर्मौखरिभिः कृतार्चनम् ।'. ग्रह...गतः as if he were the sun (ग्रहपति) come to the earth. पितु...गुणै. not inferior to his father in his virtues. एनाम्—refers to राज्यश्री. दुहितृस्नेहेन कातरतरं हृदयं यस्याः.

संवर्धन...गिन्यः useful only in nursing them (and not in determining such delicate questions as their disposal in marriage). धात्रीनिर्विशेषाः not different from (*i. e.* no better than) their nurses. प्रदाने...पितरः in bestowing them (in marriage) their fathers are the (sole) authority. कृपया कृतः विशेषः यस्मिन्—the difference being made by pity. कृपा...स्नेहः—यशोमती gives expression to the general feeling of Indian mothers that they love their daughters more than their sons and assigns the reason for this. The position of the daughter in society excites the pity of the mother more than that of the sons. Read आर्तितां for आर्तिता. यथा...जानाति my lord knows how to act so that she (राज्यश्री) will not become a lifelong (source of) anxiety to us. The reading of A 'यथा यावज्जीवमावयोरार्तिता' is not good. The meaning then would be 'my lord knows how lifelong anxiety would be caused to us'. C reads 'आवयोर्नाधितां प्रतिपद्यते', which yields the same sense as the text (न + आधिताम्).

P. 68 l. 25—**P. 69** l. 32 **राजा तु ... कुलम्.** प्रति governs the accusative according to the वार्तिक 'अभितःपरितःसमयानिकषाहाप्रतियोगेऽपि' on 'उपान्वध्याङ्वसः' I. 4. 48. विदितः अर्थः याभ्याम्. जाता मुद् (delight) यस्य—qualifies तस्मिन्, which refers to प्रधानदूतपुरुष. The principal sentence is जातमुदि...गते तस्मिन् आसन्नेषु विवाहदिवसेषु... ०लोकम्...आसीत् राजकुलम्. The author now gives a graphic description of the preparations of a marriage in a royal family. उद्दामं दीयमानानि ताम्बूलपटवासकुसुमानि तैः प्रसाधितः सर्वलोकः यस्मिन् all the people in which were decked by the betel, fragrant powders and flowers that were being given with an unrestrained hand. सकलदेशेभ्यः आदिश्यमानं शिल्पिनां सार्थस्य (समूहस्य) आगमनं यस्मिन्. Skilled artisans were invited from all countries. अवनिपालपुरुषैः (king's officers) गृहीतः समग्रैः ग्रामीणैः (villagers) आनीयमानानां उपकरणानां (useful materials) सम्भारः (collection) यस्मिन्. ग्रामे भवः ग्रामीणः. राजदौवारिकैः उपनीयमानानि अनेकनृपाणां उपायनानि यस्मिन् where the presents sent by numerous chiefs were brought (to the royal presence) by the doorkeepers of the king (प्रभाकरवर्धन). दौवारिकः—द्वारे नियुक्तः according to 'तत्र नियुक्तः' पा. 4. 4. 69. उपनिमन्त्रिताः (invited) आगताः बन्धुवर्गाः तेषां संवर्गणं (attracting, winning) तस्मिन् व्यग्राः राजवल्लभाः यस्मिन्. लब्धं मधु (wine) तस्य मदेन प्रचण्डाः (wild) चर्मकाराः तेषां करपुटैः उल्लालिताः (shaken, moved) कोणाः (drumsticks) तैः पटु (sharp) विघट्टनं (striking) तेन रणन्तः मङ्गलपटहाः यस्मिन्. Leather workers had been summoned to make drums and were plied with wine. In their intoxication they struck the drums lustily. पिष्टपञ्चाङ्गुलेन मण्ड्यमानानि उलूखलमुसलशिलाद्युपकरणानि यस्मिन् in which such utensils as mortar, pestle and grinding stones were decked with five finger-prints of powder (of turmeric probably). The five fingers were dipped in turmeric mixed with water and the mortar &c. were smeared with the finger-marks by way of मङ्गल. In the 2nd उच्छ्वास we read 'पिष्टपञ्चाङ्गुलपाण्डुरं मुखनिहितनवचूतपल्लवं पूर्णकलशमुदीक्षमाणः...प्रीतिकूटान्निरगात्' on which the Com. says 'पिष्टपञ्चाङ्गुलमाजकोक्ताभिः पंचभिरङ्गुलिभिर्मङ्गल्याय दीयते'. Even now the pestle and grinding stones are so marked. अशेषेभ्यः आशामुखेभ्यः आविर्भूता चारणानां (bards) परम्परा तया आपूर्यमाणाः प्रकोष्ठाः (quadrangles) यस्मिन्. प्रतिष्ठाप्यमानं इन्द्राणीदैवतं यस्मिन् where images of इन्द्राणी (wife of इन्द्र) were being set up. A reads ०प्रकोष्ठप्रतिष्ठाप्य०, which would mean that 'images of इन्द्राणी were being set up in quadrangles.' The works on marriage ritual lay down that शची should be worshipped. "विवाहे शचीपूजनं नारदीयसंहितायाम् 'सम्पूज्य प्रार्थयित्वा तां शचीदेवीं गुणाश्रयाम्' इति। तथा च प्रयोगरत्नाकरे। ततो दाता पात्रस्थसिततण्डुलपुञ्जे शचीमावाह्य षोडशोपचारैः पूजयेत्तां च कन्यैवं प्रार्थयेत् 'देवेन्द्राणि नमस्तुभ्यं देवेन्द्रप्रियभामिनि। विवाहं भाग्यमारोग्यं पुत्रलाभं च देहि मे।'" quoted from Mr. Nardurgikar's notes on रघु० VII. 3. The धर्मसिन्धु says 'अन्योन्यालिङ्गितगौरीहरयोः प्रतिमां सुवर्णरौप्यादिनिर्मितां कात्यायनीमहालक्ष्मीशचीभिः सह पूजयेत्।'. सूत्रधारैः (carpenters) आदीयमानः विवाहवेद्याः सूत्रपातः यस्मिन् where carpenters began to measure with their measuring line the marriage altar. सित...सत्कृतैः—the carpenters were honoured for their trouble by presents of white flowers, unguents and clothes. उत्कूर्चकः (उद्गतः कूर्चकः यस्मिन्) करः येषाम्—whose hands had brushes held up (in whitewashing). सुधायाः *(chunam)* कर्परः (pail) स्कन्धे येषाम्. अधि...रूढैः mounted on ladders. धवैः= पुरुषैः. धवलीक्रियमाणं प्रासादस्य प्रतोलीप्राकारशिखरं यस्मिन् where the top of the palace wall (प्राकारः) on the street (प्रतोली) was being whitened. आदौ क्षुण्णं पश्चात् क्षाल्यमानं कुसुम्भकं तस्य सम्भारः तस्य अम्भः— प्लवपूरेण रज्यमानाः जनपादपल्लवाः यस्मिन् where the feet of the people were coloured by the flood of the torrents of water from the heap (सम्भारः) of safflower that was powdered (क्षुण्ण) and then washed. निरूप्यमाणाः यौतकयोग्याः मातङ्गाः (गजाः) तुरङ्गाश्च तैः तरङ्गितं अङ्गनं यस्मिन् where the courtyard was surging with horses and elephants that were being examined as suitable bridal gifts. यौतक (n) is a kind of स्त्रीधन. यौतक means the gifts that are given to a woman at the time of marriage when she is seated with her husband. 'यौतकं विवाहादिकाले पत्या सहैकासने प्राप्तं युतयोर्यौतकमिति निघण्टूक्तेरिति मदनः' व्यवहारमयूख. गणने अभियुक्तः (engaged in)

गणकानां गणः तेन गृह्यमाणाः लग्नगुणाः यत्र. For लग्न see notes p. 24. A marriage was to be performed only when certain signs of the Zodiac were on the horizon and when there were no evil aspects of the planets. For example, the धर्मसिन्धु says 'त्रिषष्ठाष्टत्वर्कस्त्रिजलधनगोऽब्जः क्षितिसुतस्त्रिषष्ठस्थो शेज्यौ व्ययनिधिनवर्ज्यौ भृगुसुतः। द्वितीयाब्धीष्वङ्काभ्रतनुषु रिपुत्र्यष्टसु शनिस्तमः केतुश्चाये भवति सुखहेतुश्च सकलः॥'. This verse gives the evil aspects of the planets with the लग्न. गन्धोदकवाहिमकरमुखाः (crocodile—shaped) प्रणाल्यः (conductors Marathi पन्हळ) ताभिः पूर्यमाणः क्रीडावापीसमूहः यस्मिन्. हेमकाराणां (goldsmiths) चक्रं (समूहः) तेन प्रक्रान्तं (carried on) हाटकस्य (सुवर्णस्य) घटनं (shaping, hammering) तस्य टाङ्कारः तेन वाचालिताः अलिन्दकाः यत्र. अलिन्दकः a terrace before an outer door. उत्थापिता (constructed) अभिनवा भित्तिः तस्याः पात्यमाना बहला वालुका तस्याः कण्टकानां आलेपः तेन आकुलः आलेपकलोकः (plasterers) यस्मिन्. Read कण्टका० for कण्ठका०. चतुराणां चित्रकराणां चक्रवालं (समूहः) तेन लिख्यमानानि माङ्गल्यानि आलेख्यानि यत्र. लेप्य...वृक्षकम् where groups of clay—workers were engaged in making clay figures of fishes, tortoises, crocodiles, cocoanuts, plantain and betel trees. क्षितिपालैश्च—connect this with प्रारब्धविविधव्यापारम् four lines below. स्वय...कक्ष्यैः who girt up their own loins *i. e.* who personally engaged in physical labour. स्वामिना (प्रभाकरवर्धनेन) अर्पितानि (assigned) कर्माणि तेषां शोभा तस्याः सम्पादने आकुलैः. सिन्दू...मसृणयद्भिः who rendered glossy the pavements besmeared with red lead. विनिहिताः सरसाः आतर्पणहस्ताः येषु on which were placed sticky hand-marks of pigment for white-washing. 'आतर्पणं प्रीणने स्यान्मङ्गलालेपनेऽपि च' मेदिनी. विन्य...उत्तम्भयद्भिः who raised the pillars of the marriage (उद्वाहः) platforms, the tops of which were marked with tender mango and As'oka leaves, and which (pillars) were red with the Alaktaka dye placed on them. 'वितर्दिस्तु वेदिका' इत्यमरः. Even now mango leaves are hung up from pillars &c. as auspicious. प्रविष्टाभिः—this and the following instrumentals qualify ०सीमन्तिनीभिः below. आ सूर्योदयात् from early morn. The wives of chieftains were in the palace from the early morn engaged in various occupations. C and T translate 'from the furthest orient,' which seems far—fetched. सुवेशाभिः finely dressed. वधू...गायन्तीभिः singing auspicious (songs) pleasing to the ear (श्रुतिः) and containing in them mention of the families of the bride and bridegroom. बहु...चित्रयन्तीभिः dying neck-strings with their fingers that were smeared (आदिग्ध) with various paints (वर्णकः). चित्र...मण्डयन्तीभिः who, being clever in painting and drawing figures, decorated polished jars and groups of raw (शीतल) clayware. शालाजिर means a शराव according to हेमचन्द्र. र and ल are often interchanged in words. अभिन्न...रञ्जयन्तीभिः who reddened the threads of cotton that had not been taken out from its pod and the collections of woollen threads for making a marriage bracelet. Cotton is contained in pods. They took such cotton as had not yet been taken out of the pod, spun it into thread, which thread they dyed red. Such thread dyed red is even now required in marriage ceremonies. The Com. says 'अभिन्नपुटो वंशादिमयश्चतुष्कोणः पाटलाकृतिर्जालकैः क्रियते। तच्छिद्रान्तरपूरणाय कर्पासतूलपल्लवा रज्यन्ते'. What this means is not quite clear. It seems to mean—a square box of bamboo &c. is prepared, the interstices of which are filled in with dyed cotton thread. C and T following the Com. translate 'stained skeins of cotton thread for bamboo baskets.' The cotton and शाल्मलि both yield wool and hence the words कर्पासतूल are employed. बलाशनाघृतेन घनीकृतः कुङ्कुमकल्कः (saffron paste) तेन मिश्रिताम्. On बलाशना°, the Com. says 'बलाशना पुष्पाख्यौषधिः। तत्पक्वं घृतं रक्षार्थं क्रियते'. अङ्गरागः cosmetic. लावण्य...कल्पयन्तीभिः who were preparing unguents for the face that produced special beauty. कक्कोलम् (Marathi कंकोळ) is a kind of fragrant berry. जातीफलम् nutmeg. स्फुरन्ति स्फीतानि (abundant) स्फाटिककर्पूरशकलानि तैः खचितं अन्तरालं यासाम्. बहु...बध्यमानैः—this and the following instrumentals qualify वासोभिः (in l. 27). बहुविधानां भक्तीनां निर्माणे निपुणाः पुराणाः (old) पौरपुरन्ध्रियः (city matrons) ताभिः बध्यमानानि तैः. भक्तिः means 'texture, decoration.' बध्यमानैः बद्धैश्च many garments were in course of weaving and many were already woven. Those that were woven were dyed by रजकs. आचारे चतुराः अन्तःपुरजरत्यः ताभिः जनिता पूजा तया राजमानाः रजकाः (washermen) तैः रज्यमानैः. The old women honoured the washermen who thereupon beamed with self-complacency. उभय...शोष्यमाणैः that were waved to and fro by servants holding them by the two ends and were dried in shade. Those that were dyed were being dried. कुटिलः क्रमः यस्य तत् कुटिलक्रमं रूपं तेन क्रियमाणः पल्लवानां परभागः येषु. 'परभागः गुणोत्कर्षे' क्षीरस्वामी. Compare for परभाग, कादम्बरी उत्तरभाग (p. 267 of P) 'उपहितकान्तिपतिपरभागा लक्ष्मच्छायेव चन्द्रमसः' (श्मश्रुराजिलेखा). What the author means is not quite clear. The meaning seems to be—on the dyed and dried cloth, some paintings of the leaves of various trees were being drawn. The paintings had very great beauty (परभागः). The paintings were being drawn on the inside of the cloth and hence they were done in the reverse order of nature (कुटिलक्रम), so that the outside (that would be visible to others) would show the beautiful पल्लवs in their natural form. C and T translate 'some, now dry, were having all the charm of sprays reproduced in their twisted shapes.' This is obscure. अपरैः—अपरैः some—others. आरब्धं कुङ्कुमपङ्कस्थासकानां छुरणं येषु in which the spotting with saffron paste had commenced *i. e.* some of the textures were being marked with spots of saffron paste. स्थासकः perfuming the body with unguents. 'स्नानं चर्चा तु चार्चिक्यं स्थासकोऽथ प्रबोधनम्' इत्यमरः. उद्भुजाः भुजिष्याः परिचारिकाः ताभिः भज्यमानानि भङ्गुराणि उत्तरीयाणि येषु the fragile upper garments among which were torn by the maids that had lifted up their arms. The idea is not quite clear. The meaning seems to be :—The maids raised their hands to gather together the textures as they became ready. In doing so they tore away their own fragile upper garments. क्षौमैश्च…नेत्रैश्च—these words indicate the material of which the garments were made. क्षौमैः made of flax, linen. क्षुमायाः विकारः क्षौमम्. बादरैः mad͡ə of cotten. बदरायाः बदराफलस्य वा विकारः बादरम्. 'कर्पासी बदरेति च' इति; 'वाल्कं क्षौमादि फालं तु कार्पासं बादरं च तत्' इति च अमरः. दुकूलैः—The अमरकोश treats क्षौम and दुकूल as synonyms. C and T translate दुकूल as 'bark silk.' लालातन्तुजैः lit. 'made of the threads of saliva' *i. e.* made of spider's thread. This is otherwise called पत्त्रोर्णम् on which क्षीरस्वामी remarks 'लकुचवटादिपत्रेषु कृमिलालोर्णाकृतं पत्त्रोर्णम्'. अंशुक is used in the sense of 'वस्त्र' in general. It must here mean a वस्त्र made from a particular material. C and T translate 'muslin'. नेत्रैश्च—silk garments. The अमरकोश gives it as a synonym of अंशुक. 'स्याज्जटांशुकयोर्नेत्रम्'. निर्मोकनिभैः resembling the slough of serpents. अकठोरा रम्भा तस्याः गर्भवत् कोमलैः as delicate (or fine) as the inside of a plantain plant not fully developed. C and T translate 'soft as the unripe plaintain's fruit.' This is not correct. रम्भा means the plant and not its fruit. No one in India need be told how fine and delicate the *inside* of the plantain *plant* is. The inside of the *fruit*, however unripe, is not soft. निश्वासहार्यैः The clothes were so fine and light that even the breath-of a person made them move on the body of the wearer. स्पर्शानुमेयैः—the garments were of such fine texture that they were not visible to the eye, but were only determined to be on the body by touch. इन्द्रायुधसहस्रैः—the garments being variously tinted presented the hues of the rainbow. संछादितम् qualifies राजकुलम्. उज्ज्वलाः निचोलकाः तैः अवगुण्ठ्यमानानि हंसकुलानि यैः (*adj.* of शयनीयैः)—by the brilliant coverlets of which (beds) the swarms of Hamsas were veiled (*i. e.* were cast into the shade). हंसs are white 'हंसास्तु श्वेतगरुतः' इत्यमरः. 'निचोलः प्रच्छदपटः' इत्यमरः. शयनीयैः, कञ्चुकैः, °सहस्रैः and other nouns in the instrumental are to be connected with उज्ज्वलं and the following adjectives. तारा...कञ्चुकैः with bodices that were added to (*i. e.* overlaid) with brilliant pearls. अने...सहस्रैः with thousands of pieces of fine cloth rent asunder for various uses. अभि...तानैः with canopies of cloth that were glowing with fine silk garments freshly dyed. अभिनवः रागः येषाम् तानि °रागाणि अत एव कोमलानि दुकूलानि तैः राजमानैः. स्तवरकनिवहेन निरन्तरं छाद्यमानानि समस्तानि पटलानि येषाम्. स्तवरक... मण्डपैः with *pandals* all the thatches (पटलं) of which were covered with masses of clothes. The word स्तवरक is unusual. उच्चित्राः (having paintings prominent on them) नेत्रपटाः (fine silk cloth) तैः वेष्ट्यमानैः. औत्सुक्यं ददातीति °दम् causing eagerness or excitement.

P. 70 ll. 1–16 **देवी तु...राजकुलम्.** हृदयेन भर्तरि—connect each instrumental with the following locative. The principal sentence is देवी यशोमती एका अपि बहुधा विभक्ता इव अभवत्—she, though one, seemed to be divided in manifold ways. हृदयेन...जामातरि—her heart was with her husband, her curiosity was with the bridegroom. These clauses explain how she was विभक्त. She was curious to know what the bridegroom looked like. उपचारः respectful behaviour, courtesy. शरीरेण सञ्चरणे her body was engaged in moving about. चक्षुषा...वेक्षणेषु her eye was occupied in seeing things done and left undone. उपर्युपरि now and then, again and again. विसर्जिताभिः (despatched) उष्ट्रवामीभिः (camels and mares) जनितः जामातुः जोषः (pleasure) येन. एवं च—The principal sentence is एवं च तस्मिन्नविधवामये इव भवति राजकुले...आजगाम विवाहदिवसः. अवि...राजकुले—In marriage ceremonies only those women whose husbands are living take any prominent part. चारण...दिङ्मुखेषु—So many minstrels had come there that it seemed that the quarters contained nothing else but them. Explain the following clauses similarly. भूषण...जने—Even the domestics were loaded with so many ornaments that they seemed to be nothing but ornaments. सर्गः creation, world. Read निर्वृति° for निर्वृत्ति°. लक्ष्मी...महोत्सवे when the festival seemed to grow as if it were made of Lakshmî, *i. e.* everything in the festival was so gorgeous and splendid. निधाने (treasure)—connect this and the following locatives with वर्तमाने below. यौवने...प्रीतेः it seemed as if there was a youth of prosperity and as if there was a new regime of pleasure (प्रीति). यौवराज्यम्—from युवराज—the heir-apparent. The installation of an heir-apparent is a very important function, as will appear from the रामायण. गण्यमानः—one counts with the aid of one's fingers. आलो...ध्वजैः—the unfurled banners seemed to be looking out for the arrival (of the marriage day), as a person stretches his neck and tries to descry a person coming from a distance. प्रत्यु...शब्दकैः the echoes of the drums beaten in the palace spread far and wide. The echoes went so far, the poet fancies, to receive the coming विवाहदिवस. मौहूर्तिकैः—मुहूर्तं वेद मौहूर्तिकः (astrologer). समुत्सारितः निखिलः अनिबद्धलोकः यस्मात्. अनिबद्ध—unconnected *i. e.* strangers. विविक्तम् lonely.

P. 70 ll. 16–25 **अथ...प्राहिणोत्.** शोभनः आकारः यस्य सः स्वाकारः तम्. त—object of पप्रच्छ. दर्शितः आदरः येन. कच्चित्—this is a particle indicating 'I hope.' यथाज्ञापयसि—servants were to use the verb आज्ञापय् with reference to whatever the king said or asked. आगत...ज्ञात्वा knowing him to have come to intimate the arrival of the bridegroom. यामे=प्रहरे. विवाह...दोषः (so act) that there will be no defect due to the passing away of the hour fixed for marriage. The reading of B is better, but seems to be an emendation purposely mode. प्रतीपं प्राहिणोत् sent him back.

P. 70 l. 26—**P. 71** l. 14 **अथ...ग्रहवर्मा.** The principal sentence is अथ...समवसिते वासरे...आजगाम (p. 15 l. 33)...ग्रहवर्मा. सकल...वासरे—कमलs fade in the evening. The bride's face glowed with expectation of the hour of marriage. The poet fancies that the glory of the fading कमलs was transferred to the beaming face of the bride. समवसित ended (*past. p. p.* of सो with सम् and अव). विवाह...सवितरि when the sun looked radiant like the tender feet of the Glory of the bridal day. The sun looks red when setting. The feet of handsome young ladies are red. वधूवरयोः अनुरागः तेन लघूकृतं प्रेम तेन लज्जितेषु. विघटमानेषु separating. The ruddy goose becomes separate from its mate at the close of day and is a type of abiding love. See notes p. 10. This separation is fancied to be due to the shame felt at the fact that the चक्रवाक pairs were eclipsed in love by the bride and bridegroom. सौभाग्य...रागे when the radiance of the evening looking as delicate as a red silken garment flashed in the sky as if it were the banner of marital felicity. A banner also waves in the sky and may be of red silk. रक्तांशुकस्य इव सुकुमारं वपुः यस्य; रक्तांशुकेन &c. कपोत...तिमिरे when darkness variegated like the pigeon's throat began to obscure the faces of the quarters as if it were the dust (raised) by the arrival of the bridegroom's procession. Both तिमिर and dust are dark and obscure the face. कपोत...कबुरे should be construed with तिमिर and *not* with सन्ध्यारागे, as C and T do. कर्बुर according to अमरसिंह is a synonym of कल्माष, शबल &c., 'चित्रं किर्मीरकल्माषशबलैताश्च कर्बुरे'. कर्बुर means 'dark-white' and not 'yellow'. See उत्तरराम VI. 4 'अवदग्धकर्बुरितकेतुचामरैः &c.' लग्न...सज्जे ready to effect the लग्न (the auspicious aspect of the heavenly bodies). This applies to both the stars and the astrologers. उज्जिहान *pr. p.* of हा 3 A with उद् going up, rising. ज्योतिर्गणे (1) galaxy of luminaries; (2) astrologers. A person who is सज्ज gets up. वर्धमाना धवला छाया यस्य. The round disc of the moon resembles a round मङ्गलकलश. वर्धमानेन शरावेण धवला छाया यस्य (with ०कलशे). वर्धमानः—म् saucer, a lid. Earthen pots marked with white lines are even now required in marriage ceremonies. The Com. remarks 'वर्धमानं शरावः...तद्धि मक्कोललिप्तं विवाहे क्रियते इत्याचारः'. वधूवदनलावण्यमेव ज्योत्स्ना तया परिपीतं तमः यत्र (adj. of प्रदोषे). वृथो...वनेषु when the beds of night lotuses with their faces raised up (*i. e.* with expanding buds) as if laughed at the moon saying 'you have risen to no purpose.' The splendour of the moonlike face of the bride dispelled all the gloom of evening. As the gloom was dispelled by the beauty of the bride's face, the moon that rose in the sky had nothing left to dispel. The expanding of the buds of कुमुद is fancied to be the raising of faces by them. A person in ridiculing another also makes grimaces towards him. उल्लासित...चामरैः (*adj.* of पादातैः) that waved many flashing red chowries. उल्लासितानि स्फाराणि स्फुरितानि अरुणचामराणि यैः. उत्थितः (रागः अग्रपल्लव इव) रागाग्रपल्लवः येषाम् (with मनोरथैः); उत्थितः रागसदृशः अग्रपल्लवः येषाम् (with पादातैः). पुरो धावमानैः is common to both मनोरथैः and पादातैः. The idea is:—footmen waving red chowries ran before the bridegroom. The leaf-like red ends of the chowries were raised up. The desire of the bridegroom also ran before him. Desire had shooting from it passion (रागः). Connect पादातैः and वृन्दैः with आपूरितदिग्भागः (ग्रहवर्मा). उत्कर्णाः कटकहयाः तेषां प्रतिहेषितैः दीयमानं स्वागतं येभ्यः.

The idea is:—ग्रहवर्मा had with him troops of horses that neighed. The horses in the capital of प्रभाकरवर्धन neighed in response. This is represented as welcome offered to the horses of the son-in-law by the horses in the capital. चलानि कर्णचामराणि येषाम्. चामीकरं (सुवर्णं) तन्मयानि सर्वोपकरणानि येषाम् all whose trappings were made of gold. वर्णकलम्बिनाम्—C and T translate 'with gay housings.' वर्णकः painted cloth. करिणां...न्धकारम् with troops (घटा) of elephants, he (ग्रहवर्मा) as if made again darkness that was dissolved by the rise of the moon. Elephants are dark. नक्षत्रमालया मण्डितं मुखं यस्याः (with करिणीं and दिशम्). ग्रहवर्मा rode a female elephant whose head was decked with a necklace of 27 pearls. 'सैव नक्षत्रमाला स्यात्सप्तविंशतिमौक्तिकैः' इत्यमरः. निशा...रूढः as the moon had risen in the eastern quarter. पुरन्दर (इन्द्र) is the lord of the east, which also is decked with a line of stars (नक्षत्रमाला). See above p. 25. प्रकटितं विविधविहगानां विरुतं यैः (with ०चारणैः and उपवनैः). ताला...चारणैः क्रियमाणकोलाहलः the bards that danced to a particular time went before him and caused an uproar. बालः—ग्रहवर्मा was young. In वसन्त also the उपवनs resound with the chirping of various birds. गन्ध...लोकम् with the light of an array (चक्रवालं) of lamps, accompanied with the fragrance of perfumed oil poured on them (lamps), he rendered the whole world yellow, as if with a cloud of fragrant dust of saffron. उत्फुल्लानां मल्लिकानां (jasmine) मुण्डमाला (wreath) तस्याः मध्यं अध्यासितः कुसुमशेखरः यस्मिन् (with शिरसा). On his head he wore a wreath of jasmine, in the midst of which was a bunch of flowers. हसन्निव...प्रदोषम् he as if laughed at the moon-lit evening with its moon surrounded by a halo. सपरिवेशः क्षपाकरः यस्मिन्. The शेखर looked like the moon and the white wreath like halo. आत्मरूपेण निर्जितः (vanquished) मकरकेतुः (मदनः) तस्य करात् अपहृतेन. विरचितः वैकक्ष्यविलासः यस्य. वैकक्ष्यम् a garland worn over the left shoulder and under the right arm (like यज्ञोपवीत); hence a mantle. ग्रहवर्मा wore as an ornament a string of flowers on the left shoulder and under the other arm. He was more handsome than मदन. The bow of Cupid is flowery. A bow is also worn on the shoulder. By vanquishing मदन, ग्रहवर्मा took from his hand his flowery bow and wore it as a वैकक्ष्यक. The word कर suggests another meaning. One who is conquered has to offer tribute. कुसुमसौरभगर्वेण भ्रान्तं भ्रमरकुलं तस्य कलः प्रलापः तेन सुभगः (applies to both ग्रहवर्मा and पारिजात). As he had a garland of flowers bees hovered round him; they must have done so round पारिजात. पारिजात is one of the five trees of Paradise and was one of the 14 jewels churned out of the ocean. जातः श्रिया सह—ग्रहवर्मा had royal splendour from birth; पारिजात was produced (from the ocean) along with लक्ष्मी. पुन... मेदिनीम्—पारिजात was taken to Heaven when churned out and hence the words पुनः &c. नव...हृदयः—His heart was drawn by the curiosity to see the bride's face. One whose हृदय (*i. e.* the upper part of the body) is drawn forward may fall on his face. प्रत्यासन्नं (near) लग्नं यस्य. 'राशीनामुदयो लग्नम्' इत्यमरः.

P. 71 ll. 15-28 **राजा तु...प्रविवेश.** द्वारस्य समीपे उपद्वारम् (अव्ययीभाव). माधवः = वैशाखः (वसन्तः). यथाक्रमम्—ग्रहवर्मा embraced राज्यवर्धन first as the elder of the two. नृपतेः प्रणयी a favourite of the king. तात is often used as a term of address applied affectionately to any person, usually by a friend to a friend or by elderly persons to youngsters. राज्यश्रिया—(1) by राज्यश्री; (2) by royal glory. घटितौ goes with ०मुखरवंशौ. It was राज्यश्री who being married to ग्रहवर्मा brought about an alliance of the families of पुष्पभूति and मुखर. तेजोमयौ—applies to both सोम० and पुष्प०. सकलजगता गीयमानः बुधकर्णयोः आनन्दकारी गुणगणः ययोः—(1) whose many qualities, gratifying the ears of wise men, are sung by the whole world (with पुष्प०); (2) in which the many gratifying virtues of Mercury (बुध) and Karṇa are sung by the whole world (with सोम०). There is a further pun on the word गुण which also means 'threads, fibres' and वंश (bamboo). बुध was the son of the moon and कर्ण was the son of कुन्ती from the sun. सोम seduced तारा wife of बृहस्पति and did not give her back. Brahmâ returned Tārā to बृहस्पति. तारा was pregnant and at the command of बृ० discharged the गर्भ upon reeds. Both इन्दु and गुरु wanted the son. The gods asked तारा whose son he was, but she spoke nothing through shame. The new-born got angry, but ब्रह्मा intervened and drew from तारा the admission that he was the son of सोम, who said 'साधु साधु वत्स प्राज्ञोऽसीति बुध इति नाम चक्रे'. See विष्णु० IV. 6. The birth of कर्ण from कुन्ती when she was a maiden is well-known. आदिपर्व 64. 140 'सूर्याच्च कुन्तिकन्यायां जज्ञे कर्णो महाबलः । सहजं कवचं बिभ्रत्कुण्डलोद्द्योतिताननः ॥' (Kumbha. ed). प्रथममेव...देवस्य—the qualities of ग्रहवर्मा had already made a great impression on the heart of प्रभाकरवर्धन. The कौस्तुभ, one of the fourteen jewels churned from the ocean, is worn on his chest (हृदय) by Vishṇu. 'कौस्तुभाख्यमभूद्रत्नं पद्मरागो महोदधेः । तस्मिन्हरिः स्पृहां चक्रे वक्षोऽलङ्करणे मणौ ॥' भागवत VIII. The word is derived as 'कुं भुवं स्तुभ्नाति

व्याप्नोति इति कुस्तुभः समुद्रः तत्र भवः'. इदानीम्—now *i. e.* as a bridegroom. परमेश्वरेण = (1) शिवेन; (2) प्रभाकरवर्धनेन. Emperors had the titles परमेश्वर, महाराजाधिराज. See Introduction. S'iva has the moon on his head. A bridegroom is to be honoured by the father-in-law. समा...वेला the auspicious time (fixed for the marriage ceremony) approaches. कौतुकगृहम्—the house where the marriage thread (कौतुकं) is placed on the wrist of the bridegroom before the actual marriage ceremonies. Compare रघु० 8. 1. 'अथ तस्य विवाहकौतुकं ललितं बिभ्रत एव'. पतितानि—the eyes of women fell on him. The blue eyes resemble expanded blue lotuses. लङ्घयन् traversing, jumping over (the lotuses in the form of eyes).

P. 71 l. 29—**P. 72** l. 9 **अथ तत्र...पश्यत्.** The principal sentence is अथ तत्र...वधूमपश्यत्. कति...परिवाराम्—this and the following accusatives qualify वधूम्. कति...वाराम् who was attended by several relatives (आप्त), dear friends and her own people (*i. e.* servants), mostly women. अरुणं अंशुकं तेन अवगुण्ठितं मुखं यस्याः—whose face was veiled by a red silken cloth. The radiance of her face made the lamps pale before her. The radiant glow of morn also makes the lamps appear dim. अरुणः अंशुकमिव तेन अवगुण्ठितं मुखं यस्याः (प्रभातसन्ध्या)—the beginning of which is covered by Aruṇa that resembles a red silken garment. Or we may dissolve अरुणस्य अंशुकाः किरणाः &c. अति...गूढाम् The idea is that she was not a grown-up woman, but was almost a girl. A delicate substance if closely pressed may break. यौवन is fancied as afraid of hurting her by too close an embrace, as she was so delicate. साध्वसेन (भयेन) निरुध्यमानः (restrained) हृदयदेशः तस्मात् दुःखेन मुक्तैः—The sudden events of her marriage caused her heart to flutter and therefore she heaved sighs by way of relieving the pressure. निभृतायतैः secret and long. She tried to keep her emotion to herself. One who sorrows over anything heaves deep sighs. The sighs which she heaved for relief are fancied to be due to her lamenting her maidenhood that was leaving her. अत्युत्कम्पिनीं...धार्यमाणाम्—her heart was in a whirl of emotions; but she was kept motionless by bashfulness, as if through fear of her falling down. One who is trembling (in body) has to be supported (धार्यमाण) for fear of a fall. हस्तम् and शशिनम् are to be connected with अवलोकयन्तीम् (she was looking at her hand vacantly being absorbed in deep thought). ताम...पक्षं which was the rival of a red lotus *i. e.* her hand was red.

आसन्नं ग्रहणं यस्य the grasping of which (in marriage) was near ताम...पक्षम् (the moon) who is the enemy of red lotuses. आसन्नं ग्रहणं यस्य whose seizure (by Rāhu *i. e.* eclipse) was near. रोहिणी the favourite wife of the moon out of the 27 नक्षत्रs. भय...साम् —applies to both रोहिणी and वधू. रोहिणी would tremble at the approaching eclipse of her lord. चन्दनेन धवला तनुलता यस्याः. ज्योत्स्नादानेन सञ्चितं लावण्यं यस्य loveliness of which is accumulated by the gift of moonlight. कुमुदs thrive in moonlight. The inside of the कुमुदिनी would be white. कुसु...हारिणीम्—she (वधू) was spreading about the perfume of flowers. वसन्त is the season of flowers. निःश्वासपरिमलेन आकृष्टं मधुकरकुलं यया. Her fragrant breath drew round her a swarm of bees. मलयमारुत- the breezes from the Malaya Mountain are charged with the perfume of sandal. कृत...सरणाम् (1) who did what Love dictated (with वधूम्); (2) who was followed by Cupid *i. e.* मदन acted as his wife रति dictated; कृतं कन्दर्पेण अनुसरणं यस्याः (with रतिम्). The bride was as handsome and loving as रति, the wife of मदन. C and T translate 'love followed in the train of one who seemed a reborn Rati.' This is not correct. प्रभा...माधुर्यैः—these five are to be connected respectively with the five *Ratnas* 'कौस्तुभ...मृत.' अपरा...श्रियम् she was as if another श्री (लक्ष्मी) formed by the ocean out of wrath against the gods and demons. The author here mentions six out of the fourteen रत्नs churned out of the ocean. There is an emphasis on the word श्री. राज्यश्री can naturally be called श्री. अपराम्—this word is used because there was one already produced at the churning. The ocean, being a mine of jewels, can produce fresh ones though fourteen were already taken away by the gods and demons. The anger of the ocean is due to his being deprived of the *Ratnas*. स्निग्धेन...तंसाम् affectionate young maids (बालिका + लोक) made for her an ear-ornament with the rays of pearls as if with clusters of white सिन्धुवार flowers. सिन्धु- (न्दु) वार is a plant called in Marathi निगडी. स्निग्धेन...लोकेन may also mean 'by the glossy soft light' (॰आलोकेन). कर्णाभरणमरकतस्य प्रभा हरितशाद्वलं इव; ॰मरकतप्रभासदृशं हरितशाद्वलम्. कर्णा...च्छायाम् who as if removed (*i. e.* rendered imperceptible) the lovely (हारिणी) beauty of her eyes by her broad cheeks on which there fell the lustre of the emerald of her ear-ornament, resembling a green meadow. स्थली means a plot of ground. हारिणीं =हरिणसम्बन्धिनीम्. So the words suggest another sense 'who entertained the eyes of deer with a plot of ground covered with green grass' (resembling emerald). अधोमुखीं—through bashfulness she hung her head. कृतः मुखोन्नमनप्रयत्नः येन—her friends tried to raise her face; in her heart also she wished to raise her face (to see the bridegroom). वर...कुलम् her friends were absorbed in looking at the wonderful bridegroom; her heart fluttered to look &c. हृदयं निर्भर्त्सयन्तीम् she censured her heart for its cowardice in not succeeding in raising her face to see the bridegroom, though she so much desired to raise it.

P. 72 ll. 10-23 **प्रविशन्त...विभावसुः.** वध्वा समर्पितम् handed over (to cupid) by the bride. जग्राह कन्दर्पः Cupid seized him *i. e.* he became enamoured of the bride. A thief is handed over to proper custody and is held fast by the custodian. परिहासेन स्मेराणि (smiling) मुखानि यासाम्. अतिपेशलम् very cleverly. कृतः परिणयस्य (विवाहस्य) अनुरूपः वेशपरिग्रहः यया. जगाम—connect this with वेदीम्. ०धवलाम् and the following clauses in the accusative qualify वेदीम्. नव...धवलाम् (1) brilliant with fresh white-wash; (2) white like fresh chunam (with उपत्यकाम्). सुधा may, in the latter case, also mean 'nectar', which is also white. तुषारशैलस्य हिमालयस्य उपत्यका a land at the foot of a mountain. 'उपाधिभ्यां त्यकन्नासन्नारूढयोः' पा. 5. 2. 34 (संज्ञायामित्यनुवर्तते । पर्वतस्यासन्नं स्थलमुपत्यका आरूढं स्थलमधित्यका । सि. कौ.). भूभृद्भिः (1) by kings; (2) by mountains. सेक...दन्तुरैः that bristled with barley shoots that looked soft on account of the sprinkling of water. पञ्चास्यैः with five mouths. कोम...चित्रैः variegated with soft colours. अमित्रमुखैः—C and T translate 'gleaming around it were earthen dolls, whose hands bore auspicious fruits, and which had five-mouthed cups bristling with dew-besprent blades of barley and enemies' faces painted with soft colours.' So they think that the कलशs were in the hands of dolls. But one fails to see how the sentence yields this sense. We must connect कलशैः with उद्भासितपर्यन्ताम्. अमित्रमुखैः should be taken as an adjective of कलशैः (अमित्राः शत्रवः मुखे येषाम्). The idea seems to be this :— there were कलशs with barley blades that resembled दन्तs, the कलशs had a lion's shape, they were painted in various colours; hence the whole presented an awful aspect, so that the कलशs seemed to have some terrible enemies in them. अञ्जलिकारिका—a clay doll. 'स्यात्सालभञ्जिका स्तम्भे लेप्येनाञ्जलिकारिका' इति क्षीरस्वामी. C reads अमत्रमुखैः which means 'that had the mouth of a goblet'. This seems to be a suspicious reading adopted to obviate the difficulties of अमित्रमुखैः. उपाध्यायेन उपधीयमानानि (heaped, placed) इन्धनानि तेन धूमायमानः अग्निः तस्य सन्धुक्षणे (kindling) अक्षणिका

उपद्रष्टृद्विजाः यस्याम् (adj. of वेदीम्). उपद्रष्टृ means 'one who supervises.' अक्षणिक not having leisure, busy. कृशानोः (अग्नेः) समीपे इति उपकृशानु निहिताः अनुपहताः (new, not used) हरितकुशाः यस्याम्. संनिहितः दृषदां अजिनानां आज्यस्य स्रुचां (ladles) समित्पूलीनां (bundles of fuel sticks) निवहः यस्याम्. C reads स्रक् (garland) for स्रुक्; but it is not very appropriate in the context. नूतनशूर्पे अर्पिताः श्यामलशमीपलाशमिश्रिताः लाजाः (fried grain) तैः हसतीति हासिनीम्. The लाजs being white are spoken of as the हास of the वेदी. शमी is a sacred tree. पलाशं leaf. See रघुवंश VII. 26 'हविःशमीपल्लवलाजगन्धी पुण्यः कृशानोरुदियाय धूमः।'. कात्यायन says 'शमीपल्लवमिश्राँल्लाजानञ्जलिना वपति'. शूर्पः—र्पम् winnowing basket (Marathi सूप). सज्योत्स्नः—राज्यश्री resembled the light of the moon. See धर्मसिन्धु 'वधूवरौ पूर्वोक्तलक्षणां वेदीं मन्त्रघोषेणारुह्य &c.' समुत्ससर्प—connect this with 'शिखिनः (अग्नेः) समीपम्.' वेल्लिता...ल्लवस्य the red leaf-like flames of which were tremulous (with fire); the red flame-like leaves of which were tremulous (with रक्ताशोक). शिखिनः also may be applied to रक्ताशोक (it had a tapering foliage). कुसुमायुधः (कुसुमानि आयुधानि यस्य) इव—ग्रहवर्मा was handsome like मदन and राज्यश्री was like रति. रक्ताशोक is an excitant of love. In this sentence as well as in the preceding (आरुरोह तां दिवमिव), the author perhaps intentionally indicates the untimely death of ग्रहवर्मा. दक्षि...वृत्ताभिः that moved round to the right. Flames moving to the right are a good omen. ज्वालाभिरेव समं—the idea is :—the flames moved about; he also moved round the fire. नखमयूखैः धवलिता तनुः यस्य. When the bride let fall the oblation of parched grain into the fire from her hands, her brilliant nails brightened the fire. अदृष्टपूर्वं वधूवरयोः रूपं तेन विस्मयः तेन स्मेरः. Smile is white according to the poets; the brilliance of the nails transferred to the fire is the smile and the white लाजs are the teeth shown in smiling. For going round the fire and लाजहोम, see कुमारसम्भव VII. 80 'तौ दम्पती त्रिः परिणीय वह्निमन्योन्यसंस्पर्शनिमीलिताक्षौ । स कारयामास वधूं पुरोधास्तस्मिन्समिद्धार्चिषि लाजमोक्षम् ॥.' The आश्वलायनगृह्यसूत्र says 'वध्वञ्जला उपस्तीर्य भ्राता भ्रातृस्थानीयो वा द्विर्लाजानावपति' (I. 701). मेधातिथि on मनु० VIII. 227 remarks 'लाजहोममभिनिर्वर्त्य त्रिः प्रदक्षिणमग्निमावर्त्य सप्त पदानि स्त्री प्रक्रम्यते'.

P. 72 l. 24—**P. 73** l. 2 **अत्रान्तरे...वासगृहम्.** रुरोद वधूः—the bride wept because she was soon to be separated from her parents. स्वच्छ...यन्ती as if quenching the image of fire reflected inside her bright cheeks. स्थूलमुक्ताफलवत् विमलाः बाष्पबिन्दवः तेषां सन्दोहः (assemblage) तेन दर्शितं दुर्दिनं यया. दुर्दिनम् a rainy day. 'मेघच्छन्नेऽह्नि दुर्दिनम्' इत्यमरः. निर्वदनविकारम् without showing any emotion on her face. उदश्रु विलोचनं यासाम्. प्रविवेश—connect with वासगृहम्. द्वारपक्षे लिखितं रतिप्रीतिदैवतं यस्मिन् on the side of the door of which was painted Rati, the presiding spirit of Love. प्रणयि... कुलैः—the bees, drawn by the perfume of flowers, entered the वासगृह before ग्रहवर्मा and looked like his friends. अलि...काशितम्—the idea is:—the lamps began to flicker owing to the breezes set in motion by the bees; the poet fancies that they trembled because they were afraid of being struck with the कर्णोत्पल (by राज्यश्री in order to put them out). एकदेशे लिखितः स्तबकितः (having bunches of flowers) रक्ताशोकतरुः तस्य तलं भजतीति ॰भाक् तेन ॰भाजा. अधिज्यचापेन whose bow was strung. तिर्यक्कूणितः नेत्रत्रिभागः यस्य a third part of whose eye was obliquely contracted. Cupid is represented as having a squint eye to symbolize the fact that love is generally blind. काञ्चनाचामरुकेण is not quite clear. We should read 'काञ्चनाचामनकेन' (काञ्चन + आचामनकेन)—a golden spitting vessel. This latter is really the reading of B, as the MSS often confound च and व. Read दन्त॰ for दान्त॰. इतर... सनाथेन (शयनेन) bed that had on the other side a golden figure holding an ivory box, like Lakshmī herself having in her hand a lotus with a long stalk. The white ivory box resembled the white lotus and the golden figure was like लक्ष्मी. सोपधानेन with a pillow. स्वास्तीर्ण well covered with coverlets. कृता कुमुदैः कुमुदानां वा शोभा यस्य येन वा (1) that was decked with white lilies; (2) that gave beauty to the कुमुदs (with शशिना). The moon is the friend of love. See कुमारसम्भव IV. 13. राजतेन made of silver (and hence compared to the moon). निद्राकलशेन—auspicious jars were placed near the bed to ward off evil and to induce sleep. Compare कादम्बरी 'क्रमेण चोद्गते गगनमहापयोधिपुलिने सप्तलोकमङ्गलनिद्राकलशे कुमुदबान्धवे' (p. 178 of P.)

P. 73 ll. 3–9 **तत्र च...गमदिति.** प्रथमा...गवाक्षकेषु as if they were the faces of the family goddesses, (seen) in the jewelled lattice-windows, that had come out of curiosity to overhear the first words (of the bride and bridegroom). क्षणदाम् = निशाम्. अपुनरुक्तानि that were not monotonous. दत्त्वा...रणरणकम्—A door-keeper is always in attendance in a राजकुल; when ग्रहवर्मा went away, he left behind regret (in the heart of the members of the palace) at his departure. यौतक...लोकस्य taking with him the hearts of all people as the provisions for his journey offered to him as marriage gift. For यौतक, see above p. 52. शम्बलः—लम् पथिव्ययः (पाथेयम्). इति—shows the end of the उच्छ्वास.

Uchchhvāsa V

P. 74 Verse 1 नियतिः fate. Construe तरला नियतिः (विधिः) प्रथमं पुंसां सुखं विधाय उपरि (afterwards) दारुणं दुःखं निपातयति तरला (चञ्चला) तडित् (विद्युत्) इव आलोकं (light, flash) कृत्वा वज्रं निपातयति. This and the following verse are in the Āryā metre, for which see above p. 49. Both verses are suggestive of the misfortunes narrated in this Uchchhvāsa. Compare for the idea 'सुहृदिव प्रकटय्य सुखप्रदः प्रथममेकरसामनुकूलताम् । पुनरकाण्डविवर्तनदारुणो विधिरहो विशिनष्टि मनोरुजम् ॥' उत्तरराम॰ IV. 15.

Verse 2 सममेव—at one and the same time. अनादरेणैव without any qualm or regard. परिवर्तमानः revolving. अनन्तः—Time is without end. शैलान् परिवर्तमानः अनन्त इव (पातयति) as the serpent Ananta, moving (his hoods), makes the mountains fall. 'नागाः काद्रवेयास्तदीश्वरः । **शेषोऽनन्तः**' इत्यमरः. शेष has one thousand hoods, on which the earth is supposed to rest. It was believed that earthquakes occurred when शेष moved its hoods through weariness. See विष्णु॰ II. 5. 28 'यदा विजृम्भतेऽनन्तो मदाघूर्णितलोचनः । तदा चलति भूरेषा साद्रितोया सकानना ॥'.

P. 74 ll. 5–26 **अथ…तस्थौ.** राजा = प्रभाकरवर्धनः. कवचहरम्—of an age when he was fit to wear armour. कवचं हरतीति (affix अच्), acccording to 'वयसि च' पा. 3. 2. 10 (कवचहरः कुमारः । सि. कौ.). हूणान्—see p. 4 (notes). हरिः = सिंहः. प्रभाकर॰ is compared to the lion, राज्यवर्धन to a whelp and the Hūṇas to deer. चिरं…सारम् making him attended by advisers of long standing and devoted feudatories. अभिसारः companion, follower. अभिसारेण सह सा॰. उत्तरापथम्—to the north. This word is used in contradistinction to दक्षिणापथ. Here उत्तरापथ seems to stand for the Punjab and Kashmir, countries towards the north of Thanesar. But generally the word stands for northern India. *Vide* Introduction for the inscriptions of Pulikes'in, where हर्ष himself is styled the lord of उत्तरापथ. कतिचित्प्रयाणकानि for some marches *i. e.* stages. प्रविष्टे…भ्रातरि when his brother entered the region (ककुभ् *f.*) resplendent with the brilliance of कैलास. कैलास is one of the peaks of the Himālayas. निवर्तमानः (the reading of B) does not suit the words नवे वयसि that follow. विक्रम…रोधिनि (youth) that follows (acts according to) its liking for adventure. शरभ is a fabulous animal with eight legs and believed to be stronger than the lion. तुषारशैलस्य हिमाचलस्य उपकण्ठेषु

(confines, outskirts). उत्कण्ठमानाः वनदेवताः तासां कटाक्षाः तेषां अंशवः (किरणाः, प्रभा) तैः शारिता (variegated) शरीरकान्तिः यस्य. The nymphs of the forests were smitten by the handsome form of Harsha and cast glances at him. The dark pupils and the white of their eyes shed a dappled hue on his body. The word उत्कण्ठमान may also convey the idea that the वनदेवताs were anxious for the safety of the beasts of the forest. बहिरेव व्यलम्बत he tarried outside (the region of कैलास). C and T translate as 'away from camp'. आकर्णान्तं आकृष्टं कार्मुकं तस्मात् निर्गताः भासुराः (bright) भल्लाः तान् वर्षतीति °वर्षी. कर्मणे प्रभवतीति कार्मुकम् according to 'कर्मण उकञ्' पा° 5. 1. 103. भल्लः a crescent-shaped arrow. वास... यामे in the fourth watch of the night. वासतेयी—'पथ्यतिथिवसतिस्वपतेर्ढञ्' पा. 4. 4. 104 (पथि साधु पाथेयम् । आतिथेयम् । वसनं वसतिस्तत्र साधुः वासतेयी रात्रिः । सि. कौ.). It is believed that dreams seen in the small hours of the morning come to be true. चटुलानां (flickering) ज्वालानां पुञ्जेन पिञ्जरीकृताः (reddened) सकलककुभः येन (*adj*. of °हुतभुजा). दवहुतभुजा = दवदहनेन forest conflagration. The death of the lion and his mate suggest the death of Harsha's father and mother. यदाकृष्टाः—यत् refers to स्नेहमयाः °पाशाः. तिर्यञ्चः अपि even lower animals. Compare for the idea 'दारुभेदनिपुणोऽपि षडङ्घ्रिर्निष्क्रियो भवति पङ्कजबद्धः । बन्धनानि किल सन्ति बहूनि स्नेहरज्जुकृतबन्धनमन्यत् ॥'. दक्षिणात् इतरत्. The throbbing of the left eye in the case of men portends misfortune. विपप्रथे spread over. निर्निमित्तम् without any cause. अन्त...हृदयम् his heart as if went adrift (*lit.* moved) from its internal fastenings. गरीयसी very great (*f.* comparative of गुरु). दुःखासिका poignant despondency (दुःखं असिका इव). समुत्पन्नाः विविधाः विकल्पाः (doubts) तैः विमथिता मतिः यस्य. अपगता धृतिः (steadiness, composure) यस्य. स्तिमिता fixed, motionless) तारका यस्य. समुद्भिद्यमानं (shooting up) कमलिनीवनं (lotus-bed) यस्याम् (*adj.* of क्षौणीम्). He bent his lotus-like face in anxiety and looked fixedly on the ground. The poet fancies that his face was a lotus shooting forth from the earth (क्षौणी). चकोरेक्षणः—The eyes of a चकोर are red. Note कादम्बरी 'जरच्चकोरलोचनपुटपाटलकान्तिना' (p. 140 of P). Redness of the (corner of the) eye in men and women is a sign of beauty. आ...ह्नो when the sun had ascended to midday. हरिताः (greenish yellow) हयाः यस्य. The sun is called हरिदश्व. संवाह्यमानं तनु (small) तालवृन्तं (fan) यस्य. विततताम् spread. अतिशिशिरः मलयजस्य (चन्दनस्य) रसः तस्य लवेन लुलितं (touched) वपुः (frame) यस्याः (*adj.* of पट्टिकाम्). इन्दुवत् धवलं उपधानं (pillow) धारयतीति. वेत्रपट्टिका cane couch.

P. 74 l. 27—**P. 75** l. 8 **अथ...द्राक्षीत्.** The principal sentence is अथ दूरादेव...०दीर्घाध्वगं कुरङ्गकनामानं आयान्तं अद्राक्षीत्. लेखः गर्भे यस्याः. नीलीरागेण (indigo colour) मेचका (blue) रुक् (कान्तिः) यस्याः. चैल...मालकम् whose head was encircled by the hems of a garment. The messenger carried the letter in a piece of cloth which he wrapped round his head. This is the practice of illiterate messengers even now. The reading of A 'चीरचीरिकया' would suggest that he wore rags on his head. This would be too much for a royal messenger. C and T suggest that the colour symbolizes the bad news. This may be so; or it was probably his uniform. आरोप्यमाणः कायकालिमा यस्य. कालिमन् *m.* (काल + affix इमन्) is formed according to 'पृथ्वादिभ्य इमनिज्वा' 'वर्णदृढादिभ्यः ष्यञ्च' पा. 5. 1. 122–123 (चादिमनिच्। शौक्ल्यम्, शुक्लिमा। सि. कौ.). शोकः...नीयमानम्—the poet fancies that the darkness of body due to fatigue and exposure to the sun is due to the fact that he was being reduced to charcoal by the fire of sorrow. अति...गम्यमानम्—on his body there was dust raised by his rapid walking; the poet fancies that under the guise of dust it was the earth that followed him to learn the news about the king, her lord. अभिमुखः (beating on his face) पवनः तेन प्रेङ्खन् (waving about) प्रविततः (spread) उत्तरीयपटः तस्य प्रान्तेन (hems) वीज्यमानौ उभयपार्श्वौ यस्य. अति...पतन्तम् who approached quickly, having as if winged himself because he was in a great hurry. His upper garment waved about his flanks owing to the strong breeze blowing in his face and thus he looked as if he was winged. प्रेर्य...देशेन—The poet fancies that the quick pace of the messenger was due to the fact that he was urged from behind by his master's command. स्विद्यत् ललाटतटं तस्मिन् घटमानं (being formed) प्रतिबिम्बं यस्य (*adj.* of भास्वता). क may optionally be added at the end of all बहुव्रीहि compounds. कार्य...भास्वता whose letter was if snatched by the sun out of curiosity to know the business (on which he was sent). संभ्रम... शरीरम्—His senses were not working normally; his only thought was to walk quickly; the poet fancies that he left them behind in his haste to depart. गौरव (1) Importance; (2) weight. One who has a large weight on his head may stumble. समेऽपि वर्त्मनि on an even road (without ups and downs). काल... वज्रस्य—The idea is:—first a cloud rises in the sky and then the thunderbolt falls; so the messenger (who was also dark like the cloud owing to fatigue and exposure) appeared first and would afterwards disclose the bad news. धूम...ज्वलनस्य—Before fire is kindled, there is a cloud of smoke, which is dark; the messenger also was dark and was in a short time to kindle the fire of sorrow in हर्ष. बीज...शाले: he was as if the paddy seed of sin that was about to bear friut. There are some varieties of paddy seed that are dark. अनि...ध्वर्गम् a messenger that had become an evil omen.

P. 75 ll. 9–18 **दृष्ट्वा...प्रावर्तत.** पूर्वनिमित्तपरम्पराभिः आविर्भाविता भातिः यस्य. The reference is to his dream narrated on p. 19 of the text. प्रथम...लेखम् he first presented the dejection reigning (*lit.* sticking to) in his looks and then the letter. The idea is that before he presented the letter, his face told the whole tale. लेखा...सन्तापम्—there is a pun on the word गृहीत्वा, the idea being that he understood the contents of the letter and at the same time his heart was seized by affliction. अवग्रहरूपः—who was drought incarnate. This is not a very appropriate word. The reading 'आविग्नरूपः' of one of the MSS of B is good. It means 'whose face was dejected.' किं मान्द्यम् what is the illness? खञ्जाक्षरैः क्षरद्भिः with halting words that flowed from him. युगपत्—the idea is:—his eye, his tears, face and faltering voice, all conveyed the same tale. पफाल *perfect* of फल् to burst. कृतं आचमनं येन. Before beginning religious ceremonies, before and after meals and before and after doing many other acts, it was enjoined that a man should sip water. 'स्नात्वा पीत्वा क्षुते सुप्ते भुक्त्वा रथ्योपसर्पणे। आचान्तः पुनराचामेद्वासो विपरिधाय च॥' याज्ञ. I. 196. जन...ष्कामः desiring the long life of his father. परिबर्हः royal insignia, property. 'परिच्छदे नृपार्हेऽर्थे परिबर्हः' इत्यमरः. अभुक्तः एव who had not taken food. दापय...र्याणम् put the saddle on the horses. शिरःकृपाणम् a sword against his own forehead (by way of saluting). This is the object of बिभ्राणं, which qualifies युवानम्. परिवर्धकः groom. प्रावर्तत he started to go.

P. 75 ll. 19–32 **अकाण्ड...निशाम्.** अकाण्ड...क्षुभितं excited (startled) by the sudden (blowing of the) conch, which was the signal for a march. उद्धूतः मुखरः खुररवः तेन भरितं सकलभुवनविवरं येन (*adj.* of अश्वीयम्)—that filled all the world with the resonant tramp of the horses' hoofs. अश्वीयम्—अश्वानां समूहः—(cavalry) according to 'केशाश्वाभ्यां यञ्छावन्यतरस्याम्' पा. 4. 2. 48 (पक्षे ठगणौ। कैश्यम्, कैशिकम्। अश्वीयम्, आश्वम्। सि. कौ.). ढौकृ *1st A* to approach. प्रद...यान्तः going in the direction opposite the right one. प्रदक्षिणं means 'towards the right side, so that the right side is always turned towards the object that is circumambulated'. उपस्थितं that had approached. राजसिंहस्य—the poet says that the passing of the deer to the left of हर्ष (who was a lion among kings) was a precursor of misfortune. If deer pass the lion without circumambulating him (*i. e.* without showing respect to him), that indicates that the lion's fall is near. In the कादम्बरी we read that the passing of the deer to the right of women is an ill omen 'प्रस्थितामिवानभीष्टदक्षिणवातमृगागमनाम्' (p. 218 of P). In the case of men it must be the left and so we have 'प्रदक्षिणेतरम्' (adverb). Similarly in the गाथासप्तशती we read 'एक्को वि कालसारो ण देइ गन्तुं पहाइणवलन्तो' I. 25. अशिशिररश्मिः सूर्यः. हृदयम्—supply हर्षस्य. The cry of the crow is an evil omen. See बृहत्संहिता 95.19 'ऐन्द्यादिदिगवलोकी सूर्याभिमुखो रुवन् गृहे गृहिणः। राजभयचोरबन्धनकलहाः स्युः पशुभयं चेति ॥' and also 'एकचरणोर्कमीक्षन् विरुवंश्च पुरो रुधिरहेतुः' 30. For female jackals howling towards the sun, see रघु. II. 61. बहुदिवसम् (*acc.* of time) is to be connected with उपचित in the following समास. शिखिपिच्छा (tail of the peacock) लाञ्छनं (characteristic mark) यस्य. The Jain ascetics carry peacock feathers to sweep insects out of their path. नग्नाटकः a naked Jain ascetic (दिगम्बर). क्षीरस्वामी says 'भिक्षुः श्वेतः श्वेतपटः क्षपणर्षिर्दिगम्बरः । नग्नाटः श्रावकोऽह्रीको निर्ग्रन्थो जीवजीवकौ ॥'. In the मुद्राराक्षस Act IV the sight of a क्षपणक is said by अमात्यराक्षस to be an evil omen. 'लुञ्चिताः पिच्छिकाहस्ताः पाणिपात्रा दिगम्बराः' सर्वदर्शनसंग्रह (आर्हतदर्शन). पितृस्नेहेन आहितः म्रदिमा यस्मिन् (*adj.* of हृदयेन). For म्रदिमा (from मृदु) see notes above p. 68. on कालिमन्. तत्तदुपेक्षमाणः thinking about this and that. The reading उत्प्रेक्षमाणः of some MSS of B is much better. तुरङ्गमस्कन्धे बद्धं लक्ष्यं यस्य (*adj.* of चक्षुः). दुःसमवसिते हसितं सङ्कथा च येन who painfully brought to an end all laughter and talk. बहु...ध्वानम् a journey that was made up of many योजनs. What particular distance was covered by a योजन is a point on which there has been much divergence of opinion. Various scholars have taken it to be from 4½ miles to ten miles. उपलब्धा नरेन्द्रमान्द्यस्य वार्ता तेन विषण्णे (dejected). One who is dejected loses all spirit (तेजः) and bends down his face. In the evening the sun also lost its lustre (तेजः) and hung down on the western horizon. This is fancied to be due to sorrow at the news of the king's illness. पुरः प्रवृत्ताः प्रतीहाराः तैः गृह्यमाणा ग्रामीणपरम्परा तया प्रकटितं प्रगुणं वर्त्म यस्य to whom the best way (to reach the capital) was shown by troops of villagers that were secured by waiters who marched ahead. वहन्नेव निशाम् he passed the night riding.

P. 75 l. 33—**P 76** l. 20 **अन्य...इति.** The principal sentence is अन्यासन्नहांने मध्यन्दिने...स्कन्धावारं समाससाद. विगताः जयशब्दाः यस्मात्—bards were in the habit of uttering the words 'जय जीव' &c. in the presence of the king. See text p. 4. l. 12. But as the king was on his death-bed all this was stopped. This and the following words in the accusative qualify स्कन्धावारम् (capital). अस्त...नादम् not a drum was heard. अप्रसारितानि आपणे पण्यानि यस्मिन् in which merchandise was not exhibited (for sale) in the market. पवन...श्लिष्यमानम् that (capital) was rubbed by the waving streaks of the smoke of कोटिहोम, that (streaks) were twisted into curls by the force of the wind and which were as if the tips of the horns of Yama's buffalo. The curly smoke of the *Homa* performed for the welfare of the king is fancied to be the twisted horn of the buffalo of यम. यम rides a buffalo. As the king was on his death-bed, Yama comes in here very appropriately. कोटिहोम was a kind of offering into fire. वराहमिहिर prescribes it against दिव्योत्पातs. 'दिव्यमपि शममुपैति प्रभूतकनकान्नगोमहीदानैः । रुद्रायतने भूमौ गोदोहात् कोटिहोमाच्च ॥' बृह० 46. 6. कृतान्त...वेष्ट्यमानम्—As the city was lying under a cloud of smoke, the poet further fancies that it was encircled by the cords of Yama's net. उपरि...शुभम्—troops of crows roamed about and cawed. This portended approaching evil *i. e.* death here. The black crows resembled small bells of iron (कालायसं). It is usual to tie bells round the necks of buffalos and bulls. क्वचित्—क्वचित् and अन्यत्र—अपरत्र mean 'in one place—in another place.' प्रतिशायिताः स्निग्धबान्धवाः तैः आराध्यमानः अहिर्बुध्नः (शिवः) यस्मिन्. अहिब्रध्न also means the same. प्रतिशायित is one who lies down before a deity without food in order to secure some desired object. See कादम्बरी 'कृष्णाजिनप्रावृताङ्गैः कुरङ्गैरपि **प्रतिशयितै**रिव ... आराध्यमानाम्' (p. 226 of P). दीपिकाभिः दह्यमानाः कुलपुत्रकाः तैः प्रसाद्यमानं मातृमण्डलं यस्मिन्. For the divine Mothers, see above p. 26. The idea seems to be this:—the young nobles did not burn their limbs with lamps; they rather kept lamps on their heads to propitiate the Mothers and now and then had their skin burnt by accident. Even now worshippers of अम्बिका are in the habit of placing lamps on their heads and reverently going round the idol. Compare कादम्बरी 'ज्वलितलोहितमूर्धरत्नरश्मिभिः कृष्णसर्पैरपि शिरोधृतमणिदीपकैरिवाराध्यमानाम्' (p. 226 of P). मुण्डोपहाराहरणे उद्यतः द्रविडः तेन प्रार्थ्यमानः आमर्दकः यस्मिन्—where a man from the द्रविड country was soliciting the Vampire by being ready to bring an offering of a skull. द्रविड included the tract of the country from the Tungabhadrā to the Coromandel coast and had काञ्ची as its capital. On आमर्दक the Com. says 'आमर्दको वेतालो रौद्रदेवताभेद इत्यन्ये'. बाण refers to the offerings of skulls to चण्डिका, who was worshipped by an old द्रविडधार्मिक 'फलितामिव मुण्डमण्डलैरुपहारहिंसां दर्शयन्तीम्' (p. 224 of P). आन्ध्रेण उद्धियमाणः बाहुवप्रः तेन उपयाच्यमाना चण्डिका (दुर्गा यत्र) where Chaṇḍikā was being promised a present with his rampart-like arm raised up by a person from the Andhra country. बाहुः वप्रः इव. अन्ध्र corresponds pretty closely with modern Telingana and lay between the mouths of the गोदावरी and the कृष्णा. उपयाचनं is the same as नवस (in Marathi). शिरसि विधृतः विलीयमानः (melting) गुग्गुलुः (a kind of fragrant gum resin, गुग्गुळ in Marathi) तेन विकलाः नवसेवकाः तैः अनुनीयमानः महाकालः यस्मिन्. महाकाल is a name of शिव in his character as destroyer of the world. There is an emphasis on the words विकल and नव. Old servants would have gone through anything for the king without showing the least sign of pain; but new servants felt distressed even when hot gum slightly scorched their heads. निशिता शस्त्री (knife) तया निकृत्तं (cut off) आत्ममांसं तस्य होमे प्रसक्तः (engaged in) आप्तवर्गः यस्मिन्. प्रकाशं (openly) नरपतिकुमारकैः क्रियमाणः महामांसविक्रयस्य प्रक्रमः (beginning) यत्र. महामांसं human flesh. The शाक्त rites prescribed the offering of such horrible things. 'अष्टम्यां रुधिरैर्मांसैर्महामांसैः सुगन्धिभिः। पूजयेद्बहुजातीयैर्बलिभिर्भोजनैः शिवाम् ॥' शब्द०. It was believed that by resorting to such disgusting rites a person would attain miraculous powers or objects otherwise difficult to secure. महामांस was offered to पिशाचs also who, it was believed, would become the helpers of the man offering it in anything. See मालतीमाधव V. 12 and the comment of जगद्धर thereon. यातु... ध्वस्तम् as if rendered desolate by fiends. 'यातूनि यातनाः धीयन्ते अस्मिन्' क्षीरस्वामी on 'यातुधानः पुण्यजनो नैर्ऋतो यातुरक्षसी' इत्यमरः. कवलित devoured. अधर्म...लुण्ठितम् as if plundered by the movements of unrighteousness. अनित्यतया धिक्कारः. अनि...क्रान्तम् overpowered by the slights (heaped on it) by transitoriness. Everybody felt the transitoriness of human existence. नि...कृतम् that was subdued by the workings of fate. विलक्षितम् bewildered. छलितम् cheated. प्रविश...ददर्श—the principal sentence is प्रविशन् एव विपणिवर्त्मनि (on the market-street) परलोकव्यतिकरं कथयन्तं ०पट्टिकं ददर्श. कुतूहलेन आकुलाः बहलाः बालकाः तैः परिवृतम् (*adj.* of ०पट्टिकं). ऊर्ध्व... तते stretched out on a support (विष्कम्भः) of upright rods.

प्रेतनाथः = यमः. व्यतिकरम् incidents. इतर...कलितेन held in the other hand. In the left hand was the painted canvas and in the right a reed. शरकाण्ड: reed-stalk. यमपट्टिकं—see above p. 45 (notes).

P. 76 l. 21—**P. 77** l. 10 **तेन...कक्ष्यान्तरम्.** तेन = श्लोकेन. प्रतिषिद्धः सकललोकप्रवेशः यस्मिन्. अप्रसन्नः मुखरागः यस्य who had a dejected look (*lit.* the colour of whose face was not clear). उन्मु...द्रियैः who was as if left by his senses. अपि...न वा does father feel better to-day or not? यदि भवेत् there may be. मन्दं...विवेश—the principal sentence is मन्दं मन्दं...राजकुलं विवेश. ०सर्वस्वम्—this and the following clauses qualify राजकुलम्. प्रारब्धा अमृतचरुपचनक्रिया यत्र. चरुः is an oblation of rice or barley boiled for presentation to the gods. अमृतचरु perhaps means that milk or ghee was poured over it. क्रियमाणः षडाहुतिहोमः यस्मिन्. The Com. explains "'प्रजापतये स्वाहा' इति षण्णां देवतानां नाम गृहीत्वा षण्णामेवाहुतीनां प्रक्षेपः षडाहुतिहोम उच्यते." The six देवताs appear to be प्रजापति, सोम, अग्नि, इन्द्र, द्यावापृथिवी and धन्वन्तरि. हूयमानाः पृषदाज्यलवेन लिप्ताः प्रचलाः दूर्वापल्लवाः यस्मिन्. पृषदाज्यम्—Ghee mixed with coagulated milk. 'पृषदाज्यं सदध्याज्ये' इत्यमरः ('पृषद्भिः दधिबिन्दुभिः सहितमाज्यम्' क्षीरस्वामी). पठ्य...विधानम्—this is a curious compound. It contains three separate elements. पठ्यमाना महामायूरी यस्मिन्, प्रवर्त्यमाना (begun) गृहशान्तिः यस्मिन्, निर्वर्त्यमानं भूतरक्षाबलिविधानं यस्मिन् (where the offering of oblations for protection against evil spirits was being performed). What the author refers to as महामायूरी is not quite clear. From the context it seems to be a prayer. Among the Buddhists महामायूरी is the name of one of the five amulets and of one of the five tutelary goddesses. शान्ति means 'a propitiatory rite for averting calamity.' प्रयतैः पवित्रैः विप्रैः प्रस्तुतः (begun) संहिताजपः यस्मिन्—holy Brahmins had begun the recitation in a low voice of the Saṃhitā text of the Vedas. This is the practice even now. 'पवित्रः प्रयतः पूतः' इत्यमरः. जप्यमाना रुद्रैकादशी तया शब्दायमानं शिवगृहं यत्र where the temple of S'iva resounded with the low repetition of the hymn to Rudra. The reference seems to be to what is popularly known as रुद्र, which is a prayer in 11 अनुवाकs addressed to रुद्र. Great merit is supposed to result from repeating that prayer 11 times or 121 times. सायण in his comment on the रुद्रभाष्य quotes the वायुपुराण 'रोगवान्पापवांश्चैव रुद्रं जप्त्वा जितेन्द्रियः । रोगात्पापाद्विनिर्मुक्तो ह्यतुलं सुखमश्नुते ॥'. अतिशुचिशैवैः सम्पाद्यमानं विरूपाक्षस्य (शिवस्य) क्षीरकलशसहस्रैः स्नपनं यस्मिन् where the image of S'iva was being bathed with thousands of milk jars by very holy devotees of शिव. क्षीराभिषेक is even now resorted to to propitiate Rudra. शिव is called विरूपाक्ष because of his third eye. अजिरो०—connect this and the following instrumentals with नरपतिभिः below. अजिरं courtyard. अनासादितं (not obtained) स्वामिनः (प्रभाकरवर्धनस्य) दर्शनं तेन दूयमानानि मानसानि येषाम्. अभ्यन्तरात् निष्पतिताः (coming out) निकटवर्तिनः परिजनाः तैः निवेद्यमाना वार्ता (news of the king's condition) येभ्यः. वार्ता...शयनैः to whom bathing, eating and sleeping had become mere news *i. e.* 'who knew these only in name, who did not bathe, eat or sleep as the king was seriously ill. उज्झितः आत्मसंस्कारः तेन मलिनः वेशः येषाम् whose clothes were dirty because they had abandoned the toilet of their bodies. लिखितै...श्लैः who were motionless as if drawn in pictures. नीयमाननक्तन्दिवम् where night and day were passed. दुःखेन दीनानि वदनानि यस्य—connect this word with बाह्यपरिजनेन (p. 22. l. 6). प्रघ...मण्डलेन who were sitting in a circle in the porches before the palace-gate. The servants, not being intimately connected with the royal household, were sitting outside. 'प्रघाणप्रघणालिन्दा बहिर्द्वारप्रकोष्ठके' इत्यमरः. 'अगारैकदेशे प्रघणः प्रघाणश्च' पा. 3. 3. 79. उपांशुव्याहृतैः in whispered conversations. The servants that were outside assigned various causes for the sad plight of the king. There is a touch of humour in this description. केन...वयता some one (among the servants sitting outside) laid bare the errors on the part of doctors. असाध्य... पठता one recited passages containing the symptoms of incurable diseases. Diseases are generally classified into three classes, साध्य, दुःसाध्य and असाध्य. केन ... वृण्वता one expounded the story of a demon (as being at the root of the king's ailment). कार्तान्तिकादेशान् the prognostications of astrologers. कृतान्तं (दैवं) वेद इति कार्तान्तिकः (कृतान्त + ठक्). उपलिङ्गानि portents. अनित्य... लभमानेन one was revolving in his mind the transitoriness of life, was condemning this (everchanging) world, censured the wantonness of the Kali age and found fault with fate. धर्माय कुप्यता—he was angry with धर्म, because the latter could not do anything for such a righteous king as प्रभाकर०. क्लिष्ट...गर्हयता one censured the ill-luck of the noble youths that were afflicted. कथ्यमाना कष्टा पार्थिवावस्था यस्मिन्. विविधौषधिद्रव्याणां द्रवः (juice, exudation) तस्य गन्धः गर्भे यस्य (adj. of कक्ष्यान्तरम्). उत्क्वथतां...जिघ्रन् smelling the odour of boiling decoctions, of butter and oils that were being heated. कक्ष्या inner court. The रामायण (अयोध्या 20. 11-12) shows that the third कक्ष्या was set apart for the queen and her confidential attendants.

P 77 l. 11—**P. 78** l. 35 **तत्र...द्राक्षीत्.** The principal sentence is तत्र च...धवलगृहे स्थितं (p. 23 l. 1)...देव्या यशोमत्या शिरसि वक्षसि च स्पृश्यमानं पितरमद्राक्षीत्. अतिनिःशब्दे—this and the following clauses in the locative qualify धवलगृहे (p. 23 l. 1). गृहावग्रहणीग्राहिणः बहुवेत्रिणः यत्र where many door-keepers stood in the vestibule. 'गृहावग्रहणी देहली' इत्यमरः. गृहावग्रहणी the threshold. त्रिगुणया तिरस्करिण्या तिरोहितः सुवीथीपथः यस्मिन्—where the way to the inner part of the house was shut off (from view) by a triple screen. वीथी is गृहप्रान्त according to क्षीरस्वामी. पिहितानि पक्षद्वारकाणि यस्मिन् where the private entrances were shut. 'प्रच्छन्नमन्तर्द्वारं स्यात्पक्षद्वारं तु पक्षकः' इत्यमरः. पिहित *past p. p.* of धा with अपि with the initial अ dropped, according to 'वष्टि भागुरिरल्लोपमवाप्योरुपसर्गयोः।'. परिहृतं कपाटरटितं यस्मिन् where the creaking of the panels was avoided. घटितैः (united, closed) गवाक्षैः रक्षितः (prevented) मरुत् (gust of wind) यस्मिन्. चरणताडनेन स्वनत् (rattling, creaking) सोपानं (staircase) तेन प्रकुपिताः प्रतीहाराः यस्मिन्. When some one ascended the staircase in a noisy way, the doorkeepers got angry with him for fear that his action might disturb the ailing king. निभृताभिः (noiseless) संज्ञाभिः (signs) निर्दिश्यमानानि (indicated, ordered) सकलकर्माणि यस्मिन्. कञ्चुकिन् a person wearing armour. कञ्चुकः or कञ्चुकः breast-plate 'उरश्छदः कञ्चुकको जगरः कवचोऽस्त्रियाम्' इत्यमरः. कोणस्थितः आह्वानैः चकितः आचमनवाही यस्मिन् in a corner of which stood a servant bearing the bowl for rinsing the mouth, who was bewildered by numerous calls. चन्द्रशालिकायां लीनः मूकः मौललोकः यस्मिन्. For चन्द्र० see p. 21 above. मौलः an old or hereditary minister. मूलं प्रतिष्ठा तदस्ति अस्य इति मौलः. महान् आधिः (distraction of mind) तेन विधुरः (helpless) बान्धवाङ्गनावर्गः तेन गृहीतं प्रच्छन्नप्रग्रीवकं यस्मिन्. प्रग्रीवं or-कं a painted turret, window. सञ्जवनम् quadrangle, court formed by four houses on four sides 'सभा सञ्जवनं त्विदम्। चतुःशालम्' इत्यमरः. प्र ... णयिनि to which only a few friends (or favourites had been admitted). दुर्मनायमान *pr. p.* of दुर्मनायते, denominative verb from दुर्मनस्. मन्दायमानः (languishing) पुरोधाः (पुरोहितः) यस्मिन्. सीदन्तः (sinking into despair) सुहृदः यत्र. विद्राणाः (kept awake, without sleep) विपश्चितः (पण्डिताः) यत्र. सन्तप्ताः आप्ताः (trusted) सामन्ताः यस्मिन्. विचित्ताः (vacant-minded) चामरग्राहिणः यस्मिन्. दुःखेन क्षामाः (emaciated) शिरोरक्षिणः (body-guard) यस्मिन्. क्षीयमाणा प्रसादवित्तानां मनोरथसम्पद् यस्मिन् where the fulfilment (सम्पद्) of the desires of those that were (the king's) favourites was vanishing. प्रसादैः वित्तः ख्यातः. स्वामिभक्त्या परित्यक्तः आहारः यैः ते स्वामि...हाराः हीयमानबलाः विकलाः (faint) वल्लभभूभृतः यस्मिन्. क्षितितले पतिताः सकलरजन्यां जागरूकाः

राजपुत्रकुमारकाः यस्मिन् where the young Rajputs, that had watched during the whole night, were lying on the ground. कुलक्रमागतैः कुलपुत्रकैः उह्यमाना शुक् (शोकः) यस्मिन्. Separate ०शुचि and शोक०. निरानन्दाः (joyless) बन्दिनः (court bards) यस्मिन्. 'स्युर्मागधास्तु मगधा बन्दिनः स्तुतिपाठकाः' इत्यमरः. निःश्वसन्तः निराशाः आसन्नसेवकाः यस्मिन्. निःसृतं ताम्बूलं यस्मात् स निःसृतताम्बूलः अत एव धूसरः अधरः यासां ताः निःसृत... धराः, ०धराः वारयोषितः (dancing girls) यस्मिन्. विलक्षैः (bewildered) वैद्यैः उपदिश्यमानं पथ्यं (wholesome diet) तस्य आहरणे (fetching) अवहितः (attentive) पौरोगवः यस्मिन्. पौरोगवः superintendent of the royal kitchen. 'रसवत्यां तु पाकस्थानमहानसे । पौरोगवस्तदध्यक्षः' इत्यमरः (on which क्षीरस्वामी says 'पुरो गौर्मांसं वा जलं वास्याः सा पुरोगुस्तस्याः रसवत्याः अयं पौरोगवः). अनुजीविभिः पीयमानं उच्चषकं (उत्क्रुष्टः चषकः यस्मिन्) धारावारि तेन विनोद्यमाना आस्यशोषरुक् यस्मिन् where the pain due to dryness of mouth was removed by streaming water drunk by attendants without cups. The attendants were working hard and felt thirsty. It is common experience that thirst is allayed much more quickly if one pours a stream of water into the mouth than if one holds the cup to the lips. C and T translate 'attendants were drinking streams of water from uplifted cups in order to distract the pain of the king's dry mouth'. We cannot understand how the king's dry mouth would have been relieved if the servants drank water. So also the words of the Com. 'उच्चषकमपगतपानभाजनम्' do not mean 'empty cups'; but rather 'without a cup'. We think that the context requires that it was the king that was thirsty and *not* the servants. So we suggest that we should read पाय्यमान for पीयमान and then the meaning would be 'where the pain of the dry mouth (of the king) was removed by streams of water without cups which he was made to drink by the attendants'. The reading of B and C 'उच्चचषक' is not bad. It means that the water was poured from a cup held high up and not from a cup applied to the lips. राजाभिलाषेण (at the king's desire) भोज्यमानाः बहुभुजः (gluttons) यत्र. Or the meaning may be 'gluttons were fed with the food which the king desired but which he could not himself eat'. भेषजसामग्रीसम्पादने व्यग्राः समग्राः व्यवहारिणः (merchants) यस्मिन्. मुहुर्मुहुः आहूयमानः तोयकर्मान्तिकः (waterman) तेन अनुमिता घोरा आतुरस्य (रोगार्तस्य) तृट् यस्मिन्. कर्मान्तिकः a servant. तुषारेण परिकरितः करकः तस्मिन् शिशिरीक्रियमाणं उदश्वित् यस्मिन् where buttermilk was being cooled (frozen) in jars that were covered in ice. उदश्वित् *n* (उदकेन श्वयति) buttermilk that contains 50 per cent water. 'तक्रं ह्युदश्विन्मथितं पादाम्ब्वर्धाम्बु निर्जलम्' इत्यमरः on which क्षीरस्वामी says 'द्विगुणाम्बु श्वेतरसमर्धोदकमुदश्वितम्। तक्रं त्रिभागभिन्नाम्बु केवलं मथितं स्मृतमिति धन्वन्तरिः'. The frozen buttermilk was probably applied to the burning feet and head of the feverish king. श्वेतार्द्रे कर्पटे (piece of cloth) अर्पिताः कर्पूरस्य परागाः (रेणवः) तेन शीतलीकृता शलाका (a collyrium stick) यस्मिन्. The stick treated with camphor powder was to be applied to the eye to produce a cooling effect. नाश्यानेन (न + आश्यानेन) पङ्केन लिप्यमानं नवं भाण्डं (vessel) तद्गतं गण्डूषग्रहणाय मस्तु (sour cream, whey) यस्मिन्. We expect अनाश्यान; probably अ was elided in the MSS after °शलाके. आश्यान means 'dried' and so नाश्यान would mean 'wet'. The cool whey was probably required for relieving the dryness of the mouth of the patient who used it as a gargle from time to time. 'मण्डं दधिभवं मस्तु' इत्यमरः. तिम्यन्ति (wet) कोमलानि कमलिनीपलाशानि (lotus-leaves) तैः प्रावृताः मृदुमृणालकाः यत्र. सनालानि नीलोत्पलानि तेषां पूली (bundle) तया सनाथा (possessed of) सलिलपानभाजनभूः यत्र. The lotus leaves, fibres and flowers were all intended to produce a cooling effect. धारानिपातैः निर्वाप्यमाणं क्वथिताम्भः यस्मिन्—boiling-water was being cooled by being poured in streams (from vessel to vessel). Water first boiled and then cooled is given to a patient for drinking. पटु (sharp) पाटलशर्करायाः आमोदः तं मुञ्चतीति °मुच् तस्मिन् that emitted the sharp odour of pale-red sugar. मञ्चकाश्रिता (resting on a stand) सिकतिला (sandy) कर्करी (jar) तस्मिन् विश्रान्तं आन्तरचक्षुः यस्मिन्. It is difficult to explain what आन्तरचक्षुः means. We must read with the two MSS of B 'आतुरचक्षुः'. The eye of the ailing king rested upon a porous jar. The sight of water trickling from the porous jar had a soothing effect. For सिकतिल, see notes on सैकत p. 30. सरसेन शैवलेन वलयितं (अत एव) गलत् गोलयन्त्रकं यस्मिन् where there were globes dripping because they were surrounded by wet water-plants (moss). गल्वर्कशालाजिरे उल्लासिताः लाजसक्तवः यस्मिन्—where there were parched grain and barley-flour spread in a crystal platter. Separate °सक्तुनि and पीत°. क्षीरस्वामी says 'गल्वर्कोऽपि स्फाटिके पात्रेऽयं रूढः'. For शालाजिर, see above p. 54. The fried grain was used as light food for patients. पीता (yellow) मसारपारी (emerald cup) तस्यां परिगृहीता कर्कशर्करा (white sugar) यत्र. It is better to omit पीत with some of the MSS of B. C and T translate 'a paste of flour and curds was held in a yellow emerald cup.' शिशिरैः औषधरसैः चूर्णैः च अवकीर्णः स्फटिकशुक्तिशङ्खसञ्चयः यस्मिन्. Crystal, mother-o'pearl and conches are all cool to the touch. प्राचीनामलक myrobalans.

सुश्रुत (सूत्रस्थान chap 46) gives a long list of the fruits usually eaten. प्राचीनामलक (also called वारिबदर) had the effect of removing the three दोषs (वात, पित्त, कफ) and poison 'गरदोषहरं नीपं प्राचीनामलकं तथा' सु० 46. 158. मातुलुङ्ग citron (Marathi महाळुंग). प्रतिग्राहितैः (that were made to accept presents) विप्रैः विप्रकीर्यमाणाः शान्त्युदकस्य विप्रुषः (बिन्दवः) यस्मिन्. विप्रुष् *f.* drop. शान्त्युदकम् soothing or propitiatory water. प्रेष्याभिः पेष्यमाणः (being pounded) कल्काटलेपः तेन उपदिग्धा दृषद् (stone) यस्मिन्. पर...ज्वलनेन (father) round whom lustration was performed by the fire of fever for the conquest of the next world. राज् with निस् 'to perform the ceremony called नीराजन'. नीराजन was a military and religious ceremony performed by kings and generals in the month of आश्विन before they took the field; mantras were repeated and lights waved. Here fever is the fire and the king was about to proceed to the next world. Compare 'तस्मै सम्यग्घुतो वह्निर्वाजिनीराजनाविधौ । प्रदक्षिणार्चिर्व्याजेन हस्तेनेव जयं ददौ ॥' रघु. 4. 25. अनव...चेष्टमानम् who tossed on a bed waving (*i. e.* uneven) with his ceaseless rollings like the serpent S'esha (rolling) on the Milky Ocean on account of the fever of poison. तरङ्गिणि (1) that has waves (with उदन्वति); (2) that has wavy curls (on the bed). The bed had white coverlets and so resembled क्षीरसागर. The king was suffering from a fever (ऊष्मन्); शेष has poison in his hoods. The king was pale through serious illness and resembled the white-yellow शेष. मुक्ता...धवलितम् (1) who was made white with the dust of pearl-powder (with the king); (2) that was white with pearls and the grains of sand (with जलधि). Pearls are supposed to have a cooling effect. Pearls are found in the ocean and on its shores there is white sand. क्षयकाले शुष्यन्तम् (1) who had become withered at the time of death; (2) that dries up at the time of universal destruction (with जलधि). क्षय = प्रलय. 'संवर्तः प्रलयः कल्पः क्षयः कल्पान्त इत्यपि' इत्यमरः. A कल्प is a period of 1000 महायुगs (कृत, त्रेता, द्वापर and कलि constitute one महायुग). It is equal to a day of ब्रह्मा, the night also being of the same duration. At the end of a कल्प the whole universe (including the ocean) is destroyed. Compare भगवद्गीता 'सहस्रयुगपर्यन्तमहर्यद् ब्रह्मणो विदुः । रात्रिं युगसहस्रान्तां तेऽहोरात्रविदो जनाः ॥ अव्यक्ताद् व्यक्तयः सर्वाः प्रभवन्त्यहरागमे । रात्र्यागमे प्रलीयन्ते तत्रैवाव्यक्तसंज्ञके ॥' VIII. 17-18. For a description of कल्पान्त see विष्णुपुराण VI. 3 and 4. 'उदकावरणं यत्तज्ज्योतिषा पीयते तु तत् । ज्योतिर्वायौ लयं याति यात्याकाशे समीरणः ॥' विष्णु० VI. 4. 31. कालेन (1) by death

(with the king); (2) by the dark-coloured (दशानन). All Rākshasas are represented as dark. The king had the pallor of death and resembled the snowy कैलास. On one occasion रावण when travelling in the पुष्पकविमान near कैलास was stopped by नन्दी saying that शिव wanted to be in privacy there. Thereupon रावण in arrogance caught hold of कैलास and shook it. When पार्वती became afraid by the motion of the mountain, शिव in anger pressed the mountain with his toe and रावण's arms were crushed underneath and he began to scream. See रामायण VII. 16 for the story. 'पुष्पकस्य गतिश्छिन्ना यत्कृते मम गच्छतः । तमिमं शैलमुन्मूलं करोमि तव गोपते ॥ 23...एवमुक्त्वा ततो राम भुजान्विक्षिप्य पर्वते । तोलयामास तं शीघ्रं स शैलः समकम्पत ॥' 25. Compare कादम्बरी 'कैलासश्रियमिव दशमुखोन्मूलनक्षोभनिपतिताम्' (p. 129 of P). अविरत...स्पृश्यमानम्—the palms of the hands of the attendants were white with the sandal-paste with which they smeared his body. The poet fancies that the palms were white because they were reduced to ashes by touching the burning limbs of the king. Ashes are white. अत्युष्णावयवस्पर्शेन भस्मीभूतं उदरं येषां (*adj.* of करैः). Take away the comma after ०प्रस्थितम् and place it after स्पृश्यमानम्. लोका ... पृच्छ्यमानम् — The king was about to depart this world. When a person goes on a journey those that stay bid him farewell. The poet fancies that under the guise of the white sandal ointment, it was his spotless fame that embraced him and bade him a last farewell. Both sandal and fame are white. स्थास्नु (1) that remains on the body (with अनुलेपन); (2) remaining on the earth (यशः). There is a further suggestion. His fame would be everlasting (स्थास्नु) and not evanescent. अविच्छिन्नं (ceaselessly) दीयमानानि कमलकुमुदेन्दीवरदलानि यस्मै. Lotus petals have a cooling effect. कमलs are rosy, कुमुदs are white and इन्दीवर is blue. His body when covered with petals of various colours looked variegated. काल...शबलम्—Death was approaching him. The pupil of the eye is dark, the corner is red and the rest of the eye is white. There is a similar idea above. निबिडेन (tight) दुकूलपट्टेन निपीडिताः केशान्ताः तैः कथ्यमानः कष्टवेदनानां अनुबन्धः (continuity) यस्य. His head was bound tight with silk cloth because he was suffering from ceaseless headache. दुर्धरवेदनाभिः उन्नमत् (standing up) नीलशिराजालकं तेन करालं तेन (*adj.* of ०फलकेन). A net-work of dark veins due to unbearable pain stood up on his forehead. These the poet fancies to be the lines drawn by the fingers of Death representing the days that remained to him on the earth. In counting we draw lines on a board (फलकं) with our fingers. कालाङ्गुलिभिः लिख्यमानाः लेखाः ताभिः आख्यातं मरणावधिदिवससंख्यानं येन. अन्तःप्रविष्टा तारका यस्य the pupil of his eye had become contracted and dim owing to failing strength. The poet fancies that it was due to his agitation at the sight of approaching death. A person who is frightened by a terrible sight closes his eyes. शुष्यन्ती दशनपङ्क्तिः तस्याः प्रसृताः धूसराः (grey) दीधितयः तैः तरङ्गिणीम्. He heaved hot breaths that were mixed with ripples of grey rays from his dry teeth. Mirage (मृगतृष्णिका) is also उष्णा (due to heat) and presents waves (तरङ्गिणी). निवेद्यमानः दारुणसन्निपातस्य आरम्भः यस्मिन्. He had a dark tongue, which indicated that he was in the stage of सन्निपात. सन्निपात is the combined derangement of the three humours of the body (वात, पित्त and कफ) and is fatal. The योगरत्नाकर (आनन्दाश्रम ed p. 98) gives the general symptoms of सन्निपातज्वर, one variety of which called तन्द्रिक is described as 'प्रभूता तन्द्रार्तिर्ज्वरकफपिपासाकुलतरो भवेच्छ्यामा जिह्वा पृथुलकठिना कण्टकवृता ।'. The poet fancies that the tongue was dark because it was burnt up by his very hot breaths. उरः...कान्तं—मणि and the other things were placd on his chest to produce a cooling effect. When a person of position pays a visit, it is usual to appear in one's best dress and to put on jewels &c. Take away the comma after ०युगलम्. अङ्ग... युगलम् who tossed up his arms in putting his limbs into various contortions (through agony). When he tossed up his arms, rays flashed from his nails; the rays resemble streams of water. So the poet fancies that he constructed with the rays of his nails a showerbath for तापशान्ति. नेदिष्ठ—superlative of (अन्तिक) very near. His reflections fell in water, jewelled pavements, and mirrors, all of which are cool to the touch. The poet fancies that he entered inside them (as reflection) for their cooling effect. स्पृशन्तीं goes with मूर्च्छां and प्रणयिनीं. He welcomed a swoon when it came over (स्पृशन्ती) him, because it was a source of relief. मूर्च्छा is compared to प्रणयिनी (beloved wife), who touches her husband and is a source of comfort to him. The reading विश्राम० is much better than विश्वास०, as the latter cannot be well construed with मूर्च्छा. अरिष्टैराविष्टम् overwhelmed with very bad symptoms (of death). अरिष्ट also means 'crow'. The cawing of crows is an evil omen and may be looked upon as the summons of death. 'तक्रे मरणचिह्ने चारिष्टं वृक्षे च फेनिले । सुराणां च शुभेऽपि

स्यात्काके निम्बे च पुंस्ययम् ॥' quoted by क्षीरस्वामी. महाप्रस्थान—the great journey *i. e.* death. At his approaching death, anguish seized the hearts of relatives. The words प्रस्थान and सन्तान (1 continuity; 2 offspring) suggest another idea. When a man starts on a journey, he transfers (*i. e.* entrusts) to the care of his relatives his children. छायया मुच्यमानम् who was bereft of brilliance (of body). He was languid and had lost his bright complexion. The poet fancies that छाया had left him through jealousy, as he was wedded to अरति. अरतिः langour. उद्योग...द्रवाणाम् who was the effort of all (bad) symptoms, or supervenient diseases. The idea is that all bad symptoms had concentrated themselves on him. सर्वास्त्र...तयाः Emaciation had let fall all her missiles on him. हस्तीकृतं=वशीकृतम्. विहस्ततया by helplessness. विगतः हस्तः यस्य स विहस्तः तस्य भाव ०ता तया. विषयी...क्षयेण misery had made him its province, wasting had made him its field. गोचरीकृतम्=विषयीकृतम्. दुःखासिका—दुःखमासते अस्यामिति or दुःखमस्तिका इव—dejection. अस्वास्थ्यम् restlessness, anxiety. विधेयीकृतं made a servant *i. e.* brought under control. क्रोडः the chest; क्रोडीकृतम् embraced. लक्ष्यीकृतं made a target. दक्षिणाशया—the south is presided over by Yama. जग्ध devoured (*past p. p.* of अद् to eat). निगीर्ण swallowed (*past* P. P. of गृ with नि). वैवर्ण्यम् (विवर्णस्य भावः) loss of colour, paleness. गात्रभङ्गः *lit.* breaking of limbs *i. e.* stiffness of body. वण्ट् *1 P.* to divide. लुण्ठ्यमान being robbed. आदित्सितं (*past p. p.* of the desiderative base of दा with आ) desired to be seized. निरूपितं marked, observed carefully. अभाव death, destruction. परिकलितम् grasped all round. परासुता death. दत्तः अवकाशः येन who made room for. वैमनस्यम् (विमनसः भाव) mental depression. समीपे—connect this and the following locatives with वर्तमानम् below. अन्ति...च्छ्वासस्य who was near the last breath. मुखे...प्रवासस्य at the beginning of the great journey *i. e.* dying. Compare महाप्रस्थान above. The reading महाप्रयासस्य is not so good. जीवितेशः=यमः. विरलं वाचि broken in words. चलितं चेतसि shaken in mind. प्रचुरं प्रलापे profuse in incoherent speech. अनु...बन्धिकाभिः constantly followed by pains in the joints. Com. 'अनुबन्धिका गात्रसन्धिपीडाः' According to the मेदिनी, अनुबन्धी means 'hiccough' 'अनुबन्धी तु हिक्कायां तृष्णायामपि योषिति.' This meaning is preferable. अनवरतरोदनेन उच्छूने (swollen) नयने यस्याः (*adj.* of यशोमत्या). गृहीता चामरिका यया. गृहीत...वीजयन्त्या who fanned the king with her sighs alone, though she held a chowrie in her hand.

P. 79 ll. 1–18 **दृष्ट्वा च...थेति.** प्रथम...मतिः whose mind was overwhelmed by the first shock of sorrow. आ...भवत् he became as if afraid of fate. भागधेयेभ्यः is ablative. निरा...सीत् for a moment he was as if given up by his mind *i. e.* he became dazed. अव...धैर्येण discarded by steadiness. रिक्ती...रत्या he was made empty by delight *i. e.* there was not the least trace of gayness left in him. विषमविष terrible poison. तमसा...विशेषयन् excelling even Pātāla in darkness. पाताल as the haunt of demons is supposed to be dark. शून्यत्वे...शयानः excelling even space in its vacancy. His mind became a void. For the शून्यत्व of आकाश, compare above (text p. 2 l. 1) 'आकाशमयः शून्यतायाम्'. नाविन्दत कर्तव्यम् he did not know what to do. पस्पर्श...गाम् his heart came in contact with terror and his head with the earth. The idea is that his heart became extremely apprehensive for his father's life and he bowed low before his father (as a son should do). सा अवस्था यस्य सः तदवस्थः who was in that (terrible) condition. निर्भरेण स्नेहेन आवर्जितः influenced by deep affection. प्रधावमानः मनसा—being enfeebled, his body could not run, though his mind ran towards his son. शरी...गात् he rose from the couch with the upper part of his body. विन...न्नमय्य having raised him who bent through dutifulness. विशन्निव...मध्यम् as if plunging into the midst of the moon's disc. At the sight of his darling son, the king felt as much relief as he would have if he had plunged &c. The following clauses also suggest the cooling or comforting effect which the sight of his son produced upon the king in his burning fever. स्नाप...प्रस्रवणे as if wetting himself in a stream of Harichandana juice. हरिचन्दनः is a kind of very fragrant and yellow sandal. 'तैलपर्णिकगोशीर्षे हरिचन्दनमस्त्रियाम्' इत्यमरः (on which क्षीरस्वामी says 'हरेरिन्द्रस्य चन्दनं, हरि कपिलं वा, तच्चातिशीतलं पीतमाहुः'). तुषाराद्रिः = हिमालयः. कपोलेन...घट्टयन् rubbing his cheek against the cheek (of हर्ष). निमील...लोचने closing his eyes that let fall incessant tears that formed on the tips of his eyelashes. पक्ष्माग्रे ग्रथितं अजस्रं अस्रं तत् विस्रवति इति ०स्राविन्. He closed his eyes and shed tears through joy. विस्मृतः ज्वरस्य सञ्ज्वरः सन्तापः येन. अप...स्कारम् who drew aside and then bowed low. प्रणता जननी येन. For क see above p. 31. विगतः निमेषः यस्मात् सः वि...मेषः, ०मेषश्चासौ निश्चलश्च. क्षयेण क्षामः कण्ठः यस्य whose throat was parched by exhaustion. कृच्छ्रात् with difficulty. तृतीय...स्याद्य to-day is the third day since he took food.

P. 79 l. 19—**P. 80** l. 4 **तच्छ्रुत्वा ... करवाणीति.** बाष्पवेगेन गृह्यमाणानि अक्षराणि यथा स्युः the words being choked by the flow of tears. आयतं निःश्वस्य heaving a deep sigh. ईदृशेषु in such (times or calamities). विधुरयति—विधुरं करोति (denominative verb from विधुर)—renders helpless. सर्वप्रमाथी that overpowers everybody. यतः wherefore. नार्ह...दातुम् you will please not give yourself up to extreme sorrow. निशितं sharpened. तक्ष्णोति 5th conj. P. of तक्ष् to pierce. तनिमा emaciation (from तनु with the affix इमन्). See notes p. 68 on कालिमा. परलोकश्च—A son was supposed to free by his birth the father from a hell called Put. 'पुत्रेण लोकाञ्जयति पौत्रेणानन्त्यमश्नुते। ...पुन्नाम्नो नरकाद्यस्मात्त्रायते पितरं सुतः। तस्मात्पुत्र इति प्रोक्तः स्वयमेव स्वयम्भुवा ॥' मनु० 9. 137–138. A omits परलोकश्च and this seems better from one point of view. The next sentence is 'यथा...प्रजानाम्'. In this last, the word प्रजानां is well-connected with प्राणाः in the preceding (यथा मम प्राणाः त्वयि स्थिताः तथा सर्वासां प्रजानां प्राणाः त्वयि स्थिताः). The idea is that the subjects love you so much. With the reading परलोकश्च it is possible to say that Harsha would be a very righteous emperor and keep the people in the path of righteousness and enable them all to attain Heaven. But there is another difficulty. As सुखं and राज्यं are co-ordinated with प्राणाः, we expect स्थितानि. If however it be said that the predicate agrees with the last word, then we must have स्थितः (with the reading परलोकश्च). अकलुषस्य कर्मणः—of spotless actions *i. e.* meritorious actions. कर...लक्षणानि the marks on your body indicate that the sovereignty of the four oceans is as it were in your hand. For the लक्षणs of an emperor, see above p. 20. त्वज्ज...स्मि by your birth alone I attained all my ends. निर...जीवितव्ये I have no desire to live (longer). भिषजाम् अनुरोधः acting according to the wishes of the physicians. Mark the two accusatives माम् and औषधम् with पाययति (causal of पा to drink). सर्वप्रजापुण्यैः उत्पत्स्यमानानाम्—for the idea see above. उत्पत्स्यमान—future participle of पद् with उद् (meaning 'desiring to be born'). प्रजाभि...ज्ञातिभिः—in their subjects and not in their kindred do kings have their relatives. For a converse statement of this fine sentiment, compare शाकुन्तल VI 'येन येन वियुज्यन्ते प्रजाः स्निग्धेन बन्धुना। स स पापादृते तासां दुष्यन्त इति घुष्यताम् ॥'. कृता...पथ्यम् when you have taken your meal, I shall myself also take my diet. अस्य=हर्षस्य. धक्ष्यन् about to burn (future participle of दह्). सन्दुधुक्षे—*perfect* of धुक्ष् with सम् I A to be kindled. अकाण्डे *Adv.* all of a sudden. महाप्रलयः great destruction *i. e.* great calamity. व्यभ्रः इव वज्रपातः like a bolt from a cloudless sky. विगतं अभ्रं यस्मात्. For this idea, see above text p. 2. 'अनभ्रवृष्टिरिव वैदग्ध्यस्य'.

सामान्योपि शोकः even a common sorrow. The construction is 'सामान्योऽपि शोकः सोच्छ्वासं मरणं किमुत विशेषाश्रितः शोकः'. सोच्छ्वासं मरणम् (a common sorrow) is a living death. Sorrow is equal to death except that breathing continues in sorrow, while in death there is no breathing. अनु...व्याधिः (sorrow) is a serious disease without there being any medicine prescribed for it. अनुपदिष्टं औषधं यस्य. अ...प्रवेशः it is a leap into fire without being reduced to ashes. अनुपरत not dead. नरकवासः—a person abides in Hell after death. But sorrow causes the torments of Hell though a man be not dead. नि...वर्षम् it is a rain of charcoal without fire. Charcoal is produced by fire (*i. e.* by kindling wood). अश...दारणम् it is sawing with a saw without cutting into pieces. अन्न...पातः the stroke of a diamond needle without a (visible) wound. किमु...श्रितः (if a common sorrow is a living death &c.), then what words will describe a sorrow of a special sort (of a deeper kind)?

P. 80 ll. 5–19 **राज...आवेदयितास्मीति.** धूम...पातान्—this and the following clauses are to be connected with कवलान् (l.7). धूम... पातान् (mouthfuls) that made him shed tears as if they (कवल) were made of smoke. While partaking of food, he wept over them. Smoke causes tears in the eyes. So the mouthfuls are fancied to be धूममय. Explain the following clauses similarly. अग्नि...दाहान् that produced burning in his heart, as if they (mouthfuls) were made of fire. जनितः हृदयदाहः यैः. दत्तः मूर्च्छावेगः यैः That brought on swoon. Poison also produces a swoon. उत्पादिता घृणा (disgust) यैः. **'जुगुप्साकरुणे घृणे'** इत्यमरः. महापातकs are five. 'ब्रह्महत्या सुरापानं स्तेयं गुर्वङ्गनागमः। महान्ति पातकान्याहुः संसर्गश्चापि तैः सह ॥' मनु० 11. 54. क्षार...वेदनान् that caused pain as if they were made of corrosive substances. अगृहीतं ताम्बूलं येन without taking the betel. As he was in grief he discarded betel. उत्ताम्यता मनसा with a distressed (or faint heart). अस्ता...सवितरि when the sun was about to set (lit. was desirous of setting). उपह्वरे in private. 'रहोऽन्तिकमुपह्वरे' इत्यमरः. पुनः...पितरम् you will hear that your father is again restored to his original condition (प्रकृति). The physicians outwardly say that Harsha's father will be restored to health. But the words प्रकृति and श्रोष्यसि suggest another sense, which is 'your father will be merged in the supreme spirit from which he came or his body will be reduced to the five elements out of which it was created'. Death is natural to all beings and life is an accident. **'मरणं प्रकृतिः शरी-**

रिणां विकृतिर्जीवितमुच्यते बुधैः' रघु० 8. 87. The five भूतs (पृथ्वी, अप्, तेजस्, वायु and आकाश) are the प्रकृति of all bodies. पौनर्वसवः a descendant of पुनर्वसु or one who studies the science of medicine promulgated by पुनर्वसु. According to the चरकसंहिता (सूत्रस्थान I) Indra taught आयुर्वेद to भरद्वाज who instructed several sages of whom पुनर्वसु was one. पुनर्वसु imparted it to his pupils, अग्निवेश and five others, each of whom composed a work on आयुर्वेद. चरक edited what अग्निवेश had composed. 'अथ मैत्रीपरः पुण्यमायुर्वेदं पुनर्वसुः। शिष्येभ्यो दत्तवान् षड्भ्यः सर्वभूतानुकम्पया ॥' verse 29. अष्टा...देशीयः—for देशीय see notes p. 38. अष्टाङ्गस्य—The science of medicine is said by सुश्रुत to have eight parts *viz.* (1) शल्य (surgery), (2) शालाक्य (diseases of the eye, ear and other parts of the head), (3) कायचिकित्सा, (4) भूतविद्या, (5) कौमारभृत्यं (rearing up of children), (6) अगदतन्त्रं (antidotes), (7) रसायनतन्त्रं, (8) वाजीकरणतन्त्रम्. See सुश्रुत सूत्रस्थान Chap. I. 6–7. आयुर्वेद is an उपवेद of the अथर्ववेद. 'आयुरस्मिन् विद्यते अनेन वा आयुर्विन्दतीत्यायुर्वेदः' सुश्रुत सूत्रस्थान I. 14. सुत...लालितः cherished on the same footing as a son. पटीयसी *f.* comparative of पटु. सास्रः (अस्रेण सह, बहुव्रीहि) shedding tears. कथय...पश्यसि tell me the truth, if you perceive any thing evil (about the king's illness). यथा...यितास्मि I shall inform you (of the facts) as they are. Mark the first future आवेदयितास्मि. The young man by his profound study of the science of medicine understood that the king would not live for more than day.

P. 80 ll. 20–34 अत्रैव...नैषीत्. भवन...पालः the keeper of the palace lotus beds. कोकमाश्वासयन् encouraging or comforting a ruddy goose. 'कोकश्चक्रश्चक्रवाको रथाङ्गाह्वयनामकः' इत्यमरः. It should he remembered that Harsha called together the doctors in the evening (text p. 25 l. 10). In the evening the चक्रवाक becomes separated from its mate. For अपरवक्त्र, see notes p. 17. C and T read 'अपरवक्त्रा.' आस्स्व...वर्त्मनि remain in the path of discernment. सह...विरोचनः the sun mounts (resorts to) the top of Meru together with the glory of the beds of lotuses. सरोजिनी may mean 'bed' or 'lake' (compare the use of पुष्करिणी). 'पुष्करादिभ्यो देशे' पा. 5. 2. 135 (पुष्करिणी। पद्मिनी। सि. कौ.). कमल fades (*i. e.* its glory departs) when the sun sets. 'मेरुः सुमेरुर्हेमाद्री रत्नसानुः सुरालयः' इत्यमरः. All the planets were supposed to revolve round the fabulous mountain Meru. See व्यासभाष्य on योगसूत्र III. 25 'सप्तद्वीपा वसुमती यस्याः सुमेरुर्मध्ये पर्वतराजः...तस्य सूर्यप्रचाराद्रात्रिन्दिवं लग्नमिव वर्तते'. See also रघु० VII. 24. The verse suggests that the king (who was resplendent,

विरोचन) was going to Meru (heaven) together with his fair wife (the mother of Harsha). वा...ज्ञः who was proficient in the prognostications of words. क्षता (destroyed) धृतिः (courage) यस्य. तत्र च...नैषीत्—the principal sentence is तत्र च...एवंप्रायान् पितुरालापान् अनवरतं (ceaselessly) आकर्णयन्...निशां अनैषीत्. हारान्—pearl necklaces are cool. Notice that in this and the following clauses there is a charming resemblance of sounds between the names of the ladies addressed and the words in which they are called upon to do something for the king. मणि... वैदेहि—Vaidehî ! place jewelled mirrors on my body. धन...क्षि Dhavalākshî ! place (on me) the dust of the powder (क्षोदः) of camphor (घनसारः). 'अथ कर्पूरमस्त्रियाम् । घनसारश्चन्द्रसंज्ञः सिताभ्रो हिमवालुका' इत्यमरः ('घनस्येव सारोऽस्य शैत्यात् सिताभ्रत्वाच्च' क्षीरस्वामी). चन्दनचर्चा smearing the body with sandal. पाटय...मारुतम् cleave asunder (*i. e.* cause movement) the wind with a cloth. He wants her to cause a breeze with a piece of cloth. The Com. remarks 'पाटय पटुं कुरु'. But this it not necessary. Remove the comma after इन्दुमति and place it after अरविन्दैः. जलार्द्रा a fan wetted with water. मल्लिनाथ on शिशुपालवध I. 65 paraphrases जलार्द्राणां as 'जलोक्षिततालवृन्तानाम्'. But the अभिधानचिन्तामणि says 'जलार्द्रा क्लिन्नवाससि'. Compare कादम्बरी 'जलदेवताभिरिव सद्यःस्नातार्द्रचिकुरहस्ताभिरुपगृहीतसुरभिकोमलजलार्द्रिकाभिः' (p. 283 of P). Hence the meaning 'wet cloth' is preferable. तरलय make unsteady *i. e.* move. मूर्धानं...बधान bind my giddy (*lit.* running) head. उरसि...कुरु place on my chest the hand with spray. 'शीकरोऽम्बुकणाः स्मृताः' इत्यमरः. नैति निद्रा sleep does not come (to my eyes). अनैषीत् *Aorist* of नी.

P. 81 ll. 1–23 **उषसि ... तिष्ठत्.** भ्रातुरागमनार्थम्—It should be remembered that राज्यवर्धन had gone to vanquish the Hūṇas. उपर्युपरि one after another. क्षिप्र...ध्वगान् couriers that ran quickly. प्रज...पालान् swift camel-riders. परिजनेन उपनीतम् (brought, presented). प्रतिकर्म personal decoration, toilet. 'प्रतिकर्म प्रसाधनम्' इत्यमरः. विगतं मनः येषाम् (bewildered). अव्यक्तम् indistinct. किं रसायनः what about र० ? अनुबध्यमानाः pressed, importuned. प्लुष्ट...स्तापेन as if scorched by an inner fire. उत्पाट्यमानम् torn up by the roots. कामं...जनः A high-born (अभिजातः) person would indeed cease to exist himself rather than convey like an ordinary (इतरः) man words that are unwelcome and distressing (अरतिकर). कृच्छ्रे in a calamity. उज्ज्वली...मस्य his noble birth naturally blessed has been rendered more brilliant by his entering fire like gold. कल्याणा (blessed, lovely) प्रकृतिः यस्य (applies to कार्तस्वर and कौलपुत्र). Gold also by being heated in fire becomes more brilliant. कुलपुत्रस्य भावः कौलपुत्रम्. कृतस्वरः आकरः तत्र भवं कार्तस्वरं हेम. किमस्य...तातः was not my father his father? अन्य...लोके in this world even when other (*i. e.* ordinary) masters are taken away (*lit.* become rare), life that is sustained becomes a cause for shame (to the servant). अमृत...जीविनाम् who was like nectar to his dependents. निर्व्याजबान्धवे who was their kinsman without any cause (disinterested). अवन्ध्यः (fruitful) प्रसादः (favour) यस्य. सांप्रतम् *adv.* properly. किं वा...दह्यते or what is burnt of him who is full of glory and abides firmly to the end of the world? आकल्पम्—कल्पं मर्यादीकृत्य (अव्ययीभाव). For कल्प see above p. 78. स्थेयस् is the comparative of स्थिर. ममापि...प्रतिष्ठन्ते As for me, what is that very important work, what is that unperformed task, what is the preoccupation (व्यापृतता) of my life, so that it, cruel as it is, does not yet start off? कृतात् शेषः. अन्तरायः obstacle. उत्तरीय...गुण्ठ्य having wrapped himself together with the head by his upper garment.

P. 81 . l. 24—p. 27 l. 3 इत्थंभूते...महोत्पाताः. सर्वस्य लोकेस्य—these words are to be connected with all the locatives from कपोलेषु to हृदयेषु. सर्वस्य...कराः the hands of all people seemed as if rivetted (कीलित) to their cheeks. One who is in deep sorrow or thought sits resting his cheek upon his hand. Compare 'वामहस्तोपहितवदना' in शाकुन्तल IV. The people grieving for प्रभाकरवर्धन remained in that position so long that it seemed that their cheeks and hands were nailed together. लोचने...स्रुतयः streams of tears seemed as if plastered to their eyes. लेप्यं plaster or cement. Plaster or cement sticks to the object to which it is applied and cannot be easily removed. Tears were to be constantly seen in the eyes of the people. ग्रथिताः tied, fastened. उत्कीर्णाः engraved. Engravings are permanent. हाकष्टानि the words 'Oh! alas!!'. लपने...श्वसितानि sighs were twisting themselves like foliage on their mouths (लपन). They incessantly sighed. परि...पदानि words of lamentation. निधानीकृतानि treasured or stored up. उष्णाश्रु...निद्रा sleep came not to the hollows of their eyes, as if afraid of being scorched by the hot tears. निःश्वास...हासाः—no one smiled; the poet fancies that smiles vanished being thrown away by the wind of sighs that the people constantly heaved. निर...वाणी speech did not go on (*i. e.* no one talked anything) as if burnt by सन्ताप without leaving any remainder. सन्तापः (1) heat, (2) sorrow. कथास्व... हासाः—Not only no body cracked jokes, but nobody even told a tale containing jokes. गीतगोष्ठयः people assembled to hear music. गोष्ठी an assembly. जन्मान्तरातीतानि—what was experienced in a former life, no one remembers. लास्यानि—see notes p. 28. प्रसाधनानि decorations of the person, such as flowers &c. ख...मण्डलानि convivial parties at taverns became like sky—flowers *i. e.* absolutely non-existent. खपुष्प is an emblem of what is absolutely non-existent. Such emblems are summarised in the following verse 'एष वन्ध्यासुतो याति खपुष्पकृतशेखरः । मृगतृष्णाम्भसि स्नातः शशशृङ्गधनुर्धरः ॥'. बन्दिवाचः the words of court bards. Mark the words 'विगतजयशब्दम्' (text p. 20 l. 33). युगान्त...वृत्तयः pleasures seemed to belong to another Yuga as it were. पुन...केतुः—Kāma was once burnt by S'iva; see p. 38 above. But now at the approach of the king's death, all love-making in the world came to an end through grief. महा... पिशुनाः indicative of the fall of a great man. 'पिशुनौ खलसूचकौ' इत्यमरः. भूपतेरभावाय—is to be connected with समुदभवन्. Mark the dative. The result indicated by a portent is put in the dative, according to the वार्तिक 'उत्पातेन ज्ञापिते च' (वाताय कपिला विद्युत् । सि. कौ.). We may construe भयमुत्पादयन्तो भूतानाम् (causing terror to all beings) or भयमुत्पादयन्तो भूतानां महोत्पाताः great portents of the five elements (पृथिव्यप्तेजोवाय्वाकाश) causing fear. The महाभारत divides portents into three classes *viz.* दिव्य, आन्तरिक्ष and भौम. 'उत्पातांस्त्रिविधान्प्राह नारदो भगवानृषिः । दिव्यांश्चैवान्तरीक्षांश्च पार्थिवांश्च पितामह ॥' सभापर्व 46. 7-8. See also बृहत्संहिता 46. 2.

P. 82 ll. 4–26 **तथाहि...निशाम्.** तथाहि for instance. In the Rāmâyaṇa (अरण्य० 23) and in the महाभारत (वनपर्व 179; विराट० chapters 39 and 46; उद्योग 84) there are long lists of उत्पातs. For want of space it is not possible to quote them. But they seem to have been the source of Bāṇa's inspiration. दोलायमानं (swinging) सकलकुलाचलचक्रवालं यस्याः. The कुलाचलs (principal mountains) are seven. See notes p. 39. अचलद्धरित्री the earth quaked. पत्या...कामेव as if पृथ्वी was desirous of going with her lord (king प्रभाकरवर्धन, who was dying). Earthquakes were looked upon as portending great calamities and as punishments sent by God to chastise mankind for its sins. The poet Cowper writes in this strain in his poem 'Time-piece'. परास्परास्फालनेन वाचालाः वीचयः येषाम् the waves of which were noisy because they struck against each other. विजुघूर्णिरे *perfect 3rd plural* of घूर्ण् 1 A with वि to roll. धन्व...स्मरन्तः as though remembering धन्वन्तरि in that interval. When the sea was churned by the gods and demons, धन्वन्तरि emerged bearing the jar of nectar in his hand. 'अथोदधेर्मथ्यमानात्काश्यपैरमृतार्थिभिः । उदतिष्ठन्महाराज पुरुषः परमाद्भुतः ॥ 31....अमृतापूर्णकलशं बिभ्रद्वलयभूषितः । स वै भगवतः साक्षाद्विष्णोरंशांशसम्भवः ॥ 34 धन्वन्तरिरिति ख्यात आयुर्वेददृगिज्यभाक् ।' 35. भागवत० VIII. 8. धन्वन्तरि is also the promulgator of the science of medicine, as we learn from सुश्रुतसंहिता I. 1. 'अथ खलु भगवन्तममरवरं काशिराजं दिवोदासं धन्वन्तरिं...सुश्रुतप्रभृतय ऊचुः'. For curing the dying king, the ocean as if wanted धन्वन्तरि and lashed itself into fury as at the time of churning. Mark the genitive धन्वन्तरेः with स्मरन्तः. 'अधीगर्थदयेशां कर्मणि' पा. 2. 3. 52 (verbs having the sense of 'to remember' and the roots दय् and ईश् govern the genitive of the object). ०भीतानाम् goes with ककुभाम् (दिशाम्). भूभृ...ककुभाम् high rose up comets, appearing like the hair of the quarters, that were apprehensive of the death of the king, (hair) that was plentiful (विकट, or frightful) and curly with extended knots. The quarters are fancied to be the wives of the king and comets (that are long) as hair. Women whose husbands are dying would never think of decorating their hair by making a triple braid, but would tie it together in a knot. वितत... कुटिलाः may give two more meanings; (1) that are plentiful and curly like the peacock's outstretched tail; (2) that are terrible (विकट) and crooked with outstretching masses of flames. (शिखा). It is usual to compare the hair of beautiful women with the peacock's tail. See रघु० 9. 67. Comets have flashing tails. धूमकेतवः—compare 'उपप्लवाय लोकानां धूमकेतुरिवोत्थितः ॥' कुमार० II. 32. धूमकेतवः may also mean 'fires'. But as दिग्दाह is mentioned below, it is better to take the sense of 'comet.' धूमकेतुभिः (by comets, fires) करालितानि (rendered terrible) दिङ्मुखानि यस्मिन् (*adj.* of भुवनम्). दिक्पालैः आरब्धः आयुष्कामहोमः तस्य धूमेन धूम्रम्. The quarters had a dark (threatening) aspect on account of the comets. The poet fancies that this is due to the smoke of the sacrificial fire kindled by दिक्पालs for securing long life to the king. For the eight guardians of the quarters, see notes p. 25. भ्रष्टा भाः (lustre) यस्य (*adj.* of ०मण्डले). तप्त...बभ्रूणि reddish brown like a red hot iron jar. भानु...जहार In the sun's disc someone desiring the (continuance of) the life of the (dying) king offered as it were a human offering under the guise of a horrible headless trunk. A spot appeared on the sun's disc resembling the headless trunk (कबन्धः-न्धम्) of a man. This the poet fancies to be a human offering. Ccmpare रामायण अरण्यकाण्ड Chap 23. 11 'कबन्धः परिघाभासो दृश्यते भास्करान्तिके ।'. ज्वलितं परिवेशमण्डलं (circle of halo) तस्य आभोगः (expanse) तेन भास्वरः (*adj.* of श्वेतभानुः, the moon). जिघृक्षया (ग्रहीतुमिच्छया) जृम्भमाणः (yawning) स्वर्भानुः (राहुः) तस्मात् भयं तस्मात्. उपरचितः अग्निप्राकारः येन. The moon had a circle of blazing halo round it. The poet fancies that it was a wall of fire raised by the moon out of the fear of Rāhu that had opened its mouth wide to swallow the moon. अवनि...साधिताः (1) won over by the valour of the king; (2) decked by the brilliance of the king. अदह्यन्त...दिशः the reddened quarters were as if burnt. The quarters glowed red (this is called दिग्दाह). A loving (अनुरक्त) woman would enter fire before her husband dies (प्रथमतर &c.). A woman who wants to die by burning herself would be decked with all decorations (प्रसाधित). स्रुतः शोणितशीकराणां (रक्तबिन्दूनां) आसारः (shower) तेन अरुणिता (reddened) तनुः यस्याः. अनुमरणाय for following (her lord, the king प्रभाकर॰) in death. प्रावृतः पाटलः (red) अंशुकपटः यया. The earth was wet with a shower of blood. The poet fancies that the earth was going to be a सती and had covered herself in a red garment as a सती did. नरा...भीतैः afraid of the tumult that would arise on the king's death. कालायस... दिग्द्वाराणि the doors of the quarters were blocked by masses of untimely dark clouds as if they were iron door-panels. Though it was not the rainy season, dark clouds rose in the sky. The poet fancies them to be the doors of the sky. प्रेत... रटन्तः like the shrill (पटु) sounding drums beaten at the march of the Lord of the dead (यम). When a king marches, drums are beaten. हृदयस्फोटनाः (applies to पटहाः and निर्घोषाः) making the heart to burst. पस्फायिरे *perfect* of स्फाय् 1 A to swell. निर्घा...घोषाः the terrific sounds of whirl-winds. निर्घातः— 'पवनः पवनाभिहतो गगनादवनौ यदा समापतति । भवति तदा निर्घातः स च पापो दीप्तविहगरुतः ॥' बृहत्संहिता 39. 1. निकटीभवन् यममहिषः तस्य खुरपुटैः उद्भूताः. As the king was dying, the buffalo of यम is fancied to be near. द्युमणिः सूर्यः तस्य धाम (brilliance). This is the object of धूसरीचक्रुः (rendered dim). क्रमेलक...वृष्टयः showers of dust brown like camel hair. विरसविराविणीनाम् that howled disagreeably (so as to produce disgust). The reading विसर॰ would mean 'that howled in groups'. It is not so good.

उन्मुखीनाम् that had uplifted their faces. शिखिनो...राजयः rows of female jackals howled, receiving (प्रतीच्छन्त्यः) the flames of fire like meteors falling from the sky. The words in the text as they stand cannot be well construed. इव should have been placed after पतन्तीः or उल्काः. The idea seems to be that the jackals had blazing firebrands in their mouths and howled; meteors also blaze and fall from the sky. C and T translate 'like firebrands catching fire from flames that fell from the sky.' But then the difficulty is: what are the points of resemblance between rows of jackals and firebrands. Instead of being compared to firebrands, jackals are described as carrying firebrands. Compare 'नदन्मुखोल्काविचितामिषाभिः स वाह्यते राजपथः शिवाभिः ॥' रघु० 16. 12. If we read ज्वालाभिः with three MSS of B, all the difficulties may be removed. Then the meaning will be '(jackals) that as if received in the shape of flames of fire the meteors falling from the sky.' उल्का also means 'a firebrand.' धूमायमानः कबरीविभागः (सीमन्तः) तेन विभावितः विकारः यासाम् whose distress was shown by the fact that the parting line of their hair emitted smoke. प्रकीर्णेन केशपाशेन प्रकाशितः शोकः याभिः that as if manifested their grief by their dishevelled hair. One who is in grief has dishevelled hair. It was believed that in times of misfortune the hair of the images of goddesses in the house emitted smoke. That smoke is fancied to be dishevelled hair (both being dark). सिंहासनस्य समीपे उप० (अव्ययीभाव). भ्रामरम् — भ्रमराणामिदम्. Read विधूयमान for विदूय०. कालरात्र्याः विधूयमानः वृजिनः (curved, curling) वेणीबन्धः तस्य विभ्रमं (object of बिभ्राणम्)—(bearing) the appearance of the braided hair of कालरात्रि, that (hair) is curly and dangling (about the neck). वेणी is the hair of women twisted into a single unornamented braid (when their husbands are absent or ill). The dark and hovering bees resemble the dark and dangling braid. कालरात्रिः night of destruction at the end of the world. As the king was dying the word is appropriately used here. अटताम् goes with वायसानाम्. व्याक्रोशी the cawing (of crows). For the cry of the crow as an evil omen, see text p. 20 ll. 22-23. Compare वनपर्व 179. 44 'पृष्ठतो वायसः कृष्णो याहि याहीति शंसति'. ० मध्यात्—connect this with उच्चखान. सरस...लोहितम् as red as a piece of juicy meat. चञ्चन्ती (moving about) चञ्चुः (beak) यस्य. उच्चैः may be connected with कूजन् or with उच्चखान (tore away on high).

P. 82 l. 27—p. 28 l. 11 **अन्य...देव्या इति.** The principal sentence is 'अन्यस्मिन्नहनि समीपं अस्य (हर्षस्य) राजकुलात्...वेलेति नाम्ना यशोमत्याः प्रतीहारी आजगाम. द्रुतगतिवशेन विशीर्यमाणाः (broken) अलङ्काराः तैः झाङ्कारिणी (causing a tinkling). विज...षादस्य (she) seemed to be the triumphal proclamation of despondency. आकुलयोः चरणयोः चलन्ती तुलाकोटिः तस्याः क्वणितेन वाचालिताभिः. उद्ग्रीवाभिः that raised their necks. The Haṃsîs began to cackle when they heard the jingling of anklets and followed it. The poet fancies that they did so in order to ask the news. 'पादाङ्गदे तुलाकोटिर्मञ्जीरो नूपुरोऽस्त्रियाम्' अमरः ('तुलाकृतेर्जङ्घायाः कोटिरिव' क्षीरस्वामी). स्खलिते विशालश्रोण्यां शिञ्जाना रशना तां अनुरौति इति० राविणी ताभिः—that screamed in response to the girdle jingling on her broad hip when she stumbled. बाष्पान्धा—she stumbled being blinded by tears; when she stumbled, the bells of her girdle rang and the domesticated cranes screeched. It was their screeching that guided her. अदृष्टं कवाटपट्टं तस्य संघट्टेन (striking against) स्फुटितं ललाटपट्टं तस्य रुधिरपटलं तेन—her face was covered with blood as her forehead struck against the panels of doors which she did not observe in her weeping. The blood resembled the fringe (पटान्त) of a red silken garment (with which also women may veil their face). सन्तापबलेन विलीनं कनकवलयं तस्य रसधाराम्. She was throwing aside her cane (which she was to carry as a doorkeeper). The poet fancies that it was the stream of her golden bracelet that melted because of her सन्ताप (sorrow, heat). Both cane and gold are yellow. मुख...पटीं स्फुरन्तीं आकर्षन्ती she drew (into position) her flashing silken shawl that was waved about by her breath. मुख० and स्फुरन्तीं apply also to निर्मोकमञ्जरीम्. फणिनीव...र्षन्ती as a female serpent may draw after her a slough. Both the shawl and slough are white. नम्रां...स्रंसिना (*adj.* of ०सञ्चयेन) that hung over her bent shoulders. तमाल...वरेणेव—her dark hair resembled a tattered garment of Tamāla leaves (which are dark). धम्मिल्ल...रहितेन that was not arranged into a braid. 'धम्मिल्लः संयताः कचाः' इत्यमरः. शिरो... कुचा her bosom was covered with a dangling mass of hair. कुच... पीडया—beating the breast is a sign of sorrow. The word पीडया suggests that her breasts were hard (which is a sign of youth and beauty). समुच्छून swollen. If one were to scald his hands with boiling water (hot tears), the hands would be dark-red. निर्झरः a stream, spring. शीर्यति—that was scattered into drops (*adj.* of ०निर्झरे). स्नपयन्तीव...लोकम्—the idea is:—in her bright cheeks the people were reflected. Tears flowed from her eyes in streams on her cheeks and thus the reflections were bathed in water (tears). She was to tell the people sad news and thus plunge them into the fire of sorrow. One who kills himself by entering fire has first to perform a ceremonial bath. ०प्रवृत्तैः starting from her restless eyes. तारकांशुभिः by the rays of the pupils. श्यामा...दहन्तीव—her pupils were dark and she cast dark glances, whereby the day looked darkened. The poet fancies that the day looked dark because it was burnt by her grief. प्रत्युद्गता received, welcomed. कुट्टिमे न्यस्तं हस्तयुगलं यया she made her obeisance to the prince. गलन्तीभिः &c.—Her lip was dry through grief; when she bent her face, the rays of her gleaming teeth fell upon the lip. The rays resemble water. किमपि...देव्या the queen has resolved upon something (strange).

P. 83 ll. 12--34 ततस्त...लापान्. अपरम्—he was already grieving for his father and now he had to grieve for his mother. च्युत ... सत्त्वेन as if left by firmness of mind. द्रुतः melted. आचान्तः drunk. तुलितः weighed *i. e.* lifted up, made light of. अङ्कितः branded. आतङ्केन by pain. अप्रतिपत्तिः (अविद्यमाना प्रतिपत्तिः यस्य) who did not know how to proceed. प्रतिपन्ना संज्ञा येन who regained his consciousness. Put the dash and quotation mark after this and not before. दुःखाभिषङ्गः impact or contact of griefs. कठिने qualifies both हृदये and अश्मनि. दुत...पयति gives rise to fire. When an iron hammer falls upon hard stones (flint), sparks issue forth. When many causes for grief arise, the heart is set ablaze. निरनुक्रोशस्य = निर्दयस्य. तत्र... लापान्—the principal sentence is तत्र च...राजमहिषीणाम् अशृणोत् दूरादेव...आलापान्. The queens, being about to burn themselves, bid a last farewell to their favourite attendants, trees, pets and things. चिन्तय...जननी take care of yourself; your mother is going abroad. जातीगुच्छः a clump of jasmine. मर्षणीयाः...हाराः—It was the convention of poets that the अशोक tree blossomed when kicked by young damsels. Such conventions are summarized in the verse 'स्त्रीणां स्पर्शात्प्रियङ्गुर्विकसति बकुलः सीधुगण्डूषसेकात् पादाघाता-दशोकस्तिलककुरबकौ वीक्षणालिङ्गनाभ्याम् । मन्दारो नर्मवाक्यात् पटुमृदुहसना-च्चम्पको वक्त्रवाताच्चूतो गीतान्नमेरुर्विकसति च पुरो नर्तनात्कर्णिकारः ॥' quoted by मल्लिनाथ on मेघदूत II. 17. Compare कादम्बरी 'अशोकतरुताडनारणितरमणी-मणिनूपुरझङ्कारसहस्रमुखरेषु' (p. 138 of P). कर्ण...राधाश्च and the fautl of plucking thy tender leaves for (making them into) ear-ornaments. वारुणी...ललित naughty on account of receiving mouthfuls of wine. The बकुल blossomed by the sprinkling of mouthfuls of wine. See the verse quoted above. दातव्यो...लिः you should offer to me the handful of water. निवापः libation of water offered to deceased parents &c. at a श्राद्ध ('पितृदानं निवापः स्यात्' इत्यमरः.). अपत्यमसि gives the reason. किं व्याहरसि—why do you call me? स्वप्ने—she wishes that the *Mainâ* may dream of her departed mistress. मार्गलग्नम्—who clings to my path. सम्भावित honoured, celebrated. गृहहरिणिके domesticated doe (vocative). सौविदल्लः chamberlain. 'सुविदन्तं विवाहं जानन्तं लान्ति सुविदल्लाः ऊढाः स्त्रियः तत्र भवाः सौविदल्लाः' क्षीरस्वामी. वल्लकी lute. 'वीणा तु वल्लकी' इत्यमरः. अयं जनः—refers to the person speaking (one of the queens). कात्यायनी or—निका means 'a widow of middle age who puts on red garments'. 'कात्यायन्यर्धवृद्धा या काषायवसनाऽधवा' इत्यमरः. अलक्षणाम् who am unlucky (*lit.* not possessed of auspicious signs) धात्रेयी foster—sister. अपश्चिमाम्—अविद्यमानं पश्चिमं यस्याः—who can be seen no further hereafter. अय...लिः Here do I fold my hands by way of bidding (last) farewell. अवर...ष्वङ्गः embrace at the time of death.

P. 83 l. 35—**P. 84** l. 24 **दह्यमान...ददर्श** The principal sentence is तैः (आलापैः) दह्यमानश्रवणः प्रविशन्नेव...निर्यान्तीं मातरं ददर्श. दत्तं सर्वं स्वापतेयं (धनं) यया. स्वपतौ साधु स्वापतेयं according to 'पथ्यतिथिवसतिस्वपतेर्ढञ्' पा. 4. 4. 104. गृहीतं मरणप्रसाधनं यया who put on all the decorations of death (as सती). जानकी...वेक्ष्यन्तीम् who was about to enter fire before her husband like Sîtâ. सीता entered fire in the presence of (पुरः) her husband. For the incidents leading to the अग्निशुद्धि of सीता, see रामायण युद्धकाण्ड Chap. 115-118. After the defeat and death of रावण, राम received सीता rather coldly and said that he could not take her back as she had dwelt long in another's house. सीता then called upon लक्ष्मण to prepare the funeral pyre. Going round राम and calling upon fire not to harm her if she was chaste, she entered it. The fire assumed bodily form and handed over सीता to राम. प्रत्यग्रं (fresh) स्नान तेन आर्द्रः देहः यस्याः सा ०देहा तस्याः भावः ०देहता तया. लक्ष्मी when it rose out of the ocean at the time of churning must have been wet as the queen was. कुसुम्भ...दधानाम् who wore two garments reddish brown with safflower juice, as if she were the Heaven with two twillights. सान्ध्य *adj.* (from सन्ध्या). We must read अविधवामरण०. Her husband was yet living and therefore she was going to die like a सुवासिनी with all her decorations, with ताम्बूल in her mouth and so on. The author specifies below some of these, such as कण्ठसूत्र, हार, अङ्गराग &c. ताम्बूल...पाटलम् reddened by the mass of the brilliance of her lip that was dyed dark-red with betel. पट्टांशुकम् a silken cloth (shawl &c.). ०चिह्नम्—all the signs of a सुवासिनी that she wore on her body were tinged with the hue of her lip. कण्ठसूत्र- (Marathi मंगळसूत्र)—is an indispensable ornament always worn on the neck by all women whose husbands are living. The red कण्ठसूत्र hanging on her bosom looked like a stream of blood issuing from her broken heart. तिर्य...त्पीडयन्तीम् who pressed her throat with a necklace the threads of which were drawn aside by the thorn-like point of her ear-rings that were bent crosswise, as if it (necklace) was a halter of white silk rolled together. The idea of पाश is suggested by her approaching death. The necklace of pearls with its threads resembled a white silken rope with which one may hang oneself. सरसः (juicy, thick) कुङ्कुमाङ्गरागः (saffron unguent) यस्याः सा ०रागा तस्याः भावः ०रागता तया. कवलिता devoured. दिधक्षता—instru. of the desiderative base of दह्. Her body glowed with saffron paste and therefore appeared as if it were surrounded by flames of fire. चिता...पूरयन्तीम्—tears fell on her garment. Being white they looked like flowers which would be required as offerings to the funeral fire. गृह...विकिरन्तीम्- bracelets that she wore fell from her hands at each step; they resembled offerings presented to गृहदेवताs in bidding them a last farewell. आप्रपदीनां reaching to the feet. 'स्यात्रिष्वाप्रपदीनं तत्प्राप्नोत्याप्रपदं हि यत्' अमरः. The word is formed according to 'आप्रपदं प्राप्नोति' पा. 5. 2. 8 (पादस्याग्रं प्रपदं तन्मर्यादीकृत्य आप्रपदम्). गुण...मालाम् a wreath of flowers strung together. The wreath reaching her feet resembled a swing, which also has गुणs (ropes) resembling garlands. The swing is said to be that of यम, because she was going to die. अन्तर्गुञ्जन्तः मधुकराः तैः मुखरेण. आमन्त्र्य...कर्णोत्पलेन—the idea is:—she had a lotus on her ear as an ornament. In that lotus bees were humming. The humming of bees is fancied to be the words of farewell uttered by her कर्णोत्पल to the lotus of her eyes (that were about to perish along with her). Domestic हंसs are always represented as following the tinkling of the anklets of ladies. See above (text) p. 27 ll. 28–29. बद्धं मण्डलं यथा स्यात् तथा in a circle. संनिहितः प्राणसमः यस्मिन् (1) on which her husband dear to her as her own life was drawn; (2) in which her husband dwelt (with चित्तम्). She held fast (अविचलं) in her hand a board; her mind also was fixed fast on dying. Remove the comma after °दामकाम्. अर्चार्थं (पूजार्थं) बद्धं उह्यमानं धवलपुष्पाणां दाम यस्याम् (with पताकाम् and यष्टिम्). She had held fast to her bosom the spear-haft of her husband and had tied round it in worship a garland of white flowers. The poet fancies the प्रासयष्टि to be the banner of a पतिव्रता. The pole of a banner also has garlands of flowers hanging from it. 'प्रासस्तु कुन्तः' इत्यमरः. A सती if her husband died abroad was allowed to burn herself with his पादुकाs. Here यशोमती being the wife of a warrior appropriately takes प्रासयष्टि. बन्धोरिव—When a person in grief sees a friend or relative, tears begin to flow. Compare for the idea 'सन्तानवाहीन्यपि मानुषाणां दुःखानि सद्बन्धुवियोगजानि । दृष्टे जने प्रेयसि दुःसहानि स्रोतःसहस्रैरिव संप्लवन्ते ॥' उत्तरराम० IV. 8.; 'स्वजनस्य हि दुःखमग्रतो विवृतद्वारमिवोपजायते ॥' कुमार IV. पत्युः—is to be connected with सचिवान्. पादपतने समुद्गमत् अभ्यधिकं बाष्पाम्भः तस्य प्रवाहेण उपरुद्धा दृक् येषाम् whose eyes were choked up by the torrent of tears that welled up when they fell at her feet. कथ...देशान् who with difficulty understood the instructions (she gave). अनुनयेन (courteously) निवर्तितः अत एव विधुरः (distracted) वृद्धबन्धुवर्गः तेन वर्धमानः ध्वनिः यस्य. There was wailing in the house, which was augmented by the group of old kinsmen, who, when they followed the queen, were courteously asked by her to return to the house. भर्तृ... हृदयाम् whose heart was captivated by the roar of caged lions, that resembled the voice of her lord. धात्र्या...साधिताम् who was adorned by her nurse and by her own devotion to her lord. Her nurse had helped in decorating her person. In each of the following clauses, words like प्रसाधिताम् bear a literal and also a metaphorical meaning. जरत्या...धार्यमाणाम् she was supported by an old woman and by swoon, both being familiar. Frequent swoons gave relief to her aching heart and supported her. व्यसनसङ्गतया (1) who accompanied her in her misfortune (with सखी); (2) that was connected with (*i. e.* arose from) her misfortune (with पीडा). गृहीतसर्वावयवेन—her servants clasped her limbs; anguish pervaded all her limbs. कुल...छिताम् she was preceded by great nobles and she was full of heavy sighs. अतिवृद्धैः—the chamberlains were very old, while her sorrows were very heavy (वृद्ध grown, increased). कौलेयक a dog. Everything that pertained to her husband was dear to her and she was sorry to part even from the favourite dogs of her husband.

'कौलेयकः सारमेयः कुक्कुरो मृगदंशकः' इत्यमरः. The word is formed from कुल according to 'कुलकुक्षिग्रीवाभ्यः श्वास्यलङ्कारेषु' पा. 4. 2. 96. (ढकञ्। कौलेयकः श्वा, कौलोऽन्यः । सि. कौ.). सपत्नी...पतन्तीम्—in the hour of death, she forgot all petty jealousies.

P. 84 l. 25—**P. 85** l. 10 **दूरादेव...प्रारोदीत्.** सस्नेह...चूडः the hair on the top of whose head was as if affectionately kissed by the rays of the jewels of the anklets (of his mother). When he fell at his mother's feet, the rays of the jewelled anklets naturally fell on his hair. The poet fancies that the rays did so out of love. देवी...त्पतनम्—the sentence is देवी यशोमती...बाष्पोत्पतनं निवारयितुं न शशाक. पादयोः निहितं शिरः येन (*adj.* of तनये). विमनसि whose mind was distracted. गुरुणा...ष्टभ्यमाना arrested or enveloped by the great force of grief as by a large mountain. उद्वेगस्य आवेगः तेन. The reading of A and C 'उद्वेगवेगेन' is also good. If a torrent be arrested by a large mountain, it runs past with great force. मूर्च्छा एव अन्धतमसं (blinding darkness). 'अवसमन्धेभ्यस्तमसः' पा. 5. 4. 79 (तमस् when preceded by अव, सम् and अन्ध has अ added on to it). रसातल is one of the seven पाताल s (अतल, वितल, सुतल, तलातल, रसातल, महातल and पाताल). पाताल, as the haunt of demons, must be dark. There is also another suggestion. A torrent flows on the earth (रसातल). चिर...ण्डितेन formed into a mass by being pent up for a long time. स्नेह...भूयमाना she was overwhelmed by a tide of love that manifested itself in full strength. If a flow (of water) were pent up for a long time, it bursts forth in a flood; similarly if one checks tears for a long time, they will gush forth irresistibly. कृताः प्रयत्नाः यया सा ०यत्ना. उत्कटः (great) कुचयोः उत्कम्पः तेन प्रकटितं असह्यशोकस्य आकूतं (emotion) यया. गद्गदिकया गृह्यमाणः गलः तेन विकला who was in a distressing condition with her throat choked up (on account of tears). निःसामान्येन (unparalleled) मन्युना (grief) तरलीक्रियमाणः अधरोद्देशः (अधरप्रान्तः) यस्याः. पुनरुक्तेन (repeated) स्फुरणेन निबिडितं (tightened) नासापुटं यस्याः. We may perhaps explain differently. Her grief was so great that it could be inferred from the tremor of her lip. But her nose also was in tremor. This latter was superfluous (पुनरुक्त) so far as the inference of the grief by which she was shaken was concerned. सञ्छाद्य—connect this with ०पटान्तेन and वदनेन्दुम्. सञ्छाद्य...वदनेन्दुं she covered up her moon-like face, that was raised up a little, with the hem of her shawl (अंशुकपट) the body of which was inlaid with a row of the rays of her nails, as if with a flood of lucid tears issuing through the small interstices (of the shawl). As she held the fine shawl with her hands, the rays of her bright nails shot through the interstices of the fine texture of the shawl. The bright rays resembled tears. करनखमयूखमालया खचिता तनुः यस्य (*adj.* of ०पटान्तेन). तन्वन्तरेभ्यः निर्गच्छत् अच्छं अस्रं तस्य स्रोतसा इव. स्मरन्ती—governs शैशवम् as its object. अङ्कशायिनः अस्य (हर्षस्य) of him while he lay on her lap. ज्ञाति...हृदया as her heart thought of her parents' home. न पश्यतम् do not look at (me). विश्रान्तं भागधेयं यस्याः whose good luck has come to an end. असंनिहितं—राज्यवर्धन had been sent away on the expedition against the Hūṇas. श्वशुर०—we saw at the end of the fourth उच्छ्वास that राज्यश्री left the parental roof with her husband. किम...जनेन How have I offended you? अपराद्धं तव—the root राध् with अप meaning 'to offend' governs the genitive or locative of the person offended. मुषितास्मि I am robbed. कृतान्तं = दैवम्. मुक्तः कण्ठः यथा स्यात्तथा—lit. giving a free scope to her throat *i. e.* bitterly, loudly. प्राकृतप्रमदेव like an ordinary (or low) woman.

P. 85 l. 11—**P. 86** l. 11 **प्रशान्ते ... पतत्.** प्रशान्ते ... वेगे when the force of grief had ceased. प्ररुदितस्य—connect this with दृष्टिम्. पक्ष्मपालीषु पुञ्ज्यमानः नखकिरणनिवहः यस्याः. पक्ष्म...मार्जे she wiped his eye that as if melting only flowed the more, on the tips of the lashes of which clustered a mass of the rays of her nails. When she placed her hand on his eye the rays of her nails looked like tears. स्वयमपि connect this with लोचने...प्रमृज्य (after wiping her son's eyes, she wiped her own). कठोर...दरे the inside of which (eyes) was bereft of whiteness that was swallowed up by a deep red. On account of long weeping her eyes had grown red. धवलिम्ना instrumental of धवलिमन् (from धवल). See notes on कालिमा above p. 68. क्वथत् अस्रं तेन श्वयन् पर्यन्तः ययोः the corners of which had become swollen by hot (*lit.* boiling) tears. शुक्लशीकरेण तारं (bright) तारकितं पक्ष्म ययोः the bright eyelashes of which were starred with lucid drops (of tears). तारकित (having stars *i. e.* spotted)—तारकाः सञ्जाताः अस्य—according to 'तदस्य सञ्जातं तारकादिभ्य इतच्' पा. 5. 2. 36. The bright drops of tears on the eyelashes resembled stars. सूक्ष्मतराणां अश्रुबिन्दूनां परिपाटी (series) तस्याः पतनानुबन्धः (continuous falling) तेन विधुरे (लोचने). बाष्पार्द्र...लताम् then she placed on the top of her ear her tresses that were loosened in her sorrow and that stuck (गृहीता) to her cheek wet with tears. अधःस्रस्त...सटाम् she then pushed aside the mass of her hair that hung obliquely (on her shoulder) and that was entangled with her ear-ornament that had got loose and was dangling about. बालिका । बालायां वालुकापत्रकाहलाकर्णभूषणे ॥' मेदिनी (कान्त० 130). अश्रु...त्तरीयम्—she raised into its position the shawl covering her bosom that had slightly slipped aside. तरङ्गित...मुखकमलम्—the passage as it stands is difficult to construe. So read लावण्यं and कुब्जिकावर्जित०, as done by C and T. तरङ्गितमिव (connect with पयसा below)—the idea is:—when she washed her face, it seemed as if it were flooded with waves, as a lotus growing in a lake may be tossed by ripples. The reading of B नखांशुपटलेन yields a good sense. In washing her face, she again and again passed her hand over it. The rays of the bright nails of her hand were like water and hence her face over which the rays spread looked as if flooded with waves. मग्नः अंशुकपटान्तः तस्य तनवः ताम्राः लेखाः ताभिः लान्छितं लावण्यं यस्य (*adj.* of ०कमलम्). She had pressed the hem of her shawl against her face when she wiped off her tears. The red lines caused by the pressure of the hem marked her beautiful face. A lotus flower has also red lines on its petals which are small and deeply impressed like the hem of a shawl. (मग्नाः अंशुकपटान्तवत् तनवः ताम्राः &c.). कुब्जिकया आवर्जितं राजतं राजहंसास्यं तस्मात् समुद्गीर्णेन—(with water) that was emitted from a swan-mouthed vessel of silver inclined by a hunch-backed girl. The attendants of the harem always included hunch-backed persons, dwarfs, deaf-mutes and eunuchs. See कादम्बरी 'प्रनृत्तकलमूककुब्जकिरातवामनबधिरजडजनपुरःसरेण' (p. 74 of P); 'कुब्जकिरातबधिरवामनवर्षधरकलमूकानुगतेन परिजनेन' (p. 59 of P). A lotus may also be bent and be tossed with water emitted from the mouth of a swan that being white resembles silver. The swan may be attracted by a कुब्जिका (a fragrant flower plant). कल...धृते held by deaf-mutes. 'कलमूकोऽवाक्श्रुतिः' इति हलायुधः. वासःशकले on a piece of cloth, napkin. नासि...र्हो वा It is not that you are not loved, nor are you devoid of good qualities, nor do you deserve to be abandoned. स्तन्ये... हृदयम्—She means to say that her whole heart is with him, as if it had been drunk up by him. प्रभूताः प्रभोः (प्रभाकरवर्धनस्य) प्रसादाः तैः अन्तरिता—She means:—between you and me (that am to see you) intervene the numerous favours bestowed on me by my husband. My eye only sees them and not you. पुरुषान्तरविलोकने व्यसनं (attachment) अस्ति अस्याः. Both लक्ष्मी (sovereignty or Glory) and earth (क्षमा) pass from one brave man to another and feel no pang in leaving one to go to another. कुलकलत्रम्—I am a lady of a noble house. चारित्रमात्रं धनं यस्याः. धर्मेण धवले spotless on account of its righteousness. प्रशस्तः पुरुषः पुरुषप्रकाण्डम्. 'मतल्लिका मचर्चिका प्रकाण्डमुद्धतल्लजौ । प्रशस्तवाचकान्यमूनि' इत्यमरः. वीरजा—Unfortunately Bāṇa does not give us the name of the family in which यशोमती was born. पराक्रमक्रीता bought by valour *i. e.* who cares only for valour or whose heart is won by valour. भरत—The reference is probably to भरत, the son of दुष्यन्त and शकुन्तला. There was another भरत, son of ऋषभ and grandson of नाभि after whom India came to be called भारतवर्ष. See for his story विष्णुपुराण II. 1 and 13 and मार्कण्डेय पु. 53. 40. भगीरथ—son of दिलीप and descendant of सगर—brought down the Ganges from Heaven. नाभाग—For the story of नाभाग, see विष्णुपु० IV. 1. and मार्कण्डेयपु० 113. There is a great deal of confusion about नाभाग. The रामायण makes him the son of नहुष and grandson of अम्बरीष (अयोध्याकाण्ड 110. 33); while in the विष्णु० he is represented to be the son of नेदिष्ट and father of अम्बरीष. In the अर्थशास्त्र of कौटिल्य (p. 12) we find that अम्बरीष was the son of नाभाग. वृन्दारक best; *m.* god. सेवायां संभ्रान्ताः (flurried) अनन्तसामन्तसीमन्तिन्यः ताभिः समावर्जितैः (poured) जाम्बूनदघटैः अभिषेकः. जाम्बूनदम् gold ('जम्बूद्वीपे जम्बूफलरसोत्थनद्यां जातं जाम्बूनदम्' क्षीरस्वामी). महादेवी...ललाटेन—My forehead secured the honour of having the fillet of chief queen tied round it. पट्ट is the broad band which runs round the crown immediately above the forehead. The बृहत्संहिता (chap. 49) gives some directions about पट्टs to be worn on the crowns of kings, queens &c. अमित्राणां कलत्राणि एव बन्दीवृन्दं (troop of captives) तेन. विधूयमानं चामरं तस्य मरुता चलं चीनांशुकं (silken cloth from China) तस्य धरौ. शिरःसु निहितं चरणयुगलम्—we need not take these words literally. What she means is that she completely humbled her co-wives. नमन्त्यः निखिलकटककुटुम्बिन्यः (the matrons of the whole capital) तासां किरीटेषु (diadems) माणिक्यानि तेषां मालाभिः अर्चितम्. All the matrons of the capital bowed at her feet, as she was the Mahādevî. एवं... यवा all whose limbs have thus been blessed. किमपरमपेक्षे what else should I expect (or hanker after)? आर्यपुत्रविरहिता bereft of husband (applies to both रति and यशोमती). दग्धस्य भर्तुः—काम, the husband of रति, was burnt by शिव; the king's body also would be burnt after his death. निरर्थकान्प्रलापान्—the author seems to have in mind particularly the fourth Sarga of the कुमारसम्भव of कालिदास, where we have रतिविलाप. We know from the Introduction to the हर्षचरित that बाण was a great admirer of कालिदास. पितुश्च...धूलिः I am like the dust of the feet of thy father *i. e.* I am very much inferior to your father. There is another idea. Dust raised up by the feet of a person goes up into the sky. She says that like dust she will go to heaven before her husband to announce the arrival of a hero like him to the Apsarases, who will therefore be pleased with her as the harbinger of good news. It was a poetic convention that the Apsarases were ready to welcome to heaven the heroes that died gloriously on the battle-field. प्रत्यग्र—fresh. धूमः ध्वजः यस्य—fire. मरणा...साहसम्—not to die, but to live at this time would be a cruel thing in me. अक्षयं—स्नेहेन्धनं (स्नेहः एव इन्धनं) यस्य. The fire of sorrow for my husband is fed up by the fuel of imperishable love; while ordinary fire is fed with fuel that may be exhausted. स्नेहः also means 'oil'. कैलासात् ईषत् न्यूनः कैलासकल्पः; see notes on the affixes कल्प, देश्य and देशीय p. 38. प्रवसति...श्वरे when the lord of my life is departing on a journey (*i. e.* is dying). जरत् तृणं तस्य कणिकावत् लघीयः (जीवितं) light like a bit of old (*i. e.* rotten) grass. जीविते...घटते *lit.* where can it be possible (or proper) that one should be covetous of life? नर...पातकिनीम् that am guilty of the deadly sin of disregarding the death of the king. She means that to continue to live after the king's death would be a great sin in her. न स्प्रक्ष्यन्ति will not touch (*i. e.* I cannot enjoy the pleasures of your rule). दुःख...भवति prosperity (or grandeur) in those that are consumed by sorrow is inauspicious, accursed and useless. भूतिः means 'ashes' also. Ashes, except of the sacrificial fire, are अमङ्गल. 'भूतिर्भस्मनि सम्पदि' इत्यमरः. विश्व...वपुषा I wish to abide in this world not in flesh and blood, but in the glory of widows. The glory of widows was to burn themselves on the funeral pyre of their husbands. प्रसादयामि I beseech you. न...कदर्थनीयास्मि I should not be slighted by opposing my desire (to burn myself). कदर्थनीय *potential pass. p.* of the denominative verb from कदर्थ. कुत्सितः अर्थः कदर्थः, according to 'कोः कत्तत्पुरुषेऽचि' पा. 6. 3. 101 (when कु being the first member of a तत्पुरुष compound is followed by a word beginning with a vowel, it is changed to कत्).

P. 86 ll. 12–27 **स तु...स्त्रोद.** उभयकराभ्यां विधृतं वपुः यस्याः holding her body in both his arms. अवनितलगतं शिरः यस्याः. दुर्नि...धार्य concluding that her grief was impossible of being checked.

कुल...क्रियाम् and thinking that only that course of conduct befitting a lady of high family was better. क्रियां refers to her resolve to die. अभिनन्दति...रूपम्—the author assigns this as a reason why हर्ष acquiesced in the resolve of his mother. Noble birth, though made timorous by love, approves of what is proper to the time and place. पौरा...दिग्भिः who was as if obstructed by the quarters that were full of the echoes of the wailings of the citizens. सरस्वती—is a river on the banks of which the modern Thanesar (स्थाण्वीश्वर) in Karnal District, Panjab, is situated. It rises in the Sirmur state on the borders of the Ambala District and is lost in the sands in the great desert for several miles. स्त्री...पातैः she cast terrified glances as is natural to women. Her eyes had grown red by weeping. Therefore the glances resembled red lotus flowers. We have seen above (notes p. 13) that red lotuses were to be used in the worship of the sun. भानु...न्दवी as the form of the moon enters the sun (on the day of the अमावास्या). Note 'चन्द्रमा वा अमावास्यायामादित्यमनुप्रविशति सोऽन्तर्धीयते तं न निर्जानन्ति' ऐतरेय ब्राह्मण, 8th पञ्चिका chap. 5; compare विक्रमोर्वशीय III. 7 '**रविमावसते**&c'. चित्रभानुम्—अग्निम्. चित्रभानु also means 'the sun'. इतरोपि refers to हर्ष. स्वल्पः अवशेषः यस्याः सा ०शेषा प्राणवृत्तिः यस्य तम् which was almost ebbing away. परिवर्त्यमाना तारका यस्य (1) the pupil of whose eye was being revolved (with the king); (2) that makes the stars revolve (with the moon). अस्त...षन्तम् (1) about to die; (2) about to set. अस...द्रुतः assailed by an excess of intolerable sorrow. त्याजितः...धैर्यम् affection made him lose all steadiness. Mark the construction (हर्षः धैर्यं त्यजति primitive; स्नेहः हर्षं धैर्यं त्याजयति causal; हर्षः स्नेहेन धैर्यं त्याजितः passive causal). आश्लिष्य—governs पादपद्मौ. सकल...लालितौ fondled by the crests of all haughty kings. अन्तस्ता...भवन्तम् as if it were his moonlike face melting through an inner fire. This and the following clauses are to be connected with अश्रुस्रोतसां सन्तानं वर्षन्. दशन...पद्यमानम् as if it were the net-work of the light of his teeth reduced to water. His bright tears resembled bright water. His teeth were very white. अच्छाच्छम् very bright. अश्रु... वर्षन् showering a continuous stream of tears as if his eyes were made up of a large cloud. इतरवत् like a common man. विमुक्तः आरावः (cry) येन.

P. 86 l 28—**P. 87** l. 10 **राजा तु...लोचने**. उपरुध्यमाना दृष्टिः यस्य whose sight was obstructed (*i. e.* whose eyes could not see his son in the last moments). अविरतरुदितशब्देन आश्रितौ श्रवणौ

यस्य whose ears were affected by the incessant weeping (of हर्ष). Sight failed the dying king, but the incessant weeping arrested his ears and roused him to some consciousness. अविद्यमानं महासत्त्वं येषाम् that have no firm heart. महा...बीजिता Firmness of mind is the first (foremost) stay of the people and royal blood comes after it. People first betake themselves to the man of strong will. सर्वैः अतिशयैः आश्रितः the abode of all eminent things (or virtues). क—क—two कs denote great disparity or incongruity. कुल...करणमिव to call you the lamp of the family is to slight you whose majesty is like that of the sun. प्रदीप (1) lamp; (2) ornament. To call a man a lamp when he is like the sun would be really condemning him. शौर्येण पटुप्रज्ञया (sharp intellect) च उपबृंहितः (magnified) पराक्रमः यस्य. The lion has only physical strength (पराक्रम), but no keen intellect and no heroic heart. लक्षणैः आख्यातं (declared) चक्रवर्तिपदं यस्य. पुनरुक्त superfluous. गृह्यतां श्रीः accept royal dignity. स्वयमेव...गृहीतस्य—लक्ष्मी herself has come to you. Compare for a somewhat similar idea 'लभेत वा प्रार्थयिता न वा श्रियं श्रिया दुरापः कथमीप्सितो भवेत्' कुमार० V. उभय...गीषोः who are desirous of conquering this world and the next. अपुष्कलम् not sufficient, little. शशिनः कराणां निकरः समूहः तद्वत् निर्मलं यशः तस्य सञ्चये एकः केवलः अभिनिवेशः (fondness) अस्ति अस्य इति० वेशिनः. When हर्ष has set his heart in achieving spotless fame alone, it is useless to ask him to take the treasury. राजकम्—राज्ञां समूहः. गतार्थम् meaningless. अनुचितनियोगः an injunction that is unworthy. दीर्घाभ्यां दोर्दण्डाभ्यां अर्गलितानि (bolted, safeguarded) दिङ्मुखानि येन. अनुवादः repetition. It is a technical term in the पूर्वमीमांसा system. When a Vedic text lays down an injunction (विधि), other passages, that either reiterate, explain or illustrate the विधि, are called अनुवादs. विधिविहितस्य वचनमनुवादः. Harsha was already protecting the world. To call upon him to protect the world was simply superfluous, a mere repetition in words. आनुषङ्गिकम्—necessarily following; incidental (अनुषङ्गात् आगतः ठक्). हर्ष was like a लोकपाल. If he guarded the whole world it necessarily followed that he would protect his attendants. धनुर्गुणस्य किणः तस्य कलङ्कः तेन कालीकृतः प्रकोष्ठः यस्य whose forearm is blackened by the spot of the scar of the bow-string. निग्राह्यताम्—It would be better to have निगृह्यताम्. चापलम् rashness, levity. नूतन...वयसि in tender years. निरवकाशा has no room or scope. सहज...चिन्ता this is a thought for your inherent valour *i. e.* this is a matter which will be dealt with by your valour; I need not enjoin you to do this. The words are capable of yielding another sense. To ask you to annihilate your foes is casting a doubt (चिन्ता) on your inherent valour. C and T translate 'Annihilate your foes is a suggestion of your inborn valour'. This is not clear. अपुनरुन्मीलनाय never again to open them. The reading of B 'प्रत्यपद्यत पूषात्मजः' would mean 'the son of the sun (*i. e.* यम) came to him.'

P 87 l. 11—**P. 88** l. 2 **अस्मिन्नेवान्तरे...नीयत.** पूषापि—The force of अपि lies in this that, as the king lost his life, so even the sun lost his brilliance, which is the sun's essence. लज्जमान इव अधोमुखः the sun hung down as if ashamed. One who feels ashamed hangs down his head. The sun hung down on the western horizon. भूपालस्य अभावः (death) तेन शोकः स एव शिखी (अग्निः) तेन. A thing heated in the fire becomes red. मन्दं...द्दिवः slowly the sun descended from heaven as if for paying a visit of condolence, following the practice of worldly men. अप्रियप्रश्न is opposed to कुशलप्रश्न. दित्सुः desirous of giving. अपरजलनिधि western ocean. सद्यो दत्तः नृपाय जलाञ्जलिः येन. आलोहितम् slightly red. Water is to be offered with कर (hand, ray). In offering water, one would naturally feel sorrow. एवं च...नीयत—the principal sentence is नरेन्द्रः...सरस्वतीं नीत्वा...यशःशेषतामनीयत. निधनेन निधीयमानं विपुलं वैराग्यं यस्मिन्. शान्तं वपुः यस्य. An ascetic has distaste for the world (वैराग्य); the sun, a short time after the king's death, lost his radiance (विरागस्य भावः वैराग्यम्, विगतः रागः रक्तिमा यस्य). An ascetic must be शान्त (restrained); so also the sun's body became subdued (*i. e.* lost its colour). An ascetic enters the recesses of mountain caves; the sun set behind the western mountain. समुपोह्यमानं (increasing) महाजनस्य अश्रु तदेव दुर्दिनं (stormy or rainy day) तेन आर्द्रीकृते. निर्वाति (loc. sing. of *pr. p.* of वा with निर्) आतपे when the heat (of the sun) became extinguished (as if wet with &c.). Separate रुचा (कान्त्या) इव. लोहितायति—loc. sing. of *pr. p.* of the denominative verb from लोहित. The world was reddened by the glow of the setting sun; but the poet attributes the glow of the world to the tear-flushed eyes of the people. उष्णायमानाः (hot) अनेकनराणां निश्वासाः तैः सन्तापः तेन प्लुष्टं (scorched). नृपा...कमलिनीषु when the lotus beds were left by glory, as if the latter had started to follow the king (in death). Day lotuses fade in the evening *i. e.* their glory leaves them. That लक्ष्मी is identified with राज्यलक्ष्मी and is fancied as leaving them to perish after the king. पति...भुवि when the earth, having covered itself in shadows, became dark as if through grief for her husband. A king is poetically spoken of as the husband of the earth. The shades of evening were falling fast and so the earth seemed to be shrouded in them. श्यामायमाना (1) becoming dark; (2) behaving like a श्यामा (a handsome lady). A handsome woman would have all her brilliance (छाया) covered up (*i. e.* gone) through grief for her husband. परिवृता (concealed) छाया (कान्तिः) यस्याः; छायाभिः परिवृता परिवृतछाया (like the compound राजदन्त). C and T prefer the reading परिवृत्त for परिवृत and explain 'the shadows have retraced their course eastwards.' परित्यक्तानि कलत्राणि यैः (applies to both कुलपुत्र and चक्रवाक). The चक्रवाक becomes separate from its mate at the approach of night. See above p. 10 and 57. वनान्तान् (1) vicinity of woods (with कुलपुत्र); (2) the fringes of water (with चक्रवाक). The noble young men betook to woods out of grief; the चक्रवाकs to water. 'वने सलिलकानने' इत्यमरः. छत्र...शयेषु when the water-lilies closed their calyx, as if afraid of losing the umbrella-like expanse of their petals. कुशे जले शेते इति कुशेशयम्. 'सहस्रपत्रं कमलं शतपत्रं कुशेशयम्' इत्यमरः. The lotuses closed their buds at the departure of the sun. The poet fancies that the lotuses did so because they were afraid that their petals would fade and their umbrella-like appearance would disappear. There is another meaning. The lotuses are compared to devoted servants (lying on mere कुश grass in their grief and not on soft beds). They were terrified by the breaking of the royal umbrella (*i. e.* by the death of the king) and hide the treasure (कोश) in order to safeguard it for the rightful heir. C and T explain that lotuses are compared to queens, who hide the treasures. But कुशेशय is not feminine. Besides it is not in keeping with Indian sentiment to represent the widowed queens as hiding treasures when engrossed in grief. छत्रभङ्ग would be a very bad omen, foretelling the death of the king. Compare बृहत्संहिता 46. 74 'शक्रध्वजेन्द्रकीलस्तम्भद्वारप्रपातभङ्गेषु। तद्वत्कपाटतोरणकेतूनां नरपतेर्मरणम् ॥'. स्फुटित...तपे when the red glow (of evening) flowed away (gradually vanished) as if it were the flood of blood from the broken hearts of the quarter wives. अनु...धीशे when the lord of brilliance (the sun) remained only in अनुराग (red glow; love). The sun vanished and what he left behind was only the red glow of the western sky. The king, who also was

तेजसामधीश, had gone away, leaving behind only love. ०वितन्यमानः बहलः रागः तेन पाटलायाम्. प्रेतपताकायाम्—A banner flies in the sky. स्फुरन्तीषु...लेखासु when streaks of darkness appeared obstructing sight. The black chowries of the hearse resemble darkness and are an evil omen when seen (दर्शने प्रतिकूला). असिता...काष्ठायाम् (1) असितागुरुवत् कालाः काष्ठाः दिशः यस्याम्–in which the quarters are dark like black aloe wood (with रजनी); (2) which had the black beams of dark aloe wood (with चिता). असितागुरोः कालानि काष्ठानि यस्याम्. दन्तामल...लक्ष्मीषु—Here there are numerous puns. The principal idea is that the night lotuses (कुमुद) began to expand. The night lotuses are compared to *satîs* joyfully following their husbands in death. दन्तवत् (like ivory) अमलैः पत्रैः (petals) प्रसाधिता कर्णिका यासाम् (with कुमुदs); दन्तस्य (of ivory) अमलैः पत्रैः (thin plates) प्रसाधिता (manufactured) कर्णिका (ear-ring) यासाम् (with women). पत्र may also mean 'painting or figures' in the latter case. 'कर्णललाटात्कनलङ्कारे' पा. 4. 3. 65. Compare ललाटिका above. केसराणां (filaments) मालाभिः कल्पिता मुण्डमालिका यासाम् on whose top (मुण्ड) there were rows of filaments (with कुमुदs); (केसराणां बकुलानां &c.) whose heads were wreathed with garlands of बकुल (with Satîs). We saw above that a Satı was to die with all her ornaments &c. प्र... मुखीषु (1) with expanding buds (with कुमुदs); with smiling faces (with Satîs). A Satî was not to show that she regretted the step that she was taking. The निर्णयसिन्धु (परि० III) quotes a passage from the स्कन्दपुराण 'अनुव्रजति भर्तारं गृहात्पितृवनं मुदा। पदे पदेऽश्वमेधस्य फलं प्राप्नोत्यनुत्तमम् ॥'. अव...कूजिते when the twitter of groups of birds lying in their nests (कुलायः-यम्) at the top of trees was heard as if it were the tinkling of the bells of the descending car (विमानः-नम्) of the gods. It was believed that celestial cars were sent to take heroes and great souls to heaven. नाक...पत्रे इव–the round and bright orb of the moon resembles a white umbrella. The moon rose in the east, of which Indra (पुरुहूत) is the lord. The poet fancies that the rising moon was the umbrella of Indra, come forward to welcome the king (प्रभाकर०) who was travelling along the path of heaven. नरेन्द्रः refers to प्रभाकरवर्धन; connect the word with अनीयत. स्वयं...स्कन्धैः—the feudatories themselves took on their shoulders the bier (शवशिबिका). शिबिसमः—शिबि was a king and is referred to as an ideal of self-sacrifice. Once इन्द्र assumed the form of a श्येन (hawk) and pursued धर्म

as कपोत. The latter threw himself on the lap of शिबि for help. The श्येन asked the king to give his own flesh in return for the कपोत whom he wanted to save. When the कपोत was placed in a balance, its weight increased and शिबि had to offer his whole body. Thereupon the gods showed themselves to him. See कथासरित्सागर I. 7. 88 ff; रामायण II. 12. 43 'शैब्यः श्येनकपोतीये स्वमांसं पक्षिणे ददौ ।'. पुरोहितः पुरःसरः येषाम्—headed by the family priest. हुताश...नीयत by being honoured with fire, he was reduced (to ashes), so that nothing but his fame remained.

P. 88 ll. 3–24 **देवोऽपि ... यामिनी.** पुञ्जीभूतेन—goes with लोकेन. All the persons connected with the king formed a group and were huddled up there. They were so many that it seemed as if the whole world had gathered there in grief. अन्त... सिच्यमानः wet as if outside (in the form of tears) by the melting of affection, which though inside, was heated by the fire of sorrow. Affection is internal; tears are visible. The poet fancies that the tears he shed were melted affection. निर्व्यवधानायां धरण्याम् on bare earth. व्यवधानम् what comes between, what intercepts. Nothing came between हर्ष and the earth. उपविष्ट एव—he sat; he did not even lie down. भीमरथी—name of the 7th night in the 7th month of the 77th year of a man's life. This was believed to be a most critical point. If a man survived it, it was believed that he would live for 100 years. The Com. gives three explanations 'भीमरथी नरकनदी कालरात्रिर्वा अन्ये तु सप्तसप्तत्या वर्षैस्तत्संख्यैश्च मासैर्दिनैश्च तावद्भिर्गतैरेका रात्रिर्भीमरथी भवति तामतिक्रान्तो वर्षशतजीवी नरो भवतीति प्राहुः'. ताते...लोकः now that my father is removed, the world of mortals is only this much *i. e.* the world cannot reach hereafter a higher stage. लोकस्य...पन्थानः the ways of the people are broken *i. e.* their progress is arrested. मनो... स्थानानि the splendid goals of ambition are blocked up (or rendered impossible). खिलम् means 'barren or waste soil.' खिलीभू means 'to become barren or impossible.' स्थगितानि covered, veiled. लुप्ता...यात्रा the business of the world has come to an end. प्रोषिताः ...काराः various kinds of manly deeds (or sports) are exiled. पुरुषकारः manliness. विश्रान्ता...भूमयः places where trust could be reposed have ceased to exist. अप...दानानि noble deeds are without an abode. अपदानम् (seems to be another form of अवदानम्) a pure course of conduct; a noble deed. निर...रसता the single-minded devotion to valour has no support now. कथा...ज्ञता capacity to judge has now become a matter of legend. और्जित्यम्

(ऊर्जितस्य भावः) might, vigour. Might has ceased to exist and so people may offer water to it just as they do to the dead. प्रव्रज्या — the order of a religious mendicant. बध्नातु...मनुष्यता let excellent manhood bind the widow's single braid. The idea is:—as the king is dead, वरमनुष्यता has now nobody to resort to. We have seen above that widows used to tie their hair in a single knot. समा...पदम् (1) let royal glory resort to a hermitage; (2) let राजश्री go to a hermitage. By the great resemblance in sound between राजश्री and राज्यश्री the words suggest the misfortunes of राज्यश्री. धवले वाससी—a widow was to wear white garments. See धर्मसिन्धु (परि० III विधवाधर्म) 'वासो न विकृतं वसेत्।'. वहतु वल्कले—wearing bark garments is a sign of forest life. क्व...ज्ञतया where will gratitude go to find him? महा...माणून् atoms for the creation of great men. For atoms see above pp. 12 and 44. जगज्जा...धर्मस्य the world has become a darkness for righteousness. The idea is that righteousness cannot now find its way to anybody, as the whole world is enveloped in darkness. दिवसम् (acc. of time) for the whole day. वीरगोष्ठ्यः assemblies of heroes. असम...भित्तयः—असमः (unparalleled) समररसः (liking for fighting) तेन समारब्धाः कलहकथाः (रणकथाः) ताभिः कण्टकिताः (thrilled) सुभटानां कपोलभित्तयः यासु. दीर्घरक्ते नयने यस्य (1) whose eyes were long and red (with मुख); the roots of which are long and red (with सरोज). For this latter meaning of नयन, compare the use of नेत्र in 'दीर्घरक्तनालनेत्रामुत्पलिनीमिव सरसी' (text p. 10. l. 3). लोह...गर्भम्—लोहस्तम्भात् अभ्यधिकः गरिमा गर्भे यस्य—that possessed a massiveness greater than that of an iron pillar. लोका...श्रूयेत सा भारती might I hear that voice of his calling me 'son' even in another world? सुधा...रन्ती emitting nectar. The ocean when churned gave up सुधा (अमृत). The words of the king were sweet like nectar. मथ्यमानः क्षीरसागरः तस्य उद्गारवत् गम्भीरा (deep like the roar &c.).

P. 88 l. 25—**P. 89** l. 13 **ततः...जगाम**. ततः...हर्षः (p. 34 l. 2)—the principal sentence is ततः...चचाल उपस्थानाय देवो हर्षः. The poet now gives a graphic description of day-break. कृकवाकुः cock. 'कृकवाकुस्ताम्रचूडः कुक्कुटश्च रणायुधः' इत्यमरः. गृह...मयूरेषु when the domesticated peacocks let themselves fall from the tops of the trees growing on pleasure hills. गृहगिरि artificial eminences near the mansions. The peacocks rested in the branches of trees during the night and came down when the day broke. पत्त्ररथः a bird (पत्त्राणि पक्षाः रथः अस्य). सद्य...तमसि the darkness suddenly grew less and became exhausted. मन्दीभूतः आत्मस्नेहः येषाम् (1) in which the oil was failing; (2) whose love for their self had grown dull. A person who has lost all attachment to his self longs for death. The lamps also, as very little oil was left, were about to be extinguished. स्फुरन्तः अरुणस्य (रविसारथेः) किरणाः वल्कलमिव तेन प्रावृतं वपुः यस्य—the sky was covered with the flashing bark-like rays of early morn and therefore seemed to have taken to the life of a religious mendicant. A परिव्राजक also wears bark-garments that are red. प्रभात...तारकासु when the stars that were grey like the neck of a sparrow (कलविङ्कः) were being taken across by the morning. The idea seems to be that the vault of the sky is like a lake over which the stars were ferried and by morning found themselves on the other side. The stars looked dim in the light of morn. The grey stars resembled the fragments of the king's bones. The burnt up bones of the dead are collected on the third or fourth day in the morning and are carried to holy rivers like the Ganges and are thrown in them. See कुल्लूक on मनु° V. 59; the धर्म° (परि° III) says 'अस्थिसञ्चयनं तु दाहदिनादारभ्य प्रथमदिने द्वितीये तृतीये चतुर्थे सप्तमे नवमे वा गोत्रजैः सह स्वस्वसूत्रोक्तप्रकारेण कार्यम् ।...अस्थ्नां गङ्गाम्भसि तीर्थान्तरे वा प्रक्षेपः ।'. The reading समुच्चीयमानासु of some MSS. of B is rightly preferred by C and T. It means 'being gathered together.' Bones are first gathered and then placed in a jar (see next clause). But if we take the reading in the text, we have first a reference to the carrying of the bones and then to the jars, which inverts the natural order. भूभृ...धारिषु (1) possessing round foreheads that had on them mountain minerals (with elephants); (2) carrying jars that contained the remains (bones) of the king. भूभृतां पर्वतानां धातवः गैरिकादयः (red chalk &c.) तद्गर्भाः कुम्भाः तान् धारयन्तीति; भूभृतः राज्ञः धातवः (अस्थीनि) तद्गर्भाः कुम्भाः घटाः &c. 'कुम्भौ घटेभमूर्धांशौ' इत्यमरः. विविध...मुखेषु—applies to both the wild elephants and those that carried the ashes of the king. तीर्थम् a descent into a river (Marathi घाट); a place of pilgrimage. It is better to read शावे शुचि° with some MSS. of B. शावः (1) tawny; (2) funeral, relating to a dead body (शवसम्बन्धी). शावः शुचि... पाण्डुरश्च शाव...पाण्डुरः. शुचि...पाण्डुरः (1) pale as a ball of white wax; (2) pale with a mass of boiled rice. सिक्थः boiled rice; सिक्थम् bee's wax. The pale moon in the morning looked like a पिण्ड of boiled rice offered to the dead. *Pindas* are often offered on the sandy banks of sacred rivers and the ocean. The moon was going to dip into the western ocean. परिसरः vicinity. क्रमेण—connect this with अस्तमुपगते रजनिकरे. नृप...तेजसीव—the poet fancies that the dimness of the moon's disc in the morning is due to the mass (विसरः) of the smoke of the pyre on which the king was burnt. नरपतिशोकः एव पावकः तेन दाहः तेन किणः (scar) तस्य कलङ्केन कालीकृतं चेतः यस्य. On the dim disc of the moon was seen a dark spot, which the poet fancies to be his mind bu-nt to charcoal by the fire of sorrow for the king. प्रोषितानां (gone on a journey *i. e.* dead) समस्तानां अन्तःपुरपुरंध्रीणां मुखचंद्राः तेषां वृन्दं तस्य उद्वेगेन विद्राणं वपुः यस्य. We saw above that all the queens had prepared themselves to die (text p. 28 l. 17 तत्र च मर्तुमुद्यतानां राजमहिषीणां &c). The poet fancies that on seeing the agony (उद्वेग) of the women of the harem, the moon (as if out of compassion for the other moons-faces) vanished bodily (*i. e.* set). विद्राण run away (past p. p. of द्रा with वि). C and T translate विद्राण as 'stupefied'. प्रथमं अस्तमिता रोहिणी तया रणरणकः (eagerness, anxiety) तेन विमनाः (distracted) तस्मिन्. रोहिणी is the favourite wife of the moon out of the 27 नक्षत्रs. राजतीव... सवितरि when the sun that had mounted the sky shone like the king (प्रभाकर०). The king also mounted heaven after dying. The reading राजनीव preferred by C and T would no doubt improve the sense, but is not supported by the MSS. used by B. परि...प्रबन्धे when the continuance (प्रबन्धः) of night was turned back, like the kingdom. The kingdom also had changed hands. परिवृत्तम् exchanged; turned back. प्रबुद्ध...कर इव like a bed of lotuses roused by the awakened flamingoes. हर्ष also was advised by the circle of wise (प्रबुद्ध) swan-like kings (to give up wailing). Read नापस्नानाय for चोप०. अपस्नानम् bathing on the death of a relative. Drop the comma after ०हंसेषु. नूपुररवस्य विरामेण (cessation) मूकाः मन्दाश्च मन्दिरहंसाः येषु (*adj.* of शुद्धा०). We saw above (p. 92) that हंसs followed the jingling of the anklets of young ladies. But as all the queens had perished on the death of the king, there were no young ladies left. पतितः यूथपः यस्य. कक्ष्या...जने his father's servants stood in the courts of the palace. कक्ष्या also signifies 'the girth rope of an elephant or horse'. विषादि...कुञ्जरे when the king's sad elephant reclined against its post, motionless and dull and having its rider weeping on its back. उपरि रुदन् निषादी (हस्तिपकः) यस्य (*adj.* of ०कुञ्जरे). 'आधोरणा हस्तिपका हस्त्यारोहा निषादिनः' इत्यमरः. मन्दुरापालकस्य (stable keeper) आक्रन्दैः कथिते. अजिरं (courtyard) भजते इति. विश्रान्तः जयशब्दकलकलःयस्मिन्.

आस्थानमण्डप: Hall of audience. अपस्नात:'—अपस्नातो मृतस्नातः' इत्यमरः— one who has bathed after the death of a relative. अनि...मौलिः without wringing his hair. उद्गम...वाससी two white silken robes. 'तत्स्यादुद्गमनीयं यद्धौतयोर्वस्त्रयोर्युगम्' इत्यमरः. निरातपत्रः without an umbrella (the insignia of royalty). निरुत्सारणः without anybody to remove people from his path. समुप...सप्तौ although a horse was brought near. चक्षुषा...उद्गिरन् as if emitting from his eye the fire of sorrow through fear of burning his father who now remained only in his (हर्ष's) heart. His eyes were extremely red. The poet fancies that the redness was the fire of sorrow in his heart. हर्ष emitted it from his eye, so that his father now enshrined in the heart might not be burnt by the fire. अताम्बू... क्षालितस्य—हर्ष had not taken betel for many days and had washed his lip a long time before (yet it was red by nature). कल्प... लयस्य—the tender leaves of any tree are reddish; much more therefore of कल्पतरु. The धर्म० (परि० III) says 'तत्राशौचमध्ये माषमांसापूपमधुरलवणदुग्धाभ्यङ्गताम्बूलक्षाराणि वर्ज्यानि.' अधर...मोक्षैः on account of the brilliance of his spraylike lip, he seemed to vomit, as he sent forth hot sighs, lumps of flesh and blood, because his heart was struck. If one were beaten in the region of the heart, he may vomit blood. When he heaved up deep sighs his red lips quivered and presented the appearance of blood being vomited.

P. 89 ll. 14–27 **राज...विचेरुः**. उद्बाष्पैः (उद्गतं बाष्पं येषाम्) full of tears. आत्मानम् mark the reflexive use of आत्मानम् with the plural केचित्. भृगु...बन्धुः some tied themselves to precipices *i. e.* killed themselves by falling from precipices. 'प्रपातस्त्वतटो भृगुः' इत्यमरः. अनशनैः शुचम् असमाम् अशमयन् they destroyed their unparalleled sorrow by fasting (*i. e.* they died fasting). शलभाः moths. गृहीतवाचः that took the vow of silence. तुषारशिखरिणं = हिमालयम्. उपत्यका—see p. 63. सेवाविमुखाः disgusted with service (*i. e.* with the life of a servant at the royal court). परि...जगृहुः resorted to untenanted spots in forests subsisting on a limited number of morsels. परिच्छिन्नैः पिण्डकैः may also mean 'with thin bodies.' धर्मः एव धनं येषाम्. धमन्त्यः धमनयः येषाम् with veins fully blown up (*i. e.* all the veins appeared prominent, they were emaciated). गृहीतं काषायं (red cloth) यैः. कषायेण रक्तं काषायम्, according to 'तेन रक्तं रागात्' पा. 4. 2. 1. कापिलं—कपिलस्य इदम्. कपिल is the founder of the सांख्य system, which enumerates 25 तत्त्वs. अधिजगिरे perfect of इ with अधि to study. It is to be noted that the wearing of

काषाय is here associated with कापिलमत; but याज्ञ० prescribes काषाय for all those that desire मोक्ष 'त्यागः परिग्रहाणां च जीर्णकाषायधारणम्' ॥ III. 157. आचोटिताः चूडामणयः यैः the crest-jewels of which were torn away. शरणीकृतः धूर्जटिः (शिवः) यैः. जटाः जघटिरे tied knots of matted hair. परिपाटलं प्रलम्बं चीवराम्बरं (tattered garment) तेन संवीताः enveloped. स्वाम्य...चक्रुः—they rendered glorious their devotion to their master. अनुराग also means 'redness'. By putting on red garments, they made redness appear brilliant. तपोवनहरिणानां जिह्वाञ्चलैः (tips of the tongues) उल्लिह्यमानाः (licked) मूर्तयः येषाम्. They became वानप्रस्थs and resorted to the forest. पाणि...मृष्टैः wiped (or scoured) with their spray-like hands. आताम्रः (slightly red) रागः (colour) येषाम्. नयन...वहन्तः they bore water in their eyes and in their jars. The idea is:—they shed tears, which they wiped with their hands and their eyes were red by weeping. They also rubbed their jars with their hands and carried water in them. The baked jars were red in colour. गृहीतं व्रतं यैः who took the vow of an ascetic (संन्यासी). See वसिष्ठस्मृति Chap. 10 for the धर्मs of a परिव्राजक. 'मुण्डोऽममोऽपरिग्रहः सप्तागाराण्यसङ्कल्पितानि चरेद्भैक्षं विधूमे सन्न—मुसले । 17...यज्ञोपवीती उदककमण्डलुहस्तः शुचिर्ब्राह्मणो वृषलान्नवर्जी न हीयते ब्रह्मलोकात्' । 24.

P. 89 l. 28—**P. 90** l. 4 **देवमपि...वारयन्.** The principal sentence is देवमपि हर्षं...मुनयः...पौराणिकाः पर्यवारयन्. श्रियं शाप इति—supply मन्यमानम् (l. 32) after this pair and after each of the pairs in the following clauses. श्रियं शाप इति म० who regarded royal glory as a curse. It will be noticed that the poet is influenced in his choice of words in this passage by the jingling assonance of sounds. महीं महापातकम्—As we must shun महापातकs, he shunned the earth. For महापातकs, see above (p.84). भोगान् भुजङ्गाः—as the serpent, so charming to look at, is yet deadly, so the objects of worldly enjoyments he regarded as dangerous. निलयं निरय इति who looked upon home as Hell (because he suffered torments). जीवितमयशः—to have continued to live after the death of such a noble father was really infamy. कल्यता health. 'कल्यौ सज्जनिरामयौ' इत्यमरः. विषममृतमिति—poison he regarded as nectar, because the former, if taken by him, would have assuaged all his torments and united him by death with his father. कामं क्रकच इति—he looked upon desire as a saw *i. e.* to entertain desires for anything when his father was dead was as painful to him as sawing with a saw. पितृ...गताः

whose fathers and grand-fathers had enjoyed (court favour). कुलपुत्राः—This and the following words like गुरवः are to be connected with पर्यवारयन् below. वंशक्रमेण आहितं गौरवं येषु to whom respect was paid for generations. ग्राह्याः गिरः येषाम्—whose words were to be accepted (or acted upon)—qualifies गुरवः. श्रुति = वेद. स्मृति—like those of Manu, Yājnavalkya &c. इतिहास—this is often employed to denote the महाभारत. It is defined as 'आर्षादिबहुधाख्यानं देवर्षिचरिताश्रयम्। इतिहासमिति प्रोक्तं भविष्यद्भूतधर्मयुक्॥'. श्रुता...शालिनः possessing learning, noble birth and character. मूर्धाभिषिक्ताः—crowned. We must connect the two adjectives ०शालिनः and ०षिक्ताः with अमात्याः and राजानः respectively. C and T connect मू० with अमात्याः and take राजानः as qualifying अमात्याः and translate 'anointed counsellors of royal rank endowed with learning &c.' But this is far-fetched. यथावत् अधिगतं आत्मतत्त्वं यैः that have correctly understood the truth about the self. संस्तुताः = परिचिताः. मस्करिणः = भिक्षवः 'भिक्षुः परिव्राट् कर्मन्दी पाराशर्यपि मस्करी' इत्यमरः. 'मस्करमस्करिणौ वेणुपरिव्राजकयोः' पा. 6. 1. 154. पतञ्जलि derives the word as 'मा कृत मा कृत कर्माणि शान्तिर्वः श्रेयसीति आहातो मस्करी परिव्राजकः' महाभाष्य ed. by Kielhorn Vol. III. p. 96 (from मा + कृ). सम...नाभयः Dependent kinsmen who shared his joys and sorrows. समे सुखदुःखे येषाम्. 'सपिण्डास्तु सनाभयः' इत्यमरः ('समानो नाभिर्मूलमेषां सनाभयः' क्षीर०). चित्तज्ञाः clever in reading the thoughts (of their master or of the people). निष्का...मुनयः sages that were disinterested friends. सं...वादिनः students of the Vedānta philosophy expert in expounding the unsubstantial character of the world. 'मीमांसको जैमिनीये वेदान्ती ब्रह्मवादिनि' क्षीर०. The position of the thorough-going Vedântin is summarized in a half-verse 'ब्रह्म सत्यं जगन्मिथ्या जीवो ब्रह्मैव नापरः॥'. पौराणिकाः—पुराणानि अधीते वेद वा पौराणिकः (पुराण + ठक्). The Purāṇas are a class of works attributed to Vyāsa containing information principally on mythology, cosmogony, the legendary origin of royal families and their doings, the doctrines of various sects&c. Bāṇa in the third उच्छ्वास specifically refers to the वायुपुराण.

P. 90 ll. 5–19 **अस्व...तिष्ठदिति.** अ...तैः not being left to himself by them. तैः refers to the कुलपुत्रs, गुरुs and others referred to in the preceding paragraph. मनसापि...चरितुम् even in thought he had no opportunity to do as his grief dictated. If left to himself Harsha in his grief might have caused some harm to himself. But as he was always surrounded by numerous people who engaged his mind in various things, he could not even think of (much less actually do) any harm to himself. अपि नाम न गृह्णीयाद्वल्कले how much do I wish that he may not assume bark robes ! He is afraid that राज्यवर्धन would betake himself to a forest. We have to understand अपि नाम before अस्त्र...पृथिवीम् and the following clauses. अस्त्र...पृथिवीम्—would he whose lotus-like eyes are filled with tears see that the earth is helpless (without a lord)? One whose eyes are full of water cannot see clearly. The Com. seems to have read न in each clause 'अत्र च सर्वत्र नेत्याशङ्कायाम्'. Then the meaning would be 'I am afraid that he would not see &c'. But here the force of अपि नाम is gone and the sentences are not so striking as they are without न. प्रथम...विह्वल: overwhelmed by the terrible poison of this first calamity (father's death). पुरुषोत्तम: refers to राज्यवर्धन. It also means विष्णु, When the gods and demons churned the ocean for jewels, the first thing that came out was the poison हालाहल. See रामायण I. 44. and भागवतपु. VIII. प्रथमं व्यसनं एव विषमं विषं तेन विह्वलः. अभिषेकम् (1) coronation; (2) bath. One who is suffering from heat, would take a bath and find it very refreshing. राज...चरेत् (How do I wish) that he may not act the contrary when addressed by the princes (to assume sovereignty). पराचीनता = प्रातिकूल्यम्. पक्षपाती devoted to. तातश्लाघया by way of praising father. काञ्चन०—As प्रभाकर० was fair in complexion, the word काञ्चन is put before ताल. दिवसक...कसितम् that was upturned and expanded the whole day with love for the sun. A lotus blooms by day. The king प्रभा० was devoted to the sun (see text p. 3) and had a smiling (विकसित) face all day. हसितः मदेन अलसः हलधरः (बलरामः) तस्य इव विभ्रमः येषां (*adj.* of विलासाः)—that had the appearance of the grace of the laughing Balarāma lazy with drink. बलराम, the brother of कृष्ण, has the ploughshare as his weapon. He is described as fond of drink. See विष्णुपु० V. 25. वदान्य liberal.

Uchchhvāsa VI

P. 91 **Verse 1** The metre of this verse and the next is आर्या, for which see p. 49. उच्चित्य having collected or gathered. प्रहिताः निगूढाः आत्मदूताः तैः नीतानाम्. The king sends his spies to find out valiant men; यम also sends his दूतs. विजिगीषुः (from the desiderative base of जि with वि) a conqueror. 'सनाशंसभिक्ष उः' पा. 3. 2. 168 (the affix उ is applied to desiderative bases, to the roots शंस् with आ and भिक्ष्). This verse contains a suggestion of the fate of राज्यवर्धन who was treacherously murdered by the गौड king, whose name the com. gives as शशाङ्क 'अनेनोच्छ्वासार्थः सङ्गृहीतः। तथाहि कृतोऽन्तो विनाशो येन स शशाङ्कनामा गौडाधिपतिः शूराणां राज्यवर्धनानुचराणां तत्सहितानां संग्रहमकरोत्। ...तथाहि तेन शशाङ्केन विश्वासार्थं दूतमुखेन कन्याप्रदानमुक्त्वा प्रलोभितो राज्यवर्धनः स्वगेहे सानुचरो भुञ्जान एव छद्मना व्यापादितः।'.

Verse 2 Construe खलस्य विस्रब्धघातदोषः वीरकोपकरः स्ववधाय (भवति). वि...करः the sin of murdering the confiding produces resentment in the mighty and brings about the death (of the murderer himself). नव...करिणः—the elephant wantonly breaks a young tree, but the noise of breaking robs the sleep of the lion that kills the elephant. Here खल refers to the गौड king who killed the young राज्य०. राज्यवर्धन's death by treachery roused हर्ष (वीर) to wrath and led to the destruction of the गौड king.

P. 91 ll. 5–20 **अथ...जीवितम्.** अथ...द्राक्षीत्—the sentence is अथ...देवो हर्षः...महाजनेन...अकाले आत्मानं वेष्टयमानं अद्राक्षीत्. प्रथमं प्रेतपिण्डं भुङ्क्ते इति० भुक् तस्मिन्. प्रथम...जन्मनि when the ब्राह्मण, that takes the first oblation offered for the dead, had been fed. गतेषु अशौचदिवसेषु—the impurity due to the death of a सपिण्ड lasts for ten days. 'दशाहं शावमाशौचं सपिण्डेषु विधीयते।' मनु० V. 59. दीयमा...कलापे—even now the bed and other things of the dead are given to ब्राह्मणs. The धर्मसिन्धु (परि० III) says 'एकादशाहे शय्यादाने एष विधिः स्मृतः। तेनोपभुक्तं यत्किंचिद्वस्त्रवाहनभाजनम्॥ यद्यदिष्टं च तस्यासीत्तत्सर्वं परिकल्पयेत्।'; and 'अश्वं रथं गजं धेनुं महिषीं शिबिकादिकम्। शालग्रामं पुस्तकं च कस्तूरी कुङ्कुमादिकम्॥ दासीं रत्नं भूषणादि शय्यां छत्रं च चामरम्। दद्याद्वित्तानुसारेण प्रेतस्तत्तत्सुखं लभेत्॥.' अमत्रम् a goblet, vessel. पत्रम् vehicles. 'पत्रं वाहनपक्षयोः' इत्यमरः. C and T read 'नृपतिकट' and translate 'the various appurtenances of the royal bier.' This is not good. The personal property, as it were, of the deceased king was distributed, as, if retained, it would have reminded the survivors every now and then of the use which the departed made of those articles. कीकसम् bone. The bones of the deceased king were taken to holy places. The people's hearts also, when they heard that the bones were being taken to तीर्थs, ran thither out of devotion to the king. कल्पित...चिह्ने when the tomb on the spot of the funeral pyre had been covered with a plaster of *chunam*, which (tomb) became a dart of sorrow. कल्पितं शोकशल्यं येन—the tomb remained there to remind people of their loss, as the point of a dart may permanently remain in the body. चैत्यचिह्नम् monument, tombstone. B reads कल्पित...शल्येषु; and C and T connect it with कीकसेषु. This is not bad. The meaning would be 'the bones had been like the points of darts' (in the hearts of the people). महाजिजिति the victor in great battles (आजिः). विसर्जिते—even now on the 11th or 12th day after death a bull is let loose for the dead. As the deceased was a king, an elephant was let loose. उत्सार्य... शय्यासु when the beds used in misfortune were being cast aside. The धर्मसिन्धु says that in mourning one should lie down on a bed of mats 'तृणकटास्तीर्णभूमौ पृथक्शयीरन् न कम्बलाद्यास्तीर्णभूमौ' (परि० III). उप...क्षमेषु capable of listening to advice. अनु...योग्येषु fit to pay attention to requests (अनुरोधः). गण...गुणेषु—when everybody had become so far composed as to be able to recount the virtues of the king. प्रदेश...शोके—C and T translate 'Grief was becoming a moral theme'. It is not clear how this meaning is arrived at. The meaning seems to us to be 'when grief came to have a limited scope' *i. e.* when शोक was not to be found at all seasons and places, but only at particular times and places. कृतेषु...तकेषु when the poets had sung their dirges. Take away the comma after ०स्थाने. स्वप्नावशेषं दर्शनं यस्य—For some days after his death, the people felt as if the king was among them. उत्सृष्टः व्यापारः येन who was doing nothing. महाजनेन by a great company. मौलेन hereditary. किमन्यत् what else (can it be)? लोकानां आकरः समूहः. अधिकतरः प्रचारः यस्य who moved about more (than the others). C and T translate 'a man of distinguished bearing'. सोदर्यस्नेहे निहितः (*lit.* placed in *i. e.* added to) निरतिशयः मन्युः शोकः तेन मृदूकृतं मनः यस्य. What is p aced in स्नेह (oil) may become soft. उत्पीडः mass, flood.

P. 91 l. 21—**P. 92** l. 19 अनन्तरं...गात्. The principal sentence is अनन्तरं च...ज्येष्ठं भ्रातरमपश्यत्. द्वार...कथ्यमानम् who was announced by the lamentation of the doorkeeper, as if it (आक्रन्द) were an attendant that entered first. At the sight of राज्य० the doorkeepr wept. The द्वारपाल allows (मुक्त) high personages and their attendants to enter. The attendants precede the high personages to show them the way. दूर... बाहुल्येन—this and the following instrumentals qualify परिजनेन. दूरं द्रुतं आगमनं तेन मुषितं बाहुल्यं यस्य whose numbers were thinned (*lit.* robbed) by the long and quick march. विच्छिन्नः छत्रधारः यस्मिन् in which the umbrella-bearer was not to be found (he lagged behind). लम्बितः (lagged behind) अम्बरवाही (the man in charge of the wardrobe) यस्मिन्. भृङ्गारः a golden pitcher 'भद्रकुम्भः पूर्णकुम्भो भृङ्गारः कनकालुका' इत्यमरः. आचमनधारिन् spittoon-bearer. ताम्यन् (exhausted) ताम्बूलिकः (betel-bearer) यस्मिन्. खञ्जन् (limping) खड्गग्राही यस्मिन्. कति...प्रायेण mostly consisting of a few well-known (प्रकाश) servants. For दासेरक, see p. 28. बहुवासरान्तरितं स्नानभोजनशयनं तेन श्यामं क्षामं (emaciated) वपुः यस्य. अविरला मार्गधूलिः तया धूसरितं शरीरं यस्य सः ०शरीरः तस्य भावः ०शरीरता तया. अविद्यमानं शरणं यस्याः. The poet fancies that the earth in the form of dust resorted to him because it had become bereft of a protector by the death of प्रभाकर०. क्रमागतया (1) that was hereditary in his family; (2) that came to him (stuck to his body) by his walking (with धूलि). हूणानां निर्जयाय समरे शरैः व्रणाः तेषु बद्धैः पट्टकैः (pieces of cloth) शबलीकृतः (spotted) कायः यस्य. The long and white bandages are fancied to be the glances of राज्यलक्ष्मी that was approaching him (he was the king after his father). Long eyes is a sign of beauty. The inside of the eye is white like the bandages. हुतं मांसं येषाम्. आवेद्यमानः दुःखभारः यस्य. He had lost flesh through grief. The poet fancies that the flesh so lost had been offered into the fire of grief for preserving his father's life. When a sacrifice is performed, offerings are given in fire. There is a striking contrast presented by the inference of a heavy weight from lean (कृश) limbs. Ordinarily lean limbs do not carry heavy weights. अपगतः चूडामणिः यस्मात्. मलिनाः आकुलाः (dishevelled) कुन्तलाः यस्य. शेखरः garland of flowers on the head. His head was not decorated through grief. The poet fancies that grief had mounted on it. आतपेन गलिता स्वेदराजिः यस्मात् (*adj* of ०पट्टेन). रुदतेव—Drops of perspiration stood out on his forehead owing to heat. The poet fancies that his forehead was eager to bow at the feet of his father and wept, as it could not do so owing to the death of प्रभा०. प्रथीयस् comparative of पृथु. One who faints has water sprinkled on his face. राज्य० shed tears which fell on the earth. The poet fancies that the tears were water poured over the earth that had swooned away owing to the death of her honoured lord. निम्नीकृत dug out, made hollow. His cheeks that were once round and fleshy had become hollow. Constant dripping of water wears away even stones. The poet fancies that the constant falling of tears on the cheeks wore away the cheeks and made them hollow. गलितः ताम्बूलरागः यस्मात्. राज्य० used no betel owing to grief. So his lip had not its usual redness. The poet fancies that the ताम्बूलराग came in the way of his very hot breaths, became melted and disappeared from his lip. पवित्रिकामात्रे अवशेषः यस्याः सा ०शेषा इन्द्रनीलिका &c. पवित्रि... द्हन्तम्—the idea is:—in his यज्ञोपवीत there was a sapphire ring, the rays of which shot upwards and rendered his ear dark. The poet fancies that the darkness of the ear is due to its being burnt by the fire of the great grief at the recent news of his father's death. पवित्रकं = शणसूत्रजालं क्षत्रियस्य यज्ञोपवीतम्. The only इन्द्रनील he had was on the ring in his यज्ञोपवीत. C and T render 'his sapphire ornament of which only the amulet was left'. अस्फुटाभिव्यक्तं व्यञ्जनं (beard) यस्मिन्. **'व्यञ्जनं** लान्छन**श्मश्रु**निष्ठानावयवेष्वपि' इत्यमरः. His face had only a slight growth of beard, which was rendered darker by the light of the dark pupils of his downcast and motionless eye. One who is in mourning has to allow his beard to grow. Though he had a slight growth of beard, he seemed to have a thick growth of it owing to the rays of his eye. महा...ह्वलम् (1) overwhelmed by the fall of a great mountain (with lion); (2) overwhelmed by the death of the great king (with राज्यवर्धन). निरवलम्बनम् without refuge or support. If a mountain falls on a lion, the latter will lose a place for prowling and will be stunned. तेजःपतिः (सूर्यः, नृपतिश्च) तस्य पतनेन परिम्लाना श्रीः यस्य. दिवसमिव श्यामीभूतम्—who (राज्य०) had become dark (in complexion) like the day. The day also turns into night when the sun dips down into the sea. श्यामीभूतं means रात्रीभूतं with दिवसम्. **'श्यामा** स्याच्छारिवा **निशा'** इत्यमरः. नन्दनम्—the garden of Indra. भग्नः कल्पपादपः यस्य. If the tree in the नन्दनवन be broken there will be no shade (छाया). राज्य० also had no छाया (splendour) left, as his father, who was a veritable कल्पवृक्ष to suppliants, was dead. प्रोषितः

दिक्कुञ्जरः (दिग्गजः) यस्मात्. If the दिग्गजs went away, the quarters would be empty (शून्य). राज्य० also was शून्य (vacant-minded). The eight quarters are guarded by eight दिग्गजs. 'ऐरावतः पुण्डरीको वामनः कुमुदोऽञ्जनः। पुष्पदन्तः सार्वभौमः सुप्रतीकश्च दिग्गजाः॥' इत्यमरः. दिशां भावः दिग्भावः (the state of the quarters). गुरुः (heavy, crushing) वज्रपातः तेन दारितम् (with गिरि); गुरौ (पितरि) वज्रपातः (मृत्युः) तेन दारितम् (with राज्य०). The wings of mountains were clipped by Indra with his thunderbolt. See p. 19 above. किङ्क...रुण्येन enslaved by sorrow. दुर्मनसः भावः दौर्मनस्यम्—despondency. स्विन्न...पेन all perspiring through सन्ताप (heat, sorrow). उच्चितम् gathered, collected. लुप्तम् robbed. C and T would prefer वृतं the reading of two MSS. of B for धृतं for the sake of alliteration. प्रत्या...ख्यानेन discarded by reflection. Compare 'अवष्टम्भो ज्ञानं धैर्यं **प्रतिसंख्यान**मित्यस्तमितैषा कथा' कादम्बरी (p. 156 of P). दूरी...भवत्वेन cast aside by firmness (*lit.* the quality of being invincible). अबो...बुद्धीनाम् that was beyond the counsels of the aged. The instrumentals from अबोध्येन qualify शोकेन below. असा ... तानाम् that was not to be cured by the words of the good. अग...गिराम् that was inaccessible to the eloquence of elders. अशक्ये...शक्तीनाम् not within the reach of the power of scriptures. अ...यत्नानाम् that was beyond the way of the efforts of wisdom. The idea is that the efforts of wise men would not avail to lessen his sorrow. अभूमि...चयानाम् that was not a proper place for gradual healing up. उपचयः *lit.* increase, prosperity. आवेगेन उद्गताः कृत्स्नस्नेहस्य उत्कलिकाः ताभिः उत्क्षिप्यमाणः कायः यस्य—whose body was lifted up on the waves of the whole love that surged up through emotion. स्नेह is compared to the sea; emotion caused by the sight of राज्य० to the tide of the sea. The agitation (उत्कलिका) due to the emotion is compared to waves (उत्कलिका). A man swimming in the sea is borne on the crest of waves. Harsha's body was shaken by agitation.

P. 92 l. 20—**P. 93** l. 2 **अथ तं...स्यात्.** कलितं held in. ०सारितेन goes with ०द्वयेन. We must read संकलयन्निव (as if grasping). He stretched out his long arms to embrace हर्ष. The poet fancies that he did so in order to embrace all sorrows (*i. e.* he would thereby become full of all sorrows). सङ्कल्पयन् hardly yields any sense. पतितं क्षौमं यस्मात् from which the fine garment had fallen (or slipped away). सब...हृदयानि (their) hearts were as if uprooted together with their fastenings. A and C omit the sentence अश्रु...लोकेन. That sentence seems to mean 'the people let fall in their eyes a stream of tears resembling veins of blood'. The preceding sentence spoke of the uprooting of hearts. If that were actually done, blood would flow forth from the veins of the body. The stream of tears is fancied to be the veins of blood. स्मृतः नृपतिः (प्रभाकरवर्धनः) येन. When the princes wept, the king's favourite also wept. He seemed to be the echo of the princes. निर्वृष्टं नयनजलं येन. Rain ceases in autumn of its own accord; no one can stop it. So राज्यवर्धन stopped weeping after a long time. तोयेन—connect this with अक्षालयत्. तस्कर...लेखमिव (eye) that seemed to have a streak of foam produced by a big flood of water because of the pencils of the rays of his finger-nails. When he washed his face, he moved his hand over it. The rays of his bright nails resembled white foam and so his eye seemed to be covered with foam. पक्ष्माग्रे सङ्कलन्तः बिन्दवः तेषां वृन्दं तेन मन्दः उन्मेषः तेन मुषितं दर्शनं यस्य (his eye) the vision of which was robbed by the fact that its opening (उन्मेषः) was obstructed by the mass of tear-drops gathering on the tips of his eyelashes. वाससा...न्ममार्ज—he wiped his face with a white towel. The towel resembled moonlight in whiteness and in being cool. So the poet fancies that he wiped his face scorched by very hot tears with a piece of moonlight. विभूषं...ष्पीड्य having carelessly wrung his head (मौलिः) that was unadorned and the locks on which were disturbed and dishevelled. विगता भूषा यस्मात्. वित्रस्ताः व्यस्ताः (scattered about) कुन्तलाः यस्य. सावशेष...अधरेण—(connect this with कुर्वाणः)—by his lower lip that quivered on account of the remnants of sorrow, which (lip) therefore seemed as if desirous of living and as if desirous of kissing itself, as it was charming on account of its bath. The idea is:—when राज्य० bathed he washed his lip and eyes. As his grief had not all died out, his lip quivered. One who lives makes movements. So the quivering of the lip showed that in spite of grief it wanted to live. In kissing also the lips move. So the poet imagines that the lip quivered because it wanted to kiss itself on account of its own agreeableness due to the bath. अवशेषेण सह साव० (बहुव्रीहि), सावशेषः मन्युः तेन स्फुरितः. शारदः (शरदि भवः) शशी तस्य करैः विकसितानि विशदानि (shining) कुमुदवनानि तेषां दलावलिः एव बलिः तस्य विक्षेपैः (throwing). The कुमुदs bloom in moon-light. The moon is at its best in शरद्. His quivering lip resembled the flashes of lightning become rare when शरद् comes; his washed face resembled the clear moon of शरद्. When राज्य० cast glances in various directions, the poet imagines that he did worship to the दिग्देवताs with the offerings of petals of कुमुदs. चतुःशालम् a quadrangle enclosed by four buildings. चतसृणां शालानां समाहारः चतुःशालम्. वितर्दिका—platform, terrace. See p. 53. नीचापाश्रये विनिहितः एकः उपबर्हः यस्याम्—on which a single cushion was placed beneath a low awning. For अपाश्रय, see p. 21. 'उपधानं तूपबर्हः' इत्यमरः. जोषम् *adv.* silently.

P. 93 ll. 3-15 **देवोऽपि...मण्डलम्.** ०कुथायां प्रसारिता मूर्तिः (शरीरं) येन. कुथा a blanket or carpet. औरस...शोकस्य for the sight of a very near relative is the youth of sorrow. औरसः—उरसा निर्मितः according to 'उरसोऽण् च' पा. 4. 4. 94. The word is primarily applied to a son and extended to any close blood relation like a brother. The idea is that at the sight of one's near relations grief increases in intensity. Compare notes p. 96. सः (l. 8) refers to दिवसः. प्रत्यग्र...तनुरिव as if his body had recently (प्रत्यग्र) been chopped by the chisel of त्वष्टृ. The sun at the time of setting looked red. One whose body is recently cut would be red with blood and flesh. वहद्बहलरुधिररसं (वहन् बहलः रुधिररसः यस्मिन् तत्) मांसं तस्य इव छविः (कान्तिः) यस्य that looked like flesh moistened by plentiful blood. प्रत्यग्रत्वष्टृ०—त्वष्टृ is the architect of the gods. He had a daughter named संज्ञा that was married to the sun. She could not bear the light of the sun. त्वष्टृ, wishing to reduce the superfluous lustre of the sun, placed him on his lathe and trimmed off some of his lustre. With the portion thus taken away त्वष्टृ manufactured the चक्र of विष्णु, the त्रिशूल of रुद्र and the other weapons of the gods. Vide विष्णुपु० III. 2. 9-12 and मार्कण्डेयपु० Chap. 77. 'भ्रमिमारोप्य सूर्यं तु तस्य तेजोविशातनात्। कृत्तवानष्टमं भागं न व्यशातयताव्ययम्॥' विष्णु० III. 2. 9. Note रघु० VI. 32 'आरोप्य चक्रभ्रममुष्णतेजास्त्वष्ट्रेव यत्नोल्लिखितो विभाति॥'. अपरः (western) पारावारः ocean. मञ्जिष्ठावत् अरुणः. मञ्जिष्ठा Bengal madder. It is used as a red dye. अरुणः सारथिः यस्य. मुकुलायमानाः (closing) कमलिनीकोषाः तेन विकलम् (distressed). चकाण perfect of कण् to cry in distress, hum. The कमल closes its petals at sunset. चञ्चरीकः = भ्रमरः. On this word क्षीरस्वामी remarks 'चञ्चरीकभसनेन्दिन्दिररोलम्बा देश्याम्'. सविधः (near, approaching) विरहव्याधिः तेन विधुरा वधूः तया बाध्यमानम् (*adj.* of चक्रवालम्). विबुद्धस्य (blooming) बन्धूकस्य इव भाः (तेजः) यस्य (*adj.* of भास्वति). बन्धूकम् is a kind of red flower.

अस्रैः सह सास्राम् tearful. चक्रवालम्—group. For the separation of the चक्रवाक from its mate at sunset, see pp. 10, 57. सञ्चरन्त्याः goes with श्रियः. श्री is said to be wandering because प्रभाकरवर्धन being dead there is yet no new king installed. मधुकररवेण सह स... रवं. कैरवाकरं must be taken as the object of सञ्चरन्त्याः. The कैरवs are white lotuses that expand at nightfall. The bees buzzed over them. The poet fancies that this buz ing was the jingling of the small bells on the girdle of लक्ष्मी. कल... रमणीयम् goes with ०करम्. The कलहंसीs were there near the कैरव beds and lent their grace to them. आण—perfect of अण् to sound. The bees were like bells, the कलहंसीs like माणिक्यकाञ्ची and the white lotuses like the fair complexion of लक्ष्मी. प्रकटः कलङ्कः यस्य (*adj.* of ०मण्डलम्). उदयमानम् (*pr. p.* of अय् 1 A with उद्) rising. विशङ्कटः (large) विषाणः (horn) तेन उत्कीर्णः (scattered) पङ्कः तस्य सङ्करः (contact) यस्य सः ०सङ्करः शङ्करस्य शकुरः (tame) शक्करः (bull) तस्य ककुदकूटः (conical hump) तत्सङ्काशं तत्सदृशम्. 'विशङ्कटं पृथु बृहत्' इत्यमरः. The moon was like the hump of the white bull of शिव and the horns of the moon resembled the horns of the bull and the spot on the moon was like the mud on the horn of the bull. This passage is full of suggestions, as C and T observe. The word शशाङ्कमण्डलम् indicates the rise of the गौड king (शशाङ्क as the com. says), who murdered राज्यवर्धन. The red sunset symbolizes bloody wars.

P. 93 ll. 16—**P. 94** l. 18 **अस्यां...धरण्याम्.** नास्ति अतिक्रमणं यस्य तत् अनतिक्रमणं वचनं येषाम् whose words could not be disregarded. भूमिः...योगानाम् ycu are a proper person for the injunctions of elders *i. e.* elders enjoin you to do something because they feel sure that you would not disobey. Or गुरु may mean 'father', the sense being 'our father used to give you instruction as you were the fittest person to receive it.' अग्राहि चित्तवृत्तिः you held the heart. A person may seize a banner that has ropes. The king's mind also was गुणवत्; or the king's mind was the banner of the virtuous (गुणवतां पताका) *i. e.* he was the foremost or preeminent among the virtuous (as a banner is). विधेयम् docile, obedient. विधेः विधानेन उपनतं नैर्घृण्यं (निर्घृणस्य निर्दयस्य भावः) यस्य (my heart) that has become callous by the decrees of fate. C and T translate 'विधि०' as 'my heart, softened to compliance with the decrees of fate.' This is wrong. बिभणिषति = भणितुमिच्छति. प्रेमविलोमा which runs counter to affection. Read ०विलोमा for ०विलोपा. वामता perverseness, refractory spirit. वैधेयः fool, dullard.

'अज्ञे मूढयथाजातमूर्खवैधेयबालिशाः' इत्यमरः (विधेयः एव वैधेयः स्वार्थेऽण्). लोकवृत्तम् ways of the world. मान्धान्तृ—see for his story p. 23. प्रभाकर० was a pre-eminent चक्रवर्ती as मान्धाता was. 'यौवनाश्वोऽथ मान्धाता चक्रवर्त्यवनीं प्रभुः । सप्तद्वीपवतीमेकः शशासाच्युत तेजसा ॥' भागवतपु० 9. 6. 34. पुरुकुत्स was the son of मान्धातृ and killed the मौनेयगन्धर्वs that had ousted the Nâgas and re-instated the latter. He married नर्मदा. See विष्णुपुराण IV. 3. भ्रूलतया आदिष्टानि अष्टादश द्वीपानि येन who issued commands to the eighteen worlds with his brow. दिलीपे मृते वा रघुणा (किं कृतम्)—Bâna seems to follow the रघुवंश here in making रघु the son of दिलीप. According to the रामायण (II. 110 and I. 70) दिलीप's son was भगीरथ, whose grandson was रघु. So according to the विष्णुपुराण (IV. 4) दिलीप's son was दीर्घबाहु whose son was रघु. महान् असुरसमरः तन्मध्ये अध्यासितः त्रिदशानां (देवानां) रथः येन. Compare for the idea that दशरथ helped the gods in battle रघु० 9. 19 'स किल संयुगमूर्ध्नि सहायतां मघवतः प्रतिपद्य महारथः।'. It was in this battle with the demon शम्बर that कैकेयी, who had helped दशरथ, got two वरs from him. See रामायण अयोध्याकाण्ड 2. गोष्पदीकृताः चतुर्णां उदन्वतां अन्ताः येन—who looked upon the confines of the four oceans as a puddle. गोष्पदम् (गो + पद)—स् is inserted according to 'गोष्पदं सेवितासेवितप्रमाणेषु' पा. 6. 1. 145. (गावः पद्यन्तेऽस्मिन्देशे स गोभिः सेवितो गोष्पदः । प्रमाणे, गोष्पदमात्रं क्षेत्रम् । सि. कौ.). The four oceans were as small to him as a puddle that is as deep as a cow's hoof. तिष्ठन्तु...देते let alone these. तातेन—refers to प्रभाकरवर्धन. शतात् समधिकाः (more than a hundred) अध्वराः तेषां धूमः तस्य विसरेण (mass) धूसरितं वासवस्य (इन्द्रस्य) वयः येन—who rendered the youth of Indra grey by &c. It was believed that whoever performed a hundred अश्वमेध sacrifices would displace Indra. Indra is therefore always represented as anxious to put obstacles in the performance of these sacrifices. Indra grew old through anxiety and jealousy when he learnt of the hundred and more sacrifices of प्रभा०. सुगृहीतं नाम यस्य—of blessed memory. This is a term used in respectfully addressing or speaking of a person (particularly a deceased person). कुत्सितः पुरुषः कापुरुषः, according to 'विभाषा पुरुषे' पा. 6. 3. 106 (कापुरुषः । कुपुरुषः). स्त्रैणं womanishness. आस्पदम् = स्थानम्. भू...र्ध्वस्ते (1) the king being killed; (2) the mountain being shattered or laid low. If a mountain were shattered to pieces, all the torrents will be at once let loose; so the king being killed, all his tears flow in torrents. अस्त...तेजसि—refers to the setting of the sun and the death of the king. अन्धकारीभूताः दश आशाः (दिशः)

यस्य. प्र...लोकः the light of wisdom fails. When the sun sets, there is no light in the ten quarters. The king being dead, राज्य० cannot think wisely and looks on the whole world as dark. Remove the comma after हृदयं, which is the object of उपसर्पति. My heart is aflame with grief and therefore विवेक does not come to it, as if afraid of being burnt by the fire in the heart. सन्ताप (1) sorrow, (2) heat. जातुषम्—made of lac. जतुनो विकारः, according to 'त्रपुजतुनोः षुक्' पा. 4. 3. 138 (आभ्यामण् स्यात् विकारे एतयोः षुगागमश्च त्रापुषम् । जातुषम् । सि. कौ.). पदे पदे (1) at every word; (2) at every step. दिग्धः (poisoned) रोपः (arrow) तेन आहता. 'पत्री रोप इषुर्द्वयोः' इत्यमरः. 'विषाक्ते दिग्धलिप्तकौ' इत्यमरः. दूरेण भ्रमति (1) wanders far; (2) wanders at a distance (from the person hated). परिहरन्ती avoiding. अम्बा—refers to यशोमती. वार्धु...वित्तानि money that is employed by a moneylender or usurer. वार्धुषिक (from वृद्धि)—वृद्ध्यर्थं द्रव्यं वृद्धिः तां गर्ह्यां प्रयच्छति इति—according to वार्तिक 'वृद्धेर्वृधुषिभावो वक्तव्यः' on 'प्रयच्छति गर्ह्यम्' पा. 4. 4. 30. A very exacting moneylender would stipulate for interest to be calculated from day to day; and even without such stipulation, ordinarily every day adds to the interest that has to be paid. ०धूमसम्भारात् सम्भूतः अम्भोधरः (मेघः) तेन भरितमिव. पञ्चजनः—*lit.* people of the five races (*i. e.* the Aryans in the four quarters and the निषाद s); hence, people in general. Compare ऋग्वेद III. 59. 8 'मित्राय **पञ्च** येमिरे **जना** अभिष्टिशवसे'. 'स्युः पुमांसः पञ्चजनाः पुरुषाः' इत्यमरः. पञ्चत्वं प्रयाति is dissolved into the five elements (पृथिव्यप्तेजोवाय्वाकाश). असाम्परायिकम् not warlike, cowardly. सम्परायः = युद्धम्. अवष्टभ्य having enveloped. शोकः—connect it with दहति and the following verbs. वाडव...राशिम्—this and the following three clauses are to be respectively connected with दहति and the three following verbs. वाडवः—is the submarine fire, otherwise called और्व. The sons of कार्तवीर्य, with the desire of destroying the descendants of भृगु, killed even the children in the womb. One of the women of the family secreted the child in her womb in her thigh (ऊरु) and preserved it. Hence the child was called और्व. At sight of him, the sons of कार्तवीर्य were struck blind and his wrath gave rise to a flame which was going to burn the whole world, when at the desire of his पितृs, the भार्गवs, he cast it into the ocean. Compare शाकुन्तल III. 3 'त्वयि ज्वलत्यौर्व इवाम्बुराशौ'. See आदिपर्व for the story. पविरिव पर्वतं (दारयति)—for the clipping of the wings of mountains, see p. 19. क्षय...करं (तनूकरोति)—for showing greater favour to रोहिणी than to his other wives, the नक्षत्रs, the moon was cursed by their father दक्ष to be a consumptive. Compare 'दर्शयन्निव चिरकाललग्नं दक्षशापानलदाहचिह्नं' कादम्बरी (p. 178 of P). सुमेरुकल्पस्य resembling Meru. For Meru, see p. 85. For कल्प, see notes on देशीय p. 38. कल्प...पुरुषस्य who was a noble spirit (to be found once) in a कल्प. For कल्प, see p. 78. Another meaning also may be suggested 'a noble spirit like a कल्पवृक्ष'. अतिवाहयितुम् to get through. विरक्तं (1) disgusted; (2) tinged redder. चकोरस्य—It was believed that the eyes of चकोरs became red at the sight of poison. अर्थशास्त्र of कौटिल्य says 'क्रौञ्चो विषाभ्याशे माद्यति। ग्लायति जीवञ्जीवकः। म्रियते मत्तकोकिलः। चकोरस्याक्षिणी विरज्येते' (pp. 40–41). काम० says 'चकोरस्य विरज्येते नयने विषदर्शनात्। सुव्यक्तं माद्यति क्रौञ्चो म्रियते कोकिलः किल॥' VII. 12. बहवः मृतपटाः अवगुण्ठनं यस्याः that covers her face with many shrouds of the dead. The चाण्डालs were in the habit of taking the clothes in which corpses were shrouded. रञ्जितः रङ्गः (समाजः) यया that pleases the audience or sight-seers. People were diverted by the sight of the various shrouds worn by Chandāla females. जनङ्गमः=चण्डालः. राज्यवर्धन says he wants to give up राज्यलक्ष्मी, which he compares to the श्री of चण्डालs. 'चण्डालप्लवमातङ्गदिवाकीर्तिजनङ्गमाः' इत्यमरः. It would be better to read जनङ्गमाङ्गनाम् as C and T suggest. वंशबाह्याम्—(1) which is outside of (noble) family; (2) which is to be borne on bamboo-poles. बाह्य in the latter case is equal to वाह्य, as there is no difference between ब and व, र and ल, ड and ल in यमक, श्लेष and चित्र 'यमकश्लेषचित्रेषु बवयोर्डलयोर्न भित्। नानुस्वारविसर्गौ च चित्रभङ्गाय संमतौ॥' वाग्भटालंकार I. 20. चण्डालs carry all their belongings on poles. अनार्याम् (1) disreputable; (2) not of Aryan lineage. The चण्डालs were outside the pale of Âryan society. दग्ध...कुलिरिव as a bird in a burnt dwelling. दग्धगृहे may also mean 'in this palace accursed' (by the king's death). स्नेहमल is to be connected with मनसि and वाससि. स्नेह (1) affection (2) oil. Affection clung to his heart and he wanted to get rid of it in a hermitage. An oily and dirty spot sticks to a garment which must be washed in water. अन्तरितानि यौवनसौख्यानि यस्याम् in which the pleasures of youth cannot be had (*adj.* of जरां and ०चिन्ताम्). The cares of the kingdom would not allow हर्ष to enjoy youth as otherwise he would have done. अनभिमताम् not esteemed or liked (with जराम् and चिन्ताम्). जरामिव पूरुः—ययाति married देवयानी daughter of शुक्र preceptor of the दैत्यs. शर्मिष्ठा, daughter of the king of

दैत्यs, was her servant. ययाति fell in love with her and secretly married her. When देवयानी complained, her father शुक्र cursed him to be prematurely old. ययाति propitiated शुक्र and obtained permission to transfer his old age to any one that would accept it. He had two sons यदु and तुर्वसु from देवयानी and द्रुह्य, अनु and पूरु from शर्मिष्ठा. All his sons except पूरु refused to take up the decrepitude of their father. पूरु, the youngest, dutifully took it up and was placed on the throne by ययाति. See विष्णुपु. IV. 10; रामायण VII. 58–59; महाभारत आदिपर्व. गुरोः (1) of his father (with पूरु); (2) of me who am your elder (brother). त्यक्ताः सकलाः बालक्रीडाः येन (applies to हर्ष and हरि both). हरिणा = विष्णुना. दीयता...लक्ष्म्यै give your chest to लक्ष्मी. हर्ष is asked to accept sovereignty. विष्णु took लक्ष्मी as his wife. बालक्रीडा—these words suggest the doings of कृष्ण (the incarnation of विष्णु) in गोकुल. रुक्मिणी the wife of कृष्ण is looked upon as the incarnation of लक्ष्मी. 'राघवत्वेऽभवत्सीता रुक्मिणी कृष्णजन्मनि' विष्णु॰ I. 9. 141. निस्त्रिंशः—a sword—(निष्क्रान्तस्त्रिंशतोऽङ्गुलिभ्यः इति which is longer than 30 finger-breadths).

P. 94 l. 19—**P 95** l. 22 **अथ...तिष्ठत.** निशिता शिखा यस्य the point of which is very sharp. मामन्तरेण concerning me. It may also mean 'without me *i. e.* behind my back.' शोकात् जन्म यस्य (*adj.* of ०क्षेपः). चेतसः समाक्षेपः Distraction or aberration of mind. आहो...भवति ? Is it possible that he is not my brother ? The idea is that he speaks so unlike my brother that I am forced to doubt whether he is the same as my brother. विवक्षितं = वक्तुमिष्टम्. निपातनोपायः a means of decline or downfall. निखिलपुण्यस्य परिक्षयः तस्य उपक्षेपः (indication). कर्मणां is to be connected with निखिल॰. The idea is :—do these unexpected words of my brother indicate that all the merit I gathered by my actions has now been exhausted ? अन...लसितं वा or is it the wanton act of the group of all unfavourable planets ? तातस्य विनाशेन निःशङ्कः (fearless) कलिकालः तस्य क्रीडितम् (prank, freak). The idea is that प्रभाकर॰ had held कलि in cheek. अयं—refers to राज्य॰ यःकश्चिदिव like a low person. यत्किंचनकारिणं माम्—connect with समादिष्टवान्. यत्किंच...र्भूतमिव (he has ordered) me (thinking me) capable of doing anything, as if I were not born of the line of पुष्पभूति. अनात्मानुजमिव as if I were not his own younger brother. The reading अदृष्टदोषमपि breaks the symmetry of the clauses, all of which contain an इव; but yields a good sense. The reading दृष्टदोषमिव of A and C means 'as if I were one detected in committing a fault.' श्रोत्रियमिव—What Harsha says is this:—to ask me to assume sovereign power when my elder brother is quite competent to do it is as detestable as to ask a श्रोत्रिय to drink wine, to induce a faithful servant to prove treacherous to his master &c. सुरापान was one of the five महापातकs, for which see above p. 84. नीचोपसर्पणम् to approach or wait upon a mean person. तदे...यत् This much (out of what राज्य° does) is indeed befitting that &c. शौर्यस्य उन्मादः एव मदिरा तया मत्तं समस्तं सामन्तमण्डलं एव समुद्रः तस्य मथने मन्दरः तस्मिन्. The feudatories intoxicated by the pride of valour are compared to the ocean; as the ocean was churned with मन्दर as the churning handle, so प्रभाकर° was the churning handle of the kings (*i. e.* subdued them and made them yield tribute as the ocean had to yield jewels). For मन्दर, see above p. 42. For the technical meaning of मण्डल, see p. 42. The king प्रभा° was in the midst of the मण्डल as the handle मन्दर was in the midst of the ocean. The ocean also had मदिरा (वारुणी, one of the 14 jewels). या...वृष्टिः as for this command to me to assume sovereignty, it scorches me who am already burnt and is a shower of cinders on me who am like a desert parched by drought. अवग्रहेण (वृष्टेर्विघातेन) ग्लपितः (past p. p. of the causal of ग्लै). धन्वन् *m.* a barren or dry soil. 'समानौ मरुधन्वानौ' इत्यमरः. 'वृष्टिर्वर्षं तद्विघातेऽवग्राहावग्रहौ समौ' इत्यमरः. यद्यपि...मानः—supply जगति दुर्लभः after this and after every-one of the following clauses. विभु...मानः a person in power without pride. द्विजातिः = ब्राह्मणः. अविद्यमाना एषणा (greed, covetousness) यस्य. मुनिररोषणः a sage without anger. The Purâṇas illustrate only too well this *dictum.* वणि...रः a trader who is not a thief (knave). प्रिया जाया यस्य स° जानिः. जाया becomes जानि when it is the last member of a बहुव्रीहि compound. 'जायाया निङ्' पा. 5. 4. 134. प्रिय...हनः (it is rare to find) a husband fond of his wife who is also not jealous. कुहन *adj.* jealous. 'कुहना दम्भचर्यायामीर्ष्यालौ कुहनं त्रिषु' इति मेदिनी. कीना...गतः (it is rare to find) a poor man who is not an eyesore. 'कृतान्ते पुंसि कीनाशः क्षुद्रकर्षकयोनिषु' इत्यमरः. मृगयुः a hunter. पारा...ब्राह्मण्यः (it is rare to find) a mendicant who possesses the qualities of a (good) ब्राह्मण. पाराशरिन् originally means 'one who studies the भिक्षुसूत्र promulgated by पाराशर्य'; hence any mendicant (whether learned in the Vedānta or not). 'पाराशर्यशिलालिभ्यां भिक्षुनटसूत्रयोः' पा. 4. 3. 110 (पाराशर्येण प्रोक्तं भिक्षुसूत्रमधीयते पाराशरिणो भिक्षवः । सि. कौ.). कितवः a gambler. The reading of A and C is good. परि...क्षु: an ascetic who is not desirous of enjoying (life). गोप्य: a servant. राज...नींत: (it is rare to find) a king's son who is not wicked (or ill-educated). This last is the matter in hand. हर्ष means:—king's sons are generally badly educated; and so an ordinary prince would have done as राज्य॰ wants me to do. But I am the pupil of no less a person than राज्य॰ himself. को हि नाम—connect these words with चण्ड, कोऽपि. राज...कुञ्जरे who is a गन्धद्विप to the (elephants in the form of) kings (*i. e.* from fear of whom kings run away). For गन्धद्विप see p. 4 (notes). विफली...भुजे who has rendered useless his large thighs and arms resembling a stone pillar. Or we may take that the thighs resembled a slab of stone and the arms a pillar. सकल...पवित्रम्—people would shed tears when they would hear that राज्य॰ had abandoned the kingdom. मृद्गो...धानम् a sphere of mud called earth. वसुधा अभिधानं यस्य. मृद्गोलकं—is the object of कामयेत. धनमदेन खेलाः (playful) निखिलाः खलाः तेषां मुखविकारलक्षणैः आख्यायमानं नीचाचरणं यस्याः whose vile conduct is exposed by the indications offered by the changing features of the faces of the wicked &c. The idea is:—लक्ष्मी very often resorts to wicked men who become purse-proud and whose faces assume arrogant looks. Thus it is लक्ष्मी that is responsible for the arrogance and conceit of the wicked. कुम्भदासी a bawd, procuress. 'कुम्भो राश्यन्तरे हस्तिमूर्धांसे राक्षसान्तरे । कार्मुके वारनार्यां च' मेदिनी. लक्ष्मी goes about seeking the deeds of the valorous, and is therefore like a bawd. कथमि...र्येण how did my brother think this which is extremely improper to be possible (in me)? अनवदातम् Impure. चेतसः च्युतः passed from his mind. सौमित्रिः—लक्ष्मणः. लक्ष्मण is the Hindu ideal of a younger brother and so are भीम, अर्जुन, नकुल and सहदेव. It is to be noted that it is not a mere rhetorical touch that Bâṇa puts this sentiment in the mouth of Harsha. The inscriptions of हर्ष (for which see Introduction) show that हर्ष revered his brother as much as (or perhaps more than) his father. अनपेक्षितः भक्तजनः यया that cared not for those that loved him. प्रभविष्णुता—the position of being a lord. Harsha means that राज्य॰ was never before so heedless of the feelings of those that were devoted to him. कुलिशस्य (thunderbolt) शिखरवत् खरं (sharp) नखरं (claw) तस्य प्रचयः (mass, thickness.) तस्य प्रचण्डाचपेटा तया पाटितं मत्तमातङ्गस्य उत्तमाङ्गं (शिरः) तस्य मदच्छटा (mass or streak of ichor) तया छुरितः चारुकेसरभारः तेन भास्वरं मुखं यस्य.

निवासं...पृष्ठतः who protects behind his back the mountain cave—his dwelling? प्रतापः सहायः येषाम्. कश्यप...र्यस्य what indeed is this considerate treatment (अनुरोधः) of my brother towards लक्ष्मी which is fickle? चीवरेण अन्तरितौ (covered) कुचौ यस्याः. हर्ष's idea is:—if राज्यवर्धन wants to go to तपोवन, why does he not take राज्यलक्ष्मी which is rightfully his with him to the forest and there make her follow the life of an ascetic? Why does he press me to accept her? जराजालिनी (1) that presents the appearance of old age (with लक्ष्मी); (2) that falls into a snare which resembles old age (with मृगी). A मृगी also carries कुश and leaves in its mouth (on which it subsists) and is often caught in a net. The word जराजालिनी further suggests the idea that लक्ष्मी should remain in the forest with राज्य० till old age and then it will be time for हर्ष to think of becoming a king. In olden times, Indian kings transferred their kingdoms when they grew old to their sons and went to a forest to practise austerities. Compare रघु० 7. 71 'तदुपहितकुटुम्बः शान्तिमार्गोत्सुकोऽभून्नहि सति कुलधुर्ये सूर्यवंश्या गृहाय ॥'.; उत्तरराम० I. 22. किल्बिषम् sin (object of आपास्यति, the subject being तपः). 'पापं किल्बिषकल्मषम्' इत्यमरः. मनसा...वनम् who in thought went to the forest before (his brother.).

P. 95 ll. 23-31 **अत्रान्तरे...पातयत्.** The principal sentence is अत्रान्तरे...सहसैव प्रविश्य...राज्यश्रियः परिचारकः संवादको नाम... सदसि आत्मानमपातयत्. We have a number of nouns in the locative (absolute). पूर्वादिष्टेन—who had been previously ordered (by राज्य०). वस्त्रकर्मान्तिक—keeper of the wardrobe. कर्मान्तिकः—कर्मणि अन्तिकः or कर्मान्ते नियुक्तः—a servant. Read ०ताडनभियेव for ०ताडनमिव. निर्दय...स्त्रैणे when the women in the palace were screaming as if their heart being afraid of the rough beating with their hands had disappeared somewhere. The women in grief at the departure of राज्य० to a forest beat their bosom (हृदय) and wept. The poet imagines that they screamed because they had lost their heart. When one loses a thing, one raises a hue and cry to find it. ब्रह्मणि साधु ब्रह्मण्यम्, न ब्र० अब्रह्मण्यम्—this is an exclamation used when some calamity befalls. It originally meant 'what is not good to a Brâhmaṇa;' hence 'any calamity or misfortune.' ऊर्ध्वौ दोषौ (arms, from दोस्) यस्य. दोषन् is optionally substituted for दोस् from the accu. plural. पाद...परे—the citizens fell at the feet of राज्य० to dissuade him from his resolve. विद्राति (*loc.* sing. of the *pr. p.* of द्रा with वि) running away.

विद्रुतं चेतः यस्य whose heart was melted or agitated. पर्याकुलं वासः यस्य whose dress was disorderly. निवारणे उद्यतं मनः यस्य. नखेन लिखितं मणिकुट्टिमं (jewelled pavement) यैः—when a person is in reverie, he often scratches the pavement with his nails. प्रज्ञाततमः extremely well-known. विमुक्तः आक्रन्दः येन.

P. 95 l. 32—**P. 41** l. 8 **अथ...इति.** अस्माकं व्यसनं तस्मिन् व्यवसायः तस्य वर्धनं तस्मिन् बद्धा धृतिः येन (*adj.* of विधिः) that is fi·m in increasing its efforts (व्यवसाय) to bring down calamities on us. अधृतिकरम् causing loss of steadiness of mind. The sentence is विधिः इतः अधिकतरं अधृतिकरं किं अपरं दुःखातिशयं समुपनयति. छिद्रेषु प्रहर्तुं शीलं एषां इति छिद्र० that strike at a weak point. अवनिपतिः = प्रभाकरवर्धनः. ग्रहवर्मा मालवराजेन जीवलोकं त्याजितः—ग्रह० was made to leave this world (*i. e.* was killed) by the king of Mālvā. Dr. Buhler suggested that देवगुप्त was the name of the Mālava king and that मालव is not Mālvā in Central India, but the Mālvā in Punjab near Thanesar (E. I. Vol. I. p. 70). Vide Introduction. आत्मनः...त्याजितः—(the मालव king) in killing ग्रहवर्मा made his own (मालवराज's) merit to leave himself. The idea is that he by that act became bereft of all पुण्य if he had any. This is a fine example of the figure सहोक्ति. कालायसनिगडयुगलेन चुम्बितौ चरणौ यस्याः. निगडः chains. कान्यकुब्जे—the modern Kanoj, which seems to have been the capital of the Maukhari ग्रहवर्मा. किंवदन्ती rumour. अ...मत्वा thinking that the army is without a leader. The reference is to the army of Thanesar. 'साधनं मृतसंस्कारे सैन्ये सिद्धौषधे गतौ' इति मेदिनी. जिघृक्षुः desirous of seizing (this kingdom).

P.96 ll. 9–34 **ततश्च...दिदेश.** अनुपेक्षणीय—not fit to be treated with indifference. व्यतिकरः occurrence, calamity. 'अथ व्यतिकरः पुंसि व्यसनव्यतिषङ्गयोः' मेदिनी. अश्रुत...भवस्य humiliation not having been even heard of before (by राज्य०). The author assigns reasons why the deep-seated affliction of राज्य० at once disappeared. परिभव refers to the treatment meted out to राज्यश्री, the sister of राज्य०. वीर...जन्मनः because his birth was in a family of heroes. कृपा...भूतायाः who now became an object for compassion (because she was widowed and imprisoned). बद्धं मूलं येन that had taken deep root. ललाट...भिद्यत on his forehead a frightful frown of the eyebrow appeared. The frowning brow is compared to यमुना, the sister of यम, the waters of which are dark (श्यामायमाना). The brow also is dark. केशिनिषूदनः (कृष्णः) तस्मात् शङ्का (fear) तया आकुलं कालियकुलं तस्य भङ्गुरा भ्रूः तस्याः

भङ्गैः तरङ्गिणी—The river had ripples owing to the knitting of the brows of the family of the serpent कालिय that was afraid of कृष्ण. The eyebrow of राज्य० also presented a wavy appearance on account of the frowns it had. केशिन् was a दैत्य in the form of a horse sent by कंस to kill कृष्ण in वृन्दावन. कृष्ण put his hand in its mouth, when it increased. Kes'in was cut in two. See विष्णु पु० V. 16. कालिय—the reference is to कालियमर्दन. The serpent was in the waters of the यमुना and rendered it poisonous. No tree except a कदम्ब grew on its banks. कृष्ण threw himself from the कदम्ब into the Jumna and trod upon the hoods of the serpent. The serpent and its wives begged कृष्ण to show mercy. कृष्ण said 'नात्र स्थेयं त्वया सर्प कदाचिद्यमुनाजले । सभृत्यपरिवारस्त्वं समुद्रसलिलं व्रज ॥ मत्पदानि च ते सर्प दृष्ट्वा मूर्धनि सागरे । गरुडः पन्नगरिपुस्त्वयि न प्रहरिष्यति ॥'. विष्णुपु. V. 7. 75–76. यमुना was the daughter of सूर्य and संज्ञा and sister of यम. See मार्कण्डेयपु० 77. परामृशन् (*adj.* of ०पल्लवः) rubbing or striking. दिङ्नागस्य (दिग्गजस्य) कुम्भकूटवत् विकटः तस्य—that was as broad (or formidable) as the conical head front of a दिग्गज. For कुम्भ, see p. 109. बाहु...पल्लवः—with his left hand he stroked the upper part of his (right) arm, as wrestlers do when they get ready for a wrestling match. The word कोष is used because the upper part looked like a bud. नख...षेकमिव चकार—When he stroked his arm with his hand, the rays of the nails, which looked like water, brightened it. Hence the poet fancies that the arm was bathed in the water (rays of nails) in order to honour it preparatory to undertaking the responsibility of a fight. The com. says that कोष is an ordeal. With this sense all the words cannot be explained. But it is possible to explain some. Before the ordeal, the person charged had to bathe (अभिषेक). The कोश ordeal is described as follows in the व्यवहारमयूख 'तमाहूयाभिशस्तं तु मण्डलाभ्यन्तरे स्थितम् । आदित्याभिमुखं कृत्वा पाययेत्प्रसृतित्रयम् ॥ पूर्वोक्तेन विधानेन स्नातमार्द्राम्बरं शुचिम् । अर्चयित्वा तु तं देवं प्रक्षाल्य सलिलेन तु । एनश्च श्रावयित्वा तु पाययेत्प्रसृतित्रयम् ॥'. सङ्गलत् स्वेदसलिलं तेन पूरितं उदरं यस्य (*adj.* of पाणिरपरः). निर्मूलं...केश इव as if he had seized the hair (of the Mālava king) in order to tear him up by the roots. His wrath made him perspire and quiver and made his right hand seize his sword. The dark sword resembles केश. So the poet fancies he seized not the sword but the hair of मालवराज. दुर्मद...ण्ठयेव as if eager to seize the hair of the haughty Glory (in amorous sport). स्वेद and कम्प are two of the eight

सात्त्विकभावs; these two and रोमाञ्च are often described when lovers meet. Compare 'आसीद्वरः कण्टकितप्रकोष्ठः स्विन्नाङ्गुलिः संववृते कुमारी' रघु० 7. 22. पुनरपि—We saw above (text p. 39 l. 18) that राज्य० laid down his sword on the earth. शस्त्रग्रहणेन मुदिता राजलक्ष्मीः तया क्रियमाणा दिष्टवृद्धिः (congratulation) तस्यां विधुता सिन्दूरधूलिः. Even now at marriage celebrations and other festivities, red powder is sprinkled over people. For दिष्टवृद्धि see above p. 11. समासन्नाः सकलमहीपालाः तेषां चूडामणीनां चक्रं तस्य आक्रमणेन जातः अहङ्कारः यस्य. He sat in a posture peculiar to warriors of old. His upturned right foot he placed on his left thigh and the left foot was placed on the ground. निष्ठुरं अङ्गुष्ठेन कषणं (rubbing) तेन निष्ठ्यूता (emitted) धूमलेखा येन. निर्वी...शिख इव as if he had let loose the knot of hair on his head for making the earth void of (rival) heroes. He violently rubbed his toe against the pavement and a streak of smoke was thereby produced. This is dark and hence fancied to be a knot of hair (शिखा). An irascible person may take a vow not to tie up his hair until his enemies are uprooted, as चाणक्य did. Vide मुद्राराक्षस III. 29. 'शिखां मोक्तुं मुक्तामपि पुनरयं धावति करः'; VII. 17 'पूर्णप्रतिज्ञेन मया केवलं बध्यते शिखा ॥'. The word विमुक्तशिखः may suggest another meaning. He violently pressed his toe against the ground whereby a dark line of smoke was produced. That indicated that he was about to give out a flame (शिखा). Fire burns the earth and frees it of Arjuna trees. 'नदीसर्जो वीरतरुरिन्द्रद्रुः ककुभोऽर्जुनः' इत्यमरः. वीर also means 'reeds'. दर्पेण स्फुटिताः सरसाः व्रणाः तेभ्यः उच्छलितं (sent up, spurted) रुधिरं तस्य छटा तया अवसेकः. राज्यवर्धन's wounds were fresh and by his agitation they again cracked and blood began to flow. प्रबोधयन्निव—has two senses. When one faints through poison, water is sprinkled over to rouse him. The blood served to rouse his valour that had been inert owing to sorrow. राज्य० also wanted to give advice to हर्ष. इदं...प्रजाः—what he means is :—I leave these as they are; you must look after them; I cannot do it; I have only one task to discharge. भूपतिः (प्रभाकरवर्धनः) तस्य भुजौ परिघौ (bar, bolt) इव. अत्यन्तं अविनीतः (wicked, ill-mannered) अरिः तस्य निग्रहः. सोऽयं...वंशस्य च—The construction is यो मौखराणां मालवैः परिभवः...सोऽयं कुरङ्गकैः कचग्रहः केसरिणः—that the Mālavas should insult the Maukharas and the line of पुष्पभूति is like the seizure of the hair of the lion by deer. करपातः slapping. वत्सकैः...ग्रस्य the taking of the tiger as a captive by calves.

अलगर्दः a water-serpent. **गरुड** is the enemy of all serpents and shows no mercy to them. 'अलगर्दो जलव्यालः' इत्यमरः. अयुतं ten thousand.

P. 97 ll. 1–24 **तं च...मित्रम्.** जामिः sister. '**जामिः स्वसृकुलस्त्रियोः**' **इत्यमरः.** **०विज्ञानेन प्रकोपः** तस्य आधानं (production) **तेन दूयमाने. दूरं प्ररूढा प्रणयपीडा यस्य.** मनसि...**पीड इव** when his mind had pain due to love (for राज्य०) much augmented by the plea that he (**हर्ष**) should return (remain behind). The reading **निवर्तनादेशेन** (by the order of राज्य० to stay behind) is much better. **कमिव...गमनेन** what possible harm does my lord see in my following (my lord)? **यदि...सि** if you raise the objection that I am a mere boy, that is a greater reason why I should not be left behind. '**बाल आ षोडशाद्वर्षात्**'. This passage may be looked upon as indicating that **हर्ष** was about sixteen at this time. **रक्षणीय...स्थानम्**—If you assign for my staying behind the reason that I need protection (and therefore should not be taken on a campaign), then your arms are a cage for me. What greater protection can there be than your own powerful arm? **सं...करोति**—if you say that I am not to be taken with you because I require to be carefully brought up, then separation from you will make me thin (whatever other care may be bestowed on me in your absence). **स्त्री...सि** then I am placed among women *i. e.* I am treated just as women (who are delicate and unable to bear hardships). **तत् (सुखं) प्रयाति**—all my happiness, being centred in you, marches with you. **विरहो...तरः** separation from you is more difficult to bear (than even the toils of the journey). **कलत्रं...वसति**—the idea seems to be:—you may say that you leave me behind because you want me to guard your harem; but then Glory (which is really the only wife you care to have) dwells in your sword *i. e.* Glory, the only wife you should have, is taken by you on your sword and not placed under protection. राज्य० was to secure Glory by his sword. C and T translate 'if you would have me watch over my wife &c.'; but this does not appear to be correct. There is no connection between **हर्ष**'s watching over his own wife and the fact of Glory residing in his brother's sword. **पृष्ठ...ताप:** if you leave me behind (to guard your rear), that is unnecessary, as your valour remains behind (and will guard everything). **राज...गुणैः** if you say that the circle of princes will be without supervision, then (I say there is no need for it as) the princes are well secured by your virtues. A person is also bound (बद्ध) with ropes (गुण). न...गणयसि if you say that a great man (like yourself) does not require an outsider as a companion, then you count me as distinct from yourself. I regard myself and yourself as identical. प्रलघुः (very small) परिकरः (retinue, train). लघु also means light (in weight). पाद...भारः what great weight is there in the dust of your feet? हर्ष means that he is like the dust of his brother's feet and so there is no भार (weight, responsibility) in taking him on the expedition. द्वयो...श्रया If you argue that it is not proper that both of us should go, then favour me by ordering *me* to go (and you may remain behind). सदृशो दोषः the idea is :—if you leave me behind because you are afraid out of your affection for me (of what may befall me) then I say I am afraid of what may befall you in my absence. So this fault of कातरत्व is common to both of us and should not be urged against me alone, according to the न्यायवैशेषिक maxim 'यत्रोभयोः समो दोषः परिहारोऽपि वा समः । नैकः पर्यनुयोक्तव्यस्तादृगर्थ विचारणे ॥' तर्कभाषा. आत्मम्भरिता selfishness, greed. 'फलेग्रहिरात्मम्भरिश्च' पा. 3. 2. 26 (आत्मानं बिभर्तीति). क्षीरोदफेनपटलवत् or–पटलेन पाण्डुरम्. Fame is poetically represented as white. The foam of the milky ocean must be very white. When अमृत was churned out of the ocean, it must have been white with the foam &c. अव...देषु I have never before been deceived (*i. e.* deprived) of favours *i. e.* you always granted whatever favours I asked. अति...हितः why should a very insignificant foe be given great importance by making too great a preparation? हरि...म्भारः a host of lions for (catching) a hare causes great shame. हेपण—from ह्रेपयति, causal of ह्री 3rd *conj.* कवचयन्ति put on armour. आशुशुक्षणयः—fires. This is a word used more in the Vedas. अष्टादश द्वीपाः एव अष्टमङ्गलकं तस्य माला अस्ति अस्याः that is wreathed with the bracelet in the form of the eighteen द्वीपs. The com. says 'अष्टमङ्गलकं कङ्कणमित्यन्ये.' A horse is called अष्टमङ्गलक. कुल...वाहिनः blowing against the group of principal mountains. For the कुलपर्वतs, see p. 39. न संनह्यन्ति do not gird up their loins, do not put on armour. सुमेरोः वप्रः (slope) तस्मिन् प्रणयः (liking) तेन प्रगल्भाः (bold) or सुमेरौ वप्रः (butting) तस्मिन् &c. For सुमेरु, see pp. 8, 85. न परिणमन्ति do not stoop to strike with their tusks. Elephants and bulls are represented as butting against the slopes of hills and mounds of earth. सकलपृथ्वीपतीनां प्रलयस्य

उत्पाते धूमकेतुम् that (bow) is a comet portending the destruction of all kings. For धूमकेतु as an उत्पात, see above p. 89. मान्धाता इव—see p. 23 above. चारुः चामीकरपत्रलता एव अलङ्कारः स एव अङ्कः यस्य स०राङ्कः, ०राङ्कः कायः यस्य—the frame of which is marked with ornamental and charming figures in gold. 'चामीकरं जातरूपं महारजतकाञ्चने' इत्यमरः (चमीकरे आकरे भवम्). विं...तायाम् in the hunger for destroying my enemy that has been roused in me. एकाकिनः goes with मम. राज्य० says 'do not claim a share in killing मालवराज; let me alone secure him as my victim'. अयं कोपकवलः एकः this one morsel of my wrath. The morsel is the king of Mālvā. अभ्यमित्रम्—अमित्रस्य अभिमुखम् (अव्ययीभाव).

P. 97 l. 25—**P. 98** l. 13 **अथ...करोत्.** तथागते भ्रातरि his brother being in that condition (*i. e.* so occupied). There is another suggested meaning. तथागत is a name of बुद्ध. 'सर्वज्ञः सुगतो बुद्धो धर्मराजस्तथागतः' इत्यमरः. So the meaning is 'his brother having become a Buddha' (*i. e.* having died in the Buddhist faith). We learn from the Madhuban inscription (see Introduction) that राज्यवर्धन was a very devout Buddhist. दत्तः प्रजागरः यस्मै: who was kept awake. तृतीयो भागः त्रिभागः, त्रिभागः शेषः यस्याः. यामिकः watchman. द्वीपैः उपगीताः गुणाः (virtues, cables) यस्य. A ship also has गुणs (cables, ropes); a ship is laden with heaps of jewels or rich merchandise of every description. रत्नराशि may also mean 'the sea' (generally called रत्नाकर). Ships bring the essence of the sea *i. e.* the best things from beyond the seas. This verse is suggestive of the fall of राज्य०. अनि...वनया by the thought of the evanescent nature (of things). प्रक्षीणं भूयिष्ठं यस्याः when (night) had almost come to an end. Dreams seen in the early morning were believed to come to be true. अभ्रंलिहम् touching the clouds. This is another indication of the fall of the mighty राज्य०. अनुबध्नन्ति persistently follow. अकल्याणस्य आख्याने विचक्षणम् clever in announcing evil. The throbbing of the left eye and arm in the case of men portends evil. अक्षु...क्षाणाः declaring the downfall of no mean king. अविकलः कायबन्धः यस्य whose bodily frame is not maimed, is perfect. कबन्ध...बिम्बे in the disc of the sun that has a headless trunk. 'भास्कराहस्करब्रध्नप्रभाकरविभाकराः' इत्यमरः. राहु is a demon without trunk and is all head. In the disc of the sun a headless trunk was seen and thus राहु was as if provided with a complete body when it seized the sun. विभाव्यते is seen. See above text p. 27 l. 9. (भानुमण्डले भयङ्करकबन्धकायव्याजेन). The बृहत्संहिता says 'दण्डे नरेन्द्रमृत्युर्व्या-

धिभयं स्यात्कबन्धसंस्थाने ।' (III. 17.). सप्तर्षयः—the constellation of the Great Bear. The Great Bear emitted a dark smoke-like streak and thereby darkened all the planets. The poet fancies that the smoke emitted is what they had taken in while performing तपः. To inhale only smoke is a kind of तपः. The बृहत्संहिता (13. 7) says 'उल्काशनिधूमाद्यैर्हता विवर्णा विरश्मयो ह्रस्वाः । हन्युः स्वं स्वं वर्गं विपुलाः स्निग्धाश्च तद्वृद्ध्यै ॥'. दिशां दाहाः—Note बृहत्संहिता 'दाहो दिशां राजभयाय पीतो देशस्य नाशाय हुताशवर्णः ।' (31. 1.) and 'योऽतीव दीप्त्या कुरुते प्रकाशं छायामपि व्यञ्जयतेऽर्कवद्यः । राज्ञो महद्वेदयते भयं सः' &c. (31. 2.). तारागणः—the falling stars appear like the particles of ashes due to दिग्दाह. The falling of stars is looked upon as an evil omen. See बृहत्संहिता (33. 11) 'अम्बरमध्याद्बह्व्यो निपतन्त्यो राजराष्ट्रनाशाय ।'. तारा...शुचेव—the moon is called तारानाथ or नक्षत्रेश; the poet fancies that the moon, the lord of stars, was grieved at their fall and therefore lost colour. The उल्काs appear like so many missiles in the battle of the planets. विलोलाः तारकाः यासां or यासु (1) the pupils of which are unsteady; (2) the stars in which fall down. The quarters are compared to ladies frightened at the sight of a battle. सञ्चारयतीव क्ष्मां as if carries the earth. वहत् बहलं रजःपटलं तेन कलिलः शर्कराशकलैः सूत्कारी च whistling with bits of gravel and full of flying (वहत्) and thick clouds of dust. न ... लग्नस्य I don't see that this hour is auspicious. For लग्न, see pp. 24, 60. अस्मिन्न...पन्थी who will obstruct fate when it seizes even a delicate scion in our family as an elephant seizes the tender shoot of a bamboo (वंशः). The scion is राज्यवर्धन. करीरः—रम् shoot of a bamboo; shoot in general. 'वंशाङ्कुरे करीरोऽस्त्री' इत्यमरः. द्रवदिव—his heart melted or was wet with स्नेह (oil or affection). Another meaning is—his heart was broken inside and was as if running away (द्रवत्); but he somehow kept it firm. यथा...करोत् he performed all his various duties, as he was in the habit of doing them.

P. 98 ll. 14–23 **आस्थान ... श्रौषीत्.** असह्यं दुःखं तेन उष्णाः निश्वासाः तेषां धूमः तेन रक्ताः (coloured) तन्तवः यस्य. His body was dressed in dirty clothes. The author fancies that the mud was the smoke of his hot breaths, which (smoke) coloured the threads. जीवित...लज्जया—he was ashamed that he should continue to live after his master's death. नासा...दृष्टिम् whose eye was fixed on the tip of his long nose. दुःखेन दूरप्ररूढानि रोमाणि यस्मिन् on which there was a long growth due to sorrow. His face, though mute, told the tale by the long growth of beard. बृहदश्ववारः a great horseman, an officer of cavalry. अभिजाततम of very noble birth.. चक्षुषि सलिलेन—supply अगृह्यत—water (tears) came to his eyes. उत्सङ्गे भुवा the earth came to his lap *i. e.* he lay on the bare earth (in grief). अगृह्यत लोकपालैः—वरुण (the lord of सलिल), the wind, the fire are among the eight लोकपाल s 'सोमाग्न्यर्कानिलेन्द्राणां वित्ताप्पत्योर्यमस्य च। अष्टानां लोकपालानां वपुर्धारयते नृपः ॥' मनु 5. 96. तस्मात्—from कुन्तल. हेलया (easily) निर्जितं मालवानीकं येन. मिथ्योपचारैः उपचितः विश्वासः यस्मिन् in whom trust was increased by false civilities.

P. 98 l. 24—**P. 99** l. 4 **श्रुत्वा...यासीत्.** ॰कोपः एव पावकः तस्य प्रसरेण परिचीयमानः (increased) शोकावेगः यस्य. The principal sentence is ततश्च...परां भीषणतां अयासीत्. अमर्षेण (क्रोधेन) विधुतं शिरः तस्मात् शीर्यमाणानि शिखामणीनां शकलानि तैः अङ्गारकितम्. Pieces of jewels from his crest were scattered about when he shook his head in wrath, which (pieces) looked like the live coals of the fire of wrath he sent forth. अङ्गारकित is formed from अङ्गारक on the analogy of तारकित, for which see p. 98. रोष...च्छेदेन with his lip that was curved through wrath. When a man drinks anything he moves his lips and makes them curved. लोहितायमाने (becoming red) लोचने तयोः आलोकः (light) तस्य विक्षेपैः (casting). He cast glances with his blood-shot eyes in all directions, which were thereby made lurid. For दिग्दाह, see above (text l. 5). रोषानलेनापि—connect with वितन्यमान. असह्यः सहजशौर्योष्मदहनः तेन दह्यमानेन. वितन्यमानं ॰दुर्दिनं (स्वेदसलिलशीकराणां आसारः एव दुर्दिनं) यस्मिन्. His wrath made him perspire and drops of perspiration stood out like drops of rain on his body. When one is oppressed with heat, one sprinkles drops of water over one's body. The poet imagines that the perspiration was water sprinkled by the fire of his wrath over itself, being afraid of the hotter and unbearable fire of his inborn valour. पूर्वं अदृष्टः अदृष्टपूर्वः कोपः तस्मात् भीतैः. His limbs shook through wrath; the poet fancies that his limbs were afraid of his wrath which they had never seen before. A terror-stricken man trembles. हरः=शिवः. कृतः भैरवः भयङ्करः आकारः येन (with राज्य॰); कृतः भैरवस्य आकारः येन (with हरः) who assumed the form of भैरव. भैरव is the name of a terrible form of शिव. हरिः=विष्णुः. प्रकटितं नरसिंहरूपं येन (1) who presented the appearance of a brave man; (2) who manifested the Man-Lion form. In the latter case the reference is to the नृसिंह incarnation of Vishnu, for which see above p. 39.

Words like सिंह are employed to denote pre-eminence, bravery &c.' 'स्युरुत्तरपदे व्याघ्रपुङ्गवर्षभकुञ्जराः। सिंहशार्दूलनागाद्याः पुंसि श्रेष्ठार्थगोचराः ॥' इत्यमरः. नरः सिंह इव (कर्म०). अपरस्य तेजःप्रसरः तस्य दर्शनेन प्रज्वलितः that burst forth into flame at the sight of the spread of another's brilliance. राज्य० was fired by the action of his foe (the गौड king); the सूर्यकान्त emits fire at the sight of the sun (a second source of light). Compare for the idea 'न तेजस्तेजस्वी प्रसृतमपरेषां प्रसहते स तस्य स्वो भावः प्रकृतिनियत्वादकृतकः। मयूखैरश्रान्तं तपति यदि देवो दिनकरः किमाग्नेयग्रावा निकृत इव तेजांसि वमति ॥' उत्तरराम० VI. 14. क्षय—दिवसः = कल्पान्तदिवसः. उदिताः द्वादश दिनकराः तैः दुर्निरीक्ष्या मूर्तिः यस्य (with दिवसः). ०दिनकरवत् दुर्निरीक्ष्या मूर्तिः यस्य (with राज्य०). For कल्पान्त, see above p. 78. At the time of प्रलय, it is supposed that twelve suns simultaneously rise in the sky. Compare 'दग्धुं विश्वं दहनकिरणैर्नोदिता द्वादशार्काः' वेणीसंहार III; 'यावत्प्राणिमि तावदस्य कल्पान्तोदितद्वादशदिनकरकिरणातपतीव्रस्य' &c. कादम्बरी (p. 156 of P). महो...कारी who caused trembling to all भूभृत्s (kings, mountains) like a portentous hurricane. विवर्धमानः विग्रहस्य (शरीरस्य) उत्सेधः (sublimity, height) यस्य—(1) the grandeur of whose form increased (with राज्य०); (2) whose height increased (with विन्ध्य). The विन्ध्य wanted the sun to revolve round itself as it did round Meru. The sun refused, whereupon the विन्ध्य began to grow higher and higher in order to obstruct the sun's path. The gods in fear sent Agastya who came to the mountain and asked it to allow him to go to the south and to remain in its original state till he returned. अगस्त्य never returned and so विन्ध्य remained low in height. *Vide* महाभारत वनपर्व chap. 104. Compare रामायण 'मार्गं निरोद्धुं सततं भास्करस्याचलोत्तमः। सन्देशं पालयंस्तस्य विन्ध्यशैलो न वर्धते ॥' अरण्य० 11. 86. दुर्नरेन्द्रेण (by a wicked king; by a bad snake-charmer) अभिभवः (insult) तेन रोषितः. आशीविषः—आशीषु आशीःषु वा (तालुगतदंष्ट्रासु) विषं अस्य—a serpent. For नरेन्द्र see p. 33. पारीक्षितः = son of परीक्षित् *i. e.* जनमेजय. सर्व...द्यतः who was bent upon burning all भोगिन्s (kings, serpents). परीक्षित्, the grandson of अर्जुन, died of snake-bite and जनमेजय made a resolve to extirpate the whole serpent race in revenge. He instituted a सर्पसत्र in which all serpents were burnt except तक्षक who was saved by the intercession of the sage आस्तीक, at whose request the sacrifice was closed. See महाभारत आदि० chap. 49–58. 'उरगः पन्नगो भोगी' इत्यमरः ('भोगः सर्पदेहः कुटिला गतिर्वास्यास्तीति' क्षीर०). 'भोगी भुजङ्गमेऽपिस्याद्ग्रासपात्रे नृपे पुमान्' मेदिनी. वृकोदरः = भीमः. He took a vow to kill दुःशासन when the latter dragged द्रौपदी by her hair and called the पाण्डवs 'गौर्गौः' and killed and drank his blood. See कर्णपर्व chap. 83 'सत्यां चिकीर्षुर्मतिमान्प्रतिज्ञां भीमोऽपिबच्छोणितमस्य कोष्णम् ।' 29. सुरगजः = ऐरावतः. प्रतिपक्षस्य वारणाय प्रधावितः who ran to repel his foe (with राज्य०); प्रतिपक्षश्चासौ वारणश्च (गजश्च) तस्मिन् प्रधावितः who ran *i. e.* attacked a rival elephant. पूर्वा...षस्य who was the first advent of prowess. आगमः may also be taken in the sense of 'tradition, revealed scriptures, Veda.' It is believed that the Veda is eternal and that in each कल्प there is only a fresh manifestation. Hence the word पूर्व. उन्माद इव मदस्य—he was the fullest realization of मद. आवेग...लेपस्य the impetuous onrush of haughtiness. सर्वोद्योगः the full endeavour. यु...ष्मणः the inauguration of an era of youthful warmth. रणरसः passion for fighting. For नीराजन, see above p. 78. On the day of नीराजन, a king marches on an expedition. The idea is that he was the marching day of असहिष्णुता *i. e.* असहिष्णुता was to become active in his person from that day.

P. 99 l 5—**P. 102** l. 18 **अवादीच्च...व्यरंसीत्.** ०पुरुषं goes with आर्यम् (राज्यवर्धनम्). निर्व्याज...शस्त्रं who subdued all the kings by his valour that is free from stratagem and who had laid aside his weapon (this applies to both राज्य० and द्रोणाचार्य). कलशयोनिं = द्रोणं. As to the birth of द्रोण see आदिपर्व 63. 6 'भरद्वाजस्य च स्कन्नं द्रोण्यां शुक्रमवर्धत । महर्षेरुग्रतपसस्तस्माद्द्रोणो व्यजायत ॥'. In the great महाभारत war, once an elephant named अश्वत्थामा was killed and the report spread that अश्वत्थामा, the son of द्रोण, was killed. द्रोण asked धर्म, who replied 'हतः कुञ्जरः'. The last word was uttered in a low tone. The old man heard only the first word and in grief for his son laid aside his weapon when धृष्टद्युम्न killed him. See द्रोणपर्व chap. 190. कृष्णवर्त्मा (अग्निः) तस्मात् प्रसूतिः यस्य सः ०सूतिः धृष्टद्युम्नः. About the birth of धृष्टद्युम्नः see द्रोणपर्व chap. 191. 2 'य इष्ट्वा मनुजेन्द्रेण द्रुपदेन महामखे । लब्धो द्रोणविनाशाय समिद्धाद्धव्यवाहनात् ।'. The word कृष्ण० further means 'who is the source of dark paths *i. e.* dark deeds' (as applied to गौडाधिप and also धृष्टद्युम्न). **ईदृशेन** मृत्युना—the reference is to the treachery practised by the **गौड** king. अनार्य...पातम्—the sentence is अनार्यं तं मुक्त्वा...केषां मनःसु आर्यशौर्यगुणाः पक्षपातं न कुर्युः—Excepting that vile wretch, in whose minds would not my lord's valour and other qualities produce a favourable impression ? भागीरथी...पाण्डुराः—The waters of the Ganges are white; the foam would be whiter still. Both राजहंस and the qualities are white like the foam. The राजहंसs cause

पक्षपात (movement with or flight on their wings) in the मानस lake (मनःसु सरःसु). पर...कृतः (1) that remind one of the valour of परशुराम (with ०गुणाः); (2) that remember the valour of परशुराम (with ०हंसाः). परशुराम, while he was learning धनुर्विद्या from शिव, being jealous of the power of स्कन्द who had once by his missile called शक्ति pierced the mountain क्रौञ्च, shot an arrow through that mountain and made a passage, through which it was believed the हंसs passed from the plains to the मानस lake. बाण perhaps derived his inspiration from the मेघदूत 'प्रालेयाद्रेरुपतटमतिक्रम्य तांस्तान्विशेषान् हंसद्वारं भृगुपतियशोवर्त्म यत्क्रौञ्चरन्ध्रम् ॥'. In the वनपर्व chap. 225. 33 'बिभेद स शरैः शैलं क्रौञ्चं हिमवतः सुतम् । तेन हंसाश्च गृध्राश्च मेरुं गच्छन्ति पर्वतम् ॥', it is स्कन्द who makes a hole for हंसs. अत्युग्रस्य— applies to गौडाधिप and निदाघरवि. कम...शोषणे in drying up the water of the bed of lotuses. The summer sun dries up the water in which lotuses grow. राज्यवर्धन is compared to कमलाकर, because he was also कमलाकर (the abode of लक्ष्मी) and सलिल to जीवित. अनपेक्षिता प्रीतिः यैः that paid no heed to his friendship (with the hands of गौडाधिप); that paid no heed to the bloom (*lit.* happiness) of the lotuses (with 'the rays of the summer sun'). गतिम् fate, state (after death). कस्मिन्नरके—In the विष्णुपु० (II. 6) a large number of hells such as रौरव is mentioned. So also in the मार्कण्डेयपु० chap. 10 and 12. श्वपाकः = चण्डालः. Construe पापकारिणः अस्य नामापि गृह्णतो मे जिह्वा &c. किं...कार्यम् *lit.* undertaking what object *i. e.* with what object in view. आर्यः— connect with तेन क्षयमुपनीतः. क्षुद्रेण goes with both तेन and घुणेन. अनुप्रविश्य who worked himself into favour with my lord; that bores inside (timber). विगता घृणा (दया) यस्य. घुणः—an insect that eats into timber and produces furrowed lines thereon resembling letters. Note the word घुणाक्षरन्याय. राज्य० is compared to a sandal pillar. मधुरसास्वाद (1) taste of honey; (2) taste of wine. भावी कष्ट...द्रवः the coming trouble of the fall of distressing शिलीमुखs (arrows, bees). One who takes away honey from the honeycomb is attacked by the bees. 'अलिबाणौ शिलीमुखौ' इत्यमरः (शिली शल्यं मुखे अस्य). निज...षणं (1) that is a blot on his own family (with अयशः); (2) that renders dirty one's house (with कज्जलं). जाल...केन (1) by one who lights up a path of deceit (with गौडाधमेन); with a lamp placed in a latticed window. Lampblack sticks to windows and mars the brightness of a house. ' जालं समूह आनायो गवाक्षःक्षारकावपि ' इत्यमरः. जालं deceit. Separate न तु आशु (quickly) अस्तम्. न वेधसादिष्टः शशी is there not the moon ordered by the creator? ग्रह...पः—ग्रहाणां षण्डे (समूहे) विहारः तस्मिन् एकः केवलः हरिणाधिपः सिंहः—who is the sole lion in roaming among the cluster of planets. The moon wanders in the midst of planets. It is compared to a lion, that also roams about in the midst of thickets. There are further suggestions due to paronomasia. विहार may mean 'reducing'. The moon puts into the shade the group of planets. The lion is called मृगाधिप (lord of beasts). The moon is हरिणाधिप because the spot on the moon is supposed to be a deer. 'अब्जादिकदम्बे षण्डमस्त्रियाम्' इत्यमरः. विनयविधायिनि that lays down (*i. e.* teaches) discipline or obedience. व्यालवारणः a wicked or unruly elephant. कुवैकटिकाः bad jewellers. 'मणिकारो वैकटिकः' क्षीर°. तेज...नाशकाः (1) those that destroy the best of spirited men (with तादृशाः); (2) those that destroy brilliant jewels. 'रत्नं स्वजातिश्रेष्ठेऽपि' इत्यमरः. इत्येतदभि (p. 44, l. 22)...विज्ञापितवान् (p. 45, l. 14). The principal sentence is इत्येतत् अभिदधतः एव अस्य (हर्षस्य) पितुः मित्रं सेनापतिः... सन्निधावेव समुपविष्टः सिंहनादनामा विज्ञापितवान्. सम...हरः foremost in all battles. हरितालं (yellow orpiment) तस्य शैलवत् अवदातः (polished, bright) देहः यस्य. परिणतः (full grown) प्रगुणः (straight) सालः (a tree) तस्य प्रकाण्डं (trunk) तत्प्रकाशः तत्सदृशः. अति...गतः that had reached maturity as if on account of the warmth of his great valour. Heat makes a thing ripe; or cooking (पाकः) is effected with heat. C and T translate 'tall as if ripened by valour's exceeding heat.' This is wrong. There is no connecttion whatever between tallness and ripening by heat. गतं भूयिष्ठं यस्य. °शयने आदौ सुप्तः पश्चादुत्थितः. The सेनापति very often lay wounded with arrows but always got over his wounds. There is another sense. सेनापति (*i. e.* सेनानी) is a name of स्कन्द, who also lay on a bed of शर (reeds). शरजन्मा is a name of स्कन्द. See for the story, रामायण I. 36 and 37. शान्तनवः=भीष्मः, son of शन्तनु and the Ganges. भीष्म also lay wounded on a bed of arrows, waiting for the उत्तरायण, after the advent of which he wanted to die. See भीष्मपर्व chap. 119. 'शरतल्पे महेष्वासं शयानं पुरुषर्षभम् । 92...तानब्रवीच्छान्तनवो नाहं गन्ता कथंचन । दक्षिणावर्ते आदित्ये एतन्मे मनसि स्थितम् ॥' 104. भीष्म was the grand-uncle of the पाण्डवs and yet was the most vigorous of the combatants in the महाभारत war. दु ... तया as his body was such that it could not be subdued (by old age). प्रकटितः प्रकम्पः यया (1) that manifested shaking (in him); (2) प्रकटितः प्रकम्पः यस्याम् (2) that had shaking. A person that is afraid trembles.

Through old age, his limbs shook. The poet fancies that it was जरा (not he) that was trembling, being afraid of touching him. परा...रुहेषु touched in his stiff hair. The idea is that his hair was turning grey. शशिनः कराः तेषां निकरः (समूहः) तद्वत् सिताः सरलाः शिरोरुहाः तैः सटालः (possessed of a mane). His grey hair looked like the lion's mane. He had the same straightforwardness and valour that the lion has. संक्रान्तो...जातिम्—the poet fancies that, even while he was alive, he was transformed into the class of lions. A man may become a lion *after death* (according to the theory of पुनर्जन्म); but he became a lion while living. परिजिहीर्षा desire to avoid. भ्रू...दृष्टिः his eye (or sight) was covered by brows the skin of which was wrinkled, loose and hanging down (over the eye). वलिन—(from वलि + affix न, according to 'लोमादिपामादिपिच्छादिभ्यः शनेलचः' 5. 2. 100 लोमशः। पामनः। पिच्छिलः)—वलयः सन्ति अस्य इति. धवल...मुखेन—in this clause we have first to take विक्रमकालं as qualifying शरदारम्भं and then take शरदारम्भं as qualifying विक्रमकालम्. धवला स्थूला गुञ्जा ('उत्तरोष्ठोपरि रोमराजिः' *com. i. e.* moustache) पिच्छमिव (like a feather) तेन प्रच्छादितः कपोलभागः तेन भास्वरं (bright) तेन (मुखेन). वि...शदं bright with blooming काश thickets. The काश flowers are seen in शरदृतु and are white. वमन्निव विक्रमकालं शरदारम्भं भीमेन मुखेन—The idea is:—The beginning of शरद् is the time to start on an expedition, as the rains are then over. In शरदृतु there are white काश flowers. On his face, he had white moustache resembling काश flowers. So the poet fancies that he vomited from his mouth शरदारम्भ, the time for expedition. अकालेऽपि—the force of this is:—in his old age, his moustache is white at all seasons. So he appears to vomit शरदृतु with its काश flowers at all seasons *i. e.* even when it is वसन्त or ग्रीष्म &c. Then there is a further suggestion. The विक्रमकाल (era so called) is used in the whole of northern India except Bengal and the year commences in चैत्र (except in Gujrat where it begins in कार्तिक). Hence the word अकालेऽपि is used. To Bāna, a विक्रम year beginning in शरद् would be अकाल. For a brief resume about the origin of the विक्रम era, see I. A. vol. 30 pp 3 and 4. शरदि आरम्भः यस्य सः विक्रमकालः. His white beard reaching his navel looked like a white chowrie, whereby he as if fanned the deceased king enshrined in his heart. परिणामेऽपि even in old age. विवृतं वदनं येषां (1) that were open, not yet healed (with व्रण॰); (2) that open their mouth (with thirsty people). विषमितं (made rough or uneven) विशालं वक्षः यस्य. There were open gashes of wounds on his chest. The bright sword blade resembles water. A man suffering from thirst opens his lips when he wants to drink water. The poet fancies that the wounds were open because they wanted to drink water (sword blade) *i. e.* his chest would have welcomed more sword-cuts. निशितैः शस्त्रैः टङ्कानां (axe) कोटिभिश्च कुट्टिताः (impressed, engraved) बहूव्यः बृहद्व्रणाः एव अक्षरपङ्क्तयः ताभिः निरन्तरः (closely covered) तस्य भावः ०निरन्तरता तया. The many wounds on his chest resembled lines of letters engraved on a slab of stone. सकल...कुर्वन् as if making a calculation of the auspicious hours of victory in all battles. In calculating we have to draw lines on a board. He is compared to पूर्वपर्वत because the latter also has lines (furrows) made by chisels that are like sharp weapons (निशितशस्त्रसदृशैः टङ्ककोटिभिः &c.). The mountain also has पर्वन्s (joints, parts). पर्वन् means 'the day of new or full moon' and also 'the moment of the sun's entering a new sign.' C and T say that for calculating the ascensions of heavenly bodies the पूर्वपर्वत was used by astronomers. पादचारी (1) walking on foot (with सिंहनाद); (2) that is in the midst of the hills near it. 'पादाः प्रत्यन्तपर्वताः' इत्यमरः. वीररसः—the heroic sentiment. रामणीयकम् beauty. The महाभारत is full of warlike episodes. लघयन् (denominative verb from लघु)—casting into the shade. प्रति...निर्बन्धेन by his extreme persistence in destroying his enemies. परशुराममपि—see p. 38 above for his exploits. परशुराम killed the क्षत्रियs only 21 times; but सिंहनाद did so for times without number. अप्सु भ्रमणं तेन (1) in roving over seas (with सिंहनाद); (2) revolving in the water of the sea. अनादरात् श्रियः समाकर्षणं तस्य विभ्रमेण (लीलया)—by his ease in winning लक्ष्मी without effort. He without effort won several kingdoms for his master. The मन्दर mountain revolved in the sea at the time of the churning and helped in drawing out श्री. See notes p. 42 for मन्दर. वाहिनी...वर्तनेन (1) in acting according to the principles laid down for the commander of an army; (2) in not going beyond the limit prescribed for the lord of rivers. The sea is poetically spoken of as the husband of rivers (वाहिनी). स्थै...भिः in firmness, toughness, and elevation. अचलान् = पर्वतान्. ईश्वरभारस्य उद्वहनेन घृष्टं पृष्ठं यस्य सः ०पृष्ठः तस्य भावः ०पृष्ठता. He toiled very hard (*lit.* his back was abraded) to carry out the important tasks of his king. The back of the bull of शिव is also ground down under the weight of

ईश्वर (*i. e.* शिव). अरणि...ग्नेः who was the rubbing stick of the fire of wrath. The sacrificial fire was produced by the attrition of two pieces of S'amî wood. मदो मदस्य—the idea is that haughtiness found its fullest expression in him. विसर्पः—a dry spreading itch. In the choice of words here the poet is guided mainly by the assonance of sounds. उच्छ्वसितम् life. अङ्कुशो दुर्मदानाम् he was the goad of the unruly *i. e.* he subdued even the most unruly. नाग...भोगिनाम् he was a subduer of elephants (*i. e.* a goad) to wicked kings. There is a pun. नागदमनः means गरुड and भोगिन् means 'serpent' also. वि...ष्यतायाः he was the end of the best manhood *i. e.* he was the acme, the perfection of &c. कुल...गोष्ठीनाम्—all assemblies of warriors took their lessons from him. तुला...शालिनाम् he assessed all warriors at their true value. शस्त्रग्रामः = शस्त्रसमूहः. A village (ग्रामः) has boundaries and officers supervise them. आघोष...र्थिनाम् the proclaiming drum of those that seek battle. The drum encourages the fighters. न...श्रयया—that does not stay (long) anywhere *i. e.* that is very fickle or unsteady. न चेतयन्ते do not know. लक्ष्मी deceives कापुरुषs. लक्ष्मी is fickle and मलिन (*i. e.* secured by dark deeds). The cuckoo is dark, but the crow is darker still. The cuckoo has no fixed abode and manages to deceive the crow by placing its eggs in the latter's nest for rearing. Compare 'प्रागन्तरिक्षगमनात् स्वमपत्यजातमन्यैर्द्विजैः परभृताः खलु पोषयन्ति' शाकुन्तल V. श्रियो...काराः for लक्ष्मी possesses the faults pertaining to lotuses, *viz.* दोषान्धता. लक्ष्मी dwells in कमल; therefore the faults of कमल attach to her and consequently लक्ष्मी deceives other people. दोषान्धता—दोषेषु अन्धता or दोषायां अन्धता (1) being blind to error; (2) closing the buds at night. कमलs close their petals at night-fall. लक्ष्मी makes people blind to the errors they commit. Again कामलाविकाराः would mean 'the evil effects of jaundice' and दोषान्धता means:—a man suffering from jaundice (कामला) regards everything as yellow and may not detect his error; or he may become रात्र्यन्ध. छत्रछायया अन्तरितः रविः येषाम्. छत्र is the symbol of राज्यलक्ष्मी. सर्वातिशायी शौर्यातिशयः तस्य श्वयथुः (increase, swelling) तेन कपिलौ (tawny) कपोलौ तयोः पुलकः तेन पल्लवितः कोपानलः येषु. The cheeks of warriors were tinged by their ardent passion for heroic deeds and were thrilled. The shooting hair on the cheek is represented as the पल्लव of कोपानल. A man always turns away his face from the brilliant sun (तेजस्विन्). A wretch dares not look at the face of enraged heroes. तपस्वी miserable or helpless man. अभिचारः magical spell for securing some malevolent purpose. विप्रकृताः (1) insulted, injured (with मनस्विनः); (2) worked by Brāhmaṇas (with अभिचाराः). When high-souled (or spirited) persons are insulted they at once bring about the ruin of the whole family, as spells employed by Brāhmaṇas do. जले...तेजस्विनः—every word has double meanings here. जडेऽपि...स्विनः the mighty, when struck, become inflamed even against a dullard. Because it is a fool that strikes, they would not tolerate it. In श्लेष, ड् and ल् are identical. See above p. 125. जले...स्विनः the bright (flashes) of lightning blaze forth even in water. तडित् (विद्युत्) तस्याः इमे ताडिताः. सकल...बाह्यस्य who is outside the pale of all assemblies of heroes. He has rendered himself an outcast by this deed. Or we may also explain that he, never frequenting वीरगोष्ठी, does not know the code of chivalry. अविद्यमानः उत्तारः (crossing) यस्य स अनुत्तारः निरयः (hell) तस्मिन् पातः तत्र निपुणम्. This action will hurl him into hell from which there will be no return. प्रधने (युद्धे) प्रधानं धनं. The bow is the chief wealth in battle to the powerful. कमला (लक्ष्मीः) एव कलहंसी तस्याः केलिः (sport) तदर्थं कुवलयकाननम् (in apposition with कृपाणे) The sword being dark is compared to कुवलयकानन (as कुवलय is a blue lotus). The कलहंसी plays among lotuses. लक्ष्मी plays among swords *i. e.* it goes over to the stronger sword. मनस्विनां कृपणो...त्थानस्य to the strong the churning of the sea &c. are but vile expedients to raise Lakshmî up. We may also say 'कृपणानां देवासुराणां उपायाः' (means to be employed only by wretched persons). लक्ष्मी rose up (समुत्थान) from the sea after मथन. लक्ष्मी (fame) rises up (*i. e.* spreads) in the case of the strong, who employ only their bow and sword for achieving it. ईदृशाः—refers to the treachery of the Gauḍa king. त्रातुं नियुक्ताः गिरयः—It was believed that the mountains made the earth steady. See p. 6. ll. 8–9 (text) 'भिषजो भूधरा इव भुवो धृतिं चक्रुः'. कुलिशं (वज्रं) तद्वत् कर्कशः भुजः परिघः इव तस्मिन् प्रहरणं (शस्त्रं) तस्य हेतोः तदर्थम्. स्वयम...लोहानि the idea is :—mountains yield iron from which weapons are made. The poet fancies that mountains yield iron, because they are themselves unable to discharge the task of protecting the earth and desire that others should do their work with the weapons made of iron. येषाम्—connect with उद्गिरन्ति गिरयो लोहानि—'for whom.' °हेतोः (उद्गिरन्ति)—when the word हेतु is used for denoting 'object or purpose,' it is put in the genitive 'षष्ठी हेतुप्रयोगे' पा. 2. 3. 36 (अन्नस्य हेतोर्वसति । सि. कौ.). वि...न्धवाः friends of spotless fame. कथं ध्यायेयुः अकार्यम् how will they even think of doing an evil deed? सर्व...स्वराणान् (1) glorious by the overwhelming strength in seizing everything (सर्वस्य ग्रहः तेन अभिभवः तेन भास्वराः); (2) brilliant by overshadowing all the planets (सर्वेषां ग्रहाणां अभिभवः तेन &c.). मु...तः in front of (*i. e.* as compared with) the hands of great warriors. दि...कराः the करs (hands, rays) of the sun are crippled in grasping the quarters (as compared with &c.). The idea is:—the sun's rays take time in occupying all the directions; but the warriors seize the world by a single stroke. दिग्ग्रहणे—here there is also an allusion to पाणिग्रहण in marriage. लोक...यमस्य merely in popular report is the south the abode of Yama, but in reality it is the frowning brow of a warrior (that is the abode of यम) *i. e.* it is the wrath of the warrior that deals death. महा...ला (1) the spaces of which are rendered terrible and curling with the wavy lines of the horns of the great Buffalo (महामहिषशृङ्गस्य तरङ्गवत् भङ्गाः तै भङ्गुराणि भीषणानि अन्तरालानि यस्याः); (2) the intervening space between which (eyebrows) is terrible and wavy like the curling lines of the horns &c. (with भ्रुकुटिः, ०भङ्गवत् भङ्गुरं भीषणं च अन्तरालं यस्याः). The Com. seems to have read तरङ्गभङ्गुरभङ्गभीष०, which is good (तरङ्गवत् भङ्गुरः भङ्गः तेन तद्वत् वा &c.). For यम and his buffalo, see pp. 71, 81. चित्रम् *adv.* it is wonderful. उन्मुक्तः सिंहनादः यैः (1) who raise a war-cry; (2) who let loose सिंहनाद (the commander-in-chief of हर्ष). Separate सहसा साहस०. साहसरसेन रोमाञ्चाः एव कण्टकाः तेषां निकरेण. The idea is :—warriors raise war-cries in battle and their bodies are thrilled. When they raise सिंहनाद, the रोमाञ्च comes out (निर्यान्ति); then it is but natural to expect that manes should come out on their bodies by सिंहनाद along with रोमाञ्च. But this does not happen and hence the word चित्रम्. द्वयमेव...भाजनम् only two are (the proper) receptacles for the mass of wealth that springs from the four oceans. प्रति...दाहि that burns its enemies (applies to both ०मुखं and ०हृदयं). वडवामुख the submarine fire. See for वाडव or और्व, p. 124. The submarine fire is supposed to have the face of a horse (वडवा a mare). See महाभारत आदिपर्व 180. 'ततस्तं क्रोधजं तात और्वोऽग्निं वरुणालये । उत्ससर्ज स चैवाप उपयुङ्क्ते महोदधौ ॥ महद्धयशिरो भूत्वा यत्तद्वेदविदो विदुः । तमग्निमुद्गिरद्वक्त्रात्पिबत्यापो महोदधौ ॥' 21–22. The word भूति also means 'ashes'. Ashes are collected in a vessel (भाजनम्). तेजस्विनः...निवृत्तिः how can the inborn fire of the powerful rest without securing all the oceans? The powerful do not rest till they have conquered the world. तेजस्विनः applies to वडवाग्नि also, which did not rest till it was submerged in the ocean. वृथा विततः विपुलफणानां भारः येन. शेष the lord of serpents has 1000 hoods and hence the word विपुल. बिभर्ति...केवलम् that supports merely a clod of earth on its hood. The idea is that शेष merely supports the earth (without the oceans); while the warrior supports all (earth and oceans together). भोग may also mean 'ruling over, government.' भुजङ्गानां भर्ता may mean 'the master of gallants.' The idea is:—'the master of gallants is a king in name, he merely rules over the earth but cannot protect it.' अप्रतिहतं शासनं तेन आक्रान्तिः तस्याः उपभोगः तस्य सुखं तस्य रसः तं (object of जानन्ति) the taste of the happiness of enjoying a suzerainty over the earth in which the edict (issued) is unresisted. Connect रसायाः (of the earth) with ०आक्रान्ति in the preceding compound. दिक्कुञ्जरकरभारवत् भास्वरः प्रकोष्ठः येषाम्. There may be another idea 'the forearm of which is glorious with the tribute levied from even दिग्गजs.' This sentence distinguishes वीरs from शेष; the latter only bears the earth on its भोग (it has no उपभोग); but the warrior enjoys the earth. उन्मुखाः पद्माकराः (lotus beds) तैः गृहीताः पादपल्लवाः (rays) यस्य (with रवि); उन्मुखा (that turns her face towards them, favourable) पद्मा ('लक्ष्मीः पद्मालया पद्मा' अमरः) तस्याः करेण गृहीतः पादपल्लवः (foot) यस्य (with शूरः). अखण्डितं तेजः यस्य (with शूरः); आखण्डितं (destroyed, reduced) तेजः यस्य (with रविः). The radiance of the sun becomes less in the evening. हरिणः हृदये यस्य--the spot in the moon is supposed to be a deer. हरिणस्येव हृदयं यस्य whose heart is (timid) like that of the deer (with कातरस्य). पाण्डुरं पृष्ठं यस्य. The moon is pale in hue; as to the coward 'पाण्डुरपृष्ठस्य देशभाषया निर्लज्जस्यापि' Com. लक्ष्मीः wealth or sovereignty; splendour (of the moon). द्विरात्रमपि—the moon is not the same even for two nights. पुरःप्रवृत्तः प्रतापः तेन प्रहताः. पुरः ... पौरुषस्य the paths of prowess are beaten (*i. e.* prepared) by valour that goes in front. People hear the प्रताप of a warrior and then his way is clear; there is no obstacle. शब्देन विद्रुताः द्विषन्तः येषु. At the word of a proud warrior enemies run away. Doors creak and then the panels fly asunder. शस्त्रस्य आलोकेन (1) by the light of weapons; (2) by the sight of weapons. शून्या दिशः—the world is open to him (*i. e.* nothing comes between him and the world); the world is empty (of enemies). रिपु...रज्यते—the earth is pleased by a shower (आसारः) of rain; लक्ष्मी becomes coloured (or loves) by the shower of blood. ०पतिमुकुटेषु मणिशिलाः शाणाः इव (touchstones) तेषां कोणेषु (points, edges) कषणेन. राजता royalty. Many kings bow at the feet of the overlord and thereby the latter's glory is brightened. The nails of his feet also are brightened by being rubbed against the jewels in the crowns of kings when they fall at his feet. राजता suggests also silver (रजतस्य इयं राजता) which when rubbed against a touchstone shows off brilliant. श्यामीभवन्ति (1) become dark (with hands); (2) become pale or terrified (with रिपुमुख). कव...पात्यमानाः dealt against the panel—like chests of enemies covered with coat of mail. Swords striking against armour produce sparks and also श्री (*i. e.* the successful warrior attains glory or royalty). अहितेन हतः स्वजनः यस्य. Remove the vertical line after ०दुःखम्, मनस्विजनः being the subject of कथयति, उच्छ्वसिति, रोदिति and ददाति. परु...सिति—whose sighs are the wind caused by the fall of the piercing sword-blade. निर्गतं उच्छ्वसितं (जीवितं) यस्मात् तत् ०सितं शत्रुशरीरं तस्मिन् अश्रुधारापातः तेन—the tears he sheds are those that are shed on the body of his lifeless enemy (by the latter's relatives and friends). It would be better if we could read ०शरीरास्रधारापातेन. अस्रम् means both 'tear' and 'blood.' विपक्ष...जलम्—Water is offered to the dead. The spirited offer water to their murdered relatives by the eyes of the wives of their enemies (who shed tears when their husbands are slain in revenge). स्वप्ने आदौ दृष्टाः पश्चान्नष्टाः तेषु. प्रबुद्धाः (1) the wise; (2) those that are awake. When awake we attach no value to things seen in dreams. The wise do not regard their evanescent bodies as their own (kinsmen). Compare for the idea in this and in स्थायिनि &c. 'किमप्यहिंस्यस्तव चेन्मतोऽहं यशः—शरीरे भव मे दयालुः । एकान्तविध्वंसिषु मद्विधानां पिण्डेष्वनास्था किल भौतिकेषु ॥' रघु०-II. 57. अनवरतं प्रज्वलितः तेजःप्रसरः यस्य स चासौ भास्वरस्वभावश्च तं. A jewelled lamp (a jewel shedding light) is naturally brilliant and shoots forth rays. Hence there is no कज्जल in its case. शोक also darkens (कलुषः) a man's face. प्रष्ठो...नाम् the foremost of the nobly born. 'पुरोगाग्रेसरप्रष्ठाग्रतःसरपुरःसराः' इत्यमरः. 'प्रष्ठोऽग्रगामिनि' पा. 8. 3. 92 (प्रतिष्ठते इति प्रष्ठो गौः । अग्रतो गच्छतीत्यर्थः । सि. कौ.). एताश्च—connect with ०भूमयः and भित्तयः. सततसन्निहिताः धूमायमानाः (giving out smoke) कोपाश्रयः यासाम् (*adj.* of ०भूमयः and ०भित्तयः). In cool retreats also fires are lighted which give out smoke. सुलभा असिधारातोयेन तृप्तिः यासु. Thirst is quenched in cool places by water. The bright sword-edge resembles water and is welcomed by these warriors. विकटाः (large) बाहवः एव वनच्छाया तया उपगूढाः—the retreats may be surrounded by the shade of trees. धीर...भूमयः cool places for the abode of courage. स्वायत्ताः = स्वाधीनाः. सिंहनाद means:—such warriors are at your service. धीरता dwells in comfortable (cool) lodgings the walls of which are the broad (panel-like) chests of warriors. यतः...भूयः whence (*i. e.* this being the case) what of the vile Gauḍa king ? So act that no one else will again behave thus (treacherously). सर्वो...कामुकानाम् seeking the confidence of the whole earth; or the words may mean 'lovers of the whole earth believing that it will be theirs'. Compare 3rd उच्छ्वास 'भो विद्याधरीश्रद्धाकामुक'. ०विजि...श्वसितैः—the idea is:—kill these pretentious conquerors, so that their wives will weep and heave deep sighs. The sighs will fan them as chowries did before. रुधिरगन्धेन अन्धं गृध्रमण्डलं तेन आच्छादनं तैः. उच्छिन्धि...व्यसनानि remove their attachment to the shade of umbrellas (insignia of royalty) by the coverings made by the groups of vultures &c. Vultures hover over dead bodies and with their large wings appear like umbrellas. कदुष्णं (tepid) शोणितं उदकं इव तस्य स्वेदैः. कु + उष्ण = कदुष्ण; Vide. notes on कदर्थ p. 101 and 'कवं चोष्णे' पा. 6. 3. 107 (कवोष्णं कोष्णं कदुष्णम् । सि. कौ.). कुलक्ष्मीः एव कुलटा तस्याः कटाक्षैः चक्षूरागरोगाः (चक्षूरागाः एव रोगाः) तान्. This is a compound complicated by puns. The sinful sovereignty of other kings is compared to a harlot. A harlot casts glances by which people are enamoured. The wicked kings also are enamoured of कुलक्ष्मी. चक्षूराग (1) redness of the eye (due to some disease); (2) love as manifested by the exchange of glances. If a man is suffering from an eye disease, he is treated by the process of स्वेद (fomentation with tepid water). The idea briefly is:—kill rival kings and their tepid blood will come out and will extinguish their love for sovereignty obtained by unfair means (कुलक्ष्मी). For चक्षूराग, see उत्तरराम० V —'भूयसा जीविधर्म एष यद्रसमयी कस्यचित् क्वचित् प्रीतिः, यत्र लौकिकानामुपचारस्तारामैत्रकं चक्षूराग इति'. ०शरैः शिरावेधः तैः. अकार्ये शौर्यमेव श्वयथुः. If a part is swollen, it has to be pierced with a lancet to let out foul matter. लोहनिगडः आपीडमाला इव तस्याः मलः (dark spot due to wearing iron chains) एव महौषधं तैः. पादपीठे (foot-stool) दोहदः (longing) तेन दुर्ललितः (wanton, fondled) पादः तस्य पटुमान्द्यानि (sharp pains or stiffness). The idea is:—put iron fetters on the feet of kings that desire to rest their feet on foot-stools (which were attached to the throne of a king on which feudatories laid their heads). If a person has feet stiffened by some disease like paralysis or epilepsy, iron rings are placed round them. तीक्ष्णानि आज्ञाक्षराणि (words of command) एव क्षाराः तेषां पातैः. ०कण्डूः is accu. plural. Itch was cured by the application of क्षारs (caustic). ०मरीचयः एव चन्दनचर्चा तया ललाटलेपाः तैः. अनमितानि स्तिमितानि (stiff) मस्तकानि तेषां स्तम्भविकाराः (rigidity) तान्. If the head became rigid, some लेप had to be applied to it. Make the kings bow their unbending heads at your feet, so that the rays of your bright nails, resembling sandal paste, will be a salve to their foreheads. करदानस्य (payment of tribute) सन्देशः (message, order) एव सन्दंशः (forceps). द्रविणदर्पेण उष्णायमाणाः दुःशीललीलाः एव शल्यानि. For taking out शल्य (the point of a dart), forceps are required. Kings did all sorts of wicked and wanton deeds owing to the warmth of wealth. Send a message to them levying tribute and their pride of wealth will be gone. ०पीठस्य दीधितयः एव प्रदीपिकाः (torches or lamps). शुष्कः (vain) सुभटाटोपः (pride of being a great warriar) तेन भ्रुकुटिबन्धः एव अन्धकारः. Darkness is removed by torches. Make the vain and frowning kings bend on your jewelled पादपीठ. चरणलङ्घनं (insulting with the feet, kicking) तेन लाघवं तेन गलितं शिरोगौरवं (weight in the head) तस्मात् आरोग्यं तैः. मिथ्याभिमान is compared to सन्निपात, for which see p. 80. Remove the false pride of kings by kicking them, so that they will not hold their head high. In सन्निपात, there is a feeling of heaviness in the head, which is removed by लङ्घन (fasting). म्रदय denominative verb from मृदु. ०ञ्जलिषु मुकुलितः (closed, folded) करसम्पुटः तस्य ऊष्मभिः. इष्वसनं (इषवः अस्यन्ते अनेन) धनुः तस्य गुणः (string) तेन किणः तस्य कार्कश्यानि (hardness). If the hands be always folded together, heat is produced in the cavity. A hard callosity may become soft by fomentation. देवभूयं गते having reached the state of being a god *i. e.* having gone to heaven. 'स्याद् ब्रह्मभूयं ब्रह्मत्वं ब्रह्मसायुज्यमित्यपि । देवभूयादिकं तद्वत्' इत्यमरः. नरेन्द्रे = प्रभाकरवर्धने. वृत्ते...प्रलये when this great Pralaya (calamity) has taken place. धरणी...शेषः you alone are left to support the world. शेष also means the serpent शेष that supports the earth on its hoods. See p. 19. अविद्यमानं शरणं यासाम्. 'शरणं गृहरक्षित्रोः' इत्यमरः. शरत्सवितेव like the sun in autumn. क्ष्मापतीनां (1) of kings; (2) of mountains. ललाटन्तप—burning the forehead. पादः foot, ray. आयाहि... ताम्—become one whose feet have a variegated hue (black and white). There is another sense 'become कल्माषपाद'. King मित्रसह son of सुदास came to be called कल्माषपाद. The king killed a tiger out of two. When killed it became a राक्षस. The other vowed revenge. The king performed a sacrifice at the end of which the राक्षस came disguised as वसिष्ठ and asked for a meal of flesh. Then the राक्षस assumed the form of a cook and served human flesh. The real वसिष्ठ came and knowing what was served cursed the king to be a cannibal. The king, knowing that he was innocent, took water to curse वसिष्ठ, when his queen मदयन्ती dissuaded him from cursing the sage. He threw the water taken for the curse on his own feet, which became spotted. See विष्णुपु० IV. 4; भागवत 9. 9. 20-25 and रामायण VII. 65 (where the king's name is वीर्यसह). रामायण I. 70 gives a different story. अभिनवा सेवादीक्षा तया दुःखं तेन सन्तप्ताः श्वासाः एव धूममण्डलानि तैः. दीक्षा means 'initiating a person into some rite or work.' The kings were to be subdued and made to attend upon हर्ष for the first time. Naturally they would heave hot sighs, which are compared to धूममण्डल. नखम्पचैः scorching the nails. 'मितनखे च' पा. 3. 2. 34 (मितंपचा ब्राह्मणी । नखंपचा यवागूः । सि. कौ.). The hot breaths of kings when they bowed at his feet would scorch his nails and the jewels in their crowns that moved when they bowed would emit rays resembling the mellow light of morn (बालातप). सहजं ब्राह्मण्यमार्दवं तेन सुकुमारं मनः यस्य. चण्डेन चापवनानां अटनिः (the notched extremity of a bow) तस्याः टाङ्कारनादेन निर्मदीकृताः दिग्गजाः येन (*adj.* of राज्यन्यकम्)—(the क्षत्रिय race) that had deprived the quarter elephants of their intoxication by the terrible twanging of the extremities of the forest of (*i. e.* group of) bows. The idea is that the क्षत्रियs had subdued the whole earth. गुञ्जत् ज्यानां जालं तेन जनितः जगतः ज्वरः येन (*adj.* of राजन्यकम्). उद्यतम् making an (united) effort. कृत्ताः वंशाः यस्य the families of which were cut off (by परशुराम). वंशs (bamboos) also are cut off, produce a sound and their thickets are burnt. Or कृत्तवंशं (कृत्ताः वंशाः यथा स्युः) may be taken as an adverb modifying उत्खातवान्. कृतवंशं (कृताः संस्कृताः वंशाः यस्य) is not a good reading. राजन्यकम्—the race of क्षत्रियs. 'अथ राजकम् । राज्यन्यकं च नृपतिक्षत्रियाणां गणे क्रमात् ॥' इत्यमरः. नैसर्गिकेण कायकार्कश्येन कुलिशायमानं मानसं यस्य whose mind acts like the thunder-bolt on account of the natural hardness of his body. मूर्धन्यः foremost (मूर्धनि भवः). ०ध्वस्तये for the destruction &c. जीवितानां सङ्कलने आकुलः कालः यमः तस्य अकाण्डे यात्रा तस्याः चिह्नध्वजं—(bow) which is the banner indicating the unexpected expedition of Yama eager to gather lives. The idea is:—your bow will do terrific carnage among your foes. A ध्वज is carried in front of an army. Harsha has to resolve on fighting all of a sudden. अरातिः शत्रुः तस्य रक्तमेव चन्दनचर्चा तया शिशिरोपचारः (cooling treatment) तमन्तरेण (without that). दुःखमेव दाहज्वरः. In दाहज्वर sandal paste is applied. Blood resembles रक्तचन्दनचर्चा. निकारेण (insult) सन्तापः तस्य शान्तिः तस्याः उपायानां परिक्षये--when no other means to allay the heat of insult could be found. रिपुरुधिरं एव अमृतं. For the reference, see above p. 139. पवनात्मजेन=भीमेन. अमन्दरोपायम् (न विद्यते मन्दरः उपायः यत्र)—for being able to drink अमृत, the gods required the mountain मन्दर; see p. 42. But भीम obtained रुधिरामृत without मन्दर. हिडिम्बा was a राक्षसी, wife of भीम. भीम drank the blood of दुःशासन with zest, as if it had first been touched by the lips of his wife हिडिम्बा. Being a राक्षसी, she is appropriately mentioned in connection with blood. See आदिपर्व 155 for the union of हिडिम्बा and भीम. As to the extirpation of the क्षत्रियs by परशुराम, see above p. 38. 'त्रिःसप्तकृत्वः पृथिवीं कृत्वा निःक्षत्रियां प्रभुः । समन्तपञ्चके पञ्च चकार रुधिरह्रदान् ॥ स तेषु तर्पयामास भृगून् भृगुकुलोद्वहः ।' वनपर्व 117. 9–10; see also आदिपर्व 2. 3–5. जामदग्न्येन—परशुरामेण. शाम्यन् ०सञ्ज्वरः (मन्युः क्रोधः एव शिखी तस्य शिखानां ज्वालानां सञ्ज्वरः) तस्मिन् सुखायमानेषु स्पर्शशीतलेषु च &c. क्षत्रियाणां क्षतजं रुधिरं तस्य ह्रदेषु (lakes).

P. 102 l. 19—**P. 103** l. 13. **देवस्तु...भुवनस्य.** मान्येन refers to सिंहनाद. इतरथा—even otherwise *i. e.* even if this treachery of the Gauda king had not kindled my wrath. मे goes with भुवनस्य. गृहीत...भुजस्य. दायमादत्ते दायादः—one who shares in the ancestral estate. The idea is:—my arm does not like the idea of sharing the burden of the earth with शेष. It wants the whole to itself. गच्छति qualifies ग्रहग्रणे. The idea is:—When the stars go up (reach the zenith), my brow wants to check their rise (*i. e.* I am so ambitious as to crave not only the control of this earth but also of heavenly bodies). Explain the following similarly. अनमत्सु...कचग्रहम्—one who does not bend may be made to bend by seizing his hair. दुर्विदग्ध conceited. चामराणि—I wish to make the rays of the sun my chowrie-bearers. Chowries are held in the hand (कर, also ray). राज...रुषा As I resent the title 'king' (applied to the lion). The lion is called मृगराज. I cannot bear that anyone else should bear the title of king in this world. Compare for the idea 'नूनं तेषामभ्यसूयापरोऽभूद्वीर्योदग्रे राजशब्दे मृगेषु' रघु० 9. 64. स्व...गृहीतानाम् (*adj.* of दिशाम्) that have been seized (occupied) at their sweet will by the self-willed (uncontrolled) लोकपालs. For लोकपालs, see above p. 137. The author seems to have used the word लोकपाल in the sense of दिक्पाल, but the two are slightly different, as will be seen from pp. 25, 137. आक्षेपादेशाय for giving the order of snatching them (quarters) away (from their hands). दुर्जातं—calamity. 'दुर्जातं व्यसने क्लीबेऽसम्यग्जातेऽन्यलिङ्गकम्' मेदिनी. The construction is इतरथा हि मे...भुजस्य...किं पुनरीदृशे...जाते. Put a vertical line after जाते. हृदय...शल्ये who is a painful thorn in my heart. मुसल्ये—मुसलेन वध्यः—deserving to be pounded with a pestle. The word is formed on the analogy of विष्य (विषेण वध्यः according to पा. 4. 4. 91 which is a very long सूत्र). पोटा—Hermaphrodite 'पोटा स्त्रीपुंसलक्षणा.' प्रतिकारशून्यम् (adverb) helplessly. शुष्कः अधरपुटः यस्य (with हृर्ष) whose lips are dry (through the fever of grief). With पोटा, the word cannot be explained for reasons of propriety. अधरं स्त्रीयोनिः. अकृतं रिपुबलस्य अबलानां (wives) विलोललोचनेषु उदकं (tears) एव दुर्दिनं येन. He says he cannot offer water to his deceased brother with ordinary water, but will do so with the tears &c. Supply कुतः before अदृष्ट°. धूम causes tears. शपामि...स्पर्शेन—the thing with which an oath is taken is put in the instrumental. परिगणितैः counted *i. e.* limited. सकलचापानां चापलेन (quickness, fickleness) दुर्ललिताः (naughty, spoilt) नरपतयः तेषां चरणेषु रणरणायमानाः (resounding) निगडाः यस्याम्. The kings of the earth are quick archers. Those who are fickle are spoilt. तनूनपाति=अग्नौ. पीतं सर्पिः घृतं येन—fed with ghee. पतङ्गः a moth flies against the flame of a lamp. महा...कृतम् the great minister for peace and war. सन्धिश्च विग्रहश्च तयोः अधिकृतः. महांश्चासौ °कृतश्च. This officer is often spoken of as महासान्धिविग्रहिक (see I. A. Vol. 15 p. 304; E. I. Vol. III. p. 267, 270). Compare C. I. Vol. III. p. 35 'अन्वयप्राप्तसाचिव्यः व्यापृतसन्धिविग्रहः'. अन्तिके तिष्ठतीति °स्थः. आ is a कर्मप्रवचनीय governing a noun in the ablative and means 'up to'. चारणः—a heavenly chorister, a semi-divine being. त्रिकूटकटके (capital) कुट्टाकटङ्कैः लिखितः काकुत्स्थेन (रामेण) लङ्कालुण्ठनव्यतिकरः यस्मिन्—where the incident of the devastation of लङ्का by Rāma was engraven with cutting axes on the capital situated on त्रिकूट. त्रिकूट was a hill on which the capital of रावण was situated. 'स सागरमनाधृष्यमतिक्रम्य महाबलः । त्रिकूटस्य तटे लङ्कां स्थितः स्वस्थो ददर्श ह ॥' अरण्यकाण्ड 2. 1. कुट्टाक *adj.* that cuts. सुवेल is a mountain identical with त्रिकूट according to हेमचन्द्र. See also अनर्घराघव VI. 17. वरुण is the lord of the ocean and of the West. परिमलैः सुगन्धयः पाषाणाः तैः वासितं गुह्यागृहं यस्मिन्. गुह्यकs are semi-divine beings that are the attendants of कुबेर and guardians of his treasures. The unguents they employ perfume the caves where they dwell. गन्धमादनः name of a mountain to the east of मेरु famous for its fragrant forests. There भीम had gone to bring सौगन्धिकपुष्प for द्रौपदी. See वनपर्व 152 ff. सज्जी...ग्रहणाय वा—In this and the following clauses he offers them a choice between submitting to him and offering battle. गृह्यन्तां...चामराणि वा either seize the quarters or chowries *i. e.* either be my chowrie-bearers or hold fast by your kingdoms and fight. गृह्यन्तां दिशः may also mean 'run away, fly from your kingdoms'. नमन्तु धनूंषि—bows are bent in discharging arrows. कर्णपूरः an ear-ornament. कर्ण... मौर्व्यः either honour my commands (by listening to them) or draw the strings (मौर्वी) of your bows to the ear (in discharging arrows). शेख...शिरस्त्राणि turn the dust of my feet into chaplets or don the helmet. शेखरः a chaplet worn on the head. घटन्तां करि...बन्धाः arrange the arrays (घटा) of elephants. समा...यष्टयः either take hold of canes or lances. Canes were held by chamberlains or doorkeepers. मच्चरणनखेषु &c. He asks them either to bow at his feet, on the bright nails of which they will be reflected or to take bright swords. परा...मिति because I am come. This gives the reason why the kings should make a choice. निवृत्तिः cessation, rest. सकल...मयः consisting of the jewels in the crowns &c. *i. e.* all kings must bow at my feet. A person maimed has to apply a लेप to his feet. स्वस्थवत् like one who is at ease (as if nothing had happened). श्रुता प्रतिज्ञा येन. शाम्यन् ऊष्मा यस्य (*adj.* of दिवसः). The idea is:—the day passed away together with its heat. The poet says that it was not the heat that faded away from the day of the worlds, but it was the pride that faded (at hearing the terrible प्रतिज्ञा of हर्ष).

P. 103 l. **14—P. 104** l. 4 **ततश्च...मिच्छामीति.** Read अह्निमभासि, for अह्निम. अह्निमा भाः यस्य. निजा०—The setting of the sun is represented as due to the fear of the sun that the angered हर्ष may deprive him also of his sovereignty, just as he vowed that he would do in the case of the kings of the earth. निगूढाः शिलीमुखानां भ्रमराणां आलापाः येषु. The red lotuses closed their petals at sunset and the humming of bees was heard no more. The poet fancies that they did so through fear. One who is afraid remains silent and contracts himself (or hides). शिलीमुख also means 'arrow'. (निगूढः शिलीमुखानां आलापः twang येषु). Further a picturesque effect is produced by the words

मुख and आलाप and by reading इषुत्रासात्. समुपसंहृतः निजपक्षाणां (wings) विक्षेपः (tossing, movement) यैः ते ०क्षेपाः, ०क्षेपाश्च ते निश्चलाश्च. The birds lay in their nests and did not flap their wings. पक्ष also means 'side, partisans.' The suggested meaning is:—When the excitement of the partisans had died away and hence they were motionless. भुवनव्यापिनीम् (1) that spread over the whole world (with सन्ध्या); (2) that embraced or applied to the whole world (with प्रतिज्ञा). ०दिक्पालैः दीयमानानि अभ्रंलिहानि लोहप्राकारवलयानि यासु. Pitchy darkness began to envelope the sky and the quarters. Darkness is fancied to be iron ramparts (प्राकारः) touching the sky erected by दिक्पालs afraid of losing their position (as दिक्पालs) at the hands of हर्ष. प्रदोषास्थाने in the evening assembly. नमन् नृपलोकः तस्य लोलानि अंशुकानि तेषां पवनेन कम्पिताः शिखाः (flames) येषाम्. The lamps flickered owing to the wind set in motion by the upper garments of the kings when they bowed before departing. The poet says that the flickering was as if the bowing of lamps. उत्तानः stretched out, lying on the back. दीपः द्वितीयः यस्य He had no companion except the lamp. अभि...सरः जग्राह as an attendant (or servant) finding a proper opportunity wins (the mind of his master). 'अनुप्लवः सहायश्चानुचरोऽभिसरः समाः' इत्यमरः. C and T render 'finding its opportunity like a brigand.' तरसा (instru. of तरस् *n.*) quickly. उपर्यु...श्वासाः one after another his sighs went forth as if searching for his brother's life. धवलां...प्लवेन his bright tears resembled the hem of a white garment. परिणामः result, end. ०सङ्घातवत् or ०सङ्घातैः कर्कशः कायबन्धः यस्य (with तातात् and अचलात् respectively). इयं सा प्रीतिः this is my love for my brother (the idea intended to be conveyed being that he had no real love for his brother). अनुवृत्तिः acting according to, obedience. बालिशो...वितम् who even if a child (or fool) would think it possible that I would continue to live even after the death of my honoured brother ? ऐक्यम् Unity of hearts or thoughts. पृथक्कृतः separated. दग्धरोषेण अन्तरिता शुक् यस्य (*adj.* of मया) whose grief was intercepted (obscured) by accursed wrath (against the गौड king). गतघृणेन निर्दयेन. लूता...छिद्राः as brittle (easy to cut) as the webs of the spider (लूता). तन्तुच्छटा = तन्तुजालम्. तुच्छाः worthless. लोक...बान्धवता ties of kindred rest solely upon the conventions of the world. He means:—kinship is no reality, but is a mere conventional bond. लोकयात्रा एव ०मात्रं निबन्धनं (support) यस्याः. परस्परप्रीतिबन्धेन निर्वृतं (blessed) हृदयं यस्य. विघटिते—being separated. चन्द्र...गुणाः—the idea is :—while राज्य० was alive his qualities delighted the world like the moon, but when he passed away, the same qualities burn the world, as if through contact with the funeral fire. लग्नः चिताग्निः येषां (*adj.* of गुणाः). पर्यदेवत he bewailed. अशेष...कृतम् commander of the whole elephant host. स्कन्दगुप्त is probably the same स्कन्दगुप्त that is mentioned as a great officer of Harsha in the Madhuban inscription (E. I. VII. p. 155). *Vide* Introduction.

P. 104 l. 5—**P. 105** l. 3 अथ ... करोत्. The principal sentence is अथ...हूयमानः स्वमन्दिरात्...स्कन्दगुप्तो विवेश राजकुलम्. अप्रति...रेणुः who did not wait for his own elephant. करेणुः an elephant in general, or a female elephant. के मूर्ध्नि रेणुरस्य or अस्याः. प्रणमतः... दिशम् bowing (to him) on every side. दिशि दिशि प्रति० (अव्ययी०). वर...पृच्छन् questioning as to the night's news concerning the best elephants. पृच्छन् governs two accusatives इभभिषग्वरान् and ०वार्ताः. उच्छ्रित०—The instrumentals in this and the following clauses are to be connected with क्रियमाणकोलाहलः (l. 19), which qualifies स्कन्दगुप्तः below. Various groups belonging to the camp raised noises about him. उच्छ्रितं शिखिपिच्छैः लाञ्छितं वंशलतावनगहनं तेन गृहीतः दिगायामः यैः that measured the expanse of the sky with tall thickets of bamboos that were decked with peacock's feathers. In the विन्ध्य forest grow high bamboos on which sit peacocks. The elephant-riders had tall bamboos in their hands on which were hung peacock's feathers. वारण...गतैः that had come to undertake the encounter for capturing elephants (or the encounter for securing elephants that had got loose). C and T translate 'come for the purpose of bursting the animals' fastenings.' This is not clear. The com. read अनायत्त० and explains 'अनायत्ता हस्तिपार्श्वरक्षिणः'. C and T translate 'throngs of unemployed persons'. We take अना० as an *adj.* of ०गणैः. अनायतानि मण्डलानि येषाम् whose groups were not restrained (*i. e.* that did not run in proper order). 'आधोरणाः हस्तिपका हस्त्यारोहा निषादिनः' अमरः. नवः ग्रहः येषां ते ०ग्रहाः गजपतयः elephants recently caught. आत्मीय...वेदयद्भिः that reported the advent of rut in the elephants entrusted to them. डिण्डि...यद्भिः that made a request that a drum be mounted (on the elephants in their charge). प्रमादेन पतितः अपराधः तेन अपहृतः द्विरदः तस्मात् दुःखं तेन धृतं दीर्घश्मश्रु यैः that had a long beard due to the grief caused by their being deprived of an elephant because they were guilty of an offence committed through carelessness. अभि...स्रुतैः that had recently come (for being engaged as servants). कर्पटिभिः that were clothed in rags (because they had not yet been engaged). गणिका—'गजानां प्रतिलोभनार्था हस्तिनी' com. चिरात् लब्धं अन्तरं यैः that found an opportunity (to speak to स्कन्दगुप्त) after a long time. उच्छ्रितौ (uplifted) करौ येषाम्. Remove the comma after ०करैः. कर्मण्य...कुलैः busy in enumerating the female elephants that were clever in that act (in decoying wild elephants). कर्मणि साधुः कर्मण्यः. उल्लासितानि (tossed) पल्लवचिह्नानि यैः. Being foresters, it is but proper that their badges should be पल्लवs. Remove the comma after ०पङ्क्तिभिश्च. निष्पादितः (secured) नवग्रहाणां नागानां (गजानां) निवहः &c. उत्तम्भितं (raised up) तुङ्गं तोत्रवनं यैः. तोत्रम् (from तुद्) a goad. महामात्राः (महती मात्रा परिच्छदः येषाम्) प्रधानहस्त्यारोहाः (chiefs of elephant riders) तेषां पेटकैः समूहैः. प्रकटितं करिकर्मणे चर्मपुटं यैः. Figures of elephants made of leather were used for training elephants to fight. अभि...वृन्दैः by crowds of messengers sent by the keepers of elephant forests for conveying the news of the movements of fresh herds of elephants. प्रति...कूटैः that examined at each moment the heaps of fodder for elephants. Remove the comma after वृन्दैः. Being men from the forest, they were naturally led to examine every mouthful that they saw elephants eating before them. कट...वेदयमानैः that reported about the gleaning of corn (for elephants) in villages, towns and marts (निगमः). कटानां सस्यानां ओषधीनामिति यावत् हस्तेन भङ्गः छेदनम्. Three things combined to give an air of command to स्कन्दगुप्त even when he was indifferent (he did not intend to issue any order). ०सम्भृतेन added to, increased. महा...ऽकारेण by the appearance (outward signs *i. e.* dress &c.) of the high position he held. अव...भोगेन by the great majesty (of his form). अवष्टम्भस्य आभोगः (expanse). असंख्य...सम्पादनाय—C and T translate 'to provide a limitless supply of shells for elephants' ears.' We do not know what shells had to do with elephants' ears. असंख्यकरिणां कर्णाः शङ्खाश्च (parts between the tusks) तेषां सम्पत् (beauty) तस्याः सम्पादनाय. Conchshells are found on the sea-shore. So he as if ordered the seas to supply शङ्ख (*i. e.* beautiful temples to the elephants). कर्ण also means 'the rudder of a ship'. For the meanings of शङ्ख see p. 42. शृङ्गार...संग्रहाय for making a store of the unguents (अङ्गरागः), *viz.* red-chalk (गैरिकपङ्कः), for making marks (on the elephant's forehead). **'शृङ्गारः सुरते नाट्यरसे च गजमण्डने'** मेदिनी. दिग्ग...रैः Depriving the elephant (ऐरावत) of Indra of his authority as a दिग्गज over the quarters. स्कन्दगुप्त wielded power over the quarters with his elephants and so deprived even ऐरावत of his अधिकार, though ऐ० was patronised by the powerful इन्द्र. अपहरन् governs two accusatives, ०कारं and ऐरावतम्. C and T tranlsate 'to deprive Indra of his Airâvata's charge over the sky elephants.' This is not correct. It was *not* Indra that was deprived. For the meanings of हरि, see p. 40. हरपदभारेण नमितः कैलासगिरिः तद्वत् गुरुभिः (heavy). गुरुभार० heavy weight. गति...लम्बस्य—As he walked about, his arms moved to and fro and reached his knees. Arms reaching the knees indicated sovereignty or great position. 'करिकरसदृशौ वृत्तावाजान्ववलम्बनौ समौ पीनौ। बाहू पृथिवीशानाम्' बृहत्संहिता 67. 35. आलान...मालाम् a row of stone pillars for tying elephants. ई...लम्बेन slightly raised and pendulous. कवलेने...लोभयन्—the idea is:–a female elephant is allured by the sight of a mouthful of fresh sprays that are high up hanging from a tree. His lip was red and resembled tender leaves and so allured the करेणुका, *viz.* श्री (glory or prosperity). His lip was such as indicated the high position he had attained. The whole of chap. 67 of the बृहत्संहिता gives the सामुद्रिकलक्षणs of men. निज...दधानः having a straight (bamboo-like) nose as long as his master's pedigree. This is rather a strange simile. A long nose indicated beauty and prosperity 'दीर्घया तु सौभाग्यम्' बृहत्संहिता 67. 61. स्निग्ध glossy (with eyes); oily, sticky (with क्षीरोद). पिब...यामम् he as if drank the expanse of the quarters with the expanse of his two eyes. पीतः क्षीरोदः (क्षीरसागरः) येन. विकटं विपुलं च अलिकं (forehead) यस्य. He had a forehead that was broader than the slopes of Meru. There is a further suggestion. As मेरु is a mountain of gold, his forehead also was gold-coloured (fair). सतत...वशादिव—His hair was long, dark and soft like tendrils. The poet fancies that this was due to its growing under the shade of an umbrella (which was the sign of his authority). भङ्गुर curling. कुन्तलाः (tresses) एव बालवल्लरी तस्याः वेल्लितं (tossing) तेन विलासिना. बर्बरक (also written वर्वर or—क) means curly hair. A young creeper also may be long, green, soft and curling. लुन...करान्—His hair deprived by its darkness the rays of the sun of their light. लुप्तः आलोकः येषाम्. अरिपक्षस्य परिक्षयेण परित्यक्तं कार्मुककर्म येन सः. ०दिगन्तेषु श्रूयमाणः गुरुः गुणध्वनिः यस्य. If he had given up archery, how can the twang of his bowstring (गुण) be heard? This विरोध is removed by taking गुण in the sense of 'virtue.' आत्मस्थं (under his control) सकल-

मत्तमातङ्गसाधनं यस्य. मदेन (1) by ichor; (2) by pride. भूति...मयः— though full of भूति (ashes), he was yet full of oili-ness. Ashes can never contain oil. So we must explain 'though full of prosperity, yet possessing a sweet manner'. पार्थिवो...मयः though made up of earthy substance, yet produced from गुण. पृथ्वी is a द्रव्य according to the न्यायवैशेषिक system. What is made of द्रव्य cannot at the same time be an effect of गुण (the 2nd पदार्थ of the above system). The विरोध is got over by translating 'though he was in rank a king, yet he was full of good qualities.' The com. says 'गुणास्तन्तवोऽपि । नहि घटः पटो भवतीति विरोधः' (*i. e.* पार्थिव means a घट and गुणमय a पट). This is another way of putting forward the विरोध, but is not so striking as the one we give. दानव...स्थितः standing at the head of the generous. दानवत् also means 'full of rut' and qualifies 'करिणाम्'. स्कन्दगुप्त was superintendent (उपरिस्थितः) of elephants. भृत्य...द्वहन्—the idea is:— though he was a servant, he had never borne any humiliation, just as if he were the master (or king). भर्तृ (1) master ; (2) husband. अनन्यगम्याम् (1) not to be reached by anyone else (with प्रसादभूमि); (2) not approachable by anyone else (with कुलाङ्गना). विदग्ध learned. अभृत...भजताम् an unpaid servant of those that resorted to him (for protection). उभय...तलं he rested both his hands on the earth and touched it with his head.

P. 105 l. 4—P. 106 l. 20 उपविष्टं...निर्जगाम. Read नाति०. अस्य...तस्य of what I desire to do. प्र...र्गतानि gone out to the pastures (प्रचारः). भर्तृभक्तेः from devotion to my master. पुष्प...जनस्य (worthy) of the race sprung from पुष्प०. आभिजात्यम् (अभिजातस्य भावः) nobility of birth. उपक्रान्तम् undertaken, begun. काकोदरः अभिधानं यस्य called a snake. 'काकोदरः फणी' इत्यमरः. (काकस्येव उदरं यस्य). निकारम् insult, injury. उदन्तः 'वार्ताप्रवृत्तिर्वृत्तान्त उदन्तः स्यात्' इत्यमरः. विषयः a district. From the inscriptions we shall find that विषय is a portion of राष्ट्र. आकाराः features. व्याहारः speech. व्यवहारः dealings, pursuit. प्र...देवः your Majesty has heard everyday many stories about the disasters due to the fault of carelessness. 'अभिषङ्गः पराभवे' इत्यमरः. श्रुताः बह्व्यः वार्ताः येन. यथा—the following passage contains numerous interesting stories of love and intrigue. They appear to have a historical basis; many of them occur in the अर्थशास्त्र of कौटिल्य; a few in the कामन्दकीयनीतिसार and in the बृहत्संहिता. नागकुले जन्म यस्य. सारिकया श्रावितः मन्त्रः यस्य— whose line of policy was published (to the world) by a सारिका bird. पद्मावती—What particular city is meant, we cannot say.

The scene of the मालतीमाधव is laid in पद्मावती, which seems to have been in Malva. As to the secrecy to be observed in the case of मन्त्र, see above p. 37. The Com. says 'नागसेननामा...राजा मन्त्रिणमर्धराज्यहरमपाकर्तुं शारिकासमक्षं मन्त्रमकरोत् । स चापि मन्त्री शारिकामुखाद्विज्ञाय विस्रम्भपूर्वकं तं दण्डेनावधीत्'. शुकात् श्रुतं रहस्यं यस्य. श्रावस्त्याम्—श्रावस्ती was a famous city in the ancient kingdom of अयोध्या north of the Ganges, identified with the ruins at Sahet-Mahet. स्वप्नायमानस्य speaking in a dream. चूडामणौ लग्नं लेखप्रतिबिम्बं तस्मिन् वाचितानि अक्षराणि यया. What the king had written was reflected in his crest jewel, which the chowrie-bearer standing by his side read. यमतां ययौ became यम *i. e.* caused his death. यवनेश्वर—A Yavana king. The word यवन primarily meant the Greeks, but was subsequently applied to any non-Indian people. लोभबहुलं full of greed. बहुलनिशि on a night of कृष्णपक्ष. निधानम् a treasure. उत्खा...थिनी pounding with drawn swords. माथुरम् of मथुरा (on the Jumna). माया...र्गताः issuing from the body of a sham elephant. वत्सपति king of the वत्स country. न्ययंसिषुः—*Aorist* of यम् with नि—imprisoned. उदयन, king of वत्स, the capital of which was कौशाम्बी (modern Kosam about 30 miles above Allahabad) is a famous king in ancient legendary lore. चण्डमहासेन, king of उज्जयिनी, wanted to conquer him. उदयन was fond of catching elephants. So चण्डमहासेन prepared a wooden elephant, had warriors concealed in it and placed it in the विन्ध्य forest. उदयन was captured and brought to उज्जयिनी, but spared at the request of the citizens. उदयन taught music to वासवदत्ता, daughter of चण्ड०, and after several adventures escaped with her from prison and married her. See for a full account बृहत्कथामञ्जरी II. 2. कालिदास refers to it in the मेघदूत 'प्रद्योतस्य प्रियदुहितरं वत्सराजोऽत्र जह्रे'. अतिदयितं लास्यं यस्य. For लास्य, see p. 28. शैलूषः an actor, 'शैलालिनस्ते शैलूषा जायाजीवाः कृशाश्विनः । भरता इत्यपि नटाः' अमरः ('शिलूषस्य ऋषेरपत्यं शैलूषः' क्षीर०). The Com. says: 'सुमित्रो राजा...स्त्रीजनपरिवारे इव नटजने विस्रब्धो मित्रदेवेन नटत्वमाश्रित्य हतः । स च योगचूर्णावचूर्णितस्तिरोहितो बभूवेति । अतो व्यसनिभिः प्रकृतलोकविश्वसिभिर्न भाव्यमित्युक्तम्'. प्रियाणि तन्त्रीवाद्यानि (stringed instruments, lutes) यस्य. अलाबूः (gourd) वीणा च तयोः अभ्यन्तरे सुषिरं (cavity) तस्मिन् निहिताः निशिताः तरवारयः (swords) यैः. गान्धर्व...छद्मानः who had disguised themselves as students of music. गान्धर्वम्—the art of the गन्धर्वs *i. e.* music. अश्मक is the name of the country about the Ajanta caves. See J. B. B. R. A. S. Vol. VII p. 62. प्रज्ञादुर्बलम् weak in intelligence, foolish. बल...सैन्यः who displayed his whole army on the pretext of showing his power (to his master). मौर्यम् of the famous Maurya dynasty of Magadha, to which the great चंद्रगुप्त and अशोक belonged. In this case we are on firmer ground. According to the Purāṇas, बृहद्रथ was the last of the Mauryas. पुष्यमित्र was the founder of the S'unga dynasty. The महाभाष्य also refers to him as a contemporary (Kielhorn's ed. Vol. II pp. 34 and 123). See the विष्णुपु० IV. 24 and भागवतपु. XII. 1. for the S'ungas, where numerous dynasties of kings are mentioned. आश्च...ली being curious to know or see marvels. चण्डीपतिः seems to be the name of some king; or means 'king of चण्डी.' दण्डे उपनतः यवनः तेन निर्मितेन prepared by a यवन that had been imprisoned or that had approached for punishment. The idea seems to be that चण्डीपति had taken some यवन as captive who prepared an aerial car moving by some machinery. C and T translate 'by a यवन condemned to death' and connect काकवर्णः with अनीयत in this sentence. काकवर्णः शैशुनारिः—we must read शैशुनागिः with three MSS. of B. The विष्णुपु० (IV. 24) mentions a शैशुनागवंश of ten kings, the founder of which was शिशुनाग and the second of whom was काकवर्ण. शुङ्गम् belonging to the शुङ्ग dynasty. The name of the last शुङ्ग king was देवभूति according to the विष्णुपु०. वसुदेवः—he was the founder of the कण्व dynasty. देवीव्यञ्जनया disguised as his queen. असु...सनिनं (*adj.* of मागधं) who was very fond of mines (of treasure). The word असुरविवर is used very frequently by बाण. It is not easy to give the exact sense. In the 3rd उच्छ्वास we have 'यः...असुरविवरमिति वातिकैः (अगृह्यत)'; on p. 7 (text, 4th उच्छ्वास) we have 'असुरविवराणीवापावृतानि'; 'लब्धासुरविवरप्रवेशपिशाचेन' कादम्बरी (p. 227 of P.). One of the companions of Bâṇa's youth was 'असुरविवरव्यसनी'. We think that असुरविवर was a term applied to mines worked up in bygone days. They were believed to have been the work of असुरs and to lead to the treasures of Pātāla in hopes of reaching which many people might have endangered their lives. The Com. remarks "वातिकच्छद्मभिः 'अहिविवरं साधितं तपसास्माभिः' इत्युक्त्वा मागधो गुहाद्वारप्रतिद्वारैर्बद्धोऽभूत्". सुरुङ्गा or सुरङ्गा—a subterranean passage or tunnel. In the passage many women had been placed, whose jingling anklets allured the king onwards. मागधम् king of मगध, modern Bihar. 'गोधनः सूर्याख्यः पर्वतः' Com. The ब्रह्मपुराण mentions a mountain गोधन (27. 22). मेकल is that mountain from which the नर्मदा springs. महाकालमहे in the festival of महाकाल. महाकाल is a form of शिव. There is a celebrated shrine of महाकाल at उज्जयिनी. 'मह उद्धव

उत्सवः' अमरः. महा...वातूलम् whose head was turned by his belief in (the efficacy of) the sale of human flesh. For महामांस, see above p. 72. जघ...द्योतस्य the younger brother of प्रद्योत. रसायनरसे अभिनिवेशः अस्य ०वेशिनः (*adj.* of गणपतेः). That had set his heart upon the elixir of life. It was believed that mercury if properly treated would make men immortal. वैद्यव्यञ्जनाः persons professing to be doctors. सुबहुपुरुषान्तरैः प्रकाशिताः औषधगुणाः गैः that had advertised the virtues of their medicines through various people. विदेह was a country that comprised a part of modern Nepal, the district of Tirhut and Champaran. राजयक्ष्मन् *m.* consumption. ०श्वासिनः (*adj.* of भद्रसेनस्य). महा...भाक् who secretly found access into the wall of the chief queen's apartment. कालिङ्ग king of कलिङ्ग, which was a country between the mouths of the Godāvarī and the Mahānadî. तूलिका—a mattress filled with cotton. दध्रस्य—दध्र is the name of the king. करूष—seems to be a country near Jubbulpore. It is closely connected with Chedi. For this and the preceding, see काम० VII. 51. 'देवीगृहगतं भ्राता भद्रसेनममारयत् । मातुः शय्यान्तरालीनः कारूषं चौरसः सुतः ॥'. उत्सारके रुचिः (liking) यस्य. 'दण्डी दौवारिको वेत्री उत्सारकश्च' क्षीर०. चकोरनाथः king of चकोर. चकोर is the name of a mountain in the Purāṇas. गण्डकः a rhinoceros. उद्दण्डं high-stemmed. नडलं abounding in reeds. नलवन forest of reeds. चम्पा was the capital of अङ्ग or north Bengal. चमूं चरन्तीति ०चराः भटाः. चामुण्डी seems to have been the name of a city. बन्दि...परम् who was absorbed in his fondness for bards. परप्रयुक्ताः employed by his enemy. ०मुखरं मुखं येषाम्. मल्लाः bards. कामि...गुप्तः concealing his identity by the dress of a woman. अशातयत्—from the causal of शद्. 'चन्द्रगुप्तभ्रातृजायां ध्रुवदेवीं प्रार्थयमानश्चन्द्रगुप्तेन ध्रुवदेवीवेषधारिणा स्त्रीवेषजनपरिवृतेन रहसि व्यापादितः' Com. शकपति—the S'akes are identified with the Scythian hordes that invaded India before the beginning of the Christian era. मधुमोदितम् exhilarated with wine. मधुरकं = विषम्. Compare for the story काम० VII. 52. व्याज...दर्पा who pretended to be in a passion of love. क्षुरधारा पर्यन्ते यस्य that had the edge of a razor. परन्तप who subdued others. जारूथ--was the name of the king Supply जघान here and in the following clauses. विषचूर्णेन चुम्बितः मकरन्दः यस्य. सौह्य—king of सुह्म, Western Bengal, the capital of which was ताम्रलिप्त. योगपरागः magic powder. वैरन्त्यं king of वैरन्ती or विरन्ती. In the whole of this passage the names are corrupt and there is no agreement between the MSS on the one hand and the authorities we have quoted. Some MSS read वैरन्त्या. वृष्णिम्—belonging to the वृष्णिs, a यादव clan. विदूरथम्—

'शस्त्रेण वेणीविनिगूहितेन विदूरथं स्वा महिषी जघान। विषप्रदिग्धेन च नूपुरेण देवी विरक्ता किल काशिराजम् ॥' बृहत्संहिता 78. 1; see काम॰ VII. 54. सौवीर—seems to have been a country west of Mount Abu. अदृश्या...वदना who smeared the inside of her mouth with an invisible antidote. ॰पायनेन by making him drink &c. Note the following from the अर्थशास्त्र of कौटिल्य 'देवीगृहे हि लीनो भ्राता भद्रसेनं जघान। मातुश्शयान्तर्गतश्च पुत्रः कारूशम्। लाजान्मधुनेति विषेण पर्यस्य देवी काशिराजम्। विषदिग्धेन नूपुरेण वैरन्त्यं मेखलामणिना सौवीरं जालूथमादर्शेन वेण्यागूढं शस्त्रं कृत्वा देवी विदरथं जघान।' (p. 41).

P. 106 l. 21—**P. 107** l. 12 **देवोऽपि...वात्येति.** राज्यस्थितीः—establishment of good order in his state; or, all the usual duties of a king. प्रतिसामन्तानां rival chiefs. उदवसितेषु = गृहेषु. उपलिङ्गानि portents. अविप्रकृष्टाः not far, approaching. चटुलाः moving about, restless. कृष्ण...श्रेणयः rows of black antelopes. The spotted antelopes resembled the dark glances of यमदूतs. See about the running of deer, p. 70 above. If we read प्रविष्ट॰ then the meaning is 'the glances of यमदूत that had entered (the chiefs' palaces)'. प्रचलि...प्रतिमाः resembling the jingling of the anklets of लक्ष्मी that had started away (in order to leave them). मधुसरघा honey bees. जहादिरे *perfect* of ह्राद् 1 A to sound. चिरम् for अजिरे is not a good reading. विवृतात् विकृतात् वदनविवरात् विसृतः वह्निविसरः यासाम् from whose wide-open and terrible mouths spread flames of fire. The reading 'उपशिबिरं शवार्थं' would mean 'near the royal camp for corpses'. For howling jackals, see p. 91. शवानां पिशिते (मांसे) प्ररूढः प्रसरः येषाम् whose expansion or growth (of body) had grown out of the flesh of corpses. The idea is:—as the vultures (काननकपोताः) fed on carrion, their wings also should have the colour of rotten flesh (dark-red). The reading of A and C 'प्ररूढप्रणयेव' seems to be a mistake for ॰प्रणयाः इव, which latter C and T translate 'full well acquainted'. कपिपोतस्य कपोलवत् कपिला पक्षतिः (पक्षमूलं) येषाम्. आमन्त्रयमाणाः as if bidding farewell (to the kings who were to be defeated by हर्ष). सभाशालभञ्जिकाः the statues of females in the halls. आसन्नः कचग्रहः तस्मात् भयं तेन उद्भ्रान्तं उत्तमाङ्गं यस्य as if their heads had run away out of fear of the seizure of hair (in killing them) that was approaching. चक्रशङ्खकमलानि लक्ष्माणि (marks, चिह्नानि) येषाम्. According to the सामुद्रिकशास्त्र, चक्र, शङ्ख and कमल are some of the marks of an emperor's feet. What is indicated is that some emperor will humble their husbands. For the lines on the hands of an emperor, see above p. 20. व्यघटन्त were separated or broken. मधु...गोष्ठ्यः the honey-drinking bouts. ताम्यन्तः languid. स्तम्बकारि forming into sheaves or clusters (*i. e.* grown, ripe). स्तम्बं करोतीति. हरयः = अश्वाः. चल...लालिताः caressed (or coaxed) by the music of the clapping of the girls' hands resonant with the moving bracelets. रजनिकरः चन्द्रः तस्य हरिणः (*i. e.* the spot) तस्मिन् निहिते नयने येषाम्—the idea is—the dogs as if wanted to hunt down the deer in the moon. तोरणस्य समीपे उप० (अव्ययीभाव) near the outer gate (of the palace). कौलेयक—see above p. 97. Compare for a similar idea 'सूर्योदयेऽर्काभिमुखो विरौति ग्रामस्य मध्ये यदि सारमेयः । एको यदा वा बहवः समेताः शंसन्ति देशाधिपमन्यमाशु ॥' बृहत्संहिता 89. 2. गतायुषः—is the object of गणयन्ती—गतं आयुः येषां ते गता० तान्. तर्जन...तर्जन्या with her forefinger that was quickly moved for frightening. वाटकेषु in the gardens. कोटवी—'स्त्री नग्निका कोटवी स्यात्' इत्यमरः. दिवसम् (*accu.* of time) the whole day. कुटिल...तरङ्गिण्य wavy like the curling hair on the hoofs of deer. जनितः वेणीबन्धः येषु—in which the hair was tied in a single knot (as in the case of a widow). See above p. 108. निरञ्जनानि च तानि रोचनारोचींषि च (रोचनायाः इवरोचिः कान्तिः येषाम्) that had no collyrium (in the eyes) and had the colour of yellow pigment. A widow is not to put collyrium in the eye. The reflection appeared pale (as if through grief). If we read निरञ्जनलोचन० as C and T propose, the meaning would be 'having the appearance of eyes without collyrium.' चषकमधुनि in the wine in the goblets. समासन्ना०—the poet fancies that the earth quaked (trembled) because it was afraid of its seizure (by हर्ष from the hands of other kings) that was impending. वध्या...च्छटाः streaks of red sandal paste with which persons sentenced to be hanged were decked. विकसितं बन्धूककुसुमं तद्वत् शोणितं शोचिः (द्युतिः) यासाम्. Compare मृच्छकटिक X. 5 'सर्वगात्रेषु विन्यस्तै रक्तचन्दनहस्तकैः । पिष्टचूर्णावकीर्णश्च पुरुषोहं पशूकृतः ॥.' पर्यग्नी...श्रियम् as if carrying a torch round sovereignty that was to pass away (into the hands of हर्ष). A torch was carried round the animal to be offered in a sacrifice. श्री was going to be offered to हर्ष and the meteors served as torches for that purpose. अविरलं स्फुरन्तः स्फुलिङ्गाः तेषां अङ्गारोद्गारः तेन दग्धः तारागणः यैः that burnt the stars with the eruptions of fire due to the incessantly flashing sparks. गणशः in masses. उल्कादण्डाः—उल्काः दण्डाः इव. A torch has a staff. प्रतीहारीव—प्रतीहारी carries in her hands chowries, umbrellas, fans for the king. प्रतिभवनं (भवने भवने इति) at each house. वात्या a hurricane 'स्यात् वात्या वातमण्डली' त्रिकाण्डशेष. 'पाशादिभ्यो यः' पा. 4. 2. 49.

Uchchhvāsa VII

Verse 1 अङ्गनवेदी वसुधा—(to the hero that has taken a vow) the whole earth is a mere raised spot in his courtyard. वेदी is a quadrangular spot in a temple or courtyard. The idea is that just as one walks easily and fearlessly in his courtyard, so a hero has an easy walk-over in the case of the earth. कुल्या a canal. Verse 2. धृतं धनुः येन. We expect धृतधन्वनि, as धनुः becomes धन्वन् when it is the last member of a बहुव्रीहि. 'धनुषश्च' पा. 5. 4. 132 (धनुरन्तस्य बहुव्रीहेरनङादेशः स्यात्). कैव गणना of what account. Compare for the use of गणना, 'का वा गणना सचेतनेषु, अपगतचेतनान्यपि सङ्घट्टयितुमलं (मदनः)' काद० (p. 157 of P). रिपुः संज्ञा येषां. For क see above p. 36.

P. 108 ll. 5-22 **अथ...जंगाम.** The principal sentence is अथ व्यतीतेषु केषुचिद्दिवसेषु...भवनान्निर्जगाम (हर्षः). शत...णिते well calculated a hundred times (*i. e.* again and again, so that no mistake may be committed). दत्ते...लग्ने when an hour for the expedition was given (*i. e.* settled) that was fit for the conquest of even the four quarters (east, south &c.). For लग्न, see above p. 24. दण्डः army. यात्रा expedition. सलिल...दैः (1) that were skilled in pouring water (with कुम्भैः); (2) that were clear by the dropping of water (with अम्भोधरैः). When a cloud is full of water, it is dark; when it has poured all the water it had (as after the rains) it becomes white. कालधौतैः (1) made of silver (with कुम्भैः); (2) washed or white by time *i. e.* by the passing away of the rains (with ०धरैः). कलधौतं silver. कालेन धौतैः. शातकौम्भैः made of gold. 'तपनीयं शातकौम्भं' इत्यमरः (शतकुम्भे गिरौ भवं शातकौम्भं सुवर्णम्). स्नात्वा—this refers to the bath of coronation. नीललोहितस्य शिवस्य अर्चां पूजाम्. 'कृशानुरेताः सर्वज्ञो धूर्जटिर्नीललोहितः' इत्यमरः ('नीलः कण्ठे लोहितश्चकेशेऽतो नीललोहित इति पुराणम्' क्षीर०). उद्गतानि अर्चींषि यस्य the flames of which went up. प्रदक्षिणावर्तः शिखाकलापः यस्य the mass of the flames of which curved towards the right. This was an auspicious sign; see p. 25. Compare रघु० IV. 25 'तस्मै सम्यग्घुतो वह्निर्वाजिनीराजनाविधौ। प्रदक्षिणार्चिर्व्याजेन हस्तेनेव जयं ददौ॥'. दत्त्वा—the objects are ०पात्राणि and गाः. See for तिलपात्रदान, चतुर्वर्ग० (दानखण्ड) p. 600. कनकपत्रलताभिः अलङ्कृतानि शफाः शृङ्गशिखराणि च यासाम्—the hoofs and tips of the horns of which were decked with figures of gold. अर्बुदशः—अर्बुदम् ten crores. विततं व्याघ्रचर्म यस्मिन्. भद्रासनम्—'नृपासनं तु यद्भद्रासनं सिंहासनं तु तत्' इत्यमरः. विलिप्य

—the object is शरीरम्. प्रथमं विलिप्तं आयुधं येन—before anointing his body with sandal, he first of all anointed his weapon (by way of doing worship to it). राज...लक्ष्मणी—०मिथुनं लक्ष्म (चिह्नं) ययोः—on the silken robes was drawn a pair of राजहंस. सदृशे suited to his position (as emperor). परमे...भूताम् (1) that is the special mark of शिव (with शशिकला); (2) that became the mark of an emperor (with ०मालिका). शशिकला also is white like flowers and is placed on the head by शिव. नीत्वा कर्णगोचरतां दूर्वा-पल्लवम् having placed in the region of the ear a Dūrvâ spray. The green दूर्वा resembles the rays of emerald, that also may be worn on the ear as an ear-ornament. गोरोचनया आच्छुरितम् (blended with). For गोरोचना, see p. 36. विन्यस्य...प्रकोष्ठे having placed on his forearm an amulet-ribbon auspicious for his march together with a seal bracelet. 'भवेत्प्रतिसरो मन्त्रभेदे माल्ये च कङ्कणे। ...आरक्षे करसूत्रे च' मेदिनी. ०पूजितः प्रहृष्टः पुरोहितः तस्य करेण प्रकीर्यमाणः ०निकरः तेन अभ्युक्षितं शिरः यस्य. For शान्तिसलिल, see p. 73. संप्रेष्य—connect with भूभुजाम्. महार्हाणि वाहनानि very valuable vehicles (horses, elephants &c.). बहलः रत्नानां आलोकः तेन लिप्ताः ककुभः दिशः यैः (*adj.* of भूषणानि). संविभज्य having distributed. संविभज्य ...दानैश्च—this cannot be well construed as it stands, as no persons among whom the distribution took place are mentioned. We must read, as C and T do, ०लोकम् उचितैः for लोकमोचितैः. क्लिष्ट...लोकम् among distressed pilgrims and well-born persons. क्लिष्ट may be construed with both कार्पटिक and कुलपुत्र. कार्पटिकः (from कर्पट) one who carries water from one sacred place to another. बन्धनानि prisoners. For letting loose prisoners, see above p. 25. नियुज्य connect with भुजस्तम्भम्. तत्काल...कारे that (arm) throbbed at that moment as if to remind that it was ready for the task of conquering the 18 द्वीपs. तत्काल...रणेन (1) that appears the moment it is remembered (with a person who offers his services); (2) that throbbed at the time in order to remind हर्ष of the task undertaken by him (with भुजस्तम्भ). तत्काले स्मरणं तस्मिन् स्फुरणम्; तत्काले स्मरणार्थं स्फुरणम्. The throbbing of the right arm is a good omen in the case of men. अहमहमिकया with emulation, with eagerness. 'अहमहमिका तु सा स्यात्परस्परं यो भवत्यहङ्कारः' अमरः. Servants pressed forward to do whatever was ordered. Good omens welcomed him as he went. हिरण्य...करणाय—as हिरण्यगर्भ (emerged) from the egg of Brahmâ to start an age of holiness. For हिरण्यगर्भ, see pp. 30, 37. कृत was the first युग after हिरण्य० was born. For कृतयुग see pp. 3, 40.

P. 108 l. 23 –**P. 109** l. 9 **नातिदूरे...पटीयांसः**. सरस्वत्याः समीपे उप० (अव्ययीभाव). समुत्तम्भितानि तुङ्गानि तोरणानि यस्मिन् in which high outer gates had been erected. 'तोरणोऽस्त्री बहिर्द्वारम्' इत्यमरः. वेद्यां विनिहितः पल्लवललामः (पल्लवः ललामं चिह्नं भूषणं वा यस्य) हेमकलशः यस्मिन्. 'ललामं पुच्छपुण्ड्राश्वभूषाप्राधान्यकेतुपु' इत्यमरः. A jar with sprays at its top is an auspicious thing. Compare 'उभयपार्श्वस्थापितोत्पल्लवमुखपूर्णहेमकलशं (कायमानं)' काद० (p. 281 of P). 'वनमाला पुष्पपत्रप्रतियोजिता स्रक्' com. भ्रमन्तः शुक्लवाससः परिजनाः यस्मिन्. पठन्तः द्विजन्मानः (विप्राः) यस्मिन्. प्रस्थानम् = विजिगीषोः प्रयाणम्. ग्रामाक्षपटलिकः—the keeper of the records of the village. In the अर्थशास्त्र we have an interesting chapter headed 'अक्षपटले गाणनिक्याधिकारः'. From the description given it seems that the अक्षपटल was a record and accountant-general's office of modern times and that the ग्रामाक्षपटल was something like the modern *chavdi* in the villages of Mahārāshtra, where the village accounts were kept. 'अक्षपटलमध्यक्षः प्रत्यङ्मुखमुदङ्मुखं वा विभक्तोपस्थानं निबद्धपुस्तकस्थानं कारयेत्' (p. 62 of अर्थशास्त्र). In the Banskhera plate of Harsha we have a महाक्षपटालाधिकरणाधिकृत (E. I. IV. pp. 208, 211). सकलकरणिनः परिकरः यस्य. करणिन् or करणिक means 'a writer of documents, clerk.' करणम् a writing, document. See मनु० VIII. 52, 154. Com. 'करणिर्लेख्यं कायस्थ इत्यन्ये'. अवन्ध्यं शासनं यस्य whose edicts are never fruitless. करोतु...शासनानाम् let your Majesty this very day begin the day of your Majesty's orders (to us). He means that Harsha had come to the throne recently and that till then he had issued no royal edict and requests him to issue one that very day. वृषः अङ्कः यस्याः that had a bull as its emblem. On the Sonpat copper seal of हर्ष there is a नन्दी (see C. I. I. Vol. III p. 231 ff). अभि...निन्ये he presented a new-made golden seal. मुद्रा may also mean 'a coin' but that is not suitable here. मृत्पिण्डे—the ball of earth was presented in order that an impression with the new-made seal might be made upon it. मन्दाश्यानं पङ्कपटलं यस्मिन् on which there was mud that was nearly dry. अम...नि that thought it to be an evil omen (that the new-made seal should fall down from the king's hands). अ...दर्शिन्यः not able to see the truth. एकं (केवलं) शासनं तस्य मुद्रा अङ्कः यस्याः which will be marked with the seal of my single command. The only seal that will mark the earth will be mine. अन्य...ग्राम्याः the villagers understand it differently. This episode reminds one of what happenea to William, the Norman Duke, when he first set foot on English soil. सीरसहस्रेण संमिता

सीमा येषाम् whose boundaries were measured (*i. e.* comprised) by a thousand ploughs. Each village comprised as much land as would be ploughed by a thousand ploughs. गलति...यामे when the third watch (of the night) had passed away. Time was measured by means of a water-clock and hence the word गलति. सुप्तानि समस्तानि सत्त्वानि यस्मिन् स चासौ निःशब्दश्च. दिक्कुञ्जरस्य इव जृम्भमाणः गम्भीरध्वनिः यस्य the deep sound of which swelled like the roar of the quarter elephant. प्र...पकाः that made (the people) count the क्रोशs of that day's march. The eight strokes indicated that that day eight *kros'as* were to be covered.

P. 109 l. 10—**P. 111** l. 2 **ततो...राजद्वारम्.** The principal sentence is ततः...प्रयाणसमये (p. 55 l. 14)...राजभिः आपुपूरे राजद्वारम्. रटन्तः पटहाः यस्मिन्. This and the following locatives qualify प्रयाणसमये. नन्दन्ती (joyous) नान्दी यस्मिन्. For नान्दी see p. 17. 'नान्दी मङ्गलपटहः' com. गुञ्जन्तः कुञ्जाः यस्मिन् in which the arbours resounded. कुञ्ज is out of place here. We must read गुञ्जद्गुञ्जे as some MSS. of B do. गुञ्जन्त्यः गुञ्जाः यस्मिन्. गुञ्जा a trumpet, according to the com. "गुञ्जासंज्ञः शङ्खभेदो यत्पृष्ठे जतु परिकलितं भवति । 'सन्ना' इति यस्य प्रसिद्धिः" or 'a drum' according to मेदिनी. 'गुञ्जा तु काकचिञ्चायां पटहे च कलध्वनौ ।' मेदिनी. See भट्टिकाव्य XIV. 2. 'वेणून् पुपूरिरे गुञ्जा जुगुञ्जुः करघट्टिताः ॥'. कूजन्ती काहला (a large drum) यस्मिन्. 'काहला वाद्यभाण्डस्य भेदे चाप्सरसां भिदि' मे०. क्रमेण उपचीयमानः कटककलकलः यस्मिन्. नरिजनोत्थापने व्यापृताः व्यवहारिणः (officers) यत्र. व्यवहारिन् ordinarily means 'a trader.' द्रुतः द्रुघनघातः तेन घट्यमानः (being joined or added) कोणिकाकीलकोलाहलः तेन कलिताः ककुभः यस्मिन्. द्रुघनः a wooden mallet for striking a thick plate of iron or bell-metal (for indicating time &c.). कोणिका drum. कीलः stick. बले अधिकृतैः (commanders) बध्यमानः (collected) पाटीपतीनां पेटकः (समूहः) यस्मिन्. पाटीपतिः—superintendent of barracks 'पाटी बहुपरिवारपुरुषगृहीतो निवासभूभागः कुलपुत्रकसमूह इत्यन्ये ।...'पाठीपति' इति पाठे...प्रतिनियतस्वस्थानपरिरक्षिणः ।'. पाठीपति would mean 'those that guard the place assigned to them.' जनैः ज्वलितं उल्कासहस्रं तस्य आलोकेन लुप्यमानं त्रियामातमः यस्मिन्. यामचेट्या चरणचलनेन उत्थाप्यमानं कामिमिथुनं यस्मिन्. यामचेटी a servant of the watch, a female watchman; compare यामाकेनी above p. 16. We must read कटुककटुनिर्देश० with some MSS of B. कटुकानां कटुनिर्देशेन नश्यन्ती निद्रा तस्याः उन्मिषन्तः निषादिनः यस्मिन् when the elephant riders woke up from sleep that was dispelled by the sharp commands of their superior officers. प्रबुद्धेन हास्तिकेन (हस्तिसमूहेन) शून्यीक्रियमाणं (vacated) शय्यागृहं यस्मिन्. 'हास्तिकं गजता वृन्दे' इत्यमरः, 'अचित्तहस्तिधेनोष्ठक्' पा. 4. 2. 47. आदौ

सुप्तं पश्चात् उत्थितं अश्वीयं तेन विधूयमानाः सटाः यस्मिन्. For अश्वीय, see p. 69. रटत् कटकं (camp) तेन मुखरैः खनित्रैः (spades) खन्यमानाः क्षोणीपाशाः यस्मिन्. The tents had been fastened by ropes twisted round pegs driven into the earth. These were dug up. समुत्कील्यमानाः कीलाः तैः शिञ्जानाः हिञ्जीराः यस्मिन् where the fetters (for tying elephants' feet to posts) were rattling because their pins were being taken away. As the army was to march, the fetters were to be removed. We must read अपनीय० for उपनीय०. The reading पनीयमाम is equal to अपनीयमान, as the अवग्रह (here after हिञ्जीरे in the last clause) is very often omitted in MSS. As the fetters of elephants were removed, so also the chains with which horses' hoofs were tied for the night were removed when the army was about to march. अपनीयमानं निगडतालकं तस्य कलरवेण उत्तालाः (wild, shying) तुरङ्गाः तैः तरङ्ग्यमाणाः (curved) खुरपुटाः यस्मिन्. 'निगडार्थं तालकं तालपत्रं निगडतालकम् । लौह एवाश्वबन्धनविशेष इत्यन्ये' com. C and T take उपनीयमान. तालकं bolt, latch. लेशिकैः (हस्त्यारोहैः) मुच्यमानाः मदस्यन्दिनः दन्तिनः तेषां सन्दानशृङ्खलानां (chains for tying) खनखननिनादेन निर्भरं भरिताः दश दिशः यस्मिन्. घासपूलकप्रहारेण प्रमृष्टं पांसुलं (dusty) करिपृष्ठं तस्मिन् प्रसार्यमाणं प्रस्फोटितं (bursting) प्रमृष्टं (wiped *i. e.* clean) चर्म यस्मिन्. The dust from the backs of elephants was rubbed off with bundles of hay and then leather bags that burst because they were more than full were placed on the backs. संवेष्ट्यमानानि (being rolled up) पटकुटीनां ०मण्डपानां च परिवस्त्रा वितानकानि च यस्मिन्. गृहचिन्तकचेटकः a servant whose business was to look after the tents and lodgings of the soldiers. पटकुटी a small tent. काण्ड...मण्डपः a large tent subdivided into rooms by screens. परिवस्त्रा the screens that form the body of the tent. वितानकं the awning. कीलककलापेन आपूर्यमाणं चिपिट (flat) चर्मपुटं (leathern bag) यस्मिन्. सं... रिणि where the superintendent of the store-room was collecting the utensils (platters &c.). भाण्डागारवहने वाह्यमानाः बहवः नालीवाहीकाः यस्मिन् when many elephant attendants were made to work in carrying the stores. 'नालीवाहिकः करिणां घासग्रहणनियुक्तो हस्तिपको मेण्ठाख्यः' com. निषादिभिः निश्चलाः अनेकानीकपाः तेपु आरोप्यमाणाः कोशकलशपीडानां आपीडाः (समूहाः) तैः सङ्कटायमानानि सामन्तौकांसि यस्मिन् When the dwellings of chieftains were full of rows of boxes containing cups and jars that were being placed on numerous elephants that were held motionless by their riders. It is better to read अनेकानेकप. अनेकप means 'an elephant', as it drinks water by the trunk and mouth. अनीकप 'one that saves the army;' so by

लक्षणा an elephant. 'पिटकः पेटकः पीडा' इत्यमरः. दूरगतैः (that stood at a distance from the bad animals) दक्षैः दासेरकैः क्षिप्रं प्रक्षिप्यमाणः उपकरणसम्भारः तेन भ्रियमाणाः (filled, covered) दुष्टाः (restive, bad) दन्तिनः यस्मिन्. For दासेरक, see p. 28. तिर्यक् (side-ways) आनमन्तः (bending) जाघनिककराः तैः कृच्छ्रेण आकृष्टः (अत एव) लम्बमानः (lagging behind) परतन्त्रः चुन्दीजनः तेन जनितः जनहासः यस्मिन्. चुन्दी—a procuress. क्षीर० remarks that it is a देश्य word. The idea is:—the procuresses were very fat. Hence their legs (जाघनिक from जघन) were bent outwards (they were bandy-legged) and they could draw their bodies forward with difficulty. पीड्यमानः (tightened) शारशारिवरत्रागुणः तेन ग्राहितः (held fast, restrained) गात्रविहारः (free movement of limbs) तेन बृंहन्तः बहवः बृहन्तः मदकरिणः यस्मिन्. The root बृंह् is used for the cry of the elephant. शार of various colours. शारिः elephant's housings. वरत्रागुणः girth or strap. 'शारिर्नाऽक्षोपकरणे स्त्रियां शकुनिकान्तरे । युद्धार्थगजपर्याणे, मे०. करिघटासु (arrays of elephants) वटमानः &c. ०कण्ठालकैः (bags) कदर्थिताः (अत एव) कूजन्तः करभाः (camels) यस्मिन्. The camels disliked the placing of bags and so bellowed. अभिजातराजपुत्रैः प्रेष्यमाणाः कुप्रयुक्ताः (bad confidants) तैः आकुलानि (troubled, full of) कुलीनकुलपुत्रकलत्रवाहनानि यस्मिन्. गमनवेलाविप्रलब्धाः वारणाधोरणैः अन्विष्यमाणाः नवसेवकाः यस्मिन् where servants recently engaged, being in error as to the time of starting, were being sought out by elephant riders. C and T think that it was the elephant riders that were deceived as to the time of starting. But that is wrong. प्रसादवित्तैः पत्तिभिः (footmen) नीयमानाः नरपतिवल्लभाः वारवाजिनः यस्मिन्. प्रसादेन वित्ताः (प्रसिद्धाः) well-known as being high in the king's favour. '**प्रतीते** प्रथितख्यात**वित्त**विज्ञातविश्रुताः' इत्यमरः. पाणिनि uses the word in this sense in 'तेन वित्तश्चुञ्चुप्चणपौ' पा. V. 2. 26. वारवाजिन् *lit.* a horse for an (grand) occasion *i. e.* a show-horse. There is another reading वरवाजिनि. ०सैन्यैः न्यस्यमानाः नासीरेण (कर्पूरेण) मण्डलाडम्बरार्थाः स्थूलाः स्थासकाः यस्मिन् where gay warriors applied thick unguents of camphor to their persons for showing circular lines upon it. चारभटः warrior. मण्डल a circle. आडम्बरः show. For स्थासक see p. 55. The usual meaning of नासीर is 'the van of an army or the soldiers in the van.' नासीरं सेनामुखं नासीराः अग्रेसराः. The meaning then will be 'where gay warriors applied thick unguent paste to their body in order to show off that they formed the vanguard'. न्यस्यमानाः नासीरमण्डलाडम्बराय &c. स्थानपालानां (अश्वपालानां) पर्याणे (on the saddle) लम्बमानानि ०सनाथानि सङ्कलितानि (fastened) तलसारकाणि (martingales) यस्मिन्. The com. reads

लवणकालायी and explains 'मृगाकृतिः अश्वानां दारुमयी क्रियते' *i. e.* a wooden figure of a deer. नालीसनाथ together with hollow stalks (of reeds &c.). 'तलसारिको अश्वमुखपट्टिका ऊर्णादिसूत्रमयी । उरःपट्टिकेत्यन्ये' com. It is not clear for what purpose the wooden figure was required. कुण्डलीकृतैः (coiled) अवरक्षणीजालैः जटिलाः (confounded with, entangled in) वल्लभपालाः यासां ता० पालाः अश्वघटाः (rows of horses) तासु निवेश्यमानाः शाखामृगाः (कपयः) यस्मिन्. अवरक्षणी reins. वल्लभः 'a horse with auspicious marks' + पालः a groom. 'वल्लभपालोऽश्वपालः । अन्ये तु यो बलवान् महाकारो हयोपकरणं यवसतण्डुलादि वहति स वल्लभपालोऽश्वपाल इत्याहुः' com. According to the com. the monkeys were carried as auspicious. We think it not unlikely that they were carried by way of amusement, when the soldiers had nothing to do. परिवर्धकैः (grooms) आकृष्यमाणाः अर्धजग्धाः ०प्रारोहकाः यस्मिन्. प्रभाते भवा प्राभातिका योग्या (martial exercise) तस्यां अशनार्थं प्रारोहकाः. The grooms had thrown shoots in front of the horses before they were to be taken through some morning exercises. As the order to march was given early, the grooms took up the half-eaten shoots and started. The com. seems to have read प्रौढिके for प्रारोहके 'प्रौढिको योग्याशनार्थं प्रसेवको यो बुक्कण इति प्रसिद्धः'. प्रौढिक means 'bag'. व्याक्रोश्या (परस्पराह्वानेन) विजृम्भमाणः (growing) घासिकानां आघोषः (noise) यस्मिन्. घासिकः one who is in charge of the food of the horses. गमनसंभ्रमेण भ्रष्टाः (running away) भ्रमन्तः उत्तुण्डाः तरुणतुरङ्गमाः तैः तन्यमानः अनेकमन्दुराणां विमर्दः (breaking, devastation) यस्मिन्. उत्तुण्डाः (with their nostrils raised up, rearing). सज्जीकृता करेणुका तस्यां आरोहः तदर्थं आह्वानं तस्मिन् सत्वरं सुन्दरीभिः दीयमानं मुखालेपनं यस्मिन्. The unguents were to be applied to the face of the करेणुका. चलितेषु मातङ्गतुरङ्गेषु प्रधावितः प्राकृतः(low) प्रातिवेश्यकलोकः तेन लुण्ठ्यमानः(plundered) निर्घाससस्यसञ्चयः यस्मिन्. प्रातिवेश्यकः neighbour. The low people in the neighbourhood took away the loads of grass that were left when the army started. But no food had been left (निर्घास). The com. explains otherwise 'निर्घासो भुक्तशेषो घासः'. सञ्चरन्तः चेलचक्रेण आक्रान्ताः चक्रीवन्तः (गर्दभाः) यस्मिन्. The donkeys were laden with bundles of clothes. The com. says that चेल also means 'a boy,' the meaning being 'boys followed on donkeys.' 'चेलं वसनमंशुकम्' इत्यमरः. चेल = चेट according to the com. चक्रैः चीत्कारी गन्त्रीगणः तेन गृह्यमाणं प्रहतं (beaten) वर्त्म यस्मिन्. गन्त्री a cart drawn by oxen. अकाण्डे दीयमानैः भाण्डैः (utensils) भरिताः अनड्वाहः यस्मिन्. निकट...सौरभेये in which powerful oxen, driven in advance, tarried out of greed for fodder lying near (on their way). The com. takes differently 'लम्बमानो गर्दभदासो वणिजां कर्मकरो वा' *i. e.* oxen were driven by servants that tarried. 'अनड्वान् सौरभेयो गौः' इत्यमरः (सुरभेरपत्यं सौरभेयः). प्रमुखे (in front) प्रवर्त्यमानं etc. महानसं kitchen. पुरः प्रधावन्तः ध्वजवाहिनः यस्मिन्. ०शतैः उपलभ्यमानं आसङ्कट...रालेभ्यो निःसरणं यस्मिन् where the exit (of the soldiers) from the rather crowded inside of the huts was seen by hundreds of friends. सङ्कट crowded, full. करिचरणैः चलिता (shaken) मठिका (cell, cottage) तस्याः उत्थितेन लोकेन लोष्टैः हन्यमामाः मेण्ठाः (elephant keepers) तैः क्रियमाणाः आसन्नाः साक्षिणः यस्मिन् where the bystanders were made witnesses by &c. The reading दलित is much better. सङ्घट्टेन (collision) विघट्टमाना (crushed) व्याघ्रपल्ली तस्याः पलायमानानि क्षुद्रकुटुम्बकामि यस्मिन्. 'व्याघ्रपल्ली तृणकुटीभेदः' com. (a hut thatched with grass). कल ... वणिजि when the traders ran after their oxen laden with wealth that ran away owing to the fear of the tumult. For विद्राण see p. 75. The com. takes विद्राण in the sense of सशोक (*i. e.* that despaired). पुरःसरं... कदम्बकं यस्मिम् when the group of female elephants carrying the harem started when the crowd of people grew less owing to the light of torches that were carried in front. We may also translate 'owing to the light of torches carried by servants walking in front.' ०आहूयमानाः लम्बिताः (that tarried) श्वानः यस्मिन्. C and T 'dogs tied behind them.' But this is not proper. If they were *tied*, there was no necessity to call them up. सरभस... गणे when the groups of tall तङ्गण horses were being praised by men inured to a hard life who felt comfortable by the steady motion of the tramp of their quick feet. We must read तङ्गण and not तुङ्गण. तङ्गण is the name of a country; see बृह० X. 12 and XVI. 6. The com. says 'खक्खटाः वृद्धाः' but the meaning assigned to the word in lexicons is 'hard'. स्रस्ताः वेसरविसंवादिनः सीदन्तः दाक्षिणात्यसादिनः यस्मिन् where Deccan riders sitting on mules fell down, not being able to keep their bodies moving with the motion of the mules. There are no mules in the Deccan and the Deccan people not being accustomed to their ways and pace fell down from their backs. सीदन्तः may also mean 'dejected or sinking on the ground' (because they fell). विसंवादिन् not agreeing with. 'सादी तुरङ्गमातङ्गरथारोहेषु दृश्यते' मे०. C and T translate 'Deckhan riders disconsolately contended with fallen mules.' Our interpretation seems to be preferable. प्रति...च्छद्भिः coming from every direction. This and the following instrumentals qualify राजभिः (p. 56 l. 1) below. आधो...शार्ङ्गैः whose bows spotted (शार) with golden figures (पत्रभङ्गः) were held up by elephant riders. शार्ङ्गः—र्ङ्गम् (शृङ्गस्य विकारः) 'शार्ङ्गः कार्मुकमात्रेऽपि' मे०. अन्तरासने आसीनैः अन्तरङ्गैः (confidential persons) गृहीताः असयः येषाम्. पश्चिमासनिकेभ्यः अर्पिताः भस्त्राभरणाः (भस्त्रा आभरणं यासां) भिन्दिपालपूलिकाः यैः that had consigned to those occupying the back seats (on their elephants) bundles of javelins encased in quivers. 'भस्त्राभरणं तूणभेदः' com. आसनिक from आसन. भिन्दतः पालयति इति भिन्दि० हस्तक्षेप्यो लगुडः. पत्रलतावत् or पत्रलताभिः कुटिलाः कलधौतनल्काः तैः पल्लवितं पर्याणं येषाम् whose saddles bristled with silver arrows curved like (or with) paintings of figures. What नलक means is not clear. To us it seems the meaning is 'a cylinder, a case or quiver.' कलधौतं silver or gold. पर्याणपक्षकयोः परिक्षेपार्थं पट्टिका तया बन्धः तेन निश्चलं पट्टोपधानं तेन स्थिरं अवधानं येषाम् whose attention was fixed because the silk cushion (on which they sat) was motionless, being secured by a girth that confined both ends of the saddle. We must rather read स्थानैः for धानैः, the meaning being 'whose seat was firm &c.' प्रचला पादफलिका तस्याः आस्फालनेन (striking) स्फायमानः (increased) पदबन्धस्य (anklet) मणिशिलाशब्दः येषाम्. पादफलिका is the foot-rest on each side of the saddle. The com. reads पादबन्धः and C and T prefer it. उद्गतानि चित्राणि येषु तानि उच्चित्राणि नेत्राणि (अंशुकानि) तैः सुकुमाराणि (fine) स्वस्थाने (at the proper place) स्थगितानि (covered) जङ्घाकाण्डानि (shanks) येषाम्. उच्चित्र on which the pictures appeared prominently. For नेत्र, see pp. 37, 55. The com. says 'स्वस्थानं स्वस्थानिति यस्याः प्रसिद्धिः'. This is not clear. The other reading स्वस्थगनस्थगित conveys a good sense. The garments were so fine that they were not noticed on the body (स्व—स्थगन) and yet they covered the shanks &c. कार्दमिकपटेन कल्माषिता (variegated) पिशङ्गा (reddish brown) पिङ्गा (leg) येषाम्. कर्दमेन रक्तं का०—mud-stained. The com. says 'पिङ्गा जङ्घिका । अन्ये जङ्घालेत्याहुः' *i. e.* पिङ्गा means either 'leg' or 'trousers.' अलिवत् नीला मसृणा सतुला तया समुत्पादितः सितसमायोगस्य परभागः येषाम् whose white accoutrements were heightened by the breeches blue and glossy like bees. 'सतुला अर्धजङ्घिका, अन्ये अर्धजङ्घालेत्याहुः' com. *i. e.* सतुला either means 'the upper part of the leg' or 'breeches.' 'समायोगो व्यापृतकेषु प्रसिद्धः' com. For परभाग, see p. 54. 'परभागो वर्णस्य वर्णान्तरेण शोभातिशयः'. We must read '०मेचककञ्चुकैः'. ०वर्णे विराजमानाः राजावर्ताः तैः मेचकाः कञ्चुकाः येषां whose jackets looked dark-blue with black diamonds shining on their bright bodies. 'राजावर्ताः कृष्णपाषाणाः' com. राजावर्तः a kind of diamond or other gem of inferior quality regarded as a lucky possession, though not esteemed as an ornament.

It comes from the country of विराट. The बृह० (chap. 80. 4) speaks of a राजमणि. अपचिताः चीनचोलकाः यैः that wore China-made shawls. 'संव्यानमुत्तरीयं च चोलः कूर्पासकोऽस्त्रियाम्' इत्यमरः. Another meaning would be 'whose China-made shawls were very fine' or 'who highly thought of their shawls.' तारमुक्ताभिः स्तबकिताः स्तवरकवारबाणाः येषां whose coats made of स्तवरक cloth showed clusters of bright (तार) pearls. 'मुक्ताशुद्धौ च तारः स्यात्'. For स्तवरक, see p. 56. 'कञ्चुको वारबाणोऽस्त्री' इत्यमरः. स्तबकित—स्तबकाः (bunches of flowers) सञ्जाताः अस्य; compare तारकित p. 98. नानाकषायैः कर्बुराः कूर्पासकाः येषां whose bodices were variegated with various decoctions. 'निर्यासेऽपि कषायोऽस्त्री' इत्यमरः. कर्बुर white-grey, variegated. 'चोलः कूर्पासकोऽस्त्रियाम्' इत्यमरः. शुकपिच्छस्येव छाया येषां तानि ०च्छायानि आच्छादनानि (upper garments, shawls) येषाम्. व्यायामेन उल्लुप्तः (made thin) पार्श्वप्रदेशः (sides) तस्मिन् प्रविष्टानि (fastened) चारुशस्त्राणि येषाम्. If we read शस्त्रैः the meaning is 'fine waist bands were twisted round their flanks &c.' 'शस्त्रं पट्टिकाठोरः कटिसूत्रमित्यर्थः' com. गतिवशेन वेल्लिताः (moving) हारलताः तासु गलत् (lit. dropping *i. e.* touching) लोलं (dangling) कुण्डलं तस्य उन्मोचनाय प्रधाविताः परिजनाः येषाम्. चामीकरपत्राङ्कुरैः कर्णपूरकः तेन विघट्टमानः वाचालः बालपाशः येषाम् Whose ear-ornaments resounded as they were struck by the ear-ring made up of golden wires. बालपाशः (or वाल०) seems to be the same ornament as वालपाश्या. 'वालपाश्या पारितथ्या पत्रपाश्या ललाटिका' इत्यमरः. उष्णीषपट्टेषु विष्टब्धं कर्णोत्पलस्य नालं येषां the stalk of whose ear-lotus was fixed in their turban-cloth. कुङ्कुमरागेण कोमलं उत्तरीयं तेन अन्तरितं (wrapped) उत्तमाङ्गं (शिरः) येषाम्. चूडामणिखण्डेन खचितः (inlaid) क्षौमः (linen) खोलः (helmet, turban) येषाम्. खोलः or खोलकः '**खोलकः** पाकवल्मीकपूगकोश**शिरस्त्रके**' इति विश्वकोशः. Compare 'क्षणमप्युक्तकालकम्बलखण्डखोलेन' काद० (p. 228 of P). The reading ०चोलैश्च is not good; we have already had a description of चोलक above. ०पत्रायमाणानि शेखरषट्पदपटलानि येषां the swarms of bees on whose chaplets looked like an umbrella of peacock feathers. मायूरं आतपत्रं तद्वत् आचरतीति मायूरातपत्रायते. The shining bees looked like peacock's tails and formed an umbrella over their heads. The reading मायूरपत्रायमाण is not so good; it simply means 'that resemble peacocks' feathers.' मार्गागताः (that covered a long distance) शारिकशारिवाह्याः वेगदण्डाः येषाम्. 'वेगदण्डस्तरुणो हस्ती' com. शा...ह्याः that carried housings rendered variegated (by a long march). For शारि, see above p. 170 पुरश्चलन्ति चामराणि येषां ते ०चामराः किर्मीरं कार्दरङ्गचर्ममण्डलं मण्डनं येषां ते ०मण्डनाः, उड्डीयमानाः चटुलाः (restless) डामराः (dreadful, riotous) चारभटाः तैः भरितं भुवनान्तरं यैः. '**चित्रकिर्मीर**—

कल्माषशबलैताश्च **कर्बुरे**' इत्यमरः. चर्ममण्डलं round shield. On कार्दरङ्क (the reading of the com.), it says 'कार्दरङ्कानि कार्दरङ्गदेशोद्भवानि बहुसुवर्णसूत्ररचितानि चर्माणि. स्फोटकाः स्निग्धवर्णमांसस्फारणि कार्दरङ्गचर्माणि'. आस्कन्दन्तः (careering) काम्बोजवाजिनः तेषां शतं तस्य शिञ्जानं जातरूपायानं (golden ornament) तस्य रवेण मुखरितानि दिङ्मुखानि यैः. As to the breed of काम्बोज horses, see above p. 30. 'आयानमश्वभूषणम्' com. '**लम्बापटहाः** पटहभेदाः तमिलाः इति प्रसिद्धाः' com. उन्मुखैः पादातैः प्रतिपाल्यमानः आज्ञापातः येषाम् whose commands were awaited by footmen with upturned (*i. e.* expectant) faces.

P. 111 ll. 2–27 **उदिते…नरपतिः**. समा…शंसी declaring the time of the king's arranging his army. '**समायोगस्तु** संयोगे **समवाये** प्रयोजने' मे०. The principal sentence is अथ नचिरादिव प्रथमप्रयाणे एव दिग्विजयाय…निर्जगाम नरपतिः. प्रथम०—the idea is:—many kings start on दिग्विजय after several less ambitious expeditions; but in the case of हर्ष his very first march was for दिग्विजय. दिग्गज…कुर्वाणया that as if brought the king into the company of the *diggajas* by the graceful play of the movements of its ears waving to and fro as it went on. The flapping of ears produced a sound which caused echoes in the sky and reached the दिग्गजs who thus came in contact with हर्ष. Or समागम may mean 'assemblage' (of दिग्गजs). सिद्धयात्रया (सिद्धा यात्रा यस्याः) auspicious for expedition. वैदू…कटेन that looked formidable with its rod of *lapis lazuli*. विदूरात् प्रभवति वैदूर्यम् according to 'विदूराञ्ञ्यः' पा. 4. 8. 84. उपरि goes with ध्रियमाणेन. प्रत्युप्ताः (inlaid) पद्मरागखण्डाः तैः खचितं तस्य भावः ०खचितता तया. सूर्योदय०—The idea is:—the umbrella was inlaid with rubies; hence it looked dark-red. The poet fancies that it was angry at the sight of the red rising sun. It could not brook another round object like itself. A person's face, when angry, becomes red. Supply उपलक्षितः after मङ्गलातपत्रेण, according to 'इत्थंभूतलक्षणे' पा. 2. 3. 21. कदलीगर्भात् अभ्यधिकः म्रदिमा यस्य (*adj.* of कञ्चुकेन). See p.14 (text) '**अकठोररम्भागर्भकोमलै**'. भोगिनां अधिपतिः = शेषः. भोगिनाम् also means 'of kings'. कञ्चुकेन—हर्ष wore a tunic, which resembled the slough (कञ्चुक) of a serpent, which also is अङ्गलग्न. क्षीरोद…वाही—हर्ष wore clothes (अम्बरं) as white as the foam of the Milky Ocean. The day of churning had a sky (अम्बरं) white with the clouds of foam. So the king is compared to मथनदिवस. His white umbrella was like the sky white with foam and his fine robes were like the fine slough of Vāsuki, who served as the rope in the churning. 'शेषोऽनन्तो

वासुकिस्तु सर्पराजोऽथ गोनसे इत्यमरः. For वासुकि and अमृतमथन, see p. 46. बाल:...रूढ: who attained to the position of Indra, while still young (with हर्ष); which grew in the land of Indra (heaven) while still young (with पारिजात tree). The पारिजात tree, the moment it was churned out, was taken by Indra. विधूयमानेन चामरेण यः मरुत् तेन विधूता कर्णपूर—कुसममञ्जरी तस्याः रजसा (with the pollen). दिशः छुरयन् overspreading the quarters. The pollen spread on the earth; the poet fancies that it was the magic powder for subduing the world. अभिमुखे (turned towards the sun, or worn in front) चूडामणौ घटमानं (formed) पाटलं (reddish) प्रतिबिम्बं यस्य. As the morning sun was red, its reflection also was red. The poet fancies that हर्ष as if drank with his own lustre the sun (in the form of the reflection in his crest-jewel). बहलं ताम्बूलं सिन्दूरमिव तेन छुरितया (०मुद्रया) that was overspread with thick vermilion-like betel. ओष्ठमुद्रया by his closed lips. विलभ...रागस्य as if making a gift of the various continents to अनुराग (redness, devotion or loyalty). His lips red with betel made the world red (*lit.* gave up the world to redness). A devoted servant receives gifts which are confirmed with the stamp of the royal seal (मुद्रा) in virmilion. Vide above p. 32. स्फुरन्ति महाहारमरीचीनां चक्रवालानि. स्फुर...ग्राहयन् the idea is:—the rays of the large necklace worn by Harsha spread in all directions. The rays were white like chowries. So the poet fancies that he made the quarters hold chowries for him. राजकस्य ईक्षणे उत्क्षिप्तः त्रिभागः (तृतीयो भागः) यस्याः (*adj.* of भ्रूलतया). A command may be given by the movement of the brow. बाहुप्राकारेण by the rampart of his arms. परि...खातान् as if surrounding even the seven ocean ponds with the desire of protecting them. There is a picturesque effect. Ordinarily it is a ditch (खातं) that protects a wall (प्राकारः) against an attack. Here the seven oceans are so many ponds in the eye of Harsha, who protects them with his arms, the walls. लक्ष्म्या...गूढः he was embraced by लक्ष्मी (sovereignty; लक्ष्मी that sprang out of the ocean). The eyes of the people of the camp were fixed on him (drank him). The poet says they did so because he had become अमृतमय as लक्ष्मी embraced him taking with her all the sweetness of the ocean. हृदयेषु...मज्जन्निव he plunged into the hearts (of the kings) by the greatness of his qualities. Every thing that has गौरव (heaviness) also goes deep in a fluid. स्नेहार्द्र affectionate; fluid with oil. मज्जामपि even the marrow (of the bones). अमरपतिः = इन्द्रः. अग्र...कुलः intent upon wiping off the stain of the slaughter of his elder brother. This applies to हर्ष as well as to इन्द्र, who wanted to get rid of the sin of killing a ब्राह्मण (अग्रज). इन्द्र killed वृत्र son of त्वष्ट्‌ who was a ब्राह्मण. He became free from the sin of ब्रह्महत्या by performing an अश्वमेध sacrifice. See रामायण उत्तरकाण्ड 84 and 85. 'तमिन्द्रं ब्रह्महत्याशु गच्छन्तमनुगच्छति' 84. 16. पृथिव्याः परिशोधनस्य अवधानेन सङ्कलितान् सकलमहीभृतः समुत्सारयतीति (1) who urged forward all the assembled kings with the fixed purpose of cleansing the earth (of a कण्टक like गौड); who cast away all the gathered mountains with &c. See notes p. 1 for पृथु who levelled the earth. पुरः...कारकैः—Harsha was preceded by ushers (दण्डिभिः) that went in front and that uttered complimentary words like जय, जीव, आलोकय &c. 'आलोको जयशब्दः स्यात्' इति हलायुधः (quoted by मल्लिनाथ on रघु 17. 27). The com. explains it differently 'लोक इत्येवं ये वदन्ति ते आलोककारकाः' those who cry 'Ho! people'. This does not seem to be quite correct. The rays of the sun also go before him (before he is seen) and cause light (आलोकः). सहस्र...किरणैः—The sun is called सहस्ररश्मि; हर्ष also had thousands of servants. अधिकारचातुर्येण (cleverness in discharging their duties) चञ्चलाः चरणाः येषाम्. All the instrumentals qualify दण्डिभिः below. व्य...निष्ठुरैः rigorous in maintaining order. भय...ग्राहयद्भिः who as if made the people take to the ten quarters, that were screened (from Harsha's view) by the mass of people running through fear. They cleared the way for Harsha so well that people in fear ran far away from him. चलितानां कदलिकानां (banners) सम्पातेन (mass) पीतः प्रचारः (movement) यस्य. The wind was hemmed in by a number of waving banners and so could not blow fiercely. The poet represents this as teaching the wind discipline or humility. कदलिका also means the plantain tree, the long leaves of which might retard the motion of the wind and the leaves of which become yellow when dry. द्रुतत्वरणैः उद्धतं (raised up) धूलिपटलं तेन अवधूतान् (despised *i. e.* obscured). °लतानां आलोकेन विक्षिप्यमाणं (dispersed). The light of the golden canes in the hands of the ushers cast daylight into the shade as it were and hence daylight is fancied to be removed by the ushers.

P. 111 l. 28—**P. 112** l. 4 **अवनमति···राजकम्.** अवनमति connect with राजचक्रे (*loc. absolute*). चलनेन शिथिलाः मणयः येषां तानि °मणीनि कनकमुकुटानि तेषां किरणनिकरेण रुचिरं शिरः यस्य. विलुलितं

०शेखररजः यस्य the pollen in the chaplets on the head of which was shaken (or tossed about). It should be noticed that from अवनमति to ०कुसुम every letter is short. अवाञ्चः downwards. उदञ्चः upwards. चाष...चेलुः the rays moved like flocks of blue jays for effecting good omens. The flight of the चाष bird to the right of a person or the sight of the चाष when a man starts on a journey was an omen indicating prosperity. Compare बृहत्संहिता 'पूर्णाननः कृमिपतङ्गपिपीलिकाद्यैश्चाषः प्रदिक्षणमुपैति नरस्य यस्य ।...तस्यार्थलाभमचिरात्सुमहत्करोति ॥' 88. 23 and 'सन्दर्शनं शुभदमस्य सदैव यातुः' 88. 25. मेघायमानः रेणुः तेन मेदुरं (thick with, full off)—*adj.* of खम्. The dust raised by the marching army was like a cloud. उड्डीयमानाः applies both to शिखण्डिनः and मरीचयः (from the preceding clause). The rays of the crest jewels shooting up into the sky looked like house peacocks. The peacocks fly up towards the cloud and dance when it appears. The feathers present numerous tints. The rays were of different hues. The cloud of dust represents दिग्द्वार. The shooting rays of jewels appear like the delicate पल्लव of कल्पवृक्ष. वन्दनमाला—is an auspicious garland fixed on the outer gate of a mansion 'मङ्गलस्त्रक्तोरणोर्ध्वे भवेद्वन्दनमालिका' क्षीर०. नेत्रत्रिभागैः—glances in which only a third part of the eye is open. समग्रेक्षितैः full glances. 'भ्रवञ्चितैः भ्रूचलितैः' com. छेकालापः insinuation, *double entendre*. 'छेको विदग्धे' क्षीर०; 'छेको गृहाश्रितमृगपक्षिणोर्नागरे त्रिषु' मे०. छेक means 'clever or polished'. आ...वीराणां who as if bought the souls of the heroes consisting in honour by gifts (tokens) of his favour. The glances, smiles and jests &c. were the price he paid for what they gave, *viz.* the honour they did him. यथा...राजकम् he distributed among the kings according to their worth (his favours).

P. 112 l. 5—**P. 114** l. 16 अथ...जगाम. तस्तार spread. तारतारः very loud. दिग्गजेभ्यः is dative, according to 'क्रुधद्रुहेर्ष्यासूयार्थानां यं प्रति कोपः' पा. 1. 4. 37. The elephants of Harsha were wroth with the दिग्गजs for the latter's pre-eminence and so wanted to establish their own superiority by the flow of their rut. त्रिप्रसृतानां that emitted a flow (of rut) from three places, the trunk, the eyes and the temples. मद...स्यन्दिरे with the tracks of the streams of ichor dark with swarms of bees, thousands of the windings of the Jumna as if began to flow. The waters of the Jumna are dark and so resembled the ichor with bees on it. The word त्रि in त्रिप्रसृतानां is suggestive. Ordinarily the braid of a woman whose husband is living is triple. Further there is a striking effect produced by laying emphasis on त्रि and सहस्र. सिन्दूर०–we saw above that red powder was sprinkled over people on festive or auspicious occasions. So much red powder was used that the sun appeared red and birds (like the चक्रवाक) feared that sunset was near (though really it was not). करिणां—connect with ०निस्वनैः. मांसलैः augmented by. कर्णतालः flapping of elephant's ears. दोधूयमान (frequentative of धू pass.) being again and again waved. अश्वीयं—See p. 69. शिश्विन्दे—*perfect* of श्विन्द् 1 A. to become white. पिण्डीभूतानि तगराणि तेषां स्तबकवत् पाण्डुराणि (white). परस्परसङ्घट्टेन नष्टाः अष्ट दिशः यस्मिन् (*adj.* of दिवसम्) where the eight quarters were not to be recognised on account of the close contact (of the umbrellas). The umbrellas were so many that no space was left uncovered by them. The sunlight paled before the golden handles and white sheen of the umbrellas. उच्चः चामीकरदण्डः येषाम्. रजः (dust) एव रजनी तया निमीलितः (closed, blinded). The day was dark with clouds of dust; but had the mellow light of morning with the jewels of the coronets. मण्डनक...कृताः rendered green (or tawney) by the clanging ornaments of horses (made of gold and silver). 'स्याद्भाण्डमश्वाभरणे' इत्यमरः. ह्राद् 1 A to sound. परिह्रादाः resounding. हरितः = दिशः. शिशीकरे *perfect* of शीक् 1 A to sprinkle. चक्षुषामुन्मेषं मुमुषुः robbed the eye of the power to open. The lightning also robs the eye of this power. विसिष्मिये *perfect* of स्मि with वि. It will be noticed that from तस्तार (at the beginning of the paragraph) to विसिष्मिये the author uses the perfect tense only. बलानां stands for बलैः—(the king wondered at his own vast army). आवासस्थान camping ground. अधोक्षजः (विष्णुः) तस्य कुक्षेः (उदरात्). युगादौ = कल्पादौ. The army starting from its encampment looked like the world rising from the belly of Vishṇu at the beginning of a कल्प. Compare (text) p. 10 ll. 1–2 'यशोमती गर्भेणाधत्त नारायणमूर्तिरिव वसुधां देवीं राज्यश्रियम्.' कुम्भभुवः = अगस्त्यस्य. प्लावितं (flooded) भुवनं येन. अगस्त्य was born from a कुम्भ in which the seed of मित्र and वरुण was placed. See for the story रामायण VII 56 and 57. He drank the ocean to help the gods against the Kāleyas who hid themselves in the sea. Compare 'भूतधात्री कलशयोनिपानपरिकलितसकलसलिलं सागरमवतीर्णा' काद० (p. 124 of P.). ०सहस्रेण आदौ सम्पिण्डितं पश्चात् उन्मुक्तम् at first stemmed and then let loose. अर्जुन is सहस्रार्जुन कार्तवीर्य. 'योऽसौ भगवद्दंशमत्रिकुलप्रसूतं दत्तात्रेयाख्यमाराध्य बाहुसहस्रमधर्मसेवानिवारणं धर्मेण पृथिवीजयं धर्मतश्चानुपालनमरातिभ्योऽपराजयमखिलजगत्प्रख्यात-

पुरुषाच्च मृत्युमित्येतान्वरान् लेभे' विष्णुपु० IV. 11. See मार्कण्डेयपु. 18. While once bathing in the Narmadâ, he wanted to see the power of his thousand arms and stemmed the waters and then let them off in a flood. See रामायण VII. 32. सहस्रधा प्रवर्तमानं applies also to the army. प्रसर तात—In these and the following words (up to p. 58 l. 6) the author gives us what the soldiers and camp-followers talked among themselves. भाव—this is a word showing respect in addressing a person. 'मान्ये भावोऽपि वक्तव्यः' भरतः (quoted by क्षीर०). त्वङ्गति तुरङ्गमः—a horse is galloping. This gives the reason why the man tarried. He waited till the galloping horse passed. भग्न...पतन्ति you walk as if you were lame, while these men of the van come in furious speed upon you. वाह...ष्ट्रम् why do you drive the camel? निःशूक= निर्दय, 'शूकोऽस्त्री शुक्नदययोः' मे०. Separate निःशूक शिशुम्. रजसि...भव be near me so that you may not be missed in the dust. गलति...वकः the sack of barley-meal leaks. प्रसेवः or—कः a sack or bag. इत्वर a traveller, one who walks. सौ...वरि leaving the track of oxen, you run in the midst of horses, O fish-woman! The track of oxen would be safer for pedestrians than that of horses. We may also translate 'Oh ox! why do you leave the proper track and run in the midst of horses? Oh! fishwoman, do you wish to come along'? On this latter interpretation, we must take सौरभेय as a vocative and connect धीवरि with विशसि. गन्तु...मार्गम् Oh female elephant! do you wish to enter the way of the male elephants? अङ्ग is a term of address applied to a friend &c. गलति...रटन्तम् the bag of peas is crosswise and leaks; you don't mind my bawling. We must read अतटेन for अवटेन. अव...तरसि you are descending into a pit from a precipice. 'गर्तावटौ भुवि श्वभ्रे' इत्यमरः. 'प्रपातस्त्वतटो भृगुः' इत्यमरः. The com. says 'अवटेन. अमार्गेण'. सुख...भग्नः 'you uncontrolled female, be quiet. The jar of sour barley-gruel is broken.' This is addressed to some woman who carried a jar and, stumbling in hurry, had it broken. Or it may have been addressed to a female elephant on the back of which the jar was placed. Or we may take 'सुख...णि' by itself and regard सौवीरक as a vocative (meaning 'a man from the सौवीर country' or 'a person carrying the sour gruel'). 'आरनालकसौवीरकुल्माषाभिषुतानि तु । अवन्तिसोमधान्याम्लकुञ्जलानि च काञ्जिके ॥' इत्यमरः (सुवीरेषु प्रायो भवं सौवीरकम्). मन्थ...क्षुम्—this is addressed to some one who lagged behind while sucking sugarcane. 'You will suck it when you have finished your journey.' उक्षाणं प्रसारय drive on your bull. This should be taken with the preceding. If we read प्रसादय, we must regard it as an independent sentence. प्रसादय make quiet. दूरं गन्तव्यम् we have to go a long way. कि...यात्रा Droṇaka! why do you run even to-day (the first day of the march)? The expedition is going to be for a very long time (so you will have plenty of time to run). वि...साकम् excepting that one cruel man, this is the belief (निष्ठा) of all of us (that the expedition is going to be very long). We must read निष्ठेयं for निष्क्रेयम्. C and T translate the words किमद्यैव...साकम् as 'why do you linger, Droṇaka, now? this long expedition is at a standstill for one rascal.' One fails to see how दण्डयात्रा is connected with निष्ठेयम्. अग्रतः...स्थालीम् the road in front is uneven; स्थावरक, see you don't break the jar of raw-sugar. स्थावरक may mean 'you mountain (of flesh).' 'स्थपुटं तु नतोन्नतम्' क्षीर०. 'मत्स्यण्डी फाणितं खण्डविकारे शर्करा सिता' इत्यमरः. Separate गण्डक तण्डुल०. न... दम्यः the bullock cannot carry it (to the end of the journey). माषीणम् a field of माष (beans), according to 'धान्यानां भवने क्षेत्रे खञ्' पा. 5. 2. 1 and 'विभाषा तिलमाषोमाभङ्गाणुभ्यः' पा. 5. 2. 4. (माषाणां भवनं क्षेत्रं माष्यं माषीणं वा). अमुतः from yonder. द्राक्...लुनीहि quickly cut with a knife a bundle of a mouthful of fodder. को...गतानाम् when we are gone, who will know what happened to his crop? Or better still 'who will detect the bundle lying in the midst of the fodder, when we are gone.' The idea is that they would keep the raw beans concealed in the fodder. धव...मिदम् O man, keep away your oxen, this field is guarded by barbarians. He calls the watchmen barbarians. The com. says 'वाहीकः काष्ठकः परिपालक इत्यन्ये गोरक्षक इति चान्ये'. लम्बिता...युङ्क्ष्व the cart has lagged behind; harness to the yoke an excellent (धवल) ox (शाक्कर) capable of bearing the burden (धुरन्धर). धुरं धायतीति ०धरः or धूर्धरः. यक्षपालित may be a proper name or it may mean 'one protected by यक्ष, a man possessed by a ghost.' दीव्य...दण्डे you are playing on the trunk of the elephant (instead of minding your business as a rider). समद is addressed to an elephant. न... स्खलसि you lose your footing in the mud due to the crowd (संमर्दः). माणवक is a name very frequeutly cited in the phrase 'अग्निर्माणवकः'. घनेभ...सरणिः in the thickness of the meeting of the array of elephants, there is no way to come out (if you once get entangled therein). If we read निस्तरणम् it would mean 'there is no getting out &c.' ०प्रवर्तमानाः अनेकसंलापाः यस्मिन् (*adj.* of स्कन्धावारम् above). All the following accusatives also qualify स्कन्धावारम्. In the following long passage Bāna uses many obscure words, the meanings of which are doubtful and which are rarely found in classical works. The commentary is our only authority in some cases. स्वेच्छया (at their will) मृदितानि उद्दामानि (plentiful) सस्यघासविघसात् सुखेन सम्पन्नानि (easily obtained) अन्नानि तैः पुष्टाः तैः. सस्य...घसात् from the leavings of the grain (for horses &c.). 'अमृतं विघसो यज्ञशेषभोजनशेषयोः' इत्यमरः. केलिकलैः that were noisy with jests. मेण्ठ...मण्डलैः by groups of elephant—keepers, bachelors (वण्ठ), dullards (वठर), donkey boys (लम्बन), elephant-riders (लेशिक), thieves, servants, rogues (चाटः) and grooms. 'वण्ठा अकृतविवाहाः तरुणाः ये दण्डमादाय हस्तिनां दर्पमाकर्षयन्ति । पत्तय इत्यन्ये लम्बनाः गर्दभदासाः ।... शाटा धूर्ताः चण्डाला अश्वपालाः' Com. The com. seems to have read शाट for चाट. For लेशिक see above. चाट 'चाटाः प्रतारकाः विश्वास्य ये परधनमपहरन्ति' मिताक्षरा on याज्ञ० I. 336. आण्डीर bold, according to the com. It also suggests that the word may be राण्डीर (from रण्डा) 'harlot's sons.' असहायैः (helpless) goes with ०पुत्रकैः (l. 12). क्लेशेन आर्जिताः कुग्रामकुटुम्बिसम्पादिताः सीदन्तः (sinking, weak) सौरभेयाः तैः शम्बलस्य संवाहने आयासः तेन आवेगः तेन आगतः संयोगः येषाम् who gathered together on account of the excitement caused by the worry &c. The com. says 'आयासो योगस्तेन गतसंयोगैरुत्पन्नचित्तक्षोभैरिति समासः'. So it read आयासगतसंयोगैः. स्वयंगृहीतानि गृहोपस्करणानि यैः. As the oxen could not carry, they had to put their own shoulders to the work. We must change the punctuation. Read ०तलम् । तृष्णा...भवतु । शिवं सेवा करोतु ।. तृष्णा...भवतु let there be an end of this height of greed! न भवनं अभवनिः. 'आक्रोशे नञ्यनिः' पा. 3. 3. 112. (नञि उपपदे अनिः स्यादाक्रोशे । अजीवनिस्ते शठ भूयात् । सि. कौ.). 'अकरणिरित्यादयः शापे' अम०. शिवं०—May (this) service do us good !! भूतिः prosperity *i. e.* excess. दुःखकूटाय = दुःखराशये. 'निःस्वस्तु दुर्विधो दीनो दरिद्रो दुर्गतोऽपि सः' इत्यमरः. अति ... द्रवद्भिः by people that ran (द्रवत्) quickly in lines, as if they were tied together and as if they were on board a boat carried along by a very sharp current. जनैः goes with सर्वमेव...कारयद्भिः. कृष्णकठिनस्कन्धयोः गुरवः लगुडाः येषाम्. गृहीताः...हाः यैः. सौवर्णपादपीठी golden footstool. करङ्कः—betel-box. Compare ताम्बूलकरङ्कवाहिनी, which occurs very frequently in the कादम्बरी (*e. g.* p. 148 of P). पतद्ग्रहः a spittoon. 'प्रतिग्राहः पतद्ग्रहः' इत्यमरः. अवग्राहः = स्नानद्रोणी com. It seems that the correct reading as अवगाह and not अवग्राह.

प्रत्यास...दुर्वारैः that were hard to check in their pride for being in charge of the appurtenances (उपकरणं) of their king who was near by. सर्वे...द्भिः that pushed aside everybody. भूपति...वाहि-भिश्च and by the porters (भारिक) engaged by the king, that carried the kitchen utensils. 'भारवाहस्तु भारिकः' इत्यमरः. बद्धः वराहवध्रेण वाध्रीणसः यैः that had tied a rhinoceros by straps (वध्रं) of pig-skin. 'खड्गं शृङ्गमस्यास्तीति खड्गी वाध्रीणसोऽपि' क्षीर. But the com. says 'वाध्रीणसा यज्ञियाश्छागविशेषाः.' लम्बमानाः हरिणानां चटुकाः ('पूर्वभागाः' com.) चटकानां (sparrows) जूटाश्च (mass) तैः जटिलाः तैः. चटु means उदर according to the मेदिनीकोश. शिशु...ग्राहिभिः that had a collection of young rabbits, vegetables (शाकः), leaves and shoots of bamboo. वेत्राग्राणि = 'वंशांकुराः' com. शुष्ककर्पटेन प्रावृतं मुखं यस्य तत् ०मुखं; एकदेशे दत्ता आर्द्रा मुद्रा (seal) तया गुप्तः गोरसः यस्मिन् तत् ०गोरसं; ०मुखानि ०गोरसानि भाण्डानि येषाम्. गोरसः may mean 'cow's milk or butter-milk.' **'दण्डाहतं कालशेय**मरिष्टमपि **गोरसः**' अम०. तलक...भारिकैः carrying loads of baskets full of तलक &c. 'तलकोऽग्निशाटिका। तापकोऽपूपा-दिकरणस्थानम्। तापिका काकपालिका यत्र तैलादिना भक्ष्याः पच्यन्ते। हस्तको शूलम्' com. तापकः oven. तापिका pan. हस्तकः spit. ताम्रचरुकः a copper vessel (in which rice or barley may be boiled). कटाहः a frying pan (Marathi कढई). फलकाले at the time of reward or payment. अन्य...स्थास्यन्ते other rogues will approach or be near. पदे...पततां falling at each step. The com. says 'स्खलने प्रेरणे.' This is a sense hardly ever met with. We would translate 'who were appointed to look after the tripping of the oxen.' The reading खेटचेटकैः will mean 'servants from the hamlets.' खेद्यमानः असंविभक्तः (not separated *i. e.* whole) कुलपुत्रलोकः यस्मिन् (*adj.* of स्कन्धावारम्). The noble youths were pestered by the servants with the words 'क्लेशो—स्थास्यन्ते'. प्रजविताः प्रधाविताः ग्रामेयकजनपदाः यस्मिन्. ग्रामेयक = ग्रामीण. आग्रहरिकजाल्मैः—connect this with ०धूलिपटलम् below—the rogues that had appropriated to themselves the अग्रहारs (endowments of lands conferred on Brāhmaṇas). The lands had been granted by former kings to Brāhmaṇas and some rogues enjoyed the lands free from tax when the families of the original grantees became extinct. Or आग्र...जाल्मैः may mean 'wretches from the अग्रहार villages.' पुरःसराः जरन्तः (old) महत्तराः (headmen of villages) तैः उत्तम्भिताः (raised up) अम्भःकुम्भाः येषु (*adj.* of ०जाल्मैः). The water jars are a good omen. महत्तर as the name of an officer occurs in numerous grants (Compare I. A. VIII, p. 20 and I. A. vol. XII p. 25). खण्डः candied sugar. धनेन घटिताः पेटकाः येषाम् that had boxes full of money (as

Nazarana). प्र...द्रुतैः that fled being frightened by the angered and fierce staff-bearers. असतो...यद्भिः that laid bare the imaginary (असतः) faults of former provincial officers. असतः that did not exist. There is a touch of humour here and in many other places in this passage. भोग or भुक्ति frequently occurs as a sub-division of a country (see I. A. vol. 19 p. 303, 304). अति...शंसद्भिः praising hundreds of former (subordinate) officers (युक्तक). The reading आयुक्तक also is good. Both these occur in numerous grants. For आयुक्तक see I. A. vol. 16 p. 24; I. A. vol. 15 p. 187. As'oka's edicts mention certain officers called युता, who correspond to the युक्तकs (see the third edict in E. I. vol. II. p. 448 ff). चिरन्त... धानैः—the word चाट seems to have some technical sense. In grants of villages the word 'अचाटभटप्रवेश्यः' occurs very frequently. Dr Fleet renders it 'irregular troops' (C. I. I. III p. 98 n. 2). एकान्त...रक्षणम् in which protection of crops was sought against the coming Gauḍa king who was repeatedly thought of by a group of horsemen riding in a part (of the army). आदिष्ट...तुष्टैः who were pleased with the protecting officers to whom orders had been issued. लूयमानं निष्पन्नं (ripe) सस्यं तेन प्रकटितः विषादः यैः. Their crops had been taken for the army. क्षेत्रशुचा out of grief for (the state of) their fields. प्ररूढः प्राणच्छेदः येषाम् the destruction of whose lives had taken deep root *i. e.* whose lives were in imminent danger. Those who reviled the king were severely dealt with 'त्रैविद्यनृपदेवानां क्षेप उत्तमसाहसः' याज्ञ० II. 2 11.; राज्ञोऽनिष्टप्रवक्तारं तस्यैवाक्रोशकारिणम् । तन्मन्त्रस्य च भेत्तारं छित्वा जिह्वां प्रवासयेत् ॥' याज्ञ० II. 302. परितापेन (grief) त्याजितं भयं येषाम्. प्रारब्धा नरनाथस्य (हर्षस्य) निन्दा यस्मिन् (*adj.* of स्कन्धावारं). शशकैः—this is to be connected with कृतकलकलम् (p. 59 l. 4). प्रजः...बद्धैः (hares) pursued by swift crowds with formidable sticks in their hands. गिरिः...हन्यमानैः that were struck as if they were clods of earth (that also are struck with thick clubs in preparing the soil for crops). C and T translate 'struck like polo balls.' सञ्चरद्भिः goes with शशकैः. अपरैः—take with शशकैः. युग...तित that came upon them all at once. अनेक...कुशलिभिः (hares) clever in escaping between the legs of many animals. कुटिलिकया (वक्रगमनेन) व्यंसिताः सादिनां बहवः श्वानः यैः that gave the slip to many dogs of riders by dodges. व्यंस् *10th conj.* to foil. पतन्त्यः...यष्टयः येषु. कुद्दालः spade. खनित्रं hoe. निःस...बलात् that escaped because they were to live longer (though on them fell clods &c.). सङ्घशः in groups. घासिकैः—connect with

०धूलिपटलम्. घासे नियुक्तः one in charge of fodder. बुसधूल्या धूसरितानि घासजालेन जालकितानि (covered) जघनानि येषाम्. बुसं chaff. पुराणपर्याणस्य एकदेशात् दोलायमानानि दात्राणि (knives) येषाम्. शीर्णोर्णाशकलैः (with bits of torn wool) शिथिलाः मलिनाः मलकुथाः (dirty blankets) येषाम्. 'मलकुथैरिति पाठः। मलकुथा मलपट्टी छविरित्यर्थः । अंसोपरि वास इत्यन्ये' com. प्रभुणा प्रसादीकृतः पाटितः पटच्चरे चलन् चोलकः तं धारयन्ति इति—that wore a jacket dangling on a tattered garment, that was (once) presented by their master, (but now) all torn. 'पटच्चरं जीर्णवस्त्रम्' इत्यमरः. एकान्त...विग्रहम्—A portion of this compound occurs above (text p. 58 l. 28). The copyist was probably misled by the occurrence of the word उद्धूयमानधूलिपटलम् which in both places precedes the sentence. The proper text in the former place seems to be '०धूलिपटलम्, विमृग्यमाणसस्यसंरक्षणम्'. ०चक्रेण चर्व्यमाणः आगामी गौडविग्रहः यस्मिन् where the coming fight with the Gauḍa king was reflected upon by &c. If we read चर्च्यमाण, then the meaning is 'being discussed.' This is better. पङ्किलस्य (muddy) प्रदेशस्य पूरणाय आदेशः तेन आकुलैः सकललोकैः लूयमानाः तृणपूलकाः यस्मिन्. तलवर्तिनः (standing at the root of the trees) वेत्रिणः तेषां वेत्रैः वित्रास्यमानाः (being frightened) शाखिशिखरगताः विवादिनः ब्राह्मणाः यस्मिन्. कुलुण्ठकपाशे विवेष्ट्यमानाः (enveloped) ग्रामीणकानां (villagers) ग्रामेण समूहेन आकृष्टाः कौलेयकाः (dogs) यस्मिन्. For कौलेयक, see p. 97. 'कुलुण्ठकाः शुनां बन्धनलगुडाः' com. C and T prefer to read ग्रासाकृष्ट and translate 'village dogs, entrapped by bits of food, were being tied in leashes'. It is better to hold that powerful dogs (not village curs) were being led by villagers pressed into the service of the army. अन्योन्यविभवस्पर्धया उद्धुरैः राजपुत्रैः वाह्यमानाः वाजिनः तेषां संघट्टेन (collision, race) मण्डितम्. 'उन्नतमुद्धुरम्' क्षीर०. उद्धुर unchecked, bold. अनेक...जननम् that caused interest by its numerous incidents. जगतः ग्रासेन ग्रहणम्. The sea at the time of Pralaya engulfs (ग्रास) the world and makes it its own. The army wanted to seize the world and to hold it in its grasp. महा...गुप्तये (1) for the protection of the great serpents; (2) for the protection of great kings or rather headmen of villages. 'भोगी भुजङ्गमेऽपि स्याद् ग्रामपात्रे नृपे पुमान्' मे०. Pātāla is the abode of the Nâgas. कैलासम्—On कैलास, परमेश्वर (शिव) resides. See above p. 79. हर्ष was परमेश्वर (an emperor). दृश्यमानः सकलप्राणिनां पर्यायः यस्मिन् where all the animals were seen in succession (with ०कोशम्); in which all beings were seen to walk about (in military order). पर्यायः succession, rotation; regular order. प्रजापतीनाम्—see p. 55 for them. ब्रह्मा produced the ten प्रजापतिs, who in their turn produced the seven Manus, the Devas, demons, men, birds and beasts &c. See मनु I. 36 ff. For the four Yugas, see p. 3. For the creation of various beings see विष्णुपु. I. 5. चतु...कोशमिव like the collection (or store) of the creation of the four Yugas. There is another meaning. In a कोश (lexicon) there are seen synonyms (पर्यायः) for all beings. Perhaps Bâṇa alludes to some lexicon divided into four *sargas* (sections). चतुर्युग may itself mean कृतयुग (as कृत means four in the language of astronomers). When the world was first created, the कृतयुग began. क्लेशबहुलम् though abounding in troubles (applies to both 'army' and 'austerity'). क्रम...कल्याणानाम् The army would in the end achieve victory; तपःकरण (performance of austerities) leads gradually to happiness.

P. 114 l. 17—**P. 115** l.2 **आसन्न...सिष्ट.** आसन्नवर्तिनाम् and तत्रभवताम् qualifiy पार्थिवकुमाराणां (l. 32). 'पूज्ये तत्रभवानत्रभवांश्च भगवानपि'. It would be better to read तत्रभवता as the com. does. तत्रभवता goes with मान्धात्रा. For मान्धातृ, see pp. 23, 123. अप्रतिहतं रथरंहः (रथवेगः) यस्य. प्रसादनम् purifying, making clear (of enemies); calming down. The reading प्रसाधनम् of some mss. would be much better, being quite in keeping with Bâṇa's style. प्रसाधनम् accomplishing (conquering); ornamenting. करद one who pays tribute. For the conquest of the world by रघु, see रघुवंश IV. करदीचकार made them pay tribute. चक्रम् goes with भूभुजाम्. क्रमागतानां भुजबलं अभिजनः (noble ancestry) धनं च तेषां मदेन अवलिप्तानाम् (haughty). सव्यसाची applies to अर्जुन only out of the five पाण्डवs. 'उभौ मे दक्षिणौ पाणी गाण्डीवस्य विकर्षणे । तेन देवमनुष्येषु सव्यसाचीति मां विदुः॥' विराटपर्व 44. 19. चीनविषयं = चीनदेशम्. राज...दे for completing the राजसूय. राजसूय was a sacrifice performed by a universal monarch at the time of his coronation to mark his undisputed sovereignity. See सभापर्व 32 ff. for the incidents of the राजसूय performed by युधिष्ठिर. क्रुध्यन्तः गन्धर्वाः तेषां धनुष्कोटीनां टाङ्कारेण कूजिताः कुञ्जाः यस्य. हेमकूट was the abode of the गन्धर्वs. अर्जुन is said to have conquered the गन्धर्वs (सभापर्व 2. 58). पराजैष्ट *Aorist* of जि with परा. जि necessarily takes the Âtmanepada when preceded by वि and परा. 'विपराभ्यां जेः' पा. 1. 3. 19. सङ्कल्पेन अन्तरितः separated or screened by resolve. तरस्विन् strong. The idea is :—In the case of the strong, what comes between the conquest of the world and them is the wish or resolve. As long as they do not desire, conquest is far off. The moment they desire it, it is theirs. सहिमः हिमवान् तेन व्यवहितः—though screened by the हिमालय with its snows. बाहु...कातरः afraid of the clash of his prowess (against that of his enemy). अकृती not happy, wretched. द्रुमः—was a king of किंपुरुषs. 'द्रुमो किंपुरुषेशश्च उपास्ते धनदेश्वरम्' ॥ सभापर्व 10. 29. भगदत्त...प्रभृतयः—these are the names of various kings that were present in the great Mahâbhârata war. भगदत्त was king of प्राग्जोतिष and a partisan of दुर्योधन. He was killed by अर्जुन. दन्तवक्र was defeated by सहदेव in his दक्षिणदिग्विजय (सभापर्व 31. 3). क्राथ was a son of धृतराष्ट्र killed by भीम. शिशुपाल, कर्ण and जरासन्ध are well-known. शाल्व was a partisan of दुर्योधन and king of म्लेच्छ tribes. He was killed by सात्यकि (शल्यपर्व 20). सिन्धुराज is जयद्रथ. धनञ्जयजयेन जनितः जगत्कम्पः येन. समीप एव—The किंपुरुषs or किन्नरs are a race of semidivine beings with the face of a horse. Their country called किंपुरुषवर्ष was next to भारतवर्ष. The विष्णुपुराण (II. 2.) tells us that किंपुरुषवर्ष was next to भारतवर्ष between हिमवत् and हेमकूट. Compare 'इतश्च नातिदूरे तस्मात्साद्भारतवर्षादुत्तरेणानन्तरे किंपुरुषनाम्नि वर्षे वर्षपर्वतो हेमकूटो नाम निवासः' काद० (p. 136 of P). अलसः dull, lazy. There is a picturesque contrast between अलस and the literal meaning of the name चण्डकोश. चण्ड means 'fierce, powerful.' स्त्रीराज्यम्—see above p. 27. There is an untranslateable pun on the word चण्डकोश in relation to women. Put a vertical line after ०मादनयोः. ह्रसी...मादनयोः very short is the distance between the Himālaya and the गन्धमादन. The idea is:—When even the distant countries of the Turks and the Persians are a mere span to the persevering hero, then surely the distance between the हिमालय and the गन्धमादन is small indeed. उत्सा...विषयः to the persevering the land of the Turushkas (Turks) is but a cubit. 'किष्कुर्हस्ते वितस्तौ च' इत्यमरः. Understand उत्साहिनः in each of the following clauses. It will be noticed that in the choice of words the poet is guided only by similarity of sounds. पारसीकदेशः Persia. प्रादेशः span. 'प्रादेशतालगोकर्णास्तर्जन्यादियुते तते ॥ अङ्गुष्ठे सकनिष्ठे स्याद्वितस्तिर्द्वादशाङ्गुलः ॥' इत्यमरः ('तर्जन्या युते तते प्रसारितेऽङ्गुष्ठे मध्यं, प्रादिश्यते प्रादेशः' क्षीर०). शकस्थानम् the country of the S'akas. The S'akas are identified with the Scythians, who migrated to India and established themselves at Taxila in Punjab, at Mathurā and in Kathiawad. अदृश्यमानः प्रतिप्रहारः यस्मिन् in which there is none to give a counter-stroke. पारियात्र is one of the seven principal mountains of India. From the बृहत्संहिता (69. 11-12) it seems that it was in Malva and corresponded to the western portion of the Vindhya and the Aravali Hills. यात्रैव शिथिला an expedition (against पारियात्र) is very easy. शौर्यं शुल्कं

यस्य—the price of which is valour *i. e.* by showing valour it can be won. शुल्कं originally meant the price of a bride taken by her parents. 'शुल्कं यद् गृहीत्वा कन्या दीयते' मिताक्षरा on याज्ञ० II. 144. दक्षिणापथ—the whole of the country south of the Narmadā up to Cape Comorin; sometimes, the country between the नर्मदा and the कृष्णा. 'सेतुनर्मदामध्यं सार्धसप्तलक्षं दक्षिणापथं पालयामास' E. I. Vol. IV. p. 305 Bāṇa seems to have used it in the latter sense, as the next sentence shows. दक्षिणार्णवस्य कल्लोलाः (waves) तेषां अनिलैः चलिताः चन्दनलताः तासां सौरभेण सुन्दरीकृतानि दरीमन्दिराणि यस्य. दर्दु...मलयः—मलय is very near to the mountain दर्दुर. नेदीयसि *loc. sing.* of the comparative of अन्तिक. For मलय, see above p. 39. दर्दुर is a mountain in the extreme south of India and closely associated with मलय. Compare रघु. IV. 51 'स निर्विश्य यथाकामं तटेष्वालीनचन्दनौ । स्तनाविव दिशस्तस्याः शैलौ मलयदर्दुरौ ॥.' महेन्द्र is one of the seven कुलाचलs and corresponds to the eastern Ghauts on the Coromandel coast. उद्योगद्योतकानाम् that manifested or encouraged energetic efforts. प्रास्तः समायोगः येन who dismissed the people round him.

P. 115 ll. 3—27 **अथ तत्र ... देवस्येति.** प्राग्ज्योतिष—corresponds with modern Assam. It was also called कामरूप. कुमार is the name of the king of Assam. C and T think that he was only the heir-apparent. But the word ०श्वरेण militates against that view. Besides see text p. 63 ll. 25-26. अन्तरङ्ग confidential. दक्षतया through cleverness, promptness. क्षिति...राच्च and on account of the regard shown by the king Harsha (for the messenger). नयनानन्दसम्पादनाय सुभगः आभोगः तेन भद्रया (form) that was agreeable on account of its charming fulness (आभोगः, proportions) that caused delight to the eye. आकृत्यैव समु...गरिमा whose very personal charms exceeded the greatness of his qualities. It is the convention of Sanskrit poets to say that a noble exterior is an indication of noble qualities of the head and the heart; compare 'आकारसदृशप्रज्ञः' रघु I. 15. The exterior of हंसवेग was in comparison grander than his qualities. प्राभृतं present, *Nazarana*. आरादेव = दूरादेव. पञ्चाङ्गैः आलिङ्गितं अङ्गनं येन who fell prostrate on the courtyard with five limbs (*i. e.* hands, feet and head). Read प्रधावितोपसृतः who approached the king running. पादपीठे लुठिता ललाटलेखा येन. न्यस्त...पार्थिवेन on whose back the king laid his hand. पार्थिवेन is to be connected with न्यस्त in the compound ०हस्तः. अविप्रकृष्टं not far (from the king). तिरश्चीं...दधानः slightly bending his body on one side. संमुखीनः having turned his face towards him (हंसवेग). सप्रश्रयम् *adv.* respectfully, politely. हंसवेग continues his speech from the words 'चतुरम्भोधि०'. चतु...भूतस्य who is the (worthy) abode of the prosperity (or grandeur) due to enjoying the four oceans. Construe देवस्य अन्यत् अनुरूपं प्राभृतमेव दुर्लभं लोके another present worthy of your Majesty is difficut to find in this world. सद्भावः गर्भे यस्य. सद्भा...मेकम् excepting one thing, *viz.* a heart full of goodness. He means:—an affectionate heart is the only present that can be worthy of your Majesty. सन्दे...नयता who wanted to make his message solid. अशून्य not empty, solid. वारुणातपत्रम् an umbrella derived from Varuṇa. See text p. 63 below. आभोगः आख्या यस्य. The umbrella is appropriately named आभोगः (expanse). अनु...तत् this has been made blessed by being deposited in a proper place. He means that Harsha is a proper person to whom the umbrella (emblem of sovereignty) may be entrusted. कुतूहलं कुर्वन्ति इति०कृन्ति. शैत्य... छायायाः for the purpose of giving coolness to its shade. प्रध्यानानन्तरम् after reflection *i. e.* after the person possessing it desires. दन्तवीणा chattering of the teeth due to cold. चन्द्रभासाम् चन्द्रस्येव भाः येषां (waters) that are as bright as the moon. मणिशलाकाभ्यः from the jewelled ribs. इच्छामनतिक्रम्य यावदिच्छं as long or as much as desired. प्रचेताः 'प्रचेता वरुणः पाशी' इत्यमरः. सप्तार्चिः—fire. पृषदश्वः wind 'पृषदश्वो गन्धवहः' इत्यमरः ('पृषन्मृगविशेषोऽश्वोऽस्य पृषदश्वः, पृषन्त्यम्बुकणाः सन्त्यश्वा अस्येत्येके' क्षीर०). विस्रब्धं confidentially. We must supply देवः as the subject of श्रोष्यति or read श्रोष्यसि as C and T suggest. विवृत्य having turned round (from वृत् with वि).

P. 115 l. 28—**P. 116** l. 21 स...महच्छत्रम्. तत् = आतपत्रम्. धौ...षीत् he took it out of its case made of white silk. 'निचोलः प्रच्छदपटः' इत्यमरः. अतिसितं महः (तेजः) यस्य. ०महसि goes with यस्मिन्. In the following clauses the author makes a very imaginative effort to convey the extreme whiteness and brilliance of the umbrella. सरभ...हरेण S'iva as if laughed wildly. S'iva's laugh is called अट्टहास. Smiles and laughs are spoken of as white. अहासि Aorist passive of हस्. There are many such Aorist forms in the following clauses. रसा...मण्डलेन—शेष, the king of Nâgas, dwells in पाताल and its 1000 hoods are pale in colour. चक्रीभूय having assumed the form of a circle. The umbrella was round. The poet says it looked like the milky ocean transformed into a circle. गगनमेव अङ्गनं तस्मिन्. The clouds (बलाहकः) in S'arad are white. A गोष्ठीबन्ध (an assembly of learned men) is held in one's अङ्गन. विश्रान्त that had taken rest. वितता पक्षतिः (पक्षमूलं)

वस्य. पिता...यूथेन the swarm of swans that are the conveyance of Brahmâ. हंसs have white wings 'हंसास्तु श्वेतगरुतः' इत्यमरः. अत्रिनेत्रनिर्गतस्य—The moon is said to have sprung from the lustre of Atri's eye. See हरिवंश 25 'नेत्राभ्यां वारि सुस्राव दशधा द्योतयद्दिशः। तं गर्भं विधिना हृष्टा दश देव्यो दधुस्तदा ॥ समेत्य धारयामासुर्न च ताः समशक्नुवन्। स ताभ्यः सहसैवाथ दिग्भ्यो गर्भः प्रभान्वितः। पपात भासयंल्लोकाञ्शीतांशुः सर्वभावनः।' verses 6-8. Compare 'अथ नयनसमुत्थं ज्योतिरत्रेरिव द्यौः' रघु. II. 75. कुमुदs bloom in moonlight. उद्गमनक्षणः the moment of the emergence. पुण्डरीक has a long stalk like the handle of an umbrella and is white. आहिते...क्षणाम् as if the eyes (of people) had been satiated with the delight of seeing a moonlit evening. उदमांक्षीत्—Aorist of मस्ज् with उद्—emerged. मन्दाकिनी is the celestial Ganges and hence the word अम्बरोदरे (in the sky). महत् goes with ०मण्डलम्. The umbrella also was covered with an अम्बर (cloth). परि...निशया as if the day had been exchanged for a full moon night. The umbrella was raised up in space. But its mellow white light made the day look like night lit up by the full moon. The full moon also is white and round. इन्दूदयसन्देहेन दूयमानं मानसं येषाम् (*adj.* of मिथुनैः). As the umbrella looked like the moon, the चक्रवाकs thought that the time for separation had come. See p. 57 for चक्रवाक. विघटितं connect with ०मिथुनैः. विघटमानाभ्यः (that separated or opened) चञ्चुभ्यः च्युताः मृणालकोटयः येषाम्. The चक्रवाकs opened their beaks from grief and let fall from them the ends of fibres. आसन्नकमलिनी neighbouring lotus lake. ०पटलाशङ्कया सङ्कोचितं केकाखमूकं मुखपुटं येषाम्. The peacock is in its glory before the advent of the rains and its feathers begin to drop after the rains. The white umbrella they took to be an autumnal cloud. प्रबुद्धं कुमुदषण्डैः the beds of कुमुदs awoke (opened). आबद्धः चन्द्रात् (चन्द्रदर्शनात्) आनन्दः तेन उद्दामं उद्दलत् (opening) दलपुटं तस्य अट्टहासः तेन विशदं यथा स्यात् तथा. चित्रीयमाणं (विस्मयमानं) चेतः यस्य. चित्रीयते is a denominative verb from चित्र according to 'नमोवरिवश्चित्रङः क्यच्' पा. 3. 1. 19. The principal sentence is ०चेता...राजा दृष्टया सादरं ऐक्षिष्ट तत्...महच्छत्रम्. दण्डस्य अनुसारेण अधिरोहतीति—(eye) that mounted up following the track of the handle (of the umbrella). शैश...द्वीपस्य as if it were the babyhood of the white continent. A person, when a baby, is much fairer than when grown up. श्वेतद्वीप—In श्वेतद्वीप everything was supposed to be white; compare 'श्वेत द्वीपनिवासमिव...अनुभवति जने' का॰द॰ (p. 162). For a description of श्वेतद्वीप see शान्तिपर्व chap. 336. 'आलोकयन्नुत्तरपश्चिमेन ददर्श चाप्यद्भुत-

मुक्तरूपम् । क्षीरोदधेर्योत्तरतो हि द्वीपः श्वेतः स नाम्ना प्रथितो विशालः ॥' 8 'श्वेताः पुमांसो गतसर्वपापाः' 10. अंशावतार—partial incarnation. When a portion of a deity appears in flesh and blood, that is अंशावतार, as opposed to पूर्णावतार. धर्म must be white (pure); its heart will be whiter. दन्ताः मण्डलकमिव तस्य द्युतिः तेन धवलं. A face (मुख) is illuminated by the lustre of white teeth. The commencement (मुखं) of the regime of an emperor (चक्रवर्तिन्) is marked by a मण्डल. For मण्डल (with reference to चक्रवर्ति) see p. 42. Further the umbrella was white and round and resembled ivory (दन्त) in its whiteness; or perhaps its ribs were made of ivory. मौक्तिक... दिवः—०परिकरेण or परिकरवत् वा सितम्. The idea is:—The umbrella was white, being surrounded by a band of bunches of pearls. It resembled the parting line of the hair of the damsel (Heaven). In the सीमन्त of a woman there may be a pearl ornament. The heaven has the ring (चक्र) of the Milky Way which is white and is like a सीमन्त and the stars therein resemble pearls. बहलज्योत्स्नया शुक्लं उदरं यस्य. The fully expanded umbrella was like the halo of the moon and its centre was like the orb of the moon. शौक्ल्येन अपहसिता शङ्खश्रीः यस्य येन वा. The umbrella was whiter than a conch. It was also whiter than the head front (शङ्खः) of ऐरावत. ऐरावत is white; compare 'ऐरावतदेहच्छविमिव (महाश्वेताम्)' काद० p. 129. An elephant's ear is always flapping and hence the umbrella is compared to the motionless ear of ऐ०. आवर्तः whirlpool. त्रिविक्रमस्य = विष्णोः. The Ganges is said to have sprung from the foot of Vishṇu. Compare 'वामपादाम्बुजाङ्गुष्ठे नखस्रोतोविनर्गता । विष्णोर्बिभर्ति यां भक्त्या शिरसाहर्निशं ध्रुवः ॥' विष्णुपु० II. 8. 110. See also मार्कण्डेय 56. प्रचेतसः = वरुणस्य. मानस...वेशम् which (umbrella) was surrounded by rows of chowries made of lotus fibres from the मानस lake. The white fibres resemble the bright rays of the crest jewel of वरुण. श्लिष्ट closely stuck. उपरि लक्ष्मणा... शिखरम्—on the top of the umbrella there was the emblem (लक्ष्मन् *n*) of a हंस with wings spread out. वितते पत्रे (पक्षौ) यस्य. चक्र...निश्चलेनेव—the figure of the हंस on the umbrella was naturally motionless. The poet fancies that it was a living हंस motionless because it was intent upon listening to the jingle of the anklets of the Glory of an emperor. For हंसs listening to anklets, see p. 95. स्पर्शवता = सुखस्पर्शेन or मृदुस्पर्शेन. प्रभाव...मृणालेन नीतेन दण्डताम्— its handle was made of a lotus stalk from the मन्दाकिनी, which (stalk) was made stiff by the power (of वरुण). मुकुलिता (contracted) फणा यस्य. वासुकि the lord of serpents is pale and long and resembles the long lotus stalk. प्रथिमन् *m.* breadth. समुच्छ्राय: height. स्तबक...स्तम्भस्य it was like a bunch of flowers on the trunk (tree) of Brahmâ *i. e.* it was the pick, the cream of the world. नाभि०—As the spokes start from the round nave (नाभि) of a wheel, so from it radiated light. कीर्ति is white.

P. 116 l. 22—**P. 117** l. 13 च...**छायाम्**. कार्मा: ='स कार्मः कर्मशीलो य:' इत्यमर:. 'कार्मस्ताच्छील्ये' पा. 6. 4. 172. परार्घ्यरत्नानां अंशुभि: शोणीकृता: दिग्भागा: यै: (*adj.* of अलङ्कारान्). Remove the comma after दिग्भागान्. For भगदत्त, see above p. 187 and text p. 63. परागत come, handed down. आहतलक्षणान् = प्रसिद्धान्, 'गुणै: प्रतीते तु कृतलक्षणाहतलक्षणौ' इत्यमर: (आहतानि उद्घोषितानि लक्षणानि यस्य). प्रभा...त्कर्षान् the best of crest jewels that covered (everything) with their sheen. अनेक...क्षौमाणि— silken cloth rolled up in charming variously coloured cane boxes and bright like the rays of the autumn moon and that were capable of purifying a person. उल्लिखित carved out. For गल्वर्क, see p. 77. निचोलकै: (cases) रक्षिता रुक् (कान्ति:) येषाम्. ०भङ्गेन भङ्गुराणां wavy with charming figures in gold. अतिबन्धुर: परिवेश: (fringe, hem) येषाम्. कार्दरङ्गचर्मणाम् of कार्दरङ्ग shields. कार्दरङ्ग seems to be the name of a country. जातीपट्टिका: loin-cloths. 'जातीपट्टिका: श्रेष्ठानि जघनग्रन्थनानि' com. चित्रपट cloth with paintings or figures. समूरुक is a kind of deer. उपधानम् pillow. '**समूरुश्चेति** हरिणा अमी अजिनयोनय:' इत्यमर:. प्रियङ्गुप्रसववत् पिङ्गला त्वक् येषाम्. प्रियङ्गु: millet. प्रसव: fruit. अगुरुवल्कलेन कल्पित: सञ्चय: येषाम् the leaves of which were made of अगुरु bark. परिणतं (अत एव) पाटलं पटोलं तस्येव त्विट् (कान्ति:) येषाम्. पटोल is called in Marathi पडवळ. तरुण...हरिन्ति as green as a young pigeon. Some of the betel nuts were green and some red. क्षीरक्षारीणि from which milky juice was oozing (being recently cut from the trees). ०कपोलवत् कपिलानि कापोतिकापलाशानि तेषां कोश्या कवचितं अङ्गं यासाम् that were covered with cases of the leaves of the कापोतिका plant as tawny as the cheeks &c. स्थवीयसी *f.* comparative of स्थूल. वैणवीर्नाडी: (object of प्रकाशयांचक्रु:) tubes of bamboo. पट्ट...र्पितान् (connect with राशीन्) placed in bags made of woven silk. For प्रसेवक, see p. 180. भिन्ना...गुरुण: of black aloe (कृष्णागुरु *n.*) as dark as pounded collyrium. This and the following genitives are to be connected with राशीन्. गोशीर्षम् is a kind of very fragrant sandal. 'तैलपर्णिकगोशीर्षे हरिचन्दनमस्त्रियाम्' इत्यमर: ('तैलपर्णगोशीर्षौ गिरी आकरौ अस्य' क्षीर०). कस्तू...कानां of bags of musk. कक्कोलं a fragrant berry (Marathi कंकोळ). जातीफलं nutmeg. अतिमधुर: मधुरस:

तस्य आमोदेन निर्हारिणीः redolent of the perfume of very sweet wine. The com. takes the word to be मधुरसा. 'मृद्वीका गोस्तनी द्राक्षा स्वाद्वी मधुरसेति च' इत्यमरः. उल्लककलशीः pitchers of उल्लक. 'उल्लकः सुगन्धिफलविशेषरस : । आसवभेद इत्यन्ये' com. अवलम्बमानानि तूलिकाः (brushes) अलाबुकानि च येभ्यः—अलाबुकम् vessel made of a gourd (to hold paints). आ...टान् boxes of boards for drawing pictures. कनकशृङ्खलया नियमिताः ग्रीवाः येषां or यासाम्. For किंनर, see above p. 187. C and T suggest that some species of ape may be meant here. वनमानुषी 'ourang—outang' C and T. जीवञ्जीवक is a bird, the चकोर according to अमरकोश. Compare 'पाणितलसंवर्धितं मे जीवञ्जीवमिथुनं क्रीडापर्वते यथा न विपद्यते तथा कर्तव्यम्' काद० p. 316. परिमलेन आमोदिताः ककुभः (दिशः) यैः. गेह... चमरीः chamarî deer accustomed to move about the house. चामीकर...गतान् placed in cages of cane painted with gold. बहुसुभाषितैः जल्पाका जिह्वा येषाम्. जल्पाक garrulous. 'स्याज्जल्पाकस्तु वाचालः' इत्यमरः. 'जल्पभिक्षकुट्टलुण्टवृङः षाकन्' पा. 3. 2. 155. प्रवालः—लम्—coral. जल...कुण्डलानि rings of the long tusks of hippopotamus, bristling (दन्तुर) with rows of large (उदग्र) pearls from their headfronts. It was believed that pearls were found in the temples of elephants. 'द्विपभुजगशुक्तिशङ्खाभ्रवेणुतिमिसूकरप्रसूतानि । मुक्ताफलानि तेषां बहु साधु च शुक्तिजं भवति ॥' बृह० 81. 1. Compare 'शशिकेसरिविदार्यमाणतमःकरिकुम्भसम्भवेन मुक्ताफलक्षोदेनेव धवलतामुपनीयमान्' काद० p. 160 of P. सकल...धाम्नः that is the abode of all precious things (applies both to महार्णव and कुमार). परमे...हंस्य which is fit to be held on the head of a परमेश्वर (emperor); which is to be held on the head by परमेश्वर (शिव). शिव placed the moon on his head to lessen the fever of his body due to हालाहल. कुमुदबान्धवस्य = चन्द्रस्य. न विस्मयाय does not cause wonder *i. e.* does not make me wonder. बाल...कृतयः favours (bestowed on others) are the first lessons of the great. मङ्गलाकाङ्क्षी desiring an auspicious (conclusion to his expedition). प्राङ्मुखः with his face to the east. आभोगस्य—the umbrella was so called.

P. 117 l. 19—**P. 118** l. 9 **अथ विशत**...**वनानाम्.** अस्य = हर्षस्य. छायायाः जन्म यस्य (*adj.* of जडिम्ना). जडिम्ना...बिम्बम् by the coolness it seemed as if the disc of the moon had become his crest jewel *i. e.* under the shade of the umbrella he felt as much coolness as he would have if the moon had been placed on his crest. Explain the following similarly. Everyone of his limbs and his whole body felt the coolness. अम्बुबिन्दून् मुञ्चन्तीति ०मुचः (*adj.* of मणयः). It should be noted that all the objects mentioned are white and cool. चन्द्रकान्त—moonstone, that was believed to ooze when the rays of the moon fell upon it. कर्पू...युगले his eyes felt the coolness of camphor applied to them. गलन्तः तुहिनकणाः तेषां निकरेण कृतः नीहारः (frost, dew) येषाम्. हरि...मुरसि—हरिचन्दनम् is a kind of yellowish sandal. अन्त... दङ्गानि a concealed melting slab of ice as if smeared his limbs. अजर्यं सङ्गतम् undying or everlasting friendship 'अजर्यं सङ्गतम्' पा. 3. 1. 105 (नञ्पूर्वात् जीर्यतेः कर्तरि यत् सङ्गतं चेद्विशेष्यम् । सि. कौ.). प्रतिकौशलिका a present in return (from कुशलं). हंसवेगाय—connect with प्राहिणोत्. धवलकर्पटेन प्रावृतं धौतं (bright, polished) नालिकेरं (cocoanut shell used as a box) तस्मिन् परिगृहीतम् contained. विलिप्तशेषं चन्दनम् (object of प्राहिणोत्) sandal paste that remained after he (हर्ष) had anointed himself. This was deemed a mark of great favour and friendship. अङ्गस्पृष्टे—touched by his own person. शरदि तारकाः तेषां इव आकारः यासां ताः ०काराः ताराः (pure and bright) मुक्ताः तैः स्तबकितं पदं यस्य. The stars shine very brightly in the clear autumnal sky. कटिसूत्रम् belt. कटक...तरत्— the setting of the sun is represented as due to his desire to wash his body rendered dusky by dust. 'मलीमसं तु मलिनम्' इत्यमरः. वारुणीं दिशम्—वरुण presides over the West. अयासीत्—the subject is अंशुमाली. कमलs close their petals at sunset. प्रमुखे एव at the very beginning (of his expedition). The closing petals of the lotuses are represented as the folded hands of the earth. The earth as if submitted to him at the very start of his march. नृपा...मयः इव (the glow of twilight) was as if made up of the अनुराग (love, redness) for the king. The idea is:—the twilight made the whole world aglow; the poet fancies it was rather the अनुराग of the world that spread over it. निखिल...बन्धुः which is a kinsman (*i. e.* closely connected) with the folding of the hands of the people. People perform सन्ध्यावन्दन in the evening; people also fold their hands before a king. ०शङ्किनी afraid of. प्रचितः तिमिरस्य निवहः (समूहः) यस्याम्. निर्वाणः (extinguished) अन्यनृपप्रतापानलकलापः यस्याम्. When we quench fire, black charcoal is left. अवचकरुः *perfect 3rd plu.* of कृ with अव to spread. मेदिनी...ककुभः—clusters of stars resembling expanded *Tagara* flowers twinkled in the sky and seemed as if they were the bunches of flowers spread in the evening audience-hall of the lord of the earth. मार्गो...वतस्य the track of ऐरावत grey with dust shone in the sky. ऐरावत is the vehicle of इन्द्र, the lord of the east. The dust is represented to be raised by ऐरावत that fled from the गन्धगजs of Harsha. रजःपाण्डुः also means 'pale like or with the pollen of flowers'. The east became lit up with the rays of the moon that was about to rise. कुपितः नृपः (हर्षः) व्याघ्र इव तेन आघ्राताम् (smelt, touched). उपसृष्टामिव as if it were possessed by an evil spirit. पौरुहूतीम्=ऐन्द्रीम्. रोहिणीरमणः=चन्द्रः. For रोहिणी being the favourite wife of the moon, see pp. 9, 47, 62. The simple idea is that the moon rose up high in the sky. रोहिणीरमण also means 'a bull', that leaves a place where he smells the tiger. रोहिणी a tawny cow. 'अर्जुन्यघ्न्या रोहिणी स्यादुत्तमा गोषु नैचिकी' इत्यमरः. C and T see here a reference to the growing power of शशाङ्क the Gauḍa king. मानिनी...भेदिन्यः the rays of the moon melt the heart of proud women *i. e.* they become favourable to their husbands with whom they were displeased. प्रयाण ...भेदिन्यः as the news of the march (of Harsha's army) breaks the heart of proud women (because they are afraid of the death of their husbands when they oppose him). नवनृपस्य (हर्षस्य) दण्डयात्रा &c. चक्षुमु...हिनीनाम् the lords of rivers (oceans) became agitated *i. e.* after the rise of the moon the ocean has a full tide. This tidal agitation is fancied to be due to the fear of the expedition of हर्ष. वाहिनीनां पतयः also means 'commanders'. तरलिताः सत्त्वानां प्राणिनां वृत्तयः येषु the movements of the animals in which were made unsteady (with oceans). By the tide the aquatic animals were carried here and there. तरलिता सत्त्वस्य धैर्यस्य वृत्तिः येषाम् whose steadiness of mind was shaken. चिन्ता— anxiety entered the hearts of kings (भूभृत्). Darkness entered the caves of mountains (भूभृत्) *i. e.* only the caves were dark; the rest was lighted up by the moon. विमुक्ताः सर्वाः आशाः दिशः यया (*adj.* of सन्ततिः); विमुक्ता सर्वा आशा (hope) यस्यां (*adj.* of चिन्ता). निद्रा...वनानाम्—The कुमुद lotuses open in moon-light. प्रति...निद्रा sleep left the eyes of the rivals of हर्ष.

P. 118 l. 10—**P. 119** l. 12 **अस्यां...स्वामिन इति.** महावराह-सम्पर्केण सम्भृतः गर्भः यस्याः. महावराह refers to the Boar incarnation of विष्णु. Compare 'यदाहमुद्धृता नाथ त्वया सूकरमूर्तिना। त्वत्स्पर्शसम्भवः पुत्रस्तदायं मय्यजायत॥' विष्णुपु० 5. 29. 23. नरक was king of प्राग्ज्योतिष. कृष्ण killed him at the request of Indra. He deprived वरुण of his umbrella, took away मणिपर्वत from मन्दर, the ear-rings of अदिति &c. 'छत्रं यत्सलिलस्रावि तज्जहार प्रचेतसः।' विष्णु० 5. 29. 10. त्रिभुवनं भुङ्क्ते इति ०भुक् तस्य. भुजयोः शौण्डः प्रवीणः. The construction is यस्य... आज्ञया विना रविरस्तं न अव्राजीत्. ०वाकीभिः कोपकुटिलैः कटाक्षैः ईक्षितः. The चक्रवाकी is separated from her lord at sunset and so fearing it looks angrily at the sun. भयचकितेन अरुणेन परिवर्तितः (turned)

रथः यस्य. अरुण is the charioteer of the sun. बहि...यमिव as if it (छत्र) were his heart dwelling outside. The छत्र was as dear to वरुण as his own heart. Only the छत्र was outside his body. अन्वये in the line or family. भगदत्त was a contemporary of the Pâṇḍavas and took part in the great war. See above p. 187. वज्रदत्त was son of भगदत्त and was defeated by the Pāndavas in their अश्वमेध. See आश्वमेधिकपर्व chap. 76. कैलासस्य इव स्थिरा स्थितिः यस्य whose sense of duty was as firm as Kailâsa. अग्रजेन... कारेण who was born together with pride, as if the latter was the elder of the two. The idea is:—he and अहङ्कार were twin brothers; but अहङ्कार was the elder of the two *i. e.* he paid more regard to, subordinated everything to अहङ्कार. From his very birth he was proud. The reading अजेनेव does not yield a good sense. प्रतिग्रहान् (1) presents (with द्विजातीन्); (2) the rear of an army. अरातीन् प्रतिग्रहान् अग्राहयत् he made his enemies take to the rear of their armies *i. e.* to run from the battlefield. 'सैन्यपृष्ठे प्रतिग्रहः' इत्यमरः. यत्र परं...लक्ष्म्या in whom लक्ष्मी (royal glory) attained her greatest sweetness. There is a picturesque contradiction in saying that लक्ष्मी sprung from the *salt* ocean became *sweet.* Effects generally possess the properties of their causes. वाहिनीनाथानां (1) of commanders of armies; (2) of oceans. शङ्ख was an emblem of command. The great warriors in the महाभारत war had each a शङ्ख which they blew before beginning the fight. Both शङ्खs and jewels are found in the sea as well as with commanders. स्थैर्यः...करम् he took the steadiness of the earth, but did not levy tribute from it. He was as steady as the earth. अवनिभृतां = राज्ञां, पर्वतानां च. गौरव...नैष्ठुर्यम् —mountains have गौरव and नैष्ठुर्य both. He took the one (*i. e.* he was majestic) and not the other (*i. e.* he was not harsh). There is a suggested sense. He deprived the kings of their high position. C and T take भास्करद्युति as the name of the king. This does not seem to be correct. भास्करस्य इव द्युतिर्यस्य. The king's name was कुमार alias भास्करवर्मन्. See above text p. 60. l. 4. भास्करद्युति as the name of a king will probably be found nowhere (with the last word द्युति in the feminine gender). The word कुमार suggests another idea. भीष्म remained a कुमार (prince) all his life; he never became a king. सङ्कल्पः resolve. स्थेयाम् *nom. sing. m.* of the comparative of स्थिर. प्रचण्डेन प्रतापज्वलनेन जनितः दिशां दाहः येन. जगत्येकवीरेण who is the only (unequalled) warrior in the world. मैत्री...भृताम् the friendship of kings generally is dependent upon some purpose *i. e.* it is never disinterested. य...देवम् which when mentioned would make your Majesty a friend (of the king भास्करवर्मा). सञ्चिचीषत: desiring to collect. He now mentions several purposes which induce kings to form friendships and dismisses them all by saying that Harsha is in need of none of them. First he takes up wealth. बहिरङ्ग external *i. e.* not of the essence. बाहा...काशः As he relies solely upon his arm, the desire of even his other limbs to help him has no scope *i. e.* even his other limbs cannot offer him any help; what can a stranger do? चतुःसागराणां ग्रामः समूहः तस्य ग्रहणे घस्मरस्य (greedy). उपन्यासः proposal. The word ग्राम suggests that even the four oceans are but a small village to हर्ष. अभि...भनमपि अकिञ्चित्करम् even the allurement of the gift of a beautiful maiden is of no value. लक्ष्मीमुखारविन्ददर्शनेन दुर्ललिता (fondled) दृष्टिः यस्य. No maiden can be more alluring than लक्ष्मी. अघट...पदार्थेऽस्मिन् this being an object that is attainable by means which are all incapable of attaining it. प्रार्थनामात्रकमेव—connect with शृणोतु. अनुरुध्यमानः being favourably disposed. देवेन—connect with अजर्यं सङ्गतमिच्छति. एक...द्विषा like that of Kubera with the enemy of Cupid. He cast a glance at उमा and lost his left eye and the right became yellow. See रामायण VII. 13. 22–24. एकं पिङ्गं (नेत्रं) यस्य. The author instances five memorable friendships. For दशरथ and Indra, see p. 123. पुष्कराक्षः = पुण्डरीकाक्षः (कृष्णः). वैकर्तनः—son of विकर्तन (the sun) *i. e.* कर्ण. कर्ण was made king of अङ्ग by दुर्योधन. 'अस्य राज्यप्रदानस्य सदृशं किं ददानि ते।...अत्यन्तं सख्यमिच्छामीत्याह तं स सुयोधनः॥' आदिपर्व 136. 39–40. मलयानिल and माधव (वसन्त) are both excitants of love. मैत्रीयति—feels friendship. अवगच्छति...इति (and if your Majesty's) heart understands that friends discharge a slavery under another name. The idea is that friendship entails so many obligations that one has to work day and night for the other. तत...स्यते then why sit (silent)? अनुभवतु—the object is गाढोपगूढानि (close embraces). विष्णो...रिरिव as the mountain Mandara had the close embrace of विष्णु. मन्दर was the churning handle and विष्णु churned the ocean and the mountain rubbed against his body. विकट...मणीनां विघट्टनेन (striking against) कणितानि (jingling) कटकमणिशिलाशकलानि येषु. केयूरक is an ornament of the arm and कटक is a bracelet. In a close embrace these two ornaments will strike against each other. कटकः—कम् also means 'the slope of a hill'. 'कटकाऽस्त्री नितम्बोद्रेः' इत्यमरः. The केयूरक of विष्णु clashed against the slopes of मन्दर in churning. कामरूप is the same as प्राग्ज्योतिष. अस्मिन् goes with ०शशिनि. आ तृप्तेः till she (श्री) is satisfied. अन...झरिणि that pours forth a constant spring of nectar in the form of spotless beauty and grandeur. लालयतु let her please or indulge. The simple idea is:—let the king of प्राग्ज्योतिष see your Majesty's face. But the words चिरात्, शशिनि and श्रीः suggest another sense. लक्ष्मी sprang from the ocean as the moon did and therefore लक्ष्मी is the sister of the moon. Let the sister separated from her brother see him after a long time. नाभि...प्रणयम् If your Majesty does not welcome his love or if your Majesty does not approve of his request.

P. 119 ll. 13–24 **विरत...त्कण्ठा इति.** पूर्वोपलब्धैः which he had heard of (by hearsay). आरोपितः बहुमानः यस्मिन् in whom great regard (for कुमार) had been produced. ०व्यतिकरेण by the incident of &c. महान् अभिजनः (family) यस्य. प्राग्रहरः foremost (प्रकृष्टं अग्रं हरति). परोक्षसुहृदि who is a friend without seeing me. शिशिरायन्ते become cool. कमलाकरे on a bed of lotuses. तिग्मं तीक्ष्णं तेजः यस्य = रवेः. The idea is that the कमलs do not feel that the rays of the sun are hot. सु...सख्यस्य being bought by his numerous qualities, who am I to (form) friendship? The idea is:—his qualities have already made me his. It is not in my hands to *form* a friendship which did not exist before. सज्जन...दिशः the ten quarters are the unhired slaves of the sweetness of the good. The good make the world theirs by their sweetness. एकान्तावदातः उत्तानः स्वभावः तेन सम्भृतं सादृश्यं येन. The कुमुद is extremely white; so is the moon. The कुमुद is उत्तान (has its petals turned up towards the moon); the moon also is उत्तान (open, straightforward). Thus the two resemble each other and form friendship without anybody's intercession. Compare 'समानशीलव्यसनेषु सख्यम्'. समालम्बितं शरासनं येन. अव...हृदयस्य the heart feels great regard for the proud lion, though a beast.

P. 119 l. 25—**P. 121** l. 16 **हंसवेगस्तु...निर्जगाम.** किमप...देवेन 'What else will now give pain (to both of you)? Your Majesty has spoken noble words.' He says that nothing else but the eagerness to see one another will hereafter pain the two kings. अहङ्कारः धनं यस्य. वैष्णवो वंशः—the family of भास्करवर्मा descended from नरक, the son of the earth and महावराह. पुरुषस्य हि—the principal sentence is पुरुषस्य हि सेवां प्रति...अभिमुखीक्रियमाणस्य...राजकुलं संप्रवेष्टुं कृतचित्तस्य (p. 64 l. 33)...किं प्रायश्चित्तम्...कीदृशं जीवितम् &c. (p. 66 ll. 1–3). सेवा...क्रियमाणस्य who is induced to (enter) service by his extremely wretched state, like a bad old mother. अतिवृद्धया very old; very much aggravated. 'निरयो दुर्गतिः स्त्रियाम्' अम०. वा— It will be noticed that in each clause up to अनुवर्त्यमानस्य there is वा. These are put forward as the various reasons which led a man to accept the service of a king. कुदु...प्रेर्यमाणस्य who is urged (towards service) by greed like a discontented wife. A discontented wife always urges her husband to earn more. तृष्णा also can never be gratified to the full. All genitives in this long passage are to be connected with पुरुषस्य. असत्सङ्कल्पैः by evil thoughts. यौव...षिभिः (apply both to bad children and ०सङ्कल्प) that are born of youth and that desire many things. जरत्कु...पश्यतः who sees (*i. e.* expects) a great position like an old maid (a daughter rather advanced in age for marriage). पर...योग्याम् that is commensurate with the solicitations he addresses to others (with अवस्थाम्); that is fit to be sought by others (with ०त्कुमारीम्). परेषां मार्गणं (याचनं) तस्य योग्याम्; परैः मार्गणं तस्य &c. स्वगृहे...योगम् who is compelled to make efforts by all badly placed planets in their houses like bad kinsmen. स्वगृहे—in his own house; in their 'houses' or 'mansions' (with ग्रहैः). The planets are believed to be very powerful when they are in 'mansions' (स्वगृह) *e. g.* सिंह is the स्वगृह of रवि, कर्क of the Moon, मेष and वृश्चिक of Mars and so on. दुःस्थितैः in distressed circumstances; in evil aspects with other planets. 'आभिमुख्येन उद्यमः अभियोगः' क्षीर०. पुरातनैः of long standing; done in former lives (with कर्मभिः). अतिदुस्त्यजैः—old servants cannot be easily got rid of; the fruits of evil deeds done in past lives cannot be avoided. मलिनैः dirty (servants); sinful. It is the sinful deeds in past lives that follow a man and make him take service. सकल...करम् goes with both कारीषाग्निम् and राजकुलम्. कारीषस्य अग्निः fire of dried cowdung. Its heat is more intense than that of fire fed with wood. करीषं शुष्कगोमयं तस्य समूहः कारीषम्. कृत...कुलम् who has made up his mind to enter the palace (*i. e.* the service of a king). दुष्कृतिनः one who is guilty of some deadly sin. He may be condemned to be burnt alive. उपहता सक...शक्तिः यस्य. मिथ्यैव...लापस्य who has vain hopes of seizing the whole gamut of the sensual pleasures his heart desires. The servant vainly thinks that he would by entering service enjoy all विषयs; the old voluptuary also thinks the same. प्रथममेव शुष्यतो...रुद्धस्य first of all (before a man actually gets into royal service) he is obstructed by the doorkeepers and has to wither away at the portal for days. The वन्दनमाला also is tied to the portals and becomes dried by time. For वन्दनमाला see p. 178. करि...पुटस्य—see (text p. 49 l. 17) for ॰पुट. प्रति...मानस्य—he is driven out by doorkeepers who beat him with their hands. The leather figure also is beaten by the कर (trunk of elephants) encased in a covering. 'प्रतिहारेण वेष्टनेन मण्डलं यस्य करस्य तत्प्रहारैश्च' com. अधो...भवतः who bends down his face (*i. e.* bows low) through greed of money. निधि...रोहस्य—it was believed that a tree with treasure beneath it had boughs bending in a peculiar way. See above text p. 4 'निधिस्तरुविकारेण'. अमार्गणस्यापि (1) though he is not a suppliant; (2) though not an arrow. अतिविप्रकृष्टैः आदौ विवृत्तः पश्चात् विसर्जितः he is made to turn back by very mean (servants at the court) and then dismissed. दूरं उद्वेगं व्रजतः he becomes extremely dejected. An arrow also is अति...व्रजतः. It is drawn (विवृत्त) very far (up to the ear) and then discharged. दूरं उद्वेगं व्रजतः (an arrow) reaches a long distance very swiftly (उत्कृष्टः वेगः यथा स्यात्तथा). विवृत also will yield a good meaning. He is first thoroughly examined by low people. The arrow (*i. e.* the bow) is opened very wide. अकण्टक...माणस्य he dogs the feet of persons about the court, who draw him and throw him out quickly, though he is not a thorn. कण्टक has also a technical meaning 'a troublesome person'. The अर्थशास्त्र has a section on कण्टकशोधन. क्षेपीयः used as an *adv.* (comparative of क्षिप्र). A thorn also pierces the sole of one's feet, is taken out and thrown away. अ...केतोः (1) though he is not Cupid; though he is innocent of love affairs (being engrossed in thoughts of service). अकालोपसर्पणेनः कुपितः ईश्वरः (राजा, शिवश्च) तस्य दृष्ट्या दग्धस्य. मदन tried to influence शिव when the latter was engaged in meditation and was burnt; see p. 38. The candidate for service approaches the king at an improper moment and angers him. प्रलय...तः (1) who is destroyed (with Cupid); (2) who disappears (with पुरुषस्य). अभिन्नः मुखरागः यस्य (applies both to कपि and पुरुष)—The redness of the ape's face remains as before. The servant shows no sign on his face though soundly rated. ब्रह्मघ्नः— the murderer of a ब्राह्मण. ब्रह्महत्या was a महापातक; see p. 84. प्रतिदिवसवन्दनेन उद्घृष्टं शिरःकपालं यस्य येन वा—the aspirant after service has to bow down every day and his head is thereby rubbed off. One that murders a ब्राह्मण has to bow by way of प्रायश्चित्त before a skull. Remove the comma after ॰कपालस्य. स्पर्श...वंहतः the servant is devoid of the pleasures of senses and has to carry out degrading duties. स्पर्शः means 'pleasant feelings, pleasure'. The slayer of a Brāhmaṇa had to avoid society and had to live by unworthy means. Note '**शिरःकपाली ध्वजवान्** भिक्षाशी कर्म वेदयन् । **ब्रह्महा** द्वादशाब्दानि मितभुक् शुद्धिमाप्नुयात् ॥' याज्ञ० III. 243 ('तच्च कपालं स्वव्यापादितब्राह्मणशिरःसम्बन्धि ग्राह्यम् । ... तदलाभे अन्यस्य ब्राह्मणस्यैव ग्राह्यम्' मिताक्षरा). See मनु 11. 78, which prescribes for him a forest dwelling. अर्वाक्शिरसः—with head downwards (*i. e.* bent). The servant has day and night to bow to his master. त्रिशङ्कुः—He was a king of the solar race and father of हरिश्चन्द्र. He wished to go to heaven with his mortal body by performing a यज्ञ. His family priest वसिष्ठ declared it impossible. He went to the sons of वसिष्ठ who rejected his proposal. त्रिशङ्कु told them that he would go to another preceptor, whereupon they cursed him to be a चण्डाल. विश्वामित्र, whose family त्रिशङ्कु had saved from starvation in a famine, took pity on him and raised त्रिशङ्कु towards heaven, when Indra refused to admit him and made him fall down headlong. Thereupon विश्वामित्र called upon him to stay where he was and began to create new worlds, नक्षत्रs &c. The gods intervened and made his creations as eternal as those of ब्रह्मा and त्रिशङ्कु blazed forth as a constellation, but with head downwards. See रामायण I. 57–60. Compare 'सुरलोकमारोहतस्त्रिशङ्कोरिव कुपितशतमखहुंकारनिपतिता राजलक्ष्मीः' काद० p. 8. सुखवाह्यम् easily driven (with वाजिनः); who is bereft of happiness (with पुरुषस्य). In the latter case वाह्य is equal to बाह्य; compare वंशवाह्याम् (text p. 39 l. 12, notes p. 125). अनशनशायिनः—One who has resolved upon dying by starvation. हृदये स्थापिता जीवनस्य (of livelihood) आशा येन the man has hopes in his heart of making a livelihood by service. हृदये स्थापितः जीवनाशः येन. निज...खस्य—being engrossed in his duties, the servant has no time to bestow on his wife. The application of निज...खस्य to a dog cannot be explained for the sake of decency. जघन्ये अधमे कर्मणि लग्नं सक्तम्. जघन्यं (जघने भवं) कर्म सुरतं तस्मिन् लग्नम्. अनु...पिण्डस्य—the servant has to take his food in some dirty place. अन्नपिण्ड is offered to the dead (प्रेत) in places (*viz.* river &c.) where the deceased was never accustomed to take food. बलिभुजः = काकस्य. जिह्वायाः लौल्येन उपयुक्तं पुरुषवर्चः येन who wasted his manly spirit for satisfying his fastidious tongue. जिह्वालौल्येन उपयुक्तं (भुक्तं) पुरुषस्य वर्चः (excrement) येन (with crow). 'तेजःपुरीषयोर्वर्चः' अम. वृथा...जीवतः who lives a life applied to no purpose (applies to both). The crow is supposed to live long. 'काकोऽपि जीवति चिरं च बलिं च भुङ्क्ते'. वृथा विहितं

आयुः यस्य. The com. separates 'विभ्यः पक्षिभ्यः हितमायुः यस्य' who has a life useful to birds (with crow). दग्ध...कृताम् rendered rugged by the ashes of persons burnt (with श्म०); rendered harsh by their accursed prosperity (with ०वल्लभान्). दग्धानां भूत्या; दग्धा चासौ भूतिः तया. पिशाचs were supposed to resort to the trees of the cemetery. विपरीतजिह्वया जनितं माधुर्यं येषाम् (1) who talk sweet words by a false tongue (with kings); who talk sweetly with a tongue that is turned backwards (with parrots). ओष्ठमात्रे (ओष्ठे एव) प्रकटितः रागः (प्रीतिः, रक्तत्वं च) येषाम्. The hearts of the kings know no affection; it is only their words that are full of affection. The beak of the parrot is red. राजानः शुकाः इव. राजशुकाः—a variety of parrots. मुग्ध...मानस्य who is fooled and allured. नरेन्द्र...विष्टस्य that takes possession of a person by the power of a wizard (with वेताल); who is overcome by the power of his king (with servant). For नरेन्द्र in the sense of wizard, see p. 33. न कि...तः there is nothing that he will not do (with both) वेताल and servant. चित्रधनुष इव like a painted bow. अलीकं गुणाध्यारोपणं एव एका क्रिया तस्यां नित्यनम्रस्य—the painted bow is always bent and has a false (*i. e.* unreal, painted) string placed upon it. The servant is also humble and solely engaged in ascribing false virtues to his master. निर्वाणं (extinguished) तेजः यस्य (with धनुषः and पुरुषस्य). The pictured bow has not the force of the real one. संमार्जन्या (broom-stick) समुपार्जितं रजः (dust) येन—the servant has to scour the dust off the floor by a broom-stick; dust is accumulated by a broom-stick and thrown on अवकरकूट. अवकरकूटः heep of sweepings. 'संमार्जनी शोधनी स्यात् सङ्करोऽवकरस्तया । क्षिप्ते' अम०. निर्माल्यम् flowers used and cast off. These may be thrown on the heap of sweepings; the servant is often given what his master has worn. Besides the word may suggest that he wears no माल्य (flowers, which produce beauty and are a sign of happiness). C and T suggest that निर्माल्य may mean purity. We fail to see how; and even if it does, it cannot be made to fit in here. कटुकै...मानस्य—the servant is worried by the sharp words of his master; or कटुक has the same sense as on p. 54 l. 14 (text). A man suffering from कफ is treated with कटुक (bitters). See अष्टाङ्गहृदय I. 13. 10. 'श्लेष्मणो विधिना युक्तं तीक्ष्णं वमनरेचनम् । अन्नं रूक्षाल्पतीक्ष्णोष्णं कटुतिक्तकषायकम् ॥.' कटुकं also means 'Ginger, long and black pepper'. सौगतस्य—बौद्धस्य. सुगत is a name of बुद्ध and सौगत means a follower of बुद्ध. अर्थशून्या (धनविरहिता, बाह्यवस्तुशून्या) विज्ञप्तिः (प्रार्थना, विज्ञानं च)

तया जनितं वैराग्यं यस्य. The servant becomes despondent because his requests are not followed by the bestowal of wealth and wants to be a भिक्षु. It is the doctrine of one of the Buddhist schools, called विज्ञानवादिन्, that there is no positively existing entity in the world. All that exists is a train of momentary cognitions. Compare 'बौद्धबुद्धिमिव निरालम्बनाम्' काद० p. 131; 'न जिनस्येवार्थवादशून्यानि दर्शनानि' हर्षचरित 2nd उच्छ्वास. निशा...माणस्य—the servant is hurried off on various errands even at night. बलि is offered to the Mâtṛis at the advent of night; compare मृच्छकटिक I 'मातृभ्यो बलिमुपहर.' For the मातृs, see p. 26. कुशयनेन जनिता...दुःखवृत्तिः यस्य—the servant's worry is aggravated by having to lie down on bad beds or on the bare ground. कु=पृथ्वी. A person in mourning has very slight bedding. See above p. 116. तुलायन्त्रम् seems to mean 'the water-wheel.' पश्चात्कृतं गौरवं येन who leaves aside all ideas of self-respect (with servant). पश्चात्कृतं गौरवं (weight) यस्य. The wheel is turned by a man with his hands. In front of him are the empty pots; those that are filled are farther away from him. The servant has to bow; the wheel goes down to bring up water. अतिकृपण very wretched. शिरसा...स्पृशतः—the idea is:—the servant is not content with bowing his head at the feet of his superiors; with his words also he worships them (sings panegyrics of them). The words suggest another sense. A very miserly person may not be satisfied even with the head of his debtor. दैन्येन सङ्कोचितं (contracted, mean) हृदयं तेन हृतः अवकाशः यस्याः. आहोपुरुषिका—'आहोपुरुषिका दर्पाद्या स्यात्सम्भावनात्मनि' अम० ('अहो पुरुषोऽहमित्यस्य भावः आहो०' क्षीर०)—confident self-respect. He is bereft of self-respect because in his heart contracted through meanness there is no room for it. उन्नति elevation (of thought or mind). धन...जैयतः thinking of amassing riches, he secures trouble. स्व...वर्धयतः thinking that he is making himself prosper, he merely increases his humiliation. स्वं means 'wealth' also. सत्यपि...रचयतः who folds his hands in greed though there are forests scented with the perfume of various flowers. The idea is that the servant at a court should rather take to a life in the forest. There is a striking effect produced by taking वन in the sense of water, 'though there is water, yet he folds his hands in thirst.' The com. suggests another idea. तृष्णा stands for मृगतृष्णा; 'the servant is after a mirage, though there is water fragrant with flowers.' कृतं आगः (अपराधः) येन.

दर्श...जन्मनः—the painted flower is charming to behold, but useless; so is the court attendant. For वैधेय see p. 122. अपशब्दं (अपगतशब्दं मूकं) मुखं यस्य; अपशब्दाः मुखे यस्य. The fool has in his mouth ungrammatical (or, vulgar) words. The courtier, though he knows, cannot speak out his mind and so is silent. There is a contradiction in विदुषः and वैधेयस्य (if he is a पण्डित, he cannot be a fool). श्वित्रिन् a leper, a person suffering from white leprosy. सङ्कोचितं करयुगलं यस्य. समानां तुल्यानां समुत्कर्षेषु. सम... पच्यमानस्य when his equals are raised to a higher position (than his own), he is boiled without fire. He suffers the same torments as boiling would inflict. नीच...म्रियमाणस्य when his inferiors are brought up to his level, he is dying without actually perishing. दुःखा...वृते: on account of the wind of pain, he has no rest (he gets no happiness in service). The wind allows no rest (tranquility निर्वृति) to a lamp. ज्वलतो...भक्तस्य he is worried in attending court, he is devoted and yet not endowed (by his master with gifts). There is a suggestion of boiled rice (भक्त) also in which case अभक्त means 'without boiled rice'. निरूष्मणः०–he has no heat (pride) and yet he causes heat (pain) to his relatives (who feel for his low position). वि...कस्य though he is disrespected, yet he has no alternative (and remains where he is). There is another sense 'though a विमान (aerial car or chariot), yet he has no motion.' च्युतं गौरवं (respect, weight) यस्य. What has weight goes down. Though he is given no respect, yet he bends (in homage). निःसत्त्व spiritless; that has no being with him. महा...कुर्वतः he sells human flesh *i. e.* his own body (to his master). For महामांस, see p. 72. Without an animal, no मांस can be had and sold. नि...वृत्तेः though free from intoxication, yet not master of himself. मद also means 'pride.' The court servant is under the control of another. One intoxicated totters. ध्यानेन वशीकृतः आत्मा यस्य येन वा. The courtier's mind is absorbed in contemplating (ध्यान) how to acquire wealth. ध्यान is one of the eight *Angas* of योग. 'यमनियमासनप्राणायामप्रत्याहारधारणाध्यानसमाधयोऽष्टावङ्गानि (योगस्य)' योगसूत्र II. 29. A *Yogin* controls his mind (आत्मा). 'योगश्चित्तवृत्तिनिरोधः' योगसूत्र I. 2. अयोगिन् also means 'one that has no luck or armour.' योगः = दैवयोगः. 'योगः संनहनोपायध्यानसङ्गतियुक्तिषु' अम०. दग्धं मुण्डं यस्य— the servant's head is burnt by the heat of the sun, when going on errands. दग्धमुण्ड was the name of a sect of ascetics according to the com. शय्यायाः उत्थाय ०त्थायम्—gerund in अम् (णमुल)

from स्था with उद्. This gerund here conveys the idea of haste. 'अपादाने परीप्सायाम्' पा. 3. 4. 52. (परीप्सा त्वरा। शय्योत्थायं धावति ॥ सि. कौ). The courtier is in a hurry to bow to his master, the moment he leaves his bed. The ascetic also performs obeisance. The courtier degrades his family (गोत्र०). The विदूषक (the buffoon of the Indian stage) remains in the family of the hero, makes grimaces and makes his master laugh. The courtier dances (attendance) on his master. The servant is a blot on the fair name of his family (कु०). वंशं दहत: bamboos also are burnt by अङ्गार (live coal). नृपशोः...नमयत: a beast such as a bull bends its neck when grass is seen by it. The courtier bows even when a trifle is given by his master. The courtier is a mere mass of flesh (with no spirit or brains) who is born solely for the purpose of filling his belly. मांस also fills one's belly when eaten. गर्भरोगस्य मातुः—he is a diseased growth in the womb of his mother. There are certain diseases of the womb (*e. g.* mole) characterized by fleshy growths or knots. अपु...भृतस्य who becomes a servant because he committed sinful deeds (in past lives). प्रतिपत्तये क्रिया what action should bring exaltation (or honour) to him? क... शान्तिः whither shall he go to secure rest. कः...मानः what manly pride can he entertain? किं...श्रद्धा what sort of pleasures can he have? What means his belief that he will enjoy (life)? प्रबल...यति if once a man's feet stick in deep mud, the more he struggles to extricate himself, the deeper does he go. अभ... तस्याः may that advancement (of the courtier) come to an end! For अभवनिः see above p. 182. तस्या....र्थस्य here do I fold my hands to such grandeur (*i. e.* I bid farewell to it). परिच्छदः paraphernalia, pomp. यदर्थे...ष्यति for the sake of which the head must prostrate itself on the earth. He says that if for securing wealth, rank and pomp, one has to bow his head, then it is not worth the trouble. Put a vertical line after गमिष्यति. मुख...कलमः—the construction is (यदि) मुख...रतः क्लीबः...सेवकोऽपि मर्त्यमध्ये (गण्यते) (तदा) राजिलोऽपि वा भोगी पुलाकोऽपि वा कलमः (भवेत्). The reading of B 'अशापा०' gives a good sense. तपस्वी ascetic; wretched. तपस्वी was capable of cursing or bestowing a boon. क्लीबः coward, mean; impotent. मुखप्रियं रतं यस्य—whose affection is pleasing only in his mouth *i. e.* who expresses only lip loyalty (and his heart feels no affection for his master). With क्लीब (impotent) the meaning cannot be explained in English. मुखे प्रियं रतं (सुरतं) यस्य. See सुश्रुत शारीरस्थान chap. 2. 38. 'पित्रोरत्यल्प-

बीजत्वादासेक्यः पुरुषो भवेत् । स शुक्रं प्राश्य लभते ध्वजोच्छ्रायमसंशयम् ॥'. पूति... मयः springing from (or consisting of) rotten flesh. पूति Putrid, foul smelling. Worms are found in rotten flesh. The courtier is a despicable creature (कृमि) emitting foul smell from his body (because he has no time to bathe). अगण्यमानः—of no account; of vast dimensions (अगण्यं मानं यस्य). नरकः an insignificant man; a hell. कुत्सितः नरः नरकः, कुत्सार्थे कन्. 'कुत्सिते' पा. 5. 3. 74. पादरजसा धूसरं उत्तमाङ्गं यस्य. A courtier's head is rendered dusty by bowing at the feet of his master. A foot-stool has its top dusty because the feet rest upon it. पुंस्कोकिलः a male cuckoo; a man like a cuckoo (पुमान् कोकिल इव). काकुः *f.* is the change of voice due to different feelings such a joy, sorrow &c. 'काकुः स्त्रियां विकारो यः शोकभीत्यादिभिर्ध्वनेः' अम०. The courtier can change his voice to suit the occasion. The cuckoo cries sweetly expressing its feeling of joy (in spring). C and T read स्थलकूर्मः which is preferable. क्रोडकषणेषु in rubbing the chest. 'न ना क्रोडं भुजान्तरम्' अम०. The courtier has to toil hard; the tortoise has its chest rubbed against the earth when moving. नीच...करणेषु in mean flattery, 'अस्त्री चाटु चटु श्लाघा प्रेम्णा मिथ्या विकत्थनम्' क्षीर०. मूर्च्छना—a duly regulated rise and fall of sounds due to the letting out of the air in a particular way; modulation of voice 'क्रमात्स्वराणां सप्तानामारोहश्चावरोहणम् । सा मूर्च्छेत्युच्यते' सङ्गीतरत्नाकर I. 4. 9. मूर्च्छना also means 'fainting or delusion.' करण...शेषु in the trouble of tying the limbs of the body. The servant has his various limbs tied to work of various kinds. करणं also means 'a posture of the body; a kind of dance.' 'करणं हेतुकर्मणोः । वणिजादौ हस्तलेपे नृत्यगीतप्रभेदयोः । क्रियाभेदेन्द्रियक्षेत्रकायसंवेशनेषु च' मे०. 'कामशास्त्रोदितकरणानि' com. पलालम् husk or straw (*i. e.* as worthless). सत्त्वशालिषु among those that are possessed of manliness. शालि suggests rice. कृकलासः lizard, chameleon. 'सरटः कृकलासः स्यात्' अम० (कृकं शिरोग्रीवं लासयति). The lizard now and again raises its head. The courtier has to nod his head to whatever his master speaks. जाहकः a polecat. आत्म...नेषु in contracting the body (with जाहक); in making his mind have a narrow vision (with servant). 'जाहको गात्रसङ्कोची' क्षीर०. 'आखुर्जाहकः प्राणिभेदः; कूर्म इत्यन्ये.' प्रतिपादकः 'footstool' C and T. पाद...सु in shampooing the feet (of his master); in bearing the feet. Compare verse 20 in the introduction to हर्षचरित ' शब्दैराख्यायिका भाति शय्येव प्रतिपादकैः'. प्रतिपादक seems to mean a block on which the leg of a couch rests. कर...ताडनेषु—the servant is slapped by his master. 'कोणो वीणा-

दिवादनम्' अम०. कोणः fiddlestick; stick. वराक...भोगी if a wretched servant (is to be counted) among men, then even a राजिल will be a cobra. 'समौ राजिलडुण्डुभौ' अम० ('निर्विषो द्विमुखोऽहिः' क्षीर०). पुलाकः shrivelled grain 'स्यात्पुलाकस्तुच्छधान्ये' अम०. '**शालयः कलमाद्याश्च**' अम०. Put a vertical line after कलमः. वरं...मानवता It is better that manliness (मानवता) be shown even for a moment by the man that respects himself. मानवता *instru.* of मानवत्. The student will notice how the same letters are repeated with different senses, as in यमक. न मत...मनस्विनः. The highminded do not approve of even the enjoyment of the sovereignty of three worlds by one who bows down (for it). नमतः goes with ०भोगः and मतः with मनस्विनः. अभिनन्दितः (welcomed) अस्मदीयः प्रणयः (friendship or request). परागतः come, arrived.

P. 121 l. 17—P. 122 l. 4 राजापि...पादयोः. कुमारदर्शनौत्सुक्येन स्वीकृतं (seized, engrossed) हृदयं यस्य. आत्मा...करणम् to offer oneself heart and soul captivates the great without roots and spells. For वशीकरण (magic power over the minds of others), roots and spells were required. But the fact that Kumāra devoted himself heart and soul to Harsha captivated the mind of the latter. प्रतिप्राभृतम् gifts in return (for those received). ०दूतैः अधिष्ठितं (supervised by). आत्मनापि by himself, so far as he was concerned. अमित्रमभिलक्ष्य = अभ्य० (अव्ययीभाव)—towards his enemy (the गौड king). For साधन, see above p. 130. आवासितम् encamped. मूर्च्छा...विवेश he entered the darkness of a swoon. प्रतीहारस्य निवारणेन निभृतः निःशब्दः परिजनः यस्मिन् where attendants were motionless and speechless by the prohibition of the doorkeeper. The principal sentence is अथ भण्डिः एकेनैव वाजिना...राजद्वारमाजगाम. निखाताः बहवः लोहकीलकाः तेषां परिकरः (समूहः) तेन रक्षितं स्फुटनं यस्य the breaking of which was prevented by an array of numerous iron nails implanted in it. Nails prevent a tottering structure from giving way. The poet fancies that the numerous points of arrows on his chest were nails implanted to prevent his heart from breaking through grief (for राज्यवर्धन). Understand उपलक्षितः after हृदयेन. हृदयलग्नैः resting on or reaching his chest (with beard); deeply impressed on the heart (with ०सत्कृतैः). स्वामिसत्कृतैः the honours bestowed on him by his master. For the growing of the beard in sorrow, see p. 118. दूरीकृतः (given up) व्यायामः तेन शिथिलः भुजदण्डः तस्मिन् दोलायमानं मङ्गलवलयं एव एका केवला शेषालङ्कृतिः यस्य—The only ornament he wore was a single auspicious bracelet (on the left hand) that moved up and down owing to his arm being languid. For the wearing of bracelets by men see pp. 15, 46. अनादरेण (without particular care) उपयुक्तं (भुक्तं) ताम्बूलं तेन विरलः रागः (रक्तत्वं) यस्य. Supply उपलक्षितः after अधरेण. He was careless in taking betel; therefore his lip was faint in colour. The poet fancies that the lip was a coal from his heart burning with grief, which (coal) was pressed out by the force of his deep sighs. ०विरहे विधृतं जीवितं एव अपराधः तेन वैलक्ष्यं (विलक्षस्य भावः) तस्मात्—as if through embarrassment (or shame) at the fault of continuing to live though his master was dead. One abashed covers his face with his garment. His face was covered with tears. Tears (being bright) resemble the hem of a white garment. विशन्निव अपत्रयया स्वाङ्गं अङ्गैः Through shame his limbs appeared to be entering his own body (*i. e.* his body was shrunk). वमन्निव—he heaved deep and hot sighs, which, the poet fancies, were the warmth of his valour emitted by him because it was useless (as he could not save राज्यवर्धन). मुषितः robbed. छलितः cheated. वेग...णः a young elephant. For वेगदण्ड, see p. 174. सूर्या...करः—there is a suggested sense. सूर्य stands for राज्यवर्धन and कमला means लक्ष्मी. दुर्योधननिधनेन दुर्मनाः (sad). द्रौणिः son of द्रोण *i. e.* अश्वत्थामा. See शल्यपर्व 65 'वार्तिकाणां सकाशात्तु श्रुत्वा दुर्योधनं हतम्। हतशिष्टास्ततो राजन् कौरवाणां महारथाः। ... ततो द्रौणिर्महाराज बाष्पपूर्णेक्षणः श्वसन्।' 12. दुर्योधन...मैनाः also means 'who (Bhandin) was sad on account of the death of (राज्यवर्धन) who was hard to fight with.' अपहृतं रत्नं (राज्यवर्धनरूपं) यस्य. अपहृतानि रत्नानि यस्य (with सागरः).

P. 122 ll. 5–34 **अवनि...कैलासाम्.** उत्थाय...द्रम्य he got up and went out a few steps to receive him. For व्यतिकर, see pp. 72, 130. देवभूयं गते—see above p. 150. गुप्तः इति नाम यस्य तेन. See Introduction for the significance of this. कुशस्थलम्—seems to be the same as कान्यकुब्ज. In the रामायण (I. 32) we are told that कुश, son of ब्रह्मा, had four sons, one of whom कुशनाभ founded the city of महोदय, which is identified with कान्यकुब्ज. कुशनाभ's son was गाधि. कान्यकुब्ज is designated गाधिनगर in a grant of जयच्चन्द्र of Kanoj. See I. A. Vol. 15 p. 6, 7. किं...पदिभिः what is the use of other seekers (for राज्यश्री) ? अनुपदिन्—'अन्वेष्टानुपदी समौ' क्षीर०. परित्यक्तं अन्यकृत्यं येन. कारितं ०वपनकर्म येन who was made to shave &c. शारीरिक for the body; or rather the meaning is 'he sent flowers, unguents &c., which he had meant for himself'. सपरिबर्ह together with the equipage

(paraphernalia). 'परिच्छदे नृपार्हेऽर्थे **परिबर्हः**' अम०. करिणः, हरीन् and the following nouns in the accusative are governed by दर्शयाम्बभूव. ०गण्डान् qualifies करिणः. ०मदः मदिरा इव तस्याः आमोदेन मुखराणां मधुकराणां जूटः तेन जटिलः करटः (cheek) पट्टः इव तेन पङ्किलः गण्डः (face) येषाम्. गण्ड...ङ्गमान्—the elephants looked like moving rocks. '**गण्डशैलास्तु** च्युताः स्थूलोपला गिरेः' अमरः ('च्युताः भूकम्पादिना गलिताः' क्षीर०). गम्भीरः गर्जितरवः येषाम् (with जलधरान्); गम्भीरगर्जितवत् रवः येषाम् (with करिणः). Both clouds and elephants are dark. **सप्तच्छद** is the same as Marathi सातवीण. The odour of the ichor was like the scent of the सप्तच्छद, which blossoms in शरद्. चारु... **हरीन्** the horses had chowries with gold work on their heads. Note for the **चामर**s on horse's heads 'निष्कम्पचामरशिखा निभृतोर्ध्वकर्णाः' **शाकुन्तल** I. हरिणस्य इव रंहः (वेगः) येषाम्. बाला...वर्षिणाम् that shed a mass of light mellow like that of morn. किरणै...दिशाम् that covered the quarters with many rain-bows on account of their rays. ०कृतः (wonderful) qualifies हारान्. स्मरेण उन्मादिताः मालव्यः तेषां कुचपरिमलेन दुर्ललितान् (fondled, caressed). The necklaces had once rolled on the breasts of Malva females and rubbed off the sandal applied by them to their bosom. तारान् bright. There is a pun here. तारा means a star. A star has only a twinkling light. The हारs, though तार, flooded the world with their light. उडुपतिः चन्द्रः तस्य पादानां (किरणानां) सञ्चयवत् शुचीनि शुभ्राणि. **निज०** refers to Harsha. जातरूपमयं नालं यस्य the handle of which was made of gold. लक्ष्मी dwells in a white lotus. The white umbrella resembled पुण्डरीक and the handle resembled a lotus-stalk. वारविलासिनीः dancing girls. बहूनि समररसेण साहसानि तस्मिन् अनुरागः तेन अवतीर्णाः. The Apsarases are represented as fond of heroes and as welcoming them to heaven. See above p. 101. Here the damsels are represented as Apsarases come down on earth out of their fondness for gallant deeds. आसन्दी chair of state. 'आसन्दी पीठिका' क्षीर०. ससंख्यानि आलेख्यपत्राणि येषु which were accompanied with written records giving the number (in each chest). अलङ्काराणां आपीडस्य पीडा तया सह सा० that groaned under (the weight of) the wreaths of ornaments. If we read ०पेडापीडान् the meaning will be 'that were wreathed with small bags (पेडा) of ornaments.' यथा...कारम् according to their respective functions.

P. 123 l. 1—**P. 124** l. 24 **अथ...वसदिति.** The principal sentence is अथ प्रविशन् दूरादेव...वनग्रामकं ददर्श तत्रैव च अवसत्. दह्यमान... दधानैः—this clause qualifies वनप्रदेशैः (l. 4)—that were rendered grey by the smoke of granaries (बीजधानी) of wild corn, in which (granaries) fire flared up on account of heaps of smouldering षष्टिक chaff. षष्टिकः a kind of rice ripening in sixty days from the day of sowing. 'षष्टिका· षष्टिरात्रेण पच्यन्ते' पा. 5. 1. 90. ०विसरैः विसारी विभावसुः (अग्निः) यासु (*adj.* of ०धानीनाम्). ०शाखासञ्चयेन रचितानि गोवाटानि (cowpens) तैः वेष्टिताः विकटाः (large) वटाः येषु.०रोषेण रचितानि व्याघ्रयन्त्राणि येषु—where tiger-traps had been placed in wrath at the slaughter of young calves. वत्सस्येव रूपं येषां ते वत्सरूपकाः that were like their own children. अयन्त्रितैः (uncontrolled) वनपालैः हठेन (forcibly) ह्रियमाणाः परग्रामीणानां काष्ठिकानां (wood-cutters) कुठाराः यस्मिन्. The reading यन्त्रित० is not suitable. C and T render it by 'zealous.' ०षण्डे निर्मितः चामुण्डामण्डपः येषु. चामुण्डामण्डप seems to mean 'a flimsy structure used as a temple of Durgā.' प्रकाश्यमानम् qualifies वनग्रामकं (text p. 69 l. 24). अटवीप्रायः प्रान्तः यस्य स ०प्रान्तः तस्य भावः. ०प्रान्तता तया—as the forest settlement was bordered on all sides by forest (the villagers found it hard to secure fields for cultivation). कुद्दालप्राया कृषिः येषाम् whose agriculture depended almost on spades *i. e.* they had no ploughs and no oxen. कृषीवलैः is to be connected with भज्यमान०. अविद्यमानाः बलीवर्दाः येषाम् (*adj.* of कृषी०). अवलन्द्भिः who did not hasten, who were slow. This does not yield a good sense. A and C omit अबलीवर्दैः and read अबलवद्भिः. It is probable that अवलन्द्भिः is a mistake for अबलवद्भिः. भज्यमानानि भूरीणि शालिखलक्षेत्राणां खण्डलकानि यस्मिन्. उच्च...खण्डलकम् where many small pieces of rice-fields and threshing grounds were being divided (by farmers) in high-pitched language. खलः—लम्—threshing floor. क्षेत्र is to be connected with शालि and खल. उच्चः भागः यस्य तत् ०भागं भाषितम्. भाग seems to be redundant. The reading भज्यमानभूरिखिलक्षेत्र० is better. The meaning would be 'where many pieces of waste land (खिलक्षेत्रं) were being broken by farmers accompanied with talk on higher ground or with loud talk.' अल्पावकाशैः—of small extent. This and the following instrumentals qualify केदारैः (l. 9). काशि...कठिनैः that abounded in काश grass and that were hard with black soil resembling iron. स्थानस्थानेषु स्थापिताः स्थाणवः तेभ्यः उत्थिताः स्थूलाः पल्लवाः येषु. Trees had been cut off from the fields, leaving only the trunks imbedded in the earth, which again put forth vigorous foliage. दुरुपगमा श्यामाकप्ररूढिः येषु in which the growth of श्यामाकs was impenetrable. श्यामाक is a kind of grain. अल...क्षुपैः that abounded in अलम्बुस and were thick with कोकिलाक्ष bushes. 'ह्रस्वशाखाशिफः क्षुपः'

अम०. नातिप्रवृत्तं गतागतं (गतं च आगतं च तयोः समाहारः) तेन अप्रहता भूः यस्मिन् (*adj.* of वनग्रामकं)—where the earth was not trodden because there was not much coming and going. क्षेत्राणां समीपे उप० (अव्य०). मञ्चै...द्रुमम् where the (high) platforms (or scaffolds for watchmen to sleep on) suggested the depredations of wild beasts. The next clause is दिशि दिशि च...अटवीप्रवेशप्रपाणां शैत्येन त्याजयन्तमिव ग्रैष्मम् ऊष्माणम् (l. 20). All the genitives in this clause qualify ०प्रपाणां. प्रति...कृतानाम् (प्रपाs) made of (or, under) trees growing about the roads. पथिक...छायानाम्—Travellers walking barefooted used leaves to wipe off (प्रस्फोटन) the dust off their feet and left the leaves at the प्रपा when they started. Compare 'विश्रान्तकार्पटिकप्रस्फोटितचरणधूलिधूसरकिसलयलाञ्छितोपकण्ठैः' काद० p. 223 l. 15. अटवीसुलभानि सालकुसुमानि तेषां स्तबकैः अञ्चिता (marked, decked) नवखाता (recently dug) कूपिका तस्याः उपकण्ठे (समीपे) प्रतिष्ठिताः नागस्फुटाः यासु. नागस्फुट or–टा seems to be some kind of bush. अच्छिद्रैः (closely woven) कटैः (straw mats) कल्पितं कुटीरकं (hut) यासु. कुटिला कीटानां (insects, flies) वेणी (row, line) तया वेष्ट्यमाना शक्तुशारा (spotted with barley meal) शरावश्रेणी (lines of platters) तया श्रितानाम् (०प्रपानाम्). अध्वगजनेन जग्धानि जम्बूफलानि तेषां अस्थिभिः (stones) शबलाः समीपभुवः यासाम्. जम्बूफल is Marathi जांभूळ. उद्धूलिता धूली येषां ते ०धूलीकाः कदम्बस्तबकाः तेषां प्रकरेण पुलकिनीनाम्. C and T take धूलीकदम्ब to be a tree, which also is good. Bunches of कदम्ब flowers the pollen of which was scattered about were lying near the प्रपाs and resembled hair (पुलकः) standing on end. रोमाञ्च is often compared to कदम्ब flowers. Compare 'अनिलैरपि कदम्बकेसरोत्करवाहिभिः कण्टकितैरिवानुगतम्' काद० p. 217; 'ततोऽपि घनजलधारासीकरपुलकितकाया कदम्बकलिकेव' काद० p. 254. See also उत्तरराम III. 'सस्वेदरोमाञ्चित' &c. कण्टकितं कर्करीचक्रं तेन आक्रान्ता काष्ठमञ्चिका (wooden stand) तया मुषिता तृट् (thirst) यासु. कर्करी a water jar. The idea expressed by कण्टकित is :—the porous jars had very small particles of water (due to cooled vapour) on their outside which resembled hair standing on end. C and T translate 'bristling' and suggest that the jars contained grass stalks. तिम्यत् (wet) तलं यासां ताः ०त्तलाः शीतलाः सिकतिलाः (porous) कलश्यः ताभिः शमितः श्रमः यासु. For सिकतिल, see p. 30. आश्यानेन (partially dry, moist) शैवलेन श्यामलितः अलिञ्जरः (a large pitcher) तेन जायमानः जलस्य जडिमा (coldness) यासु. उदकुम्भेभ्यः आकृष्टानि पाटलशर्कराशकलानि तैः शिशिरीकृता दिक् यासु. What पाटलशर्करा means is not clear. C and T translate 'pink gravel'. But compare 'पटुपाटलशर्करामोदमुचि' above (text p. 22 l. 30), where पाटलशर्करा is said to have a fragrance. It was probably 'a lump of red raw sugar.' घटमुखेषु घटितानि (formed) कटहारेण (by a rope of straw) पाटलापुष्पपुटानि यासु. पाटला is a plant with red flowers. If we read करहाट it will mean 'with the fibrous root of a lotus'. शीकरेण पुलकिताः (bristling) पल्लवाः तेषां पूल्या पाल्यमानाः (preserved) शोष्याः (liable to wither) सरसाः शिशवः सहकाराः (mangotrees) तेषां फलानां जूटी तया जटिलाः स्थाणवः (pillars) यासाम् (*adj.* of प्रपानाम्). This seems to be a description of the care taken to preserve young grafted mango plants. विश्राम्यन्तः कार्पटिकाः तेषां पेटकाः (समूहाः) तेषां परिपाट्यः (successive rows) ताभिः पीयमानं पयः यासु. For कार्पटिक, see p. 166. अटवी...ष्माणम् that was made to give up the heat of summer by the coolness of the water arbours at the entrances to the forest. त्याजयन्तम् qualifies वनग्रामकम् below. प्रपा पानीयशालिका—Marathi पाणपोई. ग्राहय...व्योकारैः—we have to understand ग्रैष्ममुष्माणम् with ग्राहयन्तम्—that was made to take up the heat of summer by blacksmiths that burnt heaps of wood for charcoal. 'व्योकारो लोहकारकः' अम॰. The next clause is a very long one सर्वतश्च...व्याप्तदिगन्तरम् (text p. 69 l. 7). Read **॰वासिना** for ॰वासिनाम्. This and the following instrumentals are connected with ॰लोकेन (l. 26). प्राति...वासिना that dwelt in the neighbouring district (विषयः). समासन्नेषु ग्रामगृहेषु स्थापितैः स्थविरैः परिपाल्यमानेन पाथेयेन (provisions) स्थगितः (covered, surrounded) तेन (*adj.* of ॰लोकेन). पथि साधु पाथेयम्, according to 'पथ्यतिथिवसतिस्वपतेर्ढञ्' पा. 4. 4. 104. See p. 67 on वासतेयी. कृतः दारुण—दारुव्यायामयोग्यः अङ्गाभ्यङ्गः येन that had rubbed their body with oil befitting their hard toil in the forest. अभ्यङ्ग removes fatigue. स्कन्धं अध्यासितः कठोरकुठारः यस्य स ॰कुठारः कण्ठे लम्बमानं प्रातराशपुटं यस्य स ॰पुटः, ॰कुठारश्चासौ ॰पुटश्च तेन. प्रातराशः breakfast. पाटच्चराणां (चौराणां) प्रत्यवायेन (obstacle) प्रतिपन्नं पटच्चरं (rags) येन. 'पटच्चरं जीर्णवस्त्रं' अम॰. कालवेत्रकस्य (black cane) त्रिगुणः (triple) व्रततिवलयपाशः तेन ग्रथिता (encircled) ग्रीवा तस्यां ग्रथितैः (fastened)-qualifies पीतकुटैः. पत्रवीटया (a bundle of leaves used as a cork) आवृतं मुखं येषाम्. We must read पीतकुटैः. Compare कुटहारिका above p. 28. ऊढं (carried) वारि येन (*adj.* of ॰लोकेन). पुरःसरौ वलन्तौ (moving, quick) बलीवर्दौ तयोः युगं (pair). तेन सरतीति ॰सरेण. Or युगं may mean 'yoke'. For वलत् some read बलवत्. निकटे भवः नैकटिकः. कुटुम्बिन् a peasant. ॰लोकेन is to be connected with व्याप्तदिगन्तरम् below (p. 69 l. 7). श्वापदानां व्यधनं (shooting) तदर्थं व्यवधानानि (screens) तेषां बहली तस्यां समारोपिताः कुटीकृताः (twisted) कूटपाशाः (traps) यैः (*adj.* of व्याधैः). बहली seems to mean 'heap'. गृहीतानि मृगतन्तवः तन्त्र्यः जालवलयानि वागुराश्च यैः. The मृगतन्तुs (animal sinews) were for mending nets; the lutes (तन्त्रीs) for luring the deer. Or मृग...तन्त्री may mean 'strings made of animals' sinews.' बहिः विचरद्भिः व्याधैः (व्याप्त-दिगन्तरम्). The hunters wandered outside the वनग्रामक. अंसे अवसक्तः (attached to, fixed) वीतंसः (aviary) तेन व्यालम्बमानाः (hanging about, loitering) बालपाशिकाः येषाम् (*adj*. of शाकुनिकैः). बालपाशिकः a boy hunter. सङ्गृहीताः ०जालादीनां पञ्जरकाः (cages) यैः. ग्राहकः falcon. क्रकरः partridge. शाकुनिक—शकुनान् हन्ति इति—according to 'पक्षिमत्स्यमृगान् हन्ति' पा. 4. 4. 35 च्युतः लासकलेशः तेन लिप्ता लता तस्यां वधूलट्वाः तासु लम्पटानाम् (eagerly following). लासकः soup, broth. लट्व means a भ्रमरक according to क्षीर०. C and T translate वधूलट्वा as 'female sparrows.' पैटकैः goes with व्याप्तदिगन्तरम्. पाशिक—a fowler. तृणस्तम्बेन अन्तरितः (concealed) तित्तिरिः तेन तरलायमानं (rendered restive) कौलेयककुलं तस्य चाटुकारैः that coaxed the dogs &c. ०मृगयां is the object of क्रीडद्भिः. मृगयुयुवभिः by youths that were hunting. परिणतः (fully grown) चक्रवाकः तस्य कण्ठवत् कषाया रुक् (colour) येषाम् (वल्कलानाम्). शीध-व्यानाम्—what tree is meant is not clear. कलापान्—connect this and the following accusatives with आदाय (l. 5). धातोः इव त्विट् येषाम् the hue of which was like metallic ore (such as गैरिक). गोणीः अगणिताः countless bags. धातकीपुष्प is very red. पिचव्यानां च (गोणीः) and of cotton plants. अतसी...मूलकानां of cloth made from a quantity of flax and of radish. The reading अतसीशणपूलकानां is easier 'of bundles of flax and hemp.' मधुनो माक्षिकस्य of honey derived from bees. मयूराङ्गजस्य of peacock's tails. अक्लिष्टं (untouched by anyone else) मधूच्छिष्टं (wax) तस्य चक्रं (balls) तेषां मालानाम्. लम्बमाना लामज्जकजूटजटा येषाम् (*adj*. of ०काष्ठानाम्). लामज्जकम् is the root of a fragrant grass. अपगता त्वक् येषां (barkless). कुष्ठ—a kind of plant, with a fragrant adour. बभ्रु tawny. रोध्र a tree with white or red flowers. Construe भारकान् आदाय व्रजता लोकेन (व्याप्त०). प्रविचितैः (gathered) ०फलैः पूरिताः पिटकाः मस्तके यासाम्. अभ्य...गत्वरीभिः hastening to the neighbouring villages. The next clause is इतस्ततश्च...संस्कारम् (l. 9). युक्ताः (yoked) शूराः शकुराः (tame) शाकराः (oxen) यासु (*adj*. of श्रेणीनाम्). पुराण...हिनीनां carrying heaps of dry cowdung (करीषं) and old dust-heaps. उत्किरः heap. धूर्गताः (sitting on the poles) धूलिधूसराः सैरिकाः तैः सरोषस्वरेण सार्यमाणानाम् that were being driven with angry voices by ploughmen &c. सैरिक—सीरं वहति इति—'हलसीराट्ठक्' पा. 4. 4. 81. सैरिभ would mean 'a buffalo.' संक्रीडन्ति (creaking) चटुलानि (loose) चक्राणि तैः चीत्कारिणीनाम् (noisy). सम्पातः multitude. संपाद्यमानः दुर्बलोर्व्या विरूक्षाणां क्षेत्राणां संस्कारः यस्मिन् where the fields parched up on account of the poor soil were being prepared. आरक्ष...वृतिभिः—*adj*. of वाटैः. आरक्षार्थं (for protection) क्षिप्तः क्षिप्रः

दान्तवाहकदण्डः तेन उड्डीयमानैः हरिणैः हेलया (लीलया) लङ्घिता तुङ्गा वैणवा वृतिः (hedge of bamboos) येषाम्. दान्तः (an ox broken to the yoke) +वाहकः driver. निखातः (implanted) गौरस्य (buffalo) करङ्कः (skeleton) यस्मिन् सः ०करङ्कः'. शङ्कुः (a dart, stake) तस्मात् शङ्कितैः शशकैः शकलिताः तुङ्गाः शुङ्गाः येषाम्. शुङ्गः the sheath or calyx of a bud. प्रयत्नेन प्रभृताः (nourished) विशङ्कटाः (large) विटपाः येषाम्. वाटैः ऐक्षवैः gardens of sugarcane. ऐक्षव—from इक्षु. ०कण्ठम् (*adj.* of वनग्रामकम्). अतिविप्रकष्टं अन्तरं येषाम्. This and the following instrumentals qualify गृहैः below. स्नुहा the milk-hedge plant. कार्मुककर्मणि साधुः ०कर्मण्यः वंशः तस्य विटपैः सङ्कटानि (full of). ०गर्मुतां गुल्मैः गहना गृहवाटिका येषाम्. उरुबूकः = एरण्डः castor plant. वचा, वङ्कक and सुरस are various plants. सूरण—Marathi सुरण. शिग्रु—Marathi शेगवा or शेगट. ग्रन्थिपर्ण is a fragrant कन्द. गवेधुका a grass eaten by cattle. गर्मुत् a kind of grass. निखातानि (planted in the earth) उच्चानि काष्ठानि तेषु आरोपितः काष्ठालुकलताप्रतानः तेन विहिता छाया येषु. परिमण्डल circular. परि... रूपैः where calves were tied to pegs of Khadira &c. For वत्सरूप see above p. 210. संनिवेशः situation. अङ्गना...वापिकैः.Here the text is unsatisfactory. What क्षिप्र...पूपिका means is not clear. अङ्गनागस्ति–the अगस्ति plant in the courtyard. पूपिका a sweet cake. वापिका tank. Some MSS. read क्षिप्रपूपिका. May we read क्षिप्त for क्षिप्र (the meaning being 'where there were tanks constructed under the courtyard अगस्ति plants, on which (tanks) were thrown (क्षिप्त) cakes for birds'). विकीर्णानि बदराणां पाटलानि पटलानि (heaps) येषु. ०मयवृतिभि विहिताः भित्तयः येषु the walls of which were made of fences consisting of slips (पोटः) of bamboo, leaves (दलं), stalks and reeds (शरः). नलः means 'a kind of reed.' किंशुक...राशिभिः hardly yields a sense. So read ०रोचनाविरचितमण्डनैः बल्वज०. किंशुकैः रोचनया च रचितं मण्डनं येषाम्. किंशुक is a red flower without fragrance. बल्वजैः बद्धः अङ्गारराशिः येषु where a heap of charcoal was tied with बल्वज grass. संनिहिताः...तण्डुलाः येषु. नलशालिः rice from नल reeds (probably देवभात). शालूकं roots of waterlily. 'शालूकमेषां कन्दः स्यात्' अम०. खण्ड candied sugar. We must read with B ०हीततमालबीजैः. भस्ममलिनाः म्लानैः काश्मर्यकूटैः व्याधृताः कटाः येषु where mats were dusty with ashes and full of heaps of drying काश्मर्य plants. आश्यानानि (partially dry) ... फलानि तैः स्फीतैः abounding. 'राजादनः फलाध्यक्षः' अम०. मधूक a flower of the मधूक tree. आसवः extract or decoction. कुसुम्भकुम्भाः गण्डे यस्य सः ०गण्डः कुसूलः(granary) येषाम् the granaries of which were filled to the mouth with pots of safflower. अविरहितानि...बीजानि येषु. राजमाषः a kind of bean. त्रपुषं cucumber. कर्कटिका species of cucumber. मालुधानः a kind of serpent. 'मालुधानो मातुलाहिः' अम०. It is hard to say what शालिजात and जातक are. वनग्रामकम्-a village settlement in a forest.

Uchchhvāsa VIII

Verse 1. दैवेनापि...सेवेव Even Fate as if serves beforehand the fortunate. The idea is:–there is no wonder that people pay homage to the fortunate; even Fate serves them, which is an earnest of the good things that are to be theirs at a later stage of their career. 'फलकल्याणयोर्भव्यम्' क्षीर०. *Verse 2.* सम्पर्कः union, association. नष्टः इष्टः ज्ञातिः (बन्धुः, स्वजनः) तस्य दर्शनमेव अभ्युदयः. कस्य...भवति—the answer expected is सर्वस्यैव सुखाय भवति. It is better to read भुवने. भवने would mean 'in the house.' Both the verses are suggestive of the events narrated in this उच्छ्वास. हर्ष is to meet a sage in the person of दिवाकरमित्र, he further finds his sister and receives a wonderful necklace from दिवाकरमित्र.

P. 125 l. 5—**P. 126** l. 13 **अथापरे...गोचरमिति.** The principal sentence is एकदा तु भूपतेः भ्रमत एव...व्याघ्रकेतुर्नाम कुतोऽपि...शबरयुवानमादायाजगाम. भूप...एव while the king was wandering. आटविकसामन्तः a feudatory dwelling in the forest. अटव्यां भवः आटविकः. ललाटस्य उपरि अधिललाटम् (अव्ययीभाव). श्यामलता—is a creeper called 'गन्धप्रियङ्गु' according to क्षीर०. कृतः मौलिबन्धः यस्य—whose hair was tied. This and the following accusatives qualify शबरयुवानम् below. 'चूडाकिरीटकेशाश्च संयता मौलयस्त्रयः' अम०. अन्धकारिणीं dark (*adj.* of ललाटस्थलीं). अका...यामामिव which resembled night on account of the frown of his eyebrow divided into three branches, which (frown) was natural (not due to any particular cause). Emphasis is laid on the word त्रि. Night is divided into *three* watches; his brow was dark and naturally covered with *three* wrinkles. So it is like त्रियामा. Night causes darkness (अन्धकारिणी). तिस्रः शाखाः यस्य. साहस० applies to both. Night is the friend of adventures; his forehead was always with him in adventures. साहसानां or साहसेषु सहचारिणी. अवतंसितः (made into an ear-ornament) एकः शुकस्य पक्षकः (wing) तस्य प्रभया हरितायमानेन (looking green). पिनद्धा (tied) काचरा (glass-like) काचमणेः (crystal) कर्णिका (ear-ring) यस्मिन्. For कर्णिका, see p. 106. चुल्ल blear-eyed. 'स्युः क्लिन्नाक्षे चुल्ल—चिल्लपिल्लाः क्लिन्नेऽक्ष्णि चाप्यमी' अम. प्रविरलं पक्ष्म (eye-lashes) यस्य. सहजेन...क्षरन्तम् The blood of a hyena is employed as a medicine. His eyes were naturally red and therefore it appeared as if his eyes let fall the blood of a hyena useful in preparing Rasāyanas. रोचिः = दीप्तिः. 'तरक्षुस्तु मृगादनः'. तरक्षोः इदं तारक्षवम्. क्षतजम् = रुधिरम्. अवनाटा (नता low) नासिका यस्य.

'अवटीटोऽवनाटश्चावभ्रटो नतनासिके' अम०. चिपिटः (thick, large) अधरः यस्य. चिकिनं (flat) चिबुकं (chin) यस्य. अहीना (full) हनुः (chin) तस्यां उत्कटः (prominent) कपोलकूटास्थिपर्यन्तः यस्य—the tops of whose round cheek bones were prominent over a full chin. ईषत् अवाग्रः (अवनतः) ग्रीवाबन्धः यस्य whose neck was slightly bent. स्कन्नः (drooping) स्कन्धस्य अर्धभागः यस्य. अनवरतं कोदण्डस्य (धनुषः) कुण्डलीकरणं (bending) तेन कर्कशः (hard) व्यायामः तेन विस्तारितेन. अंसल strong 'बलवान्मांसलोंऽसलः' अम०. उरसा...गिरेः who as if laughed at the breadth of the rock on the slopes of the Vindhya by his chest that was &c. अजगरः a huge serpent said to swallow goats. लघयन्तम् ridiculing, casting into the shade. तुहिनशैलः हिमालयः तस्मिन् शालद्रुमाः तेषाम्. द्राघिमाणं (लघयन्तम्)—his arms were long like the शाल tree. वराह...प्रकोष्ठे on his forearm the back of which was thickly covered with a mass of the roots of the नागदमन plant which was fastened with the hair of a boar. ०बालैः वलितं बन्धनं यासाम्. 'नागदमनो विषहर ओषधिभेदः । जूटिका लघुमूलम् । वाटिका पूल्यः' com. गो...चित्रम् decorated with गोदन्त beads. According to the com. 'decked with the head gem of गोदन्त serpents.' गोदन्तं yellow orpiment, white fossil substance. त्रापुषं made of tin (from त्रपु, according to 'त्रपुजतुनोः षुक्' पा. 4. 3. 138). See जातुष p. 124. अतु...भम् though not fat, he had a prominent navel. 'वृद्धनाभौ तुण्डिलतुण्डिभौ' अम०. 'तुन्दिवलिवटेर्भः' पा. 5.'2 139 (वृद्धा नाभिस्तुन्दिः । सि. कौ.). तुण्डिभ also means 'fat' and hence the apparent contradiction. अहीरमणी (according to com.) a serpent with two heads. The other reading अहीरणि means the same thing. ०चर्मणा निर्मिते पट्टिके तयोः—inside (*i. e.* between) two strips of the skin of &c. चित्रा (variegated) चित्रकत्वक् तया तारकितः (spotted) परिवारः (scabbard) यस्याः (*adj.* of कृपाण्या). चित्रक seems to be a kind of serpent. सङ्कुब्जं अजिनं तेन जालकितया that was encased in a contracted deer skin. What सङ्कुब्ज means is not clear. C and T translate 'short'. शृङ्गमयः (made of horn) मसृणः (smooth, glossy) मुष्टिभागः (handle) तेन भास्वरया. मस्तकं end. कृपाण्या...प्रदेशम् whose broad loins were made formidable by a dagger. For विशङ्कट (written also as विसङ्कट), see p 122. प्रथमयौवनेन उल्लिख्यमानः (being pared or thinned) मध्यभागः (waist) तस्मात् भ्रष्टं मांसं तेन भरितौ. By exercise in youth his waist became thin and his thighs thick. The poet fancies that the flesh from the reduced waist went to the thighs. अच्छभल्लः bear. भल्ली...भृता—bearing numerous arrows most of which were crescent-shaped. All the instrumentals qualify भल्लाभरणेन. शबल...पीडितेन made fast with a broad spotted tiger skin. अलिकुलेन or कुलवत् कालानि कम्बललोमानि यस्य the blanket-like hair of which (bear's skin) was dark with (or like) &c. भस्त्रा...दर्शयन्तम् who exhibited a darkness as if blossoming with a quiver. भस्त्रा आभरणमिव. We must read कार्ष्ण्यं for कार्श्यम्. He was already dark enough and had a dark quiver and spotted tiger-skin &c., which looked like the पल्लव of darkness. उत्तर...शिखरे—this and the following locatives qualify दोषि. उत्तरत्रिभागे उत्तंसितं चाषपिच्छं तेन चारु शिखरं यस्य (arm) the top of which was charming with a blue jay's tail placed as an ornament on the upper third part of it (arm). 'पुंस्युत्तंसावतंसौ द्वौ कर्णपूरेऽपि शेखरे' अम०. खदिरजटानामिव निर्माणं यस्य the make or essence of which was (tough) like the fibres (or branches) of Khadira. The खदिर is a very tough tree. खरः प्राणः यस्य. 'शक्तिः पराक्रमः प्राणः' अम०. प्रचुरा मयूरपित्तेन पत्रलता (figures) तेन चित्रिता त्वक् यस्य. त्वचिसारः वंशः (bamboo) तद्वत् गुरुणि. वामस्कन्धे अध्यासितं धनुः यस्य. दोषि लम्बमानेन hanging from his arm. This and the following instrumentals qualify शशेन. अवाक् शिरः यस्य. शितशरेण कृतं एकं नलकविवरं तस्मिन् प्रवेशिता इतरा जङ्घा तेन जनितः स्वस्तिकबन्धः यस्य. स्वस्तिकबन्ध is a posture in योग in which the toes are placed in the inner hollow of the knee. 'जानूर्वोरन्तरे सम्यक् कृत्वा पादतले उभे। ऋजुकायो विशेन्मश्री स्वस्तिकं तत्प्रचक्षते ॥'. One leg of the hare was made to enter a cylindrical hole made in the other by a sharp arrow. For नलक, see above p. 173. बन्धूकवत् लोहिता रुधिरराजिः तया रञ्जितं (stained) घ्राणवर्त्म (nose) यस्य. वपुर्विततया व्यक्तं विभाव्यमानः कोमलक्रोडरोम्णां शुक्लिमा यस्य the whiteness of whose fine hair on the chest was clearly visible on account of its body being stretched out fully (as the hare hung from the arm of the forester). शितायां अटनीशिखायां (notched extremity of the bow) ग्रथिता (fastened) ग्रीवा यस्य—qualifies तित्तिरिणा. Separate च अपावृत &c. अपावृता (open) चञ्चुः तया उत्तानं ताम्रं तालु यस्य whose (of the partridge) red palate was displayed as its beak was wide open. वर्णकमुष्टि a handful of paints or unguents. वर्ण...दर्शयन्तम्—on his arm hung a partridge and a hare. These seemed to be unguents with which he had smeard his body when hunting. विषमेण (terrible, powerful) विषेण दूषितं वदनं यस्य (with विकर्णेन and ०हिना). विकर्ण- a kind of arrow. मूलगृहीतेन held by the tail (with arrow); caught or subdued by some drug. व्यग्रं दक्षिणकराग्रं यस्य. तमाल has dark leaves and the शबर youth also was dark. यन्त्रो...भ्रमन्तम् he was like a moving pillar of solid stone cut out (chiselled) by a machine (from a mountain). अञ्जन...छेदम् a piece of collyrium slab. अयःसारः essence of iron. पाकलम्—He worked havoc among elephants, as fever does. For पाकल, see p. 5. कालपाशम् the noose of death. काल—he was also black. धूम...चक्राणाम् he was a comet (indicating the destruction of) to the multitude of lions. There is a pun on the word राजचक्र. A comet portends evil to kings. महानवमी—is the 9th of the bright half of आश्विन. The day is sacred to Durgā. See चतुर्वर्गचिन्तामणि व्रतखण्ड chap 13 p. 903 for महानवमी. 'अश्वयुक्शुक्लपक्षस्य अष्टमी मूलसंयुता। सा महानवमी नाम त्रैलोक्येऽपि सुदुर्लभा ॥...तस्यै ये उपयुज्यन्ते प्राणिनो महिषादयः। सर्वे ते स्वर्गतिं यान्ति घ्नतां पापं न विद्यते ॥' p. 909. महः=उत्सवः. On this day goats and buffaloes were offered to the goddess Kālî or Durgā. हृदय...हिंसायाः in him one would have found the heart of destruction *i. e.* हिंसा at its highest. फलमिव—sin is represented as dark. He was the result of sin as it were. कलिकाल—Kali, the age of sin, is dark. कामु...रात्रेः the lover of the night of universal destruction. For कालरात्रि see p. 91. कालरात्रि—(also) dark night. He loved to start in pursuit of adventure on dark nights. सर्व...हरः the leader of all the chiefs of (forest) hamlets. स्वस्रीयः स्वसुरपत्यम्—sister's son. 'स्वसुश्छः' पा. 4. 1. 143. उप...यनम् he presented the present of the hare together with the partridge. उद्देशस्य=प्रदेशस्य. विहार...भवन्तः you are in the habit of wandering in the forest in these days. उदारं रूपं यस्याः of noble bearing or form.

P. 126 ll. 14–29 **निर्गतस्तु...गन्तुम्.** दर्शितः आदरः यथा स्यात्तथा. अपरिगताः without being known. अविद्यमानं अन्यत् कृत्यं येषाम्. इत...मात्रे एव only a *Kros'a* from this place. गव्यूति **'गव्यूतिः स्त्री क्रोशयुगम्'** अम०—from गो+यूति. मुनिमहिते honoured by sages. मही...षण्डे in a thicket of trees growing at the foot of a mountain chain. पिण्डपाती—पिण्डपातः अस्ति अस्य—living on alms. 'छात्रान्तेवासिनौ शिष्ये' अम०. पाराशरी—see p. 127. स...वार्ताम् perhaps he may know some news. मैत्रायणीयः—belonging to the मैत्रायणीयशाखा of the Yajurveda. त्रयी—the three Vedas. 'स्त्रियामृक्सामयजुषी इति वेदास्त्रयस्त्रयी' अम०. 'ब्राह्मणायनः द्विजवरिष्ठः' com. 'शुद्धसन्तानजो विप्रः' त्रिकाण्डशेष. उत्पन्ना समाधिः यस्य. उत्पन्न...मते who concentrated his mind on the doctrines of सुगत (बुद्ध) or who was reconciled to the doctrines of बुद्ध. काषायाणि—the red robes of a monk. इति is to be connected with श्रूयते. अभि...सर्वस्य good qualities (persons possessing) are fit to be approached by everyone. कस्य...मावः who would not look up to (with reverence) the position of an ascetic? धर्मगृहिणी the wife of धर्म *i. e.* intimately associated with धर्म. The idea is that even if a dullard takes to the life of an ascetic, respect is paid to him. ०मनांसि मुष्णातीति who wins the hearts &c. प्रास...कल्याणम् this is an accidental thing that has happened and that will be very auspicious to me. पश्यामः—governs जनम्. प्रयत्नेन प्रार्थितं दर्शनं यस्य.

P. 126 l. 30—**P. 127** l. 34 **अथ...गन्तुम्.** The principal sentence is अथ क्रमेण गच्छत एव तस्य...पुरस्तादर्शनपथं अवतेरुः तरवः. तस्य =हर्षस्य. अ...नः full of fruits. 'वन्ध्योऽफलोऽवकेशी च' अम०. कुड्मलिताः कार्णिकाराः येषु. कर्णिकार has flowers of excellent colour but without fragrance. प्रचुराः (abundant) चम्पकाः येषु. स्फीताः फलेग्रहयः येषु in which some trees had abundant fruit. 'स्यादवन्ध्यः फलेग्रहिः'—फलानि गृह्णातीति—'फलेग्रहिरात्मम्भरिश्च' पा. 3. 2. 26. नमेरु is a kind of tree. नीलानि दलानि येषां ते ०दलाः नलदानां नारिकेलानां निकराः येषु. नलदं a kind of fragrant grass. हरिकेसरसरलाः परिकरे येषाम्. सरल is a tree. हरि yellowish. केसर 'चाम्पेयः केसरो नागकेसरः काञ्चनाह्वयः' अम०. कोरकनिकुरुम्बेण रोमाञ्चिताः कुरबकराजयः येषु in which rows of कुरबक trees bristled with heaps of buds. 'कलिका कोरकः पुमान्' अम०. 'निकुरम्बं कदम्बकम्' अम०. प्रविकसिताः केसराः तेषां रजोविसरेण बध्यमानः वासरधूसरिमा येषु. स्वरजसा सिकतिलं तिलकतलं येषु where the ground underneath तिलक trees was sandy with their own pollen. हिङ्गु assafoetida plant. पूग Betel nut. प्रसवानां (flowers) पूगेन (समूहेन) पिङ्गलाः प्रियङ्गवः येषु. परागेण पिञ्जरिताः मञ्जर्यः तासु पुञ्ज्यमानाः मधुपाः तेषां मञ्जुशिञ्जया जनिता जनमुद् (जनानन्दः) येषु. मदमलेन (by the stain of ichor) मेचकिताः ०स्कन्धाः (branches) काण्डं च (trunk) तैः कथिता निःशङ्कानां करिणां करटस्य कण्डूतिः येषु. The elephants rubbed their itching temples against मुचुकुन्द trees. उड्डीयमानाः निःशङ्काः चटुलाः कृष्णशारशावाः येषु तानि सकलानि शाद्वलानि (grassy plots) तैः सुभगाः भूमयः येषु. तमोवत् कालतमा (very dark) तमालमाला तया मीलितः (covered, obscured) आतपः येषु. स्तबकैः दन्तुरिताः देवदारवः येषु. दन्तुरित bristling with. तरलैः (moving to and fro) ताम्बूलीस्तम्बैः जालकिताः (entangled) जम्बूजम्बीरवीथयः येषु. जम्बीरः citron. कुसुमरजसा धवलाः धूलीकदम्बाः तेषां चक्रेण (समूहेन) चुम्बितं व्योम येषु. बहलमधुमोक्षेण उक्षिता (sprinkled) क्षितिः येषु. परिमलेन घटिता (effected) घ्राणस्य तृप्तिः यैः. ०कुक्कुट्या कुटीकृतः कुटजकोटरः (hollow of the कुटज tree) येषु. कुटीकृत used as a hut *i. e.* tenanted. चटकाभिः (sparrows) सञ्चार्यमाणाः (being taken from one tree to another) वाचाटाः चाटकेराः (young of sparrows) तैः क्रियमाणं चाटु (प्रियवाक्यं flattery) येषाम्. We must read चाटकैर 'चटका कलविङ्कः स्यात् तस्य स्त्री चटका तयोः। पुमपत्ये चाटकैरः' अम०. 'चटकाया

ऐरक्' पा. 4. 1. 128. सहचरीणां चारणे (feeding) चञ्चुराः (expert) चकोरचञ्चवः येषु. ०भुरुण्डैः भुज्यमानानि पाकेन (ripening) कपिलानि पीलूनि येषु. भुरुण्डः a kind of bird. पीलु a kind of fruit. ०फलानां विशसने (destruction) निःशूकाः (निर्दयाः) शुकशकुन्ताः तैः शातितानि शलाटूनि येषु. सदाफल a kind of tree. कट्फल—Marathi कायफळ. शलाटु raw fruit. 'आमे फले शलाटुः स्यात्' अम०. शैलेय belonging to a mountain. शिफा fibrous root. ०विवरेषु विस्रब्धं (fearlessly) विवर्तमानाः (rolling about) गौधेरराशयः येषु. गौधेर young lizard. 'त्रयो गौधेरगौधार—गौधेया गोधिकात्मजे' अम०. निरातङ्काः (fearless) रङ्कवः (deer) येषु. निराकुलाः ०कुलस्य केलयः (play) येषु. आरामः garden, grove. ०रामेषु रोमन्थायमानं (ruminating) चमूरयूथं येषु. We must read चमूरु (a kind of deer). 'नीलाण्डजा मृगभेदाः' com. C and T suggest that by नीलाण्डज a bird is meant. निर्विकारैः (motionless) वृकैः (wolves) विलोक्यमानाः पोतैः (calves) पीताः गवयधेनवः येषु. गवयः an animal resembling an ox, Gayal. श्रवणहारी (charming to the ear) सनीडस्य (निकटस्य) गिरिनितम्बनिर्झरस्य निनादः तेन निद्रा तया आनन्दः तेन मन्दायमानाः ०दुन्दुभयः येषु. The elephants became drowsy by the murmur of the stream and stopped the flapping of their ears. ०रवं रसमानाः रुरवः येषु. We expect रसयमाणाः (tasting *i. e.* listening with appreciation). रुरु is a kind of deer. प्रमुदिततराः (very much delighted) तरक्षवः येषु. क्षता (pierced by boars) हरिता (yellowish) हरिद्रा (turmeric) तस्याः द्रवेण रज्यमानं नववराहपोतानां पोत्रवलयं येषु. पोतः young. पोत्रं snout—'मुखाग्रे क्रोडहलयोः पोत्रम्' अम०. ०कुञ्जेषु गुञ्जन्तः जाहकाः (polecat) येषु. जातीफलकेषु (nutmeg trees) सुप्तं शालिजातकवलयं येषु. For शालिजात as a pet, see text p. 69 l. 23. दशनेन कुपिताः ०पोतानां पेटकाः समूहाः तैः पाटितः पाटलमुखानां कीटानां पुटकः (hollow, nest) येषु. Some insects with red mouths bit the apes, which in anger crushed their nests. लकुचलम्पटाः गोलाङ्गूलाः तैः लङ्घ्यमानाः लवलयः येषु. लकुच the bread fruit tree. गोलाङ्गूल is a kind of monkey with a dark body and a tail like a cow's. लवली a kind of creeper. बद्धानि वालुकया आलवालवलयानि येषाम्. कुटिलाभिः कुटावलिभिः (rows of water-jars) वलितः (turned or checked) वेगः येषां तानि ०वेगानि गिरिनदिकास्रोतांसि येषु. ०काण्डेषु लम्बमानाः कमण्डलवः येषु. सूत्रशिक्येषु आसक्तानि रिक्तानि भिक्षाकपालानि तैः पल्लविताः लतामण्डपाः येषु. सूत्रशिक्यम् a loop made of threads. Compare Marathi शिकें. निकटासु कुटीषु (huts) कृताः पाटलाः मुद्रया (by a stamp or seal) चैत्यकमूर्तयः येषु. The models of small चैत्यs were pink-red (पाटल) either because the mud used was red or because the stamp was impressed on vermilion. For the latter, compare p. 32. चैत्यः a monument, pyramidal column containing the ashes of deceased persons; or a sacred tree *(e. g. figtree)* growing on a mound; hall or temple. चीवराम्बरस्य रागेण (redness) कषायं उदकं तेन दूषितः उद्देशः (प्रदेशः) येषाम्. 'चीवरं मुनिवासः' क्षीर०. मेघ...हलाः—peacocks ran wild in the forest and emitted loud notes. When a cloud is seen peacocks dance and cackle. Hence the trees are said to be मेघमय. वेद...गहनाः—the trees were full of numerous branches (शाखा); the वेद्s are subdivided into numerous schools; *e. g.* the ऋग्वेद had 21 शाखाs of which शाकल and बाष्कल were the two principal ones. Note 'एकशतमध्वर्युशाखाः, सहस्रवर्त्मा सामवेदः, एकविंशतिधा बाह्वृच्यं, नवधाथर्वणो वेदः' महाभाष्य (Kielhorn) vol. I p. 9. महानीला (very dark) तनुः येषाम्. महानीलः is also a kind of sapphire or emerald. तिमिर...मुषः—the trees attracted the eyes of all people; darkness obscures people's eyes. तिमिर is also an eye disease. ऊर्ध्वीकृताः महाह्रदाः (great lakes) यैः—There were lakes in the forest; there are deep spots in the यमुना also. ०मणिवत् श्यामलाः—the trees were green like emerald, particularly in Spring. Hence they are said to be the pleasure—hill of वसन्त, dark with emerald. अञ्जनाचलाः—as the trees were dark with shade, they are represented to be hills of collyrium. For the same reason they are fancied to be the darkness of पाताल. As पाताल is supposed to be below the earth, the author says 'भित्त्वा भुवमुत्थिताः.' What प्रतिप्रवेशकाः means is difficult to say. A and C read प्रतिवेशिकाः (neighbours). The com. reads 'प्रतिप्रसवकाः प्रतिच्छन्दकाः' *i. e.* reflections, images. प्रति...शकाः may mean 'the ushers, those that introduce.' अंशावतार—see p. 191. कृष्णरात्रीणाम् of the nights of the dark half. The trees were dark like इन्द्रनील. अदूर...भदन्तेन the venerable sage must not be far off. भदन्तः aterm of respect applied to a Buddhist. समुपस्पृश्य having sipped and ejected water as a religious act. युगपद्विश्रामेण (sudden rest) समुन्मुक्तः हेषाघोषः तेन बधिरीकृतं अटवीगहनं यया *(adj.* of वाजिसेनाम्). अवलम्ब्य...विनयं हृदयेन...मंसे having assumed in his heart humility and having leant with his right hand on the shoulder of माधवगुप्त. माधवगुप्त was the younger of the two princes from Mālava, who were the companions of Harsha in his boyhood. See text p. 12 l. 17.

P. 128 ll. 1–32 **अथ तेषां...ववन्दे.** The principal sentence is अथ तेषां तरूणां मध्ये...दिवाकरमित्रमद्राक्षीत्. The instrumentals from नानादेशीयैः are connected with आवेद्यमानम् (l. 8). स्थाणूनाश्रितैः sitting on or reclining against posts. अरण्यानी-'महारण्यमरण्यानी' अम०. निकुञ्जः bower. निलीन hidden. वीतः (विगतः) रागः (passion) येषाम्. This may be an *adj.* of आर्हतैः or may be taken independently. आर्हतैः by Jain philosophers. अर्हत्—a sanctified teacher of the Jainas, a तीर्थङ्कर. The philosophy of the Jainas is called आर्हतदर्शन in the सर्वदर्शनसंग्रह. मस्करिभिः—see above p. 113. श्वेतपटः—this probably refers to the श्वेताम्बर sect among Jains. पाण्डुरभिक्षुभिः—the com. explains that these were ascetics that had abandoned the red robes peculiar to Buddhist monks. भागवत—a devotee of भगवत् *i. e.* वासुदेव or कृष्ण. वर्णिभिः—'वर्णिनो ब्रह्मचारिणः' अम०, from वर्ण+इन्—according to 'वर्णाद्ब्रह्मचारिणि' पा. 5. 2. 134. केशलुञ्चनैः that pulled out their hair. 'लुञ्चिताः पिच्छिकाहस्ताः पाणिपात्रा दिगम्बराः' सर्व० आर्हतदर्शन. कापिलैः followers of कपिल, the founder of the सांख्य system. जैनैः—the com. renders it by बौद्धैः. Though जिन is a name of बुद्ध, the word जैन does not popularly mean बौद्ध. The word आर्हत also would mean बौद्ध as अर्हत् is a name of बुद्ध. लोकायतिक—is a materialist, an atheist, a follower of चार्वाक, who held that there was no intelligent ruler of the universe, that there was no soul, that there was no पुनर्जन्म, that only प्रत्यक्षप्रमाण was to be accepted and that all beings were created from the *four* elements. Compare 'लोकायतिकविद्ययेवाधर्मरुचेः' काद० p. 150. लोकायतं शास्त्रमस्ति अस्य इति लो०. काणादैः followers of कणाद, who was the founder of the वैशेषिक system. औपनिषदैः that were students of the doctrines of the Upanishads. The Upanishads, often called वेदान्त, are works forming the last portions of the several Vedas and are concerned with philosophical problems, such as the orign of the Universe, the relation of the individual soul to the Supreme Spirit and so on. ऐश्वर...कैः who believed in ईश्वर as the cause (or creator) of the world. This probably applies to the माहेश्वरमत, according to which ईश्वर is only निमित्तकारण and which is refuted in the ब्रह्मसूत्र (II. 2. 37–41) or to the न्याय system founded by गौतम which regards ईश्वर as the निमित्तकारण. 'कारन्धमिभिः धातुवादिभिः' com. This probably refers to the school of alchemists (called रसेश्वरदर्शन) who believed that mercury, if properly treated, would make men immortal. *Vide* सर्वदर्शनसंग्रह for this दर्शन. 'कारन्धमी कांस्यकारे धातुवादरतेऽपि च' मे०. धर्मशास्त्रिभिः those that studied the Smṛitis, like those of Âpastamba, Vasishṭha, Baudhāyana, Manu &c. पौराणिकैः—see p. 113. साप्ततन्तवैः those who studied the sacrifice. This probably stands for the students of the पूर्वमीमांसा system founded by जैमिनि, in which the most prominent place is assigned to sacrifice. 'सप्ततन्तुर्मखः क्रतुः' अम० (सप्तभिश्छन्दोभिस्तन्यते इति क्षीर०). शाब्दैः=वैयाकरणैः, whose position was that the व्याकरणशास्त्र would lead to मोक्ष 'तद्द्वारमपवर्गस्य

वाङ्मलानां चिकित्सितम् । पवित्रं सर्वविद्यानामधिविद्यं प्रकाशते ॥' वाक्यपदीय I.; compare महाभाष्य 'एकः शब्दः सम्यग्ज्ञातः शास्त्रान्वितः सुप्रयुक्तः स्वर्गे लोके कामधुग्भवति' vol III p. 58. पाञ्चरात्रिकैः followers of the पञ्चरात्र doctrines. In the महाभारत we are told that नारद promulgated the पञ्चरात्र doctrines after receiving them from नारायण 'सांख्ययोगकृतं तेन पञ्चरात्रानुशब्दितम् । नारायणमुखोद्गीतं नारदोऽश्रावयत्पुनः ॥ शान्ति० 340-112. सिद्धान्तान् dogmas, established truths. अभि...शयानैः absorbed in (the pursuit of their special philosophy), pondering, repeating, doubting. व्युत्पादयद्भिः giving etymologies. व्याचक्षाणैः expounding. आवेद्यमानम् indicated, pointed out (qualifies दिवाकरमित्रम् below). कपिभिः—this and the following nouns in the instrumental are to be connected with उपास्यमानम्. कपिभि...परैः (waited upon) even by monkeys that had taken refuge with the 'three refuges' and that were engaged in doing the menial work about चैत्यs (or of चैत्य). त्रिसरणं (Pāli तिसरणं, Sanskrit त्रिशरणं)—the three Refuges are बुद्ध, धर्म (the Law) and सङ्घ (the assembly). The formula in which faith in these three is professed may be looked upon as the *credo* of Buddhism. It consists in repeating thrice the words 'बुद्धं सरणं गच्छामि धम्मं सरणं गच्छामि संघं सरणं गच्छामि'. परमो...दिशद्भिः by parrots, greatly devoted to Buddha and skilled in his teaching, giving instruction in the कोश. According to C and T कोश is the Buddhist dictionary by Vasubandhu. ०शालिनीभिः—शिक्षापदानां उपदेशेन दोषोपशमः तेन शालन्ते इति—that had secured the extinguishment of the दोषs (sins) by instruction in the शिक्षापदs. The शिक्षापदs (Pāli सिक्खापद) are ten and are the precepts regulating the life of a Buddhist monk. They are the same as the ten शीलs for which see below. धर्मदेशना instruction in the धर्म. अनवरतश्रवणेन गृहीतः आलोकः यैः that had attained light (enlightenment) by incessant listening to instruction. Owls (कौशिक) cannot see in daylight (आलोकः). बोधिसत्त्वजातकानि—the Jātakas are the stories of the former lives of बुद्ध before he had attained perfect knowledge. जातकं is the tenth book of the Khuddakanikāya and contains 550 *Jātakas* or birthstories. बोधिसत्त्व is a term applied to बुद्ध in his various births before he attained Buddhahood. शीलं (Pāli सीलं)—There are ten moral precepts laid down by Buddha, prohibiting the destruction of life, theft, impurity, lying, use of intoxicants, eating at forbidden hours, attending worldly amusements, use of unguents and ornaments, the use of a large or ornamented couch and receiving money. जातः सौगतशीलैः शीतलः स्वभावः येषाम्

whose natures became mild by the (practice of the) moral precepts enjoined by बुद्ध. आसनोपान्ते उपविष्टाः विस्रब्धाः अनेककेसरिशावकाः यस्य सः ०शावकः तस्य भावः शावकता तया. मुनिपरमेश्वरम्—he was the foremost of sages. ०कृत्रिम...निषण्णम्—A परमेश्वर (emperor) sits on a सिंहासन (throne) which is only artificial (*i. e.* it has the *shape* of a lion); while दिवाकर० sat on a real सिंहासन (lion-seat). There is another idea. बुद्ध is called मुनीन्द्र or मुनीश्वर. So दिवाकर० seemed to be बुद्ध himself. 'मुनीन्द्रः श्रीघनः शास्ता' अम०. उप...पल्लवम्—deer licked his feet. The poet fancies that they drank from his feet tranquility of mind. नीवाराः wild rice. 'तृणधान्यानि नीवाराः' अम०. प्रियां...यन्तम् who propitiated मैत्री that was dear to his heart. मत्री means 'good will towards the whole world'. 'अपकारिण्यभिप्रीतिः मैत्री' com. The young dove looked like a lotus placed on the ear. The word प्रियां suggests another sense. मैत्री was as if his wife and he propitiated her by ०कर्णोत्पल (the पारावत). Remove the comma after व्यामोहम्. In this long passage and elsewhere Bāna shows considerable acquaintance with Buddhist dogma and technique. जनितः जनव्यामोहः येन-the people were infatuated by the rays of the nails of his right hand (as he poured water into the beak of a peacock). The shining and dark-green neck of the peacock resembled an emerald water pot. 'कमण्डलौ च करकः' अम०. The long neck of the peacock was like the neck of a jar. Take away the comma after संवीतम्. संवीत (*past p. p.* of व्ये with सम्)—'संवीतं रुद्धमावृतम्' अम०. पौरन्दर—पुरन्दरस्य इन्द्रस्य अयं पौरन्दरः. दिवाकर० was covered with a red robe and looked like the eastern quarter arrayed in the mellow light of morn. उल्लिखितः (polished, wrought) पद्मरागः तस्य प्रभा प्रतिमा यस्याः (*adj.* of देहप्रभया). रक्तावदातया red and bright (pure). The quarters were reddened by the glow of his body. The poet fancies that he taught the quarters to assume the red robes (peculiar to Buddhist monks). अनौद्धत्यम् freedom from insolence, modesty. मन्द...कारेण that resembled a night lotus slightly closed. The कुमुद is white; his eye was white. मन्द...मुदस्येव आकारः यस्य. जनेन क्षुण्णाः (trampled upon) क्षुद्रजन्तवः तेषां जीवनार्थम्. अमृत is स्निग्ध (glossy), धवल and प्रसन्न (transparent); while his eye was affectionate (स्निग्ध), धवल and प्रसन्न (quiet, unruffled). सर्व...मितम्—the idea is that he knew all the S'āstras. From परमाणुs the whole material world is produced. See above p. 12. परमसौगतः a very aealous or devout follower of Buddha. अवलोकितः ईश्वरः येन who saw (*i. e.* recognised) an ईश्वर. The Buddhists do not recognise an intelligent Supreme Ruler of the Universe. This contradiction is got over by taking अव० in another sense. अव० is a बोधिसत्त्व worshipped by the northern Buddhists. अस्ख...लग्नम् though he never faltered (in the path of धर्म), yet he clung to austerities. One who falters has to cling to something for support. आलोकः light. यथा...प्रकाशकम् he explained the proper worth of each thing; light shows objects as they are. दर्शनार्थिनाम् (1) those who want to see; (2) those who desire to have correct knowledge. सुगतस्य=बुद्धस्य. अभि...नीयम् fit to be approached. प्र...नीयमिव whose grace was to be prayed for even by Favour. आत्मनो...णीयम् who was to be longed for even by the Soul. जन्म जपस्य the source of जप (inaudible prayers). जन्म यमस्य would mean 'the source of यम.' यम is the first of the eight *Angas* of योग. 'अहिंसासत्यास्तेयब्रह्मचर्यापरिग्रहाः यमाः' योगसूत्र II. 30. नेमिं नियमस्य the circumference (*i. e.* the utmost limit or reach) of religious observances. नियम may also mean the seconed *Anga* of Yoga. 'शौच—सन्तोष—तपः—स्वाध्याय—ईश्वरप्रणिधानानि नियमाः' योगसूत्र II. 32. तत्त्वं essence. कोशं कुशलस्य the treasure of bliss or auspiciousness. सर्व...तायाः the all-in-all of good conduct. दाक्ष्यं दाक्षिण्यस्य the civility of courteousness *i. e.* the perfection of courteousness. पारं...याः the highest limit of compassion for others. निर्वृतिं सुखस्य—Happiness itself would find pleasure in him. ०गम्भीराकारेण आरोपितः बहुमानः यस्मिन् in whom high regard (for दिवा०) was produced by his &c. शिरसा...ववन्दे he uttered words of salutation and also bent his head.

P. 128 l. 33—**P. 129** l. 16 दिवाकर...विशत्. महानु...भाजा possessing the magnificence belonging to noble persons. This qualifies ०विशेषेण. अप्राकृतेन not belonging to common men. ०प्रकाशकेन goes with प्रश्रयेण. प्रश्रयेण=विनयेन. चक्षुषि...ग्रहीत् he took him (*i. e.* greeted him) by his eye and heart. We may also connect आह्लादितः with चक्षुषि and चेतसि. सम्पादितं ससम्भ्रमं अभ्युत्थानं येन who (दिवाकर०) rose up hurriedly (to receive हर्ष). सङ्कलय्य having held together. उद्ग...लोलं disordered by his rising up. उत्क्षिप्य having raised up (his hand). महा...प्रशस्तं हस्तं—see for these बृह० 67. 44–48, one of which is quoted on p. 20 above. गुरु...मानः highly thinking of हर्ष that had come as a guest, as if he were his *guru*. स्वेन आसनेन—this is the highest mark of respect that can be shown to a guest.

आध्वम् (*Imperative 2nd plural* of आस् to sit). अलोह...जातानाम् goodness is in the case of the noble a fetter for tying fast, though not made of iron. स्थाने it is quite proper. दर्शनमेव पुण्यं तेन अनुगृहीतस्य—the idea is:—your very sight adds to the store of my merit (पुण्य) and that is a great favour in itself. पुनरुक्तः superfluous. अनुग्रहः the favour (*viz.* hospitable treatment by आसनदान and पादोदक &c.). चक्षुः प्रमाणं यस्य सः °माणः प्रसादः तेन स्वीकृतस्य (मम)—I was accepted by you as your own by bestowing on me a favour whose standard is the eye *i. e.* your very eye showed me the greatest favour possible. पर...चेष्टितम् the acts of civility (उपचारः), such as offering a seat &c., make me a stranger *i. e.* these civilities are to be shown to strangers only. अति...पुरः in your presence to have the bare ground as a seat is the highest pitch (of honour). There is another meaning also 'to sit even on bare ground in the presence of a person like you is an impropriety (a violation of proper limits).' Read °वृत्ति and take away the vertical line after it. सम्भाषणमेव अमृतं तेन अभिषेकः तेन क्षालितं सकलं वपुः यस्य. प्रदेशे वृत्तिः यस्य. The idea is:—when my *whole* body has bathed in the nectar of speech with you, water for the feet, that will only wash a part (प्रदेश) of my body, is useless (अपार्थक). 'पाद्यं पादाय वारिणि' अम°. If we read अतिभूमिरेव भवादृशां...वृत्तिः the meaning will be 'when my *whole* body has been bathed &c., then my remaining here in a particular spot before you will be the height of impropriety.' This is not very happy.

P. 129 l. 17—**P. 130** l. 13 अलङ्कारो...भाव्यते इति. अल...शयः great politeness (प्रश्रयः) is really the true ornament of the powerful (and not jewels &c., which are mere stones). प्रभवत् one who rules, powerful. न प्रत्य...वचनम् when the king did not accede to the words (of the sage). °निहितं °युगलमेव निगडः (fetters) तेन निश्चलीकृतं हृदयं यस्य. कालकलाम् a portion of time. 'पापं किल्बिषकल्मषम्' अम°. मूल...वनम्—the idea is:—he subsisted on fruits and roots only; consequently his breath was fragrant. When he opened his lips, he as if sent forth (in the form of his breath) a bower of creepers fragrant with white flowers. His white teeth were like flowers. अभ्यवहारः (food, eating) तस्मात् सम्भवः यस्य (*adj.* of °वनम्). अद्य...संसारः—from this day this संसार (worldly life) is not only not to be blamed, but has become fit to be saluted (praised). प्रकाशितं सत्सारं येन that has manifested its excellent essence. संसार is often spoken of as

असार, but now it is सत्सार (सत् being opposed to असत् represented by अ in असार). Or प्रकाशितः सत्सु सारः श्रेष्ठः (हर्षः) यस्मिन्. 'सारो बले स्थिरांशे च न्याय्ये क्लीबं वरे त्रिषु' अम०. किं...द्भुतं what wonders may not living beings see? The meaning is:—your splendid form is the greatest wonder in this world. That being seen, a living person may be blessed to see many wonders, that are less marvellous. अचिन्ति...तम् presented unexpectedly. जन्मान्तरेषु अवस्थितानि सुकृतानि. दत्तमेव goes with फलम्. दर्शयता goes with तपःक्लेशेन. देवानां प्रियम् beloved of the gods. Bāṇa uses the word in the same way as As'oka does in his edicts. As'oka calls himself देवानां प्रिय. The महाभाष्य uses it in a good sense 'के पुनर्भवदादयः । भवान् दीर्घायुः देवानां प्रियः आयुष्मानिति' on पा. V. 3. 14 (Kielhorn vol. II p. 405). But later Sanskrit grammarians assign the meaning of 'fool' to this word. जातं...सुखस्य my mind has no longing for the happiness of final emancipation. We must read निर्वृति० with C. निवृत्ति० also may be made to yield (though rather in a far-fetched way) the same sense. निवृत्ति cessation of the round of births and deaths). But the com. says 'निवृत्तिश्चित्तविभ्रमः.' ०जीवितजनकम् who gives life *i. e.* who protects and supports. पुण्य...णामः blessed even are those merits, of which thou art the fruit (the fulfilment). Compare the words of प्रभाकरवर्धन 'फलमस्यनेक... अकलुषस्य कर्मणः' (text p. 24). सुकृतं तपः यैः. परिगृहीताः सर्वावयवाः यैः. ये...वाः that constitute all your limbs. भव्यः...यः fortunate is manliness in that it has resorted to you. यत्सत्यं to say the truth. पुण्यभाजं = हर्षम्. पुनः...जन्मनि Once more faith in human birth has been generated in me. He means:—up till now I had looked upon human birth as an unmixed evil, a thing to fly from; but now I think it has some inherent good in it. नेच्छद्भिः—I don't desire to see the working of Cupid; but in your person I have seen Kāma (*i. e.* you are as handsome as काम). अमृत...कार्यमेव—the idea is:—that your words are so sweet is natural; you are yourself full of अमृत and so your words (the effect) must possess the quality (माधुर्य) of the cause (you). Compare वैशेषिकसूत्र II. 1. 24 'कारणगुणपूर्वकः कार्यगुणो दृष्टः.' There is a well-known न्याय (maxim) 'कारणगुणा हि कार्यगुणानारभन्ते'. उपाध्या...यामि even though I reflect deeply I cannot fancy who your teacher could have been (in this humility). गुणग्रामः—there is a suggested idea. A village also may become शून्य (tenantless) when nobody has a long life. वंशे family; bamboo. It was supposed that pearls were found in bamboos. See above p. 193.

27

मुक्तः आमयः येन free from disease or hurt. पारिप्लवं restless. 'चञ्चलं तरलं चैव पारिप्लवपरिप्लवे' अम०. के वयम्—who are we to offer (fruits and roots that we share in common with all the foresters)? The idea is:—there is nothing in this forest that I can call my own; fruits and roots belong to the foresters as well as to me. So I cannot offer them to you as something special. अपरो...साकम् this wretched body, that was never made useful to others, belongs to us. कलि is the age of sin; so कायकलि means 'sinful body'. C and T strangely enough translate 'But this wretched body of ours is only for another's service.' सर्वे...ध्याय all that has been left to us is for the welcome of our friend (इष्ट). He says:—All that I can call my own is my wretched body, but that was never made useful to anybody. But that is all that is left to me and I shall use it for welcoming you my friend. स्वायत्ताः...कतिचित्—he means:—besides my body, I possess a few drops of learning that are completely at my disposal. उप...यति but my affection for you does not stop to consider whether they (विद्याबिन्दवः) will be of any use to you. In my affection for you I place my learning at your disposal, whether useful to you or not does not matter. C and T translate 'our friendship cannot hesitate how to make use of them.' This is not correct. Read कच्चित् for कश्चित्. यदि...लवम् He says that he would not press him to tell, if thereby he was likely to hinder even the smallest business of his (हर्ष's). अरक्षणीयानि अक्षराणि यस्य (*adj.* of कथनीयम्) the words of which are not to be kept secret. कियान् अवधिः यस्य. Separate वा अयम्. सन्तप्तरूपेव विभाव्यते is seen to be as if afflicted.

P. 130 ll. 14—P. 131 l. 6 राजा तु...कीदृशीति. दर्शितः संभ्रमः यस्मिन् (*adj.* of वचसा) that shows the flurry (of your mind due to my arrival). हृदय...करम् that supports (*i. e.* encourages, gladdens) the heart. अभ्यर्हितम्=पूज्यम्. अनु...यमपि though I do not deserve to be treated with respect. विनष्टाः निखिलाः इष्टबन्धवः यस्य. जीवि...बन्धनम् the sole tie that keeps up my life. निबन्धनम् tie, suport. अनुबन्धः continuity. He means that he continues to live because of her. विन्ध्यवनम्—is the object of अविशत्. The student will notice that all the letters from ०वन...to ०शत् are short. ०बहुलम् abounding in &c. ०कुलैः कलिलम् full of 'कलिलं गहनं समे' अम०. ०शरभेभ्यः भयं यस्मिन्. For शरभ, see p. 66. ०महिषैः मुषितं पथिकगमनं यस्मिन् where the journeys of travellers are hindered by huge buffaloes. शर reed. कुश a kind of grass. अवटः

pit. तस्याः वार्ता तद्वार्ता. अभाजनं...भवताम् we are not fit (destined) to make such presents (उपायनं) of glad tidings to you. शमि... मानः of an age when passions are restrained. जाता करुणा यस्य. प्रक्षरितं चक्षुः यस्य whose eye was full of tears. मह...वर्तते there is a very pitiable occurrence. व्यसनं misfortune. पूर्वं भूता भूतपूर्वा. भूत...रूपा who seems to have seen prosperity in former days. सम्भा...भगवान् honour her before her life leaves her. अप्रोषिताः प्राणाः यस्याः. अभ्यु...श्वासनैः favour her with suitable comforting words. अनुपरतपूर्वं कृमि...मपि आर्यस्य गोचरगतम् even insects when once within your sight have never died before. जाता अनुजायाः आशङ्का यस्य who suspected that she was his sister. अन्तर्द्रुतः इव as if melting inside. For दोदूयमान, see p 42. गद्गदिकया गृहीतः कण्ठः यस्य whose throat was choked up. विकला वाक् यस्य whose accents were broken. जीवे...वन्तम् would she be still alive? आकारतो कीदृशी what sort of woman is she in appearance?

P. 131 l. 7—**P. 133** l. 26 **तथा...निवेदितवानिति.** रोधसा by the bank. यदृच्छया by chance. हिम...कातराणां frightened by the lotus beds withering through frost. रसितं humming. He compares the weeping of females to the hum of bees and the tones of lutes. सार्यमाण being touched gently with the fingers. अति...वर्तिनीनाम्—that were tuned to a high protracted tone. वीणातन्त्रीणाम् of the strings of lutes. एकः तानः यस्मिन् in which the note was one (and not complex). तान is defined in the सङ्गीतरत्नाकर I. 4. 27 as 'तानाः स्युर्मूर्च्छनाः शुद्धाः षाडवौडवितीकृताः॥'. तान is a mode of मूर्छना, for which see above p. 206. With रुदितं, एकतानं means 'incessant.' अधृतिकरम् that caused loss of firmness *i. e.* that agitated me. The principal sentence is दृष्टवान् असि च...अबलानां चक्रवालेन परिवृताम् (l. 25)...योषितम् (p. 77. l. 22). दृष...लोहितेन—this and the following instrumentals qualify चक्रवालेन below. दृषत्खण्डैः खण्डिताः अङ्गुलयः ताभ्यः गलत् लोहितं यासाम् from whose toes shattered by pieces of stones blood was oozing. पार्ष्णिषु प्रविष्टानि शरशलाकाशल्यानि तैः शूलः तेन सङ्कोचितानि चक्षूंषि येषाम् whose eyes became contracted by the sharp pain of the points of the long *S'ara* grass that entered their heels (पार्ष्णि *m.*). अध्वनीनेन श्रमेण श्वयथुः तेन निश्चलौ चरणौ यस्य whose feet could not move owing to the swelling caused by the fatigue of the journey: अध्वनीन from अध्वन्. स्थाणवैः व्रणैः व्यथिताः गुल्फाः (ankles) तेषु बद्धा भूर्जत्वक् येन. स्थाणव due to stakes or posts (from स्थाणु). वातेन (inflammation) खुडानां (ankle-joints) खेदः (pain) तेन खञ्जा जङ्घा (leg) तया जातः ज्वरः यस्य. 'वातखुडो गतिप्रतिघातलक्षणो

वातव्याधिः' com. Or we may take वातखुड as the name of a disease like rheumatism or gout. The अष्टाङ्गहृदय describes the disease called खुड or वातशोणित as follows:—'प्रायेण सुकुमाराणामचङ्क्रमणशीलिनाम् । अभिघातादशुद्धेश्च नृणामसृजि दूषिते ॥...आढ्यरोगं खुडं वातबलासं वातशोणितम् । तदाहुर्नामभिस्तच्च पूर्वं पादौ प्रधावति ॥ विशेषाद्यानयानाद्यैः प्रलम्बौ तस्य लक्षणम् ॥' III. 16. 2, 4–5. पिण्डिका calf of the leg. ०जटया (by the twisted fibres of date-palms) जर्जरितं जानु यस्य. शतावर्या विदारितः ऊरुः यस्य. शतावरी is a plant otherwise called नारायणी. विदार्या दारितः (torn) तनुदुकूलपल्लवः यस्य. विदारी is a plant called in Marathi भुईकोहळा. उत्कटाः (prominent) वंशविटपानां कण्टकाः तेषां कोटिभिः पाटितं कञ्चुककर्पटं (bodice-cloth) यस्य. फलक्षोभेन आलम्बितानि (held) आनम्राणि ०जालकानि उद्गताः कण्टकाः येषाम् (*adj.* of ०जालकैः). उल्लिखितं (scratched) सुकुमारं करोदरं यस्य. कदर्थिताः (teased, pained) बाहवः यस्य. With the pointed horns of deer they dug up roots &c. for their food and their arms were wearied by the exertions. For कदर्थित, see p. 101. ताम्बूलविरहेण (absence of betel) विरसं (dry) मुखं तेन खण्डितं कोमलं आमलकीफलं येन. Everyone knows how welcome an आमलक fruit is in one's childhood, when one is thirsty. कुशकुसुमानां आहत्या लोहितानां. The flowers of कुश grass struck their eyes, which became red and swollen. श्वयताम्—*gen. sing.* of *present p.* of श्वि 1 P. to swell. लेपीकृता मनःशिला येन. They applied red arsenic (Marathi मनशीळ) to their swollen eyes. The अष्टाङ्गसंग्रह (उत्तरस्थान chap. 16) prescribes red assenic for swollen eyes 'दाहोपदेहरागाश्रुशोफशान्त्यै विडालकम् । कुर्यात्सर्वत्र पत्रैलामरिचस्वर्णगैरिकैः ॥ 2...मनोह्वाफलिनीक्षौद्रैः कफे सर्वैस्तु सर्वजे ॥ 3.' कण्टकिनीभिः लताभिः लूनः अलकलेशः (small curls) यस्य. किसलयैः उपपादितं आतपत्रकृत्यं यस्य to whom tender foliage served as an umbrella (against the sun). ०पुटे गृहीतं अम्भः येन. पाथेयीकृता मृणालपूलिका येन that made a bundle of the fibrous roots of lotuses their provisions (in their wanderings). For पाथेय, see p. 212. ०शिक्ये निहिता नारिकेलकोशस्य कलशी तस्यां कलितं रसालतैलं येन that placed mango oil in a cup made of the outer (hard) covering of cocoanut fruit placed in a loop (शिक्यं) made of the hems (दशा) of their China-made garments. There is another reading ०सरलतैलेन (the oil of pine). कतिपयावशेषाः ०वर्बराः तैः अविरलेन full of deafmutes, hunch-backed persons, dwarfs, deaf men and barbarians, that were helpless through grief and of whom only a few remained. We must read कलमूक (for कलामूक) for which see p. 99. These are usually described as the attendants and guardians of the ladies of the harem. बर्बरः a low person, one not an Aryan. The com. says 'कलामूकाः पण्डकाः । एवमादयोऽन्तःपुररक्षिणः बर्बरा एतद्देशजाः'. So it takes कलामूक in the sense of 'eunuch.' आप...लावण्येन—her grace which covered every thing by its brilliance did not leave her even in misfortune. A person born of a noble family does not forsake his master or friend even in adversity. प्रति...कायाम्—the tender (and therefore reddish) shoots of creepers were reflected in her bright complexion. The poet fancies that her body was reddened by the bloody wounds of sorrow (and not by red shoots). सरसैः (किसलयैः) means 'juicy.' Read पाटली° for पटली°. °ङ्कुरेण क्षतं तस्मात् क्षरतीति तेन °क्षारिणा. Her feet were red with blood from wounds caused by sharp दर्भ grass. The poet fancies that it was Alaktaka dye which ladies usually applied to their feet. In the forest they had no अलक्तक; but blood took its place. अनुसरणं habit. कृता छाया यस्य that was shaded. विगता छाया यस्य that had lost its lustre. There is a pun on छाया. आका...शयानाम् that surpassed even आकाश in शून्यता (being vacant-minded, being a void). For आकाश and शून्यता, see above (text p. 2 ll. 1-2). निश्चेतनतया she was fainting; earth has no intelligence (चैतन्य) in it (it is जड). मरु...म्पदा she heaved so many sighs that she seemed to be all sighs (*i. e.* wind). Explain the following clauses similary. सन्तापः heat; grief. निर...तया—she had no support (*i. e.* she had nothing that could keep up her drooping spirits); आकाश is also without support; it rests on nothing. पारिप्लवतया—she was trembling (through grief); lightning flashes are tremulous. मुक्तानि मुक्ताः (pearls) अंशुकं (fine silken robes) रत्नानि कुसुमानि कनकं पत्राभरणानि (paintings on cheeks &c.) यया (with योषितम्). She had no ornaments &c. on her person, as she had escaped from imprisonment and she was in grief. The com. takes मुक्तांशुक as one word 'मुक्ताख्यमंशुकं मालवदेशजमुत्तरीयम्'. The कल्पलता is a mythical plant that was supposed to yield what was desired by its votary. It may also drop down मुक्ता, अंशुक &c. In this case we must take पत्रं as equal to वाहनं (vehicles) and take आभरणं (ornaments) by itself. महावने—the woman was in a great forest; कल्पवृक्ष is in the great garden of Indra. The com. takes वन in the sense of जल. Then we may explain that पारिजात, which is one of the कल्पवृक्षs, was produced from the sea (महावन) at the time of the churning. परमेश्वरस्य (शिवस्य) उत्तमाङ्गे

पातेन दुर्ललितं अङ्गं यस्याः (with गङ्गाम्) who is insolent by falling &c.; परमेश्वरस्य (of the great king ग्रहवर्मा, her husband) उत्तमाङ्गपातः तेन दुर्ललितानि अङ्गानि यस्याः (with योषितम्) whose limbs were wayward by the fall of the head of &c. गां गताम्—the Ganges came down to the earth from the matted hair of शिव; the woman was lying on the earth (through grief) or walking on the earth (as she had no vehicle). भगीरथ brought the Ganges from Heaven, which fell on the head of शिव and which thought that by its force it would crush शिव. 'विशाम्यहं हि पातालं स्रोतसा गृह्य शङ्करम्' रामायण बाल० 43. 6. ०पादपल्लवाम्—her feet (पाद) were grey with pollen; the rays of the moon also were grey. Remove the comma after पल्लवाम्. लोकान्तर०—she wished that death might take her away to her deceased husband; the moon also goes to another sphere in the morning. निजजलमोक्षेण कदर्थिता दर्शिता धवलायतयोर्नेत्रयोः शोभा यया her long and white eyes were wearied by shedding tears and became dim. If the water of the Ganges goes very low, then the lotus bed will show its long and white roots (नेत्र). For नेत्र, see pp. 37, 53. Remove the comma after शोभाम्. निमीलिताम् she was languid by the fierce heat of the sun; a कुमुदिनी closes its petals in the sun. दग्ध...दिताम् the woman was disappointed at her wretched state (दशा); the flame of the lamp at dawn is made to fail by the wick (दशा) being burnt. पाण्डु वपुः यस्याः her body was pale; the flame also becomes dimmer and dimmer. पार्श्ववर्तिनां वारणे अभियोगः तेन रक्ष्यमाणां who was saved by the perseverance of her attendants in dissuading her. पार्श्ववर्ती वारणः तस्य अभियोगात् रक्ष्यमाणां being saved from the attack of an elephant near her (with करिणीम्). महा...स्नाम् the woman had bathed in a lake before she burnt herself in grief; the करिणी plunged in a deep lake. प्रविष्टां ध्याने she was in deep thought. स्थितां मरणे she was resolved on dying. दूरीकृताम् separated from. वि...षा she was exhausted by wandering and was empty of life (as she had resolved on dying). आकुलाम्०— her hair was dishevelled; she was absorbed in finding the means of dying. धृत... मौनेन च she had placed her hand on her mouth (in deep thought) and her lips were also silent. मन्युना = शोकेन. भ्रष्ट... लासैश्च—here and with the following instrumentals we have to supply the word उपलक्षिताम्. भ्रष्ट...लासैश्च with her kindred and graceful gestures all gone. मुक्तेन...त्मना her ears were bereft (of ornaments) and her spirit was drooping. आरम्भः effort, undertaking. भग्नैः वलयैः—because she was a widow. चरण०—her attendants fell at her feet to dissuade her from dying; and points of grass pierced her feet. हृदय—her eye was downcast; she had enshrined in her heart her husband. दीर्घैः केशैः her hair was loose and not tied into a braid. क्षीणेन...पुण्येन—She was so miserable that it seemed that the whole stock of her merit was exhausted. स्वल्पा०—she had only a few attendants left; she had not long to live. अलसामुन्मेषे she was careless (or lazy) in opening (her eyes). It will be noticed that the auther employs pairs of adjectives that are opposed in sense, such as अलसां and दक्षां, कृशां and स्थूलां, निश्चलां and चलिताम्. विच्छिन्नां आशासु broken in hopes (*i. e.* she had no hope left). रिक्तां सत्त्वेन she was empty of energy or vitality. अध्या...सेन she was full of worry (lit. tenanted by). शून्यां हृदयेन deserted by her heart. आधा...नाम् a receptacle of agonies. अव...नाम् the abode of vicissitudes. अधृतिः want of steadiness. अवसादः langour, fainting. अभियोगः effort. उद्वेगः—she was the highest pitch of despondency. पारं—the other side *i. e.* the highest point of helplessness. उपतापाः sorrows, distress. This is a favourite sentiment with Bāna; compare 'अहो दुर्निवारता व्यसनोपनिपातानां यदीदृशीमप्याकृतिमनभिभवनीयामात्मीयां कुर्वन्ति । सर्वथा न न कंचन स्पृशन्ति शरीरधर्माणमुपतापाः' काद० p. 135. सा अवस्था यस्याः सा तदवस्था. कथं...श्रये how shall I address this noble lady? Compare the end of the पूर्वभाग for a passage in a similar strain 'अतिप्रियोऽसीति पौनरुक्त्यम् &c.' काद० p. 237. वत्से...प्रणयः—He means that he is a perfect stranger and so cannot use the very affectionate mode of address 'वत्से,' which is only appropriate in parents &c. चाटु flattery. She was so young and he was comparatively so aged that there would have been no semblance of truth in calling her 'मातः.' आत्मसम्भावना honouring one's own self. He would be placing himself on an equality with her by calling her a sister. देवि...लापः—Only her attendants can call her 'your Majesty'; I am not one of them. अस्फुटम् not clear, very general (mode of address). उपासिका a lay female votary of बुद्ध as distinguished from a Bhikshunî. An उपासक is one that reveres the रत्नत्रय *viz.* बुद्ध, धर्म and सङ्घ and observes the first five शीलs for which see p. 223. मनोरथः—to call her 'उपासिका,' without knowing whether she is one already, would be only expressing my desire that she should be a follower of बुद्ध. भृत्य...गमः accepting the position of a servant of hers (which I am not). इतर...चितम् suitable to ordinary women

(and not to one so exalted as she seemed to be). अव...प्रियम्—to address her as 'longlived one' would be distasteful to her in her present condition (when she wanted to die). कल्या...रुद्धम्—to address her as 'fortunate one' would be opposed to her present state (when she was a widow). अमुनिमतम्—that mode of address is not approved of by ascetics. बाले...पेतम् to call her a girl would be disrespectful to her. जरारोपणम् attributing old age (which does not exist in her). आर्या is a suitable term for an elderly lady. फलविपरीतम् opposed to the result which she is experiencing. सर्वसाधारणम् common to all ladies (high or low). अनभिजातम् not well-bred, rude. मा...शोभते—as long as the cause of grief is not removed, so long one cannot ask her not to weep. समा...श्रित्य If I were to say 'be comforted', what is that on which she is to rely for consolation? स्वागतम्—these words are addressed to anybody and are very formal. यातयामम्—stale. 'जीर्णं च परिभुक्तं च यातयाममिदं द्वयम्' अम० ('याताः यामाः क्षपांशाः अस्य' क्षीर०). सुख...ते 'are you well or happy?' मिथ्या—because her very surroundings indicate that she is not. स्त्रैण—see p. 35. आर्यायाः इव रूपं यस्याः who had the appearance of a venerable lady. कलि...शारं variegated with partially grey hair. अतिकृपणैः very pathetic. Connect हृदयं with दहन्ती. प्रतिपन्ना (accepted) परदुःखस्य क्षपणं तस्य दीक्षा तस्यां दक्षाः skilful (or assiduous) in their vow taken by them of removing the sorrows of others. सौगताः=बौद्धाः. करुणा...गृहं—a lady is honoured and made much of in her father's house. So is करुणा in the teaching (शासन) of बुद्ध. करुणा and मैत्री are two out of the four *Appamaññas* (अप्पमञ्ञा), the other two being मुदिता and उपेक्षा. सज्जनता जैनी—the saints that follow जिन (*i. e.* बुद्ध). 'समन्तभद्रो भगवान् मारजिल्लोकजिज्जिनः' अम०. पर...मुनीनाम् it is the duty of *munis* to strive to attain the next world. C and T translate 'the religion of the Munis is a means to attain the next world.' This is not correct. The argument is:—प्राणरक्षण is the highest पुण्य, पुण्य leads to परलोक and परलोकसाधन is the धर्म laid down for मुनिs. You, being a मुनि, must therefore save the life of our mistress. विप...भूताः overwhelmed by misfortunes. आर्तं वचः येषाम् those whose words are distressed (*i. e.* convey the distress they are in). सिद्धक्षेत्र is the land of the सिद्धs *i. e.* those that have attained wonderful powers (such as the eight सिद्धिs, अणिमा, लघिमा &c.). The idea is:—those that are distressed will find that good men are their land of promise and that the good will remove their distress. The construction is यत इयं नः स्वामिनी...अग्निं प्रविशति...आर्योऽपि तावत् व्यापारयतु वाणीमस्याम्. पितुः refers to प्रभाकरवर्धन. भर्तुः refers to her husband ग्रहवर्मा. प्रवासेन by the journey (of हर्ष). The reading of B supplies a gap. The text does not refer to her mother nor to राज्यवर्धन. निरवलम्बना without support. नीचाराति refers to the king of Malva who killed ग्रहवर्मा. प्रकृतिमनस्विनी spirited by nature. कदर्थितं सौकुमार्यं यस्याः. उपर्युपरि व्यसनैः by calamities (befalling her) one after another. निवा...जनम् not minding her elders that dissuade her and whom she never disobeyed before even in dream. अख...स्वपि whose requests were not violated even in play. अविद्यमानं शरणं यस्य helpless. यथा...स्याः शोकः from what you say (I gather that) her sorrow is beyond the reach of my words. पुण्यः आशयः (अभिप्रायः) यस्याः whose thoughts are holy. उपरिष्टात् afterwards (after that moment). अभ्यर्थना request. दुःखमेव अन्धकारपटलं तस्य भिदुरैः capable of piercing &c. सौ...दर्शनैः by the sayings of बुद्ध and his own illustrated by examples. स्वकैः सुभाषितैः. दर्शितानि निदर्शनानि येषु. नाना...कौशलैः by his eloquent words weighty with various texts. कुशलं (पुण्यं) शीलं यस्याः. प्रबो...यिष्यति will place her on the path of enlightenment. अशरणानां कृपणानां (distressed) बहुयुवतीनां मरणं यस्मिन्.

P. 133 l. 27—**P. 135** l. 26 अथ...संभ्रमम्. भिक्षोरिदं भैक्षवम् (भाषितम्). निम्नीकृतं मनः यस्य—whose mind was depressed (by sorrow). सर्वैः आकारैः संवदति इति तया. सर्वा...सन्देहः whose doubts were dispelled by the very condition (of that woman) that agreed in all features with (that of his sister). श्रमणः a Buddhist ascetic. निष्कारणवैरिभिः goes with भागधेयैः. यदि...यामः if we can honour her somehow while she is alive *i. e.* if we can reach the place and find her alive. तेन शाक्यपुत्रीयेण refers to the pupil of दिवाकर० who had seen राज्यश्री. प्रदिश्यमानं वर्त्म यस्य. पद्भ्यामेव—connect with प्रावर्तत (started). तं...पिबन्निव as if drinking the distance by his rapid steps. मुमूर्षोः (from the desiderative base of मृ) desirous of dying. Read धारयसि. The root in धरणी is the same as in धारयसि. If the earth is धरणी (supporter), it must support even राज्यश्री. प्रभाकरवर्धन was धरणीनाथ. His daughter therefore is the daughter of the earth. पुष्पभूति was the ancestor of हर्ष. See p. 1 (text, 4th उच्छ्वास). मुखरवंश्य refers to ग्रहवर्मा, husband of राज्यश्री. विवि...धुराम् overwhelmed with various agonies (आधिः). न विबोधयसि why dost thou not enlighten (also why dost thou not bring to consciousness)? भक्त...सुप्तोऽसि thou art asleep when your devotees are suffering torments. पुष्प...पातिन् partial to the house of पुष्प०. राजधर्म was always associated with पुष्पभूति's line. The foremost duty of a king is to protect. The com. says 'राजधर्मो बुद्धः' पतङ्गः the sun. चारित्र is called ungrateful चण्डाल, because it does not help राज्यश्री, though she guarded it jealously. Many women are described as rising superior to all difficulties by their चारित्र (chastity). कि...लक्षणैः what have her auspicious marks settled for her? The idea is:—is this the end that the auspicious marks on her body indicated would be hers? प्रतापशील was an *alias* of प्रभाकरवर्धन (see p. 1 text). निष्ठुरः...भावः the world of the dead is cruel. संवादय declare. नितान्तनिःशूक extremely cruel. श्वपाकः = चण्डालः. सकामोऽसि thou hast secured thy desire. गान्धारि—This (गान्धारी) and the following are the names of the attendants of राज्यश्री, who are making ready to kill themselves along with their mistress. गृही...पाशः this creeper has already been taken by me. The idea is:—take another creeper for using it as a halter to kill yourself. पिशाचि—She is called पिशाची because पिशाचs are supposed to dwell on boughs. हंसि...क्रम् why do you still beat your head? The idea is there will be an end of grief soon. So don't beat your head now. मुक्तगलं = मुक्तकण्ठम्. दूरी...सार्थः your friends are going far off *i. e.* they are all going to a land whence there is no return and where you and they may never meet. शवशिबिरे in this camp of corpses (after the women have killed themselves). शबरिके—this is addressed to some *Bhil* woman of the forest who befriended them. तनूनपाति in fire. त्वमपि— there is a question here and in मातर्मातङ्गिके &c. वत्स्य... नगरे how will you dwell in the city of the dead which is hateful? विरा...सायेन you are illumined (*i. e.* made famous) by your resolve to sacrifice your life in the princess' misfortune. भृगु... भिज्ञे who know your lot *viz.* preparing to fall from a precipice. For भृङ्गार see p. 117. वीजय fan. Separate नमति इन्दीवरिका. देहि... काशम् give me room to go round the fire. कुरबककोरकैः (buds of कु०) आचिताम् (filled with). Remove the line after गृहाण. चामरं... कण्ठे Oh ! chowriebearer ! again hold the chowrie to the neck. This hardly makes any sense. So we must read चरमं for चामरम् the meaning being 'clasp me by the neck for the last time.' मर्ष...हसितानि you must forgive my unchecked laughs due to jests. अग्रामी...गिणि that lovest virtues not found among villagers (*i. e.* noble). अन्तरं room. आपृच्छते bids farewell. नाटक...धारी who managed dramatic performances for you. पश्चिमः last. कतिकृत्वः how many times? निर्माण...शः generally all creation comes to this (*i. e.* all created beings have to suffer these reverses of fortune). धीरयसि किम् why do you comfort (or encourage) me still ? केय...नानाम् what has (my present) condition to do with consolations (*i. e.* I am past all consoling words). कृताः...रोधाः I have disregarded the wooing (of my mind) by my loving friends by falling at my feet. पृष्ठतः कृ— to turn the back towards, leave behind, disregard. ग्रहिणि— you who are persistent (in dissuading me by holding my feet). 'निर्बन्धोपरागार्कादयो ग्रहाः' अम०. महत्तरिका—chamberlain. दृष्टासि I have seen you (*i. e.* I am at least fortunate enough to have seen you when departing this life). कर्मणां विपाकाः the fruit or reward of actions. आर्यचरणानाम्—she probably refers to हर्ष her elder brother. परः...प्रणामः this is my last salutation at the time of departing to the next world. 'हलहलकः उत्कण्ठा' com. It seems to be a Des'ya word. It will be perceived that here there is a change from grief to joy, which suggests the coming of Harsha, according to the common belief of Sanskrit poets expressed in the words 'आवेदयन्ति प्रत्यासन्नमानन्दमग्रजातानि शुभानि निमित्तानि'. उच्चं रोमाञ्चं मुञ्चन्तीति ०मुञ्चि. किमङ्गीकृत्य relying upon what? वामेन—the throbbing of the left eye in the case of women is a good omen. वृथा विरमसि in vain dost thou stop or stay. रम् 1 A when preceded by वि, आ and परि takes the परस्मैपद only. 'व्याङ्परिभ्यो रमः' पा. 1. 3. 82. क्षीरिणि वृक्षे on a milky tree (like the figtree, or उदुम्बर &c.). The crow sitting on milky trees was a good omen. Note 'सुस्निग्धपत्रपल्लवकुसुमफलानम्रसुरभिमधुरेषु। सक्षीराव्रणसुस्थितमनोज्ञवृक्षेषु चार्थकरः॥' बृह० 95. 33; see also 95. 16 and 1. हेषितम् neighing. उत्तरतः to the north. आर्यस्य = हर्षस्य. उपससर्प— supply हर्षः.

P. 135 l. 27—P. 136 l. 25 अथ तेन...भुवमिति. भ्रातुः is to be connected with हस्तसंस्पर्शेन (l. 31). प्रकोष्ठ...क्षरता (the touch of his hand) that as if dropped a flood of juice capable of restoring life from the herbs tied on his forearm. हर्ष had on his forearm some herbs by way of amulets. His touch revived राज्यश्री; the poet fancies that it was the juice of those herbs that revived her. वमते...भावम् (touch) that as if emitted the inconceivable power of the jewels in his bracelet. It was believed that various drugs and jewels had mysterious powers; compare 'लौकिकानामपि मणिमन्त्रौषधिप्रभृतीनां देशकालनिमित्तवैचित्र्यवशाच्छक्तयो विरुद्धानेककार्यविषया दृश्यन्ते।' शाङ्करभाष्य on वेदान्तसूत्र II. 1. 27. 'आवापकः पारिहार्यः कटको वलयोऽस्त्रियाम्' अम०. अमृत...द्विरदा—his bright nails resembled the moon's rays, which shower nectar (*i. e.* a sensation of coolness and pleasure). चन्द्रोदयेन च्युतः शिशिरः शीकरः यस्मात्. समुन्मिमील opened her eyes. असम्भावितं आगमनं यस्य whose arrival was not thought to be possible. स्वप्ने दृष्टं दर्शनं यस्य. तत्काले (हर्षस्य) आविर्भावः तेन निर्भरः तेन which was full on account of his sudden appearance. अभिभूतः सर्वात्मा येन. Connect ०सम्भारेण with उत्सृजन्ती०वारि. स्थूलः प्रवाहः यस्य (*adj.* of ०वारि). नदी...वारि—she shed such floods of tears from her two eyes that there seemed to be two river channels (प्रणालः) at their mouth let loose. A river at its mouth is very full. ०मन्युना goes with भ्राता. समुद्भूतः भगिनीस्नेहसद्भावः तस्य भारः तेन भावितः मन्युः यस्य whose sorrow became manifested by the great feeling of affection for his sister that swept over him. करेण स्थगितं (covered) मुखं यस्याः. अग्रजः elder brother. विश्रम्य...तव्यम् stop and then weep again (after some time). चिरसम्भावितः अनेकदुःखनिवहः तस्य निर्वहणं तेन बाष्पोत्पीडः तेन पीड्यमानः कण्ठभागः यस्याः whose throat was choked by a flood of tears due to the completion (निर्वहणं) of the numerous griefs that she had suffered for a long time. काहलेन resembing that of a drum (काहलं). आक्षिप्य being led away. तथा in that way *i. e.* by the incidents that had happened. मुहूर्तं...वाह्य having allowed some time to pass. नि...नीतं brought by his pupil who was informed by a secret sign. चिरप्रवृत्तं अश्रुजलजालं यस्मिन्. Her eyes red with weeping resembled a red lotus. If we read जातं for जालं then the meaning is 'her eye red with weeping was like a red lotus sprung from the water of her long continued flow of tears.' पुनरानीतं नेत्राम्भः यस्याः. पति...म्भसि whose eyes again filled with tears by the shock of hearing that he was familiar with her husband. उद्घातः allusion; blow. प्रयत्नेन रक्षितः आगत...सम्भारः तेन भज्यमानं धैर्यं तेन आर्द्रे लोचने यस्य whose eyes moistened because his serenity was broken by the flood of rising tears that he checked with effort. परावृत्त turned aside. कल्याणराशे—this is addressed to हर्ष.

P. 136 l. 26—**P. 137** l. 27 अथ भूपति...मन्दाकिनीम्. अनु...चारम् obeying the observances of the world. तस्यां=भूमौ. आहितं अवधानं येन attentively. परवती शुचा beside herself through grief. पतिपिण्डे प्रदर्शितः प्रयत्नः तेन प्रतिपन्नं अभ्यवहारकरणं यया who consented to take food when Harsha had made efforts to offer oblations to her deceased husband *i. e.* she ate when she saw that Pindas had been offered to her husband. बन्धनात् प्रभृति—she had been imprisoned in Kanoj by the king of Malva that killed her husband (text p. 41). विस्तरतः—connect with सर्वमश्रृणोत्. °सम्भ्रमं—is governed by अश्रृणोत्. गौडसंभ्रमम् the tumult of the Gauda king. What this was is not clear. The order in which the events are arranged here shows that the गौड king caused some tumult in Kanoj before राज्यवर्धन was treacherously murdered by him. But we know that the king of Malva took कान्यकुब्ज by killing ग्रहवर्मा. If we read संभ्रमगुप्तितः, the sense is not much improved. But if we read °सम्भ्रमे, then the meaning is:—'he heard how his sister was sent away from Kanoj out of her prison by a noble named गुप्त at the time of the tumult caused by the गौड king.' With this reading it is easy to say that the tumult refers to the treachery of the Gauḍa king against राज्यवर्धन whose death राज्यश्री naturally heard after escaping from imprisonment. निराकरणम् despising, giving up. पराहता struck down, faint. उपक्रमणं undertaking, commencement. यावत् up to. विविक्तभुवि in a lonely spot. लेशतः little by little. अयं refers to ताराराजः (the moon). परिभूय... भार्याः—the moon has 27 wives, the नक्षत्रs. यौ...तारेण तरलतराः very brilliant by the advent of youth (*adj.* of भार्याः). रजनी... पूरः the ear-ornament of night. पुरुहूतः इन्द्रः तस्मै पुराधाः (family priest) तस्य. धिषणस्य—'बृहस्पतिः सुराचार्यो गीष्पतिर्धिषणो गुरुः' अम०. पुरन्ध्री matron. पत्नीयन्—पत्नीं आत्मनः इच्छन्—Wishing to make her his wife. पत्नीयति is a denominative verb from पत्नी, according to 'सुप आत्मनः क्यच्' पा. 3. 1. 8. अतितरलः extremely fickle. तारा—for her seduction by the moon, see p. 60. चकितचकोरस्य इव लोचने यस्याः. अतिकामया whose love for him was excessive. सर्वाकारैः अभिरामया charming in every gesture. सर्व...गौरवात् out of respect for the words of all the gods. अविद्यमानानि इन्धनानि यथा स्युः (अव्ययी०). वरारोहा a beautiful woman (वरः आरोहः यस्याः). 'श्रोण्यामप्यारोहो वरस्त्रियाः' अम०. शै...मानः rising from the mountain in the east. 'अस्तस्तु चरमक्ष्माभृदुदयः पूर्वपर्वतः।' अम०. We often have the word उदयशैल as in 'उदयशैलो मित्रमण्डलस्य' काद०. वारुणालयस्य—सागरस्य. सस्मरः=समदनः. स्मेरं गण्डस्थलं यस्य the cheek of which was dimpled with a smile. Sanskrit poets compare the cheeks of beautiful women with the moon. Compare मृच्छकटिक I. 57. 'उदयति हि शशाङ्कः कामिनीगण्डपाण्डुः.' ससार मुखस्य—the genitive is used in accordance with the सूत्र 'अधीगर्थदयेशां कर्मणि' explained above. स्वःस्थोऽप्यस्वस्थः—स्वःस्थ means 'being in the heavens' and स्वस्थ which resembles स्वःस्थ in sound means 'at ease'. 'स्वरव्ययं स्वर्गनाक &c.' अम०. स्ववीयसः qualifies ०बिन्दून्. पीतः ०प्रवाहः तेन धवला तारा (pupil) यस्य. आचेमुः मुक्ताशुक्तयः pearl oysters drank them. विषमुचाम् = सर्पाणाम्. तैः मुक्ताफलैः—तारागण is seen in the sky and not in पाताल. But the pearls were like stars and being taken to पाताल made the latter look like the sky. एकावली a necklace with a single string of pearls. The moon is said to be the lord of plants also. 'ओषधीशो निशापतिः' अम०. हिममेव अमृतं तस्मात्सम्भवः यस्याः सा ०सम्भवा तस्याः भावः ०वत्वं. Or we may dissolve as 'हिमं च अमृतं च ताभ्यां &c'. The moon is cool and has also nectar in it. पर्यधत्त wore. नागार्जुनो नाम भिक्षुः—नागार्जुन is a famous name among the Buddhists. The राजतरङ्गिणी (I. 172–173) refers to him as a king that lived 150 years after Buddha. In the बृहत्कथामञ्जरी (XIV. 392–407) he is represented as an adept in रसायनविद्या and as the minister of a king called चिरायु. The कथासरित्सागर tells us that he was a बोधिसत्त्व. त्रिसमुद्राधिपतये—*i. e.* the lord of the Deccan, the peninsula of India, with seas to the east, south and west. C and T think that सातवाहन ruled over जम्बुद्वीप, प्लक्षद्वीप and शाल्मलिद्वीप. But that is not correct. The kings of the Deccan were represented as lords of the three oceans, while universal kings were represented to be lords of the four oceans. Compare 'चतुरम्भोधिभोगभृति०' (text p. 60 l. 16 above) and the words 'देवस्य चतुःसमुद्राधिपतेः...हर्षस्य' in the 2nd उच्छ्वास; and the words 'तिसमुदतोयपीतवाहनस' applied to king 'सातकणि' (शातकर्णि) in the Nasik Inscription (No. 2); vide Bombay Gazetteer vol. 16 p. 550. King सातकणि is there styled 'सातवाहनकुलयसपतिठापनकरस.' सातवाहन is the name of a family of kings of whom many were named शातकर्णि. यद्यपि...चारः although entertaining persons like you by gifts seems to be an insult. ओषधिबुद्ध्या looking upon it as a medicine. सर्व...प्रवृत्तेन who has set about to protect all beings. रक्षणीयं शरीरं यस्य. विष...क्षया with the object of protection against poison. अभ्याशे समीपे वर्तते इति ०वर्ती तस्य.

P. 137 l. 28—**P. 138** l. 25 उन्मुच्य...कर्तव्यानामिति. उन्मुच्यमानायाः while it was being untied. लब्धः अवकाशः येन that found their opportunity (of illuminating the world). विशदं (brilliant) महः (तेजः) यस्य. युगपत्—all the quarters were simultaneously rendered bright. मुकुलि...तरुभिः the trees as if blossomed forth from their very roots, longing for their budding brides—the creepers. The idea is that the splendour of the एकावली was the same that would be seen if trees blossomed forth even from their roots. In this and the following clauses the author tries to convey the effect of the whiteness and brilliance produced by the unveiling of the bright necklace of pearls. अभि...यूथैः—As the rays of the एकावली spread all round, it seemed as if हंसs (that have white wings) were flying for lotus fibres. भर—by the very weight of the केतकी flowers, the pollen was scattered about. गर्भभेदेन सूचितः सूचीसञ्चयः तेन शुचिभिः bright with the numerous pointed leaves made manifest by the opening of the inside (of the bud, that was at one time closed). The केतकी flower is pale-white and bright. We should read उद्दलित for उद्गलित. उद्...दिनीभिः the night lotuses seemed to wake up, bristling with their opening petals. 'दन्तुरस्तून्नतरदे तथोन्नतनते त्रिषु' मे०. There is a suggestion. The petals of (white) कुमुदs resemble the teeth. When a handsome woman gets up from sleep and yawns, her gleaming teeth are seen. सितदशनानां अंशवः तेषां माला तस्याः आलोकेन लिप्यमानं वनं यथा स्यात् तथा. प्रहसितमिव—smiles and laughs are white. The teeth of वनदेवताs would send forth rays. काश flowers are white. शिथिलितः कुसुमकोशः तस्य केसराणां अट्टहासेन निरङ्कुशं यथा स्यात्तथा they bloomed forth smiling without restraint with the filaments of their loosened buds. चमरी deer have white tails. बालाः (hair) पल्लव इव तस्य परिवेशेन (circle) श्वेतायमानैः. स्फायमानाः (swelling) फेनिलाः (foamy) तरलतराः तरङ्गाः (ripples) तान् उद्गिरति इति ०द्गारी तेन. Foam is white. The light of the full moon resembled the light of the एकावली and the pearls resembled stars (which pearls are fancied to be अपरतारागण). ०चक्रेण आक्रान्ताः ककुभः येन. दावानलधूलिना धूसरितः दिगन्तः येन. The idea is:—the quarters were obscured by the ashes of the forest fires; but if water were poured over, then the bright day would shine forth. The एकावली was like the fair faces of the women (राजश्री and her attendants) that were washed after being tear-bedewed. मांसलैः thick. आकुली...चक्षुः again and again opening and closing his eye that was overpowered by the rays &c. सर्वा...रणीं filling all the quarters (with संहतिम्); fulfilling all desires (with एकावलीम्). पङ्क्ती...हतिम्—the row of pearls resembled the spray from the trunks of दिग्गजs, when it is collected in a row (पङ्क्ति). घनमुक्ताम् (घनाः मुक्ताः यस्याम्) having pearls thickly arranged; (घनेन

मुक्ताम्) free from cloud (with ज्योत्स्नाम्). लेखीकृताम् turned into a streak. The necklace was like autumnal moonlight. प्र...चिह्नाम् (प्रकटं पदकचिह्नं यस्याम्) which is clearly marked by the central jewel (with एकावली); which is marked with clear foot-prints. सञ्चारणवीथी road for moving about. The pearls looked like the stars of the Great Bear. Only the latter change their position in the sky from evening to morning. हस्तमुक्ताम् which fell from the hand (because of the round and glossy pearls); that were without हस्त, a constellation (with सप्तर्षि). अभिभूतः ०भूषणानां (कौस्तुभादीनां) भूतेः प्रभावः यया (एकावली) that cast into the shade the powerful magnificence of the ornaments in the whole world; अभिभूतः ०भूषणस्य (शिवस्य) भूतेः (ashes) प्रभावः यया that surpassed the glory of the ashes of शिव who is the ornament of the whole world. ऐशानीं belonging to ईशान (*i. e.* शिव). शिव placed the digit of the moon on his head. 'ईश्वरः शर्व ईशानः' अम०. धवल...हीताम् possessed of the quality of whiteness (with कान्तिम्); possessed of whiteness and thread (with एकावली). क्षीरसागर is white. The एकावली was as if the whiteness of क्षीरसागर come out of it. महीभृतः राजानः पर्वताश्च. The Ganges goes round several mountains. The एकावली had passed through the hands of many kings. The Ganges purifies a man and prevents his falling into hell (दुर्गति). The एकावली would remove poverty. अनवरतं स्फुरिताः तरलस्य (मध्यमणेः) अंशुकाः यस्याम् (with एकावली); अनवरतं स्फुरितं तरलं (moving) अंशुकं (fine silk cloth) यस्याः (with पताका). A banner is carried in front (पुरःसर) and its cloth is waving. महे...गमस्य of the approach (आगमः) of the position of a great emperor. एकावली announced like a पताका the great position that हर्ष was to occupy. A banner also indicates the existence of (a temple of) शिव (महेश्वर). घनसारवत् शुक्लाम् white like camphor (with एकावली). दन्तपङ्क्ति also is घन (thickset), strong and white; or it is white like camphor. ईश्वर is हर्ष who sat facing (अभिमुख) the necklace. ईश्वर means शिव also. Or a king (ईश्वर) when favourable (अभिमुख) smiles on the man with whom he is pleased. वर = श्रेष्ठ (with एकावली). वरः a bridegroom. The garland at the time of स्वयंवर gratifies the desire of the bridegroom when thrown round his neck. The एकावली fulfilled the highest ambitions and was white like flowers (स्रज्). The world-bride as if chose हर्ष as the bridegroom by the garland-necklace. निज...लक्ष्याम्—the necklace could not be gazed at being surrounded by its own (dazzling) rays.

A laughing woman may cover her face with her own hands (निजकर) and then it would be difficult to see her smile. एकावली is fancied to be the smile (both being white) of the earth indicating its love for (हर्ष). विहसतिका gentle laughter. For चक्षूराग, see p. 149. The reading सुधाया: is not so good. सुधा is white. अक्षमाला rosary. It is राजधर्म to be absorbed in मन्त्र (state policy), कोष (treasury) and साधन (army); one who takes a rosary (*i. e.* becomes an ascetic) is intent upon mastering the numerous *Mantras* (hymns or spells). स...भूतां that (एकावली) was an ornament of the ocean (the pearls of it being found in the ocean). स...भूतां which was ornamented with the seal (of कुबेर). संख्या...काम् which was as if the board or fillet engraved with the calculations of the treasures of कुबेर. Each pearl of the necklace resembled a figure drawn in calculation. कुबेर is the lord of riches and treasures. बन्धुर high, raised 'बन्धुरं तून्नतानतम्' अम०. के...त्मनोऽपि who are we even to control our own selves? The idea is that he is not master even of his own self, that his soul has come to belong to the ascetic. किमुत...नस्य वा much more therefore have I no control in accepting or rejecting (the necklace). परवन्त: in the hands of others. अत्र...कर्तव्यानाम् you may do what you like with this (body). कामचार: acting according to one's will.

P. 138 l. 26—**P. 140** l. 12 समतिक्रान्ते...व्यरंसीत्. लब्धःविश्रम्भः यया who took courage. उपांशु *adv.* in a whisper. शुचा...विनयम् the unbearableness of her sorrows impels her and lessens her modesty, being ordered by wretched fate. हतदैवेन दत्तः आदेशः यस्यै (with असह्यता). This passage is corrupt. Some MSS read व्यापारयति, which is a good reading; others read व्याहारयति (makes her speak). Another reading is हतदैवदत्ता च दशा, which is better than the text. अवलम्बनं support; compare मनु० 9. 3. 'पिता रक्षति कौमारे भर्ता रक्षति यौवने। रक्षन्ति स्थविरे पुत्रा न स्त्री स्वातन्त्र्यमर्हति ॥'; there is a similar passage in अनुशासनपर्व 20. 21. दुः...मानं serving as fuel to the fire of sorrow. प्राणित...केवलम् to continue to live is sheer immodesty. For शालीन, see p. 28. प्रतिहत: frustrated. काषा...श्रया by being allowed to assume the red robe. पर्याय: synonym. आक्षेप: epilepsy 'आक्षेपस्यापस्मारस्य' com. This is not the usual meaning of the word. तारुण्यं तमसः (sorrow) is the youth of darkness. Darkness reigns supreme when a person gives himself up to sorrows. विशेषणं विषस्य it is a kind of poison. Or the meaning may be 'sorrow is an epithet of poison.' अनन्तकः...यकः

it is the lord of the city of the dead, but without यम. अविद्यमानः अन्तकः यस्मिन्. यम is the lord of प्रेतनगर. The विरोध is got over by taking अनन्तक in the sense of 'never-ending'. अविद्यमानः अन्तः यस्य. For क, see p. 68. प्रेत...नायकः also means 'that leads to प्रेतनगर' *i. e.* that kills a man. Explain the following विरोधs in a similar way. अनिर्वृतिः धर्मः यस्य the characteristic of which is that it is not extinguished. But fire can be extinguished. So अ...धर्मः means 'the characteristic of which is that there is no happiness in it.' अक्षयः not consumption. But राजयक्ष्मन् is the same as consumption (क्षयः). So अक्षयः means 'endless'. अ...निवासः who is not the abode of लक्ष्मी; which is the abode of distress. लक्ष्मी dwells on the chest of विष्णु (जनार्दन); शोक is जनार्दन *i. e.* torments people (जनानर्दयतीति). अपु...त्तः that is not working for पुण्य; that is due to one's sins (in former lives). A Jaina mendicant (क्षपणकः) takes to the order of mendicancy for storing merit. क्षपणक also means 'that destroys' (life). अ...धः in which there is no waking up; in which there is no discrimination (in the mind). After sleep, one gets up. निद्राप्रकारः also means '(sorrow) that scatters about *i. e.* destroys sleep.' अन...धर्मा the characteristic of which is to be active (not dull or dazed); which resembles fire (अनलस-धर्मा and अनल-सधर्मा). In सन्निपातज्वर a man becomes अलस. For सन्निपात see p. 80. सन्निपात also means 'that pulls down people.' धर्म becomes धर्मन् at the end of a बहुव्रीहि when preceded by a single word 'धर्मादनिच्केवलात्' पा. 5. 4. 124. अ...चरः that is not in the company of शिव; that is ever associated with evil. विनायकः= गणेशः. Pictures of शिव are generally represented as having गणेश on his lap. विनायक also means 'an obstacle,' or 'one that leads a man astray.' 'विनायकस्तु हेरम्बे तार्क्ष्ये विघ्ने जिने गुरौ'. Compare 'अशिवमूर्तयो महाविनायकाधिष्ठिताः' काद० p. 287. There is another meaning also. A Jaina (*i. e.* sight of a जैन) is associated with evil; compare text p. 20 'अभिमुखमाजगाम...नग्नाटकः.' अ...वितः not attended upon by mercury; not resorted to by wise men. ग्रहवर्गः the group of planets; a number of eclipses or ghosts. 'निर्बन्धोपरागार्कादयो ग्रहाः' अम०. अ...समुत्थः not caused by योग; springing from bad luck or evil conjunctions of stars. For योग, see above p. 204. ज्योतिःप्रकारः a kind of light (*i. e.* highest knowledge); a kind of fire. Higher knowledge (about ब्रह्म) cannot be had without योग (चित्तवृत्तिनिरोध). स्नेहा...कोपः it is a delirium due to स्नेह (affection, oil). वायु is one of the three humours and प्रकोप

means its excess. Oil is prescribed against वायुप्रकोप as an outward application; so in स्नेहात्...पः there is a विरोध, which is removed by taking स्नेह to mean affection. मानसात् from the मानस lake; from the mind. There can be no fire in the lake. आर्द्रभावात् from moisture; from tender feelings. रजःक्षोभः agitation of passion; scattering of dust. Dust is *laid*, not *scattered* by moisture. रसात् out of juice (or fluid); out of affection. अभिशोषः dryness (of mouth); that makes a man wither. रागात् out of affection; out of redness. कालपरिणामः that ends in death; that is transformed into darkness. Out of redness one cannot make a dark thing. तदस्या°—The construction is तत् (तस्मात्) अस्य (शोकस्य)...विदुषामपि हृदयानि न अलं सोढुं आपातं...किमुत अबलानां हृदयम्. Read अजस्रास्रस्राविणः (that makes one shed tears continuously, that makes blood to ooze forth continually). हृदयमहाव्रणस्य—शोक is a great wound of the heart. Blood comes out from a wound. बहुलाः दोषाः अन्धकारः इव तेन लब्धः प्रवेशप्रसरः येन—sorrow enters the heart that is labouring under the darkness of many faults and robs the man of his life. A robber also enters in the darkness of night. बहुलस्य (कृष्णपक्षस्य) दोषा (रात्रिः) तस्याः अन्धकारे लब्धः प्रवेशप्रसरः येन. शून्यताहेतोः which is the cause of the mind being vacant; that causes depopulation. महाभूतग्रामः (प्राणिसमूहः) तस्य घातकः तस्य—sorrow kills many beings. महान्ति भूतानि यस्मिन् स महाभूतः ग्रामः (village) &c. One who destroys a village causes depopulation. महाभूतानि पृथिव्यप्तेजोवाय्वाकाशानि तेषां ग्रामः &c. If the five elements are destroyed nothing will be left. सकल...दक्षः expert in exhausting the whole body; expert in destroying all in battles. दोष...वर्तिनः pre-eminent among faults; a bad emperor. कार्श्यम् emaciation. श्वासः sighing, hard breathing. प्रलापः lamentation; delirium. उपद्रवः affliction; bad supervenient symptoms. असद्ग्रहस्य an evil planet; which is persistence in a bad thing. सकल...केतोः which indicates the destruction of the whole world; which is fire in destroying &c. शोक is a fire (धूमः केतुः चिह्नं यस्य). 'अभ्युत्पातौ धूमकेतू' अम°. जीवि° applies to both शोक and वज्र in the same sense. अक्षणरुचेः न क्षणे (उत्सवे) रुचिः (liking) यस्मिन्. 'कालविशेषोत्सवयोः क्षणः' अम°. अविद्यमाना क्षणरुचिः (विद्युत्) यस्मिन्. विद्युत् flashes only for a moment (क्षणं रुचिः यस्याः). When a bolt falls in a cloudless sky, there is naturally no lightning. क्षणप्रभा is given by अमर as a synonym of विद्युत्. For °वज्रपातस्य, see p. 25 (text) l. 1. Compare महा° उद्योगपर्व 84. 5. 'अनभ्रेऽशनिनिर्घोषः.' स्फुरन्त्यः अनवद्याः (blameless, pure) विद्याः एव विद्युतः ताभिः उद्द्योतमानानि illumined by flashing and pure lightning-like lores. The lores are either four or fourteen. 'पुराणन्यायमीमांसाधर्मशास्त्राङ्गमिश्रिताः । वेदाः स्थानानि विद्यानां धर्मस्य च चतुर्दश ॥' याज्ञ० I. 3. (*i. e.* the four Vedas, six वेदाङ्गs, पुराण, न्याय, मीमांसा and धर्मशास्त्र). The four (in the case of kings) are आन्वीक्षिकी, त्रयी (वेदत्रयी), वार्ता and दण्डनीति (अर्थशास्त्र p. 6). विद्युत् also is flashing (स्फुरत्) and bright. गहनाः ग्रन्थाः ग्रन्थयः इव तेषां गूढः गर्भः तस्य ग्रहणेन गम्भीराणि profound by grasping the hidden meanings lying in deep works. The interior of a fleshy knot is also deep. कठोर well-developed; hard. A swelling (ग्रन्थि) is hard; a गर्भ becomes developed (कठोर). बहु...बृहन्ति big with carrying many S'āstras. A swelling makes the part swollen look big and heavy. So a गर्भ also has to be borne (उद्वहन) by the mother. न अलं सोढुं आपातं are not able to bear the onset (of sorrow). नवमालिका jasmine. सरस juicy (with बिसतन्तु); affectionate (with हृदयम्). सत्यं व्रतं यस्याः who is true to her vow. उपालभ्यते rebuked. अमूढेन without being bewildered. मर्त्यधर्मणा = मनुजेन. पुरा...कर्तुम् who can change these ancient rules of conduct ? There is a suggested meaning:—these decrees of fate due to actions in former lives, who can gainsay. In this and the following there are laboured puns everywhere. जन्म...घटनानि (union, happening) एव ०रज्जवः. For पञ्चजन, see p. 124. All people have to undergo the long round of births, deaths and old age. The ropes of the water-wheel also are very long and revolve (संसरन्त्यः) night and day. पञ्चमहाभूतान्येव पञ्चकुलः तेन अधिष्ठितः अन्तःकरणव्यवहारः तस्य दर्शने निपुणाः; पञ्चमहाभूतेषु *i. e.* ०भूतात्मके शरीरे अधिष्ठितं अन्तःकरणं. The ideas here are rather complicated. The mind presides over the body (*i. e.* regulates its movements) that is made up of the five elements. यम notes what men do and what is passing in their minds. Compare the verse 'आदित्यचन्द्रावनिलोऽनलश्च द्यौर्भूमिरापो हृदयं यमश्च । अहश्च रात्रिश्च उभे च सन्ध्ये धर्मोऽपि जानाति नरस्य वृत्तम् ॥'. 'धर्मराजः पितृपतिः... यमः ॥' अम०. यम spares none (सर्वंकष) and is terrible. A king's ordinances (राजस्थितयः) are applicable to all (सर्वंकषा). The king sees into the transactions and documents (करणं) of the पञ्चकुल officers. They seem to be the same as modern Panchait. Compare the word पञ्चमण्डली in C. I. I. vol. III. p. 31, 32. For करण, see above p. 167. धर्मसदृशो राजा तस्य स्थितयः. We must read अक्षममाणाः. क्षण...माणाः not allowing even a moment to pass (every moment is calculated by the water-clock). कालनालिकाः the Ghaṭikâs of

Death (काल); the Ghaṭikās of time. नाडिका also means 'a water-clock'. आयुष्क...कुशलाः expert in calculating the span (कला, portion) of life (allotted to each individual); expert in calculating the कलाs. निलये निलये in each house; at the time of destruction (or in each Hell). निलय is equal to निरय; see above p. 125 for identity of र् and ल्. कला, क्षण and नाडिका are measures of time 18 or 15 निमेषs are equal to a काष्ठा, 30 काष्ठाs to a कला, 30 कलाs to a क्षण and 12 क्षणs to a मुहूर्त which is equal to two घटिकाs. See अमरकोश for this. For a different table and for a water-clock, see ब्रह्मपुराण 231. 6–9 'निमेषो मानुषो योऽयं मात्रामात्रप्रमाणतः। तैः पञ्चदशभिः काष्ठा त्रिंशत्काष्ठास्तथा कला॥ नाडिका तु प्रमाणेन कलाश्च दश पञ्च च। उन्मानेनाम्भसः सा तु पलान्यर्धत्रयोदश॥ हेममाषैः कृतच्छिद्रा चतुर्भिश्चतुरङ्गुलैः। मागधेन प्रमाणेन जलप्रस्थस्तु स स्मृतः॥ नाडिकाभ्यामथ द्वाभ्यां मुहूर्तो द्विजसत्तमाः।.' आयुष्कला is proper according to 'इदुदुपधस्य चाप्रत्ययस्य' पा. 8. 3. 41. चण्डिका fierce; the goddess Durgā. The command of Yama goes forth in the world. सर्व...पातिनी—at Yama's word, the lives of beings are offered at his feet; to Durgā all sorts of animals are offered. उपहारः=बलिः. प्रेतपतिः यमः तस्य पटहाः. Drums announce the march (प्रयाण) of a king's army. The drums of Yama announce the departure of the life of all beings. पेटकैः in groups. प्रतप्तलोहवत् लोहिते अक्षिणी येषाम् whose eyes are red like heated iron. कालकूटस्य इव कान्तिः यस्य सः ०कान्तिः कालः (dark) कायः येषाम्. कालपाशः पाणौ येषाम्. कालकूट is the same as हालाहल poison, which first came out at the churning and darkened the throat of शिव. There is an allusion to gamblers, whose eyes are red through late hours, envy and hatred and who have dark dice (पाशः) in their hands. भीषणकिङ्कराणां करैः घट्टितः (struck) यम...पुटः तस्य पटुना (sharp) टाङ्कारेण भयङ्कराः. Separate घोराः घातघोषणाः the terrible proclamation of death (with यमकिङ्कर); and read घोरा...षणाः as one word (with *servants*)—proclamations in which there is fierce beating (of the drum or bell). घोरः आघातः यस्यां सा ०घाता घोषणा. King's proclamations are announced by his servants that ring a bell and collect (संहरणं) all people to listen to them. The messengers of Death (किङ्कर) destroy (संहरणं) all beings. वहन्ति—is to be connected with वीथयः. बहुचितानां धूमैः धूसरिता ०पताका तस्यां पटुपतिता गृध्रदृष्टिः यासु—where the keen eye of vultures falls on the banners of Yama darkened by the smoke of numerous funeral pyres. शोकेन कृतः कोलाहलः यामि- ताः ०हलाः ०म्बिन्यः तासां विकीर्णाः (dishevelled) ०कलापाः तैः शबलं शवशिबिकासहस्रं तेन सङ्कुलाः—

round the biers of their husbands widows scream and their hair sticks to them. किलकिलायमानाः श्मशानशिबिरे शिवाशावकाः यासु—there are howling young ones of female jackals in the cemetery. परलोकः आवसथः इव तस्य पथिकाः तेषां सार्थः तस्य प्रस्थाने विशिखाः तेषां वीथयः (rows, lines). 'रथ्या प्रतोली विशिखा' अम०. The roads lead the sojourners to the next world to their destination. There is another meaning. आवसथः a resting-place, an asylum for students and ascetics. Roads lead the intending travellers to an आवसथ (outside the town) whence they makes their प्रस्थान (start for the journey). There are heaps (चिता) of fuel and cowdung burning near it and a पताका too. Vultures hover over it in search of crumbs. Their wives scream round their palanquins (शिबिका) when they start and urchins are merry round the encampment (शिबिरं) of travellers. The student will note the chain of alliteration in the next clause. सकल...लम्पटा greedy to taste the mouthful *viz.* the whole world. He means the night of destruction (कालरात्री) threatens all and would spare no man. बहला thick. 'वहंलिहा छिद्रान्वेषिणी' com—striking at a weak point. लोहितेन आचिता full of blood. चिताङ्गारैः काली dark with the charcoal of the pyre. The words suggest the tongue of a cow. The tongue is बहला and वहंलिहा (licks the shoulder of the calf). 'स्कन्धप्रदेशस्तु वहः' अम०. The tongue licks mouthfuls of grass. It is red (लोहिता) and full (आचिता) and the cow may be dark like अङ्गार. तृप्ति...मृत्योः the hunger of Death that devours all beings never learns satiety. अति...वाहिनी flowing very quickly. महान् भूतग्रामः (भूतसङ्घः) तस्य गोष्ठ्यः (meetings). According to Buddhist philosophy everything is transitory (सर्वं क्षणिकं) and hence the group of five elements also must be so. रात्रि...देहिनाम् the sticks of the cage of the machine—like body of men are liable to break in the night. A cage set to catch wild animals may be shattered by them at night. रात्रिषु may refer to कालरात्रि. अणु...माणवः the atoms that create this body, being helpless against the oncoming (आवेशः) of good and evil, are liable to be shattered. विशरारु from शृ with वि. जीव...तन्तवः the threads of the strings that fasten the soul (in the body). The threads of पाश (snares) and the strings of lutes also are likely to break. सर्वं...नश्वरम् the whole world, which is perishable, is not independent (is not master of itself). तमसः...यातुम् to allow full scope to darkness (ignorance).तमः is the third गुण of out of the three (सत्त्व, रजस् and तमस्). मेधाविनि is addressed to राज्यश्री; it also goes with मनसि. एको...धृते: A single moment of discernment becomes the support of steadiness of mind *i. e.* makes the mind steady. For प्रतिसंख्यान see p. 119. अपेक्षणीय: to be cared for. पितृकल्प: almost like your father. For कल्प, see p. 38. काषायग्रहणं करोतीति तं. ज्याय:...वताम् this (प्रव्रज्या) is the best place for the wise (for the self-restrained). वत्सल: affectionate. सर्व...योगे by all means you must act according to his order.

P. 140 l. 13—**P. 141** l. 6 उपरत...जगाम. अन...र्मिता: created by Fate, though not requested to do so. विषम...स्तम्भा: pillars for support in serious calamities. Pillars support a house. स्नेहा...मूर्तय: who are full of affection; that are wet with oil. मोहा...ध्वंसिन: that destroy the darkness of error (delusion). धर्मप्रदीपा: that illuminate the law. A lamp also destroys darkness &c. प्रणय...लिता rendered naughty by the gift of affection; spoilt by giving what is asked for. A spoilt child may ask for what is दुर्लभ. धीर...वल्लभत्वम् the knowledge that one is loved emboldens even a steady man, the levity of his heart urging him to transgress proper limits. हृदयस्य लघिम्ना लङ्घितं (०ल्लभत्वम्). शालीन...गल्भ्यम् the desire to secure one's objects teaches even a modest man to be overbold. For शालीन, see p. 28. अभ्य...मार्या: the noble respect the limits of request, as the ocean does. The idea is:—the ocean, though so full, does not pass beyond the prescribed limits; so the noble, though galled by unreasonable requests, do not reject them but respect them. दत्तमेव च शरीरम्—See text p. 75 ll. 7–8. सर्व...लालनीया must be fondled for a while even in spite of the neglect of all my duties. ०अवधीरणं (neglect) एव उपरोध: (obstacle). बाह्वोर्विधेयै: being the servants of (*i. e.* under the control of) our arm. दीय...मिदम् Give this your body to me who am your guest *i. e.* you must be my guest and accompany me. अयं जन: refers to हर्ष himself. यावत्...प्रजा: while I lessen the burden of my vow (*i. e.* fulfil my vow) and comfort the subjects distressed by the sorrow of my father's death. तावदिमां...अस...मेव प्रतिबोध्यमानामिच्छामि so long I desire that she should be enlightened, while still remaining by my side. The instrumentals कथाभि:, उपदेशै, &c., are to be connected with प्रतिबोध्यमानाम्. कथाभि: धर्म्याभि: by righteous discourses. कुशल...रजोभि: by advice free from passion, that brings about right knowledge. अविद्यमानं रज: (रजोगुण:) यस्मिन्. शीलो...नाभि: by instruction that produces quiescence by the practice of the

S ilas. For शील, see above p. 223. क्लेश...भूतैः that are the cause of the abandonment of the क्लेशs. क्लेश means 'evil passions'. They are ten such as लोभ, मोह, मान, दृष्टि (heresy), विचिकित्सा, (doubt), स्त्यानं (sloth), औद्धत्यम् &c. क्लेशs are the causes of sinful actions and therefore of rebirth. तथागतैर्दर्शनैः by the doctrines of बुद्ध. समासं कृत्स्नं येन (*adj.* of मया). अतिसृजन्ति grant. सुरनाथम् = इन्द्रम्. दधीचः—the gods requested दधीच for his bones which were to be turned into a वज्र for killing वृत्र. See वनपर्व chap. 100. मुनिनाथः = बुद्धः. 'मुनीन्द्रः श्रीघनः शास्ता' अम०. अनपेक्षिता आत्मस्थितिः येन who cared not for the continuance of his life. अनु...कृत्वा thinking that it was an act of compassion. बठरसत्त्वेभ्यः to animals that are dull *i. e.* to beasts like the lion. The com. refers to the story of Buddha's offering himself in a former life to a hungry lioness that was about to devour its own young. This story occurs in the जातकमाला (Harward series) where it is a व्याघ्री and not a lioness. भव्याः the good or worthy. Read इमं for इमाम्. Remove the line after इमं. Mark the construction (गुणाः बलिं गृह्णन्ति primitive; असौ जनः गुणान् बलिं ग्राहयति causal; गुणाः अमुना जनेन बलिं ग्राहिताः passive causal). चेतसा...जनेन this person (*i. e.* I) already made in his mind an offer of this body to your virtues. If we read कायकलि that will be in keeping with the words on p. 75 l. 7 (कायकलिरस्माकम्). उपयोगस्तु गुणवदायत्तः the use of it is in the hands of you, a virtuous man. तस्मिन् refers to दिवाकरमित्र. अभिनन्दितः प्रणयः येन who welcomed his request or friendship. निर्घात is the शबर who gave intelligence about दिवाकर०. अनुजाह्नवि along the banks of the Ganges. जाह्नव्याः अन्वायतम् (अव्ययीभाव).

P. 141 ll. 7—29 तत्र च...नरेन्द्रायेति. प्रणयिभ्यः to his friends. ततार crossed over *i. e.* set. बहल...पिङ्गलः tawny with thick and plentiful honey (with पङ्क०); tawny like thick &c. (with दिवस). पङ्कजानां आकरः (समूहः) bed. Both the lotuses and the day are dear to the चक्रवाक. See pp. 10, 57. The sentence is पूषा रोचिषां जालकानि पुनरपि निजवपुषि सञ्जहार—the sun again withdrew in his own body the masses of his rays. प्रकीर्णानि dispersed (with rays); published or promulgated, or scattered (with यजूंषि). नवरुधिररसवत् अरुणः वर्णः येषाम् (with जालकानि) or ०रसेन अरुणाः वर्णाः (letters) येषाम् (with यजूंषि). कुपित...वान्तानि vomited from the mouth of the angered याज्ञवल्क्य. याज्ञवल्क्य was the pupil of वैशम्पायन, who was the pupil of व्यास. वैशम्पायन incurred the sin of ब्रह्महत्या. He asked his pupil to perform some sacrifice whereby he might be purified. याज्ञवल्क्य said that the Brāhmaṇas to be invited for the sacrifice had no holiness in them. At this expression of disrespert for Brāhmaṇas his teacher got angry and said 'मुच्यतां यत्त्वयाधीतं मत्तो विप्रावमन्यक ॥ निस्तेजसो वदस्येतान्यस्त्वं ब्राह्मणपुङ्गवान् ।' Thereupon याज्ञवल्क्य vomited the Yajus hymns, which the other pupils took in the form of partridges (तित्तिरि). Those hymns came to be called कृष्णयजुर्वेद; while याज्ञवल्क्य promulgated a separate recension, which he received from the sun, called शुक्लयजुर्वेद. 'मयाप्यलं त्वयाधीतं यन्मया तदिदं द्विज ॥ इत्युक्त्वा रुधिराक्तानि सरूपाणि यजूंषि सः । छर्दयित्वा ददौ तस्मै स्वेच्छया चाययौ मुनिः ॥ यजूंष्यथ विसृष्टानि याज्ञवल्क्येन वै द्विज । जगृहुस्तित्तिरा भूत्वा तैत्तिरीयास्तु ते स्मृताः ॥' विष्णुपु. III. 5. 10–12. The com. makes याज्ञवल्क्य a pupil of शाकल्य. लोका...जूंषि—लोकस्य आलोकं जुषन्ते—that like to illumine the world (with rays). लोकालोकः पर्वतः तं जुषन्ते that visit or go to the mountain लो०. लोकालोक is a mythical mountain in पुष्करद्वीप, the last of the seven द्वीपs. Beyond लोकालोक there is complete darkness and on this side of it there is light. See विष्णुपु० II. 4. 'लोकालोकस्ततः शैलो योजनायुतविस्तृतः ।...ततस्तमः समावृत्य तं शैलं सर्वतः स्थितम् । तमश्चाण्डकटाहेन समन्तात्परिवेष्टितम् ॥' 95–96. पापं मुष्णन्ति इति पाप०—applies to both. क्रमेण च—the principal sentence is क्रमेण च उष्णांशुः (सूर्यः)...मुहूर्तमदृश्यत. समुपोह्यमानः (increasing) मांसलः (thick, deepened) रागः (red colour) तेन रोचिष्णुः. The poet now puts forward many similes to convey the idea of the redness of the disc of the setting sun. It resembled the congenital crest jewel (चूडामणि) of अश्वत्थामन् (son of द्रोण) placed in his turban. उष्णीषबन्धे (उष्णीषस्य बन्धः यत्र तत्र शिरसि) सहजः. 'उष्णीषं शिरोवेष्टकिरीटयोः' अम०. वृकोदरः भीमः तस्य करेण उत्पाटितः (snatched off). प्रत्यग्रं शोणितं तेन शोणः अङ्गरागः तेन रौद्रः (looking) terrible with the red unguent of his own fresh blood. When the jewel that was on his head from birth was snatched away, blood spurted on his body. The colour of the sun's body (अङ्गरागः) was red like fresh blood. For the story see महा० सौप्तिकपर्व chap. 14 and 15. अश्वत्थामा discharged ब्रह्मास्त्र and अर्जुन in return did the same; when नारद and व्यास intervened, अर्जुन took it back, but अश्वत्थामा could not and so he had to give the jewel on his head in exchange for his life. कपाल...पैतामहः (the sun looked) like the begging skull-vessel of Brahmā (पितामह) reddish by being filled with blood from the veins and arteries of the head, that was hurled down by S'iva who is skilled (or fond of) in giving alms to the Rudras. रुद्रेभ्यो

भिक्षादानं तस्मिन् शौण्डः पुरमथनः तेन मुक्तं मुण्डं तस्य शिरानाडीनां रुधिरं तेन पूरणं तेन कपिलः. We must read ०पूरणकपिलः. We may also take रुद्रभिक्षा in the sense of terrible alms. The story alluded to is the cutting off of the fifth head of Brahmā by S'iva. The Rudras are eleven, chief of whom is शङ्कर or शम्भु. शङ्कर is called त्रिपुरान्तक or पुरमथन because he burnt down the three cities of gold, silver and iron built by Maya for demons in the sky, air and earth. See द्रोणपर्व chap. 202. 64 'असुराणां पुराण्यासंस्त्रीणि वीर्यवतां दिवि। आयसं राजतं चैव सौवर्णं परमं महत्॥'. पितृवधेन रुषितः रामः (परशुरामः) तेन रागेण रचितः. **'रागस्तु मात्सर्ये** लोहितादिषु। **क्लेशादावनुरागे** च गान्धारादौ नृपेऽपि च॥' मे०. With the sun, we may explain 'रामः तस्य रागः (redness) तेन रचितः' possessing the redness of परशुराम &c. पृथुः (broad) विकटः (formidable) कार्तवीर्यस्य अंसकूटः (the hump-like or peak-like shoulder) तस्य कुट्टाकः कुठारः तस्य तुण्डेन तष्टानि (chopped off) कण्ठकुहराणि तेषां रुधिरकुल्याप्रणालाः तेषां सहस्रेण पूरितः. दूररोधी stretching far and wide (applies to the lake and to the sun's rays also). रुधिरस्यायं रौधिरः. For the five lakes of blood and for the destruction of क्षत्रियs, see pp. 152, 38. भयेन निगूढानि (concealed) करचरणमुण्डानि यस्य स चासौ मण्डलाकृतिश्च that presented the shape of a sphere because the hands &c. were contracted through fear. The sun also is मण्डलाकृति. गुरुः गरुडस्य नखपञ्जरः तेन आक्षेपः तेन क्षपणं (smashing) तेन क्षिप्तं क्षतजं (blood) तेन उक्षितः (sprinkled). विगताः असवः यस्य (dead). Remove the comma after विभावसुः. कमठः tortoise. See महा० आदिपर्व chap 29–30. विभावसु and सुप्रतीक were brothers. सुप्रतीक the younger asked विभा० to give him his share. Thereupon विभावसु cursed him to be an elephant and सुप्रतीक cursed him to be a tortoise. They were always fighting in a lake. When गरुड set out for bringing nectar, he seized, carried into space and ate both of them. लोठ्यमानो नभसि—the sun also rolls in the sky. अरुणः गर्भः यस्य सः ०गर्भः मांसपिण्डाण्डः the egg containing a mass of flesh forming the embryo Aruṇa. The sun is also round (like an egg) and is like the red flesh of an embryo. खण्डिमानमानीतः broken into pieces (with egg); reduced in effulgence. ०पातेन दूयमाना दाक्षायणी तया क्षिप्तः thrown by विनता that was anxious by the passing away of the period fixed (for pregnancy). C and T following the com. take the clause 'नियत... क्षिप्तः' with धातुतटः. That construction does not yield a good sense. We do not know when Meru was tossed by दाक्षायणी (which com. renders by काली). कद्रू and विनता were two of the daughters of

दक्ष and wives of कश्यप. Her husband said that कद्रू would have a thousand sons and विनता only two. कद्रू gave birth to 1000 serpents. 'अण्डाभ्यां विनतायास्तु मिथुनं न व्यदृश्यत । ततः पुत्रार्थिनी देवी व्रीडिता च तपस्विनी ॥ अण्डं बिभेद विनता तत्र पुत्रमपश्यत । अप्यर्धकायसम्पन्नमितरेणाप्रकाशता ।' आदिपर्व 16. 16–17. धातु...रोः like the slope of Meru containing metallic ores. Meru is a mountain of gold; the sky suffused with the glow of evening resembled it; and the disc of the sun looked like चरु. असुरवधाय अभिचारः तस्य चरुः तस्य पचनं तस्य पिशुनः (सूचकः) indicating the cooking of an oblation in some magic rites for the destruction of the demons. For अभिचार see p. 145. A चरु (oblation of rice) may be smeared with red powder. If the gods wanted to perform any rite for असुरवध, they would do so on Meru. We may also take असुर... पिशुनः with कटाहः. In that case we have to look upon धातु... मेरोः as an independent clause by itself (the disc of the sun being red like the slope of Meru). शोणितक्वाथेन कषायितः कुक्षिः यस्य the sides of which are red with the decoction of blood. For विसङ्कट see p. 122. कटाह...त्यः the cauldron of बृहस्पति. The sun looks like a cauldron. बृहस्पति is the priest of the gods. The poet fancies that he was engaged in boiling in a cauldron an oblation for the purpose of killing the असुरs. सद्यो गलितं गजदानवस्य (गजासुरस्य) लोहितं (blood) तस्य उपलेपेन (smearing) भीषणः. मुख... भोगः the expanse of the round face. महाभैरव is a form of शिव. गजासुर was a demon, son of महिषासुर, slain by S'iva. The sun was भीषण like the application (उपलेप) of the blood &c. ०जले प्रतिबिम्बिता रविबिम्बराजिः तेन भास्वरं अभ्रं (cloud) तदवलम्बते इति. गृहीतः आर्द्रमांसभारः यया. वासरा...निभा the evening resembled a वेताल (vampire). Flesh is offered to वेताल. The idea is:—in the evening the sky was overspread with clouds which were suffused red by the lustre of the reflections of the sun in the ocean. The clouds are like वेताल and their glow is like मांस. After night-fall, वेतालs begin to appear (वेतालाः नितरां भान्ति यस्याम्). ज्वलन् सन्ध्यारागः तेन रज्यमानः जलप्रवाहः यस्य. पुराणपुरुषः (विष्णुः) तस्य पीवरं ऊरुसम्पुटं तेन पिष्टौ मधुकैटभौ तयोः रुधिरपटलं (pool of blood) तेन पाटलं वपुः यस्य. अर्णसाम् = जलानाम्. मधु and कैटभ were two demons born from the ear of Vishṇu, when he was absorbed in Yogic sleep at the end of the *Kalpa*. They were about to devour Brahmā. The latter woke up Vishṇu, who asked them to choose a boon. They asked him to choose one, when विष्णु chose that they be killed by him. He killed them between his thighs 'स्वकावनावृतावूरू दृष्ट्वा देववरस्तदा। मधुकैटभयो राजन् शिरसी मधुसूदनः॥ चक्रेण शितधारेण न्यकृन्तत महायशाः॥' वनपर्व 203. 35. See मार्कण्डेयपुराण chap. 81. Compare 'अचिरमृदितमधुकैटभरुधिरारुणेन हरिमिवोरुयुगलेन विराजमानम्' काद० p. 9. अवसिते The sentence is अवसिते ०समये समनन्तरं...श्वेतभानुः उपानीयत निशया नरेन्द्राय when the time of evening ended, immediately afterwards the moon was presented to the king (Harsha) by night. अपरि...कीर्त्या as if it were a goblet made from a pearl slab (presented) by the Glory of his family to him who had a thirst for drinking boundless fame. The bright moon resembled a goblet of pearls. His family was already glorious, just as the night may be glorious with the twinkling stars. But Harsha was not satisfied with that. He thirsted for glory that would embrace the whole world like the moon's rays. कृत...ताय who was bent on starting the कृतयुग (*i. e.* an era of perfect righteousness). हर्ष wanted to bring back in कलियुग the pristine righteousness of कृतयुग. For कृतयुग and धर्म see pp. 3, 40. The bright moon resembled a round silver coin or edict stamped with the royal seal. आदिराजस्य राजतः ०निवेशः the stamp on silver of the primeval king's seal conferring authority (on Harsha). Night is compared to राज्यश्री (royal glory). राज्यश्री originally belonged to the first king (either Manu or Pṛithu) who reigned in the Kṛita age. His authority was transferred to Harsha. Authority is conferred by a शासन (copperplate or patent) impressed with the royal seal. Compare for आदिराज 'पृथुः प्रथमपुरुषकः परिभूतवान् पृथिवीम्' हर्षचरित (3rd उच्छ्वास). Probably there is a veiled allusion. राज्यश्री, Harsha's sister, called upon Harsha to assume the sovereignty of the world including her husband's realm. सकल...चलिताय that had set off on the conquest of all the continents. For श्वेतद्वीप, see above p. 190. The people from श्वेतद्वीप are all white; so the moon is aptly compared to a messenger from श्वेतद्वीप. निशा is compared to आयति (Future; or, Glory). A दूत is sent either to encourage a person or to make peace with him. इति shows that the chapter ends here. C and T suggest that the descriptions of sunset and of moonrise indicate bloody wars and the fall of Harsha's enemy, followed by the rise of Harsha's glory.

In the third Uchchhvāsa, Bāna promised to his cousins a narrative of Harsha's career and described it thus far. The narrative is suddenly brought to a close.

Appendix

A Brief Analysis of the Harshacharita.

Chap. I & II. After the usual invocation and sympathetic references to his great predecessors, Bāṇa gives us an account of his family and of himself which has been summarised in the Introduction (pp. II–IV) and need not be repeated here.

Chap. III. When Bāṇa returned from Harsha's court, he was pressed by his cousins with the request that he should entertain them with a narrative of the life and career of Harsha. Bāṇa expressed his inability to do even the slightest justice to the remarkable career of Harsha and said that he was ready to narrate to them only a portion of the brilliant career of Harsha. He then proceeded to narrate as follows. In the country of S'rîkaṇṭha, there is a district named Sthāṇvîs'vara. In ages long past there reigned a king named Pushpabhūti. He was a great devotee of S'iva. He formed friendship with a great S'aivite teacher from the Deccan named Bhairavāchārya. The latter made a present of a wonderful sword named Aṭṭahāsa to the king. Pushpabhūti offered to help the S'aiva ascetic in a magic rite. While engaged in his task, he had a vision of Lakshmî, who promised him that he would be the founder of a mighty line of kings, one of whom Harsha would have a most glorious career.

Chap. IV. In Pushpabhūti's line, as time rolled on, was born Prabhākaravardhana alias Pratāpas'îla, who fought successfully against the Hūṇas, the king of the Gūrjaras and the lords of Sindhu, Gāndhāra, Lāṭa and Mālava. His queen was Yas'omatî. The king was a great devotee of the sun. Rājyavardhana was the first child of the king and the queen. Then was born Harsha on the 12th of the dark half of the month of Jyeshtha. The birth of Harsha was heralded by auspicious signs prognosticating his future greatness. When Rājyavardhana was in his sixth year and Harsha was an infant just beginning to take a few steps with the help of his nurse and prattling a few indistinct words, a daughter named Rājyas'rî was born to the king and queen. About the time of the birth of Rājyas'rî, queen Yas'omatî's brother handed over to the king Prabhākaravardhana his son Bhaṇḍin about eight years old as a companion to the two princes, between whom and Bhaṇḍin sprang up a close and intimate friendship. The king in course of time brought, as companions for the growing princes, two brothers, sons of the king of Mālava, named Kumāragupta and Mādhavagupta, the elder Kumāragupta being about 18 years old at the time. These two followed the princes like their shadow. When Rājyas'rî grew up an accomplished princess she was married to Grahavarman, the eldest son of Avantivarman of the Maukhari family. Rājyas'rî went with her husband to his country of Kānyakubja.

Chap. V. When Rājyavardhana was old enough to bear arms, Prabhākaravardhana sent him accompanied by hereditary ministers and devoted feudatories to the north against the Hūṇas. Harsha accompanied him for some distance and when Rājyavardhana entered the Kailāsa range, Harsha remained behind and devoted some time to hunting. A courier from Prabhākaravardhana announced his serious illness. He started in hot haste and riding day and night reached the capital on the third day. He saw the whole city given up to performing rites of various sects and faiths for the sake of his father. On entering the palace he found the king lying in the clutches of death with queen Yas'omatî weeping over him. Two days afterwards when the king's condition became hopeless, Yas'omatî ascended the funeral pyre and the king died a short time afterwards. Harsha performed the funeral rites and anxiously waited for the arrival of his elder brother to whom he had already despatched swift messengers.

Chap. VI. About a fortnight after the death of Prabhākaravardhana, Rājyavaradhana arrived wounded in his successful war against the Hūṇas and with a thin growth of hair on his chin. The next day Rājyavardhana announced his intention of refusing the throne and of taking to a life in the forest. Harsha was taken aback by the strange resolve of his brother and had a mind to follow him, when one of Rājyas'rî's attendants, named Saṃvādaka, threw himself into the hall where the brothers sat and narrated a harrowing tale. He told Rājyavardhana that on the very day on which the news of Prabhākaravardhana's death reached Kānyakubja (Kanoj), Grahavarman, the husband of Rājyas'rî, was slain by the king of Mālava, that Rājyas'rî was put into prison at Kânyakubja with fetters on her feet like a brigand's wife and that the king of Mālava had designs even against Sthāṇvîs'vara. On that very day Rājyavardhana, who did not listen to Harsha's entreaties that, though a boy, he should be allowed to accompany him, started against the king of Mālava accompanied by Bhaṇḍin with ten thousand cavalry. After many days had elapsed, Harsha saw Kuntala, a high cavalry officer and a great favourite of Rājyavardhana, coming with sorrow written on his face. He brought the news that Rājyavardhana, though he subdued with ease the Mālava prince, was treacherously slain by the king of the Gauḍas, who had induced Rājyavardhana to go alone to the former's place. Siṃhanāda, the old and faithful commander-in-chief of Prabhākaravardhana, encouraged Harsha to avenge his brother's death. Harsha took the vow of destroying the Gauḍa king and dictated to his minister for foreign affairs named Avanti a proclamation to be sent to all kings either to submit to Harsha or to offer battle. The next morning, Harsha called Skandagupta, the chief of his elephant hosts, and asked him to get ready his whole army for an expedition. Skandagupta applauded Harsha's project but implored his master to learn the lesson of distrust from the fate of Rājyavardhana and narrated for his master's edification the stories of numerous former kings that fell victims to treachery and intrigue.

Chap. VII. A few days afterwards Harsha crowned himself and set out on an auspicious day, after worshipping S'iva. The first halt was made not far from the capital (Thanesar) on the banks of the Sarasvatî. There the chief accountant of the village waited upon him with a golden seal marked with the emblem of the bull and requested Harsha to issue a charter. The next day Harsha marched on with his vast army. When the day's march was over, he gave audience to Haṃsavega, a confidential messenger of Kumāra alias Bhāskaravarman, king of Prāgjyotisha (Assam). The messenger announced that the prince of Assam desired to form an undying friendship with Harsha and offered many wonderful presents, the chief of which was a miraculous parasol that originally belonged to Varuṇa. At night Haṃsavega informed Harsha how the parasol came into the possession of the kings of Assam. He traced the descent of Kumāra alias Bhāskaravarman from Naraka and mentioned that Kumāra was the great-great-grandson of Bhūtivarman, great-grandson of Chandramukhavarman, grandson of Sthitivarman and son of Susthiravarman alias Mṛigānka from his queen S'yāmādevî. Bhāskaravarman was a devotee of S'iva and desired the friendship of Harsha. Harsha was highly pleased with the king of Assam and sent back Haṃsavega with numerous presents. Harsha then proceeded for several days against his enemy (the king of Gauḍa). On the way he met Bhaṇḍin who brought with him the booty wrested from the Mālava king by Rājyavardhana. He brought news that after Kānyakubja was seized by Gupta, Rājyas'rî escaped from prison and had betaken herself to the Vindhya forest. Harsha then asked Bhaṇḍin to march against the Gauḍa king and himself entered the Vindhya forest in search of his unlucky sister.

Chap. VIII. After roaming about in the forest for several days, he met Vyāghraketu, son of the Bhil chieftain S'arabhaketu, who presented to Harsha a young Bhil by name Nirghāta, the commander-in-chief of the Bhils. He informed the king of an ascetic named Divākaramitra who was a convert from Brahmanism to Buddhism. Harsha remembered him as the friend of Grahavarman from the latter's childhood. Harsha resting his right hand on the shoulder of Mādhavagupta went to the hermitage of Divākaramitra, where he saw the latter surrounded by pupils and students of various sects. Just then a Bhikshu came unexpectedly and informed his teacher Divākaramitra that a woman of noble birth was about to burn herself for grief in the neighbourhood. Harsha hastened with the Bhikshu leading the way and saw his sister ready to perish in fire. From his sister he learnt how she was helped out of prison by a noble named Gupta at the time of the tumult of the Gauḍa king in Kānyakubja, how she then heard of the death of Rājyavardhana, how she gave up food on hearing it, how she came to the Vindhya forest and how in despair she prepared to burn herself. Divākaramitra then made to Harsha a present of a necklace named Mandākinî, brought by Nāgārjuna from the Nāgas in Pātāla and handed over to Sātavāhana, overlord of the Deccan. Rājyas'rī expressed to her brother her wish to put on the red robe. Harsha implored her to remain with him till he carried out his vow of destroying the Gauḍa king and requested Divākaramitra to be the spiritual adviser of his sister. He further said that after fulfilling his vow, he would himself assume the red robes along with his sister. When Divākaramitra acceded to the wishes of Harsha, the latter returned to his army encamped on the banks of the Ganges.

Here the narrative of Harsha's career comes to an end.

INDEX